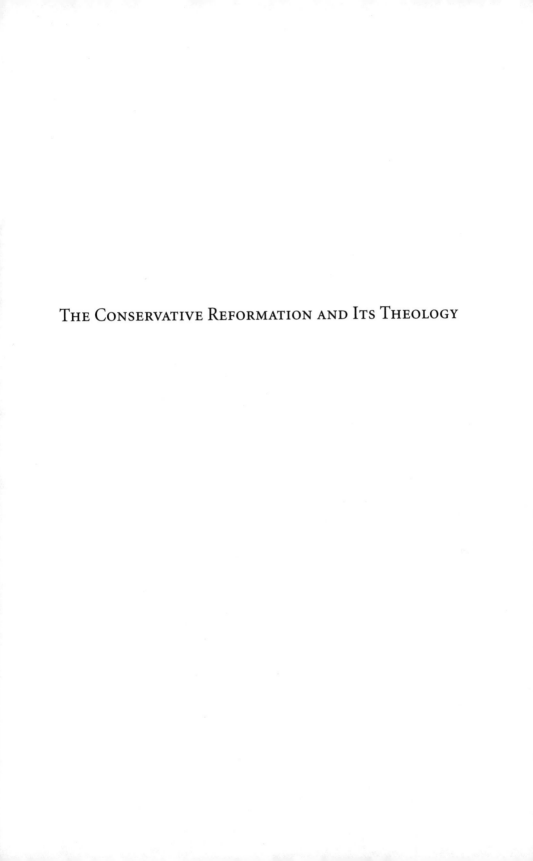

THE CONSERVATIVE REFORMATION AND ITS THEOLOGY

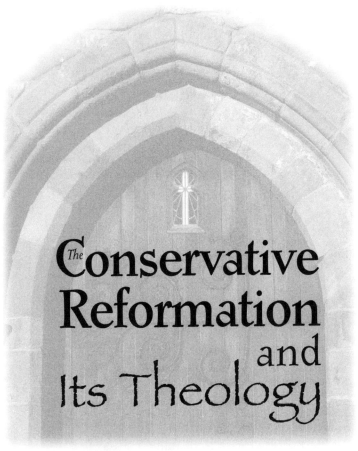

The Conservative Reformation and Its Theology

As Represented in the Augsburg Confession
and in the History and Literature
of the Evangelical Lutheran Church

Charles Porterfield Krauth
introduction by Lawrence R. Rast Jr.

CONCORDIA PUBLISHING HOUSE · SAINT LOUIS

*To the memory of Charles Philip Krauth D.D.,
my venerated and sainted father, this book is dedicated.*

 Published 2007 by Concordia Publishing House
3558 S. Jefferson Avenue, St. Louis, MO 63118-3968
1-800-325-3040 • www.cph.org

Manufactured in the United States of America

Library of Congress Cataloging-in-Publication Data
Krauth, Charles P. (Charles Porterfield), 1823-1883.
  The conservative Reformation and its theology : as represented in the Augsburg Confession and in the history and literature of the Evangelical Lutheran Church / Charles Porterfield Krauth ; introduction by Lawrence R. Rast, Jr.
    p. cm.
  Originally published: United States : s.n., 1913.
  Includes index.
  ISBN-13: 978-0-7586-0994-6
  ISBN-10: (invalid) 0-7586-0994-0
  1. Lutheran Church—Doctrines. 2. Reformation. 3. Augsburg Confession. I. Title.
  BX8065.3.K73 2007
  230'.41—dc22

                                                                    2007017360

1 2 3 4 5 6 7 8 9 10   16 15 14 13 12 11 10 09 08 07

CONTENTS

Introduction by Lawrence R. Rast Jr.   vii

Preface   xxxix

A. The Conservative Reformation:

     I. Occasion and Cause   1

     II. Chief Organ: Luther   22

     III. Chief Instrument: Luther's New Testament   88

B. Church of the Conservative Reformation: Lutheran Church   112

C. Confessional Principle of the Conservative Reformation   162

D. Confession of the Conservative Reformation:

     I. Primary Confession: Augsburg Confession   201

     II. Secondary Confessions: Book of Concord   268

E. History and Doctrines of the Conservative Reformation;
Mistakes Corrected   329

F. Specific Theology of the Conservative Reformation:

     I. Original Sin (Augsburg Conf., Art. II)   355

     II. Person of Christ (Augsburg Conf., Art. III)   456

     III. Baptism (Augsburg Conf., Art. IX)   518

     IV. Lord's Supper

         1. Thetically Stated   585

         2. Antithesis Considered   664

         3. Objections Answered   755

Index   831

Introduction

CHARLES PORTERFIELD KRAUTH

The Background and Context of *The Conservative Reformation and Its Theology*

It is vastly more important, then, to know what the Reformation retained than what it overthrew; for the overthrow of error, though often an indispensable prerequisite to the establishment of the truth, is not truth itself; it may clear the foundation, simply to substitute one error for another, perhaps a greater for a less.[1]—*Charles Porterfield Krauth*

"AMERICAN LUTHERANISM"

As the nineteenth century moved toward its midpoint, many Lutherans in the United States were decidedly antagonistic to the Lutheran Orthodoxy of the sixteenth and seventeenth centuries. The historic confessional documents of sixteenth-century Lutheranism were marginalized and, at times, deprecated by a number of Lutheran theologians, of whom Samuel Simon Schmucker and Benjamin Kurtz were the most outspoken. American Evangelicalism, with its Arminian theology and revivalistic practice, dominated the scene and shaped the life of the Lutheran Church. The New Measures of Second Great Awakening revivalist Charles G. Finney were common in American Lutheran worship.

However, during the second third of the nineteenth century, a change in the doctrinal complexion of the Lutheran Church began to unfold. A movement that looked back to the historic confessional positions of the Lutheran Church

---

1 Charles Porterfield Krauth, *The Conservative Reformation and Its Theology* (repr. St. Louis: Concordia, 2007), 202.

began to emerge and make its presence felt in the U.S. Lutheran community. The leading figure among the American-born Lutheran confessionalists was Charles Porterfield Krauth. Born March 17, 1823, in Martinsburg, Virginia, the son of Catharine and the Rev. Charles Philip Krauth, the younger Charles entered Pennsylvania College in 1834. In 1839 he entered Lutheran Theological Seminary at Gettysburg, Pennsylvania, from which he graduated in 1841. Krauth received his license to preach on October 18, 1841, from the Synod of Maryland and entered into the pastoral ministry at Canton, Maryland.

While at the Gettysburg seminary, Krauth studied under Samuel Simon Schmucker (1799–1873), one of the leading figures in the American Lutheran Church. From Schmucker, Krauth imbibed fully the tradition known as "American Lutheranism,"[2] which argued that the historic theology and practice of the Lutheran Church in Europe was inadequate in basic ways because of the historical context in which it emerged. Although Martin Luther had made a vibrant beginning at reforming the Church, the scope of his work was limited by his circumstances. Later Lutheranism—usually labeled "Orthodox"—mistakenly assumed that Luther had completed the Reformation and thus lost the reforming drive that characterized Luther's own work. More interested in abstract theological hairsplitting than in preaching an affective Gospel that changed lives, Orthodox Lutheranism stifled the spirit of Luther and threatened its future viability. The United States, with its freedom from restrictive relationships between church and state, now allowed Lutherans to recapture the revolutionary perspective of Luther and promised radical changes in theology and in practice. Indeed, argued the American Lutherans, if the Lutheran Church did not update its doctrine and practice, the Lutheran Church in the United States was doomed to irrelevance and, ultimately, death. Articulated in a variety of books and articles, Schmucker's perspective comes clearly to the fore in *Fraternal Appeal to the American Churches*, in which he offered a generic creed, based upon the fundamental articles of faith upon which all Protestants could agree and thus unite.[3]

As active as Schmucker was, no one was more forceful in promoting "American Lutheranism" than Schmucker's colleague Benjamin Kurtz (1795–1867).[4] Kurtz was a key leader in the American Lutheran movement and influenced the

---

2 Vergilius Ferm, *The Crisis in American Lutheran Theology* (New York: Century, 1927).

3 Samuel Simon Schmucker, *Fraternal Appeal to the American Churches, with a Plan for Catholic Union on Apostolic Principles*, 2d ed. (New York: Taylor & Dodd, 1839), 128–39.

4 Kurtz's necrology appears in *Proceedings of the Twenty-Second Convention of the General Synod of the Evangelical Lutheran Church in the United States, Assembled in Fort Wayne, Ind., May, 1866* (Philadelphia: Jas. B. Rodgers, 1866), 37–38. See also E. W. Hutter, *Eulogy on the Life and Character of Rev. Benjamin Kurtz, D.D., LL.D., Delivered before the Professors and Students of the Missionary Institute, and a Large Concourse of Citizens at Selingsgrove, Pa., Monday Evening, May 28th, 1866* (Philadelphia: H. G. Leisenring, 1866).

Church through the pages of the *Lutheran Observer*. Born in Harrisburg, Pennsylvania, on February 28, 1795, Kurtz studied for the ministry under George Lochman and was licensed as a minister by the Pennsylvania Ministerium in May 1815. In the most important move of his life and after serving parishes in Baltimore and Hagerstown, Maryland, and Chambersburg, Pennsylvania, in 1833 Kurtz assumed the editorial chores of the *Lutheran Observer*. As editor of this periodical, he helped shape the Lutheran experience in the United States.[5]

Although Schmucker was the theologian of the American Lutheran movement, Kurtz popularized it through the pages of the *Observer*. Where Schmucker argued in a scholarly and nuanced manner, Kurtz employed the broadside. His presentation was sensational and geared to elicit a strong response from his readers.[6] Kurtz was convinced that the greatest threat to the Lutheran Church in America was "Old Lutheranism," which, he firmly believed, was deficient in character. "Old Lutheranism," chiefly associated with The Lutheran Church—Missouri Synod (founded in 1847), subscribed unconditionally to the entire Book of Concord *quia* ("because") it was the faithful exposition of Scripture. As such, Old Lutherans looked back to the confessional documents of the sixteenth century to address contemporary issues. Because the Lutheran Symbols confessed biblical truth, they were as applicable to the Church of the nineteenth century as to that of the sixteenth. "American Lutheranism" viewed itself as the natural

5 The *Lutheran Observer* wielded an enormous influence on the Lutheran Church in the middle third of the nineteenth century. It was the first Lutheran periodical to have a distribution wide enough, both geographically and theologically, to act as the chief medium of communication within the Lutheran communion. Kurtz was well aware of this power and used it with great effectiveness. The first issue of the *Observer* appeared on August 1, 1831, and its editor at that point, John G. Morris, wrote: "May we not establish a religious semi-monthly periodical in the centre of the church, which will enlist the support of the whole denomination, be identified with its interests, and be regarded by all as its accredited organ?" ("To Our Readers," *Lutheran Observer* [August 1, 1831]).

6 Kurtz believed that if the Lutheran Confessions were used as the chief source of Lutheran identity, division would necessarily result. Rather, the Confessions should be subscribed to only in respect to their teaching "the fundamental doctrines of Scripture in a manner substantially correct." Benjamin Kurtz, "Creeds and Confessions," *Lutheran Observer* (August 21, 1840): "These documents, or standards, as they are usually termed, have been a source of strife and persecution in the Christian church, and are likely so to be, as long as they remain in force in all their accustomed minutiae of subordinate and detailed doctrine. In great and fundamental principles, the intelligent and pious may indeed be expected to coincide, but in the numerous small and unimportant points which enter more or less into the creeds of different individuals, it is impossible for all to think alike; nor is it important that they should. What does it matter whether all the members of a church or a denomination agree or not as to the precise mode of Christ's presence in the Eucharist. . . . On all such subjects men should certainly be permitted to exercise their own judgment, and to adopt those views which seem to be most consistent with reason and scripture. If, then, we must in the nature of things have creeds, let them be brief, clear and intelligible; comprehending as few articles as posssible, and only those essential to true piety and the salvation of the soul."

development and maturation of the revolutionary principles initiated by Luther. Kurtz believed that the two kinds of Lutheranism could not be more dissimilar and, further, could not be reconciled. A different spirit animated them.

> If we are permitted to judge from what appears in the *Alt-Lutheraner* and the *Lehre und Wehre*, we would be constrained to believe that they can find or see Christ nowhere but in the sacraments. They presumptuously denounce all others who do not hold to their views, and would exclude from the Lord's table any Lutheran who may be connected with the General Synod. There is scarcely a week that they do not anathematize the General Synod and the *Observer*, because it is planted upon the basis of this body. To hope for union or fraternization with such selfish, such exclusive views, would be worse than folly. They are a class of spiritual Ishmaelites; their appropriate place is in the Church of Rome, where men believe what they are told the church believes, and not what the Bible and the Holy Ghost teach them. An inanimate congregation of wax or clay might be formed by passing them through the same *iron mould*, but a community of immortal minds, whose divinely delegated prerogative it is "to search the Scriptures," "to prove all things, and to hold fast to that which is good," never, no, never! Revolutions do not go backwards; the Reformation of the 16th century was emphatically a revolution in the sentiments and dogmas of Christendom, and you will never turn the church back into that night of barbarism and spiritual bondage out of which she emerged at the Reformation, while the Holy Spirit makes men free with the liberty of Christ.[7]

Kurtz believed that the distinctively American Lutheranism that he and Schmucker were advancing was naturally superior to older expressions of the Lutheran Church, and he quickly grew frustrated with those who appealed to these older expressions. According to Kurtz, as important as sixteenth-century institutions and individuals may have been for the Church of their time, they had little or nothing to say to the Church of the present. Thus he rejected appeals on the part of both German- and English-speaking Lutherans for a return to the "Fathers" of the Lutheran Church—or the Church of any period. "The Fathers—who are the 'Fathers'?" he asked.

> They are the *children*; they lived in the *infancy* of the Church, in the early dawn of the Gospel day. John the Baptist was the greatest among the prophets, and yet he that was least in the Kingdom of God, in the Christian Church was greater than he. He probably knew less, and that little less distinctly than a Sunday-school child, ten years of age, in the present day. Even the apostle Peter, after all the personal instructions of Christ, could not expand his views

---

7 Benjamin Kurtz, *Lutheran Observer* (November 18, 1859), quoted in C. F. W. Walther, "Fidelity to the Written Word: The Burden of the Missouri Synod," *Concordia Journal* 1 (March 1975): 69–70.

sufficiently to learn that the Gospel was to be preached to the Gentiles, and that the Church of Christ was to compass the whole world. A special miracle was wrought to remove his prejudices and convince him of his folly. Every well-instructed Sunday-school child understands this thing without a miracle, better than Peter did. Who, then, are the "Fathers"? They have become the Children; they *were* the Fathers when compared with those who lived in the infancy of the Jewish dispensation; but, compared with the present and advanced age, they are the Children, and the learned and pious of the nineteenth century are the Fathers. We are *three hundred years older* than Luther and his noble coadjutors, and *eighteen hundred years older* than the primitives; theirs was the age of infancy and adolescence, and ours that of full-grown manhood. *They* were the *children*; *we* are the *fathers*; the tables are turned.[8]

In contrast to the theology of the "Fathers," Kurtz offered a progressive, up-to-date form of Lutheranism that accommodated much of the theology and practice that characterized American Protestantism around 1840. Beginning in the mid-1830s, Kurtz ran a weekly column in the *Observer* that kept his readers abreast of the latest revival happenings in Lutheranism, as well as other denominations.[9] He hoped thereby to help his denomination become a truly American Church—one that reflected the general character of American Evangelicalism in doctrine and practice. Old Lutheranism's outmoded theology and liturgical practice could not be meaningful to the advanced mind of the nineteenth-century United States. Lutheranism must change or die.[10]

The chief proponent of the New Measures was Charles Grandison Finney (1792–1875).[11] Finney was born in Connecticut, but his family moved to upstate New York two years later. It was there that he received his education in frontier schools. As a young man, he studied law and established a practice at Adams, New York, in the northern reaches of the state around Watertown. While reading

---

8 Benjamin Kurtz, "The Fathers," *Lutheran Observer* (November 29, 1849) (*original emphasis*).

9 For background on the use of the New Measures by Lutherans, see Frank H. Seilhamer, "The New Measure Movement among Lutherans," *Lutheran Quarterly* 12 (1960): 121–43; Raymond M. Bost, "Catechism or Revival?" *Lutheran Quarterly* 3 (Winter 1989): 413–21; Donald Herbert Yoder, "The Bench Versus the Catechism," *Pennsylvania Folklife* 10 (Fall 1959): 14–23.

10 For an example of Kurtz's preaching in practice, see Benjamin Kurtz, *Christ Blesses the Little Children: A Sermon Preached before the Sunday School in Funks-Town, on the 16th November, 1828* (Hagerstown, MD: William D. Bell, 1828).

11 Among the more recent biographies of Finney are Keith J. Hardman, *Charles Grandison Finney 1792–1875: Revivalist and Reformer* (Syracuse: Syracuse University Press, 1987); Charles E. Hambrick-Stowe, *Charles G. Finney and the Spirit of American Evangelicalism*, Library of Religious Biography (Grand Rapids: Eerdmans, 1996). Nathan Hatch also touches on Finney in *The Democratization of American Christianity* (New Haven: Yale University Press, 1989).

Blackstone's *Commentaries on Law*, he noted continuous references to the Scriptures, which, coupled with repeated urging from a clergyman friend, moved Finney to buy a Bible. He was soon reading it more than law. On October 10, 1821, having wrestled with the demands of the Gospel, he finally made his decision to commit his heart and life to God and to act as an "attorney for Jesus."[12]

Finney soon began conducting successful revival meetings.[13] His reputation grew from his use of the New Measures, the most famous of which was the "anxious" or "mourner's" bench, where those who were disturbed over their sin were exhorted to make the leap toward God and salvation. Finney held revivals all over the Eastern seaboard, including Rome, Utica, Auburn, Troy, Wilmington, Philadelphia, Boston, and New York City. Later, he systematized his theology during his long tenure as a professor at Oberlin College.[14]

Although Finney was not a particularly innovative thinker, he redefined the worship practice of American Protestants.[15] Through the shift in practice, he was able to reshape Protestant theology. First, he rejected the idea of original sin, as Protestants had historically understood it. Finney believed that the human will had the capability to do spiritually good works, albeit with the "help" of the Holy Spirit, thus he encouraged preachers to challenge their hearers to exercise their wills and do the good that God called them to do.[16] Second, Finney reshaped the doctrine of Christ's atoning death. Although he at times spoke of Christ's death as

---

12 Hardman, *Finney*, 43.

13 Whitney R. Cross, *The Burned-over District: The Social and Intellectual History of Enthusiastic Religion in Western New York, 1800–1850* (Ithaca: Cornell University Press, 1950), 151–208.

14 Charles G. Finney, *Lectures on Systematic Theology: Embracing Lectures on Moral Government, Together with Atonement, Moral and Physical Depravity, Regeneration, Philosophical Theories, and Evidences of Regeneration* (Oberlin, OH: J. M. Fitch; Boston: Crocker & Brewster, 1846).

15 See David Bennett, *The Altar Call: Its Origins and Present Usage* (Lanham, MD: University Press of America, 2000), for an investigation into the origins of the "invitation system." Bennett argues that the New Measures were not original to Finney, though he did offer the most complete and compelling apologetic for their use.

16 Charles G. Finney, *Revival Lectures* (Grand Rapids: Baker, Revell, n.d.), 224–25: "Let him [the preacher] go right over against them, urge upon them their ability to obey God, show them their obligation and duty, and press them with that until he brings them to submit and be saved." Finney, like the American Lutherans he influenced, denied that Baptism worked regeneration and forgiveness of sins. For Finney, Baptism was a "new measure" employed by the apostolic Church. While it had been effective in the early history of the Church, its original purpose—namely, the place where one made the decision to follow Christ—had been lost. "In the days of the apostles *baptism* answered this purpose. The Gospel was preached, and then all those who were willing to be on the side of Christ were called on to be *baptized*. It held the precise place that the anxious seat does now, as the public manifestation of a determination to be a Christian" (Finney, *Revival Lectures*, 305 [*original emphasis*]).

a payment for the sins of human beings, more frequently he defined the atonement in terms of God's "moral government," that is, Jesus' death demonstrated God's anger over sin and God's great love for humankind. Christ's atoning death did not pay for human sin once and for all; it made salvation a possibility for those who chose to follow Christ in His selfless commitment to the revealed will of God. As such, for Finney, Jesus became primarily a motivating example of complete submission to the will of God.

Finney linked doctrine with practice and argued that the way one believes forms the way one worships and that the way one worships shapes the way one believes. Finney intended his thought to be preached, and the purpose of the preaching was to get people to do something. He was not interested in abstract theories. Rather, "sinners ought to be made to feel that they have *something* to do, and that is, *to repent*; that it is something which *no other* being can do for them, neither God nor man; and something which *they can* do, and do *now*. Religion is something to *do*, not something to *wait for*. And they must do it now, or they are in danger of eternal death."[17] Thus Finney believed that

> all ministers should be revival ministers, and all preaching should be revival preaching; that is, it should be calculated to promote holiness. People say: "It is very well to have some men in the Church, who are revival preachers, and who can go about and promote revivals; but then you must have others to *indoctrinate* the Church." Strange! Do they know that a revival indoctrinates the Church faster than anything else? And a minister will never produce a revival if he does not indoctrinate his hearers. The preaching I have described is full of doctrine, but it is doctrine to be *practised*.[18]

Finney linked his style of worship to a specific theology and vice versa. For Finney, to adopt one meant to adopt the other.

Not all American Protestants accepted Finney's theology and practice. In the German Reformed Church, John Williamson Nevin (1803–1886) advocated a decidedly antirevivalistic theology and practice that emphasized the catholicity of the Reformation and the continuity of the historic Church.[19] Nevin grew up in a Presbyterian home, was catechized in the Westminster catechisms, yet also had a "conversion experience" while a student at Union College. He attended Princeton

---

17 Finney, *Revival Lectures*, 246 (*original emphasis*).

18 Finney, *Revival Lectures*, 246 (*original emphasis*).

19 Krauth wrote as follows about Nevin: "Of what our Church is, and of what she brings to this, her new home, witness has been borne by more than one thoughtful man of other communions. But among them all, there is none of more value than that given by Dr. John W. Nevin, of the Reformed Church. No amount of divergence from Dr. Nevin's views, could prevent a man of candor from acknowledging in him the presence of a great intellect, of the most unpretending simplicity and modesty, and of the most uncompromising love of truth. Our county has few men who can be classified with him" (*Conservative Reformation*, 157).

Seminary and eventually began teaching at Western Seminary in Allegheny, Pennsylvania. Throughout the 1830s, in response to what he believed were the extremes of Finney's New Measures, Nevin slowly moved toward a more "catholic" posture theologically and liturgically. He believed that the New Measures, which had affected both the Lutheran and Reformed communions, were "quackery." His book *The Anxious Bench* was one of the first sustained theological critiques of Finney's practice.[20] In contrast to evangelicals such as Finney and Kurtz, who saw the anxious bench as "God's Lever of Archimedes in converting sinners," Nevin stressed the difference between genuine and counterfeit revivals.[21] He argued that the "system of the bench" fought against the life of true Christianity; in fact, it incorporated in itself a life different from that at work historically in Christ's Church. Rather than the bench, the proper means for the cultivation of the proper Christian life was the "system of the catechism." Whether Presbyterian, German Reformed, or Lutheran, the historic catechisms were the appropriate and certain route for Christianity to create and take hold of a Christian person and integrate that person into the life of the Church. The system of the bench, with its confusion and use of false psychological methods for conversion, drowned out the still, small voice of the Spirit and replaced it with the decision of the human subject. In contrast, the system of the catechism, through the faithful ministrations of the representatives of Christ, quietly cultivated the life of the Christian. For Nevin the bench promoted radical individualism at the expense of the organic life of the Church, and in the final analysis he found the two systems entirely irreconcilable. Where one flourished, the other would fail and vice versa.[22]

As an important player on the U.S. religious scene, Kurtz kept a close watch on the happenings within the other Protestant denominations. He knew and approved of Finney's work. When Nevin, widely known for his antislavery agitation in western Pennsylvania, joined the German Reformed Church in 1839 and moved to its seminary at Mercersburg, Pennsylvania, to teach systematic theology,

---

20 John W. Nevin, *The Anxious Bench* (Chambersburg, PA: Printed at the Office of the "Weekly Messenger," 1843).

21 "Correspondence," *Lutheran Observer* (November 17, 1843), quoted in John W. Nevin, *The Anxious Bench*, 2d ed. (Chambersburg, PA: Publication Office of the German Reformed Church, 1844). Reprinted in *Catholic and Reformed: Selected Theological Writings of John Williamson Nevin*, eds. Charles Yrigoyen Jr. and George H. Bricker, Pickwick Original Texts and Translations Series Number 3, gen. ed. Dikran Y. Hadidian (Pittsburgh, PA: Pickwick Press, 1978), 22. The *Lutheran Observer* also featured a regular column for the sole purpose of reporting the various revivals in the Church. See John E. Groh, "Revivalism among Lutherans in America in the 1840s," *Concordia Historical Institute Quarterly* 43 (February 1970): 20–43; (May 1970): 59–78; Karl Koch, "The American Lutheran Scene, 1831–1841, as Reflected in the 'Lutheran Observer,'" *Concordia Historical Institute Quarterly* 37 (July 1964): 61–62.

22 Nevin, *Anxious Bench* (1st ed.), 55.

Kurtz identified him immediately as a potential ally. By the time Nevin moved to Mercersburg, the Second Great Awakening and its New Measures were making a strong impact on both the Lutheran and German Reformed Churches.[23] Thus Kurtz's distress over Nevin's changing position is understandable—an ally had become an enemy. When Nevin attacked the New Measures in *The Anxious Bench*, Kurtz responded with alacrity and vigor. Beginning in the November 10, 1843, *Lutheran Observer*, Kurtz offered a series of articles that challenged Nevin's critique of revivals. Kurtz's chief argument for the divine nature of revivals was simple: The Bible refers to them. Of course, Kurtz admitted, the revivals in the Bible were not exactly the same as those of the Second Great Awakening, but they were similar. Thus the onus was on Nevin to prove the New Measures wrong.[24]

By the time the second edition of *The Anxious Bench* appeared in 1844, Nevin's primary concern was the relation of the systems in question to the doctrine of the Church. The issue at hand was not whether the bench can be used properly. It can. But what does the system of the bench mean for the Church? A mediating Hegelian, Nevin concluded that the Lutheran and Reformed branches of the Reformation complemented one another, thus both were necessary for the constitution of an inclusive Protestantism. But the bench subsumed all under an Anabaptist radicalism, which had no organic connection to Christ's body, the historic Church. Those who held to the system of the bench compromised the true work of the reformers, particularly Luther, who had rediscovered the life of the historic Church and expressed it in the catechisms.[25]

---

23 The history of the German Reformed Church was similar to that of American Lutheranism in this period. In the United States the two denominations had a close relationship because "they used the same language, they very often worshiped in the same church building and, besides, they had a common interest in one of the educational institutions of Pennsylvania, the High School at Lancaster" (James I. Good, *History of the Reformed Church in the U. S. in the Nineteenth Century* [New York: Board of Publication of the Reformed Church in America, 1911], 182). Good details (pp. 182–86) the Reformed and Lutheran efforts toward union that occurred during the first half of the nineteenth century.

24 Benjamin Kurtz, review of *The Anxious Bench*, by John W. Nevin, *Lutheran Observer* (November 17, 1843).

25 Nevin, *Anxious Bench* (2d ed.), 31: "The cause of the Reformation was endangered more by its own caricature, namely the wild fanaticism of the Anabaptists, than the opposition of Rome. Luther saved it, not by truckling compromise, but by boldly facing and unmasking the false spirit, so that all the world might see that Lutheran Christianity was one thing, and wild Phrygian Montanism, with its pretended inspiration, quite another." Nevin, *Anxious Bench* (2d ed.), 12: "The system of New Measures lacks affinity whatever with the life of the Reformation, as embodied in the Augsburgh [*sic*] Confession and the Heidelberg Catechism. It could not have found favor in the eyes of Zwingli or Calvin. Luther would have denounced it in the most unmerciful terms." On Nevin's relationship with U.S. Lutherans, see Lawrence R. Rast Jr., "The Influence of John Williamson Nevin on American Lutheranism to 1849" (master's thesis, Concordia Theological Seminary, Fort Wayne, IN, 1990).

Nevin challenged the American Lutheran movement to define and defend itself. Kurtz took up Nevin's question and published *Why Are You a Lutheran?*[26] Kurtz used the book to identify the fundamental principles of Lutheranism and why one can, in good conscience, be a member of the Lutheran Church. First, the symbolic books of the Lutheran Church contain all the prominent doctrines of God's Word: the Trinity, the universal depravity of humankind, the proper and eternal deity of Jesus Christ. Kurtz singles out the atonement by the death of Christ, arguing that it is vicarious in nature and unlimited in its extent. Where Kurtz showed his evangelical hand, however, was in his understanding of faith. He wrote in the section "Good works involving purity of heart and life" that true "confession *requires an active faith*, a faith that produces obedience and holy living."[27] Kurtz did not sufficiently distinguish between passive, justifying faith and active faith, which works as a *result* of justification. Instead, Kurtz sounded very much like Finney, who defined religion largely as a human endeavor: "*Religion is the work of man*. It is something for man to do. It consists in obeying God. It is man's duty."[28] Faith as activity, rather than that which passively receives the gifts of God, showed how thoroughly Kurtz was influenced by American Evangelical thought. Kurtz immediately followed his discussion of the nature of faith with a citation of Article V of the Augsburg Confession and thereby redefined the ministerial office. The purpose of the preacher is to encourage his audience to a life of obedience in faithfulness to God's Law.[29] The Law replaced the Gospel.

The controversy between the German Reformed Nevin and Lutherans such as Kurtz concerning the anxious bench and its implications for the doctrine and practice of their respective traditions bore rich fruit. On the one hand, Nevin became convinced that the real problem with Lutherans in the United States was Benjamin Kurtz, who because of his rejection of historic Lutheran teaching and practice might better be labeled a "pseudo-Lutheran."[30] On the other hand,

---

26 Kurtz had already published a series of articles in the *Lutheran Observer* entitled "Why Are You a Lutheran?" When Nevin contested Kurtz's Lutheranism, the latter expanded the series and published it in book form: *Why Are You a Lutheran? or A Series of Dissertations, Explanatory of the Doctrines, Government, Discipline, Liturgical Economy, Distinctive Traits, etc., of the Evangelical Lutheran Church in the United States* (Baltimore: Evangelical Lutheran Church, 1843). The book was extremely popular and went through at least thirteen editions.

27 Kurtz, *Why Are You a Lutheran?* 18 (*original emphasis*).

28 Finney, *Revival Lectures*, 232, 246, 1 (*original emphasis*).

29 For other contemporary Lutheran commentary on the New Measures that also shows Finney's influence, see Ruben Weiser, *A Tract for the People: The Mourner's Bench* (Wm. T. Chapman, Printer, n.d.); D. F. Bittle, *Remarks on New Measures* (Staunton: Kenton Harper, 1839); Francis Jacob Ruth, *The Life and Work of Rev. Francis Jacob Ruth, a Pioneer of Lutheranism in North-Western Ohio* (Plymouth, OH: Advertiser Steam Printing House, 1888).

30 John W. Nevin, "Pseudo Lutheranism," *Weekly Messenger of the German Reformed Church* (March 22, 1848).

Nevin's writings challenged American Lutherans, especially an emerging generation trained largely at Gettysburg and regular readers of the *Lutheran Observer*, to
examine the sources for themselves and to form their own conclusions. Thus,
though he despaired of ever converting Kurtz, an optimistic Nevin looked forward
to a time when American Lutherans would regain their distinctive stance, for
Kurtz's position presented "a strange contradiction surely, which, we may trust, is
not destined always to endure."[31]

THE CONFESSIONAL MOVEMENT
IN AMERICAN LUTHERANISM

Nevin's words had barely reached print before they proved to be prophetic. During the second third of the nineteenth century, a change in the doctrinal and
liturgical complexion of the U.S. Lutheran Church took place. A movement that
hearkened back to the historic confessional positions of the Lutheran Church
began to emerge and make its presence felt.[32] The confessional movement manifested itself in two distinct groups. First, the great immigration into the United
States from Germany and Scandinavia brought significant numbers of Lutherans
who were vigorously committed to the historic theological formulations and
liturgical practices of the Lutheran Church.[33] As these immigrants arrived, American Lutherans were confused by their presence, thought, and, above all, their
practice. Ezra Keller, a colleague of Kurtz and Schmucker, offers a report of a

---

31 John W. Nevin, *The Mystical Presence: A Vindication of the Reformed or Calvinistic Doctrine of the Real Eucharist* (Philadelphia: J. B. Lippincott, 1846), 106.

32 This confessional movement had several roots. Theodore Tappert rightly assigned the primary credit to the great immigration that swelled the Lutheran population in the nineteenth century. He notes further, however, that the immigrants brought with them not only
confessional attitudes but also, and perhaps just as important, theological books and journals
that held to the same ideals. Along with the importation of Luther's writings, these sources
moved the confessionalists to express more boldly their rediscovered faith. See Theodore G.
Tappert, ed., *Lutheran Confessional Theology in America, 1840–1880* (New York: Oxford University Press, 1972).

33 Tappert, *Lutheran Confessional Theology*, 25: "Although some American churchgoers were
far more self-consciously Lutheran than Schmucker . . . it was not until after the large
immigrations from Germany and the Scandinavian countries that the views of Schmucker
were successfully challenged." The standard history for the founding of The Lutheran
Church—Missouri Synod is Walter O. Forster, *Zion on the Mississippi: The Settlement of the
Saxon Lutherans in Missouri, 1839–1841* (St. Louis: Concordia, 1953). See also E. Theodore
Bachmann, "The Rise of Missouri Lutheranism" (PhD diss., University of Chicago, 1946).
For more specialized treatments of LCMS history, see *Concordia Historical Institute Quar-
terly*, the journal of the LCMS Department of Archives and History. For an account of the
influence that the Old Lutheran immigrants had on the American Lutherans, see Carl
Mauelshagen, *American Lutheranism Surrenders to Forces of Conservatism* (Athens, GA:
University of Georgia, 1936).

meeting with the Rev. J. Wangner, a German pastor, which shows just how disconcerting the appearance of an Old Lutheran could be to an American Lutheran:

> He is an accomplished gentleman, and an ardent Christian, but a fanatical dogmatist. . . . He is quite antiquated in his views of Christian doctrine and church polity. He considers subscription to the unaltered Augsburg Confession, without note or comment, as indispensable to constitute a man a Lutheran. The Lutheran Church, based on the Augsburg Confession he considers the Apostolic Catholic Church. He believes in baptismal regeneration, and the real presence of the *body* and the *blood* of Christ in the Lord's Supper. He recommends private confession and absolution; makes the sign of the cross in the administration of the ordinance of baptism, and conforms to the various forms of the symbolists.[34]

The other source of the confessional movement was indigenous and, in line with the thinking of Nevin and the Mercersburg theology, was disenchanted with the prevailing revivalism of American Evangelicalism. These groups increasingly found the theology of American Lutheranism unsatisfactory and sought to develop a Lutheranism true to its history, confession, and practice.

When Charles Porterfield Krauth entered the ministry in the early 1840s, the American Lutheran movement was at its peak. However, signs of a transition were already beginning to appear. The revivalistic and Arminian assumptions of the American Lutherans were beginning to give way to a more churchly and confessional perspective. English-speaking Lutherans, primarily students of Samuel Schmucker, began to consider the challenges laid down by the Old Lutherans and Mercersburg. In addition to Krauth, William A. Passavant (1821–1894), Beale M. Schmucker (1827–1888), and Joseph A. Seiss stand out.[35] As they considered the historical record, they concluded that fundamental theological differences existed between the positions held by Schmucker and Kurtz and embraced by their church body, the General Synod, and that of historic, confessional Lutheranism. These differences extended to matters of both doctrine (the real presence of Christ and baptismal regeneration versus memorialism and Baptism as a public act of profession of an already existing faith) and practice (liturgical worship versus

---

34 Michael Diehl, *Biography of Rev. Ezra Keller: Founder and First President of Wittenberg College*, introduction by S. Sprecher (Springfield, OH: Ruralist Publ. Co., 1859), 260.

35 William Alfred Passavant was the missionary and philanthropist of the group. The standard biography of Passavant is George H. Gerberding, *Life and Letters of W. A. Passavant, D.D.*, 4th ed. (Greenville, PA: Young Lutheran Co., 1906). The sources on Beale Schmucker are fairly limited. See George W. Sandt, "Lutheran Leaders as I Knew Them: Rev. Beale M. Schmucker, D.D., Leader as Parliamentarian, Archivist and Liturgist," *Lutheran Church Review* 37 (January 1918): 94–100; Adolph Spaeth, "Schmucker, Beale M., D.D.," *Lutheran Cyclopedia* (St. Louis: Concordia, 1975), 431–32. For Joseph Seiss, see Lawrence R. Rast Jr., "Joseph A. Seiss and the Lutheran Church in America" (PhD diss., Vanderbilt University, 2003).

revivalism). Although the movement of these men occurred over a fairly long period of time, the beginnings of the shift showed already in the 1840s.

Under the guidance of his father, Charles Philip Krauth (1797–1867), Charles Porterfield Krauth studied the theological and historical sources of the Lutheran Confessions during the early years of his ministry in the 1840s. The early Fathers of the Church and the reformers of the sixteenth century began to attract his attention with greater frequency. He was especially interested in the doctrine of the real presence of Christ in the Sacrament. Only later did Krauth have the opportunity to develop his own thinking on the subject. By the late 1840s he had developed a real appreciation for historic, confessional Lutheranism. His good friend Beale Schmucker speculated on exactly when and for what reasons the theological shift occurred for Krauth:

> An interesting question arises as to the time at which the change in Mr. Krauth's theological views took place. I cannot definitely answer that question. ... But in 1848 and 1849 and the following years, when I was admitted to a very near intimacy, when one subject after another was by agreement studied by us both, when we compared views both personally and in regular correspondence, when the whole course and results of his studies were familiarly open to me, I may safely affirm that the change of view and conviction was substantially complete. ... It may very well be that that great masterpiece of Lutheran theology [the *Loci* of Martin Chemnitz], with its array of scriptural evidence and its clear, cogent argument, had great power with so philosophical and logical a mind as that of Mr. Krauth. But wherever the start may have been made, at the time of which I speak, he had already made himself familiar with much of patristic theology; he was engaged in following the course of thought in the Church through the ages; he was nearly as familiar with the very phrases and statements of the Book of Concord as we have all known him to be in these later years; he was then following the doctrinal disputations of the Reformation, gathering in his library the special literature of its different periods, and subjecting the whole to a most thorough examination, and the result at each successive stage of the examination was to confirm and deepen the conviction that the whole truth of the authoritative Word was nowhere set forth with such clearness, purity and fullness as in the collected Confessions of the Lutheran Church, and that in all their doctrinal teachings they were in conformity with that Word.[36]

As the 1840s waned, Samuel Schmucker and Benjamin Kurtz became increasingly vocal in their antagonism toward the confessional movement. This animosity seemed to provide the mortar to cement the relationship between Krauth and

---

36 Beale M. Schmucker, "Memorials of Deceased Minister Charles Porterfield Krauth," *Lutheran Church Review* 2 (July 1883): 260–61.

his colleagues.[37] While the likes of Krauth, Seiss, Passavant, and Beale Schmucker had begun to engage the assumptions of American Lutheranism critically, they remained for the most part within the doctrinal and practical tradition of the General Synod. Yet their increasing familiarity and interaction with one another helped prepare them for the founding of the General Council. As Samuel Schmucker and the American Lutherans became ever more bold—some interpreters would say desperate—in their doctrinal assertions, the younger men began to lose patience. For example, the elder Schmucker's clear rejection of the doctrine of the real presence led Joseph Seiss to argue as early as 1851 for a new church body.[38] In his response, Krauth urged patience and confidence in the ultimate turn of the Church toward a more confessional position.[39] Yet ultimately Krauth himself became frustrated with the boldness of the American Lutherans. In time both Seiss and Krauth found it necessary to break ties with their teacher and friend. Over the course of a little more than a decade, beginning with the *Definite Synodical Platform* and ending with the formation of the General Council, the confessionalist party within the General Synod finally broke with its teachers.[40]

---

37 Adolph Spaeth, *Charles Porterfield Krauth, D.D., LL.D.*, 2 vols. (New York: Christian Literature Co., 1898; Philadelphia: General Council Publication House, 1909), 1:146, 149: "A very warm friendship was formed in those days between Mr. Krauth and Rev. J. A. Seiss. He [Krauth] invited Mr. Seiss repeatedly to Winchester to assist him in special services in connection with a communion season. . . . He discussed with him very frankly the condition of the Lutheran Church at that critical period of her history in America."

38 Seiss to Charles Porterfield Krauth, 22 July 1851, cited in Spaeth, *Krauth*, 1:193: "I suppose you have read Dr. S. S. S.'s article on the mode of the presence in the Lord's Supper. It is specious, evasive, unfair, with great appearances of profound learning, liberality, candor, and piety. It is just calculated to have weight with such as know no better. I suppose that it is as strong and efficient an article as can be written on his view. Is it not time that some one should take S. to pieces, and show the Church what he is made of? If he continues he will yet realize his conception of the Church in 'pails,' with a squad here in a tub, and a squad there in a tub. For my own part, I am almost ripe for a re-organization now. What have you to say?" See also Spaeth, *Krauth*, 1:352, where Spaeth notes "for a time, preceding the meeting in Winchester [of the General Synod in 1853], the leaders had seriously thought of forcing the 'great question' upon the body for final decision."

39 Krauth to Seiss, 7 August 1851, cited in Spaeth, *Krauth*, 1:193–94: "Dr. Schmucker's article is a very poor one. Did it really grapple with the subject it would be worth an answer—but no advance is made on either side, by writing such articles or confuting them. . . . As regards a re-organization, I do not think that matters are ripe for any decided move. Truth is winning its way silently in our Church. Let us hold it together tightly, that we may carry it as one body into the camp of truth."

40 For a discussion of the events leading to the break, see Vergilius T. A. Ferm, *The Crisis in American Lutheran Theology: A Study of the Issue between American Lutheranism and Old Lutheranism* (repr. St. Louis: Concordia, 1987), and David Gustafson, *Lutherans in Crisis: The Question of Identity in the American Republic* (Minneapolis: Fortress, 1993).

Krauth, Seiss, Beale Schmucker, and Passavant helped the Church to transition from American Lutheranism to a more confessional position.[41] Institutional means for supporting the emerging movement began to appear in the late 1840s, once papers such as the *Lutheran Observer* began to reject submissions from confessional Lutherans. In 1848 Passavant began publishing the *Missionary*. Although chiefly committed to the extension of the Church generally and Lutheranism particularly, the *Missionary* served to advance, in popular form, the tenets of the confessional party in respect to both confessional doctrine and liturgical practice. Further, the first formal theological journal specifically designed for the U.S. Lutheran Church first appeared in 1849. Titled the *Evangelical Quarterly Review,* it was dedicated to the advancement of the confessional Lutheran position. Although it offered its pages to American Lutherans as well, it was decidedly a confessional journal. The younger theologians were frequent contributors. Krauth supported the journal in a number of ways, particularly by supplying it with original articles and translations. Although only about 30 years old, Krauth was distinguishing himself as a leader within U.S. Lutheranism.

Krauth emerged clearly as the leader of the movement when the association, led by Seiss, selected him as the editor of the *Lutheran and Missionary,* which first appeared on October 31, 1861. The full-time responsibilities of the position required Krauth's resignation from active pastoral ministry.[42] The paper's purpose was to advocate for a decidedly confessional Lutheranism within the American context. Krauth wrote:

> We are "AMERICAN LUTHERANS." We accept the great fact that God has established our Zion in this western world under circumstances wholly different from those in which her past life has been nurtured. New forms of duty, new types of thought, new necessities of adaptation, are here to tax all her strength, and to test how far she is able to maintain her vital power under necessary changes of forms. The Lutheranism of this country cannot be a mere feeble

---

41 Gerberding writes: "B. M. Schmucker was a son of Dr. S. S. Schmucker. He was a neighbor and a warm friend of young Krauth. Joseph Seiss was of about the same age and an intimate friend of both. This gifted and promising trio of young Lutherans frequently came together and also carried on regular correspondence. Krauth was the leader. He had conceived quite an interest in the Lutheran confessions and in the old dogmaticians. Through his father he secured copies of Chemnitz, Gerhard, Calovius and Schmidt. These were circulated and discussed among the three. The more these young ministers studied these writings, the more firmly were they convinced that the old Lutheran faith is the faith taught in the Scriptures; and that the theology of Gettysburg and of the Observer was without either scriptural or confessional foundation" (*Passavant,* 167).

42 "The Lutheran and Missionary," *Lutheran and Missionary* (October 31, 1861); Charles Porterfield Krauth, "How the Marriage Came About," *Lutheran and Missionary* (October 31, 1861); Joseph A. Seiss, *Notes of My Life,* transcribed and edited by Henry E. Horn and William M. Horn (Huntingdon, PA: Church Management Service, 1982), 100.

echo of any nationalized species of Lutheranism. It cannot be permanently German or Scandinavian, out of Germany and Scandinavia, but in America must be American.[43]

At the same time, argued Krauth, *"we are not American Lutherans*, if to be such, means that we are to have a new faith, a mutilated confession, a life which abruptly breaks with all our history, a spirit alien to that of the genuine Lutheranism of the past."[44] Krauth clearly rejected the teaching of his teachers—a new day had dawned in English-speaking U.S. Lutheranism.[45]

The 1860s was a turbulent decade for the Lutheran Church yet one that also held tremendous promise. Amid an escalating war that threatened to divide the country once and for all, many Lutheran synods in North America were moving toward union. The General Synod of the Evangelical Lutheran Church in the Confederate States of America was formed out of the older General Synod. The General Council emerged from the break between the General Synod and the Pennsylvania Ministerium. Certainly there were differences and even schisms, but many hoped that by the end of the decade significant movement toward Lutheran unity might be realized.

The union that appeared imminent to some in 1866 was, sadly, unrealizable in the end. In some cases doctrinal differences proved insurmountable and fellowship was broken. Within the brief span of fifteen years, Lutheranism in the United States was rocked by two controversies that continued to affect Lutheran unity well into the twentieth century. The second, which does not concern Krauth directly, was the Predestination Controversy (1878–1938), which divided the fledgling Synodical Conference, sending the Missouri and Ohio Synods on diverging paths that were never fully rejoined.[46] The first controversy, concerning altar and pulpit fellowship in the General Council (1867–1889), was more complex in many ways because it involved issues of doctrine and practice.

Krauth, Seiss, Beale Schmucker, and Passavant provided the General Council (formed in 1867) with theological leadership throughout the next several decades. Among the four, Krauth and Seiss especially provided the intellectual and practi-

---

43 Charles Porterfield Krauth, "Where Do We Stand?" *Lutheran and Missionary* (October 31, 1861) (*original emphasis*).

44 Krauth, "Where Do We Stand?" (*original emphasis*).

45 Over time Krauth realized that his other responsibilities at both Lutheran Theological Seminary at Philadelphia and the University of Pennsylvania made his continued editing of the paper impossible, thus he resigned. See Charles Porterfield Krauth, "Retirement of the General Editor," *Lutheran and Missionary* (June 27, 1867).

46 See Hans Robert Haug, "The Predestination Controversy in the Lutheran Church in North America" (PhD diss., Temple University, 1968). For a more general history of this body, see Armin W. Schuetze, *The Synodical Conference: Ecumenical Endeavor* (Milwaukee: Northwestern, 2000).

cal energy that helped make the General Council a reality. After the Pennsylvania Ministerium was denied recognition at the General Synod of 1866, Krauth and his co-workers called for a new general body of Lutherans in the United States who "confessed the unaltered Augsburg Confession."[47] Thirteen separate Lutheran synods responded favorably to the proposal to a greater or lesser degree, including the conservative Missouri Synod. However, by the time of the General Council's constituting convention in Fort Wayne, Indiana—which was held November 20–26, 1867—the Missouri Synod no longer desired to participate. A moment when confessional Lutherans in North America might have moved solidly toward unity passed—and the effects remain apparent today.

Theologically, Krauth continued to mature. The nature of the Church and its place in history emerged as a key theme in his writing. Already in 1849, in an article titled "The Relation of Our Confessions to the Reformation" (which he later incorporated into *The Conservative Reformation*), Krauth traced the lineage of the Lutheran Church from the Early Church through Roman Catholicism, out of which emerged the Reformation. Krauth believed that the Roman Catholic Church, though in error, and seriously so on a number of points, was still Church. Luther and his co-workers were neither revolutionaries nor restorationists—they were reformers. As such, their aim was not the destruction of Rome but its correction.[48] Krauth wrote:

> The spirit of the Reformation was no destroying angel, who sat and scowled with a malignant joy over the desolation which spread around. It was overshadowed by the wings of that spirit who brooded indeed on the waste of waters and the wildness of chaos, but only that he might unfold the germs of life that lay hidden there, and bring forth light and order from the darkness of the yet formless and void creation.[49]

In this principle lies the idea of a conservative reformation, not evangelical radicalism. And from this it follows that "it is vastly more important, then, to know what the Reformation retained than what it overthrew; for the overthrow of error, though often an indispensable prerequisite to the establishment of the truth, is not truth itself; it may clear the foundation simply to substitute one error for another, perhaps greater for less. . . . The overthrow of Romanism was not its object at all."[50]

---

47 S. E. Ochsenford, *Documentary History of the General Council of the Evangelical Lutheran Church in North America* (Philadelphia: General Council Publication House, 1912), 128.

48 Charles Porterfield Krauth, "The Relation of Our Confessions to the Reformation, and the Importance of Their Study, with an Outline of the Early History of the Augsburg Confession," *Evangelical Review* 1 (October 1849): 234–63.

49 Krauth, "Relation of Our Confessions," 235.

50 Krauth, "Relation of Our Confessions," 235.

Certainly Krauth recognized error in Rome's theology and practice, but Rome is no more dangerous than those rationalists who extol their own ability to interpret the Scriptures apart from the common confession of the Church. The purpose of the historic confessions, the ecumenical creeds, and the entire Book of Concord is to guard against individualistic rationalism. Furthermore, these writings are not merely histories of the Reformation, they "are parts of the reformation itself. . . . In them you are brought into immediate contact with that sublime convulsion itself." Those who define the Church apart from its symbolical books do not differ from Rome.

Krauth believed that the Lutheran Church is the "mother church of restored Christianity."[51] Thus those who want to be assured that they are within the sheepfold should come in through the Lutheran gate. Alone among all communions, the Lutheran Church holds to the pure doctrine of Christ, based upon the writings of the apostles and prophets.

Helped by his reading of John Nevin, Krauth was fundamentally concerned that Lutheranism not fall into sectarianism. However, where this led Nevin to a more inclusive posture in his idea of the Reformation tradition, it drove Krauth to a more restrictive position. Nevin saw both the Lutherans and Reformed as necessary parts of the organically developing Church. Over time these two branches would come to produce a new synthesis, a more perfect expression of the Church of God on earth. On the other hand, Krauth saw the Lutheran Church as *the* true visible Church of God on earth, for it includes in itself all the essential features of the true Church:

> Our Church is *Reformed* as against all corruptions; *Protestant* as against the assertion of all false principles in Christian faith, life, and Church government; *Evangelical* as against all legalism and rationalism, against all restricted atonement and arbitrary limitation of God's love; and by a historical necessity, created not by herself but by her enemies, she is *Lutheran*, over against all perversions, mutilations, and misunderstandings of the Word under whatever name they may come, though that name be Reformed, Protestant, Evangelical, Catholic, or Christian, or by false assumption Lutheran itself. We claim, in a word, as the explanation of the being of the Lutheran Church, and of her right to be, that Lutheranism is pure Christianity.[52]

The Lutheran faith is the true faith; it is true religion. Other groups and sects are "religionisms" because they are a "perversion" of the religion. Religionisms are of two sorts: supra-ecclesiasticism, which is an externalization of the Church, as is

---

51 Charles Porterfield Krauth, "Religion and Religionisms," *Lutheran Church Review* 26 (January 1907): 230.

52 Krauth, "Religion and Religionisms," 230.

the case with Rome and the Church of England, and sub-ecclesiasticism, which reduces "the Church to the level of a mere voluntary organization, with no divine authority to give her being."[53] Supra-ecclesiasticism is not the greatest problem facing the Church. Sub-ecclesiasticism threatens the Church more because of its tendency toward unionism, which confirms the sin of sectarianism. "It is not the division which pains, but their discomfort of it. Sects are sorry, not for the sin, but for the penalty it brings, and the unionism of the day is trying to escape from God's punishment of the sin of sectarianism without abandoning the sin itself. Unionism does not mean to remove division, but to perpetuate and hallow it."[54]

Krauth was indeed a confessionalist. The sixteenth-century Confessions were the means by which the Lutheran Church defined itself. If one wanted to be assured that one held fully to the doctrines of Scripture, then one must subscribe unconditionally to the Book of Concord. Those who refuse to do so indicate that they will not fully accept the clear teaching of God's Word:

> [Confessions] mark those who are totally not against us, who are totally on our part. Hence, in the very act of forming a bond with all other Churches, as she and they contain a part of the Church invisible, in this very act, the Confessions draw a dividing line between the part of the Church visible—between that part which is of the Church visible in consequence of all its doctrines and in spite of none, and those parts which are of the Church visible in consequence of some of their doctrines and in spite of others.[55]

The Church made visible in the former sense is the Lutheran Church, while other Christian denominations have placed themselves into the latter category.

Krauth's last years were spent embroiled in the practical implications of the position outlined above. The General Council itself nearly divided over the questions of Communion fellowship and altar fellowship with Christians of other traditions. So intense did the controversy become that the long-standing friendship of Krauth and Joseph Seiss was stretched to the breaking point. Seiss offered an olive branch in the August 2, 1877, *Lutheran and Missionary*. In an article titled "A Pair of Twin Biographies," Seiss outlined the close relationship that he and Krauth had enjoyed throughout their ministerial lives. The two served several of the same congregations (Lombard Street in Baltimore; Shepherdstown/Martinsburg, Virginia; and, while Seiss was abroad, St. John's in Philadelphia), corresponded regularly, and developed a relationship to the point that Krauth at one point suggested the two form "a mutual compact never to allow ourselves to be separated in friendship and devotion one to the other, or to suffer anything to

---

53 Krauth, "Religion and Religionisms," 237.
54 Krauth, "Religion and Religionisms," 239–40.
55 Krauth, "Religion and Religionisms," 239–40.

divide us while we lived."[56] But as close as they were, serious tension developed in their relationship. Once Seiss wrote to Krauth to ask about a note that appeared in the *Lutheran Observer* that claimed that Krauth had stated that "Dr. Seiss was the most, or one of the most un-Lutheran men" in the Lutheran Church. Krauth denied having made the statement and defended Seiss as "among the most earnest and most effective defenders of the faith of our Church."[57] But this interchange merely anticipated future deeper divisions.

When the controversy over pulpit and altar fellowship broke out in earnest following the adoption of the Akron Rule (1872) and the Galesburg Declaration (1875), the friendship the two men shared was nearly destroyed. Krauth and Seiss fell on different sides when the question was put to the Church, and they found it difficult not to allow their theological differences to interfere with their friendship. So pronounced did the animosity become that Seiss wrote to Krauth in January 1879 seeking an explanation for the rift between them. Krauth responded with great vigor and clarity. Seiss rejoiced at Krauth's frankness and responded in kind, yet ended on a note of hope that differences in conviction "need not hinder us from being personal friends." According to Seiss's account, the exchange "materially thinned and scattered" the cloud that lay between them. "We met again as friends, exchanged letters of kindness, and continued in brotherly fellowship, working together as far as his failing health permitted, until his death."[58]

Death arrived early. Charles Porterfield Krauth died on January 2, 1883.[59] His death was not unexpected because his health had clearly declined over several years preceding his death. The controversy over altar and pulpit fellowship, coupled with his intense work schedule, certainly contributed to Krauth's premature death. Still, with his passing, grief filled many. C. F. W. Walther of the LCMS captured the feelings of many:

> Herewith a heavy blow is fallen, not only upon the General Council . . . but at the same time upon the whole American Lutheran Church. For the blessed one was indeed the most prominent man in the English Lutheran church of this country, a man of unusual learning, at home not less in the old than in the new theology, and, what is the chief thing, in hearty accord with the doctrine of his Church, as he had leaned to know it; a noble man without guile.[60]

---

56 Seiss, *Notes of My Life*, 234.

57 Seiss, *Notes of My Life*, 234.

58 Seiss, *Notes of My Life*, 238. See also Rast, "Seiss and the Lutheran Church in America," ch. 4.

59 Donald L. Huber, "The Controversy over Pulpit and Altar Fellowship in the General Council of the Evangelical Lutheran Church, 1866–1889" (PhD diss., Duke University, 1971), 219–22.

60 Henry D. Steffens, *Doctor Carl Ferdinand Wilhelm Walther* (Philadelphia: Lutheran Publication Society, 1917), 392–93.

Seiss perhaps captured the loss of Krauth best: "There can be no question, that the English part of our Church, if not the entire Lutheran Church in this country, has lost its greatest and best informed theologian in the death of our deceased brother and fellow laborer DR. CHARLES PORTERFIELD KRAUTH."[61]

THE CONSERVATIVE REFORMATION AND ITS THEOLOGY

Krauth's magnum opus, *The Conservative Reformation and Its Theology*, brings two decades of his scholarship together into what he believed was a definitive statement of confessional Lutheranism, that is, restored Christianity in it purest form. Krauth interpreted the Augsburg Confession through the spectrum of the Formula of Concord, thus he came to the restrictive conclusion, not the inclusive. In the preface of this book, Krauth states his views on church history and the Reformation:

> The history of Christianity, in common with all genuine history, moves under the influence of two generic ideas: the conservative, which desires to secure the present by fidelity to the results of the past; the progressive, which looks out, in hope, to a better future. Reformation is the great harmonizer of the two principles. Corresponding with Conservatism, Reformation and Progress are three generic types of Christianity; and under these *genera* all the species are but shades, modifications, or combinations, as all hues rise from three primary colors. Conservatism without Progress produces the Romish and Greek type of the Church. Progress without Conservatism runs into Revolution, Radicalism, and Sectarianism. Reformation is antithetical both to passive persistence in wrong or passive endurance of it, and to Revolution as a mode of relieving wrong. Conservatism is opposed to Radicalism both in the estimate of wrong and the mode of getting rid of it. Radicalism errs in two respects: in its precipitance it often mistakes wheat for tares, and its eradication is so hasty and violent that even when it plucks up tares it brings the wheat with them. Sober judgment and sober means characterize Conservatism. Reformation and Conservatism really involve each other. That which claims to be Reformatory, yet is not Conservative, is Sectarian; that which claims to be Conservative, and is

---

61 Joseph A. Seiss, "In Memory of Dr. Krauth," *Lutheran and Missionary* (March 8, 1883) (*original emphasis*). The article also states: "That for which the church will ever most admire and commend our lamented brother, was, his Supreme devotion to the Gospel of Christ, and his great and lasting services in behalf of the faith, history and cultus of our own Evangelical Lutheran Church. His heart and home, his life and highest being were ever in these. He knew our Church, and he loved it. He understood the faith, and he gave his best energies to its exposition, inculcation, and defense against all assailants, of whatever name. His other works were great, and will have their future; but his productions in the special interests of our Church, which he held to be pre-eminently the realization of the Church of Christ on earth, and will ever be dear to Lutherans as among the choice products of the last thirty years, and will have their weight and influence for many a generation."

not Reformatory, is Stagnation and Corruption. True Catholicity is Conservatism, but Protestantism is Reformatory; and these two are complementary, not antagonistic. The Church problem is to attain a Protestant Catholicity or Catholic Protestantism. This is the end and aim of Conservative Reformation.[62]

Obviously, the volume is a mammoth offering. Collecting and supplementing articles authored over two decades, it united Krauth's mature thinking on the nature of the Reformation, the question of Lutheran identity, and the relationship of the Lutheran Church to the broader Christian tradition, and it emphasized what Krauth thought was the theological center of Lutheranism. Chapters 5, 6, and 7 are the heart of the book, vigorously articulating Krauth's understanding of confessional Lutheranism and its unique theological identity. These chapters are supported in careful and extended treatments of the distinctive Lutheran teaching of original sin, the person of Christ, Baptism, and the Lord's Supper. In all of them, Krauth shows that all doctrine is centered in the person and work of Christ.

What is most refreshing is how seamlessly Krauth brings together the theoretical and the practical. For him there is no abstract theology, useful only in the classroom of the theologian/philosopher.[63] Rather, these words of Christ are words of life, life for the individual and life for the Church. Krauth did not achieve this remarkable integration haphazardly but intentionally. As he wrote: "The plan of this book is, in some respects, new. It aims at bringing under a single point of view what is usually scattered throughout different classes of books. It endeavors to present the Exegesis, the Dogmatical and Confessional development, and the History associated with each doctrine, with a full list of the most important writers in the literature of each topic."[64]

Krauth had been a longtime combatant in the battle for Lutheran identity in the United States. Not surprisingly, his familiarity with polemical theology also found its way into *The Conservative Reformation*. "The life of a Church may be largely read in its controversies," he wrote.

---

62 Krauth, *Conservative Reformation*, xxxix–xl.

63 Widely known for his theological and historical expertise, Krauth was also a careful student of the Scriptures. He participated in the translation and revision work that produced the English Revised Version of the Bible (1881–1885). See Isaac H. Hall, ed., *The Revised New Testament and History of Revision* (Philadelphia: Hubbard Brothers; Atlanta: C. R. Blackall; New York: A. L. Bancroft, 1881). He also produced a fascinating hermeneutical work on typology: *Christ and His Kingdom in Shadows: or, The Christian Dispensation, as Typified in the Old Testament, and Especially in the Mosaic Rites and Ceremonies, in The Holy Bible* (Philadelphia: John Potter, 1883).

64 Krauth, *Conservative Reformation*, xliv.

As the glory or shame of a nation is read upon its battle-fields which tells for what it perilled the lives of its sons, so may the glory or shame of a Church be determined when we know what it fought for and what it fought against; how much it valued what it believed to be truth; what was the truth it valued; how much it did, and how much it suffered to maintain that truth, and what was the issue of its struggles and sacrifices.[65]

Despite its favorable reception, some of Krauth's colleagues were disappointed with the book. Much of the material had appeared in previous contexts. For example, the chapter titled "The Lord's Supper Thetically Stated" was first published in the *Mercersburg Review*; substantial portions of Krauth's "The Relation of Our Confessions to the Reformation" appeared in the *Evangelical Review*; and Krauth first wrote the section on the three phases of error's course in the Church for the *Lutheran and Missionary*.[66] However, the manner in which he synthesized these writings under the thesis of the work joined the various documents together to provide a powerful attestation to the catholicity of the doctrine and practice of the Lutheran Church. The clarity of the volume helped dissipate the disappointments, and it quickly earned its place as a classic work in the field of American Lutheranism.

Krauth's old friend John Nevin recognized *The Conservative Reformation* as just such a volume in an extended review of the book.[67] Expressing his delight over the publication of the volume, he marveled that U.S. Lutheranism had come so far in such a short time from the sectarianism of Schmucker and Kurtz. Noting rightly that "the cause here maintained is not just that of Protestantism over against the Roman Catholic Church," Nevin approved of Krauth's simultaneous critique of the "radical and unsound" Reformation.[68] In this respect, claimed Nevin, Krauth perfectly captured Luther: "In no view does the character of Luther appear so great, and his cause so worthy of admiration, as in the successful stand he was enabled to make against the fanatical and radical tendencies of his times, which, coming in like a flood, and pretending to make common cause with him in his opposition to Rome, threatened to involve the whole movement in confusion

---

65 Krauth, *Conservative Reformation*, 147.

66 Charles Porterfield Krauth, "The New Testament Doctrine of the Lord's Supper, As Confessed by the Evangelical Lutheran Church, Thetically Stated, with the Exegetical Argument," *Mercersburg Review* 17 (April 1870): 165–242; for Krauth, "Relation of Our Confessions to the Reformation," see xxiii n. 48; Charles Porterfield Krauth, "Three Stages," *Lutheran and Missionary* (June 15, 1865).

67 John W. Nevin, "Krauth's Conservative Reformation," *Reformed Church Messenger* (October 4, October 11, December 6, December 13, December 20, December 27, 1871; January 3, January 10, January 17, January 24, January 31, February 21, March 13, March 20, 1872).

68 Nevin, "Krauth's Conservative Reformation," *Reformed Church Messenger* (October 4, 1871).

and shame."[69] The key to Lutheranism, Nevin believed, was its conservative nature. Where Krauth argued that "it is more important to know what the Reformation retained than what it overthrew," Nevin stated: "The mightiest weapon which the Reformation employed against Rome was, not Rome's errors, but Rome's truths."[70]

Not all received the book with the same approval. The *Lutheran Observer* received it very coolly.[71] Other communions received the volume antagonistically. Isaac T. Hecker, a Roman Catholic priest, violently rejected Krauth's thesis. "The simple fact is, there is no defence of the so-called Reformation on catholic, church, or conservative principles," he wrote. "It sought to reform the faith, and to change the very constitution of the church, and wherever it was successful, it proved to be the subversion of the church, and the destruction of her faith, her authority and her worship."[72] Hecker concluded:

> Let our learned Lutheran professor remove the film from his eyes, and look at her in her simple grandeur, her unadorned majesty, and see how mean and contemptible, compared with her, are all the so-called churches, sects, and combinations arrayed against her, spitting blasphemy at her, and in their satanic malice trying to sully her purity or dim the glory that crowns her. Say what you will, Protestantism is a petty affair, and it is one of the mysteries of this life how a man of the learning, intelligence, apparent sincerity, and good sense of Dr. Krauth can write an octavo volume of eight hundred closely printed pages in defense of the Protestant Reformation.[73]

Time has provided the space for more balanced critiques of the work. When a reprint of the book appeared in the 1960s, Verlyn Smith noted that the volume showed its age in its vigorous polemics, a discordant note to the ecumenical tune of the late twentieth century. Nevertheless, Smith was convinced of the volume's enduring value:

> No, this book ought not die. While its chief value is its role as a window to another time, it has a contribution to make to theology today, particularly on the parish and lay level. There are parallels between the 1860's and the 1960's.

---

69 Nevin, "Krauth's Conservative Reformation," *Reformed Church Messenger* (December 20, 1871).

70 Nevin, "Krauth's Conservative Reformation," *Reformed Church Messenger* (January 17, 1871).

71 Nevin noted that "the Lutheran Observer is throwing out his anathemas against you . . . but He that has promised, that He will be with His Church and that the gates of hell shall not prevail against it, will make all their machinations come to naught" ("Krauth's Conservative Reformation," [October 4, 1871]).

72 Isaac T. Hecker, "The Reformation not Conservative," *The Catholic World* 13 (September 1871): 728–29.

73 Hecker, "Reformation not Conservative," 737.

The "sectarianism" of which Krauth spoke is still with us, though we would perhaps label it differently. Krauth was writing in opposition to a repristinatory, unhistorical, anti-sacramental, unchurchly view of Christianity and against those who would interpret the reformation in terms of radical freedom. He is trying, however successfully he achieves it, to emphasize continuity rather than discontinuity, catholicism rather than enthusiasm. . . . In the America of Billy Graham and Harvey Cox it would seem to suggest a very different way to look at the task of the Church in the world.[74]

Nevin stated that "Dr. Krauth is known as one of the first writers of our country. The gentleman, the Christian, and the scholar, are happily blended in this person. He is one of the pillars of his own Church on this side of the Atlantic, and one of the ornaments of our American Christianity."[75] For these reasons, at least, Smith is right: "This book ought not die." Thanks to the efforts of the Rev. Frederick Davison in producing the electronic text and Concordia Publishing House, especially the Rev. Mark Sell, in reducing the electronic text to paper, it will not. Through this book the voice of one of the most remarkable Lutheran theologians in the United States will continue to be heard.

May the reading of this book delight, inform, and challenge you as it has so many over the century and a quarter since it first appeared.

Lawrence R. Rast Jr.
August 31, 2006

---

74 Verlyn O. Smith, "Krauth on *The Conservative Reformation*," *Una Sancta* 24 (1967): 79.

75 Nevin, "Krauth's Conservative Reformation," (October 4, 1871).

CHARLES PORTERFIELD KRAUTH
(1823–1883)

March 17, 1823	Born at Martinsburg, Berkeley County, Virginia, son of Lutheran minister Charles Philip Krauth.
1831–1839	Attended Gettysburg Gymnasium, which later became Pennsylvania College.
1839–1841	Attended Theological Seminary at Gettysburg, Pennsylvania.
October 16, 1841	Licensed to preach by the Maryland Synod.
1841–1843	Pastor at Canton, Maryland, a mission congregation.
1843–1847	Pastor of Second English Lutheran Church, Baltimore, Maryland.
November 12, 1844	Married Susan Reynolds.
June 1847	Became pastor at Shepherdstown, Virginia. In November began to serve Martinsburg, Virginia.
March 1848	Accepted a call to Winchester, Virginia. During this general period, Krauth became more confessionally oriented.
1853	First wife died.
May 1855	Married Virginia Baker.
1855–1859	Pastor at English Lutheran Church, Pittsburgh, Pennsylvania.
1856	Awarded honorary doctorate by Pennsylvania College.
1856	Rejected Schmucker's "Definite Platform."[1]
October 1859	Became pastor at St. Mark, Philadelphia, Pennsylvania.

---

1 For more information regarding this subject, see Charles Porterfield Krauth, "Testimony of the Synod of Pittsburgh," in *Memorial History of the Pittsburgh Synod*, by E. B. Burgess (Greenville, PA: Beaver Printing, 1925), 105–8.

1861	Became editor of the *Lutheran and Missionary* (until 1867).
October 4, 1864	Installed as professor at Lutheran Theological Seminary, Philadelphia, Pennsylvania.
1866	Is named trustee of the University of Pennsylvania.
1866–1867	Played a major role in founding the General Council; contributed *Fundamental Principles of Faith and Church Polity* and *Theses on Pulpit and Altar Fellowship.*
1868	Appointed professor of mental and moral philosophy at the University of Pennsylvania.
1868–1888	The controversy in the General Council over the "Four Points," specifically altar and pulpit fellowship.
1871	*The Conservative Reformation and Its Theology* published.
1873	Appointed vice provost of the University of Pennsylvania.
1874	Awarded honorary Doctor of Laws degree by Pennsylvania College.
1882	Appointed professor of history at the University of Pennsylvania.
January 2, 1883	Died in Philadelphia and buried in Laurel Hill Cemetery.

Charles Porterfield Krauth
(1823–1883)

Select Bibliography

Books

The Altar on the Threshing Floor. Pittsburgh: W. S. Haven, 1857.

Baptism: The Doctrine Set Forth in Holy Scripture and Taught in the Evangelical Lutheran Church. Gettysburg: J. B. Wible, 1866.

The Bible a Perfect Book. Gettysburg: H. C. Neinstedt, 1857.

The Benefits of the Pastoral Office: A Farewell Discourse. Baltimore: Sherwood, 1845.

Caesar and God; or, Politics and Religion. A Sermon. Philadelphia: Lutheran Book Store, 1874.

Christian Liberty. Philadelphia: Henry B. Ashmead, 1860.

A Chronicle of the Augsburg Confession. Philadelphia: J. Frederick Smith, 1878.

The Conservative Reformation and Its Theology. Philadelphia: J. B. Lippincott, 1871.

Cosmos: In the Rhymes of a Summer Holiday Journey. Philadelphia: G. W. Fredrick, 1881.

The Evangelical Lutheran Church: Her Glory, Perils, Defence, Victory, Duty, and Perpetuity. Philadelphia: Smith, English, 1863.

The Former Days and These Days. Pittsburgh: W. S. Haven, 1856.

Infant Baptism in the Calvinistic System. Philadelphia: Lutheran Book Store, 1874.

The Liturgical Movement in the Presbyterian and Reformed Churches. Philadelphia: Lutheran Book Store, n.d.

The Lutheran Church and the Divine Obligation of the Lord's Day. Gettysburg: H. C. Neinstedt, 1856.

Oration on the Advantages Arising to the American Student from His Access to German Literature by Means of the Knowledge of the German Language. Getttysburg: H. C. Neinstedt, 1832.

Popular Amusements. Winchester: Senseney & Coffroth, 1852.

Poverty: Its Perpetuity, Causes and Relief. Pittsburgh: W. S. Haven, 1858.

The Reformation: Its Occasions and Cause. 1869.

Religion and Religionisms. Philadelphia: The Students of the Evangelical Lutheran Seminary, 1877.

Select Analytical Bibliography of the Augsburg Confession. Gettysburg: H. C. Neinstedt, 1858.

The Sunday Service according to the Liturgies of the Churches of the Reformation. Gettysburg: H. C. Neinstedt, 1853.

The Transfiguration, An Exegetical Homily. Gettysburg: H. C. Neinstedt, 1850.

The Two Pageants. Pittsburgh: W. S. Haven, 1865.

A Vocabulary of the Philosophical Sciences. New York: Sheldon, 1885.

ARTICLES

"The Person and Work of Christ." *Mercersburg Review* 1 (May 1849): 272–306.

"The Relation of Our Confessions to the Reformation, and the Importance of Their Study, with an Outline of the Early History of the Augsburg Confession." *Evangelical Quarterly Review* 1 (October 1849): 234–63.

"Luther's Translation of the Holy Scriptures: The New Testament." *Mercersburg Review* 16 (April 1869): 180–200.

"The Liturgical Movement in the Presbyterian and Reformed Churches." *Mercersburg Review* 16 (October 1869): 598–647.

"The New Testament Doctrine of the Lord's Supper, as Confessed by the Evangelical Lutheran Church, Thetically Stated, with the Exegetical Argument." *Mercersburg Review* 17 (April 1870): 165–242.

"The Western Liturgy." *Mercersburg Review* 18 (January 1871): 92–114.

"Church Polity." *Lutheran Church Review* 2 (October 1883): 307–23; (April 1884): 139–51; (October 1884): 320–34.

"Luther, Melanchthon and the Augsburg Confession." *Lutheran Church Review* 16 (January 1897): 101–4.

"The Denominational Question." *Lutheran Church Review* 26 (January 1904): 317–24.

"Religion and Religionisms." *Lutheran Church Review* 26 (January 1907): 227–63.

"One Faith." *Lutheran Church Review* 26 (January 1907): 264–75.

"Galesburg Declaration on Pulpit and Altar Fellowship, Prepared by Order of the General Council." *Lutheran Church Review* 27 (January 1908): 129; (April 1908): 321–30.

The Conservative Reformation and Its Theology

PREFACE

That some form of Christianity is to be the religion of the world, is not only an assured fact to the believer in Revelation, but must be regarded as probable, even in the judgment which is formed on purely natural evidence. Next in transcendent importance to that fact, and beyond it in present interest, as a question relatively undecided, is the question, *What* form of Christianity is to conquer the world? Shall it be the form in which Christianity now exists, the form of intermingling and of division, of internal separation and warfare? Is the territory of Christendom forever to be divided between antagonistic communions, or occupied by them conjointly? Shall there be to the end of time the Greek, the Roman, the Protestant churches, the sects, and the heretical bodies? Or shall one or other of these specific forms lift itself above the tangled mass, and impose order on chaos? Or shall a form yet unrevealed prove the church of the future? To this the answer seems to be, that the logic of the question, supported by eighteen centuries of history, renders it probable that some principle, or some combination of principles now existent, will assuredly, however slowly, determine the ultimate, world-dominating type of Christianity. Unless there be an exact balance of force in the different tendencies, the internally strongest of them will ultimately prevail over the others, and, unless a new force superior to it comes in, will be permanent.

The history of Christianity, in common with all genuine history, moves under the influence of two generic ideas: the conservative, which desires to secure the present by fidelity to the results of the past; the progressive, which looks out, in hope, to a better future. Reformation is the great harmonizer of the two principles. Corresponding with Conservatism, Reformation, and Progress are three generic types of Christianity; and under these *genera* all the species are but shades, modifications, or combinations, as all hues arise from three primary colors. Conservatism without Progress produces the Romish and Greek type of the Church. Progress without Conservatism runs into Revolution. Radicalism, and Sectarianism. Reformation is antithetical both to passive persistence in wrong or passive endurance of it, and to Revolution as a mode of relieving wrong. Conservatism is opposed to Radicalism both in the estimate of wrong and the mode of getting rid of it. Radicalism errs in two respects: in its precipitance it often mistakes wheat for tares, and its eradication is so hasty and violent that even when it plucks up tares it brings the wheat with them. Sober judgment and sober means characterizes Conservatism. Reformation and Conservatism really involve each other. That which claims to be Reformatory, yet is not Conservative is Sectarian; that which claims to be Conservative, and is not Reformatory, is Stagnation and Corruption. True Catholicity is Conservatism, but Protestantism is Reformatory; and these two are complementary, not antagonistic. The Church problem is to attain a Protestant Catholicity or Catholic Protestantism. This is the end and aim of Conservative Reformation.

Reformation is the means by which Conservatism of the good that is, and progress to the good yet to be won, is secured. Over against the stagnation of an isolated Conservatism, the Church is to hold Reformation as the instrument of progress. Over against the abuses of a separatistic and one-sided progressiveness, she is to see to it that her Reformation maintains that due reverence for history, that sobriety of tone, that patience of spirit, and that moderation of manner, which are involved in Conservatism. The good that has been is necessary to the safety of the good that is to be. There are to be no absolutely fresh starts. If the foundation were removed, the true course would not be to make a new one, but to find the old one, and lay it again. But the foundation never was wholly lost, nor was there, in the worst time of the accumulation of wood, hay, and stubble, an utter ceasing of the building of gold, silver, and precious stones upon it. The Reformation, as Christian, accepted the old foundation; as reformatory, it removed the wood, hay, and stubble; as conservative, it carefully separated, guarded, and retained the gold, silver, and precious stones, the additions of pious human hands, befitting the foundation and the temple which was to be reared upon it. Rome had accumulated greatly and given up nothing, till the foundation upheld little but perishing human traditions, and the precious things were lost in the heaps of rubbish. The revolutionary spirit of the radical Reform proposed to leave nothing but the foundation, to sweep from it everything which had been built upon it. The Conservative, equally accepting the foundation which has been laid once for all, proposed to leave on it everything precious, pure, and beautiful which had risen in the ages. The one proposed to pull down the temple; the other, to purify it, and to replace its weak and decayed portions with solid rock. The great work of the sixteenth century, which bears the generic title of the Reformation, was divided between these tendencies; not, indeed, absolutely to the last extreme, but yet really divided. The whole Protestant movement in the Church of the West was reformatory as over against papal Rome, and was so far a unit; but it was divided within itself, between the conservative and radical tendencies. The conservative tendency embodied itself in the Reformation, in which Luther was the leader; the radical, in Zwingle and his school. Calvin came in to occupy a relatively mediating position—conservative as compared with the ultraism of Zwinglianism, and of the heretical tendencies which Zwinglianism at once nurtured, yet, relatively to Lutheranism, largely radical.

The Church of England is that part of the Reformed Church for which most affinity with the conservatism of Lutheranism is usually claimed. That Church occupies a position in some respects unique. First, under Henry VIII., ceasing to be Popish without ceasing to be Romish; then passing under the influences of genuine reformation into the positively Lutheran type; then influenced by the mediating position of the school of Bucer, and of the later era of Melanchthon, a school which claimed the ability practically to co-ordinate the Lutheran and Calvinistic positions; and finally settling into a system of compromise, in which is revealed the influence of the Roman Catholic views of Orders in the ministry, and, to some extent, of the Ritual; of the Lutheran tone of reformatory conservatism, in the general structure of the Liturgy, in the larger part of the Articles, and especially in the doctrine of Baptism; of the mediating theology in the doctrine of predestination; and of Calvinism in particular changes in the Book of Common Prayer, and, most of all, in the doctrine of the Lord's Supper. The Conservatism of the Church of England, even in the later shape of its reform, in many respects is indubitable, and hence it has often been called a Lutheranizing Church. But the pressure of the radicalism to which it deferred, perhaps too much in the essence and too little in the form, brought it to that eclecticism which is its most marked feature. Lutheranizing, in its conservative sobriety of modes, the Church of England is very un-Lutheran in its judgment of ends. The conservatism of the Lutheran Reformation exalted, over all, pure doctrine as the divine presupposition of a pure life, and this led to an ample and explicit statement of faith. While the Church of England stated doctrines so that men understood its utterances in different ways, the Lutheran Church tried so to state them that men could accept them in but one sense. If one expression was found inadequate for this, she gave another. The Lutheran Church has her Book of Concord, the most explicit Confession ever made in Christendom; the Church of England has her Thirty-nine Articles, the least explicit among the official utterances of the Churches of the Reformation.

The Eclectic Reformation is like the Eclectic Philosophy,—it accepts the common affirmation of the different systems, and refuses their negations. Like the English language, the English Church is a miracle of compositeness. In the wonderful tessellation of their structure is the strength of both, and their weakness. The English language is two languages inseparably conjoined. It has the strength and affluence of the two, and something of the awkwardness necessitated by their union. The Church of England has two great elements; but they are not perfectly preserved in their distinctive character, but, to some extent, are confounded in the union. With more uniformity than any other great Protestant body, it has less unity than any. Partly in virtue of its doctrinal indeterminateness, it has been the home of men of the most opposite opinions: no Calvinism is intenser, no Arminianism lower, than the Calvinism and Arminianism which have been found in the Church of England. It has furnished able defenders of Augustine, and no less able defenders of Pelagius. Its Articles, Homilies, and Liturgy have been a great bulwark of Protestantism; and yet, seemingly, out of the very stones of that bulwark has been framed, in our day, a bridge on which many have passed over into Rome. It has a long array of names dear to our common Christendom as the masterly vindicators of her common faith, and yet has given high place to men who denied the fundamental verities confessed in the general creeds. It harbors a skepticism which takes infidelity by the hand, and a revised mediævalism which longs to throw itself, with tears, on the neck of the Pope and the Patriarch, to beseech them to be gentle, and not to make the terms of restored fellowship too difficult. The doctrinal indeterminateness which has won has also repelled, and made it an object of suspicion not only to great men of the most opposite opinions, but also to great bodies of Christians. It has a doctrinal laxity which excuses, and, indeed, invites, innovation, conjoined with an organic fixedness which prevents the free play of the novelty. Hence the Church of England has been more depleted than any other, by secessions. Either the Anglican Church must come to more fixedness in doctrine or to more pliableness in form, or it will go on, through cycle after cycle of disintegration, toward ruin. In this land, which seems the natural heritage of that Church which claims the Church of England as its mother, the Protestant Episcopal Church is numerically smallest among the influential denominations. Its great social strength and large influence in every direction only render more striking the fact that there is scarcely a Church, scarcely a sect, having in common with it an English original, which is not far in advance of it in statistical strength. Some of the largest communions have its rigidity in form, some of the largest have its looseness in doctrine; but no other large communion attempts to combine both. The numbers of those whom the Church of England has lost are millions. It has lost to Independency, lost to Presbyterianism, lost to Quakerism, lost to Methodism, lost to Romanism, and lost to the countless forms of Sectarianism of which England and America, England's daughter, have been, beyond all nations, the nurses. The Church of England has been so careful of the rigid old bottle of the form, yet so careless or so helpless as to what the bottle might be made to hold, that the new wine which went into it has been attended in every case by the same history,—the fermenting burst the bottle, and the wine was spilled. Every great religious movement in the Church of England has been attended ultimately by an irreparable loss in its membership. To this rule there has been no exception in the past. Whether the present movement which convulses the Church of England and the Protestant Episcopal Church in America, is to have the same issue, belongs, perhaps, rather to the prophet's eye than to the historian's pen. Yet to those who, though they stand without, look on with profound sympathy, the internal difficulties which now agitate those Churches seem incapable of a real, abiding harmonizing. True compromise can only sacrifice preferences to secure principles. The only compromise which seems possible in the Anglican Churches would be one which would sacrifice principles to secure preferences, and nothing can be less certain of permanence than preferences thus secured. These present difficulties in the Anglican Churches proceed not from contradiction of its principles, but from development of them. These two classes of seeds were sown by the husbandmen themselves,—that was the compromise. The tares may grow till the harvest, side by side with the wheat, with which they mingle, but which they do not destroy, but the thorns which choke the seed must be plucked up, or the seed will perish. Tares are men; thorns are moral forces of doctrine or of life. The agitation in the Anglican Churches can end only in the victory of the one tendency and the silencing of the other, or in the sundering of the two. In Protestantism nothing is harder than to silence, nothing easier than to sunder. If the past history of the Anglican Church, hitherto unvaried in the ultimate result, repeat itself here, the new movement will end in a formal division, as it already has in a moral one. The trials of a Church which has taken a part in our modern civilization and Christianity which entitles it to the veneration and gratitude of mankind, can be regarded with indifference only by the sluggish and selfish, and with malicious joy only by the radically bad.

The classification of Churches by tendencies is, of course, relative. No great organization moves so absolutely along the line of a single tendency as to have nothing in it beyond that tendency, or contradictory to it. The wilfulness of some, the feeble-mindedness of others, the power of surrounding influences, modify all systems in their actual working. There was some conservatism in the Swiss reformation, and there has been and is something of the reformatory tendency in the Church of Rome. The Reformation took out a very large part of the best material influenced by this tendency in Rome, but not all of it.

The object of this book is not to delineate the spirit and doctrines of the Reformation as a general movement over against the doctrinal and practical errors of the Roman Church, but to state and vindicate the faith and spirit of that part of the movement which was conservative, as over against the part which was radical. It is the Lutheran Reformation in those features which distinguish it from the Zwinglian and Calvinistic Reformations, which forms the topic of this book. Wherever Calvin abandoned Zwinglianism he approximated Lutheranism. Hence, on important points, this book, in defending Lutheranism over against Zwinglianism, defends Calvinism over against Zwinglianism also. It even defends Zwinglianism, so far as, in contrast with Anabaptism, it was relatively conservative. The Pelagianism of the Zwinglian theology was corrected by Calvin, who is the true father of the Reformed Church, as distinguished from the Lutheran. The theoretical tendencies of Zwingle developed into Arminianism and Rationalism; his practical tendencies into the superstitious anti-ritualism of ultra-Puritanism: and both the theoretical and practical found their harmony and consummation in Unitarianism.

The plan of this book is, in some respects, new. It aims at bringing under a single point of view what is usually scattered through different classes of books. It endeavors to present the Exegesis, the Dogmatical and Confessional development, and the History associated with each doctrine, with a full list of the most important writers in the literature of each topic. Its rule is, whether the views stated are accepted or rejected, to give them in the words of their authors. The citations from other languages are always translated, but when the original words have a disputed meaning, or a special force or importance, they are also quoted. The author has, as nearly as he was able, given to the book such an internal completeness as to render it unnecessary to refer to other works while reading it. While he has aimed at something of the thoroughness which the scholar desires, he has also endeavored to meet the wants of that important and growing class of readers who have all the intelligence needed for a full appreciation of the matter of a book, but are repelled by the technical difficulties of form suggested by the pedantry of authors, or permitted by their carelessness or indolence.

So far as the author's past labors were available for the purposes of this work, he has freely used them. In no case has a line been allowed to stand which does not express a present conviction, not simply as to what is true, but as to the force of the grounds on which its truth is argued. In what has been taken from his articles in Reviews, and in other periodicals, he has changed, omitted, and added, in accordance with a fresh study of all the topics. He has also drawn upon some of the Lectures delivered by him to his theological classes, and thankfully acknowledges the use, for this purpose, of the notes made by his pupils, Rev. F. W. Weiskotten, of Elizabethtown, Pa., and Messrs. Bieber and Foust. To Lloyd P. Smith, Esq.,

Librarian, and to Mr. George, M. Abbot, Assistant Librarian, of the Philadelphia and Loganian Libraries, the author is indebted for every possible facility in the use of those valuable collections.

An Index has been prepared, in which the effort has been made to avoid the two generic vices of a scantiness which leaves the reader in perplexity, and a minuteness which confuses him.

The positions taken in this book are largely counter, in some respects, to the prevailing theology of our time and our land. No man can be more fixed in his prejudice against the views here defended than the author himself once was; no man can be more decided in his opinion that those views are false than the author is now decided in his faith that they are the truth. They have been formed in the face of all the influences of education and of bitter hatred or of contemptuous disregard on the part of nearly all who were most intimately associated with him in the period of struggle. Formed under such circumstances, under what he believes to have been the influence of the Divine Word, the author is persuaded that they rest upon grounds which cannot easily be moved. In its own nature his work is, in some degree, polemical; but its conflict is purely with opinions, never with persons. The theme itself, as it involves questions within our common Protestantism, renders the controversy principally one with defects or errors in systems least remote in the main from the faith vindicated in this volume. It is most needful that those nearest each other should calmly argue the questions which still divide them, as there is most hope that those already so largely in affinity may come to a yet more perfect understanding.

The best work of which isolated radicalism is capable is that of destroying evil. The more earnestly radicalism works, the sooner is its mission accomplished. Conservatism works to a normal condition, and rests at last in habit. Radicalism presupposes the abnormal. Itself an antithesis, it dies with the thing it kills. The long, fixed future must therefore be in the hands of conservatism in some shape; either in the hands of a mechanical conservatism, as in the Church of Rome, or of a reformatory conservatism, as represented in that historical and genuine Protestantism which is as distinct from the current sectarianism, in some respects, as it is from Romanism in others. The purest Protestantism, that which best harmonizes conservatism and reformation, will ultimately control the thinking of the Christian Church. The volume which the reader holds in his hand is meant to set forth some of the reasons in view of which those who love the Evangelical Protestant Church, commonly called the Lutheran Church, hope to find pardon for their conviction that in it is found the most perfect assimilation and co-ordination of the two forces. It has conserved as thoroughly as is consistent with real reformation; it has reformed as unsparingly as is consistent with genuine conservatism. The objective concreteness of the old Apostolic Catholicity, Rome has exaggerated and materialized till the senses master the soul, they should serve. The subjective spirituality of New Testament Christianity is isolated by the Pseudo-Protestantism, which drags the mutilated organism of the Church after it as a body of death from which it would fain be delivered, and which it drops at length, altogether, to wander a melancholy ghost, or to enter on the endless metempsychosis of sectarianism. To distinguish without separating, and to combine without confusing, has been the problem of the Lutheran Church. It has distinguished between the form of Christianity and the essence, but has bound them together inseparably: the Reformatory has made sacred the individual life and liberty, the Conservative has sanctified the concrete order. Nor is this claim extravagant in its own nature. No particular Church has, on its own showing, a right to existence, except as it believes itself to be the most perfect form of Christianity, the form which of right should and will be universal. No Church has a right to a part which does not claim that to it should belong the whole. That communion confesses itself a sect which aims at no more than abiding as one of a number of equally legitimated bodies. That communion which does not believe in the certainty of the ultimate acceptance of its principles in the whole world has not the heart of a true Church. That which claims to be Catholic *de facto* claims to be Universal *de jure*.

A true unity in Protestantism would be the death of Popery; but Popery will live until those who assail it are one in their answer to the question: What shall take its place? This book is a statement and a defence of the answer given to that question by the communion under whose banner the battle with Rome was first fought,—under whose leaders the greatest victories over Rome were won. If this Church has been a failure, it can hardly be claimed that the Reformation was a success; and if Protestantism cannot come to harmony with the principles by which it was created, as those principles were understood by the greatest masters in the reformatory work, it must remain divided until division reaches its natural end,—absorption and annihilation.

March 17, 1871

CONSERVATIVE REFORMATION.

I.

THE REFORMATION:

ITS OCCASION AND CAUSE.*

THE immediate occasion of the Reformation seemed insignificant enough. Three hundred and fifty-three years ago, on the 31st of October, immense crowds were pouring into an ancient city of Germany, bearing in its name, Wittenberg, the memorial of its founder, Wittekind the Younger. The weather-beaten and dingy little edifices of Wittenberg forbade the idea, that the beauty of the city or its commer- _{The day before "All-Saints' Day."} cial importance drew the masses to it. Within _{Day."} that city was an old church, very miserable and battered, and

---

* On the history of the Reformation, the works following may be consulted :

BRETSCHNEIDER: Die Deutsch. Reformat. 1855.

CLAUDE: Defence of the Reformation. Transl. 2 vols. 8vo. London: 1815.

COCHLÆUS: Commentaria de Act. et Scrip. Lutheri. 1549. Fol.

CYPRIAN: Nützlich. Urkunden. z. Erl. der erst. Reformations-Geschichte. Leipz.: 1718. 12mo. 2 Parts.

D'AUBIGNÉ: Histoire de la Reform. Par.: 1835-1838. (Engl., Lond.: 1839. New York: 1841.)

FÖRSTEMANN: Archiv. f. d. Gesch. d. K. Reformation. Halle: 1831. 8vo.

GERDES: Introd. in historiam. Ev. Sec. XVI. renov. 4 vols. 4to. Groning.: 744-1752.

HAGENBACH: Vorles. üb. Wes. u. Gesch. d. Reformation. Leipz.: 1839. 8vo.

JUNIUS: Compend. Seckendorf. (1755)—Reform. Gesch. in Auszug. v. Roos. Tüb.: 1788. 2 vols. 8vo.

KEYSER: Reformat. Almanach. Erf. 4 vols. 12mo. 1817-1821.

MAI: Hist. Reformat. Frankf.: 1710. 4to.

MAIMBOURG: Hist. du. Lutheranism. Par.: 1680. 4to.

very venerable and holy, which attracted these crowds. It was the " Church of all Saints," in which were shown, to the inexpressible delight of the faithful, a fragment of Noah's Ark, some soot from the furnace into which the three young Hebrews were cast, a piece of wood from the crib of the infant Saviour, some of St. Christopher's beard, and nineteen thousand other relics equally genuine and interesting. But over and above all these allurements, so well adapted to the taste of the time, His Holiness, the Pope, had granted indulgence to all who should visit the church on the first of November. Against the door of that church of dubious saints, and dubious relics, and dubious indulgences, was found fastened, on that memorable morning, a scroll unrolled. The writing on it was firm; the nails which held it were well driven in; the sentiments it conveyed were moderate, yet very decided. The material, parchment, was the same which long ago had held words of redemption above the head of the Redeemer. The contents were an amplification of the old theme of glory — Christ on the cross, the only King. The Magna Charta, which had been buried beneath the Pope's throne, reappeared on the church door. The keynote of the Reformation was struck full and clear at the beginning, Salvation through Christ alone.

It is from the nailing up of these Theses the Reformation takes its date. That act became, in the providence of God, the

MAIMBOURG: Hist. du. Calvinisme. Par.: 1682. 4to.

MARHEINEKE: Gesch. d. Teutsch. Reform. Berl.: 1831. 4 vols. 12mo.

MYCONIUS: Hist. Reformat. Cyprian. Leipz.: 1718. 12mo.

NEUDECKER: Gesch. d. Evang. Protestantism. Leipz.: 1844. 2 vols. 8vo.

RANKE : Deutsch. Gesch. im Zeitalt. d. Reformat. Berl.: 1839. 3 vols. 8vo. (Transl. by Sarah Austin.) Philad.: 1844. 8vo.

SCULTETUS: Kirchen. Reformat. in Teutschl. d. Guolfium. Heidelb.: 1618. 4to.

SECKENDORF: Lutheranism. Leipz.: 1694. Fol. Deutsch. 1714. 4to.

SLEIDAN: de Stat. relig. et reipub. (1557. 8vo.) Boehme am Ende. Frankf. a. M.: 1785–86. 3 vols. 8vo.

SPALATIN: Annales Reformat. (Cyprian.) Leipz.: 1718. 12mo.

TENTZEL: Reformat. Lutheri (Cyprian.) Leipz.: 1718. 12mo.

VON SEELEN: Stromata Lutherana. Lübeck: 1740. 12mo

VILLERS: Ess. sur l'ésprit et l'influ. d. l. Reformat. de Luth. Par.: 3d. ed. 1808. 8vo. Ubers. von Cramer, mit vorred. v. Henke. 2d. ed. Hamb.: 1828. 2 Parts. 12mo.

WADDINGTON: Reformat. on the Contin. Lond.: 1841. 3 vols. 8vo.

starting-point of the work which still goes on, and shall forever go on, that glorious work in which the truth was raised
to its original purity, and civil and religious liberty were restored to men. That the Reformation is the spring of modern
freedom, is no wild assertion of its friends. One of the greatest Roman Catholic writers of recent times, Michelet, in the
Introduction to his Life of Luther, says: " It is not incorrect to say, that Luther has been the restorer of liberty in
modern times. If he did not create, he at least courageously
affixed his signature to that great revolution which rendered
the right of examination lawful in Europe. And, if we exer
cise, in all its plenitude at this day, this first and highest
privilege of human intelligence, it is to him we are most indebted for it; nor can we think, speak, or write, without being
made conscious, at every step, of the immense benefit of this
intellectual enfranchisement ; " and he concludes with the remark : " To whom do I owe the power of publishing what I
am now inditing, except to this liberator of modern thought?"
Our Church, as clearly, in one sense, the mother of the Reformation, as, in another, she is its offspring, the first, and for a
time, the exclusive possessor of the name Protestantism, its
source and its mightiest bulwark, our Church has wisely set
apart a day in each year to commemorate this great deliverance, and wisely has kept her great Jubilees. There are other
ways of noting time, besides by its loss. The Church Festivals note it by its gains, the Church Year marks the time which
has been redeemed for ever. An old writer describes the
Church of All-Saints at Wittenberg, as a manger, where in his
lowly glory the Son of God was born again. Blessed forever be
the day! On it, through all time, men shall gather, bringing
their offerings of praise ; remembering, treasuring, and keeping untarnished, the holy faith whose restoration was thus
begun.

It is well, then, to have added to the grand order of the
Church Year, the Festival of the Reformation, and to the
revolution of the centuries, its Jubilee. Whether as the child
or as the parent of the Reformation, whether she would awake
her heart to gratitude as its daughter, or arouse herself to an

ei rnest sense of responsibility as its mother, our Church can claim it, as pre-eminently her privilege, and acknowledge it as pre-eminently her duty so to do. When the Festival of the Reformation shall come and shall wake no throb of joy in her bosom, her life will have fled. For if the Reformation lives through her, she also lives by it. It has to her the mysterious relation of Christ to David; if it is her offspring, it is also her root. If she watched the ark of the Lord, the ark of the Lord protected and blessed her, and when it passes from her keeping her glory will have departed. Let her speak to her children then, and tell them the meaning of the day. In the pulpit, and the school, and the circle of the home, let these great memories of men of God, of their self-sacrifice, of their overcoming faith, and of their glorious work, be the theme of thought, and of word, and of thanksgiving. The Festival of the Reformation is at once a day of Christmas and of Easter and of Pentecost, in our Church year; a day of birth, a day of resurrection, a day of the outpouring of the Holy Ghost. Let its return renew that life, and make our Church press on with fresh vigor in the steps of her risen Lord, as one begotten again, and born from the dead, by the quickening power of the Spirit of her God. Let every day be a Festival of the Reformation, and every year a Jubilee.

The occasions and cause of so wonderful and important an event as the Reformation have naturally occupied very largely the thoughts of both its friends and its foes. On the part of its enemies the solution of its rapid rise, its gigantic growth, its overwhelming march, has been found by some in the rancor of monkish malice — the thing arose in a squabble between two sets of friars, about the farming of the indulgences — a solution as sapient and as completely in harmony with the facts as would be the statement that the American Revolution was gotten up by one George Washington, who, angry that the British Government refused to make him a collector of the tax on tea, stirred up a happy people to rebellion against a mild and just rule.

Specific occasion and cause of the Reformation.

The solution has been found by others in the lust of the human heart for change — it was begotten in the mere love of novelty; men went into the Reformation as they go into a menagerie, or adopt the new mode, or buy up some "novelist's last." Another class, among whom the brilliant French Jesuit, Audin, is conspicuous, attribute the movement mainly to the personal genius and fascinating audacity of the great leader in the movement. Luther so charmed the millions with his marvellous speech and magic style, that they were led at his will. On the part of some, its nominal friends, reasons hardly more adequate have often been assigned. Confounding the mere aids, or at most, the mere occasions of the Reformation with its real causes, an undue importance has been attributed in the production of it to the progress of the arts and sciences after the revival of letters. Much stress has been laid upon the invention of printing, and the discovery of America, which tended to rouse the minds of men to a new life. Much has been said of the fermenting political discontents of the day, the influence of the great Councils in diminishing the authority of the Pope, and much has been made, in general, of the causes whose root is either wholly or in part in the earth. The Rationalist represents the Reformation as a triumph of reason over authority. The Infidel says, that its power was purely negative; it was a grand subversion; it was mightier than Rome, because it believed less than Rome; it prevailed, not by what it taught, but by what it denied; and it failed of universal triumph simply because it did not deny everything. The insect-minded sectarian allows the Reformation very little merit except as it prepared the way for the putting forth, in due time, of the particular twig of Protestantism on which he crawls, and which he imagines bears all the fruit, and gives all the value to the tree. As the little green tenants of the rose-bush might be supposed to argue that the rose was made for the purpose of furnishing them a home and food, so these small speculators find the root of the Reformation in the particular part of Providence which they consent to adopt and patronize. The Reformation, as they take it, originated in the divine plan for furnishing a nursery for sectarian Aphides.

But we must have causes which, however feeble, are adapted

to the effects. A little fire indeed kindleth a great matter, but however little, it must be genuine fire. Frost will not do, and a painting of flame will not do, though the pencil of Raphael produced it. A little hammer may break a great rock, but that which breaks must be harder and more tenacious than the thing broken. There must be a hand to apply the fire, and air to fan it; it must be rightly placed within the material to be kindled; it must be kept from being smothered. And yet all aids do but enable it to exercise its own nature, and it alone kindles. There must be a hand to wield the hammer, and a heart to move the hand; the rock must be struck with vigor, but the hammer itself is indispensable. God used instruments to apply the fire and wield the hammer; His providence prepared the way for the burning and the breaking. And yet there was but one agency, by which they could be brought to pass. Do we ask what was the agency which was needed to kindle the flame? What was it, that was destined to give the stroke whose crash filled earth with wonder, and hell with consternation, and heaven with joy? God himself asks the question, so that it becomes its own answer: "Is not MY WORD like as a fire? Is not MY WORD like the hammer which breaks the rock in pieces?"

It is not without an aim that the Word of God is presented in the language we have just quoted, under two images; as fire and as a hammer. The fire is a type of its inward efficacy; the hammer, of its outward work. The one image shows how it acts on those who admit it, the other how it effects those who harden themselves against it; the one symbolizes the persuasive fervor of that Word by which it makes our hearts burn within us in love to the Son of God, the other is an image of the energy with which, in the hands of the King on the holy hill of Zion, it breaks the opposers as with a rod of iron. The fire symbolizes the energy of the Word as a Gospel, which draws the heart to God, the hammer shadows forth its energy as a law which reveals the terrors of God's justice against transgressors. In both these grand aspects the Word of God was the creator of the Reformation and its mightiest instrument. It aroused the workers, and fitted them for their work; it opened blind eyes, and subdued stubborn hearts. The Reformation is its work and its trophy. However manifold the occasions of the Reformation, THE WORD, under God, was its cause.

The Word of God kindled the fire of the Reformation. That Word lay smouldering under the ashes of The Bible in centuries; it broke forth into flame, in Luther the Middle Ages. and the other Reformers; it rendered them lights which shone and burnt inextinguishably; through them it imparted itself to the nations; and from the nations it purged away the dross which had gathered for ages. "The Word of God," says St. Paul, "is not bound." Through the centuries which followed the corruption of Christianity, the Word of God was still in being. In lonely cloisters it was laboriously copied. Years were sometimes spent in finishing a single copy of it, in the elaborate but half-barbaric beauty which suited the taste of those times. Gold and jewels, on the massive covers, decorated the rich workmanship; costly pictures were painted as ornaments on its margin; the choicest vellum was used for the copies; the rarest records of heathen antiquity were sometimes erased to make way for the nobler treasures of the Oracles of the Most High. There are single copies of the Word, from that mid-world of history, which are a store of art, and the possession of one of which gives a bibliographical renown to the city in whose library it is preserved.

No interdict was yet laid upon the reading of the Word, for none was necessary. The scarcity and costliness of books formed in themselves a barrier more effectual than the interdict of popes and councils. Many of the great teachers in the Church of Rome were devoted students of the Bible. From the earliest writings of the Fathers, down to the Reformation, there is an unbroken line of witnesses for the right of all believers freely to read the Holy Scriptures. No man thought of putting an artificial limitation on its perusal; on the contrary, there are expressions of regret in the mediæval Catholic writers that, in the nature of the case, so few could have access to these precious records.

In communities separate from the Church of Rome, the

truth was maintained by reading and teaching the Holy Scriptures. The Albigensian and Waldensian martyrs, were martyrs of the Word:

> " Those slaughtered saints whose bones
> Lie scattered on the Alpine mountains cold,
> Even those who kept God's truth so pure of old,
> Wl en all our fathers worshipped stocks and stones."

The invention of printing, and hardly less, the invention of paper made from rags — for what would printing be worth, if we were still confined to so costly a material for books as parchment — prepared the way for the diffusion of the Scriptures.

The Church of Rome did not apprehend the danger which lay in that Book. Previous to the Reformation there were not only editions of the Scripture in the originals, but the old Church translation into Latin (the Vulgate) and versions from it into the living languages were printed. In Spain, whose dark opposition to the Word of God has since become her reproach and her curse, and in which no such book as the one of which we are about to speak has come forth for centuries, in Spain, more than a hundred years before there was enough Hebrew type in all England to print three consecutive lines, the first great POLYGLOT BIBLE, in Hebrew, Chaldee, Greek, and Latin, was issued at Complutum under the direction of Ximenes, her renowned cardinal and chief minister of state. It came forth in a form which, in splendor and value, far surpassed all that the world had yet seen. We may consider the Complutensian Polyglot, the crown of glory to the labors of the Middle Ages. It links itself clearly in historical connection with the GRAND BIBLICAL ERA, the Reformation itself, for though the printing of it was begun in 1502, and finished in 1517, it was not published till 1522, and in 1522, the FIRST EDITION OF THE NEW TESTAMENT, in German, came from the hand of Luther, fixing the corner-stone of the grand edifice, whose foundation had been laid in the Ninety-five Theses of 1517.

This, then, is the historical result of the facts we have presented, that the Middle Ages became, in the wonderful providence of God, the conservators of the Word which they are charged with suppressing; and were unconsciously tending toward the sunrise of the truth, which was to melt away their mists forever.

The earliest efforts of the press were directed to the multiplication of the copies of the Word of God. The <small>Where the Bible fell open.</small> first book ever printed, was the Bible. Before the first twelve sheets of this first edition of the Scriptures were printed, Gutenberg and Faust had incurred an expenditure of four thousand florins. That Bible was the edition of the Latin Vulgate, commonly known by the name of the "Mazarin Bible," from the fact that a copy of it which for some time was the only one known, was discovered about the middle of the eighteenth century in the Library of the College of the Four Nations, founded at Paris by Cardinal Mazarin. At Mentz and Cologne, the Vulgate translation of the Holy Scriptures was multiplied in editions of various sizes. Some of these Latin Bibles had been purchased for the University Library at Erfurth at a large price, and were rarely shown even to visitors. One of them was destined to play a memorable part in the history of mankind. While it was lying in the still niche of the Library, there moved about the streets of the city and through the halls of the University, a student of some eighteen years of age, destined for the law, who already gave evidence of a genius which might have been a snare to indolence, but who devoted himself to study with an unquenchable ardor. Among the dim recesses of the Library, he was a daily seeker for knowledge. His was a thirst for truth which was not satisfied with the prescribed routine. Those books of which we now think as venerable antiques, were then young and fresh — the glow of novelty was on much of which we now speak as the musty and worm-eaten record of old-time wisdom which we have outgrown. There the city of Harlem, through Laurentius, and the city of Mentz, through Faustus, and the city of Strasburg, through Gutenberg, put in their silent claims for the glory of being the cradle of the magic art of printing. There the great masters in jurisprudence and in scholastic philosophy challenged, and not in vain, the attention of the young searcher for knowledge. Some of the most voluminous of the Jurisconsults he could recite almost word for word. Occam and Gerson were his favorites among the scholastics. The masters of the classic world, Cicero, Virgil and Livy, "he read," says a Jesuit author, "not merely as a student whose aim was to understand them, but as a superior intellect, which sought to draw from them instruction, to find in them counsels and maxims for his after life. They were to him the flowers whose sweet odor might be shed upon the path he had to tread, or might calm the future agitation of his mind and of his heart." Thus passing from volume to volume, seeking the solution of the dark problem of human life, which already gathered heavily upon his deep, earnest soul, he one day took down a ponderous volume hitherto unnoticed. He opens it; the title-page is " Biblia Sacra " — the Holy Bible. He is disappointed. He has heard all this, he thinks, in the lessons of the Missal, in the texts of the Postils, in the selections of the Breviary. He imagines that his mother, the Church, has incorporated the whole Book of God in her services. Listlessly he allows the volume to fall open at another place, in his hand, and carelessly looks down at the page. What is it that arouses him? His eye kindles with amazement and intense interest. He rests the Book on the pile of the works of Schoolmen and of Fathers which he has been gathering. He hangs entranced over it; his dreamy eyes are fixed on the page; hour after hour flies; the shades of night begin to gather, and he is forced to lay the volume aside, with the sigh, O, that this Book of books might one day be mine!

Was it accident, or was it of God, that this Book opened where it did? Could we have arranged the providence, where would we have had the Book to open? It opened at the first chapter of First Samuel, the simple story of Hannah consecrating her boy to the Lord. There are many parts of the Bible as precious as this; with reverence we speak it, there are some more precious, " for one star differeth from another star in glory," though God made them all. Why opened not

that Book at some of the most glorious revelations of the New
Testament? This might have been, and who shall say what
incalculable loss it might have wrought to the world, had it
been so? For this very portion might have been one of the
Epistles, or Gospels, or Lessons of the Romish Service, and thus
might have confirmed the false impression of the young man
that he already knew all the Bible. This was a critical period
of Luther's life. Already was his mind tending to an absorption in studies which would have given a wholly different cast
to his life. The sound of a drum upon the street was the
turning point of the spiritual life of an English nobleman. It
lifted him from his knees, and drew him again into the full
march upon everlasting death. On what little things may
God have been pleased to hang the great impulses of the man,
who proved himself capable of leading the Reformation, and
who, but for these little things, might have been lost to the
world. Nothing in God's hand is trifling. The portion on
which Luther's eye fell was not in the Church Service. It
quickened him at once with a new sense of the fulness of God's
Word. In a double sense it stood before him, as a revelation.
His eyes were opened on the altar of that inextinguishable
fire, from which a few sparks had risen into the Romish
Ritual, and had drifted along on the night-breezes of the ages.
Did the angel of the Covenant with invisible hand open that
page, or was it a breath of air from some lattice near at hand?
It matters not — God opened the Book.

That Book was to Luther, henceforth, the thing of beauty
of his life, the joy of his soul forever. He read and re-read,
and prayed over its sacred teachings, till the place of each passage, and all memorable passages in their places fixed themselves in his memory. To the study of it, all other study
seemed tame. A single passage of it would ofttimes lie in his
thoughts days and nights together. The Bible seemed to fuse
itself into his being, to become a part of his nature. Often in
his writings he does not so much remark upon it, as catch its
very pulse and clothe his own mind in its very garb. He is
lifted to the glory of the reproducer — and himself becomes a
secondary prophet and apostle. His soul ceased to be a mere

vessel to hold a little of the living water, and became a foun
tain through which it sprang to refresh and gladden others.
As with Luther, so was it with Melanchthon, his noble co-
worker, with Zwingle in Switzerland, at a later period with
Calvin in France, with Tyndale and Cranmer in England, with
Knox in Scotland. The Word of God was the fire in their
souls which purified them into Christians — and the man who
became a Christian was already unconsciously a Reformer.

The fire which the Word of God kindled in the Reformers
they could not long conceal. "They believed —
Luther's Bible. therefore they spoke." One of the first, as it was
one of the greatest, revelations of the revived power of the Word
of God, was, that it sought an audience for itself before the people, in their own language. Every new Pentecost revives the
miracle and wonder of the first Pentecost: men marvelling, say
of the apostles to whom the Holy Ghost has again given utterance: "We do hear them speak in our tongues the wonderful works of God." Foremost in this imperishable work of the
Sixteenth Century, was the man who was first and chief in
more works, and in greater ones, than ever fell to any of our
race, in the ordinary vocation of God. Great monuments has
the Sixteenth Century left us of the majesty revealed by the
human mind, when its noblest powers are disciplined by study,
and sanctified by the Spirit of God. Great are the legacies of
doctrinal, polemical, historical and confessional divinity which
that century has left us. Immortal are its confessions, its devotional, practical, hymnological and liturgical labors. It was
the century of Melanchthon's Loci and of Calvin's Institutes,
of the Examen of Chemnitz, and the Catalogus Testium of
Flaccius, and of the Magdeburg Centuries. Its confessions are
still the centres of great communions, its hymns are still sung
by devout thousands, its forms still mould the spirit of worship among millions. But its grandest achievement was the
giving of the Bible to the nations, and the centre and throne
of this achievement is LUTHER'S TRANSLATION OF THE BIBLE, the
greatest single work ever accomplished by man in the department of theological literature. The Word of God, in
whole or in part, has been translated into several hundred of

the dialects of our race. Many of these translations, as for ex
ample the Septuagint, the Vulgate, and our own authorized
version, have great historical significance; but in its historical
connections and significance, Luther's is incomparably most
important of all. Had it been his sole labor, the race could
never forget his name.

Never were a greater need and the fittest agent to meet it,
so brought together as in the production of this translation.
One of the earliest convictions of Luther was, the people *must*
have the Bible, and to this end it must be translated. It is
true, that beginning with the Gothic translation of Ulphilas,
in the fourth century, there had been various translations of
the Scriptures into the Germanic tongues. About 1466, ap
peared the first Bible, printed in German. It came from the
press of Eggesteyn, in Strasburg, (not as has been frequently
maintained, from the press of Faust and Schöffer, in 1462.)
Between the appearance of this Bible and that of Luther, there
were issued in the dialect of Upper Germany some fourteen
editions of the Word of God, beside several in the dialect of
Lower Germany. These were, without exception, translations
of a translation; they were made from the Vulgate, and, however they may have differed, they had a common character
which may be expressed in a word — they were abominable.
In a copy of one of them, in the library of the writer of this
article, there is a picture of the Deluge, in which mermaids
are floating around the ark, arranging their tresses with the
aid of small looking-glasses, with a most amphibious non-
chalance. The rendering is about as true to the idea, as the
picture is to nature. There is another of these editions, remarkable for typographical errors, which represents Eve, not
as a house-wife, but as a " kiss-wife," and its typography is
the best part of it. How Luther raised what seemed a barbarous jargon into a language, which, in flexible beauty,
and power of internal combination, has no parallel but in the
Greek, and in massive vigor no superior but the English,
writers of every school, Protestant and Romish alike, have
loved to tell. The language of Germany has grown since
Luther, but it has had no new creation. He who takes up Lu-

ther's Bible grasps a whole world in his hand—a world which will perish only, when this green earth itself shall pass away.

In all lands in which the battle of the Reformation was

The Only Rule.

fought, the Bible furnished banner, armor, and arms. It was, indeed, more than ensign, more than shield, more than sword, for " the Word of God is quick and powerful, sharper than any two-edged sword, piercing even to the dividing asunder of soul and spirit, and of the joints and marrow, and is a discerner of the thoughts and intents of the heart." The Word of God opened the eyes of the Reformers to the existing corruptions; it called them forth from Babylon; it revealed to them the only source of healing for the sick and wounded Church ; it inspired them with ardor for their holy work; it lifted them above the desire for man's favor, and the fear of man's face. The Bible made them confessors, and prepared them to be martyrs.

The Reformers knew where their strength lay. They felt that what had redeemed them could alone redeem the Church. They saw that, under God, their ability to sustain their cause depended on His Word. The supreme and absolute authority of God's Word in determining all questions of doctrine and of duty, is a fundamental principle of the Reformation — a principle so fundamental, that without it, there would have been no Reformation — and so vital, that a Reformation without it, could such a Reformation be supposed, would have been at best a glittering delusion and failure.

It is true, that there was testimony from human sources, which was not without value, in its right place, in the controversy with Rome. In a certain sense, her condemnation had already been anticipated by her own lips. In the long-gone days of her purity, the Church of Rome had men of God, who held to the truth as it is in Christ Jesus. Thirty years after our Lord's Ascension, St. Paul wrote to the Church of Rome, " I am persuaded of you, my brethren, that ye also are full of goodness, filled with all knowledge, able also to admonish one another. Your obedience is come abroad unto all men." This glorious condition did not pass away speedily. There were generations following, in which the truth was kept comparatively pure. Papal Rome could no more stand before the judgment of the early writers in the Church of Rome yet undefiled than she could before the Scriptures. Hence, the confessors declared * that, in their doctrine, there not only was nothing in conflict with the Holy Scriptures, and with the true Church Catholic, or Church Universal, but nothing in conflict with the teachings of the true Church of Rome, as her doctrines were set forth by the writers of the earlier ages. The quotations made from these Fathers, in the Confession, best illustrate the meaning of this declaration, and prove its truth. Thus, for example, they quote the Nicene Fathers, as witnesses to the doctrine of the Trinity; Ambrose is cited to show, " that he that believeth in Christ, is saved, without works, by faith alone, freely receiving remission." In the articles on Abuses, the testimony of the purer Fathers and Councils is used with great effect.

But not because of the testimony of the Church and of its writers did the Reformers hold the truth they confessed. They knew that individual churches could err, and had erred grievously, that the noblest men were fallible. Nothing but the firm word of God sufficed for them.

They thanked God, indeed, for the long line of witnesses for the truth of His Word. Within the Church of Rome, in the darkest ages, there had been men faithful to the truth. There were men, in the midst of the dominant corruption, who spake and labored against it. There were Protestants, ages before our princes made their protest at Spires, and Lutherans, before Luther was born. But not on these, though they sealed the truth with their own blood, did the Reformers lean. They joyfully used them as testimony, but not as authority. They placed them in the box of the witness, not on the bench of the judge. Their utterances, writings, and acts were not to be the rule of faith, but were themselves to be weighed in its balance. In God was their trust, and His Word alone was their stay.

When the great princes and free cities of our Church at Augsburg, in 1530, laid their Confession before the Emperor

* Augs. Confess. 47 : 1.

and potentates, civil and ecclesiastical, of the realm, they said:
" We offer the Confession of the faith held by the pastors and
preachers in our several estates, and the Confession of our
own faith, *as drawn from the Holy Scriptures, the pure Word of
God.*" * That Confession repeatedly expresses, and in every
line implies that the Word of God is the sole rule of faith and
of life. The same is true of the Apology or Defence of the
Confession by Melanchthon, which appeared in the following
year, and which was adopted by the larger part of our Church
as expressing correctly her views. † Seven years later, the
articles of Smalcald were prepared by Luther, for presentation
at a general council, as an expression of the views of our
Church. In this he says:‡ " Not from the works or words
of the Fathers are articles of faith to be made. We have
another rule, to wit: that God's Word shall determine articles of faith — and, beside it, none other — no, not an angel
even."

Half a century after the Augsburg Confession had gone
forth on its sanctifying mission, our Church in Germany, in
order that her children might not mistake her voice amid the
bewildering conflicts of theological strife, which necessarily
followed such a breaking up of the old modes of human
thought as was brought about by the Reformation, set forth
her latest and amplest Confession. This Confession, with reference to the harmony it was designed to subserve, and under
God did largely subserve, was called the Formula of Concord.
That document opens with these words: " We believe, teach,
and confess that the only rule and law, by which all teachings
and all teachers are to be estimated and judged, *is none other
whatsoever* than the writings of the prophets and the apostles,
alike of the Old and of the New Testament, as it is written:
'Thy word is a lamp unto my feet, and a light unto my path;'
and St. Paul saith (Gal. 1:8): 'Though we, or an angel from
heaven, preach any other Gospel unto you, than that which
we have preached unto you, let him be accursed.' "

" All other writings," it continues, " whether of the Fathers,
or of recent authors, be their name what they may, are by no

* A. C. Præfat. 8.   † Apol. Con. 284 : 60.   ‡ 303 : 15.

means whatsoever to be likened to Holy Scripture; but are, in such sense, to be subjected to it, as to be received in none other way than as witnesses, which show how and where, after the apostles' times, the doctrines of the apostles and prophets were preserved." "We embrace," say our confessors, "the Augsburg Confession, not because it was written by our theologians, but because it was taken from God's Word, and solidly built on the foundation of Holy Scripture."

With equal clearness do the other Churches of the Reformation express themselves on this point.

If, then, the Reformers knew the movements of their own minds, it was God's Word, and it alone, which made them confessors of the truth. And it is a fundamental principle of the Reformation, that God's word is the sole and absolute authority, and rule of faith, and of life, a principle without accepting which, no man can be truly Evangelical, Protestant, or Lutheran.

Fire not only makes bright and burning the thing it kin dles, but gives to it the power of impartation; The Providence whatever is kindled, kindles again. From the of God and His Word, working Reformers, the fire spread to the people; and from together in the cold and darkness the nations seemed to struggle Reformation. upward, as by a common touch from heaven, in flames of holy sacrifice; and here, too, THE WORD showed its divine power.

We acknowledge, indeed, with joyous hearts, that God had prepared all things wondrously, for the spread of the flame of the truth. In GERMANY, the fire was to burst forth, which was to spread to the ends of the earth. "In no event in the history of mankind does the movement of Divine Providence present itself more unmistakably, than in the Reformation in Germany."* The time, the place, the circumstances, the condition of the religious and of the political world, were in wonderful unison. They worked with each other, compensating each other's weaknesses, and helping each other's power, so as to give a sure foundation, a firm hold, a healthy direction, a high purity, a mighty protection, a wide-spread recognition, a swift and joyous progress, an abiding issue to the glorious

* Dr. H. Kurtz, K. G. ₰ 211

2

work. The soul of the best men of the time was alive to the wretched condition into which the Church had fallen. A profound longing for the Reformation filled the hearts of nations; science, literature, art, discovery, and invention were elevating Europe, and preparing the way for the triumphal march of pure religion, the queen of all knowledge. In the Papal chair sat Leo X., a lover of art and literature, careless and indolent in all things else. Over the beautiful plains of Germany wandered Tetzel, senseless and impudent, even beyond the class to which he belonged, exciting the disgust of all thinking men, by the profligate manner in which he sold indulgences. To protect the trembling flame of the truth from the fierce winds, which, at first, would have extinguished it; to protect it till the tornado itself should only make it blaze more vehemently, God had prepared Frederick, the Wise, a man of immense influence, universally revered, and not more revered than his earnest piety, his fidelity, his eminent conscientiousness deserved. The Emperor Charles V., with power enough to quench the flame with a word, with a hatred to it which seemed to make it certain that he would speak that word, was yet so fettered by the plans of his ambition, that he left it unsaid, and thus was made the involuntary protector of that which he hated. These and a thousand other circumstances were propitious.

But in vain is the wood gathered, and in vain do the winds breathe, unless the fire is applied. In vain would Luther, with his incomparable gifts, have risen — in vain would that genius, to which a Catholic writer declares Luther's own friends have not done full justice — in vain would that high courage, that stern resolve have presented themselves in the matchless combination in which they existed in him, had there not been first a power beyond that of man to purify him, and from him to extend itself in flame around him. With all of Luther's gifts, he might have been a monster of wickedness, or a slave of the dominant superstition, helping to strengthen its chains, and forge new ones, had not the truth of God made him free, had not the Spirit of God in His Word made him an humble and earnest believer. Luther was first a Christian.

and then a Reformer, and he became a Reformer because he was a Christian. "He believed, therefore he spoke." But Christian as he was, he could not have been a successful Reformer, had he not possessed the power of spreading the fire of Divine truth. The fatal defect in all the Reformatory movements in the councils and universities of Paris in the fifteenth century, was that they were not based upon the true foundation, and did not propose to attain the great end by the right means. The cry had been for a Reform "in the head and members" by outward improvement, not in the Spirit and through the Word. The Reformation was kindled by the Word; it trusted the Word, and scattered it everywhere, directing attention to it in every writing, and grounding every position upon it. The Word soon made itself felt throughout all Europe. Even in the lands most thoroughly under Papal power, sparkles of the truth began to show themselves, as in Austria, Spain, and Italy. But from Wittenberg through Germany, from Zurich through Switzerland, the first flame spread, and but a few years passed ere all Europe, which is at this hour Protestant, had received the pure faith of the Word of God.

The fire of the Divine Word destroyed the accumulated rubbish of tradition, swept away the hay, wood, and stubble, which the hand of man had gathered on the foundation and heaped over the temple, and the gold, silver, and precious stones of the true house of God appeared. The Bible, like sunshine bursting through clouds, poured its light upon the nations. The teaching of mere men ceased to be regarded as authority, and the prophecy was again fulfilled: "They shall all be taught OF GOD."

Three hundred and fifty-three years ago, the first thrill of the earthquake of the Reformation was felt in Europe. Men knew so little of its nature, that they A Lesson for our time. imagined it could be suppressed. They threw their weight upon the heaving earth, and hoped to make it lie still. They knew not that they had a power to deal with, which was made more terrible in its outburst by the attempt to confine it. As the result of the opposition to the Reformation,

Europe was made desolate. After the final struggle of the Thirty Years' War, Europe seemed ruined; its fields had been drenched with blood, its cities laid in ashes, hardly a family remained undivided, and the fiercest passions had been so aroused, that it seemed as if they could never be allayed.

Yet the establishment of the work of the Reformation has richly repaid Europe for all it endured. The earthquake has gone, the streams of desolation have been chilled, and the nations make a jubilee over the glorious anniversary of that grand movement which, by the depravity of men, was made the occasion of so much disturbance and misery. The evils of which the Reformation was the occasion, have passed away. We must go to the page of history to know what they were. The blessings of which the Reformation was the cause, abide; we feel them in our homes, in the Church, in the State; they are inwoven with the life of our life. Once feeling them, we know that this would be no world to live in without them.

And how instructive is this to us in the struggle of our day for the perpetuation of the truth restored by the Reformation. Not alone by Rome, but also by heretical or fanatical Pseudo-Protestants, is it still assailed — and when we see the guilty passions, the violence and odious spirit of misrepresentation excited, and feel them directed upon ourselves, we may be tempted to give up the struggle. But we are untrue to the lessons of the Reformation, if we thus yield.

Men tremble and weep as the molten and seething elements make the earth quake, and pour themselves out in red and wasting streams. But their outbursting is essential to their consolidation, and to their bearing part in the work of the world. What was once lava, marking its track in ruin, shall one day lie below fair fields, whose richness it has made. The olive shall stay the vine, and the shadows of the foliage of vine and olive shall ripple over flowers; and women and children, lovelier than the fruits and the flowers, shall laugh and sing amid them. The blessings from the upheaving of the heart of the world shall gladden the children of those who gazed on it with wo-begone eyes. Had a war of three hundred years been necessary to sustain the Reformation, we now know the Reformation would ultimately have repaid all the sacrifices it demanded. Had our fathers surrendered the truth, even under that pressure to which ours is but a feather, how we would have cursed their memory, as we contrasted what we were with what we might have been.

And shall we despond, draw back, and give our names to the reproach of generations to come, because the burden of the hour seems to us heavy? God, in His mercy, forbid! If all others are ready to yield to despondency, and abandon the struggle, we, children of the Reformation, dare not. That struggle has taught two lessons, which must never be forgotten. One is, that the true and the good must be secured at any price. They are beyond all price. We dare not compute their cost. They are the soul of our being, and the whole world is as dust in the balance against them. No matter what is to be paid for them, we must not hesitate to lay down their redemption price. The other grand lesson is, that their price is never paid in vain. What we give can never be lost, *unless we give too little.* If we give all, we shall have all. All shall come back. Our purses shall be in the mouths of our sacks. We shall have both the corn and the money. But if we are niggard, we lose all — lose what we meant to buy, lose what we have given. If we maintain the pure Word inflexibly at every cost, over against the arrogance of Rome and of the weak pretentiousness of Rationalism, we shall conquer both through the Word; but to compromise on a single point, is to lose all, and to be lost.

II.

LUTHER PICTURED BY PENCIL AND PEN.*

THE pictured life of Luther, by König and Gelzer, which alone we propose to notice at any length, is a charming book —a book with a great subject, a happy mode of treatment, well carried out, and combining the fascination of good pictures, good descriptions, and elegant typography. It is an offering of flowers and fruit on the altar of the greatest memory which the heart of modern Christianity enshrines. It is the whole history of Luther told in pictures, and descriptions of those

*Dr. MARTIN LUTHER der Deutsche Reformator. In bildlichen Darstellungen von GUSTAV KÖNIG. In geschichtlichen Umrissen von Heinrich Gelzer. Hamburg: Rudolf Besser. Gotha: Justus Perthes. 1851. [Dr. Martin Luther the German Reformer. In pictorial representations, and historical sketches.] 4to. (In English, Lond.: 1853.) (With Introduction by T. STORK, D. D. Philada.: 1854.)
AUDIN: Histoire de M. Luther. Nouv. ed. Louvain.: 1845. 2 vols. 8vo. (Transl. into English, Phila.: 1841. 8vo. London: 1854. 2 vols. 8vo.)
BOWER: Life of Luther. (1813.) Philada.: 1824. 8vo.
COCHLÆUS: Historia M. Lutheri. (1559.) Ingolst.: 1582. 4to.
ENGELHARD: Lucifer Wittenberg. Leb. Lauf Catherinae v. Bore.) 1747. 12mo.
FABRICIUS: Centifolium Lutheranum. Hamb.: 1728.
HUNNIUS, N.: Off. Bew. d. D. M. L. zu Ref. beruffen. n. Ap:logia Olearii. Leipz.: 1666. 12mo.
JUNCKER: Guld. u. Silb. Ehren. Ged. D. Mart. Luth. Frankf. u. Leipz.: 1706. 8vo.
JÜRGENS: Luther's Leben. Leipz.: 1846. 3 vols. 8vo.
KREUSSLER: D. M. L.'s Andenk. in Münzer. Leipz.: 1818. 8vo.
LABOUCHERE: Illustr. of the Life of Martin Luther. (D'Aubigné.) Philada. ath. Board: 1869. 4to. (Photographs.—A beautiful book.)
LEDDERHOSE: M. L. n. s. äussern u. innern Leben. Speyer.: 1836. 8vo.
LUTHER: Briefe. De Wette. Berl.: 1826 seq. 6 vols. 8vo.
    "   Concordanz d. Ansicht. etc. Darmst.: 1827–31. 4 vols. 8vo.
    "   Opera. Erlangen: 1829 seq. Jena: 1556. Wittenb.: 1545–58.

pictures, followed by a connected sketch of the Reformation as it centred in him.

The work contains forty-eight engravings, divided, with reference to the leading events of his life, or the great features of his character, into seven parts. _{Luther's child hood.}

The FIRST division embraces the years of his *childhood* — and, not uncharacteristically of the German origin of the book, presents us as a first picture Martin Luther (such we must here call him by anticipation) on the night of " his birth, 11 o'clock, November 10th, 1483." Speaking of Luther's birth, Carlyle says: " In the whole world, that day, there was not a more entirely unimportant-looking pair of people, than this miner and his wife. And yet what were all Emperors, Popes, and Potentates, in comparison? There was born here, once more, a Mighty Man; whose light was to flame as the beacon over long centuries and epochs of the world; the whole world and its history was waiting for this man. It is strange, it is great. It leads us back to another Birth-hour, in a still meaner environment, eighteen hundred years ago — of which it is fit

LUTHER: Werke. Altenburg: 1661. Erlangen: 1826 seq. (2d ed. Frankf. a. M.: 1869 seq.) Halle (Walch.): 1740–52. Leipzig: 1729–34. Wittenberg: 1539–59.

LUTHER: Table Talk. Hazlitt. Luth. Board Public., Philada.: 1868.

MATHESIUS: Dr. M. L. Leben. In XVII. Predigt. (1565.) Berlin: 1862.

MELANCHTHON: Vita et Act. Lutheri. (1546.) Ed. Förstemann. Nordhausen: 1846. 8vo.

MELANCHTHON: Aus d. Lateinischen. (Mayer.) Wittenb.: 1847.

MEURER: Luthers Leben a. d. Quellen. 2d edit. Dresden: 1852. 8vo.

MORRIS, J. G.: Quaint Sayings and Doings concerning Luther. Philada. 1859.

MÜLLER: Lutherus Defensus. Hamb.: 1658. 12mo.

NIEMEYER, C. H.: M. L. n. s. Leben u. Wirken. Halle· 1817. 8vo.

SCOTT: Luther and the L. Reformation. New York: 1833. 2 vols. 12mo.

SEARS: Life of Luther. Am. S. S. Un.

STANG: M. L. s. Leben u. Wirken. Stuttg. 1835. 4to.

UKERT: L.'s Leben, mit d. Literat. Gotha: 1817. 8vo

ULENBERG: Gesch. d. Lutherischer Reformatoren. Dr. M. Luther, &c. Mainz: 1836. 2 vols. 8vo.

WEISER: Life of Luther. Balto.: 1853.

WIELAND: Charakteristik. D. M. L. Chemnitz: 1801. 12mo.

ZIMMERMANN, K.: Luther's Leben in Reformat. Schriften D. M. L. Darmstadt: 1846–1849. 4 vols. 8vo.

that we say nothing, that we think only in silence; for what words are there! The Age of Miracles past? The Age of Miracles is forever here!"* In the second picture, Master Martin is brought to school, to a terrible-looking school-master, with a bundle of rods in his hand, and with a boy whom you can almost hear sobbing, crouching at the back of his chair. In the third, wandering with his little com rades, he comes, singing, to the door of Madame Cotta in Eisenach, (1498.) In a little niche below, his gentle protect ress brings him his lute, to win him for a while from his books.

The SECOND division leads us over his *youth*, in seven illus-
Luther's Youth. trations. In the first, Luther is seen in the Library of the University of Erfurt, gazing eagerly, for the first time, on the whole Bible — his hand unconsciously relaxing on a folio Aristotle, as he reads, (1501.) Next, the Providence is smiting, together with the Word. His friend Alexis, as they journey, falls dead at his side, by a thunderstroke. Then follows the step of a fearful heart. With sad face, and with the moon, in her first quarter, beaming on him like that faith which was yet so far from the full; with his heathen poets beneath his arm, he takes the hand of the monk who welcomes him to the cloister of the Augustinian Eremites, (1505.) Next the monk receives the solemn consecration to the priesthood, and now with the tonsure, the cowl and the rosary, barefooted, with the scourge by his side, he agonizes, with macerated body and bleeding heart, at the foot of the crucifix. We turn a leaf — he lies in his cell, like one dead — he has swooned over the Bible, which he now never permits to leave his hand. The door has been burst open, and his friends bring lutes, that they may revive him by the influence of the only power which yet binds him to the world of sense. Now a ray of light shoots in: the Spirit chafing in the body has brought him hard by the valley of death; but an old brother in the Cloister, by one word of faith gives him power to rise from his bed of sickness, and clasp his comforter around the neck. With this touching scene, ends this part.

---

* On Heroes and Hero-Worship — or Six Lectures by Thomas Carlyle - New York, 1849, p. 114.

In the THIRD period, we have illustrations of Luther's career at the *University* of Wittenberg. As a Bachelor Luther at the University. of Arts he is holding philosophical and theological prelections, (1508.) Then we have him preaching in the Cloister before Staupitz, and the other brethren of his order, as a preliminary to appearing in the Castle and City church. Luther's journey to Rome (1510) is shown in four pictures grouped on one page. In the first he is starting eagerly on his journey to the " holy city "—in the second, at first view of that home of martyrs hallowed by their blood, and not less by the presence of the vicar of Christ and vicegerent of God, he falls upon his knees, in solemn awe and exultation ; in the centre, he is gazing on the proud and godless Pope Julius, riding with pampered cardinals in his train—and in the last, he looks back, and waves over that city the hand whose bolts in after time seemed mighty enough to sink it to that realm—over which, its own inhabitants told him, if there was a hell, Rome was certainly built.* " To conceive of Luther's emotions on entering Rome, we must remember that he was a child of the north, who loved privation and fasting—who was of a meditative nature, and had vowed to the cross of Christ an austere worship. His Christianity was of a severe and rigid character. When he prayed it was on the stone; the altar before which he knelt was almost invariably of wood ; his church was time-worn, and the chasuble of its ministers of coarse wool. Imagine, then, this monk—this poor Martin, who walked twelve hundred miles, with nothing to support him but coarse bread ; think of him suddenly transported to the midst of a city of wonders, of pleasure, of music, and of pagan antiquity. What must have been his feelings: he who had never heard any greater sound than was made by the falling water of the convent fountain—who knew no recreation beyond that of his lute, when prayers were over, and who knew no ceremony more imposing than the induction of an Augustinian monk— how must he have been astonished, even scandalized ! He had fancied to himself an austere religion—its brow encircled with

---

* " So hab ich selbs zu Rom gehört sagen: ist eine Hölle, so ist Rom darauf gebaut."

care, its ministers lying on the hard ground, sating their thirst at heavenly founts, dressed as were the Apostles, and treading on stony paths with the Everlasting Gospel in their hands. In place of this he saw cardinals borne in litters, or on horseback, or in carriages, their attire blazing with jewels, their faces shaded by canopies, or the plumes of the peacock, and marking their route by clouds of dust so dense as completely to veil and hide their attendants. His dreams reverted to those days, when the chief of the Apostles, a pilgrim like himself, had only a staff to support his weakness. The poor scholar, who, in his childhood, had endured so much, and who often pillowed his head on the cold ground, now passes before palaces of marble, alabaster columns, gigantic granite obelisks, sparkling fountains, villas adorned with gardens, cascades and grottos ! Does he wish to pray ? He enters a church, which appears to him a little world ; where diamonds glitter on the altar, gold upon the ceiling, marble in the columns, and mosaic in the chapels. In his own country, the rustic temples are ornamented by votive flowers laid by some pious hand upon the altar. Is he thirsty ? Instead of one of those springs that flow through the wooden pipes of Wittenberg, he sees fountains of white marble, as large as German houses. Is he fatigued with walking ? He finds on his road, instead of a modest wooden seat, some antique, just dug up, on which he may rest. Does he look for a holy image ? He sees nothing but the fantasies of paganism, old deities — still giving employment to thousands of sculptors. They are the gods of Demosthenes, and of Praxiteles; the festivals and processions of Delos; the excitement of the forum; in a word, pagan folly: but of the foolishness of the Cross, which St. Paul extols, he appears nowhere to see either memorial or representation." *
These are the concessions, and this the apology of a Roman Catholic historian, and we permit them to pass together. After his return we see Luther with high solemnities created Doctor of the Holy Scriptures, Carlstadt as Dean of the Theological Faculty, officiating at his promotion, (1512.) The close of this era leaves Luther busy in dictating letters, and per

* Audin's Life of Luther.

forming the functions of "a Vicar-General of the Augustinian Order," with which he had been intrusted by Staupitz, (1516.) By this office he was fitted for that part which he took in giving form to the Church when it ere long began to renew its youth like the eagle's.

We come now to the Reformation itself, (1517,) the warning flash, the storm, and the purified heaven that The Reforma- followed it. This period is embraced in sixteen tion in its rise. principal pictures, with seven subsidiary ones on a smaller scale.

The first of these grouped pictures presents four scenes. Below, Luther is refusing, as the Confessor of his people, to give them absolution, while they exultingly display their indulgences; in the centre, Luther nails to the door of the church-tower the immortal theses — on the left, Tetzel sells indulgences, and commits Luther's writing to the flames, and on the right, the Wittenberg students are handling his own anti-theses in the same unceremonious way. The smoke from both fires rises to a centre above the whole, and, like the wan image in a dream, the swan whose white wings were waving before Huss' dying eyes, is lifting herself unscathed from the flames. Now Luther bends before Cajetan, and then at night, "without shoe or stocking, spur or sword," flies on horseback through a portal of Augsburg. The picture that follows is one of great beauty, rich in portraits. It represents the dispute at Leipsic between Luther and Eck, (1519.) In the Hall of the Pleissenburg the two great chieftains face each other — the one bold, cogent, overwhelming — the other sly, full of lubricity, sophistical and watchful; the one Hercules, the other the Hydra. By Luther's side sits Melanchthon, with the deep lines of thought upon his youthful face; at their feet, Carlstadt, with a book in each hand, with knit brows searches for something which his treacherous memory has not been able to retain. In the centre of the court, Duke George of Saxony listens earnestly to the dispute, till at Luther's words, that " some Articles even of Huss and the Bohemians accorded with the Gospel," he involuntarily exclaimed, " The man is mad ! " At his feet sits the court-fool, gazing with a puzzled and earnest air at Dr. Eck,

as though he dreaded remotely that he had in him a danger
ous competitor for his own office. Next we have Luther burn
ing the Papal bull, (1520,) then his reception at Worms, (1521.)
These are followed by a double picture: above, Luther is preparing by prayer to appear before the Emperor and the Diet;
his lattice opens out upon the towers of the city, and the calm
stars are shining upon him. It reminds us of the garden at
Wittenberg, where, one evening at sunset, a little bird has
perched for the night: "That little bird," says Luther—
"above it are the stars and deep heaven of worlds; yet it has
folded its little wings; gone trustfully to rest there as in
its home." His lute rests by his side, his brow is turned to
heaven and his hands clasped fervently; below, he approaches
the entrance to the Diet; the knight Frundsberg lays a friendly
nand upon his shoulder, and speaks a cheering word. In the
angles of the ornamental border appear statues of those two
heroes who declared themselves ready with word and sword,
if need were, to defend at Worms their "holy friend, the un-
conquerable Theologian and Evangelist;" Hutten rests upon
the harp and lifts the sword in his right hand; his brow is
crowned with the poet's laurel; the brave Sickingen lifts the
shield upon his arm, and holds in his right hand the marshal's
staff. Luther has entered the hall—stands before the mighty—
and is represented at the moment when he throws his whole
soul into that "good confession," surpassed in moral grandeur
but by one, in the whole history of the race. "The Diet of
Worms, Luther's appearance there on the 17th of April, 1521,
may be considered as the greatest scene in modern European
History; the point, indeed, from which the whole subsequent history of civilization takes its rise. The world's pomp and power
sits there, on this hand: on that, stands up for God's truth,
one man, the poor miner Hans Luther's son. Our petition—
the petition of the whole world to him was: 'Free us; it rests
with thee; desert us not.' Luther did not desert us. It is, as
we say, the greatest moment in the Modern History of Men—
English Puritanism, England and its Parliaments, America's
vast work these two centuries; French Revolution, Europe
and its work everywhere at present: the germ of it all lay

there: had Luther in that moment done other, it had all been otherwise."* Next follows his arrest on the way, (1521.) Next, sitting in the dress of a knight, his cap hanging on the head of the chair, his sword resting at its side, in a quiet chamber of the Thuringian castle, we see him at work on his translation of the Bible. But his active spirit prompts him to return to his former duties at any risk; now, with his book resting on the pommel of his saddle, he rides away from the Wartburg; meets the Swiss students at the hostelry of the Black Bear in Jena, who can talk about nothing but Luther, who sits unknown, and is recognized by them with astonishment when at Wittenberg they meet him in the circle of his friends.

A new stadium is now reached in this era. The danger greater than all outward dangers, that which arises within great moral movements, now begins to display itself. From applying the internal remedies well calculated to eradicate the cause of disease, men begin to operate upon the surface; instead of curing the leprosy, they com-   _{Fanaticism.} mence scraping off its scales. The war against images in the churches commenced; 'Cut, burn, break, annihilate,' was the cry, and the contest was rapidly changing, from a conflict with errors in the human heart, to an easy and useless attack on paint and stone. A harder struggle, than any to which he had yet been called, demands Luther's energy. He must defend the living truth from the false issues into which its friends may carry it. Luther arrests the storm against images. The artist places him in the centre of a band of iconoclasts in the temple. His hand and voice arrest a man who is about climbing a ladder to destroy the ornaments of the church. Near him a youth holding a chasuble is pausing to hear; on the floor, a peasant suspends the tearing of a missal in the middle of a page; an older man, with a heap of sacred vestments beneath him and a broken crosier under his foot, half relaxes his hold on the Monstrance, and looks scowlingly around. On the extreme right of the picture, there is a fine contrast between the fanatical countenance of a man who has just lifted a heavy hammer against the statue of a saint, and the placid face which he is

---

* Carlyle, Heroes and Hero-Worship, p. 121.

about to destroy. Carlstadt, with his foot propped upon the shoulder of a devout old bishop in stone, looks on Luther with an expression of impotent wrath.

The next picture leads us to a calmer scene. Luther is in his Luther and Melanchthon. quiet room. His translation of the Bible is growing beneath his hand. By his side, rendering invaluable aid, is Melanchthon: "Still," said Luther, "in age, form, and mien, a youth: but in mind a MAN." This was the time of their first love, when they were perfectly of one spirit, and full of admiration, each of the other's wondrous gifts; when Melanchthon knew no glory on earth beyond that of looking upon Luther as his father, and Luther's chief joy was to see and extol Melanchthon, (1523–24.)

Next, as if the artist would lead us through alternate Luther's marriage. scenes of sunshine and tempest, we have Luther preaching in Seeburg against the peasant war, (1525;) a noble picture crowded with varied life. Then from revelry, arson, and rapine, we are led into a private chapel in the house of the Registrar of Wittenberg. The jurist, Apel, and the great painter, Cranach, stand on either side; Bugenhagen blesses the plighted troth of Luther and Catherine, who kneel before him, she with her long hair flowing over her shoulders, and the marriage wreath on her brow, her face meekly and thoughtfully bent downward; he holding her right hand in his, his left pressing on his heart, and his eyes turned to heaven, (June 13th, 1525.)

From sunshine to storm — Luther's conference with Zwingle on the question of the Sacrament, (October 1–4, 1529.) Luther Luther and Zwingle. had redeemed the Gospel doctrine of the Supper from the gross materialism and scholastic refinings of Rome: it was now his work to maintain it against the error which violent reaction had produced, a hyperspiritualizing, which was driven to so violent a resort as confounding the benefits of our Redeemer's flesh with the feebleness of our own. It was to save the living body of Christ himself from disseverance, to rescue the Reformation from a tendency toward Sect, which an easy perversion of some of its principles might cause, that Luther struggled. As the Protestant world has receded

from the great sacramental principles which Luther maintained at Marburg, just in that proportion has it been torn
with internal dissension — and just in proportion to its return
to them, has there risen a more earnest striving toward a.
consummation of the Saviour's prayer: that all his people
might be one. No man in Luther's time, no man since, so
harmoniously blended, so kept in their due proportion all the
elements of a real Reformation. "Luther's character," says
Bengel, "was truly great. All his brother Reformers together will not make a Luther. His death was an important
epocha; for nothing, since it took place, has ever been *really*
added to the Reformation itself."

The artist closes this period fitly, with the delivery of the
Augsburg Confession, (1530,) that great providen-   - The Augsburg
tial act by which God, having brought to mature   Confession.
consciousness the leading doctrines of the Gospel, gave them
currency in the whole world. Thirteen years had passed since
the truth, like a whisper in a secret place, had been uttered at
Wittenberg; now it was to ring like a trumpet before the
Emperor and his whole realm. "In sighs and prayers," writes
Luther from Coburg, "I am by your side. If we fall, Christ
falls with us — if He fall, rather will I fall with him than
stand with the Emperor; but we need not fear, for Christ
overcometh the world." In the picture, the artist has ranged
the Evangelical party to the right, the Romish to the left of
the spectator: contrary to the historical fact, he has introduced
Melanchthon, who stands most prominently, with folded arms
and careworn face. Below him, the Elector, John the Constant, clasps his hands in silent invocation; behind whom
stands George, Margrave of Brandenburg, and by his side sits
Philip, Landgrave of Hesse, bracing himself on his sword.
In the centre sits Charles, his Spanish origin showing itself
in his features. Back of his seat is embroidered the double-
headed crowned eagle of the Empire. A crown with triple
divisions, the central one of which is surmounted by a
small cross, rests on his head — the sceptre is in his hand.
The ermine, crosiers, mitres, cowl, and cardinal's hat mark
the party to his right. Before him the Chancellor Baier reads

the Confession. Around the picture are thrown connected Gothic ornaments; in the upper arch of which Luther is prostrate in prayer. At its base an angel holds in either hand the coat of arms of Luther and Melanchthon, with an intertwining band, on which are traced the words from Luther's favorite Psalm: "I shall not die, but live, and declare the works of the Lord." From the highest point, not without significance. rises the cross, and here this part appropriately ends.

The Church thus fairly brought to a full self-consciousness, The Reforma- the FIFTH part, presents us, in four characteristic tion in its results. pictures, the *results*. In the first, Luther, with all his co-laborers, Christian and Jewish, around him, labors on that *translation* of which even a Jesuit historian speaks thus: "Luther's translation of the Bible is a noble monument of litera- Translation of ture, a vast enterprise which seemed to require the Bible. more than the life of man; but which Luther accomplished in a few years. The poetic soul finds in this translation evidences of genius, and expressions as natural, beautiful and melodious as in the original languages. Luther's translation sometimes renders the primitive phrase with touching simplicity, invests itself with sublimity and magnificence, and receives all the modifications which he wishes to impart to it. It is simple in the recital of the patriarch, glowing in the predictions of the prophets, familiar in the Gospels, and colloquial in the Epistles. The imagery of the original is rendered with undeviating fidelity; the translation occasionally approaches the text. We must not then be astonished at the enthusiasm which Saxony felt at the appearance of Luther's version. Both Catholics and Protestants regarded it an honor done to their ancient idiom."* In the picture, Luther stands between Bugenhagen and Melanchthon; Jonas, Forstensius, Creuziger, and the Rabbins are engaged in the effort to solve some difficulty that has risen.

The second result is shown in a scene in a school-room, The Catechism. in which the *Catechism* has just been introduced. Luther sits in the midst of the children teaching them the first Article of the Creed. Jonas is distributing the

---

* Audin's Luther, chap. xxiv.

book among them, and in the background a number of teachers listen that they may learn to carry out this new feature in their calling.

The third result is shown in the *pulpit.* Luther had given the Bible for all ages, and all places; he had laid The Pulpit. primal principles at the foundation of human Church Service. thought, by introducing the Catechism into the schools; now he re-creates the service of the church. In the engraving the artist has grouped happily, all that is associated with the Evangelical service. Luther, in the pulpit, is preaching to nobles and subjects, with all the fervor of his soul. The font and altar, illumined by a flood of sunbeams, recall the Sacraments; the organ reminds us of the place which the Reformation gave to sacred music, and the alms-box, of its appeals to sacred pity. The fourth picture represents the administration of the Lord's Supper in both kinds; Luther extends the cup to the Elector John Frederick, whilst Bugenhagen distributes the bread.

The SIXTH general division shows us Luther in *private life.* First we have two pictures illustrating his relations Luther in private life. Princes. to his princes. In one he is represented reading Friends. Family. from the Bible to his devoted friend, the Elector John the Constant; in the other, on his sick-bed, he is visited and comforted by the Elector John Frederick, (1537.) Secondly, we have him in his relations to his personal friends. In the first picture, Luther is sitting for his likeness, to Lucas Cranach; in the next he is rousing Melanchthon almost from the torpor of death, by the prayer of faith; the third, illustrating the introduction of the German church music, conducts us into Luther's "Chantry in the House." With his children and friends around him, he is giving voice to the first Evangelical hymns. The little choir is led by Walter, Master of the Electoral Chapel; on the left stands the Chanter, on the right, Mathesius. Thirdly. we see him in his family. The first picture shows him in the enjoyment of all that imparts delight to summer — with his household and his most familiar friends about him. It is a charming scene of innocent festivity which the artist here brings before the eye. Under a trellis mantled with vines

3

loaded with rich clusters of grapes, the party is assembled, at sunset. Luther holds out his hands to his youngest child, who, by the aid of his mother, is tottering towards his father with a bunch of grapes weighing down his little hands. The oldest boy, mounted on a light ladder, hands down the grapes, which Madeleine receives in her apron. The third boy is bringing to his father a cluster remarkable for its size; the second son is playing with the dog, perhaps that very dog which, Luther said, had "looked at many books." The ground is covered with melons. One of Luther's friends plays upon the flute, another sketches a basket of beautiful fruit; two of them sit beneath the arbor, and two others wander in the garden in friendly converse. Through an arch in the wall the river is seen winding quietly along, under the last rays of the declining sun. What a change from the time of scourging before the crucifix!

As a counterpart to this scene, we next have Luther on Luther at Christmas. Christmas Eve in the family circle. This is a picture that touches the heart. The Christmas-tides of Luther's life might indeed be considered as its epitome.

Fourteen times Christmas dawned on the cradle, or on the sports of Luther as a peasant boy. Four times Christmas found the boy in the school at Magdeburg. Long years after in his old age, he gave a sketch of those Christmas days. "At the season when the Church keeps the festival of Christ's birth, we scholars went through the hamlets from house to house, singing in quartette the familiar hymns about Jesus, the little child born at Bethlehem. As we were passing a farm-yard at the end of a village, a farmer came out, and in his coarse voice, offered us food. His heart was kind, but we had become so familiar with the threats and cruelty of the school, that we fled at the sound of harsh tones. But his repeated calls reassured us, and we returned and received his gifts."

Four times Christmas found him amid the toils of the school at Erfurt. Then came a Christmas in which the angel voice seemed no more to sing, "Peace on earth, good will toward men;" nothing but wrath seemed above him, and the pains of death around him. In the gray stone walls of the cloister he shut himself up to wrestle with dark doubts and agonizing fears.

Christmas after Christmas came. Some sunshine flickered in successive years over the cell of the monk. The gentle hand of him who came as the Babe of Bethlehem was touching and healing the heart corroded with care. Gleams of in dwelling greatness began to break forth from the cloud in which he had been folded.

The turn of the autumn leaves of 1517 reminded children that Christmas was once more drawing near; but on the gales which swept those leaves from the trees was borne, through all Christendom, the first sounds of a mighty battle for the right of the Babe of Bethlehem to sit upon the throne of all hearts as the Saviour of the race. Years followed, but Christmas and all festivals, and all waking and all dreaming thoughts of men were directed to one great life-question, were absorbed in one surpassing interest. In half of Christendom, as Christmas eve came on, the soft light in children's eyes turned to a fierce glare, as lisping amid their toys and echoing the words of the old, they spoke of the traitor to the mother of the blessed Babe, the heretic who would destroy their Christmas if he could. In the other half of Christendom the eyes of men grew bright, and those of women were suffused with tears of gratitude, and children shouted for gladness at the mention of the name of one who had led back the race to the cradle, and taught them to bow there, as did the shepherds in childlike trust — trust not in the mother, but in her holy Child.

All days were Christmas to the great Restorer. He had found the Christ, and when he was not kneeling with the shepherds, he was singing with the angels. One Christmas he spent in his rocky Patmos, but a starlight, as soft as that of Palestine on the mystic night, touched every pinnacle of the old towers. The next Christmas passed in that circle of near friends which loved and was loved by one cf the greatest and warmest hearts that ever beat in human bosoms. But-tle and storm, sorrow and sickness came, but Christmas came too.

Then came a bright year, not the most glorious, but the most happy of his life. That great home-nature had never had a home. His Christmas had been spent in the home of others. There came a Christmas, and by his side, as he thanked God once more for the great gift to whose memory it was consecrated, there knelt by him his wife, her hand in his, and her face turned with his towards the world, whose light and song is the Babe of Bethlehem. The heaven of the presence of children was in that home in the Christmas of after years. Madeleine and Martin, Paul and Margaret, immortal by their birth, were the olive-plants around the Christmas tree. In the beautiful pictures by König, one of the happiest is devoted to Luther at Christmas in the family circle. The Christmas tree blazes in all its glory in the centre; the tapers imparting a new ravishment to those inconceivable fruits, trumpets, horses, cakes, and dolls, which only Christmas trees can bear. On Luther's lap kneels his youngest child, clasping him around the neck. Its little night-cap and slip and bare feet show that it has been kept from its bed to see the wonderful sight. On Luther's shoulder, and clasping his hands in hers, leans Catherine, with the light of love, that light which can beam only from the eye of a devoted wife and mother, shining upon him. The oldest boy, under Melanchthon's direction, is aiming with a cross-bow at an apple on the tree, recalling to our mind that charming letter which his father wrote from Coburg to him, when he was only four years old, in which are detailed the glories of that paradisiacal garden, meant for all good boys, where, among apples and pears, and ponies with golden bits and silver saddles, crossbows of silver were not forgotten.*

---

* Luther's letter to his little son is so beautiful and characteristic that our readers, though they have read it a hundred times, will not pass it by as we give it here. It was written in 1530, from Coburg, when Luther's destiny, and the whole future of his work, seemed trembling in the balance. It shows that his childlike mind was at once the cause and the result of his repose of spirit in God.

"Grace and peace in Christ, my dear little son. I am very glad to know that

At the table, "Muhme Lehne" (cousin Helena, not a withered old woman, as she is generally pictured, but Luther's young niece, who was not married till Madeleine was nine years old,) is showing a book of pictures to the second boy; the third boy clasps his father's knee with one hand, in which, however, he manages to hold a string also, by which he has been drawing along a knight in full armor on horseback, while with the other hand he holds up a hobby-horse. Madeleine is clasping in her hand, in ecstasy, the little angel which always stands apeak of all orthodox Christmas trees — when it can be had — and which, when the curtain of the gorgeous child-drama of Christmas eve has fallen, is given to the angel of the household — the best of the children. Her doll by her side is forgotten, the full light from the tree is on her happy face, in which, however, there is an air of thought, something more of heavenly musing than is wont to be pictured upon the face of a child.

you learn your lessons well, and love to say your prayers. Keep on doing so, my little boy, and when I come home I will bring you something pretty from the fair. I know a beautiful garden, where there are a great many children in fine little coats, and they go under the trees and gather beautiful apples and pears, cherries and plums: they sing, and run about, and are as happy as they can be. Sometimes they ride about on nice little ponies, with golden bridles and silver saddles. I asked the man whose garden it is, What little children are these? And he told me, They are little children who love to pray and learn, and are good. Then I said: My dear sir, I have a little boy at home; his name is little Hans Luther; would you let him come into the garden too, to eat some of these nice apples and pears, and ride on these fine little ponies, and play with these children? The man said: If he loves to say his prayers, and learn his lesson, and is a good boy, he may come. And Philip and Jocelin may come too; and when they are all together, they can play upon the fife and drum and lute and all kinds of instruments, and skip about and shoot with little cross-bows. He then showed me a beautiful mossy place in the middle of the garden, for them to skip about in, with a great many golden fifes, and drums, and silver cross-bows. The children had not yet had their dinner, and I could not wait to see them play, but I said to the man: My dear sir, I will go away and write all about it to my little son, John, and tell him to be fond of saying his prayers, and learn well, and be good, so that he may come into this garden; but he has a cousin Lehne, whom he must bring along with him. The man said, Very well, go write to him. Now, my dear little son, love your lessons, and your prayers, and tell Philip and Jocelin to do so too, that you may all come to the garden. May God bless you Give cousin Lehne my love, and kiss her for me."

Oh, happy Christmas! thou mayest be the prelude to wail
ing. The little coffin may follow the Christmas tree within
our door. Thy babe, O Bethlehem, turned in the sleep of that
hallowed night, his pure, pale face toward Gethsemane. The
angel of the Christmas tree could not guard the home from
life's sorrows. Days of grief are coming thick and fast upon
that noble one, whom heaven, earth, and hell knew so well.
Carrying the weight of a wounded heart, that form was
bowed, which neither kings, nor popes, nor devils could bend.
The candles of the Christmas tree of 1542 were not mirrored
in the eyes of his beautiful and darling Madeleine. Those
gentle eyes had been closed by her father's hand three months
before—the ruddy lips parting in joy at the Christmas festival,
one year ago, had received the last kiss—their music was
hushed in the home, and the little ones grew still in the very
flush of their joy, as they thought that their sister was lying
in the church-yard, with the chill snows drifting around her
grave.

The old man's heart was longing for Christmas in heaven,
and his sigh was heard.

Through threescore and two years he had on earth opened
his eyes upon the natal day of our Redeemer. When the next
Christmas came he stood by that Redeemer's side in glory
and transfigured in heaven's light, and in surpassing sweetness, there stood with him that fair girl who had gazed upon
the angel of the Christmas tree with dreamy eyes, which told
that even then, in thought, she was already in heaven.

As we think upon the obvious meaning of the artist in her
attitude and occupation, the heart grows, not wholly unpre-
pared for the next and last of these family scenes. Luther
kneels by the coffin of this same lovely daughter. The struggle
is over; a holy serenity illumines his face. He has given her
back, with no rebellious murmur, to her God. To those who
have contemplated the character of Luther only
in his public life, it might appear strange to
assert that there never was a heart more susceptible than
his to all that is tender in human emotion, or melting in human sympathies. The man who, while he was shaking to its

Luther and Ma-
deleine.

foundation the mightiest dominion the world ever saw, remained unshaken, was in his social and domestic life a perfect example of gentleness. " Perhaps no man of so humble, peaceable disposition ever filled the world with contention. We cannot but see that he would have loved privacy, quiet diligence in the shade; that it was against his will he ever became a notoriety."—"They err greatly who imagine that this man's courage was ferocity—no accusation could be more unjust. A most gentle heart withal, full of pity and love, as indeed the truly valiant heart ever is. I know few things more touching than those soft breathings of affection, soft as a child's or a mother's, in this great wild heart of Luther. Luther to a slight observer might have seemed a timid, weak man; modesty, affectionate shrinking tenderness, the chief distinction of him. It is a noble valor which is roused in a heart like this, once stirred up into defiance; all kindled into a heavenly blaze." * How open his heart was to those influences which sanctify whilst they sadden, he showed on the death of Elizabeth, his second child, in infancy: " My little daughter is dead. I am surprised how sick at heart she has left me; a woman's heart, so shaken am I. I could not have believed that a father's soul would have been so tender toward his child." " I can teach you what it is to be a father, especially a father of one of that sex which, far more than sons, has the power of awakening our most tender emotions." Yet more touching was that event to which our artist has consecrated this picture. Madeleine, his third child, and second daughter, died in September, 1542, in the fourteenth year of her age — four years before her father. " Luther bore this blow with wonderful firmness. As his daughter lay very ill, he exclaimed, as he raised his eyes to heaven, 'I love her much, but, O my God! if it be thy will to take her hence, I would give her up to thee without one selfish murmur.' One day she suffered violent pain: he approached her bed, and taking hold of her small thin hands, pressed them again and again to his lips. 'My dearest child, my own sweet and good Madeleine, I know you would gladly stay with your father here; but in heaven there

* Carlyle's Heroes and Hero-Worship, p. 125

is a better Father waiting for you. You will be equally ready to go to your Father in heaven, will you not?' 'O yes, dear father,' answered the dying child, 'let the will of God be done.' 'Dear little girl,' he continued, 'the spirit is willing, but the flesh is weak.' He walked to and fro in agitation, and said, ': Ah, yes! I have loved this dear child too much. If the flesh is so strong, what becomes of the spirit?' Turning to a friend who had come to visit him: 'See,' said he, 'God has not given such good gifts these thousand years to any bishop as He has to me. We may glorify ourselves in the gifts of God. Alas! I feel humbled that I cannot rejoice now as I ought to do, nor render sufficient thanks to God. I try to lift up my heart from time to time to our Lord in some little hymn, and to feel as I ought to do.'—'Well, whether we live or die, we are the Lord's.'"

The night before Madeleine's death, her mother had a dream, in which she saw two fair youths beautifully attired, who came as if they wished to take Madeleine away with them, and conduct her to be married. When Melanchthon came the next morning and asked the lady how it was with her daughter, she related her dream, at which he seemed frightened, and re marked to others, "that the young men were two holy angels, sent to carry the maiden to the true nuptials of a heavenly kingdom." She died that same day. When the last agony came on, and the countenance of the young girl was clouded with the dark hues of approaching death, her father threw himself on his knees by her bedside, and with clasped hands, weeping bitterly, prayed to God that he would spare her. Her consciousness ceased, and resting in her father's arms she breathed her last. Catherine, her mother, was in a recess of the room, unable, from excess of grief, to look upon the death-bed of her child. Luther softly laid the head of his beloved one upon the pillow, and repeatedly exclaimed: "Poor child, thou hast found a Father in heaven! O my God! let thy will be done!" Melanchthon then observed that the love of parents for their children is an image of the divine love impressed on the hearts of men. God loves mankind no less than parents do their children.

On the following day she was interred. When they placed her on the bier, her father exclaimed, " My poor, dear little Madeleine, you are at rest now!" The workman had made the coffin somewhat too small. "Thy couch here," said Luther, "is narrow; but oh! how beautiful is that on which thou restest above!" Then looking long and fixedly at her, he said, "Yes, dear child, thou shalt rise again, shalt shine as the stars, yes, like the sun. . . I am joyful in spirit; but oh, how sad in the flesh! It is a strange feeling, this, to know she is so certainly at rest, that she is happy, and yet to be so sad." When the body was being lowered into the grave, "Farewell!" he exclaimed, "Farewell, thou lovely star, we shall meet again."

The people in great crowds attended the funeral, showing the deepest sympathy with his grief. When the bearers came to his house and expressed their sorrow, he replied, "Ah, grieve no more for her; I have given to heaven another angel. Oh! that we may each experience such a death: such a death I would gladly die this moment." "True," said a bystander; to whom Luther replied, "Flesh is flesh, and blood is blood. But there may be joy in the heart, whilst there is sorrow in the countenance. It is the flesh that weeps and is afflicted." At the grave the language of condolence was offered. "We know how you suffer."—"Thanks for your sympathy," said he, "but I am not sad — my dear angel is in heaven."

Whilst some laborers were singing at the grave the words "Lord remember not our sins of old," he was heard to sigh: "No, gracious Lord; nor our sins of to-day, nor of times to come."

When the grave-digger threw the earth on the coffin, "Fix your eyes," said Luther, "on the resurrection of the flesh; heaven is my daughter's portion — body and soul — all is the arrangement of God in his providence. Why should we repine? Is it not His will that is accomplished? We are the children of eternity. I have begotten a child for heaven."

On returning from the burial, he said, amongst other things, "The fate of our children, and above all, of girls, is ever a cause of uneasiness. I do not fear so much for boys; they can find a living anywhere, provided they know how to work. But it is different with girls; they, poor things, must search for employment, staff in hand. A boy can enter the schools, and attain eminence, but a girl cannot do much to advance herself; and is easily led away by bad example, and is lost. Therefore, without regret, I give up this dear one to our Lord. Children die without anguish; they know not the bitter pains of death; it is as if they fell asleep."

This affliction struck Luther to the heart. He looked upon it as an admonition of Heaven: it was another thunderbolt. The first had taken from him the friend of his youth, Alexis: the second snatched from him an idolized child, the joy of his old age. From this period, all his letters are tinged with melancholy: the raven wing of death was ever fluttering in his ear. On receiving a letter from the Elector, who wished him many years of long life, he shook his head mournfully, and in reply to his friend wrote: 'The pitcher has gone too often to the well; it will break at last.' One day, while preaching, he drew tears from his audience, by announcing to them his approaching death. "The world is tired of me," said he, "and I am tired of the world; soon shall we be divorced — the traveller will soon quit his lodging."

Soon after her death, he wrote to a friend: "Report has, no doubt, informed you of the transplanting of my daughter to the kingdom of Christ; and although my wife and I ought only to think of offering up joyful thanks to the Almighty for her happy end, by which she has been delivered from all the snares of the world, nevertheless, the force of natural affection is so great, that I cannot forbear indulging in tears, sighs, and groans; say rather my heart dies within me. I feel, engraven on my inmost soul, her features, words, and actions; all that she was to me, in life and health, and on her sick-bed — my dear, my dutiful child. The death of Christ himself (and oh! what are all deaths in comparison?) cannot tear her away from my thoughts, as it should. She was, as you know, so sweet, so amiable, so full of tenderness."

When the coffin had been covered with earth, a small tombstone was placed over it, on which was the name of the child, her age, the day of her death, and a text of Scripture. Some time after, when Luther could apply himself to labor, he composed a Latin inscription, which was carved upon a monumental slab: and which breathes a spirit of subdued melancholy, and resignation to God's will:

> "Dormio cum Sanctis hic Magdalena, Lutheri
> Filia, et hoc strato tecta quiesco meo;
> Filia mortis eram, peccati semine nata,
> Sanguine sed vivo Christe redempta tuo."

> "I, Luther's daughter Madeleine, with the Saints here sleep,
> And covered, calmly rest on this my couch of earth;
> Daughter of death I was, born of the seed of sin,
> But by thy precious blood redeemed, O Christ! I live."

"We looked," says Audin, the Romish historian, who, animated by a strange enthusiasm for the great opposer of the corruptions of his Church, followed his footsteps as a pilgrim — "we looked for this tomb in the cemetery at Wittenberg, but could not find it." The mild, regular features, the gentle eyes, the broad forehead, the flowing hair, and womanly repose, which the picture * of this child presents, are all in keeping with the image which her father's grief has impressed upon the heart; and though the searcher looks in vain for the stone which marks her lowly resting-place, her memory shall dwell sweetly in the heart of the world, with that of her more than illustrious father, to the end of time.

The next two pictures illustrate Luther's strength of character while in personal jeopardy. The first represents Luther and Kohlhase — the second, Luther among the dying and the dead, during the plague. The last three pictures present the closing scenes of his life — his journey to Mansfeld on a mission of peace and conciliation, his death and burial. During his last hours he repeated frequently the words: "Father, into thy hands I commend my spirit. Thou hast redeemed me, O God of truth." When Jonas and Coelius asked him, "Reverend father, do you die faithful

Luther's last days. Death.

* This portrait is given in Juncker's interesting work on the medals of the Reformation.

to Christ, and to the doctrine you have preached?" He replied distinctly, "I do!" These were his last words on earth, and in the first hour of February 18th, 1546, he fell asleep in Jesus. "Now," said Melanchthon, as he stood by the coffin, — "now he is united with the prophets of whom he loved to speak, now they greet him as their fell w-laborer, and with him thank the Lord who collects and upholds his Church to the end of time."

In addition to the descriptive matter that accompanies each picture, we have "Historical Sketches" by Gelzer. First we have an introduction, and then four sketches. The first sketch presents the preparation and ground-work of the Reformation — the Reformation before Luther, and the great work which took place in him before he came forth to the world. The second sketch embraces the contest with Rome; the third, "Reformation and Revolution;" the last, the Reformer and his work.

There was one picture promised us, which we would fain _{Charles V. at} have had, but which is not given. It is one which _{Luther's tomb.} connects itself with the Providence of God watching over the ashes of his servant, whose body he had protected in life. Luther had been "taken from the evil to come." The year after his death Wittenberg was filled with the troops of Charles V., many of whom were full of intense hate to the great Reformer. One of the soldiers gave Luther's effigies in the Castle-church two stabs with his dagger. The Spaniards earnestly solicited their Emperor to destroy the tomb, and dig up and burn the remains of Luther, as this second Huss could not now be burned alive. To this diabolical proposition the Emperor sternly replied: "My work with Luther is done; he has now another Judge, whose sphere I may not invade. I war with the living, not with the dead." And when he found that the effort was not dropped, to bring about this sacri- legious deed, he gave orders that any violation of Luther's tomb should be followed by the death of the offender.* Charles, it is said, died a Protestant on the great central doctrine of

---

* Bayle's Dictionary, (H. H.) Juncker's Guldene und Silberne Ehren-Ge dächtniss Lutheri. Franckf. und Leipz. 1706, p. 281

justification by faith. May we not hope that after the warfare of life, Charles, the most ambitious of the Emperors of his age, and Luther, the greatest disturber of his plans of ambition, have reached a common consummation.

It is a hopeful thing that the German heart, through all religious and civil convulsions, has remained true to the memory of Luther. Romanists have emulated Protest- Luther characterized. ants in his praise; Rationalists have seemed to venerate him whilst they were laboring to undo his work. After three centuries of birth-throes, Germany feels that she has given to the world no second Luther. The womb of Time bears such fruit but once in thousands of years. " In such reverence do I hold Luther," says LESSING, " that I rejoice in having been able to find some defects in him ; for Lessing. I have, in fact, been in imminent danger of making him an object of idolatrous veneration. The proofs, that n some things he was like other men, are to me as precious as the most dazzling of his virtues."—" What a shame," says Hamann, (1759,) " to our times, that the spirit of this man, who founded our Church, so lies beneath the ashes ! What a power of eloquence, what a spirit of interpretation, what a prophet ! "—" We are not able to place ourselves even up to the point from which he started."

" He created the German language," says HEINE. " He was not only the greatest, but the most German man of our history. In his character all the faults and all the virtues Heine. of the Germans are combined on the largest scale. Then he had qualities which are very seldom found united, which we are accustomed to regard as irreconcilable antagonisms. He was, at the same time, a dreamy mystic and a practical man of action. His thoughts had not only wings, but hands. He spoke and he acted. He was not only the tongue, but the sword of his time. When he had plagued himself all day long with his doctrinal distinctions, in the evening he took his flute and gazed at the stars, dissolved in melody and devotion. He could be soft as a tender maiden. Sometimes he was wild as the storm that uproots the oak, and then again he was gentle as the zephyr that dallies with the violet. He was full of the most awful reverence and of self sacrifice in honor of the Holy Spirit. He could merge himself entire in pure spirituality. And yet he was well acquainted with the glories of this world, and knew how to prize them. He was a complete man, I would say an absolute man, one in whom matter and spirit were not divided. To call him a spiritualist, therefore, would be as great an error as to call him a sensualist. How shall I express it? He had something original, incomprehensible, miraculous, such as we find in all providential men — something invincible, spirit-possessed."

"A fiery and daring spirit," Menzel calls him. "A hero in the garb of a monk." But the most interesting testimony is that borne by Frederick Schlegel; interesting not only because of the greatness of its source, but because based on a thorough knowledge of the person of whom he speaks, because uttered by a devoted and conscientious Romanist, and accompanied by such remarks as to show that, deep as is his admiration of Luther, he has in no respect been blinded by it. We will give extracts from his three great works: on "the History of Literature:" on "Modern History:" and on the "Philosophy of History."

Menzel.

Schlegel.

"I have already explained in what way the poetry and art of the middle age were lost, during the controversies of the sixteenth, and how our language itself became corrupted. There was one instrument by which the influx of barbarism was opposed, and one treasure which made up for what had been lost — I mean the German translation of the Bible. It is well known to you, that all true philologists regard this as the standard and model of classical expression in the German language; and that not only Klopstock, but many other writers of the first rank, have fashioned their style and selected their phrases according to the rules of this version. It is worthy of notice, that in no other modern language have so many Biblical words and phrases come into the use of common life as in ours. I perfectly agree with those writers who consider this circumstance as a fortunate one; and I believe that from it has been derived not a little of that power, life, and simplicity, oy which, I think, the best German writers are distinguished from all other moderns. The Catholic, as well as the modern Protestant scholar, has many things to find fault with in this translation; but these, after all, regard only individual passages. In these later times, we have witnessed an attempt to render a new and *rational* translation of the Bible an instrument of propagating the doctrines of the illuminati; and we have seen this too much even in the hands of Catholics themselves. But the instant this folly had blown over, we returned, with increased affection, to the excellent old version of Luther. He, indeed, has not the whole merit of producing it. We owe to him, nevertheless, the highest gratitude for placing in our hands this most noble and manly model of German expression. Even in his own writings he displays a most original eloquence, surpassed by few names that occur in the whole history of literature. He had, indeed, all those qualities which fit a man to be a revolutionary orator. This revolutionary eloquence is manifest, not only in his half-political and business writings, such as the Address to the Nobility of the German Nation, but in all the works which he has left behind him. In almost the whole of them, we perceive the marks of mighty internal conflict. Two worlds appear to be contending for the mastery over the mighty soul of this man, so favored by God and nature. Throughout all his writings there prevails a struggle between light and darkness, faith and passion, God and himself. The choice which he made — the use to which he devoted his majestic genius — these are subjects upon which it is even now quite impossible for me to speak, so as to please you all. As to the intellectual power and greatness of Luther, abstracted from all consideration of the uses to which he applied them, I think there are few, even of his own disciples, who appreciate him highly enough. His coadjutors were mostly mere scholars, indolent and enlightened men of the common order. It was upon him and his soul that the fate of Europe depended. He was the man of his age and nation." *

Let us hear another expression of the opinion of this great man. "That the Reformation did not at its very commence-

* Lectures on the History of Literature, New York, 1841, p. 348–350.

ment become a revolution of this kind, we are chiefly indebted to Luther, (a revolution in which war and the flames of popular passion took their own destructive course.) He it was who thus gave permanency to the Reformation. Had not Luther opposed with all his power the dangerous errors into which some of his adherents at the very first fell; had these fanatical doctrines of universal equality, and of the abolition of all temporal authority as a thing superfluous in the new state of things, obtained the upper hand; had the so-called Reformation of faith and of the Church become wholly and entirely a political and national revolution; in that case, the first shock of civil war would have been incontestably more terrific and more universal; but it would, probably, when the storm had blown over, have subsided of itself, and a return to the old order of things would have ensued. The princes in particular were indebted to Luther for having contributed so vigorously to stifle the flames of rebellion; and he must thereby have gained consideration even among those who disapproved of his doctrines and proceedings. His personal character in general was excellently adapted to consolidate and perpetuate his party. The great energy, which gave him such a decided preponderance over all who co-operated with him, preserved as much unity as was at all possible in such a state of moral ferment. With whatever passionate violence Luther may have expressed himself, he nevertheless, in his principles and modes of thinking, preserved in many points the precise medium that was necessary to keep his party together as a distinct party. Had he at the first beginning gone farther, had he sanctioned the fanaticism adverted to above, the whole affair would then have fallen sooner to the ground. The very circumstance, that he did not at first secede from the ancient faith more than he did, procured him so many and such important adherents, and gave such strength to his party. He was undeniably gifted with great qualities. Luther's eloquence made him a man of the people; his principles, however, despite his passionate expression of them, remained, nevertheless, in essentials, both with regard to political subjects and to matters of faith, within certain limits; and joined to that circumstance, the very obstinacy which his friends complained of, consolidated and united the new party and gave it a permanent strength."*

With some extracts from the " Philosophy of History," by the same distinguished author, we shall close the illustrations from his hand.

" In the first place, as regards the Reformation, it is evident of itself, that a man who accomplished so mighty a revolution in the human mind, and in his age, could have been endowed with no ordinary powers of intellect, and no common strength of character. Even his writings display an astonishing bold- ness and energy of thought and language, united with a spirit of impetuous, passionate and convulsive enthusiasm. The opinion, as to the use which was made of these high powers of genius, must, of course, vary with the religious principles of each individual; but the extent of these intellectual endow- ments themselves, and the strength and perseverance of char- acter with which they were united, must be universally ad- mitted. Many who did not afterwards adhere to the new opinions, still thought, at the commencement of the Reforma- tion, that Luther was the real man for his age, who had received a high vocation to accomplish the great work of regen- eration, the strong necessity of which was then universally felt. If, at this great distance of time, we pick out of the writings of this individual many very harsh expressions, nay, particular words which are not only coarse but absolutely gross, nothing of any moment can be proved or determined by such selections. Indeed, the age in general, not only in Ger- many, but in other very highly civilized countries, was char- acterized by a certain coarseness in manners and language, and by a total absence of all excessive polish and over-refinement of character. But this coarseness would have been productive of no very destructive effects; for intelligent men well knew that the wounds of old abuses lay deep, and were ulcerated in their very roots; and no one, therefore, was shocked if the knife destined to amputate abuses, cut somewhat deep. It was by the conduct of Luther and the influence which he thereby acquired, that the Reformation was promoted and

* Lectures on Modern History, London, 1849, p. 169.

4

consolidated. Without this, Protestantism would have sunk
into the lawless anarchy which marked the proceedings of
the Hussites, and to which the War of the Peasants rapidly
tended; and it would inevitably have been suppressed, like all
the earlier popular commotions — for, under the latter form,
Protestantism may be said to have sprung up several centuries
before. None of the other heads and leaders of the new re
ligious party had the power, or were in a situation to uphold
the Protestant religion: its present existence is solely and entirely the work and the deed of one man, unique in his way,
and who holds unquestionably a conspicuous place in the history of the world. Much was staked on the soul of that man,
and this was in every respect a mighty and critical moment in
the annals of mankind and the march of time."

It will, perhaps, not be wholly a thankless work to add here
some of the attestations of distinguished men of every shade
of opinion, and in the most varied positions, which demonstrate how profound and many-sided was that character which
left so great an impress on them all. "Martin Luther," says
Dr. Bancroft, "a man of the most powerful mind and intrepid
character, who persisted resolutely in his defence
Dr. Bancroft. of Christian liberty and Christian truth; and by
the blessing of God he triumphed over all opposition. His
name is identified in every country with the reformed religion,
and will be venerated and esteemed in every subsequent age,
by all who prize religious freedom, and set a value on religious
privileges." *

This is the language of a Congregational Unitarian, in New
England. Let us hear from a high-church English Bishop,
eminent for all that intellect can confer, a testimony no less
strong: "Martin Luther's life," says Bishop Atterbury, "was
a continued warfare. He was engaged against the
Atterbury. united forces of the Papal world, and he stood the
shock of them bravely, both with courage and success. He
was a man certainly of high endowments of mind, and great
virtues. He had a vast understanding, which raised him to a

---

* Sermons on Doctrines, etc., which Christians have made the Subject of Controversy. By Aaron Bancroft, D. D. Worcester, 1822. Serm. XI.

pitch of learning unknown to the age in which he lived. His knowledge in Scripture was admirable, his elocution manly, and his way of reasoning, with all the subtility that the plain truths he delivered would bear. His thoughts were bent always on great designs, and he had a resolution to go through with them, and the assurance of his mind was not to be shaken, or surprised. His life was holy, and, when he had leisure for retirement, severe. His virtues were active chiefly, and social, and not those lazy, sullen ones of the cloister. He had no ambition, but in the service of God ; for other things, neither his enjoyments nor wishes ever went higher than the bare conveniences of living. If, among this crowd of virtues, a failing crept in, we must remember that an apostle himself had not been irreproachable ; if in the body of his doctrine, a flaw is to be seen, yet the greatest lights of the Church, and in the purest times of it, were, we know, not exact in all their opinions. Upon the whole, we have certainly great reason to break out in the language of the prophet, and say, ' How beautiful on the mountains are the feet of him who bringeth glad tidings.' "*

Bayle, prince of skeptics, has devoted an article of his great Dictionary, to a defence of Luther's character from the falsehoods which have been published concern- Bayle.
ing him. His slanderers, Bayle says, have had no regard to probability or the rules of their own art. " His greatest enemies cannot deny but that he had eminent qualities, and history affords nothing more surprising than what he has done : for a simple monk to be able to give Popery so rude a shock, that there needed but such another entirely to overthrow the Romish Church, is what we cannot sufficiently admire." †

Archbishop Tennison, of the Church of England, says : " Luther was indeed a man of warm temper, and uncourtly language ; but (besides that he had his Tennison.

* Atterbury's vindication of Luther, (1687.) Burnet, in his History of his Own Times, regards this vindication as one of the most able defences of the Protestant religion. Atterbury, on his trial, appealed to this book to exculpate himself from the charge of a secret leaning to Popery.

† Bayle's Histor. and Critic. Dictionary, translated by Maizeaux, London, 1736, vol. iii., pp. 934–937.

education among those who so vehemently reviled him) it may be considered, whether in passing through so very rough a sea, it was not next to impossible for him not to beat the insulting waves till they foamed again. Erasmus tells us ' that he perceived, the better any man was, the more he relished the writings of Luther;' * that his very enemies allowed him to be a man of good life ; that he seemed to him to have in his breast certain eminent Evangelical sparks; that it was plain that some condemned things in Luther's writings which in Augustine and Bernard passed for pious and orthodox." †

Bishop Kidder, in the same interesting collection from which we have just quoted, alludes to the " Confessions of Adversaries," which Bellarmine has presented as the thirteenth mark of the Church. This weapon he turns against the great Romish author: " As for Martin Luther, whatever the Romanists say of him now, yet certain it is that Erasmus, who I hope will pass with Cardinal Bellarmine for a Catholic, who lived in his time, gives a better account of him. In his letter to the Cardinal of York, speaking of Luther, he says: ‡ ' His life is approved by all men, and this is no slight ground of prejudice in his favor, that such was the integrity of his morals, that his enemies could find nothing to reproach him with.' Again, in a letter to Melanchthon: § ' All men among us approve the life of Luther.' " ||

Even Bossuet, the eagle of Meaux, is obliged, at the beginning of his ferocious assault on Protestantism, to concede something in regard to Luther's gifts: " In the time of Luther, the most violent rupture, and greatest apostasy occurred, which had perhaps ever been seen in Christendom. The two parties, who have called themselves reformed, have alike recognized him as the author of this new Reformation. It is not alone his followers, the Lutherans, who have lavished upon him the highest praises. Calvin frequently admires his virtues, his magnanimity, his constancy, the incom-

---

* Erasm. Epist. ad Albert. Episc., etc., pp. 584, 585.

† Bellarmine's Notes of the Church Examined and Refuted, London, 1840, p. 251.

‡ Erasm. Ep., lib. xi., Ep. 1.

§ Ep., lib. vii., Ep. 43. || Bellarmine's Notes Examined, etc., p. 312

parable industry which he displayed against the Pope. He is
the trumpet, or rather, he is the thunder — he is the lightning
which has roused the world from its lethargy : it was not so
much Luther that spoke as God whose lightnings burst from
his lips.   And it is true he had a strength of genius, a vehemence in his discourses, a living and impetuous eloquence
which entranced and ravished the people." *

The judgment of Bower in regard to Luther, is, on the
whole, the most discriminating which had appeared in the English language up to his time.   Bower.
" In the personal character of Luther, we discern many qualities calculated to enable him to discharge with success the
important duty to which he was called.   A constitutional
ardor for devotion, a boundless thirst of knowledge, and a
fearless zeal in communicating it, were prominent characteristics of this extraordinary man.   An unwearied perseverance
in theological research, led him to detect errors, and to relinquish step by step, many of his early opinions.   In all situ-
ations Luther is the same, pursuing indefatigably the knowl
edge of the word of God, and never scrupling to avow his
past mistakes, whenever the confession could facilitate the
inquiries or confirm the faith of others.   It was in vain that
the head of the Church, and the chief of the German Empire
combined to threaten and proscribe him — he braved with
equal courage the very lance of either power, and continued
to denounce, with an unsparing hand, the prevalence of corruption.   In no single instance did he seek to turn to his
personal advantage, his distinctions and the influence attached
to them.   How few individuals would have possessed Luther's
power without making it subservient to the acquisition of
rank or honors?   All these were disdained by him, and his
mind remained wholly occupied with the diffusion of religious
truth.   Even literary fame had no attractions for him.   The
improvement of the condition of his fellow-creatures was the
object, which with him superseded every other consideration.
No temptation of ambition could remove him, in his days of

* Œuvres de Bossuet, (Histoire des Variations,) Paris, Didot Frères 1851, vol
iv., p. 9.

celebrity, from his favorite University of Wittenberg. While his doctrine spread far and wide, and wealthy cities would have been proud to receive him, Luther clung to the spot where he discharged the duty of a teacher, and to the associates whom he had known in his season of humility. The freedom of his language in treating of the conduct of the great, arose partly from his constitutional ardor, and partly from an habitual impression of the all-powerful claims of truth. The lofty attitude, so often assumed by him, is not therefore to be attributed to pride or vanity. In treating of the Scriptures, he considered himself as acting in the presence of God, whose majesty and glory were so infinitely exalted above all created beings, as to reduce to one and the same level the artificial distinctions of worldly institutions. Under this conviction, the prince or king, who ventured to oppose what Luther considered the word of God, seemed to him no more exempted from severe epithets than the humblest of his adversaries. However we may censure the length to which his freedom was carried, the boldness of his conduct was, on the whole, productive of much good. An independent and manly tone in regard not only to religion, but to civil liberty, literature, the arts and sciences, was created and disseminated by his example. Few writers discover greater knowledge of the world, or a happier talent in analyzing and illustrating the shades of character. It is equally remarkable that no man could display more forcibly the tranquil consolations of religion. Few men entered with more ardor into the innocent pleasures of society. His frankness of disposition was apparent at the first interview, and his communicative turn, joined to the richness of his stores, rendered his conversation remarkably interesting. In treating of humorous subjects, he discovered as much vivacity and playfulness as if he had been a man unaccustomed to serious research." His conjugal and paternal affection, his love of music, his power of throwing a charm around the topics of religion, his fearlessness in danger, and his extraordinary powers as a preacher, are dwelt upon by Bower, whose sketch is one well worthy of being read.*

* The Life of Luther, etc., by Alexander Bower. Philadelphia. 1824

In a similar strain proceeds the language of the Rev. James Brewster, who, in speaking of Luther's character as a musician and composer, mentions that "the great Handel acknowledged that he had derived singular advantage from studying the compositions of the great Saxon Reformer." * Buddeus gives us a particular account of the principal writings of Luther, and points out his great services in all the departments of theology and practical Christianity. Among the foremost of these, he places his revival of catechising and his invaluable contributions to it ; he points out how much he did for moral theology, and the great obligations under which he laid the Church, by his translation of the Bible. We will give his estimate of Luther in the department of Polemic Theology: "Here, beyond controversy, the highest praise is due to our sainted Luther, who first, when all was lost, all in despair, lifted up the standard of better hopes. Nor could one better fitted for sustaining the cause of truth have been found. Acuteness of judgment and fertility of thought were both his ; these gave to him arguments of might, overwhelming eloquence which swept everything before it like a torrent. His was an intrepid soul, which neither power, danger nor threats could turn from the right. The truth indeed fought for him ; but no less did he fight for the truth, so that no mortal could have done more to defend it, and place it beyond the reach of ts foes. You are forced everywhere to confess the accurate disputer, the exquisite Theologian, the earnest defender of the truth. His own writings leave no room for doubt that he argued from profound conviction of the truth, and that he was wholly free from the crime of men who employ a line of defence, not because they regard it as true, but because it suits their purpose. The abundance of arguments well adapted to their purpose, the copiousness and power of his language, alike arrest the attention. He so demonstrates the truth, as to leave the errorist no subterfuge ; such is the firmness of his grasp, that he seizes the assent of the reader, hurries him, forces him to his conclusion. He asks no favors, makes no effort to propitiate ; he compels by the weight of proof, triumphs by dem-

Brewster.
Buddeus.

* Edinburgh Encyclopedia, vol. xii., Philadelphia, 1832, art. LUTHER.

onstration of the truth, and forces the unwilling to do homage to sound doctrine. When we look at the effrontery and obstinacy of his opponents, and their cruel purposes, we feel that in comparison with theirs, the severest language of Luther appears mild." *

Calvin, who was far from being a hearty praiser, yet speaks thus of him, in a letter to Bullinger: " Recall these
Calvin. things to your mind: how great a man Luther is, and in what great endowments he excels, with what fortitude of mind and constancy, with what excellent address, and efficacy of doctrine he has hitherto labored and watched to overthrow the kingdom of Antichrist, and propagate the doctrine of salvation. I often say, if he should call me a devil, I hold him in such honor, that I would acknowledge him an illustrious servant of God." † Again, Calvin says of him: " We sincerely testify that we regard him as a noble apostle of Christ, by whose labor and ministry the purity of the Gospel has been restored in our times." ‡ Again: " If any one will carefully consider what was the state of things at the period when Luther arose, he will see that he had to contend with almost all the difficulties which were encountered by the Apostles. In one respect, indeed, his condition was worse and harder than theirs. There was no kingdom, no principality, against which they had to declare war; whereas Luther could not go forth, except by the ruin and destruction of that empire which was not only the most powerful of all, but regarded all the rest as obnoxious to itself." We cannot forbear quoting a few more sentences from Carlyle. " As a participant and dispenser of
Carlyle. divine influences, he shows himself among human affairs a true connecting medium and visible Messenger between Heaven and Earth; perhaps the most inspired of all teachers since the first apostles of his faith; and thus not a poet only, but a Prophet and God-ordained Priest,

---

* Buddei Isagoge Historico-theologica, Lipsiæ,1730, pp 1031, 1040.

† J. Calvini Epistolæ et Responsæ, Genev., 1576, fol., p. 383.   Life of John Calvin, by Beza, translated by Sibson, Philada., 1836, p. 86.

‡ Life and Times of John Calvin, translated from the German of Paul Henry, D. D., by H. Stebbing, D. D., New York, 1851, p. 18.

which is the highest form of that dignity, and of all dignity." *
" I will call this Luther a true Great Man ; great in intellect,
in courage, affection, and integrity ; one of our most lovable
and precious men. Great, not as a hewn obelisk ; but as an
Alpine mountain, — so simple, honest, spontaneous, not setting
up to be great at all ; there for quite another purpose than being
great ! Ah, yes, unsubduable granite, piercing far and wide
into tLe heavens ; yet in the cleft of its fountains, green beautiful valleys with flowers ! A right Spiritual Hero and Prophet ; once more, a true Son of Nature and Fact, for whom
these centuries, and many that are to come yet, will be thankful to Heaven." †   Martin Chemnitz, that most precious man
of the second generation of the great divines of our Church,
like all who spoke of Luther, immediately after his
own time, breathes the spirit of profound reverence
toward him. After the death of Melanchthon, Chemnitz was
indubitably the greatest living theologian. " What Quintilian
said of Cicero: ' Ille sciat se in literis multum profecisse, cui
Cicero plurimum placebit,' I apply to Luther. A man may tell
how far he has advanced in theology, by the degree to which
he is pleased by Luther's writings." ‡   Claude, in his famous
" Defence of the Reformation," which is still richly
worth perusal, has vindicated the character of
Luther in a very judicious manner: " We discover," he says,
" a great many excellent things in him, an heroical courage, a
great love for the truth, an ardent zeal for the glory of God,
a great trust in His providence, extraordinary learning in a
dark age, a profound respect for the Holy Scripture, an indefatigable spirit, and a great many other high qualities." §

All who are familiar with the writings of S. T. Coleridge,
know how deep was his reverence for Luther. To
this his son, Henry Nelson Coleridge, makes numerous allusions in the defence of his father's religious opinions,

Chemnitz.

Claude.

The Coleridges.

* Critical and Miscellaneous Essays, by Thomas Carlyle, Philadelphia, 1850,
p. 224.
† Heroes and Hero-Worship, p. 127.
‡ Locorum Theolog. M. Chemnitti, Pars Tertia, 1623, Witebergæ, p. 41.
§ A Defence of the Reformation, translated from the French of Monsieur
Claude, etc., London, 1815, vol. i., p. 289.

which forms part of his Introduction to the "*Biographia Lite-raria.*"—"He saw," says his son, "the very mind of St. Paul in the teaching of Luther on the Law and Justification by Faith." "My father's affectionate respect for Luther is enough to alien-ate him from the High Anglican party."—"He thought the mind of Luther more akin to St. Paul's than that of any other Christian teacher."—"It is an insult," says Henry Nelson Coleridge, speaking in his own person, "to the apostolic man's (Luther's) memory, to defend him from the charge of Anti-nomianism. He knocked down with his little finger more Antinomianism than his accusers with both hands. If his doctrine is the jaw-bone of an ass, he must have been a very Samson, for he turned numbers with this instrument from the evil of their lives; and the same instrument, in the hands of mere pigmies in comparison with him, has wrought more amendment of life among the poor, than the most eloquent and erudite preachers of works and rites have to boast, by their preaching." Coleridge is here answering some of the aspersions cast by High-Church writers on Luther. Referring to one of them, who had called the Commentary on Galatians "silly," he says, "Shakspeare has been called silly by Puri-tans, Milton worse than silly by Prelatists and Papists, Words-worth was long called silly by Bonaparteans; what will not the *odium theologicum* or *politicum* find worthless and silly? To me, perhaps from my silliness, his Commentary appears the very Iliad of justification by faith alone; all the fine and strik-ing things that have been said upon the subject, are taken from it; and if the author preached a novel doctrine, or pre-sented a novel development of Scripture in this work, as Mr. Newman avers, I think he deserves great credit for his origin-ality. The Commentary contains, or rather is, a most spirited siege of Babylon, and the friends of Rome like it as well as the French like Wellington and the battle of Waterloo."—"My father called Luther, in parts, the most evangelical write he knew, after the apostles and apostolic men." This he said in view of his "depth of insight into the heart of man and into the ideas of the Bible, the fervor and reality of his religious feelings, the manliness and tenderness of his spirit, the vehement eloquence with which he assails the Romish practical fallacies and abuses." — " It is for these things that staunch ' Catholics ' hate ; for these things that my father loved and honored Luther's name." — " How would Christendom have fared without a Luther ? What would Rome have done and dared but for the Ocean of the Reformed that *rounds* her ? Luther lives yet — not so beneficially in the Lutheran Church as out of it — an antagonist spirit to Rome, and a purifying and preserving spirit in Christendom at large." *

" Luther possessed a temper and acquirements which peculiarly fitted him for the character of a Reformer. William Coxe. Without the fastidious nicety of refined taste and elegance, he was endowed with singular acuteness and logical dexterity, possessed profound and varied erudition ; and his rude, though fervid eloquence, intermixed with the coarsest wit and the keenest raillery, was of that species which is best adapted to affect and influence a popular assembly. His Latin, though it did not rise to the purity of Erasmus and his other learned contemporaries, was yet copious, free, and forcible, and he was perfectly master of his native tongue, and wrote it with such purity, that his works are still esteemed as models of style by the German critics. He was animated with an undaunted spirit, which raised him above all apprehension of danger, and possessed a perseverance which nothing could fatigue. He was at once haughty and condescending, jovial, affable, and candid in public ; studious, sober, and self-denying in private ; and he was endowed with that happy and intuitive sagacity which enabled him to suit his conduct and manners to the exigency of the moment, to lessen or avert danger by timely flexibility, or to bear down all obstacles by firmness and impetuosity. His merciless invectives and contemptuous irony, were proper weapons to repel the virulence and scurrility of his adversaries, and even the fire and arrogance of his temper, though blemishes in a refined age, were far from being detrimenta' in a controversy which roused all the passions of the human breast, and required the strongest exer-

* Biographia Literaria, by S. T. Coleridge, edited by Henry Nelson Coleridge, New York, 1848.

tions of fortitude and courage. Such were the principles and
conduct of this extraordinary man, when the enormous abuses
arising from the sale of indulgences attracted his notice, and
involved him in that memorable controversy with the Church
of Rome, for which he seems to have been trained and adapted
by his-temper, studies, occupation, and habits of life." This is
the language of William Coxe, in his History of the House of
Austria.*

Dr. Cox, (of London,) after characterizing the Reformation,
says: " Amongst the instruments of this remark-

Cox.

able change, the name of Martin Luther stands
pre-eminent. He was not indeed the *first* or the *only* advocate
of this righteous cause, but he was, in many respects, the
greatest. Luther possessed a vigorous and fearless soul. He
was qualified to take the lead, and to head opposition in a
servile age. His mind was incessantly active; his ardor in
the pursuit of knowledge and in the propagation of what he
knew, inextinguishable; and in the holy war which he under-
took, having buckled on the armor, he was impatient for the
conflict and assured of the victory. Never scarcely did the
hand of God form a fitter instrument to do a greater work." †

The writings of D'Aubigné, contain some just and beautiful tributes to the character of Luther. " Luther

D'Aubigné.

proved, through divine grace, the living influence
of Christianity, as no preceding Doctor, perhaps, had ever felt
it before. The Reformation sprang living from his own heart,
where God himself had placed it." ‡ " Some advised the
Evangelical princes to meet Charles, sword in hand. But this
was mere worldly counsel, and the great Reformer Luther,
whom so many are pleased to represent as a man of violent
temper, succeeded in silencing these rash counsellors." § " If

---

* Hist. of House of Austria, from the Foundation of the Monarchy by Rudolph
of Hapsburg, to the Death of Leopold the Second, 1218 to 1792, 3d ed., in 3 vols.,
London, Bohn, 1847, vol. i., p. 383.

† The Life of Philip Melanchthon, comprising an Account of the most Important Transactions of the Reformation, by F. A. Cox, D. D., LL. D., 1st American from
2 l London ed., Boston, 1835. O for a Life of Melanchthon worthy of its theme!

‡ D'Aubigné's Voice of the Church.

§ Do. Confession of the Name of Christ.

.n the history of the world there be an individual we love
more than another, it is he. Calvin we venerate more, but
Luther we love more. Besides, Lutheranism is of itself dear
and precious in our eyes, and with reason. In Reform there
are principles of which we should be afraid, were it not for the
counterbalance of Lutheranism. . . . Luther and Lutheranism do
not possess, even in Germany, even in Wittenberg, friends and
admirers more ardent than we." *

Even the Article of the " Dictionnaire Historique," intensely
Romish as it is, confesses the libellous character of   Dictionnaire
many of the charges which were, for a long time,   Historique.
current among Papists, in reference to Luther. Especially does it
mention that favorite one, that the Dispute about Indulgences
arose from the jealousy of the Augustinians and Dominicans,
and confesses that it is wholly without foundation. It goes
so far as to concede that the old story of Luther's being begotten of an Incubus, is not probable. It concedes to him " a
powerful imagination, resting on intellect and nurtured by
study, which made him eloquent by nature, and insured him
the concurrence of all who heard the thunders of his declama
tion." †

D'Israeli speaks with considerable severity of Luther's vio
lence, but he has the candor to compare with it
some products of the spirit to which he opposed   D'Israeli.
himself. " Martin Luther was not destitute of genius, of learning, or of eloquence ; but his violence disfigured his works
with invectives and singularities of abuse. It was fortunate
for the cause of the Reformation, that the violence of Luther
was softened, in a considerable degree at times, by the meek
Melanchthon : he often poured honey on the sting inflicted by
the angry bee. Luther was no respecter of kings — he addresses Henry VIII. in the following style : ' It is hard to say,
if folly can be more foolish, or stupidity more stupid, than is
the head of Henry. He has not attacked me with the heart

---

* D'Aubigné's Luther and Calvin ; or, the True Spirit of the Reformed Church.
All three of these tracts are in "D'Aubigné and his Writings," with a Sketch, etc.,
by Dr. Baird, New York, 1846

† Nouv. Diction. Historique, Caen, 1783, tom. v., p. 382

of a king, but with the impudence of a knave. This rotten worm of the earth having blasphemed the majesty of my king, I have a just right to bespatter his English majesty with his own dirt. . . . This Henry has lied.' He was repaid with capital and interest by an anonymous reply, said to have been written by Sir Thomas More, who concludes by leaving Luther, in language not necessary to translate, 'cum suis furiis et furoribus, cum suis merdis et stercoribus cacantem cacatumque.' Such were the vigorous elegancies of a controversy on the 'Seven Sacraments.' Long after, the Court of Rome had not lost the taste of these 'bitter herbs;' for in the bull of the canonization of Ignatius Loyola, in August, 1623, Luther is called *monstrum teterrimum, et detestabilis pestis.*"—" Calvin was *less tolerable,* for he had no Melanchthon! His adversaries are never others than knaves, lunatics, drunkards, and assassins! Sometimes they are characterized by the familiar appellatives of bulls, asses, cats, and hogs! By him Catholic and Lutheran are alike hated. Yet, after having given vent to this virulent humor, he frequently boasts of his mildness. When he reads over his writings, he tells us that he is astonished at his forbearance; but this, he adds, is the duty of every Christian! At the same time he generally finishes a period with—'Do you hear, you dog? Do you hear, madman?'"*

" Amidst all that Luther has written," says Doederlein, " I know nothing more precious than his sermons and his letters. From both of these we can at least learn to know the man in his entire greatness, and in accordance with his genuine character, which superstition and malice, and the partizan licentiousness both of friends and foes has disfigured; from both beams forth the most open honesty, the firmness of a courage which never quailed, fearlessness of judgment, and that spirit which knew so perfectly its aim, which preserved its serenity amid all calamities, and changes allotted by Providence, and knew how to use to good purpose, sport and earnest. His letters especially bear the impress of the most artless simplicity, and of the most naïve vivacity and apart from their contrib.tions to history, and the attract-

Doederlein.

* Curiosities of Literature, by J D'Israeli, London, Moxon, 1841, p. 82.

iveness of their contents, are entertaining, rich in instruction, and worthy of descending to posterity, were there no other reason, to show that immortal man speaking, especially with his friends."* Dupin concedes that Luther's errors, as he styles them, obliged the Romanists to study The- ology upon right principles; and confesses that his version of the Bible was " elegante"—even while he brings the charge that it was " peu litterale " and "peu exacte."† Dupin.

Speaking of Luther's reply to Henry VIII., the author of the article in the " Cyclopædia of the Society for the Diffu- sion of Useful Knowledge" says: " It must be observed, how- ever, that the coarse vituperations which shock the reader in Luther's controversial works, were not peculiar to him, being commonly used by scholars and divines of the middle ages in their disputations. The invectives of Valla, Filelfo, Poggio, and other distinguished scholars, against each other, are notorious, and this bad taste continued in prac- tice long after Luther, down to the seventeenth century, and traces of it are found in writers of the eighteenth, even in some of the works of the polished and courtly Voltaire." The writer might have added ' down to the nineteenth,' for who cannot recall specimens of theological warfare in our own day, vastly more offensive to all right feeling, than anything writ- ten by Luther. The same writer goes on to say: " Luther ranks high among German writers for the vigor of his style, and the development which he imparted to his vernacular language. Schroeck, Melanchthon, and others have written biographies of Luther, and Michelet has extracted a kind of autobiography from his works. From these passages the char- acter of Luther is clearly deduced, for there was no calcula- tion, reserve, or hypocrisy about him. He was frank and vehement, and often intemperate. But he was earnest in his vehemence; he really felt the importance of the topics he was discussing; and whether he was right or wrong in his peculiar Cyclopædia of British Society.

* D. Joh. Christoph Doederlein Auserlesene Theologische Bibliothek. Review of " Schutzes Luther's Briefe," Erst. Band, Leipzig, 1780, p. 631.

† Method of Studying Divinity, London, 1720, p. 27. Dissertation Prélimi naire, etc., Paris, 1699, vol. i., p. 726.

opinions, he was a sincere and zealous believer in the Christian Revelation. Luther considered religion as the most important business of man, and because he considered it as such, he wished to ascend to its very source, unalloyed by human authority. He contended for the right of every man to consult the great book of the Christian Law. The principles of free inquiry, which he introduced, led to further results, and gradually established that liberty of conscience which now exists in the Protestant States of Europe. But Luther himself, whilst he appealed to the Scriptures against human authority, did not for a moment admit of any doubts concerning the truth of Revelation. . . . Those who judge of Luther's disposition, merely from his controversial style and manner, greatly mistake his character. He was a warm-hearted German, kind and generous; he abused and vilified his antagonists the more in proportion as they were powerful, but he could feel for the unhappy, and he even tendered some consolation to his bitterest enemy, Tetzel, when, forsaken by his employers, and upbraided as the cause of all the mischief, he was in the agonies of death and despair. Luther gave that impulse towards spiritual philosophy, that thirst for information, that logical exercise of the mind, which have made the Germans the most generally instructed, and the most intellectual people in Europe. Luther was convinced of the necessity of education, as auxiliary to religion and morality, and he pleaded unceasingly for the education of the laboring classes, broadly telling princes and rulers how dangerous, as well as unjust, it was to keep their subjects in ignorance and degradation. He was no courtly flatterer; he spoke in favor of the poor, the humble and the oppressed, and against the high and mighty, even of his own party, who were guilty of cupidity and oppression. Luther's doctrine was altogether in favor of civil liberty, and in Germany it tended to support constitutional rights against the encroachments of the imperial power. Luther's moral courage, his undaunted firmness, his strong conviction, and the great revolution which he effected in society, place him in the first rank of historical characters. The form of the monk of Wittenberg, emerging from the receding gloom of the middle ages, appears towering above the sovereigns and warriors, statesmen and divines of the sixteenth century, who were his contemporaries, his antagonists, or his disciples." *

"As long as Luther lived he was for peace; and he succeeded in maintaining it; he regarded it as impious to seek to establish the cause of God by force; and, in fact, during thirty years of his life, the principles of the Reformation gained a firmer footing, and were more widely propagated, by his unshaken faith and unwearied endeavor, than by all the wars, and treaties, and councils since." † Luther "introduced, not into Germany only, but into the world, a new and most important era, and his name can never be forgotten, while anything of principle remains that is deserving of remembrance." ‡

Bunsen contributed the article on Luther, to the eighth edition of the Britannica. It opens with these words: "Luther's life is both the epos and the Bunsen.
tragedy of his age. It is an epos because its first part presents a hero and a prophet, who conquers apparently insuperable difficulties, and opens a new world to the human mind, without any power but that of divine truth, and deep conviction, or any authority but that inherent in sincerity and undaunted, unselfish courage. But Luther's life is also a tragedy; it is the tragedy of Germany as well as of the hero, her son; who in vain tried to rescue his country from unholy oppression, and to regenerate her from within, as a nation, by means of the Gospel; and who died in unshaken faith in Christ and in His kingdom; although he lived to see his beloved fatherland going to destruction, not through, but in spite of the Reformation.

"Both parts of Luther's life are of the highest interest. In the epic part of it we see the most arduous work of the time (the work for two hundred years tried in vain by Councils,

---

* Vol. xiii., pp 206, 207, (London, 1839, fol.)

† Encycl. Americ., vol. viii., p. 153, Philadelphia, 1848. The article "Reformation" in this work is one of the best in it. It is the article "Luther," however, from which we quote.

‡ Rees' Cyclop., American edition, Philadelphia, vol. xxii., art. **Luther.**

5

and by prophets and martyrs, with and without emperors, kings, and princes,) undertaken by a poor monk alone, who carried it out under the ban both of the Pope and the Empire. In the second, we see him surrounded by friends and disciples, always the spiritual head of his nation, and the revered adviser of princes, and preacher of the people ; living in the same poverty as before, and leaving his descendants as unprovided for as Aristides left his daughter. So lived and died the greatest hero of Christendom since the Apostles ; the restorer of that form of Christianity which now sustains Europe, and (with all its defects) regenerating and purifying the whole human race ; the founder of the modern German language and literature ; the first speaker and debater of his country ; and at the same time, the first writer in prose and verse of his age."

The relations of *Erasmus* and Luther form an interesting chapter in the history of the Reformation. With all the cau-

Erasmus.

tion of Erasmus, and the difference of spirit and principle in the two men, he could not help feeling a profound though uneasy reverence for Luther. In writing to Cardinal Wolsey, in 1518, when Luther's name was just rising, he says: " As to Luther, he is altogether unknown to me, and I have read nothing of his except two or three pages. His life and conversation is universally commended ; and it is no small prejudice in his favor, that his morals are unblama ble, and that Calumny itself can fasten no reproach on him. If I had really been at leisure to peruse his writings, I am not so conceited of my own abilities, as to pass a judgment upon the performances of so considerable a divine. I was once against Luther purely for fear lest he should bring an odium upon literature, which is too much suspected of evil already Germany hath produced some promising youths, who have eloquence and learning, and of whom she will one day, in my opinion, have reason to boast, no less than England can now boast of her sons."* In a letter to Melanchthon, (1519,) he says: " All the world is agreed amongst us in commending his moral character. He hath given us good advice on certain

* Quoted by Jortin, "Life of Erasmus," London, 1728, 4to, p. 129.

points; and God grant that his success may be equal to the liberty which he hath taken." * In reply to a letter from Luther himself, Erasmus calls him his dearest brother in Christ, speaks of the excitement his works had produced at Louvain, and that he had advised the Divines of that University to answer them instead of railing against them. Though he had told them that he had not read those works, yet he owns that he had perused part of his Commentaries upon the Psalms, that he liked them much, and hoped they might be very serviceable. " There is a Prior of a Monastery at Antwerp, a true Christian, who loves you extremely, and was, as he relates, formerly a disciple of yours. He is almost the only one that preacheth Jesus Christ, whilst others preach human fables, and seek after lucre. The Lord Jerus grant you, from day to day, an increase of his Spirit, for his glory and for the public good." † In a letter to the Elector of Mentz, (1519,) he had the courage to apologize openly enough for Luther ; declines taking sides, but lashes the monks, and plainly justifies the beginnings of the Reformation. ‡ In the same year, he wrote a letter to Frederic of Saxony, highly favorable to Luther. § As the storm advanced, however, Erasmus grew more timid and sensitive to the reproaches which the enemies of Luther directed against all who showed any moderation or candor in regard to him. When the thunder of the Vatican rolled over Luther's head, Erasmus thought all was ruined, and, in a very oracular manner, told his friends that all the disaster came of not following his advice, to be mild, conciliating, and cautious, to be every thing, in short, which all men now see would have left the Church and the world precisely where they were. Erasmus spent the rest of his life, in the miserable condition of every man who is striving to compound between his convictions and his fears, too acute to miss the truth, and too selfish to confess it. He did not take open grounds against the Evangelical doctrines ; even the apologetic letter he wrote the Pope, showed that he was not very cordially

---

* Quoted by Iortin, Life of Erasmus, London, 1728, 4to, p. 156.
† Do., p. 166   ‡ Do., p. 202.
‡ Seckendorf, Historia Lutheranismi L i., p. 96.

on the Romish side. He declined the task of refuting Luther, for which his second reason was: "it is a work above my abilities," and the fourth: that he is not willing to endure the resentment it would occasion. "By the little of Luther's writings which I have rather run over than examined, I thought that I could discern in him natural talents, and a genius very proper to explain the holy Scriptures according to the manner of the fathers, and to kindle those sparks of Evangelical doctrine, from which common custom, and the doctrines of the schools upon speculations more subtile than useful, had departed too far. I heard men of great merit, equally respectable for learning and piety, congratulate themselves for having been acquainted with his books. I saw that the more unblamable their behavior was, and the more approaching to Evangelical purity, the less they were irritated against him. His moral character was recommended even by some who could not endure his doctrine. As to the spirit with which he was animated, and of which God alone can judge with certainty, I chose rather, as it became me, to think too favorably than too hardly of it. And, to say the plain truth, the Christian world hath been long weary of those teachers, who insist too rigidly upon trifling inventions and human constitutions, and begins to thirst after the pure and living water drawn from the sources of the Evangelists and Apostles. For this undertaking Luther seemed to me fitted by nature, and inflamed with an active zeal to prosecute it. Thus it is that I have favored Luther; I have favored the good which I saw, or imagined that I saw in him." * In the same tone is his letter to the Archbishop of Mentz, (1520.) In it, he shows his prevailing spirit of temporizing, which reaped its fit reward in the hatred of the Romish and the contempt of the Protestant party. "Let others affect martyrdom; for my part, I hold myself unworthy of that honor." "Luther," said Erasmus to the Elector Frederic, (1520,) † " hath committed two unpardonable crimes; he hath touched the Pope upon the crown, and the

---

* Letter to Campegius, 1520, quoted in Jortin's Life, p. 232.

† " When Charles V. had just been made Emperor, and was at Cologne, the Elector Frederick, who was also there, sent to Erasmus, desiring that he would

monks upon the belly." He then added, in a serious manner, that the doctrine of Luther was unexceptionable. He solicited the ministers of the Emperor to favor the cause of Luther, and to persuade him not to begin the exercise of his imperial dignity with an act of violence. To Frederic he presented the following Axioms for his consideration : ' That only two Universities had pretended to condemn Luther;' 'That Luther made very reasonable demands, by offering to dispute publicly once more. That, being a man void of ambition, he was the less to be suspected of heresy.' The Pope's agents, finding Erasmus so obstinately bent to defend Luther, endeavored to win him over by the offer of abbeys, or bishoprics: but he answered them,* "Luther is a man of too great abilities for me to encounter ; and I learn more from one page of his, than from all the works of Thomas Aquinas." The Lutherans acknowledged their obligations to Erasmus for these favors, by a picture, in which Luther and Hutten were represented carrying the Ark of God, and Erasmus, like another David, dancing before them with all his might.†

That Erasmus went thus far, is wonderful ; that he would have gone much farther, if he had simply acted out his convictions, is certain. "But if Luther," he says, (1521,) "had written everything in the most unexceptionable manner, I had no inclination to die for the sake of the truth. Every man hath not the courage requisite to make a martyr ; and I am afraid, that if I were put to the trial, I should imitate St. Peter." ‡ "I follow the decisions of the Pope and Emperor

come to his lodgings. Erasmus accordingly waited on him. It was in December, and they conversed at the fireside. Erasmus preferred using Latin instead of Dutch, and the Elector answered him, through Spalatine. When Erasmus was desired freely to give his opinion concerning Luther, he stood with lips compressed, musing in silence for a long time ; whilst Frederic, as was his wont in earnest discourse, fixed his eyes upon him in an intense gaze. At last he broke the silence with the words we have quoted. The Elector smiled when they were uttered, and in after time, not long before his death, recalled them. Erasmus afterwards begged Spalatine to return the manuscript of the axioms, lest it might be used to his hurt."—Seckendorf. Jortin.

* Melchior Adami, Vita Lutheri.

† Critique de l'Apol. d'Erasme, quoted by Jortin, p. 242. Seckendorf gives the same facts in still ampler detail.

‡ Letter to Pace, quoted in Jortin, p. 273.

when they are right, which is acting religiously; I submit to them when they are wrong, which is acting prudently, and I think that it is lawful for good men to behave themselves thus, when there is no hope of obtaining any more." * " There is a certain innocent time-serving and pious craft."† Lamartine says: " No great man is cunning." This was a truth to which Erasmus does not seem to have attained. On the train of circumstances which led to the controversy between Erasmus and Luther, on free will, it is no place here to dwell. Erasmus wrote to prove the freedom of the will, though his very doing so, he confesses, was a proof that his own will was not free. Through Luther he struck at the Reformation itself. "Luther replied, and had unquestionably the best of the argument."‡ " I count this," says Vaughan, speaking of Luther's reply, " a truly estimable, magnificent and illustrious treatise." " Luther did not rejoin to Erasmus' twofold reply : he well knew that Erasmus was fighting for victory, not for truth, and he had better things to do than to write books merely to repeat unanswered arguments."§

Gelzer, who wrote the sketches which accompany König's pictures, says of Luther: " If we recall, among other great names
Gelzer. in German history, the Reformers Melanchthon and Zwingle, the Saxon Electors, Frederick the Wise and John the Constant, Gustavus Adolphus and Frederick the Great ; or among intellectual celebrities, Klopstock and Lessing, Haman and Herder, Göthe and Schiller ; or turn to the great religious reformers of the last centuries, Spener, Franke, Zinzendorf, Bengel, and Lavater, they all exhibit many features of relationship with Luther, and in some qualities may even surpass him, but not one stands out A LUTHER. One is deficient in the poetic impulse, or the fulness and versatility of his nature ; another wants his depth of religious feeling, his firmness of purpose and strength of character ; others again, want his eloquence or influence over his contemporaries. Luther would

---

* Jortin, p. 274.   † Erasmus, quoted by Jortin.   ‡ Rees' Cycl., art. Erasmus
§ Martin Luther on the Bondage of the Will, translated by E. T. Vaughan, London, 1823, preface, xlix. Vaughan gives a sketch of Luther's Life, and a view of his character, a mere abridgment of Dean Milner's continuation of his brother's Church History.

not have been Luther, without these three leading features:
his strong faith; his spiritual eloquence; and firmness of character and purpose. He united — and this is the most extraordinary fact connected with him — to large endowments of
mind and heart, and the great gift of imparting these intellectual treasures, the invincible power of original and creative
thought, both in resisting and influencing the outer world."

" The history of the Reformation, which Guericke presents
in his admirable compend, is in keeping with his
strong, consistent Lutheran position, and though
$\qquad$ Guericke.
it does not contain any distinct, elaborate analysis of Luther's
character, presents a just view of his career and his qualities." *
The Twelfth Lecture of Guizot, † is devoted to the Reformation. In a note at the close of the chapter, the
remark of Robertson is quoted, that " Luther, Cal-
$\qquad$ Guizot.
vin, Cranmer, Knox, the founders of the Reformed Church, in
their respective countries, inflicted, as far as they had power
and opportunity, the same punishments which were denounced
by the Church of Rome upon such as called in question any
article of their creed." Upon this passage of Robertson,
Smythe ‡ remarks, that "Luther might have been favorably distinguished from Calvin and others. There
are passages in his writings, with regard to the
$\qquad$ Luther's Toler-
ation.
interference of the magistrate in religious concerns, that do
him honor; but he was favorably situated, and lived not to
see the temporal sword at his command. He was never tried."
The closing words of Smythe are in defiance of the facts in
the case. More than any private man in the sixteenth century, Luther *had* the temporal sword at his command. He
was tried. He was a shield to his enemies, both in person and
doctrine, when the penalties of the law were hanging over
them. Single-handed he protested against resort to violence.
He averted war when the great Protestant princes were eager

* Handbuch der Kirchengeschichte von H. E. F. Guericke, 9te Aufl., Leipzig,
1867, vol. iii., 1–778.

† General History of Civilization in Europe, from the Fall of the Roman Empire to the French Revolution, 3d American from the 2d English edition, with
occasional notes by C. S. Henry, D. D., New York, 1846, p. 248–268.

‡ Lectures on Modern History, Am. ed., p. 262.

for it.　He had a great, loving heart, as full of affection and forbearance for man, even when straying, as it was full of hatred to error in all its forms.　Bancroft makes a more correct statement of Luther's true principles in regard to persecution: [*] "Luther was more dogmatical than his opponents; though the deep philosophy with which his mind was imbued, repelled the use of violence to effect conversion in religion.　He was wont to protest against propagating reform by persecution and mas-

Bancroft.　　sacres; and with wise moderation, an admirable knowledge of human nature, a familiar and almost ludicrous quaintness of expression, he would deduce from his great principle of justification by faith alone, the sublime doctrine of freedom of conscience."　To this is added the note: "Nollem vi et cæde pro evangelia certari," (I could not wish any to contend for the Gospel by violence and slaughter.)　Luther's Seven Sermons — delivered in March, 1522.　"Predigen will ichs, sagen will ichs, schreiben will ichs, aber zwingen, dringen mit Gewalt will ichs Niemand; denn der Glaube will ich ungenœthigt und ohne Zwang angenommen werden."　(I will preach, I will talk in private, I will write, but I will force, I will coerce no man: for I will have the faith accepted, without constraint and without force.)　We have a testimony to the same effect, in the History of Germany,[†] by KOHLRAUSCH: "Shortly previous to the commencement of the sanguinary war of religion, Luther, the author of the grand struggle, breathed his last.　He had used all the weight of his power and influence in order to dissuade his party from mixing external force with

Kohlrausch.　　that which ought only to have its seat within the calm profundity of the soul; and, indeed, as long as he lived, this energetic Reformer was the warm advocate for the maintenance of peace.　He repeatedly reminded the princes that his doctrine was foreign to their warlike weapons, and he beheld with pain and distress, in the latter years of his life, the growing temporal direction given to the Holy Cause, and the increasing hostility of parties, whence he augured nothing good."

　　In that immortal work of John Gerhard (theologorum princeps, tertius à Luthero et Chemnitio, orbis Evangelici Atlan-

---

[*] Hist. United States, i. 274.　　　　　　[†] Lond., 1844, p. 402.

tis), the 'Confessio Catholica,' in which the concessions of
Romish writers are employed in defence of the truth,* he
answers in full all the calumnies directed against the life, and
the attacks on the doctrines of Luther.　He shows
that Luther was actuated by no blind fury against ⠀⠀Gerhard.
the Church of Rome, but distinguished in it the precious from
the vile, and that he was an instrument of God endowed with
extraordinary qualities for an extraordinary work.　In showing this, he cites at large the opinions of Mellerstadt, Staupitz,
the Emperor Maximilian, Von Hutten, Erasmus, Frederick,
Elector of Saxony, Langius, Fisher † (Bishop of Rochester and
Chancellor of the University of Cambridge), who afterwards
wrote against Luther, Mosellanus, Cellarius, Ulner, Podusca,
Phænicius, Schirner, Rosdialovinus, Margaret, Archduchess
of Austria, Emser, Kigelin, Masius, and Severus. ‡　These
persons were all in the Church of Rome at the time that these
favorable testimonies were given.　Portion by portion is taken
up by Gerhard, and disposed of with most eminent judgment,
sustained by incredible learning.

"It may be said," is the remark of Hagenbach, "that Martin Luther became emphatically *the* reformer of the
German Church, and thus the reformer of a great ⠀⠀Hagen'ach.
part of the Universal Church, by his eminent personal character
and heroic career, by the publication of his theses, by sermons
and expositions of Scripture, by disputations and bold controversial writings, by numerous letters and circular epistles, by
advice and warning, by intercourse with persons of all classes of
society, by pointed maxims and hymns, but especially by his
translation of the Sacred Scriptures into the German language.§

* "Doctrina Catholica et Evangelica, quam Ecclesiae Augustanæ Confessioni
addictæ profitentur."— From the title of the "Confessio Cathol., Frankfurti et
Lipsiæ, 1679," folio.

† In a letter to Erasmus he commends Luther highly, and among other things
speaks of him as "Scripturarum ad miraculum usqae peritum."

‡ Preceptor of Ferdinand, author of the distich,

"Japeti de gente prior majorve Luthero
Nemo fuit, nec habent secla futura parem." — Conf. Cathol., p. 58 seq.

§ Compendium of the History of Doctrines, by K. R. Hagenbach, Dr. and
Professor of Theology in the University of Basle, translated by Carl W. Buch,

It is . unjust . . to maintain that Luther's profound **and**
dynamic interpretation of the sacrament, which on that **very**
account was less perspicuous and intelligible, had its origin in
nothing but partial stupidity or stubbornness. The opinion
which each of these reformers (Zuinglius and Luther) enter
tained concerning the sacraments, was most intimately connected with his whole religious tendency, which, in its turn,
stood in connection with the different development of the
churches which they respectively founded."

Hallam has offered, in his "Introduction to the Literature
of Europe," a work acceptable in the great dearth,
Hallam.
in our language, of all books of the kind, but
neither worthy, in all respects, of the subject nor of the reputation of its author. For too much of it is obviously, in the most
unfavorable sense, second-hand, and even in its dependence, it
does not rest on a thorough acquaintance with the best sources
whence opinions can be had ready-made. Would it not be
thought preposterous for a man to write an introduction to
classic literature who knew nothing of the Latin language,
and depended for his information on the translations existing
in his mother tongue? Hallam has been guilty of a greater
absurdity than this; for in total ignorance of the most important language in Europe, he has pretended to give a view of its
literature — a literature almost none of which, comparatively,
exists, even in the imperfect medium of translations into English. He displays everywhere, too, an ignorance of theology
which makes his views on theological literature not only inadequate, but often absurd. There is, too, an air of carelessness
in his treatment of it, which seems, at least, to involve that
he feels little interest in it, or that a man of his position in
general letters is condescending, in touching such matters at
all. It is one of the poorest affectations of men of the world
to talk of theology, in a tone of flippancy, as if it were too

Edinburgh, Clark, 1847, vol. ii., 156, (Am. ed., edited by Dr. H. B. Smith,
1862.) Hagenbach's work has an occasional slip. An illustration lies just under
our eye: "Nor did the authors of the Symbolical Books differ from Luther, on
Transubstantiation." Very true, but half of Hagenbach's proof is a citation **from**
the Smalcald Articles. *i. e.* he proves that Luther did not differ from Luther.

vague for a thinker, too dull to inspire enthusiasm. They speak and write of it, as if they were with difficulty repressing a yawn. But Hallam is not guilty of mere listlessness in his treatment of theological topics. He is a partisan, and a very ill-informed one.

Especially is his account of the Reformation and of Luther full of ignorance and full of prejudice. He seems to have prepared his mind for a just estimate of Luther by reading, with intense admiration, Bossuet's "Variations," though, as he tells us, with great impartiality, "It would not be just *probably* to give Bossuet credit in *every* part of that powerful delineation of Luther's theological tenets." He charges on the writings of Luther, previous to 1520, various "Antinomian paradoxes," but yet he has the candor to say: "It must not be supposed for a moment that Luther, whose soul was penetrated with a fervent piety, and whose integrity, as well as purity of life, are unquestioned, could mean to give any encouragement to a licentious disregard of moral virtue, which he valued as in itself lovely before God as well as man, though in the technical style of his theology he might deny its proper obligation. But his temper led him to follow up any proposition of Scripture to every consequence that might seem to result from its literal meaning."

"Every solution of the conduct of the reformers must be nugatory except one, that they were men absorbed by the conviction that they were fighting the battle of God." — "It is hardly correct to say of Luther, that he erected his system on the ruins of Popery, for it was rather the growth and expansion in his mind of one positive dogma, justification by faith in the sense in which he took it, (which can be easily shown to have preceded the dispute about indulgence,) that broke down and crushed successively the various doctrines of the Romish Church." *

* Literature of Europe, vol. i., p. 166. Hallam, putting a different construction from Le Clerc on some theological expressions, adds: "But of course my practice in these nice questions is not great." Vol. ii., p. 41, *n.* After adjusting in the text the comparative merits of half a dozen theologians, he says he has done it "in deference to common reputation," "for I am wholly ignorant of the writings of all." Page 287.

" A better tone " (in preaching) " began with Luther. His
language was sometimes rude and low, but persuasive, artless,
powerful. He gave many useful precepts, as well as examples,
for pulpit eloquence." — " In the history of the Reformation,
Luther is incomparably the greatest name. We see him, in the
skilful composition of Robertson, the chief figure of a group
of gownsmen, standing in contrast on the canvas with the
crowned rivals of France and Austria, and their attendant
warriors, but blended in the unity of that historic picture. It
is admitted on all sides, that he wrote his own language with
force, and he is reckoned one of its best models. The hymns
in use with the Lutheran Church, many of which are his own,
possess a simple dignity and devoutness never probably excelled
in that class of poetry, and alike distinguished from the poverty
of Sternhold or Brady, and from the meretricious ornament of
later writers." — " It is not to be imagined that a man of his
vivid parts fails to perceive an advantage in that close grap-
pling, sentence by sentence, with an adversary, which fills most
of his controversial writings ; and in scornful irony he had no
superior." *

* Literature of Europe, vol. i., p. 197. The great currency which Hallam's
name gives to any view he expresses, would make it well worth while for some
one competent to the task, to review all his charges against Luther, and positive Evangelical Protestantism, as has been done, so ably, on some points, by
Archdeacon Hare. An instance of the knowing air with which a man ignorant
of his subject may write about it, occurs in the following sentence (i. 278):
" After the death of Melanchthon, a controversy, began by one Brentius, relating
to the ubiquity, as it was called, of Christ's body, proceeded with much heat."
" One Milton, a blind man," has grown into a classic illustration of happy appreciation of character. " One Brentius " ought to contest a place with it. Brentius, whose name, in the department of polemic theology, is mentioned next that
of Luther and of Melanchthon in the early history of the Reformation — Brentius, who stood so high in the judgment of Luther himself, one of the acutest
judges of character, to whom Luther applied terms of commendation which
seemed so near an approach to flattery, that he felt it necessary to protest that
he is speaking in godly sincerity, whom he compared, in relation to himself, to the
" still small voice following the whirlwind, earthquake, and fire " — Brentius,
whose contributions to sacred interpretation not only stood in the highest repute
in his own land, but several of which had sufficient reputation to lead to their
translation in England, (as, for instance, his " Arguments and Summaries,"
translated by John Calcaskie, London, 1550 ; his Commentary on Esther, by John
Stockwood London, 1554 ; his Homilies and Exegesis on John, by Richard Shirry,

Next to the Milners,* who were the first English writers who gave a large and just view of Luther's character and Luther's work, is to be placed Archdeacon Hare, who in a note to his " Mission of the Comforter," a note which grew into a volume, vindicated Luther against " his recent English assailants." † First of these is Hallam ; then follow Newman, Ward, and Dr. Mill. The last reply is to Sir William Hamilton, who has left an indelible disgrace upon his name by the manner and measure of his attack upon Luther. He has largely drawn his material from secondary sources, wholly unworthy of credit, and has been betrayed into exhibitions of ignorance so astounding as to excite suspicion that Sir William was rather a large reader than a thorough scholar. His fierceness of polemic, which his greatest admirers lament, was never more manifest nor more inexcusable than it is here. Archdeacon Hare's vindication is everywhere successful, and not unfrequently overwhelming. He has won for himself the right of being listened to respectfully, even reverently, in his estimate of Luther : ‡ "As he has said of St. Paul's words, his own are not dead words, but living creatures, and have hands and feet. It no longer surprises us that this man who wrote and spoke thus, although no more than a poor monk, should have been mightier than the Pope, and the Emperor to boot, with all their hosts, ecclesiastical and civil — that the rivers of living water should have swept half Germany, and in the course of time the chief part of Northern Europe, out of the kingdom of darkness into the region of Evangelical light. No day in spring, when life seems bursting from every bud, and gushing from every pore, is fuller of life than his pages ; and if they are not without the strong breezes

Archdeacon Hare

London, 1550 ;) and whose writings are still consulted with delight by the scholar, and republished — such a man could not have had such a seal of insignificance attached to his name by any other than a writer ignorant at least of this part of his theme.

* Hist. of Church of Christ, by Joseph Milner, with add. by Is. Milner, Lond. (1819) 1847, 4 vols. 8vo.

† Vindication of Luther, 2d ed., Lond., 1855.

‡ Mission of the Comforter, from 2d Lond. ed., Boston, 1854, pp. 281, 402, 403.

of spring, these too have to bear their part in the work of purification."—"How far superior his expositions of Scripture are, in the deep and living apprehension of the primary truths of the Gospel, to those of the best among the Fathers, even of Augustin! If we would do justice to any of the master minds in history, we must compare them with their predecessors. When we come upon these truths in Luther, after wandering through the dusky twilight of the preceding centuries, it seems almost like the sunburst of a new Revelation, or rather as if the sun, which set when St. Paul was taken away from the earth, had suddenly started up again. Verily, too, it does us good, when we have been walking about among those who have only dim guesses as to where they are, or whither they are going, and who halt and look back, and turn aside at every other step, to see a man taking his stand on the Eternal Rock, and gazing steadfastly with unsealed eyes on the very Sun of righteousness."

Hase, most eloquent, most condensed, most happy in giving the cream of things of all the writers of his school, shows a just and appreciating spirit in all he has said of Luther. Not only in his general allusions to the primal spirit of the Reformation embodied in Luther, his correct deduction of that great movement, neither from the skeptical nor scientific tendency, but from faith and holy desire, but still more fully Hase. in the happy outline of Luther's career in his Church history, has he shown that as far as one occupying so different a theological position from Luther can thoroughly understand him, he does so. Not only as a fine illustration of our theme, but as a highly characteristic specimen of the work of Hase, to which we have just alluded, we give the whole of his chapter on "Luther's death and public character." "In the last year of his life, Luther, worn out by labor and sickness, took such offence at the immorality and wanton modes at Wittenberg, that he left it, (1545,) and only consented to return at the most urgent supplications of the University and Elector. He saw a gloomy period impending over the land of his fathers, and longed to depart in peace. Over his last days sti.. shone some of the brightness of his best years—the words bold, child-like, playful, amid exalted thoughts. Having been called to Eisleben to act as arbitrator in settling some difficulty of the Counts of Mansfeld, he there, on the night of February 18th, 1546, rested in a last calm and holy sleep. The mutations of the times on whose pinnacle he stood, imparted to his life its stronger antitheses. He had regarded the Pope as the most holy, and most Satanic father. In his roused passions emotions had stormily alternated. The freedom of the Spirit was the object of his life, and yet he had been jealous for the letter. In trust on all the power of the Spirit, he had seized the storm of revolution by the reins, and yet on occasion had suggested that it would be well if the Pope and his whole brood were drowned in the Tyrrhene Sea. But throughout he had uttered with an unbounded ingenuousness his convictions, and was a stranger to every worldly interest. With a powerful sensuousness, he stood fast rooted in the earth, but his head reached into heaven. In the creative spirit, no man of his time was like him; his discourses were often rougher than his own rough time seemed to approve, but in popular eloquence his equal has never arisen in Germany. From anguish and wrath grew his joy in the contest. Where he once had discovered wrong, he saw nothing but hell. But his significance rests less upon those acts by which he searched and destroyed — others could more easily and more readily tear themselves away from the old Church— it rests much more upon his power of building up, on his earnest full faith and love; though in hours of gloom, through the temptations of Satan, he imagined that he had lost God, and Christ, and all together. Especially, in opposition to his antagonists, did he believe, and declare without reservation, that he was a chosen instrument of God, known in heaven, on earth, and in hell. But with himself, personally considered, he would have nothing to do; he would recognize no doctrine of Luther, and his sublime trust in God pointed not to his personal delivery from dangers, but to the faith that God could every day create ten 'Doctor Martins.' Insipid objections and narrow vindications are forgotten; such a man belongs not to one party, but to the German people and to Christendom."

The distinctive characteristics of Göthe and Herder displayed themselves in the difference of their feelings towards
Luther. "What seemed to Göthe narrow and partial, Herder called noble and philanthropic; while, on the contrary,
what Herder admired as the infinitude of a great idea, reveal-
ing itself to man in various godlike emanations —
in the valor of the hero, the wisdom of the legisla-
tor, the inspiration of the poet, or the events of a world — this
sort of elevation moved Göthe so little, that such characters
as Luther and Coriolanus excited in him a sort of uncomforta-
ble.feeling, which could be satisfactorily explained only on the
hypothesis that their natures stood in a mysterious sort of
opposition to his. Göthe's genius and disposition were for
the beautiful; Herder's for the sublime."

Herder.

Herder has given, in his writings, the most unmistakable
evidence of his admiration of Luther. There is no author
whom he cites so frequently, so largely, and so admiringly, as
Luther. "Luther has long been recognized as teacher of the
German nation, nay, as co-reformer of all of Europe that is
this day enlightened. He was a great man and a great patriot.
Even nations that do not embrace the principles of his religion
enjoy the fruits of his Reformation. Like a true Hercules, he
grappled with that spiritual despotism which abrogates or
buries all free, sound thought, and gave back to whole nations
the use of reason, and in that very sphere where it is hardest
to restore it — in *spiritual* things. The power of his speech
and of his honest spirit united itself with sciences, which
revived from him and with him; associated itself with the
yearnings of the best thinkers in all conditions, who, in some
things, had very different views from his own, and thus formed
for the first time a *popular literary public* in Germany and the
neighboring countries. Now men read what never had been
read; now men learned to read who had never learned before.
Schools and academies were founded, German hymns were
sung, and preaching in the German language ceased to be rare.
The people obtained the Bible, possessed at the very least the
Catechism; numerous sects of Anabaptists and other errorists
arose, many of which, each in its own way, contributed to the

scientific or popular elucidation of contested matters, and thus, also, to the cultivation of the understanding, the polishing of language and of taste. Would that his spirit had been followed, and that, in this method of free examination, other objects had been taken up which did not lie immediately in his monastic or church sphere; that, in a word, the principles on which he judged and acted had been applied to them. But what avails it to teach or reproach times gone by? Let us rise and apply his mode of thought, his luminous hints, and the truths uttered for our time, with equal strength and *naiveté*. I have marked in his writings a number of sentences and expressions in which (as he often called himself) he is presented as Ecclesiastes, or the preacher and teacher of the German nation."

"Of Luther as a preacher," Herder says: "He spoke the simple, strong, unadorned language of the understanding; he spoke from the heart, not from the head and from memory. His sermons, therefore, have long been the models, especially of those preachers in our church who are of stable minds."

Speaking of the contents of the Psalms, he says, in the same beautiful letters from which we have just quoted: "I am sure I can give you no better key to them than the exquisite preface of Luther to this, his darling book. He will tell you what is in them, how to apply them, and turn them to use."

Speaking of the romantic and moonshiny way of preaching which prevailed in his time, he closes a most severe paragraph with the exclamation: "O Luther! when we recall thee and thy pure, solid language, comprehended by all!"

"Would you hear the nature, power, and necessity of this living principle of faith, treated in a manner living and clearly defined, read Luther's writings. He shows a hundred times and at large, how little is contained in that beggar's bag of a gradual reform of our bad habits; how little of Christianity there is in it, and of how little worth it is before God. But he himself, even at that early day, mourned that so few formed a right conception of that which he called true, life-restoring faith, how few knew how to give it, in accordance with his meaning, its practical power!" "The doctrine of justification

6

is so closely associated with that of faith, that one must stand or fall with the other. On this, also, the corner-stone of Lutheranism, pre-eminently hold fast, I beg you, by Luther's writings. I think it was Spener who had felt, with reference to this system, a doubt which, it seemed to him, nothing could overthrow; he read Luther's writings and his doubts vanished. But, as I have said, Luther already mourned that not all comprehended him, and whilst every one was crying out about faith, justification, and good works, few had really grasped his meaning and his spirit; the consequences, both immediate and long after his death, were melancholy enough. When in this matter you need instruction, or long to have difficulties resolved, go to this living man of faith himself, this legitimate son of Paul. In his writing is so much sound sense, with such strength of spirit and fervor of an honest heart, that often, when worn out with the frigid refinings and speculations of a more recent date, I have found that I was revived by him alone." "Conjoin with his biography, his own writings, (O that we had a complete collection of them in the languages in which he wrote them!) read these, and you will know him differently, for he gives a picture of himself in every line."

"May the great Head of the Church revive in this land (Germany)—the cradle of the Reformation—the spirit of the reformers, so that the mantle of Luther may fall upon his professed followers and admirers, that all who pretend to teach may be taught of God, men of faith, learning, research, and above all, of ardent and unfeigned piety."

Kahnis: * "Nothing but the narrowness of party can deny that there are respects in which no other reformer can bear comparison with Luther as *the* person of the Reformation. The Romanists do but prejudice their own cause, when they undervalue a man who, with nothing but the weapons of the Spirit, shook to its lowest depths the entire Church of the Middle Ages. Every Catholic who claims to be a lover of truth, should concur in the judgment of Count Stolberg, who, though he deserted Protestantism for the Catholic Church, says·

Kahnis.

Roman Catholic Judgment. Stolberg

* Ueb. d. Principien d. Protestantismus, Leipz., 1865.

Against Luther's person I would not cast a stone. In him I
honor, not alone one of the grandest spirits that have ever lived,
but a great religiousness also, which never forsook him.'"
There have indeed been Roman Catholics, who did not breathe
toward Luther the spirit of Schlegel and Stolberg, and from
one of the greatest of these, whose sketch is peculiarly full of
genius, and has been called "an official one," by F. V. Raumer,
we quote. Palavicini, the historian of the Council Palavicini.
of Trent, thus characterizes Luther: "A fruitful
genius, but one that produced bitter rather than ripe fruits ; he
was rather the abortive birth of a giant, than a healthy child
born in due time. A mighty spirit, but better fitted for tearing down than for building up. His learning was more like a
drenching rain which beats down all before it, than like the
soft shower of summer, beneath which nature grows fruitful.
His eloquence was in its language coarse, and crude in its matter, like the storm which blinds the eyes with the dust it drives
before it. Bold in beginning strife, no man was more timor-
ous when danger was near ; his courage was, at best, that of a
beast at bay. He frequently promised to be silent, if his opponents would be silent too — a proof that he was determined by
earthly influences. He was protected by the princes, only
because they coveted the Church's goods ; he was a disturber
of the Church, to the injury of others, and without benefit to
himself. History will continue to name him, but more to his
shame than to his renown. The Church, the vine, has been
pruned, that it may shoot forth with fresh life : the faithful
have been separated from the seditious. Opposed to him
stands the major part — the more noble, the more moderate,
the more holy."

To this no better answer can be furnished than that which
the great historian and statesman, F. V. Raumer, has given
"To this judgment of Palavicini," he says, "after a conscientious
testing of all the facts, we cannot assent — but are constrained
to acknowledge the truth to be this: A fruitful F. V. Raumer's reply to Palavicini.
genius, whose fruits could not all come to a mellow
ripeness, because they were prematurely shaken down
by storms. A mighty spirit, who helped to ⌐ e the storms ;

but, had not the building been undermined by fearful abuses, a
purification might have been possible without overthrowing it.
Only because the builders who were called to the work of
reform, not only refused to perform it, but increased the evil,
did he become their master; and with success grew his boldness
or his faith in his divine vocation, and his wrath against his
opponents. In his contest with the Papacy he placed in the
van Evangelical freedom of faith, and this is the source of
Protestantism; in the establishment of his Church he often
was willing to shackle thought, lost his own clearness of perception, and became intolerant. But his hardest and least becoming language appears mild in comparison with the blood-thirsty
intolerance of his opponents, mild in comparison with the heads-
man's axe and the stake. A noble eloquence supplanted the
unintelligible prattle of the schools; through him Germany
once more learned to speak, the German people once more
to hear. He who is displeased with his style, or with his matter, must yet confess that his writings reveal everywhere the
inspiration of the fear of God and the power of faith. Luther
never dissimulated. Persuasions, promises, threats had no
power to shake his rock-firm will, his indomitable purpose; and
the seeming self-will and severity connected with this arose,
at least, from no commonplace and perverted character. No
man ever grasps the whole truth, in perfect clearness; but few
have more earnestly striven to attain it, and with more perfect
self-renunciation confessed it, than Luther. Among his oppo
nents not one can be compared with him in personal qualities:
with all his faults, he remains greatest and most memorable
among men; a man in whose train follows a whole world of
aspiration, effort, and achievement."

In affinity with that of Von Raumer is the estimate of
Ranke: "Throughout we see Luther directing his weapons on
Ranke.   both sides — against the Papacy, which sought to
reconquer the world then struggling for its eman-
cipation — and against the sects of many names which sprang
up beside him, assailing Church and State together. The
great Reformer, if we may use an expression of our days, was
one of the greatest Conservatives that ever lived."

Ernst Karl Wieland opens the last paragraph of his Characteristics of Luther with the words: " Such was he, Wieland. so great in whatever aspect we view him, so worthy of admiration, so deserving of universal gratitude ; alike great as a man, a citizen, and a scholar."

Stang, to whom we are indebted for one of the best lives of Luther, thus closes his biography : " We stand before the image of the great Reformer with the full conviction that between the first century, when Christianity appeared in its youth, and the sixteenth, when it obtained the Stang. maturity of its riper age, not one of our race has appeared, in whom the ever-creative spirit of God, the spirit of light and of law, has found nobler embodiment, or wrought with richer sequence."

But among all the tributes which the centuries have laid at the feet or on the tomb of Luther, none are more touching than the words in which Melanchthon showed that Melanchthon. Luther's death had brought back, in all its tenderness, the early, pure devotion. Melanchthon, the Hamlet of the Reformation, shrinking from action into contemplation, with a dangerous yearning for a peace which must have been hollow and transient, had become more and more entangled in the complications of a specious but miserable policy which he felt made him justly suspected by those whose confidence in him had once been unlimited. Luther was saddened by Melanchthon's feebleness, and Melanchthon was put under restraint by Luther's firmness. Melanchthon was betrayed into writing weak, fretful, unworthy words in regard to Luther, whose surpassing love to Melanchthon had been sorely tested, but had never yielded. But death makes or restores more bonds than it breaks. When the tidings of Luther's death reached Wittenberg, Melanchthon cried out in anguish: "O my father, my father, the chariot of Israel, and the horsemen thereof! " — tributary words from one of the greatest, to the greatest. He was gone of whom Melanchthon, cautious in praise, and measured in language, had said, from a full heart: " Luther is too great, too wonderful for me to depict in words." — " If there be a man on earth I love with my whole heart, that man is Luther.

And, again: "One is an interpreter; one, a logician; another, an orator, affluent and beautiful in speech; but Luther is all in all — whatever he writes, whatever he utters, pierces to the soul, fixes itself like arrows in the heart — he is a miracle among men."

What need we say more, after such eulogies?

The greatness of some men only makes us feel that though they did well, others in their place might have done just as they did: Luther had that exceptional greatness, which convinces the world that he alone could have done the work. He was not a mere mountain-top, catching a little earlier the beams which, by their own course, would soon have found the valleys; but rather, by the divine ordination under which he rose, like the sun itself, without which the light on mountain and valley would have been but a starlight or moonlight. He was not a secondary orb, reflecting the light of another orb, as was Melanchthon, and even Calvin; still less the moon of a planet, as Bucer or Brentius; but the centre of undulations which filled a system with glory. Yet, though he rose wondrously to a divine ideal, he did not cease to be a man of men. He won the trophies of power, and the garlands of affection. Potentates feared him, and little children played with him. He has monuments in marble and bronze, medals in silver and gold; but his noblest monument is the best love of the best hearts, and the brightest, purest impression of his image has been left in the souls of regenerated nations. He was the best teacher of freedom and of loyalty. He has made the righteous throne stronger, and the innocent cottage happier. He knew how to laugh, and how to weep; therefore, millions laughed with him, and millions wept for him. He was tried by deep sorrow, and brilliant fortune; he begged the poor scholar's bread, and from Emperor and estates of the realm received an embassy, with a prince at its head, to ask him to untie the knot which defied the power of the soldier and the sagacity of the statesman; it was he who added to the Litany the words: "In all time of our tribulation, in all time of our prosperity, help us good Lord;" but whether lured by the subtlest flattery or assailed by the powers of hell, tempted with the mitre, or threatened with the stake, he came off more than conqueror in all. He made a world rich forevermore, and, stripping himself in perpetual charities, died in poverty. He knew how to command — for he had learned how to obey. Had he been less courageous, he would have attempted nothing; had he been less cautious, he would have ruined all: the torrent was resistless, but the banks were deep. He tore up the mightiest evils by the root, but shielded with his own life the tenderest bud of good ; he combined the aggressiveness of a just radicalism with the moral resistance — which seemed to the fanatic the passive weakness — of a true conservatism. Faith-inspired, he was faith-inspiring. Great in act as he was great in thought, proving himself fire with fire, "inferior eyes grew great by his example, and put on the dauntless spirit of resolution." The world knows his faults. He could not hide what he was. His transparent candor gave his enemies the material of their misrepresentation ; but they cannot blame his infirmities without bearing witness to the nobleness which made him careless of appearances in a world of defamers. For himself, he had as little of the virtue of caution as he had, toward others, of the vice of dissimulation. Living under thousands of jealous and hating eyes, in the broadest light of day, the testimony of enemies but fixes the result : that his faults were those of a nature of the most consummate grandeur and fulness, faults more precious than the virtues of the common great. Four potentates ruled the mind of Europe in the Reformation, the Emperor, Erasmus, the Pope, and Luther. The Pope wanes, Erasmus is little, the Emperor is nothing, but Luther abides as a power for all time. His image casts itself upon the current of ages, as the mountain mirrors itself in the river that winds at its foot — the mighty fixing itself immutably upon the changing.

III.

LUTHER'S TRANSLATION OF THE NEW TESTAMENT.*

THE author's best vindication of his vocation to a work must, in the nature of the case, be the work itself. The

Luther's call-ing as a trans-lator of the Scrip-tures.

fact of success seems to dispense with the necessity of any argument, in advance, as to his fitness for the labor on which he entered. We need no *a priori* proof that Milton had a vocation as a poet, or Bacon as a philosopher, or Gerhard as a theologian. To argue it, is to argue in the sunlight the question of the sun's adaptation for shining. Luther's translation of the Bible is itself the invincible proof of his vocation to the work of

---

* The most important works on Luther's Bible are the following:

I. — In defence or criticism of his translation.

    ANDREÆ: Erinerung v. d. Teutschen. Bibl. Dollmetsch. Tübing. 1564.

    TRAUB: Avisa o. Warnung von Luther's Teutsch. Bib. Ingolst. 1578.

    WICELII: Annotationes. Leipz. 1536.

    ZANGER: Examen Versionis. Maintz. 1605.

    BERINGER: Rettung. 1613.

    RAITHII: Vindiciæ. 1676.

    A. H. FRANCKE: Obs. Biblicæ. 1695.

    HALLBAUER: Animadversiones in Nov. Germ. Version. Jena: 1731.

    ZEHNER: Probe. 1750.

    MARHEINECKE: Relig. Werth. d. Bibelübersetz. Luther. Berl. 1815.

    STIER: Altes und Neues. 1828. (In defence of Meyer's Revision.)

    " Darf Luther's Bibel, etc. 1836.

    GRASHOF: D. M. L's. Bibelüber. in ihr. Verhalten. z. d. Bedürfn. d. Zeit. 1835.

    HOPF: Würdig. d. Luthersch. Bibel. Verdeutscht mit Rücks. d. Alt. u. Neuen Uebersetzung. Nürnb. 1847.

    RÖSSLER: De Vers. Luth. caute emend. 1836.

preparing it. It shines its own evidence into the eyes of every one who opens it.

Nevertheless, it is not without historical interest, little as it is necessary, logically, to look at the evidence of Luther's fitness for the work. Some of the facts which naturally attract our attention here, are the following:

I. *Luther was well educated as a boy.* He went to school in Mansfeld until he reached his fourteenth year; thence he went to Magdeburg; four years he spent at Eisenach, under the tuition of a teacher of whom Melanchthon testifies that in the grammatical branches, the very ones which were so largely to become useful to Luther as a translator, he had no superior. Here he finished his school-days proper — already as a boy, by his great proficiency, giving indications of extra-ordinary talents and industry. Melanchthon says of him at this era: " As he had great genius, and a strong predisposition to eloquence, he speedily surpassed the other youths in the fulness and richness of his speech and of his writing, alike in prose and verse." Even as a boy, he was already marked out as a translator.

II. *Luther received a thorough collegiate education.* In 1501 he repaired to the college at Erfurt, where he was matricu-lated during the presidency of Truttvetter, whom he loved and venerated as a man and a teacher, and where he faithfully used all the advantages which surrounded him.

II. — Bibliography and History.

MAYER, J. F.: Hist. Vers. Luth. 1701.

KRAFT: (1705–1734.)

ZELTNER: Historie. 1727. Bertram: Giese: Nachricht. (1771.)

PALM: Historie — Götze. 1772.

" De Codicibus. 1735.

GÖZEN's: Sammlung. 1777. Vergleichung der Uebersetz. v. Luther, von 1517 — b. 1545. Erst. St. 1777; 2d, 1779. Neue Entdeckungen, 1777.

PANZER: Entwurf. 1791.

GŒTZ: Ueberblicke. 1824.

SCHOTT: Geschichte. 1835. Bindseil. (1841.)

REUSS: Gesch. d. Heil. Schriften. N. T. 1860.

FRITZSCHE: Bibelübersetzungen Deutsch. 1855. (in Herzog's Real Enc. iii. 337.)

Popular Histories: KUSTER (1824); WEIDEMAN (1834); K. MANN (1834); KRAFFT, C. W (1835)

III. *Luther was a devoted student of the Hebrew and Greek*
In 1505, after his entrance into the cloister, Luther devoted
himself, with that earnestness which marked all he did, to the
study of Hebrew and Greek. He had skilful teachers in both
languages. As professor and preacher in Wittenberg, he continued both studies with great ardor. In Hebrew, Luther
regarded the illustrious Reuchlin, the Gesenius of that day, as
his teacher, compensating for the want of his oral instruction
by a thorough use of his writings. But Luther was not of
the race of sciolists who think that, because books can do
much, they can do everything. He knew the value of the
living teacher. To obtain a more thorough mastery of Hebrew,
he availed himself of the instruction of his learned colleague,
Aurogallus, the Professor of the Oriental languages at Witten
berg. When he was at Rome, in 1510, he took lessons in Hebrew from the erudite Rabbin Elias Levita. Luther was master
of the Hebrew according to the standard of his time, as his
contemporaries, and learned men of a later date, among them
Scaliger, have acknowledged. "If Luther," says Fritzsche,[*]
" was not the greatest philologist of his time, he was yet sufficiently learned to see for himself, and to be able to form an
independent judgment. What he lacked in philological profundity was compensated for, in part, by his eminent exegetical
feeling, and by the fact that he had lived himself completely
into the spirit of the Bible." Luther's first master in Greek
was Erasmus, through his writings ; his preceptor, both by
the book and the lip, was Melanchthon. These were the
greatest Greek scholars of the age. Luther happily styles
Melanchthon, " most Grecian."

IV. With genius, the internal mental requisite, and learning, the means by which that genius could alone be brought
to bear on the work of translation, Luther united *piety*. His
soul was in affinity with the spirit of the Bible. He was a
regenerate man. A De Wette may produce a translation
which the man of taste admires, but he cannot translate for
the people. We would not give a poem to a mathematician
for translation, whatever might be his genius ; still less would

---

* Herzog's Real Encyc., iii. 340.

we give the words of the Spirit to the hand of a translator who had not the " mind of the Spirit." Luther, the man of faith, of fervent prayer, the man who was as lowly toward God as he was inflexible toward men — Luther was called to that work of translation in which generations of the past have found a guide to heaven, and for which millions of our race, in generations yet to come, will rise up and pronounce him blessed.

V. All these gifts and graces as a translator found their channel in his *matchless German.* In this he stood supreme. The most German of Germans, towering above the great, yet absolutely one of the people, he possessed such a mastery of the tongue, such a comprehension of its power, such an ability to make it plastic for every end of language, as belonged to no other man of his time — to no other man since. His German style is the model of the scholar, and the idol of the people.

The plan of a great human life is not something which the man makes — it is something which makes the man. The wide and full-formed plans which men make before they begin to act, are always failures. The achievements of the great masters in the moral revolutions of our race have invariably, at first, had the semblance of something fragmentary. The men themselves were not conscious of what their own work tended to. Could they have seen the full meaning of their own first acts, they would have shrunk back in dismay, pronouncing impossible those very things with the glorious consummation of which their names are now linked forever. So was it with Luther in the work of the Reformation. The plan of it was not in his mind when he began it. That plan in its vastness, difficulties, and perils would have appalled him, had it been brought clearly before him. So was it also in regard to his greatest Reformatory labor — the translation of the Bible. At a period when he would have utterly denied his power to produce that very translation which the genius and learning of more than three centuries have failed to displace, he was actually unconsciously taking the first step toward its preparation. Like all great fabrics, Luther's translation was a growth.

The first Protestant Version of the New Testament. Its early history.

The memorable year 1517, the year of the Theses, was also the year of Luther's first translation of part of the Holy Scriptures. It is earlier, however, than the Theses, or the controversy with Tetzel, and yet its very preface implies the Protestant doctrine of the right of the illumined private judgment of Christians. It embraced only the SEVEN PENITENTIAL PSALMS, (VI., XXXII., XXXVIII., LI., CII., CXXX., CXLIII.) He used in its preparation the Latin translation of Jerome, and another by Reuchlin, which had appeared at Tübingen in 1512. In the Annotations, however, he frequently refers to the Hebrew.

Between 1518 and the appearance of his New Testament complete, in 1522, Luther translated eleven different portions of the Bible. In 1518 appeared two editions of a translation and exposition of the Lord's Prayer. The first edition was issued without Luther's consent, by Schneider, one of his pupils. Luther himself published the second edition, which deviates very much from the other. It appeared with this title: "Exposition, in German, of the Lord's Prayer, for the simple Laity, by Dr. Martin Luther, Augustinian Monk, of Wittenberg. Not for the learned." The same year he translated the CX. Psalm. In 1519 appeared the Gospel for the Festival of St. Peter and St. Paul, and the Prayer of Manasseh. In 1520 he published his first Catechetical work, embracing the Ten Commandments.

In 1521, Luther was seized, on his way from Worms to Wittenberg, and carried to the castle of the Wartburg, where he remained from May 4th, 1521, to March 6th of the following year. These months of calm, and of meditation, led to the maturing of his plans for the promotion of the Reformation, and among them, of the most important of the whole, the giving to the people the Word of God in their own tongue. Before his final leaving the Wartburg, Luther, in disguise, made his way to Wittenberg, and spent several days there, known only to a very few of his most trusted friends. During that mysterious and romantic visit, they may have urged upon him personally this very work of translation. He had been urged to this work, indeed, before. " Melanchthon," says he, " constrained me to translate the New Testament." Various fragments of translation were published during the earlier part of Luther's sojourn in his Patmos, but not until his return from Wittenberg did he begin the first grand portion of his translation of the Bible as a whole.

Luther translated the New Testament in the first draft in about three months. It sounds incredible, but the evidence places it beyond all doubt. He was only ten months at the Wartburg; during this period he wrote many other things; did a good deal of work on his Postils, and lost a great deal of time by sickness, and in other ways, and did not commence his New Testament until his sojourn was more than half over. Never did one of our race work with First draft. the ardor with which Luther wrought when his whole soul was engaged, and never, probably, was that great soul so engaged, so fired, so charmed with its occupation, as in this very work of translating the New Testament. The absurd idea that Luther was assisted in this first work by Melanch thon, Cruciger, Amsdorf, and others, has arisen from confounding with this a different work at a different period. In this, he was alone, far from the aid, far from the co-operating sympathy of a single friend.

He did not translate from the Vulgate, though he used that ancient and important translation with sound judgment. In his earlier efforts as a translator we see more of its influence than at a later period. This influence was partly, no doubt, unconscious. His thorough familiarity with the Vulgate would shape his translation to some extent, even when he was not thinking of it. But the Vulgate was of right the most important aid, next to the sacred text The Vulgate. itself. Consequently, though Luther grew less and less dependent upon it, and saw more and more its defects, he never ceased to value it. He well knew, too, that many of the most serious faults of the received form of the Vulgate were the results of the corrupted text, the state of which before the critical labors which ran through the sixteenth century, was almost chaotic. We will give a few illustrations of the fact that in certain cases Luther followed the Vulgate, in his earliest translation, without warrant from the Greek text. We will distribute our

illustrations under these heads: I. of *Additions;* II. of *Omis*
sions; III. of *Renderings;* IV. of *Readings*, in which Luther
follows the Vulgate when the Vulgate does not represent the
Greek text — or at least that text to which alone Luther had
access.

I. — ADDITIONS of the Vulgate and of Luther to the Erasmian Text. (1516, 1519.)

Mark vi 2. Were astonished, Luther adds: Seiner Lehre:
so Coverdale: at his learning.

" xvi. 9. Luther adds: Jesus.

" xii. 3. Luther adds: Alle: all the whole world:
Cranmer.

1 John v. 12. He that hath the Son, Luther adds: Gottes
— of God.

II. — OMISSIONS of the Vulgate and Luther from the Erasmian
text. These are few, for the sins of the Vulgate
against the pure text are most frequently those of *addi-*
tion.

Matt. i. 18. Omit: Jesus.

Matt. v. 22. Whosoever is angry with his brother, omit:
without a cause.

Matt. vi. 4. Omit: himself.

III. — RENDERINGS in which the Vulgate and Luther depart
from the Greek text.

Matt. x. 42. Little ones, Luther renders: one of the least.
So Coverdale.

Mark xv. 4. Behold how many things they witness
against thee, Luther renders: Wie hart sie
dich verklagen. Coverdale: How sore they
lay to thy charge.

1 Cor. xv. 44. There is a natural body, and there is a
spiritual body, Luther renders: Hat man ein
natürlichen Leib, so hat man auch einen
geistlichen Leib. Coverdale: If there be a
natural body, there is a spiritual body also.

1 Thess. i. 7. Renders: an example: Vulg.: ensample.

IV. — READINGS in which Luther follows the Vulgate.

Matt. iii. 8. For: fruits, Luther reads: fruit.

Matt. x. 25. For: Beelzeboul, reads: Beelzebub.

John xi. 54. For: Ephraim, reads: Ephrem.

Acts ix. 35. For: Saron, reads: Sarona.

Acts xiii. 6. For: Bar Jesus, reads: Bar Jehu.

Eph. iii. 3. For: he made known, reads: was made known.

Eph. v. 22. For: Wives submit yourselves, reads: Let the wives be subject to.

1 Tim. iii. 16. For: God was manifest in the flesh, reads: Which was manifest in the flesh (in all the early editions).

Heb. iv. 1. For: any of you, reads: any of us. So Tyndale and Coverdale.

Heb. ix. 14. For: your consciences, reads: our consciences.

Rev. xiv. 13. For: I heard the voice, reads: the voice which I heard.

A number of these adhesions to the Vulgate are to be traced to his judgment that it here represented a purer text than that of Erasmus.* Luther used the Basle Edition of 1509.

To have rendered even the Vulgate into the noble German which Luther used would have been a great task. The very defects of the old German versions from the Vulgate which did not prevent their wide circulation, is a pathetic proof of the hungering of the people for the bread of life. But it was characteristic of Luther's originality, vigor, and clearness of perception, that he at once saw — what now seems so obvious, but which had not been seen for ages — that to give the people what they needed, required more than a translation of a translation. If we remember that in our own day the general feeling is, that the new translations to be prepared for the Bible Society should be conformed to our English version, and not independent versions from the original, we have before us a fact which may help us, though very imperfectly, to realize how daring it seemed, in Luther's time, to prepare a trans-

* Palm, De Codicibus: quibus Lutherus usus est. Hamburg,1735
Palm, Historie. Halle, 1772, p. 245.

lation for the people from the original, involving, as it did, the idea that the Vulgate, embalmed as it was in the reverence of ages, was not in all respects a pure representation of the Word of God. When Luther's translation appeared, there was no point which the Romanists made with more frequency, violence, and effectiveness, than that it ignored the Vulgate; though the reason for which the Vulgate was ignored was that it departed from the Greek.

There is no decisive reason for thinking that Luther used any MANUSCRIPTS of the Greek text. The Greek texts which had been published, or at least printed, when Luther was engaged in his translation of the New Testament, were:

1. The Complutensian, folio, printed 1514; not published till 1523. Though doubts have been expressed as to Luther's having used the Complutensian, to which some force is given by his nowhere citing it, yet Melanchthon, his great co-worker in the New Testament, cites it during Luther's lifetime. The copy sent to the Elector of Saxony (six hundred were printed in all) was placed in the library at Wittenberg, whence it was removed, two years after Luther's death, to Jena. His not citing it is no evidence over against the irresistible presumption of the case; and Krell (1664) asserts positively that Luther was familiar with the Complutensian.*

2. The first Erasmus, 1516, folio.

3. The Aldine, 1518, folio; follows for the most part the first Erasmus, even in its blunders, yet has some peculiarities worthy of note, as in James iv. 6. The Septuagint, in this edition, was used by Luther.

4. The second Erasmus, 1519, folio.

5. The Gerbelius, based on the second Erasmus and the Aldine, 1521, 4to.

6. The third Erasmus, 1522, folio.

It is evident that Luther's choice was confined at first to the Editions 2–5. The Complutensian and Erasmus 3 appeared too late for his earliest New Testament translation.

We might illustrate Luther's adherence to the Erasmian

Greek texts used by Luther.

---

* Hopf, Würdigung. 45.

Greek text over against the Vulgate: I. In his *additions* from the Greek of what the Vulgate *omits*. II. In his *omissions*, following the Greek, of what the Vulgate *adds*. III. Of *readings* in which he does the same. IV. Of *renderings* in which he forsakes the Vulgate for the Greek. The last head we defer for the present.

I. — *Additions* from the Greek where the Vulgate omits.
    Matt. ii. 18. *adds:* lamentation.   Tyndale: mourning.
    "   vi. 4, 6, 18. *adds:* openly.
    "   vi. 13. *adds:* For thine is the kingdom and the power and the glory forever.   So Coverdale. Tyndale *omits.*
    Matt. vi. 14. *adds:* their trespasses.
    "   vi. 25. *adds:* or what ye shall drink.
    "   vi. 32. *adds:* heavenly.
    Mark vi. 11. *adds:* Verily I say unto you, it shall be more tolerable . . . . . city.

II. - - *Omissions*, following the Greek, where the Vulgate *adds.*
    Matt. vi. 15. *omits:* your trespasses.
    "   vi. 21. *omits:* he shall enter into the kingdom of the heavens.
    "   vii. 29. *omits:* their ; and, Pharisees.
    Mark xi. 26. *omits:* But if ye do not . . . trespasses.
    Luke xvii. 36. *omits:* Two men shall be in the field . . . and the other left.
    John xix. 38. *omits:* He came therefore and took the body of Jesus.
    Jas. iv. 6. *omits:* Wherefore he saith, God resisteth . . . . the humble.   All the editions of Erasmus and Gerbelius *omit* these words, but the Asulanus (Aldine) of 1518 *has* them, and so the Complutensian.   Tyndale 1. Cov. *omit.*
    1 John v. 7. *omits:* There are three that bear record . . . and the Holy Ghost.   This text Erasmus Ed. 1, 2, Asulanus, Gerbelius *omit.*   Erasmus: Ed. 3–5 *has* it, though he did not be-
    7

lieve it to be genuine. The Complutensian
has it with slight variations. Luther rejected
it on critical grounds, and it did not appear
in any of his Bibles published in his lifetime.
The Codex Amiatinus of the Vulgate omits
it. Tyndale has it, either from the Vulgate
or Erasmus 3. Tynd. 2. and Cov. put it in
brackets.

Rev. **xii.** 10. *omits:* the accuser of our brethren.
" **xviii.** 23. *omits:* and the light of a candle . . . thee
" **xix.** 9. *omits:* the marriage.

[I] —Of *Readings* in which he follows the Greek.
Matt. **v.** 4, 5. *reads* in order of Greek. Vulgate puts ὅ
first.
" **v.** 47. *reads:* publicans; Vulgate: heathen.
" **vi.** 1. *reads:* alms; Vulgate: righteousness.
" **vi.** 5. *reads:* thou prayest; Vulgate: ye pray.
Acts **xiii.** 33. *reads:* first Psalm; so Tynd., Cov.; Vulgate
reads: second Psalm.
Rom. **xv.** 2. *reads:* Every one of us; Vulgate: of you.
Rev. **ii.** 13. *reads:* in my days; Vulgate: in those days.
" **v.** 12. *reads:* riches and wisdom; Vulgate: divinity
and wisdom.

The most important peculiarities of Luther's first version, as
we see by this minute examination, are solved at once by a
comparison of it with the text of Erasmus. The differences
in the four editions — two of them reprints of Erasmus — are
not, for the most part, important; 2 and 3 may be considered
as in the main one text, and 3 and 4 another. A minute
examination seems to indicate that Luther had them all, and
used them all; but the second Erasmus seems, beyond all
doubt, to have been his chief text, though the first Erasmus,
and the Gerbelius have both been urged by scholars for the
post of honor.
Of the Aldine edition of Erasmus, 1518, there is a copy, in
fine condition, in the City Library of Philadelphia. The

author has all the later editions mentioned, except the first Erasmus and the Complutensian,* in his own library. The admirable edition of the New Testament by Van Ess † gives all the various readings of Erasmus and the Complutensian, in the best form for comparison with each other and the Vulgate. Mill, and Wetstein, and Bengel also, give these various readings, but not in so convenient a shape. The Complutensian readings are presented very fully also in Scrivener's Plain Introduction to the Criticism of the New Testament, (Cambridge, 1861,) pp. 349–358. But the most desirable modern edition for the collation of the Complutensian text is that of Gratz, N. T. Textum Græcum ad exemplar Complutense, ed. Nova Mogunt., 1827, 2 vols. 8vo.

It may be interesting to present a few illustrations of the variations between the Complutensian (1514) and the first Erasmus (1517), comparing both with Luther and our Authorized Version.

		Complutensian, 1514.	First Erasmus, 1516.	Luther, 1522.	Auth. Engl., 1611.
I.	Matt. i. 14	Acheim	Achēn	Achin.	Achim
II.	" ii. 6	For	omits	For (Denn)	for
III.	" ii. 6	Shall come	shall come *to me*	sol mir kommen	shall come
IV.	" ii. 11	they saw	they found	they found	they saw
V.	" iii. 8	fruit	fruits	fruit	fruits
VI.	" ii. 11	the Holy Ghost	the Holy Ghost *and with fire*	m. d. h. g. u. mit feur	w. t. h. G. and with fire.
VII.	" iv. 15	*land of N.*	Nepthalim	Nepthalim	land of Nepthali
VIII.	" 17	From that	and from that	From that	From that
IX.	" 18	he walking	Jesus walking	Jesus walking	Jesus walking
X.	" v. 12	*Your* reward	*Our* reward	*Your reward*	your reward
XI.	" 27	It was said	was said by (or to) them of old time	said to (zu) them of old time.	said by (or to) them of old time
XII.	" 47	friends	brethren	Brüdern	brethren .

In these twelve examples, Luther agrees with the Complutensian in four cases; the Authorized Version agrees in seven. Erasmus retained in all his editions his readings Nos. 1, 3, 4,

* The writer has examined the Complutensian Polyglot in the library of the Theological Seminary at Princeton, and the New Testament, formerly the property of Judge Jones, of Philadelphia, now in the choice collection of Professor Charles Short, of New York.

† Tübingen, 1827.

5, 6, 7, 9, 11, 12.   He coincides in editions 2, 3, 4, 5 with the Complutensian in Nos. 2, 8, 10.

We will now illustrate the different readings of the five editions of Erasmus:

		Erasmus 1, 1516.	Erasmus 2, 1519.	Erasmus 3, 1522.	Erasmus 4, 1527.	Erasmus 5, 1535.	Luther, 1522.
I.	Matt. vi. 14	our	our	our	your	your	Your, as 4, 5
II.	" vi. 24	Mamon	Mamon	Mammon	Mammon	Mammon	Mammon, as 3, 4, 5
III.	" vi. 26	we	we	you	you	you	You, as 3, 4, 5
IV.	" viii. 25	you	you	us	us	us	us, as 2, 3, 4, 5
V.	" x. 8	raise the dead, cleanse lepers	Cleanse lepers, raise the dead	as 2	as 2	as 2	Cleanse the lepers, raise the dead, as 2, 3, 4, 5
VI	" xiii. 8	of the Sabbath	of the S. *also*	as 2	as 2	as 2	as 2, 3, 4, 5
VII	" xiii. 27	*the* tares	tares	*the* tares	*the* tares	*the* tares	as 1, 3, 4, 5
		us	us	you	you	us	us, as 1, 2, 5
VIII.	" xiii. 56	envies (phthnoi)	Murders, (phonoi)	as 2	as 2	as 2	as 2, 3, 4, 5
IX.	" xv. 19						
X.	" xv. 36	And having given thanks	*Om:* and	as 2	as 2	as 2	as 2, 3, 4, 5

This table illustrates the lack of accuracy in the printing of Erasmus—shows that Luther was not misled by typographical errors, and that he used the later editions in each case.   In none of these instances does he follow a reading for which there is no authority but the first of Erasmus.

The order of the books in Luther's New Testament varied somewhat from that of the Vulgate and Erasmus; which is the one retained in our Authorized Version.   Luther places Peter and John immediately after Paul's Epistles.   Then come Hebrews, James, Jude, and Revelation.   He based his arrangement on the relative clearness of the canonical authority of the books.   His order is followed by Tyndale (1526), and in all the editions which bear the name of Tyndale, Matthews, or Rogers.   It is also the order in Coverdale's Bible.   This is one proof, among
Order of the   a great number, of the large influence of Luther
Books of the New   upon those versions.   The " Great Bible " of 1539,
Testament.   the Cromwell Bible, frequently called the Cranmer, restores the arrangement of the Vulgate—and in this is followed by the Genevan, Bishops, and the Authorized.   Luther bestowed great care upon the division of the text into paragraphs, and as a result of this there are some changes in the division into chapters, which had been made very imperfectly in the Vulgate, in the thirteenth century.   No German New Testament appeared in Luther's lifetime with the division into

verses. Their place, nearly to the close of the century, was partly supplied by capital letters, dividing the page at regular intervals. There were Introductions to the New Testament, and to some of the books: marginal notes and parallel passages.

The same spirit which had impelled Luther to prepare this translation made him eager to have it as speedily as possible in the hands of the people. This desire, no less than the necessity of quelling the uproar and arresting the ruin which the fanaticism of Carlstadt was bringing about, led to his flight from his prison, and his final return to Wittenberg, (March 14, 1522.) Here, in the house of Amsdorff, Revision. especially with the counsel and aid of Melanchthon, he revised his translation with great care.* He interested in the work his friend Spalatin, the chaplain, librarian, and private secretary at the court; he solicited from him aid in suggesting apt words, " not words of the court or camp, but simple words; for this book wishes to be luminous in simplicity." He obtained through him the privilege of an inspection of the Electoral jewels, that he might more accurately render the names of the gems in the twenty-first chapter of Revelation. They were sent to Luther, and returned by him through Cranach, the great painter.

After a thorough revision, Luther put his New Testament to press, urging on the work of printing with all his energies. Three presses were kept going, from which were thrown off ten thousand sheets daily. Luther complained of the slowness of the progress. The steam-presses of our own day would hardly have worked rapidly enough for him. The first edition embraced probably three thousand copies, and appeared about September 21st, 1522. So eagerly was it received, Publication. that in December another edition came forth. It was hailed with delight wherever the German tongue was used, and within three months of its appearance an edition was issued at Basel by Petri. It woke a thrill of rapture everywhere among those who loved the Word of God. None received it more eagerly than the pious women of the time. The people and the evangelical part of the pastors vied with

---

* March 30, 1522   Omnia nunc elimari (to polish) cepimus, *Philippus* et ego

each other in the enthusiasm with which they greeted it;
Lange, the Senior at Erfurt, had translated several of the
books of the New Testament into German: when Luther's
translation came into his hands, he at once used and cited it
in his preaching. Lifted by his noble evangelical spirit above
the littleness of vanity, he was the first to give its true position
in the Church to the work which forever consigned his own to
oblivion.

There lie at our hand, as we write, three early impressions
of these first editions. One is a folio, dated 1523, and was
printed by Hans Schönsperger, in the city of Augsburg. It
was fitting that in that imperial city should early appear a
work from which sprang the great Confession, which was destined to be set forth in its halls a few years later. The second
is a Basel edition, in quarto, of 1523, with its pictures richly
colored. The third was printed at Strasburg, in 1525, by John
Knoblauch. All these editions have engravings. They are especially rich in pictures in the Book of Revelation; and there the
Early impres- artists have been allowed ample room for the play of
sions. their imaginations. The discolored pages, the antique type, the grotesque cuts, the strange devices of the print-
ers, the binding of stamped hogskin, the curious clasps, the
arms of the old families in whose libraries they once stood,
gilt upon the sides or engraved on book-plates, the records in
writing on margin and fly-leaf, made by men of different generations, nay, a kind of odor of the past — all these, as we
handle these ancient books, carry the mind back to days long
gone — to sore struggles, whose blessings we enjoy; to the
seed-time of weeping, whose harvest-sheaves we bear in our
bosom. In the heart of those times there comes before the
vision that immortal man to whom the world owes the eman-
cipation of the Word, and its own redemption by that Word
unbound. We see him bending over his work in the Wartburg. There are times when the text beneath his eyes fails
to reveal to him the mind of the Spirit, and in the ardor of
prayer he raises them to the Eternal Source of all illumination,
and lifts them not in vain.

Well may we take the Bible in our hands, reverently **and**

prayerfully, most of all because it was God who gave it to the Fathers. Well may we lift it tenderly and gratefully for the sake of martyrs and confessors, who toiled and died that it might be transmitted to us and to all time.

Amid the enthusiasm with which Luther's translation of the New Testament was received, there were, of course, not wanting voices whose tones were by no means in unison with the general laudation. One of these growls of disapproval came from a very august source — from a gentleman portly in form, and charged by some who professed to know him well, with exhibiting a self-will of the largest kind. He is memorable in history for winning the title of "Defender of the Faith"—a faith which he afterward had his people burned to death for receiving in a part or so which interfered with his later discoveries. Bitterly disappointed, as he had been, in his matrimonial anticipations, he yet exhibited evidences of what Dr. Johnson said was illustrated in second marriages: "The triumph of hope over experience." He had entered into controversy with Luther, and had discovered that there was one man, at least, who was bold enough to "answer a fool according to his folly," although that fool might wear a crown. Not having it in his power to relieve his feelings in regard to Luther, in his favorite mode, which would have been to have had his head taken off, he relieved himself, as he best could, by venting his wrath in savage words, and in trying to rouse the enmity of others against the man he detested and feared. Henry the Eighth wrote, in January, 1523, to the Elector Frederick and to the Dukes John and George, of Saxony, as follows: " As I was about to seal this letter, I recollected that Luther, in the silly book which he put forth against me, excused himself from giving an answer on certain points, on the ground, that the work of translating the Bible left him no time for it. I thought it well, therefore, to solicit your attention to this matter, so that he be not allowed to go on with this thing. I do not think it right, in general, that the Holy Scriptures should be read in the living tongues, and consider it specially perilous to read it in a translation by Luther. Any one can foresee how unreliable he will be; he will corrupt the blessed Scriptures by his false interpretation, so that the common reader will believe that he is drawing from the Holy Scriptures what that accursed man has derived from damnable heretical books." The German nobles, to whom this letter was addressed, received it in very different ways. Duke George replied, that he had bought up all the copies of Luther's translation which had found their way into his dominion, and had interdicted the circulation of it. The Elector Frederick and Duke John, in their reply, passed over this point with significant silence.

The mandate of Duke George spoke with special bitterness of the pictures in Luther's New Testament, pictures which it characterized as "outrageous, tending to throw scorn upon the Pope's holiness, and to confirm Luther's doctrine." Luther's comment, which he bestowed upon the Duke himself, was, "I am not to be frightened to death with a bladder:" and to inspire some of his own courage in others, he wrote his treatise "Of Civil Authority — how far we owe allegiance to it," in which he declares that rulers who suppress the Holy Scriptures are tyrants — murderers of Christ — worthy of a place with Herod, who sought the life of the infant Saviour.

Jerome Emser managed to get himself involved in the amber The counter-translation. Em- ser.* of Luther's history; and so we know of him. After Duke George had entered on his crusade against Luther's New Testament, especially against the pictures in it, (and in this latter point, we confess, something might be urged for the duke, in an artistic point of view,) he found his Peter the Hermit in a Catholic theologian, a native of Ulm, who had studied at Tübingen and Basle. He had been chaplain of Cardinal Raymond Gurk, and had travelled with him through Germany and Italy. On his return, he obtained the chair of Belles-Lettres at Erfurt. Subsequently, he became secretary and orator to Duke George. He was originally a friend of Luther, but his friendship was not permanent. It gave way at the Leipzig disputation, in 1519, and he transferred his allegiance to Eck. He had the honor of being the first literary antagonist of Luther's version. Duke George, the

* See Göz, Ueberblicke, etc., p. 300.

Bishop of Merseburg, Prince Adolphus of Anhalt, and the Bishop of Meissen, not satisfied with legal measures of suppression, called in Emser, to use the more formidable weapon, the pen, the gigantic power of which Luther was then exhibiting. About a year after the publication of the first edition of Luther's New Testament, Emser came forth with his confutation of it. Its title stated its object, which was, to show " On what ground, and for what reason, Luther's translation should be prohibited to the common people," and he claimed to have discovered in the unfortunate book about four errors and a quarter, more or less, to each page, some " fourteen hundred heresies and falsehoods," all told. Luther did not consider the work worthy of a reply; but Dr. Regius took up its defence, and confuted Emser in the robust manner which characterized that very hearty age. It seemed, however, as if Emser were about to illustrate his honesty in the very highest and rarest form in which a critic can commend himself to human confidence; it seemed as if he were about to prepare a book of the same general kind as that which he reviewed, in which he could be tested by his own canons, and his right to be severe on others demonstrated by the masterly hand with which he did the work himself. He prepared to publish a counter-translation. He had the two qualities, in which many translators have found the sole proofs of their vocation: he could not write the language into which, and did not understand the language from which, he was to translate. But his coolness stood him in better stead than all the knowledge he might have had of Greek and German. With little trouble, he produced a translation, equal, on the whole, as even Luther himself admitted, to Luther's own, and literally free from every objection which he had made to Luther's. We have had books on the Reformers, before the Reformation; on Lutheranism, before Luther, and such-like; and another might be written on the Yankees, before the sailing of the Mayflower. Emser was one of them.

The way he did the masterly thing we have mentioned was this: He adopted, not stole (he was above stealing) — he *adopted* Luther's translation bodily, only altering him where he had

had the audacity to desert the Vulgate for the original. These alterations removed nearly all the fourteen hundred heresies at a sweep. But this was not enough. As the people looked at the " outrageous " pictures, not merely in spite of Duke George's prohibition, but with that zest with which human nature always invests forbidden things, it was determined not merely to have pictures, but the happy idea, which none but men nobly careless of their reputation for consistency would have harbored for a moment, was fallen on — the plan of having the very same ones. Duke George paid Cranach forty rix thalers for copies of them, and thus secured for himself the great satisfaction of seeing the book he had denounced going forth in substance, and the pictures which he had specially assaulted, scattered everywhere by his own ducal authority. In his preface, Emser has anticipated a style of thinking which has crept into our Protestant Churches. He says: " Let the layman only attend to having a holy life, rather than trouble himself about the Scriptures, which are only meant for the learned." We have had a good deal of nonsense ventilated in our churches in this country very much in the same vein. It means about this: Be pious, be in earnest; never mind having ideas or doctrines — they only create divisions; be zealous about something, whether it be right or wrong. You may read your Bibles, but be careful not to form an opinion as to their meaning, or if you do, attach no importance to it if any one does not agree with you. The English moralist was thought to go very far when he said, " He can't be wrong whose life is in the right; " but we have something beyond him and Emser; it is in effect: " He can't be wrong whose sensations are of the right kind," and who gives himself up blindly to the right guidance, and takes the right newspaper.

Luther's New Testament, with Luther's pictures, thus adopted, and with its margin crowded with Papistical notes, which were meant, as far as possible, to furnish the antidote to the text, went forth to the world. The preparation was made for a second edition of it. Duke George furnished for it a preface, in which, after exposing the enormities of Martin Luther, he characterized Emser as his dearly beloved, the worthy and erudite, and gave him a copyright for his work, which was to reach over the next two years. Poor Emser, suffocated in such a profusion of praises and privileges, died before he could enjoy any of them. His vanity was very great. One special token of it was, that he had his coat of arms engraved for the books he published. A copy of his New Testament lies before us, in which there figures, as a part of his crest, that goat's head from which Luther — whose sense of the ludicrous was very active — derived his ordinary sobriquet for Emser, " the *goat.*"

In his Treatise on Translation, Luther thus characterizes his opponent and his work: " We have seen this poor dealer in second-hand clothes, who has played the critic with my New Testament, (I shall not mention his name again — he has gone to his Judge; and every one, in fact, knows what he was,) who confesses that my German is pure and good, and who knew that he could not improve it, and yet wished to bring it to disgrace. He took my New Testament, almost word for word, as it came from my hand, removed my preface, notes, and name from it, added his name, his preface, and his notes to it, and thus sold my Testament under his own name. If any man doubts my word, he need but compare the two. Let him lay mine and the frippery man's side by side, and he will see who is the translator in both. If any man prefers the puddle to the spring, he need not take my work; only, if he insist on being ignorant himself, let him allow others to learn. If any man can do the work better than I have done, let him not hide his talent in a napkin; let him come forth, and we will be the first to praise him. We claim no infalli bility. We shall be thankful to those who point out our mis takes. Mistakes we have no doubt made, as Jerome often made them before us."

The New Testament, in common with the rest of the Scrip tures — yet with a pre-eminence among them — continued to be the object of Luther's repeated study up to the time of his death. The last revision of the translation of the whole Bible was commenced in 1541. The last edition printed under Lu- ther's own eyes appeared in 1545. In February, 1546, he died.* The Exegetical Library — not to speak of the Fathers, and of other indirect sources — had grown around him as he advanced. The Complutensian Polyglott, (1514–18,) and the editions of the New Testament which followed its text, had <small>Growth of N.T. literature.</small> become accessible. Erasmus had carried his Greek New Testaments, with their translation and annotations, through five editions, (1516–1535.) The fifth remains to this hour the general basis of the received text. The Aldine of 1518 had been reprinted frequently. Colinæus had issued his exquisitely beautiful † edition, (Paris, 1534,) which anticipated many of the readings fixed by modern criticism. Robert Stephens, the royal and regal printer, issued the wonderfully accurate ‡ O mirificam edition of 1546, the text based upon the Complutensian, but with a collation of sixteen manuscripts, only a little too late for Luther to look upon it. Great efforts, and not unsuccessful, had been made, especially by Robert Stephens, to amend the current and greatly corrupted text of the Vulgate, (1528–1540.) Flacius had issued his Clavis, the immortal work in which he developed, as had never been done before, the principles of Hermeneutics, (1537.) Pagninus had done the same work from a relatively free Roman Catholic position, in his Introduction to Sacred Letters, (1536.) The era of Luther was an era of translations, in whose results there has been specific improvement in detached renderings, but no general advance whatever. Germany has produced no translation of the New Testament equal, as a whole, to Luher's. Our authorized English Version is but a revision of Tyndale, to whom it owes all its generic excellencies and beauties. Among the Latin translators, Pagninus (1528) took a high rank, by his minute verbal accuracy, which caused his translation, in after times, to be used as an interlinear. A Latin version of the New Testament appeared in 1529, with the imprint of Wittenberg, an imprint which is probably spurious. It has been believed, by many scholars, to have been the work of Luther; others attribute it to Melanchthon; but

---

* See Panzer's Entwurf, pp. 370–376.

† Perquam nitida. Le Long. (Bœhmer-Masch.), i, 206.

‡ Nitidissima-duodecim sphalmata duntaxat accurunt. Le Long., i, 208

the authorship has never been settled. The Zürich translators, Leo Juda and his associates, had issued their Latin
version, marked by great merits, not verbal, as Pagninus', but
more in the reproductive manner of Luther, shedding light
upon the meaning of the text, (1543.)

Luther's version had been followed by a number of rival or
antagonistic translations in German, all of them freely using
him — many of them, in fact, being substantially no more than
a re-issue of Luther — with such variations as, they supposed,
justified, sometimes, by the original, but yet more frequently
by the Vulgate. Zürich sent forth its version, (1527,) Rival transla-
Hetzer and other fanatics sent forth theirs. The tions.
Romish theologians did Luther good service by the rigorous
process, to which they subjected his translations in every way.
To the labors of Emser (1527) were added those of Dietenber-
ger, whose Bible appeared in 1534, (a compound of Emser's
Recension of Luther's New Testament, of Luther's Old Testament, and of Leo Juda's Apocrypha, with corrections of the
Hebrew and Greek from the Latin, and a body of notes,) and
of Eck, 1537. The gall of their severity was certainly sweet-
ened by the unconscious flattery of their plagiarism — and
whatever may have been the spirit in which objections were
made to his translations, Luther weighed them carefully, and
wherever they had force, availed himself of them.

It was the age of inspiration to the translator, and the
foundations of Biblical Versions, laid by its builders, will stand
while the world stands. Luther had many and great competi-
tors, in this era, for the highest glory in this grand work ; but
posterity accords him the rank of the greatest of Biblical translators. " His Bible," says Reuss,* " was, for its era, a miracle
of science. Its style sounded as the prophecy of a golden age
of literature, and in masculine force, and in the unction of the
Holy Spirit, it remains a yet unapproached model." For Luther may be claimed, that in the great edifice of the people's
knowledge of God's Word, he laid the noblest stone, the corner-stone, in his translation of the New Testament. Future
ages may, by their attrition, wear away the rougher points of

* Geschichte der Heiligen Schrift, N. T., § 47.

its surface, but the massive substance will abide, the stone itself can never be displaced.

Up to this hour, Luther's version of the New Testament has been the object of minute examination by friend and foe Protestant scholarship has subjected it to a far severer test than the enmity of Rome could bring to bear upon

Sources of defects in Luther's version.

it. That particular mistakes and defects exist in it, its warmest admirers will admit, but the evidence of its substantial accuracy and of its matchless general beauty is only strengthened by time. The facts which bear upon its defects may be summed * up in the statements which follow:

I. The influence of the Vulgate was necessarily very power-ful on Luther. It was felt when he thought not of it, felt when he was consciously attempting to depart from it where it was wrong. Imagine an English translator preparing now a version of the New Testament — and think how the old version would mould it, not only unconsciously, but in the very face of his effort to shake off its influence.

II. Luther's Greek text was in many respects different from that now received, as the received is different from the texts preferred by the great textual critics of our century.

III. Luther's words, as they were used and understood in his day, were an accurate rendering of the original, at many places, where change of usage now fixes on them a different sense. He was right, but time has altered the language. Luther, for example, used "als," where "wie" (as) would now be employed; "mögen" for "vermögen," (to be able;) "etwa" for "irgend einmal," (sometime;) "schier" in the sense of "bald," (soon).†

IV. Many of the points of objection turn on pure triviali-ties.

V. Many of the passages criticized are intrinsically difficult. Scholars in these cases are not always agreed that Luther was wrong, or yet more frequently when they agree so far, they are not agreed as to what is to be substituted for his rendering.

---

* Hopf, Würdigung, p. 214.

† On the antiquated words in Luther's Bible, see Pischon, Erklärung., Berl., 1844; and Beck, Wörterbuch z. L.'s Bibelübers., Siegen. u Wiesbaden, 1846; Hopf, 230-241.

Over against this, the felicity in his choice of words, the exquisite naturalness and clearness in his structure of sentences, the dignity, force, and vivacity of his expressions, his affluence of phrase, his power of compression, and the rhythmic melody of his flow of style, have excited an admiration to which witness has been borne from the beginning by friend and foe. When the time shall come, as come it must, when the toils and discoveries of centuries shall be brought to bear upon Luther's version, in changes which shall be recognized by the Church as just, Luther's grand work will not only remain in the new as the foundation, but will abide as the essential body of the structure itself. The German nation will never have a Bible for which, next to its great Source, they can cease to bless Luther's name.

IV.

CONSERVATIVE CHURCH OF THE REFORMATION — THE EVANGELICAL PROTESTANT (LUTHERAN) CHURCH.*

FIRST at Wittenberg, and not long after at Zurich, when, at the beginning of the sixteenth century, the fulness of God's time had been reached, "there blazed up a fire which had long been hidden beneath the ashes. It burst into a mighty flame. The farthest horizon of Northern Europe grew bright as with some glorious display of the wondrous electric light, the reflection of which touched, with its glory, the remote South — even to Italy and Spain. The truth, which had been set free, moved with bold steps to the conquest of the hearts

Restoration of the purified Church of the West.

---

*GOEBEL: D. relig. Eigenthüm. d. Luth. u. ref. Kirch. 1837.
AUGUSTI: Beitr. z. Gesch. u. Statist. der Ev. Kirch. 1838.
HERING: Gesch. d. kirch. Unionsb. 1838.
RUDELBACH: Ref. Luth. u. Union. 1839.
DORNER: D. Princip. Uns. Kirch. 1847.
WIGGER'S: Statistik. 2 vols. 1842.
ULLMANN: Z. Charakter. d. ref. Kirch. (in Stud. u. Kritik. 1843.)
HERZOG: D. Einh. u. Eigent. d. beid. Ev. Schwesterk. (Berl. 1. Zeitung, 1844.)
NITZSCH: Prakt. Theol. 1847.
SCHWEIZER: Die Glaubensl. d. Ev. Ref. Kirch. BAUR: Princ. d. Ref. Kirch. (Both in Zeller's Jahrb. 1847.)
EBRARD: Dogmatik. 1851. (2d ed. 1861.)
SCHENKEL: D. Princip. d. Protestantism. 1852. HEPPE. (1850. Stud. u. Krit.)
SCHENKEL. (1852: Prinzip. 1855: Unionsberuf. 1858: Dogm.)

of men. The princes and people of the great Germanic races were ripest for its reception, and were the first to give it their full confidence. Such a triumph of the Gospel had not been witnessed since the times of the Apostles. The corner-stone of the purified temple of the Holy Ghost was laid anew — nay, it also seemed as it were the very top-stone which was laid, while the regenerated nations shouted, ' Grace, grace! ' unto it. The Gospel won its second grand triumph over the Law, and a second time Paul withstood Peter to the face because he was to be blamed. In place of a bare, hard set of words, of a lifeless and mechanical formalism, there reappeared the idea, the spirit, and the life, in the whole boundless fulness and divine richness in which they had appeared in the primitive Church." * To comprehend the Reformation, it is necessary to trace the essential idea of Christianity through its whole history. " The Greek Church saw in Christianity the revelation of the Logos, as the Supreme Divine Reason. Christianity was to it the true philosophy. The Church of the West, the Roman Catholic Church, laid its grand stress on the Organism of the Church. There dwelt the truth, and there the life-controlling power." † " Catholicism had unfolded itself into a vast system of guarantees of Christianity; but the thing itself, the Christianity they were to guarantee, was thrown into the shade. The antithesis between spurious and

GASS: Ges. d. Prot. Dogmat. 1853.
ZELLER: Syst. Zwinglis. 1853. WETZEL: (Ztschr. Rudelb. u. Guerik. 1853.)
LÜCKE: Ueb. d. Geschicht. ein. richt. Formulirung. (Deutsch. Zeitschr. 1853.)
MULLER: 1854–63: Union.
HAGENBACH: Z. Beantw. d. F. üb. d. Princ. d. Protest. (Stud. u. Krit. 1854.)
SCHNECKENBURGER: Vergl. Darstell. d. Luth. u. Ref. Lehrbeg. 1855. 2 vols
HARNACK: Die Luth. Kirche in Licht. d. Geschicht. 1855.
RUDELBACH: Die Zeichen d. Zeit. inn. d. Ev.-Luth. Kirche. 1857.
STAHL: Die Luth. Kirche u. d. Union. 2d ed. 1861.
THOMAS: Union Luth. Kirch. u. Stahl. 1860.
HUNDESHAGEN: Beiträg. z. Kirch. Verf. etc., d. Protest. 1864.
KAHNIS: Ueber d. Princip. d. Protestantis. 1865.
LUTHARDT: Handb. d. Dogmat. 2d ed. 1866.
KAHNIS: Luth. Dogmat. iii. 1868.
SEISS: Ecclesia Lutherana: A Brief Surv. of E. L. C. 1868.

* Wigger's Statistik, i. 92.   † Luthardt, Dogm. § 11, 8.

real Christianity came more and more to be narrowed to the affirmation or denial of the validity of these guarantees — until it became the error most fundamental of all errors, to assail the infallibility of the Pope, and of the Church." * In the Roman Catholic Church a vast system of outward ordinances and institutions had grown up, a stupendous body of ritualistic legalism — under which the old life of the Gospel went out, or became dim, in the heart of millions. The powers that ruled the Church were Moses, without the moral law, and Levi, without his wife. The grand distinctive characteristic of the Reformation over against this, the characteristic which conditioned all the rest, was that it was evangelical, a restoration of the glad tidings of free salvation in Jesus Christ — and thus it gave to the regenerated Church its exalted character as "Evangelical." Both the tendencies in the Reformation claimed to be evangelical. Both, as contrasted with Rome, rested on the Gospel — Christ alone; grace alone; justification by faith alone; the Bible the only rule; but in what is now styled the Lutheran Church, the Evangelical principle, as opposed to legalistic, deterministic, and rationalistic tendencies, came to a more consistent development, both in doctrine and life.

The large body of Christians whose historical relation to the great leader of the Reformation is most direct, forms a Church, which, in the language of a writer of another communion,† Evangelical Protestant Church. Name. "is the most important, the greatest, the most weighty of the churches" which arose in that glorious revolution. It has been her misfortune to be known to English readers, not through her own matchless literature, but by the blunders of the ignorant, the libels of the malicious, and the distorted statements of the partisan. Yet it would be easy to present a vast array of evidence in her favor, which should be taken, not from the language of her apologists, but exclusively from the writings of large-minded and intelligent men in other churches; and if, in this sketch of the Lutheran Church, the reader should be struck with the fact that in sustaining our position by cita-

* Martensen, 30.

† Goebel. Die relig. Eigenthümlichk. d. Luther. u. reform. Kirch., 1837.

tions, our own authors seem to be passed by in some cases where they might appropriately be quoted, he will account for it by the preference which we naturally feel for the testimony of those who can be suspected of no partiality for the object of their eulogy.

It is a curious fact in denominational history, that, as an ordinary rule, the more large, catholic, and churchly the title of a sect, the smaller, narrower, and more sectarian is the body that bears it. In a certain respect, the Roman Catholic Church is one of the narrowest of sects, first, Denomination al Name. because of the bigotry of its exclusiveness, not only over against the Protestant bodies, but also toward the venerable Church of the Orient, with which it is in such large doctrinal and ritual affinity, and with which it was once so closely united, but in which there has been produced by irritating and aggressive acts a more than Protestant ardor of aversion to the Papal See ; and secondly, because of its building upon a solitary earthly see as a foundation. If you look round among the Protestant bodies, you will find such glorious titles as "Disciples of Christ," "Church of God," "Christians," worn as the distinctive cognomen of recent, relatively small, heretical or fanatical bodies, who have largely denounced all sectarianism, for the purpose of building up new sects of the extremest sectarianism, and who reject the testimony of ages and the confessions of Christendom, for the purpose of putting in their place the private opinion of some pretentious heresiarch of the hour. The latest assaults upon the old-fashioned denominationalism are made, every now and then, by some new church, the statistics and leading features of which are somewhat as follows: ministers, one ; members, intermittent from the sexton up to a moderate crowd, according as the subject of the sermon advertised on Saturday takes or does not take the fancy of those who spend the Lord's day in hunting lions ; churches, one (over, if not in, a beer saloon;) creed, every man believes what he chooses ; terms of membership, every one who feels like it shall belong till he chooses to leave. This uncompromising body, which looks forward to the speedy overthrow of all Christendom because all Christendom rests on human creeds, is styled " Church of the Everlasting Gospel," " Pure Bible Christians Church," or some-thing of the kind.

Had the Lutheran Church chosen her own name, therefore, it would have furnished no presumption against her — it would have only shown that, as sectarianism may take the names which point to a general catholicity, so, on the other hand, the most truly catholic of Christian bodies might be willing to submit to the historical necessity of assuming a name which seemed to point to a human originator. There was a time when the true Catholics were tauntingly called Athanasians, and could not repudiate the name of Athanasius without faithlessness to the triune God himself. But our Church is not responsible for this portion of her name. She has been known by various titles, but her own earliest and strongest preference was for the name EVANGELICAL, (1525,) and many of her most devoted sons have insisted on giving her this title without any addition. No title could more strongly express her character, for pre-eminently is her system one which announces the glad tidings of salvation, which excites a joyous trust in Christ as a Saviour, which makes the word and sacraments bearers of saving grace. In no system is Christ so much as in the Lutheran; none exalts so much the glory of his person, of his office, and of his work. The very errors with which her enemies charge the Lutheran Church are those which would arise from an excess in this direction. If she believed in a local ubiquity of Christ's whole person, (as she does not,) this would be the excess of faith in his presence; if she believed in consubstantiation, (as she does not,) this would show that though her faith in Christ was blind, yet it hesitated at nothing which seemed to rest on his word; if she denied the obligation of the Church to keep the Christian Sabbath, (as she does not,) it would show that she had carried to excess her disposition to see in Christ the substance of all shadows. Happy is the Church whose failings bear in the direction of safety, which, if it err, errs not in a legalistic direction, but in an excess of evangelism. The heart of unbelief works only too surely in reducing an excess; but how shall a Church be revived, which, in its very constitution, is

Evangelical.

defective in the evangelical element? The name Evangelical is now given, out of the bounds of the Lutheran Church, to the Christianity of the heart everywhere, to all that makes much of Christ in the right way. It is a poor trick of some extravagant party within a party—some paltry clique in Protestantism at large, or in one of its communions—to attempt to monopolize the name Evangelical. Where thoughtful men accept the word in this narrowed sense, they despise it—but it is, in its true, original compass, a noble, a glorious name, not to be lightly abandoned to those who abuse it. The true corrective of abuse, is to restore, or hold fast the right use. Our Church, to which it belongs in the great historic sense, has a claim in her actual life, second to none, to wear it. She *is* the Evangelical Church.

At the Diet of Spire, (1529,) the Evangelical Lutheran Confessors, from their protest against the government of the Bishops and against the enforced imposition of the Mass, received the name of PROTESTANTS. This continued to be the diplomatic style of the Church till the peace of Westphalia, 1648.
Protestant. "The name Protestants," says Archbishop Bramhall, "is one to which others have no right but by communion with the Lutherans." This name, in European usage, is indeed, to a large extent, still confined to them.

In Poland and Hungary, the official title of our communion is "CHURCH OF THE AUGSBURG CONFESSION," and this
Church of the Augsburg Confession. is the name which, on the title-page of the Form of Concord, and repeatedly within it, is given to our churches.*

The name LUTHERAN was first used by Eck, when he published the Bull against Luther. Pope Hadrian VI. (1522) employed it, also, as a term of reproach. It was applied by the Romanists to all who took part against the Pope.† Luther strongly disapproved of the use of his name, while he warned men at

---

* "Electors, Prince, and States of the Augsburg Confession," "who embrace the Augsburg Confession." Gerhard, in the title-page of his "Confessio Catholica": "The Catholic and Evangelical doctrine as it is professed by the churches devoted (addictæ) to the Augsburg Confession."

† In the German of the Apology of the A. C., 213, 44, it is said: "The saving doctrine, the precious, Holy Gospel, they call Lutheran."

the same time against such a repudiation of it as might seem
to imply a rejection of the doctrine of God's word preached by
him. "It is my doctrine, and it is not my doctrine; it is in
my hand, but God put it there. Luther will have nothing to do
Lutheran. with Lutheranism except as it teaches Holy Scripture
purely."* " Let us not call our Church Lutheran,"
said Gustavus Erichson, King of Sweden, "let us call it Christian
and Apostolic." The Church simply tolerates the name to
avoid the misapprehension and confusion which would arise if
it were laid aside. " We do not call ourselves Lutherans, but
are so styled by our enemies, and we *permit* it as a token of our
consent with the pure teaching of the word which Luther set
forth. We *suffer* ourselves to bear his name, not as of one who
has invented a new faith, but of one who has restored the old, and
purified the Church."† " Our faith does not rest upon Luther's
authority. We hearken to the voice of Christ in his word, to
which, as his faithful teacher and servant, Luther led us."
" We are called Lutherans only by Papists and other sectarians, as in the ancient Church the Arians styled those who held
the true faith Athanasians." In the Form of Concord, indeed,
the Church has uttered a solemn protest against all human
authority, which ought forever to remove the misapprehension
that any other position is conceded to Luther than that of a
witness for the truth. ‡

It is not indeed difficult to see why the name of Luther
should attach itself so firmly to the part of the Church in
whose Reformation he was the noblest worker. He was the *first*
Reformer — the one from whom the whole Reformation of
the Sixteenth Century evolved itself. What may be the date
Reason of the
name. of the private opinions of others has nothing to do
with this question. A reformer is not one who
thinks reformation, but one who brings it about. Men had
not only had reformatory ideas before Luther was born, but
had died for them, and in some sense, though not utterly, had
died in vain. The names of Wiclif, Huss, Jerome of Prague,

---

* See the passages collected in Cotta's Gerhard, **xi.** 229.
† Gerhard: Loci, xi. 224, 228, 230.
‡ Form. Concord, 518, 2, 8.

and Savanarola, will be forever dear to mankind. Yet the Reformers before the Reformation were only such potentially. So often did the Reformation seem to hang upon Luther's own person, that we are justified in saying that God gave him the place he filled, because there was no other man of his age to fill it. With all the literary grace of Erasmus, how feeble does he seem, " spending his life," as Luther happily said, " trying to walk on eggs without breaking them." Without Luther, we see no evidence that the Reformation of the sixteenth century would have taken place, or that the names of Zwingle, Melanchthon, or Calvin would occupy their present place in history. No position is so commanding as that of Luther. He rises above the crowned heads, above the potentates in Church and in State, and above all the Reformers of his era. In this or that respect he has had equals — in a few respects he has had superiors, but in the full circle of those glorious gifts of nature and of grace which form a great man, he has had no superiors, and no equals. He sustained a responsibility such as never rested upon any other man, and he proved himself sufficient for it. In the Reformation, of the Germanic and Scandinavian type, his views carried great weight with them. His name to this hour is revered with a singleness and passionateness of affection without a parallel. No man was able to take to the Swiss type of Reformation, the attitude Luther took to the Germanic. In its own nature, the Reformed division has no ideal embodied in an actual life; it cannot have a solitary man who is its microcosm. It can have no little Cosmos, because it has no great Cosmos; it can have no name equally revered in all its branches. Luther is more a hero to it than any one of its own heroes. It could have at best but a unity like that of those great stars which have been broken, and as asteroids are now separate in their unity. But, in fact, it has no unity, no tendency to draw around a common historical centre. It binds itself closely to the particular nationalities in which it is found. It is German, Dutch, Scotch. Out of this arises a confusion, when these churches make a transition into other nationalities. So little is there of the tendency to unity, that they keep up their old divisions

with their old names, when they have put an ocean between
them and the land of their origin. The name of the national
tongue cleaves to the body, until the vague yearning of unionistic feeling overcomes the Calvinistic positiveness, or the
sense of the living nationality completely overcomes the tradi-
tionary feeling of the old, or a broader catholicity is substituted
for the earlier denominational feeling. Then only the name
of tongue or race drops, but with it vanishes an evidence, if
not a source of fealty to the original tendency of the Zwinglo-
Calvinistic Reformation.

The Swiss Reformation, which had commenced with the
Pelagianizing and rationalistic tendency imparted by Zwingle,
was redeemed by Calvin, who, under influences originating in
the Lutheran Church, was brought to that profounder faith
which, in many of its aspects, is a concession to the Lutheran
system over against the Zwinglian. Calvin was, as compared
with Zwingle, Lutheranizing in doctrine and in worship; but,
as compared with Luther, he was Zwinglianizing in both. But
the Lutheranizing element which Calvin brought, and by
which he saved the Swiss tendency from early transition to
chaos, was not sufficient to overcome all its defects. The comparative unity of Calvinism has been broken in upon by the
nationalizing tendency showing itself in the rise of a variety
of national creeds, where there was little real difference of
doctrine; by the internal sectarian tendency producing Calvinistic denominations within the national Calvinistic churches;
and by the branching off of Arminian and other sects. The
Lutheran Church, on the other hand, has had a great relative
unity. It has not felt itself divided by the nationalities into
which it is distributed. It has a common Confession throughout the world; and while it repudiates the idea that true unity
depends upon outward uniformity, its unity of spirit has
wrought a substantial likeness throughout the world, in life,
usage, and worship. In view of all these facts, it is not surprising that the name of Luther has adhered to the Church.
It has an historical definiteness which no other of the greatest
names associated with the Reformation would have. The
system of Zwingle, as a whole, is not now the confessional

system of any denomination. The Arminians who would accept his sacramental views, reject his fatalistic ideas. The Calvinists reject his sacramental views and his Pelagianism. The name of Calvin would not define denominational character; for within the Calvinistic denominations there is so real a diversity that parts of the Reformed Churches vary more from each other than those most in affinity with the Lutheran Church vary from it. Of all the Church-names suggested by the ingenuity of men, by the enmity of foes, or by the partiality of friends, what name, in the actual state of Christianity, is preferable to the name Lutheran? The name "Christian" has no divine warrant. First used at Antioch, it may have been meant as a reproach; and St Peter alludes to it only as actually used, not as commanded. We know that "Nazarenes" and "Galileans" were the earlier names of the disciples of Christ. To assume the name Christian, or any other title which belongs to all believers, as the exclusive name of any part of Christendom, is in the last degree presumptuous. The name "Catholic" is also without divine command: it embraces the whole true Church invisible; and while our Church claims that her true members are a part of this Church Catholic, and that she confesses in all their purity its doctrines, she would repudiate the claim of any particular Church to the sole possession of this great title. The "Orthodox Church" of the East is only entitled to that name if the rest of Christendom is heterodox. "Roman Catholic" is a contradiction in terms. The Church which bears it ceases to be Catholic just in the proportion in which it is Roman. To call a church "Episcopal," is to give it a title which only marks its government, and that a government not peculiar to it: the Church of Rome, the Greek Church, the Oriental sects, are all Episcopal in government. To limit it by "Protestant" still leaves it vague. The Lutheran Church in Denmark, in Norway, and in Sweden, and the Moravian Churches are Episcopal in government and Protestant in doctrine. The name "Presbyterian" only indicates a form of government in which great bodies of Christians concur who differ in faith and usage. "Methodist" simply preserves a college nickname, and is given to a variety of bodies. "Methodist

Episcopal" unites that nickname with a form of government older and wider than Methodism. The name " Baptists " only indicates the doctrine concerning the external mode and the proper candidates for a Christian sacrament, and covers a great number of communions which have nothing else in common. The name " Reformed " applies to a species that belongs to a genus. There is, indeed, in every case, a history which explains, if it does not justify, these names: nevertheless, every one of them, as the distinctive name of a communion, is open to the charge of claiming too much, expressing too little, or of thrusting an accident into the place of an essential principle. The necessity of distinctive names arises from the indisputable divisions of Christendom, and in the posture of all the facts the name of Luther defines the character of a particular Church as no other could. It has been borne specifically by but one Church; and that Church, relieved as she is of all the responsibility of assuming it, need not be ashamed of it. No name of a mere man is more dear to Christendom and to humanity. It is a continual remembrancer of the living faith, the untiring energy, the love of Christ and of men, on the part of one who did such eminent service to the Church, that men cannot think of her without thinking of him.

The name thus given her in scorn by her foes stands, for historical reasons, in conjunction with the name she first chose for herself. As distinct from the Romish Church, and all churches which obscure the grace of the Gospel, or do not confess its doctrines in all their fulness, let her consent to be called THE EVANGELICAL LUTHERAN CHURCH, to testify, if God so please, to the end of time, that she is neither ashamed of the Gospel of Christ, nor of Christ's servant who, in the presence of earth and of hell, restored that Gospel, preached it, lived it, and died in the triumphs of its faith.

Our age has been extraordinarily fertile in efforts at defining the distinctive and antithetical characteristics of the Lutheran and Reformed Churches. One age develops principles — another speculates on them. The sixteenth century was creative — the nineteenth is an age of cosmogonies: the one made worlds — the other disputes how they were made. " The owl of Mi·

nerva," says Hegel, " always flaps her wings in the twilight." *
Göbel, Nitzsch, and Heppe affirm that in Reformed Protestantism, the formal principle of the exclusive normal authority
of the Holy Scriptures (acknowledged by both) is the dominating principle. In Lutheran Protestantism, the material
principle, justification by faith, (acknowledged by both,) dom-
inates. In the former, Scripture is regarded more exclusively
as the sole source; in the latter, more as the norm of a doc
trine which is evolved from the analogy of faith, and to which,
consequently, the pure exegetical and confessional tradition of
the Church possesses more value. Herzog says $\quad$ Distinctive
that Lutheran Protestantism is the antithesis to principle of the
the Judaism of the Romish Church — an antith- Lutheran Church.
esis which has imparted to the Lutheran doctrines a Gnos-
ticizing tinge: the Reformed Protestantism was opposed to
the paganism of the Roman Church, and thus came to exhibit
in its doctrine a Judaizing ethical character. Schweizer says:
" The Reformed Protestantism is the protestation against every
deification of the creature, and, consequently, lays its emphasis on the absoluteness of God, and the sovereignty of his will.
This is its material principle, with which coheres the exclusive
emphasizing of Scripture as the normal principle." In a similar vein of thought, Baur says: " The Reformed system
begins above, and comes down; the Lutheran begins below, and
ascends." We might perhaps phrase it: the Reformed begins
with God, and reasons down to manward; the Lutheran begins
with man, and reasons up to Godward. In opposition to
this view, Schneckenburger says that the distinction does not
arise from the predominance of the theological in the one system, of the anthropological in the other, of the absolute idea
of God upon the one side, or of the subjective consciousness
of salvation on the other, but in the different shape taken in
the two systems by the consciousness of salvation itself; from
which it results that the one system falls back upon the eternal decree, the other is satisfied to stop at justification by faith.
Stahl, approximating more to the view of Schweizer, finds in
the " absolute causality " of God the dominating principle of

* Kahnis, Princip. d. Protestant.,4.

the Reformed doctrine, and regards it as its characteristic that its line of thought is adverse to the recognition of mysteries.* "The entire structure of the Reformed Church is determined, on the one side, by a motive of opposition to the mysterious, (no actual dispensation by the means of grace,) which was imparted to it by Zwingle; and on the other side, by the evangelical theocratic impulse, (the glorification of God in the congregation,) which was derived from Calvin." † How far these estimates may be accepted as well-grounded, our readers can judge with the facts more fully before them.

The Lutheran Church has peculiar claims upon the interest of the thoughtful reader of history, as she is the oldest, the most clearly legitimate, the most extensive of Protestant Churches, and in a certain sense the mother of them all. Embracing the North of Europe, the Scandinavian kingdoms, the German States, with millions of her children in Russia, Hungary, Poland, France, Holland, and in almost every part of the globe where Protestantism is tolerated, she speaks in more tongues, and ministers in more nationalities than all the others together. She is the most conservative of them all, though she bore the first and greatest part in the most daring aggression on established error. No church has so vigorously protested against the abuses of human reason, and none has done so much for the highest culture of the human mind — she has made Germany the educator of the world. No church has been so deeply rooted in the verities of the ancient faith, and none has been marked by so much theological progression: in none has independent religious thought gone forth in such matchless ornature of learning, and under such constant control of a genuine moderation. No church has enunciated more boldly the principles of Christian liberty, and none has been so free from a tendency to pervert it to licentiousness. No church has more reverently bowed to the authority of God's Word, and none has been more free from the tendency to sect and schism. More than forty millions of the human race acknowledge her as their spiritual mother; and she gives

Claims and Character of the Lutheran Church.

* Luthardt, Dogm., § 13, 1.   † Stahl, Die Luth Kirch., 65.

them all, not only the one rule cf faith, but she *dies what no other church does: acknowledging the Bible as the only authority, she gives to her various nationalities one confession of faith,* the Augsburg Confession, of which the most popular historian of the Reformation, a French Calvinist, says: " It will ever remain one of the masterpieces of the human mind enlightened by the Spirit of God," and which Bishop Bull calls " the greatest, the most noble and ancient of all the confessions of the Reformed Churches." This immortal document furnishes an integral defining term to the Lutheran Church. Through all time and in all lands this is hers: it is her grand distinction that she is the Church of the Augsburg Confession.

It has been said with some truth that the Evangelical Lutheran development of Christianity is closely allied with that of Augustine, but it is wholly remote from his fatalistic tendencies, and from his indeterminate and often self-contradictory attitude toward many important points of doctrine. The Romish Church makes divine things objects of *sense,* the ultra-Protestant principle would make them objects of the *understanding,* the Lutheran Church holds them as objects of *faith.* The Romish Church too much *confounds* the divine and the human, as for example, in the person of Christ, in Scripture, in the Church, and in the Sacraments. Ultra-Protestantism *separates* them too much. The Evangelical Lutheran Church holds herself alike remote from confounding and from separating them, and maintains them as at once distinct in their essence, and inseparable in their union * " Zwingle's labors were from the outward to the inward, Luther's wholly from the inward to the outward. The Reformed Reformation, like all the earlier efforts, would probably have failed, if the Reformed had not received from Luther the internal element of faith. It cannot be denied that *that* Reformation which was actually brought to pass, was begun by Luther. With full justice, in this respect, he is entitled to be called the first Reformer."† " The Lutheran Church is the most glorious and most complete earthly image cf the invisible Church.

The Lutheran Church. The Radical Protestant Churches. The Romish Church.

* Kurtz, Lehrb. d. K. G ed. 6th, 1868, ⸹ 140.　　　† Goebel, 52.

The word in the spirit, the spirit in the word, the body in the idea, the idea in the body, the visible in the invisible, and this again in that, the human and natural in the divine and super-natural, and these latter elements again in the former — this is what she aims at, and this it is she has. As the Romish Church represents mere rest and stability, the Reformed mere unrest and mobility, and both are consequently defective in development and in history in the highest sense of those terms, the Lutheran Church, on the other hand, has in it the true germ of historical life, which constantly expands itself toward a higher perfection. In the Romish Church the life of history dries up, in the Reformed it is comminuted ; in the one it compacts itself to a mummy, in the other it dissipates itself into atoms. There is a Lutheran *Church*, but there are only Calvinistic or Reformed *Churches.*" *

" The Lutheran Church in its distinctive character," says a Reformed writer, † " can tolerate no sects. The number of the Reformed sects is prodigious, literally innumerable. In Edin-burgh alone there are sixteen of them, in Glasgow twenty-six. It seems as if the production of these sects, which shoot up as mushrooms in the soil of the Reformed Church, were neces-sary to the preservation of her life and health. They have all proceeded from the same principle, and have only striven to carry it out more logically, and she is therefore bound to recog-nize them as her genuine children. The Lutheran Church is like the trunk of a great tree, from which the useless branches have been cut off, and into which a noble scion (justification by faith) has been grafted. It is one complete, well-arranged, closely compacted church, which unsparingly removes all wild growths and pernicious off-shoots, (sects.) The Reformed Church has cut down the tree to the root, (the Holy Scrip-tures,) and from that healthy root springs up a wide thicket. The dying out of one of the twigs only leaves ampler nourish-ment for the others." The most powerful conservative influ-ences within the Reformed Churches have, in fact, invariably been connected more or less immediately with the Lutheran Church. With her principles is bound up the only hope of Protestant unity.

* Wiggers, i. 96.   † Goebel, 176.

In the unaltered Augsburg Confession, (1530,) the Lutheran Church has a bond of her distinctive life through- The doctrines of out the entire world. As a further development the Evangelical of her doctrines, the larger part of the Church Lutheran Church. recognizes the confessional character of the "Apology for the Augsburg Confession," (1530,) the Larger and Smaller Catechisms of Luther, (1529,) the Smalcald articles, (1537,) and the Formula of Concord, (1577,) all which were issued together in 1580, with a preface signed by fifty-one princes, and by the official representatives of thirty-five cities. The whole collection bore the title of the "Book of Concord." The fundamental doctrine most largely asserted in them is, that we are justified before God, not through any merit of our own, but by his tender mercy, through faith in his Son. The depravity of man is total in its extent, and his will has no positive ability in the work of salvation, but has the negative ability (under the ordinary means of grace) of ceasing its resistance. Jesus Christ offered a proper, vicarious, propitiatory sacrifice. Faith in Christ presupposes a true penitence. The renewed man coworks with the Spirit of God. Sanctification is progressive, and never reaches absolute perfection in this life. The Holy Spirit works through the Word and the Sacraments, which only, in the proper sense, are means of grace. Both the Word and the Sacraments bring a positive grace, which is offered to all who receive them outwardly, and which is actually imparted to all who have faith to embrace it.

Luther, in consequence of his rigid training in the Augustinian theology, had maintained, at an earlier period, a particularistic election, a view which he gradually aban- Arminianism. doned. The views of Arminius himself, in regard and Calvinism. to the five points, were formed under Lutheran influences, and do not differ essentially from those of the Lutheran Church; but on many points in the developed system now known as Arminianism, the Lutheran Church has no affinity whatever with it, and on these points would sympathize far more with Calvinism, though she has never believed that in order to escape from Pelagianism, it is necessary to run into the doctrine of absolute predestination. The "Formula of Concord " touches the five points almost purely on their practical sides, and on them arrays itself against Calvinism, rather by the negation of the inferences which result logically from that system, than by express condemnation of its fundamental theory in its abstract form. It need hardly be added that the Lutheran Church holds firmly all the doctrines of the pure Cath olic faith, and of our general Protestant and Evangelical or thodoxy.

The Evangelical Lutheran Church regards the Word of God, the canonical Scriptures, as the absolute and only law of faith and of life. Whatever is undefined by its letter or its spirit, is the subject of Christian liberty, and pertains not to the sphere of conscience, but to that of order ; no power may enjoin Rule of faith and Creed. upon the Church as necessary what God has forbid den, or has passed by in silence, as none may for bid her to hold what God has enjoined upon her, or to prac tise what by His silence he has left to her freedom. Just as firmly as she holds upon the one hand that the Bible is the rule of faith, and not a confession of it, she holds, on the other hand, that the creed is a confession of faith, and not the rule of it. The pure creeds are simply the testimony of the true Church to the doctrines she holds ; but as it is the truth they confess, she, of necessity, regards those who reject the truth confessed in the creed, as rejecting the truth set forth in the Word. While, therefore, it is as true of the Lutheran Church as of any other, that when she lays her hand upon the Bible, she gives the command, " Believe ! " and when she lays it on the confession, she puts the question, " Do you believe ? " * it is also true, that when a man replies " No," to the question, she considers him as thereby giving evidence that he has not obeyed the command. Believing most firmly that she has the truth, and that her testimony to this truth is set forth in her creeds, she is distinguished among Protestant churches by her fidelity to her Confession. "During the time of unbelief, the State Church of Holland, the Church of the Palatinate, and the Re formed Synod of Lower Saxony, renounced all confessions of faith. No Lutheran Church, however, ventured to do this." †

---

* See Goebel, 122, note.   † Do., 123.

Very great misrepresentations have been made in regard to certain doctrines of the Evangelical Lutheran Church, which it may be well to notice. No doctrine can be _{Doctrines mis-} charged upon her as a whole unless it is set forth, ^{represented.} or fairly implied in a Confession to which she gives a universal recognition. The only creeds which have this attribute are the œcumenical creeds and the Augsburg Confession. The large majority of the Church which explicitly receives the other Confessions does so on the ground that one system is embraced in the whole, that to accept one *ex animo* intelligently, is logically to accept all, and that it is wise for the Church so fully to state her faith, and its grounds, that as far as human preventives can go, the crafty shall not be able to misrepresent, nor the simple to mistake her meaning. As the Church did but the more surely abide by the Apostles' Creed in setting forth the Nicene, and did but furnish fresh guarantee of her devotion to the Nicene in adopting the Athanasian, and gave reassurance of her fidelity to the three œcumenical creeds in accepting the Augsburg Confession — so in the body of symbols in the Book of Concord she reset her seal to the one old faith, amplified but not changed in the course of time.

The doctrines in regard to which she has been misrepresented, may be classed under the following heads:

I. *Baptism.* The Lutheran Church holds that it is necessary to salvation to be born again of water (baptism) and the Spirit, (John iii. 5, and Augsburg Confession, Art. II. and IX.;) but she holds that this necessity, though absolute as regards the work of the Spirit, is, as regards the outward part of baptism, ordinary, not absolute, or without exception; that the contempt of the sacrament, not the want of it, condemns; and that though God binds us to the means, he does _{Baptism.} not bind his own mercy by them. From the time of Luther to the present hour, the Lutheran theologians have maintained the salvability and actual salvation of infants dying unbaptized. The rest of the doctrine of the Lutheran Church, as a whole, is involved in her confessing, with the Nicene creed, " one baptism for the remission of sins,'' and that through

9

it the grace of God is offered, that children are to be baptized and that being thus committed to God, they are graciously received by him.   At the same time she rejects the theory of the Anabaptists, that infants unbaptized have salvation because of their personal innocence, and maintains that the nature with which we were born requires a change, which must be wrought by the Spirit of God, before we can enter into heaven (A. C., Art. IX. and II.,) and that infants are saved by the application of Christ's redemptory work, of which Baptism is the ordinary channel.

II. *Consubstantiation.* The charge that the Lutheran Church holds this monstrous doctrine has been repeated times without number.   In the face of her solemn protestations the falsehood

Consubstantiation.   is still circulated.   It would be easy to fill many pages with the declarations of the Confessions of the Evangelical Lutheran Church, and of her great theologians, who, without a dissenting voice, repudiate this doctrine, the name and the thing, in whole and in every one of its parts.   In the " Wittenberg Concord," (1536,) prepared and signed by Luther and the other great leaders in the Church, it is said : " We deny the doctrine of transubstantiation, as we do also deny that the body and blood of Christ are locally included in the bread." *   In the " Formula of Concord," † our confessors say : " We utterly reject and condemn the doctrine of a Capernaitish eating of the body of Christ, which after so many protestations on our part, is maliciously imputed to us ; the manducation is not a thing of the senses or of reason, but supernatural, mysterious, and incomprehensible.   The presence of Christ in the supper is not of a physical nature, nor earthly, nor Capernaitish, and yet it is most true."   It would not be difficult to produce ample testimony of the same kind from intelligent men of other communions.   One or two of the highest order may suffice.   Bishop Waterland, in his great work on the Doctrine of the Eucharist, speaks thus : " As to Lutherans and Calvinists, however widely they may appear to differ in words and names, yet their ideas seem all to concentre in what I have mentioned.   The Lutherans deny

* In Rudelbach, 664.   † Müller's ed., 543, 547.

every article almost which they are commonly charged with by their adversaries. They disown assumption of the elements into the humanity of Christ, as likewise augmentation, and *impanation*, yea, and *consubstantiation* and concomitancy; and if it be asked, at length, what they admit and abide by, it is a *sacramental* union, *not a corporal presence.*" * D'Aubigné says: " The doctrines (on the Lord's Supper) of Luther, Zwingle, and Calvin were considered in ancient times as different views of the same truth. If Luther had yielded (at Marburg) it might have been feared that the Church would fall into the extremes of rationalism . . . Taking Luther in his best moments, we behold merely an essential unity and a secondary diversity in the two parties."

III. *Ubiquity.* The Lutheran Church holds that the essential attributes of the divine and of the human natures in Christ are inseparable from them, and that, therefore, the attributes of the one can never be the attributes of the other. But a large part of her greatest theologians hold, also, that as His human nature is taken into personal union with the divine, it is in consequence of that union rendered present *through the divine*, wherever the divine is; that is, Ubiquity. that the human nature of Christ, which as to its finite presence is in heaven, is in *another sense*, equally real, everywhere present. " Our Church rejects and condemns the error that the human nature of Christ is locally expanded in all places of heaven and earth, or has become an infinite essence." † " If we speak of geometric locality and space, the humanity of Christ is not everywhere." " In its proper sense it can be said with truth, Christ is on earth or in His Supper only according to his divine nature, to wit, in the sense that the humanity of Christ by its own nature cannot be except in one place, but has the majesty (of co-presence) only from the divinity." " When the word corporeal is used of the mode of presence, and is equivalent to local, we affirm that the body of Christ is in heaven and not on earth."

" Of a *local* presence of the body of Christ, in, with, or under the bread, there never was any controversy between the Luther-

* Works, Oxford, 1843, iv. 642.   † Form of Concord, p. 548, 695

ans and Calvinists; that local presence we expressly reject and condemn in all our writings. But a local absence does not prevent a sacramental presence, which is dependent on the communication of the divine Majesty."

IV. *The Lord's Day.* The Augsburg Confession touches on this subject only incidentally in connection with the question of Church power. It teaches that the Jewish Sabbath is abolished; that the necessity of observing the First day of the week rests not upon the supposition that such observance has in itself a justifying power, as the Romanists contended, but on the religious wants of men. It teaches, moreover, that the Lord's day is of apostolic institution. The prevalent judgment

Lord's Day. of the great theologians of our Church has been that the Sabbath was instituted at the creation of man; that the generic idea it involves, requires the devoting one day of the week as the minimum, to rest from labor and to religious duties, and so far pertains to the entire race through all time; and that the law of the Sabbath, so far as it is not determinative and typical, but involves principles and wants of equal force under both dispensations, is binding on Christians.

An ample discussion of all the points here summarily presented will be found in their place in this volume.

Perhaps no stronger testimony to the general purity of the doctrines of the Lutheran Church could be given, than that which is presented in the statements of the great divines of the Reformed Communion. ZWINGLE* says: "Luther has brought

Reformed testimony to the Lutheran Church.
1. Zwingle.   2. Calvin. forth nothing novel, (*nihil novi;*) but that which is laid up in the unchanging and eternal Word of God, he has bountifully drawn out; and has opened to Christians who had been misled, the heavenly treasure." CALVIN:† "Call to mind with what great efficacy of teaching Luther hath to this time been watchful to overthrow the kingdom of Antichrist, and speak the doctrine of salvation." Anthony de Bourbon, King of Navarre,‡ (1561,) said: "Lu-

3. King of Navarre. ther and Calvin differed in forty points from the Pope, and in thirty-eight of them agreed with one another; there were but two points on which there was con-

---

* Explan. Art. XVIII.   † Ep. ad Bullinger.   ‡ Thuanus, lib. xxvii

troversy between them, but in his judgment they should unite
their strength against the common enemy, and when he was
overthrown it would be comparatively easy to harmonize
on those two points, and to restore the Church of God to its
pristine purity and splendor." HENRY ALTING * says, that
one great object of his writing his book is to show " to
those into whose hands it may come how truly both the
Palatinate Church (which has always been regarded as
the mother of the other churches of Germany,) and the
other Reformed Churches with her, still adhere to the
Augsburg Confession, and have by no means departed from
the old profession of faith." He then takes up article by
article, claiming that the Heidelberg Catechism and the
Helvetic Consensus are in unity with the Augsburg Confession.   Quoting the Second Article, (of original
sin,) he says: " The Palatinate Catechism teaches

4. Alting.

the same thing in express words — we are all conceived and
born in sin — and unless we be regenerated by the Holy Spirit,
are so corrupt, that we are able to do no good whatever, and
are inclined to all vices. It is a calumny that the Reformed
teach that the children of believers are born holy, and without original sin." On the Third : "It is a calumny that the
Reformed Churches dissolve the personal union of the two
natures in Christ ; and abolish a true and real communion of
natures (communicatio idiomatum)." In the Tenth Article (of
the Lord's Supper): " This is a manifest dissent of the Confession — but not of such a character that it ought to destroy
the unity of the faith, or distract with sects the Evangelical
Christians — so that the dissent is not total in the doctrine of
the Lord's Supper, neither as regards its principal thing, nor
much less, as regards a fundamental article of faith and of the
Christian religion." Of the Eleventh Article (of private absolution): " The Heidelberg Catechism never condemns or abrogates Confession and Private Absolution, but leaves it as a
thing indifferent and free." "And this," he says in conclusion, " is a collation of the Augsburg, Palatinate, and Helvetic Confessions, in all the articles, which most clearly exhibits

₂ Exegesis Log. et Theol. Augustan. Confess. Amstel., 1648, 4to.

and demonstrates their orthodox agreement in every article, except the Tenth, and there the disagreement is not entire."

The illustrious Dr. Spanheim, (d. 1701,) one of the greatest Calvinistic divines of the seventeenth century, in his work on Religious Controversies, preparatory to a discussion of the point on which Lutherans and Calvinists differ, gives a sketch of the points on which they agree. 1. "Both Lutherans and Calvinists have the same RULE and PRINCIPLE, to wit: Holy Scripture; rejecting human and Papistical
. 5. Spanheim.
In General. traditions, and the decrees of the Council of Trent. 2. Both have the same FUNDAMENTAL DOC- TRINE as to the cause of our salvation, both the efficient and the meritorious cause; as it relates to the person, verity of the natures and their union, the office and benefits of Christ our Lord; in fine, as to the mode of justification, without the merits or causality of works. 3. Both have the same WOR- SHIP, of the one true and triune God, and of Christ our Saviour, remote from all idolatry, superstition or adoration of the crea- ture. 4. Both hold the same DUTIES of the Christian man, the requisites to sanctification. 5. Both make the same PROTESTA- TION against papal errors, even in the matter of the Lord's Supper. They protest alike against all papal idolatry, foul superstitions, Romish hierarchy, cruel tyranny, impure celi- bacy, and idle monkery. 6. Both are under the same OBLIGA- TIONS to forbear one another in love, in regard to those things which are built upon the foundation and treated in different ways, while the foundation itself remains unshaken. 7. Both finally have the same INTERESTS, the same MOTIVES for estab- lishing Evangelical peace, and for sanctioning if not a concord in all things, yet mutual TOLERATION forever. From such a toleration would flow a happier propagation of the Gospel, the triumph of Evangelical truth, the mightier assault on Anti- Christ, and his final fall; the repression of tyranny, the arrest of Jesuitical wiles, the assertion of Protestant liberty, the removal of grievous scandals, the weal of the Church and of the State, and the exultation of all good men.

"I. Both Lutherans and Calvinists agree in the Article of the Lord's Supper, that the spiritual eating of Christ's body is necessary to salvation, and to the salutary use of the Sacrament; by which eating is understood the *act of true faith*, as it directs itself to the body of Christ delivered to death for More specific us, and his blood shed for us, both apprehended ally. and personally applied with all Christ's merits.

"II. In the Articles of PREDESTINATION, GRACE, and FREE WILL, both agree: 1. That after the fall of man, there were *no remaining powers* for spiritual good, either to *begin* or to *complete:* 2. That the whole matter of the salvation of man depends *alone* on the will, good pleasure, and grace of *God.* 3. Neither approves the *Pelagian* doctrine, but each condemns it, and both reject Semi-Pelagianism.

"III. In the Article of the PERSON OF CHRIST, both agree: 1. That the *divine and human* natures are truly and *personally united*, so that Christ is God and man in unity of person; and that this union is formed, *without confusion or change, indivisibly and inseparably:* 2. That the *names of the natures* are reciprocally used; truly and in the literal sense of the words, God is man, man is God; the *properties* of each of the natures are affirmed truly and really, of the whole person in the concrete; but *according to* that nature to which those properties are peculiar, which is called by theologians, *communicatio idiomatum* (com munion of properties.) 3. That the human nature of Christ is not *intrinsically omnipotent* nor *omniscient;* that in the union, the natures conjoined remain distinct, and the essential proper- ties of each are secure. 4. That the human nature was lifted to *supreme* glory, and sitteth at the right hand of God. 5. Both reject the heresies of Nestorius, Eutyches, Marcion, Arius, Plotinus, Paul of Samosata, and their like.

"IV. In the Article of HOLY BAPTISM, both Lutherans and Calvinists agree: 1. That *infants* are to be baptized: 2. That the *object* of baptism is that they may be inserted into Christ, and spiritually regenerated: 3. That baptism is necessary, yet not *absolutely*, but so that the *despising* of baptism is damning: 4. That infants have the capacity of receiving *regenerating grace*, and 5. That these things pertain to the *essentials* of this Sacrament.

"V. As to the CEREMONIES, especially as regards EXORCISM in

the baptismal formula, both are agreed: 1. That it is not to be imagined that an infant is *corporeally* possessed by Satan: 2. That the rite of exorcism may not be employed for any other end than to signify the habitual inherence of *original sin:* 3. That these formulæ of *exorcism* may be omitted, and special prayers be substituted therefor."

It may be well to note that the practice of exorcism even with these safeguards and limitations, never was universal in the Lutheran Church; never was regarded as essential by those who practised it, always had strong opposers among the soundest men in the Church, and long ago fell into general disuse. It never could have been styled, without qualification, a Lutheran usage. All that could with truth have been said, at any time, was that the Lutheran Church *in this* or *that country*, retained it in the exercise of church liberty, among things indifferent. Lutheran unity is based upon heartfelt consent in the doctrines of the Gospel, and in the essential parts of the administration of the Sacraments, and consistency, as Lutherans, requires no more than that we should maintain and defend these. So much it does demand, but it demands no more.

CLAUDE,* one of the greatest theologians of the French Reformed Church, says: "Those of the Augsburg Confession (who are called Lutherans) are in difference with us only about the point of the real presence, and about some questions of the schools which we cannot yet impute to their whole body; and as for the rest, they reject with us the invocation of saints, religious worship of images, human satisfactions, indulgences, purgatory, worship of relics, the public service in an unknown tongue, the merit of good works, transubstantiation, the sacrifice of the mass, the supremacy of the Pope, the opinion of the infallibility of the church, and the principle of blind obedience to the decisions of councils. They acknowledge the Scriptures to be the only rule of faith; they carefully practise the reading of them; they own their sufficiency; they believe their authority, inde-

٩. Claude.

* Defence of the Reformation, 1673, translated by T. B., London, 1815, vol. i., p 291.

pendent of that of the Church; they distinctly explain the doctrine of justification, and that of the use of the Law, and its distinction from the Gospel; they do not conceive amiss of the nature of faith, and that of good works; and as for popular superstitions, we can scarce see any reign among them."

JOHN ALPHONSUS TURRETIN * has collected a great body of witnesses whose testimony tends to the same general point: the possibility and desirableness of concord between the Lutherans and the Reformed. He argues for the same position at great length, on the same general grounds with the divines we have quoted.

7. J. Turretin.

The pastors of the church at Geneva, and the Professors in its Academy, in their letter to Wake, Archbishop of Canterbury, (1719,) say: "As regards our Lutheran brethren, we doubt not that you are aware what exhibitions of love, what ardent desire (*cupidinem*) of having concord with them our Church has shown at all times."

8. Church of Geneva.

PICTETUS (d. 1724) thus addresses the theologians of the Augsburg Confession: † "Let the names of Lutherans and Calvinists be blotted out, let altar no more be set up against altar. O happy day, in which all your churches and ours shall embrace each other, and with right hands joined and with souls united we shall coalesce into one body, (*in unum corpus coalescimus,*) with the benediction of God, the plaudits of angels, the exultation of holy men."

9. Pictetus.

The object of these citations is to show that, judged by candid and great men who are not of her communion, the Lutheran Church is pure in all the fundamental doctrines of the Christian faith, a Church to be revered and loved even by those who cannot in all respects unite in her Confession.

According to the simple and sublime principles of the New Testament, accepted by the Evangelical Lutheran Church, true church unity rests upon the common acceptance of the fundamental doctrines of the Gospel in the same sense, and in agreement in the Scriptural essentials of the administration of the Sacraments. On the second point we are in unity with

---

* Nubes Testium, Genevæ, 1719, 4to.

† Dissert. de Consens. ac Dissens. int. Reform. et Aug. Conf. Fratres, 1697.

all Evangelical and Protestant bodies except the Baptists, **and**
with them we here fail of unity not because of their
practice of immersion, which, as a free mode, might
be allowed simply as a matter of preference, but in
regard to their doctrine of its necessity, and in
that they deviate from the Scripture essential of baptism as to
its proper subjects, excluding from it children, to whom God
has given it. In regard to the externals of the Lord's Supper,
the Lutheran Church has nothing to prevent unity with the
rest of the Evangelical Protestant world. To her, questions
of kneeling, sitting, standing, of leavened or unleavened
bread, or of its thickness, are questions dismissed from the
sphere of essentials into that of the liberty of
the Church. They have nothing to do with the
essence of unity. The Presbyterian is none the less one with
us because he sits at the table while we kneel or stand, unless
he construes into a matter of conscience a thing in itself
indifferent, neither enjoined nor forbidden. Luther * says:
"Fix steadfastly on this sole question, What is that which
makes a Christian? Permit no question to be put on a level
with this. If any one brings up a matter, ask him at once:
'Do these things also make a man a Christian?' If he answer,
No, let them all go." If Luther's life seemed largely one of
warfare, it was not that he did not love peace much, but that
he loved truth more. He could not take Zwingle's hand at
Marburg, (1529,) because that would have meant that the great
point which divided them was not an article of faith, and Luther
believed in his inmost heart that it was; but he prepared and
signed his name to the Declaration then set forth, "that both
sides, to the extent to which the conscience of either could
bear it, were bound to exercise mutual charity — both were
bound earnestly and unremittingly to implore Almighty God,
that through his Spirit he would vouchsafe to confirm us in
the true doctrine." The Wittenberg Concord, between Luther, Melanchthon, and others, upon one side, and Capito,

Side notes: Relations of the Lutheran Church to other Christian communions. — True unity.

---

* Epistle to the Strasburgers, (1524,) occasioned by Carlstadt's doctrine of the
Lord's Supper, and his fanaticism. **Briefe, De Wette,** ii. 514, Leipz., xix. 225.
Walch., xv. 2444.

Bu er, and their associates, (1536,) on the other, filled the heart
of Luther with pure joy.   When no principle was endangered
Luther could be as gentle as Melanchthon.   When the intelligence reached Luther that the Swiss had accepted the Wittenberg Concord, he wrote to Meyer, the burgomaster of Basel
(February 17, 1537): "I have marked with the greatest joy
your earnestness in promoting the Gospel of Christ   God
grant us increasing grace that we may harmonize more and
more in a true, pure unity, in a sure accordant doctrine and
view . . that to this end we forgive one another, and N. B.,"
(the *nota bene* i L ther's,) "bear with one another as God the
Father forgives us and bears with us in Christ.   We must forget the strifes and smarts of the past, and strive for unity with
patience, meekness, kindly colloquies, but most of all with
heartfelt prayer to God, the Father, the Father of all concord
and love."*   On December 1, of the same year, Luther wrote an
official reply to the letter of the representatives of the Swiss
Church.   He addresses them as "venerable, dear sirs, and
friends," and wishes them "grace and peace in Christ our
Lord and Saviour," and goes on to say: "I rejoice that the
old bitterness and suspicion, between us, have been laid aside,
and that you propose, in great earnestness, to promote concord.
God himself will graciously consummate a work so well begun.
It cannot indeed but be that so great a schism will not heal
easily, and leave no scar.   There will be some, both with you
and with us, who will not be pleased with this Concord, but
will regard it with suspicion.   But if there be earnestness and
diligent effort on both sides, by God's grace, the opposition will
die out, (zu Tod blut,) and the raging waters will be calmed.
Certainly, if strife and clamor could accomplish anything, we
have had enough of them.   God is my witness that nothing
shall be wanting on my part to promote concord.   This discord has never benefited me or others, but has done great mischief.   No good ever was, or ever is to be hoped from it."   On
the Lord's Supper, on which the Concord had seemed to embody
a substantial agreement, Luther, in a few words, shows how
greatly he had been misunderstood, and then adds: "Yet, as

* Luther's Briefe, De Wette, v. 54, Walch. xxi. 1282.

I said before, where we in this point (hierin) have not come
fully to an understanding, (wir nicht gänzlich verstünden,) the
best thing for the present (itzt) is that we be friendly to each
other, that we put the best construction on each others' acts,
(das beste zu einander versehen,) till the mire (Glüm) that has
been stirred up settles.   On our side, and I speak especially for
my own person, (sonderlich mein person halben,) we will, from
the heart, dismiss all unkindness and regard you with confidence and love.   When we have done all in our power, we still
need God's great help and counsel.   We need not indulge the
disposition to suspect each other, and stir up strife, for Satan,
who hates us and the Concord, will find his own, to throw trees
and rocks on the way.   Let it be our part to give each other
our hearts and hands (die herzen und hand einander reichen)
to hold fast with equal firmness, lest the after state of things
be worse than the first.   May the Holy Ghost fuse our hearts
together in Christian love and purpose, and purge away all the
dross of suspicion, to the glory of His sacred name, and to the
salvation of many souls." *

A similar spirit is breathed in Luther's letter of reply to the
Council of the Reformed Churches of Switzerland held in Zurich,
1528 : "I beseech you that you go on, as you have begun, to
aid in consummating this divine work, of the peace and unity
of the Christian Church, as I doubt not ye are ready with all
joyfulness to do." †   To the Council at Strasburg, Luther had
written (May 29, 1536) : "There shall be nothing lacking on
my part, whether of act or of suffering, which can contribute to a
genuine, thorough, steadfast unity, for what are the results of
the dissensions of the Churches, experience, alas ! has taught
us." ‡

Luther's cordial spirit toward the Waldenses, his fervent
appeals to them when it was rumored that they were about making peace with Rome, his noble witness to his fellowship with

---

* Luther's Briefe, De Wette, v. 83 : Leipz. xxi. 107. Walch. xvii. 2594. In
Latin: Hospinian. H. S. i. 275. Buddeus : 258.

† L.'s Briefe, De Wette, v. 120. Leipz. xxi. 110. Walch. xvii. 2617. Latin,
Hospin. H. S. ii. 164. Buddeus, 292.

‡ Briefe, De Wette, iv 692. Leipz. xxi. 106. Walch, xvii. 2566. Latin : Buddeus, 251.

Huss and Jerome of Prague, reveal his large catholic heart. Nor even in the ardor of his bitterest conflict with Rome did he ignore the truly Christian elements and great blessings which had been perpetuated in the Church of the West. He distinguished between Popery in the Church of Rome, and the Church of Rome herself, and between the false living representatives of the Roman Church, and her ancient, true representatives. From the true ancient Roman Church as known in the writings of the earliest Fathers, neither Luther nor the Lutheran Church ever separated. It was the true old Roman Church which in the Reformation revived, over against the modern corrupted Church of Rome. Not destruction, not revolution, but reformation, was that at which Luther aimed, and reformation is not revolution, but the great preventive of it. If Europe passed through revolutionary convulsions in and after the sixteenth century, it was not because Reformation was accepted, but because it was resisted.

Against the High-Churchism, which makes dividing walls of forms, ceremonies, modes of government, the Lutheran Church enters a living protest. "Where," says Luther, "the Gospel is rightly and purely preached, there must be a Holy Christian Church."* "The Holy Church Universal is preeminently a fellowship whose internal bond is faith and the Holy Spirit in the heart, and whose outward token is the pure Word and the incorrupt Sacraments. The Church is a communion of saints, to wit, the assembly of saints who are in the fellowship of the same Gospel or doctrine, and of the same Holy Spirit, who renews, sanctifies, and governs the heart."† The unchanging marks of the Church are "the pure doctrine of the Gospel and the Sacraments. That Church which has these is alone properly the pillar of the truth, because it retains the pure Gospel, and as St. Paul saith, the foundation, that is the true knowledge of Christ, and true faith in him."

With every external human thing alike there is no unity if the parts of a communion are alien in faith. On the other hand, with every external human thing diverse, there *is* unity

* Werke, Jena, vi 109, (103.)   † Apology, (Art. IV.)

if there be harmony in faith. Our Church desires uniformity not as if it were itself unity, or could be made a substitute for it, but because it illustrates unity, and is one of its natural tendencies and its safeguard. If there be a High-Churchism genuinely Lutheran, it is a very different thing from that which bears that name in other churches. The Lutheran Church does claim that it is God's truth which she confesses, and by logical necessity regards the deviations from the doctrines of the Confession as deviations from divine truth, but she does not claim to be the whole Church. " The Christian Church and Christian holiness, both name and thing, are the common possession of all churches and Christians in the world."* It is enough for her to know that she is a genuine part of it, and she can rejoice, and does rejoice, that the Saviour she loves has his own true followers in every part of Christendom. She says :

Liberality and Charity of the Lutheran Church. " The Catholic [Christian] Church consists of men scattered throughout the whole world, from the rising of the sun to the going down thereof." † She unchurches none of other names, even though they may be unsound. It is not her business to do this. They have their own Master, to whom they stand or fall. She protests against error ; she removes it by spiritual means from her own midst ; but she judges not those who are without. God is her judge and theirs, and to Him she commits herself and them. Our Church confesses " that among those who are upon the true foundation there are many weak ones, who build upon the foundation perishing stubble, that is, empty human notions and opinions, and yet because they do not overthrow the founda- tion, are still Christians, and their faults may be forgiven them, or even be emended."‡ " An error," says Luther, " however great it may be, neither can be called heresy, nor is heresy, unless it be held and defended obstinately as right." " Erring makes no heretics ; but the defending and protecting error with stiffness of neck, does." " There never has been a heresy which did not also affirm some truth. Wherefore we must not deny the truth (it contains) on account of the falsehood (it mixes with it)."§ " Heretics not merely err, but refuse to be

---

* Luther.   † Apology, Art. IV.   ‡ Apology, Art. IV.
§ Werke, Walch. xxi. 120; xviii. 1771; iii. 2294.

taught; they defend their error as right, and fight against known truth, and against their own consciences — self-willed and consciously they remain in their error." "It is not right, and I am truly sorry that these miserable people are murdered, burnt, and executed. Every one should be left to believe what he will, (man sollte ja einen jeglichen lassen glauben was er wollte.) How easy is it to err! Let us ward against them with the Scripture, not with fire." *

It is not charity to bear with others because the differences between us are trifling; it is charity to bear with them although the differences are great. Charity does not cover error; because error is the daughter of sin, and charity is the daughter of God. Charity covers errorists so far as she may without palliating their errors, for the errorist, as a man, is God's child. Charity is the reflex of love to God, and our Church, therefore, is loyal to his truth even when she is most tender to those who err from that truth. If there have been bigoted, inquisitorial, and harsh judges of others who bear her name, it is not from her they derived these peculiarities, and such men know not the spirit they are of. Never are great systems more cruelly misrepresented than by some who claim to be their friends. While, therefore, many of the pretended representations of Lutheran theology have been gross misrepresentations, they have not always been the result of ignorance, or of malice, but have proceeded from nominal friends, sometimes from timidity of character, and sometimes from a harsh, fierce spirit, which delights to aggravate differences, and make them hopeless. This aggravation has been made by enemies from hatred of the system. They wished to excite disgust at it. But the same sort of representation has also been made by a different class, who were moved by hatred to other systems, quite as much as by ove to the system they espoused. They considered the Lutheran system not only as true, but as in such sense having all the truth, that no other church has the least share of it. They were not satisfied with showing that others are less scriptural than ourselves, or in important respects depart from the teachings of the Word, but they were determined to show that

* Werke, Walch. xvii. 2624.

they are scriptural in nothing. Such hopeless errorists are not sound, on the showing of these polemics, even on the general truths of the Apostles' Creed: they are doubters of the very elements of Christianity: they are on the way to Atheism, only kept from running into it by their fear or by their inability to follow their premises to their fair conclusions. It is true, the most extravagant of this school in the Lutheran Church have been far outstripped in their exclusiveness by sectarians of different kinds: but this is no apology for them. A Church so large-hearted, so truly catholic in her genius, and so mild in her spirit as is the Lutheran, expects better things of her children. As she does not rear them with a sectarian bias, she cannot allow them to plead sectarian excesses as an offset to their own. In treating of the doctrines of such a Church, men should be thoroughly acquainted with them, deeply convinced of their truth, and transformed by their power; and men of this stamp will develop them not in a little, sectarian spirit, but with a largeness and nobleness of mind, which will attest the moral power of the truth they hold. If our Church ever could have been moved to a different spirit, it would have been during those exasperating controversies with open enemies, and still more with false brethren, which led to the preparation of the Formula of Concord. Yet, in the Preface to the book in which that Formula was embodied, the Electors, Princes, and Orders of the Empire thus declare themselves: "It is by no means our will and intent, in the condemnation of false and impious doctrines, to condemn those who err from simplicity, and who do not blaspheme the truth of God's Word. Still less do we wish to condemn *whole churches* either within the bounds of the German Empire or beyond it, . . . for we entertain no doubt whatever (ganz und gar keinen zweifel machen) that many pious and good people are to be found in those churches also, which to this time have not thought in all respects with us ; persons who walk in the simplicity of their hearts, not clearly understanding the points involved, . . . and who, it is to be hoped, if they were rightly instructed in the doctrine, through the guidance of the Holy

Official protest against the persecution of other churches.

Spirit, into the unerring truth of God's Word, would consent with us. . . . And on all the theologians and ministers of the Church is the duty specially incumbent to admonish, and teach out of God's Word with moderation those who err from the truth through simplicity or ignorance, lest the blind leading the blind, both perish. Wherefore, in this our writing, in the presence of Almighty God and before the whole Church, we testify that it was never our purpose, by this Christian Formula of conciliation, to create trouble or peril for those poor oppressed Christians who are now enduring persecution. . . . For, as moved by Christian love, we long ago entered into the companionship of suffering with them, so do we abhor and from our soul detest the persecution and most grievous tyranny which has been directed against these hapless persons. In no degree or respect do we consent to this shedding of innocent blood, which doubtless, in the awful judgment of God, and before the tribunal of Christ, will be strictly demanded at the hands of their persecutors." This plea and protest of the Lutheran Princes and Estates was made specially in behalf of the Huguenots, the French Calvinists, whose bitter sufferings had culminated in the frightful massacre of St. Bartholomew, (August 24, 1572.)

The Princes and Estates add, to show that their charity was a heavenly love, and not the indolent passiveness of laxity in doctrine: "Our intent has been . . . that no other doctrine than that which is founded in God's Word, and is contained in the Augsburg Confession and its Apology, accepted in their genuine sense, should be set forth in our lands, provinces, schools, and churches, . . . in order that among our posterity also the pure doctrine and confession of the faith may be preserved and propagated, through the aid of the Holy Spirit, until the glorious coming of our only Redeemer and Saviour Jesus Christ." These are words to stir the inmost heart. Alike in their revelation of faith, hope, and charity, they are words without a parallel in the history of churches. Where, among Confessions, but in the Confession of the Lutheran Church, is there so tender, so apologetic, a reference to those differing in faith? Where, but in it, is there so noble a confession of the

10

fellowship of saints, and so hopeful an expression of confidence in the better mind and sincerity of those who err; where is there so brave, earnest, and heartfelt an allusion to the trials of those of another communion? so sublime a protest against their persecution, and consequently against all persecution for conscience' sake? God grant that the spirit of these holy men may be perpetuated in the church which they so signally served in their generation, and that their devout aspirations may be fulfilled, that when the Son of Man cometh, he may find faith on the earth still shedding its holy light in the midst of those whose fathers loved him so purely, loved his Truth so fervently; and yet, like their Master, refused to call down fire from heaven on those who followed not with them.

In affinity with this spirit, a great living theologian in Germany has said: "I think I may say, I am not conscious of *belonging to any party*, but have followed truth alone. In the pathway of my search for truth, I was led to Jesus Christ, who is the truth, and by him was led to the Lutheran Church, which I have held, and do now hold to be NOT THE ONLY TRUE CHURCH, BUT THE PILLAR OF THE TRUTH IN THE CHURCH UNIVERSAL. I know, moreover, that he only who has received *the spirit of this* Church, who stands immovably on the foundation of the Apostles and Prophets, who lives in the fixed *conviction* that the *Confession* of the Lutheran Church is in *its very essence* in consonance with the pure gospel, and who yet has felt the influence of the past three centuries, I know that *he only has an œcumenical mind and catholic heart for that which is true in all churches;* he only has an ear for the harmonies of truth which still ring out from the dissonances of the countless varieties of the notes of our times. I have never shrunk from the reproach of orthodoxy, so far as its cause is the cause of Christ, and yet I have constantly said that I could not be the defender of those who seek in the faith of the Church that only which is old, fixed, and finished. With justice, we withdraw our confidence from a theological writer who violently rushes from one extreme to another. But can we, on the other hand, trust a theologian of whom we know that, having once taken a position, it is entirely impossible for him forever after to doubt its correctness. Truth gives itself only to him who seeks it, but he who seeks it will not find it, if he can let nothing go."

The life of a Church may be largely read in its controversies. As the glory or shame of a nation is read upon its battle-fields which tells for what it perilled the lives of its sons, so may the glory or shame of a Church be determined when we know what it fought for and what it fought against; how much it valued what it believed to be truth; what was the truth it valued; how much it did, and how much it suffered to maintain that truth, and what was the issue of its struggles and sacrifices. Tested in all these ways, the record of the Lutheran Church is incomparably glorious. It has contended for great truths at great sacrifices, and in every conflict in which it has borne a part, truth has ultimately been victorious. A Church which contends for nothing, either has lost the truth, or has ceased to love it. Warfare is painful, but they whose errors create the necessity for it are responsible for all its miseries. At times, especially in the early history of the Lutheran Church, there arose controversies, the most important of which were: 1, the Philipistic, arising from the excessive desire of Melanchthon and his school to harmonize with the Roman Catholics and the Reformed; 2, the Antinomistic (1537–'40, 1556), caused by the effort of Agricola to introduce what has been called a " Pelagianism of the Gospel;" 3, the Osiandrian (1550–'67), so called from Osiander, who confounded sanctification with justification; 4, the Adiaphoristic (1548–'55); 5, the Majoristic (1551–'52), on the necessity of good works; 6, the Synergistic (1555–'67), on the co-operation of the human will in conversion, in the course of which Flacius spoke of original sin as substantial, not accidental; 7, the Crypto-Calvinistic (1552–'74). The view of Calvin in regard to the Lord's supper was so much profounder than that of Zwingli, (which Calvin strongly condemned,) and indeed in some aspects so Lutheranizing that Melanchthon, without abandoning the Lutheran view, thought that Calvin's might be tolerated, and the points of difference ignored in the Confessions. This position was assailed by the

stricter Lutherans.   In the course of controversy the more
general questions connected with the person of Christ were
discussed.   All these questions were settled in the " Form of
Concord," (1577.) So deeply was the church grounded in fun
damental unity of faith, that none of these controversies, violent as some of them were, were able to rend it into denominational fragments.   The subsequent controversies have been on
syncretism (1655), pietism (1686), ·and rationalism (1751), and
those connected with the Union and the revival of Lutheranism (from 1817, Harms's *Theses,* to the present hour).

Theological science flourished in the sixteenth century most
of all in the universities of Wittenberg, Tübingen, Strasbourg,
Marburg, and Jena.   To this era belong Luther, Melanchthon,
Flacius, Chemnitz, Brentius, and Chytræus. In the seventeenth
century occur the names of Glassius, Pfeiffer, Erasmus Schmidt,
Hakspan, Gier, Seb. Schmidt, Calovius ; in dogmatics, Hutter,
Gerhard, Quenstedt, Calixtus, Hunnius ; in church history,
Rechenberg, Ittig, Sagittarius, Seckendorf, and Arnold.   In
the eighteenth century, Löscher closes the ancient school ; and
the *Pietistic* school, practical rather than scientific, is illustrated
by Lange.   The *Conservative Pietistic,* avoiding the faults of the
others and combining their virtues, embraces Hollazius, Starck,
Buddeus, Cyprian, J. C. Wolf, Weismann, Deyling, Carpzov,
J. H. and C. B. Michaelis, J. G. Walch, Pfaff, Mosheim, Bengel, and Crusius.   The school which treated theology after the
philosophical method of Wolf numbers S. J. Baumgarten, Rein-
beck, and Carpzov ; to the *transitional* school belong Ernesti,
J. D. Michaelis, Semler, who prepared the way for rationalism,
and Zöllner ; the principal members of the *rationalistic* school

Theological Sci-   were Greisbach, Koppe, J. G. Rosenmüller, Eich-
ence in the Lu-   horn, Gabler, Bertholdt, Henke, Spittler, Eberhard,
theran Church.   and A. H. Niemeyer.   Of the *supranaturalistic*
school, abandoning the ancient orthodoxy in various degrees,
but still maintaining more or less of the fundamentals of general Christianity, are Morus, Döderlein, Seiler, Storr, Knapp,
Reinhard, Lilienthal, and Köppen ; and in church history,
Schröckh, C. W. F. Walch, Stäudlin, and Planck.   The
founder of the *distinctive theology* of the nineteenth century was

Schleiermacher (died 1834), the greatest of the defenders of the union between the Lutheran and Reformed Churches of Germany. Influencing all schools, he can be claimed for none. Neander may be classed as pietistic supranaturalist, De Wette as historico-critical rationalist, Hase as philosophico-æsthetic rationalist. The chief defenders of the *vulgar rationalism* are Röhr, Paulus, Wegscheider, Bretschneider, and Ammon; of *historico-critical rationalism*, Winer, Fritzsche, Credner, Schulz, Von Cölln, Rückert, Gesenius, Tuch, Knobel, Hupfeld, Hitzig, Ewald, Bertheau, and Lengerke. The *rational supranaturalistic* school is represented by Tzschirner, Tittmann, C. F. K. Rosenmüller, and Baumgarten-Crusius; *supranaturalism proper*, or suprarationalism, by E. G. Bengel, Flatt, Heubner, Augusti, Hahn, Böhmer; *pietistic supranaturalism* by Tholuck (who approached more closely in the course of his studies to a thoroughly Lutheran position), Hengstenberg, Olshausen, Stier, Hävernick, Steiger, and Bunsen in his early position, though in his latest years a rationalist. The representatives of the "*new*" or "*German*" theology, of the school of Schleiermacher, of Lutheran origin, are Lücke, Nitzsch, Julius Müller, Ullmann, Twesten, Dorner, Liebner, and Martensen; also Rothe, I. T. Beck, Auberlen, Umbreit, Bleek, H. A. W. Meyer, Huther, Wieseler, and Tischendorf. The writers of the nineteenth century whose names we have given are or were within the "Union," and defenders of it, with a few exceptions.

The representatives of the *Lutheran theology*, for the most part, in its strictest sense, are Claus Harms, who struck the first decisive blow at rationalism (1817), Scheibel, Sartorius, Rudelbach, of Denmark, Guericke, Harless, Höfling, Thomasius, Philippi, Harnack, Dieckhof, Löhe, Vilmar, Krabbe,Kliefoth, Delitzsch, M. Baumgarten, Luthardt, Dreschler, Caspari, Oehler, Keil, Zöchler, and J. H. Kurtz. Two distinguished jurists, K. F. Göschel and F. J. Stahl, are to be included among the defenders of the Lutheran confession.

Among the names which once took undisputed place in this part of the roll of honor, are three which have dropped from it, J. C. K. v. Hofmann, Thiersch, and Kahnis—the last by his assent to the rationalistic Criticism of the Canon, his rejection of the Church Doctrine of the Trinity, and his denial of the supreme divinity of the Son and the Spirit (subordin- atism), and by his rejection of the Lutheran Exegesis of the Words of the Institution of the Supper, while he yet professes to hold fast to the substance of the Lutheran Doctrine of the Eucharist.

If the Nineteenth Century has not been an era of the most safe and solid thinking, it has, beyond all dispute, been the most brilliant era in the history of theological science; and alike of the inventiveness that glittered, and of the sobriety that restrained, the theological impulse which the world owes to the Lutheran Church, has been the spring.

In the United States the energies of the best men in the Church have been directed mainly into the channels of prac- tical activity; yet there has nevertheless been an honorable exhibition of theological ability and learning. Among the names of those to whom we owe books, either as writers, translators, or editors, may be mentioned: Anspach; Bach- man; S. K. Brobst; F. W. Conrad; Demme; G. Diehl; L. Eichelberger; Endress; Goering; Greenwald; S. W. Harkey; Hazelius; Helmuth; the Henkels, Paul, D. M., Ambrose, and Socrates; J. N. Hoffman; Hutter; M. Jacobs; Henry Jacobs; E. W. G. Keyl; C. Philip Krauth; Krotel; Kunze; B. Kurtz; Lape; Lintner; the Lochmans, J. G. and A. H.; Loy; W. J. Mann; P. F. Mayer; John McCron; Mealy; F. V. Mels- heimer; C. B. Miller; J. G. Morris; the Muhlenbergs, H. M., H. E., F. A.; Norelius; Officer; Oswald; Passavant; Peixoto; Pohlman; Preus; Probst; Quitman; Reynolds; Salyards; the Shaeffers, F. D., D. F., F. C., C. F., C. W.; H. I. Schmidt; J. G. Schmauck; the Schmuckers, J. G., S. S., B. M.; Seiss; Seyffarth; Sheeleigh; G. Shober; C. A. Smith; J. Few Smith; M. L. Steover; F. C. Stohlman; T. Stork; P. A. Strobel; Stuckenberg; Titus; Van Alstine; Vogelbach; Wackerha- gen; C. F. W. Walther; Weiser; D. Worley; F. C. Wyne- ken. There are others worthy of a place in our list of authors, but as they have not put their labors into the permanent shape of books, it does not fall within our plan to enumerate them.*

The imperfect list we give of the great names in our Church, especially in Germany, may serve to explain the strong terms in which writers of other churches have felt themselves constrained to speak of Lutheran theology: " The Lutheran Church has a great pre-eminence over the Reformed in regard to its internal theological development. German theological science comes forth from the Lutheran Church. The theology of the Lutheran Church supported by German diligence, thoroughness, and profundity, stage by stage, amid manifold struggles and revolutions, arose to an amazing elevation, astounding and incomprehensible to the Swiss, the French, and the English." † " The Lutheran Church," says Lange, " is the Church of theologians." ‡

At once as a cause and a result of this greatness in the highest form of learning, may be regarded the fact that the Lutheran Church is an Educating Church from the humblest sphere of the children of the poor to the highest range of the scholar's erudition.

The early efforts of Luther in behalf of education were continued by his successors through the means of catechetical instruction, congregational and public schools, and universities. There are no exclusively Reformed universities in Germany proper. The universities which the Lutheran Church has in part or in whole may be classified as follows: 1, those in which the three confessions are represented — Tübingen, Giessen, Breslau, and Bonn; 2, the two confessions, Lutheran and Reformed — Heidelberg, Greifswalde, Marburg, Königsberg, Halle, Erlangen, (the professors Lutheran with one exception,) and Berlin; 3, exclusively Lutheran — Leipsic, Rostock, (Wittenberg, transferred to Halle in 1817, now a seminary for candidates for the ministry,) Jena, Kiel, and Göttingen; in Denmark, Copenhagen; in Norway, Christiania; in Sweden, Lund and Upsal; in Russia, Dorpat.

Education in the Lutheran Church.

---

* For the completest list of " Publications by Lutherans in the United States." up to 1861, see Evangelical Review, April, 1861, 542.

† Goebel, 263, 277.   ‡ Kurtz, § 176, 6.

In the United States she has fourteen Theological Seminaries, sixteen Universities and Colleges, nine Female Academies, sixteen Academies, and various societies for Education and Publication. The Periodicals devoted to her interests are, nine English, fifteen German, two Norwegian, two Swedish.

Nor has the Lutheran Church been satisfied with meeting the wants of her own children. She has been, and is a Church of Missions. In 1559, Gustavus Vasa, of Sweden, founded a mission among the Laplanders, which was continued with renewed earnestness by Gustavus Adolphus, Denmark also aiding. Thomas von Westen (died 1727) was the apostle of this mission. Heyling, of Lübeck, without any aid, labored as a missionary in Abyssinia, (1635,) and others, of the circle of his friends, engaged in the same cause in various parts of the East. Frederick IV., of Denmark, established the East India mission at Tranquebar, (1706,) for which Francke furnished him two devoted laborers, Plützschau and Ziegenbalg, the latter of whom translated the New Testament into Tamil, (1715.) The labors of this mission were also extended to the English possessions. From the orphan-house at Halle went forth a succession of missionaries, among whom Schwartz (died 1798) is pre-eminent. An institution for the conversion of the Jews was established at Halle, in 1728. Egede of Norway (died 1758) commenced his labors in Greenland, in 1721. In 1736, he returned, and established in Copenhagen a mission seminary. Though the larger part of the Lutheran Church is unfavorably situated for Foreign Missions, the work has ever been dear to her — and her missions have been, and are now among the most successful in the world.

Many embarrassing circumstances prevented the Lutheran Church from developing her life as perfectly in her church constitution as in her doctrines and worship. The idea of the universal priesthood of all believers at once overthrew the doctrine of a distinction of essence between clergy and laity. The ministry is not an order, but it is a divinely appointed office, to which men must be rightly called. No imparity exists by divine right; an hierarchical organization is unchristian, but a gradation (bishops, superintendents, provosts) may be observed, as a thing of human right only. The government by consistories has been very general. In Denmark, Evangelical bishops took the place of the Roman Catholic prelates who were deposed. In Sweden the bishops embraced the Reformation, and thus secured in that country an "apostolic succession" in the high-church sense; though, on the principles of the Lutheran Church, alike where she has as where she has not such a succession, it is not regarded as essential even to the order of the Church. The ultimate source of power is in the congregations, that is, in the pastor and other officers and the people of the single communions. The right to choose a pastor belongs to the people, who may exercise it by direct vote, or delegate it to their representatives.

The Lutheran Church regards preaching as an indispensable part of a complete divine service. All worship is to be in the vernacular; the wants of the heart as well as of the reason are to be met. Whatever of the past is spiritual, beautiful, and appropriate, is to be retained. The church year, with its great festivals, is kept. With various national diversities there is a substantial agreement in the liturgical services of the Lutheran Church throughout almost all the world The hymns are sung by all the people with the organ accompaniment. The clergymen in their Divine Worship. official functions wear a distinctive dress, usually a black robe, with the bands, though the surplice has also been largely retained. In Denmark and Sweden, the chasuble is also worn in the altar service; and in Sweden, the mitre and bishop's crosier are retained. A preparatory service precedes communion. The doctrine and practice of auricular confession were rejected at the beginning. The "private confession," which was established in some parts of the Church, involves no enumeration or confession of particular sins whatever, unless the communicant desires to speak of them; and the "private absolution" is simply the annunciation of the gospel promise with the gospel conditions to the individual penitent, a promise which in its own nature is collative, that is, actually confers remission, when it is received in faith. The "Exorcism" in the shape in which it existed in some of the Lutheran Churches, involved little more than "the Renunciation," and can be defended on some of the same grounds. Simply as a rite long established, and which might be tolerated if regarded as no more than a symbolical representation of the doctrine that our nature is under the dominion of sin, it was practised in parts of the Church, but has fallen everywhere into oblivion. Persons are received to the communion of the Church by confirmation performed by the pastor, after thorough instruction in the Catechism. But especially in sacred song has the Lutheran Church a grand distinctive element of her worship. "The Lutheran Church," says Dr. Schaff, "draws the fine arts into the service of religion, and has produced a body of hymns and chorals, which, in richness, power, and unction, surpasses the hymnology of all other churches in the world." "In divine worship," says Goebel, "we reach a point in which the Lutheran Church has one of its most glorious features of pre-eminence. The hymns of the Church are the people's confession, and have wrought more than the preaching. In the Lutheran Church alone, German hymnology attained a bloom truly amazing. The words of holy song were heard everywhere, and sometimes, as with a single stroke, won whole cities for the Gospel."

What has been the practical working of the Lutheran system in the *life* of the Church? This question is an extensive one, and we offer but a fact or two bearing on the answer to it. In the Lutheran system the word of God works from within to the outward. The Romanic nations are characteristically less contemplative and more radical and inclined to extremes than the Germanic, and the Swiss Reformation had a large mingling of political elements. The Lutheran type of Reformation and of religion is consequently milder and less demonstrative, less obtrusive and more averse to display, than the Zwinglian and Calvinistic; but the piety it matures is unequalled in firmness, calmness, earnestness, joyousness, and freedom. The character of Luther himself, is largely mirrored in the Church which

Practical working of Lutheranism in the life.

cherishes his memory as one of her most precious possessions. The Lutheran Church is very rich in devotional works for the people. It is more in affinity with high æsthetic culture than other Protestant Churches. It is less open than others to excessive tendencies to voluntary (especially to secret) association not under the control of the Church. It may be claimed for it that it is the most healthfully cautious of Churches, and, therefore, most sure to make the most permanent, if not the most rapid progress. Gœbel, a Reformed writer, says: "That charming, frank good-humor, and that beneficence which rise from the very depth of the soul, and which so advantageously distinguish the German nation from others, are wanting among the Reformed — even among the Germans of the Reformed Church. The piety of the Lutherans is deep, fervent, heart-felt." And a far greater theological scholar, (Dr. Schaff,) also of another communion, has said: "The Lutheran piety has also its peculiar charm — the charm of Mary, who sat at Jesus feet and heard his word. . . . It excels in honesty, kindness, affection, cheerfulness, and that gemüthlichkeit for which other nations have not even a name. The Lutheran Church meditated over the deepest mysteries of divine grace, and brought to light many treasures of knowledge from the mines of revelation. She can point to an unbroken succession of learned divines who devoted their whole lives to the investigation of saving truth. She numbers her mystics who bathed in the ocean of infinite love. She has sung the most fervent hymns to the Saviour, and holds sweet, child-like intercourse with the Heavenly Father."

A fair construction of the whole history of the past will inspire faith in the character of the people whom God has given to our Church to be gathered under her banners and to fight her battles. Not all the havoc which state-meddling, war, and infidelity have made with the true German character in Europe can efface the evidence of the past and the present, that of all nations the German is the most simply and profoundly religious, that the Germans are what Dr. Arnold calls them: "the regenerating race — the most moral race of men," and a large part of this glory is due to that Church which so faithfully exhibits and nurtures the genuine Germanic life.

And not unworthy of a place with this noble element is the other great family of Lutheran nations, which next to the Germans, are adding to the greatest treasure of this New World, thousands of Christian men. The name of Scandinavians recalls great Lutheran nationalities which have deserved well of the The Scandinavian Lutherans, Swedes, Danes. world. With it is connected the name of Gustavus Vasa, King of Sweden, who pleaded for the Reformation with tears, who laid down his sceptre and refused to take it again until the love of his people for him made them willing to receive the Reformation, and who founded, among the poor Laplanders, one of the first Protestant Missions. It recalls the name of the martyr-hero, Gustavus Adolphus, whose name should be dearer to Protestants, and most of all to Lutherans, who justly claim to be the most Protestant of Protestants, dearer than the name of Washington to Americans, for a part of the price he paid for the rescue of the religious liberty of Europe was his own blood. But for him, our Protestantism might have been borne down, and swept away from the world in a torrent of blood and fire. He, too, was zealous in the cause of missions. It was a Scandinavian king, Frederick IV. of Denmark, who established at Tranquebar, the East India Mission, which was blest with the labors of Ziegenbalg, and of the greatest of missionaries of all time, Christian Frederic Schwartz. It was a Scandinavian Lutheran preacher, Hans Egede, of Norway, who, amid toil, peril, and suffering, planted a pure Christianity among the Greenlanders.

"In the eighteenth century," says Wiggers, "Denmark shone in the eyes of Evangelical Europe as a fireside and home of missions." "In Sweden," says the same distinguished writer, "the Lutheran Church won a noble and pure people, full of a vigorous and steadfast faith, a people marked by clearness and brightness of intellect, by pure and simple morals, and the soul of chivalry; a people always ready fearlessly to wage warfare for the Gospel with the sword of the spirit, and if necessity urged, with the temporal sword. United with the state by the most intimate ties, not of bondage, but of mutual love, entering thoroughly into every part of the national life, exercising through its control of the schools the mightiest and holiest influence in the training of the young, with a ministry whose fidelity and wisdom accomplish the more, because they are sustained by high temporal position and adequate support, with a people who exhibit a calm and pious humility, and an unlimited confidence in their pastors, the Church of Sweden shines, like a star with its pure mild light, in the northern sky."

For the Anglicized and English portion of our Church, which best represents it, we claim a character in consonance with its great antecedents — a character of simplicity, earnestness, devoutness. In the departments of business, the calm of home, the sacred duties of the Church, the sphere of citizens, they show a solid worth, which testifies to the thoroughness of the Christian nurture of the communion they love.

Of what our Church is, and of what she brings to this, her new home, witness has been borne by more than one thoughtful man of other communions. But among them all, there is none of more value than that given by Dr. John W. Nevin, of the Reformed Church. No amount of divergence from Dr. Nevin's views, could prevent a man of candor from acknowledging in him the presence of a great intellect, of the most unpretending simplicity and modesty, and of the most uncompromising love of truth. Our country has few men who can be classified with him. In originality and general vigor of conception and of style, Bushnell and Parks would be thought of as most like him; but we do not think that on any just estimate of the men, they could be claimed as his superiors. Dr. Nevin's range of thought is at once broader and deeper than that of most of our theological thinkers. It is comprehensive without becoming shallow. For the Lutheran Church in its genuine life he expresses great affection and reverence, and his witness is of peculiar value, for no man out of our Church knows more fully than he what is in it. He says, in speaking of the cultivation of an historical spirit in his own Church: " But this cannot fail to bring with it, at the same time, the power of understanding and appreciating

also the vast historical significance which belongs to the other
great Protestant Confession, the Lutheran Church. In recognizing our identity with the Reformed Confession in general,
while we yet discard the peculiarity of our position in it as a
German Reformed Church, we come necessarily into the feeling of what Lutheranism is for the church at large, in a way
that is not by any means so easy for the thinking of other
branches of the Reformed Communion in this country. In
understanding ourselves and in learning to do justice to our
own historical character, we are made conscious not simply of
our difference from the Lutheran Church, but also of our old
nearness to it, and of what we owe to it for our universal church
life. The power of estimating intelligently the merits of the
Value of the Lu- Heidelberg Catechism, must prove for us the power
theran Church to of honoring also the Augsburg Confession, as it
Christianity at
large. Dr. J. W. was honored in the beginning by the framers of
Nevin.   the Catechism. We can have no sympathy with
hat type of Reformed thought, whether in New England or
elsewhere, which has fallen away entirely from the original
Spannung of the two great Protestant Confessions; which has
lost all sense for the old theological issues, that threw them
asunder in the sixteenth century; and for which Lutheranism,
in the profound distinction which then belonged to it, has
become an unmeaning memory of the dead past. We are in
the way more and more, it may be hoped, of knowing better
than this. We can have no wish to have the Lutheran Church
overwhelmed in this country by the reigning unhistorical spirit
of our American Christianity — no wish to see it *Americanized*,
in the sense of anything like a general rupture with its original
theological life. The whole Reformed Church here, whether
it be perceived or not, has a vast interest at stake on the power
of the Lutheran Church to remain true and faithful to her confessional mission. For all who are capable of appreciating at
all the central and vital character of the questions that shook
the Protestant world in the age of the Reformation, and who
are able to make proper account of the unsacramental tendencies of the present time, it must be a matter for congratulation
that German Lutheranism has grown to be so numerically

powerful within our borders, and that it is coming to be in every way so vast an ecclesiastical power in the land; while it ought to be the prayer of all, that this power may be so exercised more and more as to be a principle of wholesome redemption and preservation for the universal Protestantism of the nation."

That such a Church has a mission of extraordinary importance in this land in which exist such dangerous tendencies to sectarianism and radicalism, and whose greatest need is the cultivation of historical feeling, under the restraint of a wholesome conservatism, requires Mission of the Lutheran Church in America. no argument. The Lutheran Church daily becomes better known through the translations of her literature, though most of them are very bad ones; but her work of good cannot be consummated till she renders her genius and life themselves into the idiom of the new nationality into which she is here passing. Protestant to the very heart, yet thoroughly historical, happy in her liberty of adaptation in things indifferent, while she is fast anchored in the great doctrine of justification by faith and the doctrines which cluster around it, popular in her principles of church government, which, without running into Independency, accord such large powers to the congregation, principles free from the harshness of some systems, the hierarchical, aristocratic, autocratic tendencies of others, the fanaticism and looseness of others, possessing liturgical life without liturgical bondage, great in a history in which all mankind are interested, her children believe that she bears special treasures of good to bless the land of her adoption.

Immovable in her faith and the life it generates, our Church, the more heartily and intelligently, on this very account, accepts the great fact that God has established her in this western world under circumstances greatly different from those in which her past life has been nurtured. New forms of duty, new types of thought, new necessities of adaptation, are here to tax all her strength, and to test how far she is able to maintain her vital power under necessary changes of form. The Lutheranism of this country cannot be a mere feeble echo of any nationalized species of Lutheranism. It cannot, in the national sense, be permanently German or Scandinavian, out of Germany and Scandinavia, but in America must be American. It must be conformed in accordance with its own principles to its new home, bringing hither its priceless experiences in the old world, to apply them to the living present in the new. Our Church must be pervaded by sympathy for this land; she must learn in order that she may teach. She must not be afraid to trust herself on this wild current of the quick life of America. She must not cloister herself, but show in her freedom, and in her wise use of the opportunity of the present, that she knows how robust is her spiritual life, and how secure are her principles however novel or trying the tests to which they are subjected.

The catholicity of the range of our Church among nations, in which she is entirely without parallel among Protestant Churches, does, indeed, make the problem of the fusion of her elements very difficult; but it is the very same problem which our nation has had to solve. In spite of all the difficulties of inflowing nationalities, we consider their presence in our country as politically a source of strength, even though a collision of them has sometimes brought about riot and murder. The Lutheran Church, if she can solve her problem, will be repaid by a result richly worth all her toil and endurance.

Though the descendants of Lutherans have often been lost to the Lutheran Church, she, on the other hand, embraces in her membership thousands not of Lutheran origin; and though in the nature of the case these gains are far from counterbalancing her losses, they show that the losses have not resulted from want of adaptation to the genius of our time and of our land. The Lutheran Church, where she is understood, has proved herself a popular Church, a true church of the people.

She has a wonderful power of adaptation, and of persistence, and of recuperation. Her tendency to unite is so great, that although there have been difficulties which, in churches of a separatistic character, would have originated a dozen of sects, the Lutheran Church in this country still retains her denominational unity. Many of the difficulties of our Church were, in their own nature, inevitable. So extraordinary have they been, that nothing but a vitality of the most positive kind could have saved her. A calm review of her history in this country up to this hour, impresses us with a deeper conviction that she is a daughter of God, and destined to do much for his glory in this western world. Let her be faithful to her faith, in the confession of the lip, the love of the heart, the devotion of the life; let her soul invest itself with the body of a sound government; let her ministers and people be knit to her, and to one another, with the love which such a church should command from her children, and should infuse into them, one to another, and God helping her, the glory of her second temple shall not be unworthy of the great memories of the first.

The signs of the times must be lost on our people if they are not waked up to a more just appreciation of their Church. And though not known by others as she should be, she is better known and wins increasing respect. The importance of the aid she brings in evangelizing this western world is more deeply felt, and before the eyes of those even who would not see her when she sat mourning in the dust, she rises more brightly and beautifully, an acknowledged power in the land. Our parent tree may shed its foliage, to renew it, or its blossoms may fall off to give way to fruit, parasitic creepers may be torn from it, storms may carry away a dead branch here and there — but there is not strength enough in hell and earth combined to break its massive trunk. Till the new earth comes, that grand old tree, undecaying, will strike its roots deeper in the earth that now is: till the new heavens arch themselves, it will lift itself under these skies, and wave, in tempest and sunshine its glorious boughs.

11

V.

THE CONFESSIONAL PRINCIPLE OF THE CONSERV-
ATIVE REFORMATION.*

IN the statement of fundamental and unchangeable principles
of Faith, which the General Council of the Evangelical
Lutheran Church in America lays as the basis of its Constitution, it is declared:

I. There must be and abide through all time, one holy Christian Church, which is the assembly of all believers, among
whom the Gospel is purely preached, and the Holy Sacraments
are administered, as the Gospel demands.

To the true unity of the Church, it is sufficient that there
be agreement touching the doctrine of the Gospel, that it be
preached in one accord, in its pure sense, and that the Sacraments be administered conformably to God's word.

---

* BLACKBURNE: The Confessional: Inquiry into the right, etc., of Confessions
of Faith, etc. Lond. 1770.
  BÜSCHING: Üb. d. Symbol. Schriften d. Evang. Luther. Kirche. Hamb. 1771.
    "   Wenn und durch wen die Symbol. Schr. ausgel. werd. Berl. 1789.
  EBERHARD: Ist die Augsb. Confess. eine Glaubensvorschr., etc. 1795-97.
  HEUSINGER: Würdigung der S. B. n. d. jetz. Zeitbedürf. Leipz. 1799.
  FRITZSCHE: Über. d. unveränd. Gelt. der Aug. Confess. Leipz. 1830.
  MÄRTENS: Die Symb. Büch. der Ev. Luth. Kirche. Halberst. 1830.
  JOHANNSEN: Untersuch. der Rechtmässigk. d. Verpfl. a. S. B. Altona. 1833.
  HÖFLING: De Symbolor. natur. necessit. auctor. atque usu. Erl. 1835.
  BRETSCHNEIDER: Die Unzulässigk. d. Symbolzwanges. Leipz. 1841.
  SARTORIUS: Nothwendigk. u. Verbindlichk. d. Kirch. Glaubensbekenntn
Stuttgart. 1845. (See Review by Dr. J. A. SEISS: Evang. Rev. July, 1852.)
  KÖLLNER: Die gute Sache d. Luth. Symbole. Göttingen. 1847.

II. The true unity of a particular Church, in virtue of which men are truly members of one and the same Church, and by which any Church abides in real identity, and is entitled to a continuation of her name, is unity in doctrine and faith in the Sacraments, to wit: That she continues to teach and to set forth, and that her true members embrace from the heart, and use, the articles of faith and the Sacraments as they were held and administered when the Church came into distinctive being and received a distinctive name.

Fundamental principles of faith.

III. The Unity of the Church is witnessed to, and made manifest in, the solemn, public, and official Confessions which are set forth, to wit: The generic Unity of the Christian Church in the general Creeds, and the specific Unity of pure parts of the Christian Church in their specific Creeds; one chief object of both classes of which Creeds is, that Christians who are in the Unity of faith, may know each other as such, and may have a visible bond of fellowship.

IV. That Confessions may be such a testimony of Unity and bond of Union, they must be accepted in every statement of doctrine, in their own true, native, original and only sense. Those who set them forth and subscribe them, must not only agree to use the same words, but must use and understand those words in one and the same sense.

V. The Unity of the Evangelical Lutheran Church, as a portion of the holy Christian Church, depends upon her abiding in one and the same faith, in confessing which she obtained her distinctive being and name, her political recognition, and her history.

VI. The Unaltered Augsburg Confession is by pre-eminence the Confession of that faith. The acceptance of its doctrines and the avowal of them without equivocation or mental reservation, make, mark, and identify that Church, which alone in the true, original, historical, and honest sense of the term is the Evangelical Lutheran Church.

VII. The only Churches, therefore, of any land, which are properly in the Unity of that Communion, and by consequence entitled to its name, Evangelical Lutheran, are those which sincerely hold and truthfully confess the doctrines of the Un altered Augsburg Confession.

VIII. We accept and acknowledge the doctrines of the Un-altered Augsburg Confession in its original sense as throughout in conformity with the pure truth of which God's Word is the only rule. We accept its statements of truth as in perfect accordance with the Canonical Scriptures: We reject the errors it condemns, and we believe that all which it commits to the liberty of the Church, of right belongs to that liberty.

IX. In thus formally accepting and acknowledging the Un-altered Augsburg Confession, we declare our conviction, that the other Confessions of the Evangelical Lutheran Church, inasmuch as they set forth none other than its system of doctrine, and articles of faith, are of necessity pure and scriptural. Pre-eminent among such accordant, pure, and scriptural statements of doctrine, by their intrinsic excellence, by the great and necessary ends for which they were prepared, by their historical position, and by the general judgment of the Church, are these: The Apology of the Augsburg Confession, the Smalcald Articles, the Catechisms of Luther, and the Formula of Concord, all of which are, with the Unaltered Augsburg Confession, in the perfect harmony of one and the same scrip tural faith.

In accordance with these principles every Professor elect of the Theological Seminary of the Evangelical Lutheran Church at Philadelphia, in the act of investiture and before entering on the performance of the duties of his office, makes the following affirmation:

'I believe that the Canonical Books of the Old and New Testaments are given by inspiration of God, and are the perfect and only Rule of Faith; and I believe that the three General Creeds, the Apostles', the Nicene, and the Athanasian, exhibit the faith of the Church universal, in accordance with this Rule.

'I believe that the Unaltered Augsburg Confession is, in all its parts, in harmony with the Rule of Faith, and is a correct exhibition of doctrine; and I believe that the Apology, the two Catechisms of Luther, the Smalcald Articles, and the

Formula of Concord, are a faithful development and defence of the doctrines of the Word of God, and the Augsburg Confession.

'I solemnly promise before Almighty God that all my teachings shall be in conformity with His Word, and with the aforementioned Confessions.'

The thetical statements of the Council and the declaration which follows, exhibit, as we believe, the relation of the Rule of Faith and the Confessions, in accordance with the principles of the Conservative Reformation. Accepting those principles, we stand upon the everlasting foundation — the Word of God: believing that the Canonical Books of the Old and New Testament are in their original tongues, and in a pure text, the perfect and only rule of faith. All these books are in harmony, each with itself, and all with each other, and yield to the honest searcher, under the ordinary guidance of the Holy Spirit, a clear statement of doctrine, and produce a firm assurance of faith. Not any word of man, no creed, commentary, theological system, nor decision of Fathers or of councils, no doctrine of Churches, or of the whole Church, no results or judgments of reason, however strong, matured, and well informed, no one of these, and not all of these together, but God's word alone is the rule of faith. _{The Rule of Faith.}

No apocryphal books, but the canonical books alone, are the rule of faith. No translations, as such, but the original Hebrew and Chaldee of the Old Testament, and the Greek of the New, are the letter of the rule of faith. No vitiation of the designing, nor error of the careless, but the incorrupt text as it came from the hands of the men of God, who wrote under the motions of the Holy Spirit, is the rule of faith. To this rule of faith we are to bring our minds; by this rule we are humbly to try to form our faith, and in accordance with it, God helping us, to teach others — teaching them the evidences of its inspiration, the true mode of its interpretation, the ground of its authority, and the mode of settling its text. The student of theology is to be taught the Biblical languages, to make him an independent investigator of the word of the Holy Spirit, as the organ through which that Spirit reveals

His mind. First of all, as the greatest of all, as the ground-work of all, as the end of all else, we are to teach God's pure word, its faith for faith, its life for life; in its integrity, in its marvellous adaptation, in its divine, its justifying, its sancti-fying, and glorifying power. We are to lay, as that without which all else would be laid in vain, the foundation of the Apostles and Prophets — Jesus Christ himself being the chief corner-stone.

Standing really upon the everlasting foundation of this Rule of Faith, we stand of necessity on the faith, of which it is the rule. It is not the truth as it lies, silent and unread, in the Word, but the truth as it enters from that Word into the human heart, with the applying presence of the Holy Ghost, which makes men believers. Faith makes men Christians; Confession of but Confession alone marks them as Christians. Faith. The Rule of Faith is God's voice to us; faith is the hearing of that voice, and the Confession, our reply of assent to it. By our faith, we are known to the Lord as his; by our Confession, we are known to each other as His chil-dren. Confession of faith, in some form, is imperative. To confess Christ, is to confess what is our faith in him. As the Creed is not, and cannot be the Rule of Faith, but is its Con-fession merely, so the Bible, because it is the Rule of Faith, is of necessity not its Confession. The Bible can no more be any man's Creed, than the stars can be any man's astronomy. The stars furnish the rule of the astronomer's faith: the Principia of Newton may be the Confession of his faith. If a man were examined as a candidate for the chair of astronomy in a university, and were asked, " What is your astronomical sys-tem?" and were to answer, " I accept the teaching of the stars," the reply would be, " You may think you do — so does the man who is sure that the stars move round the world, and that they are not orbs, but ' gimlet-holes to let the glory through.' We wish to know what you hold the teachings of the stars to be? Do you receive, as in harmony with them, the results reached by Copernicus, by Galileo, by Kepler, by Newton, La Place, and Herschel, or do you think the world one great flat, and the sun and moon mere pendants to it?"

" Gentlemen," replies the independent investigator, " the theories of those astronomers are human systems — man-made theories. I go out every night on the hills, and look at the stars, as God made them, through a hole in my blanket, with my own good eyes, not with a man-made telescope, or fettered by a man-made theory ; and I believe in the stars and in what they teach me: but if I were to say, or write what they teach, that would be a human creed — and I am opposed to all creeds." " Very well," reply the examiners, " we wish you joy in the possession of a good pair of eyes, and feel it unnecessary to go any further. If you are unwilling to confess your faith, we will not tax your conscience with the inconsistency of teaching that faith, nor tax our own with the hazard of authorizing you to set forth in the name of the stars your own ignorant assumptions about them."

What is more clear than that, as the Rule of Faith is first, it must, by necessity of its being, when rightly used, generate a true faith ? But the man who has true faith desires to have it known, and is bound to confess his faith. The Rule cannot really generate two conflicting beliefs ; yet men who alike profess to accept the Rule, do have conflicting beliefs ; and when beliefs conflict, if the one is formed by the Rule, the other must be formed in the face of it. Fidelity to the Rule of Faith, therefore, fidelity to the faith it teaches, demands that there shall be a Confession of the faith. The firmest friend of the Word is the firmest friend of the Creed. First, the Rule of Faith, next the Faith of the Rule, and then the Confession of Faith.

What shall be our Confession ? Are we originating a Church, and must we utter our testimony to a world, in which our faith is a novelty ? The reply is easy. As we <small>What shall be</small> are not the first who have used, with honest hearts <small>our Confession?</small> and fervent prayers, the Rule, so are we not the first who have been guided by the Holy Ghost in it to its faith. As men long ago reached its faith, so long ago they confessed it. They confessed it from the beginning. The first adult baptism was based upon a " human creed," that is, upon a confession of faith, which was the utterance of a belief which was based

upon a human interpretation of divine words. The faith has
been confessed from the beginning. It has been embodied in a
creed, the origin of whose present shape no man knows, which
indeed cannot be fixed; for it rose from the words of our
Saviour's Baptismal Commission, and was not manufactured,
but grew. Of the Apostles' Creed, as of Him to whom its heart
is given, it may be affirmed that it was "begotten, not made."
The Confession has been renewed and enlarged to meet new
and widening error. The ripest, and purest, and most widely
used of the old Confessions have been adopted by our Church
as her own, not because they are old and widely received, but
because they are true. She has added her testimony as it was
needed. Here is the body of her Confession. Is her Confession ours? If it be, we are of her in heart; if it be not, we are
only of her in name. It is ours — ours in our deepest conviction, reached through conflicts outward and inward, reached upon
our knees, and traced with our tears — ours in our inmost hearts.
Therefore, we consecrate ourselves to living, teaching, and defending the faith of God's word, which is the confessed faith of
the Evangelical Lutheran Church. Fidelity to the whole truth
of God's word requires this. We dare not be satisfied simply
with recognition as Christians over against the Jew, because
we confess that the Rule of Faith, of which the New Testament is a part, has taught us faith in Jesus Christ: we dare
not be satisfied simply with recognition as holding the Catholic
Faith as embodied in the three General Creeds, over against heresies of various forms and shades. Christian believers holding
the faith Catholic we are — but we are, besides, Protestant,
rejecting the authority of the Papacy; Evangelical, glorying
Distinctive con- in the grace of the Gospel; and Lutheran, holding
fession necessary. the doctrines of that Church, of which the Reformation is the child — not only those in which all Christendom or a large part of it coincides with her, but the most distinctive of her distinctive doctrines, though in the maintenance
of them she stood alone. As the acceptance of the Word of
God as a Rule of Faith separates us from the Mohammedan,
as the reception of the New Testament sunders us from the
Jew, as the hearty acquiescence in the Apostles', Nicene, and

Athanasian Creeds shows us, in the face of all errorists of the earlier ages, to be in the faith of the Church Catholic, so does our unreserved acceptance of the Augsburg Confession mark us as Lutherans; and the acceptance of the Apology, the Catechisms of Luther, the Schmalcald Articles, and the Formula of Concord, continues the work of marking our separation from all errorists of every shade whose doctrines are in conflict with the true sense of the Rule of Faith — that Rule whose teachings are rightly interpreted and faithfully embodied in the Confessions afore-mentioned. Therefore, God helping us, we will teach the whole faith of His word, which faith our Church sets forth, explains, and defends in her Symbols. We do not interpret God's word by the Creed, neither do we interpret the Creed by God's word, but interpreting both independently, by the laws of language, and finding that they teach one and the same truth, we heartily acknowledge the Confession as a true exhibition of the faith of the Rule — a true witness to the one, pure, and unchanging faith of the Christian Church, and freely make it our own Confession, as truly as if it had been now first uttered by our lips, or had now first gone forth from our hands.

In freely and heartily accepting the faith of our Church, as our own faith, and her Scriptural Confession of that faith, as our own Confession, we do not surrender for ourselves, any more than we take from others, the sacred and inalienable right of private judgment. It is not by giving up the right of private judgment, but by the prayerful exercise of it, not by relinquishing a just independence of investigation, but by thoroughly employing it, that we have reached that faith which we glory in confessing. Could the day ever come, in which we imagined that the Evangelical Lutheran Church had abused her right of private judgment, so as to reach error, and not truth by it, we should, as honest men, cease to bear her name, or to connive at what we would, in the case supposed, believe to be error. On the other hand, should the Evangelical Lutheran Church ever have evidence, that we have abused our right of private judgment into the wrong of private misjudgment, so

Fidelity to the Confessions not inconsistent with the right of private judgment.

as to have reached error, and not truth by it, then, as a faithful Church, after due admonition, and opportunity for repentance have been given us in vain, she is bound to cast us forth, to purify her own communion, and to make it impossible for us, in her name, to injure others. As the individual, in exercising the right of private judgment, is in peril of abusing it, the Church has the right, and is bound by the duty, of self-defence against that abuse. The right of private judgment is not the right of Church-membership, not the right of public teaching, not the right of putting others into an equivocal attitude to what they regard as truth. A free Protestant Church is a Church, whose ministry and membership, accepting the same rule of faith, have, in the exercise of their private judgment upon it, reached the same results as to all truths which they deem it needful to unite in confessing. After all the intricacies into which the question of, What are fundamentals? has run, there can be no practical solution better than this, that they are such truths, as in the judgment of the Church, it is necessary clearly to confess; truths, the toleration of the errors opposing which, she believes to be inconsistent with her fidelity to the Gospel doctrine, to her own internal harmony and highest efficiency. The members and ministry of such a Church must have "one faith," as they have one Lord, one Baptism, and one God. Apart from the "unity of the faith," and the "unity of the knowledge of the Son of God," every striving to reach "unto a perfect man, unto the measure of the stature of the fulness of Christ," will be vain; thus only can Christian men "henceforth be no more children, tossed to and fro, and carried about with every wind of doctrine, by the sleight of men, and cunning craftiness, whereby they lie in wait to deceive."

A great deal is claimed under the right of private judgment, which is a most impudent infringement of that right. A man is a Socinian, a Pelagian, a Romanist. Very well. We maintain, that no civil penalties should restrain him, and no ecclesiastical inquisition fetter him. Give him, in its fullest swing, the exercise of his right of private judgment. But your Socinian insists on such a recognition by Trinitarians as logically implies, that they either agree with him in his error, or that it is of no importance. What is this but to ask thousands or millions to give up or imperil the results of their well-used right of private judgment, at the call of one man, who abuses his? Could impudence go further? 'Go,' they may rightly say, 'with your right of private judgment, go where you belong, and cease to attempt the shallow jugglery, by which one man's freedom means his autocracy, and every other man's slavery. If your right of private judgment has made you an Atheist, don't call yourself a Believer; if it has made you a Jew, don't pretend to be a Christian; if it nas made you a Papist, don't pretend to be a Protestant; if it has made you a Friend, don't call yourself a Churchman.'

Use and abuse
of the right cf
private judg
ment. .

When we confess, that, in the exercise of our right of private judgment, our Bible has made us Lutherans, we reither pretend to claim that other men shall be made Lutherans by force, nor that their private judgment shall, or will, of necessity, reach the results of ours. We only contend, that, if their private judgment of the Bible does not make them Lutherans, they shall not pretend that it does. We do not say, that any man shall believe that the Confession of our Church is Scriptural. We only contend, that he should neither say nor seem to say so, if he does not believe it. The subscription to a Confession is simply a just and easy mode of testifying to those who have a right to ask it

Meaning of
subscription to a
Confession.

of us, that we are what we claim and profess to be. So to sign a Confession as to imply that we are what we are not, or to leave it an open question what we are, is not the just result of the right of private judgment, or of any right whatever, but is utterly wrong. For it is a first element of truth, with which no right, private or public, can conflict, that names shall honestly represent things. What immorality is more patent than the pretence that the right of private judgment is something which authorizes a man to make his whole life a falsehood; is something which fills the world with names, which no longer represent things, fills it with black things, that are called white, with bitter things, that are called sweet, and with lies, that are called truths, with monarchists, who are called republicans, with Socinians, who are called Trinitarians, with Arminians, who are called Calvinists, with Romanists, Rationalists, fanatics, or sectarians, who are called Lutherans?

We concede to every man the absolute right of private judgment as to the faith of the Lutheran Church, but if he have abandoned the faith of that Church, he may not use her name as his shelter in attacking the thing she cherishes, and in maintaining which she obtained her being and her name. It is not enough that you say to me, that such a thing is clear to your private judgment. You must show to my private judgment, that God's word teaches it, before I dare recognize you as in the unity of the faith. If you cannot, we have not the same faith, and ought not to be of the same communion; for the communion is properly one of persons of the same faith. In other words, your private judgment is not to be my interpreter, nor is mine to be yours. If you think me in error, I have no right to force myself on your fellowship. If I think you in error, you have no right to force yourself on mine. You have the civil right and the moral right to form your impressions in regard to truth, but there the right stops. You have not the right to enter or remain in any Christian communion, except as its terms of membership give you that right. So easy is this distinction, and so clearly a part, not of speculation, but of practical morals, that the law of the land recognizes it. If certain men, under the style and title of a Church, which imply that it is Calvinistic, call an Arminian preacher, the law takes that Church from an Arminian majority which calls itself Calvinistic, and gives it to a Calvinistic minority which is what it calls itself. Does this mean that the majority must sacrifice their right of private judgment, that the law wishes to force them to be Calvinists? Not at all. It simply means, that the right of private judgment is not the right to call yourself what you are not, and to keep what does not belong to you. Put your Arminians under their true colors, though in minority, and your Calvinists under false colors, though in majority, and you will soon see how easily the principle of this law of morals and of this law of the land adjusts itself.

Before the plain distinctions we have urged, in regard to private judgment, go down all the evasions by which Rationalism has sought to defend itself from the imputation of dishonor, when it pretended to bear the Lutheran name, as if Lutheranism were *The abuse of private judgment not to be restrained by persecution.* not a positive and well-defined system of truth, but a mere assertion of the right of private judgment. It is the doctrine of the Reformation, not that there should be no checks upon the abuse of private judgment, but that those checks should be moral alone. The Romanists and un-Lutheran elements in the Reformation were agreed, that the truth must be maintained and heresy extirpated by the sword of government. Error is in affinity with the spirit of persecution. The first blood shed within the Christian Church, for opinion's sake, was shed by the deniers of the divinity of Jesus Christ, the Arians. So strong was the feeling in the primitive Church against violence toward errorists, that not a solitary instance occurs of capital punishment for heresy in its earlier era. The Bishops of Gaul, who ordered the execution of the Priscillianists, though the lives of these errorists were as immoral as their teachings were abominable, were excluded from the communion of the Church. As the Western Church grew corrupt, it grew more and more a persecuting Church, till it became drunken with the blood of the saints. The maxims and spirit of persecution went over to every part of the Churches of the Reformation, except the Lutheran Church. Zwingle countenanced the penalty of death for heresy. What was the precise share of Calvin in the burning of Servetus is greatly mooted; but two facts are indisputable. One is, that, *before* the unhappy errorist took his fatal journey, Calvin wrote, that, if Servetus came to Geneva, he should not leave it alive, if his authority availed anything; the other is, that, *after* the burning of Servetus, Calvin wrote his dissertation defending the right of the magistrate to put heretics to death (1554.) The Romish and Calvinistic writers stand as one man for the right and duty of magistrates to punish heresy with **death,** over against Luther and the entire body of our theologians, who maintain, without an exception, that heresy is never to be punished with death. The Reformed portion of Protestantism has put to death, at different times and in different ways, not only Romanists and Anabaptists, but its terrible energies have been turned into civil strife, and Episcopalians, Presbyterians, and Independents put each other to death, especially in the great civil wars of England, whose origin was largely religious. Strange as it may sound, Socinians themselves have been persecutors, and yet more strange is the ground on which they persecuted. The original Socinians not only acknowledged that Jesus Christ was to be worshipped, and characterized those who denied it as half Jews, but, when Francis David, one of the greatest of their original co-workers, denied it, the old man was cast into prison, and kept there till he died. The Lutheran Church alone, of all the great Churches that have had the power to persecute, has not upon her skirts one drop of blood shed for opinion's sake. The glorious words of Luther were: "The pen, not the fire, is to put down heretics. The hangmen are not doctors of theology. This is not the place for force. Not the sword, but the word, fits for this battle. If the word does not put down error, error would stand, though the world were drenched with blood." By these just views, centuries in advance of the prevalent views, the Lutheran Church has stood, and will stand forever. But she is none the less earnest in just modes of shielding herself and her children from the teachings of error, which takes cover under the pretence of private judgment. She would not burn Servetus, nor, for opinion's sake, touch a hair of his head; neither, however, would she permit him to bear her name, to "preach another Jesus" in her pulpits, to teach error in her Universities, or to approach with her children the table of their Lord, whom he denied. Her name, her confessions, her history, her very being protest against the supposition of such "fellowship with the works of darkness," such sympathy with heresy, such levity in regard to the faith. She never practised thus. She never can do it. Those who imagine that the right of private judgment is the

But by denial of Church recognition.

right of men, within the Lutheran Church, and bearing her hallowed name, to teach what they please in the face of her testimony, know not the nature of the right they claim, noi of the Church, whose very life involves her refusal to have fellowship with them in their error. It is not the right of private judgment which makes or marks a man Lutheran. A man may have the right to judge, and be a simpleton, as he may have the right to get rich, yet may remain a beggar. It is the judgment he reaches in exercising that right which determines what he is. By his abuse of the " inalienable rights of life, liberty, and the pursuit of happiness," a man may make himself a miserable slave. The right of property belongs as much to the man who makes himself a beggar as to the man who has become a millionaire. Rights, in themselves, give nothing, and cannot change the nature of things. The right to gather, gathers nothing; and if, under this right, the man gathers wood, hay, stubble, neither the right nor its exercise makes them into gold, silver, and precious stones. The Church will not put any violence upon him who chooses to gather what will not endure the fire; but she will not accept them as jewels, nor permit her children to be cheated with them. The right of private judgment and the right of Church discipline are co-ordinate and harmonious rights, essential to the prevention, each of the abuse of the other. To uphold either intelligently, is to uphold both. In maintaining, therefore, as Protestants, the right and duty of men, in the exercise of private judgment, to form their own convictions, unfettered by civil penalties in the State, or by inquisitorial powers in the Church, we main-.ain, also, the right and duty of the Church to shield herself from corruption in doctrine by setting forth the truth in her Confession, by faithfully controverting heresy, by personal warning to those that err, and, finally, with the contumacious, by rejecting them from her communion, till, through grace, they are led to see and renounce the falsehood, for which they claimed the name of truth.

The faith of the Church, drawn from the rule by the just exercise of private judgment, illumined by the Holy Ghost, bas been tested and developed in three ways: First, by science;

next, by history; and thirdly, in the practical life of the Church. Science has shown, in the glorious edifice of our doctrinal theology, that our faith has the grand criterion of truth, the capacity of arrangement in a self-harmonizing system. Order is Heaven's first law. As the law of the physical universe is mathematical, the law of the spiritual universe is logical. That which has no place in system, is not of God, is not truth. All his works reflect his unity and self-consistency.

Intelligent fidelity to the Confessions an essential object of theological training.

To fit for their whole work, men, whom God shall call, through his Church, to teach the Gospel and administer the Sacraments, involves, in its most perfect form, that they shall understand, in its own tongues, the Holy Book, to the teachings of whose truths they are to devote themselves, that they should see those truths in their relations, as well as in their isolation, should thoroughly comprehend the faith of the Church, which is built upon them, and should be able to defend the truth, and the faith, which is its inspiration. The student of theology must be taught the history of the Church, in order to comprehend prophecy, in order to test all things, and hold fast to the good, and in order to comprehend the force and value of the decisions, on disputed points, which the Church maintains over against all errorists. He must know the history of the past in order to live in the life of to-day, which is the outflowing of the life of yesterday, and in order to reach beyond the hour into that solemn to-morrow of the future, which is to be the outflowing of the life of to-day. For all these and for many other reasons, the student of theology must master the great facts in the history of the Church of all time; but most of all, the history of our own Church, the richest, the most suggestive, the most heart-inspiring of the whole.

Looking forward to the position of a *Bishop* in the Church, and of a *Counsellor* in the Synod, the student of theology needs to be master of the great principles of Church government, a sphere specially important to our Church amid the radicalism and anarchical tendencies of the hour. The Christian *Pastor* of the future should be master of the principles which are to guide him in his vocation as guardian of the flock; the *Preacher* of the future should understand the theory. and be practically trained in the power of that simple but mighty eloquence, which becomes the preaching of the cross; the *Catechist* of the future should be trained for the great work of feeding the lambs; the future *Ministrants at the altars* of the Most High should be shaped in the tender, trusting, and all-prevailing spirit of worship, which God, the Holy Ghost, kindles in his saints, the devotion, whose flame trembles upward to its source, in the humble confessions, in the holy songs, and in the fervent prayers of the Church, all hallowed by the memories of ages of yearning and aspiration. If we are to have men "mighty in the Scriptures," "able and faithful ministers of the New Testament," they must be, "not novices," but men who "know how they ought to behave themselves in the house of God," "perfect, thoroughly furnished unto all good works," "holding fast the faithful word as they have been taught, that they may be able, by sound doctrine, both to exhort and to convince gainsayers," "in doctrine showing incorruptness."

In the true Christian minister, the priesthood, which he holds in common with all believers, intensifies Ministerial efficiency dependent on it. itself by his representative character. He is a priest, whose lips keep knowledge, at whose mouth they should seek the law, for he is the "messenger of the Lord of hosts." We want men apt to teach, in meekness instructing those that oppose themselves. We want men of decision, ready to confront those "whose mouths must be stopped; who subvert whole houses, teaching things which they ought not, for filthy lucre's sake." We want men, who will "hold fast the form of sound words; who will take heed unto themselves and the doctrine, and continue in them, knowing, that, in doing this," and alone in doing this, "they shall both save themselves and them that hear them;" men, who shall "stand fast in one spirit, with one mind striving together for the faith of the gospel," "earnestly contending for the faith once delivered to the saints;" men, "like-minded one toward another, speaking the same thing, with no divisions

12

among them, but perfectly joined together in the same mind and in the same judgment."

But, with all, and in all, and above all, we wish to send forth men, who shall be living illustrations of the power of the gospel they preach; men, who shall show the oneness and stability of a true faith, ready to yield preferences to secure principles, to make the sacrifices of love to the consciences of the weak in things indifferent, and to stand as the anvil to the beater under the strokes of obloquy and misrepresentation. We wish men, who will have the mind of Jesus Christ, thrilling in every pulse with love to souls; men that will seek the lowliest of the lowly, men filled with the spirit of missions, men of self-renunciation; men open as the day, men that abhor deceit, who use great plainness of speech, who speak the truth in love; men who are first pure, then peaceable, "gentle to all men," not self-willed, not soon angry, yet in conflict with the "many unruly and vain talkers and deceivers, rebuking them sharply, that they may be sound in the faith;" men so glowing with love of the gospel, so clear in their judgment as to its doctrines, so persuaded that life and death, heaven and hell, hang upon its pure proclamation, that they shall be ready to say: "Though we or an angel from heaven preach any other gospel unto you, let him be accursed," and again, in the very power of the apostle's iteration: "As I said before, so say I now again, If any man preach any other gospel unto you than that ye have received, let him be accursed." It is in the simple Biblical faith, in the incorrupt, profound, and self-harmonizing system of doctrine, in the historical caution and thoroughness, in the heart-felt piety, in the reverential spirit of worship, in the holy activity which reaches every want of the souls and bodies of men, in fidelity in the pulpit and pastoral life, in uncompromising maintenance of sound government, in all these, which belong to our Church, it is in these the men of the future should be shaped. We would have them grounded in a thorough knowledge, an ardent love, a practical exhibition of all that belongs to the true idea of the Evangelical Lutheran Church, of the Evangelical Lutheran Christian, and of the Evangelical Lutheran pastor. But to be worthy of the Church of Christian purity and of Christian freedom to which they be.ong, the Church of Luther and Melanchthon, of Arndt and Gerhard, of Spener and Francke, of Schwartz and Oberlin, of Muhlenberg and Harms, and of departed worthies, whose voices yet linger in our ears, they need a faith whose Confession shall be as articulate, as its convictions are deep.

This, then, is a summary of the result we reach : The basis of the Evangelical Lutheran Church is the Word of God, as the perfect and absolute Rule of Faith, and because this is her basis, she rests of necessity on the faith of which that Word is the Rule, and therefore on the Confessions which purely set forth that faith. She has the right rule, she reaches the right results by the rule, and rightly confesses them. This Confession then is her immediate basis, her essential char- Summary of acteristic, with which she stands or falls. The result. Unaltered Augsburg Confession and its Apology, the Catechisms and Schmalcald Articles, and the Formula of Concord, have been formally declared by an immense majority of the Lutheran Church as their Confession of Faith. The portion of the Church, with few and inconsiderable exceptions, which has not received them formally, has received them virtually. They are closely cohering and internally consistent statements and developments of one and the same system, so that a man who heartily and intelligently receives any one of the distinctively Lutheran Symbols, has no difficulty in accepting the doctrine of the whole. They fairly represent the Reasons for the faith of the Church, and simply and solely as so Confessional Ba- representing it are they named in the statement of sis. the basis of the Evangelical Lutheran Church. The real question, then, is this : Ought the Church to rest unreservedly and unchangeably on this faith as her doctrinal basis ? To this question, which is but the first repeated in a new shape, we reply, as we replied to the first, She ought.

I. She ought to rest on that basis, because that Faith of our Church, in all and each of its parts, is founded on 1. It is founded the Word of God, which she will not permit to be on God's Word. overruled, either by the speculations of corrupt reason, or by the tralition of a corrupted Church, but which Word she interprets under the ordinary, promised guidance of the Holy Spirit, as a Word in itself absolutely perfect for its ends, giving law to reason, and excluding tradition as any part, direct or indirect, of the Rule of Faith.

II. The proposition we have just advanced, no Lutheran, in the historical sense of the word, can deny; for the man who

2. It belongs to historical Lutheranism.

would deny it, would, in virtue of that denial, prove that he is not in the historical sense Lutheran ; for he, and he only, is such who believes that the doctrine of the gospel is rightly taught in the Augsburg Confession. We do not enter into the question, whether, in some sense, or in what sense, a man who denies this may be some kind of a Lutheran. We only affirm that he is not such in the historical sense of the word; that he is not what was meant by the name when it was first distinctively used — that is, not a Lutheran whom Luther, or the Lutheran Church for three centuries, would have recognized as such, nor such as the vast majority of the uncorrupted portions of our Church would now recognize.

III. That many of the Articles of Faith set forth by our Church are pure and Scriptural, is acknowledged by all nominal Christendom ; that an immense proportion of them is such, is confessed by all nominal Protestants. Zwingle declared that

3. Commended by other Communions.

there were no men on earth whose fellowship he so desired as that of the Wittenbergers. Calvin subscribed *the unaltered Augsburg Confession*, and acted as a Lutheran minister under it. "Nor do I repudiate the Augsburg Confession (which I long ago willingly and gladly subscribed) as its author has interpreted it." So wrote Calvin, in 1557, to Schalling. Two mistakes are often made as to his meaning, in these much-quoted words. First: The Confession he subscribed was not the Variata. Calvin subscribed at Strasburg, in 1539. The Variata did not appear till 1540. Second: He does not mean nor say that he *then* subscribed it as its author *had* explained it. There was no word of its author then, which even seemed in conflict with its original sense. Calvin means: Nor do I now repudiate it, as its author *has* interpreted it. The great Reformed divines have acknowledged that it has not a fundamental error in it. The only error they charge on it, they repeatedly declare to be non-fundamental. Testing all Churches by the concessions of their adversaries, there is not so safe and pure a Church in existence as our own. But not only in the Articles conceded by adversaries, but in those which are most strictly distinctive of our Church, and which have been the object of fiercest assault, is she pure and Scriptural, as, for example, in regard to the Person of Christ and the Sacraments.

IV. To true unity of the Church, is required hearty and honest consent in the *fundamental doctrine* of the gospel, or, in other words, in the Articles of Faith. It may surprise some, that we qualify the word doctrine by the word "*fun-* 4. Essential to *damental;*" for that word, in the history of the union in funda- Church, has been so bandied about, so miserably mentals. perverted, so monopolized for certain ends, so twisted by artifices of interpretation, as if a man could use it to mean anything he pleased, and might fairly insist that its meaning could only be settled by reference to his own mental reservation at the time he used it, that at length men have grown afraid of it, have looked upon its use as a mark of lubricity, and have almost imagined that it conveyed an idea unknown to our Church in her purer days. Nevertheless, it conveys a good old-fashioned Biblical and Lutheran idea — an idea set forth in the Confession of the Church, constantly presented by our old Theologians, and by no means dangerous when honestly and intelligently used. Thus the Apology says: " The Church retains the pure gospel, and, as Paul says, (1 Cor. iii. 12,) the *foundation*, (fundamentum,) that is, the true knowledge of Christ and faith. Although in this Church there are many who are weak, who ' build upon this *foundation*, wood, hay, stubble,' who, nevertheless, do not overthrow the *foundation*, they are still Christians."*

It is utterly false that Evangelical Lutherans are sticklers for non-fundamentals, that they are intolerant toward those who err in regard to non-fundamentals ; on the contrary, no Church, apart from the fundamentals of the gospel in which her unity and very life are involved, is so mild, so mediating

* Apology, (Müller,) p. 156.

so thoroughly tolerant as our own. Over against the unity of
Rome under a universal Head, the unity of High-Churchism
under the rule of Bishops, the unities which turn upon like
rites or usages as in themselves necessary, or which build up
the mere subtleties of human speculation into articles of faith,
over against these the Lutheran Church was the first to stand
forth, declaring that the unity of the Church turns upon
nothing that is of man. Where the one pure gospel of Christ
is preached, where the one foundation of doctrine is laid
where the " one faith " is confessed, and the alone divine Sacraments administered aright, there is the one Church ; this is
her unity. As the Augsburg Confession * declares : " The
Church, properly so called, hath her notes and marks, to wit:
the *pure and sound doctrine* of the gospel, and the right use of
the Sacraments. And, for the true unity of the Church, it is
sufficient *to agree upon the doctrine* of the gospel, and the
administration of the Sacraments."

Our fathers clearly saw and sharply drew the distinction
between God's foundation and man's superstructure, between
the essential and the accidental, between faith and opinion,
between religion and speculative theology, and, with all these
distinctions before them, declared, that consent in the doctrine
of the gospel and the right administration of the Sacraments
is the only basis of the unity of the Church. This basis, the
Lutheran Church has defined and rests on it, to abide there,
we trust, by God's grace, to the end of time.

In this basis of unity is implied, first of all, that, in a really
united Church, there shall be agreement as to what ·subjects
of the gospel teaching are to be considered its doctrine, or
articles of faith, or fundamentals, (for all these terms are here
practically synonymous,) and not either mere matters of opinion, or of secondary importance.

It is no evidence that two men or two parts of a Church are
really in unity because they say a certain creed is right on *fundamentals*, if it be not certain that they *agree as to what subjects of the gospel teaching are fundamental*. The Socinian and
Trinitarian are in unity of faith, and could alike accept the

---

* Art. VII.

Augsburg Confession as their creed, if it be granted that the Trinity is no doctrine of the gospel, no article of faith, no fundamental, but a mere nicety of theological speculation, or something, which the Scripture, if it sets it forth at all, sets forth in no vital relation to its essential truths. Before a Socinian and Trinitarian, therefore, can honestly test their unity by a formula, which declares that they agree in fundamentals, they must settle what are fundamentals. Otherwise the whole thing is a farce. Any formula of agreement on " fundamentals," which leaves it an open question what are fundamentals, is delusive and dishonest, and will ·ultimately breed dissension and tend to the destruction of the Church. We protest, therefore, alike against the basis which does not propose the fundamental doctrine of the gospel as essential to unity, and the basis, which, professing to accept the gospel fundamentals as its constituent element, is, in any degree whatever, dubious, or evasive, as to what subjects of gospel-teaching are fundamental, or which, pretending to define them, throws among non-fundamentals what the Word of God and the judgment of His Church have fixed as Articles of Faith. On such a point there should be no evasion. Divine Truth is the end of the Church; it is also her means. She lives for it, and she lives by it. What the Evangelical Lutheran Church regards as fundamental to gospel doctrine, that is, what her existence, her history, her Confessions declare or justly imply to be her articles of faith, these ought to be accepted as such by all honorable men, who bear her name.

But it is sometimes said, by very good men, as a summary answer to the whole argument for Confessions of Faith, that the very words of Scripture are a better Creed, than any we can substitute for them ; better, not only, as of course they are, on the supposition that our words are incorrect, but better even if our words are correct ; for our best words are man's words, but its words are the words of the Holy Ghost. But this argument, although it looks specious, is sophistical to the core. The very words of Scripture are not simply a *better* Rule of Faith than any that can be substituted for them, but they are the absolute and only Rule of Faith, for which nothing can be substituted. But the object of a *Creed* is not to find out what God teaches, (we go to the Bible for that,) but to show what we believe. Hence the moment I set forth even the very words of the Bible as *my Creed*, the question is no longer what does the Holy Ghost mean by those words, but what do *I* mean by them. You ask a Unitarian, What do you believe about Christ. He replies: "I believe that he is the Son of God." These are the very words of the Bible; but the point is not at all now, what do they mean in the Bible? but what do they mean as a Unitarian creed? In the *Rule of Faith*, they mean that Jesus Christ is the second person of the Trinity incarnate; in the Unitarian *Creed*, they mean that there is no Trinity, and that our Lord is a mere man. All heretics, if you probe them with the very words of the Bible, admit that these words are the truth. The Universalists for example, concede, that the "wicked go away into everlasting punishment." Now I know that in the Bible, *the Rule of Faith*, these words mean, a punishment without end; and I know just as well, that these identical words as a Universalist creed, mean, no future punishment at all, or one that does end. Yet with the fallacy of which we speak, do men evade the argument, for a clear, well-defined, and unmistakable creed.

The truth is that *correct human explanations* of Scripture doctrine are Scripture doctrine, for they are simply the statement of the same truth in different words. These words are not *in themselves* as clear and as good as the Scripture terms, but as those who use them can absolutely fix the sense of their own phraseology by a direct and infallible testimony, the human words may more perfectly exclude heresy than the divine words do. The term "Trinity," for example, does not, in itself, as clearly and as well express the doctrine of Scripture as the terms of the Word of God do; but it correctly and compendiously states that doctrine, and the trifler who pretends to receive the Bible, and yet rejects its doctrine of the Trinity, cannot pretend that he receives what the Church means by the word Trinity. While the Apostles lived the Word was both a rule of faith, and in a certain sense, a confession of it; when

Marginal note: Fidelity to the Confession not inconsistent with the Supreme Authority of the Rule of Faith.

by direct inspiration a holy man utters certain words, they are
to him both a rule of faith, and a confession of faith —they at
once express both what he is to believe and what he does
believe ; but when the Canon was complete, when its authors
were gone, when the living teacher was no longer at hand to
correct the errorist who distorted his word, the Church entered
on her normal and abiding relation to the Word and the Creed
which is involved in these words: the Bible is the rule of faith,
but not the confession of it ; the Creed is not the rule of faith,
but is the confession of it. A Lutheran is a Christian whose
rule of faith is the Bible, and whose creed is the Augsburg
Confession.

To what end then is the poor sophism constantly iterated,
that the Confession is a "human explanation of divine doctrine"? So is the faith of every man — all that he deduces
from the Bible. There is no personal Christianity in the world
which is not the result of a human explanation of the Bible
as really as the Confession of our Church is. It is human because it is in human minds, and human hearts, — it is not a
source to which we can finally and absolutely appeal as we can
to God's word. But in exact proportion as the word of God
opened to the soul by the illumination of the Holy Spirit, is
truly and correctly apprehended, just in that proportion is the
" human explanation " coincident with the divine truth. I explain God's truth, and if I explain it correctly, my explanation
is God's truth, and to reject the one in unbelief, is to reject
the other. " Our Father who art in heaven," is a human explanation by certain English scholars of certain words used
by our Lord ; but they are correct explanations, and as such
are as really divine as those sounds in Aramaic or Greek which
fell from the lips of our Lord. The difference is this : His
words are absolutely final ; they are themselves the source of
truth, beyond which we cannot rise. Our English words are
to be tested by his — and when we believe they truly represent
his, we receive them as his. For the essence of the word is not
its sound, but its sense.

Our English translation of the Bible is a human explanation
of a certain humanly transcribed, humanly printed text, the

original; which original alone, just as the sacred penman left it, is absolutely in every jot and tittle God's Word; but just in proportion as our translation is based upon a pure text of the Hebrew and Greek, and correctly explains the meaning of such an original, it too, is God's Word. Our sermons are human explanations of God's Word, but so far as they explain it correctly, they do set forth God's Word, and he who hears us, hears our Lord. Our Confession is a human explanation of God's Word, but so far as it correctly explains it, it sets forth God's Word. The man who regards it as a correct explanation, or as " a summary and just exhibition " of the doctrines of which it treats, is consistently a Lutheran. No other man is. If any man can define Lutheran consistency in any better way, we should be glad to have him do it; and if he thinks human explanations are something antagonistic to scriptural doctrine, we wish to know, if he be a clergyman or a Sunday-school teacher, or a father, why he spends so many Sundays in the year in setting forth his " human explanation " to his people or his class or his children, instead of teaching them Hebrew and Greek. If he says that he believes that the " human explanations " of the authorized version he reads, and of the sermons he preaches to his people, or the instructions he gives to his pupils or his children, are scriptural, because they agree with Scripture, we ask him to believe that his church in her faith, that the " human explanations " of her Confession (framed in earnest, prayerful study of the Holy Scriptures, and in the promised light of the Holy Spirit) are correct and scriptural, may have as much to justify her as he has in his confidence in his own sermons, or his own lessons. We do not claim that our Confessors were infallible. We do not say they could not fail. We only claim that they did not fail.

Those who smile at the utterance of a devout Father of the Church: 'I believe it, because it is impossible '— Fidelity to the Confessions, not Romanizing. smile because they do not understand him; yet there would seem to be no solution but that given in the absurdest sense of his words, for an objection sometimes made to a hearty acceptance of the Lutheran Confession — to wit, that such an acceptance is Romanizing. Yet there are those who affect to believe that men who maintain the duty of an honorable consistency with the Confessions of our Church, are cherishing a Romish tendency. If this meant that the doctrines of our Church really have this tendency, then it would be the duty of all sound Protestants to disavow those doctrines, and with them the name of the church with which they are inseparably connected. While men call themselves Lutherans, that fact will go further before the unthinking world in favor of the Lutheran Confessions, than all their protestations will go against them. If the Lutheran Church be a Romanizing Church, we ought neither to bear the stigma of her name, nor promote her work of mischief by giving her such aid as may be derived from our own. But if the charge meant that those stigmatized have this Romish tendency, because they are not true to the Confessions of our Church, the thing really implied is, that they are not Lutheran enough — in other words, that the danger of apostasy is connected, not with fidelity to the Confession, but with want of fidelity. If this were the point which it is meant to press, we would heartily agree with those who press it ; and we would help them with every energy, to detect and expose those who would cloak their Romanism under a perversion of our Confession, as others defend their fanaticism and heresies, under the pretence that the Confession is in error. As genuine Lutheranism is most Biblical among systems which professedly ground themselves on the supreme authority of God's word ; as it is most evangelical among the systems that magnify our Saviour's grace, so is our Church at once most truly Catholic among all churches which acknowledge that the faith of God's people is one, and most truly Protestant among all bodies claiming to be Protestant. She is the mother of all true Protestantism. Her Confession at Augsburg, is the first official statement of Scriptural doctrine and usage ever issued against Romish heresy and corruption. Her confessions are a wall of adamant against Romanism. The names of Luther and her heroes who are among the dead still hold the first place among those of the opponents of Rome. The doctrines of our Church have proved themselves the most mighty of all doctrines in winning men from Rome, **and**

strongest of all doctrines in fixing the hearts of men, as a bul
wark against all her efforts to regain the ground she had lost.
The anathemas of the Council of Trent are almost all levelled
at our Church ; her soldiers have poured forth their blood on
the battle-field, and the spirits of her martyrs have taken
flight from the scaffold and the stake, in preserving, amid
Romish conspiracies and persecution, the truth she gave them.
Without our Church, there would be, so far as human sight
may pierce, no Protestantism on the face of the earth at this
hour, and without her Confession she would have perished
from among men.   It cannot be that loyalty to the Protestantism she made and saved, can demand treachery to that by
which she made and saved it.   It cannot be that fidelity to the
truth which overthrew Romanism, can involve connivance
with Romanism itself.

But there are others who, acknowledging for themselves the
force of all that can be urged for the Confessions, and not unwilling for themselves to adopt them, look with desponding
eye on the facts which seem to them to show that there can
be no large general acceptance in this country, so unchurchly
and unhistoric as it is, of these Confessions.   Were we to grant
the gloomiest supposition possible, that would not affect our
duty.   Suppose it were true, that the arguments for the pure
doctrine of the Confessions seem to have little weight with men,
shall we cease to urge them ?   After Nineteen Centuries of
struggle, Christianity is in minority in the world.   After the
evidences of Christianity have been urged for some three centuries, there are many deists, more open and avowed even than
at the Reformation.   After centuries of argument for the
Trinity, there are, perhaps, more Socinians than ever.   After
three centuries, in which the pure doctrine of justification has
been urged, millions in the Romish Church and very many
nominal Protestants reject it.   With all the arguments for infant baptism, with the proofs urged so long and so ably for the
validity of other modes of Baptism than immersion, how many
millions of Baptists there are !   With the clear testimony of
Scripture and History for the perpetual obligation of the two
Sacraments, how many Friends there are (and their number is

increasing in Great Britain,) who deny it altogether! How little headway a pure and consistent faith in the gospel makes, after so many centuries! But what have we to do with all this? Our business is to hold and urge the truth in all its purity, whether men will hear, or whether they will forbear. Truth will, at length, reach its aim and do its work. The faithful defence of the most bitterly contested doctrines has, for centuries, helped to keep millions sound in the faith, and has reclaimed many that had wandered. This very time of ours has seen the revival of the faith of our Church from all the thraldom of rationalism. In the masses of the people, and among the greatest theologians of the age, intense faith has been reproduced in the very doctrines of the Confession, which find the greatest obstacles in the weakness of human nature or in the pride of the heart of man.

But if we must have a Creed, it is sometimes urged, why have one less comprehensive than Christianity in its widest sense? Why have a Creed which will exclude from a particular church, any man whom we acknowledge possibly to be a Christian? Why exclude from the Church militant, or from our part of it, the man we expect to Wide Creeds. meet in the glories of the Church triumphant? Does not such a course set up a claim for the particular Church, as if it were the Church universal? Does it not substitute a sectarian orthodoxy for a Christian one? This theory, which logically runs into the assertion that no particular church should exclude from its communion any but those who, it is prepared to assert, will certainly be lost, is, if fairly put, hardly specious, and in the adroitness of the many ways in which it actually meets us is merely specious. It goes upon a body of false assumptions. The Church is not merely designed, as this theory assumes, to bring into outward association, men who are to get to heaven, but its object is to shed upon the race every kind of blessing in the present life. The Church is bound to have regard in her whole work, and in her whole sphere, to her entire mission — even though it should require the exclusion of a man whose imbecility, ignorance, and erratic perverseness God may forgive, but which would ruin the Church.

What is Christianity in its "widest" sense? How "wide' must it be? Is Mohammedanism a corrupt Christianity? Is every Unitarian, every Pelagian, every Swedenborgian, lost? Has a "wide" Christianity, Baptism, and the Lord's Supper? If it has, it excludes Elizabeth Fry, and Joseph John Gurney, because they were Friends. If it has not, it tramples on our Lord's commands. Can a particular Church which holds that Immersion is not a necessary mode, be the home of a man who teaches that it is? As long as there is a man in the world who wishes to make Christianity "wider" than you do, you must yield, unless you feel sure that the man must be lost. What! will you have your Church so narrow, that he who is to get to heaven shall not be of it? Never, if you wish to be consistent. The moment you do it, you have your Church militant which excludes a part of the Church triumphant.

But the theory assumes another great fallacy — which is, that there is some fixed standard of responsibility, some ascer-
Fallacies of the argument. tainable minimum of what is necessary to salvation, in the case of *each man.* But there is no such standard: the responsibility has a wide range, for it embraces, except in the extremest cases of ignorance and weakness, far more than is necessary for the salvation of *every man. Much* is required from him to whom *much* is given. He only has merely the responsibility which belongs to *every man,* who has no more than that which is given to *every man.* He who has all the opportunity of knowing God's whole truth, and God's whole will, will not be saved on the standard of the Caffre or the Digger. To make that which is essential to *every* man the standard, to put it at the minimum at which *any* creature could be saved, would be to encourage the lowering of the faith and life of millions, to reach at best a few cases. But even in this minimum, particular Churches would differ — and still some would exclude from the Church militant, those whom others regarded as possibly part of the Church triumphant.

There is another fallacy involved in this theory. The Creed does not, as this theory assumes, exclude from membership those who merely have a defective faith — it is only those who teach against a part of the faith or deny it publicly whom it shuts out. Ignorance and mental imbecility may prevent many from comprehending certain parts of a system, but no particular church, however rigid, designs to exclude such from its Communion.

The theory ignores the fact that the Church should make the standard of faith, and morals, the highest possible, not the lowest. She should lead men, not to the least faith, the least holiness which makes salvation possible, but to the very highest — she should not encourage the religion whose root is a selfish fear of hell, a selfish craving of heaven, but she should plant that religion to which pure truth is dear for its own sake, which longs for the fullest illumination, which desires not the easy road, but the sure one.

This theory, too, in asserting that there is a false assumption of catholicity in such exclusions as it condemns, forgets that the only discipline in the Church Universal is that now exercised by the particular Churches. A pure particular Church is not a sect, but is of the Church Catholic. The particular Church must meet its own responsibility — it claims no more than the right to exclude from its own com- Force and ex-munion — and does not pretend to force any other tent of excommunication. particular Church to respect its discipline. If we exclude a man for what we believe to be heresy, that does not prevent his union with another part of the Church which regards his view as orthodox. The worship of what we believe to be a wafer, may exclude a man from our Communion, but it will prepare for him a welcome to the Church of Rome, which believes that wafer to be incarnate God. There such a man belongs. His exclusion does not deny that a man may believe in Transubstantiation and yet be saved. Nor let it be forgotten that no excommunication is valid unless it be authorized of God. All the fulminations of all the particular Churches on earth combined cannot drive out of God's kingdom the man he is pleased to keep in it. If the excommunication be righteous, no man dare object to it; if it be unrighteous, the man has not been excluded by it from the Church militant. No man can be really kept or forced out of the Church militant except by God's act or his own.

Let us now test the principle by a particular case. The doc. trine of the Lord's Supper is the one which in the whole com. pass of Lutheran doctrine has been most objected to on the ground just stated. The objector to specific Creeds asks, whether the Lutheran doctrine of the Sacrament is a part of *Christian* orthodoxy, or only of *Lutheran* orthodoxy? We reply, that it is a part of both. *Lutheran* orthodoxy, if it be really orthodoxy, is, of necessity, *Christian* orthodoxy, for there is no other. The Lutheran doctrinal system, *if* it be orthodox, is, of necessity, Scriptural and Christian. If we admit that the doctrine of the Sacrament taught by our Church is taught also in the New Testament, the error to which it is opposed is, of course, inconsistent with the New Testament, and, therefore, with Christianity. Either the Lutheran doctrine on the Sacrament is Christian, or it is not. If it be not Christian, then it is not orthodoxy ; if it be Christian, then the opposite of it is, of necessity, not Christian. As we under- stand the questioner to reason with us on our own ground. and to grant our supposition, for argument's sake, we regard his question as really answering itself, as we cannot suppose that he maintains, that two conflicting systems can both be sound, two irreconcilable statements both truthful, two doc- trines, destructive of each other, both orthodox.

But, inasmuch as this exact construction of the drift of the question makes the answer to it so obvious, we are inclined to think that its point is somewhat different, and that what is meant, is, Whether it be necessary to a man's being a Christian in general, or only to his being a Lutheran Christian, that he should be sound in this doctrine? To this we reply that, to

Whom may the perfect ideal of a Christian in general, it is we recognize as essential that he should embrace the whole faith Christians? of the gospel, and that defective or false faith in regard to the sacraments, so far mars, as defective faith on any point will, the perfect ideal. *All other things being equal,* the Christian, who does not hold the New Testament doctrine of the Sacrament, is by so much, short of the perfect ideal reached, on this point, by the man who does hold that doc- trine ; or, supposing, as we do suppose, that this doctrine is purely held by our Church, by so much does the non-Lutheran Christian fall short of the full life of faith of the Lutheran Christian. It is in the "unity of the faith" that we are to "come to the *fulness* of the stature of perfect men in Christ Jesus." But the question still seems so easy of solution, that we apprehend another point may be: Can a man be a Christian, who does not receive what, on our supposition, as a Lutheran, is the New Testament orthodoxy in regard to the Sacrament? If this be the point, we unhesitatingly reply, that a man may here be in unconscious error, and be a Christian. A man, who sees that the New Testament teaches a doctrine, and yet rejects it, is not a Christian. The man who never has thoroughly examined the New Testament evidence on the subject, and this is the position of many, is so far lacking in honesty. The man who grossly misrepresents the doctrine, and coarsely vilifies it, is guilty of a great crime. Here the decision involves no difficulty, and yet it is one of the hardest practical questions to determine, what amount of inconsistency with the demands of Christianity is necessary to prove a man to be no Christian; and this difficult question pertains not alone to the faith of the Christian, but to his life; it is both doctrinal and practical. Certainly, there are many points of a self-consistent New Testament morality, in which men come fearfully short, whom we yet think we are bound to consider as Christians — weak, inconsistent, and in great peril, yet still Christians. It is hazardous, indeed, to provide for any degree of aberration in Christian morals or in Christian faith. Our Church is a liberal Church, in the true sense; she is liberal with what belongs to her, but not liberal in giving away her Master's goods, contrary to His order. The truth, in its minutest part, she does not trifle with. For herself and her children, she must hold it with uncompromising fidelity. But she heartily believes, that, even where some portion of the truth is lost or obscured, God may, through what is left, perpetuate a Christian life. She believes that God has His own blessed ones, kept through His almighty grace, through all Christendom. She believes, that, in the Romish Church, Pascal and Fenelon, and many of the obscure and unknown, were

13

true followers of Jesus; she believes that Christ may preserve many of His own there now. Even in considering the Pope as in his claims and assumptions an Antichrist, she does not exclude him as a person from the possibility of salvation; but she dares not let go her truthful testimony against Romish Christians in the Church of Rome. errors. She dare not let her children think that it is a matter of indifference, whether they hold to justification by faith, or justification by works, or, as regards the Sacrament, hold to the *opus operatum*, Transubstantiation, and the Mass, or to the pure doctrine she confesses. And here we throw back upon such an objector his own question. He acknowledges that Luther was a Christian before he left the Church of Rome, and that God has His own saints, even under the corrupt system of that Church. Are his own views, then, against the *opus operatum*, against Transubstantiation and the Mass, a part of *Christian* orthodoxy, or only of *Protestant* orthodoxy? Shall our *Protestant* creeds exclude a man from our Protestant Churches and Pulpits, because he is a *Romanist*, who, we yet acknowledge, may be God's child, and an heir of heaven? As to the great Communions, whose distinctive life originated in the Era of the Reformation, the case is no less clear. We need hardly say how heartily we acknowledge, that, in the Evangelical Protestant Churches, in their ministry and people, there are noble exemplifications of Christian grace. Nevertheless, we do not believe that there is a Christian living, who would not be more perfect as a Christian, in a pure New Testament faith in regard to the Sacraments, than he can be in human error regarding them, and we believe that pure New Testament faith to be the faith which is confessed by our Church. At the same time, we freely acknowledge, that, as Channing, though a Unitarian, was Christians in the Protestant Churches. more lovely morally than many a Trinitarian, so, much more, may some particular Christians, who are in error on the matter of the Sacraments, far surpass in Christian grace some individuals, who belong to a Church, whose sacramental faith is pure. Some men are on the level of their systems, some rise above them, some fall below them.

A human body may not only live, but be healthy, in which one lobe of the lungs is gone; another may be sickly and die, in which the lungs are perfect. Nevertheless, the complete lungs are an essential part of a perfect human body. We still truly call a man a man, though he may have lost arms and legs; we still call a hand a hand, though it may have lost a finger, or be distorted. While, therefore, we freely call systems and men Christian, though they lack a sound sacramental doctrine, we none the less consider that doctrine essential to a complete Christian system, and to the perfect faith of a Christian man. The man who has lost an arm, we love none the less. If he has lost it by carelessness, we pity his misfortune, yet we do not hold him free from censure. But, when he insists, that, to have two arms, is a blemish, and proposes to cut off one of ours, then we resist him. ⌐Somewhere on earth, if the gates of hell have not prevailed against the Church, there is a Communion whose fellowship involves no departure from a solitary article of Christian faith — and no man should be willing to be united with any other Communion. The man who is sure there is no such Communion is bound to put forth the effort to originate it. He who knows of no Creed which is true to the Rule of Faith, in all its articles, should at once prepare one that is. Every Christian is bound either to find a Church on Earth, pure in its whole faith, or to make one. On the other hand, he who says that the Church is wrong, confesses in that very assertion, that if the Church be right, he is an errorist; and that in asking to share her communion while he yet denies her doctrine, he asks her to adopt the principle that error is to be admitted to her bosom, for as an errorist and only as an errorist can she admit him.

But the practical result of this principle is one on which there is no need of speculating; it works in one unvarying way. When error is admitted into the Course of Error in the Church. Church, it will be found that the stages of its progress are always three. It begins by asking *toleration.* Its friends say to the majority: You need not be afraid of us; we are few, and weak; only let us alone; we shall not disturb the faith of others. The Church has her standards of doctrine; of course we shall never interfere with them ; we only ask for ourselves to be spared interference with our private opinions. Indulged in this for a time, error goes on to assert *equal rights*. Truth and error are two balancing forces. The Church shall do nothing which looks like deciding between them ; that would be partiality. It is bigotry to assert any superior right for the truth. We are to agree to differ, and any favoring of the truth, because it is truth, is partisanship. What the friends of truth and error hold in common is fundamental. Anything on which they differ is *ipso facto* non-essential. Anybody who makes account of such a thing is a disturber of the peace of the church. Truth and error are two co-ordinate powers, and the great secret of church-statesmanship is to preserve the balance between them. From this point error soon goes on to its natural end, which is to assert *supremacy*. Truth started with *tolerating ;* it comes to be merely tolerated, and that only for a time. Error claims a preference for its judgments on all disputed points. It puts men into positions, not as at first in spite of their departure from the Church's faith, but in consequence of it. Their recommendation is that they repudiate that faith, and position is given them to teach others to repudiate it, and to make them skilful in combating it.

So necessary, so irresistible are these facts, and the principles they throw into light, that we find in history the name of the Evangelical Lutheran Church, from the hour of its first distinctive use, linked for centuries with one unvarying feature everywhere. Divided among nationalities, speaking diverse tongues, developing different internal tendencies within certain Fidelity of the limits, and without absolute identity as to the Lutheran Church universal recognition of certain books as standards to her Confession. of doctrine, we find one unchanging element ; the Evangelical Lutheran Church accepted the Augsburg Confession as scriptural throughout. Such a phenomenon as an Evangelical Lutheran claiming the right of assailing a doctrine taught in the Augsburg Confession was unknown.

When Spener, Francke, and the original Pietistic school sought to develop the spiritual life of the Church, they did it by enforcing the doctrines of the Church in their living power.

They accomplished their work by holding more firmly and exhibiting more completely in all their aspects the doctrines of the Reformation, confessed at Augsburg. The position of them all was that the doctrines of our Church are the doctrines of God's Word, that no changes were needed, or could be allowed in them; that in doctrine her Reformation was complete, and that her sole need was by sound discipline to maintain, and by holy activity to exhibit, practically, her pure faith. These men of God and the great theologians they influenced, and the noble missionaries they sent forth, held the doctrines of the Church firmly. They wrought those great works, the praises of which are in all Christendom, through these very doctrines. They did not mince them, nor draw subtle distinctions by which to evade or practically ignore them, but, alike upon the most severely controverted, as upon the more generally recognized, doctrines of our Church, they were thoroughly Lutheran. They held the Sacramental doctrines of our Church tenaciously, and defended the faith of the Church in regard to Baptism and the Lord's Supper, as they did all her other doctrines. It was Semler and Bahrdt, Gabler, Wegscheider and Bretschneider, and men of their class, who first invented, or acted on, the theory that men could be Lutherans, and assail the doctrines of the Church. Better men than those whose names we have mentioned were influenced and perverted in different degrees by the rationalistic spirit of the time. They did not assail the doctrines of the Church, but they either passed them by in silence, or defended them with a reservedness practically equivalent to a betrayal. It looked as if the edifice of our fathers' faith might be utterly overthrown. As Deism was eating away the spiritual life of the Episcopal Church of England and of the Presbyterian Church of Scotland; as Socinianism was laying waste the Independent Churches of the same lands, as at a later period it rolled over New England; as Atheism swept away Romanism in France; so did Rationalism rear itself in the Lutheran Church. Established as our Church was on God's Word, what could move her but to take from her that Word, or to lead her to some new and false mode of interpreting it? This was the

Character of Rationalism.

work of Rationalism — to pretend to hold the Word, but to corrupt its sense, so that the Confession and the Word should no longer seem to correspond. The mischief seemed to be incurable; but God did not forsake his own work. The evil brought its own cure. The mischief wrought until it was found that the idea of men calling themselves by the name of a Church, and yet claiming the right to assail its doctrines, was the idea of Infidelity in the bud — it was Belial allowed to take shelter under the hem of the garment of Christ. Any man who will read thoughtfully the history of Rationalism in Europe, and of the Unionism which is now too often its stronghold, will not wonder at the earnestness of true Lutheranism in Germany, and of Synods which are in affinity with it, in maintaining a pure Confession. He will have no difficulty in comprehending their indisposition to tolerate indifferentism, rationalism, and heresy, under the pretencé of union. They cannot call bitter sweet, while their lips are yet wet with the wormwood which was forced upon them.

The history of Rationalism in our Church will show certain phases, of which we will offer a hint:

I. In the first place, the doctrine of the Church was conceded to be true, but its relative importance was detracted History of Rationalism. from. It was argued that doctrinal theories should be thrown into the background, and that directly practical and experimental truths, separated from their true connections in the profounder doctrines, should be exclusively urged. (Pseudo-Pietism and Fanaticism.)

II. From an impaired conviction of the value of these conceded doctrines, grew a disposition to ignore the doctrines which divided the Lutheran and Reformed Communions. The Divine Word was not to be pressed in cases in which there was a reluctance to accept its teachings. From this arose Urionistic efforts on the basis of a general Protestant orthodoxy, and an assimilation on the part of the Lutheran Church to the Reformed basis, tendency, and doctrine.

III. From the disposition to undervalue and ignore these doctrines, arose the feeling that if they could be entirely set aside, there would be a great gain to the cause of unity. Why ugree to differ, when, by a free criticism, the very causes of differences could be thrown out of the way? These distinctive doctrines originated in too strict a conception of the inspiration and weight of the Bible language. Why not liberalize its interpretation? Thus arose the earlier and more moderate rationalism of Semler and of his School.

IV. Then came the beginning of the end. Men, still in the outward communion of the Church, claimed the right to submit all its doctrines to their critical processes. Refined and Vulgar Rationalism, mainly distinguished by their degrees of candor, divided the ministry, carried away the Reformed Church, and, to a large extent, even the Romish, with our own, broke up the liturgical, catechetical, and hymnological life, and destroyed the souls of the people. Unblushing infidelity took on it the livery of the Church. Men had rejected the Faith of the Rule, and were still good Lutherans. Why not reject the Rule of Faith, and be good Lutherans? The Faith of those men of the olden time, men who were, by more than two centuries, wiser than their fathers, had proved to be mere human speculation. Why might not the Rule be? They soon settled that question, and the Bible was flung after the Confession, and men were allowed to be anything they pleased to be, and to bear any name they chose. The less Lutheran they were in the old sense of the word, the more were they Lutherans in the new sense. They not only insisted on being called Lutherans, but insisted they were the only genuine Lutherans. Had not Luther disenthralled the human mind? Was not the Reformation simply an assertion of the powers of human reason, and of the right of private judgment? Was it not an error of Luther's dark day, that, when he overthrew the fear of the Pope, he left the fear of God — which simply substitutes an impalpable Papacy for a visible one? Would not Luther, if he had only been so happy as to have lived to read their writings, certainly have been brought over to the fullest liberty? Who could doubt it? So out of the whole work of the Reformer, the only positive result which they regarded him as having reached was embraced in the well-known lines, which there is, indeed, no evidence that he wrote, but which are so far in advance of everything in his indubitably genuine works, as to be, in their eyes, supra-canonical, to wit:

Wer nicht liebt Wein, Weib und Gesang,
Der bleibt ein Narr sein Leben lang.

This is all they have left as fundamental in the Reformer's creed. Such is the Genesis, and such the Revelation of the European History of the sort of Lutheranism which claims the right to mutilate and assail the faith of the Church. Ought we not to tremble at it and take heed how we make a single step toward its terrible fallacy and its fearful results?

In the great mercy of God a reaction and revival in the true sense is taking place. It goes on in the Old World. It goes on in the New. The work is going on, and will go on, until the old ways have been found — till the old banner again floats on every breeze, and the old faith, believed, felt, and lived, shall restore the Church to her primal glory and holy strength. God speed the day! For our Church's name, her history, her sorrows, and her triumphs, her glory in what has been, her power for the good yet to be, all are bound up with the principle that purity in the faith is first of all, such a first, that without it there can be no true second.

Restoration of the Church Faith.

VI.

THE CONFESSIONS OF THE CONSERVATIVE REFORMATION.

THE PRIMARY CONFESSION. THE CONFESSION OF AUGSBURG.*

--- ———

IT is with a solemn and holy delight we have learned to traverse the venerable edifice, which the hands of our fathers erected in the sixteenth century. There is none of the glitter which catches and fascinates the childish eye, but all possesses that solid grandeur which fills the soul. Every part harmonizes with the whole, and conspires in

Spirit of the Reformation.

* The Bibliography we propose to give, in the notes to this dissertation, is not a general one, but is confined to the works which are in the hands of the writer, and, with a few exceptions, in his library. It will be found, however, to embrace all that are of the highest importance, so far as the diligence of the collector, stretching itself over years, has been able to bring them together. We give in this note only the Bibliography of the Bibliography of the Confession.

I. Notices in works of a *general* character.

BUDDEI Isagoge (1730) 426, 437.—NOESSELT, J. A.: Anweisung (3d ed. 1818) ii. 272. — PLANCK, G. J.: Einleitung (1795) ii. 592. — DANZ: Encyclopædie (1832) 415. — WALCH: Bibliotheca Theologica (1757) i. 327–362, iv. 1099. — NIEMEYER: Prediger Bibliothek (1784) iii. 63–69. — NOESSELT: Kenntniss Bücher (1790) § 507, 508. — FUHRMANN: Handbuch der Theolog. Literat. (1819) ii. a. 500, 507.— ERSCH: Literatur der Theologie. (1822) 119. — DANZ: Universal Wörterbuch (1843) 96, 186, 921. Supplem. 22. — WINER: Handbuch. (3d ed. 1838) i. 323, 572 ii. 316. Supplem. (1842) 53.—KAYSERS: Index Librorum, Confession, etc.

II. *Special* notices of its Literature.

PFAFF, C. M.: Introd. in Histor. Theolog. Liter. Tubing. 1726. iii. 385–416.— Jo. ALB. FABRICIUS Centifolium Lutheranum (Hamb. 1728–30. ii. 8) i. 104–144,

the proof that their work was not to pull down, but to erect
The spirit of the Reformation was no destroying angel, who
sat and scowled with a malignant joy over the desolation which
spread around. It was overshadowed by the wings of that
Spirit who brooded indeed on the waste of waters and the
wilderness of chaos, but only that he might unfold the germs
of life that lay hidden there, and bring forth light and order
from the darkness of the yet formless and void creation. It
is vastly more important, then, to know what the Reformation
retained than what it overthrew; for the overthrow of error,
though often an indispensable prerequisite to the establishment
of truth, is not truth itself; it may clear the foundation, simply to substitute one error for another, perhaps a greater for a
less. Profoundly important, indeed, is the history of that
which the Reformation accomplished against the errors of
Romanism, yet it is as nothing to the history of that which it
accomplished for itself. The overthrow of Romanism was not

ii. 583–606.—Bibliotheca REIMANNIANA (1731) p. 403.—WALCHII, J. G.: Intro-
ductio in Libr. Symbol. Jena, 1732. 196–257.—WALCHII, J. G.: Religions-
streitigkeiten der Evang. Luth. Kirche. Jena, 2d ed. 1733–1739. i. 35. iv. 4.—
WALCH, J. G.: Chr. Concordienb. Jena, 1750. p. 21.—BAUMGARTEN, S. J.: Er-
läuterungen der Symb. Schriften. Halle, 1761. p. 54–60.—WALCHII, C. G. F.:
Breviar. Theolog. Symb. Eccl. Luth. Göttingen, 1765. p. 69–75.—BAUMGARTEN,
S. J.: Geschichte der Religions-partheyen. Halle, 1866. p. 1150–1153.—J. W.
FEUERLEN: Bibliotheca Symbolica—edid. J. BARTH. RIEDERER (Norimb. 1768.)
8. p. 70 seq.—KOECHER: Bibliotheca theologiae symbolicae et catecheticæ item-
que liturgica. Guelferb. 1751. 114–137.—H. W. ROTERMUND: Geschichte, etc.,
(1829) p. 192–203.—SEMLERI: Apparatus ad Libr. Symbol. Eccl. Luth. Halae
Mag. 1775. pp. 39, 42.—BECK, C. D.: Commentar. histor. decret. relig. chr. et
formulae Lutheriae. Leipz., 1801. p. 148, 794.—TITTMANN, J. A. H.: Instit.
Symbolic. ad Sentent. Eccles. Evang. Lipsiae, 1811. p. 92.—UKERT: Luther's
Leben. Gotha, 1817. i. 227–293.—FUHRMANN: Handwörterbuch der Christ.
Relig. u. Kirchengesch. Halle, 1826. i. 537.—YELIN: Versuch einer histor-
liter. Darst. der Symbol. Schriften. Nürnberg, 1829. p. 67.—PFAFF, K.: Ge-
schichte des Reichst. zu Augsburg. Stuttg., 1830. p. v.-x.—BRETSCHNEIDER: Sys-
temat. Entwickelung. Leipz., (1804). 4th ed. 1841. 81–86.—C. A. HASE: Libr.
Symb Lips., 1827 (1845) proleg. iii.—J. T. L. DANZ: Die Augsb. Confess., etc.
(1829) 1–4.—KÖLLNER: Symb. der Luther. Kirche. Hamburg, 1837. p. 150–
152.—GUEREKE, H. E. F.: Symbolik (1839), 3d Aufl. Leipz., 1861. 104–110.—
MÜLLER, J. T.: Symb. Bücher. Stuttg., 1848. xv. xvii.—MATTHES, K.: Compar.
Symbolik. Leipz., 1854. p. 76.—HERZOG: Real Encyclop. Hamb., 1864. i.
234.—HOFMANN: Rud. Symbolik. Leipz., 1857. p. 284.—CORPUS REFORMATO-
RUM, (1857), vol. xxvi. Pars Prior. 101–111. 201–204.

its primary object; in a certain sense it was not its object at all. Its object was to establish truth, no matter what might rise or fall in the effort. Had the Reformation assumed the form which some who have since borne the name of Protestants would have given it, it would not even have been a splendid failure; the movement which has shaken and regenerated a world would have ended in few miserable squabbles, a few *autos da fe;* and the record of a history, which daily makes the hearts of thousands burn within them, would have been exchanged for some such brief notice as this: that an irascible monk, named Luder, or Luther, and a few insane coadjutors, having foolishly attempted to overthrow the holy Roman See, and remaining obstinate in their pernicious and detestable heresies, were burned alive, to the glory of God and the Virgin Mary, and to the inexpressible satisfaction of all the faithful. The mightiest weapon which the Reformation employed against Rome was, not Rome's errors, but Rome's truths. It professed to make no discoveries, to find no unheard-of interpretations but taking the Scriptures in that very sense to which the greatest of her writers had assented, uncovering the law and the gospel of God which she retained, applying them as her most distinguished and most honored teachers had applied them, though she had made them of none effect by her traditions, the Reformation took into its heart the life-stream of sixteen centuries, and came forth in the stature and strength of a Christianity, grown from the infancy of primitive ages, to the ripened manhood of that maturer period. There was no fear of truth, simply because Rome held it, and no disposition to embrace error, because it might be employed with advantage to Rome's injury. While it established broadly and deeply the right of private judgment, it did not make that abuse of it which has since been so common. From the position, that the essential truths of the word of God are clear to any Christian mind that examines them properly, it did not leap to the conclusion, that a thousand generations or a thousand examiners were as likely, or more likely, to be wrong than one. They allowed no *authority* save to the word of God, but they listened respectfully to the witness of believers of all time.

The tone which is imparted to the mind and heart, by the theology of the Reformation, is just what we now most need. But where are we to commence, it may be asked, in the infinite Importance of variety of works that have been written about the the Confessions. Reformation and its theology? "Art is long and life is fleeting." And how is the clergyman to find the books, or buy them when found, or read them when bought, destitute, as he is too wont to be, alike of money and time? We reply, that an immense treasure lies in a narrow compass, and within the reach of every minister in our land. By a careful study of the symbolical books of our Church, commencing with the Augsburg Confession and its Apology, a more thorough understanding of the history, difficulties, true genius, and triumphs of the Reformation will be attained, than by reading everything that can be got, or that has ever been written *about* that memorable movement. It is, indeed, too much the fashion now to read *about* things, to the neglect of the great original sources themselves. In general literature much is written and read about Homer and Shakspeare, until these great poets attract less attention than their critics. In theology it is the prevailing practice to have students read introductions to the Bible, and essays on various features of it, to such a degree that the Bible itself, except in an indirect form, is hardly studied at all, and the student, though often introduced to it, never fairly makes its acquaintance. All these illustrative works, if well executed, have their value; but that value presupposes such a general acquaintance with the books to which they serve as a guide, as is formed by every man for himself who carefully examines them. The greatest value of every work of the human mind, after all, generally lies in that which needs no guide, no critic, no commentator. Their labors may display more clearly, and thus enhance, this value, and are not to be despised; but their subject is greater than themselves, and they are useful only when they lead to an accurate and critical knowledge of that with which a general acquaintance has been formed by personal examination. It is now conceded, for example, that in the order of nature the general knowledge of language must precede an accurate, grammatical acquaintance with it. They may be formed indeed together, part preceding part, but if they must be separated, the general is better than the scientific. If, in a library, there were two cases, one containing all the Latin grammars and the other all the Latin classics, and one boy was kept six years to the classics and another six years to the grammars, the first would understand the language practically, the second would understand nothing, not even the grammar.

And this principle it is easy to apply as regards its bearings on those great masterly treatises which form our Symbolical books. *They are parts of the Reforma-* Relations to the Reformation. *tion itself:* not merely witnesses in the loose sense in which histories are, but the actual results, the quintessence of the excited theological and moral elements of the time. In them you are brought into immediate contact with that sublime convulsion itself. Its strength and its weakness, its fears and its hopes, the truths it exalted, the errors and abuses it threw down, are here presented in the most solemn and strongly authenticated form in which they gave them to posterity. They are nerves running from the central seat of thought of that ancient, glorious, and immortal time, to us, who form the extremities. To see the force of every word, the power of every allusion, requires an intimate acquaintance with the era and the men, in forming which the student will be led delightfully into a thorough communion and profound sympathy with that second greatest period in human history. The child of our Church will find occasion to exult, not only in those brighter parts of our history and of our doctrines, whose lustre fills every eye, but even in those particulars on which ignorance, envy, and jealousy have based their powerless attacks; — will find, when he reaches a thorough understanding of them, new occasion to utter, with a heart swelling with an honorable pride, " I, too, am a Lutheran." We are not such gross idolaters, nor so ignorant of the declarations of these great men themselves, as to imagine that they left nothing for their posterity to do. Whether their posterity has done it, and done it well, is, however, a very distinct question. To assume that, merely because we follow them in order of time,

we have gone farther than they in truth, is to lay the foundation of a principle more absurd and pernicious than the worst
doctrine of the Church of Rome, and is as foolish as to say, that
the child of to-day, four years of age, is a greater astronomer
than Newton, because he lives in the century after him.

But while we concede that we may and ought to advance,
we wish explicitly to say, that we mean by advance, *progress
in the same direction.* We are aware of no particular in which
advance demands, or is even compatible with a desertion of
the fundamental principles of our fathers. They *may* have
Nature of true made mistakes, and nothing but mistakes; they
progress. *may* have known nothing, and we may know every
thing; but we have seen no evidence that such is the case, and
until it be brought before us, we must beg indulgence for our
skepticism. This much we can safely assert, that those who
understand best the theology of the Reformation, have most
confidence in it, and the strongest affection for it; to them it
seems still to stand in its original glory, firm as the eternal
mountains. That which strikes them painfully, as they grow
more and more familiar with that stout heart, whose life-
blood is warming us, is that we have not advanced as we
should; that though we have the shoulders of these giants of
a former world, from which, alas! a flood of infidelity and
theological frivolity seems to separate us, on which to stand,
there are so many things in which we do not see as far as they.
It is because slothfulness or ignorance prevents us from occupying that position to which they would lift us, because taking
a poor and narrow view of their labors, and measuring them
by some contemptible little standard, sometimes one set up by
their enemies, and yet oftener by those who are more injurious
than their enemies, their superficial and injudicious professed
friends, we permit our minds to be prejudiced against them.
A simple heart is of more value than mere science in the
apprehension of religious truth; and never has there been witnessed such a union of gigantic powers, with such a child-like
spirit, as among the theologians of the sixteenth century. In
vain do we increase the facilities for the attainment of knowledge, if we do not correspondingly strengthen the temper **of**

mind and heart essential to its acquisition. It by no means, therefore, follows, that even minds of the same order in our own day, would go beyond the point to which the Reformation was carried; because circumstances more embarrassing than those of the sixteenth century may now lie around the pathway of theological truth. Flattery is a more dangerous thing than bodily peril; a vain and superficial tendency will do more mischief than even an excess of the supernatural element, and the spirit of the Romish Church, and the prejudices insensibly imbibed in her communion, are not more pernicious as a preparation for the examination of divine truth, than is a cold, self-confident, and rationalizing mind. If we do not contemptuously reject all aid in search after truth, to whom can we go with more confidence than to the great authors of the Reformation? We know them at least to be sincere; no hireling scribblers, writing to tickle the fancy of the time; we know them to be the thorough masters of their subjects, conscious that every word would be examined and every argument fiercely assailed by their foes. Every doctrine they established by the word of God, and confirmed by the witness of his Church. Every objection which is now urged, was then brought to bear upon the truth. Controversy has added nothing to its stores; they knew perfectly those superficial, miscalled reasons which make men now so confident in saying, that had the Reformers only lived in our time, they would have abandoned much to which they held. They knew them, but they lived and died unchanging in their adherence to what they had taught as truth. It is a cheap and popular way of getting rid of anything in the theology of the Reformation which is not palatable, by pretending that it is a remnant of Popery, as Rationalists evade the force of Scripture declarations, by saying they are accommodations to Jewish prejudices. Among these remnants of Popery, have for instance been enumerated the doctrines of the Trinity, and the deity of Christ, of the Atonement, of eternal punishment, in short, of every thing which is distinctive of Evangelical Christianity. No position could be more violent in regard to all the doctrines of our Confession. They

Spirit of our time adverse to thoroughness.

not only can be demonstrated from Scripture, but can be shown to have been fully received in the Church before Popery had a name or a being. It would be far more natural to suppose, that in the fierce and imbittered strife with that gigantic system of Error, a part of the Protestant party would be driven to deny some truths, by whose abuse the Church of Rome strove to maintain her power. The insinuation of Romish influence is a sword with a double edge, and is almost sure to wound those who handle it; it is, in fact, ordinarily but the refuge of a sectarian spirit, which tries to accomplish by exciting odium, what it failed to do by argument.

But are those Confessions, after all, of any value to the American and German. *American* Lutheran preacher? it may be asked. We cannot conceal our sorrow, that that term, " American," should be made so emphatic, dear and hallowed though it be to our heart. Why should we break or weaken the golden chain which unites us to the high and holy associations of our history as a Church, by thrusting into a false position a word which makes a national appeal? Is there a conflict between the two, when carried to their very farthest limits? Must Lutheranism be shorn of its glory to adapt it to our times or our land? No! Our land is great, and wide, and glorious, and destined, we trust, under the sunlight of her free institutions, long to endure; but our faith is wider, and greater, and is eternal. The world owes more to the Reformation than to America; America owes more to it than to herself. The names of our Country and of our Church should excite no conflict, but blend harmoniously together. We are placed here in the midst of sectarianism, and it becomes us, not lightly to consent to swell that destructive torrent of separatism which threatens the welfare of pure Christianity on our shores more than all other causes combined. We are surrounded by the children of those Churches, which claim an origin in the Reformation. We sincerely respect and love them; we fervently pray that they may be increased in every labor of love, and may be won more and more to add to that precious truth, which they set forth with such power, those no less precious doctrines which, in the midst of so wide an abandonment of the faith once delivered to the saints, God has, in our Confession, preserved to us. But how shall we make ourselves worthy of their respect, and lift ourselves out of the sphere of that pitiful little sectarianism which is crawling continually over all that is churchly and stable? We must begin by knowing ourselves, and being true to that knowledge. Let us not, with our rich coffers, play the part of beggars, and ask favors where we have every ability to impart them. No Church can maintain her self-respect or inspire respect in others, which is afraid or ashamed of her own history, and which rears a dubious fabric on the ignorance of her ministry and of her members. Whatever flickerings of success may play around her, she will yet sink to rise no more, and, worse than this, no honest man will lament her fall; for however such a moral dishonesty may be smoothed over, every reflecting man sees that such a Church is an organized lie, with a ministry, congregations, churches, and societies united to sustain a lie. From this feeling a gracious Providence has almost wholly preserved our Church in this country. To whatever extent want of information or the pressure of surrounding denominations may have produced the practical departure of individuals from some of the principles of our Church, our common origin and our glorious annals have formed a bond of sympathy. Struggling against difficulties which would have crushed a church with less vitality, the Lutheran Communion in this country has always preserved some honorable feeling of her own dignity and proper value. *The salt which has preserved her is Germanic.* On these shores she has yet, properly, little history, comparatively; when she looks toward the realm of her might and glory, she must cast her eye over the Atlantic wave, and roll back her thoughts over the lapse of two centuries. She has been, and is yet, passing through a period of transition from one language and one national bond to another. The question of language has interest only so far as it concerns the question of Church life, and in its bearings on this should be watched with a tender and trembling interest. No doubt there were cases in which the opposition of the earlier Lutherans in this country, to the introduction of the English

14

language in our Church, arose from narrow views and feelings simply as Germans, but in yet more instances did it spring from fears, which our subsequent history has shown not to be wholly groundless, that Lutheranism itself — our life, our doctrines, our usages — so dear to their hearts, might be endangered by the change.

Whatever, then, may be our sentiments as to the judgment they displayed, let us do honor, at least, to their motives. They saw that the language of our land contained no Lutheran literature, no history just to the claims of our Church, no spirit which, on the whole, could be said fully to meet the genius of our Church. They feared that, under these circumstances, Lutheranism would melt away, or become the mere creature of the influences with which it was surrounded. They clung to their language, therefore, as a rampart which could shut out for a time the flood which was breaking upon them each day with increasing force. For what, then, do we blame them? Not for their intense love to the Church, or their ardent desire to preserve it in its purity, nor for that sensitive apprehension which is always the offspring of affection; not, in a word, that they were Lutherans indeed. If we blame these venerable men at all, it is that they *were not Lutheran enough;* that is, that, with all their devotion to the Church, they had not that inspiring confidence which they should have had in the power of her principles, to triumph eventually over every obstacle. Would that they could have realized what we believe most firmly, (though part of it yet lies in the future,) that, after all the changes of national existence, and of language, all pressure from the churches and the people around us, our holy faith shall come forth in all her purity and power, eventually to perform, in the great drama in our western realm, a part as important as that which she bore in her original glory in the history of the world.

And having spoken thus freely in regard to a misapprehension on one side of this question, we shall be equally candid in speaking the truth upon the other.

It is evident that our American fathers clung to the German language from no idea that there was any connection between

Lutheranism and that language *as such* — some mysterious coherence between its sounds and inflections, and the truth₁ of our Church ; so that, in the very nature of the case, and by an essential necessity, the English language and Lutheranism could not harmonize together. It is fanaticism to attempt to narrow our great Church into an English sect or a German one. The Lutheran Church is neither English nor German ; and though both should cease to be the tongues of living men, *she* cannot pass away. The greatest works of her original literature, some of her symbols, part of her Church service and hymns, were in the Latin language ; and surely if she can live in a dead language, she can live in any living one. She has achieved some of her most glorious victories where other languages are spoken. She sought at an early period to diffuse her principles among the Oriental Churches, and we will add, that she is destined, on these shores, in a language which her fathers knew not, to illustrate more gloriously, because in a more unfettered form, her true life and spirit, than she has done since the Reformation.

If the question may be mooted, How far shall we *adopt* the principles of the Reformation, and of our earlier Church ? — *this* admits of no discussion : Whether we should make ourselves thoroughly acquainted with those principles ; — for the rejection even of error, unless it result from an enlightened judgment, and a mature intelligent conviction, has no value whatever — nay, is in itself a worse error than any which it can possibly reject, for it rests on the foundation on which almost all moral falsehood has arisen. Let our ministry enter upon a profound study of the history and of the principles of our Church, and if the result of a ripe judgment shall be any other than an increased devotion to the first, and an ardent embracing of the second, we shall feel ourselves bound to re-examine the grounds on which such an examination has led us to repose with the confidence of a child on that maternal bosom, where so many, whose names are bright on earth and in heaven, have rested their dying heads, and have experienced that what she taught

Importance of an acquaintance with the Church.

them was sufficient, not only to overcome every trial of life, but every terror of the grave.

First in place, and first in importance among those great documentary testimonies of the Church which came forth The Augsburg Confession.* in the Reformation, is the Augsburg Confession. The man of the world should feel a deep interest in a document which bears to the whole cause of freedom as close a relation as the " Declaration of Independence " does

---

*Works connected with the history of the Augsburg Confession, chronologically arranged.

1530, (and the works of contemporaries.)

1. LUTHER: Werke (Walch.) xvi. 734–2145. Leipz. xx. 1–293. — Briefe: De Wette, iv. 1–180. vi. 112–128. — 2. MELANCHTHON: Epistolae etc. (Corp. Reform.) ii. 1–462. — 3. NURENBERG ENVOYS: Briefe: Strobels Miscellan. lit. inhalt. ii. 3–48. iii. 193–220. cf. Fikenscher. — 4. Pro. Relig. Christ. res gestae in Comit. Augustae Vind. hab. 1530. in Cyprian, Beylage vii. Written by a Roman Catholic during the Diet, and published with the Imperial privilege. — 5. BRUCK: (Pontanus, Heinse) Verzeichniss der Handlung. herausgeg. von Foerstemann. Archiv. Halle 1831. (Apologia MS.), in refutation of the work just mentioned. — 6. OSIANDRI, PHILIPPI HASSIAE: Senat. Noremberg. Literae in Camerarii Vit. Melanchthonis, ed. Strobel. 407–414. — 7. SPALATIN: Berichte, in Luther's Werke, Leipz. xx. 202–212. — 8. SPALATIN: Annales Reformationis, published by Cyprian. Leipz. 1718. 131–289. — 9. MYCONIUS: Historia Reformationis, from 1517–1542, published by Cyprian, 1718, p. 91, very brief. — 10. CAMERARIUS: Vita Melanchthonis (1566) Strobel. Noesselt, Halae 1777. 119–134. — 1555. SLEIDAN: The General History of the Reformation, Englished and continued by Bohun. London, 1689. Fol. 127–140. — 1574. WIGAND: Histor. de Augustana Confessione. Regiomont. 1574, in Cyprian Beylag. x. — 1576. CHYTRAEUS: Histor. der Aug. Conf. Rost. 1576. Frankfort 1580. — 1578. Do. Latin. Frcf. ad Moen. — 1582. Do. Histoire de la Conf. d'Auxpourg. mise en Francois par le Cop. Anvers. — 1576. COELESTINUS: Historia Comitiorum. Frankf. on the Oder, 1576–77. — (Kirchner, Selnecker, and Chemnitz): Solida ac vera Confess. August. Historia (against Wolf) translat. ꝑer Godfried. Lipsiae, 1685, 4to. — 1620. SARPI: Histor. Concil. Trident. London, 1620. 40–45. — 1630. BAKIUS, R.: Confessio Augustana triumphans· das ist die trefflich-schöne Geschicht der Wahr. Ungeend. Augsburg Confession. Magdeb. 1630. — 1631. SAUBERT: Miracula Aug. Conf. Norimb. 4to. — 1646. CALOVIUS: Criticus sacer vel Commentar. sup. August. Conf. Lips. 1646, 4to. p. 19–45. — 1654. GOEBEL: Predigten, 1–119. — 1665. CARPZOV: Isagoge. 2d ed. 1675. 90-107. — 1669. ARNOLD: Unparth. Kirchen u. Ketzer Historien. Schaffhausen, 1740. 3 vols. Folio. i. 809. 1230. — 1681. MAIMBOURG: Historie der Lutheranisme. Paris, 1680. 178–209. — 1686. Du PIN: Bibliotheque. A new Ecclesiastical History of the sixteenth century. London, 1720. Fol. ch. xxii. — SECKENDORF: Commentarius de Lutheranismo, 1686. Franc. and Lips. 1692. p. 150-209. übers. Frick. — 1714. Do. Reformations Geschichte von Roos, 1781. — 1705. MÜLLERI, J. J.: Historia von . . . Protestation . . wie auch Augspurgische Confession, 1705, 4tc. —

to our own as Americans. The philosopher should examine
what has formed the opinions and affected the destinies of
millions of our race. To the Christian it presents itself as the
greatest work, regarded in its historical relations, in which
pure religion has been sustained by human hands. The theologian will find it a key to a whole era of fervent, yet profound
thought, and the Lutheran, to whom an argument on its value,
to him, must be presented, is beyond the reach of argument.

— 1706. JUNKER : Ehrengedächtniss Lutheri. Lipsiae, 1706, 8vo. § 30. — 1708.
LOESCHER : Historia Motuum. 2d ed. 1723, 3 vols. 4to. i. 158–180. — 1715. HIL-
DEBRAND : Historia Conciliorum. Helmstadii, 1715, 311–314. — 1716. FLEUTER's
Historischer Katechismus. 3d ed. 1718. 339–365. — 1719. CYPRIAN : Hilaria Evan-
gelica. Gotha, 1719. Nachricht, von der Augspurg Confession, p. 551–555. — 1727
BUDDEUS : De Colloq. Charitat. Secul. xvi. (Miscellan. Sacra) 1727. — 1730
CYPRIAN : Historia der Augsb. Conf. aus den Original-Acten — mit Beylagen.
Gotha, 1730, 4to. Racknitz : Flores in Aug. Conf. 1730. — PFAFF : Lib. Symb.
Introd. Histor. cap. iii. — HOFFMANN,C. G. : Summar. Betrachtung. der auf Augsp.
Reichstage, 1530. Actorum Religionis, 1730. — SALIG : Vollständige Historie der
Aug. Conf. 3 vols. Halle, 1730, 4to. — Do. Geschichte der Aug. Conf. aus Sleidan,
Spalatin, Coelestinus, Chytraeus, Hortleder, Seckendorff u. Müller. 1730. In the
form of a dialogue. — 1732. WALCH, J. G. : Introd. in L. S. Jena, 1732. 157–482.
—HANE : Historia Crit. A. C. — 1740. MORERI : Le Grand Dictionaire Historique,
1740. 8 vols. Folio. Art. Confession d'Augsburg, and Diete. — 1745. WEISMANN :
Introduc. in memorab. eccles. Histor. Sacr. Halae, 1745. i. 1498–1504. — 1751.
BOERNERI : Institut. Theolog. Symbolicæ. 23–55. — 1761. BAUMGARTEN : Erleu
terungen. 45. — 1765. WALCHII, G. F. : Breviarium Theolog. Symb. Ec. Luth.
Götting. 1765. 57–75. — 1775. SEMLERI : Apparatus ad Libr. Symb. 36. — 1781.
PLANCK : Gesch. Protestant. Lehrbegriffs. Leipz. 1781. 8 vols. 8vo. iii. 1. 1–178.
— 1791. HENKE : Geschichte der Chr. Kirche. 4th ed. 1806. iii. 139–143. ix.
(Vater) 94–97. — 1782. WEBER : Kritische Gesch. d. Aug. Conf. Franf. 1782. 2
vols. 8vo. — 1804. SCHRÖCKH : Kirchengesch. seit der Reformat. Leipz. 1804. i.
442–482. — 1811. TITTMANN : Instit. Symbol. 80–90. — 1826. SCHÖPFF : Symb.
Büch. i. 24. — 1827. HASE : Libr. Symb. Lips. 1827. Prolegom iii–cxiv. — 1829.
ROTERMUND: Geschichte des . . zu Augsb. übergeb. Glaubensbek. nebst. . Lebens-
nachrichten. Hannover, 1829. 8vo. — CUNOW : Augsb. Confession, 1829. — HAAN :
Darstellung, 1829. — DANZ : Die Augspurg. Conf. nach ihrer Geschichte, etc. Jena,
1829, 8vo. — YELIN : Versuch, 55–60. HAMMERSCHMIDT : Gesch. d. Augsb. Con-
fess. 1829. von Ammon: Jubelfestbuch, 1829. — 1830. SCHIEBLER : Reichstag zu
Augsburg, 1830. — SPIEKER : Confessio Fidei, etc. LOEBER. FACEUS. — PFAFF :
Geschichte des Reichst. zu Augs. u. des Augsb. Glaubensbek. Stuttg. 1830. —
TITTMANN : Aug. Conf. — FIKENSCHER : Geschichte des Reichst. zu Augsp. Nurnb.
1830, 8vo. — MÄRTENS: Ueber die Symb. Bücher. Halberstadt, 1830. 8vo. 63–80.
— 1831. TITTMANN : Die Evangelische Kirche im 1530 und 1830. Leipz. 1831. —
MARHEINEKE : (1831.) — 1833–1835. FOERSTEMANN : Urkundenbuch. 2 vols. —

It is our shield and our sword, our ensign and our arming, the constitution of our state, the life of our body, the germ of our being. It is the bond of our union throughout the world, and by it, and with it, our Church, as a distinct organization, must stand or fall. Her life.began, indeed, before it, as the vital point of the embryo exists before the heart and brain are formed, but having once evoked the Confession into which her own life flowed — they live or perish together, as that embryo grows or dies, as the vital organs expand in life or shrink in death.

In the Symbolical books of the Lutheran Church, the first place, indeed, is justly held by those general Confessions, in which the pure Church has united, in every age since their formation, and in which, throughout the world, it now concurs.   These are the Apostles', the Nicæno-Constantinopolitan, and Athanasian creeds.   She thus vindicates her true catho licity and antiquity, and declares that the name of Lutheran does not define her essence, but simply refers to one grand fact

1835. Bretschneider : Annales vitae Melanchthonis. a. 1530. (2d vol. of Corpus Reform.) — Cox : Life of Melanchthon. Boston, 1835. Ch. viii. — 1837. Köllner : Symb. d. Luth. Kirche. 150–226. — D'Aubigne : Reformation (1837.) — 1838. Audin : Histoire de la vie, etc., de Martin Luther. Paris, 1845. Chap. xxiv. xxv. Translated from the French. Philadelphia, 1841. Chap. xlvii. xlviii. Translated by Turnbull. London, 1854. Vol. ii. 319–353. — 1839. Stang : M. Luther : Sein Leben u. Wirken. Stuttg. 1839. 600–687. — Ranke : Reformation (1839.) — 1840. Wessenberg : Kirchenversammlungen des 15ten und 16ten Jahrhunderts. iii. 115. — 1841. Rudelbach : Histor. kritisch. Einleitung in die Augsb. Conf. Dresden, 1841. — 1842. Stebbing : History of the Church from the Diet of Augsburg, etc. London, 1842. i. 9–56. — Neudecker : Die Hauptversuche zur Pacification der Ev. Prot. Kirche Deutschlands, von der Reformation bis auf unsere Tage. Leipz. 1846. 57–62. — 1846. Michelet : Luther ; translated by Smith. New York, 1846. p. 147. — 1847. Francke : Lib. Symb. xiii–xx. — 1848. Müller : Symb. Büch. liv. Translated : The Book of Concord ; New Market, 1851. xxxiii–xxxviii. 2d ed. 1854. 37–43. — 1849. Zimmermann : Luther's Leben (Ref. Schr. iv.) 471–481. — 1853. Sartorius : Beiträge. 2d ed. 1–21. "The Glory of the Augsburg Confession."— 1854. Herzog's Real Encyclop. Hamb. 1854. i. 603–610. — Matthes : Comparat. Symbolik. 61–67. — 1855. Ledderhose : Life of Melanchthon, translated by Krotel. Philadelphia, 1855. Chap. xi. — 1857. Hofmann : Rud. Symbolik. 229–231. — Bindseil, H. E. : Corpus Reformatorum. xxvi. Pars. Prior. — 1866. Guericke : Handb. der Kirchen-Gesch. iii. ₰ 176. (9th ed.) 1866. — Winer : Darstellung. 3d ed. ii. 1866. — 1868. Kurtz : Lehrbuch d. K. C. ₰ 182. 6. 7.

in her history, her restoration in the great Reformation. The most splendid phase of that portion of her annals is to be found in the Diet of Augsburg, and the " Good Confession " which she then " witnessed " before the mighty of the world. The city of Augsburg has not been wanting in historical associations of high interest, but they are dim before its chief glory. Its ancient spires, on which the soft light of many a sinking sun had rested, were then illumined by a milder radiance, which shall never set. It slopes towards two considerable rivers, between which it lies embosomed, but never had that " river which makes glad the city of God," so poured through it its stream of life, as on that eventful day. Thrice since that period the thunder of artillery and the clash of arms have sounded around and within it — but it is our heroes whose glory still keeps its name fresh in the memories of men, and shall keep it when its palaces have crumbled into dust.

An age of darkness is a creedless age ; corruption in doctrine works best when it is unfettered by an explicit Romanism and statement of that doctrine. Between the Athana-   its Creed. sian Creed (probably about A. D. 434) and the sixteenth century, there is no new General Creed. Error loves ambiguities. In the contest with Rome the Reformers complained bitterly that she refused to make an explicit official statement of her doctrine. " Our opponents," says the Apology,* " do not bestow the labor, that there may be among the people some certain statement of the chief points of the ecclesiastical doctrines." Just in proportion to the blind devotion of men to Popery were they reluctant to have its doctrines stated in an authorized form, and only under the compulsion of a public sentiment which was wrought by the Reformation, did the Church of Rome at length convene the Council of Trent. Its decisions were not completed and set forth until seventeen ye irs after Luther's death, and thirty-three years after the Augsburg Confession. The proper date of the distinctive life of a particular Church is furnished by her Creed. Tested by the General Creeds, the Evangelical Lutheran Church has the same claim as the Romish Church to be considered in unity with the early

* 231, 43.

Church, — but as a particular Church, with a distinctive bond and token of doctrinal union, she is more than thirty years older than the Romish Church. Our Church has the oldest distinctive Creed now in use in any large division of Christendom. That Creed is the Confession of Augsburg. Could the Church have set forth and maintained such a Confession as that of Augsburg before the time over which the Dark Ages extended, those Dark Ages could not have come. There would have been no Reformation, for none would have been needed.

The mighty agitations caused by the restoration of divine truth by Luther and his great co-workers, had led

The Augsburg Confession: Preliminaries to preparation of.*

to attempts at harmonizing the conflicting elements, especially by action at the Diets of the Empire. At the Diet of Worms (1521) Luther refuses to retract, and the Edict goes forth commanding his seizure

---

* I. Official writings which prepared the way for the Augsburg Confession.

1. The visitational articles : the Saxon visitation articles.

a. The Latin Articles by Melanchthon, 1527. These are extremely rare, and are found in none of the older editions of Melanchthon or Luther. Given in the Corpus Reformatorum. Vol. xxvi. (1857.) 7.

b. Melanchthon's Articles of Visitation in German, with Luther's Preface and some changes by him. 1528. (Last Edition 1538.) Given in Melanchthon's Werke (von Koethe) i. 83–130. Corpus Reformatorum xxvi. 49 — in Luther's Werke. Jena iv. 341. Leipzig, xix. 622. Walch. x. 1902. Erlangen xxiii. 3. These articles are not to be confounded with the Saxon visitation articles of 1592, which are given as an Appendix in various editions of the Symbolical Books (Müller, p. 845.)

2. The fifteen articles of Marburg. (October 3d, 1529.) cf. Feuerlin 42. These articles are given in Luther's Werke, Jena iv. 469. Leipzig xix, 530. Walch. xvii. 2357. Erlangen 65, 88. Reformatorische Schriften von Zimmermann (1847) iii. 420. In all these editions the fourteenth article (on Infant Baptism) has been omitted, so that they make only fourteen articles. Walch, however, (xxiii. 35,) gives the fourteenth article among the omissions supplied (compare do. Pref. p. 6.) — In the Corpus Reformatorum. xxvi. 121–128. xiv.article given. — Zwingle's Werke (Schuler u. Schulthess) ii. iii. 44–58. xiv. article given. — Chytraei Historia. 355. The fourteenth article omitted. — Müller J. J. Historie. p. 305–309. Fourteenth article given. — Rudelbach. Reformation Lutherthum und Union (Leipzig, 1839) Appendix 665–668. from Müller, of course with fourteenth article. — They have been *translated* into Latin: Solida ac vera Confess. August. Histor. p. 128–131. — Zwinglii Opera (Schuler et Schulthess) iv : ii. 181. cf. Seckendorf ii. 138. — In *French* in Le Cop's **Chytræus** 463–466. — Into English by Dr. *Lintner*. Missionary, 1857. (Without the fourteenth article.)

and the burning of his books; at the Diet of Nuremberg (1522) Cheregati, the Papal Nuncio, demands the fulfilment of the Edict of Worms, and the assistance of all faithful friends of the Church against Luther. The first Diet at Spires (1526) had virtually annulled the Edict of Worms, by leaving its

3. The xvii. articles of Schwabach, 1529, (miscalled frequently the Torgau articles.) For the special Bibliography of these articles, cf. Walch. Bib. Theolog. Select. i. 330, and Introd. in L. S. 163.—Feuerlin 78, cf. Layritii : De Articulis Suobacens. Wittenb. 1719. 4to.—Weber, Kritisch. Gesch. i. 13. K. Pfaff. i. 94. Evangelical Review, i. 246–249 (which presents the confused view of Walch. Introd. in L. S., and of the older writers.)

1. In June 1528, the first convention was held in Schwabach. The xxiii. articles of that convention are not to be confounded, as they have been, with the xvii. articles of the second convention.

2. The second convention at Schwabach was fixed for October 16th, 1529.

a. At this convention the xvii. articles were presented.

They are given in Luther's Werke, Jena v. 14. Leipzig xx. 1–3. Walch xxi. 681, 778. Erlangen xxiv. 322.—Corpus Reformatorum xxvi. 151–160.—Chytraeus, 22–26, Müller, Historie 442–448. Cyprian, Beylag. 159, most critically in Weber, Krit. Geschicht. Beylagen i. and Corp. Reform.

They have been translated into *Latin*: Coelestinus i. 25. Pfaff, Lib. Symb. Adpend. 3.—French: Le Cop's Chytraeus, p. 19.—English: Evangelical Review, ii. 78–84. (With the old title, " Articles of Torgau.")

b. Reply of Wimpina, Mensing, etc., to these articles, 1530. This is given in Luther's Werke, Jena v. 16. Leipz. xx. 3–8.

"   "   Walch. xvi. 766.

Cf. Seckendorf, lib. ii. 152. Cyprian 52. Evangelical Review, ii. 83.

c. Luther's answer to the outcry of the Papists on the xvii. articles, given in Luther's Werke, Leipz. xx. 8.

"   "   Walch, xvi. 778.

"   "   Erlangen, 24, 319.

Cyprian, Beyl. 159.

4. The Articles of Torgau, 1530. (confounded frequently with the articles of Schwabach.)—Cf. Seckendorf, ii. 151. Müller 441. Cyprian 52, who suppose what we have called the "Articles of Swabach" to be in fact the articles sent to Torgau.—Cf. Salig: i. 158. Walch: Luther's Werke xvi. 681, who suppose the articles of Schwabach to have been somewhat changed and sent to Torgau.— Cf. Weber: Krit. Gesch. i. 16–19. Foerstemann: Urkundenbuch i. 40–41.—Köllner: Symbolik. i. 156–168.—Corpus Reformator. xxvi. 161–170, who prove the Articles of Swabach and those of Torgau to be totally distinct. The Articles of Torgau, truly entitled to that name, bear, in a large degree, to the second part of the Augsburg Confession, the relation which the Schwabach Articles bear to the first part.—The Articles of Torgau were discovered by Foerstemann (1833) and given to the world by him, in his Urkundenbuch, i. 66–84.—Given also in Corpus Reformatorum, xxvi. 171–200.

execution to the unforced action of the different Estates, and it promised the speedy convocation of a General Council, or at least of a National Assembly. The second Diet at Spires (1529) quenched the hopes inspired by this earlier action. It decreed that the Edict of Worms should be strictly enforced where it had already been received; the celebration of the Romish Mass protected, and the preachers bound to confine themselves to the doctrine of the Romish Church in their teachings. The Protest of the Evangelical Princes against this decision, originated the name PROTESTANTS.

The Protestant Princes made their appeal to a free General Council. Charles V., after vainly endeavoring to obtain the consent of the Pope to the convocation of a General Council, summoned the Diet at Augsburg, promising to appear in person, and to give a gracious hearing to the whole question, so that the "one only Christian truth might be maintained, that all might be subjects and soldiers of the one Christ, and live in the fellowship and unity of one Church." To this end the Emperor directed the friends of the Evangelical faith to prepare, for presentation to the Diet, a statement on the points of division.

In consequence of this order of the Emperor, the Elector of Saxony, who was the leader of the Evangelical Princes, directed Luther, in conjunction with the other theologians at Wittenberg, to draw up a summary of doctrine, and a statement of the abuses to be corrected. The statement drawn up in consequence of this, had, as its groundwork, Articles which were already prepared; and as the Augsburg Confession is the ripest result of a series of labors, in which this was one, and as much confusion of statement exists on the relations of these labors, it may be useful to give the main points in chronological order.

1. 1529. October 1, 2, 3. The Conference at Marburg took place between Luther and the Saxon divines upon the one side, and Zwingle and the Swiss divines on the other. Luther, in conjunction with others of our great theologians, prepared the XV. Marburg Articles, October, 1529. These Articles were

meant to show on what points the Lutherans and Zwinglians agreed, and also to state the point on which they did not agree, and as a fair statement of the points, disputed and undisputed, were signed by all the theologians of both parties.

2. 1529. Oct. 16. On the basis of these XV. Articles were prepared, by Luther, with the advice and assistance of the other theologians, the XVII. Articles of Schwabach, so called from the place at which they were presented.

3. 1529. Nov. 29. From the presentation of these XVII. Articles at Smalcald, they are sometimes called the Smalcald Articles.

4. 1530. March 20. These XVII. Articles of Luther revised were sent to Torgau, and were long called the Torgau Articles, though they are in fact the revised Articles of Schwabach. These Articles are mainly doctrinal.

5. March 20. In addition to these, a special writing, of which Luther was the chief author, in conjunction with Melanchthon, Jonas, and Bugenhagen, was prepared by direction of the Elector, and sent to Torgau. These articles are on the abuses,* and are the *Torgau Articles proper.*

6. The XVII. doctrinal articles of Schwabach *formed the basis* of the doctrinal articles of the Augsburg Confession; the Articles of Torgau are the basis of its articles on abuses, and both these are mainly from the hand of Luther.

In six instances, the very numbers of the Schwabach Articles correspond with those of the Augsburg Confession. They coincide throughout, not only in doctrine, but in a vast number of cases word for word, the Augsburg Confession being a mere transcript, in these cases, of the Schwabach Articles. The differences are either merely stylistic, or are made necessary by the larger object and compass of the Augsburg Confession; but so thoroughly do the Schwabach Articles condition and shape every part of it, as to give it even the peculiarity of phraseology characteristic of Luther.

To a large extent, therefore, Melanchthon's work is but an elaboration of Luther's, and to a large extent it is not an

* For the latest and amplest results of historical investigation of these points, see Corpus Reformat., vol. **xxvi.** (1858,) cols. 97–199.

elaboration, but a reproduction. To Luther belong the doctrinal power of the Confession, its inmost life and spirit, and
to Melanchthon its matchless form. Both are in some sense its
authors, but the most essential elements of it are due to Luther,
who is by pre-eminence its author, as Melanchthon is its composer. If the authorship of the Confession should be claimed
for Melanchthon to the exclusion of Luther, it would open the
second great Reformer to the charge of the most unscrupulous
plagiarism. Even had Luther, however, had no
direct share in the Augsburg Confession, the assertion would be too sweeping that he was in *no sense*
its author. Not only as great leading minds are in some sense
the authors of all works that have germinated directly from
their thoughts, but in a peculiar sense Luther was the author
of Melanchthon's theological life; he was, as Melanchthon loved
to call him, "his most dear father." All the earliest and
purest theology of Melanchthon is largely but a repetition, in
his own graceful way, of Luther's thoughts; and the Augs-

Its Authorship:
Luther's relations
to *

* Collected works, having an importance in the Interpretation and History of
the Augsburg Confession.

LUTHER. Opera Omnia (Latin) (1556–58.) Jena 1579–83. 4 Tom. Folio. — In
primum Librum Mose Enarrationes. 1555. Fol. — Schriften und Werke (Boerner
u. Pfeiffer.) Leipz. 1729–34. 22 vols. Folio. Greiff's Register. 1740. Fol. —
Sämmtliche Werke. (Walch) Halle 1740–52. 24 vols. 4to. — Sämmtliche Werke.
(Ammon, Erlsperger, Irmescher, Plochmann) Erlangen, 1826–1857. 65 vols.
(German) and 2 vols. Register. Invaluable for critical purposes. — Geist, oder
Concordanz der Ansichten, etc. Darmstadt, 1827–31. 4 vols. — Briefe, Sendschrei-
ben u. Bedenken (De Wette), Berlin, 1826–56. 6 vols. (The last edited by Seide-
mann.) — Reformatorische Schriften, in Chronologischer Folge. (Zimmermann)
Darmstadt, 1846–49. 4 vols. 8vo. — (Lutherus Redivivus, oder des fürnehmsten
Lehrers der Augspurg. Confess. D. M. Luther's hinterlassene Schriftliche Erklär-
ungen . . . was der Augspurg. Confess. eigentliche Meinung u. Verstandt in allen
Articuln allezeit gewesen. (Seidel) Halle 1697.) — MELANCHTHON. Opera Omnia
(Peucer.) Wittenb. 1562–64. 4 vols. Fol. — Opera quae supersunt omnia. (Bret-
schneider) Halle 1834–1856. 28 vols. 4to. Indispensable to the student of the
Augsburg Confession, or of the Reformation in general. The Loci Theologici
especially, are edited with a completeness unparalleled in the Bibliography of
Dogmatics. — MELANCHTHON. Corpus Doctrinae Christianae, das ist, Gantze Summa
der rechten Christlichen Lehre, etc. Leipzig, 1560. Fol. — Corpus Doctrinae
Christianae quae est summa orthodoxi et Catholici Dogmatis. Lipsiae, 1563.
Folio. — ZWINGLII Huldr. Opera, Completa Editio prima cur. Schulero et Schul-
thessio. Zurich 1829–1842. 8 vols. 8vo.

ourg Confession is in its inmost texture the theology of the
New Testament as Luther believed it.   Melanchthon had no
creativeness of mind, and but for Luther, his name would
hardly have taken a place among great theologians.   He was
a sculptor who cut with matchless grace after the model of the
master.

For the absence of Luther from Augsburg, the reasons constantly assigned in history are obviously the real ones.   Luther
was not only under the Papal excommunication,
but he was an outlaw under the imperial ban.   In
the rescript of the Emperor he was styled "the
evil fiend in human form," "the fool," and ".the blasphemer."
His person would have been legally subject to seizure.   The
Diet at Spires (1529) had repeated the Decree of Worms.   The
Elector would have looked like a plotter of treason had Luther
been thrust by him before the Emperor, and with the intense
hatred cherished by the Papistical party toward Luther, he
would not have been permitted to leave Augsburg alive.   The
Elector was so thoroughly anxious to have Luther with him,
that at first he allowed his wishes to obscure his judgment, —
he attached such importance to the mild language of Charles
V., that he allowed himself to hope, yet, as his letter of March
14th shows, rather feebly, that even Luther might be permitted to appear.   Luther left Wittenberg on the assumption
that he perhaps might be permitted to come to Augsburg.
But a safe-conduct was denied him.   Had it been desired by
the Elector to have Luther out of the way, it would have been
far easier to the Elector, and pleasanter to Luther, to have kept
him at Wittenberg.

That Luther came to Coburg, is proof of the ardent desire
to have his counsel and co-operation; that he stopped there,
shows the greatness of the peril that would have attended his
going farther.   But Luther's safety was not merely provided
for by his detention here, but by placing him in the old castle
of the Duke of Coburg, which occupies a commanding height,
more than five hundred feet above the town, and which is so
well fortified by nature and art, that during the Thirty Years'
War, Wallenstein besieged it in vain.   The arrangements

were planned by loving friends for his safety : Luther perfectly understood the character and object of the arrangements, before they were made, while they were in progress, and after all was over. Thus, April 2d, writing before his journey, he says: "I am going with the Prince, *as far as Coburg*, and Melanchthon and Jonas with us, until it is known what will be attempted at Augsburg." In another letter of same date: "I am not summoned to go to Augsburg, but for certain reasons, I only accompany the Prince on his journey through his own dominions." June 1, he writes: "I am waiting on the borders of Saxony, midway between Wittenberg and Augsburg, for it was not *safe* to take me to Augsburg."

The expressions of impatience which we find in his letters during his stay at Coburg, only show that in the ardor of his great soul, in moments of intense excitement, the reasons for his detention at the castle, which had commended themselves to his cooler judgment, seemed reasons no longer — death seemed nothing — he would gladly face it as he had faced it before, only to be in body where he was already in heart. "I burn," he says, "to come, though uncommanded and uninvited." His seeming impatience, his agony, his desire to hear often, his refusal for the moment to listen to any excuses, were all inevitable with such a spirit as Luther's under the circumstances ; yet for places some days' journey apart, in those troublous times, of imperfect communication, with special couriers carrying all the letters, there was an extraordinary amount of correspondence. We have about seventy letters of Luther written to Augsburg during the Diet, and we know of thirty-two written by Melanchthon to Luther, and of thirty-nine written by Luther to Melanchthon in the five months of correspondence, during the Diet, or connected with it in the time preceding.*

Luther and Melanchthon went in company to Coburg, and at
Correspondence with Luther. Melanchthon's Letters of May 4th. Coburg the "Exordium" of the Confession was written. At Augsburg, Melanchthon, as was his wont, elaborated it to a yet higher finish. May 4, he writes to Luther: "I have made the exor

---

* Luther's Letters, De Wette's ed., iii. iv.

ᴅium of our Apology somewhat more finished in style (reto-rikoteron) than I wrote it at Coburg." Speaking of his work he says: "In a short time, *I myself will bring it*, or if the Prince will not permit me to come, *I will send it.*"

By the Apology or Defence is meant the Confession, which was originally designed to be in the main a defence of the Evangelical (Lutheran) Confessors, especially in regard to their practical application of their principles in the correction of abuses. The second part was the one which at the time of the preparation of the Confession was regarded as the more difficult, and for the immediate objects contemplated, the more import-ant. The articles of faith were designed as a preparation for the second part, and the judgment of Foerstemann and others that by the " Exordium," Melanchthon meant not the Preface, which there seems to be evidence was written in German by Brück, and translated into Latin by Jonas, " but the whole first part of the Confession, is not without much to render it] robable."

If we take Melanchthon's language, in his letter of May 5, g ʾammatically, it seems to settle it, that the Exordium was the whole first part, for it is inconceivable that he would desire to come all the way to Coburg to show Luther merely the Pre-face, more especially as we know that the Confession itself was nearly finished at the time. In a letter of the same date, (May 4th,) to Viet Dietrich, who was with Luther, he says: " I will shortly run over to you, that I may bring to the Doctor (Luther) the Apology which is to be offered to the Emperor, that he (Luther) may examine it."

For very obvious reasons, Melanchthon could not be spared from Augsburg at this time even for an hour, to say nothing of the hazards which might have been incurred by the journey, which his great anxiety ^{The Elector's Letters of May 11th.} for a personal conference with Luther inclined him to make. But on May 11th, the Elector sent to Luther the Confession, with a letter, in which he speaks of it as meant to be a careful revision of those very articles of which Luther was the main anthor. He says to Luther (Augsburg, May 11th): " As you and our other theologians at Wittenberg, have brought into summary statement the articles of religion about which there is dispute, it is our wish to let you know that Melanchthon has further revised the same, and reduced them to a *form*, which we hereby send you." "And it is our desire that you would further revise the same, *and give them a thorough examination*, and at the *same time* (daneben) you would also write how you like it, or what you think proper to add about it or to it, and in order that, on his Majesty's arrival, which is looked for in a short time, we may be ready, send back the same carefully secured and sealed, without delay, to this place, by the letter-carrier who takes this."

Luther had been the chief laborer in the articles of which the Elector declared the Confession to be but a revision and re-ducing to shape — there could be little room for large changes, and as the Emperor was expected speedily, the time was too pressing to allow of elaborate discussions, which were indeed unneeded where all were so absolute a unit in faith as our Con-fessors were. That margin would have been narrow, and that time short, indeed, on which and in which Luther could not have written enough to kill any Confession which tampered with the truth.

The Elector's whole letter expressly assigns the natural and cogent reason, that Luther's judgment might be needed at once, in consequence of the expected advent of the Emperor, a point which Melanchthon's letter of the same date also urges. The haste is evidence of the anxiety to have Luther's opinion and approval, as a *sine qua non*.

The Diet had been summoned for April 8th. It was soon after postponed to the 1st of May, and at this later date, had it not been for the delay of the Emperor in appearing, the arti-cles of Luther, on which the Confession was afterwards based, would themselves have been offered. As it was, it was need-ful to be ready at any hour for the approach of Charles. The letter of the Elector implies that the original of the Confession was sent to Luther. Great care was taken to prevent copies from being multiplied, as the enemies were eager to see it. Even on June 25th, the day of its presentation, the Latin Con fession, in Melanchthon's own handwriting, was given to the Emperor.

With this letter of the Elector was sent a letter from Melanchthon addressed "to Martin Luther, his most dear father." In it he says: "Our Apology Melanchthon's Letter of May 11th. is sent to you, although it is more properly a Con- fession, for the Emperor will have no time for protracted dis- cussion. Nevertheless, I have said those things which I thought most profitable or fitting. With this design I have embraced nearly all the articles of faith, for Eck has put forth the most diabolical slanders against us, to which I wished to oppose a remedy. I request you, in accordance with your own spirit, to decide concerning the whole writing (*Pro tuo spiritu de toto scripto statues.*) A question is *referred to you*, to which I greatly desire an answer from you. What if the Emperor . . should prohibit our ministers from preaching at Augsburg? I have answered that we should yield to the wish of the Em- peror, in whose city we are guests. But our old man is diffi- cult to soften." (The "old man" is either the Elector John, so called to distinguish him from his son, John Frederick, or the old Chancellor Brück.) "Whatever therefore you think, I beg that you will write it *in German on separate paper.*"

What Luther was to write was his judgment both as to the Confession and the question about preaching, and the "sepa rate paper," on which he was particularly requested to write, must mean separate from that which held the Confession. One probable reason why Luther was so particularly requested not, as was very much his wont, to write upon the margin, was, that this original draft of the Confession might have been needed for presentation to the Emperor. The original of Lu- ther's replies to the Elector on both points (for to the Elector and not to Melanchthon they were to be made, and were made,) still remains. Both are together — neither is on the margin of anything, but both are written just as Melanchthon specially requested, "in German," and on "separate paper." * It shows

---

* Cœlestinus, i., p. 40. Luther's Epistol. supplem. Buddei, 93. Salig. Hist. d Aug. Conf., i. 169. Cyprian, Beylage xiv. Ex Autographo. Luther's Briefe: De Wette (Lett. 1213) himself compared the original in the Weimar Archives.

the intensest desire to have the assurance doubly sure of Luther's concurrence, that under all the pressure of haste, the original of the Confession was sent him.

That the highest importance was attached to Luther's judgment on this form of the Confession, is furthermore proved by the fact that after the Confession was despatched, (May 11,) *everything was suspended at Augsburg*, till he should be heard from. "On the 16th of May, the Elector indicated to the other States, *that the Confession* was ready, but was not entirely closed up, but had been sent to Luther for examination." Shortly after, Luther's reply of May 15, heartily indorsing the Confession, without the change of a word, was received at Augsburg.*

It is called "*form* of Confession," in the Elector's letter to Luther, because the *matter* of the Confession had been prepared by Luther himself. Melanchthon's work was but to revise that matter, and give it "form," which revised form was to be subjected to the examination of all the Lutheran authorities and divines at Augsburg, and especially to Luther.

As to the articles of faith, and the abuses to be corrected, the matter of the Confession was already finished and furnished — much of it direct from Luther's hand, and all of it with his co-operation and approval. It was only as to the "form," the selection among various abuses, the greater or less amplitude of treatment, that all the questions lay. The "form of Confession" sent on May 11th was the Augsburg Confession, substantially identical with it as a whole, and, in all that is really essential to it, verbally identical. We have copies of it so nearly at the stage at which it then was as to know that this is the case. Melanchthon's letter expressly declares that nearly all the articles of faith had been treated, and the Augsburg Confession, in its most finished shape, only professes to give "about the sum of the doctrines held by us."

But we need not rest in inferences, however strong, in regard to this matter. We have direct evidence from Melanchthon himself, which will be produced, that Luther did decide, before its presentation, upon what, in Melanchthon's judgment, was

*Corpus Reform., No. 700. Köllner, pp. 171, 175.

the Augsburg Confession itself. His words prove that the changes which Luther did not see were purely those of niceties of style, or of a more ample elaboration of a very few points, mainly on the abuses; in fact, that Luther's approval had been given to the Confession, and that without it the Confession never would have been presented.

The Elector's letter of May 11th was answered by Luther, who heartily indorsed the Confession sent him, without the change of a word. Nothing was taken out, nothing was added, nothing was altered. He speaks admiringly, not reprovingly, of the moderation of its style, and confesses that it had a gentleness of manner of which he was not master.

As the Emperor still lingered, Melanchthon used the time to improve, here and there, the external form of the Confession. He loved the most exquisite accuracy and delicacy of phrase, and never ceased filing on his work. What topics should be handled under the head of abuses, was in the main perfectly understood, and agreed upon between him and Luther. The draft of the discussion of them was largely from Luther's hand, and all of it was indorsed by him.

The main matters were entirely settled, the principles were fixed, and the questions which arose were those of style, of selection of topics, of the mode of treating them, or of expediency, in which the faith was not involved. In regard to this, Luther speedily hears again from his son in the Gospel.

May 22d, Melanchthon wrote to Luther: * "In the Apology, we daily change many things; the article on Vows, as it was more meagre than it should be, I have re- moved, and supplied its place with a discussion a little more full, on the same point. I am now treating of the power of the keys also. I wish you would run over the Articles of Faith; if you think there is no defect in them, we will treat of the other points as we best may (*utcunque.*) For they are to be changed from time to time, and adapted to the circumstances." In the same letter he begs Luther to write to George, Duke of Saxony, because his letter would carry decisive weight with him: "there is need of your letters."

Melanchthon's Letter of May 22.

---

* Corpus Reformatorum, ii. Epist., No. 680.

This letter shows :

1. That Melanchthon desired Luther to know all that he was doing.

2. That the Articles of Faith were finished, and that the changes were confined to the Articles on Abuses.

3. That in the discussions on Abuses, there were many questions which would have to be decided as the occasions, in the providence of God, would determine them.

From three to four days seems to have been the ordinary time of the letter-carrier between Augsburg and Coburg. The Elector sent the Confession May 11th. Luther replied May 15th, probably the very day he received it; his reply probably reached Augsburg May 20th, and two days after, Melanchthon sends him the Articles of Faith, with the elaboration which had taken place in the interval, and informs him of what he had been doing, and designs to do.

In part, on the assumption that Luther was not permitted to receive this letter, a theory was built by Rückert, a Rationalistic writer of Germany, that the Augsburg Confession was meant to be a compromise with Rome, and that it was feared that if Luther were not kept in the dark he would spoil the scheme. But even if Luther did not receive Melanchthon's letter and the Articles of May 22d, we deny that the rational solution would be that they were fraudulently held back by the friends of the Confession at Augsburg. Grant that Luther never received them. What then? The retention of them would have been an act of flagrant immorality ; it was needless, and foolish, and hazardous ; it is in conflict with the personal character of the great princes and leaders, political and theological, who were as little disposed as Luther, to compromise any principle with Rome. The Elector and Brück were on some points less disposed to be yielding than Luther. The theory is contradicted by the great body of facts, which show that Luther, though absent in body, was the controlling spirit at Augsburg. It is contradicted by the Confession itself, which is a presentation, calm in manner, but mighty in the matter, in which it overthrows Popery from the very foundation. It is contradicted by the fierce replies of the Papists in the Council, by the assaults of Popery upon it through all time, by the decrees of the Council of Trent, whose main polemical reference is to it. It is contradicted by the enthusiastic admiration which Luther felt, and expressed again and again, for the Confession.

The millions of our purified churches have justly regarded it for ages as the great bulwark against Rome, and the judgment of the whole Protestant world has been a unit as to its fundamentally Evangelical and Scriptural character over against Rome. Its greatest defenders have been the most able assailants of Popery.

It might as well be assumed that the Bible is a compromise with the Devil, and that the Holy Ghost was excluded from aiding in its production, lest he should embarrass the proceedings, as that the Augsburg Confession is, or was meant to be, a compromise with Popery, and that Luther was consequently prevented from having a share in producing it.

If the letter really never reached Luther, the theory that it was fraudulently kept at Augsburg by the friends of the Confession, that the whole thing was one of the meanest, and at the same time, most useless crimes ever committed, is so extreme, involves such base wickedness on the part of its perpetrators, that nothing but the strongest evidences or the most overwhelming presumptions justify a man in thinking such an explanation possible.

If this letter, or others, never reached Luther, it is to be attributed either to the imperfect mode of transmission, in which letters were lost, miscarried, or destroyed by careless or fraudulent carriers, of which bitter complaints constantly occur in the letters of Luther and others at that time, or if there were any steps taken to prevent Luther's letters reaching him, these steps would be taken by the Romanists, who were now gathering in increasing force at Augsburg. The difficulty in the way of communicating with Luther increased, as his being at Coburg was kept secret from his enemies, and at his request, in a letter which we shall quote, was kept secret in June even from the body of his friends.

So much for the theory, granting its fact for argument's sake.

But the fact is that Luther did receive Melanchthon's letter of the 22d. The letter was not lost, but appears in all the editions of Melanchthon's letters, entire,* and in the earliest histories of the Augsburg Confession, without a hint, from the beginning up to Rückert's time, that it had not been received. When we turn to Luther's letters, complaining of the silence of his friends, we find no evidence that Melanchthon's letter had not been received. They create, on the contrary, the strongest presumption that it had been received. As it was sent at once, (Melanchthon says that he had hired a letter-carrier before he began the letter,) it would reach Luther about May 25th.

Luther's letter of June 1st to Jacob Probst, in Bremen,† shows that he had intelligence of the most recent date from Augsburg, that he was sharing in the cares and responsibilities of what was then passing: "Here, also, I am occupied with business for God, and the burden of the whole empire rests upon us." He then uses, in part, the very language of Melanchthon's letter of May 22d, as to the time when the Emperor would be at Augsburg.‡ He quotes from that letter Melanchthon's very words in regard to Mercurinus: § "He would have nothing to do with violent councils — that it had appeared at Worms what violent councils would do. He desired the affairs of the Church to be peacefully arranged." He closes his account of things at Augsburg by saying: "You have an account of matters now as they *are to-day* at Augsburg" (*hodie habet.*)

Luther did receive Melanchthon's letter of the 22d, and on June 1st quotes largely from it.

Up to this time, too, there is no complaint of suspension of

* In the original Latin, in Corpus Reform., ii., No. 698. In German, in Walch's Luther's Werke, xvi., No. 927.

† De Wette's Briefe, No. 1217. Buddeus, Suppl., No. 123.

‡ Melanchthon: vix ante Pentecosten. Luther: forte ad Pentecosten.

§ Melanc.: Nolle se violentis consiliis interesse. Luth.: Se nolle interesse violentis consiliis. Mel.: Wormatiæ apparuisse, quam nihil proficiant violenta consilia. Luth.: Wormatiæ vidisset, quid efficerent violenta consilia. Mel.: Vir summus Mercurinus. Luth.: Summus Mercurinus. Mel.: Res ecclesiasticæ rite constituerentur. Luth.: Ecclesiæ res cum pace constitui.

communication with Augsburg, but, on the contrary, he reports up to the day on which he writes.

On June 2d, Luther writes to Melanchthon.* There is no word of complaint in this letter of any silence on the part of Melanchthon, or of others at Augsburg. He complains that he is so overrun with visitors as to be compelled to leave Coburg for a day, to create the impression that he is no longer there. " I beg of you, and the others with you, in future to speak and *write* so that *no one* will seek me here any longer; *for I wish to remain concealed*, and to have you, at the same time, to keep me concealed, both in your words *and letters.*" He then speaks of the report that the Emperor would not come to Augsburg at all, and of his deep anxiety. This letter shows what was the subject of Luther's intense solicitude on the following days. A thousand alarming rumors reached him, and he was anxious to hear, by every possible opportunity, from Augsburg; at the same time, wishing to be concealed, he had requested Melanchthon and his other friends to avoid sending etters in a way that would make it known that he was at Coburg. These two facts help to solve Luther's great solicitude to hear news, and also, in part, as we have said, to account for the irregularity in his receiving letters, as they would, in accordance with his direction of June 2d, be sent with secrecy. In Luther's letter of June 5th, he complains not that there had been a long delay, but that they did not write by every opportunity. These were sometimes quite frequent. In some cases more than one opportunity occurred in a day. None of Luther's anxiety is about the Confession. In Luther's letter to Melanchthon, of June 7th, he complains of the silence of his friends at Augsburg, but in a *playful tone.* In his letter of June 19th, to Cordatus,† he says: " We have no *news* from Augsburg. Our friends at Augsburg write us none." In his letter to Gabriel Zwilling,‡ June 19th, he says: " You will, perhaps, get the *news* from Bernhard, for our friends have not

* De Wette, Briefe, No. 1219. Buddeus, No. 124. In German, Walch xvi., p. 2826.

† De Wette, Briefe, No 1229. Buddeus, No. 125. Walch xvi. 2833.

‡ De Wette, No. 1230. Buddeus, No. 126. Walch xvi. 2836.

answered our letters through the whole month," (June.) Luther's letter of *June 20th*, to Justus Jonas,* gives direct evidence how long the interruption of correspondence continued: " Your letters have come at last, my Jonas, after we were well fretted for *three whole weeks* with your silence." The period, therefore, does not embrace May 22d, but only the first three weeks in June. There is no reason whatever, therefore, for doubting that Luther received Melanchthon's letter, and the Articles of Faith of May 22d. On June 1st, the Elector, John, sent Luther secret advices of an important proposition which he had received from the Emperor. If, therefore, there were any furtive and dishonorable course pursued toward Luther, the causes and results of it must, in some special manner, be found between the Elector's secret advices of June 1st and the letter to Luther from Augsburg, June 15th; but there is nothing in the course of events to suggest any such reason, even if there were a fact which seemed to require something of the sort — but there is no such fact. On the contrary, we shall produce a fact which will sweep away all necessity for any further discussion of this point.

We have seen, 1st, that the Confession was sent by the Elector, May 11th, to Luther, at Coburg, for his written judgment upon it, in its *first form.*

2d. That it was sent again, on the 22d of the same month, by Melanchthon, and was received by Luther, in its *second form.*

3d. We shall now show that it was sent as nearly as possible in its complete shape to Luther, for a *third time*, before it was delivered, and was approved by him in what may probably be called its *final form.*

The evidence to which we shall appeal is that of Melanchthon himself. It is first found in the Preface to his Body of Christian Doctrine, (Corpus Doctrinæ,) 1560, and also in the Preface to the first volume of the Wittenberg edition of his works in folio. It is reprinted in the Corpus Reformatorum, vol. ix., No. 6932. He there says, in giving a history of the Augsburg Confession:

---

* De Wette No. 1232. Buddeus. No. 127.

I. "I brought together the principal points of the Confession, embracing pretty nearly the sum of the doctrine of our Churches."

II. "I assumed nothing to myself, for in the presence of the Princes and other officials, and of the preachers, it was discussed and determined upon in regular course, sentence by sentence."

III. "The complete form of the Confession was *subsequently* (*deinde*) sent to Luther, who wrote to the Princes that he had read the Confession and approved it. That these things were so done, the Princes, and other honest and learned men, *yet living*, well remember."

IV. "*After this* (*postea*,) before the Emperor Charles, in a great assemblage of the Princes, this Confession was read."

This extract shows, 1, that this complete Confession — the *tota forma* — the Articles on Doctrines and Abuses, as contrasted with any earlier and imperfect form of the Confession, was submitted to Luther.

2. This is wholly distinct from Luther's indorsement of the Confession as sent May 11th, for that was not the "*tota forma*," but relatively unfinished; that had not been discussed before Princes, officials, and preachers, for they were not yet at Augsburg. Nor was it then meant that the Confession should be made in the name of all the Evangelical States. It was to be limited to Saxony. Luther's reply to the letter of May 11th was not to the Princes, but to John alone. Up to May 11th, the Elector (with his suite) was the only one of the Princes at Augsburg. On the 12th, the Landgrave of Hesse came ; on the 15th the Nurembergers. Not until after May 22d did that conference and discussion take place, of which Melanchthon speaks. After the whole form of the Confession had been decided upon, it was sent to Luther, received his final indorsement, and was presented to Charles. This complete form was identical in matter with the Confession as exhibited, although verbal changes were made by Melanchthon up to the very time of its delivery.

On LUTHER's *opinion of the Augsburg Confession*, we propose to let Luther speak for himself.

1. 1530, May 15. In Luther's reply to the Elector, he says

"I have read the Apology (Confession,) of Philip, from begin
ning to end; it pleases me exceedingly well, and I know of
nothing by which I could better it, or change it, nor would I
Luther's opin- be fitted to do it, for I cannot move so moderately
ion of the Augs- and gently. May Christ our Lord help, that it
burg Confession. may bring forth much and great fruit, as we hope
and pray.   Amen."*

These words of admiration for Melanchthon's great gifts,
came from Luther's inmost heart.   Less than six months before
he had written to Jonas: † "All the Jeromes, Hillarys, and
Macariuses together, are not worthy to unloose the thong of
Philip's sandal.   What have the whole of them together done
which can be compared with one year of Philip's teaching, or
to his one book of Common Places?" Had Luther been at
Augsburg, he would have allowed the work of finishing "the
form of the Confession" to be given to no other hands than
Melanchthon's. "I prefer," he says, "Melanchthon's books to
my own, and would rather have them circulated than mine.
I was born to battle with conspirators and devils, therefore my
books are more vehement and warlike. It is my work to tear
up the stumps and dead roots, to cut away the thorns, to fill
up the marshes. I am the rough forester and pioneer. But
Melanchthon moves gently and calmly along, with his rich
gifts from God's own hand, building and planting, sowing and
watering."‡

2. Between June 8th and 25th, we have Melanchthon's declaration, cited in our former extracts, as to Luther's approval of
the Confession in the form it took after the discussion.

3. June 3d. Luther to Melanchthon : "I yesterday re-read
your Apology entire, with care (*diligenter,*) and it pleases me
exceedingly." §

4. July 6th, to Hausman : ‖ he speaks lovingly of "*our* Confession which our Philip hath prepared."

---

* Luther's Briefe, De Wette, 1213, Walch xvi, 785. In Latin: Cœlestinus i,
40, Buddeus 93. In French: (Le Cop's) Chytraeus, p. 29.

† Buddeus, No. 100.   ‡ Pref. to Melanchthon on Colossians.

§ In Latin : De Wette, No. 1243. Buddeus, No. 187. German : Walch xvi
1082.

‖ De Wette, No. 1245.

5. July 6, to Cordatus : * " The Confession of ours was read before the whole empire. I am glad exceedingly to have lived to this hour, in which Christ through h'.s so great Confessors, in so great an Assembly, has been preached in so glorious a Confession, and that word has been fulfilled : ' I will speak of thy testimonies in the presence of kings,' and this also has been fulfilled : ' and shall not be ashamed,' for ' him who confesseth me before men ' (it is the word of him who cannot lie,) ' I also will confess before my Father who is in heaven.' "

6. July 6, to the Cardinal Albert, Archbishop of Mentz, Primate of Germany : † " Your Highness, as well as the other orders of the empire, has doubtless read the Confession, delivered by ours, which I am persuaded is so composed, that with joyous lips it may say with Christ : ' If I have spoken evil, bear witness of the evil ; but if well, why smitest thou me?' It shuns not the light, and can sing with the Psalmist : ' I will speak of thy testimonies before kings, and will not be ashamed.' But I can well conceive that our adversaries will by no means accept the doctrine, but much less are they able to confute it. I have no hope whatever that we can agree in doctrine ; for their cause cannot bear the light. Such is their bitterness, with such hatred are they kindled, that they would endure hell itself rather than yield to us, and relinquish their new wisdom. I know that this our doctrine is true, and grounded in the holy Scriptures. By this Confession we clearly testify and demonstrate that we have not taught wrongly or falsely."

7. July 9, to Duke John, Elector of Saxony : ‡ " Our adversaries thought they had gained a great point in having the preaching interdicted by the Emperor, but the infatuated men did not see that by this written Confession, which was offered to the Emperor, this doctrine was more preached, and more widely propagated, than ten preachers could have done it. It was a fine point that our preachers were silenced, but in their stead came forth the Elector of Saxony and other princes and lords, with the written Confession, and preached freely in sight

* De Wette, 1246. Walch xvi, 1083.
† De Wette, No. 1247. Walch xvi, 1085. In Latin : Buddeus, No. 139.
‡ De Wette, No. 1050. Walch xvi, 969. Latin : Buddeus, No. 142.

of all, before the Emperor and the whole empire. Christ surely was not silenced at the Diet, and mad as they were, they were compelled to hear more from the Confession, than they would have heard from the preachers in a year. Paul's declaration was fulfilled: ' The word of God is not bound: ' silenced in the pulpit, it was heard in the palace; the poor preachers were not allowed to open their lips — but great princes and lords spoke it forth."

8. July 9, to Jonas:* "There will never be agreement concerning doctrine " (between the Evangelical and Romish Churches,) "for how can Christ and Belial be in concord? But the first thing, and that the greatest at this Council has been, that Christ has been proclaimed in a public and *glorious Confession ;* he has been confessed in the light and to their face, so that they cannot boast that we fled, or that we feared, or concealed our faith. My only unfulfilled desire about it is that I was not present at this noble Confession. I have been like the generals who could take no part in defending Vienna from the Turks. But it is my joy and solace that meanwhile *my Vienna* was defended by others."

9. July 15. Luther addresses a letter to his "most dear brother in Christ, Spalatine, steadfast Confessor of Christ at Augsburg;"† and again, July 20th, "to Spalatine, faithful servant and Confessor of Christ at Augsburg."‡

10. July 20, to Melanchthon: "It was a great affliction to me that I could not be present with you in the body at that most beautiful and holy Confession of Christ "§ (*pulcherrima et sanctissima.*) August 3d, he sends a letter to Melanchthon, "his most dear brother in Christ, and Confessor of the Lord at Augsburg."

11. But perhaps nowhere has Luther's enthusiastic admiration for the Augsburg Confession blazed up more brightly than in his eloquent summary of what our Confessors had done at the Diet. It is in the last letter he wrote to Melanchthon, before they again met at Coburg (September 15th): "You have confessed Christ, you have offered peace, you have obeyed the Emperor, you have endured injuries, you have been drenched

* De Wette, No. 1251.   Walch xvi, 1098   ‡ Buddeus, No. 154.
† Buddeus, No. 150.   § Buddeus, No. 155.

in their revilings, you have not returned evil for evil. In brief, you have worthily done God's holy work as becometh saints. Be glad then in the Lord, and exult, ye righteous. Long have ye borne witness in the world, look up and lift up your heads, for your redemption draweth nigh. *I will canonize you as faithful members of Christ*, and what greater glory can ye have than to have yielded Christ faithful service, and shown yourself a member worthy of him?"

12. In his Table Talk Luther said: "Such is the efficacy and power of God's word, that the more it is persecuted, the more it flourishes and spreads. Call to mind the Diet at Augsburg, where the last trumpet before the judgment-day sounded. How the whole world then raged against our doctrine! Our doctrine and faith were brought forth to light in our Confession. Our doctrines fell into the souls of many of the noblest men, and ran like sparks in tinder. They were kindled, and kindled others. Thus our Confession and Defence came forth in the highest glory."*

13. In the year 1533,† Luther united in demanding of candidates as a pre-requisite to entering the ministry, the declaration, "that they embraced the uncorrupted doctrine of the Gospel, and so understood it, as it is set forth in the Apostles', Nicene, and Athanasian Creeds, and as it is repeated in the Confession, which our Churches offered to the Emperor at the Diet of Augsburg, 1530, and the promise that with God's help they will remain steadfast in that conviction to the end, and will faithfully perform their duty in the Church."

It is not wonderful that Melanchthon himself considered the Confession as rather Luther's than his own, and called it "the Confession of the revered Doctor Luther."‡

This, then, is the result of the whole: The Holy Ghost in His ordinary illumination through the Word, is the true source and original of the Augsburg Confession; its secondary source is the whole Evangelical Church of 1530, the main organ

* Leipz., xx, 200. Tischreden (Fœrstemann,) iv, 351.

† Buddeus, No. 178.

‡ Melanchthon Orat. (1553.) Pref. to Confessio Doctrinæ, 1551, in Corp Ref., lib. xii, No. 5849

of whose utterance was, as to the *matter* and the substance of the form, Luther; as to the finish and grace of the form, Melanchthon: both acting with the advice, co-labor, and full approval of the clerical and lay representatives of the Church. Just as we accept this or that point of view, we may say that the Augsburg Confession is the work of the Evangelical Church, or of the theologians and laymen at Augsburg, or of Melanchthon, or of Luther. "The Confession of ours," "our Confession which our Philip prepared," "your Confession," "my Confession," are all terms employed by Luther. All these statements are true, and perfectly harmonious—just as we may say that the Declaration of Independence was the work of the Thirteen Colonies, or of the Continental Congress, or of its Committee, or of Thomas Jefferson. Melanchthon, then, was by pre-eminence the composer of the Confession, not as a private individual, but as chief of a body of advisers, without whose concurrence nothing was fixed,* Luther, by pre-eminence, as the divinely called representative of the Church, its author. Hence all candid writers have most heartily indorsed Luther's own declaration, in which he not only claims the Augsburg Confession as in one sense his own, but ranks it among his most precious works: † "The Catechism, the Exposition of the Ten Commandments, and the *Augsburg Confession are mine.*" This claim he puts in, in no sense which conflicts with the public character of the document, or of Melanchthon's great merit, as in part the compiler, and as in part the composer of the Confession. Kœllner adds: "And he had the right to say so." Weber ‡ says: "As to its matter, Luther was the author of the Confession, not indeed the only one, but the primary one." "Melanchthon," says Danz, § "was the composer, the editor, not the author, (Redacteur, nicht Urheber.)"

But are there not a few words of Luther in regard to the Confession, which are in conflict with this enthusiastic approval? We reply, there is not one word of the kind. The

* Melanchthon, June 26. "I would have changed more things if my counsellors would have permitted it."

† Werke (Walch,) xxii, 4532. Kœllner 181 (45.)

‡ L. S. prol. ad C. A. p. viii.   § A. C. § 8.

passages which have been cited to show that Luther was not satisfied with the Confession, in some respects, are the following:

1. June 29,* (to Melanchthon.) "On my side more than enough has been yielded in that Apology, which if they refuse, I see nothing more which I can yield, unless they furnish clearer reasons and Scripture proofs than I have yet seen them furnish." In this citation it is manifest that Luther does not mean that any concessions have been made, by others, for him. It is his own concessions of which he speaks, concessions not of doctrine or of principle, but of preferences, very dear to him, which might be renounced if the truth itself were not periled. "Day and night" he adds, "I am occupied with the matter, thinking over it, revolving it in my mind, arguing, searching the entire Scriptures, and there grows upon me constantly that fullness of assurance, in this our doctrine, and I am more and more confirmed in the purpose, that I will yield nothing more, come what may." "I am offended at your writing, that ir this cause, you follow my authority. I will not be, nor be called, author in this cause. If it is not equally your cause, it shall not be said that it was mine, and was imposed on you. If it be my cause alone, I will manage it alone." "If we be not the Church, or a part of the Church, where is the Church? If we have not the Word of God, who has it?" "As I have always written, so I now write, I am ready to concede to them everything, provided only, that the Gospel be left free to us. But what conflicts with the Gospel I cannot concede." This shows that Luther felt that no concession in conflict with the Gospel had been made in the Confession.

2. The letter of July 3d,† to Melanchthon, is one which Rückert, with the prosiness characteristic of the Rationalistic mind, is completely puzzled with, but he can make nothing of

Luther's alleged objections to the Confession.

---

* In Latin: Epistol. Mar. Luth. Buddeus, 113. Cœlestin. i. 198. De Wette, No. 1236. German: Jena (ed. 1566) 40. Leipz. xx. 185. French: Chytræus (Le Cop) 131.

† Latin: Ep. M. L. Budd. 127. Cœlestinus, 204. German: Walch xvi. 1092 De Wette, No. 1243.

it, if it be not meant to censure the Confession. It must be granted, that it opens in an extraordinary manner for a letter of censure: "Yesterday, I read again carefully your Apology, and it pleases me vehemently." Now come the supposed words of stricture: "But it errs and sins in one thing, that it acts contrary to the Holy Scripture, where Christ says of himself, 'We will not have this man to reign over us'; and falls upon that reproof 'the stone which the builders rejected.' But where there is so great blindness and obstinacy, what can you expect but to be rejected. For they do not grant us the name of builders, a name which they arrogate to themselves, and with justice; but we ought to glory in the name of destroyers, scatterers, and disturbers; we should glory in being counted with the wicked, as that stone itself was counted with thieves and condemned with them." To one familiar with Luther's style and vein of thought, it is at once apparent that these words are ironical: they burlesque, and hardly burlesque, the absurd arguments and use of texts of which some of the Romish Controversialists of that day were guilty. Luther begins by playfully personating such an objector. The Confession will have Christ to reign over us, but the objector urges this is contrary to Scripture, which says: 'We will not have t is man to reign over us.' The Confession moreover is reproved by Scripture for making a corner-stone of the very thing which the builders rejected. We are the builders, and you reformers are the pullers down. The humor of the passage consists in making the opponents represent that as approval which the Scripture condemns, that as reproach which the Scripture approves, and in throwing upon them their own claims to be builders. You are the builders, no doubt, the builders who rejected the stone which has become the head-stone of the corner, in the Confession.

3. The letter of July 21,[*] to Justus Jonas, speaking of the question which had been put, 'Whether the Confession had more articles to present,' says: "Satan still lives, and has observed that your Apology, treading softly, has passed over

---

[*] Latin: Budd. 169. Cœlestinus, 233. German: Wa'ch xvi. 2843. De Wette. No. 1266.

the Article of Purgatory, of the Worship of the Saints, and most of all of the Pope as Antichrist. Unhappy Emperor, if he proposes to give up the Diet to listening to confutations of Luther, as if the present Apology did not give them enough to answer." This means that although the Confession, by not making a longer enumeration of abuses, had led to this demand, yet that it had quite enough. The words moreover, in the most unfavorable sense, would only show that Luther wished that among the Articles of Abuses there should have been a declaration that the Pope is Antichrist, and a full handling of the doctrine of Saint-Worship and Purgatory. But the Confession, as a conjoint public document, could only discuss what a majority of those who were to unite in it thought best to present. Melanchthon himself was overruled in regard to matters he desired to introduce. The Augsburg Confession was no private document, but in the labors of both Luther and Melanchthon in connection with it, both were the organs of the whole Church, and were compelled to sacrifice their mere private preferences to the common judgment. Every sentence, every word of the Augsburg Confession as it stands, embodies the faith of Luther, and received his unqualified, repeated, and enthusiastic assent.

If, in the Declaration of Independence, Thomas Jefferson, in preparing his statement of the political abuses which justified our separation from Great Britain, had wished to specify one or two more than the Committee thought necessary, and which were consequently not inserted, it would not weaken his claim to the authorship of that document. Nor would the fact, that he continued to think that it would have improved it to have specified the one or two additional abuses, affect the conscientious heartiness with which he indorsed that document, nor impair the value of his testimony. But even the preference of Luther, to which this is a fair parallel, was but transient, and he came to see clearly what the whole world has since seen, that in its silence, the Augsburg Confession is a model of exquisite judgment, as in its utterances it is a masterpiece of style.

The occasion of the Augsburg Confession was the command
16

of the Emperor, — not that he demanded such a Confession, but that under the leadings of God's providence it grew ou

Object of the Augsburg Confession. of his summons. The last was destined to become first, and the first last. The Confessors themselves did not at first realize the full value of the opening which had been made for the proclamation of the truth, but when it dawned upon them they showed themselves worthy of their great position. They at first meant but an Apology. The faith they cherished, and the usages they practised, they simply wished to defend from the current libels This object they did not lose sight of, but it became secondary. Their distinctive object soon became the setting forth the great points in the whole system of heavenly truth, and the showing how, in its light, they had endeavored cautiously, and gently, yet firmly, to remove the abuses which had arisen in the Church of the West. The Apology was transfigured into a Confession. It was not only not meant to be a compromise with Popery, but it clearly showed, and was designed to show, that such a compromise is impossible. Our Reformers had indeed cherished a noble hope, which bitter experience was constantly rendering feebler, that the whole Church of the West, redeemed from the thrall of the Pope, might return to her ancient Scriptural faith, and, abjuring Roman Catholicism, attain once more to Christian Catholicity, and become a Communion of saints. If such a return had been possible, the Augsburg Confession, alike in the simplicity and purity of its statement of doctrine, the conservatism of its whole tone, its firmness and .ts gentleness, would have helped to facilitate it; but the bridge it made was not meant to open the way back to error, but to aid men to come over to the pure faith.

The Confession, in Latin and German, was presented to the

The presentation of the Confession : Latin and German Text.* Diet on Saturday, June 25th, 1530. Both texts are originals; neither text is properly a translation of the other; both present precisely the same doctrines, but with verbal differences, which make the

---

* Manuscripts of the Augsburg Confession in the Archives. Cf. Köllner, 321 -336.

A. Latin manuscripts. Köllner 323–329. Corpus Reformatorum, xxvi, 213–226.

one an indispensable guide in the full understanding of the other; both texts have, consequently, the same authority. The German copy was the one selected, on national grounds, to be read aloud. Both copies were taken by the Emperor, who handed the German to the Elector of Mentz, and retained the Latin. It is not now known where either of the originals is, nor with certainty that either is in existence. In addition to seven unauthorized editions in the year 1530, the Confession was printed, under Melanchthon's own direction, both in Latin and German, while the Diet was still sitting. Authorized editions of this year, both in Latin and German, are in the hands of the writer, and have been examined in preparing this work. The Confession began to be multiplied at once. Innumerable editions of the originals, and translations into the chief languages of Europe appeared. Its enemies have helped its friends to circulate it, and to preserve the re-issues of these originals from any change involving more than questions of purely literary interest.

When Melanchthon, in 1540, issued a varied Edition of the Latin, though he declared that the changes were but verbal, and that he designed only to state more clearly the precise doctrine of the Confession in its original shape, the changes were marked by foe and friend. In Melanchthon's Edition

1. The Weimar MS: (Vin. Weim.) cf. Corp. Reform. l. c. 223. Köllner 323. Foerstemann, Urkundenb. i. 444. Weber i. 79–81. The variations are given in Weber, Foerstemann, Hase, Müller, Corp. Reformat. — 2. The Anspach: (Onold. Ansb.) ut supra. — 3. The Hannoverian. Köllner 324. Weber i. 84. — 4. Hessian I. Köllner 325; Foerstemann i. 442, gives the variations. — 5. Hessian ii. Foerstemann i. 444, gives the variations. — 6. Dessau (Anhalt.) Cf. Weber i. 87, who gives the variations. — 7. The Nuremberg. Köllner 336; Weber i. 94, gives the variations. — 8. The Ratisbon. Köllner 327; Foerstemann 446, gives the variations (Reg.) — 9. The Würzburger, Köllner 329; Foerstemann (i. 446) gives the variations.

B. German Manuscripts.

1. The Mentz copy in the Protocoll of the Empire. This was long regarded as the original, and as such found a place in the Book of Concord (1580.) Cf. Weber i. 165; Köllner 306. — 2. Spalatin's (Weimar i.) — 3. Weimar (ii.) — 4. The first Anspach (i.) — 5. The second Anspach (ii.) — 6. The third Anspach (iii.) — 7. The Hannoverian. — 8. The Nuremberg. — 9. The Hessian. — 10. The Munich [Münch.] — 11. Nordlingen. — 12. Augsburg. Of all these Köllner, Foerstemann and Weber give full descriptions, and the two latter the variations; so also Müller, under the text of the Editio Princeps.

of 1531, trifling changes of a verbal nature had been made, but in antithesis to both this Edition and the Original of 1530,

The Augsburg Confession Al- tered.* that of 1540 is called the *Variata*, because it has elaborated anew some of the articles, and has made important changes. The first articles so treated is the Article on Original Sin, (II) in which the changes are these as given in brackets:

" They also teach that after Adam's fall all men propagated after the common course of nature [*the natural mode*] are born with sin [being born have sin of origin] that is without fear of God, without trust toward God. [But by sin of origin, we understand, what the Holy Fathers so call, and all the orthodox and piously instructed in the Church, to wit, liability (reatum) by which those born, are on account of (propter) Adam's fall, liable to (rei) the wrath of God and eternal death, as also, the corruption itself, of human nature, which (corruption) is pro-pagated from Adam,] and with concupiscence. [And the corruption of human nature, defect of the original righteousness, or integrity, or obedience, embraces concupiscence.]

---

* Melanchthon's varied edition of the *Latin* Confession of three kinds.
I. 1531, 8vo.   II. 1540, 4to.   III. 1542, 8vo.   Weber ii. 32–116.

I. Edition of 1531, 8vo.   The variations slight.   It has never been pretended that they affect the meaning.   Weber ii. 82–102.   Corpus Reformat. xxvi. 337. – Lutheri Opera, Jena (1583) iv, 191–203.—Melanchthon's Opera, Wittenb. 1562, p. 27–38. — Corpus doctrinæ, Leipz. 1563, given with that of 1542. — This edi-tion has often been confounded with the edition of 1530, 4to. (1. *a*.,) and was actually introduced by Selnecker into the first Latin edition of the Book of Con cord. Cf. Weber ii. 102; Köllner 348.   The variations are given in Hase: Pro-legomena xv. Confess. Variat. Varietas, and are marked (A.)

II. Edition of the Latin Confession, 1540, 4to.   The *variata*.   Weber ii. 103–107. — Corpus Reformat. xxvi, 339.— It is given in Corpus Reformatorum xxvi, 351–416, with the various readings. (Edit. of 1535, 1538. — The variations are given in Hase: Prolegomena xv–lxxiv and are marked (B.) — It is translated in "An Harmony of Confessions," &c., Cambridge, 1586. It is there called the "first edition." Cf. Weber ii. 103, Köllner 349.

III. Latin Confession of 1542, 8vo.   The variata varied. — Weber ii. 108–116, Corpus Reformat. xxvi, 345. — Given in Corpus Doctrinae, Lipsiæ, 1563. 1–56. — Fabricii Harmonia 1573. — Melanchthonis Opera (Peucer) Witt. 1562. i. 39–58. This has been frequently reprinted, and is sometimes confounded with the Vari-ata of 1540.—The variations are given in Hase, and are marked (C.) and in Corp. Reform. (ed. 4.) Cf. Weber ii. 108; Köllner 349.   It is translated in "an Harmony," &c.   It is there called " the second edition."

"And that this disease or vice of origin [And this defect is a horrible blindness and non-obedience, to-wit, to lack that light and knowledge of God which would have been in nature, in integrity; likewise to lack that rectitude, that is perpetual obedience, the true, pure and highest love of God, and like gifts of nature in integrity. Wherefore these defects and concupiscence, are things condemned, and in their own nature worthy death; and the vice of origin] is truly sin . . . [They condemn the Pelagians who deny the sin of origin, and think that those defects, or concupiscence, are things indifferent or penalties only, not things to be condemned in their own nature, and who dream that man can satisfy the law of God, and can on account of this obedience of his own be pronounced just before God.]"

The Fourth Article (on Justification) is greatly enlarged, and the treatment of the topic is very fine. The Fifth on the Means of Grace asserts more distinctly than the original Confession the *universality* of the offer of Remission in the Gospel, and is thus more positively Anti-Calvinistic in its expression on this point. The Sixth amplifies the doctrine of Holiness, in its relations to Justification. In the Ninth it is said: Baptism is necessary to salvation [as a ceremony instituted by Christ.] Infants through Baptism, being [committed] to God, are received into God's favor, [and become children of God, as Christ testifieth, saying of the little ones in the Church, Matt. xviii, 'It is not the will of your Father in heaven, that one of these little ones should perish'.] They condemn the Anabaptists who affirm that infants are saved without Baptism [and outside of the Church of Christ.] This is yet more decidedly than the original Article incapable of a Calvinistic construction. The Articles on Free Will (xviii,) the Defence of Justification by Faith (xx,) the Worship of Saints (xxi,) are all ably amplified. The Articles on Abuses are recast and re-arranged. It is not to be disputed that in various respects, as a statement of doctrine, the Variata has great beauty and great value, and that where it indisputably is in perfect harmony with the original Confession, it furnishes an important aid in its interpretation. Had Melanchthon put forth the new matter purely as a private

writing, most of it would have received the unquestioning admiration to which it was well entitled.   But he made the fatal
mistake of treating a great official document as if it were his
private property, yet preserving the old title, the old form in general, and the old signatures.   How would Jefferson have been
regarded if in 1786, ten years after the Declaration, he had sent
forth what he called the Declaration of Independence, enlarged
here, abridged there, with new topics and new treatment, and
with what seemed at least a concession to the power from
whom we had separated, had added to this the names of the
Committee and the vouchers of the Continental Congress, that
this was its act and deed for the nation?   Melanchthon did
worse than this.   The Declaration of Independence was the
mere form of an act consummated.   The Augsburg Confession
was a document of permanent force, and of continuous use.
To alter any of its doctrines, was to acknowledge that so far
the Confessors had erred, and to excite the suspicion that they
might have erred in more ; and to alter the phrases, no matter
what explanation might be given, would be construed as involving alteration of doctrine.   Nor were the adversaries of our
faith slow in taking advantage of Melanchthon's great mistake.   The first public notice of the change came from the
Roman Catholic side.   Melanchthon brought the Variata with
him to the Colloquy at Worms, at the beginning of 1541.*
The Augsburg Confession was by the request of the Protestants
(Lutherans) to be the basis of the discussion.   Eck brought
to the Colloquy, from the Imperial Archives of Mentz, the
German Original, which had been read at the Diet in 1530, and
had been given to the Emperor.   He opened with these words:
" Before all else I would prefer one thing . . Those of the other
part have offered to us a copy of the Confession and Apology,
not at all (minus) in conformity with the Hagenau Recess, in
virtue of which the *Confession itself*, as it was given (exhibita)
to his Imperial majesty, and the Princes, ought to have been
given to us also, nakedly and truly . . . waiving that point however, with a protest, we turn to the matter in hand."   To this

* Corpus Reformator. iv. No. 2132.   P. Melanchthon. Leb. u. ausgewählt.
Werke, von Dr. Carl Schmidt. Elberfeld. 1861. 879.

Melanchthon replied, "As to the dissimilarity of copies, I answer that the *meaning of the things is the same* (rerum eandem esse sententiam,) although some things here and there, in the later edition, are more freed from harshness, (mitigata) or are more explicit." To this Eck replied : " As to the variation of copies, I could easily overthrow his reply, and show by ocular inspection, that not only in words, but in the things themselves, these copies depart from the Augsburg Confession. For brevity's sake I defer what I have to say, to the Articles as they come up in the colloquy, when I will make clear what I have alleged, as in the *Tenth* Article, etc." To this Melanchthon said : " We can reply more fitly elsewhere to what has been urged in regard to copies — and let there be some moderation to charges of this sort." To this Eck said : " As to the change of copies, I now purposely pass it by." If Melanchthon consciously made a change of meaning in the Confession, it is impossible to defend him from the charge of direct falsehood. For ourselves we do not hesitate for a moment. With all the mistakes into which Melanchthon fell through his great love of peace, we regard him as above all suspicion in any point involving Christian character. If the doctrine of the Variata differs from that of the Confession, the change was not designed by Melanchthon. We go further and say, that to accept it as a Canon, that the interpretation of the Variata is to be conditioned by a belief that Melanchthon designed no changes, will involve the interpreter in no absurdity. The Variata can be so interpreted as to be in sufficient harmony with the Unaltered Confession, to leave Melanchthon's statement credible. Of the changes in the Tenth Article (the Lord's Supper) we shall speak in another place. The Calvinists and Crypto-Calvinists acted as if they did not believe Melanchthon's statement that no alteration of doctrine had been intended. In the Lutheran Church different views were taken of the matter. Those who believed Melanchthon's declaration that the changes were purely verbal, the better to express the very doctrine set forth at Augsburg, either passed them over without disapproval, or were comparatively lenient in their censure. Every instance of the seeming toleration of them in the Lutheran Church was connected with the supposition that the Altered Confession in no respect whatever differed from the doctrine of the Unaltered. There never was any part of the Lutheran Church which imagined that Melanchthon had any right to alter the meaning of the Confession in a single particular. Melanchthon himself repeatedly, after the appearance of the *Variata*, acknowledged the Unaltered Augsburg Confession as a statement of his own unchanged faith, as for example, at the Diet of Ratisbon in 1541. In 1557, at the Colloquy at Worms, he not only acknowledged as his Creed, the Unaltered Augsburg Confession, the Apology, and the Smalcald Articles, but by name, and in writing, condemned the Zwinglian doctrine. But a few days before his death (1560), he said : "I confess no other doctrine than that which Luther propounded, and in this will abide to the end of my life." Any man who professes to accept the Altered Confession, therefore, though he rejects the Unaltered, either is dishonest, or assumes that Melanchthon was, and shows himself willing to take advantage of his moral weakness.

The history of the Altered Confession demonstrates that not only is it no gain to the peace of the Church, but produces a yet more grievous disturbance of it, when the effort is made to harmonize men by an agreement in ambiguous phraseology, the adoption of terms which are to be accepted in one sense by one set of men, and in another sense by another.

The Current Edition of the Augsburg Confession in LATIN, the one which is found in the Book of Concord, is the reprint of Melanchthon's own first Edition of 1530. The Current Edition of the Confession in GERMAN, however, which is the one found in the Book of Concord, is not a reprint of Melanchthon's first Edition, and this fact requires some explanation.

The Current Editions of the Augsburg Confession: Latin and German. *

* Editions and Translations of the Augsburg Confession.

For the Literature see FABRICIUS : Centifol. 109, 585–589.FEUERLIN : Bibl. Symb. [1st ed. 44–69] p. 40 seq. MASCH : Beyträge zur Geschichte merkwürdig. Bücher, [1769] i. 159. — SALIG : i. 695–737. KOECHER : Bibliotheca theol. Symbol. 145–149. WEBER : Kritisch. Geschichte. Vol. ii. — KÖLLNER : Symbol. Luth. Kirch. 226–237. 344–353. — Corpus Reformatum xxvi. 201–264. 337–350. On the translations, cf. Weber ii. 4. Feuerlin 60–64 [66–69.] Rotermund, 184. Danz. 38

The original German was, as we have seen, deposited in the imperial archives at Mentz. The Emperor had forbidden the Confession to be printed without his permission; nevertheless, it appeared surreptitiously several times in the year, printed

The work of Weber, which is classic in the department of the criticism of the text of the Confession, arranges the different editions according to the order of their publication thus:

A. The unauthorized editions of the Augsburg Confession in 1530. These were issued contrary to the order of the Emperor, and without the knowledge of the Protestant Princes. Weber i. 353–408. Danz. 35–40. There were *seven* editions of this kind.

I. Latin: There was *one* Latin edition. This is described by WEBER i. 405–408, and the variations (ED. ANT.) from Melanchthon's are given by him in the Beylagen to the second part of the Krit. Gesch. cf. Corpus Reformatorum xxvi 231–234.

II. German.

1. Described by WEBER i. 357–366, and the various readings (Ae. Ex. 1.) given. Beylag. z. Erst. Theil. iii. — 2. Described by WEBER: i. 367–372, more correct than the former. — 3. Described by WEBER: i. 372–375, closely conformed to No. 1. — 4. Described by WEBER: i. 376–381, closely follows No. 1. cf. Reimmani Catalog. 403. Feuerlin 41. — 5. Described by WEBER: i. 381–387. cf. Salig. i. 711. Feuerlin 41. — 6. Given by ZEIDLER in the supplemental volume of Luther's Werke. Halle 1702, p. 346–363. Described by WEBER: i. 387–400, who given the variations (Ae. Ex. 2.) Compare in addition, KÖLLNER Symbolik 228–231. The whole of these, Weber has shown (400) are probably based on but one MS.

B. Melanchthonian Editions: cf. KÖLLNER, 231, 345. Melanchthon's Præfatio. Salig. i. 471. Weber ii. 6.

I. The first of these, the EDITIO PRINCEPS, is the 4to edition, Latin and German. Wittenberg, 1530 (1531.) Copies of the Confession in this edition came to Augsburg while the Diet was still in session. WEBER i. 356. ii. 11. HASE Proleg. v. 3, KÖLLNER 234, cf. FEUERLIN No. 253 (205) and above all, Corpus Reformator. xxvi, 234–258.

1. The LATIN, accurately reprinted, with various readings, in WEBER's Kritisch. Gesch. ii. Beylage i. Nothwend. Vertheidig. 1629. 24–223. The Latin of the ed. princeps is also the Textus receptus of the Symbol. Books. REINECII Concord, Lips. 1708. Do. Lips. 1730. (A. C. Germ. et Latina cum vers. Graeca.) PFAFF: Lib. Symb. Tübing. 1730 first critical edition. WALCH. Christlich. Concordienb. Jena 1750. RECHENBERG: Concordia Lips. 1732 (1677.)—TWESTEN: 1816. WINER: 1825. HASE: Libr. Symb. (1827) with various readings. —FRANCKE: Lib. Symb. 1846, with various readings, and compared with the German: MÜLLER: Die Symb. Bücher, 1848. — TITTMANN: Confessio Fidei &c., ex prima Melanchthonis editione, Dresden 1830; 8vo. with notes. WEBER, 1830, with notes — FOERSTEMANN: Urkundenbuch i. 470–559, with various readings. — CORPUS REFORMATORUM xxvi. 263–336, with various readings. From this edition we have the doctrinal articles in Schmucker's Pop. Theolog., 1834. Appendix i. Do. Lutheran Manual, 1855 TRANSLATIONS It has been translated into French·

in no case from a copy of the original, but from copies of the Confession made before it had reached the perfect form in which it was actually presented to the Diet. These editions of the Confession not only being unauthorized, but not pre-

Histoire de la Conf. d'Auxpourg (Chytraeus) mise en Francois par Luc le Cop. Anvers, 1582, 72–106; cf. Weber ii. 212–216. Fabricius, Cent. Luth. 588. —In English : An harmony of Confessions, &c. Cambridge 1586. — S. S. SCHMUCKER, D. D., Popular Theology, 1834. In the doctrinal articles the condemnatory clauses are omitted, except in Art. xii, xiii, xvi, xvii. — E. HAZELIUS, D. D., Discipline, etc., 1841. 5–56. The doctrinal articles only, but with the condemnatory clauses. — C. P. KRAUTH : Augsburg Confession with notes. Philada. 1868. On the translations of the Augs. Confess. into English, cf. WEBER ii. 216–218. Under the direction of Thomas Cromwell, "who died a Lutheran" (Burnet) the Augsburg Confession and Apology were translated by RICHARD TAVERNER into English, and were printed in London, 1536.

2. The GERMAN of the Editio princeps (*not* the Text. recept. of the Symbol. Books) cf. WEBER ii. 16–54; KÖLLNER 346 (Cyprian Cap. x.) Given in Luther's Werke, Jena vi, 387. Leipzig, xx, 9. — TWESTEN : 1816. — TITTMANN : Die Augsburg Confess. nach den Original Ausgab. Melanchthon's. Dresden 1830, with notes. —MÜLLER : Symb. Bücher, 1848. Abdrücke von Melanchthon's erster Ausgabe der Augsb. Confess. 861–904, with various readings. The variations from the German Text. recept., as given in Baumgarten's Concord. (*Rh*, from Rhaw — the printer of the original edition,)and in Walch : Concordienbuch (Wittenberg i.) Weber i. Beylag.iii.

II. Melanchthon's "improved" edition of the German Confession, 1533, 8vo. Cf. Weber K. G. ii. 55–81. Feuerlin, 44, 45 (48,) Köllner 347. Given in Corpus Doctrinæ. Leipz. 1560. i–xlii. — WEBER : Augspurg. Confession nach der Urschrift im Reich's Archiv, nebst einer Ehrenrettung Melanchthon's, Weimar,1781. 8vo. The mistake of Weber, which led to the issue of this edition, is one of the curiosities of Theological Literature. (cf. Köllner Symb. 294.) It became the occasion of the preparation of his masterly work : The Critical History of the Augsburg Confession.

C. The Augsburg Confession (German) from a collation of the copy in the Imperial Archives (The received German text of the Book of Concord.) Köllner 349 ; Weber ii. 117–192. — Given in Chytræus : Histor. der Augspurg. Confess. (1576) 1580. 59–94. — CŒLESTINUS : Historia Comit. August, 1577. ii. 151–167. — Concordia. Dresden 1580. Fol. 3–20. Nothw. Vertheidig. 1629. 24–223. Müller, Historia 595–649. Reineccius 1730. Cyprian, Historia 1730. — WEBER's Krit. Gesch. 1783, i. Beylage iii, with various readings. Schott 1829, and in most of the histories of the Augsburg Confession. — It is to be found in all the German, and German-Latin editions of the Symbols. With various readings in Reineccius 1708. Baumgarten 1747. Walch 1750. Twesten 1816. Ammon 1829. Müller 1848 Schmucker : Lutheran Manual, 1855. 325–339, gives the doctrinal articles and the Epilogue. TRANSLATIONS : The abridged translation of the articles on abuses in Dr. Schmucker's Popular Theology, p. 337, is from this edition. In the Lutheran Manual, 283–309, a complete translation is given of the articles

senting it in the shape in which it had actually been delivered, Melanchthon issued the Confession both in German and Latin. The German was printed from his own manuscript, from which the copy had been taken to be laid before the Diet. It reached Augsburg, and was read and circulated there, while the Diet was still in session. Melanchthon issued it expressly in view of the fact that the unauthorized editions were not accurate.

The first authorized edition, the Editio Princeps, coming from the hand of its composer, and presenting not only in the nature of the case the highest guarantee for strict accuracy, but surrounded by jealous and watchful enemies, in the very Diet yet sitting, before which it was read, surrounded by men eager to mark and to exaggerate the slightest appearance of discrepance, was received by Luther and the whole Lutheran Church. Luther knew no other Augsburg Confession in the German than this. It was received into the Bodies of Doctrine of the whole Church. It appears in the Jena edition of Luther's works, an edition which originated in the purpose of having his writings in a perfectly unchanged form, and was

on abuses, also from this edition. The Unalt. Aug. Conf. New York, 1847, do. 1848. Phila. 1855, for the Lutheran Board of Publication. — The Christian Book of Concord. New Market, 1851. Second edition revised, 1854. The Confession was translated by Revs. A. and S. Henkel, for the first edition, and revised by C. Philip Krauth, D. D., for the second.

D. Combined editions. Cf. Weber ii. 193–206. Köllner 351.

I. Latin. Fabricii Leodii: Harmonia Aug. Conf. Colon. 1573, Fol. It contains 1. A text claiming to be the original. 2. The variata of 1542. 3. Various readings from the 4to edition of 1530, and the 8vo of 1531. Cf. Corpus Reformat. xxvi, 225–229. — Corpus Doctrinae, Lips. 1563. 1. The Confess. of 1542. 2. The 8vo of 1531. Translation: An Harmony of Confessions, Cambridge, 1586.

II. German. Chytræus: Historia (1580.) 1. The received text from the archives. 2. The text of the Editio Princeps where it differs from the other.

III. German and Latin. Nothwendige Vertheidigung des Aug. Apffels. Leipz 1619. 24-223. Editio princeps of Latin, Textus recep. of the German. Reineccius 1708. Do. 1730. Walch 1750. Müller 1848. Do. Tittmann 1830, Editio princeps of both. Twesten 1816. 1. ed. princ. of Latin and German. 2. German of the ordinary edition.

IV. Greek, Latin and German (Dolscii) ed. Reineccius, 1730.

E. Versified. —Augspurgisches Lehr-lied. The Doctrinal articles only. In Greek and Latin verse (Rhodomann) 1730. There is also an English versification of the Doctrinal Articles in the oldest Moravian Hymn Books.

there given as the authentic Confession in antithesis to all the editions of it in which there were variations large or small.

In the Convention of the Evangelical (Lutheran) Princes at Naumberg in 1561, among whóm were two of the original signers, this edition was declared to be authentic, and was again solemnly subscribed, and the seals of the signers appended. Nothing could seem to be more certainly fixed than that this original edition of Melanchthon presented the Confession in its most perfect form, just as it was actually delivered in the Diet.

But unhappy causes, connected largely with Melanchthon's later attempts to produce unity by skilful phrases and skilful concealments, led to a most groundless suspicion, that even in the original edition there might be variations from the very letter of the Confession as actually delivered. That there were any changes in meaning was not even in those times of morbid jealousy pretended, but a strong anxiety was felt to secure a copy of the Confession perfectly corresponding in words, in letters, and in points, with the original. The original of the Latin had been taken by Charles with him, but the German original was still supposed to be in the archives at Mentz. Joachim II., in 1566, directed Cœlestinus and Zochius to make a copy from the Mentz original. Their copy was inserted in the Brandenburg Body of Doctrine in 1572.

In 1576, Augustus of Saxony obtained from the Elector of Mentz a copy of the same document, and from this the Augsburg Confession as it appears in the Book of Concord was printed. Wherever the Book of Concord was received, Melanchthon's original edition of the German was displaced, though the corresponding edition of the Latin has been retained. Thus, half a century after its universal recognition, the first edition of the Augsburg Confession in German gave way to what was believed to be a true transcript of the original.

Two hundred years after the delivery of the Confession, a discovery was communicated to the theological world by Pfaff, which has reinstated Melanchthon's original edition. Pfaff discovered that the document in the archives at Mentz was not the original, but a copy merely, and the labors of Weber have demonstrated that this copy has no claim to be regarded as made from the original, but is a transcript from one of the less-finished copies of the Confession, made before it had assumed, under Melanchthon's hand, the exact shape in which it was actually presented. While, therefore, the ordinary edition of the Augsburg Confession, the one found in the Book of Concord, and from which the current translations of the Confession have been made, does not differ in meaning at all from the original edition of Melanchthon, it is, nevertheless, not so perfect in style, and where they differ, not so clear. The highest critical authority, then, both German and Latin, is that of Melanchthon's own original editions.*

The current edition of the German, and the earlier edition of Melanchthon, are verbally identical in the larger part of the articles, both of doctrine and of abuses. The only difference is, that Melanchthon's edition is occasionally somewhat fuller, especially on the abuses, is more perfectly parallel with the Latin at a few points, and occasionally more finished in style. When the question between them has a practical interest, it is simply because Melanchthon's edition expresses in terms, or with greater clearness, what is simply implied, or less explicitly stated in the other.

The structure of the Augsburg Confession bears traces of the mode of its growth out of the Articles which formed its groundwork. It contains, as its two fundamental parts, a positive assertion of the most necessary truths, and a negation of the most serious abuses. It comprises : I. The Preface ; II. Twenty-one Principal Articles of Faith ; III. An Epilogue-Prologue, which unites the first part with the second, and makes a graceful transition from the one to the other; IV. The Second great Division, embracing Seven Articles on Abuses ; V. The Epilogue, followed by the Subscriptions.

The Articles are not arranged as a whole with reference to a system. They may be classified thus :

---

* For the facts here presented, compare Weber Krit. Geschichte: Hase, Lib Symb., Francke do. Köllner Symb., Luther. Kirch., 342.

I. The Confessedly Catholic, or Universal Christian Art·
icles, — those which Christendom, Greek and Roman, have
confessed, especially in the Apostles' and Nicene Creed. These
were the doctrines of the Trinity (I), the Incarnation (III), the
Second Coming of Christ, the General Resurrection, the Eternity of Rewards and Punishment (XVII), the Validity of Ad·
ministration by Unworthy Ministers (VIII), the Offer of Grace
in Baptism, and the Right of Children to it (IX), Church Gov
ernment (XIV), Civil Government (XVI), Free Will (XVIII),
and the Cause of Sin (XIX).

II. The Protestant Articles, — those opposed to the errors
in doctrine, and the abuses in usage, of the Papal part of the
Church of the West. To this the Confession, in its whole
argument, based upon the Holy Scriptures as a supreme rule
of faith, was opposed. But more particularly to the Pelagianism of Rome, in the doctrine of Original Sin (Art. II): its corruption of the doctrine of Justification (Art. IV): its doctrine
of Merit in Works (Art. VI, XX), of the Ministerial Office, as
an Order of Priests (Art. V), of Transubstantiation (Art. X),
of Auricular Confession (Art. XI), of Repentance (Art. XII),
of the Opus Operatum in Sacraments (Art. XIII), of Church
Order (Art. XX), of the true nature of the Christian Church
(Art. VII), and of the Worship of Saints (Art. XXI).

The entire second part was devoted to the argument against
the Abuses in the Church of Rome, especially in regard to Communion in One Kind (Abus., Art. I), Celibacy of the Priesthood (Art. II), the Mass (Art. III), Confession (IV), Human
Traditions (V), Monastic Vows (VI), Church Power, and especially the Jurisdiction of the Bishops (VII).

III. The Evangelical Articles, or parts of Articles, — those
articles which especially assert the doctrines which are connected most directly with the Gospel in its essential character
as tidings of redemption to lost man, — the great doctrines of
grace. These articles are specially those which teach the fall
of man, the radical corruption of his nature, his exposure to
eternal death, and the absolute necessity of regeneration (Art.
II); the atonement of Christ, and the saving work of the Holy
Spirit (Art. III); justification by faith alone (IV), the true

character of repentance, or conversion (XII); and the impotence of man's own will to effect it (XVIII).

IV. The CONSERVATIVE Articles, the Articles which set forth DISTINCTIVE BIBLICAL doctrines which the LUTHERAN Church holds in peculiar purity, over against the corruptions of Romanism, the extravagance of Radicalism, the perversions of Rationalism, or the imperfect development of theology. Such are the doctrines of the proper inseparability of the two natures of Christ, both as to time and space (Art. III), the objective force of the Word and Sacraments (Art. V), the reality of the presence of both the heavenly and earthly elements in the Lord's Supper (Art. X), the true value of Private, that is, of individual Absolution (Art. XI), the genuine character of Sacramental grace (Art. XIII), the true medium in regard to the rites of the Church (Art. XV), the freedom of the will (XVIII), and the proper doctrine concerning the Cause of Sin (XIX). On all these points the Augsburg Confession presents views which, either in matter or measure, are opposed to extremes, which claim to be Protestant and Evangelical. Pelagianizing, Rationalistic, Fatalistic, Fanatical, unhistorical tendencies, which, more or less unconsciously, have revealed themselves, both in Romanism and in various types of nominally Evangelical Protestantism, are all met and condemned by the letter, tenor, or spirit of these articles.

Through the whole flows a spirit of earnest faith and of pure devotion. The body of the Confession shows the hand of consummate theologians, the soul reveals the inmost life of humble, earnest Christians.

The Augsburg Confession has incalculable value as an abiding witness against the Errors of the Roman Catholic Church. The old true Catholic Church was almost lost in pride, avarice, and superstition. The great labor of the body of the clergy was to defend

The Augsburg Confession: its value. 1. As a protest against Romanism.

* Interpretation of the Augsburg Confession, in Commentaries, Notes and Sermons.

Histoire de la Confess. d'Auxpourg (Chytraeus) par le Cop. Anvers 1582. p. 107–114. The notes are occupied with the citations, and historical allusions of the Confession.

An Harmony of the Confessions, etc. "There are added in the ende verie

the errors by which they were enriched.   Two false doctrines
were of especial value to this end : The first, that the Church
tradition is part of the Rule of Faith ; the second, that good
works can merit of God.   With both the formal and material

short notes in which both the obscure things are made plaine, etc." Cambridge,
1586. p. 593, ad fin.
Mentzer : Exegesis Augustanae Confessionis (1613) Frankfort, 1690.   Still
retains its position as a work of the highest value. — Calovius : Criticus Sacer
vel Commentar. in August. Confess. Lips. 1646. 4to. pp. 920. Do. Theologia sec.
tenorem August. Confess., etc. 4to. pp. 1900.   These two works only get as far as
the first article of the Confession. — Alting H. : Exegesis Logica et Theologica
August. Confess. Amstelod. 1647. 5–114. — Goebel : Augustana Fidei Confess.
das ist die xxi Artikel. . erkläret. Frankf. a. M. 1654, Fol. pp. 1400.   Under the
title of Sermons, an elaborate Commentary on the Confession. — Calovius : Synopsis Controversiarum etc. secund. seriem Articul. August. Confess. Wittenberg,
1685, 4to. pp. 1104. Lutherus Redivivus. Halle 1697. — Hoffman G. : Commentarius in August. Confessionem. Tubing. 1717. 4to. pp. 400. A work of great
value. The portions of the other symbols parallel with the different articles of
the Augs. Confess. are brought together ; the Wirtemberg Confession is also
brought into the harmony. — Cyprian : Historia der Augspurg. Confession. Gotha,
1730. p. 208–227. Specimens of a commentary on the i. xiii. xxii. xxviii. articles.
— Von Seelen : Stromata Lutherana sive var. Script. ad. . . Augustan. Confess.
On the v. and vi. art. on abuses. xii.   On the citations of the Fathers. xvi.—
Carpzovii : Isagoge in L. Eccl. Luth. Symb. Lips. 1675. 95–763.   After the lapse
of nearly two centuries, still the best of the eclectic works on the symbols.   The
Confession and Apology are treated together. cf. Fabricii Histor. Biblioth. iv.
264. — Pfaff : Eccles. Evang. Libri Symb. Loca difficilia explanavit et vindi-
cavit. Tubing. 1730. p. 28–86.   The notes are very brief, and very valuable. —
Walch : Introductio in L. S. . . observat. histor. et theolog. illus. 1732. 157–408.
Classic, among the older works. — Reinecii : Concordia — adjectis, locis, etc.
notisque aliis. Lips. 1735. 7–74.   The notes mostly critical, or connected with
the scriptural and patristic quotations in the Confession. — Boerneri : Institutiones Theologiae Symbolicae. Lipsiae, 1751. — Baumgarten : Erleuterungen.
2d. ed. 1761.   Compendious and rich. — Walchii : Breviarium (1765,) p. 75–116.
— Semleri : Apparatus (1775,) p. 42–127.   Tittmann : Institut. Symbol. (1811)
p. 91–134. — Tittmann : Die Augsburg. Confession : Confessio Fidei. Dresden
1830. Winer (1825.) — Schöpff : Die S. B. mit historischen Einleit. kurz. An-
merk. u. ausführlichern Erörterungen. Dresden, 1826. 24–103. — Yelin : Versuch (1829) p. 70–77. — Schott C. H. : Die Augsb. Conf. mit historisch. Einleit.
u. erläuter. Anmerkungen. Leipz. 1829.   The Unaltered Augsburg Confession.
To which is prefixed a historical Introduction to the same, by C. H. Schott. New
York, 1848. — Weber : Conf. August. animadversionibus, historicis, exegeticis,
dogmaticis et criticis. Halis 1830, 4to. — Spieker : Confessio fidei. . . varii gen-
eris animadversionibus instruxit. Berolini 1830. — Tittmann : De summ. princip. A. Conf. 1830. — Lochman G., A. M. The History, Doctrine, etc., of the
Evang. Luth. Church.   Part II, the Augsburg Confession, with explanatory notes

principles of the Church corrupted, what could result but the wreck of much that is most precious in Christianity? The protest needed then is needed still. The Roman Church has indeed formally abrogated some of the worst abuses which found their justification in her false doctrines; the pressure of Protestant thinking forces, or the light of Protestant science, wins her children to a Christianity better than her theories; but the root of the old evil remains — the old errors are not given up, and cannot be. Rome once committed, is committed beyond redemption. It needs but propitious circumstances to bring up any of her errors in all their ancient force. The fundamental principle of infallibility, the pride of consistency, the power which these doctrines give her, make it certain that they will not be abandoned. Against all of Rome's many errors, and pre-eminently against those doctrines which are in some way related to them all, the Augsburg Confession must continue to hold up the pure light of the sole Rule of Faith, and of its great central doctrine of justification by faith.*

The Augsburg Confession had, and has great value, in view of the sound *political* principles it asserted and guaranteed. Signed by the princes and free cities, it was a sovereign ratification, and guarantee of the rights of the 2d. Its political Church and of the individual Christian in the value. State. It asserted the independence on the State of the Church, as a Church, the distinctness of the spheres of the Church and State, the rights of the State over the Christian, as a subject, the Christian's duty to the State, as a

and remarks. Harrisburg, 1818. — SCHMUCKER S. S., D. D. Elements of Popular Theology, with special reference to the doctrines of the Reformation, as avowed before the Diet at Augsburg in 1530. Andover, 1834. Do. Lutheran Manual, or the Augsburg Confession illustrated and sustained. Philadelphia, 1855. — HAZ-ELIUS E. L. : The Doctrinal Articles of the Augsburg Confession, with notes ; in the Discipline etc. of the Evangelical Lutheran Synod of South Carolina. Baltimore, 1841. — BECK : Sammlung Symbol. Bücher — Evangelisch. Reform. Kirche. 2d ed. Neustadt, 1845. ii. 353–406. — FRANCKE: Libri Symb. Eccles. Lutheranæ. Lipsiae 1847, 9–50. — The Unaltered Augsburg Confession. Philada. 1855. (for Luth. Board.) A few valuable notes by Prof. Schaeffer. — Sermons by Bakius, Goebel, Tholuck, Schleiermacher, Harms, and Sartorius.

* Fikenscher. Gesch. d. R. z. Augsb. 208. KÖLLNER ii. 395.

subject, and the supremacy of God's law and of the demands of conscience over all unrighteous enactments of man. It defined in brief, yet ample statements, the entire relation of ecclesiastical and civil power.* It overthrew the conception of the Church as a great world-dominating power — taught the obligation of legitimate civil ordinances, the lawfulness of Christians bearing civil office, the right of the State to demand oaths, to enact penalties, and to wage "just wars," and the obligation of the Christian citizen to bear part in them. It asserts that "God's command is to be more regarded than all usage — that custom introduced contrary to God's command is not to be approved." "Christians should render obedience to magistrates and their laws in all things," "save only those when they command any sin, for then they must rather obey God than men." It overthrew monasticism and enforced celibacy, those weaknesses of the State; curbed the insolence of Pope, Bishop and Clergy, and restored the normal and divine relations of man to man, of subject to ruler, of Church to State, of God's law to human law, of loyalty to the rights of conscience. The Lutheran Church gives to every State into which she enters, her great voucher of fidelity to the principles on which alone free governments can stand.

The Augsburg Confession was exquisitely adapted to all its 3. Its value as objects, as a confession of faith, and a defence of a confession and it. In it the very heart of the Gospel beat again. apology. It gave organic being to what had hitherto been but a tendency, and knit together great nationalities in the holiest bond by which men can be held in association. It enabled the Evangelical princes, as a body, to throw their moral weight for truth into the empire. These were the starting points of its great work and glory among men. To it, under God, more than to any other cause, the whole Protestant world owes civil and religious freedom. Under it, as a banner, the pride of Rome was broken, and her armies destroyed. It is the symbol of pure Protestantism, as the three General Creeds are symbols of that developing Catholicity to which genuine Protestantism is related, as the maturing fruit is

* Art. vii., xvi., xxviii.

related to the blossom. To it the eyes of all deep thinkers have been turned, as to a star of hope amid the internal strifes of nominal Protestantism. Gieseler, the great Reformed Church historian, says:* " If the question be, Which, among all Protestant Confessions, is best adapted for forming the foundation of a union among Protestant Churches, we declare ourselves unreservedly for the Augsburg Confession." But no genuine union can ever be formed upon the basis of the Augsburg Confession, except by a hearty consent in its whole faith, an honest reception of all its statements of doctrine in the sense which the statements bear in the Confession itself. If there be those who would forgive Rome her unrepented sins, they must do it in the face of the Augsburg Confession. If there be those who would consent to a truce at least with Rationalism or Fanaticism, they must begin their work by making men forget the great Confession,which refused its covert to them from the beginning.

With the Augsburg Confession begins the clearly recognized life of the Evangelical Protestant Church, the purified Church of the West, on which her enemies fixed the name Lutheran. With this Confession her most self-sacrificing struggles and greatest achievements are connected. It is hallowed by the prayers of Luther, among the most ardent that ever burst from the human heart ; it is made sacred by the tears of Melanchthon, among the tenderest which ever fell from the eye of man. It is embalmed in the living, dying, and undying devotion of the long line of the heroes of our faith, who, through the world which was not worthy of them, passed to their eternal rest. The greatest masters in the realm of intellect have defended it with their labors ; the greatest princes have protected it from the sword, by the sword ; and the blood of its martyrs, speaking better things than vengeance, pleads for ever, with the blood of Him whose all-availing love, whose sole and all-atoning sacrifice, is the beginning, middle, and end of its witness.

But not alone on the grand field of historical events has its power been shown. It led to God's

4. Its value as a centre of great associations.

5. Its value as a guide to Christ.

* Theolog. Stud. u. Kritik, 1833, ii, 1142. Schenkel takes the same view.

Word millions, who have lived and died unknown to the great world. In the humblest homes and humblest hearts it has opened, through ages, the spring of heavenly influence. It proclaimed the all-sufficiency of Christ's merits, the justifying power of faith in Him ; and this shed heavenly light, peace and joy, on the darkest problems of the burdened heart. "It remains forever," says Gieseler, "a light to guide in the right path those who are struggling in error." It opened the way to the true unity of the Church of Christ ; and if it has seemed to divide, for a little time, it has divided only to consolidate, at length, the whole Church under Christ's sole rule, and in the one pure faith.

Its history, in its full connections, is the history of the centuries midway in the fourth of which we stand, and the future of the Church, which is the future of the race, can unfold itself from the present, only in the power of the life which germinates from the great principles which the Augsburg Confession planted in the world.

6. Its value for the future.

Can we honorably bear the name of Evangelical Lutherans, honestly profess to receive the Augsburg Confession as our Creed, and honestly claim to be part of the Church of our fathers, while we reject, or leave open to rejection, parts of the doctrine whose recep-

The Augsburg Confession as a Creed: what is involved in a right reception of it? *

* Works on *Dogmatics, and the history of Dogmatics,* of value in the interpretation or defence of the Augsburg Confession, or in illustration of the theology based upon or deviating from it.

MELANCHTHONIS : Opera Dogmatica in the Corpus Reformatorum, vol. XXI.-XXIII.   *a.* Loci Theologici (1521). *b.* Examen ordinandorum. *c.* Catechesis puerilis. *d.* Explicatio Symboli Niceni. *e.* Repetitio Augustanae Confessionis sive Confessio doctrinae Saxonicarum ecclesiarum. — Cf. GALLE : Melanchthon (1840) and Augusti's, Edit. of the Loci (1821), for Melanchthon's changes in doctrine. — FLACCII : *a.* Catalogus Testium veritatis (1556). *b.* Centuriæ Magdeburgenses. *c.* Clavis. *d.* Scholia in N. Test. — CHEMNITZ : *a.* de vera et substantiali præsentia. *b.* de duabus naturis. *c.* Loci Theologici. *d.* Examen Concil. Trident. *e.* Theologiae Jesuitic. praecipua capit. — HUTTER : Compendium Locor. Theo logic (1610) ed. Schutze 1772. — OSIANDER L: Enchiridion Controvers. (1614.) - HUNNIUS N: Epitome Credendorum (1625). — GERHARD J : *a.* Loci Theologici (1610) (Cotta). *b.* Confessio Catholica (1633). — CALOVIUS : *a.* Apodixis (1684). *b.* Synopsis Controversiarum (1653). *c* Mataeologia papistica (1647). *d.* Biblia Illustrata. — KOENIG : Theologia positiva (1664). — QUENSTEDT: Theologia didactico-polemica (1685). — BECHMANN : Adnotationes in Compendium

tion gave our Church her separate being and distinctive name, and led to the formation of her Confession, and which are embodied in its articles, and guarded in their condemnatory clauses, and which our whole Church, for centuries, in every official act, maintained as principal and fundamental? This is the real question. All others are side issues. This question, once agitated, can never be laid till it is fairly settled ; and to it, every conscientious man, every lover of our Church, should bend his prayerful thoughts. A testimony bearing upon the great question, a testimony of the highest importance, and entitled to be heard first of all, is the CONFESSION itself, about whose claims so much is now said.

In what light is the Augsburg Confession regarded in the Augsburg Confession itself? This is a primary question for an honest man who thinks of subscribing it : for if the Confession itself, in its origin, its history, its letter, protests against certain ideas, it would seem that its witness against them is of more value than any other. Look, then, at a few facts:

I. The Confession exhibited the one, undivided faith of the entire Lutheran Church in the Empire. It was not the work of men without authority to represent the Church ; but was

Hutteri (1690). — BUDDEUS: *a.* Theologia Dogmatica (1723). *b.* De veritate religionis evangelicae (1729). *c.* Religions-Streitigkeiten 1724. *d.* Isagoge (1727). — SCHMID J. A.: Breviarium theolog. polemic. (1710).—LANGE: Oeconomia salutis (1728). — REINHARD L. Theologia Dogmat. (1733). — WALCH J. G. *a.* Dogmatische Gottesgelahr. (1749). *b.* Polemische (1752). *c.* Religions-Streitigkeiten (1724). — CARPOV. (1737). — BAUMGARTEN S. J. *a.* Evangelische Glaubenslehre (1759). *b* Theologisch. Streitigkeiten. (1762) *c.* Religions-Parteyen (1766). — MOSHEIM : *a.* Streit-Theologie (1763). *b.* Theolog. Dogmat. (1758). — CARPZOV J. B. Jr. Liber doctrinalis (1767). — WALCH C. W. F. *a.* Geschichte der Lutherischen Religion (1753). *b.* Bibliotheca Symbolica (1770). — SEMLER : Institutio (1774). — DOEDERLEIN (1780). — SEILER : *a.* Theolog. dogmat. polemica (1780). *b.* Doctrin. Christian. Compend. (1779). — MORUS : *a.* Epitome Theol. Christianae (1789). *b.* Commentarius in Epitom. (1797). — BECK: (1801). — STORR & FLATT : Dogmatik (1803). — REINHARD F. V. (1801). — SCHOTT (1811). — BRETSCHNEIDER: *a.* Dogmatik (1814). *b.* Entwickelung (1804). — WEGSCHEIDER : Institutiones (1815). — TWESTEN (1826). — KNAPP (1827). — NITZSCH (1829). — (Schuman): Melanchthon Redivivus, 1837. — HASE : *a.* Dogmatik (1826). *b.* Hutterus Redivivus (1829–1868). — KLEIN : (1822) Ed. LANGE (1835). — SCHMID H. Dogmatik d. Evang. Luth. Kirche, (1843–1863). — MARTENSEN (1855). — SARTORIUS (1861). — THOMASIUS (1863). — PHILIPPI (1863). — HOFMAN (1860). — KAHNIS (1868).— LUTHARDT (1868).

the voice of all the Churches. Its groundwork was laid by Luther ; materials were brought together by the great theo-logians of the whole Lutheran Church — by Brentius, Jonas, Spalatin, and others, who carefully examined and tested each other's work. The matchless hand of Melanchthon was em-ployed in giving the most perfect form, the most absolutely finished statement of the faith ; the Confession was subjected to the careful examination of Luther, by whom it was heartily approved. Melanchthon's own account is : " I brought to-gether the heads of the Confession, embracing almost the *sum of the doctrine of our Churches.* I took nothing on myself. In the presence of the Princes and the officials, every topic was discussed by our preachers, *sentence by sentence. A copy of the entire Confession* was then sent to Luther, who wrote to the Princes that he had read, and that he approved the Confes-sion." Every position of the Confession had been pondered again and again, had been tried in the crucible of the Word, had been experienced in its practical power in the life, and had been maintained against sharp attacks, by our great Confessors, as well as by thousands of humble and earnest private Chris-tians. For the immediate work of its preparation, there were at least four months. It was on the 11th of May the Confes-sion was first sent by the Elector to Luther, and it was not read in Diet till the 25th of June ; so that *six weeks elapsed* between the time of its substantial completeness and of its presentation. Every touch after that time was the result of striving after absolute finish of style and perfection of handling. Never was a Confession more thoroughly prepared, more carefully and prayerfully weighed, more heartily accepted.

II. As various kingdoms, states, and cities embraced the faith of God's word, as our Church had unfolded it, they accepted this Confession as their own, and were known as Evangelical Lutherans because they so accepted it. The Church was known as the Church of the Augsburg Confession, and that great document became a part of the defining terms of the Church. The Lutheran Church was that which unreservedly held the Unaltered Augsburg Confession in its historical sense.

III. The arguments on which men rely now to shake the

faith of the Church, had all been used before the Confession was prepared. In fact, the Rationalistic argument had been brought out with far more vigor and plausibility than usually attend it now, and those who renew the unsuccessful attempts of the original opponents of our faith, might with advantage to their cause study those old errorists. Nothing has been added to the argument of that day in the great substantial points on either side. After the learning and insinuating statement of Œcolampadius, whose work, Erasmus said, " might, if possible, deceive the very elect," and which Melanchthon considered worthy of a reply—after the unflinching audacity of Carlstadt, and the plausible argument of Zwingle, which was so shallow, and therefore seemed so clear, it is not probable that the feeble echo of their arguments, which is now alone heard in the maintenance of their views, would shake our fathers were they living. The Scripture argument stands now where it stood then, and the Word, which was too strong for Luther's human doubts then, would prove too strong for them now. It is not the argument which has changed : it is as overwhelming now as then ; but the singleness of faith, the simple-hearted trust —these have too often yielded to the Rationalizing spirit of a vain and self-trusting generation. If our fathers, with their old spirit, were living now, we would have to stand with them on their confession, or be obliged to stand alone. Luther would sing now, as he sung then :

> "The Word they shall permit remain,
> And not a thank have for it."

IV. The very name of AUGSBURG, which tells us WHERE our Confession was uttered, reminds us of the nature of the obligations of those who profess to receive it. Two other Confessions were brought to that city : the Confession of Zwingle, and the Tetrapolitan Confession : the former openly opposed to the faith of our Church, especially in regard to the Sacraments ; the latter ambiguous and evasive on some of the vital points of the same doctrine. These two Confessions are now remembered only because of the historical glory shed by ours over everything which came into any relation to it. But can it be, that the doctrine which arrayed itself against the Augsburg Confession at Augsburg can be the doctrine of that Confession, or capable of harmonizing with it anywhere else ; that what was not Lutheranism there is Lutheranism here ; that what was Lutheranism then is not Lutheranism now ; that Zwingle or Hedio of Strasburg could, without a change of views, honestly subscribe the Confession against which they had arrayed themselves, that very Confession, the main drift of some of whose most important Articles was to teach the truth these men denied, and to condemn the errors these men fostered, or that men, who hold now what they held then, can now honestly do what they would not and could not do then ? What could not be done then, cannot be done now. A principle is as little affected by the lapse of three hundred years as of one year. It cannot be, that, consistently with the principles of our fathers, consistently with Church unity with them, consistently with the Church name which their principles and their faith defined, men holding Romish, or Rationalistic, or Zwinglian error, should pretend to receive the Confession as their own. Such a course effaces all the lines of historical identity, and of moral consistency, and opens the way to error of every kind.

V. The language of the Confession, when it speaks of itself, is well worthy of attention.

1. It calls itself a *Confession*, not a rule. The Bible is the only rule of faith, and this document *confesses* the faith of which the Bible is the rule.

2. It calls itself a Confession of *faith ;* of *faith*, not of men's opinions or views, but of that divine conviction of saving truth, which the Holy Ghost works through the Word. It speaks of that with which it has to do as "the holy faith and Christian religion," "the one only and true religion," "our holy religion and Christian faith." The title of the doctrinal portion of the Confession is, "*Principal* Articles of Faith."

3. The Confessors speak of this Confession of faith as "the Confession of their *preachers*, and *their own* Confession," "the doctrine which *their preachers* have presented and taught in the *Churches*, in their lands, principalities, and cities." The

Preface closes with the words : " This is the Confession of *our-selves* and of *ours*, as now distinctly follows, Article by Article." They separate *their* faith alike from the errors of Rome and of the fanatical and rationalizing tendencies of the day.

4. The Confession declares that : " The CHURCHES among us teach " the doctrines set forth in the Articles. It is not simply great princes, nor great theologians ; it is the CHURCHES which teach these doctrines. The private opinions of the greatest of men are here nothing. It is the faith of the Churches which is set forth, and those who acted for them spoke as their representatives, knowing the common faith, and not mingling with it any mere private sentiments or peculiar views of their own, however important they might regard them.

It is a great mistake to suppose that our Evangelical Protestant Church is bound by consistency to hold a view simply because Luther held it. Her faith is not to be brought to the touchstone of Luther's private opinion, but his private opinion is to be tested by her confessed faith, when the question is, What is genuinely Lutheran? The name Lutheran, as our Church tolerates it, means no more than that she heartily accepts that New Testament faith in its integrity, in whose restoration Luther was so glorious a leader. When, at the conferences at Augsburg, Eck produced certain passages from Luther's writings, Brentius and Schnepf replied : " We are not here to defend Luther's writings, but to maintain our Confession." In showing that the Augsburg Confession is the Symbol of our time, the Formula of Concord rests its authority on its being " the unanimous consent and declaration of our faith." The private opinions of individuals, however influential, can in no sense establish or remove one word of the Creed of the Church. Any man who, on any pretence, gives ecclesiastical authority to private opinions, is robbing the Church of her freedom. She is to be held responsible for no doctrines which she has not officially declared to be her own.

5. The Confessors say, at the end of the doctrinal Articles : " This is almost *the main portion* (*summa : chief points, principal matters*) *of the doctrine* which is preached and taught in our Churches, in order to the true Christian instruction and

comfort of the conscience, as also for the edification of believers." It calls the things it sets forth " the one, simple truth,"
and styles them " the chief," or fundamental, " Articles"
(Hauptartikeln.)

The Confessors style and characterize the Confession as
" our Confession," as " the *chief points* of the doctrine taught
in our Churches," as " the main (or fundamental) Articles,"
as " the Articles of faith." They say : " *Those things only
have been recited* which seemed *necessary* to be said, that it
might be understood, that, in *doctrine* and ceremonies, *nothing*
is received by us *contrary to Scripture ;* " and they declare, at
the close of their work, that it was meant as " a sum of doctrine," or statement of its chief points, " for the making
known of our Confession, and of the doctrine of those who
teach among us."*

6. The Confessors say of this statement of the main points
of doctrine : " In it may be seen, *that there is* NOTHING *which departs from the Scriptures ;* " " it is clearly founded in the holy
Scriptures,"† " in conformity with the pure, Divine word and
Christian truth." They declare, that, in these " main" or
fundamental " Articles, no falsity or deficiency is to be found,
and that this their Confession is godly and Christian (göttlich
und Christlich)." They open the Articles on Abuses by reit-
erating that their Confession is evidence, that, " in the *Articles
of faith,* NOTHING is taught in our Churches contrary to the
Holy Scripture,"‡ and the Confessors close with the declaration, that, if there be points on which the Confession has
not touched, they are prepared to furnish ample information,
" in accordance with the Scriptures," " on the ground of holy
Divine writ."

7. The Confessors say that in the Confession : " There is
NOTHING which departs from the *Church Catholic, the Universal
Christian Church.*"§

8. The Confessors moreover declare, that they set forth

---

* Epilogue, 69. 5   † Epilogue, 70, 6.

‡ Nihil inesse, quod discrepat a Scripturis — in heiliger **Schrift klar**
gegründet.

§ Ab Ecclesia Catholica — gemeine, Christlicher Kirchen.

their Confession that they may " not put their soul and conscience in the very highest and greatest peril before God by
abuse of the Divine name or word."

9. They declare, moreover, that it is their grand design in
the Confession, to avoid the " transmission as *a heritage* to
their *children and descendants of another doctrine,* a doctrine
not in conformity with the pure Divine word and Christian
truth."

Our fathers knew well that human opinions fluctuate, that
men desert the truth, that convictions cannot be made hereditary ; but they knew this also, that when men assume a name,
they assume the obligations of the name, that they may not
honestly subscribe Confessions unless they believe their contents ; and they knew that after this, their great Confession,
men could not long keep up the pretence of being of them
who were anti-Trinitarian, Pelagian, Romish, Rationalistic, or
Fanatical. They could transmit the heritage of their faith to
their children, trusting in God that these children would not,
for the brassy glitter of Rationalism, or the scarlet rags of
Rome, part with this birthright, more precious than gold.

Our fathers believed, with St. Paul, that the true faith is
" one faith," and therefore never changes. It is the same from
age to age. The witness of a true faith is a witness to the end
of time. When, therefore, Brück, the Chancellor of Saxony,
presented the Confession, he said : " By the help of God and
our Lord Jesus Christ, this Confession shall remain invincible
against the gates of hell, TO ETERNITY."

VII.

THE SECONDARY CONFESSIONS OF THE CON-
SERVATIVE REFORMATION.

THE BOOK OF CONCORD.

IN the Symbolical Books of the Evangelical Lutheran
Church, the Augsburg Confession is followed by five other
statements of doctrine: the Apology; the Schmalcald Articles;
the two Catechisms; the Formula of Concord, in epitome, and
ampler declaration, with an appendix of testimonies: the six,
in conjunction with the three general Creeds, forming the Book of Concord. The Augsburg Confession, the Smaller Catechism, and the Epitome, may
be regarded as the texts, respectively, on which the Apology,
the Larger Catechism, and the Declaration are Commentaries.
The whole of these books can be embodied in a fair type in
an ordinary duodecimo volume. When we think of the space
which a minister covers with the words in which during a
single year he states the sacred doctrines — when we look at
the many volumes in which particular authors have presented
the results of their labors on Scripture, the folios which have
been devoted to single topics, it hardly seems an excessive
demand on the part of the Church that she should ask ministers to study one small volume to reach the official expression
of her judgment on the greatest questions, which pertain to
pure doctrine, sound government, and holy life. Yet the Book
of Concord has been denounced apart from the character of its
contents on the ground that it contains so much. Be it right

Contents and bulk of the Book of Concord.

268

or wrong, be its teachings truth or falsehood, its bulk is sufficient to condemn it.

The very right of the Book to a hearing, at least as regards
its last five parts, has been further denied on the ground, that
a Church having once announced its Creed has no authority to
change it by adding to it — and that to change by *adding*, involves the same fallacy as to change by *subtraction ;* that consequently those who at one extreme accept the whole Book of
Concord, and those who reject the Augsburg Confession in
whole or part, at the other, are alike illogical. — In reply to
this these facts might be urged :

I. The use of the word " Creed," in the objection is open to
misapprehension. If, by it, is meant WHAT a pure church believes, the faith and doctrine of a pure church, it is true that
these cannot be changed. WHAT a pure church   May a Church
believes is Scriptural, for a pure church means a   change its Creed?
                                                    1. Creed as *what*
church whose faith is Scriptural. If it be Scrip-   is believed.
tural, then to *change* it, is to abandon the truth, and to cease
to be a pure church. Moreover, the *faith* of any church is her
identifying point — losing that, she loses her spiritual identity.
If the Catholic Church had abandoned her faith in the Trinity,
she would have ceased to be the Catholic Church, and would
have become the Arian sect. If the Protestant Episcopal
Church were carried over into the Romish faith, she would
cease to be the Protestant Episcopal Church, and would be a
part of the Romish apostasy. If the Evangelical Churches
were to abandon the Evangelical faith, they would become
Socinian or Universalist bodies, and if the Lutheran Church
were to change her faith, she would cease to be the Lutheran
Church, and would become either a new sect, or a part of this,
that, or other of the old sects. It is a contradiction in terms
to talk of a pure Church, as such, changing her faith.

II. But if by " Creed," be meant an official *statement* of the
faith held, it is a great mistake to assert that there can be no
Church authority to add to it. As the Rule of   2. Creed as a
Faith, the written revelation of God, has been en- statement of be-
                                                    lief.
larged by successive additions from the early records
which form the opening of Genesis, on through the Old and

New Testaments, until the finished temple stands before us in the Bible; so may the Church, as God shall show her her need, enlarge her Confession, utter more fully her testimony, and *thus* "change her Creed," to express more amply her one unchanging faith. If the Rule of an unchanging faith can be added to, the Confession of an unchanging faith can also be added to.

The identity of the Church faith resembles not the sameness of a rock, but rather the living identity of a man. The babe and the adult are identical. They are the same being in different stages of maturity : that which constitutes the individual does not change. The child does not grow to adult maturity by any change in personal identity — but retaining that identity grows by its attraction to itself, of what is consonant with its own unchanged nature. Adult perfection is reached not by amputations and ingraftings, but by growth, in which the identifying energy conforms everything to its own nature. The faith of the Church now is identical with what it was in the Apostolic time, but the relation of identity does not preclude growth — it only excludes change of identity. That faith must always be its essential self — whether as a babe receiving milk, or as a man enjoying strong meat. In a word, the advances are wrought, not by change in the Church faith, but by the perpetual activity of that faith, a faith which because it is incapable of change itself, assimilates more and more to it the consciousness of the Church, her system of doctrine, her language, and her life.

To subtract from a pure faith differs as largely from a healthy development of that faith in enlarged statements, as the cutting off of an arm differs from the expansion of its muscles, by healthful exercise. The whole history of the Church illustrates the truth of this principle. The *creeds* recorded in the New Testament were generally confined to one point. The Apostles' Creed, in the earliest form Growth of the known to us, is a *change* of these primal creeds, Creed. in so far that it *adds* to their statements to make the faith itself more secure. The Apostles' Creed, as we have it now, is a *change* of the earliest form, adding to its words to secure more perfectly its things. The Nicene Creed, in its earliest shape was a *change* in the same way from the Apostles'. The Nicene Creed, (Niceno-Constantinopolitan) in the Greek, is a change of the earliest Nicene, by addition. The Nicene Creed of the Churches of the West (both Roman and Protestant) adds the " filioque " to the Nicene of the East. The Athanasian Creed, though but the expansion of two main points, is about six times as long as the Apostles' Creed. Then through ages the Church lay fallow; the soil resting and accreting richness for the time of a new breaking up, and of a glorious harvest. The first great undeniable token that the warm rains from above were responsive to the toils of the husbandman below, in the field of the Lord, was the up-springing of the blade of the New Confession. The New Confession in its opening Word shows that it germinates from the old seed: " The Churches among us, with great accord, teach that the decree of the Nicene Council is true, and, without any doubting, to be believed." (A. C. I.) " Christ shall return again, as saith the Apostles' Creed." (A. C. III.) The other Confessions mark the same connection with the ancient Creeds: " Shall sanctify believers — as teach the Apostles' and Nicene Creed." (Ap. III.) " As the Apostles and Athanasian Creeds teach." (Smal. Art. II, 4.). " Since immediately after the time of the Apostles, nay, while they were yet on earth, false teachers and heretics arose, against whom, in the primitive Church, were composed Symbols, that is brief and categorical Confessions, which embraced the unanimous consent of the Catholic Christian faith, and the Confession of Orthodox believers and of the true Church, to wit: the Apostles', Nicene, and Athanasian Creeds ; we profess publicly that we embrace them, and reject all heresies, and all doctrines which have ever been brought into the Church of God, contrary to them." (Formul. Concord. 517, 3.) — " Those three Catholic and General Creeds are of the highest authority — brief, but most holy Confessions, solidly founded in God's word, most glorious Confessions." (Do. 569, 4.)

The Augsburg Confession, itself, was a " change of creed, by addition," inasmuch as it more amply confessed all the points of the Apostles', Nicene, and Athanasian Creeds, and added a confession on manifold points, held, indeed, potentially and implicitly in the *faith* of the pure Church, but never before formally confessed by her.

But, furthermore, the Augsburg Confession, even as a Lutheran document, is an abiding witness of the right and duty of Christian men, and a portion of the Christian Church to amplify the confession of the faith, according to the leadings of God's providence. For the Augsburg Confession is really not first, but *fourth* in the Genesis of our Church's first official statement of her distinctive faith. For first were the XV Marburg Articles, in which the great representatives of our Church made a statement of points of faith ; then the XVII Articles of Swabach, then the Articles of Torgau, and as the outgrowth of the whole, and their noble consummation, last of all, the Augsburg Confession.

The Augsburg Confession, itself, grew from its earliest shape, at the beginning of the Conference at Augsburg, up to the day of its delivery to the Emperor. The one faith which it confessed in its infant form, shaped its phrases, added to its enumerations, guarded against misapprehensions more perfectly, until it reached its maturity.

III. The right to " change a creed," " by *addition*," is, if it be fallacy at all, not a *common fallacy*, with the assumption of a right to " change by *subtraction*." The mistake here involved

To define is not is in using the word " change" ambiguously, and
to change.   in making it falsely emphatic. We deny the right of a pure Church to *change* the faith : we hold that her *creed* should not be changed ; but we maintain, first, that to *cut out* articles of faith bodily *from* her creed, and to mangle and change the meaning of what remains, *is* to change her creed ; and secondly, that to leave her earlier creed untouched and unvaried, to cling to it heart and soul, in its original and proper sense, and in order to the maintenance of the faith it treasures, to witness again, in ampler form, by adding clear and Scriptural statements of doctrine, is *not* to change the creed, but is the act of wisdom to prevent its *change*. If a clergyman, on one Lord's Day, should succinctly set forth the

doctrine of justification by faith, and should find, that owing to the brevity of his statement, the uncultured had misunderstood it, or the malicious had taken occasion to pervert it, he might very properly, on the next Lord's Day, amplify his statement, and thus " change his creed by addition," for every sermon is a minister's creed. If his doing so is a fallacy, it is surely not a *common* fallacy with his retractation, denial or evasion on the second Lord's Day, of what he taught on the first ; not a common fallacy, even if his second statement were needlessly extended, and though it introduced many statements on other closely associated doctrines.

IV. We object also to all *unnecessary* multiplication of the number or extension of the bulk of creeds. So does the Lutheran Church, as a whole. For nearly three centuries, no addition has been made to her Symbolical Books; and although it is quite possible that, for local reasons, parts of our Church may enunciate more largely particular elements of her faith, we do not think it likely that the Lutheran Church, as a whole, will ever add to her Symbols, not merely anything which can have such relations to them as the Augsburg Confession has (which would be impossible), but not even such as the Formula of Concord has.

General judgment of the Church as to desirableness of ample definition

But this does not settle the question now before us. We think we have shown, that to have creeds additional to the Augsburg Confession, is not in itself inconsistent or wrong. Now to the point : Is it necessary or desirable that there should be any such additional statements? To this question, our whole Church, without a solitary exception, which we can recall, certainly with no important exception, has returned the same reply, to wit: that it is desirable and necessary. For while it is a fact, that no creed, exclusively hers, except the Augsburg Confession, has been formally accepted in every part of the Lutheran Church, *it is equally true that there is no important part of that Church which has not had, in addition, some other Creed.* No national, or great Lutheran Church, from the beginning of her full organization, to this hour, has had nothing but the Augsburg Confession as a statement of her faith. For not

18

to speak of the three General Creeds to which the Lutheran Church pays higher reverence than to the Augsburg Confession itself, many of the Lutheran Churches before the preparation of the Book of Concord, had their Bodies of Doctrine, as bulky as the collection which has been so much decried for its vast extent, and sometimes more bulky. There lies before the writer, for example, the first of these, the Corpus Doctrinæ, the Symbolical Books of Saxony and Misnia, printed in 1560, edited by Melanchthon, which, in addition to the General Creeds and the Augsburg Confession, has the Apology, and four other extensive statements of doctrine, forming a folio of more than a thousand pages. Every one of the seven ponder. ous Corpora Doctrinæ has additions to the Augsburg Confession, as, for example, the Apology, both the Catechisms of Luther, and the Schmalcald Articles, in fact, everything now in the Book of Concord which had appeared up to the time of their issue. The Church Orders and Liturgies of the Sixteenth Century embraced Creeds. We have examined nearly all of them in the originals, or in Richter's Collection. We have not noticed one which has the Augsburg Confession alone.

It is an historical fact easily demonstrated, that the Book of Concord diminished both the *number* of doctrinal statements and the *bulk* of the books containing them, in the various Lutheran Churches. It not only removed the Corpora Doctrinæ, but the yet more objectionable multiplied Confessions prepared by various local Reformers, and pastors, of which not only lands, but cities and towns had their own. So far from the Book of Concord introducing the idea of addition to the Augsburg Confession, it, in fact, put that idea under the wisest restrictions. But, not to dwell on this point further, it is certain that the Lutheran Church, with a positive, almost absolute unanimity, decided, both before and after the Book of Concord, that it is desirable to have more than the Augsburg Confession as a statement of doctrine.

The Lutheran Church in America is no exception to this rule. Her founders confessed to the whole body of the Symbols. The General Synod recognizes, in addition to the Augsburg Confession, the Smaller Catechism for the people, and in its Theological Seminary, originally, both Catechisms were mentioned in the Professor's oath. In its present form the Smaller Catechism is retained. But if the Smaller Catechism be adopted, and an ampler statement of doctrine be an unlawful change, that Catechism alone must be adopted, and the Augsburg Confession which appeared a year later, be thrown out.

The Book of Concord may be divided generically into two parts: the first part selected, the second part original. The first is formed by our Church Creeds, which it simply collected. The second is the Formula of Concord, in two ^{Book of Concord, Contents of.} parts, Epitome and Declaratio, which it first set forth. Every part of both these divisions, except the first part of the first, would be rejected on the principle we now discuss; in fact, if the principle were pressed through, logically, not only would the Augsburg Confession, but the Apostles' Creed itself be sacrificed to it. The Church would have to recover the earliest form of the Creed, or be creedless altogether.

First of all, then, let it be remembered, that *five-sevenths* of what now forms the Book of Concord, were accepted in the Lutheran Church before that Book was compiled: secondly, that the directly confessional part of the Formula (the Epitome) is very little larger than the Augsburg Confession, the " Solid Declaration" being simply an exegesis and defence of the Epitome. Let us for the present look at these earlier parts of the Book of Concord. Taking then, one by one, the Symbols which follow the Augsburg Confession in the Book of Concord, let us ask whether it be *wrong*, to acknowledge officially, that they set forth the faith of our Church? To begin with the first of these,—

IS IT WRONG TO ACKNOWLEDGE THE APOLOGY AS A SYMBOL OF THE LUTHERAN CHURCH? This question we will answer by a few facts.

I. It will not be denied that it presents one and the same system of faith with the Augsburg Confession. It is in its first sketch the Answer from the hand of the great Melanchthon, with the advice and co-labor of the other theologians,

to the Roman Catholic Reply to the Augsburg Confession. Pre
pared under the direction of the same authority that had origi-
The Apology. nated the Confession, it was designed to present
it to the Emperor in the same way. Happily, the Emperor
refused to allow its presentation: for that refusal has substituted for Melanchthon's sketch the Apology as we now have it.
Melanchthon, on receiving the Papal Confutation, at once
gave himself to the work of answering it in full. On the
journey from Augsburg to Wittenberg, he labored on it.
At Altenburg,. in Spalatin's house, he was engaged upon it on
Sunday, till Luther took the pen from his hand, telling him
that " on *this* day he should rest from such labor. We can
serve God, not only by labor, but by rest ; therefore he has
given us the third Commandment and ordained the Sabbath."*
No longer amid the confusion and disadvantages of a strange
place, but at home, Melanchthon prepares this defence, expansion and explanation of the Confession. What can be more
obvious than the Providence which reveals itself in the
occasion and character of the Apology ?

II. Köllner, confessedly a most able writer, but not Lutheran in doctrine, says of the Apology : " It had from the very-
beginning, and has had *without dispute* up to the recent times,
the *validity* of a Symbol." Winer, that princely scholar,
whose laxity of doctrinal views gives more value to his testimony on this point, says : " Beyond dispute, with reference to
the matter it contains, this work takes *the first rank* among the
Symbols of the Lutheran Church." We might multiply citations like these, but it is not necessary.

III. The Apology has been regarded indeed in our Church
as one of her noblest jewels. In making it one of her Symbols,
she confessed her profound love for it. In reply to one of the
fiercest assaults made upon her by the Jesuits, the Apology
without note or comment, was reprinted, as in itself an ample
reply to all the falsehoods that Romish malignity could invent
against our Church.

IV. In modern times, the attacks upon it have come first

* Salig: Hist. d. Augsp. Conf. I, 375. Ledderhose's Melanchthon. Transl
by Dr. Kretel, 115.

from the covert infidels who crept into the Church under the pretentious name of rationalists, and secondly from unionistic theologians. Over against this, the unvarying witness of the Lutheran Church has been given to the pure teaching, the great importance, and the symbolic validity of the Apology. Let a few facts illustrate this.

1. The Lutheran States whose names are subscribed to the Augsburg Confession, offered the Apology to the Diet, and the sole reason why it did not take its place at once, symbolically co-ordinate in every respect with the Confession, was that *Romish bigotry refused it a hearing.* The fierce intolerance of the hour anticipated the objection to hearing anything further in the way of explanation or vindication of the Confession. Was it a fallacy of the same sort, for the Lutheran States to prepare the Apology, as it would have been for them to have come back to the Diet, having taken out everything in the Confession, which Eck and his co-workers did not relish? Prepared by the author of the Augsburg Confession, and adopted by its signers, is it probable that the Apology was in any respect out of harmony with the work it defended?

2. In 1532, the Evangelical Lutheran States presented it at the Schweinfurth Convention as their Confession of Faith.

3. In 1533, Luther, in a consolatory, printed, public and official letter, refers the Christians who were driven out of Leipzig, to the Confession and its Apology, as setting forth his faith and that of the Church. Both are incorporated in all the old editions of Luther's works, as so thoroughly an exhibition of his faith, of his thoughts and even of his phraseology, as really in an important sense to be considered his.

In the letter to the persecuted Lutherans at Leipzig,[*] Luther says : " At Augsburg, our general (allgemeine) Confession sounded in the ears of the Emperor and of the whole realm ; and then, by the press, in all the world . . Why should I say more? There are my writings and public Confessions — our Confession and Apology : in the Churches, our usages are before men's eyes ; wherein we superabundantly show what we believe and hold as certain, not alone in these Articles con

[*] Werke : Leipz. xxi. 20.   ch : x. 2228.

cerning the Sacrament, but in all parts of the faith . . There-fore, Dear Friends, be firm, let no one mislead you, give ear to no empty talk (Geschwätze), even though it should come from our own side : but hold fast to our Confession and Apology . . . Hold fast to the Gospel, and to St. Paul's doctrine, to which also our Apology and our Church usage hold fast."

4. In 1537, at Schmalcald, the *Apology*, at the request of the Princes, was *thoroughly compared* with the Augsburg Confession by the theologians, and then, as consonant with the Holy Scriptures and the Confession, *formally subscribed* by them with the declaration, that they " believed and taught in their Churches in accordance with the Articles of the Confession and Apology." *

5. In 1539, in Denmark, it was prescribed as a doctrinal guide to the Lutheran pastors.

6. In 1540, it was delivered to the Conference at Worms, as a statement of Lutheran doctrine, and as a basis of discussions.

7. In 1541, it was solemnly confirmed by the " Evangelical Princes," " the Allied Estates of the Augsburg Confession," " the Protestant Princes and States," who say to the Emperor : " And that no man may doubt what kind of doctrine is set forth in our Churches, we again testify, that we adhere to the Confession which was presented to your Majesty at Augsburg, and to the Apology which has been added to it, nor do we doubt that this doctrine is truly the Consent of the Catholic Church, which has been delivered in the writings of the Prophets and the Apostles, and has firm testimonies of the Apostolic Church, and of the learned fathers — and in this faith and acknowledgment of Christ we shall ever call upon God and show forth His praise, with His Catholic Church." †

8. It was incorporated in all the " Bodies of Doctrine," the " Corpora Doctrinæ " proper, of the various parts of our Church, without exception; and

9. In 1580, it took its due place in the Book of Concord.

* In all the editions of the Symbolical Books at the end of the Schmalcald Articles.

† Melanchthon's Opera. Witeberg. iv. 752. Corp. Reformat. iv. col. 483. In German : Walch : xvii. 865. (Bucers translation) Corp. Ref. iv. 493, 494. (Melanch-thon's Original.)

V. It *deserves* the place our Church has given it. On the merits of the Apology Köllner * says : " In considering its value for its immediate purpose, *it is difficult to praise this work enough*, alike as to its form and the entire composition of it, and its doctrinal matter. It is written with an inimitable   <small>Value of the</small> clearness, distinctness and simplicity, which must <small>Apology.</small> carry conviction alike to the learned and the unlearned. Its moderation and modesty are worthy of the good cause it vindicated. The mild and pious character of Melanchthon so sheds its lustre on the whole, as to force the conviction that the noblest views and purest piety, with no particle of unworthy aim, here struggle in behalf of religion.

As to its matter, it is undeniable, that it presents the truth in the clearest light, and successfully maintains the Evangelical doctrine over against the Romish system. Its *effectiveness for the interests of the Gospel in its own era, is beyond description* (unbeschreiblich.)   Historically considered, therefore, the Apology may claim in the formation and confirmation of the Evangelical Church an *infinitely high* (unendlich hoher) value. To the Apology belongs an eternal value. If the Church should make to herself new symbols, she will take over her fundamental doctrines from this symbol, and to it will be due a holy reverence to the end of time."

The same distinguished writer says in another work : † " Not only for the immediate aim of its own time, but as absolutely now as in the era of the Reformation, the Apology has its value and importance for religious truth, inasmuch as it wrought all that (indescribable effect), alone by the deepest and weightiest truths of the Gospel, as the Augsburg Confession witnesses to them, and the Apology more amply unfolds and establishes them. The Augsburg Confession was an erudite State-paper, composed with equal diplomatic foresight and caution, and Evangelical simplicity, and for this very reason needed a fuller exposition . . Hence it was and is of inexpressible importance, that the illustrious man, to whom, to say the least, the superintendence of the preparation of the Augsburg Confession had been given,

---

* Symbol. d. Luth. Kirch. 436.

† Die gute Sache d. Luther. Symbol. geg. ihreAnkläg. Göttingen. 1847. p 153.

should himself set in a yet clearer light its brief propositions, in this second jewel of Evangelical Lutheran testimony; that he should explain and establish them from the entire complex of Evangelical Biblical truth. The fundamental and essential doctrine of the Evangelical Church, in its separation from the human additions of the Romish priestly caste, consists in this, that we are justified, not by the righteousness of works, but by regeneration in the faith of the Gospel. And as this was the centre from which the heroes of the faith in the Reformation fought out their triumphs, so is it now, not only profoundest truth, but is the chief doctrine of Christianity itself, a doctrine which insures to Christianity and to the Evangelical Church with it, a perpetual endurance — for it is the very truth eternal itself. This doctrine in which is the ground and essence of all Christianity, is established by Melanchthon in the Apology with a greater accuracy than anywhere else." "To its importance testimony is borne in the attacks of its enemies, who felt deeply the injury to their cause, connected with the clear, luminous, and Scriptural argument, the dialectic skill, the combination of repose and thoroughness, with a beneficent warmth which characterize this writing. In the grand thing, the doctrine, it is as pure as the Confession to whose vindication it is consecrated." *

The next great Confession in the Book of Concord is the SCHMALCALD ARTICLES. The very existence of these Articles is a proof that neither the Lutheran authorities, who caused them to be written, nor Martin Luther, who is their author,

The Schmalcald Articles. nor the great theologians who advised in their preparation, nor Melanchthon, Jonas, Bugenhagen, Creutziger, Amsdorf, Spalatin, Brentius, and the other great theologians and pastors of our churches who subscribed them, imagined that to confess the Church's faith more fully involves a fallacy.

The Articles were occasioned by the expectation that a free General Council, so ardently desired from the beginning by the Reformers, and so often promised, was at length about to be convened. The Pope convened a Council, to be opened at

* Müller lxxix.

Mantua, on the 23d of May, 1537. To this Council the Evangelical (Lutheran) States were invited to come; and until it became manifest that it was not to be a free Council, they showed a strong desire to be represented in it.

In consequence of the expectation that the truth would have a hearing, the Elector desired to have a new statement of the great doctrinal principles of our Church, touching those questions which would arise at the Council as matters of discussion between Lutherans and Romanists. This desire How they orig-led him to commit to Luther the composition of inated. new Articles as a basis of Conference. The Articles thus prepared were taken to the Convention of the Evangelical States, held at Schmalcald, in February, 1537. There they were thoroughly examined by our great theologians, and by them subscribed, and, from the place where they were signed, came to be called the Schmalcald Articles.

The question at once suggests itself, Why was a new Confession prepared? Why was not the Augsburg Confession considered sufficient, in itself, or as sufficient in conjunction with the Apology? Was our Church giving way, or Why they were changing her ground, or dissatisfied with her first necessary. great Confession? Far from it. The reasons were these:—

I. *The Augsburg Confession had too much*, in some respects, for the object in view. The object in view, in 1537, was to compare the points of controversy between the Lutherans and the Romanists. The Augsburg Confession is in large measure a Confession of the whole faith of the Church universal, and hence embraces much about which there is no controversy between our Church and the Romish; as, for example, the doctrine concerning God and the Son of God. It was as much an object of the Augsburg Confession to show wherein our Church agreed with the Roman Church in so much of the faith as that Church had purely preserved, as to show wherein, in consequence of her apostasy from parts of the truth, our Church departed from her. The Augsburg Confession had done its great work in correcting misrepresentations of our Church on the former points. It was now desirable that omitting the discussion of what was settled, she should the more clearly ex press herself on the points of difference. This was the more needful, because in the efforts to come to an agreement at Augsburg, which followed the 25th of June, Melanchthon, in his great gentleness, had made concessions, whose real point the Romanists perverted, so as to find a warrant in them for false interpretations of the Confession in its distinctive doctrines. They understood well the two counter-tricks of polemics: the one, to exaggerate differences until innocence looks like crime; the other to diminish differences until truth seems nearly identical with error. The Church wished the deck cleared for action, that the truth disputed might put forth its whole strength, and the truth obscured reveal its whole character. But

II. *The Augsburg Confession has too little* for a perfect exhibition of the full position of our Church as to the errors of Rome. In 1530, our fathers rightly avoided an *unnecessary* opening of points of difference; for there was yet hope that many in the Church of Rome would be drawn by the gentler power of the truth, and that the fierceness of the conflict might be allayed. But the providence of God had made it imperative that the Church should more amply set forth now what she had succinctly confessed in 1530.

III. *The Augsburg Confession was not in the right key* for the work now to be done. That Confession was the Church's embodiment of the Spirit of her Lord, when he is tender with the erring. Now the time had come when she was to embody the Spirit of that same Lord, when he speaks in tones of judgment to the wilful and perverse.

Through the Augsburg Confession, even in the night of conflict which seemed to be gathering, the Church sang, " Peace on earth," but in the Schmalcald Articles, the very Prince of Peace seemed to declare that He had come to bring a sword — the double-edged sword of truth — the edge exquisitely keen, and the scabbard thrown away. Therefore, wise and heaven-guided, the Church which had committed the olive branch to Melanchthon, gave the sword to Luther.

The motion of the Augsburg Confession was to the flute, the Schmalcald Articles moved to the peals of the clarion, and the roll of the kettle-drum. In the Augsburg Confession Truth makes her overtures of peace, in the Schmalcald Articles she lays down her ultimatum in a declaration of war.

That which was secondary in the Augsburg Confession is primary in the Schmalcald Articles. At Augsburg our Church stood up for the Truth, that error might die by the life of Truth ; at Schmalcald she stood up against .the error, that Truth might live by the death of error. To utter her new testimony, to take her new vantage ground, was to use conquests made, as a basis for conquests yet to be made.

The Jesuits, indeed, set up the cry, that the Schmalcald Articles are in conflict with the Augsburg Confession. Our Church, by an overwhelming majority, has answered the falsehood, by placing them among her crown jewels. And there they deserve to be. "Not only were the doctrines of the Church presented clearly, but they were stated so thoroughly in Luther's style, might and spirit, that the era

Their value.

which he moved so profoundly, could not but recognize in them, alike a faithful image of the Truth, and a new point of support for it. In these Articles Luther presents directly the principles of the Evangelical (Lutheran) Church, and of the Romish See, in their conflict. In the name of the Evangelical Church he has spoken against the whole Papacy a bold and manly word, the word of refutation, with nothing to weaken its force. And this fact is decisive in establishing their high value for our own time. The impossibility of uniting the Evangelical (Lutheran) Church's pure life with Rome's worldly aims, is set in so clear a light, that the Evangelical Church will ever look upon this Symbol with the greatest reverence, and cling to it with true devotion. Melanchthon's Appendix to the Articles is classic alike in form and matter. For our Church these writings must ever remain very weighty, and the more because outside of them there is nowhere else in the Symbols so ample a statement *about* the Papacy, and what is to be noted well, so ample a statement *against* it." (Köllner.)

"They form," says Müller,* "with the earlier Symbols a complete whole, yet have, for the reasons given, an indepen-

* Die Symb. Bücher, lxxxii.

den. value, because in them the Lutherans for the first time, expressly and at large, define their relations to the Pope and the Papacy. We may say, that in and with them the Reformation closes, and the final separation from Rome is pronounced."

The compassion which moved our Lord when He saw the multitudes, fainting and scattering abroad, as sheep having no shepherd, was breathed by Him into the heart of Luther, and originated the CATECHISMS. The yearning to provide for the religious wants of the neglected people, early showed itself in Luther's labors,* and during the visitation in the Electorate of Saxony, 1527–1529, matured in the decision to prepare the Catechisms: " This Catechism, or Christian instruction, in its brief, plain, simple shape, I have been constrained and forced to prepare by the pitiful need of which I have had fresh experience in my recent work of visitation." In its general idea, Catechizing, the oral instruction, of the young especially, in the elements of divine truth, is as old as religion itself, and has always been in the Church; but to Luther belongs the glory of fixing the idea of the Catechism, as the term is now used. He is the father of Catechetics proper, and the most ancient Catechism now used in the world is Luther's Shorter Catechism of 1529. In the Catechisms he retained what the Ancient Church had used as the basis of the elementary instruction, to wit: the Decalogue, the Creed, and the Lord's Prayer: only adding the explanation of the Two Sacraments. " In this he showed far more Catechetical, Churchly-Didactic tact, than all the authors, whose thread is that of a system, be this system what it may. There is in the Catechisms a genuine conservatism, a holding fast and development of that which already had its home as the Christian Confession in the heart of the people. In the explanations which follow his questions, What does this mean? How does this take place? he has retained, almost word for

Marginal note: Luther's Catechisms: their occasion and character.

---

* See Luther's Catechetical Writings, beginning with the Exposition of the Lord's Prayer for the simple laity, 1518. Werke: Leipz. xxii. Walch x. Erlangen xxi–xxiii. Luther's Catechisms. By John G. Morris, D. D. Evang. Rev July, 1849.

word, language found in Kero (the Monk of St. Gall, A. D. 750), in his exposition of the Lord's Prayer, in fact, found yet earlier, in the Sacramentary of Gelasius (Pope 492–496.) It shows he self-renunciation, with which Luther held aloof from the formulary manner of Dogmatics and from Polemics ; it reveals the art of saying much in little, yet with all its pregnant richness never becomes obscure, heavy, unfit for the people. These qualities, in conjunction with that warm, hearty tone, in virtue of which Löhe " (who simply repeats an expression of Luther himself) " says the Catechism can be *prayed*, these — despite the barbarism of times and tendencies, whose nature it has been to have the least comprehension of the highest beauty — have preserved to this little book its exalted place of honor." *

The love of the Church anticipated the orders of Consistories in the universal introduction of Luther's Catechisms, and authority could come in only to sanction what was already fixed. So truly did the Shorter Catechism embody the simple Christian faith, as to become by the spontaneous acclamation of millions, a Confession. It was a private writing, and yet beyond all the Confessions, the direct pulsation of the Church's whole heart is felt in it. It was written in the rapture of the purest Catholicity, and nothing from Luther's pen presents him more perfectly, simply as the Christian, not as the prince of theologians, but as a lowly believer among believers.

In the Preface to the Book of Concord the " Electors, Princes, and Orders of the Empire, who adhere to the Augsburg Confession," declare in conclusion : " We propose in this Book of Concord to make no new thing, nor in any Confessional respect to depart from the truth of the heavenly authority. doctrine, as it has been acknowledged by our pious fathers and ourselves. By this divine doctrine we mean that which is derived from the writings of the Prophets and Apostles, and embraced in the three Ancient Creeds; the Augsburg Confession, delivered in 1530 to the Emperor Charles V.; the Apology which followed it; the Schmalcald Articles, and the CATE-CHISMS of Dr. Luther. Wherefore, it is our purpose in nothing

* Palmer in Herzog's: R. E. viii. 618. Do : Evang. Katechetik. Stuttg. 5. ed 1864

to depart from these in things or words, but by the grace of the Holy Spirit, with one accord, to abide in this pious Consent, and to regulate all decisions in controversies on religion, in accordance therewith."* "And because this matter of religion pertains also to the laity, as they call them, and bears upon their eternal salvation," says the Formula of Concord, "we publicly profess that we also embrace the SMALLER AND LARGER CATECHISMS of Luther, regarding them as a sort of Bible of the laity, wherein all those things are briefly comprehended which in the Holy Scripture are more largely treated, and the knowledge of which is of need to a Christian man unto his salvation " "These CATECHISMS have been received and approved by all the churches of the Augsburg Confession, and are everywhere used in the churches and schools publicly, and in private houses — and in them the Christian doctrine, taken from God's Word, is set forth with the utmost clearness and simplicity for the use of the unlearned and of the laity." †

In chronological order, as writings, the Catechisms, which appeared in 1529, would have preceded the Augsburg Confession, and this is the order in the Thuringian Corpus of 1561: but the chronology, so far as the Book of Concord preserves it in its arrangement, is that of acceptance as Confessions.

It would seem as if by preëminent necessity the Catechism of a Church should have an unmistakable indorsement as _{Opinions of} official and confessional. It is the Catechism by _{eminent men, in} which her future ministers and her people are _{regard to.} trained in the faith, in early life. If the Church puts into the hands of her children statements of doctrine in any respect false, she is the betrayer of their souls, not their guardian. A Catechism which embodies the pure faith in the form best adapted to preserve and diffuse it among the people is of inestimable value. Such a Catechism, if we may accept the judgment of the wisest and best men, our Church possesses. "It may be bought for sixpence," said Jonas, "but six thousand worlds would not pay for it." "Luther," says Polycarp Lyser, ‡ "has written a short Catechism, more precious than

---

*Müller. 21: 299 : 518.5.   † Do. 570.8.
‡ In the Dedication of Chemnitzii Loci.

gold and gems. In it the purity of the Church doctrine, drawn from prophets and apostles, is so compacted into one entire body of doctrine, and set forth in such luminous words, as not unworthily to be esteemed a Canon, as that which is drawn entire from the Canonical Scriptures. I can affirm with truth, that in this one little book are embraced so many and so great things, that if all faithful preachers, throughout their lives, should confine themselves in their sermons to the hidden wisdom of God shut up in these few words, explaining them rightly to the people, and opening them at large from the Holy Scriptures, they could never exhaust that boundless abyss."

"If," says Matthesius, * " Luther, in his whole course, had done nothing more than to introduce these Catechisms into the family, the school, and the pulpit, and to restore to the home the blessings at meat, and the prayers for morning and night, the world could never thank him enough, or repay him."

"Such," says Seckendorf, † " is the union of pure doctrine and of spirituality in the Lesser Catechism, that in its kind it has no equal.. Above all is its explanation of the Apostles' Creed admirable." " Is there an eloquence which is sufficient — not to do full justice to the theme — but in some degree to vindicate the value of the book? As I look upon the Churches everywhere, in the enjoyment of the blessing it brings, I confess that it surpasses all the range of my thought. If I must make the effort to express my regard for it, I acknowledge that I have received more consolation, and a firmer foundation of my salvation from Luther's Little Catechism, than from the huge volumes of all the Latin and Greek Church writers together. And although excellent theologians, not without success, have imitated Luther and written Catechisms, Luther's Cate-' chism in the judgment of all good men deserves the palm." ‡ Matthes, § who urges various objections to the Catechisms, nevertheless adds: " The little Catechism of Luther, with its explanations, brief, adapted to the people, childlike, and at the same time profound, meeting the wants of the mind and of the

---

* Sermons on the Life of Luther.   † Historia Lutheranismi. i. ? 51.

‡ Heshusius, quoted in Fabricii: Centif. Luther. ad Cap. lxxxii.

? Comparative Symbolik all. Christl. Confession. 1854.

heart, is still the Catechism which impresses itself most readily on the memory of children, and more than any other produces the spirit and life of religion in them. If this be still the case, who can measure the blessing it brought in the era of the Reformation, when a new epoch of the religious nurture of the people and of their children began with it?" "There are as many things in it as there are words, as many uses as there are points." * "It is a true jewel of our Church, a veritable masterpiece." † "It is impossible to estimate," says Köllner,‡ "the value of these Catechisms for their time. Luther gave in them not only a brief sketch of the fundamental truths of the Gospel, but restored to life the actual Catechizing, the primary instruction in religion. The form of the Catechism was as fitting as its matter. Luther was a man of the people; like Paul he had the gift of speaking to the masses, as no one else could, so that the simplest understood him, and heart and soul were alike touched. And this language of the heart, sustained by Luther's whole mode of thinking as a theologian, is the key-note of his Catechisms. They bear the true impress of his joyous assurance, of the earnest heartiness in which he was unique, and of all that true piety which here presents in conjunction the light and kindling which illumine the mind and revive the affections." Ranke's words ‖ may fitly close these eulogies: "The Catechism which Luther published in 1529, and of which he says that, old a Doctor as he was, he himself used it as his prayer, is as childlike as it is profound, as easy of grasp as it is unfathomable, as simple as it is sublime. Happy he who nourishes his soul with it, who clings fast to it! For every moment he possesses a changeless consolation — he has under a thin shell that kernel of truth which is enough for the wisest of the wise."

We now approach the part of the Book of Concord, with the acceptance or rejection of which, the Book as a whole is Formula of Concord. likely to stand or fall. If the Book of Concord did not contain the FORMULA OF CONCORD, it is very cer-

---

* Dr. I. F. Mayer.   † Baumgarten.
‡ Die gute Sache, 157.
‖ Deutsche Gesch. im Zeitalt. d. Reformat. Berl. 1839. ii. 445.

tain that the most decided and persistent opposition it has experienced would never have been raised. There is no instance on record in which any State, city, or individual, accepting the Formula of Concord, rejected or objected to any other of the Symbols. To decide upon acknowledging it, is to decide really upon the acknowledgment of the whole. Was it needed? Was it a restorer of concord, or a promoter of discord? Is it a pure witness of the one unchanging faith? Has it been stamped by the Church as an authoritative witness of her faith, and is it as such of force and value still? On these questions it is impossible to form an intelligent opinion without recalling the main facts in the his- tory of this great document. This History may be divided into FOUR parts. FIRST: The events which rendered necessary the preparation of a new Confession. SECOND: The events terminating in the preparation of the Torgau Formula. THIRD: The development of the Torgau Formula into the Bergen Book, which in its revised form appeared as the Formula of Concord, in the Book of Concord, Dresden, 1580. FOURTH: The subsequent reception of the Book of Concord. *

FIRST: Among the necessitating causes and preliminaries of the preparation of the Formula, may be mentioned:

I. Melanchthon's vacillations, real and seeming. These were due to his timidity and gentleness of character, tinged as it was with melancholy; his aversion to controversy; his philosophical, humanistic, and classical cast of thought, and his extreme delicacy in matter of style; his excessive reverence for the testimony of the Church, and of her ancient writers; his anxiety that the whole Communion of the West should be restored to harmony; or that, if this were impossible, the Protestant elements, at least, should be at peace. The coworking of these, in different proportions at different eras, produced inconsistencies of the most extraordinary kind, and, when Luther was gone and the intellectual headship of the Reformation devolved upon Melanchthon, the lack of self-consistence and firmness, which had been his misfortune as a man assumed the character of a public calamity. The whole work

* C. G. F. Walch: Breviarium L. S. E. L. 198–219.

19

of the Reformation, as represented in Melanchthon, seemed destined to fall into chaos. Everywhere, his works in their various editions, were in the hands of the friends and foes of the Conservative Reformation. The friends of that Reformation were embarrassed and confounded, and its enemies delighted and encouraged, by perceiving endless diversities of statement in the editions of books, rapidly succeeding each other, books which, in their first form, Luther had endorsed as of Canonical purity and worthy of immortality. The very Confessions of the Church, determined by her authorities, and signed by her representatives, were emended, enlarged here, abridged there, changed in structure and in statement, as the restless spirit of refining in thought or style moved Melanchthon. All his works show the tinge of his mind at the time of their issue, whether affected by his hopes that Rome would be softened, or roused by the elusive prospect of real union with the less radical part of the Zwinglians. Melanchthon fell into a hallucination by which his own peace of mind was wrecked, his Christian consistency seriously compromised, the spirit of partisanship developed, the Church distracted and well nigh lost. This was the hallucination that peace could be restored by ambiguous formulas, accepted indeed by both parties, but understood in different senses. It is a plan which has often been tried and which never succeeds, where men are in earnest. It not only does not bind men more closely, but leaves them more widely alienated, more full of bitter mistrust. Men must be honest in their difference, if they are ever to be honest in their agreement.

The three works of Melanchthon in which the changes were most noted and most mischievous, are 1: the Augsburg Confession; 2: the Apology; and 3: the Loci Communes.

II. Connected closely with Melanchthon's vacillations, various Controversies rose among the theologians of the Augsburg Confession, which may be stated as generically the conflict between the PHILIPPISTS, or adherents of Melanchthon, and the more consistent LUTHERANS. The great name of Melanchthon was used to shield much which there is no reason to believe he would have approved. Much that he wrote could be taken in two senses. The Lutheran-Philippists, who took the more charitable view, put the best construction on them, and were reluctant to abandon one to whom the Church owed so much, and whom Luther had loved so dearly. The Reformed put upon Melanchthon's words the construction most favorable to themselves. The Crypto-Calvinists made them their covert. The enemies of the Reformation appealed to them as proof that the first principles and doctrines of the Reformers had been abandoned. Whatever may be the meaning of Melanch thon's words in the disputed cases, this much is certain, that they practically operated as if the worse sense were the real one, and their mischievousness was not diminished but aggravated by their obscurity and double meaning. They did the work of avowed error, and yet could not be reached as candid error might. We have twenty-eight large volumes of Melanch thon's writings — and at this hour, impartial and learned men are not agreed as to what were his views on some of the profoundest questions of Church doctrine, on which Melanchthon was writing all his life.

III. 1560. A great centre of this controversy was furnished in the PHILIPPIC CORPUS DOCTRINÆ, 1560, to which the Philippists, especially in the Electorate of Saxony, desired to give Confessional authority, an effort which was resisted by the consistent Lutherans on the ground that it contained very serious errors. It was in the unionistic part of our Church, not the consistent part, that the tendency first appeared to put forth bulky Confessions, and the necessity for the Book of Concord was largely generated by the greatly larger Bodies of doctrine which were set forth by the Philippists.

The Philippic or Meissen German Corpus of 1560, contained. 1. The three General Creeds; 2. The Augsburg Confession from the Wittenberg ed. 1553, enlarged and altered; 3. The Apology; 4. The Repetition of the Augsburg Confession, written in 1551, to be sent to the Council of Trent; 5. The Loci Theologici; 6. The Examen Ordinandorum; 7. The Answer to the idolatrous Articles of Bavaria; and 8. A Confutation of the Mahometan Error of Servetus. The corresponding Latin Corpus of the same date, contains all the writings em-

braced in the German: the Augsburg Confession is the Va
riata varied of 1542; and there is added to the whole Melanchthon's Reply to Stancar.

As this Corpus became the special rival of the Book of Con
cord, and the controversy so largely clustered around the question, Which should be preferred, this Corpus, or that Book?—
t may be well to note:

1. That the Corpus is greatly more bulky than the Book of
Concord.

2. With the exception of the General Creeds it is entirely
composed of Melanchthon's writings. Not a line exclusively
Luther's is in it. The Catechisms are not there; not even the
Schmalcald Articles are there. It was a silent dishonor put
upon Luther, and his faith and work, apparently in the name
of the Lutheran Church, by the men who afterwards clamored
that Melanchthon was not treated with due respect in the Book,
which yet gives the place of honor to Melanchthon's greatest
confessional works, the Augsburg Confession and the Apology
and contains also his Tractate on the power of the Pope.

3. It is largely composed of private writings on which no
official action of the Church was taken.

4. The texts of its most important parts are changed greatly,
and corrupted.

5. There is much in it cumbrous, and wholly unsuited to
form a Confession.

6. It is ambiguous on some vital points, and unsound on
others.

7. A treachery and double-dealing unworthy of our holy
faith, and especially condemned by the frank directness, characteristic of Lutheran Christianity, underlies the whole concep
tion of the issue of such a Corpus.

IV. The earlier Saxon CRYPTO–CALVINISM, which the Wittenberg theologians embodied in various publications. Confessing one system of faith, it held and furtively promoted the
doctrines of another, or ignored the truths it did not openly
assail. Many were involved in its meshes, who imperfectly
understood its nature, and were slow to believe the worst of it.
This greatly complicated the difficulties, and embittered the

controversies of this century. Again and again it circumvented and deceived the very men who were engaged in the effort to expose and overthrow it.

V. 1569. The alarming state of things led to various consultations on the part of our theologians, who heartily desired to save the Church from being choked with the upspringing of error, or from being trodden down and torn to pieces in the effort to root it out. Chief among them were JAMES ANDREÆ, of Tübingen, who at an early stage of his efforts made a journey into Lower Saxony, 1569, MARTIN CHEMNITZ, DAVID CHYTRAEUS, and NICHOLAS SELNECCER, all of them great theologians, moderate in spirit, earnest Christians, and intensely devoted to the purity and peace of the Church.

VI. 1570. A Convention was convened at ZERBST, by the Electors of Saxony and Brandenburg, and by Julius, Duke of Brunswick, for the promotion of concord among the theologians, 1570. Andreæ was satisfied with the results of the Convention, but they did not correspond fully with the expectation of others. Heshus wrote against the Convention and against Andreæ. So much had men in fact come to distrust what was most specious, that Andreæ was suspected by some of secret connivance with the errors, to the casting out of which he was devoting his life.

VII. 1573. Two BOOKS, designed to promote peace, were prepared by Andreæ and sent to the theologians of Lower Saxony for subscription: 1. Six sermons on the divisions which had arisen between 1548 and 1573; 2. An exposition of the existing controversies. The first was sent in print. The second, prepared by advice of Chemnitz, remained in manuscript.

VIII. 1574. The ELECTORAL-TORGAU ARTICLES were written by the Saxon divines, by order of the Elector Augustus, 1574. These Articles were suspected, perhaps not without reason, of making concessions to Calvinistic errors. And yet upon the surface no charge seemed more groundless. He who reads them, supposing them to have been written in good faith, will be apt to see in them a thorough rejection and confutation of the Calvinistic Sacramentarianism. So perfect is the deception, if it be one, that Selneccer, on a first reading, was delighted

with them, and congratulated the Church of God, that at Torgau, so pure and sincere a Lutheran Confession had been set
forth. He who reads them now, is more likely to be surprised
at Selneccer's change from this opinion, than at his having
formed it. The Calvinists themselves complained bitterly of
the severity of these Articles against them. Their leaders are
named, their views stated and refuted. Beza, who was named
in them more than once, wrote an answer to them. Hospinian
regards them as the basis of the Formula of Concord. Even
Hutter * says that " the something of the Calvinistic jugglings
latent in them is found in very few places," and attributes
their defects either to the writers' want of full information
about the points at issue, or to a charity which hoped by softness of style to win the enemies of truth to accept it. In a
time in which sad experience had found no reason for jealous
care, these Torgau Articles would probably have been regarded
by all as Selneccer first regarded them. A long succession of
causes of distrust can alone account for their being suspected.

IX. 1575. The SUABIAN-SAXON FORMULA OF CONCORD, mainly
the work of Chemnitz and Chytraeus, appeared in 1575.
This is not to be confounded with the Confession of the
Churches of Lower Saxony, prepared by the same hands, 1571.
The " Exposition " of Andreæ was well received by the Würtemberg theologians, but the Doctors of Lower Saxony, dissatisfied with it, desired Chemnitz and Chytraeus to elaborate on
it as a basis the Suabian-Saxon Formula, which was sent back
after careful revision by the representatives of the churches to
Würtemberg. This Formula became a general ground-work
of the Formula of Concord.

THE SECOND PERIOD of the history of the Book of Concord
follows the preparation of the Suabian-Saxon For-
Second Period. mula (1575) and ends with the completion of the
Torgau Formula. The most important points embraced in it,
are these :

I. 1576. Feb. *The Convention at Lichtenberg.* Augustus,
Elector of Saxony, saw that though the work of uniting the
Church was begun, it was very far from completion. Under

---

* Concordia Concor. ch. v.

the influence of this feeling, (Nov. 21, 1575) he sent to his Privy Council, in his own hand-writing, a paper, worthy of a Christian prince. It took just views of the peril of the time and of its source, and so wisely marked out the principles, afterwards acted on, on which alone peace could be restored, that it may be regarded as having laid "the first foundation-stone of the Work of Concord." "We are to look," said he, "more to the glory of God, than to that of dead men." "Unity among us who claim to receive the Augsburg Confession, is impossible, while every land has a separate Corpus Doctrinæ. In this way many are misled: the theologians are embittered against each other, and the breach is constantly widened. If the evil be not cured, there is reason to fear that by this embittering and confusion on the part of the theologians, we, and our posterity, will be utterly carried away from the pure doctrine. My plan is that we who confess the Augsburg Confession, shall unite and compare views in a friendly way ; that three or four peace-loving theologians, and an equal number of Civil Counsellors nominated by the heads of the States, meet together, bringing with them the different Corpora Doctrinæ ; that they take the Augsburg Confession as their rule (Richtschnur); that they compare the Corpora, and take counsel together how, out of the whole, to make one Corpus, which shall be the common Confession of us all." This paper led to the assembling, (Feb. 1576,) of the Convention at Lichtenberg, composed of theologians marked by that love of peace on which the noble Elector justly laid so much stress. These twelve theologians, among whom were Paul Crell of Wittenberg, and Selneccer, determined upon three things as essential to the establishment of concord :

1. All private self-seeking and ambition, all personal griefs and contentions, all suspicions of injury and desire of revenge, all the controversies and controversial writings between orethren, in the past, were to be given to eternal oblivion — were to be "as if they had never been."

2. The Philippic Corpus Doctrinæ was confessed to have been the occasion of misunderstanding. "That useful and good book, written by the sainted Philip, had been commended

oy us, and introduced into the churches and schools; **some** had styled it a Norm of doctrine and Confession This ha1 been understood as designed to take the useful and admirable spiritual writings of Luther, of precious memory, out of the hands of pastors and people. ·Certain points in the Corpus, as Free Will, Definition of the Gospel, the Lord's Supper, want of sufficient explicitness toward the Sacramentarians, had been understood in a sense, or distorted to it, of which our Churches have known, and now know, nothing."   While they therefore regard it as " an admirable, good and useful book," they renounce it as a " Symbol, Norm, or Rule."   " The Norm of our doctrine and Confession is this, We set and name, first of all, and unconditionally, the Writings of the Prophets and Apostles, the three Œcumenical Creeds, and then the Augsburg Confession, the first, Unaltered, its Apology, the Catechisms of Luther and the Schmalcald Articles. If any one, because of the doctrine of justification, desires to add Luther on the Epistle to the Galatians, we would heartily agree with him."   They then speak with severity of Crypto-Calvinistic books which had been furtively prepared and circulated, and advise the repression of them.

3. They proposed that a Commission of theologians loving truth and peace, taking the Augsburg Confession as a rule and following its order, should prepare a clear statement in regard to the doctrines involved in controversy.   They expressed their approval of the great divines who had already done so much in this direction, Chytræus, Chemnitz, and Andreæ, and added the name of Marbach.

II. 1575. Nov. 14. *The Saxon, Henneberg and Würtemberg union of action.* Though the earlier steps of this concerted action preceded the Lichtenberg Convention, it yet, because of its close connection with the Maulbrunn Formula, is more naturally placed here.

1. It was said by an old French Chronicler, that the English are sad even in their mirth. It might be said of our pious Princes of the Sixteenth Century that they were religious even at their amusements. The Elector Augustus met George Ernest, the old Count of Henneberg, at the hunt, and in a con-

versation on the troubles of the time, said that he would gladly correct the evils, especially those charged upon the Wittenberg theologians, if he could be furnished with a distinct statement both of the false doctrines charged, and of the truths opposed to them. The Count promised to have a paper, of the kind desired, drawn up.

2. The Count of Henneberg (Nov. 1575,) met Louis Duke of Würtemberg, at the nuptials of the Duke to the daughter of Charles, Margrave of Baden. When the festivities were over and the other princes had departed, the Count, the Duke, and the Margrave, agreed to commit to Luke Osiander and Bidembach the preparation of such a writing as the Count had promised.

3. These divines laid as the groundwork of their paper the Suabian-Saxon Formula (see Divis. First viii.), compressing it and adding proof passages from Scripture, and citations from Luther. Their work was finished Nov. 14, 1575.

III. 1576. Jan. 19. *The Maulbrunn Formula.*

1. The document thus prepared was submitted to a number of theologians, delegates of the princes. They tested and approved it in the Convention at the Cloister of *Maulbrunn* (Jan. 19, 1576.)

2. The Maulbrunn Formula was sent, Feb. 9, 1576, by the Count of Henneberg to the Elector of Saxony. The Elector had meanwhile obtained (Jan. 17, 1576) a copy of the Suabian-Saxon Formula (Div. First. viii.) from Duke Julius. The Elector now placed both the Formulas, the Maulbrunn and Suabian-Saxon, in the hands of Andreæ, for his advice.

3. Andreæ pursued a course in the matter worthy of his venerable name, and of the confidence reposed in him at the great crisis. Though the Suabian-Saxon Formula was built so largely upon his own labors, he confessed that it was unfitted for its end by the irregularities of its style, its copious use of Latin words, and its diffuseness, while its indeterminateness toward Melanchthon's writings might give rise to new controversies. The Maulbrunn Formula, on the other hand, which was in some sense an abridgment of the Suabian-Saxon, was too brief. His counsel, therefore, was that the two should be

made the basis of a third Formula, which, combining the virtues of both, should avoid their faults.

4. This counsel of Andreæ was thoroughly approved of by the Elector. As the great function of the Formula of the future was to guard the true doctrine of the Augsburg Confession, and to this end it was necessary to fix and preserve its uncorrupted text, the first movement of the Elector was toward the securing of the copy of the Augsburg Confession, in German, made by Spalatin during the Diet, in 1530.

IV. 1576, May. *The Convention at Torgau.* The Elector did not delay the now promising movement toward unity. He made the arrangements for a convention of theologians, of different lands, at Torgau. Eighteen, out of twenty invited, appeared. Eleven of the twelve delegates at Lichtenberg were of the number, of whom Selneccer was the most distinguished. The other names of greatest renown are Andreæ, Chytraeus, Chemnitz, Musculus, and Corner. The deliberations were held at the Castle of Hartenfels, the Rock of Hardness, a name of happy suggestion for confessors of the truth in troublous times. The inspection of the two Formulas, the Suabian-Saxon and the Maulbrunn, produced at once a concurrence in Andreæ's opinion, that the one was too diffuse, the other too brief, and an adoption of his advice to fuse both into a new Formula. They laid as the basis of the new, the Suabian-Saxon Formula, departing occasionally from its arrangement, pursuing, as nearly as possible, the order of Articles in the Augsburg Confession, and inserting an Article on the Descent into Hell.

V. Thus originated the Book *or Formula of Torgau,* (1576), after the toils and anxieties of seven years. The Lichtenberg Convention had determined the general principle on which the Concord should be established ; the Suabian-Saxon Formula had furnished its basis ; the Maulbrunn Formula had aided in the superstructure ; the necessary combinations, additions and emendations, had been happily made at Torgau. Varied as had been the difficulties, and wide as had been the gulf which once yawned as if it would swallow up the Church, the accord of spirit had now been such, that in ten days the work of

Torgau was finished. The theologians who met May 29, **were ready** with the Torgau Opinion (Bedenken) June 7th, 1576. All the theologians had borne an active part in its preparation, but Andreæ and Chemnitz are justly regarded as its authors.

The THIRD PERIOD of the history of the Formula of Concord opens with the sending forth of the Torgau Form- Formula. His- ula for examination by the Churches, (1576), tory of Third and ends with the publication of the Book of Period. Concord, 1580.

I. The Elector AUGUSTUS, (June 7, 1576), having carefully examined the Torgau Formula, and having laid it before his counsellors, submitted it to the Evangelical orders of the Empire, in order that it might be thoroughly tested in every part.

II. The work was everywhere received with interest. Twenty conventions of theologians were held in the course of three months. The Formula was scrutinized in every part. The work found little favor with the Calvinists, whether secret or avowed. The Reformed held a Conference at Frankfurt, Sept., 1577, to avert what they considered a condemnation of their party. Delegates were there from other countries. Elizabeth, Queen of England, sent ambassadors to several of the Evangelical States, and especially to the Elector Augustus, to avert the imaginary condemnation. The Elector, in a courteous but firm letter, assured the Queen, through the King of Denmark, that the object of the Formula was to correct and prevent errors within the Churches of the Augsburg Confession, not to pass condemnation on other Churches. Some of the friends of Melanchthon thought that the Formula failed in not recognizing his merits. On the part of a few theologians, there was a scarce suppressed ill-humor that they had not been consulted in the preparation of the Formula. But the great mass of the twenty-five responses testified to a general approval of the Formula, and showed that the pure faith still lived. Many opinions of great value were expressed involving no change in doctrine, but suggesting various additions, omissions, and alterations of language. It was clear that the book had not yet reached the shape in which it could fully meet the wants of the Church.

III. As soon as the answers were received, the Elector Augustus, with the concurrence of Brunswick and Würtemberg, called together the three greatest of the co-workers, Chemnitz, of Brunswick, Andreæ, of Tübingen, and Selneccer, of Leipzig, to revise the Torgau Formula in the light of the expressed judgments of the Churches. They met, with the cordial consent of the Abbot Ulner, at the Cloister of Bergen, near Magdeburg.

1. Here the Torgau Formula was submitted to its *first revision*, March 1 – 14, 1577. The work was done very conscientiously. Every suggestion was carefully weighed, and estimated at its real value, the treatment was made more compact, and an Epitome of the Solid Declaration was prepared. The theory, that a second revision was made in April, at Bergen, has little to sustain it.

2. The *second and final* revision of the Torgau Formula took place at Bergen, May 19–28, 1577. To the "first Triumvirate" Brandenburg added Corner, and Musculus, of Frankfort on the Oder, and Mecklenburg, at the special request of Augustus, sent Chytræus of Rostock. Though they passed over the Formula with minute care, they found little to change.

IV. The last touches were put to the work. At this stage, (May 28, 1577,) we know it as the *Bergen* Formula. It was to be known in history as the Formula of Concord, for this it was. Between this time and its publication in 1580, no change was made in it. There waited in it a silent might which the magic touch of the press was to liberate, to its great mission in the world.

V. But wonderful as had been the work done, much yet remained to be done. When the Church first saw clearly the way in which peace was to be won, she saw that it involved four problems: 1. The determination what writings were to be her standard of teaching; where was to be found a statement of doctrine which the Lutheran Church could accept unreservedly as her Confession. 2. The preparation of a Confession which should apply the doctrines of holy Scripture, and of the earlier standards of teaching, to the new issues which convulsed the Church, and should protect the older standards

from corruption and false interpretations. 3. The securing
for both classes of Confession, the subscriptions of the teachers
of the Church, as representatives of its faith, and 4. The
solemn sanction of the norm of teaching by the Political
Estates, which would shield it against violence.*

Two of these problems had now been happily solved : The
Augsburg Confession ; its Apology : the Schmalcald Articles
and the Catechisms had been fixed upon as the standard of
teaching ; and the Bergen Formula had determined the new
questions, in accordance with that standard. Two problems
remained. It was first contemplated to settle them by holding
a General Convention, a plan, wisely abandoned. The plan
adopted was, to submit the book for signature to the representatives of the Church in the various lands. In far the larger
part of the Lutheran States and Cities, the subscription was
promptly made. It was throughout voluntary. A free expression of opinion was invited. Force was put upon no man.
Not even the enemies of the Formula pretended that such was
the case. The Apostates from it, at a later period, did not pretend that they had acted under constraint in signing it. It
was signed by three Electors, twenty-one Princes, twenty-two
Counts, twenty-four Free Cities, and by eight thousand of the
teachers of the Church.

VI. It was impossible, nevertheless, in the nature of the case
that there should be no dissenting voices. Few and feeble as
they were when contracted with the joyous response of a
major part of the Church, they were listened to with respect,
and no effort was spared to unite the whole Church. But as
one class of objections was often of the pettiest and most pitiful
nature, for the most part the merest effusions of the ill nature
of men who were too little to lead, and too vain to follow, and
as another class, though of a more dignified nature, were
drawn from mere motives of political jealousy, or State interest,
the gentleness and patience failed of their object. Those who
loved the Church best had hoped rather than expected, that
all the Estates would accept the bond of union. This holy hope
was not indeed consummated, but great beyond all expectation

* Anton : Gesch. d. Conc. formel. I. 214.

were the results, nevertheless. If the Church's vote was not absolutely unanimous, it was that of an immense majority. A Church threatened with destruction, from the insidious working of error, had risen out of the chaos created by heresy which pretended to be orthodox. The darkness in which no man could tell friend from foe had been swept away. Deliverance had come from a state of pitiful strife and alienation, over which the enemies of God were already exulting as hopeless, and which would have ended in the overthrow of the Reformation. But for the Formula of Concord it may be questioned whether Protestantism could have been saved to the world. It staunched the wounds at which Lutheranism was bleeding to death, and crises were at hand in history, in which Lutheranism was essential to the salvation of the whole Reformatory interest in Europe. The Thirty Years' War, the war of martyrs, which saved our modern world, lay indeed in the future of another century, yet it was fought and settled in the Cloister of Bergen. But for the pen of the peaceful triumvirates, the sword of Gustavus had not been drawn. Intestine treachery and division in the Church of the Reformation would have done what the arts and arms of Rome failed to do. But the miracle of restoration was wrought. From being the most distracted Church on earth, the Lutheran Church had become the most stable. The blossom put forth at Augsburg, despite the storm, the mildew and the worm, had ripened into the full round fruit of the amplest and clearest Confession, in which the Christian Church has ever embodied her faith.

The FOURTH DIVISION of the History of the Formula of Concord embraces the *events which followed* its publication. Among them may be enumerated, as most important, the following:

I. A number of Estates, not embraced in the first subscription, 1580, added their signatures, in 1582. There was now a grand total of eighty-six Evangelical States of the Empire united in the Formula of Concord.

II. As regards its reception, *out of Germany*, may be noted these facts:

1. The Princes and theologians by whom the Formula of Concord had been given to the world, had made no effort to

procure the subscription and coöperation of the Churches outside of the German Empire. The reasons for this course were
various. First, To have invited the co-working of other nationalities, would have complicated, to the degree of impracti-
cability, what was already so tangled. Second, The
difficulties which originated the necessity for the Fourth Period.
Formula of Concord were comparatively little felt outside of
Germany. The whole doctrinal Reformation, outside of Germany, was in a certain sense secondary. Germany was the
battle-ground of the great struggle, and others waited, knowing that the decision there would be a decision for all. Third,
Political barriers existed. In some lands where the Lutheran
Church had strength, the rulers were Reformed or Roman
Catholic. One of the Reformed monarchs indeed, King Henry
of Navarre, desired to form an alliance with the Evangelical
States against the Roman Catholics, but the States, setting the
pure faith before all political considerations, declined the alliance, except on the basis of the Formula of Concord.

2. Denmark was the solitary exception to the rule in regard
to foreign lands, an exception due, probably, to the fact that
the wife of Augustus of Saxony was the sister of the King,
Frederick the Second. The feeling of Frederick II. was probably a mingling of aversion, inspired by some of his theologians
who were Crypto-Calvinistic or Philippistic, and of dread, lest
the Formula of Concord should introduce into his land the
controversies from which it had hitherto been free. How
blind and irrational the feeling of Frederick was, is shown by
the fact, greatly disputed but apparently well established, that
without reading it, or submitting it to his theologians, he threw
into the fire the superbly bound copy sent him by his sister, the
Electress. On July 24th, 1580, he sent forth an order forbid-
ding the bringing of a copy of the Book into Denmark, under
penalty of the confiscation of all the property of the offender,
and of his execution. Ministers and teachers, if convicted of
having a copy in their houses, were to be deposed. In spite
of this fierce opposition, the Formula came to be regarded in
Denmark with the highest reverence, and in fact, if not in
form, became a Symbol of the Danish Church.

3. In HOLSTEIN, it was speedily introduced and greatly prized, and, in 1647, was formally accepted as a Symbol.

4. In SWEDEN, John II. (1568–1592) was on the throne. To the cruel murder of his insane brother Eric, he added the crime of persistent efforts to force Romanism on his people. There of course, for the present, the Formula could not hope for a hearing. But in 1593, the year after his death, the Coun cil of Upsala determined upon its subscription, and its authority as a Symbol was still further fixed by later solemn acts of official sanction.

5. In POMERANIA, LIVONIA and HUNGARY (1573–1597), it was accepted as a Symbol.

III. It is worthy of note that some of the nominally Lutheran Princes and States either 1, never accepted the Formula as their Confession, or 2, having accepted it, subsequently withdrew.

1. The city of Zweibrücken which had not received the Formula, went over, in 1588, to the Reformed Church. Anhalt, about the same time, the Wetterau, in 1596, and Hesse, in 1604, made the same change.

2. In the *Electoral Palatinate*, Louis had been a devoted friend of the work of Concord. On his death, 1583, John Casimir introduced the Reformed faith. In *Brandenburg*, in 1614, under John Sigismund, an Electoral Resolution was set forth, full of coarse abuse of the Formula and of its authors. The Formula, nevertheless, continued to be loved and reverenced in Brandenburg. In part of Brunswick, the Corpus Julium took the place of the Book of Concord. It embraced everything in the Book of Concord except the Formula, and had in addition a work on doctrines by Chemnitz, and another by Urban Regius. In the part of Brunswick which had had the Corpus Wilhelminum, the Book of Concord and the Corpus were both received as symbolical. The Corpus had all the matter of the Book except the Formula.

IV. As might be anticipated, appearing in so controversial an age and involving all the greatest questions of the time, the *Formula of Concord was assailed* by the Reformed and the Roman Catholics, and by a few nominal Lutherans. Most renowned among these earlier assaults were the "Christian Admonition" by Ursinus, 1581, the Anhalt Opinion, 1581, the Reply of the Bremen Preachers, 1581, Irenæus' Examen, 1581, and Ambrose Wolff's History of the Augsburg Confession, 1580. To these bitter libels, for they were little else, the three great divines, Kirchner, Selneccer, and Chemnitz, by order of the three Electors, of the Palatinate, Saxony, and Brandenburg, replied. In 1599, appeared the Staffort Book (naméd from the place of its publication,) in which the Margrave of Baden assigned his reasons for rejecting the Formula of Concord. They were so convincing to his own mind that he persecuted his Lutheran subjects for not seeing the force of them. The Book was answered by the Würtemberg and Electoral-Saxon theologians, in 1600–1602.

Several Roman Catholic writers also assailed the Formula. The most renowned of these was Cardinal Bellarmin in his "Judgment on the Book of Concord," Cologne, 1589. It now forms the Fourth Part of his work on the Controversies of his time, the master-piece of the Romish Polemic of the Sixteenth Century. It was answered by Hoe of Hoenegg (1605) and others.

In forming an estimate of the MERITS AND VALUE OF THE FORMULA OF CONCORD, for which we have been prepared by the glance taken at its history, the following facts may be worthy of consideration:

I. The controversies which the Formula of Concord was meant to settle, had produced incalculable mischief in the Church, and absolutely needed settlement, if the Church were to be saved.

Formula of Concord. Its merits and value.

1. The time was one of mighty agitations and of strong convictions. Every question involving doctrine was regarded with an intensity of feeling, which a cold and skeptical age is unable to understand. God's least word was something for which men would spend their years in battle, would take joyfully the spoiling of their goods, would abandon their homes for exile, and would ascend the scaffold. They resisted unto blood on the division of a hair, if they believed the hair to belong to the head of Truth.

20

2. The age was one of vast upheaval, and of rapid reconstruction. The superstitions of centuries had been overthrown and the temple of a pure Scriptural faith was to be reared upon their ruins. Every man was a polemic and a builder, eager to bear part in the wonderful work of the time. It was an age of feverish excitement, and many passed through the delirium of weak mind overwrought, and fancied their ravings, inspirations. It was the age of antitheses, in which extravagances, by a law of reaction, rose in hostile pairs. Two errors faced each other, and in their conflict trampled down the faith which lay prostrate between them. Extremists treated truth as if it were habitable only at one pole, and the proof that the one pole was untenable at once involved to them the necessity of going to the other.

3. The controversies which followed Luther's death, arrested the internal development of the Church, and brought the processes of its more perfect constitutional organizing almost to a close. The great living doctrines, which made the Reformation, were in danger of losing all their practical power in the absorption of men's minds in controversies. War, as a necessary evil to avoid a greater, just war, as the preliminary to a pure peace, is to be defended; but war, made a trade, treated as a good, pursued for its own sake, and interminable, is the curse of curses, and much of the controversy of the second half of the Sixteenth Century was making a rapid transition to this type of strife. The Church was threatened with schisms. Her glory was obscured. Her enemies mocked at her. Her children were confounded and saddened. Weak ones were turned from her communion, sometimes to Zurich, or Geneva, sometimes to Rome. Crafty men crept in to make the Lutheran Church the protector of heresy. There was danger that the age which the Conservative Reformation had glorified, should see that grand work lost in the endless dissensions of embittered factions. Hence it is that the *peculiar* characteristic of the Formula, on which its necessity and value depend, goes so far in solving — what might otherwise seem mysterious — that while the larger part of the Lutheran Church received it with enthusiasm, some did not accept it. The reason is: that while

the Confessions set forth the faith of our Church, in her antagonism to the errors *outside of her*, the Formula, if not exclusively, yet in the main, is occupied in stating the truth, and defending it, over against the errors *which had crept into her*, and corrupted some of her children. *Romanism*, with its artifices, had misled some. *Fanaticism, sectarianism,* and *heresy,* had lured others ; and the ardor of controversy against the wrong, had led others, as, for example, the noble and great Flaccius, to extravagance and over-statement, which needed to be corrected. The Lutheran Church was assailed by open war and direct persecution, by intrigue, Jesuitical device, and conspiracy. Romanism was active on the one hand, and sectarianism on the other. False brethren, pseudo-unionists, endeavored by tricks of false interpretation to harmonize the language of the Augsburg Confession, and of the earlier Confessions, with their errors. The mighty spirit of Luther had gone to its rest. Melanchthon's gentleness sometimes degenerated into utter feebleness of purpose, and alike to the Romanists and the sectarians he was induced to yield vital points.

Not yet compacted in her organism, living only by her faith, and centred in it, as her sole bond of union, the Lutheran Church, in Germany especially, which was the great battleground, was called to meet an awful crisis.

No man who knows the facts, will deny that something worthy of the responsibility involved in such great and cogent issues had to be done. About the means there may be dispute, about the end there can be none. The world is very much divided between men who do things, and men who show that they could have been done better, but the latter class, at least admit that they had to be done.

II. The Church in this time of trial used the *best means* for the needed end. She availed herself of the labors of the best men, who proposed and carried out the best means for the preparation of the Formula of Concord.

1. First and greatest among these men, was the Elector AUGUSTUS, of Saxony, (1533–1588,) son of Duke Henry, the Pious. In 1548 he married Anna, daughter of Christian III. of Denmark, who was universally beloved for her devoted adhe-

rence to Lutheranism, and for her domestic virtues. Augustus assisted in bringing about the religious peace of Augsburg, in 1555, by which the Protestants (Lutherans) obtained important rights in common with the Roman Catholics. The fact that these benefits were confined to the " adherents to the Augsburg Confession," was one dangerous source of temptation to the Reformed. It led men to pretend to adhere to that Confession, simply to secure the civil benefits connected with it.

The Elector was in advance of his time in the principles of constitutional sovereignty. In an arbitrary age he governed by law. He consulted his parliament on all great questions, and raised no money by taxation without their advice. His edicts were so just that he has been called the Saxon Justinian. His subjects regarded him with peculiar love and reverence. By his skilful internal administration, he raised his country far above the rest of Germany, introducing valuable reforms both in jurisprudence and finance, and giving a decided impulse to education, agriculture, and manufactures. The Dresden Library owes to him its origin, as do also most of its galleries of arts and science.

Augustus bore a part in the Formula of Concord worthy of him. To meet the necessary expenses connected with the Formula, the Elector himself paid a hundred thousand dollars in gold. His gifts and efforts were unceasing till the great end was attained. Noble and unsuspicious, he had been slow to believe in the possibility of the treachery of the false teachers, whose mischievous devices he at length reluctantly came to understand. The troubles they brought upon the Church whitened untimely the Elector's head, but so much the more did he toil and pray till the relief from the evil was wrought. While the theologians were engaged in conferences, the Elector and his noble wife were often on their knees, fervently praying that God would enlighten His servants with His Holy Spirit. In large measure, to the piety, sound judgment, and indefatigable patience of this great prince, the Church owes the Formula of Concord.*

2 Next to the name of AUGUSTUS, is to be placed that of

* Hutter: Conc. Conc. ch. xi.   Anton: i. 147, 148.   Köllner: 533.

JACOB ANDREÆ, (1528–1590,) Professor and Chancellor of the University at Tübingen, and Provost of the Church of St. George. He was the pupil, friend, and colleague of Brentius. " He was," says one who had no reason to tempt him to ex-travagance of eulogy, " a man of excellent genius, of large soul, of rare eloquence, of finished skill — a man whose judg-ments carried the greatest authority with them." * At the age of eighteen he was Dean at Stuttgart —and when, on the capture of that city by the Spaniards, the Protestant preachers were driven out, Andreæ remained, and exercised an influ-ence in moderati g the victors. He resigned, at the age of twenty, his earliest place as a clergyman, rather than accept the Interim, with its concessions to Romanism. His labors as a Reformer, both in doctrine and discipline, and afterward as a Conservator of the Reformation, were unwearied. He was " in journeyings oft," and all his journeyings were directed to the good of the Church, and the glory of God. The estimate which Planck makes of Andreæ, is confessedly an unkind and unjust one, yet he says : " Andreæ belongs not merely to the learned, but to the liberal-minded theologians of his era . . . It was not in his nature to hate any man merely because that man was not orthodox . . . It was not only possible for him to be just, at least at the beginning, toward those who were in error, but he felt a something to which it is not easy to give a name, which attracted him to those that erred." " His writings," says Hartmann, " over one hundred and fifty in number, are among the most interesting memorials of the characteristics of the theological effort of the era. He was a man of rich erudition, and of unflagging diligence. His eloquence bore his hearers resistlessly with it. As a preacher, he was full of fire and life. His sermons were pre-eminently practical. In negotiations, he was skilful and captivating."

3. Worthy of association with the venerable names of Augus-tus and Andreæ, is that of CHEMNITZ, (1522–1586,) Melanch-thon's greatest pupil. At the age of fourteen, already reveal-ing " a peculiar genius," he was sent to school at Wittenberg.

---

* Weismann : H. S. N. T. i. 1455. See Andreæ, in Herzog's R. E. i. 310, by Hartmann. Planck : Gesch. d. Protest. Theol. vi. 372

There he received his first deep impressions of Luther, whom he often heard in the pulpit, in the fullest glory of his power. When, nine years later, Chemnitz came to Wittenberg as a University student, Luther was living, but the young scholar had not yet decided on the theological studies with which his renown was to be identified. To these Melanchthon drew him. The learning of Chemnitz was something colossal, but it had no tinge of pedantry. His judgment was of the highest order. His modesty and simplicity, his clearness of thought, and his luminous style, his firmness in principle, and his gentleness in tone, the richness of his learning and the vigor of his thinking, have revealed themselves in such measure in his Loci, his Books on the Two Natures of our Lord, and on the True Presence, in his Examen of the Council of Trent, his Defence of the Formula of Concord, and his Harmony of the Gospels, as to render each a classic in its kind, and to mark their author as the greatest theologian of his time — one of the greatest theologians of all time.

4. The third man in the great theological " triumvirate," as its enemies were pleased to call it, was NICHOLAS SELNECCER (1530–1592). He too was one of Melanchthon's pupils (1549). In 1557 he became Court preacher at Dresden. He was a great favorite with the Elector Augustus. His simple, earnest Lutheranism led him to defend Hoffman against the persecutions of the Melanchthonian-Calvinistic party. So little did Augustus at that time understand the real character of the furtive error against which, in after time, he was to direct the most terrible blows, that Selneccer was allowed to resign his place, (1561). The exile sought refuge in Jena. There the Flaccian troubles met him, and led to his deposition, but Augustus recalled him (1568) to a position as Professor at Leipzig, in which he labored on, in stillness, not unobservant, however, of the mischiefs connected with the Crypto-Calvinistic movements in Saxony. Finally the Elector, with his aid, had his eyes opened to these evils, and the movements began which terminated in the Formula of Concord. In all these movements, Selneccer was very active and useful. To him we owe the Latin translation of the Formula. Like all who bore part

in that noble work, he was very fiercely assailed. When the Reformed party came into power, at the death of Augustus, Selneccer was deposed, and not even allowed to remain in Leipzig as a private citizen. His family was harassed by Crell, and Selneccer himself was reduced to poverty. But such a man could not long be crushed. He was called to the superintendency in Hildesheim. Lying upon the bed of sickness, in 1592, he was summoned to Leipzig, as its Superintendent. Crell had been overthrown. Selneccer was borne back, dying but vindicated, and breathed his last, in Leipzig, May 24, 1592. The Church will sing his precious hymns, some of them set to his own melodies, to the end of time, and his memory will be treasured as that of one of her great defenders in the time of darkness.*

5. Nor were the three men who were associated with Andreæ, Chemnitz, and Selneccer, unworthy to bear part with these three chiefs in their great work. CHYTRAEUS (1530–1600), of Würtemberg, was one of Melanchthon's favorite pupils. Professor at Rostock, and Superintendent, renowned for his solid judgment, his large culture, his moderation, his deep insight into the needs of his time, his desire for the peace of the Church, his fame was great in his own communion, but was not confined to it. His history of the Augsburg Confession is classic in its kind. He was a " great and renowned teacher, who had few equals."† ANDREW MUSCULUS (1514–1581) was of Saxony. In 1538, he was among the devoted young men of the Reformation who surrounded Luther None were more devoted to the great leader than Musculus. He says of Luther: " Since the Apostles' time, no greater man has lived upon earth. God has poured out all His gifts on this one man. Between the old teachers (even Hilary and Augustine) and Luther, there is as wide a difference as between the shining of the moon and the light of the sun." He was an earnest defender of the faith, a fearless and powerful preacher, unsparing of wrong, and active in all the works of love. CHRISTOPHER CÖRNER (1518–1594) was of Franconia. He was a Doctor and Professor of theology, at Frankfort on

---

* Herzog's R. : **xiv**, 226. (Hollenberg).   † Weismann: H. E. i. 1457.

the Oder, and General Superintendent of the Electorate of Brandenburg, and author of a number of learned works. He was styled the " Eye of the University."*

6. With these chief laborers were associated, at various stages, a number of others. In some shape, the whole learning and judgment of the Lutheran Church of that era had an opportunity of making itself felt in the Formula of Concord.

7. The *plan* on which the work was carried through, was of the best kind. The plan involved careful preparation of the proper documents by the ablest hands, repeated revision, comparison of views, both in writing and by colloquy, the free expression of opinion by the various parts of the Church, the concurrence of the laity and ministry, and the holding of a large number of conventions. So carefully and slowly was the work carried on, that in the ten years between its opening and its close, the gifts and contrasts of the great men engaged in it were brought to the most perfect exercise. Never was a work of this kind so thoroughly done. The objections made to the plan and its working are of the weakest kind. A General Synod of all the Lutheran Churches was impossible, and if it could have been convened, could not have sat long enough for the needed discussions. The General Consent, which is the only thing of value which a General Synod could have given, was reached in a far better way. The Formula, though prepared by a committee of great divines, was the act and deed of the Lutheran Church, in its major.part. The Formula of Concord brought peace and blessing wherever it was honestly received. The evil that remained uncorrected by it, remained because of the factious opposition to it. All good in this evil world is but proximate. Even the divine blessing which lescends direct upon the world from the hand of God, is marred by the passions of bad men, and the infirmities of the good. The divine rule of faith does not force upon the unwilling a perfect faith, nor should we expect a Confession of faith, however pure, to compel the unwilling to a consistent confession.

IV. The DOCTRINAL RESULT reached in the Formula of Concord is in conformity with the pure truth of the divine Word.

---

* Jöcher: Gelehrten Lexic. Vol. i: col. 2106

The doctrines which the Formula was meant to settle, were settled aright. As preliminary to the whole discussion proper, the Formula

1. Lays down, more sharply and clearly than had yet been done, the principle, that *Holy Scripture* is the only and perfect *rule* of faith. The *Rule* sets forth the *credenda* — the things that are to be believed.

2. It defines the proper functions of the pure *Creed* as the Church's *testimony* and Confession of the truth derived from the rule. The *Creed* sets forth the *credita* — the things that are believed.

In consonance with this Rule, and by necessity in consonance with the pure Creeds of the past, the Formula determines over against the errors of the time:

i. In regard to *original sin*, that it is not the essence, or substance, or nature of man, (Flaccius,) but a corruption of that nature.

ii. Of *free will*, that there are not *three efficient* causes of conversion, of which one is man's will, (Philippistic,) but two only, the Holy Spirit, and, as His instrument, the Word.

iii. Of *justification*, that Christ is our righteousness, not merely according to his divine nature, (Andrew Osiander,) nor merely according to his human nature, (Stancar,) but according to both natures: and that justification is not an infused righteousness, (Osiander,) but a pardon of our sins — is not physical, but forensic.

iv. Of *good works*. Here are rejected the phrases: that good works are necessary to salvation, (Major,) and that good works are injurious to salvation, (Amsdorf,) and the truth is taught First, that good works most surely follow true faith, as the good fruit of a good tree; that it is the necessary duty of regenerate men to do good works, and that he who sins knowingly loses the Holy Spirit; but that, nevertheless, men are neither justified nor saved by their good works, but by "grace through faith." In a word, justification and its consequent salvation are necessary to good works, not the converse. They precede, the good works follow. Second: "We reject and condemn the naked phrase, 'that good works are injurious to salvation, as scandalous and destructive of Christian discipline. That the works of a man who trusts in them are pernicious, is not the fault of the works themselves, but of his own vain trust, which, contrary to the express Word of God, he puts in them. Good works in believers are the indications of eternal salvation. It is God's will and express command that believers should do good works. These the Holy Spirit works in them. These works for Christ's sake are pleasing to God, and to them He hath promised a glorious reward in the life that now is, and in that which is to come. In these last times it is no less necessary that men should be exhorted to holy living, should be reminded how necessary it is that they should exercise themselves in good works to show forth their faith and gratitude toward God, than it is necessary to beware lest they mingle good works in the matter of justification. For by an Epicurean persuasion about faith, no less than by a Papistical and Pharisaic trust in their own works and merits, can men come under condemnation." *

v. Of the Law and the Gospel. When the word Gospel is taken in its general and widest sense, as embracing the entire teaching of Christ and of His Apostles, it may be rightly said that it is a preaching of repentance and remission of sins. But when the word Gospel is used in its *specific* and *proper* sense, so that Moses as the teacher of the Law, and Christ the teacher of the Gospel are contrasted, the Gospel is not a preaching of penitence, and of reproof of sins, but none other than a most joyful message, full of consolation, a precious setting forth of the grace and favor of God obtained through the merits of Christ.

vi. Of the third use of the Law. The Law of God has not only a *first* use, to-wit, to preserve external discipline, and a *second* use, to lead men to the knowledge of their sins, but has also a *third* use, to wit, that it be diligently taught unto regenerate men, to all of whom much of the flesh still clings, that they may have a sure rule by which their entire life is to be shaped and governed.

vii. Of the Lord's Supper. This was by pre-eminence the

* Epitome 588–591.   Solid. Declarat: 699–708.

question which led to the preparation of the Formula, and it is answered with peculiar di tinctness and fulness. The statements in which it embraces the pure doctrine of the Lord's Supper, are these:

The true body and true blood of our Lord Jesus Christ are truly and substantially * present in the Holy Supper, and are truly imparted with the bread and wine:

"They are truly received orally with the bread and wine, but not in the manner imagined by the men of Capernaum, (John vi. 52,) but in a supernatural and heavenly manner, by reason of the Sacramental union, a manner which human sense and reason cannot understand. We use the word ' Spiritual ' in order to exclude and reject that gross, fleshly manner of presence which the Sacramentarians feign that our Churches hold. In this sense of the word spiritual, we also say that the body and blood of Christ, in the Holy Supper, are spiritually received. . . For though that participation be oral, the manner of it is spiritual:"

They are received by all those who use the Sacrament : by the worthy and believing, to consolation and life ; by the unbelieving, to judgment.

Hence the Formula *rejects and condemns :*

The Popish Transubstantiation ; the Sacrifice of the Mass ; the Communion in one kind ; the adoration of the external elements of bread and wine in the Supper:

The errors of the Zwinglians and Calvinists, such as these: that the words of the Testament are not to be taken as they sound ; that only bread and wine are orally received ; that the body of Christ is received merely spiritually, meaning by this merely by our faith ; that the bread and wine are only tokens by which Christians acknowledge each other ; or that they are figures, types, and similitudes of an absent body ; that in the Supper, only the virtue, operation, and merit of the absent body and blood of Christ are dispensed ; that the body of Christ is in such sense shut up in heaven, that it can in no manner whatever be on earth when the Holy Supper is observed:

"All language of a gross, carnal, Capernaitish kind, in regard to the supernatural and heavenly mystery :

* German: wesentlich. Latin: substantialiter.

" That Capernaitish eating of the body of Christ, as if it were rent with the teeth and concocted as other food, which the Sacramentarians, against the witness of their consciences, after so many protestations on our part, maliciously feign, that they may bring our doctrine into odium." *

viii. The Person of Christ. The handling of this great theme connects itself closely with the Lord's Supper. The doctrine of the person of Christ presented in the Formula rests upon the sublimest series of inductions in the history of Christian doctrine. In all Confessional history there is nothing to be compared with it in the combination of exact exegesis, of dog matic skill, and of fidelity to historical development. Fifteen centuries of Christian thought culminate in it. The doctrine of the " Communicatio Idiomatum" is indeed but the repetition which Christian science in its last maturity presents, of the truth that " the Word was made flesh." The Apostle's Creed already has it, when it says that God's " *only Son, our Lord*, was conceived, born, suffered, was crucified, dead, buried, descended into hell, ascended to the heavens, and sitteth at the right hand of the Father Almighty." The " idiomata" are inseparable from the natura, the attributes are inseparable from the nature, and if there be a " communicatio" of natures, there must be a " communicatio " of these attributes ; that is the nature personally assumed must, in that assumption, be participant of the attributes of that nature to whose person it is assumed. If an Eternal Being was actually *conceived* and *born*, if the impassible actually suffered, if the infinite was actually fastened to the cross, if the immortal was dead, if He whom heaven, and the heaven of heavens, cannot contain, was hidden in a grave, — if all this be not a riddle, but a clear direct statement of doctrine — to accept the Apostles' Creed is to accept the presupposition which necessitates the reception of the doctrine of the Communicatio Idiomatum. If the Apostles' Creed does not mean that Jesus Christ is *one person* in whom there is an inseparable connection of the natures, so that the one person really does all that is done, whether through one nature or through both, and the

* Epitome, 597–604. Solid. Declaratio. 724–760.

one person really suffers all that is suffered, though it can suffer only through the sole nature which is passible — if it means that God's only Son did not die, but that another and human person died; if it means that He who was born, and suffered, and died, does not sit at the right hand of God, and is not the judge of the quick and the dead, but that only another and divine person so sits and shall so judge; if, in a word, the Apostles' Creed means that Jesus Christ was *not* God's only Son, but that one of His natures was God's Son, and the other nature was not God's Son, and that Jesus Christ is not in fact one person in two natures, but two persons, then does the Apostles' Creed persistently say what it does not mean, and the faith Catholic is a chaos of contradictions. The Nicene Creed asserts the same great doctrine at an advanced point of scientific ripeness. The only begotten, the Eternal Son, Maker of all things, descends from heaven, is made man, is crucified (though infinite), suffers, (though impassible). He is one person, to whom is referred all the glory that is divine, and all the shame and pain that are human. The Athanasian Creed witnesses still further: " Though he be God and man, He is not two, but one Christ — one, not by the conversion of Divinity into flesh, but by the assumption of humanity to God; one altogether, not by confusion of substance, but by unity of person. For as the rational soul and flesh is one man, so God and man is one Christ, who " (God and man, one Christ,) " suffered for our salvation, descended into hell, rose the third day." The Augsburg Confession takes up this thread of witness : " God the Son became man, so that there be two natures, the divine and human, in unity of person *inseparably* conjoined, one Christ, truly God and truly man, who was born, truly suffered, was crucified, dead and buried."

The Scripture faith represented in these witnesses, the Formula sets forth at large in these propositions :

1. The divine and the human nature are personally united in Christ. These natures are not commingled into one substance, nor is one changed into the other, but each nature retains its essential properties, which can never become the properties of the other nature.

2. The properties of the divine nature are, to be *essentially, naturally, and of itself* omnipotent, eternal, infinite, everywhere present. These neither are, nor can be, the attributes of the human nature. The attributes of the human nature neither are, nor can be, the attributes of the divine nature.

3. Those things which are proper to the one nature only, are attributed to the other nature not as separate, but to the whole person. The divine nature does not suffer, but that person who is God, suffers in His humanity. All works and all sufferings are attributed not to the nature, but to the person. Each nature acts, with the communion of the other, what is proper to it.

4. The human nature in Christ, because it is personally united with the divine nature, beside and above its natural, essential, and permanent human properties, has *received* peculiar, supernatural, unsearchable, unspeakable prerogatives of majesty, glory, and power. .

5. This impartation is not made by any essential or natural outpouring of the attributes of the divine nature upon the human nature, as if the humanity of Christ could have them *per se* and separated from the divine essence, or as if through that communication the human nature of Christ had laid aside its natural and essential properties, and was either converted into the divine nature, or was made equal in itself, or *per se*, to the divine nature by these communicated attributes, or that the natural and essential properties of each are the same, or at least equal.

6. Inasmuch as the whole fulness of the Godhead dwells in Christ, not as in holy men and angels, but bodily, that is, *as in its own proper body,* that Godhead, with all its majesty, virtue, glory, and operation, where and as Christ will, shines forth in that human nature; and in it, with it, and through it, reveals and exercises its divine virtue, majesty, and efficacy.

7. Thus there is and abides in Christ *one only* divine omnipotence, virtue, majesty, and glory, *which is proper to the divine nature alone;* but this same, which is one only, shines forth and fully, yet voluntarily, exerts its power in, and with, and through the assumed humanity in Christ.*

* Formul. Concor. Epit. et Sol. Declarat. art. viii

8. To make more clear the train of reasoning which results in the doctrine of the Communion of properties, certain logical presuppositions, and certain definitions should be held in mind. In the incarnation it is not two persons, to wit, a divine person and a human person, which assume each other, as if there were two co-ordinates, which equally took each other; nor does one person, to wit, the divine, take another person, to wit, a human person, so that there are two persons in the union, the divine person assuming, and the human person assumed: but one person, having the divine nature, assumes a human nature, so that there results a person in which two natures are constituent, but in different ways — the divine nature absolutely and independently personal, and the human nature secondarily and dependently personal; the divine nature still has, as it ever had, its own intrinsic personality; the human nature is assumed to the divine nature, and neither had, nor has any other personality than the one divine personality, which it has in virtue of the union. The human nature of Christ does not subsist *per se*, as does the humanity of every other one of our race, but subsists in the person of the Son of God. Hence, though the natures be distinct, the person is inseparable. This complex divine-human person did not exist before the union, and cannot exist except in and by the union.; and the second nature in the complex person has not existed as a nature before or separate from this union, and never had, nor has, nor can have, personality apart from that union. The Communicatio idiomatum is therefore no giving away, so that the giver ceases to have, and the receiver retains for itself apart henceforth from the giver, but is the fellowship of attributes, which the two natures possess in the one person, the divine nature having these attributes intrinsically, and the human nature having them in and because of its personal iden tification with the divine nature. In this relation the word " communicate " employed actively, means to " confer a joint possession," that is, the divine nature confers on the human a joint possession of attributes *in the person*. The word " com municate," used as a neuter verb, means to " have something in common with another;" the human nature has the attri-

butes in common with the divine nature, but derivatively only in and through its personal union with the divine. The "Communication, or Communion of properties" is therefore the participation of these properties by the two natures in common in the one person, the divine nature having the attributes intrinsically, the human nature having them through the divine and dependently. Though the *Logos unincarnate* was a proper person before he took a human nature, the personality of the *Logos incarnate* involves the two natures. That person which is not both human and divine is not Christ's person, and that act or presence which is not both human and divine is not Christ's act, nor Christ's presence.

The Errors rejected by the Formula are, on the one hand, all that involve a confusion or transmutation of the natures; the presence of Christ's human nature in the same way as deity, as an infinite essence, or by its essential properties; all equalizing of its essential properties with those of God, and all ideas of its local extension in all places. The Errors, on the other hand, are, that the human nature of Christ was alone in the redemptory suffering and work, with no fellowship with it on the part of the Son of God; that the presence of Christ with us on earth is only according to His divinity, and that his human nature has no part whatever in it; that the assumed human nature in Christ has, in very deed and reality, no communication nor fellowship with, or participation in the divine virtue, wisdom, power, majesty and glory, but that it has fellowship with the divinity in bare title and name.

IX. OF THE DESCENT OF CHRIST INTO HELL. The treatment of this difficult point is a model of comprehensiveness, brevity, simplicity, and modesty. The doctrine may be arranged as a reply to these questions:

1. *Who* descended? *Christ*, Son of God, our Lord, therefore divine, who was crucified, dead and buried, therefore human; consequently, not the body alone, nor the soul alone, nor the divinity alone, but Christ, the whole person, God and man. This is the precise affirmation of the Apostles' Creed: "God's only Son, our Lord, who was conceived of the Virgin Mary, born, suffered, died, descended into hell."

2. *When?* Not before his death, (Calvin and Ursinus,) nor at his burial, as identical with it, (Oecolampadius, Beza,) but *after* his burial.

So the order of the Apostles' Creed : " Dead, buried, He descended into hell."

3. *Whither ?* Not into a *metaphorical* hell, of pains of soul, or of pains like those of the damned, (Calvin, Ursinus,) not into the grave, (Oecolampadius, Beza,) nor the limbus patrum, a subterranean place of souls, (Bellarmin, and the Romanists generally, with some of the Fathers,) but into hell.

4 *Why ?* To give to our Lord a glorious victory and triumph, to overcome Satan, and to overthrow the power of hell for all believers.

5. *How ?* How it was done we may not curiously search, but reserve the knowledge of it for another world, when this and other mysteries shall be uncovered, which in this life surpass the power of our blind reason, and are to be received in simple faith.

No Antitheses are added to this Article.

X. OF ECCLESIASTICAL CEREMONIES; THE ADIAPHORÆ. Usages, which are neither commanded nor forbidden in God's word, are in themselves no part of divine worship proper ; in them the Church may make such changes as are needed, due regard being had to prudence and forbearance ; but such changes may not be made to avoid persecution, nor so as to impair the clearness of the Church's testimony against the Papal religion. No Church should condemn another because of unlikeness of ceremonies, if they agree in doctrine and in all its parts, and in the legitimate use of the sacraments.

XI. OF PREDESTINATION. " For this article," says Köllner, " the Lutheran Church owes an eternal debt of gratitude to the authors of the Formula." The doctrine, it is true, had not been the subject of controversy within the Lutheran Church itself, but it was so vitally connected with the whole range of theological truth, that it was wise to set it forth in its Scriptural fulness.

The doctrine may be summed up in these theses :

1. " The *foreknowledge* or prevision of God, is that whereby

21

he foresees and foreknows all things before they come to pass, and extendeth to all creatures, whether they be good or evil."[*]

2. "*Predestination* or *election* is the purpose of the divine will, and the eternal decree, whereby God out of pure mercy hath chosen in Christ unto eternal life, and hath determined to save all those who truly believe in Christ, and endure in that faith unto the end."

3. "The whole doctrine concerning the purpose, counsel, will and ordination of God (all things, to wit, which pertain to our redemption, calling, justification, and salvation), is to be embraced together in the mind . . . to wit, that God in his counsel and purpose hath decreed these things following:

"That the human race should be truly redeemed, and should be reconciled unto God through Christ, who, by his innocence and most perfect obedience, by his passion and most bitter death, hath merited for us that righteousness which avails before God, and life everlasting:

"That the merits of Christ and his blessings should, through the Word and Sacraments, be brought, offered, and apportioned unto us:

"He hath decreed also, that by His Holy Spirit, through the Word announced, heard, and remembered, he will be efficacious in us, to bend our hearts to true repentance, and to preserve us in true faith:

"It is His eternal purpose, that all who truly repent, and embrace Christ in true faith, shall be justified, received into favor, and adopted as sons and heirs of eternal life:

"And they that are justified by faith he will sanctify in true love, as the Apostle testifies, (Ephes. i. 4 :) 'According as he hath chosen us in Him, before the foundation of the world, that we should be holy and without blame before him in love:'

"God hath also determined in His eternal counsel, that in their manifold and various weaknesses he will defend them that are justified, against the world, the flesh, and the devil, will lead and direct them in their way, and if they should fall, will uphold them with His hand, that under the cross and in temptation they may receive strong consolation, and may be preserved unto life.

* Formula Concordiæ, 728.

"It is His eternal decree that He will carry forward and strengthen, and preserve unto the end that good work which He hath begun in them, if only they steadfastly lean upon His Word as their staff, beseech his aid with ardent prayers, continue in God's grace, and well and faithfully employ the gifts they have received of Him:

"God hath also decreed that those whom He hath chosen, called and justified, He will, in another and eternal life, save and endow with glory everlasting."*

4. "Many receive the Word of God in the beginning with great joy, but afterward fall away. The cause thereof is not that God is not willing to give His grace to enable them to be steadfast in whom He hath begun that good work, for this is in conflict with the words of St. Paul, (Phil. i. 6;) but the true reason of their falling away, is that they again turn themselves away from God's holy command wilfully, and that they grieve and provoke the Holy Spirit, that they again entangle themselves in the pollutions of this world, and garnish again the guest-chamber of their heart for Satan."†

5. "God hath from eternity most exactly and surely foreseen, and knoweth, who of the number of them that are called will or will not believe in Christ, who of them that are converted will or will not remain steadfast in the faith, and who of them that have fallen into grievous sins will return, and who of them will perish in their wickedness. . . But because the Lord hath reserved such secret things for his own wisdom alone, nor hath revealed anything of this matter in His Word, much less hath commanded us to occupy our imaginations with these mysteries, but rather hath forbidden us to take them in hand: it doth not become us to give liberty to our imaginations, to establish anything, argue thereon, or wish to search out those most hidden things, but we should rest in his revealed Word to which He hath referred us." ‡

6. "If any one set forth the doctrine of the eternal predestination of God in such manner that distressed minds can derive no consolation from it, but rather occasion of despair is given unto them, or so that impenitent persons are confirmed

---

* Formula Concordiæ, 802.   † Ibid. 809.   ‡ Ibid. 812.

in their security, wickedness and wilfulness, then nothing is more sure than that this article is not taught by him according to the Word and will of God." *

7. "Not only the preaching of repentance, but the promise of the Gospel is also universal, that is, belongs to all men. For this reason Christ hath commanded ' that repentance and remission of sins should be preached *among all nations ;*' ' God so loved the *world* that he gave his only begotten Son ;' ' Christ taketh away the sin of the *world ;*' ' He gave his flesh for the life of the *world ;*' ' His blood is the propitiation for the sins of the *whole* world ;' Christ says : ' Come unto Me *all* ye that labor and are heavy laden, and I will give you rest.' ' God hath concluded them all in unbelief, that he might have mercy upon *all.*' ' The Lord is not willing that any should perish, but that *all* should come to repentance.' ' The same Lord over *all* is rich unto *all* that call upon Him.' ' The righteousness of God which is by faith of Jesus Christ unto *all,* and upon *all* them that believe.' ' And this is the will of the Father that every one which believeth on Christ should have everlasting life.' And Christ wisheth that in general unto all to whom repentance is preached, this promise also of the Gospel should be set forth."†

8. "This calling of God, which he offereth to us through the word of the Gospel is not feigned and pretended, but God by that calling revealeth to us His will, to wit, that in those whom He calls in this way He wisheth to be efficacious through His word, that they may be enlightened, converted and saved." ‡

9. "The reason why many are called but few chosen, is not the divine calling, which is made through the Word, as if God's intent were this: ' I indeed call outwardly to a participation in my heavenly kingdom, all to whom that word is set forth : but it is not the thought of my heart that all should be seriously called to salvation, but that a few only should be so called ; for my will is this, that a larger part of those whom I call through the Word, shall neither be enlightened nor converted, although through my Word, by which they are called, I signify my mind unto them otherwise,' for this would be to

* Formula Concordiæ, 728.   † Ibid. 804.   ‡ Ibid. 805.

impute to God contradictory wills, as if He who is the eterna!
truth, were divided against Himself, or spake one thing and
designed another." *

10. " As God in His eternal counsel hath ordained, that the
Holy Spirit shall, through the Word, call, enlighten, and convert the elect, and that He will justify and eternally save all
those who embrace Christ in true faith: so also in that same
counsel He hath decreed, that He will harden, reprobate, and
consign to eternal damnation those who being called through
the Word put it away from them, and resist the Holy Spirit,
(who wisheth through the Word efficaciously to work and to
be efficacious in them,) and obstinately remain steadfast in that
rebellion." †

11. " The cause of this despising of the Word is not the foreknowledge or predestination of God, but the perverse will of
man, which refuses or wrests that mean and instrument of the
Holy Spirit which God offers to man in that He calls him, and
which resists the Holy Ghost . . as Christ sayeth: ' How often
would I have gathered together and *ye would* not.' " ‡

Finally, *x* . The Formula treats *of various factions, heresies
and sects*, which have never embraced the Augsburg Confession.
The Errors enumerated and rejected are those of the Anabaptists, " who are divided into a number of sects, of whom some
defend more, some fewer Errors; " of Schwenkfeldians; of the
New Arians; and of the New Antitrinitarians, who, as here
characterized, are either Tritheists, or Subordinationists.

Such is the doctrine, such are the antitheses of the Formula
of Concord. They are in every part consonant with Holy
Scripture, with the General Creeds, and with the earlier Confessions of the Lutheran Church. The Formula is but the old
doctrine repeated, systematized, applied and defended. The
chief charge against the Formula of Concord is that it caused
a *complete separation between the Lutheran and the Zwinglian-
Calvinistic Churches.* This is a great mistake. The *cause* of
the separation was the divergent convictions and principles on
both sides. The Formula did not originate a single one of the
questions it settled. But the Formula of Concord was not

* Formula Concordiæ, 807.   † Ibid, 808.   ‡ Ibid, 809.

even the *occasion* of the separation. So far was this from being the case, that after the controversies which necessarily attended the first appearance of the Formula of Concord, a far healthier and kindlier feeling prevailed between the two Communions. Before the Formula, many things existed in their relations which tended to demoralize the Reformed Church, as much as it did to disorganize and distress the Lutheran Church. Truthful separation is far better than dishonest union, and two Churches are happier, and more kindly in their mutual relations, when their differences are frankly confessed, than when they are clouding with ambiguities and double meanings the real divergencies. And even if two Communions are in downright conflict, it is better that the battles should be on the sides of clearly marked lines, or well understood issues — should be the struggles of nationalities, under the laws of war rather than the savage, ill-defined warfare of the border, and of the bush. That the open transitions to the Reformed side of a few nominally Lutheran States were really occasioned by the Formula, is not true. Most of these movements were those of political force, in the face of the bitter regrets of the people. No State which honestly held the Augsburg Confession went over to the Reformed. If the Formula uncovered and shamed out of the pretence of Lutheranism any who were making a mere cloak of the Augsburg Confession, it is something to love it for. It is charged upon the Formula of Concord that it repressed the *Melanchthonian tendency* in our Church, and substituted the fossilization of the letter and of the dogma for the freedom of the spirit and of the Word. This again is not true. It is not true that the spirit within our Church which the Formula encountered, was that of genuine freedom. It was rather the spirit which was making a real bondage under the pretences of liberty, a spirit which was tolerant only to vagueness and laxity, not to well-defined doctrinal conviction. It was a spirit which softened and relaxed the Church when she needed her utmost vigor and firmness. It was a spirit of false deference to antiquity and human authority over against the Word. It yielded now to a false philosophizing, now to the Reformed, now to Rome. It tried to adjust some of the most vital doctrines to the demands of Rationalism on the one side, of Romanism on the other. In the "Interims," it came near sacrificing all that had been gained in the struggle with the Papacy. It confessed in effect, that the principle of the Reformation could reach no definite result, that the better path it claimed to open, led forever toward something which could never be reached. So far as Melanchthon's great gifts were purely and wisely used, the Formula fixed these results in the Church. It did not overthrow the Confessional works in which Melanchthon's greatest glory is involved. It established the Confession and Apology forever as the Confession of the Church as a whole. The Book of Concord treats Melanchthon as the Bible treats Solomon It opens wide the view of his wisdom and glory, and draws the veil over the record of his sadder days. Melanchthon's temperament was more exacting than Luther's. He made his personal gentleness a dogmatism and demanded impossibilities. The time of the deluge had come,—a world had to be purified; and it was useless to send out the dove till the waters had passed away. The era of the Reformation could not be an era of Melanchthonian mildness. To ask this, is to ask that war shall be peace, that battles shall be fought with feathers, and that armies shall move to the waving of olive branches. The war of the Formula was an internal defensive war; yet, like all civil wars, it left behind it inevitable wounds which did not at once heal up. The struggle in Churches or States, which ends in a triumph over the schism of their own children, cannot for generations command the universal sympathy, with which the overthrow of a common foe is regarded. All England is exultant in the victories over France, but even yet there are Englishmen, to whom Charles is a martyr, and Cromwell a devil. The war of the Formula was fought for great principles: it was bravely and uncompromisingly fought; but it was fought magnanimously under the old banner of the Cross. It was crowned with victory, and that victory brought peace.

Most surely will time bring all that love our Church to feel, that without the second war and the second peace, the war and peace of Conservation, the richest results of the first, the war of Reformation, would have been lost. Hopeless division, anarchy, ruin and absorption, were the perils from which the Formula of Concord saved our Church. The loss of Germany would have been the loss of Lutheranism throughout the world, and with it the loss of Protestantism itself.

Feeling the responsibility of their position, not without consciousness of the greatness of the work they had done, the authors of the Formula of Concord humbly, yet joyously, closed it with these solemn words: " Wherefore, in the presence of Almighty God, and of Christ's whole Church, both of the living, and of the generations which shall follow us, it has been our purpose to testify, that of the Articles in Controversy, the Declaration we have now made, and none other, is in very deed our doctrine, faith and Confession. In this Confession, by God's grace, we are ready with fearless hearts to appear and render an account before the judgment-seat of Jesus Christ. Against this Declaration we will speak nothing, and write nothing, openly or secretly, but, the Lord helping us, will remain steadfast in it to the end. In testimony thereof, with mature deliberation, in the fear of God, and calling upon His name, we have with our own hands set our names to this Declaration."

VIII.

SOME MISTAKES IN REGARD TO THE HISTORY AND DOCTRINES OF THE EVANGELICAL LUTHERAN CHURCH.

A REVIEW OF DR. SHEDD'S HISTORY OF CHRISTIAN DOCTRINE.*

IT cannot be claimed for Dr. Shedd's book that it is the profoundest and most exhaustive history of Christian doctrine, but it may be asserted with justice that it is eminently pleasant and readable. But if it be not as profound as is conceivable, it is as profound as its general aim permits it to be, and if it does not always exhaust its subjects, it never exhausts its readers. We cannot concede to Dr. Shedd all that he seems to claim, and we are sure with perfect sincerity, in regard to the originality, or even the self-origination of his method. It varies so little from that of some of the German works to which he confesses his obligations, that without presupposing their plan, we can hardly conceive that he would have fallen upon his. He investigates " each of the principal subjects by itself, starting from the first beginnings of scien- Dr. Shedd's History of Doctrine. tific reflection upon it, and going down to the latest forms of statement." Dr. Shedd accepts, at the very out-start, the idea of doctrinal development, and one of the best features of his book and of its plan is, that he so clearly and satisfactorily exhibits the processes and results of this development. Revelation is unchanging, but the science

* History of Christian Doctrine. By William G. T. Shedd, D. D. In two Volumes. New York: Charles Scribner.

which classifies, and adjusts in their due relations to each other its doctrines, which sees each in the light of all, and under whose guidance, to use the vigorous words of Dr. Shedd, " the objections of the heretic or latitudinarian only elicit a more exhaustive,and, at the same time, more guarded statement, which carries the Church still nearer to the substance of revelation and the heart of the mystery," this science, in its own nature, must have growth.   The man who takes up the Bible now, without reference to what the minds of generations have done towards its elucidation, is exactly as foolish as the man who would effect to take up any great branch of science without regard to what has been done before.   The botanist's Rule of faith was Eve's carpet and canopy, but not until Linnæus was the botanist's Confession of faith set forth.   Dr. Shedd has well stated and well guarded the doctrine of development. He shows that development is not creation, nor improvement. Botany neither creates the plants, nor improves upon the facts connected with them; but it develops into a more perfect knowledge of them, and out of that higher knowledge into a more perfect science.   The plants themselves furnish the Rule of the botanist's faith, but the Systema Plantarum is its creed. The science develops, but it develops toward the absolute truth, not away from it ; and the more perfect the doctrinal development is, the nearer has it come to the ideal of God's mind, which has its image in His word.

    Much of Dr. Shedd's mode of thinking is certainly not the outgrowth of anything characteristic of New England.   The attitude of the original extreme Puritanism to the history of the ancient Church, was very different from his.   Puritanism, as separatism, had no history for it, and hence it repudiated history.   It has lived long enough to have a history, to recede from its extreme positions, and to receive new elements of life ; and Dr. Shedd's book is one among many evidences that Puritanism seeks a history, and begins to appreciate its value — the value not only of its own history, but of the history of the whole Church.   After all the diversities and terrible internal strifes of the nominally Christian Church, there is not any great part of it that can safely ignore absolutely any other great part. Puritanism cannot say, even to Romanism, "I have no need of thee," still less can it say so to the grand portions of evangelical Protestantism. Dr. Shedd's book shows that he has escaped from many of the narrownesses which obscured the genuine glory of Puritanism, for genuine glory it has, and a great deal of it. No book of which we know, emanating from a New England mind, shows as much acquaintance as this book does with the character and weight of Lutheran theology.

Nevertheless, one of the greatest weaknesses of the book is its lack of a thorough and independent knowledge of our Church. Dr. Shedd, especially in his exhibitions of the Patristic and English views, shows independent research; but in the treatment of the Lutheran theology he gives unmistakable evidence that his reading has been comparatively slight among the masters, especially the old masters of our Church. He has trusted too much to manuals, and yet has hardly used them enough. He exhibits views as characteristic of Calvinistic divines, or of the Calvinistic symbols, which are mere resonances of the Lutheran theology, whose glory it is, first to have brought into the distinct sphere of science the great Biblical truths of which we speak. The scientific development of the doctrine of the redemptory character of the *active* obedience of Christ, is due to the Lutheran theologians. The true and profound views of the person of Christ, which Dr. Shedd presents in the language of Hooker and Hopkins, though involved in the Athanasian Creed, received their full scientific shape from the Christological labors and Controversies of the Lutheran Church in the Sixteenth Century. The Lutheran Church has been the ultimate spring of almost all the profound theological thought of modern times. Even Calvinism, without it, would not have been. Calvin was saved, we might almost say created, by being first Lutheranized.

It is refreshing to find in Dr. Shedd's book so much that is sound, and deep, and old; but which will, to the mass of thinkers in New England, seem like novelty. Nothing, indeed, is so novel in New England as the old theology, in some of its aspects. How, for example, must the doctrine of the true sacramental presence mystify them? Dr. Shedd, perhaps wisely, has spared them this. There are, indeed, great departments of the history of doctrine on which he does not enter. He gives us, for example, nothing direct on the doctrines of the Church, of Baptism and of the Lord's Supper; yet these involve many of the most vital questions of the hour. On the other hand, he has gone, we think, beyond the bound, in devoting a whole book to the history of Apologetics, and another to an account of Symbols. He has done it so well, however, that we not only forgive him, but thank him for it.

One very interesting feature of the book is its presentation of many of the Calvinistic doctrines in their coincidence with the Lutheran; as, for instance, in the paragraphs on the "Lutheran-Calvinistic Theory of Original Sin," "The Lutheran-Calvinistic Theory of Regeneration;" and on other points. Dr. Shedd seems to fear that "the chief criticism that may be made upon the work is, that it betokens subjective qualities unduly for an historical production." On the contrary, we think, that so far as is consistent with fidelity to conviction, his book is remarkably free from the offensive obtrusion of merely personal opinions. There is not a page in it whose tone is unworthy of the refined candor of a Christian gentleman. We are struck, indeed, as we have said, with what we regard as mistakes in reference to the Lutheran Church, but the statements of Dr. Shedd are made in a tone which relieves them of all asperity; and he knows so much more about our Church than most writers of English who have attempted to describe it, that we feel that his mistakes are involuntary. They are fewer than might have been anticipated. Dr. Shedd speaks of the Augsburg Confession as "the symbol which was to consolidate the new evangelical Church into one external unity, in opposition to that of Rome." "But the doctrines of sin and redemption had been misstated by the Papal mind at Trent; and hence the principal part of the new and original work of the Lutheran divines was connected with these." This collocation might mislead the reader, who forgets that the Augsburg Confession was prepared fifteen years before the first convention of the Council of Trent. Dr. Shedd speaks of the

Augsburg Confession as "the first in time" among our symbols. Twelve pages after, he corrects himself by mentioning that the Two Catechisms were published in 1529, a year before the Augsburg Confession. Dr. Shedd says appreciatively: "The general tone and spirit of the first creed of the Reformation is a union of firmness and mildness. The characteristics of Luther and Melanchthon, the two minds most concerned in its formation, are harmoniously blended in it."

In Dr. Shedd's interesting volumes, we naturally look with most interest for that which bears upon our own Church. His remarks upon the origin, character and supposed imperfections of the Augsburg Confession, may require some examination. Dr. Shedd speaks of the Augsburg Confession as a The origin of the Augsburg Confession. public and received Confession of the common faith of the Protestant Church. Taking the word "Protestant" in its original and strictly historical sense, this is true, but it is not, nor was it ever the received Confession of all whom we now call "Protestants." Two counter Confessions, Zwingli and the Tetrapolitan, were prepared for the Diet of Augsburg. There are some defects too in Dr. Shedd's statement of the origin of the Confession. He says: "The process began with a commission from John, Prince of Saxony, given in March, 1530, to his favorite theologians Luther, Justus Jonas, Bugenhagen, and Melanchthon, to prepare a series of succinct and comprehensive articles to be discussed and defended as the Protestant form of doctrine." Dr. Shedd's statement in this sentence is defective, for it does not furnish the reason of this commission, and it seems inaccurate in making this commission the beginning of the process which was completed in the laying of the Confession before the Diet of Augsburg. The ultimate ground-work of the Augsburg Confession is the Fifteen Articles of Marburg, which were the result of the conference between the Zwinglians and Lutherans, October, 1529. These are more closely related to the Seventeen Articles of Schwabach than the Schwabach Articles are to the Augsburg Confession. The real immediate beginning of the process was in the summons of the Diet by the Emperor Charles V., dated January, 1530, in which he stated as one of the objects of the Diet, the comparison and harmonizing of the conflicting views which were dividing the Church, and to this end required of the evangelical princes a statement of their doctrine. The Elector of Saxony, the leader of the Evangelical States, foresaw that for any such comparison a clear and judicious statement in writing, both as to doctrines and abuses, would be necessary on the part of the Protestants, (Lutherans,) and gave the command to the four theologians, to prepare the needed statement, and present it to him in eight days at Torgau. The shortness of the time allotted is the solution of the fact, that "these theologians joined upon the work that had already been performed by one of their number," though it is not strictly accurate to say that the work had been performed by one of their number, as Luther says, in so many words, in his Preface to these Articles, that they were not his exclusive work.* His co-laborers in preparing them were Melanchthon, Jonas, Osiander, Brentius and Agricola. "In the preceding year, (1529,) Luther, at a Convention of Protestants, at Schwabach, had prepared seventeen Articles, to be adopted as the doctrinal bond of union. These Articles, this body of Commissioners appointed by Prince John adopted, and, having added to their number some new ones that had respect to certain ecclesiastical abuses, presented the whole to the Crown Prince, in Torgau, in March, 1530. Hence, they are sometimes denominated the '*Articles of Torgau.*'" The reader must not suppose, as he might, that "Prince John" was one person, and "the Crown Prince" another. We do not know why Dr. Shedd prefers the title "Prince" to the more definite and historical term Elector, unless as a resident of New York, there is special music to his ear in the style and title of that old time pet of the Empire State, "Prince John" Van Buren. And why does he style the Elector the "Crown Prince?"

In the nomenclature of the best recent writers on the history of the Augsburg Confession, the title "Schwabach Articles" is confined to those of the 27th of October, 1529, and the name of "Torgau Articles" is restricted to the Articles prepared by

---

* Sie sind nit von mir allein gestellet. The whole are given in Cyprian's *Historia*, (Gotha, 1730,) Beilage, p. 159. Corpus Reformatorum, xxvi. 138.

the four theologians at Wittenberg, March, 1530, and presented at Torgau. Dr. Shedd goes on to say : ." This draft of a Confession was then brought before the Imperial Diet, at Augsburg, for examination and adoption. Here it received revision, and some slight modifications, under the leadership of Melanchthon, who was present at the discussion before the Diet, and was aided during the progress of the debate, by the advice and concurrence of Luther, then at Coburg, in a free and full correspondence. The Symbol having been formed in this manner, was subscribed by the princes and authorities of the Protestant interest, and in their name publicly read in German, before the imperial assembly, and a copy, in both German and Latin, presented to the Emperor. The Augsburg Confession thus became the authorized doctrinal basis of Protestantism in Germany." In this account we are compelled to say there is more than one mistake. Neither this draft of a Confession, nor any other draft, was ever brought before the Imperial Diet, either for examination and adoption, or for any other purpose. Of course, therefore, it received no revision there, or modification. None of the processes connected with the formation of the Confession, took place in the presence of the Diet. The Diet knew nothing of its contents up to the time of the reading of it. After the Elector had received, at Torgau, the Schwabach, and the Torgau Articles proper, he started for Augsburg, leaving, for prudential reasons, Luther at Coburg, with the understanding that nothing final should be done without consulting him. The Elector and his retinue entered Augsburg, May 2nd, and remained there. During the rest of the month, and for the first half of June, the secular and ecclesiastical dignitaries were gathering for the Diet. In this interval, from May 26th to June 20th, the Emperor not having arrived, and no sessions of the Diet having taken place, Melanchthon, with the aid and advice of the other theologians, and of all the representatives of the Evangelical interest, given in, sentence by sentence, did the work of composing the Confession which was to be submitted to the Diet, laying, as the ground-work, the Articles of Schwabach and Torgau, but doing far more than would be generally understood in Dr. Shedd's

statement, that these Articles " received revision and some
slight modifications." This Confession, when finished, was
sent by the Elector to Luther, by whom, without a solitary
change, or suggestion of a change, it was approved, May 15th,
one month previous to the entrance of the Emperor into Augsburg. The first session of the Diet was held June 20th, and it
was determined that the religious questions should be taken
up first.

On the 23d of June, the Protestant Princes signed the Confession. On the 24th they received permission to present the
Confession on the following day. The material labor on the
Augsburg Confession was finished and approved by Luther
more than a month before the Diet met. In the intervening
weeks, Melanchthon elaborated the style, and gave higher
finish to the form of the Confession, and before the Diet met,
the Confession was finished. It was then no draft, but the
perfect Confession, which was in the hands of the Confessors,
when the Diet met ; but neither draft nor Confession was ever
submitted for adoption to the Diet. It received, and could in
the nature of the case receive, no revision or " slight modification before the Diet." Melanchthon was not present at the
discussion before the Diet, not only, although this would seem
to be enough, because there was no such discussion, but he was
not, in fact, present in the Diet at any discussions of any sort.
Melanchthon did not hear the Augsburg Confession read.
Justus Jonas was the only evangelical theologian who heard
the Confession read, an honor which may have been thought
due to his juristic skill, or to his official position. There was
no discussion of the Articles of the Confession before the Diet,
and no debate in regard to them to make any progress, to be
shared in by Melanchthon, or to require the aid of Luther.
The Symbol was not formed in this manner, as we have seen,
but was finished before the Diet began. Equally mistaken is
the statement, that Melanchthon entered upon a detailed refutation of the Romish Confutation, " so far as he could recon-
struct the document from his own recollection on hearing it
read," as he did not hear it read, and was at first entirely dependent on " notes that had been taken by others who were

present at the reading." Dr. Shedd has evidently either been following very inaccurate guides, or, for some reason, has misunderstood his authorities on these points. His bibliography of the literature of the History of Symbols does not, indeed, seem to indicate that he has made it a matter of very thorough study ; for there is no mention made in it of works of the very highest rank, as for example, of Carpzov, Baumgarten, Boehmer, and Semler, among the older writers ; of Plank, Marheineke, Tittmann and Marsh, in the first quarter of the present century ; of Möhler and Köllner, whose merits are of the most distinguished order; or of Matthes and Rudolph Hoffman, and others, who, as good writers of the most recent date, deserve mention. The selectest bibliography ought to embrace all of these. The truth is, however, that the separate History of Symbols is not more properly in place in a history of Doctrines, than a history of Polemics, of Patristics, or of Biblical Interpretations would be, for all these are, incidentally, sources of illustration of the History of Doctrine. Each of them is, moreover, comprehensive enough for a distinct treatment. Dr. Shedd has made his plan too comprehensive, and necessarily renders it relatively weaker at certain points. The plan which Dr. Holmes has rendered so renowned, of making the weakest point as strong as the rest, is exquisite in theory, but difficult in practical realization.

" The Augsburg Confession," says Dr. Shedd, " is divided into two parts : the one, positive and didactic in its contents ; the other, negative and polemic." *The Augsburg Confession not Romanizing. Consubstantiation no doctrine of the Lutheran Church.* The Augsburg Confession, as it is usually and was most anciently divided, consists of the Preface, Chief Articles of Faith, The Articles on Abuses, and the Epilogue. Köllner makes a fifth part of the Epilogal Prologue, which separates and unites the Articles on Abuses. Nevertheless, Dr. Shedd very properly divides it, in a general way, into two parts. The first of the chief parts, however, in addition to its positive statements of doctrine, has negative antitheses on the doctrines of the Trinity, Original Sin, the Efficacy of the Ministry, Baptism, the Lord's Supper, Repentance, the Use of Sacraments, of Civil matters, the Second Coming of Christ,

22

and Free Will. On a number of the points, arguments are urged, Scripture is quoted and Patristic authorities appealed to, and in the Article on Good Works, the prevailing character is entirely Apologetic. The Doctrine of Good Works had been stated in the sixth article, the twentieth is devoted to the defence of it.

Dr. Shedd exhibits the thoroughly catholic and evangelical character of the Augsburg Confession in regard to the Trinity, Sin, Salvation, and the Last Things. He goes on, however, to make some strictures on certain points, and says: "Though decidedly Protestant upon the cardinal points, the Augsburg Confession contains some remnants of that unscriptural system, against which it was such a powerful and earnest protest." He admits, that upon the *cardinal doctrines*, the Augsburg Confession is Protestant and sound. He maintains, however, that the same Confession contains some remnants of Romanism.

We feel at this point no little surprise in regard to Dr. Shedd's admissions. He speaks of matters as of little moment, which we could have supposed he, as a Calvinist, would esteem as highly important. Is Dr. Shedd safe, for example, in conceding that the doctrines concerning the Eucharistic presence and Absolution are not cardinal; for if the doctrines are not cardinal, the errors in regard to them, cannot be; on his premises, then, Transubstantiation itself is not a cardinal error, and the Romish doctrine of priestly absolution is not a cardinal error. We, as Evangelical Lutherans, hold that, as error on these points is cardinal, so must the truth, in regard to them, be cardinal. Fundamental errors are the antitheses of fundamental truths only, and we Evangel ical Lutherans actually cherish, on Dr. Shedd's own showing, a stronger, and, as he would perhaps regard it, an extremer opposition to the Romish errors on these points, than he does — we do regard the Romish errors on these doctrines as cardinal, but it seems he does not. He will find in our divines, through centuries, this stern opposition to these very errors as cardinal, and among no men, at this hour, is this feeling deeper, than among the most tenacious adherents to the Augsburg Confession. How does he account for it then, that under the nurture of this very Confession, which he supposes to be sympathetic with Romanism at some points, there has been nursed a deeper and more radical anti-Romish feeling on these very doctrines, than his own?

Dr. Shedd goes on to say : " These Popish elements are found in those portions particularly, which treat of the sacraments ; and more particularly in that article which defines the Sacrament of the Supper. In Article XIII, the Augsburg Confession is careful to condemn the Papal theory, that the sacraments are efficacious, *ex opere operato*, that is by their intrinsic efficacy, without regard to faith in the recipient, or to the operation of the Holy Spirit ; but when, in Article X, it treats of the Lord's Supper, it teaches that ' the body and blood of Christ are truly present, and are distributed to those who partake of the Supper.' This doctrine of *Consubstantiation*, according to which there are two factors, viz. : the material bread and wine, and the immaterial or spiritual body of Christ united or consubstantiated in the consecrated sacramental symbols, does not differ in kind from the Popish doctrine of Transubstantiation, according to which there is, indeed, but one element in the consecrated symbols, but that is the very body and blood of Christ into which the bread and wine have been transmuted." Nothing is more difficult, than for a thinker or believer of one school, fairly to represent the opinions and faith of thinkers and believers of another school. On the points on which Dr. Shedd here dwells, his Puritanical tone of mind renders it so difficult for him to enter into the very heart of the historical faith of the Church, that we can hardly blame him, that if it were his duty to attempt to present, in his own language, the views of the Lutheran Church, he has not done it very successfully. From the moment he abandons the Lutheran sense of terms, and reads into them a Puritan construction, from that moment he wanders from the facts, and unconsciously misrepresents.

In noticing Dr. Shedd's critique on this alleged feature of Romanism, we would say in passing, that the Augsburg Confession does not teach the doctrine of Consubstantiation. From first to last, the Lutheran Church has rejected the name of Consubstantiation and everything which that name properly

implies. Bold and uncompromising as our Confessors and
Theologians have been, if the word Consubstantiation (which
is not a more human term than Trinity and Original Sin are
human terms,) had expressed correctly their doctrine, they
would not have hesitated to use it. It is not used in any Confession of our Church, and we have never seen it used in any
standard dogmatician of our communion, except to condemn
the term, and to repudiate the idea that our Church held the
doctrine it involves. We might adduce many of the leading
evidences on this point ; but for the present, we will refer to
but a few. Bucer, in his Letter to Comander, confesses that
" he had done injustice to Luther, in imputing to him the
doctrine of Impanation," and became a defender of the doctrine
he had once rejected. Gerhard, that monarch among our
theologians, says : " To meet the calumnies of opponents, we
would remark, that we neither believe in *Impanation* nor *Consubstantiation*, nor in any physical or local presence whatsoever.
Nor do we believe in that consubstantiative presence which
some define to be the inclusion of one substance in another.
Far from us be that figment. The heavenly thing and the
earthly thing, in the Holy Supper, in the physical and natural
sense, are not present with one another." Baier, among our
older divines, has written a dissertation expressly to refute this
calumny, and to show, as Cotta expresses it, " that our theologians are entirely free from it (*penitus abhorrere.*)" Cotta, in
his note on Gerhard, says : " The word *Consubstantiation* may
be understood in different senses. Sometimes it denotes a local
conjunction of two bodies, sometimes a commingling of them,
as, for example, when it is alleged that the bread *coalesces* with
the body, and the wine with the blood, into one substance.
But in *neither sense* can that MONSTROUS DOCTRINE OF CONSUB-
STANTIATION be attributed to our Church, since Lutherans do
not believe either in that local conjunction of two bodies, nor
in any commingling of bread and of Christ's body, of wine and
of His blood." To pass from great theologians to a man of the
highest eminence in the philosophical and scientific world,
LEIBNITZ, in his Discourse on the Conformity of Reason with
Faith, says: " Evangelical (Lutherans) *do not approve* of the

doctrine of *Consubstantiation* or of *Impanation,* and no one could impute it to them, unless he had failed to make himself properly acquainted with their views." To return again to theologians, REINHARD says: "Our Church has never taught that the emblems become one substance with the body and blood of Jesus, an opinion commonly denominated *Consubstantiation.*" MOSHEIM says: "Those err who say that we believe in *Impanation.* Nor are those more correct who charge us with believing *Subpanation.* Equally groundless is the charge of *Consubstantiation.* All these opinions differ very far from the doctrine of our Church."

The insinuations of Rationalism against this doctrine of our Church only strengthen the affirmations of her great divines. If all the great Congregational authorities of New England, of the past century and the present, were quite agreed that a certain doctrine was *not* taught in the Saybrook Platform, and the "liberal" gentlemen of the Theodore Parker school were very zealous in showing that it *was* taught there, would not Dr. Shedd consider the affirmation as sealing the negation? Would he not think that, if it were possible to make a mistake in believing the great divines, there could be no mistake possible in disbelieving the "liberal" polemics? We beg him therefore, as he desires to do, as he would be done by, not to think that our Lutheran Church, historically the mother of pure Churches, in some sense even of his own Church among them, has ever believed in the doctrine of Consubstantiation.

One word more on the allegation of Dr. Shedd, that there are Romanizing elements in our Confession. Nothing is more easy, and few things are more perilous, than for Protestants to insist that some peculiarity of this, or that part of a denominational system of doctrine, is a relic of Romanism. Dr. Shedd makes this the solvent of our doctrine of the Lord's Supper, just as the Baptist makes it the solvent of Dr. Shedd's doctrine of infant baptism, and as the Socinian makes it the solvent of Dr. Shedd's doctrine of the Trinity, of the divinity of Christ, and of his propitiatory sacrifice. Not everything we learn from Rome is Romish. Not only so, but, as earnest Evangelical Protestants, we may admit, that deep and vital as

are the points in which we differ from Romanists, they are not
so vital as those in which we agree with them, and that Evangelical Protestants are not so remote from Romanists as they
are from false and heretical Protestants.   Dr. Shedd (we use

Romanizing   his name simply as giving concreteness to ortho-
elements.   dox New England Congregationalism,) agrees with
the Romanists as to the sole object of supreme worship, but
he does not so agree with his Socinian New England contemporaries, Protestant, *par excellence*, as these Socinians assume to
be.   Hence he is generically of the same religion with the Romanists, and would concede a fraternal affinity with Pascal, or
Fenelon, which he could not with any Unitarian, however
lovely in his personal character.   We are not so much alarmed
therefore, as some men pretend to be with mere coincidence
with elements existing in the Romish Church.   If anything in
our Protestant doctrines or usages be, indeed, a perpetuation
of what is *unscriptural* in the Romish system, it should be
weeded out; but it does not follow, that because a thing is in
Rome, it is of Rome.   Once a pure Church of Christ, the
Church of Rome never lost all of her original endowments.
We feel that Dr. Shedd is altogether too conscientious and
noble a man to attempt to excite this kind of anti-Romish
odium as a cheap way of dispensing with argument.   Nevertheless, so far as the authority of his name will carry weight
with it, he has helped, by the sentences he has written, to increase the weight of unjust reproach which has been heaped
upon our Church for centuries, for no other reason than for unswerving fidelity to what she is persuaded is the truth of God.
Our Church does hold, as Dr. Shedd also does, without change,
the great Trinitarian and Christological doctrines which were
preserved in their purity in the Church of Rome, but our
Church does not hold a view of the Lord's Supper coincident
with that of Rome, derived from it, or sustained by the same
kind of evidence, or open to the same invincible objections,
scriptural, historical and practical.   Dr. Shedd says: "This
doctrine of Consubstantiation does not differ in kind from the
Popish doctrine of Transubstantiation."   We need not stop
here to repeat that our Church does not hold, and never did

hold the doctrine of "Consubstantiation." Be that as it may, and waiving any further consideration of it for the present, we cannot agree with Dr. Shedd, that in the sense in which he seems to employ the words, our doctrine "does not differ in *kind* from the Popish doctrine of Transubstantiation." So far we concede that there is an agreement in *kind*, that over against a merely ideal presence of Christ, wrought by the human mind in its memory, or by its faith, our Church in common with both the Roman and Greek Churches, does hold to a true presence of the whole Christ, the factor of which is not our mind, but his own divine person. We do not think him into the Supper, but he is verily and indeed there. Faith does not put him there, but finds him there. So profoundly was Luther impressed with the importance of holding to a presence which did not play and fluctuate with the emotions and infirmities of man, but which rested on the all-sufficiency of the person of Christ, on which hangs the all-sufficiency of his work and promise — that deeply as he felt, and triumphantly as he combated the Romish error of Transubstantiation, he nevertheless declared that this error was not so radical as that of Zwingli (whose view Calvin himself stigmatized as *profane*,) and said, that if he must be driven to one extreme or the other, he would rather, with the Pope, have Christ's true body without the bread, than with Zwingli have the true bread without the true body. Surely, that is a glorious error, if error it be, which springs from trusting too far, too implicitly, in too child-like a way in the simple words of our adorable Lord! If the world divides on his utterances, we will err, if we err, with those who, fettered by the word, bring every thought into captivity to the obedience of Christ. It was not the power of education, not the influence of Romanistic leaven, but the might of the Word of God, interpreted in regard to the Lord's Supper by the very laws by which Luther was controlled in reaching the doctrine of justification by faith, and every other cardinal doctrine, it was this, and this only, which fixed his conviction. After the lapse of centuries, whose thoughts in this sphere we have striven to weigh, whether for, or against, the doctrine of our Church, with everything in the character of our times and of our land unfavorable to a community in the faith of our fathers, after a conscientious, prayerful examination of the whole ground, we confess, and if need were, through shame and suffering, God helping us, would continue to confess, our profound conviction that this doctrine which Dr. Shedd considers a relic of Romanism is Scriptural to its core, and that no process can dislodge it, which will not, carried logically through, bring the whole temple of Evangelical truth to the ground. No man can defend the doctrine of the Trinity, and assail the Lutheran doctrine of the Eucharist on the same principles of interpretation.

Nevertheless, he who is persuaded that the Romish doctrine of Transubstantiation is unscriptural, is not thereby in the remotest degree logically arrayed against the Scriptural character of the doctrine of our Church. They are not, in such sense, of one kind as to warrant this species of suspicion. They are the results of greatly different modes of interpreting Scripture, Romanism and Zwinglianism, being of one kind in this, that they depart from the letter of God's Word, interpreted by just rules of language. The Lutheran and Romish views differ most vitally in their internal character and position, the one taking its harmonious place in Evangelical doctrine, the other marring its grace and moral consistency ; Romanism and Zwinglianism being of one kind in this, that both, in different ways, exhibit dogmatic superficiality and inconsequence. The Lutheran and Romish views are differently related to the doctrinal history of the Church, the one having its witnesses in the earliest and purest ages, the other being unknown to the ancient Church and generated in its decline ; Romanism and Zwinglianism here being of one kind, in that both are unhistorical. The Lutheran and Romish views differ in their devotional and practical working ; Romanism and Zwinglianism here being of one kind, in that both generate the common result of a feeble faith — the one, indeed, by reaction, the other by development. Nothing could be more remote from a just representation of the fact than the charge that, in any undesirable sense, the Romish and Lutheran views of the Lord's Supper are one in kind.

Dr. Shedd, after leaving the Augsburg Ccnfession and its Apology, enumerates the "series of symbolical writings," "which constitute a part of Lutheran Symbolism," and mentions — 1. The *Confessio Saxonica;* and, 2. The *Confessio Würtembergica.* Neither of these Confessions can be regarded as a proper part of the symbolical books of our Church. They were for temporary ends, and were confined in their official recognition to a very small part of the Church. If Dr. Shedd is correct in supposing that the altered Confession of Melanchthon of 1540 is Pelagianizing in regard to Regeneration, and more or less Calvinistic in regard to the Sacraments, it is not very likely that the Saxon Confession of 1551, from the same hand, would be received by the Lutheran Church without suspicion; and neither the claim made for it in its title, nor Dr. Shedd's endorsement of that claim, would completely overcome the innate improbability of its being without reservation "a repetition of the Augsburg Confession."

The Würtemberg Confession of Brentius, which was written before Melanchthon's, is sound enough, but never has obtained any general recognition. There are several writings which could have been classed among our symbols with more propriety than those mentioned by Dr. Shedd, as, for example, Luther's Confession of Faith, (1528;) the Articles of Visitation, (1592,) which are still authoritative in Saxony — often confounded in this country with the earlier Saxon Articles of Visitation, (1527;) and the *Consensus Repetitus* of 1664. Not one of them, however, belongs to the Confessional writings of the Evangelical Lutheran Church.

Dr. Shedd's account of the Formula Concordiæ strikes us as peculiarly unfortunate. No hint is given of the occasion for the Confession, of the urgent necessities out of which it arose, of the earnest desire for peace and unity which prompted its formation, of the patient labors running over many years, in which its foundations were laid, and of its masterly completion and the enthusiastic spontaneousness of its reception. The reader might imagine from Dr. Shedd's statements that this book was an effect without any just cause. He says: "It was

[marginal note: The Confessions of the Lutheran and of the Reformed Churches]

drawn up by Andreæ and others in 1577." The truth is, that the labors of 1577, in which Chemnitz was a greater worker than Andreæ, were merely the finishing labors of years — labors whose results were embodied in the Torgau Book. The work of 1577 was, in reality, that of thorough revision. Dr. Shedd says the Formula Concordiæ was " presented to the Imperial Diet." We are at a loss to guess out of what misconception this statement could have originated. Not only is there no historical voucher for any such statement, but the thing itself, to any one who will recall the history of the times, will be seen at once to be absolutely impossible; and yet, Dr. Shedd, as if to show that there are degrees in the absolute, adds that this Imperial Diet " sought to secure its adoption by the Lutheran Church." All this is purely aerial. There was no such Diet, no such presentation, and no such recommendation. Dr. Shedd's pen is the magician's wand which has con jured up the whole. This is a serious charge to bring against so eminent a scholar; but, feeling the full responsibility involved in it, truth compels us to make it.

Dr. Shedd, still in his aerial movement, says of this empirical Imperial Diet: " In this they were unsuccessful." Dropping any consideration of the lack of success of this hypothetical Reception of Diet, in its phantasmagorial Decrees, we might say the Formula Con- that no official effort from any source has ever been cordiæ. made to secure the adoption of the Formula Concordiæ by the entire Lutheran Church. The great German princes and theologians to whom the Formula owed its existence made no effort to bring it to the attention of the Lutheran Church in other lands, with the solitary exception of Denmark. Nevertheless, by its own internal merits this Formula secured from the first a reception by an immense majority of the Lutheran Churches, won its way against the deadliest opposition, was finally received, almost without exception, where it was at first rejected, has been acknowledged virtually in the few cases in which it has not been acknowledged officially, and is received now in almost every part of the Lutheran Church, in which her proper doctrinal life has not been disturbed by rationalistic or pseudo-unionistic principles. It was originally signed by three Electors, three Dukes and Princes, twenty-four Counts four Barons, thirty-five imperial cities, in all by eighty-six States of the Empire, and by eight thousand ministers of the Gospel. In Denmark, where it was received by the King with brutal violence, and its introduction prohibited under penalty of death, it has long since been accepted, in fact, if not in form, as a Symbol.* In Holstein it was formally adopted in 1647. In Sweden, because of the powerful influences tending to the restoration of Popery under the king, it could not at first secure an entrance; but in 1593, at the Council of Upsala, the States determined upon its subscription, and its authority as a Symbol was confirmed by later solemn acts. In Pomerania and Livonia it obtained symbolical authority. In Hungary it was approved in 1593, and formally adopted in 1597. In France, Henry of Navarre desired to form a league with the Lutherans against the Catholics, but the acceptance of the Formula of Concord was made a condition on the part of the Evangelical States, and the negotiations were broken off. "The symbolical authority of the Formula of Concord for the Lutheran Church, as such," says Köllner, "can hardly be doubted. By far the larger part of those who regarded themselves as belonging to the Lutheran Church received it as their Symbol. And as, to use the words of the Elector Augustus, we have no Pope among us, can there be any other mode of sanctioning a Symbol than by a majority? To this is to be added, and should be especially noted, that a larger part of those who did not receive it, objected to doing so, not on doctrinal grounds, but partly for political reasons, freely or compulsorily, as the case might be, partly out of attachment to Melanchthon, partly out of a morbid vanity, because they had not been invited early enough to take part in framing the Concordia, and had consequently not participated in it — and partly because, in one land, those who had the most influence were Calvinistically inclined, although a large majority of the clergy approved of the doctrines of the Formula. The inference, therefore, is by no means to be made that there was a deviation in doctrine, because there was not an acceptance of the Formula."

* Köllner, p. 575.

It will be seen from this that Dr. Shedd har lly does justice to the historical dignity of this great Confession, when Its character and contents. he says: " It was a polemic document, constructed by that portion of the Lutheran Church that was hostile to the Calvinistic theory of the Sacraments." Cer· tainly, although the Formula is polemic in meeting error, its main end is irenical, and its general tone exceedingly moder· ate. When Dr. Shedd leaves the reader to imagine that this Confession was not only, as it would seem from his representa- tion mainly, but was exclusively directed against the Calvin- istic theory of the Sacraments, he does injustice to the Form- ula and to the reader. Of the twelve Articles, but one is de- voted to either of the Sacraments, and in the others there is much in which true Calvinists would feel a deep sympathy — much that nobly defends great points of doctrine common to the whole Evangelical faith. In the first Article, which treats of Original Sin — in the second, of the Freedom of the Will — in the third, of Justification — in the fourth, of Good Works — in the fifth, of the Law and the Gospel — in the sixth, of the third use of the Law, the most rigid Calvinist would be forced to confess that there is a noble and Scriptural presentation of those great doctrines. They defend what all pure Christendom is interested in defending. In many of the antitheses of the twelfth Article a Calvinist would heartily join, as he would in the masterly discussion of the adiaphora in Article tenth. In Article eleventh, of the eternal foreknowledge and election of God, the Calvinist would find the distinctive doctrine of Calvin rejected, but he could not but be pleased with the profound reverence and exquisite skill with which the doctrine is dis- cussed, and by which it is redeemed from the extreme of Cal- vinism without running into the opposite and far more danger- ous one of Pelagianism, or of low Arminianism. In the Articles, seventh and eighth, a Calvinist might discover much in regard to the Lord's Supper and the Person of Christ, in which he might not concur ; and in Article ninth, on the Descent of Christ into Hell, he would find a view very different from Calvin's, which Calvinists themselves now almost universally reject. Nevertheless, he would discover in such a perusal, as he certainly would not from Dr. Shedd's account, that this supposed polemic document, originating in opposition to the Calvinistic theory of the Sacraments, really defends much more than it attacks that which Calvinists love.

Dr. Shedd says : " It carries out the doctrine of Consubstantiation" (which our Church never held) " into a technical statement," (every part of which had long before been   The Doctrine made.)   " Teaching the ubiquity of Christ's body,"   of Ubiquity. says Dr. Shedd, though the Formula itself never speaks of the " ubiquity" of Christ's body. " Ubiquity" was a term invented by those who wished to fix upon our Church the imputation of teaching a local omnipresence or infinite extension of the body of Christ — errors which the Formula, and our whole Church with it, reject in the strongest terms. The doctrine of the Formula is that the body of Christ has no intrinsic or essential omnipresence as the divinity has ; that after its own intrinsic manner, and in virtue of its own essential qualities, it has a determinate presence, and in that mode of presence is not upon earth ; but that, after ANOTHER MODE, supernatural, illocal, incomprehensible, and yet real, it is rendered present, " where Christ will," through the divine nature, which has received it into personal union.

If the question were asked : How is God omnipresent ? How can the undivided totality of His substance be in each part of the universe ? How can it be all in heaven and a.. on earth, and all on earth without ceasing in any measure to be all in heaven, and without motion or extension, without multiplication of presences, and so that there is no more of God in the whole universe than there is in each point of it ? If such a question were asked Dr. Shedd, we presume that, bowing before the inscrutable mystery, he would reply : God is present after the manner of an infinite Spirit — a manner most real, but utterly incomprehensible to us. Grant, then, that this infinite Spirit has taken to itself a human nature, as an inseparable element of its person, the result is inevitable. Where the divine is, the human must be. The primary and very lowest element of a personal union is the co-presence of the parts. To say that the divine nature of Christ is personally present without his humanity, is to deny that this humanity is a part of that personality, and the doctrine of the incarnation falls to the dust: Christ becomes no more than the organ of a special revelation of Deity: His humanity is no more properly one person with God than the burning bush was one person with Jehovah. Accepting the doctrine of a real incarnation, the omnipresence of the human nature of Christ, not in itself, in which respect its presence is determinate, but through the divine, is a necessary result and involves no new mystery. If that whole Godhead which dwells in Christ's body can, without motion, without leaving heaven, or extending itself, be present with us on earth, then can it render present with us, without motion or extension, that other nature which is one person with it. What the divine nature of Christ has of itself, his human nature has *through* the divine, which has taken it to be one person with itself. This is one result of that doctrine of the *Communicatio idiomatum*, of which, as we shall see in a moment, Dr. Shedd offers so extremely inaccurate a definition. If the Evangelical Lutheran is asked, how can Christ's human nature be present with us? he can reply: After the manner in which an infinite Spirit renders present a human nature, which it has taken to be an inseparable constituent of its own person, a manner most real, but utterly incomprehensible to us. This is the doctrine at which Dr. Shedd levels, as has often been done before him, the term Ubiquity. It was the *whole* Christ — the man as well as the God — who said: " Where two or three are gathered together in my name, there am I in the midst of them." It was the *whole* Christ who said: " Lo! I am with you always, even unto the end of the world." And what the whole Christ promised, the whole Christ will perform. On any other theory, the Christian on earth has no more a personal Christ with him than the Patriarchs had; the New Dispensation has made no advance on the Old; the divine nature, the second person of the Trinity, was just as much on earth then as he is now; and all the light, peace and joy, which a sense of the actual nearness, tender guardianship, and personal sympathy of an incarnate Christ sheds upon the soul, vanish in a haze of hyperboles, a miserable twilight of figures of speech, and the vigorous and soul-sustaining objectivity of Faith faints into a mere sentimentalism. Cold speculation has taken our Lord out of the world he redeemed, and has made heaven, not his throne, but a great sepulchre, with a stone rolled against its portal.

Dr. Shedd says, moreover, in his extremely compact statement of the doctrinal essence of the Formula, of which our readers, with the close of this sentence, will have every word, that it teaches " the *communicatio idiomatum,* or the presence of the divine nature of Christ in the sacramental elements." We cannot refrain from expressing our amazement that the writer of a History of Christian Doctrine should give such a definition of so familiar a term. We are forced almost to the conclusion — and it is the mildest one we can make for Dr. Shedd — that he has ventured to give a statement of the doctrine of our Formula, without having read it with sufficient care to form a correct judgment as to the meaning of its most important terms.

The Doctor closes this paragraph with these words, which certainly exhibit no very deep insight into the internal history of our Church : " The Lutheran Church is still divided upon this Symbol. The so-called High Lutherans insist that the Formula Concordiæ is the scientific completion of the preceding Lutheran Symbolism," (Dr. Shedd seems to us constantly to use the word " Symbolism " inaccurately ;) " while the moderate party are content to stand by the Augsburg Confession, the Apology, and the Smalcald Articles." We can assure Dr. Shedd, if we know anything of the Lutheran Church, that it is not to be classified in this way. A man may hold very firmly, that the Formula is the scientific completion of the system of the earlier Symbols, and may reject it and them, or receive them with a reservation ; on the other hand, a man may be satisfied with the Augsburg Confession alone, but receiving it in good faith, will be as high a Lutheran as Dr. Shedd would like to see. The real point of classification as to the relation of nominal Lutherans to the Confession seems to us to be mainly this : Evangelical Lutherans, who are such in the historical sense, heartily receive as Scriptural statements of doctrine, the Confessions of the Church in their proper meaning as reached by the laws of language ; while others who wear the name, claim the right, in varying degrees of practical latitude, to set aside, at their pleasure, part of these doctrines. This is the vital issue, and its character is substantially the same, whether a few of the Symbols or all of them are in question. We might add that, under this latitudinarian claim, there have actually been sheltered in the Lutheran Church such soul-destroying errors as Socinianism and Universalism, and that, where the tendency has not run into the grosser heresies, the pervading characteristic of those who represent its extremes is that of laxity in doctrine, government, and discipline. There is yet a third class, who, largely revealing practically the spirit of a genuine Lutheranism, and more or less sympathizing with its controverted doctrines, yet, without a positive acceptance of them, confess that the logic of the position is with historical Lutheranism, and are never consciously unjust to it. This class are regarded with affection and respect by the thoroughly conservative part of the Church, and are bitterly assailed, or noisily claimed by the fanatical element, as the anger produced by their moderation, or the hope inspired by their apparent neutrality, predominates.

Dr. Shedd, after disposing of the Lutheran Confession in what, our readers will have seen, we do not consider a very satisfactory manner, next discusses the " Reformed Calvinistic Confessions. (Calvinistic) Confessions." In this whole section he assumes the identity of the Zwinglian and Calvinistic systems, in which we are forced to regard him as mistaken. In the heart of doctrine and tendency, pure Calvinism is often more Lutheranizing than Zwinglianizing, for Zwingli was largely Pelagian. Dr. Shedd seems to recognize nothing of the mediating tendency of the school of Bucer, nor of the Melanchthonian type of doctrinal statement ; but with a classification which seems too sweeping and inaccurate, considers the Tetrapolitan, which was prepared several years before Calvin was known as a theologian, (and which seems to be the first confessional statement of that doctrine of the Lord's Supper which now bears Calvin's name,) the *Fidei Ratio* of Zwingli, the

Heidelberg Catechism, the Canons of Dort and the Thirty-nine Articles of the Church of England, all as belonging to the same class of Confessions. Certainly, if the words Reformed and Calvinistic are synonyms, as Dr. Shedd makes them, this grouping is open to very serious objections. When Dr. Shedd reaches the Heidelberg Catechism, he bestows so little care upon the arrangement of his facts, that the incautious reader might be led into very serious mistakes. He might suppose, for instance, that Frederick the First was a successor of John Casimir. He is told, in express terms, that Louis the Sixth brought the Palatinate under the Formula Concordiæ in 1576, (four years before it was published,) and if he is not on his guard, will be sure to imagine that the troubles which followed the mutations of 1576, and the subsequent ones under John Casimir, (1583–1592,) led to the formation of the Heidelberg Catechism in 1562. Dr. Shedd continues to call the Electors (we know not why) "Crown Princes," and in general seems to stumble from the moment he gets on German ground. What will intelligent preachers and laymen in the German Reformed Church think, for instance, of this eulogy with which the notice of the Heidelberg Catechism closes: "In doctrine, it teaches justification with the Lutheran glow and vitality, predestination and election with Calvinistic firmness and self-consistency, and the Zwinglian theory of the Sacraments with decision, ... and is regarded with great favor by the High Lutheran party of the present day." We will not undertake to speak for our German Reformed friends, except to say, that this is not the sort of thing they talked, at their Ter-Centenary, and put into their handsome volume. As to "the High Lutherans of the present day," if we are of them, as we are sometimes charged with being, Dr. Shedd is right: the Heidelberg Catechism *is* regarded by them with great favor — all except its doctrines. It is a neat thing — a very neat thing — the mildest, most winning piece of Calvinism of which we know. One-half of it is Lutheran, and this we like very much, and the solitary improvement we would suggest in it would be to make the other half of it Lutheran, too. With this slight reservation, on this very delicate point, the High Lutherans

23

are rather fond of it than otherwise, to the best of their knowl edge and belief.

We have not proposed to ourselves a general review of Dr. Shedd's book, but simply to look at it with reference to its statements in regard to our own Church. Nevertheless, we cannot avoid an allusion to what strikes us an extreme statement in apparent conflict with sound Theology. It is in his declaration that " sin is *in the strictest sense* a creature." " The

Sin not a crea- original act of self-will is *strictly* creative from
ture. nothing." Dr. Shedd here seems to labor to show that he is not speaking in a popular and rhetorical way, but that over against such a style of language, he wishes to be understood rigidly — sin is a creature — but God is not its creator. Man is as really and as strictly a creator as God is — and sin is his creature. Such language, if pressed, seems inconsistent with the nature of God, of man, of sin, and of creature. It denies that God is the alone Creator of all things ; it maintains, almost after a Manichean style, that evil is a primal principle and that a man is the Ahriman of it ; it makes sin an objective reality, not the condition or act of a subject, and elevates the mutilation and disease of the creature to a rank in being with the creature itself. No more than the surgeon creates by cutting off the leg of a man, does man *create* sin by a self-originated destruction of his original righteousness, on which follows that inordinate state of the natural reason and appetites which theologians call concupiscence. The impulse to theft, to lying, to impurity, is not a substance, not a creature, but is the result of inordinate desire in which self-love now unchecked by original righteousness and kindled by the fomes of the self-corrupted will, reveals itself. It is not a creature, but a moral phenomenon of the creature -- desire and purpose are not creatures, but exercises of the faculties of the creature. If sin be strictly a creature, it must be the creature of God, and this part of Dr. Shedd's theory really would make God the author of sin, an inference, which, we are sure, no one could more earnestly resist than himself. The finite will can corrupt the creatures, but it cannot add to them.

IX.

THE SPECIFIC DOCTRINES OF THE CONSERVATIVE REFORMATION

ORIGINAL SIN.

(AUGSBURG CONFESSION, ART. II.)

THE foundation of the second Article of the Augsburg Confession, which treats of Original Sin, was laid in the Articles of the Colloquy at Marburg. This colloquy took place October 3d, 1529, and was designed to bring about, if possible, an agreement between Luther and Zwingli, Documentary and their adherents. Fifteen Articles were drawn History of the second Article of up by Luther. Fourteen of these were adopted the A.Confession. entire by both parties, and the fifteenth was received with the exception of one point, to which the Zwinglians objected. In these fifteen Articles are the roots of the Augs- I. Articles of burg Confession. The fourth Article was on Orig- the Colloquy at Marburg. inal Sin, and is as follows:

"In the fourth place, we believe that original sin is from Adam, inborn and inherited to us, and is a sin of such kind that it condemns all men, and if Jesus Christ had not come to our help, by his death and life, we must have died therein eternally, and could not have come to God's kingdom and blessedness." *

---

* J. J. Müller's Historie, 306. Corpus. Reform. xxvi. 123. Compared with Hospinian His. Sacr. ii. 77. On the whole Colloquy, cf. : Corp. Reform. i. Nos. 631–642. Seckendorf. Hist. Luth. ii. 139. Luther's Werke: Walch xvii. 2361, 2374, xxiii. 6, 35. Jena: iv. 469. Leipz. xix. 530. Erlangen: lxv. 88. Zimmermann: Ref. Schr. M. L. iii. 426. Luther's Briefe (De Wette, iii. 508.) Zwingli's Werke (Zürich, 1830.): Germ. Vol. ii. P. iii. 44–58. Lat. iv. 173–204. Historia v. d. Augsburg Confess. (Chemnitz, Selneccer, Kirchner) Leipz. 1584. Fol. 92–107. Do. Lat. 1585. 113–133. Sculteti Annal. ad ann. 1529. 199. Chytræi : Histor

In an ampler form the same doctrine presents itself in the Schwabach Articles. These seventeen Articles are also from the hand of Luther. They are largely an elaboration of the *Marburg* Articles, and are the direct groundwork of the doctri-
II. The Schwa-bach Articles. nal articles of the Augsburg Confession. The fourth Article runs thus: " That original sin is a true, real sin, and not merely a weakness or defect, but such a sin as would condemn all men who spring from Adam, and would separate us from God forever, if Jesus Christ had not interceded for us, and taken upon himself this sin, with all other sins which follow therefrom, and by his suffering made satisfaction therefor, and thus utterly taken them away, and blotted them out in himself, as in Psalm li. and Rom. v. is clearly written of this sin." *

III. The Article in the Augsburg Confession. In the Latin and German texts of the earliest authorized Edition of each, we have as follows, the

ARTICLE ON ORIGINAL SIN.

Literal Translation of the Latin.†	*Literal Translation of the German.‡*
II.	**The Second.**
Also they teach, that after Adam's fall, all men begotten after the common course of nature are born with sin; that is without the fear of God, without trust in God, and with	Further is taught, (I) that after the fall of Adam, (II) all men who are born naturally, are conceived and born in sins, that is, that they all from the mother's womb, are full of evil

d. A. C. 159. Lat. 643–646. Rudelbach: Ref. L. u. Un. 665–668. Ebrard: Abendmahl, 345–347.

* Corpus Reformat. xxvi. 153. Compared with the Latin in Pfaff. L. S. Appendix 4. Luther's Werke Walch: xx. 1–3. Chytræi: Hist. (1576) 19; Do, Lat. (1578) 21; J. J. Müller's Histor. 442. Cœlestinus: i. 25. Scultetus: Annal.

† For the Latin here translated, the writer has before him the original Wittenberg Edition of 1530–1531. He has compared it word for word with the text of the Book of Concord (Müller's ed.), and finds that they do not differ in a word or *a letter.*

‡ For the German we have translated from the original Editio Princeps of Melanchthon, the Wittenberg 4to 1530, 1531.

fleshly appetite, and that this disease or original fault is truly sin, condemning and bringing now also eternal death upon all that are not born again by baptism and the Holy Spirit.

They condemn the Pelagians, and others, who deny this original fault to be sin indeed: and who, so as to lessen the glory of the merits and benefits of Christ, argue that a man may by the strength of his own reason be justified before God.

desire and inclination, and can have by nature, no true fear of God, no true love of God, (VII) no true faith in God. That also the same inborn plague and hereditary sin is truly Sin, and condemns all those under God's wrath, who are not born (IV) again (III) through baptism and the Holy Ghost.

Here (V) are rejected the Pelagians, and others, who do not hold (VI) original sin to be sin, in order that they may show that nature is holy, by natural power, to the reproach of the sufferings and merit of Christ.

As the text of the German Ed. Princ. of Melanchthon, and that in the Book of Concord, are not critically identical, and as the distinction of the two texts will be alluded to occasionally in these dissertations, and is sometimes misunderstood, it may be well at this point to illustrate more particularly the nature of the differences. The causes which led to the substitution of the Formula text for the Melanchthonian have been given elsewhere.* Taking the Second Article, we present a

* p. 248–253.

Tabular View of the Critical Differences between the Melanchthonian and the Formula Texts.

	Weim.	Mentz.	Nurem.	Nordl.	Ansp.	Ed. ant.
I.						
1: is taught 2: adds: among us, 3: adds: and preached in our churches.	Weim. 1.	Mentz.	Nurem.	Nordl.	Ansp. 2.	
II.						
1: fall of Adam. 2: Adam's fall.	Weim. 1.	Mentz.	Nurem.		Ansp. 2, 3.	
III.						
1: wieder. 2: widerum.	Weim. 1.	Mentz.	Nurem.		Ansp. 2.	Ed. ant. 5.
IV.						
1: geborn. 2: neu geborn.		Mentz.	Nurem.	Nordl. Aug.	Ansp. 1, 2, 3.	Ed. ant. 1,2,3, 4, 5,6.
3: von neuem geborn.	Weim. 1.					
V.						
1: Hie.					Hie, Ansp. 2. Corrected.	
2: Hieneben.		Mentz.			Hie (neben). Ansp. 2. First so written: a line drawn over *neben.*	
3: Daneben.	Weim. 1.					
VI.						
1: halten. 2: haben.		Mentz.				Ed. ant. 6.
VII.						
1: Keine wahre Gottes-lieb. 2: Omit:					All the MSS.	Ed. ant. 1, 6.

In this tabular view, the Nos. I, II, III, IV, V, VI, VII, refer to the parts of the Article similarly marked. The reading marked 1, is that of Melanchthon's Edit. Princeps; the reading marked 2, that of the text in the Book of Concord; 3, a reading different from both. When the readings of the MSS. and the editions surreptitiously printed before Melanchthon's Ed. Princeps *differ* from Melanchthon's, they are given in this table. *For* Melanchthon's readings are all the rest, in each case. The complete list of the Codices in alphabetical order is as follows:

Codices: 1, Aug(sburg); 2, Cass(el); 3, Dresd(en); 4, Hanov(er); 5, Mentz; 6, Mun(ich); 7, Nurem(berg); 8, Nord(lingen); 9, Ansp(ach); 10, Ansp. 2; 11, Ansp. 3; 12, Weim(ar) 1; 13, Weim. 2. Printed Ante-Melanchthonian editions, (Edit antiq.) 1, 2, 3, 4, 5, 6, of 1530.

To give an example of the mode of using the Table, under various readings: I, all the codices and editions sustain Melanchthon's reading, except Mentz, Nur., Nordl., Ansp. 2, and Weim. 1 ; under II, all but Weim. 1, Mentz, Nur., Ansp. 2, 3 ; under III, all but Weim. 1, Mentz, Nur., Ansp. 2., Ed. ant. 5. The most remarkable is VII. It is found alone in the Editio Princeps, and Melanchthon's editions of the German. Taking the aggregate of the testimony of Codices and Editions, it is about in the ratio of more than two for Melanchthon's Editio Princeps, to one for the text of the Book of Concord, and this too includes the readings of the earliest, and, consequently, immaturest of the Codices. The Codices we have given in alphabetical order, have been arranged *chronologically*, thus: 1, Weim. 1 (Spalatin's autograph); 2, Ansp. 1 ; 3, Hannov. ; 4, Mentz, (long believed to be the original, and, as such, was taken for the text of the Book of Concord); 5, Weim. 2 ; 6, Dresd. ; 7, Ansp. 2 ; 8, Ansp. 3 ; 9, Cass. ; 10, Mun. ; 11, Nur. ; 12, Nord. ; 13, Augs. These Codices are copies of the Confession made during its preparation, and, *cæteris paribus*, the later the time at which the copy was made, the greater the probability of its exact conformity with the text actually handed in. An important mark of maturity is the addition of the subscriptions. The first three are incomplete, the first six are without the subscription. Beginning with 7, Ansp. 2, the rest have the subscription except Mun., which is a fragment terminating in the Articles on the Mass. The facts we have presented demonstrate four things: First, that the question of the two German texts which have had Confessional authority in our Church, is purely critical. For all doctrinal and practical ends the two texts are one. Any principle which would really unsettle the text of the Confession of Faith, *as a Confession*, would much more unsettle the text of the Rule of Faith, as a Rule. The two texts of the German Confession differ *much less* than the texts of the Textus Receptus of the Greek, and of Tischendorf's Eighth Edition. It does not disturb our faith that we have critically diverse texts of the Rule, for they teach the same faith, **nor** will it disturb our confession that we have slightly diverse, critical texts of the German form of the Creed, for they confess the same faith. Second: The differences, even of a critical kind, are of a very trifling character. Third: The Editio Princeps of Melanchthon is the highest critical author-ity. Fourth: While the text of the Book of Concord has the highest Confessional authentication, and ought not to be changed, except by authority of the Church, it is perfectly consistent with this, that the Editio Princeps be used as an aid in interpreting it. Identical as the two texts are, for the most part, in their very words, absolutely identical in doctrine, we may thank God that we have in the two the historical evi dence of the untiring conscientiousness of effort on the part of our Fathers, to give the most perfect form of sound words to the one faith, and that the two texts, so far from disturbing, fix more absolutely that one sense of the Confession, the percep-tion of which is essential to real unity on the part of those who profess to accept it.

The Papal Confutation was read before the Emperor, Aug. 3d. The second Article was approved so far as, 1: "they confessed with the Catholic Church, that the fault of origin is truly sin-IV. The Papal condemning and bringing eternal death to those Confutation. who are not born again of Baptism and the Holy Ghost; as also in their condemnation of the Pelagians, ancient and modern, whom the Church had already condemned."

2. "But the declaration of the Article, that original sin is this, that men are born without the fear of God, without trust toward God, is to be entirely rejected, since it is manifest to every Christian that to be without the fear of God, and trust in Him, is rather the actual offence of the adult, than the fault of a new-born babe, which is not yet able to exercise reason, as the Lord saith unto Moses, (Deut. i. 39:) 'Your little ones, which in that day had no knowledge between good and evil.'"

3. "But that declaration is also rejected in which they call the fault of origin, fleshly appetite (*concupiscentia*), if by this they mean that fleshly appetite is sin, which also remains sin in a child after Baptism."

4. "For long ago the Apostolic See condemned two Arti-cles of Martin Luther, the second and third, concerning si ı

remaining in a child after Baptism, and in regard to the *incentive* (fumes) which prevents the soul from entering heaven."

5. "But if, as St. Augustine uses the term, they assert that the fault of origin is carnal appetite, which in Baptism ceases to be sin, their doctrine is to be received, since St. Paul also teacheth, Eph. ii. 3, we are all born the children of wrath, and, Rom. v. 12, in Adam we have all sinned." *

Seven persons on each side were appointed to compare the views of the Protestants (Lutherans) and Romanists. On each side the commission consisted of two princes, two jurists, and three theologians. The Romish theologians were Eck, Wimpina and Cochleus: the Protestant theologians were Melanchthon, Schnepf and Brentius. Spalatin was added to the commission as notary. {V. A commission of fourteen persons.}

1. Before this commission, the Lutheran Confessors presented the following explanation of the part of the second Article which had been objected to: "When it is said in the second Article, in the Latin, that man is born by nature without trust in God, and without fear of God, the language is to be understood not alone of children who are too young to have these emotions, but it means that when they are grown they cannot, by their natural powers, have the fear of God, and trust in Him. *And to be born thus*, without this power and gift, is a defect of that righteousness which ought to have been derived to us from Adam (had he not fallen). In the German this Article is so clearly stated, that it cannot be impugned, for it is there said that ' We are not by nature able to fear God, and trust in Him, in which words adults are also embraced.'

"In regard to the natural inclinations, we maintain, that the nature of sin remains, but the condemnation is removed by baptism." †

2. In regard to the second Article, Dr. Eck remarked that, in the main part, it was in conformity with the teaching of the Christian Church, but was defective in the definition, and in calling fleshly appetite original sin, and in maintaining

---

* Latin in Hase's L. S. Proleg. lxxviii. German in Chytræus, H. A. C. 236, b.
† Müller's Hist. Protestat. 746. Latin: Cœlestinus, iii. 55.

that it remained sin before and after baptism ; though, if the terms were employed as St. Augustine used them, there would be a logomachy, rather than an actual diversity between the parties.

Melanchthon, in reply, begged leave to make an explanation in regard to two points — first, as to the words " without fear and trust ; " and second, as to the incitement (*fomes*) to sin. His explanation was, that he had wished to avoid the scholastic phraseology, in which original sin is styled, *the defect of original righteousness* (carentia rectitudinis originalis), which he had expressed in the words, " without fear and trust," but the sense was the same.

Dr. Eck replied, that Melanchthon's form and mode of expression were new, otherwise they would already have agreed on the Article; but as there had been only an avoidance of the ordinary term, the views of the two parties might be considered as harmonized. On the second point, Dr. Eck acknowledged that the material of sin remains. The two parties were considered therefore as having agreed upon this Article.* The statement of the result in this point, made by the Romish portion of the commission to the Emperor (August 23d), is as follows: — " In this Article they agree with us, and rightly condemn the Pelagians and others, as, for example, the Zwinglians and Anabaptists, who deny original-sin. But in the definition of original sin they did not agree with us. The Lutherans, finally agreeing with our opinions, say, that original sin is a want of original righteousness, that the condemnation of this sin is removed in baptism, but that the incitement (*fomes*), or fleshly appetite, remains in men even after baptism."

An ample and admirable vindication of the Article against the Romish Church, the Church which canonizes and deserts Augustine, and reprobates and follows Pelagius, is found in the Apology of the Confession.

In beginning the analysis of the Second Article of the Augsburg Confession, its relations to the Articles between which it is placed are worthy of notice. The First Article

* From Spalatin's Protocol. in Müller's Hist., 748.

treats of God in His essence, and in His creation or creative work. The Third Article treats of Christ, and of His redemptory work. These two Articles are naturally, and indeed necessarily, connected by the Second Article, which shows how the creature of God, formed originally in the moral likeness of God, comes to need a Redeemer. <small>Relation of the Second Article to the First and Third. The Analysis.</small>

This Article of the Confession, if analyzed, will be found to present either in so many words, or by just inference, the following points :

I. The doctrine of original sin is taught with great UNANIMITY by our Churches.

II. The true doctrine of sin presupposes a right ANTHROPOLOGY, a true doctrine of man.

III. The TIME of the operation of original sin is the whole time subsequent to the fall of Adam.

IV. The PERSONS affected by it are all human beings born in the course of nature.

V. The MODE of the perpetuation of original sin is that of the natural extension of our race.

VI. The great FACT asserted in this doctrine is this, that all human beings are conceived in and born with sin.

VII. This sin RESULTS or reveals its working in these respects :

1. That all human beings are born without the fear of God

2. That they are born without trust and love toward God.

3. That they are born with concupiscence, i. e., that from their birth they are full of evil desire and evil propensity.

4. That they can have by nature no true fear, nor love of God, nor faith in God.

VIII. The ESSENCE of original sin involves that this disease or vice of origin is TRULY SIN.

IX. The natural CONSEQUENCE of this original sin is this, that it condemns and brings now also eternal death.

X. The natural consequence is actually incurred by all who are not BORN AGAIN.

XI. When the new birth takes place it is invariably wrought by the HOLY SPIRIT.

XII. This new birth by the Holy Spirit has baptism as an ORDINARY MEAN.

XIII. Baptism is the ONLY ORDINARY mean of universal application.

XIV. Our Church CONDEMNS:

1. The Pelagians.

2. All others who deny that the vice of origin is sin.

3. All who contend that man by his own strength as a rational being can be justified before God.

4. Who thus diminish the glory of the merit of Christ, and of his benefits.

In enlarging upon this analysis of the Second Article, it is to be noticed then,

I. It affirms the *unity* of the Evangelical Church in the doctrine of Original Sin. The first words of the First Article are understood before all the articles, to wit: "The Churches among us teach, with great accord" (magno consensu). "It is taught and held with unanimity."

Unity of the Church in the doctrine of Original Sin.

The Augsburg Confession avoided all minor matters, and all statements of doctrine, in regard to which there was any difference among those who presented it, who were the authorized representatives of their Churches. It embraces only the leading fundamental articles of the Evangelical system, and the minimum of detail in regard to these.

A *Lutheran*, historically and honestly such, cannot therefore *hold less than the Augsburg Confession;* hence it is as true *now*, as it was when the Confession *was given*, that our Lutheran Churches hold, confess, and teach the same doctrine of Original Sin, among themselves, to wit, the very doctrine confessed by our Fathers at Augsburg.

If men like Wegscheider, Bretschneider, and other Rationalists, or if Arminians, or Pelagians, or Semi-Pelagians, or for the matter of that Demi-semi-pelagians, who choose to call themselves Lutherans, reject the doctrine, it only proves that they are willing to bear a name to which they have no just claim whatever. It is the distinctive position of the Reformation with which, over against Rome, it stands or falls, that that which properly constitutes, defines, and perpetuates in unity a Church, is its *doctrine*, not its name or organization. While a Church retains its proper identity it retains of necessity its proper doctrine. Deserting its doctrine it loses its identity. The Church is not a body which bears its name like England, or America, which remain equally England and America, whether savage or civilized, Pagan or Christian, Monarchical or Republican. Its name is one which properly indicates its faith — and the faith changing, the Church loses its identity. Pagans may become Mohammedans, but then they are no longer Pagans — they are Mohammedans. Jews may become Christians, but then they are no longer Jews in religion. A Manichean man, or Manichean Church, might become Catholic, but then they would be Manichean no more. A Romish Church is Romish ; a Pelagian Church is Pelagian ; a Socinian Church is Socinian, though they call themselves Protestant, Evangelical, or Trinitarian. If the whole nominally Lutheran Church on earth should repudiate the Lutheran doctrine, that doctrine would remain as really Lutheran as it ever was. A man, or body of men, may cease to be Lutherans, but a doctrine which is Lutheran once, is Lutheran forever. Hence, now, as from the first, that is not a Lutheran Church, in the proper and historical sense, which cannot *ex animo* declare that it shares in the accord and unanimity with which each of the Doctrines of the Augsburg Confession was set forth.

II. The doctrine of the Second Article rests upon the presuppositions of a sound general *Anthropology.*

1. It presupposes a sound view of man as the proper *subject* of redemption, capable of it and needing it. This is implied in the very location of the Doctrine. Man is the subject of redemption, and hence appears, not as the angels do, simply as a creature of God, and within theology in its strictest sense (as the doctrine concerning *God*), but in a place, which is bounded upon the one side by Theology, on the other by Soteriology. Man, in his two states of integrity and corruption, touches the Theology which goes before, the soteriology which follows after. He stands in the Augsburg Confession where he now stands in nature, in history, and

in grace, between God the Creator, and Christ the Redeemer.

2. It presupposes a sound *definition* of man, as God's last and highest earthly creature, consisting of body and soul, having personality, freedom, moral accountability, and immortality. It rests upon the old idea of man expressed in the definition of Hollazius : "Man is an animal, consisting of a rational soul and an organic body, formed by God, endowed with his image, in the first creation, that he might unfeignedly worship his Creator, might live in holiness, and attain eternal blessedness."

3. It presupposes that the *Biblical History* of man's creation is literally true, that the first pair were the direct immediate creation of God, and that all mankind have sprung from this one pair. All the dignity and possibilities of humanity rest upon its derivation in an extraordinary manner from God. The creation of the first man is narrated in general, in Gen. i. 26 seq., and more fully delineated in Gen. ii. 7 seq. The seeming diversities of the account arise from the difference of their objects. The derivation of all mankind from a single pair, is distinctly taught in the Holy Scriptures, and we find nothing whatever in the facts of natural science to render it doubtful. Science establishes the fact, that the whole human race is of one species. It of course cannot say whether the race has sprung from one pair or not, but science demonstrates that the race might have sprung from one pair, inasmuch as they all belong to one species ; what science shows to be possible, revelation distinctly teaches. Science moreover exhibits the following facts :

i. That nature is economical in its resources ; that there is no waste of means, and as one pair is sufficient to have originated the population of the globe, the scientific presumption is strong, that there was but one pair.

ii. Natural science shows, that only animals of the *same species* produce a permanently fertile offspring. Where animals, though not of the *same species*, are sufficiently near in species to have offspring, that offspring is invariably either absolutely sterile, or the power of propagation runs out speedily. Thus, to take a familiar example, the *mule* is the offspring of the horse and the ass, and the mule is barren. But the children resulting from the union of the most widely diverse human races are permanently fertile ; their posterity is extended from generation to generation, so that in all countries, where there is a mingling of races, extreme in their diversity, there are terms indicative of near, and of increasingly remote relations. Such terms, for example, are : Mulatto, Quadroon, Octoroon, Mestizo, and many others.

iii. *The traditions of the races* largely point to a common origin. The *history* of man accounts for some of the most difficult facts, in regard to the distribution of mankind from one centre, and overthrows the very hypotheses which seem to have the largest amount of à *priori* probability.

iv. *The languages of mankind* contribute a great deal of evidence as to the original unity of the races, which have become widely sundered. We ourselves cannot speak a sentence of our native tongue, be it German or English, without giving evidence that the whole of the Germanic race, of which the English is a part, are of East Indian origin. The population of this New Continent, and the demonstrably oldest race of the Old Continent, speak languages which had a common origin. Both drew their language from that primitive tongue, of which the Sanscrit is the oldest existing remnant.

The doctrine of the "Unity of the Human Race" is important in its bearing on the recognition of the equality and fraternity of all mankind. It is essentially connected with just views of original sin, and the true view of the nature of redemption. Although modern science has sometimes been perverted to the weakening of man's faith in this great doctrine, yet the most eminent men of science, whether Christian or not, have united in the judgment, that *science does not weaken, by any of its facts, the Scripture witness to the unity of the human race.*

The hypotheses which are opposed to the Scripture doctrine of the Unity of the Human Race, are in general these:

The theory of *the Coadamites,* i. e. of the creation of several original races.

The theory of *the Preadamites,* of men before Adam. This

was specially developed by Isaac Peyrerius, in his work, *Præ-adamitæ*, Amsterdam, 1655. He took the ground that in Gen. i. 26 is narrated the creation of the first man, and in Gen. ii. is narrated the later creation of Adam, from whom the Jews spring.

The theory of *Autochthons*, which is the prevalent view of skeptical naturalists, is that the race came from the earth, in its original condition, by what is called " *generatio equivoca:* " or that man is the result of the development of a lower organization into a higher.

4. This Second Article presupposes that subsequent to the first creation of man, which was *immediate*, all human beings are the *mediate* creatures of God, and that consequently neither the body nor soul of children results from an immediate creation by God, but that both are mediated in the divine order of nature, through the parents.

As the first of our race were the immediate creation of God, so the Bible teaches that their descendants are the mediate creation of God. Ps. cxxxix. 13 ; Acts xvii. 26 ; Heb. xii. 9.

The derivation of man *from God*, now, may therefore be described as a *mediate creation, through omnipotence exercised ordinarily*, while the *creation of Adam was immediate*, by omnipotence in its absoluteness.

The propagation, or origination of the human soul, has The propaga- been explained by three theories, viz : *Preëx-*
tion of the soul. *istence : Creationism : Traducianism.*

The theory of *Preëxistence* was maintained by Plato, who dwelt upon a seemingly dim recollection of a former condition, anamneesis. It went over from Plato through Philo, to Origen, but never met with general acceptance in the Church, and was expressly condemned in the Council of Constantinople in 543. In recent times, it has been defended by *Kant*, who thinks, in his work " *Religion within the bounds of Pure Reason*," that to the explanation of the radical evil in man is required the intelligible fact of a decision made by him at some former time. *Schelling* has maintained the same view in his "*Philosophical Investigation, in regard to the Essence of Freedom*," 1809.

It has also been most ably defended by *Julius Mueller*, in his great work "*On Sin*" (4th Ed., 1858), (translated into English, Clark's For. Libr.,) who employs it to solve the problem of Original Sin. Nowhere, however, has the theory been put more beautifully, than in the lines of one of our great English poets, *Wordsworth*, in his "Intimations of Immortality, from the Recollections of Childhood." In that poem he makes this noble statement of the Platonic theory :

> " Our birth is but a sleep and a forgetting;
> The soul that rises with us, our life's star,
> Hath had elsewhere its setting,
> And cometh from afar.
> Not in entire forgetfulness,
> And not in utter nakedness,
> But, trailing clouds of glory, do we come,
> From Heaven, which is our home."

But beautiful as is this theory, and not without speciousness, it will not bear the test of logic, nor of the witness of Scripture. It only cuts the knot; it simply throws back the question, puts it out of sight, and does not answer it. It is an obvious subterfuge to get rid of a perplexity, and is like the hopeless cosmography of the Hindoos, except that it stops at the elephant. It is opposed to the great fact of our human experience, as to the similarity between the soul of the parent and child, and is contradicted by the general drift of Scripture, and specially by Gen. iii. and the whole argument in Rom. v. 12, seq. It in truth involves simply an undeveloped metempsychosis, a transmigration of the soul. Its latest defender is an American, Dr. *Edward Beecher*, who lays this theory as part of the basis of what he claims to be the solution of the "Conflict of Ages." (1854.)

The theory of Preëxistence in another form asserts simply that all souls were created at the beginning, by the word of God, and are united, at conception, with the human organism.

Immediate Creationism maintains that there is a direct creation of the soul by God, and that about the fortieth day after conception it is united with the embryo. The passages of Scripture which have been appealed to sustain this view are Jer. xxxviii. 16: Isa. lvii. 16; Zach. xii. 1; Acts xvii. 28; Ps. cxix. 73; Job x. 12; Do. xxxiii. 4; Numb. xvi. 22;

24

Do. xxvii. 16; Heb. xii. 9, and in the Apocryphal books, 2 Macc. vii. 22. Jerome asserts that this was the view of the Church, but this is an over-statement of the fact, although it certainly was the view of a number of the Fathers. Clemens Alexandrinus says: " Our soul is sent from Heaven." Lactantius says: "Soul cannot be born of souls." It is the predominant view of the Roman Church. Most of the Reformed (Calvinistic) theologians maintain it, and usually with the theory that by the union of the soul with the body the soul becomes sinful.

But this theory is really untenable. The strongest of the Scripture passages quoted to sustain it, imply no more than that the *spirit of man has higher attributes than his body,* is pre-eminent as God's work, and the chief seat of his image, without at all implying that His creation of the soul is a direct one. It would be quite as easy, not only to show from other passages, but to show from a number of these, that the body of man is the direct creation of God, which, nevertheless, no one will maintain.

To Pelagians, and the Pelagianizing Romanists, this theory indeed is not encumbered with the great moral difficulty arising from the acknowledgment of Original Sin, but to all others, this view involves, at its root, unconscious Gnosticism. It makes *matter* capable of sin and of imparting sinfulness. It represents the parents of a child as really but the parents of a mere material organism, within which the nobler part, all that elevates it, all that loves and is loved, is in no respect really their child. On this theory, no man could call his child really his own. He has no more relation, as a parent, to its soul, which is the child, than any other man in the world, and is as really the father of that which constitutes a human being, to every other person's children as he is to his own. Moreover, with all the explanations and ingenious resorts which have been found necessary in retaining this theory, there is no escaping the inference, that it makes *God the author of Sin.* According to this theory, God creates a perfect, spotless, holy soul, and then places it in a polluted body; that is, He takes what is absolutely innocent, and places it, where it inevitably, not by choice, but of necessity, is tainted with sin, justly subject to damnation, and in a great majority of cases actually reaches eternal damnation. We do not hesitate to say, that though the doctrine has been held by good men, who have guarded with great care against obvious abuse, it could be pressed until it would assume almost the character of a " Doctrine of Devils."

The third view is that of *Traducianism*, or mediate Creationism: the theory that both body and soul are derived from the parents. This theory corresponds with the prevailing and clear statements of the Holy Scriptures, as, e. g. Gen. v. 3 ; Acts xvii. 24–26. It is a doctrine absolutely demanded by the existence of original sin, and the doctrine that God is not the author of sin. This view is defended, among the Fathers, especially by *Tertullian, Athanasius, Gregory of Nissen,* and many others. Augustine remained undecided, confessing his ignorance, yet leaning strongly to the Traducian View. *The Lutheran Divines,* with very few exceptions, are *Traducian.* The expressions in the Symbolical Books, such as in the Catechism, " I believe that God has created me," and in the Formula of Concord, " God has created our souls and bodies after the fall," are meant of the mediate creation, not of the direct.

The *true theory of Traducianism* is, *that it is a creation by God, of which the parents are the divinely ordained organ.* The soul of the child is related mysteriously, yet as closely, to the soul of the parent as its body is to theirs, and the inscrutable mystery of the eternal generation of God's Son from the absolute Spirit, mirrors itself in the origin of the human soul.

5. This Article presupposes, antecedent to all human sin, a *state of integrity.* God said, Gen. i. 26, " *Let us make man in our image, after our likeness.*" This image of God in man Status integritatis, or the state is something which is not absolutely lost, but is of integrity. fearfully marred. See 1 Cor. xi. 7; James iii. 9; Eph. iv. 24; and Col. iii. 10. The *traditions* of the race preserve the memory of a golden age, a time of innocence and happiness; the *Confession* implies that the race has fallen from a condition of glory and bliss. Man was created with an ability not to sin, which, had he been faithful, would have been merged into a condition, in which he could not sin: the "*posse*

non peccare " would have become a " *non posse peccare*," and the
" *posse non mori* " would have been merged into " *non posse mori.*"
The abode of unfallen man was the Garden of Eden, or
Paradise. " The state of integrity was that happy condition of
man in which he was conformed to the image of God. The
' image of God ' is natural perfection, consisting, in conformity
with God the prototype, in wisdom, righteousness, purity, immortality, and majesty. It was concreate in the parents of our
race, so that they rightly knew and worshipped our Creator, and lived in holiness, and would have obtained a yet more
glorious blessedness." *

" In the *widest* conception of the image of God, there pertains to it everything which marks man as a rational being.
In this general sense, the image of God is not lost entirely,
though obscured. In its more *specific* sense, it embraces the
religious element in man, and its chief part is original righteousness. This involves the conformity of the *understanding* with
the *knowledge* and *wisdom* of God ; conformity of the *will* with
the *holiness* of God, *and with freedom ;* conformity of the *affections* with the *purity* of God. The *secondary conformity* consisted,
partly, in the *conformity within man*, and *partly*, in that which
was *without man.* The body of man unfallen was an image of the
immortality of God. It was free from suffering and from calamity. It imaged the eternity of God by its immortality, its freedom from necessity of dying. Rom. v. 12 ; vi. 23. The perfection *without man*, which belongs to the image of God, was conformity of his outward dominion, with the power and majesty
of the Creator. He was Lord of the world, in which he had
been placed ; all the creatures of the world, in which he had
been placed, were under his dominion. Gen. i. 26, ib. ii. 19." †

Over against just and Scriptural views of the image of God
are arrayed first the views which suppose it to have been one of
corporeal likeness. This was the view of the Anthropomor-
phites. Next the Socinians and many Arminians, conceding
that it was in conjunction with immortality, yet restricted it
to the dominion over the animal world. The Pelagians and

---

* Hollazius.

† Quenstedt. See Hutterus Rediv. (Hase) ₹ 80, and Luthardt Komp. d. Dogm. ₹ 41

Rationalists suppose the image of God in its religious aspect to have been little, if at all, injured. The Romish theology has a Pelagianizing tendency. The Fathers of the Greek Church distinguish between the image of God and his likeness, referring the *one* to the *rational nature of man,* and the *other* to *the spiritual nature of man.*

The Reformation found a deep corruption in this, as in other doctrines. Low views of justification prevailed because men had low views of sin. Over against the spurious theology of the Church of Rome, the *Apology* says: " Original righteousness was not only a just blending of the qualities of the body, but, moreover, these gifts, the assured knowledge and fear of God, trust in God, and the power of rectitude." The Formula Concordiæ :* " Original righteousness is the concreate image of God, according to which, man in the beginning was created in truth, holiness, and righteousness." Hollazius says, " The principal perfections constituting the image of God, are excellence of understanding, perfect holiness, and freedom of will, purity of desires, and a most sweet consent of the affections, with the dictates of the understanding, and the government of the will, all in conformity with the wisdom, holiness, and purity of God. The less principal perfections of this image were: freedom from every taint of sin in the body, immunity from corrupting passions in the body, its immortality, and the full power of ruling all earthly creatures."

6. To a correct conception of original sin it presupposes correct views of *sin* in general, as having its proper cause in the finite will, not in the infinite will, and as embracing the *condition* of the finite will, as well as its *overt* acts.

The need of redemption rests upon the fall from God through sin. *Sin* is the transgression of the law, or rather, it is that which is not consonant with the law, it is the anti-legal, the unlegal, and the non-legal ; John iii. 4, ἀνομία. *Melanchthon* defines sin to be : " a defect, or inclination, or action, conflicting with the law of God." *Calovius* defines it still more compactly, but with the same sense, as : " Illegality, or deformity from the law: that is, the opposite to conform-

* "Solida Declaratio," p. 640.

ity with the law." Deformity, as here used, means a "*wan*
of conformity." *Müller*, in his great work on "The Christian
Doctrine of Sin," defines it to be a turning away from the love
of God to selfishness. In the Holy Scriptures, *sin* is considered
as enmity against God ; the carnal mind is enmity against God,
Rom. viii. 7. By the general consciousness of sin is derived
the general consciousness of the need of redemption. Gal. iii. 22.
It pertains to the very essence of religion, that *sin*, which is the
opposite of religion, takes its origin not from the Creator, but
from the creature; and however systems may have tended logically, actually to make God the author of sin, no system has unreservedly admitted such a conclusion. St. James says : "Let
no man, when he is tempted, say, 'I am tempted of God,' for
God is incapable of being tempted of evil, and he truly tempts
no one; but every man is tempted, when he is drawn away by
the desire, which is his own, that is, by his own lust." The argument of St. James is, that God's incapacity of being himself
tempted to sin, is evidence that he abhors it, and no being voluntarily causes that which he abhors. If God could be the
cause of sin in others, he would necessarily be the cause of it
in himself; in fact, to be the cause of sin in others is to be
sinful ourselves. If God be the cause of sin, he would himself
be a sinner; but as it is conceded that God is himself free from
sin, he cannot be its cause. Hence, the *Augsburg Confession*,
Art. XIX., says : "Although God creates and preserves nature, yet the cause of sin is the will of the evil, i. e. of the
Devil and of wicked men, which, God not assisting, turns itself
from God; as Christ says, John viii. 44, when he speaketh a
lie, he speaketh of himself." When the Confession says "*non
adjuvante Deo*," it does not mean that God does not assist in
the repression of this sin, and that consequently it takes place,
but means that God in no sense assists to the production of
sin; *that* proceeds from the will of the evil in its independent
self-moving power. The German expression parallel with this
is, that "the cause of sin is the will of the Devil and of all the
godless, which, so soon as God has taken away his hand, turns
itself from God to the evil." But, by "the hand of God"
here is not meant the moral power by which he sways the *will*

to good, but simply his repressive external power, and the meaning is, that the sinful will consummates itself in sinful act, wherever it is not repressed by the Providence of God. *Quenstedt* embodies the faith of our Church, when he says emphatically : " God is in no respect whatever the efficient *cause* of *sin* as such, neither in part, nor in the whole ; neither directly, nor indirectly ; neither *per se,* nor by accident ; neither in the species of Adam's fall, nor in the genus of sin of any kind. In no respect is God the cause or author of sin, or can be called such. See Ps. v. 5, ib. xlv. 12, Zach. viii. 17, 1 John i. 5, James i. 13–17. But, whatever there is of want of conformity with the law, ἀνομια, *that* is to be ascribed to the free will of the creature itself, acting of its own accord. See further, Hosea xiii. 9, Matt. xxiii. 37."

In regard to these passages, which speak of a hardening on the part of God, such as Exod. vii. 3, John vii. 10, Rom. ix. 18, *Hollazius* says : " God does not harden men causally, or effec- tively, by sending hardness into the hearts of men, but (*judi- cialiter,*) judicially, permissively, and desertively."

The standing sophism against just views of original sin is that nothing is sin except it be voluntary ; and that nothing is voluntary, unless it be done with a distinct consciousness and purpose of the will. But, over against this, the Scriptures and sound logic teach, that to a true conception of what is vol- untary, i. e. is of, or pertains to the will, belongs the state of the will previous to any act. Before there can be a voluntary act, there must be a state of the will which conditions that act. Original sin, therefore, is voluntary sin on this broader and more Scriptural conception of what is voluntary. The New England theology, in our country, has laid special stress upon the false conception of what is voluntary. The *Apol- ogy of the Augsburg Confession* says : " The adversaries (i. e. Pelagianizing Romanists,) contend that nothing is sin ex- cept it be voluntary. These expressions may hold good among philosophers, in judging of civil morals, but they have nothing to do with the judgment of God." *Hollazius* says : " The element of the voluntary does not enter into a definition of sin, generically considered. A sin is said to be voluntary, either *subjectively*, as it inheres in the will, or *efficiently*, as it results from the deliberate will. In this last respect, not all sin is voluntary. This is held over against the Papists and Socinians, who define sin exclusively as the voluntary transgression of the law."

7. It presupposes that from the original state of integrity there was a FALL OF MAN into a state of sin.

The original Fall of man from God resulted, according to The Fall of Gen. iii., from external temptation and inward Man. desire, leading to doubt of the Divine goodness, and transgression of the Divine command. The consequences of this Fall were: terror before the presence of God, not filial reverence, but servile fear; the expulsion from Paradise; the troubles of earthly life — temporal death only prevented by the mercy of God — from passing into eternal death.

The Fall of man is, throughout, presupposed as a fact, in the whole Biblical teaching in regard to original sin. Rationalism and Pseudophilosophism have treated it as a fable; an allegorical delineation of the passing away of the golden age, a myth of the transition from instinct to moral freedom, or of the pernicious result of longing after a higher condition. " Without the Fall," says Hegel, " Paradise would have been but a park for beasts." The literal historical sense of the narrative of the Fall is, nevertheless, the only one consistent with the obvious intent of the Holy Scriptures. There is nothing in the narrative unworthy of God, or out of keeping with the laws of the human soul. God gave the commandment, allowed the temptation, that, by it, man's natural holiness might be strengthened, if he *would*, by his free will. The serpent was but the organ of the Devil; the essence of the divine command lay in its setting forth love to God, and acquiescence to His will, as that which should be supreme in man. The transgression was an apostasy from this. The simpler the test, the clearer was its issue, the sublimer its moral meaning. The more insignificant the outward act, the more certain it is that the grandeur of the principle will not be confounded with the grandeur of the circumstances. The *principle* of the necessity of the absolute acquiescence of the will of the creatures in

the will of the Creator has none of the splendor of drapery in
Paradise that it has in the revolt of the angels in heaven, and
it stands out, for this reason, more nakedly, sharply, and legibly
in the history of the Fall of Adam, than in that of the fall of
Satan. The littleness of the spirit of sin may readily be forgotten in the dazzling array of its raiments, or in the baleful
dignity of its mischievous results.

Hollazius defines the first sin thus:—" The *first sin of man,
or Fall*, is the transgression of the law of Paradise, in which
our first parents violated the divine interdict which forbade them to eat the fruit of the ' tree of knowledge of
good and evil,' being persuaded thereto by the Devil, and
abusing the freedom of will, and thus brought on themselves, and on their posterity, born of them in the order
of nature, the loss of the divine image, grievous fault (culpam),
and liability (reatum) to temporal and eternal punishment. The
cause of the first sin is not God, but the Devil, who persuaded,
and man who transgressed the Divine law, being overcome by
the persuasion of the Devil, and abusing the freedom of the will.
Our first parents, in the Fall, directly violated a *positive law*, but
indirectly and virtually, by their disobedience, broke through
the restraints of the *whole moral law*. The Fall of Adam was
not *necessary* to manifest the justice and mercy of God."

" This deflection," says Quenstedt, " embraces in its course
certain distinct acts of sin, which may be classed as follows :
i. *Incredulity*, — not having faith in the word of God. ii. *Af-
fectation* of the likeness of God. iii. *A purpose* springing from
this transgression of the law. iv. A carrying out of this purpose into *action*." In the Fall of our first parents began original
sin. " It is called," says Quenstedt, " original sin, not because
it existed either from the beginning or origin of the world, or
of man, but partly, because it takes its origin in man, with the
origin of each man ; partly, because it is the fount and origin
of all actual sin." Tertullian probably first introduced the term.

A distinction is drawn between " peccatum originale origi-
nans," and " peccatum originale originatum." The latter is by
preëminence styled " original sin." Thus " original sin," if not
by imputation, yet by some form of association, passed over to

all the posterity of Adam and Eve. The *Formula Concordia* says : " The hereditary evil is that fault (culpa) or liability (rea tus) whereby it comes that we all, because of (propter) the disobedience of Adam and Eve, are under God's abhorrence, and are by nature children of wrath." * The *Apology* † says: " Some dispute that original sin is not a vice or corruption in the nature of man, but only a servitude or condition of mortality, which they, who are propagated from Adam, without vice of their own, but on account of another's fault, inherit. We, that we may show that this doctrine displeases us, make mention of concupiscence, and declare that a *corrupt nature is born.*" Whatever, therefore, may be the relation of imputation to original sin, our Church holds it to be an impious opinion, that our misery and liability are merely the results of imputation. The primary point is, that we do actually participate, in our nature, in the corruption wrought by the Fall. " Original sin is that vitiation of human nature arising from the fall of our first parents, accidental, (in the theological sense,) propagated by human conception, proper and real in all men, whereby they are destitute of the power of rightly knowing and worshipping God, and are constantly impelled to sin, and exposed to eternal death."

III. The Second Article of the Confession sets forth the ɣᵀᴹᴇ
Time. of the operation of original sin, to wit, *that of the whole period commencing with the Fall of Adam.*

This implies :—

1. That man was created holy. He had original righteousness Gen i. 26, " Let us make man in our image, after our likeness." In these words image is not one thing, and likeness another, but the *word likeness defines the word image.* An image may be like that of a mirror, a mere reflection ; but this image is one which makes real likeness or similitude. The grand element of the image of God in man, as created originally, is that which conforms him to what is most essentially Godlike in God ; that is, to His moral perfection, His holiness, purity, and truth. In a certain sense, the spirituality of man's nature, his immortality, his noble endowments of

---

* Page 639. p. 9. '   † P. 51. p. 9.

intellect, affection, and active power, and his place in creation, as lord and ruler of the world, are associated with and bound up with his bearing the image of God; hence, in Gen. i. 26, immediately after the words " *Let us make man,*" we have the words, "*Let him have dominion,*" where " dominion" is not identified with the " image," as some expositors would make it, but is dependent on the image and likeness, and is conditioned by it, for the ground of man's rule over the world is not his merely intellectual gifts, in which probably the devils, certainly the angels, surpass him, but the presumption and desire, on God's part, of his ruling it in righteousness and holiness. His intellectual powers are but the means by which his moral powers carry out their ends.

The image of God is, preëminently, then, man's original holiness; the conformity of his mind to the mind of God; of his will to the will of God; in short, whatever is most completely and sharply antithetical to original sin. Just what he lost by sin, is preëminently what he possessed most completely in the image of God, and in the original righteousness, which was its vital part. That man's moral nature is that which has suffered most in the Fall, that his intellectual abilities, and his power of outward rule over nature, are left in comparative strength, is evidence that it was in his moral nature he stood nearest to God. The more glorious the image, the completer was its wreck. That this judgment as to the image of God is correct, is shown by various passages of Scripture; as, Eccl. vii. 29; 2 Cor. iii. 18; Eph. iv. 24; Col. iii. 10.

2. That he lost this righteousness. From the exalted position nearest to God, he descended to the degradation of misery and sin. In short, as original righteousness made him like God in that which is most Godlike, so the Fall plunged him into that which, in its essence, is most remote from God. Now nothing is so completely in antagonism to God as sin. Ignorance is the counterpart to divine knowledge and wisdom; weakness to divine omnipotence; but *sin* is set against the very heart and moral glory of God. The ignorant and the weak may be children of God, and bear his image, but the sinful are sundered from Him by an impassable gulf; though

they had the knowledge of an archangel, and a might as near that of God as the creature's might can be, yet with sin, their image is that of the Devil, and not that of God.

3. That with this loss, originated human sin.

4. That man's nature thereby became a sinful one. Adam remained in the state to which the original or primary sin reduced him. All human nature at the time of the Fall was embraced in Adam and Eve; they were then the human race; they actually formed all human creatures; therefore of necessity, when Adam and Eve fell, all human nature, then existing, fell; all human creatures, actually existing, fell then as completely as if there had been millions instead of two; hence the human race and human nature fell.

5. Lastly, under this thesis is asserted that original sin has continued in the world from that hour to the present.

It is worthy of note that the Confession speaks of the Fall of *Adam* only ; Eve is not mentioned, though she was first in the transgression. Why at least is not the phrase, " Fall of our Why is Adam *first parents?* " In this the Confession strictly fol- alone mentioned? lows the line of Scripture representation : " By *one man* sin entered into the world, and death by sin ; and *so* death passed over upon all men." Rom. v. 12. In the Apostle's sense, sin did not enter into the *world* in Eve's transgression ; nor did death enter into the *world* by her sin ; at most, sin and death entered her. While she was yet alone in the transgression, sin had not yet entered the world, nor death by sin What had been possible for Adam, even as to the restoration of Eve, at this point, belongs perhaps to a sphere of speculation into which it is not wise to enter, but it is certain that the race yet stood in Adam. It was yet in his power to save mankind. The prohibition of the fruit of the tree of knowledge was given directly only to Adam, and took place before the creation of Eve, (Gen. ii. 17–21.) It bound the woman, not because God repeated it to her, but because she was, in the nature of the case, under the same law with her husband. After the Fall, God says to Adam : " Hast *thou* eaten of the tree whereof I commanded *thee* that *thou* shouldst not eat ?" — but to Eve, while His words imply her great guilt,

He speaks of no such direct command. Eve was not co-ordinate with Adam, but represented in him. She sinned, personally, in her own personal act, but, in the full sense, she *fell* only when Adam fell.

Adam's body was first formed — the entrance of the breath of God made man, body and soul. Eve was taken from Adam, but this was no new inbreathing from God. She was the emanation, so to speak, of the whole man — the effluence of his body and soul, and the life of the whole race is that one united life. Eve is called the *mother* of all living ; but Adam is the source of all living, including Eve. There is then but one human life in the world — perpetuated and extended through the generations — the emanation of the first life — that of Adam. Hence the race has not fallen in Eve as well as in Adam — because her life also was derivative. The one primal life derived from Adam brings with it the impress of Adam's fallen nature. Our nature is his very nature in emanation, as our life of body and soul is his life in emanation — and as the very life and nature are transmitted, so are the Fall and its penalty transmitted. Adam's life and nature is the *sine qua non* of our life and nature — Adam's sin the *sine qua non* of our sin.

IV. The Confession teaches that the persons affected by original sin are *all human beings* born in the course of nature.

This implies that, without exception, all the children of our race, alike all the children of the most holy and of the most godless, have original sin. The *character* of the parent may, within a certain limit, benefit or injure the innate tendencies to character in the child ; but character is not nature. All human beings have the same nature. In this nature original sin inheres, and all alike *inherit* it. With reference to this inherited character, it is sometimes called hereditary sin. In German its usual title is "Erbsünde."

In the doctrine that all men (omnes homines), born in the course of nature, have this sin, is implied the falseness of the Romish figment, in regard to the sinlessness of the mother of our Lord. It rejects the idea of the immaculate conception of Mary, which has been established in our own time as a doctrine of the Romish Church. The doctrine of the immaculate conception, to wit: that the Virgin Mary *was conceived and born* without sin, had been for centuries maintained by the Franciscans, and denied by the Dominicans, but was set forth authoritatively by Pius IX. in 1854, as a doctrine of the Catholic Church.* The birth of Mary was a human birth, and hence, hers was a nature with the taint of original sin.

In this thesis, moreover, is implied the freedom of our Lord from original sin, for his birth was not in the course of nature. He was conceived by the Holy Spirit (Apostles' Creed, Art. II.); He was incarnate by the Holy Spirit, of the Virgin Mary (Nicene Creed, Art. III.); and his birth was divine and supernatural.

And here, it is impossible not to be struck with the beautiful, Scripture-like reticence of our Confession, for while it most clearly either states or implies that original sin has been in the world since Adam's Fall; that without that Fall it would not have been; that our natural descent from him actually is accompanied, in every case, by the inheritance of the moral nature, into which, so to speak, he fell, it does not define *how*, THEORETICALLY, the sin of Adam is related to us; does not touch the question of imputation at all. The Augsburg Confession sets forth the chief Articles of Faith, the Faith of the Church universal, that is of the true Catholic Church, but the doctrine of *imputation*, AS A THEORY, belongs to scientific theology. The Augsburg Confession presents the whole question, only in its great practical elements, as these in some form or other are grasped by faith, and take part in the general belief of the Church.

We cannot recall a single passage, in any of our Confessions, in which the imputation of Adam's sin is alluded to, even in passing, as an Article of Faith. The Confessions say no more than that our fallen condition was "*through the disobedience of Adam*," or "*on account of it*," and expressly reject the idea that "*original sin is derived to us by imputation* only."† "We

---

* See Preuss on the "Immaculate Conception," which has been translated into English, and Pusey's Irenicon.

† Formula Concordiæ, 575

reject," says the Formula, "and condemn that doctrine which asserts that original sin is only a liability and debt derived to us, by the fault of another, without any corruption of our own nature." These expressions, however, do not exclude the doctrine of imputation in every shape. It is a question of theology, as distinguished from the sphere of faith proper, and to that it should be referred.

That all men are embraced in the operation of original sin, is clearly taught in the Holy Scriptures.

1. It is taught in direct and positive assertion of the universality of original sin. Rom. v. 12, " Wherefore, as by one man, sin entered into the world, and death by sin; and so death passed upon all men, for that all have sinned." Mark in the passage the sphere of original sin; the word " men," and the word "all," i. e. " all men." Death itself is declared to be the token and evidence, that all have sinned. The dominion of sin is as wide as the dominion of death, that is, it is universal. It shows that the operation is not limited to adults; and that there may be no mistake in regard to this, as if men might suppose that infants were regarded as exceptions, it says in verse 14, " death reigned . . . even over them that had not sinned after the similitude of Adam's transgression," i. e. over infants, who had not sinned by conscious acts of transgression, as Adam and Eve did; but, if infants come under it, *à fortiori* all others must. It adds in verse 15, "for if through the offence of one *the many* be dead," (Greek,) and in verse 18, " as by the offence of one, judgment came upon *all men* to condemnation," and in verse 19, " as by one man's disobedience, (the) *many* were made sinners."

2. In the specification of the classes embraced in this universal operation of original sin. Eph. ii. 3: " We all were by nature children of wrath, even as others." By " we all," is meant the Jewish Christians. " We Jews ' even as others,' " i. e. Gentiles. Jews and Gentiles embrace mankind, and if even the members of God's elect race are subject to this law, *à fortiori* the Gentiles would be, if there were any distinction.

3. In the Scriptural negation of any limitation of the uni-

versality of original sin. Job xiv. 4, "Who can bring a clean thing out of an unclean? not one."

4. In the exceptional character of Jesus Christ, as *alone* free from original, as well as actual sin, in which is implied that all but He are born in sin. "He knew no sin," 2 Cor. v. 21, was "without sin," Heb. iv. 15. "He was holy, harmless, undefiled, and separate from sinners," ib. vii. 26. In all this is implied more than our Saviour's freedom from acts of sin. To our Lord, and to Him alone belongs, among men, an untainted nature; to every other child of Adam pertains the curse of original sin. To the freedom of our Lord's nature from original sin, it was essential that his conception should be of the Holy Ghost, and his birth *out of* the course of nature. They who are not thus conceived and born must have the taint of original sin, that is, as the Confession affirms: The whole race, whose conception and birth are in the sphere of nature, are conceived and born in sin.

V. The next thesis of the Confession pertains to the MODE of perpetuation of original sin.

It connects *this* with the natural extension of our race. Not only are human beings born with it, but it originates with their natural life, and before their natural birth; and hence, with reference to each human being, it comes to be called "original sin." It is the sin which is so mysteriously original with man. Its origin, and our origin, are simultaneous. It is originated when man is originated, and because he is originated, and by his origination. Hence, the term *original*, which has been objected to in the statement of the doctrine, is more expressive and accurate than any that could be substituted for it. The great point in this thesis, is that sin passes into the life of the race, not by imitation, as the Pelagians contend, but by hereditary congenital transmission, and that this propagation is its natural source.

Over against the doctrine of Calvin and other speculators, who maintain that: " the progeny of Adam do not derive their corruption *naturally* from him, but that corruption depends upon the ordination of God," (see Calvin, on Gen. iii. 6,) the Augsburg Confession distinctly connects original sin with

.he natural process of descent, " *secundum naturam*," i. e. with natural propagation, and natural birth ; and such is the clear teaching of the Holy Scriptures. Ps. li. 5, " Behold! I was shapen in iniquity." See Gen. v. 1 & 3 : in the first verse we have, " in the likeness of God made he him ; " and in the third verse this *antithesis*, " and Adam begat a son, after his image." So our Lord Jesus says, (John iii. 6,) " That which is *born* of the flesh is flesh, and that which is born of the spirit is spirit." Eph. ii. 3, " We all were by *nature* children of wrath," that is, as Tyndale, Cranmer, and others say, " were natural children of wrath." The sin of Adam is so related to the condition of the race, that by and because of our natural descent from him, sin and its penalty passes over to us. Rom. v. 12, " By *one* man sin *entered* the world."

VI. Next the great fact is asserted, That all human beings are conceived and born in sin and with sin, — " Nascantur cum peccato," "In Sünden empfangen und geboren werden." ^{Fact.}

This fact can be mentally separated from the particular theory upon which it rests. Even Pagans have acknowledged the fact. And those whose theory seemed irreconcilable with it, and those who have even denied it in downright terms, have been forced virtually to concede it. All the refinement in terms, in philosophy, in the mode of statement or of argument, has not been able to conceal the fact, that *in*, *with*, and *under* our human nature, there lies something evil ; foreign to the original condition of man ; foreign to the divine ideal, and *to man's own better ideal;* something derived from parent to child, producing misery, death, and despair ; something that is the power of all sinful results, and the seed of all sinful growths.

The Scripture testimony to this great fact is very explicit. Gen. viii. 21, " The imagination of man's heart is evil from his youth," i. e. inclusively in his youth and ever after. Gen. vi. 5, " God saw that the wickedness of man," etc., " *was only evil continually.*" (Heb. lit. " *evil all the day ;* " margin —" The whole imagination.") The Hebrew word signifies not only the imagination, but also the PURPOSES AND DESIRES.

The actual condition of the race is depicted in the 14th Ps.,

25

vs. 1, 2, 3, " They are corrupt, they have done abominable works, there is none that doeth good," (an absolute negation.) " The Lord looked down from heaven upon the children of men, to see if there were any that did understand, and seek God. They are ALL gone aside, they are altogether become filthy, there is NONE that doeth good, NO NOT ONE." St. Paul quotes these words as of universal application, covering Jews as well as Gentiles, and although the Psalmist makes exception of God's people, yet the exceptions are made by grace, and do but confirm the rule. So in Job xv. 14, " What is man that he should be clean ? and he which is born of a woman, that he should be righteous." So Jer. xvii. 9, " The heart is deceitful above all things, and desperately wicked ; who can know it ? '

An absolute identity of result in all men in FACT implies the existence of a common cause of that result. If all men, always from earliest infancy to extremest old age, everywhere, under all diversities of race, education, and outward circumstances, in short, of everything in which they can differ, are sinful, then must the root of sin be, not in any one thing, nor in all things in which they differ, but in the thing or things which they have in common. But the sole things which men have in common, are their human nature, and their common original inborn moral condition. In one of these must lie the spring of universal sinfulness; but it cannot lie in their nature as such ; for nature as such is the work of God, and cannot therefore be sinful. Sin is the perversion of nature, the uncreating, as it were, of what God has created, a marring of His work. It must lie then in man's moral *condition*, as *fallen* and *inheriting* original sin. The great acknowledged *facts* in the case then are logically and necessarily connected with the theory of original sin which is maintained in the Confession.

VII. The *results* or revelations of the workings of this original sin are, *first*, privative or negative, and *second*, positive.

Seventh Thesis. i: *Privative* or negative showing itself in what we The results. have lost ; we are *without* fear, *without* trust, " sine metu, sine fiducia." ii : *Positive* in what we have, " cum concupiscentia, *with* concupiscence."

i: 1. *Privatively or negatively* original sin shows itself, first

in this, that all human beings are born without the *fear* of God.
Conf. "Sine metu Dei;" "Keine wahre Gottesfurcht haben."
This means not only that an infant does not and cannot consciously fear God, but that there is in it a lack of anything
which can potentially, or through any process of self-develop-
ment or of natural education, exercise *such a fear of God* as He
demands of the creature. We can by nature have a false fear,
or an instinctive fear of God, but not a true fear, hence the
emphasis of the German of the Confession, "Keine *wahre*,"
"no *true* fear."

2. A second element of the *privative result* is, that they are
born without *trust* in God, without *faith* in Him or *love* for Him.
In the fear of God there is a just contemplation of His natural
attributes, and that reverential awe which inspires the spirit of
obedience. In trust, faith, and love, there is a contemplation
of His moral attributes, drawing the heart to Him. Neither
our just fears, nor our just hopes toward God, are left untouched by original sin. Conf., "Sine fiducia erga Deum;"
"Keinen wahren Glauben an Gott, keine wahre Gottesliebe."

There is innate in a child, before conscious exercise, a potential, true trust, faith, and love, toward its mother, and that trust
unfolds itself out of the potential into the actual. Before a
child's first act of love toward its mother, there must be a
power of loving, and that power of loving must exercise itself.
There must be something in a child that *can* love before it *does*
love, and that something is born with the child. In other
words, a child may be said, with reference to this innate power,
to be born with trust toward its mother. But it lacks in its
nature that which would enable it to exercise a true trust in
God, such as He demands. Man may by nature have a false
trust in God, or an intellectual and natural trust, but not that
higher and true trust which is in perfect keeping with God's
nature and His holy law. In order to this, grace must impart
something with which we are not born.

The Roman Catholic theologians, in their confutation of the
Augsburg Confession, say that the statement in this article in
regard to original sin is to be utterly rejected, since it is mani
fest to every Christian that to be without the fear of God, and

without trust toward God, is rather the actual fault of the adult than the fault of a new-born infant, which is destitute of the use of reason, as the Lord says to Moses, Deut. i. 39, " Your children, which in that day had no knowledge between good and evil." Melanchthon, in the Apology, replied by referring to the German form of the Confession, which brings out more clearly than does the Latin, that it is not the act, but the power of fearing God and trusting in Him, which is referred to, or as Melanchthon expresses it, not the act only, but the gift and power of doing these things. The Apology is the best commentary on the disputed parts of the Augsburg Confession, as well as an able defence of them.

ii. The *positive* result is that they are born with *concupiscence*, that is, that from their birth they are all full of evil desire and evil propensity. The Confession says, " Et cum concupiscentia." German: " Dass sie alle von Mutterleibe an voller böser Lust und Neigung sind." The term concupiscence is a New Test. term, Rom. vii. 7, 8, " I had not known *lust* (margin, ' or concupiscence')" etc., " wrought in me all manner of *concupiscence*." So Col. iii. 5, " Mortify therefore your members which are upon the earth ; fornication, uncleanness, inordinate affection, *evil concupiscence*, and covetousness, which is idolatry." 1. Thess. iv. 5, " Not in the lust of *concupiscence*." The Greek word which it translates, and which is used in a number of places where it is not translated concupiscence, has the general meaning of earnest and intense desire. Thus our Saviour, Luke xxii. 15, says, " With desire (epithumia) I have desired (epithumeo) to eat this passover with you before I suffer." St. Paul says, (Phil. i. 23,) " Having a *desire* (epithumia) to depart ; " 1 Thess. ii. 17, " Endeavoured with great *desire*." These are the only cases, three out of thirty-seven, in which the word epithumia is used without implying something inordinate and sinful. The natural epithumia of an unsanctified nature is always inordinate, carnal, sensual, impure : it is desire, lust, concupiscence. The word is also applied by metonymy to objects which kindle such desires. Every epithumia except that of our Lord, and of the natures conformed to His nature, is represented as sinful. In the passage in Romans vii. 7, 8, concupiscence is represented as the motive power in covetousness. In Col. iii. 5, it is distinguished from inordinate affection and covetousness, to which it is related as the root to the tree, or as the trunk to the branches. In 1 Thess. iv. 5, the "lust of concupiscence" is mentioned, that is, the lust or positive desire generated by the evil propensity inherent in our own nature; that is, the actual evil desire by the original evil desire, or concupiscence; sin by sin; sin the offspring by sin the parent, the actual sin of our character be.ng related to the original sin of our nature, as child to mother. The Pelagianizing Romanist says, Lust, or concupiscence, brings forth sin, therefore it cannot be sin, because the mother cannot be the child. We reply, Concupiscence brings forth sin, therefore it must be sin, because child and mother must have the same nature. The grand sophism of Pelagianism is the assumption that sin is confined to acts, that guilty *acts* can be the product of innocent *condition*, that the *effect* can be sinful, yet the *cause* free from sin — that the unclean can be brought forth from the clean.

The word concupiscence, therefore, as the representative of epithumia in its evil sense, very properly designates that moral *condition* which is antecedent to positive and conscious moral acts. It is the first phenomenon of personality in morals, and no better practical definition can be given of it, than the simple one of our Confession. It is " evil desire" and "evil propensity," " böse Lust und Neigung."

The grand idea here lies in this, that sin is in us *potentially* before it comes to the act; *that the moral nature of the infant is born with it*, and does not originate in, nor date its origin from, any conscious movement of the infant's will, any purpose of its heart, any act of its hands; but that, on the contrary, the general character of that movement, purpose, and act of will, heart, and hand, *apart from Divine grace*, is inevitably conditioned as *actually sinful*, and that this *actual sinfulness* is merely on the one side the result and token of a defect, and on the other the positive exhibition of an evil tendency already in being, from the time of the origin of the human nature of the child. Hence, in a new sense, this sin may be called original. It is that in which all other sins in some sense take their origin. It throws its life into them; without it they might not be; it is not only original, it is also the originating sin, or that sin which gives the original to all others.

Negatively, then, original sin is the lack of original right-eousness, that is, of the righteousness which man originally had as God's creature, bearing His image, and is the perpet uation morally of original unrighteousness, that is, of the non-righteousness which fallen man, as fallen, originally had. *Positively*, original sin is evil desire and propensity, first exist-ing potentially and seminally, so to speak, the power of all sinful results, and the seed of all sinful growths; and then re-vealing itself invariably and necessarily in conscious and actual sin, if not checked by the Spirit of God.

iii. As we *have* by nature no true fear of God, no true love of God, no true faith in God, so neither can we *get* them by nature. Conf., "Keinen von Natur haben können." Original sin is not only retrospective, looking back to the origin of our race, but it is prospective, covering the future as it covers the past, a pall upon the face of the nations. In the sphere of nature it renders our condition utterly hopeless. A man may by nature have a weak body, a feeble constitution, an imperfection of speech, but in nature he may find relief for them all. Strength may come by natural exercise, flu-ency by repeated efforts, but there is no power in man, in his reason or in his will, none in education, none in the whole store of the visible, or intellectual, or moral world, which can repair this fatal defect, and render him God's reverent, loving, and trusting child. There is no surf-beaten shore on which man may go forth and train himself amid its thunders and its whispers, to speak in true faith and love into the ear of God words which may remove His righteous disapproval of our sinful and sinning nature. In other words, in the sphere of nature, original sin leaves us in utter and hopeless ruin. Without faith it is impossible to please God; without holiness no man shall see the Lord; and by nature we are destitute of faith and holiness potentially. In our conscious, moral life there can be no development of them actually. We neither have, nor can have them, unless something not of us, nor of nature, supervenes. " The natural man receiveth not the things of the Spirit of God ; for they are foolishness unto Him : neither can he know them, because they are spiritually discerned." 1 Cor. ii. 14.

VIII. The essence of original sin involves that this disease or vice of origin is truly sin. Conf. Latin : " Quodque hic morbus seu vitium originis vere sit peccatum." German: " Dass auch dieselbige angeborene Seuche und Erbsünde wahrhaftiglich Sünde sei." Eighth Thesis. Original Sin is truly sin.

The application of a particular name to a thing raises the question, *first*, whether that name has more than one sense, and *secondly*, if it have, in what sense it is applied in the particular case under consideration. Is the name to be taken literally or figuratively ? On the names by which original sin is designated in the Confession.

The following names are applied to original sin in the Augsburg Confession : In the Latin, " *vitium, morbus, peccatum*" ; in the German, " *Seuche* " and "*Sünde.*" As these names have been most carefully employed, we must weigh them to realize their full force, and to reach with precision the doctrine which they are designed to convey.

These terms may be classified thus:

1. The terms that are used metaphorically, or by adaptation. 2. The terms used literally. To the first of these belong " vitium," and " morbus," and " Seuche"; to the second, " peccatum" and " Sünde."

I. Morbus. The word " morbus" is nowhere used in the Vulgate. The word used where we might anticipate " morbus" is usually " languor," and sometimes " ægritudo." Morbus is defined by lexicographers as a " sickness, disease, evil affection of body contrary to nature." Original Sin as " morbus " is, in general, sickness in spirit, analogous to disease in body. The metaphorical transfer is very easy and obvious. The Confession does not at all mean that original sin is literally a sickness or morbus. The Apology,* with just severity, characterizes the scholastic absurdities : " Of the fomenting inclination (fomes) — they maintain that it is a quality of body,

* 79, 7.

and inquire whether it came by contagion of the apple, or from the breath of the serpent? and whether medicines make it worse?"

II. VITIUM. The word vitium is used in the Vulgate five times. It has the sense, "fault" of a bodily kind, even in animals; "moral fault, vice," as in Job xx. 11: "Sin of his youth." Vulgate, "vices of his youth." Gal. v. 24: "The flesh with the affections (margin 'or passions') and lusts." Rheims' transl. of Vulg., "vices and concupiscences." With the Vulgate agrees in general the classic usage of the word vitium.

III. THE DISTINCTION BETWEEN MORBUS AND VITIUM. The use of these two words in the Confession is not tautological, but in the highest degree delicate and discriminating. They are not synonyms, but are used not only to convey a different idea, but with a certain degree of antithesis. Cicero, in the Tusculan Questions, Book 4, says, "Morbus is the corruption of the whole body, such as is fever for example; vitium is when the parts of the body are at variance among themselves, from which results pravity of the members, distortion, deformity." So Nonius says, "Vitium is an abiding impediment of the body, such as blindness, lameness, unsoundness."

Morbus in German would be "Krankheit." *Vitium* would be "Fehler." The one term may be said to be derived from *medicine*, the other from *surgery*.

Morbus, in a theological sense, is moral sickness, disease, or plague; vitium is moral vice, fault, or defect, maiming, mutilation, or distortion.

IV. THERE IS A CORRESPONDENCE therefore between the two names vitium and morbus, and the two parts of the definition of original sin: *a.* VITIUM corresponds with the negative part of the definition. Original sin as a defect of original righteousness, the mutilation of the moral man, the lack of something essential to his moral perfection, is vitium. *b.* MORBUS corresponds with the positive part of the definition. Original sin as the presence of a corrupting element infecting the moral man, the indwelling of a pervading and positive evil added to his constitution, is morbus.

In a word, the vitium takes away the good, the morbus

brings in the bad. The vitium is the lack of the true fear and trust, the morbus is the concupiscence.

V. Seuche. The word Seuche does not translate either morbus or vitium. Its Latin equivalent would be " lues," and it is one of the most generic words in German to express sickness. Its proper English equivalent is plague, and it is related to pestilence and to disease as genus is related to species. Luther uses the word "Seuche" thirteen times in the New Testament. Once he translates by it the word *noseema*, in John v. 4, the only place at which it occurs. In the twelve other cases he uses it to translate " nosos," which is the synonym of " noseema," and is translated in the authorized version by the word " sickness" five times, " disease" six times, "infirmity" once. In the New Testament the word " nosos " is used literally for bodily disease, except, perhaps, in Matt. viii. 17, " He bare our sicknesses," where it has been taken, though without necessity, metaphorically for pain, sorrow, evil of a spiritual kind. In the Old Testament, Luther uses "Seuche," first, to translate " Madveh," in the only two places in which that word occurs, Deut. vii. 15, and xxviii. 60, where it means literally " disease," and in the first of which the Septuagint renders it " nosos." Secondly, Luther uses it to translate "Quehtev," Psalm cli. 6. Authorized Version, " the destruction which wasteth at noon-day," but Coverdale, Cranmer, and the Liturgy Version of the Church of England, following Luther, translate it " sickness," and the Genevan, and, among recent translators, Noyes, " plague," and Ainsworth, "stinging *plague.*"

The metaphorical idea of sickness is found in the Old Testament, as Hosea, v. 13, "Ephraim saw his sickness," i. e. his political weakness and wretchedness. Psalm ciii. 3, " Who healeth all thy diseases," seems to be used metaphorically for spiritual disorders in accordance with the parallelism of the first part, " Who forgiveth all thine iniquities." So Psalm xli. 4, " Heal my soul ; for I have sinned against thee." There sin is represented as the disease of the soul, God as a physician, grace as healing. The word " holiness" is only another way of pronouncing the word " wholeness." So Isa. vi. 10, " And convert and be healed," that is, be healed of sin, which is the disease of the soul. The Chaldee Paraphrase and the Syriac render: " and be *forgiven.*"

The metaphorical transfer of the idea of disease and fault to express moral condition is so obvious, that we find it in all cultivated languages. Cicero says, " As in the body there is disease, sickness, and fault, so is there in the soul."

We have this triple parallel therefore:

body,	health,	sickness
mind,	sanity,	insanity,
spirit,	holiness,	sin.

The analogies between MORBUS, disease and sin are very many

Analogies between Morbus and Original Sin. 1. Morbus is in conflict with the original perfection of body with which man was created, the original rightness or wholeness of body.

2. Morbus is a potency before it is revealed as a fact.

3. Morbus in its tendency is toward death. The slightest morbus developed to the last degree would destroy the body. There is no morbus so slight that it has not brought death. Strike out two letters, and morbus, " disease," becomes mors, " death."

4 Morbus is common to the whole race. Cicero, in the Tusculan Questions, 325, translates from Euripides this sentence, " Mortalis nemo est quem non attingit dolor morbusque," " There is not one of our race untouched by pain and disease."

5. Morbus is the spring of pain, grief, and misery to the body.

6. Morbus rests on an inborn tendency of the body. It could not touch the body of a sinless being without his permission. Our Lord Jesus Christ could only endure it by the act of His own will.

7. Morbus is primarily in the world, not because we sinned, but because Adam sinned ; he is the spring of original morbus, as he is of original peccatum.

8. Morbus depraves and corrupts the substance of the body, but is not itself substance ; it is not a creature of God, but a defect in, and vitiation of, that which He created. The body is His work, morbus the result of sin.

9. Morbus is negatively the antithesis to health, the absence of health ; and secondly, in consequence of that lack, that which was originally useful and pleasant becomes morbid and works misery. Take, for example, a healthy tooth ; everything in it is meant for use, and is promotive of comfort. Take away its healthy state, and although no new thing is created, there is misery and uselessness in place of its former healthy condition ; there is positive pain there.

10. Morbus is real morbus, vere morbus, before it comes to symptom. A man *is* sick before he *shows* himself sick, and he shows himself sick because he is sick. He may be sick for a time, and neither he nor others be aware of it. The symptom is not the morbus, nor the cause of it, but the result, the effect, the revelation of the morbus. The fever is before the fever-heat ; the small-pox before the pustule ; the obstruction of the pores before the cough ; there is morbus originis in the body before there is morbus manifestus in it.

11. Morbus may be wholly independent of any act of ours. We may have morbus because our neighbor has it. A child may have it because the father has it, or the father may con-tract it from the child. One has typhoid-fever or small-pox, and another takes it from him. There is endemic morbus, epi demic morbus, contagious morbus, infectious morbus. With the mystery of disease staring us in the face in the physical world, it becomes us to l e humble and reverent in regard to God's teachings in reference to the mystery of His permission of hereditary sin in the moral world.

12. Morbus, not only as a generic tendency, but in specific shape, may be hereditary. There is an Erb-seuche as well as an Erbsünde. When the skeptic shall thoroughly sound the mystery of that arrangement of Providence by which the child of consumptive parents may be born not only with a tendency to consumption, but with actual consumption, then may he with more show of reason ask us to sound for him the fathom-less depths of the Divine permission of hereditary sin in our world.

13. Morbus in some forms defies all the curative powers of nature and of art. Men will be so sick as to die, despite all

original energies of the constitution, all medicines, and all physicians.

14. Whatever be the philosophy of morbus, the great facts are indisputable. Men may wrangle as to how and why it is, but they cannot deny that it is. They may believe that they relieve difficulties by abandoning the old phraseology and coining new; but all the resources of language leave the facts and the difficulties substantially where they were. The medical theorists have new names, new theories, new medicines, but men have continued to die, and will continue to die. The theological charlatan may try a new nomenclature, and assail with sugar- and rose-water what the old doctors treated with the most potent medicines, but sin will reveal itself in the world with the old signs of virulence, and, trifled with, will work death.

15. He who has false views of morbus, is not likely to obtain a thorough cure of it. His determination to call a plague-boil a pimple, will not make it a pimple; tubercular consumption is not a trifling cough, nor a cancer a corn, because men may think them such. We can neither think facts out of being, nor into being.

16. Morbus is ordinarily relieved by means. Sickness can not heal itself, nor is it ordinarily healed by miracle.

17. The wrong remedy will not cure morbus, however sincere the misguided physician may be in recommending it, and the deluded patient in using it. It is the dream of a Rationalism close upon Deism, that error is practically as good as truth, if a man heartily believes it to be the truth; that you can substitute arsenic for salt with safety, if you believe it to be salt. The kingdom of nature and of grace are both under law. Things will be done after God's ordinance, or they will not be done at all.

Analogies between Vitium and Original Sin. The analogies between Vitium and Original Sin are also many and obvious.

1. Vitium is universal. Every body has some defect. Thrasea (Pliny's Epistles 8, 22,) was wont to say, " Qui vitia odit, homines odit," " Who hates faults, hates all mankind."

2. Vitium in some of its forms is, as Nonius says, " perpetua et insanabilis atque irrevocabilis causa," " a cause which works always, beyond healing and beyond revoke."

3, and last. Vitium is privative, yet the privation is productive of positive misery. Blindness is not a thing, but the want of a thing. When the first blindness took place, there was no creation of blindness, but the mere privation of that light which was given in the first creation : The absence of an arm is not a thing, but the defect of a thing ; God did not create blindness or armlessness, nor does a man become a creator by making himself or his child armless or sightless. These conditions are in themselves but negations, yet what positive ill results from these negations. The ignorance of the blind, the helplessness of the maimed, result from these privative vitia. Though blindness be, *per se*, not something, but nothing, though the want of an arm be nothing, the deep grief is that where something should be there is nothing. The sophistry, therefore, that mere negation, mere defect, is inoperative, is exposed even by nature, for lack of operation is often the greatest of ills, and to say that because original sin is not substance or essence there can be no result from it, is in the last degree shallow and false. This point has been felicitously stated by Melanchthon : " It is useful to mark clearly the difference between the things created by God, and sin, which is the disturbance or confusion of the divine order : hence it is rightly said, Sin is a defect or privation... And here lies the answer to the sophistical question, Inasmuch as a defect is nothing, that is, is not a positive thing, how can God be angry at nothing ? The answer is, there is a broad distinction between *nothing privative* and *nothing negative*. For *nothing* taken in the *privative* sense requires a *subject*, and is a certain *destruction* in that subject, on account of which that subject is rejected, as the ruins of an edifice are a destruction or scattering of parts in the mass. Thus Original Sin is a defilement and confusion of the parts of man, and God hates it, and on account of it is angered at the subject. In disease *nothing* has the sense of *privation*, inasmuch as the *subject* remains, and disease is a certain disturbance in the subject. The wounded man looks upon his wound sorrowfully, and knows that the wound is not *nothing negatively*, but that the parts are torn. Thus Paul grieved when he saw the crimes of Nero, for he knew that they were not *nothing negatively*, but the awful ruins of the work of God." *

The Thesis on the introductory terms to which we have been dwelling, asserts that this disease or fault of origin, this inborn plague and hereditary sin is *truly* and *really* sin. The *verè* and *wahrhaftiglich* are opposed :

1. To the false, incorrect, or fictitious ;

2. To the verbal.

To the 1st they are opposed, as the true; to the 2d, as the real. When we affirm that original sin is truly and really sin, we affirm the doctrine of the Church :

1. Against those who deny that human nature is in any respect different from the condition in which it was at its origin ; who deny that original sin exists.

2. Over against those who concede that there is a real defect in human nature since the Fall, but who deny that this defect is sin.

3. Over against those who concede that original sin is, in some sense, sin, but who, either in terms, or virtually, deny that it is truly and really sin. Over against these is affirmed :

1. The true and real existence of original sin.

2. The true and real sinfulness of its character.

The doctrine is asserted against its deniers, and defined against its corrupters.

Of original sin we say :

1. It is; 2. It is sin; 3. It is truly and really sin.

In these words lies a grand distinctive feature of the doctrine of the Church, as opposed to the Pelagians or Pelagianizing tendencies of a large part of the Roman communion, and of Zwingli, as well as by anticipation of more recent heresies. In these words is the very heart of just views of original sin :

We argue that ORIGINAL SIN IS TRULY SIN :

1. Because it has the *relations* and *connections* of sin.

---

* Loc. Theolog. ed. 1545. Opera. Witteburg. 1580. Fol. vol. i. 163. Chemnitii Loc. Theol. 1653. Fol. i. 128. Corp. Reformator. xxi, 646. This striking distinction is not drawn in any of the earlier editions of the Loci.

2. It has the *name* and *synonyms* of sin.

3. It has the *essence* of sin.

4. It has the *attributes* of sin.

5. It does the *acts* of sin.

6. It incurs the *penalties* of sin.

7. It needs the *remedies* of sin.

8. Consequently, and finally, it is conformed to a true *defini-*
n. *n* of sin.

1. We argue that original sin is truly sin because its
RELATIONS and CONNECTIONS are those of sin. One _{1. The relations}
of our great old divines* adopting a distinction _{and connections.}
made by Bonaventura, says, "Sin is wrought in three ways:

"When person corrupts nature, as was done by Adam and
Eve."—Two persons corrupted their own nature, and all human
nature with it.

"When nature corrupts persons, as in the propagation of
original sin."—The nature of the parents corrupts the child
who is born of them.

"When person corrupts person, as in actual sin."—The influence of one person over another by example, by corrupting
words, and other ways, leads man into acts of sin.

"At the beginning, actual sin took the precedence, and
original sin followed it; now, original sin takes the precedence,
and actual sin follows it." As original sin, however, is presupposed as the internal force which opens itself in actual sin,
its relations are very direct, even with the forms of origin
which can in any sense, though but ideally, be separated from
its own. It is begotten of sin, and hence is of necessity of the
nature of its parent, and therefore truly sin. It is the begetter
of sin, and hence is of the nature of its child, and therefore
truly sin, for in nothing can a thing be more truly this or that,
than in its nature. It is the true child of true sin; the true
parent of true sin, and hence is itself true sin. Alike then in
the relations and connections of its Genesis and of its Revelation, original sin is truly sin.

2. Original sin, we argue further, is truly sin, because it has
the NAME and SYNONYMS of sin. It receives the names and syn-

---

* Quenstedt, Theologia Dogmatico-Polemica, I Vol. col. 914.

onyms of sin in the Word of God. Psalms li. 5, " In *sin* diα my mother conceive me," where David speaks not of the sin of his mother, but of a sin pertaining to himself, and regards his moral condition, which he calls sin, as antecedent to his birth — and as beginning with the beginning of his being.* So the German of the Confession: "In Sünden *empfangen*." Rom. v. 12, "By one man sin entered into the world, and death by sin, and so death passed upon all men for that all have sinned." Here the generic moral state of all of our race is considered as sin. "Sin dwelleth in me." "In me, that is in my flesh, dwelleth no good thing." "The law of *sin* which is in my members." " Let not *sin* reign in your mortal body." Psalm li. 5, " I was shapen in *iniquity.*" John iii. 6, "That which is born of the flesh is *flesh.*" In these passages original sin is called " sin," " iniquity," and the " flesh."

2. The name and synonyms.

In the phraseology of the early Christian writers, of the Reformers, of the Confessions of all pure Churches, of the profoundest later theologians, as well as of private Christians, the names and synonyms of sin are confessedly applied to original sin.

When men profess to believe in the reality of that which is called original sin, yet object to the term, they have failed to find or invent another term as expressive and less open to objection. In the very act of opposing the doctrine that original sin is truly sin, they drift into the use of terms whose natural force involves that it is truly sin. If a general consciousness ever embodied itself in the unhesitating application of a term, then does the name of original sin prove that it is truly sin.

3. It has the *essence* of sin, which is deviation from the will of God. In physical, irrational, or non-moral nature, as such, there can be no deviation from the will of God. To deviate from His will, personal will is necessary. Hence all deviation from God's will is sin, and all sin is deviation from His will. When matter is said to be perverted from its right use by the corrupt will, it is still true that, as matter, it obeys the law under which God has placed it. Fire is not

3. The essence.

* The Chaldee paraphrase renders Yahham by a yet more radical term : impræguat a est.

deviating from the will of God in burning, though it surrouun ls and consumes the body of Huss. All the deviation from God's will, and all the sin, is in the will of devils and men, which has brought the martyr to the stake. Whatever is not in accordance with His will, has in it the essence of sin. But not only conscious sins, but that condition of nature also in which they originate, is the result, not of God's will, but of the abuse of the will of the creature. Whatever exists of which God cannot be said to be the author, is sinful. But God is not the author either of the fall of Satan, the temptation and lapse of Adam, the corruption of his nature, or of the consequent defect of righteousness, and the evil desire inherited in human nature. Hence all of these have in them the essence of sin.

We ask, is the moral condition in which man is born in conformity with the will of God, or in conflict with it? If it be in conformity with it, it is not depravity — it is a good thing. If it is a deviation from it, it is not depravity merely, but truly sin. There is no logical consistency at any point between the extremest Pelagianism and the strictest adhesion to the faith of the Church on this point.

Not only, however, is original sin essentially sin, but it is such preëminently. It might be questioned whether a seed is essentially vegetable, because in it, undeveloped, none of the obvious distinctive characteristics of vegetation meet the eye; so that a grain of mustard-seed might be mistaken for a grain of sand, and a skilful imitation of an acorn actually be regarded as an acorn. But the answer could be truly made that not only is the seed vegetable in its essence, but preëminently so, as it is the necessary presupposition to all other veg etable existence; enfolds in it all vegetable capacity; determines all vegetable character. The nature of its potencies makes the vegetable world.

And thus in the infant the dim traces of moral character can be easily overlooked. Sceptical sciolism may maintain that there is nothing discernible in an infant which marks it, any more than a kitten or a lamb, as a personal and moral agent; nevertheless, it has a moral *nature*, which is to reveal itself in moral *character*. That moral nature is marked by a defect and

26

an evil propension which will affect the whole of its spiritual life, and that defect and propension have in them the essential element of sin ; they are not in conformity with the will of God.

This inborn something, which is not in conformity with the will of God, is related to temptation, incitement, and the power of example, as the seed is related to the soil, the dew and the sunshine which evolve it into germ, tree, flower, and fruit. It may be affirmed of the kingdom of darkness, which has its parallels so often in the kingdom of God, that its course also is, first the blade, then the ear, then the full corn in the ear.

The question here, to give it shape from our figure, is not, " Is a seed truly a tree ?" but, " Is it truly vegetable ? " " Has it really the same nature as the tree ? " And the reply is, It has. Nay, rather the tree is but a phenomenon of the seed ; it is itself the parent seed developed, and its own perfect potency ends in a seed. If the first seed that ever ripened was a phenomenon of the first tree, this was because the first tree was a direct creation, not a mediate growth; but under the law of mediate growth, the seed is the proper presupposition of the tree — the condition of its nature. On the vegetable seed depends the vegetable nature. If you may call a seed yet un-grown truly vegetable, then you may call the seminal sin yet ungrown truly sin. Original sin, therefore, has not only the essence of sin, but it has that essence by preëminence. Nay, it may be said to be that essence, and relatively to it all other sins may be said to be in some sense phenomenal, deriva-tive, and dependent. There is an important sense, therefore, in which even beyond the sins of act, original sin may be affirmed to be truly sin. It is not *a* sin, it is sin.

4. We argue that original sin is truly sin because it has the ATTRIBUTES of sin.

Is sin EVIL? so is original sin. "God saw that every 4. The attri- imagination of the thoughts of man's heart was butes of sin. only *evil* continually." Gen. vi. 5.

Is sin UNCLEAN? so is original sin. " Who can bring a clean thing out of an *unclean ?* not one." Job xiv. 4. " What is man, that he should be clean? and he which is born of a woman, that he should be righteous?" Job xv. 14.

Is sin ABOMINABLE and LOATHSOME? so is original sin. "The heavens are not clean in His (God's) sight. How much more abominable and filthy is man, which drinketh iniquity like water." Job xv. 15, 16.

Is sin UNRIGHTEOUS? so is original sin. "What is he which is born of a woman, that he should be righteous?" Job xv. 14.

Is sin IMPURE? so is original sin. "The stars are not pure in His (God's) sight, how much less man, that is a worm." Job xxv. 4. Here the contrast is between the highest purity imaged in the stars, and the deepest corruption embodied in man, who, not in physical characteristics, nor in intellect, but in moral nature, is a worm before the judgment of God—"man," paraphrases the Targum, "in life a reptile, in death a worm."

5. We argue that original sin is truly sin, because it does the ACTS of sin.

"When we were in the flesh" ("that which is born of the flesh is flesh"), "the *motions of sin* which were by the law, did *work* in our members to *bring forth fruit* unto death." Rom. vii. 5. "So then with the mind I myself *serve* the law of God; but with the flesh, the law of sin." Rom. vii. 25. "The flesh *lusteth* against the spirit." Gal. v. 17. "Now the *works* of the flesh are manifest, which are these: Adultery, fornication, uncleanness, lasciviousness, idolatry, witchcraft, hatred, variance, emulations, wrath, strife, seditions, heresies, envyings, murders, drunkenness, revellings, and such like." Gal. v. 19–21. The works of the flesh are not works done in the flesh, that is in the body, but works wrought *by* the flesh, that is by the corrupt nature characteristic of all that are born of the flesh. "The carnal mind is enmity against God, for it is not subject to the law of God, neither indeed can be." Rom. viii. 7. "If I *do* that I would not, it is no more I that *do* it, but sin that dwelleth in me." Rom. vii. 20. "I see another law in my members, *warring* against the law of my mind, and bringing me into captivity to the law of sin which is in my members." Rom. vii. 23. "The spirit that dwelleth in us lusteth to envy." "Let not sin reign in your mortal body, that ye should obey it in the lusts thereof.ᵀ Rom. vi. 12.

6. We argue that original sin is truly sin because it incurs the PENALTIES of sin.

"How then can man be *justified* with God? or how can he be *clean* that is born of a woman?" "The stars are not *pure* in His sight; how *much less* man, that is a worm?" Job xxv. 4, 5, 6. "When we were in the flesh, the motions of sins, which

6. The penalties of sin. were by the law, did work in our members to bring forth fruit unto *death*." Rom. vii. 5. "O, wretched man that I am! who shall deliver me from the body of this *death?*" Rom. vii. 24. "God .. *condemned* sin in the flesh." Rom. viii. 3. "To be carnally minded is *death*." Rom. viii. 6. "By one man sin entered into the world, and *death* by sin; and so *death* passed upon *all* men, for that all have sinned." Rom. v. 12. "Death reigned from Adam to Moses, even over them that had not sinned after the similitude of Adam's transgression." Rom. v. 14. "Through the offence of one, many (oi polloi, 'the many,' that is 'mankind') be dead." Rom. v. 15. "The judgment was by one to *condemnation*." Rom. v. 16. "By one man's offence *death reigned* by one." Rom. v. 17. "Judgment came upon *all* men to *condemnation*." Rom. v. 18. "They that are in the flesh cannot please God." Rom. viii. 8. "We all were by nature the children of *wrath*, even as others." Eph. ii. 3.

In these passages original sin comes before us in three aspects as to penalty:

1. As punished by the penalty which comes upon the sins of act, which original sin originates. The stroke which is aimed at them, of necessity, strikes it also.

2. As punished together with the sin of act. Each is aimed at, and each is smitten simultaneously.

3. As subject to punishment in itself antecedent to and separate from all sin in act. It bears the penalty which comes *by* the sin of act; it bears the penalty which it meets in conjunction *with* the sin of act, and it is subject to punishment *in itself* considered. The range of penalty in which it is involved, is, in one respect, larger than that of actual sin; for while, in

no case, can the penalty fall on actual sin without involving original sin, there is one case, the third, in which it could fall upon original sin, where there was as yet no sin of act.

If penalty then can mark its character, original sin is truly sin.

7. We argue that original sin is truly sin, because it needs the REMEDY of sin.

" Create in me a clean heart, O God ! " Psalm li. 12. " Who shall deliver me from the body of this death ? I thank God, through Jesus Christ our Lord." 7. The remedy Rom. vii. 24.

This remedy is needed. 1, As to its essence ; 2, as to its author; and 3, as to its means. " Putting off the body of the sins of the flesh by the circumcision of Christ." Col. ii. 11. " Except a man be born again he cannot see the kingdom of God." " Except a man be born of water, and of the Spirit, he cannot enter into the kingdom of God." " That which is born of the flesh is flesh ; and that which is born of the Spirit is spirit." John iii. 3, 5, 6. " Christ loved the Church, and gave Himself for it ; that He might sanctify and cleanse it with the washing of water by the word." Eph. v. 25, 26.

1. The texts we have cited show *who* need the remedy of sin ; to wit, all human beings. " Except a *man*," that is, a human being — every human being, old or young. Furthermore, *all* that is born of the flesh, to wit, every human being, old or young. Furthermore, in regard to Eph. v. 25, " Christ loved the Church," etc., it may be said : Children are either a part of the Church, or they are not. If they are not of the Church, they are not loved approvingly, and have no interest in Christ's work, nor application of it. But this no one will maintain. Then they are in the Church ; but if in the Church they are, according to St. Paul, in common with others, sanctified, and of course regenerate, washed with water, and reached by the word. But as the word cannot reach an infant didactically, it must reach it sacramentally. Infants then need, and receive the remedy of sin, and as they have original sin only, *it* must need the remedy of sin.

2. These passages show that, as to the *essence* of the remedy

of sin, it is needed by original sin ; to wit: The putting off the body of the sins of the flesh ; the being born again ; the being sanctified and cleansed.

3. These passages show that original sin needs the remedy of sin as to its *author* — He who acquires it, Christ; He who applies it, — the Holy Spirit ; in general, God.

4. These passages show that original sin needs the remedy of sin as to its *means*.

a. The *circumcision of Christ*, i. e. Christian circumcision ; to wit, that which in the Christian system answers to, and fulfils what was shadowed by circumcision under the Jewish system, to wit, Holy Baptism, which is the washing of water con joined with the Word and the Holy Ghost, in the absence of any one of which three elements there is no baptism.

b. The Word of God: didactically, that is, by preaching, teaching, reading, meditation ; and the same word set forth and sealed by the sacraments. Without these things, to wit, Baptism and the Word, the body of the sins of the flesh cannot be put off ; but the body of the sins involves original sin.

8. We argue, finally, that original sin is truly sin, because it is conformed to a true *definition* of sin. When the inspired 8. The defini- writers call the moral taint of our nature sin, they tion. give evidence in this, that as they define the term, it is applicable to that taint. Their idea of sin is of something which man has ; something which *dwells* in him ; something which is *separate* in ideal from his consciousness not only of his own essence, but from the consciousness of his truer nature, his more real self.

This sin is something inborn, which is first to be pardoned, then controlled, and finally annihilated by a new birth, by the grace of God, by the work of the Holy Spirit, by the entrance on the glory of heaven, by the mighty power by which a risen Saviour is to raise these vile bodies and make them like His own body. These ideas underlie or rise upon every New Testament doctrine, duty, and hope.

Rationalism has made it a reproach that the doctrine of original sin lies at the foundation of the evangelical system. We accept the reproach as in fact a concession that the evangelical system grounds itself, where alone a just system in regard to human restoration can be grounded; for the first question, when disease is to be cured, is, What is that disease? Is it so trifling as to need no physician? Can a man heal it himself? Will it heal itself simply by the general energy of the system? or is it radical true disease, mortal in its tendency? Does it require for its treatment a physician of the highest order, and remedies of the most exquisite adaptation and potency? To all of these questions, with characteristic simplicity and practical force, our great Confession replies, when it says: " Original sin is truly sin."

If it be asked, in what sense did our confessors use the worl sin? we reply, in what we have seen and shown to be its scriptural sense. Is it asked what did they, and what do we, regard as its scriptural sense? we reply, the language of the Confession tells us most explicitly what they meant by true sin and by that Confession in firm faith we abide. Yet it ma) not be useless to give, as a further illustration of its meaning the definition of sin by Melanchthon, not only because of h˙ relation to the Confession as its composer, but yet more because in his purest and happiest period, his definitions were as sound in their substance as they were discriminating and felicitous in their form. It may be doubted whether, before Melanchthon, in his Loci of 1535, any successful attempt had been made to define sin generically. The definitions of the fathers are either of specific sin, original or actual, or are too vague for the purposes of science. Pelagius tried to show, from some of Augustine's definitions of sin, that original sin is not really sin. What Augustine had said of sins of *act*, Pelagius applied to sin of nature. Melanchthon, in his Loci of the Second Era,* (1535-1541), says: " Sin in Holy Scripture does not merely mean something *done* (factum aliquod), but it signifies also a perpetuated fault (perpetuum vitium), that is a corruption of nature conflicting with the law of God. Sin therefore, generically taken, is a perpetuated fault, or act, conflicting with the law of God. Sin is divided into original and actual." In the Loci of the Third Era (1543–1559), he says that in Scripture the

---

* Corpus Reformatorum. xxi. 284, 878. In German: Do. xxii. 159.

name " sin properly signifies any thing *liable* (ream), and condemned by God, unless remission be made. This general
description suits both original and actual sin. But as the
definition only embraces what is relative, to wit, *liability*
(reatus), the mind naturally seeks for that on account of which
man is *liable* (reus)." Melanchthon then gives what may be considered the standard definition of sin in the Lutheran Theology.
It is almost verbally the definition which, first endorsed by
Luther's hearty approbation, and by our divines in general,
had been presented in opposition to Eck at the Colloquy at
Worms in 1541, and runs thus: " Sin is either a defect (defec-
tus, want, lack, failure,) or inclination, or act conflicting with
the law of God, offending God, condemned by God, and making us liable (faciens nos *reos*) to eternal wrath and eternal
punishments, had not remission been made." " In this
definition," adds Melanchthon, in the Loci, " the ' *defect* '
and ' inclination' correspond with original sin ; the ' act ' embraces all actual sin, internal and external."* In his Definitions,† he repeats the same idea a little more compactly.
" Sin is whatever conflicts with the law of God — a defect, or
inclination, or act conflicting with the law of God, and making
the creature liable (ream) to eternal wrath, unless remission be
made for the Mediator's sake." In the Examen Ordinandorum,‡
the definition is in substance the same ; the most remarkable
difference is in the closing words: " And *fully meriting* (com-
merens) eternal wrath, unless remission were made for the
Son, the Mediator's sake."

If this definition of sin be a just one, then original sin is
truly sin, for it is, as we have shown, a defect, and an inclination in conflict with the law of God, offending God, and condemned by God.

IX. The natural consequence of this original sin is this,
that it " condemns and brings now also eternal
death ; " " damnans et afferens nunc quoque æter-
nam mortem," " und verdamme. . unter ewigen
Gottes Zorn."

Ninth Thesis.
The natural con-
sequence of orig-
inal sin.

1. The best key to the meaning of this declaration is found

---

* Corpus Reformator. xxi. 667.   † Corp. Ref. xxi. 1077.   ‡ Corp. Ref. xxiii. 12.

ın the XVII. Swabach Articles of Luther. In the fourth of these articles of Luther, are these words : "Original sin is a true real sin, and not merely a fault or a blemish, but a sin of such kind as *would* condemn, and separate eternally from God, all men who spring from Adam, *had not Jesus Christ appeared* as our substitute, and taken Some histori-
cal illustrations
of this Thesis. upon Himself this sin, together with all sins which result from ıt, and by His sufferings made satisfaction therefor, and thus utterly removed, and blotted them out in Himself, as in Ps. li., and Rom. v. 5. is clearly written of this sin."

2. The fourth Article of the Swabach series is evidently based upon the fourth of the Articles prepared at the Marburg Colloquy. That Article says: In the fourth place, we believe that original sin is inborn, and inherited by us from Adam, and *had not Jesus Christ come* to our aid by his death and life, *we must have died* therein eternally, and could not have come to God's kingdom and blessedness.*

3. In Melanchthon's edition of the Confession in German, published in 1533, the part of the Second Article now under consideration, reads thus: " This inborn and original sin is truly sin, and condemns under God's eternal wrath all who are not born again through Baptism and faith in Christ, through the Gospel and Holy Spirit."†

4. In Melanchthon's Latin edition of the varied Confession of 1540 and 1542, occur at this point these expressions: " Condemned to the wrath of God and eternal death." " Those defects and that concupiscence are a thing criminal, in its own nature worthy of death."‡

1. The great proposition that original sin condemns and brings now also eternal death, i. e. that, left to its natural consequences, unchecked in any way by God, this condemnation and death would be the The Scripture
evidence of the
truth of the The-
sis. result, is *already involved* in the previous Thesis. The present Thesis was meant by the confessors to be the practical inference from that, and that Thesis was mainly set forth in order to this, and the emphasis of the connection is this, that origi-

---

* Rudelbach's Ref. Luth. u. Union, p. 626.

† See Weber's ed. Weimar, 1781.   ‡ Hase, L. S., p. 15,

nal sin is so truly sin as to bring its last and most fearfu.
result, the wrath and condemnation of God, and eternal death.
If original sin be truly sin, then, unchecked, it of necessity
involves men in the final results of sin If in itself, in its own
essence and nature, it be sin, then is it in itself criminal, and
in its own nature deserving of condemnation, and if condemned
at all, it must, apart from God's grace, be condemned forever,
for nature has in it no power of moral self-recuperation. The
guilt of original sin would expose men to wrath, and its helplessness would prevent them forever from rising from that
wrath. It is said that this sin " *now also* " (nunc quoque)
" brings eternal death." This is true as over against the idea
that original sin brought death only to Adam, not to all his
posterity ; or, that its effect was confined to the Old Dispensation, so that Christ's redemptory work *per se*, and without
the *application* of its benefits by the Holy Spirit through the
appointed means, releases the whole race from the liability pertaining to original sin ; or, that children, because they are born
in Christendom, or of Christian parents, are *ipso facto* free from
the penalty. " *Now also*," as when Adam sinned ; " *now also* "
in the New Dispensation, as under the Old ; " *now also*," though
Christ has " been made a propitiation, not only for original,
but for all the actual sins of men " (C. A. iii. 3) ; " *now also* "
that there is a Christendom — original sin " brings eternal
death " to all that are not born again.

2. With this general presumption the language of *Scripture*
strictly agrees: " The wages of sin is death." Rom. vi. 23. The
Apostle, in these words, is speaking not only inclusively, but
by preëminence, of the inherent sin of our nature. He uses
them in logical connection with the proposition, " by one man
sin entered into the world, and death by sin, and so death
passed upon all men, for that all have sinned." Rom. v. 12.
There is no break in the argument, and no change in the sense
of the words. It is confessed that the sin of the first man
reduced all the race to the *condition* of his fallen nature. It
follows, then, that without some Divine arrest of natural consequence, the *penalty* which attended that condition in him
would attend it in us. In his case the penalty was death, so

then must it be in ours. Death is so tenaciously allied to sin that only God can separate them.

3. Nor is the moral mystery of this fact so deep *relatively* as it is often regarded. Death, even eternal death, as the endurance of suffering, is not essentially so fearful a thing as sin. It would be more in keeping with divine holiness to permit suffering in the highest degree than to permit sin in the least degree. Suffering is the removal of a lesser good than that which sin removes, and the bringing in of a lesser evil than that which sin brings in. Those, therefore, who admit that the natural consequence of Adam's sin was, that sin entered the world, and fixed itself there by God's permission, admit a far greater mystery even than would be involved in the doctrine that God would allow suffering to enter an unfallen world. It would not so sorely test our *a priori* anticipation in regard to God to know that He allowed suffering in an innocent world, as to know that He allows a race to lose its moral innocence.

If we had been told that in one of the stars above us the people are innocent, but that suffering is there; and that in another, sin came in (by God's permission) to destroy the innocence of its people, the former statement would not shock our moral sense, or create the same difficulty of harmonizing the fact with God's spotless holiness and love of what is best as the latter would. But the case is even stronger, vastly stronger, than this supposition would imply, for the difficulty that presses us is not that suffering exists apart from sin, but that God, having allowed sin to enter the world, allowed the penalty of death to follow that sin.

Furthermore, if it were a doctrine of the Bible that the race is actually lost forever because of original sin, the mystery of the loss would be a less mystery than that of the permission of sin. Those who admit the existence and perpetuation of original sin, admit therefore a mystery greater than the doctrine of the absolute loss of this sinful race in consequence of original sin would be. Here, as in all other mysteries of Revelation, Rationalism, touching with its plausible, but weak hand, the less mystery is compelled to acknowledge the greater.

4. But the doctrine of the Confession is not that this loss of the race actually takes place, but that original sin, unchecked by God, tends to this, and that such, apart from the provisions of his grace in Christ and the Holy Spirit, would be the result. This is made very clear by the historical citations with which our discussion of this Thesis opens.

5. If it be argued that it is impossible before any moral act, or moral choice, a human creature should have an element which, unchecked in its results, would produce *death*, we reply, that it would much more seem impossible that before any moral act, or moral choice, a human creature should have an element which, not only unchecked, but with the mightiest checks, actually results in conscious sin, and is itself sin. But the latter is admitted by all who acknowledge the existence of original sin. Much more then should they admit the former. If we have sin without an act of our will, much more may we have death, the result of that sin, without an act of our will.

6. We see, furthermore, that all the *visible* results of Adam's sin to Adam are perpetuated to us his descendants, and this creates a powerful presumption that the *invisible* results of that sin are also perpetuated to us. The sorrows of Eve are the sorrows of her daughters; the sorrows of Adam are the sorrows of his sons; the curse of the ground, the curse of temporal death, the exclusion from Paradise, all are perpetuated to us. But the principle on which God allows the perpetuation of a fellowship in these *visible* results of Adam's fall is the principle on which He would also allow the natural tendency of our sin to run out into the *invisible* results of the Fall, that is, into eternal death. If God had no right to allow the one tendency, He had no right to allow the other. If He has no right to allow Adam's sin to bring upon us, apart from His grace, Adam's spiritual curse, He has no right to allow Adam's sin to bring upon us Adam's temporal curse. But confessedly, He does the latter, and has the right to do it; equally therefore has He the right to do the former, and if he does not, it is on another ground than that of abstract justice.

It is not anything *I did* which places me in a sorrowful world, with a frail body, a clouded mind, a sad heart, and under subjection to death ; it is not what *I did*, but what *I am*, that subjects me to these, and I am what I am because I spring from Adam, and because he fell. And on that same mysterious, but indubitable principle, that what we *are*, as well as what we *do*, determines our destiny, God might, in keeping with the justice which nature reveals, actually subject the race to the eternal destiny which was the result of sin, apart from the Divine arrest of its tendency, to Adam. No human logic, which acknowledges the Providence of God in nature, could overthrow the proposition, even were it absolute, that original sin brings eternal death to the race.

7. Nor is the language too strong, that original sin is, in its own nature, worthy of death. The word of God teaches that there are but two states possible, one of life, the other of death. Death is always the result of what is due. Life is always the result of grace. Death is the *wages* of sin. Eternal life is the *gift* of God through Jesus Christ our Lord.

Death is the natural due then of every human creature as a creature of sin, and eternal life can only come to man as a gracious and free gift. Nature, as well as voluntary character, is regarded as properly subject to penalty. "We were by nature children of wrath, even as others," Eph. iii. 3, that is, we who are Jews by nature, by our natural descent ; we who are born Jews are, by our natural birth, just as the Gentiles are, subject to wrath, because in both cases men are born with a sinful nature. Death is the due of sin.

8. That *infants* are included is not only necessary, logically, and involved in the words of Paul just quoted, but is expressly taught. " Death reigned from Adam to Moses, even over them that had not sinned after the similitude of Adam's transgression."

9. The results of *Adam's fall*, and of *Christ's mediation*, are represented as entirely parallel in the range of their subjects ; the one embraces exactly the same persons as the other. " If Christ died for all, then were all dead." " As in Adam all died, so in Christ shall all be made alive," (in the resurrection). " Our Lord Jesus Christ, by the grace of God, tasted death for every man." " By the offence of one, judgment came upon all

men to condemnation ; even so by the righteousness of one the free gift came upon all men unto justification of life. For as by one man's disobedience many (oi polloi, ' the many,' mankind,) were made sinners, so by the obedience of one shall many, (' the many,' mankind,) be made righteous."

10. The reply might be made, however, that not all men are actually justified through Christ, and that hence the parallel is to be restricted, and that not all men are necessarily actually involved in the death of sin. But in fact this limitation only makes the parallel more perfect. Not all embraced in the ideal of Christ's work are actually saved, because the work is arrested in its tendency either negatively by lack of the means appointed for its application, or positively by the natural will of those who have the means, but resist their power. So, on the other hand, not all embraced in the ideal of sin's work are actually lost, because that work is arrested on God's side by the means appointed as its antidote, and on man's side by the divinely enlightened will of those who, having these means, do not resist their power. Nature, so to speak, undoes Christ's work in the one case, as grace undoes sin's work in the other. God's work in grace in the one case, if unarrested, is ample for the salvation of every human creature, as sin's work, in the other case, if unarrested, is ample for the loss of every human creature. Thus the all - embracing work of love on the one hand, freely giving life, and the all-pervading power of sin on the other, meriting death, rest in the same generic mode of Divine dealing. Take away Christ, and every human creature dies in Adam ; take away Adam, and every human creature lives in Christ. But though the range of Adam's work and of Christ's work be the same, the power of Christ's work tranecends that of Adam's. God's love in Christ outweighs all. " Not as the offence, so also is the free gift." (The Apostle takes a new point of view : he had shown wherein the offence is as the free gift, to wit, in its range ; now he looks at a point in which the free gift transcends the offence.) " For if through the offence of one, many (' the many,' man- kind,) be dead, *much more* the grace of God, and the gift by grace, which is by one man, Jesus Christ, hath abounded

onto many." " Where sin abounded, grace did *much more* abound."

Thus the cloud of death which hung upon the horizon of our world in its morning parts before the beaming of the Sun of Righteousness, and then, transfigured by His ray, billows around His rising, purpling in His glory. Nothing can magnify His brightness, but this cloud diffuses it. That cloud lifts itself more and more with the ascending Sun, and at His full noon shall have melted away forever.

X. This natural consequence of original sin, to wit, condemnation and eternal death, is actually incurred by all *who are not born again.* Conf., " His qui non renascantur." " Alle die so nicht wiederum neu geboren werden."

Tenth Thesis The necessity of the new birth for the pardon and removal of original sin.

1. If the natural tendency and consequence of original sin be death, one of two results is inevitable. Either sin actually goes on and results in death, or its natural tendency is in some way arrested. Our tenth Thesis affirms that the only way in which it can be arrested is for its subject to be *born again.* By nature we are born to sin, and through sin to eternal death. By grace we are born again to a renewed heart, and through a renewed heart to eternal life.

2. The relative innocence of any human being cannot in itself save him. The innocence of any human being can only be relative. There is a great difference in the *character* of unregenerate persons relatively to each other, but there is no difference whatever in their *nature.* A thousand things mould and modify character, but the corrupt heart is untouched by them all. The phenomena of a corrupt heart are infinitely diversified, not only in their number, but in their intensity. The young man whom Jesus loved, and Judas who betrayed his Lord, were diverse in their *character.* The one was lovely, the other as odious as it was possible for unregenerated character to be. But they had alike an unchanged heart — their *nature* was the same. The innocence of the young man, relatively to Judas, could not save him. The so-called innocence of the best man falls infinitely more short of absolute innocence than it rises above the deepest absolute criminality

relatively. Every man is more guilty absolutely than he is innocent relatively.

3. There is a relative innocence in the *infant* as contrasted with the adult ; this the Scriptures freely allow: " In malice be ye children." 1 Cor. xiv. 20. Even the first budding of sin seems only to lend the charm of vivacity to the little creature. The baleful passion which, in the matured Cain, darkens all time with its deed of murder, may have made his father and mother smile as it flushed and sparkled in the miniature lines of anger traced on his face in childhood. But the nature of Cain was the same in the first glow of anger as in the last, and the nature which was *in* the first glow of anger was in Cain before that anger arose. That anger did not make his moral nature, but was made by it. The great need of the human creature is indeed to be saved *from* that moral nature, and this can only be done by giving him a new heart. The moral *nature* of the new-born infant is as truly a sinful one as that of the grey-haired old reprobate, even as the physical nature and mental nature of that babe are as really a human nature, its body as really a human body, its soul as really a human soul, as those of the ripe adult. God can no more save sin in nature than he can save it in character, and hence a new nature is as absolutely needed by an infant as by an adult. To deny that an infant is capable of regeneration is to deny that it is capable of salvation. The tree is *known* by its fruit, not *made* by it. While the tree is corrupt, the fruit must be corrupt. If the tree be made good, the fruit will be good. Our proposition, then, clothing it in the guise of our Saviour's figure, would be this : That the outgrowth and fruit of this tree of our human nature must inevitably be deadly, unless the nature of the tree itself be changed. The oak-*nature* is the same in the acorn as in the monarch of the forest who has cast his shade for centuries. If the acorn grow, it inevitably grows to the oak.

4. For the same great reason the relative innocence which arises from *ignorance* cannot save men. There are some in nominal Christendom whose privileges are so few that their accountability is relatively diminished. The millions of Jews

Mohammedans, and Pagans are relatively innocent in character, as compared with the unregenerate who have the full light of the Gospel. Yet, however few and light, relatively, their stripes may be, as they knew not their Master's will, it is evi. dent that they too can never reach heaven with an unchanged nature. Their disqualification is none the less real because it is relatively less voluntary than that of others. Man is born with a moral nature, which unfits him for heaven. More than this, the moral nature has in it something which God abhors and condemns. Unless in some way another moral nature is given him, he not only must negatively be excluded from heaven, but must, positively, come under God's wrath. It is said, " As many as have *sinned* without law shall also *perish* without law ; " but it is nowhere said, " As many as have been holy without law, shall be saved without law." On the contrary, the Apostle's whole argument is designed to prove " all the world " " guilty before God."

5. If the relative innocence, either of adults or of infants, could save them from death and take them to heaven, their natures being still under the power of inborn sin, heaven itself would simply be, in one respect, earth renewed ; it would be the abode of sinful beings. In another respect it would be worse than earth, for its sinful beings, unrestrained by the fear of death, would yield themselves without check to the thoughts and desires of their corrupt natures. Going to heaven would, in the case supposed, make no more change in the heart than going to church. A bad heart may have its worst thoughts in the best places. If sin could be self-generated in heaven, as in the case of angels once holy but now fallen, much more might and would it, already existing, reveal itself there. If angels kept not their first estate in heaven, much more would man there reveal his last and fallen estate ; and it might as well be said that to put Lucifer back in heaven unchanged is to be thought of, as that our human nature unchanged is to be placed there.

6. Hence the testimony of Scripture is of the most explicit kind as to the *absolute necessity of the new birth to every human creature.* Our Lord Jesus says : " Except a man (that is any
27

one and every one) be born again, he cannot see the kingdom of God." If our blessed Lord had, however, anticipated that there might be an effort to evade the all-comprehending force of his words, he could not more completely have made that effort hopeless than by adding, as he did: "That which is born of the flesh is flesh," that is, every human being born naturally into our world is fleshly, and needs a new birth.

7. There is one absolute characteristic of all God's children: "They were born not of blood, nor of the will of flesh, nor of the will of man, but of God," that is, no human creature, in and by his natural birth, is God's child, but must, in order to this, be born of Him. The "new creature" alone avails. "*Every one* that doeth righteousness is *born of Him.*"

8. Before these invincible necessities of the case, and this irresistible witness of God's Word, goes down the delusive idea that the *work of Christ covers the case either of Pagans or of infants, without their being born again.* Semi-Pelagianism and Arminianism, acknowledging some sort of original sin, and some sort of a need of a remedy, have said that for Christ's sake infants, having no conscious sin, are forgiven, and without anything further being needed, pass at death into heaven. There are many who imagine that this view gives relief to the great difficulty of the subject, that it avoids the doctrine that infants may be lost, and yet concedes that they all are so far sinners as to need a Saviour; that it proposes something that shall be done for them, and yet escapes the obnoxious theory of the *possibility and necessity of infant regeneration.* This view has been mainly devised indeed to evade the last-mentioned doctrine. But it is far from escaping the pressure of the difficulty. That difficulty is, that the nature of the child is a sinful nature. To forgive absolutely that sin of nature simply for Christ's sake, would be to remove the penalty, while the guilty thing itself is untouched. It would be to suppose that the child is removed from the penal curse of sin, yet left fully under the power of sin itself. It involves the justification of an unrenewed nature. It supposes Christ's work to operate apart from the applying power of the Holy Spirit, and on this theory an unregenerate human creature, forgiven for Christ's

sake, in its untouched sin, would pass into heaven still unregenerate. The theory errs utterly either by excess or by lack. If a child has not a sinful nature, it needs no Saviour. If its sin is not a proper subject of condemnation, it needs no forgiveness. But if it has a sinful nature, it needs not only a Saviour from penalty, but a renewing power to save it from the indwelling of sin; if it is subject to condemnation, it not only needs forgiveness, but the exercise of a gracious power which will ultimately remove what is condemnable. In other words, it needs to be born again.

9. Nothing but downright Pelagianism of the extremest kind can save any man logically from the conclusion we are urging. Original sin must be counteracted in its natural tendency to death, first, by a power which removes its penalty, and secondly, by a power which ultimately removes the sin itself. The power which removes the penalty is in our Lord Jesus Christ, who made atonement for original sin, as well as for the actual sins of men; the power which can remove the sin itself is in the new birth. The former, to use the old theological terminology, is necessary to remove the *reatus* of original sin, that is, its present guilt and immediate liability; the latter is necessary to remove its *fomes*, the inciting fomenting power itself, or, as it is sometimes called, the *materiale*, or essence of sin, which would, left to itself, ever renew the guilt and its curse. It is as impossible to separate the justification of an infant from its regeneration, as it would be to justify an adult while his heart is unchanged. These two things, justification and regeneration, may be separated mentally, and are really distinct, but they are never separated in fact. Unless there be regeneration, there will be no forgiveness. A regenerated man is always justified, a justified man is always regenerated; and unless a man be both, he is neither. A justified infant, unregenerate, is inconceivable in the kingdom of God; such justification would belong to the kingdom of darkness. Alike then to the attainment of both forgiveness and sanctification, or of either, there is a necessity which is most absolute; no human being has been, or can be, saved from eternal death unless he be born again.

10. On this point, all sound theology of every part of our common Christianity is a unit. It is not distinctively a Lutheran doctrine. The Romish and Greek Churches recognize the impossibility of the salvation of any human creature without a change from that condition into which he is born. The Calvinistic theory (including that of the Calvinistic *Baptists,*) involves the doctrine that infants need regeneration to fit them for heaven; that they are capable of regeneration, that it actually takes place in the case of elect infants, and that it takes place in this life. Calvin : * "How, say they (the Anabaptists), are infants regenerated, who have neither the knowledge of good or evil? We answer, that it does not follow that there is no work of God, because we are incapable of grasping it, for it is clear that *infants who are to be saved* (as certainly *some* of that age are saved) *are previously regenerated* (ante .. regenerari), by the Lord." That milder school of Calvinism, which mercifully, and perhaps illogically, departs from the rigor of the older and more self-consistent Calvinism, and believes that none but elect infants die in infancy, does not, nevertheless, depart from the old and true view, that the saved infant is regenerate, and can only as regenerate be saved.

This great fact must not be forgotten, that on the main difficulty of this part of the doctrine of original sin, all but Pelagians are in unity of faith with our Church. The testimony of the Church through all ages is most explicit on this point : That no unregenerate human being, infant or adult, Pagan or nominal Christian, can be saved. Without holiness, no man shall see the Lord — but no man can be holy with his natural heart unchanged. Except we have the Spirit of Christ we are none of His ; but this Spirit is given to us in and by the new birth alone.

XI. We have seen the absolute necessity of the new birth to Eleventh Thesis. The Holy Spirit the sole author of the new birth. every human creature, and we now affirm as our Eleventh Thesis : That as the new birth is absolutely essential to the salvation of every one of our race, so the Holy Spirit is absolutely essential to the new birth. "Durch heiligen Geist," "Per spiritum sanctum."

* Instit. (IV, xvi. 17.)

When the new birth takes place, it is invariably wrought by the Holy Spirit. This proposition sounds like a truism. Theoretically, all Christians, with any pretensions to the name Evangelical, would accept it, and yet, practically, it is constantly ignored. Let our faith rest on this, that whether with means or without means, the Holy Spirit is the author of regeneration, simply and absolutely; that the human being can accomplish no part of it whatever. It is not man's own work, it is not the work *of* his mind, *of* his heart, *of* his will, but it is God's work *in* his mind, *in* his heart, *in* his will. The power of an adult human being in the matter of his regeneration is absolutely negative. He can resist, he can thwart, he can harden himself, but in and of himself he cannot yield, or consent, or make his heart tender.

The adult is as helpless positively, in the power of producing his own regeneration, as the infant is. The adult *can*, indeed, go, and *must* go to the preached word, and *can* and *must* go to the Bible: he can use the means, and with them conjoin fer vent prayer; but it is the Spirit of God who regenerates the man through the means, not the man who regenerates himself, either through the means or apart from them. The adult, indeed, with the means, may either resist the Holy Spirit or cease to resist. He may refuse to let Him work, or he may suffer Him to work. The difference in the course pursued here makes the difference of result between two adults, one of whom becomes regenerate, and the other does not. It is not that the one regenerates himself, and the other refuses to regenerate himself. It is, that one suffers the Holy Spirit to regenerate him through the Word, and the other refuses to permit Him. But even this negative power is derived from the presence of grace and of its means, for a man to whom the Word is set forth is *ipso facto* not in a condition of pure nature. Even in the low realm of mere nature there are not wanting analogies to this spiritual fact. Man has, for example, physically no self-nourishing power. The nutritive property of food exerts itself on him. The food itself is the medium or means of nutrition. Man receives the food outwardly, and the mysterious power of nutrition exerts itself tl rough the food thus received. One man lives, the other starves; not that the first has any power of self-nutrition, but that he received the outward thing through which the power of nutrition is exercised, and did not counteract its effect; the other did not receive the food, and consequently failed to receive the nutritive energy, or receiving the food outwardly, like the first, presented something in his system which resisted the working of its nutritive power. The dependence of the adult on nutriment is the same as that of the infant. The adult can, indeed, ask for nutriment, an asking which is prayer, and the infant cannot. The adult, with reflective consciousness, craves, and with reflective consciousness receives nutriment, which the infant cannot do; but the life of neither is self-sustained. Both must be nourished of God by means of food. The mystery of regeneration lies in this central mystery, that the new man is a creature, not a manufacture; he is born, not self-made; his moral condition is the result, primarily, essentially, and positively, of the divine will, not of his own — he is the child of God " Which were born, not of the will of the flesh, nor of the will of man, but of God." With God all things are possible. " God is able of the very stones to raise up children unto Abraham; " and if of the hard rock we tread upon, He could make tender and faithful hearts, who shall attempt to limit His energy in regard to any of our race, to whom his promises are given? If God could, from inanimate Nature's hardest shapes, raise up faithful children to faithful Abraham, much more can He raise them up from infants, the children of His people — the children of the covenant. The internal processes of regeneration are hidden from us. " The wind bloweth where it listeth (the Spirit breathes where He will), and thou hearest the sound thereof, but canst not tell whence it cometh and whither it goeth. So is *every one* that is born of the Spirit." God claims for Himself the whole work of our regeneration. " Not by works of righteousness which we have done, but according to His mercy He saved us, by the washing of regeneration, and renewing of the Holy Ghost." Titus iii. 5.

The absolute essential in regeneration, and the only absolute essential in the way of an agent, is the Holy Spirit. Not even the means belong to this absolute essential, but merely to the ordinary essentials. The only previous condition in the human soul positively necessary when the Holy Spirit approaches it, is that it shall not resist His work. Before the *The absolute* true doctrine of the supreme and sole necessity of *Essential.* the Holy Spirit's work, as the author of regeneration, the great mystery of infant regeneration and of infant salvation passes away. The Holy Spirit can renew the infant because it does not resist His work. If, therefore, the Holy Spirit *wishes* to regenerate an infant, He *can* regenerate that infant. Who will dispute this proposition? We do not here affirm that He will regenerate, or wishes to regenerate one of the many millions who die in infancy. We simply ask now for toleration to this proposition, that the Holy Spirit, if He wishes, can renew the nature of a child. Admit this, and there is nothing more to settle but the question of fact, and the decision of that question rests, not on speculation, but on the witness of the Word of God.

If the Holy Spirit alone can produce this new birth, then it is evident,

1. That the *work of Christ* cannot produce that new birth in itself, *separate* from the applying power of the Holy *Christ's Work.* Spirit. It is the gracious Spirit who "takes of the things that are Christ's, and makes them ours."

2. The relation to Christian parents can, in itself, have no regenerating power. The child of the holiest of *Christian Pa-* our race has the same nature as the child of the *rents.* most godless, and needs the same work of the Holy Spirit.

3. Nor can birth, in the midst of covenant privileges, have in itself a regenerating power. The child whose *Covenant Priv-* parents are Christians, or who has one Christian *ileges.* parent, is indeed "holy" (ἅγιος), that is, is separated by the fact of such birth from heathendom. The children of Christendom are, in virtue of that fact, generically Christian; not indeed members of the Christian Church, as separated from the world, as some imagine, and receiving in their baptism merely a recognition of a relation existing apart from that baptism, but members of the Christian world, considered as separated

from the Pagan or Jewish world. The child of Christian parents, or of a Christian parent, is, so to speak, constructively and provisionally, and by a natural anticipation, to be considered Christian, but is not actually such until it is baptized. Thus a resident foreigner in our land is, constructively and provisionally, an American citizen, but not actually such until he is naturalized.

This is the true force of the passage to which we are alluding (1 Cor. vii. 14), and which is mainly relied on by those who think that infants are born of the flesh into the earthly kingdom of God — the Church. This is apparent on a careful examination of the text. The question before the Apostle was this: If one of a married couple became Christian, the other remaining Pagan, would this diversity of religion necessitate a divorce? The Apostle replies it would not. " If any brother hath a wife that believeth not, and she be pleased to dwell with him, let him not put her away. And the woman which hath an husband that believeth not, and if he be pleased to dwell with her, let her not leave him. For the unbelieving husband is SANCTIFIED ($\dot{\eta}\gamma\acute{\iota}\alpha\sigma\tau\alpha\iota$) by the wife, and the unbelieving wife is SANCTIFIED ($\dot{\eta}\gamma\acute{\iota}\alpha\sigma\tau\alpha\iota$) by the husband. Else were your children UNCLEAN ($\dot{\alpha}\kappa\dot{\alpha}\vartheta\alpha\rho\tau\alpha$); but now are they HOLY ($\ddot{\alpha}\gamma\iota\alpha$)."

Let it be noted, that three classes of persons are here spoken of as holy or sanctified:

1. The unbelieving husband is sanctified; that is, is holy, because his wife is a Christian.

2. The unbelieving wife is sanctified; that is, is holy, because her husband is a Christian.

3. The children are sanctified; that is, are holy, because one of the parents is a Christian. It is evident then that this sanctification is not a MORAL one. The Pagan husband is not, by virtue of having a Christian wife, any less a godless man; neither then can the Apostle mean that his child is holy morally because its mother is holy. It is evident, furthermore, that the sanctification is not an ECCLESIASTICAL one. The Pagan wife is not a member of the Church because her husband is a Christian, neither then is her child holy ecclesiastically, separated to the Christian Church, because its father is

a Christian. It necessarily follows then that the sanctification being neither moral, nor ecclesiastical, is GENERIC, and that this generic character has a limitation in the nature of the question and of the case. The question was: Do the children belong to Christendom or Heathendom ? The one parent is Christian, the other Pagan. Where is the generic relation of the child, or offspring, whether infant or adult, of these parents ? The reply of the Apostle is : That God decides mercifully, what could not be decided logically, and gives the children the benefit of His goodness in considering them as generically related to the better system, not to the worse.

The unbelieving father is, so far as this question is concerned, constructively in Christendom, so that his child is no more a Pagan child than if both parents were Christians. On the other side, the child is so far constructively in Christendom as if both parents were Christians. The unbelieving father is so far a Christian that his child is a member of Christendom, not of Pagandom. The child is so far holy that it is now one of the children of Christendom, not one of the children of Pagandom. Within the great world there is the generic aggregate of persons belonging to the world of Pagandom, and to the world of Christendom. The world of Christendom is *generically* holy, that is, as Christendom, it is separate generically from Pagandom. But within the world of Christendom there is a further separation. The Church is sanctified, or holy, as separate from the nominally Christian world ; this is an *ecclesiastical* holiness. But within this Church there is yet a further separation of genuine Christians from merely nominal ones, and this HOLINESS is MORAL. The answer of the Apostle is, not that the children (adult as well as infant) are MORALLY holy, nor that they are ECCLESIASTICALLY holy, but that they are GENERICALLY holy,— in a word, that they are just as little of Pagandom, just as much children of Christendom, as if both parents were Christians. All children who have either both parents, or but one parent, Christian, alike belong, not to Christian saints, nor to the invisible church, not to the Christian body in the visible church, nor to the Christian family, in a word, they belong not to the Christian species, but simply to the Christian genus or Christian world, which we call Christendom. The real question settled then by the Apostle is no more than this, that the child of one Christian parent has the same spiritual relation as the child whose parents are both Christians, leaving it in the main an open question what those relations are. Hence the inference from this passage goes to the ground, that children are members of the visible church by their birth, and much more the inference that they are born again by virtue of their relation to Christian parents.

4. Nor is there any power in death to regenerate. There are those who seem to think that the body is the seat of original sin, and that all that is necessary to redeem the soul from the power of sin, is to separate it from the body. But the true primary seat of sin is the soul. The body can be spoken of as the seat of sin only in a secondary sense, and because of the soul's connection with it. The mere separation of the soul from the body, cannot in itself change the soul's moral condition. He that is unregenerate before death, remains unregenerate after death, unless after death the Holy Spirit make the great change. Death in itself can have no such power, and no such tendency. But if the Holy Spirit can work this change in an infant after death, He can just as readily do it before its death, and the whole idea of purgation after death, of a change of relation to God after the departure of the soul, of a renewal of probation in an eternal world, is utterly foreign to the entire tendency of the New Testament doctrine. To admit it, is to admit the existence of a purgatory; it would grant the Romish doctrine in its main point, and the controversy would narrow itself to the comparative trifles of the duration and modes of that purgatory. No such refuge is necessary. The great change is wrought by the Holy Spirit alone, and the possibilities and probabilities of human regeneration are limited by nothing but His purpose and His power. Any regeneration for which infinite power is adequate, and which divine goodness purposes and promises, may and will be wrought.

XII. This new birth by the Holy Spirit has Baptism as one of its ordinary means. Conf., "Durch die Taufe," "per Bap tismum." The part of the Second Article of the Augsburg Confession which comes under discussion in this thesis is that which asserts that original sin brings eternal Twelfth Thesis death to all those who are not born again OF BAP- Relations of bap-
tism to original TISM and of the Holy Spirit. We have shown the sin. absolute necessity of being born again; we have seen that the Holy Spirit is absolutely essential to that new birth; it now remains to explain and vindicate our Confession in its declaration that the new birth must also be of Baptism.

As this is one of the points specially objected to, and as these words have been omitted in the "Definite Platform," which, so far as its omission is evidence, denies not only the necessity of baptism, but the necessity altogether either of the new birth, or of the Holy Spirit to remove the results of original sin, we may be pardoned for dwelling at some length upon it. The doctrine of our Church in regard to baptism is one of the few fundamental points on which any part of evangelical Christendom avowedly differs with her. We propose to give, first, some historical matter bearing upon the origin and meaning of these words in our Confession. We shall present these chronologically.

1529. The fifteen doctrinal articles of Luther, prepared at the Colloquy at Marburg, on this point run I. The Mar- thus: burg Articles.

" In the FOURTH place, we believe that original sin is a sin of such kind that it condemns all men, and if Jesus Christ had not come to our help with His life and death, we must have died eternally therein, and could not have come to the kingdom and blessedness of God."

" In the FIFTH place, we believe that we are redeemed from this sin, and from all other sins, and from eternal death, if we believe on the Son of God, Jesus Christ, who died for us; and without this faith we cannot be absolved from a single sin by any work, condition, or order."

" In the SIXTH place, that this faith is a gift of God, which we can gain by no antecedent work or merit, nor can reach by any power of our own, but the Holy Ghost gives and furnishes it where He will; in our hearts, when we hear the Gospel or word of Christ."

"In the SEVENTH place, this faith is our righteousness before God." *

1530. The Marburg Articles which were signed by Luther, II. The XVII Melanchthon, Zwingli, and Oecolampadius, and the Doctrinal Articles. other leading theologians on both sides, were laid by Luther as the ground-work of the XVII Doctrinal Articles, which were prepared the same year, and which appeared in 1530. These XVII Articles are the direct basis of the doctrinal portion of the Augsburg Confession. In the fourth of these Articles, Luther says: "Original sin *would* condemn all men who come from Adam, and *would* separate them forever from God, *had not* Jesus Christ become our representative and taken upon Himself this sin, and all sins which follow upon it, and by His sufferings made satisfaction therefor, and thus utterly removed and annulled them in Himself, as is clearly taught in regard to this sin in Psalm li., and Rom. v." †

1533. In Melanchthon's German edition of the Confession, III. The German Edition of in 1533, the only edition in the German in which 1533. any variations were made by him, and which has never been charged with deviating in any respect in meaning from the original Confession, this part of the Article runs thus: "(Original Sin) condemns all those under God's wrath who are not born again through Baptism, and faith in CHRIST, through the Gospel and Holy Spirit." ‡

From these historical parallels and illustrations certain facts IV. Meaning of are very clear as to the meaning of the Confes-the Confession. sion.

1. The Article teaches us what original sin would do if there Drift of the were no redemption provided in Christ. The mere Article. fact that Christ has wrought out His work provides a sufficient remedy, *if it be applied*, *to save every human creature* from the *effects of original sin*. Let not this great fact

---

* The Articles are given in full in Rudelbach's Reformation, Lutherthum und Union, p. 665.

† Luther's Werke: Jena v. 14. Mentzer: Exeges. Aug. Conf. 42.

‡ Weber's Edit. Weimar, 1781. Corpus Reformator. xxvi. 725.

be forgotten. Let it never be left out of the account in looking at the mystery of original sin, that there is an ample
arrangement by which the redemption of every human creature from the results of original sin could be effected; that
there is no lack in God's PROVISION for saving every one of our
race from its results. "Our Lord Jesus Christ, by the grace
of God, tasted death for *every man.*"

2. It is not the doctrine of our Confession that any human
creature has ever been, or ever will be, lost purely   Is any man lost
on account of original sin. For while it supposes for original sin
that original sin, if UNARRESTED, would bring death, only?
it supposes it to be arrested, certainly and ordinarily, by the
Holy Spirit, through the divine means rightly received, and
throws no obstacle in the way of our hearty faith that, in the
case of infants dying without the means, the Holy Ghost, in
His own blessed way, directly and extraordinarily, may make
the change that delivers the child from the power of indwelling sin. Luther, in his marginal note on John xv. 22, says:
"Denn durch Christum ist die Erbsünde auffgehaben, und ver-
damnet nach Christus zukunfft niemand. On wer sie nicht
lassen, das ist, wer nicht gleuben wil." "Through Christ
original sin is annulled, and condemneth NO MAN since Christ's
coming, unless he will not forsake it (original sin), that is, will
not believe."

3. It seems very probable from the parallels, that the confessors had mainly, though not exclusively, in their   Who are main
eye, in this particular part of the Article, original ly referred to in
sin as developing itself in *actual sin in the adult*, this Article?
and requiring the work of the Holy Ghost to save men from
its curse. Hence the illustrious Pfaff, in his brief but very
valuable notes on the Confession, says: "The language here
has *chiefly* (maxime) reference to *adults* who despise baptism;"
and such is, unquestionably, the drift of the form in which
Melanchthon puts it in the edition of 1533. The Larger Catechism* argues to the adult on the necessity of Baptism:
"Baptism is no plaything of human invention, but has been
instituted by God Himself, who has earnestly and strictly com-

* 486, 6.

manded that *we should cause ourselves to be baptized* (**wir uns müssen taufen lassen**), or *we cannot be saved* (**oder sollen nicht selig werden**). No man is to think of it as a trifling matter — the mere putting on of a new coat."

GRAUER (who was styled "the shield and sword of Lutheranism"), in commenting on the words of the Confession, says: * "Inasmuch as Baptism is necessary to salvation, it is carefully to be noted what, and of what sort, is that necessity. When the Augsburg Confession teaches that Baptism is necessary to salvation, it refers to the *ordinary mode* which God observes in saving men. For in that respect (ibi) Baptism is necessary, and, indeed, in such measure (ita) that if *any one is unwilling* to be baptized, *when it is in his power* to obtain Baptism, he shall surely be condemned; for the contempt of the Sacrament condemns. The meaning of the Augsburg Confession, therefore, is this, that Baptism is not a thing indifferent, which any one may use at his liberty, but that it is an external mean of such kind that every one embracing the Christian faith is bound (debet) to use it, if it is possible for him to obtain it. But the matter is different in a case of necessity, when any one cannot obtain it."

4. The Confession does not teach that the *outward part* of *Baptism* regenerates those who receive it. It says that it is necessary to be born again of Baptism *and of the Holy Spirit.* It is evident from this that it draws a distinction between the two. It implies that we may have the outward part of Baptism performed, and not be born again; but confessedly we cannot have the saving energy of the Holy Ghost exercised upon us without being born again, whether ordinarily in Baptism, or extraordinarily without Baptism. The very order of the words is significant, for the confessors do not say, and would not say, "born of the Holy Spirit and Baptism:" but the order is the very reverse, "of Baptism and of the Holy Spirit." Hence, while the doctrine of the Confession is that the new birth itself is absolutely essential to salvation, and that the energy of the Holy Spirit is absolutely essential to the new birth, it is not its doctrine that

Baptism, in what sense necessary.

* Prælect. Academic. in August. Confess. Ed. Tert. Jena. 1659. p. 818.

the outward part of Baptism is essential absolutely, nor that regeneration necessarily attends it. The necessity of the outward part of Baptism is not the absolute one of the Holy Spirit, who Himself works regeneration, but is the ordinary necessity of the precept, and of the means. It is necessary because God has enjoined it, and voluntary neglect to do what God has enjoined destroys man. It is necessary because God has connected a promise with it, and he who voluntarily neglects to seek God's promises in God's connections will look for them in vain elsewhere. It is necessary because God makes it one of the ordinary channels of His grace, and he who voluntarily turns from the ordinary channel to seek grace elsewhere, will seek it in vain. It is so necessary on our part that we may not, we dare not, neglect it. But on God's part it is not so necessary that He may not, in an extraordinary case, reach, in an extraordinary way, what Baptism is His ordinary mode of accomplishing. Food is ordinarily necessary to human life; so that the father who voluntarily withholds food from his child is at heart its murderer. Yet food is not so absolutely essential to human life that God may not sustain life without it. God's own appointments limit us, but do not limit Him. Man does live by food alone on the side of God's ordinary appointment; yet he no less lives, when God so wills, *not* by bread alone, but by every word that proceedeth out of the mouth of God.

5. Hence, of necessity, goes to the ground the assumption that the Augsburg Confession teaches that unbaptized infants are lost, or that any man deprived, without any fault of his own, of Baptism is lost. *Is Baptism absolutely necessary?*
When we say *absolute*, we mean that which allows of no exceptions. The *absolute* necessity of Baptism, in this sense, has been continually denied in our Church.

The language of LUTHER is very explicit on this point.* In his "Christliches Bedenken" (1542), in reply to anxious Christian mothers, he (1) refutes and forbids the practice of the Romish Church, of baptizing a child not fully born, a practice based upon the idea of the absolute necessity of Bap-

* Leipzig ed. of Luther's Works, Vol. xxii. pp. 400–422.

tism to the salvation of a child. (2) He directs that those who
are present should hold firmly to Christ's words, " unless a
man be born again, he cannot see the kingdom of God," and
shall kneel down and pray that our Lord God may make this
child partaker in His sufferings and death, and shall then not

Luther. doubt that He knows full well how, in his divine grace
and pity, to fulfil that prayer. Wherefore, since that
little child has, by our earnest prayer, been brought to Christ,
and the prayer has been uttered in faith, what we beg is established with God, and heard of Him, and he gladly receiveth it,
as He Himself says (Mark x. 14): " Suffer the little children to
come unto me, and forbid them not ; for of such is the kingdom
of God." Then should we hold that the little child, though it
has not obtained Baptism, is not, on that account, lost ? " Dan
das Kindlein, ob es wohl die rechte Taufe nicht erlanget, da-
von nicht verloren ist."

This " Bedenken " of Luther was accompanied by an expo.

Bugenhagen. sition of the 27th Psalm, by Bugenhagen, which
Luther endorsed. The main object of Bugenhagen
in this treatise is to give consolation in regard to unbaptized children, over against what he calls the shameful error, drawn not
from God's Word, but from man's dreams, that such children
are lost. Bugenhagen, after teaching parents to commit to
God in prayer their child which cannot be baptized, adds:
" Then shall we assuredly believe that God accepts the child,
and we should not commit it to the secret judgment of God.
To commit it to the secret judgment of God, is to throw to the
wind, and despise the promises of God in regard to little children," (pp. 400–422). Both Luther and Bugenhagen discuss
at large the argument for, and objections against, the doctrine
of the salvation of unbaptized little children, and demonstrate
that it is no part of the faith of our Church, that Baptism is
absolutely necessary : that is, that there are no exceptions or
limitations to the proposition that, unless a man is born again
of the Water of Baptism, he cannot enter into the kingdom
of God.

Luther and Bugenhagen condemn those who refuse to
unbaptized children the rites of Christian burial, and who

object to laying their bodies in consecrated ground, as if they were outside of the Church. " We bury them," say they, " as Christians, confessing thereby that we believe the strong assurances of Christ. The bodies of these unbaptized children have part in the joyous resurrection of life."*

HOFFMAN (Tuebingen, 1727), to whom we owe one of the most admirable of the older expositions of the Confession, says : " It does not follow from these words that all children of unbelievers, born out of the Church, are lost. Still less is such an inference true of the unbaptized children of Christians; for although regeneration is generally wrought in infants by Baptism, yet it may be wrought extraordinarily by an operation of the Holy Spirit without means, which the Augsburg Confession does not deny in these words. It merely desires to teach the *absolute* necessity of the new birth, or regeneration, and the *ordinary* necessity of Baptism. On the question whether the infants of the heathen nations are lost, most of our theologians prefer to suspend their judgment. To affirm as a certain thing that they are lost, could not be done without rashness." †

FEUERLIN (Obs. to A. C. p. 10,) says : " In regard to the infants of unbelievers, we are either to suspend our judgment or adopt the milder opinion, in view of the universality of the salvation of Christ, which can be applied to them by some extraordinary mode of regeneration."

CARPZOV, whose Introduction to our Symbolical Books is a classic in its kind, says : " The Augsburg Confession does not say that unbaptized infants may not be regenerated in an *extraordinary* mode. The harsh opinion of Augustine, and of other fathers, in regard to this, was based upon a misunderstanding of John iii. 5, for they regarded those words as teaching an *absolute* necessity of Baptism, when, in fact, that necessity is only *ordinary* — a necessity which binds us, and will not allow us to despise or neglect Baptism, but does not at all bind God to this mean, as if He *could* not, or *would* not, in a case of necessity arising in His own providence, perform that in an *extraordinary* way, which, in other cases, He per-

* P. 418.   † Pp. 36, 37.
28

forms in an *ordinary* one, through means instituted by Him self. As, therefore, the texts of Scripture speak of an *ordinary* necessity, so also of that same sort of necessity, and of no other, do Protestants speak in the Augsburg Confession."

It would be very easy to give evidence on the same point from all our most eminent Lutheran writers on the doctrine of our Church, but it is not necessary. No one who has read them will need any citations to establish a fact with which he is so familiar. They who tell the world that it is a doctrine of our Church that Baptism is absolutely essential, and that all unbaptized persons are lost, can only be defended from the charge of malicious falsehood on the plea of ignorance. But ignorance, if it assume the responsibilities of knowledge, is not innocent.

6. The truth is, no system so thoroughly as that of the Lutheran Church places the salvation of infants on the very highest ground.

<small>Infant salvation in the Lutheran system.</small>

The PELAGIAN system would save them on the ground of personal innocence, but that ground we have seen to be fallacious. The CALVINISTIC system places their salvation on the ground of divine election, and speaks of elect infants, and hence, in its older and more severely logical shape at least, supposed not only that some unbaptized, but also that some baptized infants are lost.

<small>The Calvinistic System.</small>

1. In the Westminster Assembly's Confession, chap. vi., it is said: "Our first parents . . sinned. . . . The *guilt* of this sin was *imputed*, and the same *death*, in sin and corrupted nature, *conveyed* to all their posterity. Every sin, both *original* and actual, . . doth in its own nature bring guilt upon the sinner, whereby he is bound over to the *wrath* of God and *curse* of the law, and so made subject to *death*, with all miseries, spiritual, temporal, and *eternal*." The infant, then, Christian or Pagan, is born in "guilt," "bound over to the wrath of God and the curse of the law, and so made subject to *eternal* death." How does Calvinism relieve it from this condition? The answer to this is given in what follows.

2. The election of God rests upon nothing whatever foreseen in the creature (ch. iii. 5), "as causes or conditions moving

Him thereunto." The foreseen Christian birth, or early death, of a child can, therefore, in no respect bear upon its election. To assume that all children dying in infancy, even the children of Christians, are elect, and yet that the prevision of their being so born and so dying has no relation to their election, is illogical.

3. "As God hath appointed the elect unto glory, so hath He . . . foreordained all the *means thereunto.* Wherefore *they who are elected . . .* are *effectually called* unto *faith* in Christ by His Spirit working in due season; are *justified*, adopted, sanctified, and kept by His power *through faith* unto salvation. Neither *are any other* redeemed by Christ, effectually called, justified, adopted, sanctified, and saved, *but the elect only.*" (Westm. Conf. iii. 6.)

According to this Article, where the "*means* thereunto" are not, the election is not. But in the Calvinistic system Baptism is not the means of grace, but only the sign or seal of grace (xxvii. 1). What is the mean whereby "elect infants" are effectually *called* unto "faith in Christ"? and do infants have "*faith* in Christ?" are they "justified, sanctified, kept through *faith* unto salvation"? Only those who have the means are among the elect, and only the elect have the effectual means. Then Pagan, Mohammedan, and Jewish adults and infants are of necessity lost. But has even a baptized infant the *means* of effectual calling, of faith, of justification? The Lutheran system says, It has. The Calvinistic system says, It has not. Either, then, the elect infant is saved without means, or there are none elect who die in infancy. But Calvinism denies both propositions, and is involved in hopeless contradiction. Either Baptism is properly a means of grace, and not its mere seal, or, according to Calvinism, logically pressed, no one dying in infancy is elect, and *all infants are lost.*

4. "*All those* whom God hath predestinated unto life, and *those* ONLY, He is pleased effectually to call by His Word and Spirit . . " (x. 1). "This effectual call is not *from anything at all foreseen* in man" (x. 2). "*Elect infants*, dying in infancy, are regenerated and saved by Christ through the Spirit, who worketh when, and *where*, and *how* He pleaseth. So also are

all other elect persons, who are incapable of being *outwardly* called by the ministry of the Word " (x. 3). " Faith is *ordinarily* wrought by the ministry of the Word " (xiv. 1). Here the system comes again into direct self-contradiction. In the face of chap. iii. 6, it is taught that there is an " effectual call," without means, without anything outward, without the ministry of the Word, or Sacraments, utterly out of the ordinary channel. " It might be lawful," says Peter Martyr, " to affirm that young children be born again by the Word of God, but yet by the *inward Word*, that is by the comfortable power of Christ and his Holy Spirit."* But if the Holy Ghost, without any means, regenerates some of the elect, why may there not be elect Pagans reached in the same way ? and if it be said that only those born in Christendom are elect, and, of consequence, extraordinarily called, is not that an admission that the mere fact of birth in Christendom in some sense influences the election? The BAPTIST system, which totally withholds Baptism from the infant, and every system which, while it confers the outward rite, denies that there is a grace of the Holy Spirit of which Baptism is the ordinary channel, are alike destitute, on their theory, of any *means* actually appointed of God to heal the soul of the infant.

The ROMISH system, too Pelagian to think that original sin could bring the positive pains of eternal death, and too tenacious of the external rite to concede that an infant can be saved without that rite, leaves its theologians, outside of this general determination, in a chaos of doubt. Some of them reach the middle theory, that the unbaptized infant is neither in heaven nor hell, but in a dreary limbo. Others consign it to hell. The COUNCIL OF TRENT declares: " If any one shall say that the Sacraments of the New Law are not necessary to salvation, and that without them, or a desire for them, men obtain . . . the grace of justification . . . ; let him be anathema." " If any one shall say that Baptism . . is not necessary unto salvation, let him be anathema."† The CATECHISM of the Council of Trent (Quest. xxx): " Nothing

Romish System.

---

* Common Place.   Transl. by Anthonie Marten. 1583. Lond. Fol. iv. 136.
† Sess. vii. Can. 4.   De Baptism, Can. 5.

can seem more necessary than that the faithful be taught that this Law of Baptism is prescribed by our Lord to all men, insomuch that they, unless they be regenerated unto God through the grace of Baptism, are *begotten* by their parents *to everlasting misery* and destruction, whether their parents be believers or unbelievers." In exposition of the doctrine of Trent, BELLARMIN says: " The Church has always believed that if infants depart from this life without Baptism, they perish. The Catholic faith requires us to hold that little ones dying without Baptism are condemned to the penalty of eternal death." " Yet are they not punished with the penalty of sense or of sensible fire." " It is *probable* that those little ones suffer an internal grief (although a most mild one), forasmuch as they understand that they are deprived of blessedness, are separated from the society of pious brethren and parents, are thrust down into the prison of hell, and are to spend their life in perpetual darkness."* DOMINICUS A SOTO says that " in the (Roman) Church it is a most fixed point that no little one without Baptism can enter into the kingdom of heaven." MALDONATUS† says "they are condemned, with the goats, to the left hand; that at once upon their death they descend into hell." CANUS‡: " Their souls, with the bodies resumed, are thrust out into darkness."

How beautiful and self-harmonious, over against all these, is the view of our Church. Over against the Calvinist, it knows of no non-elect infants, but believes that our children are alike in the eyes of Infinite mercy. Over against the Pelagians it confesses that all children are sinners by nature, and believes that the Holy Spirit must change those natures. Over against the Anabaptists, and the school which is at heart in sympathy with the Anabaptist theory, though it retains infant Baptism as a form, our Church believes that God has appointed Baptism as the ordinary channel through which the Holy Spirit works a change in the nature of a child. In the fact that there is an ordinary means appointed, our Church sees the guaranty that

Lutheran System.

---

* Lib. I. De Bapt. ch. iv.   Lib. VI. ch. ii., iv., vi.   † On Matt xxv. 23.
‡ Cited in Gerhard Confessio Catholica, 1679. Fol. 1110.

God wishes to renew and save children, and *what so powerfully as this* prompts the blessed *assurance that if God fails* to reach the child in His ordinary way, He will reach it in some other? The Calvinist *might* have doubts as to the salvation of a dying child, for to him Baptism is not a sure guaranty, and its grace is meant only for the elect; the Baptist *ought* logically to have doubts on his system as to whether an infant can be saved, for his system supposes that God has no appointed means for con- ferring grace on it, and as we are confessedly under a system of grace and providence which ordinarily works by means, the presumption is almost irresistible, that where God has no *mean* to do a thing He does not intend to do it. But the con- servative Protestant cannot doubt on this point of such tender and vital interest. The baptized child, he feels assured, is actually accepted of the Saviour, and under the benignant power of the Holy Ghost. In infant Baptism is the gracious pledge that God means to save little children; that they have a distinct place in His plan of mercy, and that He has a dis tinct mode of putting them in that place. When, then, in the mysterious providence of this Lover of these precious little ones, they are cut off from the reception of His grace by its ordinary channel, our Church still cherishes the most blessed assurance, wrought by the very existence of infant Baptism, that in some other way God's wisdom and tenderness will reach and redeem them. Our confidence in the uncovenanted mercy of God is strong in proportion to the tenacity with which we cling to Baptism as an ordinary mean most neces- sary on our part, if we may possibly have it, or have it given. Because in the green valley, and along the still waters of the visible Church, God has made rich provision for these poor sin-stricken lambs,—because He has a fold into which He gathers them out of the bleak world, therefore do we the more firmly believe that if one of them faint ere the earthly hands which act for Christ can bring it to the fold and pasture, the great Shepherd, in His own blessed person, will bear to it the food and the water necessary to nurture its undying life, and will take it into the fold on high, for which the earthly fold is meant, at best, but as a safeguard for a little while. But the earthly fold itself, reared in the valley of peace, which lies along that water which ripples with something of a heavenly music, is a sure token of a love which will never fail of its object — a visible pledge that it is not the will of our Father in heaven that *one* of these little ones should perish.

The Augsburg Confession, to sum up, affirms, as we have seen, that there is an *absolute* necessity that every human being should be born again. It affirms, moreover, that the work of the Holy Spirit is absolutely essential to the production of this change. These points we have endeavored to develop. It affirms or implies, moreover, that Baptism is *one* of the *ordinary* means by which the Holy Spirit works the change, and that Baptism is the only ordinary means of *universal* application, that is, the only means applicable alike to adults and *infants.*

In this is implied:

1. That the Holy Spirit ordinarily works by *means.*

2. That the Water and Word of Baptism is *one* of those means.

3. That the Water and Word of Baptism operates not as the proper agent, but as the *means of that agent.*

4. That the Holy Spirit *may*, and where He *will, does work* the new birth in, with, and under the Water and Word of Baptism, so that Baptism, in its completest sense, is the inseparable complex of Water, Word, and Spirit, bringing heavenly grace.

5. That this grace is *offered* whenever Baptism is administered, and is *actually conferred* by the Holy Spirit, whenever the individual receiving it does not present in himself a conscious voluntary barrier to its efficacy. This barrier, in the case of an individual personally responsible, is unbelief. In the case of an infant, there is no conscious voluntary barrier, and there is a divinely wrought receptivity of grace. The objector says, the infant cannot voluntarily receive the grace, therefore grace is not given. We reverse the proposition and reply, the infant cannot voluntarily reject grace, therefore the grace is given. When we speak of a divinely wrought receptivity of grace, we imply that whatever God offers in the Word or element bears with the offer the power of being received

When He says to the man with a withered arm, "Reach forth thine arm!" that which was impossible by nature is made possible by the very word of command. The Word and Sacraments *per se* break up the absoluteness of the natural bondage; they bring an instant possibility of salvation. Grace is in them so far prevenient that he who has them may be saved, and if he be lost, is lost by his own fault alone.

Is our Confession warranted by Holy Scripture in presenting these views of Baptism? We answer, unhesitatingly, It is.

The washing of Naaman (1 Kings v. 14) in the Jordan, may be considered as a foreshadowing of the baptismal idea. A promise was given to Naaman, to wit, that his leprosy should be healed. This promise was conditioned upon the presupposed faith of Naaman, but this faith was not sufficient; a mean was appointed for the fulfilment of the promise, and faith in the mean was as absolutely prerequisite in Naaman as faith in the promise. Faith in God always involves faith in His means as well as faith in His promises. If Naaman had not believed the promise he would not have gone to the Jordan; but if Naaman had believed the promise, and had yet refused to go and wash — which was the attitude he actually assumed at first — he would not have been saved from the leprosy.

The washing of Naaman was not an arbitrary association, but was made of God a real and operative mean, so that in, with, and under the water, the divine power wrought which healed his leprosy. Naaman was bound to the means, so that no element but water — no water but that of Jordan — would have availed to cleanse him. His faith would not cleanse him without the water. Abana and Pharpar, and every river that rolled, and every sea that lifted its waves, would have rolled and risen in vain, for the water that was to do such great things was not mere water, but that water which God had enjoined, and with which his promise was bound up (Luther: Smaller Catechism). Yet if Naaman, earnestly striving to reach the Jordan after the promise, had been providentially prevented, we may believe that God would have wrought the cure without the means.

Let us look at the representations of the New Testament.

1. MARK XVI. 16. "He that believeth, AND IS BAPTIZED, shall be saved ; but he that believeth not shall be damned." (The Saviour does not repeat the allusion to Baptism in the second part of this sentence, because he that does not believe is already condemned, whether baptized or not.) Here is something mentioned as a MEAN, to wit, Baptism, and salvation is IN SOME SENSE conditioned upon it. When men read : " He that believeth, and is *not* baptized, shall be saved," they separate what God has joined, and contradict our Lord. But here, doubtless, our Lord draws the distinction in which our Church follows Him : faith is ABSOLUTELY essential to salvation, baptism ORDINARILY essential only.

2. ACTS II. 38. "Then Peter said unto them, Repent and BE BAPTIZED, every one of you, in the name of Jesus Christ, for the remission of sin, and ye shall receive the gift of the Holy Ghost." Here Baptism is represented as one mean, and for those who could have it, as the indispensable mean, to the remission of sin, and the receiving of the Holy Spirit.

3. ACTS XXII. 16. "Arise and be baptized, and wash away thy sins, calling on the name of the Lord."

4. ROMANS VI. 3. "Know ye not that so many of us as were baptized into Jesus Christ, were baptized into His death? Therefore we are buried with Him by baptism into death."

5. 1 COR. XII. 13. "For by one Spirit are we all baptized into one body." Here the agency of the Holy Spirit in Baptism, and the fact that in Baptism rightly received we are ingrafted into the one body of Christ, are distinctly taught.

6. GAL. III. 27. "For as many of you as have been baptized into Christ, have put on Christ." Baptism, in its whole compass and intent, is not meant to introduce into mere outward relations, but bears with it a grace by which he who rightly uses it is invested with the righteousness of Christ.

7. COL. II. 12. "Buried with Him in Baptism, wherein (i. e. in Baptism) also ye are risen with him through the faith of the operation of God."

8. 1 PETER III. 20. "The ark . . . . wherein few, that is, eight souls, were SAVED BY water. The like figure whereunto

even BAPTISM doth also now save us;" or, mcre literally, "Which (that is, water) doth now save you also, (that is) the antitype Baptism (doth now save you)."

9. JOHN III. 5. "Except a man be born of water, and of the Spirit, he cannot enter the kingdom of God." It is on this verse preëminently the phraseology of the part of the Confession now under consideration is based. It embraces the same class of persons of which our Confession speaks. The Confession speaks of "all men naturally born after Adam;" the Saviour speaks of "that which is born of the flesh," that is, all our race, infant and adult. Our Confession says they have sin; our Saviour says they are FLESH, that is, are corrupt. The Confession says they must be born again, in order to be saved; our Lord says that unless they are born again, they cannot see the kingdom of God. The Confession attributes the new birth to the Holy Spirit as agent, so does our Lord; the Confession attributes a part in the new birth to Baptism, so does our Lord. We must be born again of *water*.

ALFORD, not a Lutheran, does not go too far when he says: "There can be no doubt, on any honest interpretation of the words, that ' to be born of water,' refers to the token or OUT-WARD SIGN OF BAPTISM: ' to be born of the Spirit,' to the thing signified, or inward grace of the Holy Spirit. All attempts to get rid of these TWO PLAIN FACTS have sprung from DOC-TRINAL PREJUDICES, by which the views of expositors have been warped. Such we have in Calvin, Grotius, Cocceius, Lampe, Tholuck, and others. ALL THE BETTER AND DEEPER EXPOSITORS have recognized the co-existence of the two — WATER. and the Spirit. So, for the most part the ancients: So Lücke, in his last edition, De Wette, Neander, Stier, Olshausen. Baptism, complete, with WATER and the Spirit, is the admission into the kingdom of God. Those who have received THE OUTWARD SIGN AND THE SPIRITUAL GRACE have entered into that kingdom. . . . It is observable that here as ORDINARILY, the outward sign comes first, and then the spiritual grace, vouchsafed in and BY MEANS of it, if duly received."

10. EPHES. V. 25–27. "Christ loved the Church, and gave Himself for it, that He might SANCTIFY AND CLEANSE IT WITH

THE WASHING OF WATER by the Word, that He may present it to Himself a glorious Church."

11. HEB. X. 22. " Let us draw near with a true heart, in full assurance of faith, having our hearts sprinkled from an evil conscience, and our BODIES WASHED WITH PURE WATER."

On this verse Alford remarks: " There can be no reasonable doubt that this clause refers directly to Christian baptism. The ' washing of water,' Eph. v. 26, and ' the washing of regeneration,' Titus iii. 5, and the' express mention of ' our bodies ' here, as distinguished from ' our hearts,' stamps this interpretation with CERTAINTY, . . . for ' our bodies ' confines the reference to an outward act. And so Theophylact, Theodoret, Œcumenius, etc., Böhme, Kuinoel, Tholuck, De Wette, Bleek, Lünemann, Delitzsch, and the majority of commentators. Still, in maintaining the externality of the words, as referring, and referring solely to Baptism, we must remember that BAPTISM ITSELF IS NOT *a mere external rite*, but at every mention of it carries the thought further, to wit, to that spiritual washing of which it is itself symbolical and sacramental."

According to DELITZSCH, " THE WASHING THE BODY WITH PURE WATER is purely sacramental, the effect of baptism taken in its whole blessed meaning and fulfilment as regards our natural existence. As priests we are sprinkled, as priests we are bathed . . . washed in holy Baptism."

12. 1 JOHN v. 6–8. " This is He that came by WATER and blood, EVEN Jesus Christ; not by water only, but by WATER and blood. And there are three that bear witness in earth, the Spirit, the water, and the blood: and these three agree in one."

13. 1 COR. VI. 11. " But ye are WASHED, but ye are sanctified, but ye are justified in the name of the Lord Jesus, and BY the Spirit of our God."

14. TITUS III. 5. " Not by works of righteousness which we have done, but according to His mercy He saved us by the WASHING OF REGENERATION, AND RENEWING OF THE HOLY GHOST, which He shed on us abundantly."

ALFORD says: " Observe that here is no figure: the words are literal: Baptism is taken as in all its completion, the outward, visible sign accompanied by the inward spiritual grace; and as thus COMPLETE, it not only represents, but IS the new birth, so that, as in 1 Pet. iii. 21, it is not the mere outward act or fact of Baptism to which we attach such high and glorious epithets, but that complete Baptism by water and the Holy Ghost, whereof the first cleansing by water is, indeed, the ordinary sign and seal, but whereof the glorious indwelling Spirit of God is the only efficient cause and continuous agent. Baptismal regeneration IS THE DISTINGUISHING DOC TRINE of the new covenant (Matt. iii. 11,) but let us take care that we know and bear in mind what 'Baptism' means: not the mere ecclesiastical act, not the mere fact of reception, by that act, among God's professing people, but that completed by the Divine act, manifested by the operation of the Holy Ghost in the heart and through the life."

The words of CALVIN on this same passage deserve to be produced: "It ought to be accepted as a principle among good men, that God does not trifle with us by empty figures, but by His own power performs that inwardly which by the external sign he exhibits outwardly. WHEREFORE BAPTISM IS FITLY AND TRULY CALLED THE LAVER OF REGENERATION. He rightly holds the power and use of the Sacraments, who so connects the thing and the sign, that he neither makes the sign empty and inefficacious, nor, on the other hand, for the sake of its honor, detracts from the Holy Spirit what is due to Him."

This will suffice to show how amply, by the very text of Holy Scripture, and even by the confession of interpreters who are not of our Church, her Confession is authorized in declaring that Baptism is one of the ordinary means of the Holy Spirit in working the new birth.

XIII.   That Baptism is the only ordinary means of univer-
Thirteenth sal application will be denied by two classes alone.
Thesis. Baptism The first class are those who deny that Baptism is
the only ordinary
means of univer- a mean of grace at all, and those errorists are
sal application. already sufficiently answered by the passages we
have given from the Word of God. The second class are those who deny that infants should be baptized, and who, consequently, maintain that there is no mean of grace provided

ʀor them. This error, so far as its discussion properly comes under the head of Original Sin, has already been met. The ampler discussion of the question belongs to the Article on Baptism.

Here then we reach the close of the positive part of the Article of the Augsburg Confession on Original Sin: the rest is antithetical. This Article of the Confession, as we have seen, is grounded in every line, and in every word, on God's sure testimony, and proves, in common with the other parts of that matchless Symbol in which it stands, that when our fathers sought in God's Word for light, sought with earnest prayer, and with the tears of holy ardor, for the guidance of the Holy Spirit into the deep meaning of His Word, they sought not in vain.

XIV. In maintaining the true doctrine of Original Sin, our Church, of necessity, condemns: Fourteenth Thesis. Pelagianism in antithesis to the Scriptural doctrine of Original Sin.

1. The Pelagians; that is, it condemns them in their doctrine, not by any means in their person, so far as that is separable from their doctrine.

2. It condemns, in the same way, all others who deny that the vice of origin is sin; and

3. It condemns all who contend that man, by his own strength, as a rational being, can be justified before God; and who thus diminish the glory of the merit of Christ, and of His benefits.

Pelagius was a British monk, who flourished under the Emperors Arcadius, Theodosius, and Honorius. About the year 415 he began to teach unscriptural I. Pelagius. views in regard to the freedom of the human will. Violently opposing the Manichæans, who supposed a corruption in man which involved an essential evil in his very substance, he ran to the opposite extreme.

The errors of Pelagius, which our fathers had in view in this solemn rejection of them in the Confession, are not difficult to ascertain. Our confessors knew the views of Pelagius mainly from the powerful confutation of them in the works of Augustine, who styled him the enemy of grace, and to these we must go to ascertain what they meant to condemn in condemning Pelagianism. This is the more necessary, as there are modern writers who maintain that Pelagius was not the errorist Augustine supposed him to be, and that much of the controversy was really a war of terms. We do not believe this theory to be correct ; we are satisfied that in all the main points, Augustine perfectly understood and fairly represented the position of Pelagius. But be this as it may, it cannot be disputed that, to understand the meaning of our Confession, we must take what was the accepted meaning of terms when it was framed. The characteristics we now give of Pelagianism are based mainly upon the statements of Augustine, and, for the most part, are literally translated from his very words.

1. The Pelagians " denied that little children born after Adam contract from their very birth the contagion of the old death." The Augsburg Confession maintains, on the contrary, that " after the fall of Adam, all human beings, born in the order of nature, are conceived and born in sin."

2. " Little children are born without any fetter of original sin." They neither contract nor have it from their parents.

3. " There is, therefore, no necessity that they, by a second or new birth, should be released from this."

4. The Pelagians did not deny the duty of baptizing infants, nor did they dare to go so violently against the consciousness and faith of the entire Church as to deny that Baptism is a mean of regeneration. Those who deny this in our day are more Pelagian than Pelagius himself. The Pelagians contended that infants " are baptized, that by regeneration they may be admitted to the kingdom of God, being thereby transferred from what is good to what is better, not that by that renewal they were set free from any evil of the old obligation."

5. " If children were unbaptized, they would have, indeed, a place out of the kingdom of God, yet, nevertheless, a blessed and eternal life," in virtue of their personal innocence.

6. " If Adam had not sinned he would, nevertheless, have died bodily, his death not being the desert of his sin, but arising from the condition of nature." Death is, therefore, not the penalty of sin. These illustrations are extracted from Augustine's Book on Heresies (chap. lxxxviii).

In the Second Book of Augustine on Perseverance (chap. ii.), he says: "There are three points on which the Church Catholic mainly opposes the Pelagians.

7. "One of these doctrines with which she opposes them is, that the grace of God is not given because of our merits.

8. "The second is, that whatever may be the righteousness of a man, no one lives in this corruptible body without sins of some kind.

9. "The third is, that man contracts liability by the sin of the first man, and would come under the fetter of condemnation were not the accountability which is contracted by generation dissolved by regeneration."

10. In the same book he attributes to the Pelagians the doctrine that "Adam's sin injured no one but himself."

The following statements, drawn from other reliable sources, will further illustrate the characteristics of Pelagianism:

1. Pelagius originally asserted that man without grace can perform all the commands of God. Under the pressure of the urgency of his brethren he subsequently admitted that some aid of Divine grace is desirable, but only that we might more EASILY do God's commands.

2. That concupiscence or desire, which is in man by nature, is good, and that the whole nature of man, even after the fall, remains entire and incorrupt, so that even in spiritual things he could do good, and fulfil the will of God.

3. That sin is contracted entirely by example and imitation, not at all by propagation.

The confessors, in the Antithesis, may have had reference, moreover, to the Anabaptists, who maintained: II. The Anabaptists.

1. "That sin was so taken away by the death of Christ that infants, under the New Testament, are born without sin, and are innocent, the servitude of death alone excepted;

2. "And, therefore, deny that infants are to be baptized, since they are born subject to no sin."

It is not a matter of perfect agreement among the writers on our Confession, whether Zwingli is alluded to III. Zwingli. in the Antithesis. Our old standard writers are almost unanimous in believing that he was, at least, one of those alluded to. Such is the view, for example, of Ment. zer, Gerhard, Hoffmann, Carpzov, Walch, and Baumgarten. Among recent writers CŒLLN* devotes a considerable part of a special treatise to the establishing of this point, and places it beyond all reasonable doubt. It is true that Zwingli signed the Articles of the Marburg Colloquy (1529), which were prepared by Luther, the fourth of which treats of Original Sin, but which shows, in common with the others, that Luther designed to make the way to harmony of view as easy as could be consistent with principle. In the Confession which Zwingli prepared to be presented to Charles V. at the Diet of Worms, he says: "Whether we will, or will not, we are forced to admit that original sin, as it is in the sons of Adam, is not properly sin, as has just been explained. For it is not a deed contrary to the law. It is, therefore, properly a disease and a condition." "Infants have not guilt, but have the punishment and penalty of guilt, to wit, a condition of servitude, and the state of convicts. If, therefore, it is right to call it guilt, because it bears the inflictions of guilt, I do not object to the term." That is he did not object to the term, provided it was clearly understood that the term meant nothing. In his book on Baptism, Zwingli says: "There is nothing in the children of believers, even before Baptism, which can properly be called sin."

ALTING, the distinguished Reformed divine who wrote an Exegesis, Logical and Theological, of the Augsburg Confession, declares that it is a calumny to assert that Zwingli denied that original sin is truly sin, and says that he merely denied that it was ACTUAL sin. But if by denying that it is actual, he merely meant that it is not a sin committed by deed, he denied what no one affirms; but if he meant that it was not a real sin, then he denied the very thing which, according to Alting, it is a calumny to charge upon him. Zwingli was a patriot, and as such we admire him, but he was, as compared with Œcolampadius, not to mention Calvin, an exceedingly poor theologian. Justus Jonas says of him that he occupied himself with letters in the face of the anger of the Muses and of the unwillingness of Minerva — "Iratis Musis et

---

* Confess. Melanchthonis et Zwinglii, etc., 1830.

ınvita Minerva." It is not for their intrinsic value, but for historical reasons, that it is important to follow him in his views.
He certainly did not hold, thoroughly and consistently, the doctrine which is couched in the language of our Confession, that
" original sin is truly sin." His fallacy is the ordinary one, that
the character of sin is in the deed, not in the essence of moral
nature, which originates the deed; that sin cannot *be*, but
must always *be done*. In other words, he makes a real, not a
merely phenomenal difference between sin *in* us, and sin *by* us;
the sin we *have*, and the sin we *do*. Every such distinction is
Pelagian. Zwingli illustrates the condition of the race as that
of the children born to one who has been captured in war.
" Those born of him are slaves, not by their fault, guilt, or
crime, but by the condition which followed a fault, for the
parent from whom they are born deserved this by his crime.
The children have no guilt." All this naturally means that
our race inherits the penalties of guilt, but not guilt itself.
They are innocent, but are treated as guilty. In God's thoughts
they are spotless; in God's acts they are polluted. The providence of God, and the actual course of His administration, are
not a reflection of His judgment, but a perversion of it. Zwingli's illustration only aggravates the case. He takes one of
the most atrocious acts of human cruelty towards enemies in
war, and finds in it a parallel to God's dealings with man.
His theory leaves the most difficult facts untouched, while it
removes the only possible solution of them. Of all modes of
.ooking at the subject, this seems to be the most confused and
objectionable. It is simply self-conflicting Pelagianism. Pelagianism denied both the effect and the cause. Zwingli leaves
the effect and denies the cause. In Zwingli's letter to Urban
Rhegius (1525), he says: " What could be clearer than that original sin is not sin, but a disease? What could be weaker and
more alien to Scripture than to say that this calamity is alle-
viated by the laver of Baptism, and is not merely a disease? "
In the Book on Baptism, written the same year, he says:
" We affirm that original sin is only that disease which we
derive by inheritance. Therefore, original sin does not merit
damnation. How can it be that that which is disease and
29

contagion MERITS THE NAME OF SIN, OR IS SIN IN REALITY (revera)?."

The language of the condemnatory clause also refers to the Pelagianism of the Scholastics, and of many of the Romish Church contemporary with the confessors. The Romish Church praises Augustine, and follows Pelagius.

IV. Other Pelagianizing teachers.

It also, by anticipation, condemns the Pelagianizing tendencies of the Council of Trent, and of the theologians who defended its decisions, among whom the Jesuits were preeminent.

It also, in the same way, condemns the Socinian, Arminian, and Rationalistic Theology, and the schools which approximate it. In short, all teaching which denies that the fault of origin is sin — all teaching that favors the idea that man by his own power of reason can be justified before God — all teaching that tends to diminish the glory of the merit and of the benefit of Christ, is here condemned.

In fairly estimating much of the plausible sophistry by which Pelagianism is maintained, it is well to remember that even when actual sin takes place, the *condition* or *state* of sin must be antecedent to the *act*. A being who has ever *been* holy, must cease to *be* holy, *before* he can *will* or *do* sin. This is the necessary order of succession and of conception, even if it be granted that these stages are synchronal. Not all real precessions are precessions in time. The *doing* originates in the *willing*, the *willing* presupposes the *will* as a faculty, the will as a faculty must be in a determinate *condition* antecedent to a determinate act, and the act takes its being and character from the condition. There can be no moral act without antecedent moral condition. The *condition* of the will may result in four ways:

I. It may be *concreate*, as God establishes it: or,

II. It may be *affected* by influences *from without,*—it may be tested, tried, or tempted in the nature of things, or by another will: or,

III. It may result from a *self-determining power* in the will as a faculty: or,

IV. It may be *innate* and connate.

I. The first condition of the will of angels, and of Adam, was concreate; it was holy and untempted.

II. Its second condition was that of the angels, tested in the nature of things by the essential character of virtue, which, on one side, is the negative of moral evil, the possibility of which evil is implied in the very denial of it, and by moral freedom, which is not continuously possible without choice. It is also the condition of Eve's will affected by the nature of things within and without her, and by the will of the serpent. It is also the condition of Adam's will tested by the nature of things, by the now corrupted will of his wife, and through her by the will of the serpent. So far as the fruit attracted Eve simply as pleasant to eat, and beautiful to look upon, the attraction was purely natural, and morally indifferent. The prohibitory command meant that the natural instincts, even of an unfallen creature, are not sufficient for the evolution of the highest moral *character*, but that to this *character* it is essential that there shall be the voluntary and continuous conformity of the will of the creature to the will of the Creator. Original righteousness is, *per se*, a *condition* of the will, and is antecedent to the first *act* of will. *How* a will, whose original *condition* is holy, can come to a sinful condition, as it involves an ultimate principle, cannot be grasped by man, yet, whatever may furnish the occasion, the cause is the will itself: " The *cause* of sin is the *will* of the wicked " (causa peccati est voluntas malorum). " The *perverted* will (verkehrte Wille) *worketh* sin . . . which will has *turned itself* from God to evil (zum Argen)." These words imply that sin the act, is the result of sin the condition. The *condition* of the will is the cause of the moral act as moral, and the *perverted* condition of the will the cause of the moral acts being *perverted*, that is, sinful. We reach the last point to which the mind of man can go, when we assert that in the self-determining power of a finite holy will lies the possibility of its becoming an unholy will. We may say that the finite is, in the *nature of* things, liable to the possibility of sin, that the positive good of freedom in the

* Aug Conf. Art. xix.

creature involves the incidental evil of the power of abuse
It is easy to multiply these common-places of the argument.
But none of these solutions bear upon the *process* of the change
of condition. They may show that the change is possible, but
they do not show *how* it takes place. Nor, indeed, is a solution
of the question of the *how* necessary here. The philosophy of the
mode in no way affects the certainty that the moral *condition* of
the will precedes and determines its acts. While a will is holy
in *condition*, it is impossible that it should be unholy in *act*. The
act is what the condition is. The act has no moral character
except as it derives it from the condition of the will in which
it originated. Things are not moral or immoral, only *persons*
are. The essential sin never comes to being *in* the thought or
act, but is, and must be, in being *before* there can be a sinful
thought or sinful act. The thought or act is not the root of
sin, but sin is the root of the thought and act. "Out of the
heart proceed evil thoughts"—that is, evil thought is the out-
going from an evil heart—act from condition. "Every imagination of the thoughts of his heart was only evil." "Heart"
implies will in condition, and to this the "imagination of
the thoughts" is secondary and derivative. The act is determined, the will is determining, and the self-existent cause of
its particular determination, beyond which cause we cannot go,
is its condition. Each of the *derivative* conditions supposes a
preëxistent one, and when we reach, as we soon must in this
retrospection, the first condition, which is the *sine qua non* of
the second, as the second is of the third, we reach a point at
which we are forced to acknowledge that all actual sin, in some
measure, results from a primary condition of the will. As in
the order of nature there must be the process of thinking before
the result of thought, and there must be mind before thinking,
and a particular and specific condition of mind before the particular and specific thinking which eventuates in the particular and specific thought, so must there be the process of moral
activity before the resulting moral act, and a faculty of will
before the process of moral activity, and a particular and specific condition of the faculty of will before the particular and
specific willing which reveals itself in the particular moral act.

When we say that the morality of an act is conditioned by the will, we mean simply that the character of the act is derived from the condition of the will. The sin is really *in* the condition of the will. The sin done is but phenomenal to the real sin. In this respect all sin is essentially original; and of the two extremes of statement, it would be more logical to assert that all sin is in its own nature original, and no sin in proper essence actual, than to assume that all sin is actual, and no sin original. LUTHER: * "Original sin, or sin of nature, sin of person, is the *real cardinal sin* (Hauptsünde). Did it not exist, no actual sin would exist. It is not a sin which is *done*, like all other sins, but it *is*, it *lives*, and *does* all sins, and is the *essential* (wesentliche) sin."

If this estimate of the bearing of the *condition* of will upon the controversy between the Church and Pelagianism be correct, it is evident that the great question at issue is, In which of the four *conditions* enumerated is the will of man now?

I. It is Pelagian to assert that the *primary condition* of the will of man now is that of *concreate* holiness, as it was endowed in the beginning by God. "Every man is born in the same perfection wherein Adam was before his fall, save only the perfection of age."

II. It is Pelagian to assert that the *primary condition* of the will is now made by *influences from without*. "Adam endamaged . . his posterity only by his example, so far forth as they imitate him." "There is no original sin, or corruption of human nature."

III. It is Pelagian to assert that the *primary condition* of the will now is, or results from, a *self-determining* exercise of the will. "Man of himself is able to resist the strongest temptations." "The well-using of free-will and of natural powers is the cause of predestination."

IV. It is Pelagian to *deny* that the present condition of our will is inherited by natural descent: "Adam by his sin endamaged only himself," or, to *assert* that though our present condition of will may be connate, yet that this connate condition is either

---

* Hauss-postilla on the Gospel for New Year.

1. Like that of concreate holiness; or,

2. Like that of Adam when his condition was that of tempted holiness, with the natural power of successful resistance; or,

3. That of self-determination, which still freely exercises itself; or,

4. That of non-moral passivity, neutrality, or indifference.

Over against these, the Scripture view is:

I. That man's will is not in a condition of *concreate* holiness, but has lost that condition.

II. That the positive element which affects its condition is not *external*, as example, education, or temptation, but internal, corrupt desire, or concupiscence.

III. That its condition allows of no *self-determining* power in the sphere of grace.

IV. That this condition is *connate*, is *properly called* sin, *is really sin*, justly liable in its own nature to the penalties of sin; that without the work of grace wrought, it would have brought eternal death to the whole race, and does now bring death to all to whom that work of grace is not, either ordinarily or extraordinarily, applied by the Holy Ghost.

Faithful to these doctrines, and over against all the tendencies which conflict with them, our Confession, both in its Thesis and Antithesis, holds forth the truth of the exceeding sinfulness and the utter helplessness of man's nature, the goodness of God, the all-sufficiency of Christ, and the freeness of justification.

Looking at original sin as God's Word and our Church teaches us to regard it, we shall

See its true character, and deplore the misery it has wrought.

We shall go to Christ, the great Physician, to be healed of it, and to the Holy Spirit, who, by His own means, Baptism and the Word, applies for Christ the remedy we need; taking of the things that are Christ's, and making them ours.

We shall be led to maintain a continual struggle against it; we shall watch, pray, and strive, knowing that through grace we are already redeemed from its curse; that by the same grace we shall be more and more redeemed here from its power, and at last be wholly purged from it, and shall form a part of that Church, loved and glorious, which shall show no spot, or wrinkle, or any such thing, but shall stand before her Lord holy and without blemish.

And now, in the language in which the incomparable Gerhard closes his discussion of original sin, let our words be: " To Him that hath died for us, that sin might die in us; to Him who came that He might destroy the works of the Devil, and might restore to us the blessings lost by the Fall; to Jesus Christ our Saviour, be praise, honor, and glory, world without end. Amen!"

X.

THE PERSON OF OUR LORD AND HIS SACRAMENTAL PRESENCE. — THE EVANGELICAL LUTHERAN AND THE REFORMED DOCTRINES COMPARED.*

(AUGSBURG CONFESSION. ART. III.)

IN the January number of the Bibliotheca Sacra, for 1863, the opening article is a very elaborate one, from the pen of
I. Dr. Gerhart's
Article.
Rev. E. V. Gerhart, D. D. Its subject is the " German Reformed Church." It was read at the time with special interest, as the Puritanism of New England, which has been supposed to carry out the Reformed principles to their furthest extreme, and the German Reformed Church in which those principles were more modified and subdued than in any unquestionably Calvinistic Church, were brought

---

* BRENTIUS: De Personali Unione. Tubing. 1561. 4to.; Sent. de Lib. Bullinger. Tubing. 1561. 4to.; De Majestat. Domin. nostri. Frankf. 1562. 4to.; Recogn. proph. et Apostol. doctrin. Tubing. 1564. 4to. — BULL: Defens. Fid. Nicænæ. Oxon. 1688. 4to. — CALIXTUS: F. U. Ref. ad Calov. Theses. (De Christo. 67.) Helmst. 1668. 4to. — CALOVIUS: Harmonia Calixt. Hæret. (De Christo. 938.) Witteb. 1655. 4to.; Colleg. Disput. Controv. (De Christo. 62.) Witteb. 1667. 4to. — CHEMNITZ: De duab. nat in Christo. Jena. 1570. 8vo. — DORNER: Entw. gesch. d. L. v. Person Christi. 1845–56. 8vo. — GESS: Die L. v. d. Person Christi. 1856. 8vo. — HUNNIUS AEG.: De Persona Christi. Frankf. 1597. 12mo. — LIEBNER: Christol. 1849. — LŒSCHER C.: Cons. Orthod. de Christo. Wittenb. 1699. 4to. — MEISNER: De Artic. Fid. Fundament. (p. 339.) Wittenb. 1675. 4to. — OSIANDER: Informat. Theologica. Tubing. 1620. — SARTORIUS: D. L. v. Christi Person u. Werk. 1845. — SCHNECKENBURGER: Zur Kirchl. Christol. 1848. — STRAUCH: Consens. Repetit. Vindicat (190.) Witteb. 1668. — THOMASIUS: Christi Person u. Werk. 1857. — THUMMIUS: Majestas Jesu Christi. Tubing. 1621. 4to.; De maj. Chr. doctr. Repetit. Tubing. 1624. 4to — WEBER: Doctr. Bib. de nat. Corp. Christi. Ha.is. 1825. 4to.; De natura Christi. Halis. 1825. 4to. — WOLF: Eutychianism. Lutheranor. Wittenb 1680 4to.

456

into apparently intimate fellowship by Dr. Schaff's temporary engagement at Andover. The article of Dr. Gerhart is a very able one, and we rejoiced that so full, and, in many respects, so satisfactory an exhibition of the doctrines, usages, and history of the German Reformed Church had been given. At the time, however, we entered a kind, but most decided protest in general, against what Dr. Gerhart believed it necessary to say in regard to the Lutheran Church, in exhibiting the contrast between her doctrines and those of his own communion.

It is our desire, in the Dissertation which we now submit to the reader, to place in a more permanent shape some facts which were then drawn together, bearing upon the great doctrines of our Lord's person and presence. They are doctrines of the profoundest importance in themselves, and derive additional interest from the fact that on them, primarily, the great division took place between the two Reformatory movements of the Sixteenth Century. It is a division which has been fruitful in unspeakable mischiefs, and which, more than all other causes, has made the struggle against Rome prolonged and dubious. The responsibility of the division is a serious one, and rests upon those who were in the wrong upon the great questions themselves.

"The differences of Zwingli and Luther in temperament, psychological organization, moral character, education, and political as well as social relations," do not, in our judgment, satisfactorily account, as Dr. Gerhart supposes, for their divergence in the Reformation. II. Difference of the Lutheran and Calvinistic Systems. Its Source. The root of the divergence lies in the very nature of Christianity; and there can be no satisfactory solution of the differences between the Zwinglio-Calvinistic, and the Lutheran Reformations, and the Churches which were established upon them, except this, that the one accepted the true, the other a mistaken meaning of God's Word, on certain points. That is, and will forever remain, the real question between them.

We have no less serious objection to Dr. Gerhart's statement of the Lutheran doctrine of the presence of Christ in the Lord's Supper. He states a number of important respects, in which he supposes the two Churches to agree touching Christ's sacramental presence. He then goes on to say : " But they differ as to the mode." The inference here might seem

III. Doctrine of Christ's Presence.

to be natural that the Churches agree as to a fact, but not as to its philosophy, but this representation is inadequate, for the point of difference is as to the fact, and, indeed, in a very important sense, not at all as to the mode. Our controversy with Socinians is not as to the *mode* of the Trinity, for we confess that we cannot explain *how* the Trinal Unity exists, but it is as to the fact, whether there be a *true* Trinity in Unity, and not a mere ideal distinction. So in regard to the presence of Christ, our dispute is not as to *how* he is present, which, like the whole doctrine of His person, is an inscrutable mystery, but as to whether there be a *true*, not an ideal presence. It is the *essence* of the doctrine, not its form, which divides us from the Reformed. Let them satisfy us that they accept the *fact*, and we shall have no quarrel as to the philosophy of the mode, so far as the question of mode is separable from that of fact. Let us agree as to the *kind* of presence, its objective reality ; let us agree that the true body and true blood of Christ are truly present, so that the bread is the communicating medium of the one, the cup of the other, and use these terms in one and the same sense, and we can well submit the *mode* of the mystery to the Omniscient, to whom alone *mode* is comprehensible.

The next statement of Dr. Gerhart seems to us entirely a

IV. The Lutheran Church teaches no Local Presence of Christ.

mistaken one. He says : " The Lutheran Church teaches that the veritable flesh and blood of Christ are locally present, being in, with, and under the consecrated bread and wine." On the contrary, the Lutheran Church denies that there is a *local* presence of Christ's body and blood, and if such a presence be meant, she would deny that there is any presence of them "in, with, and under the consecrated elements." Between us and the Reformed there never has been, there never can be, a controversy on so simple a point as this. The Lutheran Church maintains that there is a *true* presence of Christ's human nature, which is neither local nor determinate. The body of Christ which, in its own nature, is determinately in heaven, and is thus present nowhere else, nor will be thus present on earth till His second coming, has also another presence, diverse from the determinate, yet nc less true. It is present through that Divine nature into whose personality it has been received, and with which it has formed an inseparable union, whose lowest demand is the co-presence of the two parts. If there be a place where the human nature of Christ is not united with the second person of the Trinity, then there is a place where the second person of the Trinity is not incarnate. If this be granted, then the whole second person of the Trinity is unincarnate, for where God is, He is not in part (for He is indivisible), but He is entire. Then the second person of the Trinity is either not incarnate at all, or He is both incarnate and unincarnate ; or there are two second persons of the Trinity, with one of whom the human nature of Christ is one person, the extent of the incarnation being commensurate with that of our Saviour's body in heaven, and the other second person of the Trinity omnipresent, but not incarnate, all of which suppositions are absurd, and yet one or other of them must be accepted, if the Lutheran doctrine be denied. The truth is, that when we admit the personal union of the human nature of Christ with a divine nature, we have already admitted the fact, in which the mystery of Christ's Sacramental presence is absorbed. The whole Divine person of Christ is confessedly present at the Supper, but the human nature has been taken into that personality, and forms one person with it ; hence the one person of Christ, consisting of the two natures, is present, and of necessity the two natures which constitute it are present.

As the divine nature, without extension, expansion, or locality, has a presence which is no less true than the local presence, from which it is wholly diverse, so does it render present the human, which is now in one personality with it, — renders it present without extension, expansion, or locality ; for, as is the presence which the divine *has,* so must be the presence of the human which it *makes.* If we are asked what is the kind of the presence of the Divine nature of Christ, we reply, it is a true, illocal presence, after the manner of an infinite Spirit, incomprehensible to us: and if we are asked, what is the kind of the presence of the human nature of Christ, we reply, it is a true illocal presence after the manner in which an infinite Spirit renders present a human nature which is one person with it — a manner incomprehensible to us. Nor is the idea at all that the human nature of Christ exercises through anything inherent in it this omnipresence, for it remains, in itself, forever a true human nature, and is omnipresent only through the divine. The physical eye sees through the essential power of the soul, and the soul sees by the eye as its organ. So are the powers of the human Christ conditioned by the essential attributes of the Godhead, and the Godhead works through the Manhood of Christ as its organ. The eye never becomes spirit, and the soul never becomes matter. So in Christ the divine forever is divine, the human forever human, without absorption or confusion, though the human acts through the divine, and the divine acts by the human.

The Lutheran Church does not hold to any local presence of the body of Christ *in*, or any local conjunction of the body of Christ *with*, or any local administration of the body of Christ *under* the bread, or of His blood in, with, and under the wine. The sphere of the reality of the sacramental mystery is not of this world. The sphere in which our Lord sacramentally applies His redeeming work is that in which He made it. That sphere was indeed on this earth, but not of it. Our Lord made His propitiatory sacrifice; it was a true and real sacrifice, but its truth and reality are not of the nature of this earth, nor comprehensible by any of its modes of apprehension. Judged by the world's standards, the blood of the Lamb of God has no more efficacy than the blood of animal sacrifices. But there is a *sphere* of reality in which the shedding of Christ's blood was an actual ransom for the sins of the race. The atonement is of the invisible world, and hence incomprehensible to us, who are of the visible. In the same order of verities is the sacramental presence which applies what the atonement provided. It is a most true presence, but not in the sphere of this life. If presence means location; if sacramental is a convertible term with fleshly, earthly, natural, (as the opposite of spiritual,) then the Lutheran Church would deny that there is a sacramental presence of Christ. But a presence of the whole person of Christ, of the divine by its inherent omnipresence, and of the human through the divine — a presence, not ideal or feigned, but most true; not fleshly, but spiritual; not after the manner of this earth, but of the unseen world; not natural, but supernatural — this presence the Lutheran Church maintains, and, God helping her, will maintain to the end of time.

Dr. Gerhart goes on to say that the Lutheran Church holds that "communicants, unbelievers as well as believ- ers, partake of the human nature of Christ with the mouth; the one class of persons eating and drinking damnation to themselves, not discerning the Lord's body, and the other class eating and drinking unto sanctification and everlasting life." We have looked a little into Lutheran theology, and must confess that the expression, "partaking of the *human nature* of Christ with the mouth," is one which we never met, and which is to us incomprehensible. No such phrase occurs in the citations made from our Confessions by Dr. Gerhart, and no such phrase, we think, can be found in them. If there be such a phrase in any of our approved theologians, we should have been glad to have Dr. Gerhart quote it. But waiving this, does the Lutheran Church, *as a whole*, present in her Confession the words " with the mouth," as an essential part of the definition of the sacramental reception of the body and blood of Christ? We reply, *She does not.* THE AUGSBURG CONFESSION, the only distinctive symbol universally recognized in the Lutheran Church, has no such expression, although it was in part prepared to show that our Church was free from the Zwinglian error on this very question of the sacramental presence. The Apology, which amplifies and defends the disputed statements of the Confession, has not these words. The Smaller Catechism has no such words. The Larger Catechism has no such words. The Smalcald Articles have no such words. In Luther's Fourteen Articles drawn up at the Colloquy at Marburg, for the

v. Is sacramental communion oral?

express and sole purpose of comparing the conflicting views of Zwinglians and Lutherans, not a word is said of a reception "by the mouth." The same is true of the Wittenberg Concord, drawn up with like aims. The fact is, therefore, that the defining term "by the mouth," cannot be demonstrated to be an essential part of the Lutheran Confessional statement. Entire national bodies of Lutherans have existed for centuries, and now exist, who have no such expression in their Confessions.

It is true that the Formula of Concord, which appeared thirty-four years after Luther's death, does use and defend the term, and that this Formula, not without good reason, has been generally received in the Germanic Churches, and either formally or virtually by an immense majority of all our Churches, and that it is confessedly a just and noble scientific development of the Lutheran faith. But when the Formula and our theologians speak of a reception by the mouth, they speak, as we may, of the reception of the Holy Spirit in, with, and under the preached Word, by the ear, not meaning at all that there is, or can be, a physical grasping of the Holy Spirit by the organ of sense, but that the Word is the medium, through which His presence is operative, and that the Word, and by Divine appointment, the Holy Spirit, in, with, and under the Word, is received by the soul through the ear. Our Gerhard, of whom the Professor of Franklin and Marshall College is almost a namesake, defines the words in question in this way: "The sacramental eating of the body of Christ is none other than *with the mouth* to receive the eucharistic ' bread, which is the communion of the body of Christ,' (1 Cor. x. 16). This sacramental eating is said to be *spiritual*, because the body of Christ is not eaten naturally, and because the mode of eating, like the presence itself, is neither natural, carnal, physical, nor *local*, but supernatural, divine, mystical, heavenly, and spiritual. . . The Word of God is the food of the soul, and yet is received by the bodily ear." If, indeed, there be such a thing as a *Sacrament*, a something distinct from *language*, as means of grace, it must be received in some other way than by hearing, or sight, or in the mode in which language addresses itself to them. If Baptism be a sacrament; if the water, by its conjunction with the Word, becomes also bearer of the grace which the Holy Spirit in His substantial presence, in, with, and under both water and Word, confers, then is the reception of the Holy Spirit mediated, in some sense, through the body which is touched by the water, as well as through the ear, which hears the Word. If, in the Lord's Supper, the distinctive element is something to be received by the mouth, then the mouth acts some essential part in the reception of the thing offered in the Supper, be that thing what it may. Any theory which rejects the idea of oral reception in every sense, really denies the whole sacramental character of the Lord's Supper. If the bread communicates the body of Christ, and the bread is to be received orally, the result is inevitable that the sacramental eating is with the mouth. Nor is this so isolated a marvel. The Holy Ghost is personally and substantially present in, with, and under the Word. When the blind, therefore, as they can and sometimes do, read the Word by pressing the lips, instead of the fingers, to the raised characters, there is, in some sense, an oral reception of the Holy Ghost.

As to the doctrine that believers and unbelievers partake sacramentally, though believers alone partake savingly, it seems to us that any doctrine which concedes a responsibility in man, and an impartiality VI. Who receive Christ sacramentally? in God, must suppose that the sacrament *offers* to all who receive it the same thing; the difference in the result being made by the faith or unbelief of the recipient.

Dr. Gerhart, indeed, himself says, that the Reformed Confessions *deny*, "That the *objective efficacy* of the sacrament depends on the faith, or any frame of mind of the communicant." These words, as we understand them, involve the doctrine that there is a positive object in the sacrament, which exists apart from the faith of the communicant. If the Doctor uses the word " efficacy " in its ordinary acceptation, he must either mean " efficacy " for good, in which case he goes beyond the Lutheran doctrine, and falls into the *opus operatum* of Rome; or he must mean " efficacy " for evil or judgment, in the case of the unbelieving, in which case he practically takes ground with the Lutheran Church on this point. Nor does it seem to us that this doctrine of our Church can be successfully denied. When the Word of God is preached, the sinner who is melted to penitence, and the sinner who hardens himself against it, receive precisely the same Gospel. What the ear receives in each case is exactly the same. The Gospel is not made Gospel by our faith, nor made mere sound by our unbelief. Our unbelief cannot make the promise of God cease to be His promise. Faith accepts, and unbelief rejects what *is*: the one no more unmakes it than the other makes it. The responsibility of the hardened hearer turns upon this very thing, that receiving God's Word he does not discern it, but treats it as if it were man's word; and so in the Lutheran view the criminality of the unworthy communicant is preëminently this, that partaking of that bread, which is the communion of Christ's body, he does not " discern the body of the Lord." If the words "partake" or "receive" are so used as to imply a salutary acceptance with the heart, then our Church would say that believers alone partake in the Lord's Supper. But faith must have an object, and the object of faith can always, in the nature of things, be an object of unbelief. Our Church maintains that the object on which the faith of the worthy communicant, and the unbelief of the unworthy communicant, rest, is the same. *Sacramentally* they receive the same thing, which *efficaciously* the believer alone receives, and the difference at the table of the Lord originates, not in the arrangement of God, but in the state of the recipient. Bread is bread, although the diseased state of the man who receives it may make it act like a poison. The presence of Christ is an absolute verity, and is no more affected in its reality by our unbelief, than a wedge of gold ceases to be gold because it may be neglected or spurned as if it were brass. A man may throw away the wedge of gold, but it is no less gold, and has none the less truly been placed in his hand.

Dr. Gerhart then goes on to say, contrasting the doctrines of the two communions: " The Reformed Church, *on the contrary*, teaches that the divine-human Saviour is present, not ιocally, nor carnally, but spiritually." To this we reply that it is not *on the contrary.* The Lutheran Church repeatedly and unequivocally has denied all local or carnal presence of Christ's body, and has affirmed that, as antagonistic to any such conceptions, His presence is "spiritual." When the word "spiritual," however, is used as the opposite of "true," and means that His presence is one which rests on our intellectual operation, or on our faith, and not on the nature of His own person, then our Church denies that it is "spiritual." Dr. Gerhart, however, defines the words differently from either of these meanings. He says: "Not locally, nor carnally, but spiritually; that is, by the Holy Ghost." The Reformed Church maintains that Christ's sacramental presence is mediated by the Holy Spirit. The Lutheran Church, on the contrary, maintains that it is through the divine nature in Christ's own person, and that Christ is present, not because the Holy Spirit enables Him to be present to faith, though absent in reality, but because, in His own inseparable person, the Godhead is of itself present, and the humanity is rendered present through the Godhead. The Trinity is indeed indivisible, and the Holy Spirit is present at the Supper. But the persons of the Trinity have their distinctive work. It is the work of the Holy Spirit to illumine the mind and kindle the heart to the reception of the great gift which the glorious Saviour, present in His own person, offers to the soul. The whole Christ is truly present after the incomprehensible manner of that world of mystery and of verity in which He reigns. He applies, to faith, at His table, the redemption which he wrought upon the cross. Through His body and blood He purchased our salvation — truly and supernaturally; through His body and blood He applies salvation — truly and supernaturally. In Christ's Supper, as in His person, the human and natural is the organ of the divine and supernatural which glorifies it. As is the redemption, so is its sacrament. The foundation of both is the same, and lies forever inapproachable by man, in the lowest depth of the eternal mind. In the redemption, nature furnished the outward organ of the divine, in the frail body and the

VII. The Reformed and Lutheran doctrines of the Lord's Supper.

flowing blood of our crucified Lord. Through this organ an infinite ransom was accomplished. In the Supper, the organ of the redemption becomes the organ of its application. With an artlessness which heightens its grandeur, this redemption, which forever centres in Christ's sacred and undivided person, veils its supernatural powers under the simplest elements which sustain and revive our natural life. But faith none the less clearly sees that the bread which we break is the communion of Christ's body, and that the cup of blessing which we bless is the communion of His blood.

In illustrating and defending the doctrine of God's Word, we shall quote with some fulness from Chemnitz as illustrative of the Lutheran doctrine of the person of Christ, as bearing on His presence in the Lord's Supper, and with reference to various misapprehensions of it. We desire to present the views of Chemnitz, the greatest of the dogmatic theologians of the Sixteenth Century, not because of the weight which his name bears, nor merely because of the exquisite combination of sound judgment, erudition, profound thought and clear reasoning, with great mildness, and a simple and scriptural piety which characterized him, but mainly for two reasons. First, because he bore so distinguished a part in the preparation of the Formula of Concord, and in the subsequent masterly defence of it ; and secondly, because he was of the school which, in order to narrow the ground of controversy, had preferred *waiving* the question of a general omnipresence of Christ in His human nature, and confining attention mainly to that presence in which His people are most directly interested, His presence with His Church — everywhere and at all times, and especially at His Supper.

Chemnitz on the personal presence of Christ.

" The words in the History of the Ascension are rightly taken in their *simple*, *literal*, and *natural* signification ; for, when Christ ascended, according to the description of the Evangelists, He was, by a visible motion, lifted up on high, in a circumscribed form and location of the body, so that, by a visible interval, He departed further and further from the presence of the Apos-

I. On the Ascension and Return of Christ.

1. The Ascension strictly Literal.

tles. For such is the force of the words ' to go up,' ' to be taken up,' ' to be parted from them,' ' to be received up,' which are employed in describing His ascension."

" That visible, manifest, bodily, or sensible intercourse or sojourning, therefore, which, in a circumscribed and visible form He had hitherto had with His disciples on earth, *He has by His ascension with-* *drawn from us who are on earth,* so that in that form, *and in that mode of presence, He does not now have intercourse with us* in the world." " But (in the form and mode of presence just de- scribed) thus He appears in heaven to the angels and saints " (Rev. xiv. 1). " In that form also in which the Apostles saw Him ascend, He shall *descend from heaven,* in glory, to the judg ment (Acts i. 2 ; iv. 16), in a visible and circumscribed form."

2. The Ascen- sion in a certain respect removing Christ from us.

" So far, (that is, on all the points above specified,) as I con- ceive, WE (Beza and Chemnitz) AGREE, but the point to be decided is this : Whether from what is true in a *certain respect* (*secundum quid*), an inference may be drawn which involves EVERY *respect* — whether from the admission of a fact in *one and a certain sense,* an inference may be drawn as to the same fact in *another and a different sense* — whether because Christ, in a *visible form, and a mode of pres-* *ence perceptible by human senses, does not in His body, locally,* have intercourse with His Church on earth, we are, therefore, to infer that in NO MODE is He present with His Church on earth according to the human nature He has assumed — whether Christ neither knows, nor can have any other than that local, visible, and sensible mode by which He can perform what the words of His testament declare." These words show clearly why the famous expression of Beza, " that the body of Christ is as remote from the Supper as the highest heaven is from earth," gave such offence. It was not that our theologians denied it, in a *certain* respect (*secundum quid*), but that Beza denied it absolutely in *every* respect (*simpliciter*). Hence the Formula Concordiæ (672), commenting on this language, ex- presses the offensive point of it thus : " That Christ is, in *such manner* (*ita, als*) received in heaven, as to be circumscribed and

3. Points of Agreement and of Disagreement with the Re- formed. State of the question as regards the rela- tion of Christ's Ascension to His personal pres- ence.

shut up in it, so that IN NO MODE WHATEVER (*nullo prorsus modo —
keinerlei Weise*) He can or will be present with us on earth in
His human nature."

"I cannot see the connection between the premises and the

4. The sophism
involved in the
Denial of Christ's
Personal Pres-
ence, because of
His ascension. conclusion, when, though Christ says He will be
present in the use of His Supper, it is argued, that
because this cannot be in any way of this wo ld,
(*for in this mode Christ has left* the world, AND IS NO
LONGER IN THE WORLD) therefore He is present there
IN NO OTHER MODE, though the words declare He is."   "A comparison of the parts in John xvi. will show in what sense
Christ has left the world, for He says (18): 'I came forth
from the Father, and am come into the world,' not that He had
left the Father, for He says (ch. viii. 29): 'He that sent me is
with me : the Father hath not left me alone,' or as if the Father,
who fills heaven and earth, were not in this world, but because
He had humbled Himself, though He was in the form of God.
From the *antithesis*, therefore, we may rightfully gather what
Christ means when he says: 'Again I leave the world and go
to the Father,' to wit, that after His work was finished, His
humiliation removed, all infirmity and sorrow laid aside, He
would be exalted to the highest glory and power of the Father,
and would be transferred from the mode of this world's life to
a heavenly mode of existence with the Father.   This explana
tion John himself gives (ch. xiii. 1–3), for when he tells us:
'Jesus knew that His hour was come that He should depart
out of this world unto the Father,' he subjoins this explanation: 'Knowing that the Father had given all things into His
hands, and that He was come from God, and went to God.'
Nay, Christ Himself gives us the explanation of these declarations of His.   For when by His Resurrection He had passed
into another mode of existence, though He offered Himself
then present to be seen and touched by the Apostles, yet He
says (Luke xxiv. 44), 'These are the words which I spake unto
you, WHILE I WAS YET WITH YOU.'   He shows, therefore, that
the sayings were already fulfilled, ('Yet a little while I am
with you,' 'I am no more in the world,' 'I leave the world,')
and that they are to be understood, NOT OF AN ABSENCE IN EVERY

SENSE (*omni modo*), but of another mode of life, of intercourse, and of presence."

"Though, therefore, this presence be not in any way of this world, which we can understand or comprehend, 5. General con-yet He can fulfil (the sacramental promise) in clusion. ANOTHER MODE, though it be incomprehensible to us. 'Christ is united and conjoined with us who are yet on earth, not indeed in any gross mode of this life, a mode which would make Him an *object of touch* (*attingentiæ*), but IN A SUPERNATURAL AND HEAVENLY MODE, YET TRULY.' 'The Article of the Ascension, therefore, not only does not overthrow the simple and genuine sense of the institution (of the Lord's Supper), but, on the contrary, rightly explained, confirms the verity of it.' "

" We believe and confess that the Son of God assumed the true and entire substance of a human nature, with II. The Body those essential properties which naturally accom- of Christ. pany and follow the substance of human nature. . . That substance, with its essential properties, He retained also after His Resurrection, though its infirmities were laid aside, which also, though He is in glory, we believe He retains true and entire. And according to those natural or essential properties, and on account of the natural mode of a true body, we have such sayings in Scripture as these: 'I was not there,' 'He is not here, but is risen.' According also to those properties, and agreeably to the mode of a true body, Luther, with Augustine and the Scholastics, believes that the body of Christ is now in glory, in that circumscribed form in which He showed Himself to Paul and Stephen; in which also He shall return to judgment, and in which He is seen in heaven by angels and saints."

" When Christ says: 'Where two or three are gathered together in my name, there am I in the midst of III. The Pres-them,' we rightly understand the promise of the ence of Christ. 1. The promise WHOLE CHRIST, *or of His entire person*, for He says of Christ's pres-that He, in whose name we are gathered, is present. ence. But no one will dare to say that the name of Christ is His divine nature alone. It is His whole person, in each nature, and according to each nature, and, indeed 'n His office of

Mediator and Saviour, for it is admitted that when the Scripture says a thing is done in the name of Christ, it denotes that this pertains to the person according to each nature."

"In regard to that presence of the whole Christ in the Church, there are special promises in the Word of God. For (Matt. xxviii.) when Jesus, after His Resurrection, had appeared upon a mountain in Galilee to more than five hundred of His disciples at once, when He was before them, *not in His divinity alone,* but whole and entire, in both natures, so that by that very presence on that mountain He gave the demonstration and the confirmation of the fact that He had risen in His true body, so that His disciples, when they saw Him, worshipped him, and when some doubted, as if there were a spirit, or a spectre appearing in an outward and visible form, Jesus approached and spake to them — all which, beyond controversy, pertains to the human nature which Christ assumed. And when He gave the command to His disciples to gather a Church throughout the whole world, He added the promise, 'Lo! I am with you always, even unto the end of the world. That promise, therefore, is rightly understood of the whole Christ, God and man, according to both natures; *for He who was then and there before them, promised His presence with His Church through all time* — but He was then present, not in His Divinity alone, but showing that even after His Resurrection, in glory, he had and retained the verity of His human nature. And He who was then entire in each nature, by a sure word and peculiar promise, says: 'I am present with you' (wherever, to wit, my Church shall be, throughout the whole world). And there is no reason whatever, in that most sweet promise of the presence of Christ in His Church, why we should separate and exclude that nature which was assumed by Him in which He is our kinsman and brother, and by which we 'are members of His body, of His flesh, and of His bones,' (Eph. v. 30,) since He, in giving the promise, marks and describes, by many circumstances, the nature he assumed, as we have shown from the text."

With similar conclusiveness does Chemnitz reason in regard to other passages, as, for instance, Mark xvi. 19, 20.   " · The

Lord . . sat on the right hand of God, and they went forth
and preached *everywhere*, the Lord working with them and
confirming the word with signs following.' They preached
everywhere, the Lord working with them: therefore the Lord
Jesus worked with them *everywhere*." So, also, in regard to
the words: " The Son of man which is in heaven " (John iii. 13).

" That Christ, according to His divine nature, is present with
His Church, and with all other creatures, is not
questioned. The divine essence is infinite, immeasurable, illimitable, uncompounded: the operation
of God proceeds from His power. . . Wherefore
it is usual and right to say that God is everywhere,
or in all things essentially, or by essence, presence, and power,
without mingling, circumscription, distraction, or mutation
of Himself. Because the divine nature is incapable of parti-
tion, not having part separate from part, it is total totally,
wherever it exists; nor is there part in part, but it is total in
all, total in each, and total above all, as Damascenus says. And
the old writers say: The divine essence is within all, yet is not
included — it is out of all, yet not excluded." Luther, in a
passage so closely parallel with the one we have just quoted
from Chemnitz, that we cannot forbear placing the two side by
side, says: " God is not a Being with extension, of whom we
can say, He is so high, so broad, so thick; but He is a supernatural, unsearchable Being, who is total and entire in every
granule, and yet in, and over, and apart from all creatures. . .
Nothing is so small that God is not smaller, nothing so great
that God is not greater. . . He is, in a word, an ineffable
Being, over and apart from all that we can speak or think."

" Since, however, in the person of Christ, there subsists
not only the divine, but the human nature, the
question at present concerns the *latter*, to wit,
where and how the person of Christ, according to
both natures, or in His assumed human nature, is present — or
wills, and is able to be present ? "

After dwelling on Christ's presence at the Supper, Chemnitz
says:

" But not alone in that place — not at that time alone when

2. The Point of Agreement as to Christ's Presence. Nature of Divine Omnipresence.

3. The mooted question as to Christ's presence.

the Supper of the Lord is observed in the public assembly of the Church, is the whole Christ, in both His natures, present with the Church militant on earth, as if when that celebration was over He withdrew His presence, and the members of His Church, apart from that public assembly, were, while in their vocations, their trials, and temptations, deprived of that most sweet presence of Christ, their High Priest and King, their Head and their Brother. On the contrary, there is in the observance of the Lord's Supper a public, solemn, and peculiar attestation and sealing of the truth, that Christ, our Mediator and Saviour, wishes mercifully to be present with His Church, which is war-ring in the world, to be present, *not with the half, or with one part of Himself only, to wit, His divinity alone,* BUT WHOLE AND ENTIRE, that is, in THAT NATURE ALSO WHICH HE HAS ASSUMED, IN which He is of like nature with us, our Kinsman and our Brother — that nature in which He was tempted, so that He might have compassion on us in our griefs — that nature in which, by His sufferings and death, He finished the work of our redemption, so that thus we may be rendered members of His body, of His flesh, and of His bones (Eph. v. 30). And because our reason cannot grasp or comprehend this, St. Paul adds: 'This is a great mystery: but I speak concerning Christ and the Church.' "

"The humanity which Christ assumed was not, by that union with Deity, converted or transmuted into an infinite or immense essence, but has and retains in that very union, and after it, the verity of a human nature, and its physical or essential properties, by which a true human body consists in a certain, finite, and cir-cumscribed symmetry (dimension) of members, and which. consisting in a local or finite situation and position of mem-bers, has one part distinct from another in a certain order. The body of Christ, therefore, with the property of its own nature, is essentially or naturally finite, that is, according to its natural properties, which it has and retains even in that union, IT LOCALLY AND CIRCUMSCRIPTIVELY OCCUPIES A CERTAIN PLACE."[*]

IV. Modes of Presence. 1. The body of Christ in its own nature local.

* De duab. Nat. 174

" That mode of visible converse, and that circumscribed and local form of the presence of His body, according to the condition and mode of this earthly life, according to the flesh, He has by His ascension TAKEN FROM US WHO are on earth. And this is what He means when He says : ' Again I leave the world,— me ye have not always.' These words, therefore, speak OF A MODE OF PRESENCE, according to the respect and condition of this world, A MODE VISIBLE, SENSIBLE, LOCAL, AND CIRCUMSCRIBED, according to which mode of presence CHRIST IS NOW NO LONGER ORDINARILY PRESENT WITH HIS CHURCH ON EARTH." *

2. And as to its locality is no longer on earth.

" Since the body of Christ, neither in the (personal) union, NOR IN GLORY, is transmuted into an infinite or immense substance, therefore through itself (*per se*), and of itself (*ex se*), EVEN IN GLORY, IT IS FINITE in the property of its nature, AND BY THE MODE OF GLORIFIED BODIES IS SOMEWHERE (alicubi), the prerogative of the personal union, as I have said, being excepted. And in this visible form or condition of glorified bodies, Christ, in His body, IS NOT PRESENT to us in this life, in the Church militant on earth, but is in the heavens, whence He shall return to judgment, in that form in which He now offers Himself to be seen by the souls of the blessed, and by angels."†

3. Is not present through the properties of a glorified body, but in that mode is in heaven.

"According to the natural properties of a true body, or by any essential attribute, the body of Christ (which is by the property of its nature finite) IS NOT PRESENT in all places where the Supper is administered, EITHER BY LOCAL CIRCUMSCRIPTION, OR BY ANY VISIBLE, SENSIBLE, OR NATURAL MODE, respect, or condition of this world.   This mode has been taken from the world."

4. Modes of presence rejected.

" Nor is the presence such as that of glorified bodies : in that form He will not appear till the final judgment."

" We by no means teach that the body of Christ, as a boundless mass, is expanded, distributed, diffused, drawn out, or

---

* De duab. Nat. 175.   The limitation which Chemnitz designs to make by the word " ordinarily," has reference to such cases as the appearing of Christ to Saul on the way to Damascus, to Stephen, etc., as he shows at large. **Do. 176, 177.**
† Do 1C. Cf. 177.

extended through all places (or as Damascenus expresses it, that the flesh of Christ is corporeally co-extended with the Deity assuming it,) so that IN THIS WAY IT IS PRESENT."

"Nor by multiplication, or replication — as the image of one body in many pieces of a broken mirror. The body of Christ is one, not many."

"By no means, also, do we think that the body of Christ, either in (the personal) union, or in glory, its substance being lost, and its essential properties abolished, is converted or transmuted into a spiritual substance, infinite, immense, and now in its essential property uncircumscribed, so that by reason of its essential, infinite immensity, it is in all places, and fills all things, as divinity in this mode, and in this respect is present everywhere; for the substance of the natures and their essential properties remain in Christ unaffected, in that very union and glory."

"Nor that the divine nature alone, and not the human also is present."

"Nor that it agrees with the words of the institution, that we should understand the presence of the merit, virtue, and efficacy merely of the body of Christ, the substance of it being excluded and separated."*

"Christ, according to His human nature, wills to be present in His Church, where His Supper is celebrated on earth, and through the humanity He has assumed, as by an organ connate with us, as the ancients express it, wishes to apply, confirm, and seal to us His benefits, and thus to execute in the Church His office of life-giving, according to both natures, through His life-giving flesh."†

5. The mode of presence affirmed.

The premise which is conceded is that "in a physical respect, in a natural mode and condition of this world, one body, according to its essential or natural properties, is not at the same time in different places, nor is there an essential or natural property in the body of Christ of being in different places, nor is it by any essential or natural attribute of Christ's body that it is present at the same time in all those places where the Supper of the Lord is

6. The premise which is conceded, and the inference which is denied.

---

* De duab. natur. 173.   † Do. 178.

celebrated, as in divinity it is the essential attribute of infinite immensity to be everywhere. ALL THESE THINGS WE CONCEDE."

The inference which is denied is this : " But it *by no means follows* from this that the divine power of the Son of God cannot effect THAT, IN ANOTHER MODE than that which is natural and according to the physical properties of a body, or in the sensible manner of this world, with His body remaining safe in its substance, and its essential properties abiding HE SHOULD BE PRESENT WHERESOEVER HE WILLS, IN A MODE WHICH IS SUPERNATURAL, DIVINE, OR HEAVENLY, INCOMPREHENSIBLE TO US."

" Nor is there a contradiction involved when the same body is said to be in one place, IN THE NATURAL MODE, according to its essential properties, and if it is maintained that beyond its physical attributes, through the will and power of God, it is present not in one, but in MANY places, in a SUPERNATURAL, HEAVENLY, OR DIVINE MODE ; for there is no contradiction when what is contrary is attributed to the same thing IN DIFFERENT RESPECTS AND MODES. And Justin rightly says: We commit the things of nature to nature, the things of art to art, and the things of God to God ; but Him all things obey."

These extracts, as they throw light upon the Sacramental questions discussed by Dr. Gerhart, may also be useful in illustrating yet more directly the point next raised. After finishing his parallel between the doctrines of the two Churches on the Lord's Supper, He takes up the " Reformed (and he might have added, the Lutheran,) Doctrine of the Person of Christ." On this great point, according to Dr. Gerhart, " the Lutheran view is in the line of the ancient Eutychian, and the Reformed in the line of the ancient Nestorian method of thought, though it would be unjust to charge either Confession with holding the corresponding ancient heresy." God manifest in the flesh. The Lutheran doctrine of the Person of Christ.

We shall not attempt to question the Doctor's position as to the Nestorianizing element in the Reformed view, but we think that the idea that the Lutheran view of the person of Christ is in the " line of the ancient Eutychian," proceeds from a wholly incorrect judgment The Lutheran view not Eutychian.

of what the Lutheran view is. On the contrary, the statements of Lutheran doctrine, beyond every other, are guarded with extraordinary care against the Eutychian tendency. We maintain, further, that no system is more thoroughly antagonistic to Eutychianism than the Lutheran system, properly understood. Even the Reformed doctrine itself has a point of apparent contact with it, which Lutheranism has not. Eutyches taught that Christ has but one nature. The Lutheran Church holds " that the two natures, divine and human, are inseparably conjoined in unity of person, one Christ, true God and true man."* Eutyches taught that the body of Christ was not of the same substance as ours. The Lutheran Church teaches that " Jesus Christ is man, of the substance of His mother, born into the world, perfect man, of a rational soul and human flesh subsisting. One Christ, not by the conversion of divinity into flesh, but by the assumption of humanity to God; one, indeed, not by confusion of substances, but by unity of person, for as the rational soul and flesh is one man, so God and man is one Christ."† The doctrine of Eutyches is, moreover, expressly rejected in several passages of the Formula Concordiæ. But is not the Reformed doctrine, that Christ's *personal* presence at the Lord's Supper is only in one nature, a concession logically so far to Eutyches, that it seems to admit that sometimes, and somewhere, nay, rather always, almost everywhere, Christ has but one nature?

Alike removed from Nestorianism and Eutychianism, the <small>Illustration of</small> doctrine of the Evangelical Lutheran Church may <small>the Lutheran</small> be thus illustrated : The essential properties of <small>doctrine.</small> each nature of our Lord are undisturbed by their union in Him, but as these two natures form one inseparable person, the whole person is involved in the acts of each part of it. Everything that the Saviour did and suffered is both divine and human, that is, it is personal. *He* did, and suffered all, and *He* is both human and divine. Every act, indeed, is done, every suffering endured, *through* or *by* the one or the other nature, but not without the personal presence of the other. Jesus Christ wrought miracles *through* the divine

* Augsburg Confession, Art. III.   † Athanasian Creed, 29–35.

nature, but they were wrought *by* the human nature. *Through* His divine omnipotence sight was given to the blind, but His divine omnipotence wrought it *by* His human touch. Jesus Christ died according to His human nature, but His death was the death of a divine person. *Through* His human infirmity He was crucified, but that human weakness wrought *by* His divine majesty an infinite sacrifice. Godhead cannot bleed, but the Church is purchased by the blood of God ; for He who bleeds is in one inseparable person, God as well as man, and His blood has efficacy, not because of the properties of the nature according to which He bleeds, but because of the attributes of His whole person, which is divine. Had not He who bled been personally God as well as man, His blood would not have availed. Jesus Christ is essentially and necessarily omnipresent according to the divine nature, but His human nature not of its own essence, or by a necessity resulting from its own attributes, but because the divine has taken it into personal union with itself, is rendered present *through* the divine. The divine neither loses nor imparts any essential attribute, nor does the human lose any essential attribute of its own, nor receive any essential attribute of the divine ; but the divine, omnipresent of itself, renders present the human which has been taken into its own person. The doctrine on which this rests is known in theological technology as the " *Communicatio idiomatum*," that is, the *common participation* of properties, the doctrine that the properties of the divine and human natures are actually the properties of the whole person of Christ, and actually exercised by Him in the unity of His person. We Lutherans affirm that there is a real *common participation* of the whole person in the properties of both natures. The Reformed deny it, and say that there is no real *common participation*, but that each nature is isolated from the other in its attributes, and that the person of Christ has only the common participation in the names of the two sets of attributes, the human and divine. In other words, the question which divides us is between a *communicatio idiomatum*, and a *communicatio nominum*, the question whether the two natures enjoy a common participation of properties in the one person, or merely a common participation of names. To Lutherans, the view we reject seems logically to run out into a denial of the unity of Christ's person, and of the reality of the incarnation.

It may tend to give a clearer view of the doctrine to present Four points in four points in it, in the order in which they stand the doctrine. in the Formula of Concord.

1. The Lutheran Church holds that from a *personal* union of the divine and human, it follows that there are not two Christs, outwardly conjoined, one of whom is God, and the other a man, but one Christ, who is both God and man in one person.

2. These two natures are not fused into one substance, nor is the one absorbed by, or transmuted into the other, but each nature retains its essential properties, neither losing its own, nor receiving those of the other.

3. Dr. Gerhart, in defining the true doctrine as he regards it, says: "The Reformed predicated the essential attributes of divinity of the divine nature only." So do we. Dr. Gerhart is entirely mistaken in imagining that the doctrine of our Church is in conflict with this position. In the very statement of our doctrine over against its opposite, the Formula Concordiæ says :* "The attributes of the divine nature are, to be omnipotent, eternal, infinite, and of itself, according to the attribute of its nature and of its own natural essence, to be present everywhere, and to be omniscient. All these attributes neither are, nor ever can become, the attributes of the human nature."

4. Nor is Dr. Gerhart more happy in stating a point of difference between the doctrine of our Church and his own, when he says: "The Reformed predicated the essential attributes of humanity of (Christ's) human nature only." So do we. The paragraph of the Formula of Concord next to the one we have quoted, says: "The properties of human nature are: To be a corporeal creature, to consist of flesh and blood, to be finite and circumscribed, to suffer, die, ascend, descend, to move from place to place, to hunger, thirst, grow cold, suffer from heat, and such like. These never are, nor can become the attributes of the divine nature."

* Page 606.

Our Confessions teach that the essential attributes of Christ's human nature belong to it forever. He remains a true man, with every essential property of the nature of a true man. The divine nature loses no essential attributes of deity, and the human nature receives none. To be *essentially, or by virtue of its own nature*, everywhere present, omnipotent, and omniscient, is something divine; Summary of the view of our Church. and hence the Lutheran Church holds that the Godhead alone is essentially, and by virtue of its own nature, everywhere present, allwise, and almighty. So also to be essentially, or by virtue of its own nature limited, in presence, in power, and in wisdom, pertains to the human nature, and hence the Lutheran Church holds that the humanity of Christ is neither omnipresent, omniscient, nor omnipotent, *essentially or by virtue of its own nature*. The humanity of Christ has all the essential (by no means, however, all the accidental) properties of ours, and in and of itself is finite. God became man, but Godhead does not become humanity. A man is God — but humanity does not become Deity. In this aspect the Lutheran Church draws a distinction, total and all-comprehending, between the presence of the Godhead of Christ and the presence of His humanity. Omnipresence is the essential attribute of the divine, and hence His Godhead is necessarily, in and of itself, in virtue of its own nature, present. But the essential attribute of the human is to have a determinate presence, and hence the human nature of Christ has such a determinate presence, nor in and of itself would the human nature have any other presence; but as it is in one person with the divine, it is in that one person rendered present with and through the divine. In other words, what the divine has in its essence and of itself, the human has and exercises through the divine, in consequence of its personal union with it. We might imitate one of our Lord's own deep expressions in characterizing it, and might suppose Him to say: " As my divine nature hath omnipresence in itself, so hath it given to my human nature to have omnipresence in itself."

From what has been said, our readers will be prepared to answer for themselves the most specious objection which is

brought against the doctrine of our Church. That objection
is this: That to be omnipresent is an essential attribute of
Godhead, and, therefore, the humanity of Christ cannot be
omnipresent; for that would be to suppose humanity to have
Answer to the an essential attribute of divinity. The reply is
leading objection
to the Lutheran easy: To be omnipresent *of itself, in virtue of its*
doctrine.   *own essence,* is an attribute of the divine, and, therefore, the humanity of Christ is not, and cannot be omnipresent
of itself, in virtue of its own essence; but the Godhead can render
it present *through* the divine, with which it is one person. The
one humanity of Christ can be present in two modes: one, finite
and independent, in which mode it is present *of itself, by virtue
of its own essence;* the other, infinite and dependent, in which
it is not present *of itself, in virtue of its own essence,* for that, we
admit, would be to claim for it a divine attribute, but is rendered present by the divine. In other words, the Godhead,
which of itself *is* present, *makes* present the human, which is
one person with it. So, to be conscious in its own essence, or of
its own nature, is an essential property of soul, not of matter;
therefore, the human eye, in its own essence or nature, has no
power of being conscious of light; but when the eye is united
as a part of the body, in one person with the soul, the eye has
a real sight *through* the soul, as the soul has its sight *by* the
eye; but there are not two consciousnesses. The soul does not
give up its consciousness, nor does the eye receive it. Both
retain their essential attributes. The eye does not become
spirit, nor the soul become matter; nor has the soul one consciousness, nor the eye another; but the whole person has its
one consciousness, through the soul and by the eye. There is
a common participation of the two natures in the act of the
one person; and not verbally, but really, the man sees through
his soul and by his eye; the eye itself really receiving a distinct set of powers, from its union with the soul, and the soul
exercising its own essential power, under a wholly new set of
conditions, in consequence of its union with the eye. But if
some minute philosopher persists in saying: You then attribute
to matter the consciousness which alone pertains to mind, we
reply: An independent, self-originating consciousness belongs

to mind; but a dependent, soul-originated consciousness belongs to matter. There is no transfer of properties; but there is a common participation in them. And so, in some sense, and yet with the infinite difference made by the nature of the subjects in this case, we reply to the sophism against the doctrine of our Church: The divine in Christ is forever divine; the human forever human; but as they can never be confounded, so can they never be separated; and the one person participates in both, and each has a personal communication with the attributes of the other. "Great is the MYSTERY of Godliness: GOD WAS MANIFEST IN THE FLESH."

In Dr. Gerhart's further development of the doctrine of the German Reformed Church, especially as related to that of the Lutheran Church, he goes on to say, in immediate connection with the words on which we have already dwelt: "The Reformed . . thus emphasizing especially the difference of the two natures, though affirming them to be inseparably and eternally united in one person." The German Reformed Church certainly does not affirm more emphatically than the Lutheran that the two natures are different, although it may exaggerate the difference until it obscures the doctrine of the unity. But when Dr. Gerhart says that his Church affirms the two natures to " be *inseparably* and *eternally* united in the one person," he strikes the very rock which is fatal to the logical consistency of the whole un-Lutheran view of this great subject. For at the Lord's Supper he admits that the divine nature of Christ is present. Now, either the human nature of Christ is united with the divine there, or it is not. If it be there united with it, it must be there present with it, for personal union implies not only presence, but the most intimate species of presence. If it be not united with it there, it is separated from it there, and consequently not *inseparably* united. Except in the locality in which the human nature of Christ is confined, on the Reformed theory, the human is separated from the divine and the divine from the human. So far then from the union, on this theory, being inseparable, there is but a solitary point at which the two natures are not separated. As is infinity to a

The Reformed and Lutheran doctrines of the Person of Christ.

31

space of a few feet, so is the separateness of the two natures of Christ to their unity on the Reformed theory. And this shows that the divergence of the Reformed and Lutheran views on the Lord's Supper originates in a radical diversity on one point of doctrine, of the highest importance, in regard to the person of Christ. When the Augsburg Confession* says that the two natures are "in unitate personæ *inseperabiliter* conjunctæ," (in unity of person *inseparably* conjoined,) it *asserts* what *in its sense* the Reformed doctrine *denies*. The connection of the two doctrines of the inseparableness of Christ's person, and the co-presence of them in the Supper, is no afterthought of the stricter Lutheran theology, but was distinctly before Melanchthon's mind in the whole era of the composition of the Confession. Thus, January 30, 1529, Melanchthon wrote: " It is not to be imagined that the *divinity of Christ is anywhere* where His humanity is not ; for what is this but to *separate* Christ ? "†
And a little later, April, 1529: " Why should there be these contentions in regard to the Lord's Supper ? As all confess that Christ is present in the communion (*synaxi*), according to His divine nature, *to what purpose is it to separate the humanity from the divinity ?* "‡ In a similar strain he writes to Œcolampadius, April 8, 1529: " I look at Christ's promises of this kind, ' Lo, I am with you alway, even unto the end of the world ! ' where there is no need to *tear away the divinity from the humanity. Hence* (proinde) I believe that this sacrament is the testimony of a true presence. . . It is *a sentiment unworthy of Christians*, that Christ in such a way occupies a part of heaven — that He sits in it as if shut up in prison. . . We are to form our judgment of heavenly things not from geometry, but from the Word of God."§ These extracts show that Melanchthon meant by an "inseparable" union, one which excluded the separation in space as well as in time, and that the doctrine of the Formula of Concord on the personal co-presence

---

* Art. III. 1.

† Corp. Reform. I. No. 585. Non est fingendum, alicubi esse divinitatem Christi, ubi non sit humanitas. Quid hoc est aliud, quam seperare Christum ?

‡ Corp. Ref. I. No. 596. Quid attinet discerpere humanitatem a divinitate ?

§ Corp. Ref. I. No. 598.

of both natures of Christ is but the doctrine of the Augsburg Confession amplified.

Dr. Gerhart goes on to state very fairly the doctrines which are necessarily involved in the view of his Church. He says: "Before the Ascension, the human was located on earth." With this proposition as a Our Saviour's presence on earth.
positive one, we agree; but if it means that even when on earth the human nature of our Lord had no capacity of a higher presence through the divine in the one person, our Church would deny it. Our Lord speaks of Himself to Nicodemus as "He that came down from heaven, even the Son of man which is in heaven." The difference between our Lord on earth and in glory was not in what He had intrinsically, nor in what He had the ability to do, but in what He voluntarily exercised, or chose to forego. His humiliation consisted in the ordinary abnegation of the use of the powers which abode in Him intrinsically; but at times He chose, even on earth, to reveal that glory. He allowed the form of God to manifest itself in His transfiguration, and in His miracles, but His equality with God was none the more positive then than when His sweat, mingling with His blood, fell to the ground in Gethsemane. He moved on earth in the ordinary voluntary suspension of the exercise of His great prerogatives. While our Church, therefore, holds most firmly that His human nature was on earth locally, she denies that it had no other power of presence than the local, and that in every sense, necessarily and unchangeably, it was on earth only.

But Dr. Gerhart states still more fully, and with even more transparent fairness, the doctrine of his Church thus: "After the ascension it (the human) was located at the right hand of God, and nowhere else, Our Saviour's presence in heaven. The Reformed theory.
being *excluded* from the earth, and *limited* to the place of exaltation in heaven." The symbolical orthodoxy of this position he proves by a citation from the Genevan Catechism, which is all very well, if the German Reformed Church is in the whole unity of the Calvinistic faith; but is not so satisfactory, if that Church, as we understand some of its ablest divines now to contend, is not Calvinistic.

In Dr. Gerhart's statement, if it be analyzed, are the following propositions: 1. That the human nature of Christ is *localized*. 2. That its locality is at the right hand of God. 3. That by necessary consequence the right hand of God is a locality. 4. That the human nature of Christ is nowhere else; but is, 5. Excluded from the earth; and, 6. Limited to the place of exaltation in heaven.

On every one of these points the Lutheran Church differs from the Reformed, if Dr. Gerhart presents the Reformed view correctly, as we think, in the main, he does.

The Lutheran Antithesis.

1. The generally received view in our Church is that even the finite presence of our Saviour's human nature is not *local*, but *definitive*, that is, that its mode of presence is more closely analogous to that in which a created spirit is present, than to that of unglorified matter. St. Paul declares that the resurrection body "is a *spiritual* body," that is, a body analogous in its properties to spirit, and, as the antithesis to "natural," a body with supernatural properties. That our Saviour at His resurrection entered on the plenary use of the powers whose exercise He had foregone in His humiliation, is so well known as the doctrine of our Church, that we need cite no passages to prove it. But we might cite many passages from Calvinistic writers to show that not all of them sympathize with the disposition to narrow the power of our Saviour's humanity. We will give a single extract from one of the most finished and thoughtful Calvinistic writers of our day, the late Dr. James Hamilton. It will be found in his delightful little volume, "A Morning beside the Lake of Galilee," which dwells upon one scene in our Saviour's resurrectionlife on earth. He says: "Christ came in the morning. So at first we are apt to say; but it would be putting it more correctly, if we said that Christ, who had been present all the night, allowed Himself to be seen in the morning. He was now risen from the dead, and had put on that glorious body which evades our grosser sense, and needs an act of will to make it visible.* In His ubiquitous Godhead everywhere

1. The Saviour's resurrection-life Hamilton

---

* After His resurrection, Christ's body was only visible by a distinct act of His will. — *Chrysostom, quoted by Trench.*

present, at any moment, or in any place, He could emerge to view and reappear in corporeal guise, so that former intimacy was able to exclaim, ' It is the Lord,' and so that He Himself was able to say, ' Reach hither thy hand, and thrust it into my side ;' and as soon as the purpose was fulfilled, without necessarily quitting the spot, the glorified body ceased to be seen. In its escape from the sepulchre, more entirely trans-figured than it had been on the Holy Mount, it was only when the Lord Jesus so willed, that in flesh and blood, as of old, that body stood revealed ; and when the design was accom-plished, it again retired into the super-sensual sphere of its habitual invisibleness. It was ' on this wise that Jesus showed Himself,' when, at any period after His resurrection, He was seen at all. It was not by entering an apartment, or by arriving from a journey, but by coming forth from the impalpable and viewless, that, whether to longing disciples or to the startled persecutor, He stood disclosed ; no phantom, no mere vision, courting severest scrutiny : ' Handle me and see,'— and *into* that materialism, reëmbodied by His own divine volition, the normal state of His glorified humanity was such as mortal sense cannot grasp ; and just as when the body was ' earthy,' the thing super-natural was for His ' face to shine as the sun,' so now that it was ' heavenly,' the thing supernatural was for that body to come out appreciable by untransfigured organs — perceptible to eyes and ears which were not yet immortal like itself."

If such was the nature of the manifestations of Christ's spiritual body in what we might style the provisional inter-vals, what might we expect when it entered upon all the pleni-tude of its glory at the right hand of God ?

2. For to us the right hand of God is not a place, nor is the ascension to His right hand the rising to a place. If the right hand of God means a place, we might well ask, Where is His .eft hand ? To sit at the right hand of God is to be associated in His sovereign rule, and to share in His sovereign power. The right hand of God, if you relate it to presence, 2. The right is everywhere ; if you take it in its Scriptural use, ^{hand of God.} it either means the omnipotence of God, or His regal majesty, and has no reference to space at all. When we teach that

Christ sitteth at the right hand of God, we mean that He rules in co-sovereignty with the Father, in a potency which, as it is exercised on all things, must be in all places, a potency which, as it is inseparable from the substance of His whole person, in which it inheres, implies the presence of that whole person, and, therefore, of His humanity, which is an essential and inseparable constituent of that person.

3. Hence the Lutheran Church, while it firmly believes that the presence which the human nature of Christ has in and of itself is determinate and limited, believes that there is a presence of that human nature no less real, in and through the divine nature with which it is one person, and that in this mode of presence it is as really on earth as in heaven. God has *given* Him the uttermost parts of the earth for His possession; His mediatorial dominion is from sea to sea, and from the river unto the ends of the earth. God has said: "I will set His hand in the sea, and His right hand in the rivers," and we devoutly rest in the faith that our Saviour rules not by vicars, but in His own glorious and all-sufficient person, true God and true man inseparably. When we remember that the 3. Spirit and only absolute essence is Spirit, that all matter is matter. thought into being by the infinite Spirit, rests on that essence for its continued existence, derives all its attributes from, owes all its properties to, the will which gave and continues its being; when we remember that the body of our Lord is in personal union with the absolute essence which creates all things, we can easily draw the inference not only that any properties which it was possible for God to will that His body should have, should belong to it, but that it would have an adaptation as a personal organ of the divine nature, and properties necessary for that adaptation which would infinitely transcend the sublimest forms of all other matter. If such subtle matter, as the etherial medium which undulates into light, be the mere raiment of God, what may be the exquisite subtlety of that matter which is assumed into His very person?. Science detects a form of matter whose undulations, in forming one color, are seven hundred and twenty-seven millions of millions in a second, and it is within the power of God

to give to matter properties which transcend those of light, infinitely more than the properties of light transcend those of lead or clay. When we think of matter with this amazing range of qualities, taken as the very organ of incarnate Deity, we may realize that the demands of the "spiritual body" of our Lord, on faith, pertain to-the highest mysteries and sublimest trust with which it called to justify its work of bringing every thought into captivity to the obedience of Christ.

Dr. Gerhart goes on to illustrate his position: "The Heidelberg Catechism," he says, "inquires in the forty- seventh Question: 'Is not then Christ with us, as He has promised, unto the end of the world?'" It seems as if it were felt that the Reformed position was open to the suspicion of seeming to empty Christ's promise of its fulness. Nor does the answer of the Catechism relieve this suspicion. Its answer is: "Christ is true man and true God. According to His human nature, He is not now upon earth; but according to His Godhead, majesty, grace, and Spirit, He at no time departs from us." The reply wears to us the air of a certain evasiveness, as if it parried the question rather than answered it. It seems to answer a certain question, but really answers another; or rather, it seems to answer affirmatively, but actually answers negatively. If Christ *be* true man and true God, then humanity and divinity are inseparable elements of His essence; where either is wanting, Christ is wanting. If the question be, Is the divine nature of Christ present? the Heidelberg Catechism answers it, affirming that it is. If the question be, Is the human nature of Christ present? the Heidelberg Catechism answers, and says it is not. But if the question be, as it is, Is Christ present? the Heidelberg Catechism does not answer it, for it leaves the very heart of the query untouched: Can Christ, in the absence of an integral part of His person, really be said to be present? As far as the Heidelberg Catechism implies an answer to this question, that answer seems to us to be, Christ is *not* present. Ursinus, in His explanation of the Catechism, is compelled virtually to concede this, for on the thirty-sixth Question, in reply to the objection, that on His theory, as "the divinity is but half Christ, therefore only

[marginal note:] The Heidelberg Catechism.

half Christ is present with the Church," he replies: "If by nalf Christ they understand one nature which is united to the other in the same person, *the whole reason may be granted:* namely, that not both, *but one nature only of Christ*, though united to the other, that is, His Godhead, *is present with us.*" Leydecker, in commenting on this Question, says: "The *absence of the human nature* does not take away the presence of the Deity." Heppe (himself Reformed) indeed declares that it is the Reformed doctrine that "the humanity of Christ is not a part of His person," and quotes to sustain this position, Polanus, Heidegger, Zanchius, and Cocceius, but it does not strike us that Dr. Heppe has understood his authorities, or the natural force of his own terms.

Nor does the Heidelberg Catechism relieve the grand difficulty of its theory by its next question and answer, which Dr. Gerhart also quotes. "Question forty-eight: But if His human nature is not present wherever His Godhead is, are not the two natures in Christ separated from one another? By no means; for since the Godhead is incomprehensible and everywhere present, it must follow that the same is both beyond the limits of the human nature He assumed, and yet none the less in it, and remains personally united to it." This reply, as we understand it, runs out logically into this: The Godhead is inseparably connected with the humanity, but the humanity is not inseparably connected with the Godhead; that is, one part of the person is inseparably connected with the other, but the other is not inseparably connected with that one part: the whole second person of the Trinity is one person with the humanity in one point of space, but everywhere else it is not one person with it. There is, in fact, apparently no personal union whatever, but a mere local connection — not a dwelling of the fulness of the Godhead bodily, but simply an operative manifestation; two persons separable and in every place but one separated, not one inseparable person — inseparable in space as well as in time. As God dwells in His substantial presence everywhere, as He has a special and gracious presence in the bodies and souls of believers, as He so dwelt in inspired men as to make them miraculous organs of truth and of supernatural powers, it is exceedingly difficult to prevent this low view from running out into Socinianism, as, indeed, it actually has run in Calvinistic lands, so that it became a proverb, often met with in the older theological writers — "A young Calvinist, an old Socinian." This peril is confessed and mourned over by great Calvinistic divines. New England is an illustration of it on an immense scale, in our own land. Even the Socinianism of other parts of the Protestant world illustrates the same tendency, for these communions have either developed out of Calvinistic Churches, as, for example, the Arminians, or have first gone over, practically, to the Reformed basis, and on it have built their later Rationalism, as in the apostate portions of the Lutheran Church. Just those portions of the Reformed Churches which have been most free from Socinianism, are those which have been characteristically Lutheranizing, as the German Reformed and the Church of England. And it seems to us that the most dangerous consequences might be logically deduced from the Reformed theory. The divine nature is a totality and an absolute unit, in which there can be no fractions. It does not exist, and is not present, by parts, but as a whole. It is present not by extension nor locality, but after another manner, wholly incomprehensible to us, not less real, but if there may be degrees of reality, more real than the local. If the divine nature is present at all without the human nature of Christ, the whole of it is present without that human nature. If the whole divine nature of Christ be present on earth without His human nature, then the whole divine nature is unincarnate here. If it be unincarnate here, then it could take to itself another human nature on earth, or, for the matter of that, an infinite number of human natures, each of them as really one person with it apparently, on this theory, as the human nature of Christ now is. If, moreover, such a conjunction as this theory asserts is really a unity of person, then this infinitude of human natures being one person in the divine, would be one person with each other also. Nor is this supposition of the evolution of such a theory from these premises purely imaginary. Dr. Brewster, in his Defence of the Theory of the Plurality of Worlds, has actually tried to solve certain difficulties by suggesting the idea of multiplied cotemporaneous incarnations of the Son of God in different worlds. "May not the divine nature," he says, "which can neither suffer nor die, and which in our planet, *once* only, clothed itself in humanity, resume else-where a physical form, and expiate the guilt of unnumbered worlds?"* This is giving us Hindoo mythology for divine theology, and substituting Vishnu for Christ.

This, then, is the result which our Church, guided by God's Spirit in His Word, has reached: That a unity The Result. which does not imply the co-presence of its con-stituent parts cannot be called a personal unity, that unity which is so perfect that the very identity of the subject of it centres in it. With this result our faith reverently coincides, and our reason is in harmony with our faith. To us there seems no real incarnation possible, *logically*, on any other theory; but if logic allowed it, the Word of God would not.

Dr. Gerhart goes on to say: "The question arises logically: The Lord's Sup- Since the humanity of Christ is limited to the right per — Reformed hand of God, and believers on earth commune, in and Lutheran views. the Lord's Supper, with the flesh and blood of Christ, no less than with His Spirit, how is the communion established and maintained?" As a voucher for the doctrine which underlies the question, Dr. Gerhart gives, in a note, a sentence from Calvin's Confession of Faith, concerning the Eucharist, 1537, which, literally translated, runs thus: "When, therefore, we speak of the communion which believers have with Christ, we mean that they commune not less with His flesh and blood than with His Spirit, so that they thus possess the whole Christ." Dr. Gerhart goes on to say, in answer to the question given above: "In opposition to the Ubiquitarian theory of the Lutherans, the Reformed theologians replied: By the mysterious agency of the Holy Spirit, elevating the hearts of believers to Christ in heaven, who feeds and nour-ishes them with the life-giving power of His flesh and blood." If we analyze these sentences, we find that they express or imply the following propositions:

* More Worlds than One. N. Y. 1854. p. 148.

1. "The humanity of Christ is limited to the right hand of God." We have tried to show that the right First Proposi tion. hand of God is not limited, but, on the contrary, involves omnipresent and omnipotent rule. Whatever effect, therefore, being at the right hand of God may have on the humanity of Christ, it certainly does not limit it.

2. "Believers, on earth, commune, in the Lord's Supper, with the flesh and blood of Christ." If by this Second Proposition. is meant that none but those who receive the Lord's Supper in faith share in its blessings, the statement is entirely Scriptural and Lutheran. The Augsburg Confession expressly rejects the idea of those who teach that "the Sacraments justify by the outward work wrought, (*ex opere operato*,) and who do not teach that faith is required in the use of the Sacraments."

But as the communion is not based upon something ideal, but on a supernatural verity, upon a presence spiritual, heavenly, and incomprehensible in its manner, yet most true, a presence of the human nature of Christ, as the mystery of this presence has its heart not in us, but in the Incarnate Mediator, we believe that alike to those who receive the Supper in faith, and to those who receive it in unbelief, the object sacramentally received is the same. The believer embraces it in faith, to his soul's health; and the unbeliever, "not discerning the Lord's body," but treating that which he receives as if it were mere bread, "eateth and drinketh damnation to himself," but it is the same thing which is salutary to the one and judicial to the other. When a Paine, or a Voltaire, takes a Bible into his hand to turn its life-giving nourishment to poison in his own soul, the Bible is no less the Bible, no less really the organ of the Holy Ghost, than when an Arndt or an Edwards bends over it in the deepest devotion. When the great Kohinoor diamond shone in the head of the Hindoo idol, or when it was in the hand of the soldier who stole it, it was no less a diamond than it is now, lying amid the jewels of a great empire. When the Ark of the Lord sat in Dagon's temple, it was no less the Ark than when it was enshrined in the Holy of Holies; and the judgment which went forth from it against

the fishy idol, equally with the joyous light which gladdened
the High Priest when he went within the veil, attested it to
be the earthly throne of the Most High.   It might as well be
said, that because the Romanist does not discern the bread in
the Supper, he receives no bread, as that the unbeliever,
because he does not discern the body of our Lord, does not
commune with it sacramentally.   Here is a grand distinctive
element in the Lutheran view, that, apart from all qualities in
the recipient, the presence of Christ's humanity in the Lord's
Supper is a positive reality.   The Sacramental communion
rests on His person, not on our ideas.   To a sick man, the food
he receives may be as poison, but it is none the less food, with
all the powers of nutriment which inhere in food.   The reason
that it does not nourish is in him, not in it.   So the bread of
life, whether offered in the Word or in the Sacrament, is the
same intrinsically, and in its proper virtue, though unbelief
converts that heavenly food to its own poison — changing,
indeed, its effect, but leaving its substance unchanged.

3. The communion, according to Dr. Gerhart, with the flesh
_{Third Proposi-} and blood of Christ, takes place *in the Lord's Sup-*
_{tion.}   *per.*   But why, we may ask, limit such a commu-
nion as he defines by the Lord's Supper?   The bread and wine
are not the medium of it — and, as mere reminders of it, they
have not the power which the Word has.   On the Reformed
view, the Sacramental elements have a function limited by
their didactic or suggestive power over us ; for, up to this
point, the Zwinglian and Calvinistic views are coincident.   If
it be answered, that the whole transaction of the Supper, the
Word, and outward signs and special prayers, has extraordinary power, still it is the same in kind with the other means
of grace, however much it may differ from them in degree.
Such a communion, in a word, as the believer has with Christ,
in the Holy Supper, through the Holy Spirit, he can have, and
does have, on this theory, elsewhere.   If the Lord's Supper
has no special organ of communion, (and if it has the Holy
Spirit only, it has no special organ, for He is the general organ
of all grace,) then it has no special character.   If the bread
and wine are acknowledged as special organs, the external

appointed media of the distinctive blessings of the communion, then you accept the Lutheran doctrine that Sacramental
communion is oral, for by oral communion is meant no more
than this — that that which is the organic medium of the
communion is received by the mouth, that through the natural we reach the supernatural. Our theologians, when they
speak of a reception by the mouth, mean no more than this —
that he that receives the bread and wine by the mouth naturally, thereby, as by an organ, receives the humanity of Christ
sacramentally and supernaturally, just as when faith cometh
by hearing, the ear receives the outward word naturally, and
thereby organically receives the Holy Spirit, mediately and
supernaturally, who conveys Himself in, with, and under that
word.

4. Dr. Gerhart says that the view of his Church is that the
communion "in the Lord's Supper" is "with *the*   Fourth Propo-
flesh and blood of Christ *no less* than with His   sition.
Spirit." Here there seems to be a great advance on the Zwinglian view. A communion involves communication on the
one part, and reception on the other. It is the Reformed doctrine apparently that the flesh and blood of Christ are communicated and received no less than His Spirit. The Reformed
have insisted that to the question, What is communicated and
received in the Lord's Supper? their answer is identical with
ours. Christ's body and blood are given and received. This,
Dr. Gerhart says, "was not at issue in the sixteenth century.
On this point, Reformed and Lutherans were agreed." Even
Zwingli, in his letter to the German princes, says: "We have
never denied that the *body* of Christ is in the Supper." Far
more strongly, Calvin, in his Institutes, says: "We are fed
with the *flesh and blood* of Christ. Christ refreshes us with
the eating of *His flesh* and the drinking of *His blood*. There
is a *true* and *substantial* communication of the *body* and *blood* of
our Lord." "This mystery is in its own nature *incomprehensible*. . . The body of our Lord was once offered for us that
we may now eat it (*nunc eo vescamur*), and by eating, may
experience in us the efficacy of that one only sacrifice. . . Thus
sound the words of promise. . . We are commanded, therefore,

to take and eat that body which was once offered for our salvation: that while we see ourselves participants of this, we
may trust that the virtue of His life-giving death is strong
within us."* "There are those who say that to eat Christ's
flesh and drink His blood is nothing else than believing in
Calvin on the Christ Himself. But to me it seems that Christ
Lord's Supper. meant to teach something clearer and sublimer
than this. . . He meant to teach us that we have life given us
by true participation of Himself. . . By true communication
of Himself His life passes over into us and becomes ours, . . .
if so great a mystery can be embraced in words — a mystery
which I cannot even grasp in thought. . . I confess this lest
any should mete its sublimity with the measure of my infancy.
. . . Though the mind can reach what the tongue cannot
express, yet here the mind itself is overcome and overwhelmed
with the greatness of the thing. . . The mystery of the Holy
Supper consists of two things: the bodily signs . . and the
spiritual verity, which, through those symbols, is at the same
time figured and imparted (exhibetur). . . I say, therefore,
that in the mystery of the Supper, through (per) the symbols
of bread and wine, Christ is truly imparted (exhiberi) to us,
even His body and blood, in which he fulfilled all obedience
to obtain our justification: by which, to wit, we first are
united into one body with Him, then being made partakers of
His substance, we experience a virtue in the communication
of all good things. . . Those absurdities " (of inclusion, circumscription, and immensity,) " being set aside, I willingly
receive whatever it is possible to frame (facere potest) to
express a true and substantial communication of the body and
blood of Christ, which, under the sacred symbols of the Supper, is imparted (exhibetur) to believers. . . If any one ask me
in regard to the *mode*, I am not ashamed to confess that the
secret is too high to be grasped by my mind, or to be set forth
in words. . . I experience rather than understand it. . . In
His Holy Supper He commands me, under (sub) the symbols
of bread and wine, to take, eat and drink His body and blood.

* Institut. Lib. IV. ch. xviii. ? 1. Ed. 1543. seq. Corp. Reformat. xxix. 199.
Ed. Amstel. ix. 864.

I doubt not but that He truly offers them, and 1 receive them." *

We could continue to fill pages with citations, of equal force, from Calvinistic writers. Whatever interpretation we put upon them, they at least make it clear that a large part of the phraseology which our Church uses is accepted as sound and Scriptural by those who do not receive her doctrine. Those who shrink back from the terms of our Church, as carnal, will find that her antagonists are compelled to use terms just as open to misconstruction. It is just as Calvinistic, on the showing of Calvinistic standards, to speak of eating the body and drinking the blood of Christ, in the Eucharist, as it .s Lutheran. The question then lies fairly before the Chris tian — Which view, Calvinistic or Lutheran, more honestly accepts the natural meaning of the premises, which is in more logical harmony with their necessary issues, and which more frankly stands by the obvious meaning of the terms chosen by itself to embody its faith ?

As both parties start with the same form of words as to the premises, the first question here is, Do both accept them in the same sense? On one point we admit that both do — that is, that by the "flesh and blood of Christ," both mean His true human body and blood — the body which hung upon the cross, and which still maintains its identity, though glorified in heaven. But when the question arises, Do both mean the same thing when they speak of communing with this body and blood of Christ, the reply is, They do not. Here the Reformed Church seems to us to take away with one set of terms all that it had conceded with another. But although it differs from us, we cannot accept all of Dr. Gerhart's phraseology in regard to our Church as accurately marking the difference. He characterizes our doctrine as the "Ubiquitarian theory of the Lutherans." We can conceive no reason why Dr. Gerhart applies the word "Ubiquitarian," unless it is that he imagines that there is some ground for the reproach against our doctrine, which was originally couched under this word, which is, indeed,

"The Ubiqui tarian theory."

* Institut. ch. xviii. 19, 22, 30. Corp. Ref. vol. xxix. ¹003–1010. Ed. Am-stelod. 1667. ix. 370. seq.

a barbarous and unnecessary one, and was devised by the enemies of our Church to injure it. When our Church is charged with the doctrine of the " Ubiquity " of Christ's human nature, it is usually meant, either, 1 : that the human nature in Christ is everywhere present, in the same way as the divinity, as an infinite essence, or by some essential virtue or property of its own nature; or, 2 : that the human nature has been made equal to the divine, in its substance, essence, or essential prop- erties; or, 3 : that the humanity of Christ is locally expanded in all places of heaven and earth — *one and all of which our Church rejects in the most unqualified terms.* The Godhead alone has an *essential omnipresence.* The human nature has a per- sonal omnipresence — that is, a presence not in or of itself, but through the divine, in virtue of its personal union with it. It is present not by extension or locality. The Godhead itself is not present by extension or locality; neither does it render the human thus present. The divine nature is present after the manner of an infinite Spirit, incomprehensible to us; and the human is present after the manner in which an infinite Spirit renders present a human nature which is one person with it — a manner not less, nor more, incomprehensible to us than the other. The true designation of the Lutheran doc- trine, on this point, would be, " The *personal omnipresence* of the human nature of Christ."

In opposition to the Lutheran theory, Dr. Gerhart says :

The Reformed "The Reformed theologians (in answer to the Theory. Some question : How is this communion with the flesh objections to it. and blood of Christ established and maintained ?) replied : By the mysterious agency of the Holy Spirit, elevat ing the hearts of believers to Christ in heaven, who feeds and nourishes them with the life-giving power of His flesh and blood." To this view, thus placed in antithesis to that of our Church by Dr. Gerhart, we have many objections, some of which, because of the antagonism in which he has placed the two views, we feel it our duty to state. The Reformed view acknowledges a mystery — " the *mysterious* agency " it says — and so far concedes that, *a priori*, it has no advantage over against the Lutheran view, on the general ground that our view involves mystery. Rising, as it seems to us, in an unconscious rationalism, it yet concedes that it cannot bring the question into the sphere of reason; it simply takes it out of one part of the realm of mystery to lay it down in another. We suppose the mystery of the Supper to be that of the person of Christ; the Reformed view supposes its mystery to be that of the work of the Holy Spirit. But we dread lest the rationalizing that fails to take the subject into the sphere of reason may carry the thinker thither, and that the Reformed view, which shifts the mystery, will run out into the Arminian or Socinian view, which sets it entirely aside; for while the Reformed view acknowledges a mystery, it is evident that it hopes to find its account in the measurable relief of that mystery. It is a theory which seems to be reluctant to strain the text, and yet has a bribe for the reason over against the literal construction of that text. It is an uncomfortable thing, for it lays more on the heart than it lifts off the mind. We object to it, furthermore, that it seems to us to confound the distinctive work of two persons of the Trinity. It is the distinctive work of the incarnate Son of God to redeem, and to apply His redemption in His own person. It is the distinctive work of the Holy Spirit to work in us that faith which will savingly use what Christ offers. We, no less than the Reformed, recognize the necessity of the work of the Holy Spirit in the Lord's Supper; not, however, to do Christ's work, but to do His own. The Holy Spirit makes us savingly partakers in what is received by the outward organs of the soul. Christ is intercessor for us with the Father, and so secures for us the possibility of partaking in the blessings which centre in His person. The Holy Spirit is intercessor for the Father and the Son with us, and thus leads us actually to accept with the heart those most blessed gifts which the Father and Son offer us. In the Lord's Supper, Christ gives to us Himself, and the Holy Spirit, if we do not resist His sacred work, enables us, from the person of Christ thus given us, to draw those benefits of which that person is the sole spring. That the sacramental giving of Christ is the work of His own person, and not of the Holy Spirit, is most explicitly taught in the portions of the New

32

Testament which speak of the Lord's Supper. That it is the work not of the Spirit, but of Christ, to impart to us Christ's body and blood sacramentally, is demonstrated by the fact, that when the Lord's Supper was instituted, the Holy Ghost was not given in any of the distinctive functions allotted to Him under the New Dispensation. These, it is distinctly taught, were not to be exercised till Christ was glorified and had gone to the Father. But whatever the words of the institution mean now, they meant when the Supper was instituted. As they could not mean then that the Holy Ghost mediated Christ's presence, which, if it were done at all, would be in the highest degree a work of the New Dispensation, they cannot mean it now. There is not a solitary passage in which the sacramental impartation of Christ's body is associated with the work of the Holy Spirit. For a true presence of Christ on earth the Reformed view substitutes an imaginary presence of the believer in heaven. The view seems to derogate from the personal sufficiency of Christ. It seems to separate properties from the substance in which they inhere, to sunder the efficacy from the Omnipotent Being who has that efficacy, to segregate the merits of Christ from His undivided person, in which they were wrought out. According to it, Christ's body can be truly eaten without being truly present; it is rather we who are communicated to Christ than He to us; the Holy Spirit lifts us to heaven; the bread which we break is the communion of our spirit to Christward, not the communion of the body of Christ to usward. We are the centre of the mystery. Christ's body is at one point on its circumference, and the Holy Spirit its radius; the Holy Ghost can lift us to the body of Christ, but the divine nature of Christ cannot bring that body to us — our faith, with the aid of the Holy Ghost, can do what incarnate omnipotence cannot do. How tangled is that which promised to be so simple — how vague that which meant to be so sharp and clear. The terminology of the Reformed view is, in the last degree, perplexing, and wears the air of a want of candor. If it be accepted loosely, it runs out into the old Zwinglian·theory, which is also the view of a low Arminianism, and of Rationalism. If it be accepted rigidly, it is less intelligible, even to reason, than any other, and seems to us, when thoroughly sifted, to have, at some point, all the difficulties of all the other views, without their internal harmony. These weaknesses have been noted by others than Lutherans. The great Remonstrant divine, Limborch, whose clearness of thought, learning, and gentleness, are deservedly renowned, and who certainly, as between the two views, is impartial enough, says of the Calvinistic view: " It seems to have been invented by Bucer, who, in his desire for peace, in order that he might reconcile the Lutherans and the Zwinglians, devised ambiguous expressions, which both sides might subscribe, without changing their opinion. But the attempt was a failure. The Lutherans complained of the deceitful dealing of the Reformed, who took back with one hand what they gave with the other. . . The Reformed held that in the Supper there is a communion with the physical substance of Christ's body, which they teach is there *truly*, though not substantially present. But the doctrine *involves no less an absurdity than that of the Lutherans.* For that communion with the substance of Christ's body is either a communion with the body of Christ as it remains in heaven, or as it is verily present on earth, and in the use of the Supper. If they say the latter, they must admit the ubiquity of the body of Christ, and go over openly to the camp of the Lutherans. If they say the former, they affirm contradictory things ; for how is it possible that the body of Christ, which is in heaven, and nowhere else (as Beza says), should be truly communicated and be food to us who are on earth, and nowhere else ? They say: Our conjunction with the body of Christ is made as by a spiritual mouth through faith, by which we can render present to us many things which are absent. We answer: 1. The conjunction, through faith, with Christ, ought to precede the use of the Supper; otherwise the man is unworthy who celebrates the Supper ; for by the celebration of it he testifies that he already has that communion. 2. That union which takes place through faith they expressly distinguish from the union which takes place in the Supper, which latter they would have to embrace something more sublime

Limborch's judgment of the Calvinistic Doctrine.

and express. 3. The union by faith is not incomprehensible. 4. Nor does faith really render present things which are absent, but only represents them to itself as if they were present, though they are actually absent, for it is ' the substance of things hoped for.' Heb. xi. 1. Moreover: 5. Our soul can receive no spiritual fruit from communion with the very substance ᴣf the physical body and blood of Christ."*

Calvinism is forced to admit that its view does not solve the mystery after all, but leaves it in its fathomless depth. It requires Christ's person, the Holy Spirit, and the faith of the believer, — three factors, confusing each other. The first factor is sufficient, and if justice is done it, the other two are not needed for the objective substance of the Sacrament ; they come in at their proper place, not to help Christ to make what He has perfectly made already, but to enable the recipient to receive savingly what he is receiving sacramentally. The Calvinistic view puts too much upon man, who is nothing, because it concedes too little to Christ, who is everything. There is more than wit, there is solemn argument in the illus-tration of a great old divine: " When Christ says, ' Behold, I stand at the door and knock: if any man hear my voice, and open the door, I will come in to him, and will sup with him, and he with me,' a Calvinist might answer, O Lord, there is no need for you to wait so long at the door. Return to your heaven, and when I wish to sup with you, I will fly up with my wings of faith, and meet you there."† With its great advance upon the rationalism of Zwingli, the doctrine of Calvin still bore with it the fatal taint of the very view which he calls " profane." All that he gained in depth, as contrasted with Zwingli, he lost in clearness. He does not as flatly as Zwingli contradict the text, but he does what Zwingli did not, he contradicts himself. But two views will remain in the ulti-mate struggle, the rationalistic, Zwinglian, Arminian, Socinian view, which fully and consistently denies the whole mystery, ᴣn the one side, and the Scriptural, Catholic view, which

* Theologia Christiana. Ed. Tert. Amstelæd. 1700. Fol. Lib. V. ch. lxxi.

† Dannhauer: Reformirten Salve. u. Friedens-Gruss, quoted in Scherzer: Collegium Anti-Calvinianum. Lipsiæ. 1704. 4to. 603.

fully and consistently recognizes it on the other. This is
the view of the objective reality of the presence held in its
purity in the Lutheran Church, and held in the Roman and
Greek Churches, though with the rubbish of human additions heaped on it. The advance of either view presses out the
Calvinistic — and both views are advancing. In some parts
of the Reformed Church, as in the Church of England, the
Episcopal Church, and the German Reformed Church, the
Catholic view is more and more in the ascendant. In other
parts of the Reformed Churches, the Zwinglian view has long
since so completely triumphed over the Calvinistic, that men
who imagine themselves defenders of the purest Calvinism,
reject contemptuously its fundamental doctrine of the Supper.
Calvinism has really at least six points. Its most ardent
defenders usually think it enough to maintain five. In their
dropping of Calvin's doctrine of the Lord's Supper, if we deny
their consistency, we cannot but praise their sagacity. The
rigid logic which so wonderfully marks Calvin, in the other
parts of his system, seems to fail him here, and it is not surprising that the Churches which maintain the views of that
masterly thinker on almost every other point, have either positively rejected, or quietly practically ignored his sacramental
theories, which were, indeed, but an adaptation of the views
of Bucer, which their originator ultimately abandoned for those
of the Lutheran Church. They were grafted on Calvin's system, not grown by it, and they fall away even when the trunk
retains its original vigor, or are retained, as the Unionistic
theology, though with great changes, now retains them,
when everything, ordinarily embraced in Calvinism, is utterly
abandoned.

Our object in this dissertation is by no means to sit in judgment on the doctrines of the Reformed Church. The Lutheran
We have touched upon them only so far as Dr. doctrine of the
Person of Christ
Gerhart has thought it necessary to bring them a Scriptural doc-
into a disparaging contrast with the faith of our trine.
Church — in a word, we have had no desire to attack them,
but simply to defend ourselves. We have dwelt upon the two
great doctrines of the person of Christ, and of the Lord's Sup-

per, because these doctrines are of the highest importance, are vitally connected, and have been most frequently misunderstood. The pure truth in regard to these grand themes, as our Church holds it, is one of her highest glories, and she must be forgiven if she is unwilling that any man should take from her her crown.

Dr. Gerhart, in the paragraph which follows the one on which we have been dwelling, goes on to say: "The Lutheran Antithesis, (that is, in regard to the person of Christ,) was developed from the Lutheran theory of the Sacrament." If Dr. Gerhart means no more than that God in His Providence made the discussions in regard to the Lord's Supper the means of bringing more fully and harmoniously into a well-defined consciousness, and into clearer expression the doctrine of the Scriptures in regard to the person of Christ, we do not object to it; but if he means that the doctrine of our Church on the person of Christ originated in the necessity of defending her doctrine in regard to the Lord's Supper, we think he is wholly mistaken. The doctrine of our Church rests upon the direct testimony of God's Word, and her interpretation of the meaning of that Word is not one of her own devising, but had been given ages before her great distinctive Confession, by the Fathers and Councils of the pure Church. We offer to our readers some testimony on both these points.

John taught the doctrine of Christ's person which our **I. All things are given to Jesus according to His human nature. John xiii. 3.** Church confesses, when he said (John xiii. 3), "Jesus knowing that the Father had given all things into His hands, and that He was come from God, and went to God; He riseth from supper . . . and began to wash the disciples' feet."

1. These words teach us what Jesus had: "ALL THINGS." So in John iii. 35: "The Father loveth the Son, and hath given ALL THINGS into His hand." So in Matt. xi. 27, and Luke x. 22: "ALL THINGS are delivered unto me of my Father." What a plenitude of possession is here involved, and what supernatural characteristics of person are necessary to their reception. Unlimited possession involves supreme power —and he cannot be omnipotent who is not omnipresent. The

Lutheran need not fear to attribute too much to his adorable Saviour when God himself gives to Him "all things."

2. In these words of John is implied that Christ, ACCORDING TO HIS HUMAN NATURE, has all things. The name JESUS is not a name drawn from His divine nature, but was given to Him in His individuality after His incarnation. The text says, moreover, that the Father had GIVEN all things into His hand. Now, according to the *divine nature* of Christ, God can give Him nothing, for that divine nature in its own essence has all things absolutely. Hence, here, and everywhere that God is said to give Christ anything, or Christ is said to receive anything, it is given to Him *according to His human nature*, and received by Him *according to His human nature*. Christ, then, has received according to the one nature, to wit, the human, what He intrinsically possessed in the other, to wit, in the divine, or, as it has been expressed, Whatever Christ has in the one nature by essence, He partakes of in the other by grace — and this is the doctrine of our Church.

3. The whole point of John's antithesis, indeed, turns upon this view of the person of Christ; for his vein of thought is evidently this — that Jesus performed this act of touching lowliness, the washing of His disciples' feet, the act of a servant, not in forgetfulness of His glorious majesty, and of the plenitude of His gifts, but fully conscious of them. Though He knew His own supreme glory as the one to whom the Father had given ALL THINGS, He yet girded Himself, and bent to wash the feet of His loved ones. Now, if He had ALL THINGS only according to the divine nature, there was no humiliation involved, for according to the nature which had the glory, He did not wash their feet — but as, confessedly, it was according to His human nature, bending His human form, and using His human hands to wash their feet, so must it have been according to that nature that He here humiliated Himself; and the point is, that though as a man He had given into His hands ALL THINGS, and was thus as man infinitely glorious, yet as man, and in full consciousness of the glory which He shared as man, He humbled Himself to wash His disciples' feet.

That the expressions which attribute the plenary possession

of ALL THINGS to Jesus according to His human nature, are
not to be deprived of the very fullest significance, becomes yet
more clear when we look at the passages which specify in
detail what are some of the things, " ALL " of which the
Father has delivered to Him. Our blessed Lord
says, for example (Matt. xxviii. 18): " ALL POWER
is given unto me in heaven and on earth." Now
mark of *whom* this affirmation is made. It is made
of One who stood before them confessedly a true man, coming
with the step of man, speaking through the lips of man, with
the voice of man, and saying: "All power is given unto *me.*"
Surely, if He had meant that His human nature was to be
excluded from this personality He would have told His disciples so, for nothing could seem more clear than that the undivided Christ, the man as well as the God, affirmed this of Himself. But it is furthermore manifest that what Christ here says,
He says by preëminence of the human side of His person, for
He says: " All power is *given* unto me," but to His divine
nature, in its essence, nothing could be given. In virtue of that
essence, it was necessarily omnipotent. Supreme power, therefore, was conferred on the Mediator as *to His human nature.*
And yet there could not be two omnipotences in the person of
Christ, the one belonging to His divinity, the other to His
humanity. The divine did not part with its omnipotence to
the human, so that the divine now ceased to be omnipotent, and
the human became in its own essence omnipotent. This would
involve that the Godhead really ceased to be divine, and the
human became essentially divine — both of which are absurd.
As the Godhead, therefore, retains its essential omnipotence,
and yet the human receives omnipotence as a gift, the result
is inevitable. The one omnipotence pertains to the whole person — the divine possessing it essentially and of necessity, and
in itself; the human having a communion or participation
in it, in virtue of its personal union with the divine. Omnipotence becomes no essential attribute of the human nature of
Christ, but inheres forever in the divine, and is exercised by
the human only because it is taken into the one person of the
divine.

(II. Jesus is omnipotent according to His human nature. Matt. xxviii. 18.)

This power which is given to the human nature of Christ is supreme — " all power *in heaven and in earth ;* " it is all-comprehending, involving every kind of power throughout the universe. It is a true omnipotence. To have *all* power, implies that the power shall be *everywhere* — but the power is not separable from presence of some kind. If the Saviour is almighty everywhere, He must exercise that omnipotence directly in His own person, or through a secondary agency — but as His person is a divine one, He needs no secondary agency, the very same person that is mighty to all things is present to be mighty. Yet, as if no conjecture, however direct or irresistible, might be the ground of our hope, He closes His glorious address to His disciples with the words: " Lo! I am with you always, even unto the end of the world." He who uttered the promise fulfils it, but He who uttered it was man as well as God — and in fulfilling it, He fulfilled it as man as well as God. So irresistible is the necessity for this view, that writers who are not of the Lutheran Church have acknowledged it. Alford, for example, commenting on the words, Matt. xxviii. 20: " Lo! I am with you," says, " I," in the fullest sense: " not the *divine presence,* as *distinguished from the humanity* of Christ. His humanity is with us likewise. The presence of the Spirit is the effect of the presence of Christ." But inference is hardly necessary. The power of omnipresence is a part of *all* power.

In Matt. xi. 27, Christ defines the *sphere* of His possession. He has " *all things* " without exception ; He indicates the *manner* in which they are derived : " All things are *delivered* unto me," possessing them from eternity as God, I have received them in time as man ; He marks the *person* of the recipient : " All things are delivered unto *me,*" the one divine-human person, whose natures form one inseparable person ; He draws the inference : " Come," therefore, " unto *me,*"— the inseparably divine and human — " ALL *ye that labor* and are heavy laden, and *I* will give you rest." This one person, inseparably human and divine, calls to Him the sorrowing of every place and of every time, and promises in His own person, man as well as God, everywhere and evermore to give them rest. And there is no meaning, and no comfort in an incarnate Christ which does not rest in the conviction that He is approached and approaches both as man and as God.

In John xvii. 5, our Lord says: " And now, O Father, glorify thou me with thine own self, with the glory which I had with Thee before the world was."

The perpetual identity of Christ's person. John xvii. 5. In this text is implied, 1. That the person of Christ is *divine* — His glory is a common glory with that of the Father ; " with thine own self," " with thee ;" and like the Father's, it is from eternity, before the world, that is, the creation, either in whole or in part " was." It is implied, 2. That the human nature is taken into the unity of this divine person. For Christ, true man, speaks of a glory which He had with the Father before the world was. The identity of person is involved throughout. The same person who was then incarnate, was once unincarnate ; the same person which was simply and unchangeably glorious in its essence, was now humbled according to the nature which it had assumed into its personality. It is implied, 3. That there is a true communion of properties, for we have Christ praying according to His human nature, that the Father may glorify Him according to that nature. According to His divine nature He could not pray, nor have anything given to Him. His prayer, then, means that He desires to be glorified according to His human nature, as He had been glorified in His divine nature before the world was. And this glory is not declarative, but essential, for it is a glory which He had antecedent to the creation with the Father Himself, not with angels, but before the world of men and angels had being. But even if it were declarative glory, all real declarative glory presupposes essential perfection. Our Saviour, then, prays that the plenary exercise of the attributes, and the plenary enjoyment of the majesty which belonged to Him as God, may be shared in by His human nature.

In Colossians ii. 9, it is said : " In Him [Christ] dwelleth all the fulness of the Godhead bodily." The " fulness of the Godhead " is wholly different from the "fulness of God." The " fulness of God " is that fulness of gifts and graces which

God imparts, and which believers have from Him. The fulness of the Godhead is the plenitude of the divine nature in all its attributes. This is here intensified by the word " all:" " *all* the fulness." The Godhead is incarnate through the second person of the Trinity, and the whole second person of the Trinity dwells in Christ's humanity, which it has united to itself *as its own body.* All the fulness of the Godhead cannot *personally* dwell in Christ The Godhead dwelling in Christ bodily. Col. ii. 9.
and also personally be separate from Christ, for personality implies not simply presence, but far more ; it involves the most absolute union. If all the fulness of the Godhead in the second person of the Trinity dwells in Christ bodily, then there is no fulness of that Godhead where it is not so dwelling in Christ ; and as the human in Christ cannot limit the divine, which is essentially, and of necessity, omnipresent, the divine in Christ must exalt the human. The Godhead of Christ is everywhere present, and wherever present, dwells in the human personally, and, therefore, of necessity renders it present with itself.

So thoroughly does this idea of the personal unity underlie the New Testament conception of Christ, that we find it constantly assumed where no formal statement of it is made. Two examples of this may suffice. The Doctrine implied where there is no formal statement. Matt. xvii. 25 ; xii. 8.

When (Matt. xvii. 25) our Lord claimed, as man, the exemption from the duty of paying the Temple-tax, on the ground that He had the receiving right of royalty, and was exempt from the paying duty of the subject; it implied that His humanity was in such unity with His Godhead, that He could argue from the one to the other. If there were two persons, He must have argued : My Godhead is exempt, but my humanity is bound to the payment. But His argument is the very reverse : I am not bound as God, therefore I am not bound as man ; the logical link, of necessity, being : Because my Godhead has taken my humanity into personal unity with it. But if Christ participates in divine rights according to His humanity, He must participate in the divine attributes which condition those rights. This is the presupposition of that. That is the result of this.

" The Son of man is Lord even of the Sabbath-day," (Matt. xii. 8; Mark ii. 28; Luke vi. 5,) that is, He has the dispensing power of the Law-giver in regard to the ceremonial law. But this He cannot have as Son of man, unless as Son of man He has a personal identity with the Son of God.

These texts are but a little part of the testimony which might be cited. The faith of our Church grounded upon them had been the faith of the Universal Church for ages. The earliest ages of the Church are not, indeed, marked by dogmatic precision of language. The sciolist who is not deeply read into their testimony is sure to misunderstand it, and in any case it is necessary to allow for lax phraseology and defective thinking. No existing system can find a perfect guaranty in the exact terms used by the ancient Church. Its testimony is to be construed on broader principles than those of a mousing verbal criticism. We must read the life of the ancient Church before we can comprehend its letter — and its letter, construed by its life, shows, with ever-increasing clearness, the underlying Christological system which reached its scientific perfection in the theology of the Augsburg Confession, as developed in the Formula of Concord. The Church all along was feeling after an adequate confession of her faith in regard to the inseparable unity of the person of her Lord. EPIPHANIUS had said: " The flesh acquired the glory of Deity, a heavenly honor, glory, and perfection, which it had not from the beginning, but received it in its union with God the Word." CYRIL had said: " The Word had made common with its own body the good of its own nature." " As the Word is of God, so is the man of the woman — there is, therefore, of both one Christ, indivisible in Sonship, and in divine majesty." * THEODORET had said: " The nature assumed for us was participant of the same honor with that which assumed it." DAMASCENUS had said: " The divine nature communicates its own excellencies to the flesh. The divine works are wrought through the body

The Lutheran interpretations not novel. Views of the Fathers.

---

* Cyril in Joan. L. II. ch. xlix. Cyril means that the humanity of Christ, " man," is derived from his mother, " woman," as his divine nature, " Word," is begotten of the Father from eternity.

as their organ." ATHANASIUS had said: "Whatever the Scripture declares that Christ had received in time, it affirms with reference to His humanity, not with reference to His deity." BASIL THE GREAT had said: "When it is declared by our Lord: 'All power is given unto me,' the words are to be understood of Him in His incarnation, not in His Deity." "As the Son of God has been made participant of flesh and blood, so the human flesh of our Lord has been made participant of Deity."* AMBROSE had said: "All things are subject to Him according to His flesh. Christ, according to His humanity, shares the throne of God." "Thou art everywhere (ubique), and standing in our midst art not perceived by us." "One Christ is everywhere (ubique); here existing complete (plenus), and there complete."† CHRYSOSTOM had said: "The angels are commanded to adore Him according to the flesh." "Christ is beyond the heavens, He is beyond the earth, He is wherever He wills to be; wheresoever He is, He is entire; wheresoever He is, and wheresoever thou art who seekest Him, thou art in Him whom thou seekest."‡ THEOPHYLACT had said: "The Father hath given all things into the hand of the Son according to His humanity." "He fills all things with His rule and working, and this He does in His flesh, for He had filled all things before with His divinity."§ "The holy body of Christ . . is communicated in the four parts of the world. . . He sanctifies the soul of each with His body, through His flesh, and exists entire and undivided in all everywhere."‖ ŒCUMENIUS had said: "He received as man what He had as God. As man it was said to Him: 'Sit at my right hand,' for as God he had an eternal government." "By His divinity He had aforetime filled all things, but being incarnate He descended and ascended, that with His flesh He might fill all things."¶ JEROME** had said: "The Lamb is everywhere (ubique)."

* Basilius in Homil. de Nativ. Christi.
† Ambrosius on Luke x. Lib. vii. ch. 47, and on Heb. iv.
‡ Hom. de John Bapt.
§ Theophylact on Eph. iv. 10.
‖ In cap. xix. John.
¶ Œcumenius on Eph. iv. 10.
** Adv. Vigilantium.

AUGUSTINE had said : " The humanity itself after the resurrection obtained divine glory." " 'The Son of man which is in
heaven.' He was on earth, and yet said that He is in heaven
— and what is more, that ' *the Son of man* is in heaven,' that
He might demonstrate that there is one person in two natures.
. . There are not two Christs, two Sons of God, but one person, one Christ." " Why shouldst thou separate man from
God, and make one person of God, another of man, so that
there would be, not a Trinity, but a Quaternity — for thou, a
man, art soul and body, and as soul and body is one man,
so God and man is one Christ ? "* The Church grounds
herself, then, in this great doctrine, on the direct testimony
of God's Word, accepted in the sense in which it had long
been understood by the best interpreters of the Ancient
Church.

So irresistible, indeed, is the logic of the case, and so strong
is the historical testimony by which the argument is sustained,
that we find the truth conceded in whole or in part by some
of the ablest representatives of the Churches which have most
violently opposed the Lutheran doctrine of the person of
Christ. Bellarmine, and other Polemics of the Church of
Rome, in the blindness of their purpose to stamp our doctrine with the reproach of heresy, have violently assailed the
Lutheran doctrine of the personal omnipresence of Christ
according to both natures. But, in addition to the Fathers,
Lutheran doc- men whose names have been held in honor in that
trine; 1. Admis- Church at a later period have acknowledged, in
sions of some wri- whole or part, what modern Romanists deny.
ters of the Church
of Rome. HUGO DE S. VICTORE † says : " From the nature of
its union with divinity, the body of Christ has this dignity, that
it is at one time in many places." BIEL ‡ says : " Not only can the
body of Christ be in diverse places definitively and sacramentally,
but . . can by divine power be in many places circumscriptively."
Nor have there been entirely wanting, even among modern
Romanists, some who have conceded the truth of the Lutheran

* Augustine : De verb. Apostol. Serm. xiv.; Do. De Tempore. Serm. cxlvii.
† Lib. II. de Sacram. Pars viii. ch. xii.
‡ IV. Sent. Dist xi.

doctrine of the fellowship of properties. FABER STAPULENSIS says: "Wherever Christ is, He is incarnate. But without His body He is not incarnate. That is a great faith which knows that Christ is bodily where He is sacramentally. But that is a greater faith that knows that He is absolutely everywhere bodily." "The body of Christ is wherever the Logos is, for 'the Word was made flesh.' The Word is never without the flesh, nor the flesh without the Word."* PAUL KEMER affirms: "It is most easy, by many and firm reasons, to prove that Christ is everywhere with His body," and so also ERTLIUS, FRANCUS, and BARRADIUS.†

BIEL held, indeed, in common with many of the scholastics, that by divine power any natural body could be simultaneously present in many places. ^{2. Admissions of Metaphysicians.} Nor has this theory lacked supporters of great name in modern times. Among the Calvinistic metaphysicians, the proposition that "the existence of one and the same body in many places is not contradictory," has been maintained by GISBERT VOETIUS, and defended by his sons, PAUL and DANIEL. LEIBNITZ,‡ the greatest metaphysician, in many respects, since Aristotle, says that it cannot with reason be affirmed that a real presence of the body of Christ in many places involves a contradiction, inasmuch as no one has yet explained in *what the essence of body consists.* This theory, maintained, as it has been, by some of the acutest thinkers of our race, shows, at least, that here is a question which cannot be determined by mere speculation.

Nor are we destitute of admissions, on the part of Calvinistic writers, which, in spite of the explanations which seem meant to take away with one hand what is granted by the other, are virtual concessions of ^{3. Admissions of Calvinistic writers.} the truth of the Lutheran view. Thus BEZA § says: "If you will, I grant beside, that the humanity of Christ is also present, but in another respect, that is, not in itself, or by its

---

* Faber Stap. in 1 Cor. xii.

† Quoted in Gerhard's Loci (Cotta). iii. 517.

‡ See Letters of Leibnitz and Pelisson, and L.'s Discours d. l. Conform. de la fois avec la raison, § 18, and Cotta's Note on Gerhard. iv. 548.

§ Opera. 659.

own essence, but inasfar as it coheres by personal union with the Logos, which is everywhere." ZANCHIUS *: " The flesh of Christ can be said to be . . omnipotent, . . everywhere present . not in its own proper essence, . . but in the person which is common to it, with the divine nature." " All the learned and pious grant that the human nature of Christ is personally omnipotent, everywhere present. Not incongruously is it said that the flesh is personally omnipotent and everywhere present, . . for it is such in the person." The ZURICH THEOLOGIANS† say: " Christ, that is, that person who is at the same time true God and true man, is present with all things, governs heaven and earth, and that according to each nature (utramque naturam). For the Son of God, after He assumed human nature, wheresoever He is present and acts, is present and acts as Christ, that is, as a person who is at once God and man." SOHNIUS: " If the humanity is not wherever the divinity is, to wit, personally, or in personal subsistence, that is, if there be not everywhere one person of the two natures, or if these two natures be not everywhere united, there must, of necessity, be two persons." That these writers are consistent with these premises, in their inferences, we do not pretend; but this does but the more show how great is the pressure of that truth, which, knowing the difficulty of explaining it away, they are yet obliged to concede.

In the great practical question of the undivided adoration Worship of of the humanity and Deity of Christ, there is no Christ according consistent position between the Lutheran doctrine to His human nature. and the Socinian. The Calvinistic divines, while they show in various ways that there is great difficulty in har- monizing their view of the person of Christ with the worship of Him in His human nature, are yet, for the most part, happily inconsistent. No man can really pray to the undivided Christ without in heart resting on the Lutheran doctrine of His per- son. Either the human nature of Christ is in inseparable unity of person with the divine nature, or it is idolatry to worship Christ according to the human nature. This the Socinian con- troversialists in New England saw at once, and their arguments,

---

* Lib. de Relig. Præfat. ad Lect. Lib. II. de Incarnat. 201.   † Apolog. 108

which assumed the Nestorianizing views of New England as orthodox, and which the Orthodox there defended as Scriptural, were consequently never fairly met. One source of the rapid and deadly triumphs of Socinianism in New England was the unscriptural and lax views which the system claiming to be orthodox held of the person of Christ.

From the views which have been presented of the Lutheran doctrine of Christ's person, our readers will understand with what reservation they must accept Dr. Gerhart's statement, which follows the one on which we have dwelt. He says that the Lutheran doctrine "involved the communicating of divine attributes to the human nature of Christ, in virtue of which His human nature was not limited to heaven, nor to any place at a time, but, *like the divine nature*, was present in all places at the same time where the Sacrament of the Altar was instituted and administered." For evidence of the correctness of this proposition, the reader is referred to "Herzog's Encyclopædia, by Dr. Bomberger." We would protest against the authority of Herzog's Encyclopædia on any question involving a distinctive doctrine of Lutheranism. Great as are the merits of that almost indispensable work, it is yet an unsafe guide on any question which involves in any way the so-called Evangelical Union. The article on the *Communicatio Idiomatum* is written by Dr. Schenkel, who is one of the last men to be selected for such a work. In its whole texture it is Unionistic, and in some of its statements, demonstrably incorrect. The article has been very admirably translated by Rev. Dr. Krotel, for the Abridgment of Herzog, edited by Dr. Bomberger. We do not find, however, in the part of the article cited by Dr. Gerhart, nor indeed in any part of it, a voucher for his definition, especially for the statement that our Church holds that the human nature of Christ is present "*like the divine nature.*" Dr. Schenkel, however anxious he might be to make out a case against our doctrine, could not have ventured on a statement which is not only inconsistent with the whole theory of our Church, but is contradicted, in express terms, in the Formula of Concord. Here we will say, as we said before, if Dr. Gerhart will show

The Person of Christ; a great misapprehension corrected.

33

us a solitary passage in our Confession, or in any approved author of our Church, which says that the human nature of Christ is present "*like the divine nature*," we will confess that we have too hastily pronounced upon his statements, and will consent to sit at his feet as a learner in the doctrines of our Church. Our Confessions, as we read them, again and again assert the very opposite, and we will undertake, for every line in the Heidelberg Catechism which repudiates the doctrine that the human nature of Christ is present like the divine, to produce twenty from our Confessions which repudiate it with equal strength.

As Dr. Gerhart has cited no passage from any Lutheran authority which asserts the doctrine he imputes to us, it might be sufficient for us simply to meet his statement with this denial, but we will go further, and cite some passages of the Formula of Concord in which it is expressly repudiated.

The Formula of Concord, in its VIIIth Article, after asserting that the " divine virtue, life, power, and majesty are given to the human nature assumed in Christ," goes on to say: 1. "This declaration, however, is NOT to be accepted in such sense, as if these were communicated, as the Father has communicated to the Son, according to His divine nature, His own essence, and all divine properties, whence He is of one essence with the Father, and co-equal."

2. " For Christ only according to His divine nature is equal to the Father: *according to His human nature He is under God.*"

3. " From these statements it is manifest that we imagine no confusion, *equalizing* or abolishing of the natures in Christ. For the power of giving life IS NOT IN THE FLESH OF CHRIST IN THE SAME WAY IN WHICH IT IS IN HIS DIVINE NATURE, to wit, as an essential property: *this* we have never asserted, never imagined."

4. " For that communion of natures, and of properties, is not the result of an essential, or natural effusion of the properties of the divine nature upon the human: *as if the humanity of Christ had them subsisting independently and separate from divinity; or as if by that communion the human nature of Christ had*

laid aside its natural properties, and was either converted into the divine nature, or was *made equal* in itself, and *per se* to the divine nature by those properties thus communicated ; *or that the natural properties and operations of each nature were identical, or even equal. For these and like* ERRORS have justly been rejected and condemned by the most ancient and approved councils on Scriptural grounds. FOR IN NO RESPECT is there to be made, or admitted, any conversion, or *confusion*, or *equalizing, either* of the natures in Christ, or of their essential properties."

5. " By these words, ' real communication, really to communicate,' we never designed to assert any physical communication, or essential transfusion (by which the natures would be confounded in their essences, or essential properties), in the sense in which some, craftily and maliciously, doing violence to their conscience, have not hesitated, by a false interpretation, to pervert these words and phrases, only that they may put upon sound doctrine the burden of unjust suspicion. We oppose these words and phrases to a verbal communication, since some feign that the communication of properties is no more than a phrase, a mode of speech, that is, mere words and empty titles. And they have pressed this verbal communication so far that they are not willing to hear a word of any other."

6. " There is in Christ that one only divine omnipotence, virtue, majesty, and glory, *which is proper to the divine nature alone.* But this shines and exerts its power fully, yet most freely in, and with, the humanity assumed."

7. " For it is so as in white-hot iron, — the power of shining and burning is not a twofold power, as if the fire had one such power, and the iron had another peculiar and separate power of shining and burning, but as that power of shining and burning is the property of the fire, and yet because the fire is united with the iron, and hence exerts that power of burning and shining in and with the iron, and through that white-hot iron, so, indeed, that the glowing iron has from this union the power both to burn and to shine, and yet all this is without the *change of the essence or of the natural properties either of the iron or of the fire.*"

The reader will please observe that this illustration is neither designed as a proof of the doctrine, nor as an exhibition of the mode of the union, but simply as an aid in removing a misunderstanding of the definition of terms.

8. " We believe, teach, and confess that there occurred no such effusion of the Majesty of God, and of all His properties, on the human nature of Christ, or that anything was withdrawn from the divine nature, or that anything from it was so bestowed on another, that in this respect it no longer retained it in itself; or that the human nature, in its own substance and essence, received A LIKE MAJESTY, separate from the divine nature and essence."

9. " For neither the human nature in Christ, nor any other creature in heaven or in earth, is capacious of divine omnipotence in that way, to wit, that of itself it could have an omnipotent essence, or have the properties of omnipotence in itself and *per se*."

10. " For in this way *the human nature in Christ would be denied and completely* changed into divinity, which is repugnant to our Christian faith, and the teaching of the prophets. and apostles."

11. " We reject, therefore, and with one consent, one mouth, one heart, condemn all errors departing from the sound doctrine we have presented ; errors which conflict with the writings of the apostles and the prophets, with the received and approved Ancient Creeds, and with our cherished Augsburg Confession. THESE ERRORS we will briefly and summarily recite :

" That the human nature of Christ, because of the personal union, is confounded with the divinity, or transmuted into it :

" That the human nature in Christ IN THE SAME WAY AS DIVINITY, as an infinite essence, and by an essential virtue or property of its own nature, IS EVERYWHERE PRESENT :

" That the human nature in Christ has become equal to the divine nature in its substance or essence, and essential properties :

" That the humanity of Christ is locally extended in all places of heaven and earth, an affirmation which cannot be made with truth, even of divinity :

"THESE ERRORS, and all others in conflict with sound doctrine, we reject, and we would exhort all devout people not to attempt to scrutinize this deep mystery with the curious search of human reason, but rather with the Apostles of our Lord to exercise a simple faith, closing the eyes of human reason, and bringing every thought into captivity to the obedience of Christ. But most sweet, most firm consolation, and perpetual joy may they seek in the truth that our flesh is placed so high, even at the right hand of the majesty of God, and of His almighty power. Thus shall they find abiding consolation in every sorrow, and be kept safe from every hurtful error."

With these beautiful words our Formula of Concord closes its matchless discussion of the doctrine of our Redeemer's person, and with them we close, imploring the pardon of that ever-present and ever-precious Saviour for our poor utterances on such a theme, and beseeching Him to bless even this unworthy offering to the strengthening of some faint heart in the faith once delivered to the saints.

XI.

BAPTISM.

(AUGSBURG CONFESSION. ART. IX.)

THE Lutheran doctrine of Baptism may be stated summarily in the following propositions:

I. "We confess one Baptism for the remission of sins."[*]

II. "The vice of origin — the inborn plague and hereditary sin — is truly sin, condemning, and bringing now also eternal death upon all that are not born again by Baptism and the Holy Spirit."[†]

III. "The ministry has been instituted to teach the Gospel and administer the Sacraments; for by the Word and Sacraments, as by instruments, the Holy Spirit is given."[‡]

IV. "Unto the true unity of the Church it is sufficient to agree concerning the doctrine of the Gospel and the administration of the Sacraments."

V. "It is lawful to use the Sacraments administered by evil men — and the Sacraments and Word are efficacious by reason of the institution and commandment of Christ, though the priests who impart them be not pious."[§]

VI. "The churches among us with common consent *teach* concerning Baptism:

"1. That it is necessary to salvation.

"2. That by Baptism the grace of God is offered.

"3. That children are to be baptized.

"4. That by Baptism they are offered and committed unto God.

---

[*] Symb. Nicænum.   [†] Aug. Conf. ii. 2.   [‡] Do. v. 1, 2.   [§] Do. vii. 2; viii. 1, 2

"5. And that thus offered by Baptism, they are received into God's favor."

VII. The churches among us, with one consent, *condemn* the Anabaptists, who

"1. Allow not the Baptism of children, and who teach that it is not right;

"2. And who affirm that children are saved without Baptism."*

Our Lord, in the course of His earthly ministry, authorized His disciples to baptize (John iv. 1, 2), and previous to His ascension, commanded them to make disciples of all the nations, by baptizing them in the name of the Father, and of the Son, and of the Holy Ghost (Matt. xxviii. 19).

The rite of Baptism, thus enjoined by our Lord, Baptism. has been the subject of various disputes in the Christian world. It is the object of this Dissertation to exhibit the faith of the Evangelical Lutheran Church in regard to the points of dispute. Over against all who deny the divine institution and perpetuity of Baptism, our Church maintains that " God has instituted it," and that it is obligatory and necessary throughout all time (Aug. Conf., Art. V., VII., VIII., IX., XIII., XIV.), so that without it the Church cannot exist in the world. Serious differences of opinion, however, exist in Christendom, even among those who recognize the perpetuity and obligation of Baptism, as to what are *essential* to Baptism, even as to its outward part. For, while all are agreed that the use of water, and of the Word, is essential, some parts of the Christian world maintain that the essential mode of Baptism is that of the *total immersion* of the body, insomuch that this *immersion is absolutely necessary*, and *positively demanded by our Lord*, and the application of water in any other way whatsoever is no Baptism. THE LUTHERAN CHURCH DOES NOT HOLD that immersion is ESSENTIAL TO BAPTISM.

That the Augsburg Confession uses the word " Baptism " in its then current sense is indisputable. Baptism was commonly administered in the sixteenth century by pouring, and sprinkling, as well as by immersion. In the Roman Catholic Agenda (Mentz), 1513, the Rubric says: " He shall pour (fundat) the

* Aug. Conf. Art. ix.

water thrice upon the head of the child, so that it shall reach his head and shoulders." The Augsburg Ritual (1587) directs that the priest, "taking water from the font with his right hand, shall gently pour it (perfundat) over the head and body of the child three times." The Roman Ritual directs, as the normal mode, that the water shall be poured. If immersion had been regarded by the confessors as a divine element of Baptism, they could not but have so stated. They declared that men could not be in Church unity who did not agree as to the administration of the Sacraments. That they do not object to the existing ideas of the mode of Baptism shows that they received them. The Augsburg Confession speaks of the various washings, made in various ways, under the Old Dispensation, as " the Baptisms of the Law."* Melanchthon, in the Instruction to the Visitors (1528), says: " Baptism shall be observed as hitherto."†
Luther, in the XVII. Schwabach Articles (1529), designates the prevailing mode, that mode which he had in his own mind in using the word Tauf, as " Begiessen," pouring or sprinkling.‡ These articles are the basis of the doctrinal part of the Augsburg Confession, and fix the sense of its terms. In Luther's own form of Baptism (1523), which is not to be confounded with his abridgment and translation of the Romish form, he directs that the water shall be poured upon the child. " It was the custom," says Funk,§ " at that time, to pour water all over the child, as Bugenhagen tells us: 'The pouring (Begiessen) in Baptism — the pouring over (übergiesset) the head and shoulders of the child . . is seen among us over all Germany.'"

Attempts have, indeed, been made to show that Luther, at
_{Luther and the} least, held the necessity of immersion, and that the
_{Jewess.}   Lutheran Church either held it with him, or was inconsistent in rejecting it. We shall show how groundless these statements are. One of the passages most frequently appealed to, in the attempt to implicate Luther, is found in

* Augs. Conf. xxvi. 22. "The Baptisms of the Law washed the members, garments, vessels." Luther. Oper. Lat. Jen. 524.

† Corp. Ref. xxvi. 64.   ‡ Do. do. 156.   § P. 115.

Walch's Edition of his works, X., 2637. In regard to this, the following are the facts :

1. The passage referred to is from a letter of Luther, written from Coburg, July 9th, 1530, in reply to an Evangelical pastor, Henry Genesius, who had consulted him in regard to the Baptism of a Jewish girl. It will be noted from the date that the letter was written a few months after the issue of the Catechisms, in which it has been pretended, as we shall see, that he taught the necessity of immersion.

2. The letter given in Walch, is also in the Leipzig edition of Luther (XXII., 371), and is not in either edition in the original language, but is a translation, and that from a defective copy of the original. The original Latin is given in De Wette's edition of Luther's Briefe (IV., 8), and contains a most important part of a sentence which is not found in the German translation. The letter in Walch cannot, therefore, be cited in evidence, for it is neither the original, nor a reliable translation of it.

3. The whole letter shows that the main point of inquiry was not as to whether the girl should be baptized in this or that mode, but what precautions decency demanded during the baptism, provided it were done by immersion.

4. Luther says: " It would please me, therefore, that she should . . modestly have the water poured upon her (*Mihi placeret, ut, . . verecunde perfunderetur*), or, if she sit in the water up to her neck, that her head should be immersed with a trine immersion." (*Caput ejus trina immersione immergeretur.*)

5. An *immersionist* is one who contends that Baptism *must* be administered by immersion. The passage quoted is decisive that Luther did not think Baptism *must* be so administered. He represents it as pleasing to him, best of all, that the girl should have the water applied to her by pouring ; or that, if she were immersed, greater precautions, for the sake of decency, should be observed, than were usual in the Church of Rome. It is demonstrated by this very letter, that LUTHER WAS NOT AN IMMERSIONIST.

6. In suggesting the two modes of Baptism, Luther was simply following the Ritual of the Romish Church. In the

Romish Ritual the direction is: " Baptism may be performed either by pouring, immersion, or sprinkling; but either the first or second mode, which are most in use, shall be retained, according as it has been the usage of the churches to employ the one or the other, so that either THE HEAD OF THE PERSON to be baptized shall have a trine ablution — that is, either the water shall be POURED UPON IT (*perfundatum* — Luther quotes the very word), or the HEAD shall be immersed (*ut trina ablutione caput immergatur*) — Luther again quotes almost verbatim. In the Roman Ritual, furthermore, for the Baptism of adults, it is said: " But in the churches where Baptism is performed by immersion, either of the *entire body*, or of the head only, the priest shall baptize by thrice immersing *the person*, or his head " (*illum vel caput ejus*). It is a mistake, as these words demonstrate, to suppose that even if immersion be practised, there must needs be a submergence of the whole body. The Roman Ritual leaves the choice between the immersion of the whole body, and the immersion of the head. The immersion of the head was performed in the case of infants, usually by dipping the back of the head into the font. Thus in the Ambrosian Ritual: " He shall dip the back of the child's head (*ter occiput mergit*) three times in the water." In the case of adults, the solemn immersion of the head could take place, in the same way, without any sort of immersion of the rest of the body; or, the person could go into the water up to the neck, and the solemn immersion of the head alone be made by the minister. It is evident that in the second case, equally with the first, the baptismal immersion was of the head only. The submergence to the neck was a mere natural preparation for the other. It is in this second manner that Luther directs, in case the Jewess was immersed at all, that the officiating minister should immerse her head only. She was to seat herself in the bath, and the only religious immersion was not that of her whole body (as Rome permits, and the Baptists, if consistent, would prescribe), but of her *head* only (*ut caput ejus immergeretur*). Luther, so far as he allowed of immersion at all, was not as much of an immersionist as the Ritual of Rome might have made him, for he does not hint at the immersion of the *whole*

body of the Jewess by the minister. An immersionist contends
that the whole body must be immerged by the officiating minister; not, indeed, that he is to lift the whole body and plunge
it in, but the whole immersion is to be so conducted as to be
clearly his official work, the person being led by him into the
water, and the immersion completed by his bending the body,
and thus bringing beneath the surface what was up to that time
uncovered. Luther preferred, if there was to be an immersion,
that the *head* only, not the *body*, should be immersed by the
minister (not *illum sed caput ejus*). Even to the extent,
therefore, to which he allowed immersion, *Luther was no
immersionist.*

7. If Luther could be proved, by this letter, to be an immer
sionist, it would be demonstrated that he derived his view
from the Romish Church, and held it in common with her.
In like manner, the Church of England, the Episcopal
Churches of Scotland and of the United States, and the
Methodist Churches, would be carried over to the ranks of
immersionists, for they allow the different modes. But these
Churches are confessedly not immersionist; therefore, *Luther
was no immersionist.*

8. Whatever Luther's personal preferences may have been
as to mode, he never even *doubted* the validity of Baptism by
pouring. But immersionists do not merely doubt it, they absolutely deny it; therefore, *Luther was no immersionist.*

9. An immersionist is one who makes his particular mode
of Baptism a term of Church communion, and an article of
faith. Luther was in a Church which did not prescribe
immersion as necessary — never made it an article of faith;
therefore, *Luther was no immersionist.*

10. Finally, the letter of Luther shows that he *preferred
pouring.* He says expressly that it would please him that the
water should be poured upon her, and gives this the first place;
and his directions in regard to the immersion, are given only
in the supposition that that mode might be decided upon — "*if*
she sit, etc., her head shall be immersed," etc., *si sedens.*

Whatever, therefore, may be the difference between the
doctrine of the necessity of immersion, and the "doctrine

of immersion," we feel safe in affirming that Luther held neither.

From Luther's Larger Catechism, by confounding the very plain distinction between allowance, or even prefer-ence of a mode, and a belief in its necessity, the evidence has been drawn that our Confessions teach the Baptist doctrine of immersion.

Luther's Cate-chisms.

Yet this very Catechism, in express terms, repudiates any such doctrine, and acknowledges, in the most decisive manner, what the Baptist doctrine denies — the validity of other modes than immersion. Mark these two sentences from the Larger Catechism: "Baptism is not our work, but God's. For thou must distinguish between the Baptism which God gives, and that which the keeper of a bath-house gives. But God's work, to be saving, does not exclude faith, but demands it, for without faith it cannot be grasped. For in the mere fact that *thou hast had water poured on thee*, thou hast not so received Baptism as to be useful to thee ; but it profits thee when thou art baptized with the design of obeying God's command and institution, and in God's name of receiving in the water the salvation promised. This neither the hand nor the body can effect, but the heart must believe."* In these words there is an express recognition of pouring or sprinkling (for the word used by Luther covers both, but excludes immersion) as modes of Baptism.

But there is another passage yet more decisive, if possible : "We must look upon our Baptism, and so use it, as to strengthen and comfort us whenever we are grieved by sins and conscience. We should say: I am baptized, therefore the promise of salvation is given me for soul and body. For to this end *these two things are done in Baptism,* that the body, which can only receive the water, *is wet by pouring,* and that, in addition, the word is spoken that the soul may receive it."† Here not only is the recognition of pouring (or sprinkling)

---

* Catech. Maj. Müller, 490, 36, *das Wasser über dich giessen.* The Latin is, " *aqua perfundi.*"

† Do. 492, 45. German: "*Der Leib begossen wird.*" Latin: " *Corpus aqua perfundatur.*"

explicit, but if the words were not compared with other expressions of Luther, it might be argued, that he and our symbols went to the opposite extreme from that charged upon them, and, instead of teaching that immersion is necessary, denied its validity. So far, then, is the charge from being verified, that we are authorized to make directly the opposite statement. Luther and our Confessions repudiate utterly the Baptist doctrine of the *necessity* of immersion.

In the *original* of the Smaller Catechism there is not a word about immersion in a passage sometimes referred to. It is simply, "What signifies this *Water-Baptism?*" (Wasser Tauffen.) "Immersion" is but a translation of a translation. The same is the case with the Smalcald Articles. The original reads: "Baptism is none other thing than God's Word *in the water* (*im Wasser*)." There is not a word about immersion. We do not rule these translations out because they at all sustain the allegation built on them. Fairly interpreted, they do not; but we acknowledge the obvious rule accepted in such cases — that the originals of documents, and not translations of them, are the proper subjects of appeal. A translation can carry no authority, except as it correctly exhibits the sense of the original. Even the general endorsement of a translation as correct, by the author of the original, is not decisive on a minute point which he may have overlooked, or have thought a matter of very little importance. A clergyman of our country translates the commentary of an eminent German theologian, and receives from him a warm letter of thanks, strongly endorsing the accu racy of the translation. Yet, not only in a possible deviation of the translation from the original, but in any matter of doubt, however slight, the original alone would be the source of appeal. As the Lutheran Church accepts Luther's version of the Bible, subject to correction by the original, so does she accept any translation of her symbols, however excellent, sub ject to correction by the original.

But, even if the principle were not otherwise clear, the facts connected with the translation of the different parts of the Symbolical Books would be decisive on this point. The translation of the Smalcald Articles, made in 1541, by Generanus, a young Danish student of theology, at Wittenberg, and who was an intimate friend of Luther, was confessedly admirable, pithy, and Luther-like. The translation which Selneccer pre pared, or selected, for the Book of Concord, 1580, was an *entirely new one*, very inferior to the old,* and this, after undergoing two sets of changes, is the one now ordinarily found in the Latin editions of the Symbol. *This* is one of the translations to which appeal is made, in the face of the original, and language is used which leaves the reader under the impression that these articles were translated under Luther's eye, and the translation approved by him.

The German translation of the Apology, found in the *Editio Princeps* of the German Concordia, and in most other editions, adds some things which are not in the Latin, and omits some things which are there. Which is the authority, Melanchthon's Latin, or Jonas' German, if a dispute arise as to the meaning of the Apology?

3. The Larger Catechism was first translated by Lonicer, faithfully, and into good Latin. The second translation was made by Opsopæus, and this was *changed* in various respects by Selneccer, and thus changed, was introduced into the Book of Concord.

4. The Smaller Catechism was first rendered into Latin by an unknown hand, then by Sauermann. "This translation *seems* to have been introduced into the Concordien-buch, *but with changes*," says Köllner

The principle involved, which no honest scholar would try to weaken, is well stated by Walch, in these words: † "It is by all means proper to know what was the *original language* of each of our Symbolical Books, since it is manifest that from *that, not from translations*, we are to judge of the genuine and true meaning of any book. What they teach we ought to see, not in versions, but in the original language itself, especially where the matter or meaning seems involved in some doubt. Versions do not always agree entirely with the writings as

---

* "Diffuse and feeble." F. Francke: L. S. Eccl. Luth. Pars Sec. xi Luther's ideas are often inundated in it." — Hase.

† Introd. in Lib., Symbol, 61.

their authors composed them ; as the facts themselves show is the case in our Symbolical Books also."

The allusions of Luther to the outward mode are never found in his *definition* of Baptism. His allusions to immersion come, in every case, long after he has defined Baptism. His *definition* of Baptism, in the Smalcald Articles, is: "Baptism is none other thing than the Word of God in the water, enjoined by his institution." His *definition* of Baptism in the Larger Catechism, is thus: "Learn thou, when asked, What *is* Baptism? to reply, It is not mere water, but water embraced in God's word and command. It is a mere illusion of the Devil when our New Spirits of the day ask, How can a *handful of water* help the soul?" And then comes his powerful vindication of this "handful of water" in its connection with the Word. In the Smaller Catechism, to the question, "What is Baptism?" the reply is: "Baptism is not mere water, but that water which is comprehended in God's command, and bound up with God's Word." Nowhere does any Symbol of our Church say that Baptism *is* immersion, or even allude to immersion when it speaks of that which consti tutes Baptism.

That the word "begiessen," by which Luther indicates one of the modes of Baptism, can only indicate pouring or sprink· ling, and by no possibility immersion, every one even moderately acquainted with German very well knows. The proper meaning of *begiessen*, as given by Adelung, is, "*Durch Giessen nass machen,*" *i. e.*, to wet by pouring or dropping. Campe's definition is, "*Durch Darangiessen einer Flüssigkeit nass machen,*" *i. e.*, to wet by the pouring on of a fluid. Frisch defines it: "*Perfundi, affundendo madefacere,*" *i. e.*, to pour over, to wet by pouring upon. The Grimms define it by, "*Perfundere,*" to pour over. When followed by "*mit,*" governing a noun, the "*mit*" is always to be translated "*with,*" "*mit Wasser begiessen,*" "to wet with water by pouring it." When followed by "*auf,*" the "*auf*" means "upon." When Adler, Meissner, and others give "moisten," "bathe," "soak," and similar words as an equivalent, it is in such phrases as, "to bathe or moisten (*begiessen*) the hand with tears." You may use "*begiessen*" when the hand is bathed by the tears which pour or drop upon it; but if the hand were bathed by immersing it in water, a German would no more use "*begiessen*" to designate that act than we would use "pour." We affirm what every German scholar knows, that with any allusion, direct or indirect, to the mode in which a liquid can be brought into contact with an object, "*begiessen*" never means, and never can mean, either in whole or inclusively, "to immerse." It is so remote from it as to be antithetical to it, and is the very word used over against the terms for immersion, when it is desirable distinctly to state that Baptism is not to be performed by immersion.

But if "*begiessen*" could ever mean to immerse, or include that idea, we shall demonstrate specially that it has not that force in Luther's German. Luther uses the word *giessen* upwards of fifty times in his translation of the Bible, and invariably in the primary sense of pour. The word "*begiessen*," in which the prefix "*be*" simply gives a transitive character to the "*giessen*" — as we might say "bepour," — he uses five times. Twice he uses it in the Old Testament, to translate "Yah-tzak," which, in twenty other passages he translates by "*giessen*," to pour. The two passages in which *begiessen* is used are, Gen. xxxv. 14, "Jacob *poured* (*begoss*) oil thereon," — hardly, we think, immersed his pillar of stone in oil; Job xxxviii. 38, "Who can stay the bottles of heaven, when the dust groweth (Marg. Hebr. is poured, *begossen*) into hardness," — hardly meaning that the compacting of the mire is made by immersing the ground into the showers. Three times Luther uses "*begiessen*" in the New Testament, 1 Cor. iii. 6, 7, 8, "Apollos watered: he that watereth (*begossen, begeusst*)" — referring to the sprinkling, or pouring of water on plants. So Luther also says: "Hatred and wrath are poured over me (*ueber mich begossen*)," Jena Ed. v. 55.

We have shown that the general usage of the language does not allow of the interpretation in question. We have shown that, if it did, Luther's German does not. We shall now show that if both allowed it anywhere, it is most especially not allowable in the Catechism, nor in Luther's use of it any-where, with reference to Baptism.

Now for "*giessen*" and "*begiessen*," in their reference to Baptism by Luther, in the Catechism and elsewhere, can they *include* not *exclude* immersion? Let us try this.

1. Larger Catechism: *Dass du lässest das Wasser über dich giessen* (*quod te aqua perfundi sinis*). We affirm that these words have, to any one who knows anything of German, but one possible meaning, and that, like the verbal English translation of the words "that thou lettest the water pour over thee," the German cannot mean "thou lettest thyself be dipped into the water."

2. What *mode* of Baptism Luther had in his mind is clear, furthermore, from the words in immediate connection with those we have quoted, for he says: "This (the work of the heart) the bent hand (Faust*) cannot do, nor the body," the connection showing the thought to be this: neither the bent hand of the administrator of Baptism,—bent to gather up and pour the water,—nor the body of the recipient, can take the place of faith, in securing the blessings of Baptism.

3. This is rendered clear again, from the words, "*Was sollt ein hand voll Wassers der Seelen helfen?*" What can a *handful* of water help the soul? This shows that the "hand ful of water" was connected with a received mode at that time in the Lutheran Churches.

If the sense of *begiessen*, as applied to Baptism, were obscure, (as it is not — no word more clearly excludes immersion) this passage would settle it.

4. But there is abundance more of evidence on this point. In Luther's own Ritual for Baptism, the officiating minister "pours the water," (*geusst Wasser auf*) and says: "*Ich taufe dich.*"

5. In the Article of Torgau, the fanatics, who in the Cate-chism are characterized as asking, "What can the handful of water do," are represented as calling Baptism "miserable water, or pouring" (*begiessen*).

---

* As in Isaiah xl. 12, "*Wer misset die Wasser mit der Faust.*" Eng. Ver.: "Who hath measured the water in the *hollow of his hand?*"

34

6. In the letter of July 9th, 1530: "That standing, she should have the water poured upon her (*perfunderetur*), or sitting, her head should be immersed (*immergeretur*)," surely not both the same.

7. In the Wittenberg Liturgy of 1542, those are spoken of who do "not dip (*tauchen*) the infants in water, nor (*noch*) pour it upon them (*begiessen*)."

But Luther says *the body* is baptized; therefore, of necessity, it is urged, by immersion. When St. Paul describes Baptism in the words "having our bodies washed with pure water," he can hardly be said to prove himself an immersionist. Luther's words are: "These two things are done in Baptism, that the body, which is able to receive nothing besides the water, is wet by pouring, and, in addition, the Word is spoken, that the *soul* may embrace it." Body and soul are two things in Luther's mind, and it is not hard to see that the body does receive what is poured on the head.

But if the criticism of the word "body" stood, it would do no good, for water can be applied to the entire body by pouring (or even by sprinkling), as was largely, though not universally, the usage in our Church. The water was poured so copiously in some cases as to wet the entire body of the infant.

Luther, in speaking of the permanence of the Baptismal Covenant, and of the power of returning, by repentance, to its blessings, even after we fall into sin, says: "*Aber mit Wasser ob man sich gleich hundertmal lässet ins Wasser senken, ist doch nicht mehr denn Eine Taufe.*" This has been thus translated and annotated: "'But no one dares to *begiessen* us with water again; for if one should be sunk in water (*ins wasser senken*) a hundred times, it is no more than one Baptism.' Here *senken* is used along with *begiessen*, and to explain it."

But neither the translation, nor interpretation, is accurate. "*Darf*" does not mean "dares," but means "needs," as the Latin has it, "*non est necesse.*" The "*ob gleich*" has been dropped, those important words which the Latin properly renders "*etsi*," "for *even though* one should be sunk." "*Senken*" is not used to explain *begiessen*. Luther does not mean that to "*pour* upon *with* water" is equivalent to being "*sunk in* water a *hundred* times." The point is this: After the one Baptism, the repentant sinner needs not that water should be poured upon him again. No re-pouring can make a re-baptism. Nay, if he were not merely *poured* upon, but *sunk* into the water, not *once*, but a *hundred* times, still, in spite of the quantity of the water, and the manifold repetition of the rite, there would be but one Baptism. There is an ANTITHESIS, not a PARALLEL, between " POUR " and " SINK," and between " ONCE " and a " HUNDRED TIMES."*

Luther's translation of the words connected with *Baptism,* proves that he was no immersionist.

1. Immersionists say that *Baptisma* should *al-* Luther's translation of the Bible. *ways* be translated *immersion.* Luther, throughout his translation of the Bible, NEVER translates it *immersion* (*untertauchung*), or *dipping* (*eintauchung*), or *plunging* (*versenkung*), but always and exclusively, Baptism (*Taufe*).

2. Immersionists translate *Baptismos* immersion. Luther translates it either Baptism or washing. Mark vii. 4 — Baptist Version: *Immersion* of cups, etc. Luther: *washing.* Do. 8 — Baptist Version: *immersions ;* Luther: *washing.*

3. *a.* Immersionists say that *Baptizo* should always be translated to immerse. Luther *never* translates it by immerse, nor any of its equivalents, but with the exceptions we shall mention in a moment, by *Taufen,* to baptize.

b. Immersionists say, moreover, that *en* following *baptizo,* should be translated *in,* " I immerse you *in* water ; " " he shall immerse you *in* the Holy Ghost," etc. Luther translates as does our English version: " I baptize you *with* (*mit*) water ; " " he shall baptize you *with* the Holy Ghost," etc.

c. Luther translates 1 Cor. xv. 29, " What shall they do which are baptized *above* the dead," and explains it † of administering Baptism " *at the graves of the dead*," in token of faith in the resurrection. The words of Luther are: " They are baptized at the graves of the dead, in token that the dead who lay buried there, and *over whom* they were baptized, would rise again. As we also might administer Baptism publicly in the common church-yard, or burial place."‡ Immersionists

* 497. 78 † Leipz. Ed. X. 884. ‡ Auslegung, Anno 1534.

generally prefer to consider the Baptism here as metaphorical, and immerse the live saints in sorrows.

4. Immersionists say that the *radical* idea of *Baptizo*, in its New Testament use, is not that of *washing*. Luther repeatedly translates it *to wash*. We will present some of these translations in contrast. Translation on Immersionist principles: Judith xii. 8, "Judith went out and *immersed* herself at a spring near the camp;" Luther: "*and washed* herself in the water." Ecclesiasticus xxxiv. 25 — Immersionist: "He that *immerses* himself after touching a dead body;" Luther: "That *washeth* himself." Mark vii. 5 — Immersionist: "(The Pharisees and all the Jews,) when they come from the market, unless they *immerse* themselves, eat not;" Luther: "*wash* themselves." Luke xi. 38 — Immersionist: "That he had not *immersed* himself;" Luther: "*washed* himself."

5. The Baptist version renders *Baptistes, Immerser;* Luther, always *Täuffer, Baptist.*

6. Immersionists say that *Bapto* always properly means, to *dip.* Luther translates Rev. xix. 13: "He was clothed with a vesture *sprinkled* with blood."

These proofs are enough to demonstrate that, judged as a translator, *Luther was no immersionist.*

But it has been urged that Luther has used *taufte,* where our translators have "dipped," 2 Kings v. 14. The fact is, however, that this verse alone is enough to dispose of the false theory. Our translators have "dipped," it is true; but as Luther did not translate from our authorized version, that proves nothing. That same authorized version has "dipped" in Rev. xix. 13, where Luther has "*besprenget,*" "sprinkled." The fact is, that if the ravages in the German, on the part of those who are determined to make Luther a Baptist, or an Anabaptist, against his will, are not arrested, they will not leave a word in that language, once deemed somewhat copious, which will express any mode of reaching the human body by water, except by dipping; "*begiessen*" and "*taufen*" are disposed of, and "*besprengen*" can be wiped out exactly as "*taufen*" has been. The question, however, is worth a moment's attention, Why Luther used the word "*taufte,*" in 2 Kings v.

14 ? The word " *ta-bhal* " is used sixteen times, but Luther never translated it " *taufen*," except in this place. It is also noticeable that in this place alone does the Septuagint translate " *ta-bhal* " by " *baptizo*." The Vulgate considers it as equivalent in meaning to " *ra-hhatz* " of the preceding verses, and translates it " *lavit*," washed. The Targum considers the two words as equivalent. So does the Syriac, and so the Arabic. Pagninus' version gives to both the same meaning, but marks the distinction between their form by translating " *ra-hhatz*," " *lavo*," and " *ta-bhal*," " *abluo*." In his Thesaurus, he gives as a definition of " *ta-bhal*," " *lavare, baptizare*," and translates it in 2 Kings v. 14, " *lavit se*," washed himself. Origen, and many of the Fathers, had found in the washing of Naaman a foreshadowing of Baptism. De Lyra, Luther's great favorite as an expositor, expressly calls this washing (2 Kings v. 14) a receiving of Baptism. Luther saw in it the great idea of Baptism — the union of water with the Word, as he expressly tells us, in commenting on the passage, in his exposition of the cxxii. Psalm.* The word " *taufte*," therefore, is to be translated here, as everywhere else in Luther's Bible, not by immerse, but by " baptize." Naaman baptized himself, *not* dipped himself in Jordan, is Luther's meaning. The Hebrew, *ta-bhal*, Luther translates fourteen times, by *tauchen*, to dip, in accordance with its accepted etymology. But he also translates what he regarded as its participle, by color or dye, Ezek. xxiii. 15. According to the mode of reasoning, whose fallacy we are exposing, wherever Luther uses " *taufen*," we may translate it " to dye ; " for the etymological force of a word, according to this, is invariable, and all true translations of it must have the same meaning.

Bapto Luther translates by " *tauchen* and *eintauchen*," to dip, dip in ; but he also translates by " *besprengen* " (Rev. xix. 13), to sprinkle: but, according to this mode of reasoning, *tauchen* and *taufen* both being equivalents, *taufen* is sprinkling, and Baptism is sprinkling, and dipping is sprinkling. By the way in which it is proved that *Taufe* is immersion, may be proved that both *Taufe* and immersion are sprinkling. *Baptizo* Luther never

* Leipz. Edit V. 461.

translated by *tauchen*, nor by any word which would be under-stood by the readers of his version to mean immersion. What-ever may be the *etymology* of *Taufe*, its *actual use* in the German language did not make it equivalent to *immersion.* Sprinkling *Besprengen*) or pouring (*Begiessen*) were called *Taufe.* If Luther believed that the *actual* (not the primary or etymo-logical) force of the word made immersion necessary, he was bound before God and the Church to use an unambiguous term. It is not true that "*tauchen*" or "*eintauchen*" had, either then or now, that very trifling and vulgar sense which, it is alleged, unfitted them over against "*taufen*," to be used to designate immersion. Luther uses them in his Bible, and, when in his Liturgies he means to designate immersion, these words are the very words he employs.

Luther used the ancient word *Taufen*, because, in the fixed usage of the German, *Taufen* meant to baptize. Whatever may have been the etymology of it, we find its ecclesiastical use fixed before the ninth century. Otfried so uses it, A. D. 868. Eberhard and Maass, in their great Synonymik of the German, say: "After *Taufen* was limited to this ecclesiastical signification, it was no longer used for *Tauchen*, and can still less be used for it now that *Taufen* (Baptism) is no longer per-formed by *Eintauchen* (immersion)."

The prepositions which Luther used in connection with "*taufen*," show that he did not consider it in its *actual use* as a synonym of immerse: to baptize *with* water (*mit*), *with* the Holy Ghost (*mit*). John baptized *with* water (*mit*); baptized under Moses (*unter*) *with* the cloud (*mit*). It is not English to talk of immersing *with* water; nor would it be German to fol-low "*tauchen*" or "*eintauchen*" by "*mit;*" nor any more so to use "*mit*" after "*taufen*," if *taufen* meant to immerse.

Furthermore, Luther has twice, 1 Cor. xv. 29, "To baptize *over* the dead (*über*)," which he explains to refer to the baptism of adults over the graves of the martyrs.

But Luther has not left us to conjecture what he considered the proper German equivalent for *baptizo* and *baptismos*, in their *actual use* — how much their actual use settled as to the *mode* of Baptism. *Five* times only he departs from the rendering by *Taufe*, or *Taufen*, but not once to use "*tauchen*," but invariably to use *Waschen*, to wash.

Judith xii. 8: *Und wusch sich im Wasser*, washed herself; (Gr.: *Ebaptizeto ;* Vulg.: *Baptizat se*).

Sir. xxxiv. 30 (25): *Wer sich wäscht*, he who washes himself; (Gr.: *Baptizomenos ;* Vulg.: *Baptizatur*), what avails him this washing? *sein Waschen?* (Gr.: *Loutron*).

Mark vii. 24: *Ungewaschen (aniptois) Hönden — sie waschen (nipsontai), sie waschen sich (baptizontai), Tische zu waschen (baptismous) ;* vii. 8: *Zu waschen (baptismous)*.

Luke xi. 38; *Dass er sich nicht vor dem Essen gewaschen hatte (ebaptiste)*.

He translates *baptizo* as he translates *nipto* and *louo*.

Here is the demonstration, that while Luther believed, in common with many philologists, that the *etymological force* (*Laut*) of *baptismos* and *baptisma* is "immersion," its actual force in Biblical use is "washing," without reference to mode. Luther treats it as having the same *generic* force with *louo*, *pluno*, and *nipto*, all of which he translates by the same word, *waschen*, just as our authorized version translates every one of them, *baptizo* included, by wash. With the etymology of the Greek goes also the etymology of the German. The primitive mode of washing, in nations of warm or temperate countries, is usually by immersion. Hence the words in many languages for the two ideas of dipping and washing come to be synonyms — and as the word washing ceases to designate mode, and is equally applied, whether the water be poured, sprinkled, or is plunged in, so does the word which, etymologically, meant to dip. It follows the mutation of its practical equivalent, and comes to mean washing, without reference to mode. So our word, bathe, possibly implies, *primarily*, to immerse. But we now bathe by "plunge," "douch," or "shower-bath," and we know that the wider use of the word "bathe" is very old in English, as, for example, Chaucer* says:

> "His heart-blood hath bathed all his hair."

If the baptismal commission had been given in English, and

* Knightes Tale, v. 2,009.

the word used had been Bathe, the person who admitted that
the word "bathe" covered all modes of applying water, but
who, in a case confessedly a matter of freedom, would prefer
immersion as the mode, because it corresponds with what he
believes to be the *etymology* of bathe, as well as with its actual
use, would do what Luther did in a cognate case, in 1519, of
which we are about to speak; but the inference that either
regarded the word in question as *meaning* to immerse, or as a
synonym of it, would be most unwarranted.

An attempt has been made to show that Luther was an
immersionist, by citing his views of the etymology
both of the Greek and German words involved.
The citation relied on for this purpose, is from the
sermon: *Vom Sacrament der Taufe*,* which has been thus
given: "*Die taufe* (baptism) is called in Greek, *baptismos;* in
Latin, immersion, that is, when anything is wholly dipped
(*ganz ins wasser taucht*) in water which covers it." Further,
"according to the import of the word *Tauf*, the child, or any
one who is baptized (*getauft wird*), is wholly sunk and immersed
(*sonk und tauft*) in water and taken out again; since, without
doubt, in the German language, the word *Tauf* is derived from
the word *Tief*, because what is baptized (*taufet*) is sunk deep in
water. This, also, the import of *Tauf* demands."

This translation is not characterized by accuracy. For
example, it renders both "*Laut*" and "*Bedeutung*," by the
one word *import*, when Luther expressly distinguishes between
"*Laut*" and "*Bedeutung*;" the former referring to the *etymo-logical* or primary literal force of a word, and the latter to the
moral significance of a rite.

Further, it mutilates and mistranslates the words, which,
literally rendered, are: "Yet it should then be, and WOULD BE
RIGHT (*und wär recht*) that one sink and baptize entirely in the
water, and draw out again, the child, etc." How different the
air of Luther's German from that of the inaccurate English.

There is another yet more significant fact. It OMITS, out of
the very heart of the quotation, certain words, which must
have shown that the idea that "*begiessen*" includes immersion

---

* Leipzig Edition, **xxii**. 139.

Luther's ety-
mologies of the
words.

is entirely false. The two sentences which are quoted are con
nected by these words, which are NOT QUOTED: "And although
in many places it is no longer the custom to plunge and dip
(*stossen und tauchen*) the children in the font (*die Tauf*), but
they are poured upon (*begeusst*) with the hand, out of the font
(*aus der Tauf*)." Here, over against immersion, as the very
word to mark the opposite mode, is used that "*begiessen*,"
which, it is pretended, refers to immersion. It seems to us
inconceivable that any one could read the passage in the original, without having the falsity of the former position staring
him in the face.

On the whole passage we remark:

First. That the sermon was published in 1519, among the
earliest of Luther's writings, ten years before the Catechism,
and when he had not yet made the originals of Scripture the
subject of his most careful study, and when his views were
still largely influenced by the Fathers and Romish theology.
It was published five years before he began his translation of
the New Testament, and more than twenty before he gave his
Bible its final revision. This raises the query whether his
views, after the thorough study of the Bible, connected with
his translating it, remained unchanged. We have given, and
can give again, ample proof that if Luther's meaning in 1519
implies the necessity of immersion, his opinion had undergone
a total change before 1529, when the Larger Catechism, whose
words are in question, was published.

Secondly. The passage is not pertinent to the proof of that
for which it is urged. Luther designs to give what he supposes to be the *etymological* force of *Baptismos* and *Taufe* — not
to show their force in ACTUAL USE. That Luther affirms, not
that *Baptismos* and *Taufe* in actual use mean "immersion,"
but only etymologically, is clear. 1. From the whole vein
of argument. As an argument concerning the etymology of
the words, it is pertinent; as an argument on the actual use
of either, it would be in the highest degree absurd. 2. From
his limitation by the word "*Laut*," which means "Etymology," as Luther himself translates it in the Latin, "*Etymologia*." 3. By the fact that, twice, in these very sentences,

Luther uses *Taufe* not in the sense either of immersicn or of Baptism, but of " font." 4. That in his translatior of the Scriptures he uses " *Taufe* " for " Baptism," without limitation to mode. 5. That in his translation of the Romish Ritual, and wherever else he wishes to indicate the idea of immersion, he never uses *taufe* or *taufen*, always *tauchen* or *untertauchung*. 6. That in the only Baptismal Service properly Luther's own, he directs the water to be poured, with the words, *Ich taufe*. 7. That he repeatedly recognizes the validity of *Taufe* by pouring, which would be ridiculous, if *Taufe* in actual use meant immersion.

Third. The Latin of Luther's Sermon on Baptism, in the Jena Edition, an edition which excludes everything of his which was not officially approved, makes very plain the drift of the words quoted. It says: " The noun, Baptism, is Greek, and *can* be rendered (*potest verti*) in Latin, *Mersio*," — "That (*i. e.*, the immersion and drawing out) the *etymology* of the word (*Etymologia nominis — Laut des Wörtleins*) *seems* to demand (*postulare videtur*)." From Luther's opinion on the etymology of the words Baptism and Taufe, the inference is false that he held that Baptism, in the ACTUAL USE of the word, meant immersion, and that the German word Taufe, in ACTUAL USE, had the same meaning. To state the proposition is to show its fallacy to any one familiar with the first principles of language.

1. That the etymological force and actual use of words are often entirely different every scholar knows. Carnival is, etymologically, a farewell to meat. Sycophant, etymologically and properly, means a fig-shower; miscreant is a misbeliever; tinsel means "sparkling," (Thetis, with the "tinsel-slippered feet," Milton); carriage (Acts xxi. 15) means things carried , kindly, in the Litany, according to kind; painful, involving the taking of pains ; treacle, something made from wild beasts. The German *schlecht*, bad, originally meant good ; *selig*, blessed, is the original of our English word silly ; the word courteous has its root in a word which meant a cow-pen.

2. The very essence of the philological argument against the necessity of immersion, turns upon this fact. If to admit that

Bapto and *Baptizo* may, etymologically, mean to dip in, is to admit that, in their ACTUAL USE, they mean exclusively to dip in, then the argument against the Baptists, on the part of many, is over.

3. The English words Baptism and baptize are simply Greek words in an English shape. As this argument puts it, they also mean, throughout our authorized version and our whole usage, exclusively immersion, or to immerse. So the Baptists contend as to their etymological and native force; but as they concede that such is not the actual use of them in English, even they, when they translate anew, give us "immersion" and "immerse."

4. If the interpretation of Luther, we are contesting, stands, Luther was an immersionist, did teach that immersion is the synonym of Baptism and is necessary, did hold the "Baptist doctrine of immersion;" but it is admitted that Luther did none of these, therefore this interpretation cannot stand. The argument makes Luther to be theoretically an immersionist, and only saved by hypocrisy, or glaring inconsistency, from being an Anabaptist in practice. The Martin Luther which this new philology has given us is a disguised Anabaptist. The positions are inconsistent with each other, and the argu ments for them self-confuting.

What is the real meaning of Luther's words? It is that in its *etymological* and *primary* force (*Laut*), the German term *Taufe*, like the Greek *baptismos*, the Latin *mersio*, means immer sion, but he does NOT say, and there is abundant evidence that he did not believe, that in ACTUAL USE, either *Taufe* or *baptisma* means exclusively immersion, but, on the contrary, means "washing" without reference to mode. We believe that many scholars of anti-Baptistic schools will concede that Luther was right in his position as to etymology, as all intelligent Baptists will, and do, concede that the etymological and primary force of any word, may be entirely different from that it has in actual use.

2. Luther, in 1519, drew the inference that it would be right and desirable that the mode of washing should conform to the etymological and primary force, as well as to the actual

use of the word. That it would be right, if the Church pre
ferred so to do, is, we think, undisputable ; that it is desirable,
is, we think, very doubtful, and we can prove that such was
Luther's attitude to the mode when the Catechisms were written. That immersion is necessary, Luther denied in express
terms, in his book on the Babylonish Captivity of the same
period (1519).

3. Luther, in 1519, under the influence of the Romish Liturgy, and of the writings of the Fathers, believed that the
symbolical significance of Baptism, as pointing to the drown
ing and death of sin, though essentially unaffected by the
mode, is yet brought out more clearly in immersion, and at
that era *so far* preferred it. In his later Biblical Era, to which
his Catechism belongs, there is ample evidence that this preference was no longer cherished.

This, then, is in brief the state of the case. The point of
Luther's whole argument, in 1519, is, that inasmuch as immersion corresponds with the *etymology* of Baptism, as well as with
its actual general use, which embraces every kind of washing,
and as a certain signification common to all modes, is most
clearly brought out in immersion, it would be right, and *so far*
desirable, that *that* mode, though not necessary, but a matter
of Christian freedom, should be adopted. Then, as always, he
placed the mode of Baptism among the things indifferent, and
would have considered it heresy to make the mode an article
of faith. In the Church of Rome, some of the older rituals
positively prescribe immersion ; and in the ritual now set forth
in that Church, by authority, there is a direction that, " Where
the custom exists of baptizing by immersion, the priest shall
immerse the child thrice." Luther, in his Sermon in 1519,
expresses his preference for immersion, not on the ground of
any superior efficacy, but because of its etymology, antiquity,
and significance as a sign: and when he alludes to the fact
that the children, in many places, were not so baptized, he
does not express the least doubt of the validity of their
Baptism.

In his book on the Babylonish Captivity, which appeared
in 1520, declaring his preference again for the same mode, he

expressly adds: "Not that I think it (immersion) necessary."[*]
But this claim of necessity, and this only, is the very heart of
the Baptist doctrine. The strongest expressions in favor of
immersion occur in Luther's earliest works, and his maturer
preference, as expressed in later works, seem to have been no
less decided for pouring as an appropriate mode. Thus in his
Commentary on Genesis, one of his latest and ripest works,
he says: "The water which is poured (quæ funditur) in Baptism is not the water given by God as the Creator, but given
by God the Saviour."[†]

We will now look at the testimony furnished on the point in
question by the Liturgies of Luther and the Lutheran Church.

1. The *Taufbüchlein* of Luther, 1523, is not a Lutheran
Ritual, but avowedly only a translation of a The Liturgies
Romish service. He declares, in the Preface to it, of Luther and of
that there was much in it which he would have the Lutheran
desired to remove, but which he allowed to remain Church.
on account of the consciences of the weak, who might have
imagined that he wished to introduce a new Baptism, and
might regard their own Baptism as insufficient. That in this
Ritual, therefore, the direction given to dip the child (*tauchen*)
only proves that the particular Romish Ritual followed by
Luther had that Rubric.

2. But after this Translation, later in this same year, 1523,
Luther issued his own directions for Baptism: *Wie man recht
und verständlich einen Menschen zum Christenglauben taufen
soll.*[‡] This document, in the older editions of Luther's works,
has been erroneously placed under 1521. The Erlangen edition, the latest and most critical ever issued, gives it its true
place, under 1523. In this direction, how RIGHTLY (*recht*) and
INTELLIGENTLY (*verständlich*) to baptize, Luther says: "The
person baptizing POURS THE WATER (*geusst wasser auff*), and
says, *Ego Baptizo te*," that is, in German, *Ich tauf dich* (I baptize thee). POURING, and pouring alone, is described as Bap-

---

* De Captiv. Babylon. Eccles. Jena Edit., II. 273. "*Non quod necessarium
arbitrer.*"

† On ch. xxviii. Vol. iii. 91.

‡ Leipz. xxii. 227. Walch, x. 2,622. Erlangen xxii. 168.

tism, and positively prescribed in the only Ritual of **Baptism**
which is properly Luther's exclusive work.

3. In 1529, the year in which the Catechisms of Luther
appeared, in which it is pretended that "the Baptist doctrine
of immersion " is taught, he wrote the Seventeen Articles of
Schwabach, or Torgau,* which became the basis of the doctrinal Articles of the Augsburg Confession. In the Ninth
Article of these, he says: We baptize WITH water (*mit Wasser*),
— and Baptism is not mere *miserable water*, or SPRINKLING and
POURING (*begiessen*)." Here again the *begiessen*, the applying of
the water to the person, not the immersing of the person in
water, is exclusively spoken of as the mode of Baptism.

4. In the Liturgy of Wittenberg,† Luther's own home
(1542), dipping and pouring are placed on the same footing in
every respect. " Ins wasser tauchen — sie damit begiessen."

5. In the Liturgy of Halle, 1543,‡ the administrator is
expressly left free to use either pouring or dipping. " Zwis-
chen dem Begiessen und Eintauchen wird die Wahl gelassen."

6. Bugenhagen, in the conjoined work from Luther and
himself (1542), designing to comfort mothers who had lost
their children, says that Baptism of children, by pouring, was
prevalent in the Lutheran Churches of Germany (*das begiessen,
siehet man noch bei uns über ganz Deutschland*).

7. The Liturgy of the Palatinate of the Rhine, etc., 1556, of
which the original edition lies before us, says: " Whether
the child shall have water poured on it once or thrice, be
dipped or sprinkled, is a MATTER OF INDIFFERENCE (*mittelmässig*).
Yet, that all things may be done in the Church in good order,
and to edification, we have regarded it as proper that the child
should not be dipped (*gedaucht*), but have the water poured
upon it (*begossen werden*)." And in the Rubric: " Then shall
the minister pour water (*begiesse*) on the child."

8. The Liturgy of Austria, 1571, directs the Baptism to be
performed by copious pouring or sprinkling.§ The later usage
is so well known, that it is not necessary to multiply citations.

---

* Leipz. xx. 22. Walch xvi. 778. Erlangen xxiv. 321.
† Consistorial Ordnung, 1542; Richter K. O. I 369.   ‡ Do. Il. **15.**
§ " Mit Wasser reichlich begiessen, besprengen."

We shall close this part of our discussion with the words of two well-known authors of the Lutheran Church in America. Dr. Schmucker, in his Popular Theology, says, very truly: "The question is not whether Baptism by immersion is valid; this is not doubted. . . But the question is whether immersion is enjoined in Scripture, and consequently is an essential part of Baptism, so that without it no Baptism is valid, though it contains every other requisite. On this subject the Lutheran Church has *always* agreed with the great majority of Christian denominations in maintaining the *negative*, and in regarding the *quantity* of water employed in Baptism, as well as the mode of exhibiting it, not essential to the validity of the ordinance." "The controversy on this subject (the mode of applying water in Baptism) has always been regarded by the most enlightened divines, *including Luther*, Melanchthon, and Chemnitz, as of comparatively inferior importance."

Dr. Benjamin Kurtz, in his work on Baptism, after showing very conclusively that Luther was not an immersionist, closes his discussion with these words: "We leave our readers to judge for themselves, from the foregoing extracts, what amount of credit is due to the objection made by *some of our Baptist brethren*, that Luther believed in the necessity of submersion to *the exclusion of effusion*, or that he was not decidedly in favor of children's being baptized. To our more *enlightened readers we may owe an apology for making our extracts so copious*, and dwelling so long on this subject; but *the less informed*, who have been assailed again and again by this groundless objection, without ability to refute it, will know better how to appreciate our effort."

It is hardly necessary to show that these views of the mode of Baptism were held by all our old divines. A few citations will suffice:

CHEMNITZ: * "The verb *Baptizein* does not necessarily import immersion. For it is used, John i. 33, and Acts i. 5, to designate the pouring out of the Holy Spirit. And the Israelites are said, 1 Cor. x. 2, to have been baptized unto Moses, in the

* On Matt. xxviii. 19. Exam. Concil. Trid. Ed. 1653. See, also, Harmon. Evang. C. xvi.

cloud and in the sea, who, nevertheless, were not immersed
into the sea, nor dipped into the cloud.	Wherefore, Paul, a
most safe interpreter, says that to baptize is the same as to
purify or cleanse by the laver of water in the Word, Eph. v.
26.	Whether, therefore, the water be used by merging, dip-
ping, pouring, or sprinkling, there is a baptizing.	And even
the washing of hands, couches, and cups, in which water was
employed, whether by merging, dipping, or pouring, Mark vii.
4, is called Baptism.	Nor in the Baptism instituted by Christ,
is there needed such a rubbing of the body with water as is
needed to remove the filth of the flesh, 1 Pet. iii. 21.	Since,
therefore, our Lord has not prescribed a fixed mode of employing the water, there is no change in the substantials of Baptism, though in different Churches the water is employed in
different modes."

FLACIUS ILLYRICUS:* "Baptizo, by metalepsis, signifies, to
wash, bathe (abluo, lavo).	Hence, Mark vii. 4, says: ' The Jews
have various Baptisms (i. e. washings) of cups and pots;' and
1 Peter iii. 21, says: 'Our Baptism is not the putting away
of the filth of the flesh.'	Heb. vi. 2, the word Baptism refers
to the purifications and washings under the old dispensation."

STEPHEN GERLACH† says: "Herein Baptism is analogous to
circumcision, which, though local, yet availed, by its internal
action, to render the entire person acceptable to God.	Thus
the laver of regeneration and renewal is most efficacious,
whether the person baptized be entirely merged, or dipped, or
some portion only of the body be sprinkled, only so that he be
baptized with water, in the name of the Father, and of the
Son, and of the Holy Ghost."

GERHARD:‡ "Baptismos and Baptizein are employed to designate any kind of ablution, whether.it be done by sprinkling,
pouring, or dipping."

QUENSTEDT: "Baptism, in general, signifies washing, or
ablution, whether it be done by sprinkling, pouring, dipping,
or immersion."

The question of the outward mode in Baptism, is **far less**

---

*Clavis, S. S.	† On Matt. xxviii. 19, in Osiander
‡ Loci. Ed. Cotta ix. 68.

serious than the questions as to the internal efficacy of Baptism, its essence, its object, and results. As closely connected with the view of our Church on these points, we shall present some facts in connection with that fundamental Scriptural phrase in regard to Baptism. Our Saviour says to Nicodemus, John iii. 6: "Except a man be born of water and of the Spirit, he cannot enter into the kingdom of God." Does he refer in these words to Baptism? We think that no one ever could have doubted that there is such a reference, unless he had some preconceived theory of Baptism with which the natural meaning of these words came in conflict. The context and the text alike sustain and necessitate that interpretation which was the earliest, which was once and for ages universal, and to this hour is the general one, — the interpretation which accepts these words as setting forth the Christian doctrine of Baptism. We have said the CONTEXT proves this. We will give a few illustrations which seem to us perfectly conclusive on this point: 1. Baptism, in consequence of the ministry of John the Baptist, was, at the time of the interview between our Lord and Nicodemus, the great absorbing matter of interest in the nation. The baptizing of John was the great religious event of the time. The subject of Baptism, in its relation to the kingdom of God, was the grand question of the hour, and there was hardly a topic on which Nicodemus would be more sure to feel an interest, and on which our Lord would be more likely to speak.

2. The fact that John baptized was regarded as evidence that he might claim to be the Christ; in other words, it was a settled part of the conviction of the nation that the Messiah would baptize, or accompany the initiation of men into His kingdom with the use of water. "The Jews sent priests and Levites to ask John, Who art thou? And he confessed, and denied not; but confessed, I AM NOT THE CHRIST," John i. 20. Not a word had they uttered to imply that they supposed that he claimed to be the Christ, but his answer, to what he knew to be their thought, all the more potently proves that it was considered that THE CHRIST WOULD BAPTIZE, that the beginning of His

Internal efficacy of Baptism. "Born of water and of the Spirit." 1. The Context.

35

kingdom would be in Baptism, that He preëminently wou.ɔ be the Baptizer. "They asked him, and said unto him, Why baptizest thou, then, if thou be not that Christ?" Nicodemus came to settle in his mind whether Jesus was the Christ. Nothing would be more sure to be a question with him than this: Whether Jesus would claim the right to baptize? The answer of John implied that he baptized by authority of the Messiah, as His divinely appointed forerunner and provisional administrator of this right of Baptism, whose proper authority lay in Christ alone. Nicodemus would be peculiarly alive to any allusion to Baptism, would be likely to understand as referring to it any words whose obvious meaning pointed to it, and our Lord would the more carefully avoid whatever might mislead him on this point.

3. John continually characterized his work in this way: "I baptize with *water*," Matt. iii. 2; Mark i. 8; Luke iii. 16; John i. 26, 31, 33; Acts i. 5. At this time, and under all these circumstances, the word "water" would be connected specially with Baptism.

4. John had said of Jesus, shortly before this interview of Nicodemus, Mark i. 8: "I, indeed, have baptized you with water; but He shall baptize you with the Holy Ghost. . . " Here, before the Ruler of the Jews, was the very person of whom this had been uttered; and when he takes up these words "water" and "the Spirit," it seems impossible that Nicodemus should doubt their allusion to, and their close parallel with, John's words.

5. John had made two kinds of utterances in regard to Christ's work, and we beg the reader to note the great difference between them, for they have been confounded, and gross misrepresentation of them has been the result.

The first of these utterances we have just given, Mark i. 3. It was made to the body of John's disciples, and the two things he makes prominent are Baptism with water, and Baptism with the Holy Ghost; that is, water and the Spirit.

The other utterance, Matt. iii. 7–12, was made to those to whom he said: "O generation of vipers, who hath warned you to flee from the wrath to come?" John knew that, as a class, the Pharisees and Sadducees who came to him were unworthy of Baptism, yet as there were exceptions, and as ne could not search hearts, he baptized them all. Nevertheless, he says: "Every tree which bringeth not forth goou fruit, is hewn down and cast into the *fire*. I, indeed, baptize you with water, but He that cometh after me shall baptize you with the Holy Ghost, and with *fire*. Whose fan is in His hand, and He will thoroughly purge His floor, and gather the wheat into His garner, but He will burn up the chaff with unquenchable *fire*." When we look at these words in their connection, remember the class of persons addressed, and notice how the Baptist, in the way in which the word "fire" runs, fixes its meaning here, nothing seems clearer than this, that John has in view not the work of the Holy Spirit in the individual, but His great work in the mass, and not His purifying power in those who are blessed by it, but His purifying power shown in the removal and destruction of the evil. The wind created by the fan descends alike upon the wheat and the chaff; both are alike baptized by it, but with wholly different results. The purifying power of the air is shown in both. It is a single act, indeed, which renders the wheat pure by removing the impurity of the chaff. "You," says the Saviour to the generation of vipers, "shall also be baptized with the Holy Ghost." His work shall be to separate you from the wheat. You, too, shall be baptized with fire; the fire which *destroys* the impurity which has been separated by the Spirit. See also Luke iii. 9-17. The addition of the word "fire" marks, with awful significance, what is the *distinction of the Baptism of the wicked ; and such an idea, as that the children of God are baptized with fire*, is not to be found in the New Testament. The only thing that looks like it is Acts ii. 3, where it is said, "There appeared unto them cloven tongues like as of fire, and it sat upon each of them," but the fire here was symbolical of the character of the TONGUES of the Apostles, of the fervor with which they glowed, and of the light which they shed, in the varied languages in which they spoke. John spoke of the Holy Spirit and fire, when he addressed those who were not to enter the kingdom of God. When he addressed true disciples, he associated water and the Spirit. When he spoke to the former, it was of the Spirit first, and then of the fire. When he speaks to the latter, it is of water first, and then of the Spirit; the one class is to be baptized with the Spirit and with fire, and are lost; the others are baptized with water and with the Spirit, and will enter the kingdom of God. When John contrasted his Baptism with that of the Saviour, he meant not this: I baptize with water only, without the Spirit, and He will baptize with the Spirit only, and not with water; he meant: I baptize with water; that is all I can do in my own person, but He who in His divine power works with me now, and baptizes with the provisional measure of the Holy Spirit, will yet come in His personal ministry, and then He will attend the Baptism of water, with the full gospel measure of the Spirit. When our Lord, therefore, taking up, as it were, and opening still further the thought of John, adopts his two terms in the same connection in which he had placed them, He meant that Nicodemus should understand by "water" and the "Spirit" the outward part of Baptism, and that Divine Agent, who in it, with it, and under it, offers His regenerating grace to the soul of man.

6. It is not to be forgotten that Nicodemus was asking for a fuller statement of the doctrine of the new birth. He asked: "How can a man be born when he is old?" The emphasis is not on the word "*can*" alone, as if he meant to express a doubt of the truth of our Saviour's proposition; the emphasis rests also on the word "*how*." He meant to say: "A man cannot be born again in the natural sense and ordinary way. *How*, then, in what sense, and by what means, *can* he be born again?" It is impossible that one interested in grace itself should not be alive to its means. For our Saviour not to have made an allusion to any of the divine modes, as well as to the Divine Agent of the change, would seem to make the reply a very imperfect one. But if any one of the means of grace is alluded to, the allusion is certainly in the word "water;" and admitting this, the inference will hardly be resisted that "Baptism" is meant.

7. The entire chapter, after the discourse with Nicodemus,

is occupied with *baptisms, baptismal questions,* and *baptismal discourses.*

a. In verse 23, the word " water " occurs : " John was baptizing in Ænon, because there was much *water* there."

b. It is not unworthy of notice, that immediately following the conversation of our blessed Lord with Nicodemus, come these words, " *After these things* came Jesus and his disciples unto the land of Judea, and there he tarried with them *and baptized.*"

c. John's disciples and the Jews came to him and said : " Rabbi, he to whom thou bearest witness, *behold the same baptizeth,* and all men come to him." Then John replies : " Ye yourselves bear me witness that I said, *I am not the Christ,* but that I am sent before him." The authority for John's Baptism was secondary, derived from Christ. Christ now takes it into His own hands, and prepares to endow it with the fulness of the gifts of His Spirit.

The context of these words demonstrates that by " water " our Saviour meant Baptism. The evidence of the text itself is equally decisive that this is his meaning. 2. The Text. It is conceded by all, that if the word " water " be taken literally, it means " Baptism ; " hence, all those who deny that it refers to Baptism understand it figuratively, and in that fact acknowledge that to prove that it is to be taken literally, is to prove that it refers to Baptism.

We remark, then,

1. That to take the word " water " figuratively makes an incongruity with the idea of a birth. It is said that water here is the figure of the cleansing and purifying power of the Holy Spirit. But there is an incongruity in such an interpretation. Had the Saviour meant this, he would naturally have said : Except a man be *cleansed,* or *washed* with water, not " born of " it.

2. One of the figurative interpretations is in conflict with the evident meaning of the word " Spirit " here. For it is clear from the whole connection, that the Spirit here means the Holy Spirit as a person. In the next verse it is said : " That which is born of the SPIRIT is Spirit," and in the 8th

verse: "So is every one that is born of the Spirit." No sound interpreter of any school, so far as we know, disputes that the word "Spirit," in these passages, means the Holy Spirit as a person; and nothing is more obvious than that the word in the 5th verse means just what it does in the following ones. But if "water" is figurative, then the phrase water and Spirit means, in one of the figurative interpretations, "spiritual water;" that is, the substantive Spirit is used as an adjective, and not as the name of a person. This false interpretation makes the phrase mean "spiritual water," and Baptism and the Holy Spirit both vanish before it. In its anxiety to read Baptism out of the text, it has read the Holy Spirit out of it, too.

3. Another figurative interpretation turns the words the other way, as if our Saviour had said: "Born of the Spirit and water," and now it means not that we are to be born again of "spiritual water," but that we are to be born again of the "aqueous or water-like Spirit." But not only does such a meaning seem poor and ambiguous, but it supposes the one term, "Spirit," to be literal, and the other, "water," to be figurative; but as they are governed by the same verb and preposition, this would seem incredible, even apart from the other cogent reasons against it. In common life, a phrase in which such a combination was made, would be regarded as absurd.

4. The term "to be born of" leads us necessarily to the same result.

a. The phrase is employed in speaking of natural birth, as in Matt. i. 16: "Mary *of* whom *was born* Jesus."

Luke i. 35: "That holy thing which shall *be born of* thee, shall be called the Son of God." So in this chapter, "that which is *born of* the flesh."

b. It is employed to designate spiritual birth. Thus John i. 13: "(the sons of God) *were born* not of the blood, nor of the will of the flesh, nor of the will of man, but of God." Here no symbolical title is used, but the literal name of the Author of the new birth. So in this chapter, v. 8: "So is every one that is *born* of the Spirit." John, in his gospel and epistles, uses the phrase "to be born of" fifteen times. In fourteen of

them, it is not pretended that any of the terms used to desig
nate the cause of the birth is symbolical. The fifteenth
instance is the one before us.

The phrase to " be born of " is never connected elsewhere in
the New Testament with terms indicative of the means or
cause of birth, which are symbolical in their character. The
whole New Testament usage is in conflict with the supposition
that it is here linked with a symbolical term.

" Born of God " is used some eight or nine times. " Born
of the Spirit " is used twice, and these, with the words before
us, exhaust the New Testament use of the phrase.

Without the context, then, the text itself would settle t'
question, and demonstrate that our Lord referred to Baptism.

The words of our Lord Jesus to Nicodemus are the keynote
to the whole body of New Testament representa-
tion in regard to the necessity and efficacy of Bap- 3. The parallels.
tism. The view which regards the words " Born of water and
of the Spirit," as referring to Baptism, is sustained and necessitated by the whole body of PARALLELS in the gospels and
epistles. Let us look at a few of these:

1. In Titus iii. 5, Paul, speaking of God our Saviour, says:
" He saved us, by the washing of regeneration, and renewing
of the Holy Ghost." Here the subject is the same as in
John iii. 5, the new birth, or regeneration. There is a parallel
between "born of God," and "regeneration," and "renewing;"
between " water " and " washing," or laver. " The Spirit "
in the one is parallel with " the Holy Ghost " in the other,
and " Entering into the kingdom of heaven " in the one has
its parallel in the other, in the words, " He saved us." What
a beautiful comment does Paul make on our Lord's word!
Take up the words in John, and ask Paul their meaning.
What is it to be " born again? " Paul replies, " It is to expe
rience regeneration and renewing." What is the " water," of
which our Lord says we must be born? It is the washing of
regeneration. What is the Spirit? Paul replies, " The Holy
Spirit." What is it to enter the kingdom of God? It is to be
saved.

2. Ephes. v. 26: " Christ loved the Church and gave Him-

self for it, that He might sanctify and cleanse it with the wash-ing of water by the Word." In these words the new birth is represented as sanctifying and cleansing; the "water" is expressly mentioned; to be "born of water" is explained as a "sanctifying and cleansing with the washing of water," and the "Word" as a great essential of Baptism and organ of the Holy Spirit in it, is introduced.

3. Hebrews x. 21: "Let us draw near with a true heart, in full assurance of faith, having our hearts sprinkled from an evil conscience, and our bodies washed with pure water." Here Baptism is regarded as essential to having a true heart and full assurance of faith, and the mode in which "water" is used is defined in the words, "having our bodies washed with pure water."

4. In 1 John v. 6–8, speaking of Jesus: "This is He that came by *water* and blood, not by *water* only, but by water and blood. And it is the Spirit that beareth witness, because the Spirit is truth. And there are three that bear witness on earth, the Spirit, and the water, and the blood." Here is a most decisive confutation by John himself of the glosses put upon his Master's words. They demonstrate that "water" and "Spirit" are not one. "There are *three* that bear witness, the Spirit, *and* the water, and the blood."

5. The parallel in St. Peter is also very important. 1 Pet. iii. 21, 22: "The Ark, wherein few, that is, eight souls were saved by water. The like figure whereunto *even* Baptism doth now save us." The water lifted the Ark above it, away from the death which overwhelmed the world. It separated the eight souls from the lost, and saved them while it destroyed the others. Here the Apostle, speaking of "souls saved by water," declares that Baptism, in such sense, corresponded with the deluge, that we say of it also, "It saves *us*," — the implication being irresistible — that the whole thought in-volved is this: in the Church, as in the Ark, souls are saved by water, that is, by Baptism. Having said so great a thing of Baptism, the Apostle adds: "Not the putting away of the filth of the flesh, but the answer of a good conscience toward God." That is, it is not as a mere outward purifier, or cere-

monial washing, Baptism operates. Its gracious effects are conditioned on the state of the heart of him to whom they are offered. He who in faith accepts Baptism in its purifying energy through the Spirit of God, also receives it in its saving result.

6. The words of our Lord Jesus, elsewhere, fully sustain the view which the Church takes of His meaning in John iii. 5 In his final commission he charges the Apostles " to *baptize* " the nations, Matt. xxviii. 19, and connects with it the promise: " He that believeth, and is baptized, shall be saved ; " and adds : " but he that believeth not shall be damned," Mark xvi. 16. These words should be pondered. We are not to separate what God hath joined together. Who shall be saved? First, He only that *believeth*. That is decisive against the idea that Sacraments operate apart from the spiritual state of the recipient. It is a death-blow to formalism — a death-blow to Rome and to Oxford. We are justified by faith ; that is written with a sunbeam in the words : " He that believeth . . shall be saved." But is that all the Saviour said? No! He adds. " AND IS BAPTIZED, shall be saved." Who dares read a " NOT " in the words, and make our Saviour say, " He that believeth, and is NOT baptized, shall be saved "? But the man who says, " Baptism *is in no sense* necessary to salvation," does contradict the words of our Lord. But if it be granted that *in any sense* our Lord teaches that Baptism is necessary to salvation, then it makes it highly probable that the same doctrine is asserted in John iii. 5. The reader will please notice that we are not now attempting to settle the precise meaning of either the words in John or the parallels. Our question now simply is, What is the *subject* when our Saviour speaks of water and the Spirit ?

7. In the minds of the Apostles, the doctrines of our Lord, of the necessity *in some sense* (we are not inquiring now in *what* sense or with what limitations,) of Baptism to salvation, was ever present. When the multitudes said to Peter, and to the rest of the Apostles, " Men and brethren, what shall we do ? " then Peter said unto them, " Repent, and be baptized, every one of you, in the name of the Lord Jesus Christ, for

the remission of sins, and ye shall receive the gift of the Holy
Ghost." Now, mark — first, that Baptism and the Holy Spirit
are separately spoken of, as in John iii. 5 ; second, that Baptism is represented as a means or condition of receiving the
gift of the Holy Ghost; third, that besides repentance Bap
tism is enjoined as necessary ; fourth, that it is clearly set forth
as in *some sense* essential to the remission of sins.

8. The Apostles and other ministers of the Lord Jesus bap
tized all persons: " When they believed Philip preaching the
things concerning the kingdom of God, they were baptized,
Acts viii. 12. When Philip preached Jesus to the eunuch, he
said: " What doth hinder me to be baptized?" And Philip
said, "If thou believest with all thine heart, thou mayest;"
not, as some would say now, "If thou believest with all thine
heart, there is no need of being baptized." Thus, Lydia and
her household; the jailer and his household. No matter
where or when the Spirit of God wrought His work in men,
they were baptized, as if for some reason, and in some sense it
was felt that this was necessary to an entrance on the kingdom
of God.

9. Ananias said to Saul, after announcing to him the commission which God gave him : " And now, why tarriest thou ?
Arise and be baptized, and wash away thy sins, calling on the
name of the Lord," Acts xxii. 16. Here Baptism is represented
as necessary, in *some sense*, even to a converted man, as a means,
in some sense, of washing away sins.

10. As resonances of the wonderful words of our Lord, we
have the Apostle's declaration: "So many of us as were baptized into Jesus Christ, were baptized into His death, therefore, we are buried with Him, by Baptism, into death. By
one Spirit are we all baptized into one body. For as many of
you as have been baptized into Christ have put on Christ."

Thus comparing God's Word with itself do we reach a sure
ground. Context, text, and parallel, the great sources of a
sound interpretation of the living oracles, all point to one
result, in determining what our Lord spoke of when he said
" Except a man be born of water and of the Spirit, he cannot
enter into the kingdom of God."

The form of speech to which recourse has most frequently been had here to put a figure into the words, is that which is called "HENDIADYS;" that is, the phrase in which *one* (hen) is presented *by* (dia) *two* (dys). That is to say, *two* nouns are used where one noun would answer, if the idea of the other were presented in an adjective form. Thus Virgil says: "We offered drink in bowls and gold;" that is, in golden bowls, or bowl-shaped gold. By this hendiadys, the Saviour is said here to have meant "spiritual water," or "the water-like Spirit."

4. The resorts of interpreters. Hendiadys.

Now let us look at this "hendiadys" by which it is pro posed to set aside the natural meaning of our Saviour's words We remark:

1. That after a careful search, we cannot find a solitary instance (leaving this out of question for a moment) in which it is supposed that the Saviour used the form of speech known as hendiadys. It was not characteristic of him.

2. Neither is it characteristic of John the Evangelist, whose style is closely formed upon that class of our Lord's discourses which he records in his Gospel.

3. Nor is it characteristic of the style of any of the New Testament writers. But three instances of it are cited in the entire New Testament by Glass in his Sacred Philology, and in every one of those three, the language is more easily interpreted without the hendiadys than with it. Winer, the highest authority on such a point, says, in regard to hendiadys in the New Testament: "The list of examples alleged *does* not, when strictly examined, *furnish one* that is unquestionable."*

4. The passage in Matt. iii. 11: "He shall baptize you with the Holy Ghost and with fire," is the only one in which it is pretended that a parallel is found with the one before us; but we have shown in a former part of this Dissertation, that there is no hendiadys here; the fire and the Holy Ghost are distinct subjects. The persons addressed were neither to be baptized exclusively with the Holy Spirit-like fire, or the fire-like Holy Spirit, but just as our Lord says, with both; with the Holy

* Gramm. of N. T. Diction. Transl. by Masson. Smith, English & Co. 1859 p. 652. Seventh Ed. by Lünemann. (Thayer.) Andover. Draper. 1869. p. 630

Spirit *and* with fire — the former, in His personality, separating them as the breath of the purifier's fan, and the latter consuming them as the purifier's flame.

5. But we have a little more to say in regard to this hendiadys ; and that is, that if we even concede that it is used here, it does not help the figurative interpretation at all. For look at its real character a moment. Hendiadys does not affect at all the question of the *literalness* or figurativeness of the terms embraced in it ; it does not change their *meaning*, but simply their form. Take, for example, the illustration we gave from Virgil : " bowls " and " gold " are both literal ; and to have " golden bowls," you must have literal gold as well as literal bowls ; not gold analogous to a bowl, or a bowl like to gold. So Lucan says of a horse : " He champed the brass and the bit ; " that is, the brass-formed bit ; but the brass was real, and the bit was real ; it does not mean the brass-like bit, or the bit-like brass. So, in Acts xiv. 13, it is said that the expression " oxen and garlands," is a hendiadys, and means " garlanded oxen." We are not sure that it does ; but if it does, it means there were literally garlands and literally oxen. Oxen is not figurative, meaning strength, of which the ox is a symbol ; nor does " garlands " mean " honored," though garlands are an image of honor. It does not mean that they brought honored strength, or strong honor, to the gates ; but hendiadys or no hendiadys, it involves equally that there were oxen and garlands. So here, even supposing a hendiadys, we must none the less have literally water, and literally the Spirit.

The only thing hendiadys proves, is, that the things it involves are not separated ; and if we suppose a hendiadys here, it leaves both the water and the Spirit as literal terms, and only involves this, that they are conjoined in the one birth. In other words, hendiadys only makes a slight bend in the route, and brings us after all to the same result as the most direct and artless interpretation, to wit, that our Saviour referred to Baptism in His words to Nicodemus.

Another resort, more extreme than the one we have just disposed of, is that of the EPEXEGESIS, that is to suppose that the " AND " gives the words this force : " Born of water, THAT

IS TO SAY, of the Spirit. ' It is contended that it is parallel to such an expression as this: "God and our Father," which means: "God, *that is to say*, our Father." In the epexegesis, one thing is spoken of in more than one aspect, and, hence, under more than one term. For instance, in the phrase we have quoted: "God and our Father"   Epexegesis. means: That Being who is God, *as to his nature*, and Father, *as to his relation to us*, God essentially, and Father relatively; in a word, *both* God and Father. It does not make the term God metaphorical, and the term Father the literal substitute for it. If an epexegesis, therefore, were supposable in John iii. 5, the phrase could only mean: Born of that which is water, as to its outer part, and Spirit, as to its internal agent, that is, *both* water and Spirit. It is, therefore, of no avail to resort to the epexegesis here, even if it were allowable. But it is not allowable. There is not an instance, so far as we know, in human language, in which a noun used metaphorically is conjoined by a simple "and" with a term which is literal and is meant to explain it. In a word, the resorts of a false interpretation, which are sometimes very specious, utterly fail in this case. Our Lord has fixed the sense of his words so surely, that the unprejudiced who weigh them calmly cannot be at a loss as to their meaning.

The Augsburg Confession (Art. IX. 1) declares that Baptism "is necessary to salvation." Is it justified in so   Is Baptism doing? Can we accept a statement apparently so necessary to salvation? sweeping? Is it a Scripture statement?

In order properly to answer these questions, it is necessary to determine what the Confessors meant. In all human writings, and in the Book of God, occur propositions apparently universal, which are, nevertheless, in the mind of the writer, limited in various ways. What is the meaning of the proposition of our Confession? Is it absolute, and without exceptions, and if it meant to allow exceptions, what are they? The first question we naturally ask, in settling the meaning of our Confession, is, What is Baptism?

The Platform, in defining *what* Baptism it supposes the Church to connect with salvation, designates it as "such

WATER BAPTISM." But what our Church affirms of the bless ings of Baptism, she does not affirm of " water Baptism,' that is, of the application of water *per se.* The total efficacy of the Sacraments is defined in the Augsburg Confession (Art.

1. What is Bap- V. 2), thus, that through them and the word, " as tism? instruments, or means, God gives His Holy Spirit, who worketh faith." It would at once remove much of the grossest prejudice against the doctrine of our Church, if it were known and remembered that the Baptism of whose bless ings she makes her affirmation, embraces not merely the exter nal element, but yet more, and pre-eminently, the word and the Holy Spirit. She regards it as just as absurd to refer any blessings to Baptism, as *her enemies define* it, as it would be to attribute to swords and guns the power of fighting battles without soldiers to wield them.

Her first lesson on the subject is : " Baptism is not mere water," (Cat. Min., 361, 2). " Wherefore," says Luther (Cat. Maj., 487, 15), " it is pure knavery and Satanic scoffing, that now-a-days these new spirits, in order to revile Baptism, sepa rate from it the Word and institution of God, and look upon it as if it were mere water from the well, and then, with their childish drivelling, ask, ' What good can a handful of water do the soul ? ' Yes, good friend, who does not know that when you separate the parts of Baptism, water is water ? " " Bap tism cannot be sole and simple water (do. 26), mere water can not have that power." " Not by virtue of the water" (do. 29). " Not that the water (of Baptism) is in itself better than any other water," (do. 14.) So in the Smalcald Articles : " We do not hold with Thomas and the Dominican friars, who, forget ful of the word and the institution of God, say, That God has conferred a spiritual power on water, which washes away sin through the water " (320, 2).

" Baptism," says Gerhard,* " is the washing of water in the Word, by which washing the whole adorable Trinity purifieth from sin him who is baptized, *not by the work wrought (ex opere operato) but by the effectual working of the Holy Ghost coming upon him, and by his own faith."* Such is the tenor of all the

* Loci (Cotta) ix. 318.

definitions our Church gives of Baptism, from the simple ele mentary statements of the Catechism up to the elaborate defini tions of the great doctrinal systems.

The assumption, then, that what the Church says of Baptism, she affirms of mere water Baptism, rests on a fundamental misapprehension. Whatever is wrought in Baptism, is wrought by the Holy Ghost, through the Word, with the water, in the believing soul.

"That some adults, by actual impenitence, hypocrisy, and obstinacy, deprive themselves of the salutary effi- cacy of Baptism, we freely admit." Gerhard (IX. 170).

2. Baptism is not always followed by regen-eration. Regen-eration not al-ways preceded by Baptism.

Just as clear as they are in their judgment that Baptism is not necessarily followed by regeneration, are our Church and her great divines in the judgment that regeneration is not necessarily preceded by Baptism, or at-tended by it.

The Augsburg Confession (Art. V.) declares the gospel (as well as the Sacraments) to be the means whereby the Holy Ghost works and confers faith, and (Art. VII.) presents the gospel purely preached (as well as the Sacraments) as that whereby the true Church is marked out and made. "As we come alone through the Word of God to God, and are justi-fied, and no man can embrace the Word but by faith, it fol-lows that by faith we are justified." Apol. 99, 68. "The natural man is, and remains, an enemy of God, until, by the power of the Holy Ghost, through the Word preached and heard, he is converted, endowed with faith, *regenerated* and renewed." Form. Concord, 589, 5. "We cannot obey the law unless we are *born again* through the gospel." Apol. Conf. 140, 190. "Faith alone brings us to a new birth." Do. 119, 61. "This faith alone justifies and regenerates." Do. 138, 171. "Regeneration is wrought by faith in repentance." Do. 253. "When, therefore," says Gerhard,* "they are bap-tized, who have already been regenerated through the Word, as a spiritual seed, they have no need of regeneration through Baptism, but in them Baptism is a confirmation and sealing of regeneration."

* Loc. viii. 325.

When Nicodemus asked, "How can a man be born when he is old?" Jesus replied, "Of water and of the Spirit," and extends the proposition to all "that which is born of the flesh;" that is, to "all men after the fall of Adam, who are 3. Men may be born in the course of nature." (A. C., Art. II.) unbaptized and The necessity of the new birth He clearly predi-
be saved. cates upon the fact that the flesh, which is such by virtue of fleshly birth, requires this change.

That in John iii. 5, water means Baptism, the Platform concedes: "The language of the Saviour, *doubtless*, refers also to *Baptism*." But even critics who deny this, concede that in John iii. 6, man is contemplated as the subject of original sin. Those who concede this (and this all concede), and who concede that "water" means Baptism (and this the Platform concedes), concede that, not only in the phraseology, but in the connection, application, and argument of that phraseology, the Augsburg Confession is perfectly justified by the Saviour's language, when it says (Art. II.) "this original sin" ("that which is born of the flesh is flesh") "brings now also eternal death" ("cannot see the kingdom of God") "to those who are not born again of Baptism ('water') and of the Holy Ghost." If the case is made out from these words, against the Confession of the Church, it is also made out against the Saviour, to whose words it so closely adheres. The dilemma, then, is irresistible, either that both teach it, or that neither does. As regards the effectual overthrow of their own position, it matters little which horn the objectors take. If they take the one, then, on their own concession, the Saviour teaches Baptismal regeneration; if they take the other, on their own concession, the Confession does not teach Baptismal regeneration. Is, then, the inference warranted, that our Saviour, in His words, and our Confession, in its use of them, mean to affirm an absolute and unconditional necessity, that a man shall be born of water, before he can enter into the kingdom of God? We reply, that neither the Saviour nor the Confession meant to affirm this, but simply an *ordinary* necessity. "The necessity of Baptism is not *absolute*, but ordinary." (Gerhard IX. 383.) Bellarmine had argued from John iii. 5, for the Romish doctrine, that unbaptized infants are lost. Gerhard (IX. 287) replied: " 1. The warning of Christ bears not upon the privation of the Sacrament, but the contempt of it. 2. He describes the ordinary rule, from which cases of necessity are excepted. We are bound to the use of the means, but God may show His grace in extraordinary ways."

How touchingly and consolingly LUTHER wrote upon this topic is known to all admirers of his writings. Bugenhagen, in the admirable Treatise already referred to, which is incorporated in Luther's Works, and was issued with a Preface by him, shows at large that neither to infants nor adults is the necessity of Baptism absolute. " Rather should we believe that the prayers of pious parents, or of the Church, are graciously heard, and that these children are received by God into His favor and eternal life."

4 Are unbaptized infants saved?

On the whole dark question of the relation of the heathen world to salvation, the early writers of our Church generally observe a wise caution. Yet even in the school of the most rigid orthodoxy we find the breathings of tender hope. " It is false," says Mentzer,* " that original sin in infants out of the Church is an adequate cause of reprobation; for men are never said in Scripture to be reprobated on that account solely. But as faith alone justifies and saves, so also, as Luther says, unbelief alone condemns."

Ægidius Hunnius, whom Gerhard pronounced the most admirable of the theologians of his period, and of whom another great writer affirms, that by universal consent he holds the third place of merit after Luther, says:† " I would not dare to affirm that the little children of heathen, without distinction, are lost, for God desireth not the death of any — Christ died for them also," etc.

Our Church, then, does not teach that Baptism " is necessarily and unavoidably attended by spiritual regeneration,' but holds that a man may be baptized, and remain then and forever in the gall of bitterness, and in the bonds of iniquity,

* Oper. I. 959, quoted in Gerhard. Cotta.
† *In Quaest.* in Cap. VII. Gen., quoted in Gerhard IX. 284.

36

and therefore holds as heartily and fully as the Platform,* "that Baptism in adults does not necessarily effect or secure their regeneration."

In the next place, our Church regards Baptism not as 5. Baptism not "*essential*" in its proper sense, but as "necessary." essential. That which is properly "essential," allows of no degree of limitation; but that which is "necessary," may be so in various degrees with manifold limitations. It is "*essential*" to our redemption that Christ should die for us; therefore, without limits of any kind, we affirm that no human being could be saved without His atoning work. It is "necessary" that we should hear the gospel, for it is the power of God unto salvation; but the necessity of hearing is limited in various ways. It does not comprehend both infants and adults, as that which is essential does.

The Augsburg Confession (Art. IX.) says, not that Baptism 6. But neces- is essential, but simply that it is necessary — to sary. which the Latin, not to show the *degree* of necessity, but merely its *object*, adds "*to salvation.*"

In later editions of the Confession, Melanchthon, to remove the possibility of misconstruction, added a few words to the first part of the Ninth Article, so that it reads: "Of Baptism, they teach that it is necessary to salvation, *as a ceremony instituted of Christ.*" So far, at least, we think all could go in affirming its necessity. And with such mild expressions, even those who were most remote from the Melanchthonian spirit were satisfied.

"Among all orthodox Lutherans, Hutter is among the most orthodox; no one has remained more thoroughly within the bounds of the theology authorized and made normative by the Church than he — no one has adhered with more fidelity, not merely to the spirit, but to the very letter of the Symbols, especially of the Form of Concord."† Yet Hutter exhausts, in the following answer, the question: "Is Baptism necessary to salvation?" "It is; and that *because of God's* command. For whatever God has instituted and commanded, is to be done, is precious, useful, and necessary, though as to its out-

---

* P. 29.   † Herzog's Encyclop. fuer. Theol. VI. 346.

ward form it be viler than a straw."* So much and no more
does this great theologian say of the *necessity* of Baptism in his
Compend. Later theologians have properly given prominence
to its necessity as a *mean*, but never have ascribed to it a necessity *per se*.

For, finally, on this point, the Church never has held, but
has ever repudiated the idea that Baptism is   7. Yet not un-
" *unconditionally* essential " or necessary " to sal-   conditionally.
vation."

She has limited the necessity, first of all, by the " *possibility*
of having it " — has declared that it is not *absolutely* necessary,
and that not the deprivation of Baptism, but the contempt of
it condemns a man† — that though God binds us to the means,
as the ordinary instruments of His grace, He is not Himself
limited by them.‡ She teaches, moreover, that all the blessings of Baptism are conditioned on faith. C. M., 490: 33 – 36.

The " Shorter Catechism " of Luther teaches that whatever Baptism gives, it gives alone to those " who believe that
which the Word and promises of God assure us of." " The
water cannot do such a great thing, but it is done by the
Word of God, and faith which believes the Word of God,
added to the water." We shall not give the reference for this,
as even the little children are supposed to know it by heart,
nor stultify ourselves or our readers by adducing authorities
for the catechetical doctrines of our Church.

The Lutheran Church holds that Baptism is necessary to
salvation, inasmuch as God has commanded it, and obedience
to His commands is necessary to salvation; and, furthermore,
because He has appointed Baptism, as one ordinary and positive channel of His grace, through which channel we are to
seek the grace He offers. But our Church denies that, where
the command cannot be carried out, because of a necessity
which is of God's creating, the lack of the sacrament involves
the loss of the soul.

On the more difficult question, whether infants born out of
the Church are saved, many of our old divines, of the strictest

* Compendium Loc. XX. 3.   This answer is taken from Luther's Larg. Cat.
† Luther's Werke: Leipz. Edit. XXII. 400 – 422.   ‡ Do. p. 412.

school, have maintained, as we have already seen,* that it would be harsh and cruel to give over, absolutely, to condemnation, the infants of pagans, for the lack of that which it was impossible for them to have. This view has been defended at large, by Dannhauer, Hulsemann, Scherzer, J. A. Osiander, Wagner, Musæus, Spener, and very many others. Some of our best theologians, who have not considered the argument on either side as decisive, have suspended their judgment in the case, as did Gerhard, Calixtus, Meisner, Baldwin, Bechman, and others. HUNNIUS, whom Gerhard quotes approvingly, makes the statement of this middle view, in these words: "That the infants of pagans are saved, outside of the Church, is a matter on which the silence of Scripture forbids us to pronounce with assurance on the one side, yet I would not dare to affirm, on the other, that those little ones, without distinction, are lost.

8. Our theologians in general. Cotta.

"For, 1. Since God desires the death of none, absolutely, it cannot rightly be supposed that he takes pleasure in the death of these little ones. 2. Christ died for them also. 3. They are necessarily excluded from the use of the Sacraments. Nor will God visit the children with eternal death, on account of the impiety of the parents. Ezek. xviii. We commit them, therefore, to the decision of God."

COTTA approves of the most hopeful view of their condition, and argues for it — "1. From the infinite pity of God. 2. The extent of the benefits wrought by Christ. 3. The analogy of faith — no one absolutely reprobated, but actual unbelief alone condemns. 4. Not the absence, but the contempt of Baptism condemns. 5. God can operate in an extraordinary way. 6. Though original sin, *in itself*, merits damnation, and is a *sufficient* cause of it, yet it is not (because of God's *infinite goodness*) an *adequate* cause of the actual infliction of that condemnation."

The facts we have dwelt upon dispose of another charge against our Church — the charge of teaching an unscriptural doctrine in regard to regeneration, and the relation of Baptism to it.

9. Baptismal regeneration.

* See Dissertation on Original Sin.

The Definite Platform says of "Baptismal Regeneration:" "By this designation is meant the doctrine that Baptism is necessarily and invariably attended by spiritual regeneration, and that such *water Baptism* is *unconditionally* essential to salvation." "Regeneration, in its proper sense of the term, consists in a radical change in our religious views — in our religious feelings, purposes, habits of action." The Miami Synod, in 1858, set forth what they suppose to be meant by the charge, when "they utterly repudiate and abhor" (as well they may) the following error: "Baptismal regeneration — that is, that Baptism is necessarily connected with, or attended by, an internal spiritual change *ex opere operato*, or from the mere outward performance of the act."* Their definition and that of the Platform are substantially the same, though we do not understand them to charge such a doctrine upon their Church or its Confession.

The charge against our Church of teaching "Baptismal Regeneration," as those who make the charge define it, is, as we have seen, utterly ungrounded. It is not true in its general statement nor in its details; it is utterly without warrant in the whole, or in a single particular. We have presented a few facts in elucidation and defence of the Scripture doctrine of Baptism, as confessed by our Church, and as misrepresented and assailed in the Definite Platform. It is always an interesting question, often a very important one, If we give up that which is assailed, what shall we have in the place of it? This question is of great importance in the present case. What equivalent do those propose to the Church, who ask her to give up her most cherished doctrines? What is the doctrine which the Definite Platform proposes as the true one, in place of that theory of "Baptismal Regeneration" which it denounces? It is this, "Baptism in adults is *a pledge* and CONDITION of obtaining those blessings purchased by Christ, and offered to all who repent, believe in Him, and profess His name by Baptism."

Now, is not that which is a CONDITION of obtaining a thing

The counter-theory of Baptism.

1. Baptism of adults. The Confession and the Platform compared.

---

* Luth. Observ. xxvi. 29.

necessary to it — and is not " salvation " the generic term for
the " blessings purchased by Christ ? " How, then, can the
Platform take offence at the Ninth Article of our Confession ?
Just put them side by side :

Aug. Conf.:	Baptism	is necessary	to salvation.
Def. Plat.:	Baptism	is a *condition* of obtaining	those blessings purchased by Christ.

Then comes the question of the Baptism of *infants*. What
2. Baptism of here is the view which is to supersede that anni-
infants. hilated theory (if that may be said annihilated
which never existed,) " that Baptism is a *converting ordinance*
in infants ? "

The theory is this (p. 31): " Baptism, in infants, is the *pledge
of the bestowment* of those blessings purchased by Christ, for all.
These blessings are, forgiveness of sins, or exemption from the
penal consequences of natural depravity (which would at least
be exclusion from heaven) on account of moral disqualification
for admission," etc.

Look now at this, and compare it with what our Confession
says on the Baptism of *Infants*. (Art. IX.) All that it says
on the subject is :

1. " That children are to be baptized." Here the Platform
assents fully.

2. " That by this Baptism they are offered and committed
to God."

Here, too, we apprehend, there will be no dissent, for it is
said : " Baptism in infants, is the pledge of reception into the
visible Church of Christ, grace to help in every time of need."

3. " Being offered in Baptism to God, they are well-pleasing
to God, (that is,) are received into the favor of God," says the
Confession, and here it ceases to define the blessings of Baptism ; but the Platform goes much further. " Baptism in
infants," it says, " is a pledge." The first blessing of which it
declares it to be a pledge is " forgiveness of sins," conceding
this, that infants have sins ; that they need the forgiveness of
sins ; that *baptized infants* have the *pledge* of the forgiveness of
their sins, and, of necessary consequence, that *unbaptized* infants

have no pledge of the forgiveness of *their* sins ; in other words that there is no *pledge* that the sins of unbaptized infants are forgiven ; for if they have the pledge, too, though they have no Baptism, how can Baptism be the pledge of forgiveness ?

The words that follow now, are explanatory of the preceding ones. " These blessings are forgiveness of sins, or exemption from the penal consequences of natural depravity." For giveness is defined to be " exemption from penal consequences." Sins are defined to be " natural depravity."

Now wherein does this doctrine differ from the old one, that in Baptism the " *reatus*," or liability of original sin is taken away, although the " *materiale* " remains ?* except, perhaps, in this, That Luther supposes God graciously to do it by His Holy Spirit *through* the Baptism, while the Platform may mean, that Baptism is only the *pledge* that it is done, but it is done either way, and in both Baptism is the proof, at least, that it is done.

But we have, furthermore, a statement of what " the penal consequences of natural depravity " are : " Which would, at least, be *exclusion* from *heaven*, on account of moral disqualification for admission."

Now, analyze this proposition, and you have the following result :

1. That infants have natural depravity, which is a moral disqualification for heaven.

2. That this *natural depravity has penal consequences*, that is, is a *punishable thing ;* that infants, *consequently, have moral character*, and some sort of *moral accountability ;* are the subjects of law, as to its obligation, for they have sins to be forgiven ; and of law as to *its pains*. for they are subject to " penal consequences."

3. That this punishment would be exclusion from heaven. But this statement is qualified in a very remarkable way — " would, *at least*, be exclusion from heaven," — that is the *minimum*. The words " *at least*," seem to mark this train of thought : " They would, *at least*, be excluded from heaven, even if they were not sent to hell." Now this style of thinking as

* Apolog. Confess., 83, 35.

it has in it, unconsciously to its author, we trust and believe
— as it has in it a tinge of Pelagianism — so it trembles, logically, upon the very border of that figment to which the Pelagianism of the Church of Rome, combined with her strong
sacramenta ism, leads her — the doctrine of a *limbus infantum.*
She was too *sacramental* to admit that the original sin of a
child could be removed without Baptism ; too Pelagian to concede that original sin must, in its own nature, apart from God's
grace, *bring death* eternal.   Her *sacramentalism*, therefore, kept
the *unbaptized child out of heaven ;* her *Pelagianism kept it out
of hell*, and the conjunction of the two generated a *tertium quid*
— the fancy of a " *limbus infantum*," or place which, without
being hell, was yet one of exclusion from heaven, a mild perdition, whereby infants not wholly saved were, nevertheless,
not totally lost.   And the shadow of this very tendency shows
itself in the words we have quoted from the Platform.

Connecting the three propositions now, with what has preceded them, we reach, then, furthermore,

4. That God grants forgiveness of the sins of the baptized
infant, forgives its natural depravity, exempts it, of course,
from the penal consequences thereof, and thus, if it is not saved
from a liability to eternal death, it is, " *at least*," saved from
exclusion from heaven.   If the Platform means that the sin of
an infant, unforgiven, would bring eternal death to it, then it
goes as far as the extremest views of the nature of original sin
can go, and vindicates the very strongest expressions of the Confession on this point ; and if it means that original sin would
exclude it from heaven without consigning it to despair, it has
virtually the doctrine of the *limbus infantum.*

5. And finally, Baptism in infants is the pledge of all this
— they have the *pledge* — and, of consequence, unbaptized
infants have not.   In other words, there is an *assurance* that
every baptized child has this great thing, " forgiveness of
sins."

It is not surprising that, after all this, the Platform closes
its discussion on this point with these words (p. 31): " It is
proper to remark that the greater part of the passages in the
former Symbols, relating to this subject, are, and doubtless

may be, explained by many, to signify *no more than we above inculcate.*" We understand the author in this to concede, not simply that they are so explained, but that they are, in fact, susceptible of this explanation, and that this *may be* really their meaning.

It is our sincere belief, that if the energy which has been expended in assailing as doctrines taught by our Confessions what they do not teach, had been devoted to ascertaining what is their real meaning, these years of sad controversy would have been years of building up, and of closer union, not years of conflict, years in which our ministry and members have had their minds poisoned against the truth of God as held by our Church.

But, while there are apparent points of identity with the Church doctrine in that of the Platform, there is one *chasm* in its theory which nothing can bridge over, a contradiction of the most palpable and fatal character. That vital defect is this, that while this theory secures the *forgiveness* of an infant's sins, it makes no provision whatever for the *change* of its sinful nature. While it provides for its *exemption* from *penalty,* it leaves utterly out of sight the *correction* of its depravity, which is a more fearful thing than the penalty which follows it; for in the pure judgment of sanctified reason, it would be better to be holy and yet bear the penalty of sin, than to be sinful and have the immunities of holiness; better to be sinless, although in hell, than to be polluted and in heaven. The theory concedes that there is in "infants a *moral disqualification* for heaven." It absolutely needs, therefore, before an infant can have a *pledge* in Baptism of its salvation, that there shall be a pledge provided for its moral qualification for heaven, and this moral qualification must be REGENERATION.

But the theory not only does not provide for this, but as far as it is stated in the Platform, absolutely excludes it. It says, "Baptism in infants is a pledge of the forgiveness of sins," but it says not a word of the *removal* of sins in whole or in part. The cardinal defect, therefore, is, that it provides a pledge that the *blessings which follow regeneration* shall be given, but provides none that the regeneration itself shall be given — it provides that the child shall be saved from the *penalty* of sin without being saved, in whole or in part, from *the sin itself;* saved, in fact, *in* its sins, not *from* them. To what end would a child enter heaven if its nature were unchanged *Forgiving* a sin in no sense changes its character. And where in the Word of God is there the shadow of that baleful doctrine, that *the sins of an unregenerate person are forgiven;* where the shadow of that deadly error, that God has provided a Church, into which, *by His own ordinance, and at His command,* millions are brought, without *any change* in a nature whose moral evil is such as would condemn them forever to exclusion from heaven — where is the shadow of that fatal delusion, that the curse of sin can be removed while the sin itself remains dominant?

But if a refuge is sought in saying that infants are regenerated, but that Baptism, in all its parts, element, Word and Spirit, is not the ordinary channel of this grace, this is to accept a theory which has every difficulty which carnal reason urges against the doctrine of the Church, but which has nothing that even looks like a warrant for it in God's Word, and which, run out logically, would destroy the whole character of Christianity as a system of wonderful means to beneficent ends.

Dr. Heppe, in his Dogmatik of the Evangelical Reformed Church (1861), presents the doctrines of the Calvinistic Churches, and illustrates his text with citations from their *standard theologians.* The doctrine of the Lutheran Church, in regard to Baptism, is often very severely spoken of by Calvinists — it is, indeed, one of the main points of attack. Perhaps it may not be without some interest to compare the Lutheran and Calvinistic views in regard to this important subject.

Calvinistic and Lutheran views of Baptism compared.

The definitions of Baptism which Heppe gives as purely Calvinistic and Reformed, are as follows: "Baptism is a sacrament, in which those *to whom the covenant of grace pertains,* are washed with water in the name of the Father, Son, and Holy Spirit, that is, that to those who are baptized, it is *signified and sealed,* that they are received into the *communion* of the covenant of grace, *are inserted into Christ* and His mystic body, the Church, are *justified* by God, for the sake of Christ's blood shed for us, and *regenerated* by Christ's Spirit." This definition he gives from POLANUS. Another and shorter one he furnishes from WOLLEBIUS, as follows: " Baptism is the first sacrament of the new covenant, in which *to the elect* received into the family of God, by the outward application of water, *the remission of sins and regeneration by the blood of Christ, and by the Holy Spirit, are sealed.*" He gives only one other, which is from HEIDEGGER, thus: "Baptism is *the sacrament of regeneration, in which to each and to every one embraced in the covenant of God, the inward washing from sins through the blood and Spirit of Christ*, is declared *and sealed.*"

The doctrine thus stated, and correctly stated, for it is the doctrine of all genuine Calvinists, involves several things, which the detractors of our Church may do well to ponder. First, It draws a line between baptized *infants* as well as between baptized *adults*, representing some as belonging to the elect, some to the non-elect, some as belonging to the class to whom the covenant of grace pertains, others as not of that class. Shall we prefer this part of the doctrine to that which teaches that God is the Father of all, and Christ the Saviour of all, heartily loving all and desiring to save them? Can a *mother* believe it *possible* that between her two beloved little children prattling at her knee, there may be, in *God's love, will, and purpose, a chasm cleft back into eternity, and running down to the bottom of hell?* Can she believe this when her conscience tells her that the slightest *partiality on her part*, for the one or the other, would be a crime? Can she believe that God's absolute sovereignty elects absolutely one of her children to eternal glory, and passes by the other, when that passing by necessarily involves its ruin forever? Can it be wondered at that High Calvinism has, in so many cases, been the mother of Universalism — that men who start with the premise, that the absolute sovereignty of God determines the eternal estate of men, should draw the inference, not that He elects *some* to life, and leaves the mass to go to perdition, but that He elects *all?* Shall we give up this part of the baptismal doctrine of the Church? And yet if we surrender it — if we say the doctrine of Baptism is not a fundamental one in our system, men may teach among us on this point what they please. What is to prevent these views from being preached in our pulpits and taught in our houses?

A second feature of the Calvinistic view of Baptism 'is, that *to those perfectly alike in all personal respects, Baptism comes with entirely different functions.* To one infant it signs and seals *communion in the covenant, insertion into Christ, justification and regeneration;* to another, perfectly alike in all personal respects, it signifies and seals *nothing.* No parent knows what his child receives in Baptism, whether it be a mere handful ot water on its hair, or the seal of blessings, infinite like God, and irrevocable to all eternity. The minister does not know what he has done; whether he has sealed the everlasting covenant of God with an immortal soul, or thrown away time and breath in uttering mocking words, to that little being which smiles and prattles, in utter unconsciousness that it is abandoned to a destiny of endless pain, of unspeakable horror. Can we give up the baptismal doctrine of our Church for this? Our Church tells us that Baptism makes the offer of the same blessing to every human creature who receives it; that a difference in the result of Baptism depends upon no lack of the divine grace, on no secret counsel of God, but upon the voluntary differences of adults — and that as there are no such differences in infants, there is no difference in the effects of Baptism to them. Surely Lutherans should stand shoulder to shoulder in this, that whatever be the blessing of Baptism, be it little or great, vague or well-defined, it is offered alike to all, and *conferred* alike upon all who do not present in themselves the voluntary barrier to its reception. Yet if we say the doctrine of Baptism is non-fundamental, these very errors may be set forth in our theological chairs, taught in our Catechisms, and set forth in our pulpits.

A third element of the Calvinistic doctrine of Baptism is, that to those for whom any of the blessings of Baptism are designed, it supposes the sealing of as *great blessings,* as on the strongest sacramental theory, even that of the Church of

Rome herself, is conferred by Baptism; it seals to the elect, to whom alone its blessings belong, reception into the "communion, that is the fellowship in, the participation in, the cove. nant of grace," "insertion into Christ and His mystic body," "justification," "regeneration," and "the inward washing of sin." Two infant brothers, twins, we will say, are offered for Baptism; whatsoever is to come to pass has been unchangeably ordained by God from eternity in regard to them; one of the twins may be "*elect*," may have been predestinated unto everlasting life; the other is non-elect, is foreordained to everlasting death, particularly and unchangeably. The twins die in infancy, the elect one, by the terms of the theory, is regenerated, the non-elect is unregenerate; the one is saved, the other is lost; the grace of Baptism belongeth to the elect infant according to the counsel of God's own will, and therefore "baptismal grace,"—that is a Calvinistic idea, too,—therefore baptismal grace is "not only *offered*, but *really conferred on that infant.*" To an elect infant dying soon after its Baptism, the Calvinistic theory seems to give as much as the highest theory of "baptismal regeneration." Let Lutherans remember that it is here conceded that the highest blessings which our Church teaches us are connected alone with a *worthy* entrance into the baptismal covenant, and a *faithful continuance* therein, are acknowledged by Calvinists to be actually *sealed* therein — that is, that God sets his hand to it, by the act of baptizing, that the elect do *then* have, or shall *yet* have, if they have not then, justification, regeneration, and inward washing from sin. Shall we take offence at the doctrine of our Church, wh ch asks us to receive as an article of faith, in regard to the efficacy of Baptism, no more than is summed up in the words of our Confession, that "through Baptism the grace of God is offered, that *children* are to be baptized, and being through Baptism offered to God, are received into His favor?"

Here, then, we rest the case. The doctrine of Baptism held and confessed by the Evangelical Lutheran Church is, as we believe all her doctrines are, absolutely accordant in every part with the Word of God. To abide by her Confession, is to abide ·by the Word, and there she and her true children will rest. If we destroy the historical life of our Church, and abandon her Confession, whither can we go? What system can we accept which will meet so fully our wants? If we destroy or rend the Lutheran Church, or allow as normal and final just as much deviation as the individual may wish from all to which she has been pledged in her history, from all that is involved in her very name, from all that gave her distinctive being, what may we hope to establish in her place to justify so fearful an experiment, and to indemnify the world for so great a loss?

The final proposition of the Confession is antithetical, and The Antithesis arranges itself into three parts: of the Confession. 1. "On this account the Anabaptists are condemned." "Derhalben werden die Wiedertäufer verworfen." "Damnant Anabaptistas."

2. "Who disapprove of the Baptism of children and teach that it is not right." "Welche lehren dass die Kindertauf nicht recht sei." "Qui improbant baptismum puerorum."

3. "And affirm that children are saved without Baptism." "Et affirmant pueros sine baptismo salvos fieri."

I. The Anabaptists took their name from their repetition of The Anabap- Baptism in the case of those who had been baptists. tized in infancy. (*Ana* in composition indicates repetition.) They have also been called Katabaptists from their opposition to the Baptism of children. The early Anabaptists with whom our Reformers had to contend, made their main opposition to infant Baptism, and although they immersed, they certainly gave little prominence (if they gave any) to the question of mode, as compared with modern Baptists. The sect of Anabaptists made their appearance in history soon after the beginning of the Reformation, and excited disturbances in Saxony in 1522. The roots of the Anabaptist movement, especially on its political side, strike deep into the Middle Ages. The Reformation was not its cause, although Anabaptism often made the Reformation its occasion. Fanaticism always strives to corrupt the purity of faith in one direction, as Formalism strives to stifle it in the other. A pure

Church stands in living antagonism to the formalism of Rome, and to the fanaticism of all pseudo-Protestantism. It has the body, but disavows the flesh; it has spirituality, but carefully guards it against running into spiritualism.

The most renowned of the Anabaptists in history was THOMAS MUENZER, who was originally preacher in Allstaedt. He was deposed on account of his fanaticism, and uniting himself with the Anabaptists, became their leader. He published a bitter attack upon the Baptism of children. Leaving Saxony, he passed through a large portion of Germany with his associates, everywhere finding, among a population degraded by the current Romanism, abundance of adherents. Returning to Saxony, he established himself at Muehlhus, where he aroused the peasantry, claimed princely authority, gathered an army, abolished the magistracy, proclaimed that in future Christ alone was to be king, and made war in 1525 upon the princes themselves. The rebel bands were defeated at Franckenhus, and Muenzer was put to death. Prominent also among the Anabaptists were those who were led by JOHN OF LEYDEN, so called from his having seized upon that city, where he overthrew the magistracy, assumed the government with the title of king, made laws to suit himself and his followers, and practised great cruelties toward those who did not yield themselves to him. The city was besieged in 1526; an immense number of his adherents were slain, and he himself was put to death. It is evident that the Anabaptist movement was political as well as religious, and was largely a reaction, blind and ignorant, against gross abuses. The Anabaptists are condemned in the Confession, not in their persons, but in their errors; the man was not condemned — the errorist, or more strictly the error in the errorist, was condemned.

II. The SECOND point is: "Who disapprove of the Baptism of children, and teach that it is not right."

It is natural here to look at the grounds on which the Anabaptists object to Infant Baptism, and say that it is not right. The most plausible arguments which they urge against it, have been in a large part anticipated in

our discussion, but we shall, nevertheless, notice the **three**
strongest, the only ones which seem to carry any weight with
them.   Much of the earlier Anabaptist argument has been
abandoned, as, for example, that as our Saviour was baptized
in the thirtieth year of his age, infants ought not to be baptized.   The three arguments which have been urged with
most plausibility are:

1. That there is no express command for infant Baptism.

To this we reply: *a.* That there is an express command.
Our Lord commands his Apostles to make disciples of all
nations by baptizing them.   The word "nations" embraces
infants.   "God hath made of one blood all nations of men."
(Acts xvii. 26.)   The redemption is as wide as the creation,
and the power of application as wide as the redemption.   The
"nations," therefore, which God has made, redeemed, and desires to gather into His Church, are nations of children as well
as of adults.   "It is most certain," says the Apology,* "that
the promise of salvation pertains also to little children.   But
the promises do not pertain to those who are out of the Church
of Christ, for the kingdom of Christ cannot exist without the
Word and Sacraments.   Therefore it is necessary to baptize
little children, that the promise of salvation may be applied to
them, according to Christ's command (Matt. xxviii. 19), 'Baptize all nations,' in which words as salvation is offered to all,
so Baptism is offered to all — to men, to women, to children, to
infants.   It clearly follows, therefore, that infants are to be
baptized, inasmuch as salvation is offered in Baptism — in and
with Baptism the common grace and treasure of the Gospel is
offered to them."

b. When Jesus says: "That which is born of the flesh is
flesh," and "Except a man be born again of water and of the
Spirit he cannot enter into the kingdom of God," He teaches
that infants, inasmuch as they are flesh, must be born again of
water and of the Spirit, that is, must be baptized and become
regenerate.

c. If the express term were necessary, men and women
equally with infants would be excluded from Baptism, because

* 163, 52.

none of them are specifically mentioned in the baptismal com mission; in other words, there is a generic express command to baptize infants on the one hand, and there is no specific express command on the other either as regards sex or age.

d. Infant membership, sealed by a sacramental rite, was established under the Old Testament. If it had been designed to abolish infant membership under the New Dispensation, it would have been necessary to do it in so many words. The question fairly put, then, is not, " Where is infant Baptism enjoined in the New Testament? " but, " Where is it forbidden? "

e. Infant Baptism was practised by the Jews in New Testa ment times. Lightfoot, the greatest of the old rabbinical schol- ars, says, in his Harmony on John: * " The baptizing of infants was a thing as commonly known and as commonly used before John's coming, and at the time of his coming, and subsequently, as anything holy that was used among the Jews, and they were as familiarly acquainted with infant Baptism as they were with infant circumcision." And this he proves by abundant citations from the Talmud and the old rabbinical writers. It is inconceivable, therefore, that in such a state of things the Apostles should not have forbidden infant Baptism, if it were not meant that it should be administered.

f. The argument, *a fortiori:* If in the Old Testament, com- paratively restricted as its range was, infants were embraced in the covenant, much more in the New Testament, broader and more gracious than the Old as it is, would they be em- braced. But infants are embraced in the Old, much more than in the New.

g. That is as really Scriptural which is by just and necessary consequence deduced from Scripture, as that which is stated in it in so many words. When the Bible says: " There is but one God," it means just as much that the gods of the heathen are false, as if it were said in so many words.

2. It is urged that a covenant requires consciousness and intelligence on the part of those whom it embraces; but infants can have no consciousness of a covenant, therefore they cannot be embraced in one.

* Opera, 1686. Vol. I. p. 390.

37

We reply to this : *a.* DIVINE covenants do not require con-sciousness and intelligence on the part of all whom they embrace.   On the contrary, they embrace not only infants, but prospectively generations unborn, as, for example, the cove-nant with Abraham and his seed after him, sealed by the sac-rament of circumcision.

b. HUMAN covenants do not necessarily require consciousness and intelligence on the part of all embraced in them, but rest on the right of the adult generation to represent, and act for their children and posterity.   We are bound by the constitu-tional compact made by our fathers — bound by the covenants and treaties with foreign nations made before we were born.

c. The baptismal covenant *is* a voluntary covenant in one sense, that is to say, the child's will is presumed in the case. If the child cannot consciously accept the covenant, neither can it, nor does it, reject it.   In another sense, however, the baptis-mal covenant is not voluntary.   All human creatures are bound to be children of God, and have not the right to say whether they will or will not be His children.   If my child has not the right of self-decision as to whether it shall honor me as its parent, but is absolutely bound so to do, though it never was consulted, much more is that same child bound to honor God, and I usurp no right pertaining to it, when, as its representa-tive, I bind it by covenant to that to which it is bound with-out covenant.

3. It is urged that sacraments do not benefit without faith ; but the infant has no faith, therefore Baptism can do it no good.

We reply to this : *a.* If infants demonstrably have no faith, it would still be possible that in their Baptism there is a treas-ure of blessing, the full understanding and use of which is reserved for them when they can have faith, even as a father provides for his babe, or bequeaths to it many things which it cannot use till it reaches adult life, though they belong to it from the beginning.

b. But infants do have receptive faith.   " When we say that infants believe or have faith, it is not meant that they under-stand, or have consciousness of faith, but the error is rejected that baptized infants are pleasing to God, and are saved, *without any action of the Holy Spirit in them*. This is certain, that the Holy Spirit is efficacious in them, so that they can receive the grace of God and the remission of sins. The Holy Spirit operates in them in His own way, which it is not in our power to explain. That operation of the Spirit in infants we call faith, and we affirm that they believe. For that mean, or organ, by which the kingdom of God, offered in the Word and Sacraments, is *received*, the Scripture calls faith, and declares that believers *receive* the kingdom of God. And Christ affirms, Mark x. 15, that adults receive the kingdom of God in the same way that a little child receives it; and, Matt. xviii. 6, He speaks of the little ones which believe in Him." These are the words of Chemnitz,* and they mark the distinction we make in the term receptive faith. Faith as an act, like sin as an act, presupposes a *condition* of mind, which condition is the *essential* thing in both cases, to which the act is merely phenomenal. The act is intermittent, the condition is continuous. The worst of men does not cease to be a sinner merely because the act of sinning ceases. He may be in stupor, or in sleep, or his present thoughts may be absorbed in something morally indifferent, and yet he is a sinner through the whole. He is not always sinning, but he is always sinful, because the essence of character lies in the *condition* of the soul. The believer may be in stupor, or sleep, or his present thoughts be entirely absorbed in the necessary cares, or duties, or innocent enjoyments of life, but he is a believer through the whole. He is not always consciously exercising faith, but he is a believer always, because the essence of character is the condition of the soul. In the case of the infant, both on the side of nature and of grace, there must be, and is, a stronger and more protracted separation between the essential condition of sin and faith, and the phenomenon of conscious sin and of conscious faith, than in the case of the adult, but the condition is as real. By nature the infant is as really a sinner, and by grace as really a believer, as the adult is, though it can neither *do* sin nor *exercise* faith. It *has* sin by nature, and *has* faith by grace. Working out

* *Examen. Conc. Trid.* II. ii. x. 14.

under the law of the first condition, it will inevitably *do* sin, as under the law of the second it will *exercise* faith. Faith justifies by its *receptivity* alone. There is no justifying merit in faith as an act, nor is there any in the acts it originates. In the adult it is divinely wrought: it is "not of ourselves, it is the gift of God." In the infant there is wrought by God, through the Holy Ghost, by means of the water and the Word, that receptivity of condition which it has not by nature. The Holy Ghost offers grace, and so changes the moral nature of the child that this nature becomes receptive of the grace offered. This divinely wrought condition we call receptive faith, and though its phenomena are suspended, it is really faith, and as really involves what is essential to justification, as does the faith of the adult. The hand of an infant may as really grasp a diamond as if the infant knew the value of the treasure it held, and if the natural hand can be the minister of acts whose force it comprehends not, how much more may the supernatural hand? To accept the doctrine of original sin, and deny the doctrine of a divine counterwork — the doctrine "that where sin abounded, grace did much more abound" — is to make nature potent, and grace weak — it is an aggravation of Manicheism, and gives us a Devil mightier than God. Many of the Calvinistic divines have felt the difficulty under which their system labors, and have modified it in various degrees, so as to approximate the Lutheran view. Calvin acknowledges "a seed of faith in infants." Ursinus [*] says they have an "inclinatory faith, or inclination to faith." Voetius says "there is in them a root, faculty, supernatural principle, seed, or nursery, from whence, in its own time, faith rises up. It is related to faith as seed is to the tree, the egg to the bird, the bulb to the flower." Peter Martyr says that faith in infants is "incipient, is in its principle and root, inasmuch as they have the Holy Spirit, whence faith and all virtues flow forth. . . The age of infancy is capable of the motions of faith, and Jeremiah and John are witnesses that this age can be graced by the Holy Ghost." [†]

Nor was this great truth unknown in the Ancient Church.

[*] In Cateches. Q. 57.   [†] Quoted in Quenstedt. Theologia. II. 1142, 1145.

Thou must number baptized infants among believers," says Augustine* to a Pelagian: "thou darest not judge in any other way, if thou art not willing to be a manifest heretic." " In baptized infants, the Holy Spirit dwells, though they know it not. So know they not their own mind,—they know not their own reason, which lies dormant, as a feeble glimmer, which is to be aroused with the advance of years."†

c. Over against the proposition that nothing benefits without faith, we put the complementary proposition that nothing condemns but unbelief; but infants who by nature are condemned, because of the unbelief of nature, though they are not conscious of it, are by grace received into covenant, because by grace they have faith, though they are unconscious of it. If infants can be regenerated and have remission of sins, then can they have faith, which is an element in regeneration, and necessary to remission.

d. The Word does not profit, without faith, in the adult, and yet it is the Word through which the Holy Ghost excites the faith which secures the benefit. So is it in Baptism. It offers the faith which receives, and offers to that faith the grace of God; as the word of our Lord to the man with the withered hand bore the power which made obedience to the command possible. If Baptism offers grace to a child, then may we be well assured that God, who does not mock us, gives to that child what by nature it cannot have — a receptive faith. All divine commands bear with them the power of their fulfilment under the law of grace.

e. The Apostles in their original ignorance reasoned about children somewhat as the Anabaptists do. But Jesus said: " Suffer little children, and forbid them not, to come unto me, for of such is the kingdom of heaven." But the kingdom of God is not a kingdom of unbelievers, or of unregenerate persons. All the tares in that kingdom are sown by the Devil.

III. The THIRD and last point in the antithesis is that the Anabaptists " affirm that children are saved without Baptism," " et affirmant pueros sine baptismo salvos fieri."

---

* De Verb. Apostol. Serm. xiv. Vol. X. 221.
† Do. Epist. 57. Op. IV. 180.

We have seen that our own Confessors did not maintain the absolute necessity of Baptism to salvation, and it may, therefore, seem surprising that they charge upon the Anabaptists as an error what they themselves appear to concede. But if we see the true force of their language, the difficulty vanishes, for

1. The Anabaptists contended that Baptism was not the ordinary channel of salvation to the child. Our Confessors maintained that it is.

2. The Anabaptists contended that in fact children are not saved by Baptism. Our Confessors maintained that in fact children are saved by it.

3. The Anabaptists contended that no child is saved by Baptism. Our Confessors maintained that children are saved by Baptism.

4. The Anabaptists contended that a baptized child who is saved, is saved without respect to its Baptism. Our Confessors maintained that it is saved of God by it as a mean.

5. When our Confessors conceded that an unbaptized child might be saved, they rested its salvation on a wholly different ground from that on which the Anabaptists rested it. The Anabaptists contended, on a Pelagian basis, that the child was saved because of its innocence, and without a change of nature. Our Confessors maintained that it was saved as a sinful being for Christ's sake, and after renewal by the Holy Ghost. Our Confessors, in a word, maintained that children are ordinarily saved by Baptism; that this is God's ordinary channel of salvation to them. The Anabaptists contended that children are in no case saved by Baptism; that it is not the ordinary channel of salvation; and this error of theirs is the one condemned in the Confession. The Formula of Concord * makes all these points very clear in its statement of the errors of the Anabaptists, which it enumerates thus: 1. " That unbaptized children are not sinners before God, but are righteous and innocent, who, without Baptism (of which, according to the opinion of the Anabaptists, they have no need,) are saved in their innocence, inasmuch as they have not yet attained to the use of their reason. In this way they reject the entire doctrine of Original

* Epitom. 558. 6, 7, 8. Solid. Declarat. 727. 11, 12, 13.

Sin, and the doctrines which are dependent on it. 2. That children are not to be baptized until they attain the use of reason, and can make a profession of faith for themselves. 3. That the children of Christians, because of their birth of Christian and believing parents, are holy, and children of God, without Baptism, and previous to it."

In summing up the doctrine of Baptism we are to remember:

1. The necessity of a true definition of Baptism. Baptism is not mere water, but embraces also the command of God; the promise of God; the effectual work of the Holy Ghost, offering to faith, in connection with the outward part of Baptism, the grace of God. Whatever is wrought in Baptism, is wrought by the Holy Ghost, through the Word, with the water, in the believing soul.

2. That in adults Baptism is not always followed by regeneration, and that regeneration is not always preceded by Baptism; that men may be baptized and be lost, and may be unbaptized and be saved.

3. That unbaptized infants may be saved, and that the infants of heathen may be saved; that Baptism, though not absolutely essential in the theological sense, is yet necessary.

The whole doctrine of our Church, then, on, the question, "What is Baptism, and what are its blessings?" may be summed up in these words:

By Christian Baptism our Church understands not " MERE WATER " (Small. Cat. 361, 2), but the whole divine institution (Larger Cat. 491, 38 – 40), resting on the command of the Saviour, Matt. xxviii. 19 (Sm. Cat. 361, 2), in which He comprehends, and in which He offers the promise (Mark xv. 15; Sm. Cat. 362, 8), and which is, therefore, ordinarily necessary to salvation (A. C. ii. 2; ib. ix. 1, 3); in which institution, water, whether by immersion (L. C. 495, 65), sprinkling or pouring (L. C. 492, 45), applied by a minister of the Gospel (A. C. v. 1; ib. 14), in the name of the Trinity (Sm. Cat. 361, 4), to adults or infants (A. C. ix. 2), is not merely the sign of our profession, or of our actual recognition as Christians, but is rather a sign and testimony of the will of God toward us (A. C. xiii. 1), offering us His grace (A. C. ix.), and not *ex opere operato* (A. C. xiii. 3), but in those only who rightly use it, i. e. who believe from the heart the promises which are offered and shown (A. C. xiii. 2; L. C. 49, 33), is one of the instruments by which the Holy Ghost is given (A. C. v. 2), who excites and confirms faith, whereby we are justified before God (A. C. iv.; ib. v. 3), so that they who thus receive or use it, are in God's favor (A. C. ix. 2), have remission of their sins (Nicene Creed, 9), are born again (A. C. ii. 2), and are released from condemnation and eternal death (A. C. ii. 2; Sm. C. 361, 6) so long as they are in a state of faith, and bring forth holy works (A. C. xiii. 1–6; Sm. C. 362, 11–14); while, on the other hand, where there is no faith, a bare and fruitless sign, so far as 'blessing is concerned, alone remains (L. C. 496, 73), and they who do not use their Baptism aright, and are acting against conscience, and letting sin reign in them, and thus lose the Holy Spirit, are in condemnation, from which they cannot escape, except by true conversion (A. C. xiii.), a renewal of the understanding, will, and heart (L. C. 496, 68, 69; F. C. 605, 70).

This is the doctrine of our Church, and not one letter of it is destitute of the sure warrant of God's Word. The intelligent examiner will soon discover that, while the whole sum and tendency of the Romish and Romanizing doctrine of the Sacraments is to make them a substitute for faith in the justification of man, the doctrine of the Lutheran Church, in consonance with the Holy Scriptures, makes them a guard and bulwark of the great central truth that "by grace we are saved, through faith, and that not of ourselves,—it is the gift of God." Her view of the nature of the efficacy of the Word and Sacraments, is the only one which solves the mysterious question how God can be sovereign, and yet man be accountable; and how the Church can at once avoid the perilous extreme of Pelagianism on the one hand, and of uncorditional Election and Reprobation on the other.

XII.

THE DOCTRINE OF THE LORD'S SUPPER THETICALLY STATED.

(AUGSBURG CONFESSION. ART. X.)

IN approaching one of the highest, if not the very highest, of the mysteries of our faith, it becomes us to prepare ourselves for a most earnest, patient, and candid investigation of the Scriptural grounds on which that faith rests. The Lord's Supper has been looked at too much as if it were an isolated thing, with no antecedents, no presuppositions, no sequences; as if there were nothing before it, nothing after it, helping to determine its true character; while, in fact, it links itself with the whole system of Revelation, with the most vital parts of the Old and New Testament, so that it cannot be torn from its true connections without logically bringing with it the whole system. There is no process by which the doctrine of the Lutheran Church, in regard to the Lord's Supper, can be overthrown, which does not overthrow the entire fabric of the Atonement. No man can deem our distinctive doctrine of the Lord's Supper non-fundamental who thoroughly understands it in all its relations.

The first thing worthy of note in regard to the sacramental mystery is its antiquity. It meets us at the threshold of the divine history of our race. In Eden we see already the idea of natural and supernatural eating. We have there the natural eating terminating in the natural, in the words: "Of every tree of the Garden thou mayest freely eat." Closely following

The Lord's Supper. I. Old Testament Foreshadows. 1. The Sacraments in Eden.

585

upon this we have the idea of supernatural eating, with **the** natural bodily organ: " Of the tree of the knowledge of **good** and evil thou shalt not eat; for in the day thou eatest thereof thou shalt surely die." Man did eat of it, and found it a sacrament of death. In, with, and under that food, as a divine means judicially appointed, was communicated death. That

> " mortal taste
> Brought death into the world and all our woe."

The great loss of Paradise Lost was that of the Sacrament of Life, of that food, in, with, and under which was given immortality, so objectively, positively, and really that even fallen man would have been made deathless by it: " Now lest he put forth his hand, and take also of the tree of life, and eat, and live forever," Gen. iii. 22. The great gain of Paradise Regained is that of the Sacrament of Life. Christ says: " I am the life;" " The bread that I will give is My flesh, which I will give for the life of the world." The cross of Christ is the tree of life, and He the precious fruit borne by heavenly grace upon it. The cross is the centre of Paradise Regained, as the tree of life was the centre of the first Paradise. Christ's body is the organ of the life purchased by His obedience and death. The Holy Supper is the sacrament of that body, and, through the body, the sacrament of the life which that body brings. But that same body is also a sacrament of death to the unworthy recipient. The whole sacrament on its two sides of death and life is in it united: salvation to the believer, judgment to the unworthy. After the creation of man, God's first provision was for the generation and birth of the race, the foreshadowing of regeneration and of the new birth, for which, in Holy Baptism, the first provision is made in the new creation of the New Testament. The next provision made for man was that of sustenance for the life given, or yet to be given. In the Garden of Eden was a moral miniature of the universe; and with the act of eating were associated the two great realms of the natural and the supernatural; and with this was connected the idea of the one as a means of entering the other, **of** the natural as the means of entering into the supernatural

There were natural trees, with purely natural properties, whose fruit was eaten naturally, and whose benefits were simply nat ural; bodily eating, terminating in a bodily sustenance. But there was also the natural terminating in the supernatural. There were two trees, striking their roots into the same soil, lifting their branches in the same air — natural trees — but bearing, by Heaven's ordinance, in, with, and under their fruitage, supernatural properties. One was the sacramental tree of good. We call it a *sacramental* tree, because it did not merely symbolize life, or signify it; but, by God's appointment, so gave life — in, with, and under its fruit — that to receive its fruit was to receive life. The fruit which men there would have eaten was the communion of life. On Gen. iii. 22, the sound old Puritan commentator, Poole, thus paraphrases: " Lest he take also of the tree of life, as he did take of the tree of knowledge, and thereby profane that *sacrament of eternal life.*"

With this tree of life was found the tree which was the sacrament of judgment and of death, and by man's relations to that tree would be tested whether he were good or evil, and by it he would continue to enjoy good or plunge himself into evil. By an eating, whose organs were natural, but whose relations were supernatural, man fell and died. This whole mystery of evil, these pains and sorrows which overwhelm the race, the past, the present, and the future of sin, revolve around a single natural eating, forbidden by God, bringing the offender into the realm of the supernatural for judgment. We learn here what fearful grandeur may be associated in the moral government of God, with a thing in itself so simple as the act of eating. The first record of Revelation is a warning against the plausible superficiality of rationalism. It was the rationalistic insinuation of Satan, as to the meaning of God's Word, which led to the Fall. Abandon faith in the letter of God's Word, said the Devil. Our first parents obeyed the seductive insinuation and died.

In the Lord's Supper three great ideas meet us as they met in Paradise. There is in it, 1, *Bread*, which, as bread, is the natural food of man, and belongs to all men. But there is also, 2, The supernatural element of *life:* "My flesh, which I will give for the life of the world." The natural bread, as the sacramental bearer of this heavenly food, is the communion of the body of Christ, that is, the medium by which the body is communicated or imparted. There is also in the Lord's Supper, 3, The supernatural element of *judgment,* and that of judgment unto death: "He that eateth and drinketh unworthily, eateth and drinketh damnation (or, judgment) unto himself, not discerning the Lord's body." The tree of life, as our theologians well observed, was not a memorial, a symbol, a suggestive emblem or sign; but was a supernatural, efficacious, and energetic means of life. "This tree," says Osiander (1589), "by the divine ordination and will, bore fruit which could preserve the bodily vigor of him who partook of it ('in perpetual youth') until man, having completed the term of his earthly life, would, without dying, have been translated to his life in heaven." So also the tree of the knowledge of good and evil did not symbolize a result, but brought it. *Life* was in, with, and under the fruit of the one tree; death, in, with, and under the fruit of the other.

This view is not a modern invention. It is found in Irenæus, St. Chrysostom, and Theodoret. Gregory Nazianzen enlarges upon the idea of "being made immortal by coming to the tree of life." St. Augustine says: "In the other trees there was nourishment; in this one, a sacrament" ("*in isto autem Sacramentum*"). Vatablus (1557), a very judicious Roman Catholic expositor, fairly expresses the general sense of the Fathers in stating his own: "The tree of life was a *sacrament,* by which God would have sealed immortal life to Adam, if he had not departed from His commandment." Delitzsch: "The tree of life had the power of ever renewing and of gradually transfiguring the natural life of man. To have used it after the Fall would have been to perpetuate forever the condition into which he had fallen."

Nor is the true view without support from sources whence we might least expect it. Rosenmüller (Rationalistic): "This writer means that the weakened powers were to be revived by eating of that tree, and this life was to be preserved forever."

Knobel (strongly Rationalistic): "This passage (Gen. iii. 22) teaches that man, after partaking of the tree of life, would have become immortal." Dr. Bush, both in his earlier and later notes on Genesis (1833, 1852), says: "Adam might frequently have eaten (ed. 1859, 'undoubtedly often ate') of the tree of life before the Fall — sacramentally, as Christians eat of the Lord's Supper. In regard to the driving from Paradise, 'lest he also eat of the tree of life and live forever,' Irenæus said: 'God has so ordered it that evil might not be immortal, and punishment might become love to man.'" Dr. Bush, who, had his judgment been in the ratio of his other endowments, would indisputably have taken the first rank among American commentators on the Old Testament, says, Gen. iii. 22, 23: "The language, it must be acknowledged, seems to imply, that had man tasted of the tree of life, even after his rebellion, he would have lived forever, and that he was expelled from Paradise to prevent such a consequence." The conclusion, however, is so little in keeping with Dr. Bush's theology, that he undertakes to reason it away in a very feeble and rationalistic manner, in the face of what he concedes to be the obvious meaning of the passage.

Another hint toward the true view of the sacramental mystery is given us in the divine declaration, Gen. ix. 4: "But flesh with the life thereof, which is the blood thereof, shall ye not eat." Literally: "But flesh with its soul (*i. e.* life), its blood, ye shall not eat." Still more literally: "in its soul." At the root of this prohibition lay a great typical idea, which can be fully understood only in the light of the finished sacrifice of our Lord Jesus Christ, and in the light of His sacramental Supper, in which we participate in, or have communion with that sacrifice. The command was repeated again and again, and the reason most generally assigned was that the blood is the life of the flesh. But this reason seems itself to require an explanation, and this we find fully given in Leviticus, the book in which there is the amplest display of the typical element of sacrifice. In Lev. xvii. 10-14, we have a full explanation of the meaning of the reservation of the blood. It is especially the 11th verse in which the typical force of the prohibition is made manifest. Under the Old Testament they actually ate of the body of the sacrifice, but only drank a symbol of its blood. It is manifest that the reservation of the blood pointed to something yet to be accomplished, and hinted that the perfect communion in the whole sacrifice was reserved for another dispensation. Only in the light of this can we fully appreciate the startling character of our Lord's command, when, for the first time in the history of the chosen race, He gave the command to drink that which He declared to be blood — and solved the mystery by calling it the blood of the New Covenant.

When the three men, Gen. xviii., one of whom is called 3. The Supernatural and Natural eating. Jehovah, appeared to Abraham, the patriarch set before them bread, flesh, butter, and milk, and they did eat; Verse 8. Here was the supernatural eating of the natural; the eating of natural food with the natural organ of an assumed body, and that body of course supernatural. These same three heavenly persons did eat (Gen. xix. 3) of unleavened bread in the house of Lot.

Is there a greater mystery in the sacramental eating, in which the supernatural communicates itself by the natural, by the natural bread to the natural mouth, than there is in this true eating, in which the supernatural partakes of the natural? If God can come down and partake of human food by human organs, so that it is affirmed of Jehovah that He did eat, He can lift the human to partake of what is divine by a process which, though supernatural, is yet most real.

The relations of sacrifice to covenant in the Old Testament 4. The relations of covenant to sacrifice. suggest instructive parallels to the Lord's Supper. In Gen. xv. we have the covenant between God and Abraham sealed with sacrifice. In Gen. xxxi. 44–46, is presented the idea of eating as an act of covenant. Laban said to Jacob: "Let us make a covenant," "and they did eat there upon the heap;" where eating is the crowning act of the covenant. But more than this is presented in this chapter, for in the particulars of the ratification of the covenant, we are told (verse 54), "Then Jacob offered sacrifice upon the mount, and called his brethren to eat bread: and they did

ea bread." Here is the idea, first, of sacrifice as the inseparable constituent in the covenant; then, of joint participation in
the sacrifice by eating of it, by the parties partaking in the
covenant through it.

The idea of sacrifice under the Old Dispensation sheds light
upon the nature of the Lord's Supper. "Without
the shedding of blood is no remission." The slaying of the victim by shedding its blood, by which
alone its death could be effected, was properly the sacrifice.
After the sacrifice was made, two things were essential to
securing its end: first, that God should receive it; second, that
man should participate in it. The burning of the sacrifice
by fire from heaven was the means of God's accepting it on
the one side; and eating of it, the means of man's participating on the other. The truth is, that the sacrifice of the
Old Testament resolves itself into the very elements which
we find in the Lord's Supper. The Altar was the Table of
the Lord, and the whole conception of sacrifice runs out
into this, that it is a covenanting Supper between God and
man.

The sacrifice, through the portion burnt, is received of God
by the element of fire; the portion reserved is partaken of by
men, is communicated to them, and received by them. The
eating of one portion of the sacrifice, by the offerer, is as real
a part of the whole sacred act as the burning of the other part
is. Man offers to God; this is sacrifice. God gives back to
man; this is sacrament. The oblation, or thing offered, supplies both sacrifice and sacrament, but with this difference,
that under the Old Dispensation God received part and man
received part; but under the New, God receives all and gives
back all: Jesus Christ, in His own divine person, makes that
complete which was narrowed under the Old Covenant by the
necessary limitations of mere matter. But in both is this
common idea, that all who receive or commune in the reception of the oblation, either on the one part as a sacrifice, or on
the other as a sacrament, are in covenant; and in the light of
this alone is it, that not on Calvary, where the sacrifice was
made, but in the Supper, where the sacrifice is applied, the

5. The relations
of sacrifice to sac-
rament.

Saviour says: " This is the New Testament (the new covenant, in My blood."

The New Testament strikes its roots down into the very heart

6. The Passo-
ver is a type of
the Supper. of the Old Dispensation, and to understand either we must study both together.   Let us compare, in the case of the paschal lamb and paschal supper, the type and the fulfilment, and we shall see how the earlier sheds light upon the later, and how both placed in their true relation illustrate each other.   The following are but a part of the points of illustration, but they may be sufficient to lead the attentive student of God's Word to search for himself.

1. The passover was to be a *lamb*, and Christ is the true *Lamb*. " They shall take to them every man a *lamb*," are the words of the institution of the passover; Ex. xii. 3.   The key to the typical reference of the lamb is already given in the words of Isaiah (liii.) " He " (the man of sorrows) " is brought as a *lamb* to the slaughter."   But the New Testament unfolds the typical reference in all its clearness.   " Behold the *Lamb* of God " (John i. 29, 36) ; " the blood of Christ, as of a *lamb ;*" 1 Pet. i. 12.   It is by this name that Christ is revealed in the glories of the apocalyptic vision : " In the midst of the elders stood a *Lamb*," " the elders fell down before the *Lamb:* " " Worthy is the *Lamb* that was slain."   The title " lamb " is applied to our Lord between thirty and forty times in the New Testament.

2. The paschal lamb was to be *typically perfect*, and Christ was *truly perfect*.   The typical characteristics of the paschal lamb it is not necessary here to dwell upon.   It was to be perfect and unblemished in every respect to typify Him, who both in body and soul was spotless, " holy, harmless, undefiled, and separate from sinners."   " Ye were redeemed . . . . with the precious blood of Christ, as of a *lamb without blemish and without spot ;* " 1 Pet. i. 12.

3. The paschal lamb was to be *slain* as a type of redemption, and Christ was to be slain for the verity of redemption. " The whole assembly shall *kill* it;" Ex. xii. 6.   " Who *killed* the Lord Jesus;" 1 Thes. ii. 15.   " Lo, in the midst of the throne stood a Lamb as *it had been slain*.   And they sung a new song, saying, Thou wast *slain*, and hast redeemed us to

God by Thy blood. Worthy is the Lamb that was *slain*." Rev. v. 6–12.

4. The Passover was a typical sacrifice in the realm of the natural, and Christ is a true sacrifice in the realm of the supernatural. " It is the sacrifice of the Lord's Passover." Exodus xii. 27. " Christ, our Passover, is sacrificed *for us*." Christ hath given Himself for us, an *offering* and *a sacrifice* to God. " When He said : Sacrifice and offering, and burnt-offering, and offering for sin, Thou wouldst not, neither hadst pleasure therein ; which are offered by the law ; *then* said He, Lo, I come tò do Thy will, O God ! He taketh away the first, that He may establish the second. By which will we are sanctified through *the offering of the body* of Jesus Christ once for all." Psalm xl. 6–8 ; Heb. x. 8–10. " How much more shall the blood of Christ, who, through the Eternal Spirit, offered Himself without spot to God, purge your conscience from dead works?" Heb. ix. 14.

5. The Paschal Supper was a typical, natural eating of the typical, natural lamb ; the Lord's Supper is a true, supernatural eating of the true, supernatural Lamb : " And they shall *eat the flesh* in that night;" Exod. xii. 8. " The bread that I will give is My flesh, which I will give for the life of the world. Except ye eat the flesh of the Son of man, ye have no life in you. Whoso eateth My flesh hath eternal life. He that eateth My flesh dwelleth in Me. My flesh is meat indeed ;" John vi. 51–56. " Thus shall ye eat it," said Jehovah ; Exod. xii. 11. " Take, eat," said our Lord.

6. The Paschal Supper was a typical, natural *act ;* the Lord's Supper is a true, supernatural *act*. " The cup of blessing which we bless, is it not the communion of the blood of Christ ? The bread which we break, is it not the communion of the body of Christ ? Whosoever shall eat this bread and drink this cup of the Lord unworthily, shall be guilty of the body and blood of the Lord — he that eateth and drinketh **unwor** thily, eateth and drinketh damnation (or judgment) to **himself.** NOT DISCERNING THE LORD'S BODY !" 1 Cor. x. 16 ; xi.

7. The Paschal Supper was a *natural communion* of the

38

type ; the Lord's Supper is a *supernatural communion* of the *substance.*

8. The Paschal Supper was a feast by which the *typical* was presented in, with, and under the natural ; the Lord's Supper is a feast by which the *true* is presented in, with, and under the natural.

9. In the Paschal Supper the body of the typical lamb was received, together with the bread, after a natural manner ; in the Lord's Supper the body of the true Lamb is received, together with the bread, after a supernatural manner.

10. The natural eating of the typical Paschal lamb belongs to the sphere of *lower reality* — that is, of mere earthly and carnal fact ; the supernatural eating of the true Paschal Lamb belongs to the sphere of *higher reality* — that is, of heavenly and spiritual truth.

Thus does the dim twilight of the dawning Old Testament, if rightly used, open to us a purer vision of truth than unwilling eyes can find in the sunlight of the New Testament. How does the parallel run out into the minutest particulars between these representative institutions of the two great dispensations !

11. Of the Paschal festival, Jehovah said : " This day shall be unto you for a *memorial;* " of the Lord's Supper, the incarnate Jehovah said : " This do in *remembrance* of Me." Luke xxii. 19.

12. " The *blood* shall be to you for a token," says Jehovah. " This is My *blood* of the New Testament "— " the communion of the *blood* of Christ " — " is guilty . . . of the *blood* of the Lord."

13. " When I see the blood I will pass over you, and the *plague shall not rest* upon you," says Jehovah. " This is My blood," says our Lord, " shed for you and for many for the *remission of sins.*"

14. " Ye shall keep it a *feast,*" says Jehovah. " Christ our passover is sacrificed for us, therefore let us keep the *feast,*" 1 Cor. v. 8, or as Luther, bringing out still more clearly this element in words, renders them : " We also have a Paschal lamb, that is Christ, offered for us, wherefore let us keep passover." (*Oster-lamm, Ostern.*)

15. " Ye shall keep it to the Lord . . throughout your generations." " Ye do show the Lord's death till He come ; " 1
Cor. xi. 26.

16. " The man that . . forbeareth to keep the passover,
even the same soul shall be *cut off* from among his people."
" Except ye *eat the flesh* of the Son of man, *and drink* His blood,
ye ·have no life in you." " Whosoever eateth *leavened* bread,
that soul shall be cut off from Israel." " He that eateth and
drinketh *unworthily*, eateth and drinketh *damnation* [*or judg
ment*] to himself, not *discerning the Lord's body.* For this
cause many are weak and sickly among you, and many sleep."
1 Cor. xi. 29, 30.

17. " *Strike* the lintel . . with the blood." " This is My
blood which is *shed* for many." " Ye are come to the blood
of *sprinkling*," — " elect . . through *sprinkling* of the blood of
Jesus Christ."

18. " In one *house* shall it be eaten." " Having an high
priest over the *house* of God " — " Christ whose *house* are we."
" Ye come into *one place.*" " The members of that *one body*,
being many, are one body." " The bread which we break, is
it not the communion of the body of Christ? For we being
many are *one bread*, and *one body :* for we are all partakers of
that one bread."

19. " *Thou* shalt not *carry* forth aught of the flesh *abroad* out
of the house ; " Ex. xii. 46. " We have *an altar* whereof they
have no right to eat who serve the tabernacle ; " Heb. xiii. 10.

20. " When a *stranger* shall sojourn with thee, and will keep
the passover to the Lord, let all his males be circumcised, and
then let them come near and keep it ; " Exod. xii. 48. " For by
one Spirit are we *all baptized into one body*, whether we be *Jews
or Gentiles*, whether we be bond or free ; and have been *all*
made to *drink into one* Spirit ; " 1 Cor. xii. 13.

21. " *One law* shall be to him that is *home-born*, and unto
the stranger that sojourneth among you ; " Exod. xii. 49. " As
many of you as have been baptized into Christ, have put on
Christ. There is *neither* Jew nor Greek, there is *neither* bond
nor free, there is *neither* male nor female : for ye are all one in
Christ Jesus."

22. "*All* the congregation of Israel shall keep it," (Hebrew do it.) Exod. xii. 48. "Drink ye *all* of this; this do ye, as oft as ye drink it, in remembrance of Me;" Matt. xxvi. 27; 1 Cor. xi. 25.

ORIGEN:* "Christ our passover is slain, and this feast is to be kept by eating the flesh of the Logos:" "ὅτι το πασχα ημων εθυθη χριστος και χρη εορταζειν εσθιοντα της σαρχος του λογου." Beza on 1 Cor. v. 7.: "Our whole life should be in conformity with Christ, that feast of unleavened bread, in which we were made partakers of that spotless Lamb who was slain." Grotius: "As by the blood of the Paschal lamb the Israelites were delivered from destruction, so also Christians, by the blood of Christ, are liberated from the common ruin of mankind. That lamb was to be without fault, and Christ was without fault. (See Luke xxii. 16.) Christ, therefore, is the mystic passover, that is, the Paschal Lamb." On 1 Cor. v. 7.

Amid all these transitions from type to fulfilment the change is never from the more true to the less true, nor from the real to the ideal, but there is either a coincidence in the natural with an elevated use in the New Dispensation, or a higher natural with a true supernatural attached to it. There is in both, for example, a coincidence in a *real shedding* of blood though in the shedding of Christ's blood there is a supernatural efficacy; there is in both a *real eating*, but in the one the communion effected is earthly, in the other it is heavenly. This then is the point to which these great Biblical truths irresistibly lead us, that CHRIST IS THE TRUE PASCHAL LAMB, AND THE SUPPER OF CHRIST IS THE TRUE PASCHAL SUPPER. What the paschal lamb of the Old Dispensation typified, Christ is; and what the Paschal supper of the Old Dispensation typified, the supper of Christ is; and that which is promised and shadowed in the Paschal supper is given in the Lord's Supper, in very deed and substance. The supernatural presence of Christ's body and blood cannot be less true, but is more true, than the natural presence of the body and blood of the Paschal lamb.

That the true relation between the two Paschal lambs and the two Paschal suppers should be most clear, it pleased God

* Cont. Celsum VIII.

that there should be a coincidence in point of time between the ending of the shadow and the full appearing of the substance. The Sun of Revelation stood at its perfect zenith, and the shadow was cast no longer by the substance, because the shadow lay beneath Christ's feet. The sun stands henceforth, at its noontide, and we are done with shadows forever. Therefore it was written in God's purposes that the true Paschal Lamb should be slain at the feast of the old Passover. Our blessed Lord dwelt upon the time as in itself an essential ele ment of the perfectness of His work: " With desire have I desired to eat *this* Passover with you before I suffer." Luke xxii. 15. " Before the feast of the Passover, Jesus knew that His hour was come." John xiii. 1.

It was at the Passover time, in a Passover family group of disciples, in a room prepared for the Passover, that the Lord's Supper was instituted. The bread which our Lord brake was bread provided for the Passover. The cup which He blessed was filled with wine prepared for the Passover. It is a new Paschal Supper. But where is the *slain lamb* of this new Paschal? Where is that *verity* in it of which the unspotted lamb of the first Paschal is the type? Where is that shed blood of which the shed blood of the first Paschal is the type? Is it to be characteristic of the New Testament Paschal Supper that it shall have *no Paschal lamb ;* that there shall *be bread and wine,* but that the great element of the *soul's nourishment,* the *lamb itself,* of which these were but the accompaniments, and as *attendants* of *which* alone they were given, that the *lamb* shall be wanting? " Christ our *Passover, our Paschal Lamb, is slain for us ;* therefore let us keep the feast ; " 1 Cor. v. 8. To feed upon the Paschal Lamb is the *grand object of the feast, and if the Lord's Supper be but the taking of bread and wine, the true Paschal Lamb not being truly present, and not truly received,* then is the substance more shadowy than the shadow, and the Christian at his Supper has less than the Jew at his Passover. Well might a childlike faith breathe a sigh, as it were an echo of the innocent words of Isaac: " My father ! behold the fire and the wood ; but WHERE IS THE LAMB ? " — but a faith like that of Abraham, in the light of a new dispensation, will answer: "My son, God has provided Himself a lamb. '

"They said one to another: It is manna. (*Sept.:* What is 7. The manna this? *Ti esti touto.*) And Moses said unto them, In the desert. This is the bread (*Sept.: outos o artos*) which the Lord hath given you to eat. This is the thing (*Scpt.: Touto to rema*) which the Lord hath commanded;" Exod. xvi. 15. "I am the bread of life. Your fathers did eat manna in the desert, and are dead. This is the bread (*outos estin o artos*) which cometh down from heaven, that he that eateth of it may not die. I am the living bread which came down from heaven; if any man eat of this bread, he shall live forever; and the bread that I will give is My flesh, which I will give for the life of the world;" John vi. 49–57. "All (our fathers) did eat the same spiritual meat;" 1 Cor. x. 3. *Cyrill* (*Lib.* iv. *in John* xvi.): "The manna was not, therefore, the living food, but the sacred body of Christ is the food which nourisheth to eternal life." *Lombard* (*Lib.* iv. *Sentent.*): "That bodily bread brought the ancient people to the land of promise through the desert; this heavenly food will carry the faithful, passing through the desert, to heaven." *Gerhard, John* (*Loci* xxii. *ch.* ii.): "By that bread which came down from heaven, that is by Christ's body, we are nourished, that we perish not with hunger in the desert of this world."

In quoting the sixth chapter of John, as bearing on the Lord's Supper, it may be well, once for all, to say that it is quoted not on the supposition that it speaks of the Lord's Supper specifically, but that in stating the general doctrine of the life-giving power of Christ's flesh and blood, it states a doctrine under which the benefits of the sacramental eating come as a species. If we come into supernatural, blessed participation of Christ's flesh and blood, in the act of faith, without the Lord's Supper, *a fortiori* we have blessed participation of them in the act of faith with the Lord's Supper. The sixth of John treats of the grand end of which the Lord's Supper is the grand means. We partake of Christ's body and blood sacramentally, in order that we may partake of them savingly. Of the latter, not of the former, the sixth of John speaks.

The doctrine of the Lord's Supper, as the Lutheran Church believes it to be set forth in the New Testament, is thus defined in her great general Symbol, the Augsburg Confession:

Of the holy Supper of our Lord, our Churches, with one consent, teach and hold

1. That the *true* body and blood of Christ are the sacramental objects.

2. That the sacramental objects are *truly* present in the Lord's Supper.

3. That this true presence is under the form or species of *bread and wine.*

4. That present, under this form or species, they are *communicated.*

5. That thus communicated, they are *received by all communicants.*

6. That the opposite doctrine is to be rejected.

On each and all of these we affirm that the doctrine of the Evangelical Lutheran Church is the Scriptural doctrine.

We affirm, first, then that it is a Scriptural doctrine, that the true body and blood of Christ are the sacramental objects; that is, that apart from any questions on other points, the true body and true blood of our Lord

are the objects set before us in the sacramental words, and whether their presence be offered to contemplation, to memory, to faith, or after a substantial, supernatural manner, it is the true body and true blood of Christ, of which we are to make our affirmation, or denial, when we state the doctrine of the Lord's Supper.

By *true* body, we mean that body in which our Saviour was actually incarnate, as opposed to His mystical body, which is the Church, or any ideal or imaginary body. It is conceded that it was His true body, not His mystical body, which was given for us; but Christ, in the Lord's Supper, says: " This is My body, *which is given for you:*" therefore the sacramental object is His true body. As neither His mystical body, nor the Holy Spirit dwelling in His body, nor a sign nor symbol of His body, nor a memorial of His body, nor faith in His body was given for us, but His true body itself was given, it and it alone, and neither one nor other of all the objects substituted for it, is the first sacramental object.

By His true blood, we mean that blood which was the actual seat of His human vitality, that " precious blood ' wherewith we are bought. It was confessedly His true blood which was shed for the remission of sins; but Christ, in the Lord's Supper, says: " This is My blood, *which is shed* for the remission of sins." Now, as neither a doctrine about His blood, nor the efficacy of His blood, nor the Holy Spirit uniting us with His blood, nor a sign, symbol, nor memorial of His blood, nor faith in His blood was shed for sins, and as His true blood alone was so shed, it, and none other of all the objects substituted for it, is the second sacramental object.

Hence the objection is groundless that our Confession adds to Scripture by saying that Christ's *true* body is the sacramental object, for although that adjective *true*, is not used in the words of the institution, the idea is there, if the body which was broken for us is Christ's true body, and His blood shed for us His true blood. Calvin, and even Zwingli, were compelled to concede so much.

Hence also falls to the ground the charge of conflicting representations, when our theologians speak sometimes of the *natural* body, and sometimes of the *glorified* body of Christ as present. Christ's *true* body, His *natural* body, and His *glorified* body, are one and the same body in identity. The words *true* and *natural*, refer to its *essence ;* the word *glorified* refers to its *condition.* The *glorification* of His body neither made it cease to be *true* nor *natural.* That is, it was no more an unreal, ideal, or imaginary body, after the glorification than before. It was identically the same body, but with a constant and plenary exercise of glorious properties. What He possessed, but did not ordinarily use in the days of His humiliation, He now constantly and fully exercises, and this new condition is called His glorification. Though His natural and true body is present, its condition is glorified. But though its condition is glorified, it is not in virtue of that glorification, but because of, and through its union as one person with God, that it is

present. This presence is *spiritual*, when that word is opposed
to carnal, but it is not spiritual when that word is opposed to
true, as if His presence were something wrought by our spirits.
His body is a spiritual body, as opposed to the present conditions and limitations of flesh and blood, but it is not spiritual
as opposed to real and natural. All the pretended contradictions of our theology vanish when the terms of that theology
are taken in the sense in which it uses them.

We affirm it, secondly, to be a Scriptural doctrine that these
sacramental objects, to wit: the true body and true 2. The true
blood of Jesus Christ, are *truly present* in the Lord's presence.
Supper: *Vere adsint — wahrhaftiglich gegenwartig sei.*

We oppose a true presence, first, to the Zwinglian theory,
that the presence of these objects is simply ideal, a presence to
our memory or contemplation: secondly, to the theory set forth
by Bucer in the Tetrapolitan Confession, further elaborated by
Calvin, and now generally known as the Calvinistic, to wit:
that the body and blood are present in efficacy through the
working of the Holy Spirit, in the believing elect. In opposition to the first, we affirm it to be Scriptural, that the presence
is one wrought not by our ideas, memories, or contemplation,
but is a presence equally true, whether we do or do not think,
remember, contemplate, or believe. In opposition to the
second, we affirm, that the efficacy of Christ's body and blood
is not separable from them, but is wrought by them truly
present; that this efficacy is direct and personal, not mediated
by the Holy Ghost, but by Christ Himself, substantially present; that this presence does not depend for its reality (but
alone for its salutary results) upon the faith of the receiver,
and that its sole causes are the divine personality and beneficent will of the Institutor of the Supper.

We prove this, first, by the demands of all those types of the
Old Testament which contemplate Christ as the Paschal Lamb,
who is to be present in that nature in which He was slain, not
after the shadowy mode of the old dispensation, but after the
true mode of the new, in the New Testament Paschal. It is
through His human nature that Christ is our Paschal Lamb
sacrificed; and, therefore, it must be through His human

nature that Christ, our Paschal Lamb, is eaten. If it was not through His divinity, separate from His humanity, that He was sacrificed upon the cross, it cannot be that through His divine nature, separate from His humanity, He is given to us at His table.

We prove it, secondly, by the demands of the type of Old Testament sacrifices, which were not only to be offered to God, but to be partaken of by the priests and offerers. That body and blood which were offered to the Father, and by Him accepted, must also be partaken of by those for whom they were offered, and the partaking must be a *true* one, as the offering itself was true — but in order to a true partaking, there must be a true presence.

Thirdly, the words of the institution force us to this conclusion. For if it even be granted for a moment, for argument's sake, that these words might be taken symbolically, the symbol only postpones, by one process, the general result, but by no means sets it aside. A symbol must be the symbol of some real thing; and there must be a point of analogy to constitute a symbol; a sign must point to the reality of which it is a sign; a symbolical act presupposes a real corresponding act; and something symbolically done to a symbol implies that something, to which that is analogous, is to be, or ought to be, really done to a real object. Why, then, is *bread* the symbol of Christ's *body* — not (as we have already shown) the symbol of a doctrine about that body, or of its efficacy, but of the *body* itself? What is the point of analogy? It must be that both are food. Then Christ's body must be conceded to be true food, or bread cannot be the symbol of it. But if Christ's true body be conceded to be true food, then the symbol has brought us to the acknowledgment of a true presence somewhere — but if there be a true presence anywhere, it will not be denied that it is in the Lord's Supper. Furthermore, if bread be the symbol of a true body, breaking bread the symbol of a true breaking of a true body, then the eating of that bread must be the symbol of a true eating of a true body; but if it be granted that this takes place anywhere, it will not be denied that it takes place in the Lord's Supper

Thus is the theory of the symbol really subversive of itself, unless it be contended that we eat symbolically in the Supper what we eat truly elsewhere, which no one is likely to maintain. The parallelism may be made more obvious by present ing it in a tabular view:

SYMBOL.	REALITY.
1. Bread.	1. True Body.
2. Breaking of Bread.	2. True Breaking of True Body.
3. Eating of Broken Bread.	3. True Eating of True Body, truly Broken.
4. Cup (Contents).	4. True Blood.
5. Pouring Out.	5. True Blood, truly shed.
6. Drinking.	6. True Drinking of True Blood, truly shed.

But it is impossible, on sound principles of interpretation, to find a symbol in the words of the Institution. The Eucharist combines three characters which forbid such an idea. 1. It is a *Supper*. 2. It is *Testamentary*. 3. It is a *Covenanting Rite*.

1. When at a *Supper* a guest has offered to him anything, with the request to eat, and with assignment of the reason, This is so and so — all laws of language lead us to expect that the thing so offered shall be not the sign, symbol, or memorial of that which is to be eaten, but shall be the very thing designated. If the words of the Institution had been: "Jesus said, Take, eat, this is *bread*," would not the man be thought to trifle who would urge that He gave them, not bread, but a sign, symbol, or memorial of bread? Would he help himself by appealing to interpretations of dreams, to parables, metaphors, figures, and symbols? By no means. Men would ask him for an instance in which, at a *supper*, any one had said: "Take, eat, this is bread," meaning that it was not bread, but a symbol of bread. Who would say, seriously, at a supper, handing a man a book: "Take, eat, this is sponge-cake," meaning that, as a sponge-cake is light and pleasant to the body, so is the book of which it is a symbol a light work, and pleasant to the mind? Why is it that the Supper of our Lord

stands separate in the world in this, that in it alone, **in any** sense, symbolical or sacramental, imaginary or real, the guests are invited to participate in the body of Him of whom it is the memorial? Does not this fact alone demonstrate that Christ's body is solitary in its powers and relations to men; that language in regard to it belongs to a wholly different sphere from that which pertains to the bodies of other men; that we can affirm of it what would be worse than blasphemy, what would be incoherent raving, if made in regard to any but Christ? Would any man at a supper devoted to the memory of Washington offer bread, and say: "Take, eat, this is Washington's body"? Would he use such language at all, or, if he did, could he mean thereby that the spirit of Washington, or his principles, or the efficacy of the work he had wrought through his oody, are the support of our civil life, as bread supports the natural life? These suppositions look so monstrous that we can hardly think of them gravely as they really are, that is as actual parallels to the mode of interpretation substituted for that of our Church, by men who pronounce our doctrine unscriptural. It is not overstating the fact to declare that as a question of the laws of language, apart from philosophical speculation or doctrinal system, the meaning of the words: "Take, eat, this is My body," are as clear as any passage from Genesis to Revelation. Dr. Hodge says that the words have been the subject of an immense amount of controversy, but so have been the clear words which teach the Trinity, the Divinity of our Lord, the eternity of future punishments; not that they are not clear, but that men will not admit them in their obvious sense. A doctrine is not proved to be disputable simply because it is disputed.

Finally, to put this point in a just light, suppose that our Lord at the Supper had said: "Take, eat, this is bread," and that men had arisen, who, in the face of this clear testimony, had said it was not bread of which He spoke, but His body, and His body only, how would the patrons of the Zwinglian theory, which in that case would have been related to the words supposed, as the Lutheran view now is to the words used, how would they have received such an interpretation? They would have received it with astonishment and reprobation, just as their own interpretation deserves to be regarded, when our Lord Jesus, stating what is that very thing for the reception of which the Supper was instituted, says: "Take, eat, this is My *body*." If our Master's words would have been clear according to the laws of language, in the terms we have, for illustration's sake, supposed Him to have used, then equally clear, according to the same laws, are the words which He did use. He who believes that the words *supposed* would have proved that our Lord desired to communicate to His disciples *bread*, must believe, if he be consistent, that the words He actually *used* prove that He desired to communicate to them His *body*. If he objects to the latter inference, then his objection is derived, not from the laws of language, but from philosophical or rationalistic principles, which he is determined shall override the clear word. Hence, we repeat the thought, and close this part of the argument with it, that the meaning of the terms of the Institution, as a pure question of language, is as clear as the meaning of any part of the Word of God — and that meaning is the one which our Church accepts and confesses. If the absolute authority of God's Word stands, the sacramental doctrine of our Church stands, for if it be incontrovertible that it is unsound to interpret, "This is bread," as meaning, "This is *not* bread, but is My body only," it is equally incontrovertible that it is unsound to interpret, "This is My body," as meaning, "This is not My body, but bread only."

2. The words of the Eucharist are also Testamentary — they are the *Words of the Will* of our Lord, who is about to die, and who invests His heirs with that whose possession gave them all that He desired to secure to them. But who ever heard of a *will* which bequeathed signs or symbols — not real possessions — to the heirs? If a will were produced in which the Testator had said: It is my wish and will that M. N. should have such and such a tract of land and so many thousand dollars; and when M. N. came to claim land and money, he was told that this "tract of land" was a sign or symbol of the Heavenly Canaan, which is the home of the soul, as an earthly

tract of land may be the residence of the body ; and that the thousands of dollars were simply a sign of incorruptible treasures in the other world ; and that the testator meant only that it was his wish and will that M. N. should have these good things of the other world, would he consider this sound interpretation ?   When Christ gives us Himself, He gives us everything.   His body and blood are the organs of His Deity.   In giving them to us He gives all to us; but in giving to us the mere signs of them, He would give us very little.   All bread is, as such, equally a symbol of His body ; all wine is a symbol of His blood.   Give us but these symbols at His Testamentary Supper, and we have at the Lord's Supper only what we may have at every meal.   What we want is Christ Himself, not symbols of Him.

But were the case less clear in regard to the Testamentary words, were it possible with equal propriety to embrace a strict or a loose acceptation of them, still the law holds good, that where a dispute arises in which it is impossible to settle which one of two meanings is the correct one, the preference shall be given to the more literal of the two ; and this rule is good here.   If we run the risk of erring, let it be by believing our Lord too far, too closely, too confidingly, rather than by doubting or by trying to explain away the natural import of His words.

3. The Lord's Supper is a *Covenanting* Institution.   But in a Covenant as in a Testament, the things mutually conveyed and received are not the signs nor symbols of things, but things themselves.   Whenever, as in the case of a will, disputes arise as to a literal or a laxer meaning, that interpretation, other things being equal, is always safest which adheres most closely to the very letter of the terms.

But the character of the covenanting words is yet further settled by their obvious allusion to the terms of the Old Covenant.   "Moses took the blood of calves and of goats, and sprinkled both the books and all the people, saying: This is the blood of the Testament which God hath appointed unto you."   It is with these words in His mind that our Lord says : "This is *My* blood (not the blood of calves and of goats) of the

New Testament" (not of the Old). Surely, if in the forming of the Old Covenant, which is a covenant of shadows, types and symbols, there was true blood, not the sign or symbol of blood, much more in the forming of the New Covenant, which is one of body, substance, and reality, we have not the symbol of blood, but the true blood of the great sacrifice.

4. Let us now look for a moment at the words of the Institution singly: "Take, eat; this is My body given for you." The Lutheran Church confesses that each word in this sentence is to be understood literally. The taking is a true taking, the eating a true eating. "This" means this — this which I tell you to take, this which I tell you to eat, this is, truly is, "My body," My true body truly given for My disciples. How have those who favored a symbolical interpretation evaded the natural force of these words?

Against a sense so natural, so direct, so universally received by the Holy Church of all ages, in its great assertion of an objective presence of Christ's body and blood, its opponents were bound to produce, not merely as probable a sense, but one more probable. They were bound in undertaking to shake the faith of Christendom, to produce an interpretation capable of a clear statement, and of invincible proofs. They were morally bound to have some agreement as to what was to be substituted for the received interpretation, and by what principles its necessity was to be demonstrated from God's Word. This they have attempted for nearly three centuries and a half, and up to this hour the failure has been total in every respect. Luther records seven of their conflicting interpretations. At the beginning of the seventeenth century there were twenty-eight contradictory views urged by Calvinists. Vorstius confessed that "he hardly knew whether the figure is in the copula or the predicate" — a confession really that he did not know that it is in either. But Zwingli happily suggests that among all their diversities, the opponents of the doctrine are agreed in the effort to throw down the citadel. So that is done, it matters little what arms are used. The efforts of our century have brought the opponents of the literal interpretation no nearer together. They are as far as ever from a fixed sense of the words, or a principle by which the sense can ever be fixed. There is no position midway between the implicit acceptance of the literal sense, and the chaos of eternal doubt.

The first view which was arrayed against that of our Church was the view of Carlstadt. He admitted the literal force of every term in the Institution, and interpreted thus: The Saviour said, "Take, eat," and came to a full pause. Then pointing, as it were, with His finger to His body, He uttered as a distinct proposition, "This body is My body." It is hardly necessary to add that so preposterous an interpretation found few friends. Zwingli himself rejected it, and Carlstadt withdrew it.*

The word TAKE these interpreters have usually construed literally, though why an imaginary body, or the symbol of a body, might not be taken mentally, they cannot say. Men do not open doors because a door is a symbol of Christ: why should they take and eat bread because it is a symbol of His body? A symbol is addressed to the mind; it derives its being and takes its shape from the mind of the user, and is intellectually received by the person to whom it is addressed. The mere symbol cannot be so identified with its object, as that an inference from the object is logically applicable to the symbol, or from the symbol, logically applicable to the object. We cannot say of one door more than another, "That door is Christ," but still less could we draw an inference from the symbol to the object, or from the object to the symbol.

The symbolic theory, even were we to grant its assumption, can give no intelligible reason for the statement, "*This* bread is My body; *This* cup is My blood," for as a symbol, this bread is no more Christ's body than any other bread; as one lamb, one vine, or one shepherd, is no more a symbol of Christ than another. The symbol is founded on the common quality of the thing symbolizing; the innocence of all lambs, the nutritious character of all bread, the means of access furnished by every door. It is evident that as it is only after Christ's blessing the bread, that it is true that "This," which He now commands us to "Take, eat," is His body — and that this

* Walch: Bibl. Theol. II. 419.

bread was just as much a symbol of His body before the blessing as after it, and was and is, just as much a symbol out of the
sacrament as in it — that the " this " cannot refer to the bread
merely, nor can the bread in the Supper be no more than a
symbol. There is true body and true bread, so related that
the true bread is the medium of the sacramental communion
of the true body, and for this reason only could it be true, that
" *this* " bread, more than any other, could be called the body
of our Lord. Just as it would be blasphemy to say, " Man is
God," and is yet literally true of Christ, " *This* man is God,"
so would it be blasphemy to say, " Bread is Christ's body," and
yet it is literally true, " *This* bread is Christ's body." *This*
man is God personally, because of the personal union, and *This*
bread is the body of Christ sacramentally because of the sacramental union. We cannot hand an *empty* purse and say,
" This is a thousand dollars ; " but we can hand a *full* one and
say so.

The word EAT they have interpreted literally, though why
the eating ought not to be done symbolically or mentally, to
correspond with the symbolical or mental character of the
body, they cannot say. Certainly there are plenty of instances
of a figurative use of the word " Eat," while there are none of
such a use of the word " is." The Quakers are more consistent.

The word "THIS," they have interpreted variously. The
renowned Schwenckfeld gets at its meaning by reading the
Saviour's words backwards thus: My body is this, that is,
My body is bread — nourishes the soul as real bread nourishes
the body. That is, he makes the subject " this," the predicate ;
and the predicate " My body," the subject. Those who have
entered the lists against the doctrine of our Church, usually
insist that " this " qualifies " bread " understood, that is, the
pronoun *touto*, which is neuter, qualifies the noun which is
masculine. Determined to be fettered by no laws of language,
they abrogate the rule — that a pronoun shall agree with the
noun it qualifies in gender.

Some theologians who have attacked the faith of our Church,
have, in order to make their work easy, been pleased to invent
arguments and positions for her. They have, of course, been

39

able to do with their imaginary arguments for her what they could not do with her real arguments for herself. They have found that upsetting the men of straw, of their own making, was very different from uprooting the everlasting foundations of the temple reared by God. One of these weak inventions is, that our Church adopts this ungrammatical construction of a neuter pronoun with a masculine noun, and that hence she after all deserts the literal sense of the word, and that her interpretation really is: "This (bread) is *not* My body, but *in*, *with*, and *under* it My body is given." But as the Church does not consider the neuter pronoun as qualifying the masculine noun, and does not interpolate the word bread, but takes our Lord's words precisely as He utters them, all this ingenuity is thrown away. It only shows how she might have argued, had she possessed as little grammar, as little logic, and as little reverence for her Master's words as is exhibited by such antagonists. From the words: "This is My body," she only gathers this: "This is Christ's body;" and neither on the one hand that the bread is not His body, nor on the other that His body is given in, with, and under it. She acknowledges that the *ecclesiastical* (not Biblical) phrase "*This* bread is Christ's body," sets forth a truth, as the Church uses and understands it; and from a comparison of text with text, she knows that the bread is the medium by which, in which, with which, under which the body is imparted, but she reaches this by no reading out of the text what is in it, nor reading into it, what is no part of it; but by interpreting every word in that natural and proper sense, which is fixed by the laws of language. Our Saviour says, Take, and we take; He says, Eat, and we eat; He says: This (which He has just told us to take, eat) is My body, and we believe it. The affirmation is as literal as the command, and we believe the one as we obey the other, to the letter, no more understanding His affirmation to be, This is *not* My body, than we understand His command to be, Do *not* take, Do *not* eat.

"*My body*," some have interpreted to mean "symbol of My body," but as this would make the Saviour say that the "symbol of His body," not His body itself, was given for us, the symbol of His blood, not His blood itself was shed for us, this view is generally abandoned. It was the view of Œcolampa dius, the Melanchthon of Zwingli in the Swiss Reformation, but far greater than his master. He was too good a scholar to be ignorant that the metaphor, if there be one, must lie in one of the nouns connected, and not in the substantive verb which connects them. As the bread was indubitably literal bread, he saw that he must either make " body " metaphorical, or aban don the idea of metaphor. The later divines of this general school rejected this theory with an earnestness which shows that they were ashamed of it. Thus BEZA :* " The v.ords which follow, to wit, ' which is given for you ' and ' which is shed for you,' compel us to understand the words of the very substance itself of the body and blood of Christ." " We do not doubt that by the term body is meant that very body which was assumed for our sakes and crucified." This view of Beza was, indeed, the view of the whole body of Calvinistic theologians, with few and inconsiderable exceptions. The sole refuge left, therefore, for the disputer of the doctrine of our Church, is in the word " IS." The word " is," Zwingli † and those who follow him say means " represents, signifies, is a symbol

---

* Epis. 5, ad Alaman. III. 202, and Adv. Illyricum, 217.

† Zwingli did not originate this interpretation. He adopted it from Honius, a contemporary whose name is now almost forgotten. Zwingli's account of the growth of his own theory is very interesting. He says: " I saw that the words ' This is My body,' are figurative, *but I did not see in what word the figure lay.* At this point, by the grace of God, it happened that two learned and pious men came to consult on this matter; and when they heard our opinion (for they had concealed their own, for it was not then safe to express opinions on the subject freely) they thanked God, and gave me an untied package, the letter of a learned and pious Hollander (Honius). *In it I found this precious pearl that ' is ' here means ' signifies.'* When we were compelled to explain our opinions openly it seemed more discreet to open with that key the word in which the figure lies, than sim ply to say: It is a figure."—*Opera, Turic.,* 1832. *Vol. III.* 606.

This frank history shows that Zwingli framed his theory first, and cherished it for some time before he could see how the Word of God was to be harmonized with it. Even when he came to see that " is " means " signifies," he could find no evidence of it, till it was revealed to him in that extraordinary vision of the man of dubious color, wb`   ·s so mercilessly ridiculed in the old contro versies.

of." Hence they draw the inference that our Saviour means :
" This [bread] [represents, is a symbol of] My body." Because
then it is to be a symbol of His broken body, He breaks this
bread, and because it is to be a symbol of His body given, He
gives this bread, and because it is to be a symbol of His body
taken, they take this bread — and what then? — because it is
to be a symbol of His body eaten, they eat this bread. The
symbol does not help its friends very far nor very long.

We have shown, that the laws of language forbid the application of the symbol here, even if the words in the abstract
would allow of it. We now go farther, and maintain that the
word " is " cannot have the sense of " signify or be a symbol
of." Taking the two terms as convertible, as they have
always been taken in this controversy by those who defend
them, we prove this : *

1. By the fact that no translations, ancient or modern, with
any pretension to character, so render the word. We assert,
after a careful examination of all of those that have most
reputation, that not one so translates the word, whether they
originate in the Eastern, Western, Lutheran, or Reformed
Churches. No man of character has ever dared to insert into
the text of his translation : This *is a symbol of* My body.
Where such terms as " means," " amounts to," or " signifies "
are used, though a superficial reader might imagine that they
are substituted for " is," they are really designed to express an
idea involved in the predicate. This use of them rests on the
fact that " is " always means " is." Twice two *amount to* four
means that twice two *are* four. Leo *signifies* lion, means that
Leo *is* lion. But we can neither say twice two signify four,
nor Leo amounts to lion, still less that twice two are a symbol
of four, or Leo is a symbol of a lion.

---

* Zwingli (De Vera et Falsa Relig. Opera, Turici., 1832. III. 257, 258): " This
signifies (significat) My body. . . This thing, to wit, which I offer you to eat, *is the
symbol* (symbolum est) of My body. . . This which I now command you to eat and
drink shall be to you *a symbol* (symbolum erit). . . As often as ye eat this *symbolic* bread (panem symbolicum) " — and so innumerably. " To be a symbol of,'
or " to signify " in the sense of " be a symbol of," is the characteristic, fixed
Zwinglian interpretation of the word " is."

2. No impartial dictionary of the Greek, whether general or New Testament, assigns such a meaning to the word. Where such a meaning is assigned, it is manifestly for the very purpose of promoting this false view, for doctrinal reasons, either rationalistic, as in such dictionaries as Schleusner's, or Zwinglian, as in Parkhurst's.

3. No good dictionary of the English assigns such a meaning to the English verb " to be ; " no good dictionary of the Hebrew or of any language of which we know anything, assigns such a meaning to the verb corresponding in each with our verb to be, or with the Greek Eimi.

4. The expositors and dogmaticians who, for philosophical or theological reasons, have been forced to maintain that the word " is " means " is a symbol of," have utterly failed to produce a *solitary instance* in which the word is so used.

Let us look at some of the passages that have been cited to prove that " is " may mean " is a symbol of." Passages such as these are favorites : " I *am* the vine, ye *are* the branches." " I *am* the door." " I *am* the bread of life." But if the word " **is** " means " is a symbol of," then Christ would say : " I *am the symbol* of a vine," " I *am the symbol* of a door," " I *am the symbol* of bread," which is absurd.

Nor do such passages as 1 Cor. x. 4, help the symbolical theory at all : " They all drank of that Spiritual Rock that followed (or went with them) : and that Rock was Christ." The meaning of that passage is, that the real spiritual Rock which attended them was the manifested Jehovah, that is, the second person of the Trinity, Christ Himself in His preëxistent state. God is a rock ; God is our true support ; our true support is God. The resolution into the literal *Metaphor.* lies in the word rock, not in the word " is." So when we say, Christ *is* the door, the vine, the foundation, the corner-stone, the resolution of the expression into what is absolutely literal, turns not upon the word " is," but on the word " door," " vine," or other noun, as the case may be. If you take Webster's Dictionary, or any other good dictionary, you will not find that the substantive verb " to be " means to signify, but you will find that the fifth meaning given to the word door is

" means of approach ; " and you will find it quotes, as proof of that meaning : " I am the door ; by Me if any man enter in, he shall be saved." But if when we say, Christ *is* the door, we do not mean Christ is the symbol of the door, neither can we mean, when we say the door is Christ, that the door is the symbol of Christ. We mean in the one case, that Christ is really and truly, not symbolically, the door — that is, He is the real means of approaching God ; and in the other, that the true and real means of approach, the real door, is truly (not symbolizes) Christ, That is, the predicate and subject are just the same in the second form of the sentence as in the first. " Christ " is the subject, " door " the predicate, in both ; but in the second there is an inversion of the more common order, in which the subject comes first. When I point to a particular door, and say, that door *is a symbol of* Christ, the word door is literal, and means a door of wood ; but when I say the door is Christ, the word door is not taken literally, but the word *is* must be so taken. Christ is the vine, the vine is Christ — Christ is not a symbol of the vine, but is the true vine itself; the true vine is not a symbol of Christ, but is Christ. We say that Washington was the pillar of his country, or the pillar of our country was Washington ; no more meaning that the pillar was a symbol of Washington, than that Washington was the symbol of a pillar ; but meaning that Washington was the true pillar of our country, and that the true pillar of our country was Washington ; the word pillar meaning in each case a support. We could not lay hold of a literal pillar and say : Lean on this, trust in this ; this is that General Washington who fought for our country. We could not bring a man to a vine and say : Attach yourself to this vine ; this is Christ: or direct him to a particular door, and say : Go through, enter in ; this door is Christ.

There is no parallel in the interpretation of DREAMS. " The three branches (are) three days." Gen. xl. 12. " The seven good kine (are) seven years, and the seven good ears (are) seven years." Gen. xli. 16. " The seven thin kine (are) seven years of famine." 1. There is no " are " in the original. 2. The " branches," " kine," and " ears " are not real branches, real kine, nor real ears, but the ideals of a dream. It is not three branches, but the three branches of the dream that are three days. The seven dream-branches, dream-kine, and dream-ears are, to speak literally — to drop the idea of a dream — seven years. 3. If "is," in interpreting Dreams. a dream, and because it so interprets, meant "signifies," it would have no bearing on the Lord's Supper, which is not the interpretation of a dream. 4. "The seven empty ears *shall* be seven years of famine." Does that mean "shall signify," as if they did not equally signify then? or does it mean that the empty ears, if we express what they really are and are to be, shall be "seven years of famine"? 5. Would the inference be justifiable from this dream, that: Take, eat; these are seven ears prepared for your food — means that there were no ears, but only symbols of ears? Pluck and strip; these are branches covered with delicious fruit — that there were no branches, no fruit, but symbols of them? If it would not, there is no parallel.

When Zwingli supposed that he saw that "is" means "signifies, is a symbol of," a formidable difficulty still stood in the way. He could not find a passage in the Old or New Testament in which it had that sense, when, as he expresses it, "it was not conjoined with a parable." "We began, therefore, to think over the whole, revolve the whole; still the examples which occurred were the same I had used in the Commentary (on True and False Religion), or of the same kind. I am about to narrate a fact — a fact of such a kind that I Zwingli's Reve-
lation. Ex. xii. 11. would wish to conceal it, *but conscience compels me to pour forth what the Lord has imparted, though I know to what reproach* and ridicule I am about to expose myself. On the thirteenth of April I seemed to myself, in a dream, to contend with an adversary, a writer, and to have lost my power of speech, so that what I knew to be true my tongue failed me in the effort to speak. . . Though, as concerns ourselves, it be no more than a dream we are telling, yet it is no light thing that we were taught by a dream, thanks be to God, to whose glory also we are telling these things. We seemed to be greatly disturbed. At this point, from a machine," (the theatrical appa ratus by which supernatural persons were made to appear in the air,) "an adviser was present (whether he was black or white I do not at all remember; for it is a dream I am telling), who said: You weakling! answer him that in Exod. xii. 11, it is written: ' *It is the Phase*—that is, the Passing over of the Lord.' On the instant that this apparition showed itself I sprung from my couch. I first examined the passage thoroughly in the Septuagint, and preached upon it before the whole congregation with all my strength. This sermon dispelled the doubts of the students, who had hesitated because of the obstacle of the parable " (that " is " meant " signify " only when a Parable was explained). " Such a Passover of Christ was celebrated on those three days as I never saw, and the number of those, it is thought, who look back to the garlic and flesh-pots of Egypt is going to be far less."* This narrative speaks for itself. Zwingli confesses that he came to the Scripture to find argument for opinions already formed — opinions held, while the search in which he was engaged for something to sustain them was still fruitless. He claims, evidently, the character of a supernatural revelation for his dream; and there is something inimitable in the simple egotism of his expectation that his discovery is going to damage the cause of the hankerers after the flesh-pots of Egypt, by which he gracefully designates Luther and the Conservative Church of the Reformation. And yet the passage which to Zwingli seemed so decisive does not help him in the least. In the words, Exod. xii. 11, " It (*is*) the Lord's Passover," Zwingli assumes that " it " means " the lamb," and that the sentence consequently results: " The lamb is the Passover," that is, the lamb signifies, or is the sign or symbol of the Passover. But 1: The word " is " is not there. This was at once objected to Zwingli's view by those whom he styles " the brawlers " (vitilitigatores). He meets it by maintaining that " no one, unless he be ignorant of Hebrew, is unaware that Hua and Hayo, Hamah and Hanah, are constantly taken for ' he *is*,' ' it *is*,' ' they are,' where they are not conjoined with the verb."† But the answer was not to the point. Zwingli was to furnish a passage from the Word of God in

* Zwinglii Opera. Turici. 1832. III. 341.   † Opera. III. 344.

which "is" means "a symbol of." The passage on which he relies does not have the word "is" at all. He replies in effect, the Word is understood, and *if it were there it would have that sense.* But the fact that it is not there shows that it is the mere substantive copula, and can have no such sense as Zwingli claims. If "is" be involved in the subject, then all symbolical possibility *must* lie in the predicate. Zwingli makes no appeal to the Septuagint on this point: First, because the thing demanded was an instance of a *divine* use of "is" in the sense "be a symbol of." It was acknowledged, on the conservative side, that the Hebrew substantive verb has the same general force in the Greek, and, therefore, Zwingli appealed to the Hebrew. He could not appeal *here* to the Septuagint, for it is but a human translation. The question was not one of Greek, but of the divine use of the substantive verb, common to both Hebrew and Greek. Second: Apart from this, the Septuagint is decisive against Zwingli, for it makes the proposition imper sonal: "Passover is to the Lord," not at all: "The Lamb is the passover." 2: The "it" does not refer to the lamb — but to the whole transaction which takes place with girded loins, and the eating of the lamb. The "it" is used indefinitely, as if we would say, "Let us gather round the cheerful hearth, let us light up the children's tree, for it is Christmas." The reason of the name "Passover" follows in the twelfth verse. "It is the Lord's Passover. For I will pass through the land." What sense is there in the words: The lamb is a symbol of the Passover, for I will pass through it? 3: In no sense in which the word "Passover" could hold, whether in the act of angelic transition, or the feast instituted to commemorate it, could the lamb signify, or be a symbol of it. The lamb was that whose body was literally slain, and whose blood was literally shed, in making the Passover Covenant. It was not a symbol of the passing over of the angel, for there is no analogy between a slain lamb and a passing over. It was not a symbol of the Feast of the Passover, but the chief material of the feast. Nor was the lamb a memorial of the original passing over. The Passover feast itself, as a whole, was. Nor was the lamb a memorial of this feast, but simply a chief ele-

ment in it. 4: The word " Passover " here means the festival,
not the transition itself. 5: If the lamb could be called the
Passover feast, it would be so called, not because the lamb signified the feast, but because the feast was made on the lamb.
6: If the words had been used at an actual supper, and had
been " Take, eat, This is the body of the Paschal Lamb slain
for you," could Zwingli's interpretation of the verse in question overthrow the literal meaning of " is " in them ? If not,
there is no parallel.

The ALLEGORY seems no better as a parallel. The allegory
leads us into a world where a being or thing is the designed
ideal representative of another. The bundle on
Christian's back is the burden of sin. The lions
are terrors in the way. Vanity Fair is the godless world, the
dark river is death — that is, says the slovenly interpreter, sig
nifies or is a sign of. Now an actual burden in real life may
be a symbol of a spiritual burden ; living lions may be symbols
of the terrible ; a real river a symbol of death ; but the bundle,
lions, river of the allegory are as ideal as the symbol. In an
allegory, moreover, the framer has the reality in his mind
before the ideal representative. The real is throughout the
subject, the allegorical representative the *predicate*. Hence, to
put them in their proper attitude both as to time and logical relation, we should say the burden of sin is the bundle on Christian's back ; the terrors are the lions ; death is the dark river.
That is the meaning even in the inverted order in which we
first put them — but the burden of sin is not the symbol of a
bundle — death not the symbol of a river. Hence the structure of an allegory not only does not sustain the Zwinglian
interpretation of the words of the institutor, but overthrows
it — for it demonstrates that the subject is not the symbol of
the predicate, but Zwingli's theory assumes that it is. But
were it otherwise, the Lord's Supper is no allegory.

A more dangerous falsity in interpretation, than the assumption that the word " is " may be explained in the sense of " sig
nify," or " be a symbol of," is hardly conceivable. Almost
every doctrine of the Word of God will melt under it. " The
Word *was* God " would mean " The Word signified was a

Allegory.

symbol of God." "God is a Spirit" would mean "God is the symbol of a Spirit." When it is said of Jesus Christ: "This is the true God," it would mean that He is the symbol or image of the true God. By it Christ would cease to be the way, the truth, and the life, and would be a mere symbol of them ; would no longer be the door, the vine, the Good Shepherd, the Bishop of Souls, but would be the symbol of a door, the sign of a vine, the figure of a shepherd, the representation of a Bishop This characteristic of the use of "is" is essential to the very morality of language, and language itself would commit suicide if it could tolerate the idea that the substantive verb shall express not substance but symbol. Creation, Redemption, and Sanctification would all fuse and be dissipated in the crucible of this species of interpretation. It would take the Bible from us, and lay upon our breasts, cold and heavy, a Swedenborgian nightmare of correspondences. The Socinian, and the Pelagian, and all errorists of all schools, would triumph in the throwing of everything into hopeless confusion, and the Infidel would feel that the Book he has so long feared and hated, deprived, as it now would be, of its vitality by the trick of interpreters, could, henceforth, be safely regarded with contempt.

Well might Luther write upon the table at Marburg: "This is My body ;" simple words, framed by infinite wisdom so as to resist the violence and all the ingenuity of men. Rationalism in vain essays to remove them with its cunning, its learning, and its philosophy. Fanaticism gnashes its teeth at them in vain. They are an immovable foundation for faith in the Sacramental mystery, and the gates of hell cannot shake the faith of the Church, that our Lord Jesus with the true body and true blood which He gave for our redemption on the Cross, is truly present in the Holy Supper, to *apply* the redemption through the very organs by which it was *wrought out.* The sacrifice was made once for all — its application goes on to the end of time. The offence of the Master's Cross now rests upon His table, and thither the triumph of the Cross shall follow it. On the Cross and at the table the saints discern the body of the Lord, and in simple faith are determined to know in both nothing but Jesus Christ and Him crucified.

The Tenth Article of the Augsburg Confession declares that
the true body and blood of Christ are truly present
in the Supper " UNDER THE FORM (*unter der Gestalt*)
OF BREAD AND WINE." The word " form " and the
German word " *Gestalt*," which it translates, are
renderings, confessedly, of the Latin term " species." The Apology (164, 54, 57: illis rebus quæ videntur,
sichtbaren Dingen), giving an equivalent of the word " species "
or " form," defines it, " those things which are seen, the visible things, bread and wine," and the Formula of Concord (674,
126) speaks of " the elements or visible species or form of the
consecrated bread and wine." The word " species " belongs to
the common terms of Theology, and is used by Roman Catholic, Lutheran, and Zwinglian authors It is used, for example,
in the articles of the Marburg Colloquy, which were signed by
Zwingli. In classic Latin, " species " not only means " a form,"
but " an object presented to the sight; " not only " figure,"
but the " nature of a thing." It also has the meaning " kind; "
hence the phrase " communion in both kinds," " both species.'
So in English we use the words " species " and " kind " as
convertible.

*III. The Spe-
cies of Bread and
Wine. Transub-
stantiation; Ro-
manism; and Ra-
tionalism.*

The emphasis in the Tenth Article is not on the word *species*,
but on *bread* and *wine* — not as if it meant the *species, not the
reality ;* but, on the contrary, the species or kinds of *true bread*
and *true wine*, not *of the accidents* of them. In a word, it asserts
that the visible objects in the Lord's Supper are real bread and
real wine. The doctrine of the Confession is that the visible
and earthly *element* in the Lord's Supper is *true bread* and *true
wine* (*not* their *accidents*), as the invisible and heavenly element
is the body and blood of Christ (not their *symbols*, nor the
memory of them, nor *their spiritual virtue*).

The words, FIRST OF ALL, reject the doctrine of *Transubstantiation.*

SECONDLY : They repudiate the Romish doctrine of *sacramental concomitance*, to wit: that because of their *natural association*, or concomitance, both the body and blood of Christ are
given, with each of the species *sacramentally*, that is, with the
bread both body and blood are given *sacramentally*, and with

the wine both blood and body are given *sacramentally*. The Confession implies that the body only is given *sacramentally* by the bread, the blood only is *sacramentally* given by the wine, that from a natural concomitance we cannot argue to a *sacramental* one, for the *sacramental* is wholly supernatural, and its character depends on the will of Christ, who has appointed one species for the *sacramental* impartation of His body, the other for the *sacramental* impartation of His blood. If *natural* concomitance were identical with *sacramental* impartation, it would follow that our Lord had appointed the cup needlessly; that the priest receives in the Mass the body and blood twice, the blood by concomitance with the species of bread, and the body by concomitance with the species of wine. And if a *natural* concomitance holds good for the *sacramental* character of the bread in communion, it would hold equally good for its *sacrificial* character in the Mass. One kind in the Supper would logically justify one kind in the Mass.

THIRDLY : In this the Confession implies that the two species or kinds, bread and wine, must both be used in order to having a complete communion, and thus the doctrine is set forth, which involves a rejection of the Romish abuse of the denial of the cup, a denial which applies not only to the laity, but to the *communicant*, whether lay or priestly. The priestly offerer of the *sacrifice* of the Mass drinks of the cup, in making the *sacrifice*, but when the same man approaches the table as a communicant, he receives only the bread.*

* As this distinction, though very important, is so little noticed, even by controversialists, and is so little known, as often to excite surprise among intelligent Protestants, the author addressed a note to Prof. George Allen (whose accuracy as a scholar can only be equalled by his courtesy as a gentleman), asking of him for the facts of the usage in the Roman Catholic Church, of which he is a member, which illustrate what we have asserted. From him we obtained the following statements: 1. There is not so properly a denial of the cup to the laity, as such, as a restriction of it to the celebrant in the Mass. 2. When a priest receives the Viaticum, the Communion on his death-bed, he does not receive the cup. 3. On Holy Thursday, in each diocese, the bishop celebrates, and the priests receive the Holy Communion only in one kind — they do not receive the cup. 4. In the Mass of the Presanctified (on Good Friday), the celebrant himself receives only in one kind. 5. The only occasion on which the cardinals receive the cup in communing, is when the Pope celebrates on Holy Thursday; and this is done on the ground "that in the Feast of the Institution of the Blessed Sacrament,

FOURTHLY: In limiting the presence of the body and blood first to the communicants (*vescentibus*), and secondly, to them *in* the Lord's Supper (*adsint in Cœna*), the Confession implies that nothing has a sacramental character apart from its sacramental use: That the presence of the body and blood of Christ is such that only the communicants can actualize it — it is not a presence for mice and worms, but for man: and that this presence is limited to the Supper: The body and blood of Christ cannot be reserved, laid up in monstrances, or carried in procession, any more than the Holy Ghost can be laid up in a Bible, or carried about in one.

FIFTHLY: In this denial of a change of the elements, and in the maintenance that the presence is one to be actualized *solely* by the *sacramental eating and drinking*, is involved the rejection of the doctrine that the species in the Supper are to be worshipped, or that Christ Himself is to be worshipped as in the species. We can and should worship Christ at His table, but precisely as we worship Him away from it. He did not say, Take, worship, but, Take, eat. He did not say, This is My Divinity, but this is My body, and the bread which we break is not the shrine of His Deity, but the "Communion of His body." The presence of Christ, which is *distinctive* of the Sacrament, is *sacramental* only, that is to say, we reach Christ there as we reach Him nowhere else, only as His will makes a specific difference. We commune in His broken body and His shed blood there, as it is impossible to commune with them elsewhere, but we can worship Christ there in no other mode than we worship Him everywhere.

On the FIRST of these points, as conditioning all the rest, we

they, on that day, represent the chosen disciples." 6. The canons of the Council of Trent, Sess. XXI., Can. II., say: "Si quis dixerit, sanctam ecclesiam catholicam non justis causis et rationibus adductam fuisse, ut laicos *atque etiam clericos non conficientes* sub panis tautummodo specie communicaret, aut in eo errasse: anathema sit."

These facts compel a candid Protestant to admit, upon the one hand, that simply as a communicant, as distinct from an offerer of the Sacrifice, simply as one who comes to receive and not, also, to impart a benefit, the priest is put by the Roman Catholic Church precisely on the same level as the layman; but they also do much to intensify the feelings of a Protestant that there is both to priest and people an exclusion from the *communion* in both kinds — the people never receive the cup, and the priesthood never receive it as communicants.

shall dwell more fully than on the others. The word " Tran-substantiation " was as unknown to pure antiquity as the doctrine couched under it. It first appears in the Twelfth Century. The first official use of the term was made in the Lateran Council of 1215. The doctrine of Tran- Transubstantia- ubstantiation affirms that at the consecrating tion rejected. words the substance of bread and wine ceases to be, and in their place, clothed with their accidents or properties, are the body, blood, soul, and divinity of our Lord Jesus Christ; no bread, but simply Christ's body, looking like bread, tasting like bread, feeling like bread, nourishing the body like bread, corrupted like bread, eaten by mice like bread, conjoined with poison killing the body like poisoned bread, bearing on it the baker's mark like bread; but no bread, only body; that there is no wine, but Christ's blood, smelling like wine, red if the wine have been red, white if the wine have been white, intoxicating like wine, spilling like wine, leaving permanent stains like wine, poisoning, if mixed with poison, like poisoned wine, pronounced by chemical analysis to be wine, depositing the acids and salts like wine, but throughout no wine. The doctrine of Transubstantiation is a doctrine not only untaught in the Scriptures, but directly in conflict with their letter. It is in conflict with the analogy of faith, overthrowing logically indubitable parts of the faith; it is in conflict with the nature of a sacrament, to which are required two real elements, the real earthly as well as the real heavenly; it is in conflict with a fair parallel with Holy Baptism, in which it is not pretended by the Church of Rome that there is any transubstantiation of the water; it is a doctrine utterly unknown to Christian antiquity, the demonstrable invention of ages of corruption, resisted by many of the greatest theologians even under the Papacy, and the nurse of superstition, and of the grossest idolatry; it is in conflict with the testimony of the senses, subversive of all the laws of moral evidence, and by overstretching faith into credulity, tends to produce by reaction, universal skepticism. An acute nation which swings into Transubstantiation, may swing out of it into Atheism.

This doctrine of the mediæval Church of Rome was very early, and very positively, rejected by Luther, and our other

great Reformers. In 1520, Luther, in his book on the Baby-
.onish Captivity, says: "For more than twelve hundred years
the Church held the right faith," (in regard to the Lord's
Supper,) "and never do the holy *fathers* make mention of that
portentous word and *dream*, Transubstantiation." In 1522, in
his book against Henry VIII., he says, "What they (the
Romanists) hold in regard to *Transubstantiation* is the merest
figment of the godless and blind Thomists;" and again, "I
declare it to be *impious* and *blasphemous* for any one to assert
that the bread is transubstantiated." It were easy, if need
were, to fill pages with testimony of this kind; but it is
needless.

The Romanists, in their Confutation, objected to the Tenth
Article that it does not teach Transubstantiation, and, what
they there say, or what was said by their great theological
representatives at the Diet, is most important as showing how
the Confession was there understood, and, of course, how it is
to be understood now. An examination of their official Confutation at once silences the pitiful old libel that the Roman
Catholics accepted the Tenth Article *without reservation*. The
latest repeater of this ignorant, if not malicious, assertion, is
Rev. Wm. Good, by whom it has been the great misfortune
of the Low Church Party in England to seem to be represented. He quotes, at second hand we judge, (from the pages
of one of the bitterest zealots against the Lutheran Church,)
four words, drawn from the Papal Confutation, which would
lead his readers to suppose that the Papists simply assented
to the Tenth Article as being sound, and hence he draws the
inference that the Article teaches the Romish view. All this
is built on an isolation of four words out of more than a hundred. The Romish Confutation, so far as it bears upon this
point, literally translated, runs thus:

"The Tenth Article *in words* offends nothing, when they
confess that in the Eucharist, after consecration legitimately
made, the body and blood of Christ are substantially and truly
present, *provided that* (*si modo*) they believe, that under *each*
species, the entire Christ is present, so that by *concomitance*, the
blood of Christ is no less under the species of bread than it is
under the species of wine, and so of the other. Otherwise in

the Eucharist, the body of Christ would be bloodless, contrary to St. Paul, that Christ, being raised from the dead, dieth no more. Rom. vi.

" *One thing is to be added as an Article exceedingly necessary* (*valide necessarium*) to this Confession, that they shall believe the Church (rather than some who falsely teach otherwise), that by the omnipotent Word of God, in the consecration of the Eucharist, the *substance of the bread is changed into the body of Christ.*"

Here it is clear, first, that so far as the Romanists give their approval at all to the Tenth Article, it is of the most reserved kind. First, they speak of the " words " only, as not offensive on the one point that there is a true presence. It is the only case in which they qualify their approval by terms which imply a suspicion that " the words " may not fairly convey what is meant. Hoffmeister, indeed, expresses this insinuation, " unless, indeed, they wish to impose upon us by a likeness of words."

Second, They declare that even these words are not offensive, solely, if they be so interpreted as to include the idea of concomitance, which it is not pretended they express ; they carefully note that the Article *does not teach Transubstantiation*, in this acknowledging that the doctrine is not implied, as has been pretended, in the word " species." In fact, as the Confession does not teach concomitance, but by implication rejects it, the Romish Confutation does not really endorse heartily a single word of it.

The discussion of the Tenth Article by John Cochlæus, sheds no less light on the understanding of the Article by the Romanists at the time. This bitter enemy of the Reformation, who was one of those who drew up the Confutation, says : " Though that Article be brief, *there are many things of which we complain as wanting in it* (*multa tamen in eo desideramur*). Luther frivolously denying Transubstantiation, though in words he disputes at large against Zwingli and Œcolampadius, *yet in the thing itself,* he thinks with them, and is in collusion with them (*cum eis colludit*). And Luther's followers have reached such a pitch of madness, that they *refuse longer to adore the Eucharist,* because Luther has impiously taught that it is safer not to

40

adore, and has openly *denied the doctrine of concomitance.* **And**
now they have proceeded in the fury of their impiety to such
a degree as to deny that the body of Christ remains in the
consecrated Host, except in the use at the altar (*extra altaris
usum*). Hence they falsely and impiously call us idolaters,
because we retain the body of the Lord in the consecrated
Host in the Tabernacles (*Cibariis*) for infirm Communicants, or
when we bear it (the body) about in monstrances and processions." He quotes Melanchthon's words in the Apology, "with
those things which are seen, the bread and wine," as flagrantly
contradictory of Transubstantiation (*turpiter contradicit sibi
ipsi*).*

In this connection it is worth noticing that, widely as Romanism, with its Transubstantiation, and Rationalism, with its
Symbol, differ in their results, they run into their error by the
same fallacious principle of interpretation — each applying it
with the same arbitrariness, but to different objects. The
Romanist wishes to do away with the Scripture testimony
in regard to the bread and wine; and, although they bear

*On the History and Literature of the Papal Confutation, which has great
value in the interpretation and defence of the Augsburg Confession, see the works
following:

BRILL: Auf d. evangel. Augapfel, 1629. 4to. (the German translation of the work
of Fabricius Leodius mentioned below). — DANZ: Augsburg Confess., Jena, 1829.
12mo. § 6. — CHYTRÆUS. Hist. Aug. Conf., 119. (Confutation, 173, seq.) Ger.
Edit., 1577, p. 191. — CŒLESTINUS l. 192 seq. Confutation III. — CYPRIAN. 87
seq. — FEUERLIN: Biblioth Symbol. — FICKENSCHER: Gesch. d. Reichst. z. Augsburg, 1830, III. 324. — FOERSTEMANN: Urkundenbuch, 2 vols. 8vo. Halle, 1835,
II. 133–176. — FRANCKE: Lib. Symb. Eccl. Luth. Lips. 1847. Proleg. 12mo.
xxx.-xxxiii. (Confutation, Append. 43–69.) — GABLER: Nst. Theol. Jour., 1801,
443 seq. — HASE: Lib. Symb. Eccles. Evangel. Lips. 1827, 2 vols. 12mo. Proleg.
lxxiv.-lxxvi. The Confutation, lxxvi.-cxiv. — HOFFMAN: Comment. in A. C.
Tubing., 1727. 4to. 205–213. — KÖLLNER: Symb. d. Luther. Kirche. Hamb. 1837,
p. 397–416. — MÜLLER, C. C.: Formulæ Confutationis A. C. Lat. German. Lips.,
1808, 8vo. — MÜLLER, J. J.: Hist. v. Protest. u. A. C. Jena, 1705, 4to. p. 653. —
PFAFF: Lib. Symbol. Eccl. Luth. — PLANCK: Protest. Lehrbeg. III. I. 52 seq. —
ROTERMUND: Gesch. d. z. Augsb. übergeb. Glaubensbek. Hannov. 1829, 8vo.
109–116. — SALIG: I. 224 seq. 378 seq. — SECKENDORF: Hist. Luth. II. 171. —
SEMLER: Apparat. in L. S. p. 73. — SPIEKER, C. G.: Conf. Fidei. Confutatio., etc.
Berlin, 1830. 8vo. 149–204. — WALCHII, J. G.: Introd. in L. S. 416. Miscel-
lan. Sacra. 205. — WEBER: Krit. Gesch. II. Vorred., and p. 489.

their name *before* the Lord's Supper, *during* the Lord's Supper, and *after* the Lord's Supper, he insists that there is neither bread nor wine there, but only their accidents. While our Lord says: " This is my body," the Romanist in effect makes it : This seeming bread is no longer bread, but has become, has been transubstantiated into, My body. He deserts the letter and reaches Transubstantiation. The Rationalist wishes to retain the bread and wine, and therefore holds that what the Scripture *calls* bread and wine, *is* bread and wine; but he wishes to do away with the Scripture testimony in <small>Romanism and</small> regard to the body and blood; and although the <small>Rationalism. Their principle</small> Scripture says, that of that which the Saviour tells <small>here the same.</small> them to Take, eat, He declares most explicitly, This is My body; and of that which He tells them to drink, He says, This is My blood — though it says that the bread is the communion of His body and the cup the communion of His blood — though it declares that the guilt of the heedless communi' cant is that he does not " discern the Lord's body," and that he that eateth and drinketh unworthily is guilty of the body and blood of Christ; in the face of all this he insists that there is in the Lord's Supper only the shadow, image, or sign of the body and blood of Christ, not the true body and true blood. With what face can a Rationalist meet a Romanist, or a Romanist meet a Rationalist? No wonder that the Rationalist, after all, is less violent against Romanism than against the pure doctrine of our Church. There is the secret affinity of error between them; and Romanism does not so hate Rationalism, Rationalism does not so hate Romanism, as both hate unswerving fidelity to the Word of God. That the Romish and rationalizing modes of interpretation are nearer to each other than either is to the Lutheran, is admitted by both Rationalists and Romanists. The rationalizing interpreters make it one of the common-places of objection to the Lutheran view that it has *less* in a literal interpretation of the Scripture to sustain it than the Romish view has: that is, the Romish view is less decisively opposed than the Lutheran is to rationalistic modes of literal interpretation.

On the Romish side, Bellarmine and others take the ground

that right principles of interpretation lead either to Romanistic or Calvinistic views of the Supper. As both these have the common ground that the proposition of the Supper is: "This bread is Christ's body," and as both argue that real bread cannot be real body, the one escapes the difficulty by maintaining that there is no real bread in the Supper, the other that there is no real body there: or, in other words, the Romanist, Zwinglian, and Calvinist agree in an exegetical principle, and simply vary in the application of it.

A single citation from two great authorities, the first Roman Catholic, the second Calvinistic, will demonstrate this. BEL-LARMINE, in his Discussion of the Sacrament of the Eucharist, ch. xix., says, "These words: 'This is My body,' necessarily lead to the inference either that there is a *true mutation of the bread*, as the CATHOLICS will have it, or a *metaphorical mutation*, as the CALVINISTS will have it; but in no way admit of the LUTHERAN view."

URSINUS, in his Explanation of the Catechism, II., Q. 78: " As it is not true that the Papists retain the verbally literal, so it is *much less true (multo minus verum)* that those (Lutherans) retain the letter and true sense of the words." " The letter is: ' This, that is, this bread, is My body ; ' the meaning is, ' That visible, broken, and distributed bread is My true and essential body.' But as this cannot be by essential conversion, but mystically or by sacramental metonomy, because the words, according to the verbally literal, have a sense repugnant to the verity of the Christian faith, therefore we say, that in the words of Christ a fitting (*conveniens*) meaning is to be taught." Do. p. 541. This, then, is the genesis of the two views: Body cannot be bread, but as there *is* body there is no bread: bread cannot be body, but as there *is* bread there is no body.

With such a principle, only a third possibility remains: it is to apply it rigidly and consistently to every part of the Institution, to take away the bread with the Romanist, and the body with the Rationalist, and then we have the Lord's Supper of the Quaker and other mystics, with neither supernatural reality nor outward element—all idea, all spirit. The extravagance of the Romish materializing of the presence of Christ's body, and of the rationalistic exaggeration, which leaves only natural matter, run into the nihilism of the mystic. You can. not annihilate either element in the Lord's Supper without annihilating both.

In the doctrine of Transubstantiation, nevertheless, as in almost all of her corruptions, the Church of Rome has not so much absolutely removed the foundation, as hidden it by the wood, hay, and stubble of human device. Truth can sometimes be reached by running the corruptions of it back to the trunk on which they were grafted. Such an error as that of Transubstantiation could never have been grafted on an original faith like that of Zwingli in regard to the Lord's Supper. The tendency of the Zwinglian view, if it be corrupted, is to laxer, not to higher, views of the sacramental mystery. Such an error as the doctrine of the immaculate conception of the Virgin Mary never could have been grafted on a faith originally Socinian. It is a corruption which presupposes as a truth, to be corrupted in its inference, the divinity and sinlessness of our Lord Jesus Christ; and just as the comparatively modern corruption of the worship of the Virgin is a proof that faith in the Godhead of Jesus Christ was part of the primitive faith, so does the comparatively modern corruption of Transubstantiation prove that faith in the objective supernatural presence of the body and blood of our Lord was part of the primitive faith. A rotten apple always presupposes a sound apple. However corrupt a fig may be, we know that it grew on a fig-tree, and not on a thistle.

Our fourth proposition in the analytic exhibition of the doctrine of the Augsburg Confession is:

That the true body and blood of Christ, truly present in the Lord's Supper, under the species of bread and wine, *are communicated.**

IV. The Sacramental Communion of the Body and Blood of Christ — Zwinglian and Calvinistic Views—Concessions of unLutheran writers.

We have virtually proved this proposition in proving the three which preceded it. Nevertheless, in the affluence of Scripture evidence sustaining the doctrine of our Church, we can well afford

* German, ausgetheilt: Lat., distribuantur. In the Apology; Lat., exhibeantur; German, dargereicht.

to give this thesis a distinct vindication. We affirm, then, that this fourth proposition is explicitly taught in 1 Cor. x. 16: " The cup of blessing which we bless, is it not the communion [κοινωνία] of the blood of Christ? The bread which we break, is it not the communion [κοινωνία] of the body of Christ?" This passage, in its express terms and in its connection, is what Luther calls it — a thunderbolt upon the heads of error-ists in regard to the Lord's Supper. The figment of Transub-stantiation is overthrown by it, for it expressly mentions bread, and that which communicates cannot be identical with that which is communicated by it. St. Paul expressly mentions the two elements; the bread, which is the earthly; the body of our Lord, which is the heavenly; the sacramental union, and the impartation of the heavenly in, with, and under the earthly. The passage equally overthrows all the Rationalistic corruptions of the doctrine. Zwingli says: The bread is the *sign* of the body; Paul says: The bread is the *communion* of the body; Zwingli says: The wine is the *sign* of the blood; Paul says: The cup is the *communion* of the blood. On Zwingli's theory, any and all bread is, as such, the sign of Christ's body; on Paul's theory, it is the bread which *we break*, that is, the sacramental bread only, which is the communion of Christ's body; on Zwingli's theory, any wine and all wine is, as such, the sign of Christ's blood; on Paul's theory, only the cup *of blessing, which we bless*, in the Supper, is the com-munion of Christ's blood; on Zwingli's theory, the relation of the bread and body is that of symbol and of reality ; on Paul's theory, it is the relation of communicating medium and of the thing communicated; on Zwingli's theory, we receive the cup to be reminded of the blood; on Paul's theory, we receive the cup to receive the blood. On Zwingli's theory, the argument of the Apostle is sophistical and pointless in the last degree, for as all bread is equally an emblem of Christ's body as food for the soul, and all wine equally an emblem of Christ's blood as the refreshing of the soul, any and every eating of bread, and any and every drinking of wine, would be the communion of His body and blood; therefore, to eat bread and to drink wine at the table of Demons, would be, on Zwingli's theory of symbol, to have communion with Christ's body and blood; for bread is a symbol of nourishment, wine a symbol of refreshing, without reference to the time or place of receiving them; their whole character as symbols depends on what bread is, as bread — on what wine is, as wine; and the Corinthian could make the table of Demons a Lord's Supper by the simple mental act of thinking of the bread and wine as symbols of Christ's body and blood. A vine, as a symbol of Christ, is equally a symbol, whether it grows on the land of devil-worshippers or of Christians; bread, as a symbol of Christ's body, is equally a symbol, whether baked by Atheist, Jew, or Pagan; whether eaten at the table of Demons or at the table of the Lord. The logic of Zwingli's position is, then, exactly the opposite of that of the Apostle, and would make his conclusion in the last degree absurd.

Equally do the words overthrow the Calvinistic theory. Calvin's theory is, that the Holy Spirit communicates the body of Christ; Paul's is, that the bread communicates it; he mentions but two elements, bread and body. Calvin says, the Holy Spirit communicates the blood of Christ; Paul says, that the cup communicates it, two elements only again, cup and blood, not three: cup, Holy Spirit, and blood. Calvin makes faith the communicating medium; Paul says, the bread we break, the cup we bless, is the communicating medium. Calvin makes the communion of the body and blood of Christ, one which is confined to worthy recipients, true believers, while to all others there is but the communication of bread and wine; Paul is speaking of what the communion also is to some who "eat and drink unworthily," "not discerning the Lord's body," "eating and drinking damnation to themselves," "guilty of the body and blood of the Lord," and yet he affirms that to them the bread communicates the body, the cup, the blood of Christ. Calvin's communion is one which can take place anywhere and always, inasmuch as the Holy Spirit is always present, and faith can always be exercised; Paul's is expressly limited to that with which the bread and cup are connected. Calvin's is a communion of the virtue and efficacy of the body and blood of Christ; Paul's is a communion of the body and blood themselves. Calvin's is the communion of an absent body and blood; Paul's the communion of a present body and blood, so present that bread, broken and given, imparts the one, and the cup, blessed and taken, imparts the other. Calvin talks of a faith by which we spiritually eat an absent body, Paul of elements by which we sacramentally eat a present body.

As by Zwingli's theory, so by Calvin's also, the argument of the Apostle here is emptied of all force. For the argument of the Apostle is addressed to those who eat and drink unworthily, that is to those who had not faith. The very necessity of the argument arises from the presupposition of a want of true faith in the Lord, on the part of those to whom it was addressed. But on the Calvinistic theory the communion of the body and blood of Christ, and participation in them, are confined to those who have faith. These Corinthians, therefore, had St. Paul taught them a theory like that of Calvin, might have replied: "Oh, no! as we are without true faith, and are receiving unworthily, we receive nothing but bread and wine, but as bread and wine were not the sacrifices which Christ offered to God, we do not come into fellowship with God's altar by partaking of *them* — therefore we are not guilty of what you charge on us, to wit, the inconsistency of eating and drinking at the same time, of the sacrifices offered on God's altar, and of the sacrifices offered on the altar of Demons." The Calvinistic theory makes the argument of the Apostle an absurdity.

Two parallels in the connection help to bring out very vividly the Apostle's idea. One is the parallel with Israel: v. 18. " Behold Israel after the flesh: are not they which *eat of the sacrifices* partakers of the altar?" The point seems to be most clearly this: that the communion of the body of Christ in the Supper is as real as the eating of the animal sacrifices in the Jewish Church. Christ's body is the true sacrifice which takes once for all the place of the Jewish sacrifices, and the sacramental communion, in which that body is the sustenance, in ever-renewing application of the one only sacrifice, takes the place of the Jewish eating of the sacrifice. The other parallel is with the eating the sacrifices and drinking of the cup offered to idols, v. 21. The communion of the body and blood of Christ is represented as no less real in its nature and positive in its results than the other communication of the sacrificial flesh and cup.

The parallel may be offered thus to the eye, as regards the Jews and the Christians.

Israel after the flesh, or	Israel after the spirit, or
the Jews,	Christians,
have the typical sacrifice	have the real sacrifice
of the body	of the body
and blood	and blood
of animals,	of Christ,
on the typical altar,	on the true altar,
and eat	and eat
of the typical sacrifice	of the true sacrifice
of animal body and blood	of Christ's body and blood
at the Jewish Festival,	at the Christian festival,
the sacrificial supper,	the Lord's Supper,
and thus partake	and thus partake
of the typical altar.	of the true altar.

Here the parallel is between type and truth—in the parallel between Pagans and Christians it is between falsehood and truth.

In a word, the whole argument involves a parallel between three things:

I. The Sacrificial meal of the Jews.

II. The Sacrificial meal of the Pagans.

III. The Sacrificial meal of the Christians, or Lord's Supper.

The common idea that underlies the triple parallel is, that in each of these meals there is a true communion, communication, or impartation of the thing sacrificed, whereby the receiver is brought into the fellowship of the Altar, on which it was sacrificed, and thus into fellowship with the being to whom it was sacrificed — the Pagan with the Demons, the Jew with God as hidden in type, the Christian with God unveiled, and incarnate in Christ.

The parallel in the thought in Heb. xiii. 10–12 is also well worthy of notice: " We have an *altar*, whereof they have no right to *eat*, which serve the tabernacle. For the *bodies* of those beasts, whose *blood* is brought into the sanctuary by the High Priest for sin, are burnt without the camp. Wherefore, Jesus, also, that He might sanctify the people with His own blood, suffered without the gate." Here is altar over against altar, body over against body, blood over against blood, sacrifice over against sacrifice, eating over against eating. We have the true altar over against the typifying altar, the true body, blood, and sacrifice of Christ over against the typifying body, blood, and sacrifice of beasts, the true sacramental and communicating eating over against the typifying eating, which foreshadowed, but could not consummate a communion.

If language can express a thought unmistakably, the words of Paul (1 Cor. x.) imply that, in the Lord's Supper, there is a supernatural reality, a relation between the bread and the body of Christ, which makes the one the medium of the reception of the other; that our atoning sacrifice, after a different manner, but a manner not less real than that of the sacrifice of Jew and Pagan, is communicated to us in the Holy Supper, as their sacrifices were given in their feasts. The Lord's Supper, indeed, may be regarded as a summing up of the whole fundamental idea of Old Testament sacrifice, a covenant consummated by sacrifice, and entered into by the covenanting parties, receiving, each after the mode appropriate to him, that which is sacrificed; the Almighty Father accepting His Son, as the Victim offered for the sins of the whole world, and the world accepting in the Holy Supper the precious body and blood which apply in perpetual renewal, through all generations, the merits of the oblation made, once for all, upon the Cross.

The interpretation of these passages implied by our Church in her Confession is sustained by the universal usage of the Church Catholic, by the judgment of the greatest of the fathers, Greek and Latin, by the opinion of the most eminent dogmaticians and expositors, ancient and modern, and even by the concessions of interpreters who reject the Lutheran faith.

1. The whole Church from the earliest period has called, and now calls, the Lord's Supper the Communion. That Supper alone has this name. But what solution of the sole application of this name can be given except that in it the body and blood of Christ are communicated and received as they are nowhere else. The universal Christian consciousness and language attest the supernatural reality of the presence of the body and blood of Christ.

2. The drift of *patristic* interpretation may be gathered from the extracts which follow:

IGNATIUS (Ordained by the Apostle Peter, ab. A. D. 43, d. 107): "The Eucharist is the flesh of our Saviour Jesus Christ. There is one cup for the uniting (ἕνωσιν) of His blood."

JUSTIN MARTYR (d. 165): "The food over which the Eucharistic prayer has been made is the flesh and blood of the incarnate Jesus."

IRENÆUS (d. 202): "When the mingled cup and the broken bread receive the words of God, it becomes the Eucharist of the body and blood of Christ."

AMBROSE (d. 307): "We receiving of one bread and of one cup, are receivers and partakers of the body of the Lord."

CHRYSOSTOM (d. 407): "Very persuasively and fearfully He speaks: For what He says is this, That very thing which is in this cup is that which flowed from His side, and of that we are partakers. Not only hath He poured it out, but He hath imparted of it to us all. What is more fearful than this? Yet, what more kindly affectioned? The bread which we break, is it not the communion (κοινωνία) of the body of Christ? Why does He not say Participation (μετοχή)? Because He wished to signify something more (than participation), and to indicate the greatness of the joining together." THEOPHYLACT* and JOHN, of Damascus, adopt and repeat these words of Chrysostom.

JEROME (d. 420): "Is it not the Communion of the blood of

---

* THEOPHYLACT (1078): "Non dixit participatio, sed communicatio ut aliquid excellentius indicet puta summam unionem. Quid autem dicit hujusmodi est, hoc quod in calice est, illud est quod effluxit de latere Christi, et ex eo accipientes communicamus, id est ·inimur Christo."

Christ? As the Saviour Himself saith: He who eateth My flesh and drinketh My blood, abideth in Me, and I in him."

THEODORET (d. 456): " Enjoying the sacred mysteries, are we not partakers with Him, the Master?"

JOHN OF DAMASCUS (d. 750): " As the body is united with the Logos, so also we are united with Him by this bread." " The Lord's Supper is called, and is, in very deed, a communion (κοινωνία), because through it we commune (κοινωνεῖν) with Christ and become partakers of His flesh." Orthod. Fidei, lib. IV. xiv.

3. The Reformers of the Non-Lutheran tendency make important concessions.

CALVIN: " The thing itself is also present, nor does the soul less receive (percipiat) the communion of the blood, than we drink the wine with the mouth." " The wine is no longer a common drink, but dedicated to the spiritual nourishment of the soul, inasmuch as it is a token (tessera) of the blood of Christ."

PETER MARTYR: " Ye are of the body of Christ, His members, participants (participes) of His body and blood." " Christians have association and conjunction with one another, which hath its seat in this (in eo sita est), that they are participants of the body and blood of Christ."

But no witness to the cogency of the passage is perhaps so striking as that of ZWINGLI, who, in the effort to explain away a text so fatal to his theory, falls upon this violent and extraordinary interpretation: " What, I ask, is the cup of blessing which we bless, EXCEPT OUR OWN SELVES (quam nos ipsi)? HE GIVES THE NAME OF THE BLOOD OF CHRIST TO THOSE WHO TRUST IN HIS BLOOD. In this passage the communion of the blood of Christ are those who exult that they have obtained liberty in Christ's blood. ALL WE who are participants of one bread and one cup, ARE THE BLOOD OF CHRIST AND THE BODY OF CHRIST We have treated this point somewhat more verbosely, but we have done it because this passage, either NOT UNDERSTOOD, OR BADLY INTERPRETED, even by many learned men, has given to the simple, occasion of believing that in the bread the body of Christ is eaten, and in the wine His blood is drunk." Who does not feel that Zwingli would have weakened his cause less by saying honestly, " I cannot harmonize this text with my view " than he has by an interpretation so forced as to look like evidence of purpose to make, in any way, God's words square with a certain assumption?

4. A few distinguished names among English and American writers may be quoted. On these words, POOL, the great master among the old Puritan commentators, says: " The cup which we bless, is it not the communion of the blood of Christ? that is, it is an action whereby and wherein Christ communicates Himself and His grace to us." " The bread is the communion of the body of Christ; an action wherein Christians have a fellowship and communion with Christ." It will be noticed that, in the face of the text, POOL substitutes " Christ " for " body of Christ," and again for " blood of Christ." Substitute the very term of the sacred Word for his substitute, and POOL is forced to say of the Lord's Supper: " It is an action whereby and wherein Christ communicates His blood to us," " an action whereby Christians have a fellowship and communion with the body of Christ," and this is, as far as it goes, the very doctrine of our Church.

Bishop WILSON'S paraphrase is: " The bread which we break, after consecration, is it not that by which we have communion with Christ, our Head? "

HUSSEY explains the " communion " " by spiritually partaking of the blood and body of Christ in the Eucharist."

The OLDER TRANSLATORS in English bring out the true sense very clearly: " Is not the cup of blessing, which we bless, partaking of the blood of Christ? " " Is not the bread, which we break, partaking of the body of Christ? " Such is the rendering of the earliest and latest Tyndale, of Coverdale, of Cranmer, and of the Bishops. The first English translation, and for more than half a century the only one, which used the word " communion " was the Genevan, which was made at Geneva by English religious fugitives who were strong Calvinists, and who here followed Beza, evidently for doctrinal reasons, as the marginal note shows. From the Genevan (1557) it went into the Authorized Version (1611), which obscures the Apostle's reasoning by rendering koinonia, in the sixteenth verse, communion, and koinonos, in the eighteenth verse, "partakers" and "fellowship."

HAMMOND translates the word κοινωνια "communication," and paraphrases it: "The Christian feast of bread and wine in the Lord's Supper is .. the making us partakers of the body and blood of Christ," and refers to his note on Acts ii. 42, in which he says: "The word koinonia is to be rendered, not *communion*, but *communication*, by that, meaning distribution .. or participation, by which any are made partakers of some gift. In this notion is the word generally used in Scripture for .. some kind of distributing or dispensing to others. .. So in 1 Cor. x. 16, the participating of the body and blood of Christ."

Bishop HALL (d. 1656): "That sacred cup .. is it not that wherein we have a joint communion with Christ, in partaking of His blood? The bread .. is it not that wherein we . have communion with Christ, in a joint receiving of His body?"

Archbishop SHARP: "St. Paul here plainly teaches us that these sacred signs make those who use them to have communion with Christ crucified."

The WESTMINSTER ASSEMBLY's Annotations represent the communion as "a sign or pledge of the spiritual communion which we have together, who by faith *participate* in the body and blood of Christ."

MATTHEW HENRY says: "He lays down his argument from the Lord's Supper, *a feast on the sacrificed body and blood* of our Lord."

MACKNIGHT translates: "Is it (the cup of blessing) not the joint participation of the blood of Christ? Is it (the loaf which we break) not the joint participation of the body of Christ?"

ADAM CLARKE gives this as the force of the words: "We who partake of this sacred cup, in commemoration of the death of Christ, are *made partakers of His body and blood*, and thus have fellowship with Him."

CONYBEARE and HOWSON thus paraphrase the words: "When

we drink the cup of blessing which we bless, are we not all partakers in the blood of Christ? When we break the bread, are we not all partakers in the body of Christ?" and say in the note: "Literally, the cup of blessing which we bless, is it not a common participation in the blood of Christ? The bread which we break, is it not a common participation in the body of Christ?"

PARKHURST, in his Greek Lexicon, gives as the proper defi nition of koinonia in this passage, "a partaking, participation."

Dr. ROBINSON defines the word, "a partaking, sharing," and cites 1 Cor. x. 16 as an illustration of the meaning "participation."

ALFORD: "Koinonia, the participation (*i. e.* that whereby the act of participation takes place) of the blood of Christ. The strong literal sense must here be held fast, as constituting the very kernel of the Apostle's argument. . . . . If we are to render this 'estin,' *represents* or *symbolizes*, THE ARGUMENT IS MADE VOID."

Dr. JOHN W. NEVIN, in his Mystical Presence, speaking of the language in this place, says: "This much it does most certainly imply, that the communion is something *more than figurative or moral.* It is the communion of Christ's *body* and *blood*, a real participation in His true human life, as the one only and all-sufficient sacrifice for the sins of the world."

GILL, the great Baptist Rabbinist, on the words: "The bread which we break, is it not the communion of the body of Christ?" says: "It is; for not only believers by this act have communion with His mystical body, the Church, *but with His natural body*, which was broken for them; they, in a spirituaʼ sense, and by faith, eat His flesh, as well as drink His blood, and partake of Him."

Dr. SCHMUCKER, in his Catechism says, that "worthy communicants, *in this ordinance*, by faith spiritually feed on the body and blood of the Redeemer, thus holding communion or fellowship with Him," and cites 1 Cor. x. 16 to prove it.

Dr. HODGE, of Princeton, says: "It is here assumed that partaking of the Lord's Supper brings us into communion with

Christ. . . . The Apostle's argument is founded on the assumption that a participation of the cup is a participation of the blood of Christ; and that a participation of the bread is a participation of the body of Christ. Is it not the communion of the blood of Christ; that is, is it not the *means of participating* in the blood of Christ? He who partakes of the cup partakes of Christ's blood. . . . By partaking of the bread, we partake of the body of Christ."

5. We will cite as representative of GERMAN INTERPRETATION four names: the first representing the Ancient Lutheran Orthodoxy; the second the intermediate Lutheran Theology of the 18th Century; the third the Unionistic Theology of our own era; and the fourth, a witness to the irresistible character of the text, which compels a rationalistic commentator to acknowledge its true force.

CALOVIUS: "The earthly thing, to wit, the bread, is taken in an earthly manner: the heavenly thing, to wit, the body of Christ, is taken and eaten in a manner fitting it, that is, a heavenly or mystical manner. As that union is *sacramental* and is in mystery, and hence called *mystical*, the manner of eating which depends upon it, is as regards the body of Christ '*plainly mystical, sacramental,* and *incomprehensible* to human reason,' as *Hunnius* correctly observes."

S. J. BAUMGARTEN: "The communion of the cup with the blood of Christ, can here be taken in a twofold mode: 1. The cup stands in communion with the blood of Christ — is a means of offering and imparting it. 2. The cup is a means of uniting the participants with the blood of Christ — a means whereby they are made participants of it. The second presupposes the first."

OLSHAUSEN: "Were there in the Supper no communion with Christ but in spirit, the words would be 'Communion of Christ,' not 'communion of the body,' 'communion of the blood of Christ.' As of course the language refers to Christ in His state of exaltation, it is of His glorified flesh and blood it speaks: these come, in the Supper, into attingence with the participant, and thus mediate the communion."

RUECKERT is the last name we shall cite, and, as a witness on the point here involved, no name could carry more force with it. Rueckert is one of the greatest scholars of the age, a historico-critical rationalist, at the furthest extreme from the Lutheran position, making it his peculiar boast that, rising above all Confessions and parties, he accepts the results of scientific exegesis. He professes to make it his law, " that you are to lend nothing that is yours to your author, and omit nothing that is his—you are not to ask what he ought to say, nor be afraid of what he does say." Rueckert, in his work on the Lord's Supper,* after a very thorough investigation of the sense of 1 Cor. x., says: " Paul . . sees in the Supper Christ's body and blood . . as supersensuous and heavenly, which He gives as food and drink at His table to believers, and indeed without any exception, and without distinction between worthy and unworthy participants." He then shows that there is no possibility of evading the acceptance of the doctrine except by rejecting the authority of Paul, and by appealing to " the decision of rational thinking." Rationalism itself, in the person of one of its greatest representatives, being judge, it has no foothold in the text. Rueckert, moreover, confesses that the earliest faith of the Church agrees with this result of the latest scientific exegesis: " That in the Supper the body and blood of Christ are given and received, *was the universal faith*, from the beginning. . . . This faith abode in the aftertime; the Christian *people* (Gemeinde) never had any other, and in the Ancient Church it had not a solitary person to oppose it; the extremest heretics themselves never did it."

The Fifth Proposition in the analytical view of the doctrine of the Augsburg Confession is : That the true v. The Com- body and blood of Christ, truly present and truly munion of th communicated under the species of bread and Unworthy.† wine, are *received by all communicants.*‡

" He that eateth and drinketh unworthily, eateth and drinketh damnation (*or*, judgment) to himself, not discern-

---

* 1856. Pages 241, 297.

† See Seb. Schmidt : De princip. s. fundam. praes. Corpor. et. Sanguin. Christi Argentor, 1699. Chap. xi.

‡ German : da . . genommen wird. Latin : vescentibus. Apology : his qui sacramentum accipiunt.

41

ιng (διαχρινων) the Lord's body," (because he hath not distinguished the body. . . Syr. Ether. Eateth and drinketh condemnation on himself, by not discerning. . . Syr. Murdock):
" Whosoever shall eat this bread, and drink this cup of the
Lord unworthily, shall be guilty (ἕνοχος) of the body and blood
of the Lord," (is guilty of the blood of the Lord and of His
body). Syr. Etheridge. 1 Cor. xi. 27–29.

From the four propositions already established it is a necessary inference, and in the cogent texts just quoted it is expressly taught, that, while none but those who receive in faith
receive savingly, all who come to the Supper receive *sacramentally*, the body and blood of Christ. As those to whom the
gospel is a savor of death unto death, receive in common with
those to whom it is a savor of life unto life, one and the same
thing outwardly, to wit: the gospel ; so do those who abuse,
to their own condemnation, the Lord's Supper, and those who
rightly use it to their soul's welfare, receive one and the same
thing sacramentally. It is the very essence of the sin of the
rejection of the gospel, that, receiving it outwardly, with the
attendant energy of the Holy Spirit in, with, and under it, the
rejector has not received it inwardly, and thus makes it not
merely practically void, but pernicious to his soul. So is it
the very essence of the sin of unworthy treatment of the Lord's
Supper, that, receiving it in its sacred and divine element, as
well as in its outward one, the communicant makes no inward
appropriation of the benefit there offered, but turns, by his
unbelief, the food of his soul to its poison. In the passages
quoted immediately after the Thesis, men, whose unworthiness
is such that their condemnation is sealed by their eating, are
represented as guilty of the body and blood of Christ ; that is,
the object of their abuse is specifically declared to be, not bread
and wine, either in themselves or as symbols, but the body and
blood of Christ. That which they are treating with contumely
is said to be the body of the Lord, and their crime is that
they do not discern it: " not discerning the body of the Lord."
But unbelief would be its own safeguard, if it were the com
municant's faith, and not the will and institution of Christ,
which is the ground of the presence. The unbeliever could

say: " As I have no faith, there is no body of Christ to discern ; there is no body and blood of which I can be guilty." Of such men, moreover, the Apostle, in the previous chapter, declared that the broken bread and the cup of blessing are to them also the communion of the body and blood of Christ.

Let any man weigh solemnly the import of the thought: He that eateth unworthily of this bread is guilty of the body of the Lord; he that drinketh unworthily of this cup is guilty of the blood of the Lord ; and then let him ask himself, before the Searcher of hearts, whether he dare resolve the Lord's Supper into a mere eating of a symbol of Christ's body, the drinking of a symbol of Christ's blood? Let it be remembered that in the case of the Corinthians, deeply as they had sinned, there was no designed dishonor of the sacramental elements, still less of Christ, whom they set forth ; there was no hatred to Christ, no positive infidelity, and yet an unworthy drinking of the sacramental cup made them " *guilty of the blood of Christ.*" The Apostle expressly tells us, too, whereon the fearfulness of their guilt and the terribleness of their penalty turned : " They ate and drank damnation to themselves, *not discerning* (making no difference of) *the Lord's body.*" But on all the rationalistic interpretations there is no body of the Lord there to discern.

To " discern " (diakrinein), elsewhere translated to " make or put differences between," involves a correct mental and moral judgment ; it means to distinguish between two things which there is a liability of confounding, to mark the distinction between one thing and another. " Can I *discern* between good and evil ? " " That I may discern between good and bad." " Cause them to discern between clean and unclean," that is, to mark and make the distinction, in mind, feeling, and act. To " discern the body of the Lord," is, therefore, to discriminate between it and something which is, or might be, confounded with it, to mark its difference from some other thing, to believe, feel, and act in the conviction that it is not that other thing, but is the body of the Lord. The point is, That which you receive in the Lord's Supper is not mere bread and wine, as your conduct would imply that it is, but is also the body and blood of Christ ; therefore, your guilt (taking its root in a failure to discern this body and blood) is not that of the abuse of bread and wine, but of the indignity offered to His body and blood which they communicate; therefore your punishment is not simply that of men guilty of gluttony and drunkenness, but that of men guilty of a wrong done to the body and blood of Christ; therefore sickness and death have been sent to warn you of your awful crime, and if these warnings be not heeded, your final doom will be to perish with the world (v. 32).

The *sacramental* communion was ordained of Christ as the means of the *spiritual* communion. In its divine essence, that is, in its sacramental character, the Lord's Supper is unchangeable, but its *effects* and *blessings* are conditioned upon the faith of the recipient. The same sunlight falls upon the eye of the blind and of the seeing alike; both eyes alike *receive* it, but the eye of the seeing alone *perceives* it; it is communicated to both; it is "discerned" by but the one. But the analogy fails at an important point: In spirituals the lack of the perception with the reception is voluntary, and, therefore, while the blind eye suffers privation only, the blind soul comes under condemnation. It is the blind man's *misfortune* that he does not see, it is the unbelieving man's *guilt* that he does not *discern*. The diseased and the sound eat of the same natural bread; but to one it brings strength, to another it is without effect, and to yet another it brings nausea and agony. The difference of result is owing to the difference of condition in the recipient. The Holy Spirit breathes forever on and in the word, and is, with it, received by all who hear the word, quickening the yielding heart, and hardening the heart which resists Him.

Jesus said to every one of the disciples present, probably to Judas, who betrayed, certainly to Peter, who soon after denied Him: "Take, eat, this is My body given for you;" and the ministers of Christ for eighteen centuries have said to every communicant, believing or unbelieving, "Take, eat, this is the body of Christ given for you," and what Christ said, and they say, is unchangingly true. So far there is no distinction made by the character of the recipient, for as much as this depended upon Christ's will, and is therefore unchanging. "The gifts of God are without repentance," that is, there is no vacillation, repentance, or fluctuation of mind in God. But when to these absolute words is added: "*Do* this in remembrance of me," there comes in something dependent upon man's will, and which may, therefore, fluctuate. As it is true, even of the man that perishes, that Christ's body was broken and His blood shed for him, "for our Lord Jesus Christ, by the grace of God, tasted death for *every man ;* " as it is true that every man in the Resurrection shall be called forth from the grave, for " as in Adam all die, so in Christ shall all be made alive," though some shall rise to glory, and others to shame; so is it true that every man, however unworthy, sacramentally partakes of the body and blood of Christ in the Supper, though it be to his own condemnation. As the unbelieving, under the Old Dispensation, were, equally with the believing, outwardly sprinkled with the blood of the covenant, though they received not, for lack of faith, its blessings; as those who are unbelieving and baptized receive the baptism itself in its sacramental entireness, though they do not appropriate its blessings, so do the communicants in the Holy Supper confirm the testimony, that, although unbelief shuts us out from the blessings of the promises and ordinances, we cannot thereby make them of none effect. Our faith does not make, and our unbelief cannot unmake them. The same objective reality is in every case presented, and in every case it is one and the same thing, whose benefits faith appropriates, and unbelief rejects.

That Judas was at the Supper of the Lord seems highly probable. Matthew and Mark, after telling us that our Lord " sat down with the *twelve*," describe the Institution of the Supper without giving a hint of the departure of Judas. Luke, who proposed to write " in order," and who is generally regarded as most precise in his chronology, in direct connection with the words of the Supper, immediately *after* them, tells us our Lord said: " But, behold ! the hand of him that betrayeth Me is with Me on the table." (Luke xxii. 21.) The force of the word " immediately," in John xiii. 30, is not such as to exclude the possibility of what Luke seems so distinctly to assert, and what the two other synoptical evangelists more than imply, to wit, that Judas was present at the Lord's Supper, and such is the judgment of the oldest and best commentators, and, among them, of Calvin himself, and of others, who, in common with him, had a doctrinal interest in denying the presence of Judas. Moreover, as John does not give an account of the Institution of the Supper, we may naturally settle the chronological and other questions connected with it from the synoptists. But if our Lord could say to Judas also, "Take, eat, this is My body," then the sacramental character of the Supper cannot depend upon the worthiness or faith of the receiver.

In all divine provisions for the salvation of man, we must discriminate between the *essence*, which is of God, and is, like Him, unchanging, and the *use* of them, which is by man, and is conditioned on his faith. The divine reality is neither affected by the character of the giver, nor of the receiver, as a gold coin does not cease to be gold, though the giver hands it away carelessly as a piece of brass, and the receiver takes it as brass and casts it into the mire. Faith is not a Philosopher's Stone; it cannot convert lead into gold; it can only grasp what is. Nor can unbelief by a reverse process convert gold into lead; it can only reject what is. " Unto *us* was the *gospel* preached, as well as unto *them;* but the word preached did not *profit* them, not being mixed with faith in them that heard it." The gospel, the word, the sacrament, remain one and the same, but the *profit* connected with them depends upon the faith of those that receive them.

God is not far from any one of us, yet none but the believing realize the benefits of His presence. The multitude thronged and pressed upon Jesus; His presence was equally real in its *essence* to all, but the saving efficacy of it went forth in virtue only to the woman who touched His clothes in faith. (Mark v. 30.) So Christ is present in the sacramental drapery alike to all communicants, but the touch of faith is needed to participate in the virtue of His healing. The touch of those who crucified our Lord was no less real than that of the woman whose touch brought healing; but their touch, like the unworthy eating and drinking, made them " guilty of the body and blood of the Lord." And as no indignity which they could offer to the raiment of our Lord could make them guilty of His body and blood, so may we reason that no indignity offered to bread and wine, even if they were the sacramental medium of the body and blood of Christ, and still less if they were but bread and wine, could make those who offered it guilty of the body and blood of Christ. The truth is, that the terms in which the guilt of the unworthy communicants is characterized, and the fearful penalties with which it was visited, to wit, temporal judgments, even unto death, and eternal condemnation with the world, if the sin was not repented of, make it inconceivable that the objective element in the Lord's Supper is bread and wine merely; but if the body and blood be there objectively, then must they be received sacramentally by all communicants. If it be said Christ cannot be substantially present to unworthy communicants according to His human nature, otherwise they must derive benefit from it, it might be correctly replied, neither can He be substantially present with them according to His divine nature, otherwise they must derive benefit from that; but the latter is conceded by the objector, therefore he must concede that his argument is of no weight against the possibility of the former. Christ is a Saviour, but He is also a judge.

But if it be granted that the presence of the body and blood of Christ in the Supper is one which is fixed, absolute, and unchanging, then must it be substantial, and not imaginary; not a thing of our minds, but of His wonderful person; not ideal, but true; faith does not make it, but finds it, unto life; unbelief does not unmake it, but, to its own condemnation, fails to discern it. The sacramental presence is fathomless, like the Incarnation; like it, also, it is in the sphere of supernatural reality, to which the natural is as the shadow. The presence of the communicant at the Supper belongs to a lower sphere of actuality than the presence of the undivided Christ in it; and the outward taking and eating is the divinely appointed means whereby the ineffable mystery of the communion of Christ's body and blood is consummated, a communion heavenly and spiritual in its manner over against all that is earthly and fleshly; but in its essence more true than all earthly truth, more real than all earthly reality, more substantial than all earthly substance. The body and blood of Christ are more truly present in the Supper than are the bread and wine, because their sphere of presence is divine; the bread and wine are but the gifts of the hand of God, the body and blood of Christ are inseparable constituents of God's incarnate person.

The Non-Lutheran interpreters have made concessions of great importance in their interpretation of these texts. GUAL-THER, one of the greatest of the Zurich divines (d. 1586), says: "Shall be held guilty of the same crime with Judas who betrayed Christ, with the Jews and soldiers who scourged Him, spit upon Him, wounded, crucified Him, and shed His blood."

PAREUS: Heidelberg (d. 1622): "Judas betrayed, the Jews condemned, the soldiers pierced Christ's body and shed His blood upon the Cross. They who abuse the sacrament are absolutely partakers in their crime (*sceleri prorsus communicant*)."

SEBASTIAN MEYER, of Berne: "They commit murder (*cædem committere*) and shed the Redeemer's blood," "incur the dreadful crime of parricide."

One more proposition remains to be touched, but it is negative in its character, and in this dissertation we have proposed to confine ourselves to the positive and thetical. Here, therefore, we reach the end of our exhibition of the positive propositions in which our great Confession sets forth the faith of our Church. We have the five simple propositions which are yielded by the analysis of the Tenth Article. We have viewed them purely as Scriptural questions. We have treated them very much as independent propositions, establishing each on special evidence of its own. But, while the argument for the faith of our Church is so strong on each head as well as on the whole as to bear even this severe process, it should not be forgotten that none of these are, in fact, isolated. They cling together with all the internal coherence of divine truth. The truth of any one of them implies the truth of all of them. If we have failed in establishing four separately, yet have succeeded in establishing one, then have we in establishing that established the five.

The sense of the words of the Institution which our Church confesses, which is derived from the words themselves, is sustained by every Scripture allusion to them. Not only is there not the faintest hint anywhere that they are figurative, but every fresh allusion to them gives new evidence that they are to be taken as they sound. If the *offering* of the ancient sacrifices pointed to a true offering of Christ, the eating of the sacrifices necessarily points to a true, though supernatural, communion of the body and blood which He offered. If the slaying of the Paschal Lamb pointed to the slaying of Christ's body, the sacramental reception of the body of the Lamb of God must be a part of the New Testament Passover; the Lord's Supper cannot substitute an unreality for a reality, but must substitute a higher reality for a lower one. If Moses meant what he said when he declared, as he sprinkled the book and the people: " This is the blood of the Testament which God hath enjoined unto you " (Heb. ix. 20), then must our Lord be accepted at His word, when, with the covenanting terms of the Old Testament, the Testament of Moses, so clearly in his eye, and meaning to mark the New Testament antithesis, He says: " This is *My* blood, of the New Testament." Every Scripture declaration in regard to the Supper of the Lord points, with an unvarying tendency, to the great result which is treasured in the faith of our Church. When we ask, What *is* it which Christ tells us to Take, eat? He replies, This is My body, not This is a sign of My body. When we ask, What does the bread communicate? St. Paul replies, The bread which we break, is it not the communion of the body of Christ? not the communion of the sign of His body. When we ask, What is he guilty of who eats and drinks unworthily? the answer is, He is guilty of the body and blood of Christ, not of the sign of the body or sign of the blood. When we ask, How did the unworthy communicant come to incur this guilt? what did he fail to discern? the reply is, Not discerning the Lord's body, not that he failed to discern the sign or symbol of Christ's body. We cannot tear from its place the sacramental doctrine of our Church without tearing up the whole Evangelical system. The principles of interpretation which relieve us of the Eucharistic mystery take from us the mystery of the Trinity, the Incarnation, and the Atonement. We cannot remove Christ from the Supper and consistently leave Him anywhere else, and we can take no part of Christ from the Supper without taking away the whole. The very foundations of our faith give way under the processes which empty the Lord's Supper of its divine glory. The Sacramental Presence is the necessary sequel, the crowning glory of the Incarnation and Atonement; and the illumination of the Holy Spirit in the word which enables the eye of Faith to see God in the body, and redemption in the blood, enables it to see the body in the bread, and the blood in the cup, not after the manner of the first man, who is of the earth, earthy, but after the manner of the second Man, who is the Lord from heaven.

The Lutheran Church believes, on the sure warrant of God's word, that the body of our Lord Jesus remains a VI. Summary true human body, and as to its natural and deter-View of the Lutheran Doctrine minate presence has been removed from earth, and of the Sacramental Presence of is in the glory of the world of angels and the re-Christ, on three Points. 1. Modes deemed. She also believes that in and through the of Presence. divine nature with which it forms one person, it is present on earth in another sense, no less true than the former. She believes that the sacramental elements are divinely appointed through the power of the Saviour's own benediction, as the medium through which we participate, after a spiritual, supernatural, heavenly, substantial, objective, and true manner, " in the communion of His body and of His blood." (1 Cor. x. 16.) Our Church never has denied that the ascension of Christ was real, literal, and local; never has denied that His body has a determinate presence in heaven; never has maintained that it has a local presence on earth. Neither does she impute to Him two bodies — one present and one absent, one natural and the other glorified — but she maintains that one body, forever a natural and true body as to its essence, but no longer in its natural or earthly condition, but glorified, is absent, indeed, in one mode, but present in another. As she believes that God is really one in one respect, and no less really three in another respect, so does she believe that the body of our Lord Jesus Christ is really absent in one respect, and just as really present in another. Christ has left us, and He never leaves us — He has gone from us, and He is ever present with us; He has ascended far above all heavens, but it is that He may fill all things. As His divine nature, which in its totality is in heaven, and in its fulness is in Christ bodily, is on earth while it is in heaven, as that divine nature is present with us, without extension or locality, is on earth without leaving heaven, is present in a manner true, substantial and yet incomprehensible, so does it render the body of Christ, which is one person with it, also present. That body in its determinate limitations is in heaven, and in and of itself would be there alone, but *through the divine,* in *consequence of the personal conjunction,* and in virtue of that conjunction, using in the whole person the attributes of the whole person in both its parts, it is rendered present. It is present without extension, for the divine through which it is present is unextended — it is present without locality, for the divine through which it is present is illocal. It is on earth, for the divine is on earth — it is in heaven, for the divine remains in heaven, and like the divine it is present truly and substantially, yet incomprehensibly.

In other words, as our Church believes that the one essence of God has two modes of presence, one general and ordinary, by which it is present to all creatures, and the other special and extraordinary, by which it is present, so as to constitute one person, after which mode it is present to none other than to the humanity of Jesus Christ, and that both modes of presence, although unlike in their results, are equally substantial; so does she believe that this one humanity taken into personal and inseparable union with this one essence, has two modes of presence: one determinate, in which it is related to space, through its own inherent properties; the other infinite, in which it is related to space in the communion of the divine attributes, and that both modes of presence, though unlike, are equally substantial.

Is it said that to deny that Christ's sacramental presence is local is to deny it altogether; that to affirm that His determinate presence is in the realm of angels and of the glorified, is to affirm that He has no presence at all on earth? Be it said; but then, at least, let the odious libel that our Church teaches consubstantiation, or a physical presence, or a corporeal or carnal mode of presence, be forever dropped. Our Church never has denied that, in the sense and in the manner in which our Lord was once on earth, He is no longer here, but she maintains that the illocal is as real as the local, the supernatural is as true as the natural. " A local absence," as Andreæ said, in his argument with Beza at Montbeillard, " does not prevent a sacramental presence; " the presence of Christ's humanity on earth, through the Deity, with which it is one person, is as real as is its presence through the properties of its own essence in heaven. The soundest theologians do not hesitate to declare in propositions which seem contradictory, but are not, " God is everywhere," and " God is nowhere," — everywhere in His fathomless omnipresence — nowhere locally or determinately; and as is the presence of the divine, such is the presence it imparts to the humanity which is personally united with it. The man Christ Jesus is with us after one manner, and He is not with us after another manner; He is with us through the plenary exercise of His divine majesty, not with us in the local or determinate restrictions of space. "There is no contradiction in attributing contrary things to the same subject, provided they be affirmed in different respects and modes."*

The current view of un-Lutheran Protestantism practically is, that all we need for our redemption is a *dead Christ.* We are to look back to Calvary to find peace in thinking of what was there done, and at the Lord's Supper we are to look back to the sacrifice once made for our sins. The current view excludes the necessity of a living Saviour in our redemption. According to it, we redeem ourselves, or the Spirit of God redeems us, by what Christ once did, and without any personal work on His part now. To the

2. A Living Saviour.

---

* Chemnitz, De duab. Naturis, 179.

theology of a large part of the Church it would be no disturbing element if the divine nature of Christ had been separated from the human after the resurrection. Instead of a robust and mighty faith which hangs upon a living Saviour, and lives by His life, we have a religion of sentiment verging away into sentimentality; a religion which lives by its own thoughts about a Saviour of bygone times. We have had in our hands a book on the Lord's Supper, by an American preacher, the frontispiece of which represents a lonely tombstone, and on it the words: "To the memory of my Saviour." Nothing could more sadly, yet vigorously, epitomize the tendency of which we speak — the graveyard tendency, which turns the great festival of the redemption into a time of mourning, and coldly furnishes forth the marriage tables with the baked meats of the funeral. The glory of the Lutheran system in all its parts, and especially in its doctrine of the Lord's Supper, is, that it accepts, in all its fulness, the Apostle's argument, "If, when we were enemies, we were reconciled to God by the death of His Son, MUCH MORE, being reconciled, we shall be saved by His LIFE." Never, indeed, has the human heart been so taught as by our system in its purity to turn to the death of Christ for hope; but our Church has been led by the Holy Spirit too deeply into all the fulness of truth to make an antagonism between the death of her Saviour and His life.

If Christ must die to make our redemption, He must live to apply it. If the Lord's Supper is a sacrament of the redemption made by His death, it is also a sacrament of the same redemption applied by His life. If it tells us that His body and blood were necessary to make our redemption, it tells us also that they are still necessary to apply the redemption they then made. He made the sacrifice once for all — He applies it constantly. We live by Him, we must hang on Him — the vine does not send up one gush of its noble sap and then remain inert. It receives the totality of life, once for all, but the sap which sustains it must flow on — its one, unchanging and abiding life puts itself forth into the new offshoots, and by constant application of itself maintains the old branches. If the sap-life ceases, the seed-life cannot save. Cut the branch off, and the memory of the life will not keep it from wither. ing; it must have the life itself — and this it must derive suc cessively from the vine. It could not exist without the origi- nal life of the vine, nor can it exist without the present life of the vine, be its past what it may. Faith cannot feed on itself, as many seem to imagine it can—it must have its object. The ordinances, the Word, and the sacraments give to it that by which it lives. Faith in the nutritious power of bread does not nourish — the bread itself is necessary.

The man who feels a moral repugnance to the Scripture doc-

**3. The Propitia-
tion and the Sac-
ramental Pres-
ence.**

trine of the Eucharist, will find, if he analyzes his feelings thoroughly, that they take their root in a repugnance to the doctrine of the atonement by Christ's body and blood. The man who asks what use is there in a sacramental application of them in the Lord's Supper, really asks, what use was there in a redemptory offer- ing of them on Calvary. He may be using the terms of Scrip- ture, but if He takes his inmost thoughts before his God, he will probably find that he has been denying the true vicarious character of the sacrifice of our Lord — that he has fallen into that conception of the sacrifice on Calvary which is essentially Socinian, for everything which brings down the oblation of the Son of God into the sphere of the natural *is* essentially Socinian. He will find that in his view his Lord is only a glorious mar- tyr, or that the power of His sacrifice is only a moral power; that the cross is but a mighty sermon, and that those awful words, which, in their natural import unbare, as it is nowhere else unbared, the heart of Deity in the struggle of its unspeak- able love and fathomless purpose; that all these are oriental poesy — figures of speech — graces of language. The theory of the atonement, which pretends to *explain* it, is rotten at the core. The atonement, in its whole conception, belongs to a world which man cannot now enter. The blessings and adap- tations of it we can comprehend in some measure. We can approach them with tender hearts full of gratitude; but the *essence* of the atonement we can understand as little as we understand the essence of God.

If Christ, through His body broken, made remission of sins,

why do we ask to what end is the doctrine that the same body through which He made the remission is that through which He applies it? His body *as such* could make no remission of sins, but, through the Eternal Spirit, with which it was conjoined in personal unity, it made redemption — His body, *as such*, may have no power to apply the redemption or to be with the redeemed, but, through the same relation by which it entered into the sphere of the supernatural to make redemption, it reveals itself now in that same sphere to apply it. All theology, without exception, has had views of the atonement which were lower or higher, as its views of the Lord's Supper were low or high. Men have talked and written as if the doctrine of our Church, on this point, were a stupid blunder, forced upon it by the self-will and obstinacy of one man. The truth is, that this doctrine, clearly revealed in the New Testament, clearly confessed by the early Church, lies at the very heart of the Evangelical system — Christ is the centre of the system, and in the Supper is the centre of Christ's revelation of Himself. The glory and mystery of the incarnation combine there as they combine nowhere else. Communion with Christ is that by which we live, and the Supper is "*the* Communion." Had Luther abandoned this vital doctrine, the Evangelical Protestant Church would have abandoned him. He did not make this doctrine — next in its immeasurable importance to that of justification by faith, with which it indissolubly coheres — the doctrine made him. The doctrine of the Lord's Supper is the most vital and practical in the whole range of the profoundest Christian life — the doctrine which, beyond all others, conditions and vitalizes that life, for in it the character of faith is determined, invigorated, and purified as it is nowhere else. It is not only a fundamental doctrine, but is among the most fundamental of fundamentals.

We know what we have written. We know, that to take our Saviour at His word here, to receive the teachings of the New Testament in their obvious intent, is to incur with the current religionism a reproach little less bitter than if we had taken up arms against the holiest truths of our faith. We are willing to endure it. Our fathers were willing to shed their blood for the truth, and shall we refuse to incur a little obloquy? The fact that we bear the name of a Church which stood firm when rationalizing tendencies directed themselves with all their fury against this doctrine of the Word of God, increases our responsibility. When, at a later and sadder period, she yielded to subtlety what she had maintained successfully against force, and let her doctrine fall, she fell with it. When God lifted her from the dust, He lifted her banner with it, and on that banner, as before, the star of a pure Eucharistic faith shone out amid the lurid clouds of her new warfare, and there it shall shine forever. Our Saviour has spoken; His Church has spoken. His testimony is explicit, as is hers. The Lutheran Church has suffered more for her adherence to this doctrine than from all other causes, but the doctrine itself repays her for all her suffering. To her it is a very small thing that she should be judged of man's judgment; but there is one judgment she will not, she dare not hazard, the judgment of her God, which they eat and drink to themselves who will not discern the Lord's body in the Supper of the Lord.

We do not wish to be misunderstood in what we have said as to the *moral* repugnance to our doctrine of the Supper. We distinguish between a mere intellectual difficulty and an aversion of the affections. How New Testament-like, how Lutheran have sounded the sacramental hymns and devotional breathings of men whose theory of the Lord's Supper embodied little of its divine glory. The glow of their hearts melted the frost-work of their heads. When they treat of sacramental communion, and of the mystical union, they give evidence, that, with their deep faith in the atonement, there is connected, in spite of the rationalizing tendency which inheres in their system, a hearty acknowledgment of the supernatural and incomprehensible character of the Lord's Supper. On the other hand, the evidence is overwhelming, that, as low views of the Lord's Supper prevail, in that proportion the doctrine of the atonement exhibits a rationalizing tendency. We repeat the proposition, confirmed by the whole history of the Church, that a moral repugnance to the doctrine that the body and blood of

Christ are the medium through which redemption is *applied*, has its root in a moral repugnance to the doctrine that His precious body and blood are the medium through which redemption was *wrought*.

It is now admitted by dispassionate scholars, who are not Lutheran in their convictions, first, that the Zwinglian doctrine was unknown in the most Ancient Church. Second: that the doctrine of our Church in regard to the Lord's Supper, was certainly the doctrine of the fathers in the Church Catholic,

VII. The Logic of the Exegesis sustained by its History. The Testimony of the Ancient Church.*

---

* ALBERTINUS: De Eucharistiæ Sacram. Libri tres. Sec. ex Patribus. Pav. 1654. Folio. Still the greatest of the defences of the Calvinistic view.— BELLARMINUS: De Controv. Chr. Fidei. Paris. 1620. Folio. De Euchar. Lib. II. Chap. I. xxxix., Testimon. Patrum. The greatest single piece of Polemic in defence of the Church of Rome. — CLAUDE: The Catholick Doctrine of the Eucharist in all ages (in answer to Arnaud) touching the belief of the Greek, Moscovite, Armenian, Jacobite, Nestorian, Coptic, Maronite, and other Eastern Churches. From the French. London, 1683, Folio. (Calvinistic.) — COSIN: The History of Popish Transubstantiation, to which is premised and opposed the Catholick Doctrine of . . the Ancient Fathers. London, 1676, 8vo. (Vigorously Anti-Romish in its negations, and decidedly Lutheranizing in its affirmation.) — EUCHARIST: A full view of the Doctrine and practice of the Ancient Church relating to London. 1668, 4to. (Calvinistic.) — FABER, G. S.: Christ's Discourse at Capernaum fatal to the Doctrine of Transubstantiation. London, 1840. 8vo. (Copious Patristic Citation.) — GOODE, WM.: Nature of Christ's Presence in the Eucharist: 2 vols. 8vo. London. 1856. Chap. V. The Testimony of the Fathers. (A tissue of partisan falsification. Anglican Low Church.) — HOSPINIAN: Histor. Sacramentariæ Pars Prior. Exp. Coen. Domin. in primitiv. et Veter. Eccles. Genev. 1681. Folio. --MARHEINECKE: Sanct. Patrum de Praes. Chr. in Coen. Dom. Senten. Triplex. Heid. 1811. 4to. — MELANCHTHON: Sententiæ veterum aliquot Scriptorum de Coena Domini. (1530.) Corpus Reformat. xxiii. 727–753. — ŒCOLAMPADIUS: De Genuina verb. Dom. juxta vetustissimos auctores expositione Bas. 1525. 8vo. Quid de Eucharistia veter. tam Graeci, tum Latini senserunt. Dialogus. (1530) in Œcolampad., et Zwingli Epistola. Lib. III.—PUSEY, E. B.: The Doctrine of the Real Presence, as contained in the Fathers from the death of St. John the Evangelist to the Fourth General Council, vindicated. Oxford and London. 1855. 8vo. — WATERLAND: Review of the Doctrine of the Eucharist, as laid down in Scripture and antiquity. Oxford, 1868. 8vo. (Abundant patristic citation.) — The recent German works which present more or less copiously the patristic history of the doctrine are: 1. Doctrines and History: Ebrard, 1845; Kahnis, 1851; Rückert, 1856; 2. History: Döllinger, 1826; Engelhardt (Ztschr. für histor. theol. 1842. Steiz, Jahrb. f. dtsche Theol. 1864–65. Meier, 1842. Baur, Tertullian, Doctr). Tüb. Ztschr. 1839. 2. See Kahnis Dogm. ii. 182. Luthardt Dogm. § 74.

42

from the Fourth to the Ninth Century—the second theological
age, the golden, or, as it is called, the classic age of Christian
antiquity, to wit : that "the presence of the Lord in the Eucharist" is "real, according to substance, in, with, and under
the species," (Marheinecke).   The first age, from the Apostolic
writings to the end of the third, is, we believe, no less decided
in its unity on the same doctrine.   To this conviction the
studies of the greatest of the English patristic scholars of our
age has led him.   His testimony, given as the final result of
years of close-investigation, has probably as great weight as
human testimony is capable of having on a point of this kind.
Of his vast patristic scholarship there is no dispute.   Of his
great personal purity there is no question.   Reared in a Church
which confesses the Calvinistic view of the Supper, his education was adverse to the perception of the force of testimony
sustaining the Lutheran view.   If he be charged with Romanizing views, in some parts of his theological thinking, it may
heighten the value of his testimony here, where he maintains
the Catholicity of the Lutheran view, over against the Romish
corruption in the doctrine of Transubstantiation, and the force
of the whole is heightened by his unconcealed aversion, in
many respects, to the Lutheran Church.   We mean, as the
reader has already anticipated, Dr. Pusey.   In his vindication
of the doctrine of the real Presence, as contained in the fathers
from the death of St. John the Evangelist to the Fourth General Council, he demonstrates that "the belief that the elements
remain after consecration in their natural substance was not supposed of old to involve any tenet of consubstantiation : " that,
"Consubstantiation was not held by the Lutheran body : "
which he demonstrates from the symbols of the Lutheran
Church, and from Luther himself.   By a most patient examination of evidence, which he cites in full, he shows, upon the
one hand, that the doctrine of Transubstantiation is no doctrine of the earliest Church, and that the doctrine of a true,
objective presence of the body and blood of Christ, and under
the bread and wine, is its doctrine.   No better summary of his
labors, and of the conviction they strengthen in his mind, can
be given than that with which he closes his book :

" I have now gone through every writer who in his extant works speaks of the Holy Eucharist, from the time when St. John the Evangelist was translated to his Lord, to the dates of the Fourth General Council, A. D. 451, a period of three centuries and a half. I have suppressed nothing; I have not knowingly omitted anything; I have given every passage, as far as in me lay, with so much of the context as was necessary for the clear exhibition of its meaning. Of course, in writers of whom we have such large remains as St. Augustine and St. Chrysostom, or in some with whom I am less familiar, I may have overlooked particular passages. Yet the extracts are already so large, so clear, and so certain, that any additional evidence could only have coincided with what has been already produced. Albertinus did his utmost on the Calvinistic side. His strength lies in his arguments against a physical doctrine of Transubstantiation; his weakness, in the paradox which he strangely maintains, that the Fathers did not believe a real Objective Presence. In so doing, he treats the Fathers as others of his school have treated Holy Scripture on the other Sacrament. When his school would disparage the doctrine of Baptism, they select passages from Holy Scripture, in which it is not speaking of that Sacrament. In like way Albertinus gains the appearance of citing the Fathers on the orthodox side (as he calls it), *i. e.*, the disbelief of the Real Presence, by quoting them when they are not speaking of the Holy Eucharist, but, *e. g.*, of the Presence of our Lord's Human Nature in Heaven, or the absence of His Visible Presence upon earth; of the natural properties of bodies; or of spiritual, as distinct from sacramental Communion, or of the Eucharistic and outward Symbols, under which the Sacramental Presence is conveyed. Supported, as he thinks, by these, he proceeds to explain away, as he best may, the clear and distinct passages which had hitherto been alleged from the Fathers, in proof of the Doctrine of the Real Presence. Yet the very diligence of Albertinus on the one side, or of Roman Catholic controversialists on the other, obviously gives the more security that nothing can have been overlooked which could seem to support either side.

Summary of Patristic Testimony by Dr. Pusey.

"In the present collection, I have adduced the Fathers, not as original authorities, but as witnesses to the meaning of Holy Scripture. I have alleged them on the old, although now, on both sides, neglected rule, that what was taught ' everywhere, at all times, by all,' must have been taught to the whole Church by the inspired Apostles themselves. The Apostles planted; they watered ; they appointed others to take their ministry, to teach as they had themselves taught from God. A universal suppression of the truths which the Apostles taught and the unmarked substitution of falsehood, is a theory which contradicts human reason, no less than it does our Lord's promise to His Church. There is no room here for any alleged corruption. The earliest Fathers, St. Ignatius, St. Justin Martyr, St. Irenæus, St. Clement of Alexandria, Tertullian, or St. Hippolytus, state the doctrine of the Real Presence as distinctly as any later Father.

"And now, reader, if you have got thus far, review for a moment from what variety of minds, as of countries, this evidence is collected. Minds the most simple and the most philosophical ; the female martyrs of Persia, or what are known as the philosophic Fathers ; minds wholly practical, as Tertullian or St. Cyprian, St. Firmilian, St. Pacian, or St. Julius ; or those boldly imaginative, as Origen ; or poetic minds, as St. Ephrem, or St. Isaac, or St. Paulinus ; Fathers who most use a figurative and typical interpretation of the Old Testament, as St. Ambrose, or such as, like St. Chrysostom, from their practical character, and the exigencies of the churches in which they preached, confined themselves the most scrupulously to the letter ; mystical writers, as St. Macarius ; or ascetics, as Mark, the Hermit, or Apollos, or the Abbot Esaias ; writers in other respects opposed to each other ; the friends of Origen, as St. Didymus, or his opponents, as Theophilus of Alexandria and St. Epiphanius ; or again, St. Cyril of Alexandria or Theodoret ; heretics or defenders of the faith, as Eusebius and Theodorus, Hereacleotes, Arius, or St. Athanasius ; Apollinarius or St. Chrysostom, who wrote against him, Nestorius or St. Cyril of Alexandria — all agree in one consentient exposition of our Lord's words, ' This is My body, this is My blood '

Whence this harmony, but that one spirit attuned all the various minds in the one body into one; so that the very heretics were slow hereiu to depart from it?

"There is a difference ofttimes in the setting, so to speak, of the one jewel, truth. We may meet with that truth where *we* should not have expected it; some may even be deterred, here and there, by the mystical interpretations of Holy Scripture, amid which they find it. That mystical interpretation is no matter of faith. But a mode of interpretation which presupposes any object of belief to be alluded to, when scarce anything is mentioned which may recall it to the mind, shows at least how deeply that belief is stamped upon the soul. It is a common saying, how 'Bishop Horne found our Lord Jesus Christ everywhere in the Psalms, Grotius nowhere.' Certainly our Lord must have been much in Bishop Horne's heart, that everything in the Psalms spoke to his soul of Him. So much the more, then, must our Lord's gift of His body and blood have been in the hearts of the early Fathers, that words which would not suggest the thought of them to others spoke it to them.

"But however different the occasions may be upon which the truth is spoken of, in whatever variety of ways it may be mentioned, the truth itself is one and the same — one uniform, simple, consentient truth; that what is consecrated upon the altars for us to receive, what, under the outward elements is there present for us to receive, is the body and blood of Christ; by receiving which the faithful in the Lord's Supper do verily and indeed take and receive the body and blood of Christ; by presuming to approach which, the wicked (*i. e.* those who with impenitent hearts wilfully purpose to persevere in deadly sin, and yet venture to 'take the sacrament') become guilty of the body and blood of the Lord; *i. e.* become guilty of a guilt like theirs who laid hands on His divine person while yet in the flesh among us, or who shed His all-holy blood.

"Now, we have been accustomed to value Ante-Nicene Testimonies to the divinity of our Lord; we are struck when St. Cyprian (while deciding as to the baptism of infants on the eighth day) lays down the doctrine of the transmission of original sin as clearly as St. Augustine amid the Pelagian con troversy.

"Yet the principle of these questions is one and the same. The argument is valid for all or for none. Either it is of no use to show that Christians, before the Council of Nice, did uniformly believe in the divinity of our Lord, as the Church has since, or it *is* a confirmation of the faith, that they did receive unhesitatingly in their literal sense our blessed Lord's words: 'This is My body.'

"This argument, from the consent of those who had handed down the truth before them, was employed as soon as there were authorities which could be alleged. So rooted was the persuasion that certain truth must have been known to those who received the faith from the first, that even heretics resorted to the argument, and garbled and misrepresented the Fathers before them, in order to bring them to some seeming agreement with themselves. The argument was used by minds in other respects of a different mould. Theodoret and St. Leo appended to works on controversial points of faith citations from the Fathers before them. St. Augustine vindicated against Pelagius, and St. Athanasius against Arius, authorities which they had misrepresented. Even the Fathers, assembled from the whole world in general councils, have, in proof of their decisions, wherein all were agreed, alleged the authorities of yet older Fathers, who were known in previous ages to have handed down the Apostolic truth.

"Yes, along the whole course of time, throughout the whole circuit of the Christian world, from east to west, from north to south, there floated up to Christ our Lord one harmony of praise. Unbroken as yet lived on the miracle of the day of Pentecost, when the Holy Spirit from on high swept over the discordant strings of human tongues and thoughts, of hearts and creeds, and blended all their varying notes into one holy unison of truth. From Syria and Palestine and Armenia, from Asia Minor and Greece, from Thrace and Italy, from Gaul and Spain, from Africa Proper and Egypt and Arabia, and the Isles of the Sea, wherever any Apostle had taught, wherever any martyr had sealed with his blood the testimony of Jesus, from the polished cities or the anchorites of the desert, one Eucharistic voice ascended: ' Righteous art Thou, O Lord, and all Thy words are truth.' Thou hast said, ' This is My body, this is My blood.' Hast Thou said, and shalt not Thou do it? As Thou hast said, so we believe.

" Truly, O Lord, ' Thy holy Church throughout all the world doth acknowledge Thee.' "

But not alone from the hand of one who, though in a non-Lutheran Church, has become Lutheran on this point, have we testimony as to the identity of our faith with the faith of the early Church of the Fathers. We have the same testimony from others within the Reformed Church, whose concessions are the more striking because those who make them still refuse to accept the Lutheran faith. On this point, one citation may suffice. It is from Peter Bayle,* the unrivalled general scholar of his age. He says: " There are Protestants who, without holding the opinions of the Lutherans, are, Peter Bayle. nevertheless, convinced that, in forming hypotheses (to harmonize the statements of the Fathers on the Eucharist), the view of the Augsburg Confession is preferable to all others in furnishing a reason for the phrases of antiquity. For, as the expressions in regard to Jesus Christ which seem most directly in conflict with each other are best harmonized — so that not even a shadow of contradiction remains, by the supposition that he is *both* God and man in unity of person — in the same way all the terms, difficult, inflated, hyperbolic, simple, and direct, which the Fathers used in speaking of the Holy Sacrament, can be easily harmonized on the supposition that, in the Supper, is present at once *both* the humanity of Christ and the substance of the bread."

* Nouv. de la Rep. des Lettres, 1687, Febr. Art. II., 129–181.

XIII.

THE DOCTRINE OF THE LORD'S SUPPER CONSIDERED IN ITS ANTITHESIS.

(AUGSBURG CONFESSION. ART. X.)

WE have, in our previous dissertation, discussed the thetical part of the Tenth Article, and now reach the closing words, in which, very briefly stated, we have the antithesis.

The Antithesis.

It is in these words: *first*, in the Latin, " et improbant secus docentes," " and they disapprove of those who teach otherwise;" *second*, in the German, "derhalben wird auch die gegenlehr verworfen," " therefore also the opposite doctrine is rejected." In the Latin, the errorists are spoken of; in the German, the error. The Latin was designed more especially for the learned classes, the German was meant for the people, and is therefore more cautious even than the Latin against phraseology, which might be misconstrued as a warrant for personal animosity. Our confessors carefully avoided all appeals to the passions of men. Everything harsh and revolutionary was contrary to the spirit of Conservative Reformation, which is wholly distinct from that of radicalism and revolution. This conservative spirit prompts the softness of the language toward persons: "improbant," *they* "are disapproved of;" while it bears, in all its force, the decisiveness toward error; *it* "is rejected." The errorists, moreover, are regarded as errorists, not as individuals. We may love, esteem, cherish, see their virtues, stand in any relation of amity, which does not imply approval of error, or connivance at it: out in so far as errorists are " secus docentes," teaching other

664

wise than the truth, we disapprove of them, "improbamus."
So far as their doctrine is "gegenlehr," — counter to the
truth, — it is rejected (verworfen). It has been asked why the
" damnant," or harsher condemnatory word, is used   "Improbant"
in the antitheses to the other Articles, and the seem- —why used?
ingly milder "improbant" is used here? The answer to this
is that the heresies condemned are more directly in conflict
with the general faith confessed by the whole Catholic or Universal Church in the Œcumenical Creeds, and that the persons
specially had in view in this "improbant," professed to hold
with our confessors on every other point than that of the Supper, and some of them, as the Tetrapolitans, declared that even
on this point the differences were more verbal than real. Therefore our confessors, in the exercise of that charity which
" hopeth all things," and to avoid closing the door upon all
prospect of bringing those who professed to be so near them to
perfect accord, used the mildest term consistent with truth —
a term which, however, was none the less strong in the thing,
because of its gentleness in the form.

The question now arises, who are they that are here alluded
to, and why are they disapproved of, and their doc-   Who are meant
trine rejected? We might make various classifica- in the Antith-
tions of them. One of the most natural is derived esis?
from the various parts of the Divine testimony against which
their error is arrayed. And here it must be remembered that
the antithesis is, in its logical sequence, prospective as well as
retrospective. It involves in its rejection all future errors
against the truth confessed, as well as errors then past or then
present. If a new form of error were to arise to-day in conflict with the testimony of the Confession, it is disapproved of
by that anticipation with which truth, in its simple unity,
reaches the Protean forms of errors. New heresies are, for the
most part, but the shifting of masks. The errors classified
after the plan which we suggest may be arranged under *three*
generic heads: The errors, *first*, of those who are arrayed
against the Scripture testimony as to the *outward* element, to
wit, the *Romish* and *Greek* Churches, which, by their doctrine
of transubstantiation, deny the presence of true bread and true

wine in the Lord's Supper. *Second*, of those who deny the Scripture testimony in regard to the *internal* or heavenly element, the Zwinglians, Calvinists, Socinians, and Rationalists, who deny the objective presence of the true body and blood of our Lord Jesus in his Supper. *Third*, of those who deny both, who, combining, as it were, the two erroneous extremes, contend that in the Lord's Supper there is neither bread nor body —wine nor blood—and maintain that the Supper is not an objective, permanent institution, but a purely ideal, spiritual thing. Such are the Quakers, and certain schools of mystics.

The long array of what claims to be argument in behalf of the various mistaken views which are rejected in the Antithesis to the Tenth Article may be classified under these heads: Arguments from a false grammar; a false lexicography; a false rhetoric; a false philosophy; a false dogmatic; a false construction of history; a false presumption as to the effect of the Scriptural doctrine on the Christian life.

In regard to these various genera of error, and the arguments for them, some of the species have been abandoned — some have been already sufficiently noticed in the thetical treatment of the doctrine — some are unworthy of notice. We may, therefore, confine ourselves to the form of error in regard to the Lord's Supper which we are, practically, most frequently called to meet. It is not likely that we will meet a Carlstadtian, who will maintain that the key to the words is that Christ pointed to His body, when He said, "This is My body;" or an "Œcolampadian," who will say that the word "body" is metaphorical; or a "Schwenkfeldian," who will argue that the subject is predicate, the predicate subject, and that the words are to be inverted, "My body is this." The modern argument against the true doctrine of the Lord's Supper rests ordinarily on two exegetical assumptions, both of which have the common feature that whereas the truth rests on what Christ actually said, in its direct sense, these assume that the interpreter is justified in adding to our Saviour's words, and in modifying their natural force.

Two chief centres of the most recent controversy, as to the exegesis of the words of the institution, are "touto" and

" **esti.**" Does "to ıto" mean "this bread "? does "esti" mean
" signifies, is a symbol of "?

Of " *touto*,"—"*this*,"—Capellus, a Reformed divine, says, " the
entire controversy hinges on the meaning of ' this.' "
 "Touto"—"This."
In regard to the proper grammatical force of " tou-
to," the truth seems to be very simple. The Saviour breaking bread and giving it to His disciples, and saying, " Take,
eat," commenced with the word " touto," a proposition which
might, in conformity with the truth, have ended either with the
word " artos," or, as it actually did, with the word " soma."
He might, looking at the thing given simply on its natural
side, have said, " This is bread," or might have said, as He
actually did say, contemplating it on its supernatural side,
" This is My body."   Hence, apart from all other reasons, it is
evident that neither the word " bread," nor the word " body,"
is to be supplied after " touto," as it is inconceivable that our
Lord should have uttered an identical proposition — a proposition whose two parts are tautological repetitions of each other,
or would be self-involved. In the first case the proposition
would be " This bread is bread ; " in the other it would be
" This body is My body."   Hence, if there were no other
reason whatever for the interpretation, it is evident that the
" touto " is used here, as it is used in all phrases fairly parallel with this — indefinitely indicating simply " this thing," —
" this," whose definite character is to be stated in the words
which follow. The grammatical question in hand here is
really this, and no more, whether the demonstrative pronoun " touto," in the neuter gender, standing where it does,
and used as it is, may be considered as qualifying " artos,"
" bread," in the masculine understood ; in other words,
whether we may read *in* " artos " after " touto," so as to make
the sense " This bread is My body "?   In advance of the direct
grammatical argument, we might settle the question by asking
of the reasoner to state his argument in Greek.   Now, stating
it in Greek, he will write what no educated Greek ever wrote —
" Touto artos."   What is not logical in Greek is not so in
English.   Now, then, we affirm, *first*, that it is the rule that a
pronoun shall agree with its antecedent, or the noun it *quali*

fies, in gender; *second,* that in the seeming exceptions to this rule, in which the demonstrative pronoun is of a different gender from the thing alluded to, that exception arises from the fact that the thing is thought of *as* a *thing,* and not in the grammatical force of its name; *third,* that in such cases, consequently, we may not supply the grammatical name of the thing, but must conceive of it indefinitely *as* a thing, so that in no case whatever is it lawful to read *in* after a demonstrative, a noun of a different gender from its own. The general rule, therefore, stands in this case, and decides it. The rule specifically applied here is, that a demonstrative pronoun qualifying a noun agrees with that noun in gender. Now " touto " does not agree in gender with " artos," and " artos " may, therefore, not be supplied.

Against the critic who maintains that we may reach *grammatically* the construction: " This *bread* is," some of the points which we consider decisive in the case are here: 1. The word artos (bread) had not been used by our Lord at all. He had simply said: " Take, eat, this is My body." The word *artos* the critic gets from Matthew's narrative. No such *word* as he reads in was used antecedently to our Saviour's declaration. He says that, as our Saviour uttered the words: " This is My body," the " this " refers to the word *artos.* Our reply in brief is, *there was no word artos to refer to.* That word is Matthew's word, written long after our Lord's ascension. The *artos expressed* cannot be the antecedent to our Saviour's *touto,* for the simple reason that there *was no artos* expressed.

2. Our second point is this, that as there is no precedent *artos* standing in any *possible grammatical relation* to the *touto,* if we get the *artos* in at all, we must get it in by supplying it by conjecture from the mind of the speaker, and adding it after the *touto,* thus: *touto artos,* a neuter pronoun qualifying a masculine noun.

3. Our third point is, that the pronoun never varies from the gender of the noun *it qualifies,* or agrees with. Our inference, therefore, is, that as on the critic's theory, *touto,* a neuter pronoun, must *qualify artos,* a masculine noun, that theory is

false, and is utterly overthrown by the RULE that a pronoun shall agree with its antecedent in gender.

To every text cited or referred to by such a critic, one and the same answer will apply. *In not a solitary one does the pronoun differ in gender from the noun it qualifies,* or which must be supplied to make the desired sense. In not a solitary case does a demonstrative pronoun differ in gender from the noun which must be supplied in order to make a required rendering. Not one instance can be found from Genesis to Malachi, in the Septuagint, or from Matthew to Revelation, in the New Testament, in which such a conjunction must be made as that of *touto neuter* with *artos masculine,* in order to reach the full sense of a passage.

Many of the supposed examples, in addition to the general lack of adaptation to their end, have a peculiar infelicity. One is Galat. iv. 24: " Which things The Scriptural Examples. are an allegory; for these are the two covenants." " These," it is said, is feminine, corresponding in gender with covenants, though the antecedent is "which things." " Which things," we reply, is neuter, it is true, but " which things " is a pronoun, and not the antecedent of the feminine " these." Nor has " covenants " anything to do with the gender of " these." The true antecedents are " bondwoman " and " freewoman," v. 22, 23, and the meaning is, " these women " are the two covenants. So clear is this, as the whole connection will show, that Luther, in the first twelve editions of his New Testament, and following him Tyndale and Coverdale, translate: " these women;" the Genevan: " these mothers," and so the best interpreters of all schools, as Henry, De Wette, Fausset, Noyes. But if the critic were right in his exegesis, the text would not help him, for he could not read in "things," neuter, after "autai," feminine, so as to translate " these which things " *autai atena.*

The second example given is Rev. xx. 14: " This is the second death." " ' This ' is masculine, and agrees with ' death,' though it really refers to the antecedent clause, which is, of course, neuter!" If the critic has a Greek Testament with a reliable text, he will find that *autos does* agree with *thanatos,* and that the text literally runs: This death is the second. Even with the received text, a good sense is: This (death) is the second death. How, too, can he imagine, even on his ground, that a "this" which refers to a previous sentence is parallel to a "this" which has no sentence or word on which it grammatically depends. Where is the parallel to *touto artos?*

In Matt. xxvi. 28: " This is My blood of the New Testament " is not parallel; for it is not independent, and is connected with what precedes by the *gar* "*for:*" Drink of *it, for this* is My blood. The pronoun *autou* (hereof, of it, of this) is connected with what follows: Drink *of it, for this is My blood*, and moreover *does agree in gender with the noun poterion* (cup), if a word is to be supplied, the word which is actually supplied in Luke xxii. 23: *This cup is.* Now, the critic will not deny that in Luke xxii. 20, the gender of *touto* is *determined* by *poterion* (cup), not by *aima* (blood), and if it is so there, so must it be in Matt. xxvi. 27, where we know, on divine authority, that if we supply a noun at all, *poterion* is to be supplied, and where consequently the gender of *touto* would be determined, not by the noun in the predicate, but by the noun understood. If, then, *artos* were the noun understood here, as the critic supposes, the very principle of the text to which he appeals is decisive that the pronoun should be *autos*, masculine, not *touto*, neuter. If St. Luke had supplied a noun understood, as he does in the case of *poterion*, he would, according to the critic's principles, have written *touto artos*, which even he will not contend would be Greek. Yet, into this actually runs what he is now contending for, and what he has to prove, to wit, that the demonstrative pronoun *requiring a noun to be supplied* does not agree in gender with that noun. Not a solitary example adduced even contemplates the disproof of this position. Yet this is the very thing which is to be disproved.

A true parallel in the main matter is found in 1 *Cor. x.* 28: " If any of those that believe not bid you to a feast, . . if any man say unto you: This is offered in sacrifice to idols, (more literally, This is idol-sacrifice, ' a thing offered to a god,') eat not." Here is a real as well as a verbal example; for it speaks of the very eating of which St. Paul makes a contrasting parallel with the " communion of the body of Christ." What does

" *this* ' mean here? Not the idol-sacrifice, for that would make an identical proposition: This idol - sacrifice is idol - sacrifice. But there is no noun whatever in the context to which *touto* can refer; the force of "this" is, therefore: This which you are about to eat is idol-sacrifice. If a translator, on the ground that he knew that *flesh* was used for sacrifice, should insist on rendering, or on building on the rendering: This flesh is idol-sacrifice, it would be *decisive* against him that *touto* is *neuter*, and *sarx* (flesh) is feminine. We need not multiply examples. Our principle is so simple and easy of application, that even the English reader can run it out for himself in these and other passages. The testimony is unvarying, complete, and over-whelming, that in every case really parallel with the *present* the view we take is correct, which is, that when Jesus says, "Take, eat, this is My body," He means, This which I tell you to Take, eat, is My body.

The correct view in regard to *touto*, to wit, that it cannot qualify or refer *grammatically* to *artos*, has been maintained by a large majority of the best scholars in all parts of the religious world.

The accepted view of the *Lutheran* theologians is that *touto* cannot refer grammatically to *artos*. This is espe- _{Lutheran The-} cially illustrated among those we have examined _{ologians.} by Gerhard, Quenstedt, Calovius, Carpzov, Oliarius, Scherzer, Bengel, and the best both of our earlier and later commenta tors. Gerhard, for example, says, in his Harmonia: "The whole argument for transubstantiation from the words of the institution rests upon the hypothesis that by the pronoun 'this' is denoted the bread. But the 'this,' used deictically, has not reference to the bread alone, but to the whole complex. If the bread alone were meant, what sort of a grammatical construction would result? — 'Touto artos.' When Paul, 1 Cor. x. 16, makes bread the subject, then the predicate is not 'body of Christ,' but 'communion of the body of Christ;' when Luke places the 'cup' as the subject, the predicate is not 'blood of Christ,' but the 'New Testament' in His blood. The pronoun 'this' is therefore used, not adjectively, but substantively, so that there is an exhibitive proposition."

The true view is accepted even by some of the ripest Roman

Catholic scholars, much as the concession embarrasses the argu ment for transubstantiation. Maldonatus, whose Commentary on Matthew is regarded by Romanists as the very best ever written on that Gospel, is especially worthy of examination on **Roman Catho- lic Expositors.** this point.   When Romish testimony agrees with the Protestant, it has special value.

It is the view of many of the most thoughtful and reliable Protestants who are not Lutherans, and who have a strong dogmatic temptation to overcome, in order to be faithful to the truth.   We will give a few of these, as they come from sources where we might least expect them.

Dr. HENRY HAMMOND, a classic among the older commentators of the Church of England, says: "It must here be observed that the word *touto*, *this*, is not the relative to *artos*, bread, but of the neuter, whereas that is of the masculine, and consequently it is not here said, This bread is My body."

The best interpreters of the Calvinistic Unionistic School have abandoned the theory that "touto" can refer grammatically to "artos."

Dr. JOHN J. OWEN in his Notes on Matthew (New York, **Reformed Di- vines.** 1857), on this point, says: "The form of words in the original does not refer so much to the *bread*, which is not mentioned, as to the *thing*."

LANGE, the latest commentator of eminence on Matthew, confessedly one of the greatest scholars of the age, but strongly anti-Lutheran, says: "This is My body.   This, in the *neuter, therefore not* directly ὁ ἄρτος (the bread)."

STIER, who was Unionistic, says, in regard to τοῦτο: "If *anything be certain* in regard to this matter, it is the sober word of Bengel, *which is faithful to the simple letter, and has, therefore, become classical,* 'hoc quod vos sumere jubeo,' this which I command you to take."   With this HENGSTENBERG, originally from the Reformed side in the Union, concurs with what Stier calls an "almost Lutheran approval."   STIER says further in the note: "The Lutheran divines maintain this as the force: This which I command you to eat.   They are right."   And again, in the text: "There is good reason why our Lord does *not* say *this bread.*"

ALFORD: "The form of expression is important, not being ' αυτος ο αρτος,' not the bread, but the thing itself." Dr. SCHAFF quotes these words of Alford as confirming the view of Lange, and thus endorses the judgment of these two interpreters. We may, therefore, say that the theory that "this," the confessed subject in the sacramental proposition, means grammatically "this *bread*," is a theory abandoned by the best scholars of the school which is most interested in maintaining it.

But even if it were granted that the true resolution of the grammatical form is into "This *bread* is My body," the desired inference, that the meaning is, "This *bread* is a symbol of My body," is as remote as ever.

In what sense This bread is the body of Christ.

For, first, if Christ had said, "*This* bread is My body," He would have implied that no other bread is His body: but as a symbol all bread is equally Christ's body. Second: the reason why *this* bread is His body must lie in something which has taken place, since there was simply bread upon the table at the Lord's Supper. It must be something which has taken place, since that bread was in the mere natural sphere of all bread. When it thus lay, it was not true of it that it was Christ's body any more than all other bread is. Between the lying of that bread on the table, a mere thing of nature in all its relations, and the affirmation "This is My body," six things had occurred. 1. *He* "took" it, the incarnate Almighty, after whose taking (Matt. xiv. 19) five loaves and two fishes had satisfied the hunger of five thousand men, besides women and children, and had left twelve baskets full of fragments. *He* "took" it, after whose taking (Matt. xv. 36) four thousand men, besides women and children, were fed, and seven baskets of fragments remained. 2. He "*gave thanks*," as He had done in the stupendous miracle of creation in which He fed the thousands (Matt. xv. 36). 3. He "*blessed*" the bread, as in the supernatural feeding (Matt. xiv. 19), and in virtue of that word of omnipotent benediction, the border of the realm of nature was passed, and all that followed was under the powers and conditions of the infinite supernatural. 4. He "*brake* it," as He had broken the mystic loaves and fishes (Matt. xv. 36). 5. He "*gave* it" to His disciples, as He had given the loaves and

43

fishes to His disciples for the multitude (Matt. xiv. 19 ; xv. 36).
6. He had said, "Take, eat," and had assigned as the reason
why this solemn preparation had taken place, and this command was now given: " *This* is My body." If " this " means
" *this* bread," it means not *that* bread which was *before* the six
acts, but *this* bread, which is eaten *after* the six acts ; and if it
be called the body of Christ *now*, it is not because it is a symbol of the body, for this it was *then*, but because it is now what
St. Paul expressly calls it, " the communion," or medium of
the communication of Christ's body. Conceived in this way
the word bread would mean the complex result of the sacramental union, the sacramental bread in its supernatural conjunction with the sacramental body. *This* bread, this complex,
is not symbol but reality. It is literally Christ's true body, as
it is literally true bread. As the words, " This man is God,'
applied to Christ, means, This man is literally God personally,
(in virtue of the personal union), yet is literally man naturally,
Christ is true man and true God ; so the words, This bread is
Christ's body, mean, This bread is literally Christ's body sacramentally, (in virtue of the sacramental union,) yet is literally
bread naturally. The Eucharist is true bread and true body.
Before the miraculous blessing of the five loaves and the fishes
it was true, *That* food is *not* food for thousands ; *after* the blessing, it was true, *This* food *is* food for thousands: *before* the
blessing *that* bread was *not* the body of Christ ; *after* the blessing, *This* bread *is* His body.

Hence the Ancient Church and the Lutheran Church, holding
the same faith, have not hesitated at all to use the
expression, " This bread, or the sacramental bread,
is Christ's body," while both would repudiate as error the idea
that bread, as bread, can be called Christ's body. The fathers
are very explicit in affirming that it is *not* bread, as bread, of
which they affirm that it is Christ's body, but that bread
whose character is conditioned by the six sacramental acts of
our Lord. Thus Jerome*: "The bread *which our Lord brake
and gave to His disciples is His body.*" Gaudentius†: " When
our Lord reached the *consecrated* bread and wine to His disci-

The Ancient Church.

---

* Epist. ad Hedebiam. † In Exod. Tract 2.

ples, He said: This is My body." Facundus*: "Our Lord called the bread and cup *which had been blessed, and which He delivered to His disciples,* His body and blood." Maxentius †: "The bread *which the whole Church partakes of in memory of the Lord's passion* is His body." Theodoret ‡: "*After consecration,* we call the mystic fruit of the vine the Lord's blood." Tertullian §: "Christ, when He had *taken* bread, and *distributed* it to His disciples, *made* it His body by saying, 'This is My body.'" Cyril of Jerusalem ‖: "*When the invocation is made,* the bread becomes the body of Christ and the wine His blood." Gregory Nyssen ¶: "*At first* the bread is common bread, *but after the mystery has consecrated* it, it is both called and becomes the body of Christ." Augustine **: "*Not all bread, but only that* which receives the blessing of Christ, becomes Christ's body." The author of the Book on the Sacraments, imputed to Ambrose (L. IV. ch. iv.): "Perhaps thou wilt say, My bread (the bread of which I speak) is ordinary bread; but though that bread is (ordinary) bread *before* the sacramental words, yet, *when the consecration takes place,* the bread becomes the body of Christ. . . How can that which is bread be the body of Christ? By consecration. By whose words is this consecration? By the words of the Lord Jesus. Whatever else may have gone before, as praise to God, and prayers, yet when the venerable sacrament itself is to be consummated, the priest no longer uses his own words, but uses the words of Christ. Wherefore it is Christ's word by which the sacrament is consummated. What is Christ's word? That by which the universe was made out of nothing. . . *It was not the body of Christ before consecration,* but after consecration it is the body of Christ. He hath said, and it is done. Wine and water are put into the cup; but it becomes blood by the consecration of the heavenly word."

The Lutheran Church, holding the same Eucharistic faith with the Ancient Church, does not hesitate to employ the

---

* In Defens. 3. Capit. Lib. IX. c. ult.   † Dialog. 2. c. 13.
‡ Dialog. 1.   § Catech. Mystag. 2.
‖ Cont. Marc. L. IV. ch. 40.   ¶ Orat. in Christ. Baptisms.
** Serm. de diversis. 87.

same language in the same sense. Luther often uses the expression: "This bread, or the sacramental bread, is the body of Christ." He does this with respect to three objects. First, to assert the reality of the bread over against the error of transubstantiation. Second, to deny the exclusion of the sacramental bread from the complex of the Saviour's meaning, as was done by Carlstadt; and, third, to assert the character of the bread as the medium of a true impartation of the body of Christ, involving a true presence of that body. Thus of the first he says * : " The gospel calls the sacrament bread. *Consequently*, the bread is the body of Christ. By this we abide; it is sure over against the dreams of the sophists, that it is bread which *it* (the gospel) calls bread." He is not speaking of *touto* in its relation to *artos*, or to anything bearing upon it in any way. Luther is arguing against transubstantiation. Over against the theory that it is the accidents of bread which are the Sacrament, on its earthly side, he says that bread itself is. He says: " Consequently, that is, logically, over against transubstantiation, the bread, not its accidents, is the body of Christ." While Luther and the Lutheran Church deny that the expression " bread is the body of Christ " is found in the Bible, they admit that there is a sense in which it may be allowed as a part of human terminology,and, where the Romanist says the accidents of the bread, and not bread itself, are the visible part of the Sacrament of Christ, Luther replies: No; the bread, true bread, is that Sacrament; and over against the Romish theory that the mere species of bread, and not its substance, is the communion of Christ's body, Luther maintains that true bread is that communion, or, in virtue of the sacramental union, that, in a certain sense, it is (not is like) the body of Christ. On the second point, Luther demonstrates in his whole argument against Carlstadt that the proposition cannot mean " This body, to which I point, is My body, broken for you," but "This which I tell you to take, eat, is My body." This sacramental complex, in a word, is both bread and body ; and, because of the sacramental union, we can say, This bread is

Luther.

* Werke. Leipzig Edi. Vol. XVIII. p. 421.

Christ's body. Hence, in the third place, Luther makes the point: "It is no longer mere bread of the oven, but bread of flesh, or bread of body, that is, a bread which is *sacramentally one* with the body of Christ. . . It is no more mere wine of the vintage, but wine of blood, that is, a wine which has come to be a *sacramental unit* with the blood of Christ." *

In conformity with the ancient phraseology the Formula of Concord declares: "The bread does not signify the absent body of Christ, and the wine the absent blood of Christ; but by means of (propter) the sacramental union, the bread and wine are truly the body and blood of Christ."† Gerhard ‡ has so admirably explained the meaning of the ecclesiastical phrase "The bread is the body of Christ," that a citation from him will render any other unnecessary. "Although the proposition, 'The bread is the body of Christ,' does not occur in so many words in the Scripture, we do not, by any means, disapprove of it, inasmuch as the church-writers, ancient and recent, frequently employ it From the words of Christ, 'Take, eat, this is My body,' and the words of Paul, 'The bread which we break is the communion of the body of Christ,' we are to estimate its meaning and explain it, and hence it is usual to call it a *sacramental* proposition. This may be more clearly understood by noting what follows. In all regular affirmative predications, it is required that there shall be a mutual agreement and coherence between the subject and the predicate. If this agreement be intrinsic and essential, the predications are *essential ;* if it be extrinsic and accidental, the predications are *accidental.* From the rule in logic, that one thing cannot be affirmed literally and without type to be another thing (disparatum de disparato proprie adfirmate non posse predicare), the adversaries draw the inference that the proposition 'The bread is the body of Christ' is figurative. But they ought to know that besides those ordinary predications, which conform to the rules of logic, there are in

Formula of Concord. Gerhard.

---

* Werke. Leipzig. xix. 497: "Fleisches-brod oder Leibs-Brod so mit dem Leibe Christi ein Sacramentlich Wesen . . worden ist . . ein Wein, der mit dem Blut Christi in ein Sacramentlich Wesen kommen ist."

† Epitome. Art. VII. ii. ‡ Loci. Cotta. x. 155. 240 seq.

theology predications not in ordinary use (inusitati), in which, on account of the mystic union, one thing is said, without a trope, to be another thing. Such propositions are of two kinds, personal and sacramental. The *personal* are those in which the human nature is predicated of the divine nature of the *Logos*, and, on the other hand, the divine nature of the *Logos* is predicated of the human nature assumed, *in the concrete*, to wit, on account of the personal union. Such expressions are these, God is man, Man is God, the Son of Mary is the Son of God. *Sacramental* propositions are those in which the heavenly thing is predicated of the earthly element, on account of the sacramental union, such as these, the bread is the body of Christ, the wine is the blood of Christ. As *in the abstract* the divine nature of the *Logos* is *not* predicated of the human, nor the human of the divine, but *only in the concrete*, which is a manifest proof that the personal union is the cause and source of these predications; so also it is not predicated of the bread, as such, but only in its sacramental use, that it is the body of Christ; and hence it is usual to add to the subject, and say the eucharistic bread, the consecrated bread, the bread which we break is the body of Christ, and this again is a manifest proof that the sacramental union is the cause and source of the latter predication. If the adversaries say that the bread must be the body of Christ either in a *literal* or a *figurative* sense, we answer that there is a third sense, to wit, the *sacramental*, by which is meant that the bread is the *collating organ*, the *exhibitive* symbol and vehicle, by which the body of Christ is communicated, or as St. Paul expresses it, it is the communication (koinonia) of the body of Christ. The bread is not transmuted into the body of Christ, nor is it a bare sign of the body of Christ, but is the organ and mean whereby the body of Christ is communicated."

The new view of KAHNIS in regard to the Lord's Supper has,

View of Kahnis.

for various reasons, excited an interest beyond anything in its kind in our day; and as it links itself with a confused perception of the points which are so clearly put by Gerhard, we shall introduce it here, and, as an act of justice to its author, shall give it entire, instead of breaking it into fragments to fit the parts of it into their most natural place in our own discussion. The view of Kahnis has aroused extraordinary feeling, not merely nor mainly because of his distinguished ability as a theologian, but because, in various writings, but especially in his work on the Lord's Supper (1851), he had appeared as the defender of the distinctive Lutheran faith — a faith to which he had shown his devotion in 1848, by leaving the State Church of Prussia, to take part with the persecuted Old Lutherans. This faith, in more than one vital respect, he has recently abandoned. Most conspicuous among these changes are two, the first of which really necessitated the second. Kahnis abandons the doctrine of the proper and supreme divinity of Jesus Christ, and gives Him the place assigned by the theory of Subordination. In doing this he, of necessity, gives up the true doctrine of the Sacramental Presence — a presence which presupposes the Godhead of Christ, and the personal union of His human nature with it. In Kahnis' work, in which he aims at presenting an historico-genetical delineation of the Lutheran Dogmatics, he unfolds these changes of view. His presentation of his theory and argument on the Lord's Supper * is as follows:

" The fact that in the exposition of the words of the Institution the teachers of the Church, in all ages, have been divided into two camps, the one holding to a verbal sense, the other to a metaphorical sense of the decisive words, is in itself enough to set bounds to too confident a security on either side. Where difficulties exist of the character which here meets us, it is well to lay down propositions to which assent may, with justice, be demanded. FIRST: It is beyond dispute, that the proposition, The bread is the body, the wine is the blood of Jesus, literally taken, is impossible. As in every proposition the subject is placed in identity with the predicate, by means of the copula, in such a way that the subject stands to the predicate in the relation of the individual to the general, it follows that there can be no logical meaning except in a proposition in which the subject stands to the predicate as the individual stands to the

* Die Lutherische Dogmatik historisch-genetisch dargestellt. Leipz. 1861. Vol L 616–626.

general. Now the bread (as bread) is not the body of Christ
(as body). Bread and body are heterogeneous ideas, which can
no more be united in one than the propositions: Wood is iron,
Hegel is Napoleon, and such like. So soon as a proposition
cannot be taken literally, as, for example, in the one just given,
'Hegel is Napoleon,' the figurative exposition is in place—
Hegel is a Napoleon in the sphere of science.

"So, also, in the SECOND place, it is beyond dispute that the
proposition, This is My body, *may be* figurative (metaphorical).
The Scripture contains innumerable figurative propositions.
From the copula 'is' it is alike impossible to demonstrate the
figurative or the literal character of the proposition. The copula
allows of no change of meaning. Those who say that 'is' is
equivalent to 'signify' mean to say that either the subject or
the predicate of a proposition is to be taken figuratively.

"THIRDLY, as to the words of the Institution as they sound,
it may be affirmed, without contradiction, that in them the
body of Christ is regarded as a body which is to be delivered to
death. Though the body of the risen Saviour bore on it the
marks of the crucifixion (John xx.), and men shall recognize
Him at His second coming as Him whom they pierced (Rev. i.
7), from which it follows that the slain body and the glorified
body are identical, yet the words of the Institution contemplate the body, not as glorified, but as put to death. That the
blood which was to be shed, that is, literally, the blood of
Jesus, which in His death left His body, has to be understood
of the death of Christ, is shown by the proposition as Paul and
Luke have it: This cup is the New Testament in My blood.
The blood which has mediated a new covenant is that which
was shed upon the cross, to wit, is the sacrificial death of Christ.
If, then, these propositions stand, we have a sure basis for
exposition. The Lutheran Church has the indisputable fundamental principle of hermeneutics, that the literal exposition
has the first claim, if the literal sense be at all tenable—a principle of special force in this case, in which the words are of
such great importance — words which were given of the Lord
to Paul by special revelation. 1 Cor. xi. 25. (See Kahnis, Lehre
v. Abendm. 14 seq.) But this is only possible when in the

proposition, This is My body (My blood), the subject is not bread (wine). When the determination of the subject is involved, it is decided upon the one hand by the connection, on the other, by the predicate. The connection demands as subject bread (wine), as predicate, body (blood); and in this way the exposition found itself directed to the supposition of an internal connection of bread and body, and of wine and blood, in which the predicate gives prominence to the chief substance. Thus the physician, in giving an essence in water, says: This is a cordial. The 'this,' in such a sentence, is 'essence and water,' the predicate is the chief substance. When Christ says, 'My words are spirit and life,' from words as the subject, which are partly spirit, partly letter, He educes the essential substance. This mode of speech, to which Luther gives the name Synecdoche, is, in itself, admissible. The only question to be raised is, Is it admissible here? To a renewed investigation which we have given the subject, on the principle 'day teacheth unto day,' the difficulties connected with this view have presented themselves with increasing force. According to the connection, the 'this' is that which Jesus took, brake, gave them to eat, that is, the bread. In the case of the cup, the subject is expressly specified as 'this cup.' Now cup (chalice), by the familiar metonomy 'container for thing contained,' stands for that which it contains. But what the chalice contains is wine. Christ does not say, 'That which ye now eat is My body, that which ye now drink is My blood, but that which I *give* you to eat and drink,' consequently is such in advance of the eating and drinking. The *potēerion* is the drink, as it was in the chalice before the disciples drank. But *before* the eating and drinking it is still, according to the Lutheran doctrine, bread and wine, not the body and blood of Christ. But that *potēerion* means the wine. Yet undrunken is affirmed in Paul's exposition (1 Cor. x. 16): 'The cup of blessing which we bless, is it not the communion of the blood of Christ? the bread which we break, is it not the communion of the body of Christ?' in which, beyond doubt, the bread, as broken for eating, the cup, as blessed for drinking, is called the communion. That which places us in communior with the body and blood of Christ (Abendm. 127 seq.), consequently is such before the eating and drinking. But if bread (wine) be the subject, the literal meaning has to be abandoned. To this we are necessitated by the proposition, 'This cup is the New Covenant in My blood,' inasmuch as it is impossible that a chalice of wine can itself be the covenant relation between God and man established by Christ in His death. The only exposition, therefore, is: This cup is a sign of the new covenant in My blood. The supposition that body and blood stand, by metonomy, for sign of body, sign of blood (Œcoiampadius, Calvin) is untenable. No such metonomy can be shown. The proposition is like countless others, in which the predicate is figurative. Thus we say of a statue, This is Blucher; of a serpent with his tail in his mouth: This is eternity. The supposition of a symbol is justified by the manifest symbolical character of the whole transaction. The bread which is *broken* is the body which is *broken* (*klōmenon*) for us; the wine which is *poured* out of a large vessel into the chalice is the blood which is *shed* for us (*ekchunomenon*). That the breaking of the bread has a special significance is shown by the designation of the bread which we *break* (1 Cor. x. 16), parallel with the cup *which we bless*. So, also, in Baptism, the submergence beneath the water is a symbolical act (p. 615). Had it been the glorified body which Jesus, at the Institution, offered in the bread, it might be imagined that somehow, though still in a mysterious and obscure manner, there was an impartation of it. But the body which was to be put to death, which stood before the disciples, could not be the object of the participation.

"To this point the exposition of *Zwingli* is justified. But that it is impossible to stop here *Calvin* acknowledged, yet failed, because he rested the lever of his sacramental theory on hypotheses destitute of Scriptural support. In the words 'This do in remembrance of Me,' our Lord commanded that this Supper should be celebrated from that time on in commemoration of Him; and it has been so done to this day. As often as it is celebrated Jesus dispenses, by the hand of the ministrant, bread and wine, as signs of His body and blood.

ordained by Him. But signs ordained and dispensed by God, through Christ, are not symbols — which would leave it undetermined how much or how little we are to impute to them, but are *a visible word of God* (p. 613). With the words of Christ, ' This do ye, as oft as ye drink it, in remembrance of Me,' the apostle links the declaration : ' For as often as ye eat of this bread and drink of this cup, ye do show the Lord's death till He come.' Inasmuch as the Supper is a participation of bread and wine as signs of the sacrificed body and blood, it is a memorial feast in which the guest confesses his faith in the sacrificial death of Christ. But he who makes such a confession before the Church, in reality must do it in a state of mind fitting it. ' Wherefore, whosoever shall eat this bread, or drink this cup of the Lord unworthily, shall be guilty (*enochos*) of the body and blood of the Lord ' (v. 27). *Enochos*, literally, bound for, when it has the sense of guilty, is conjoined with the genitive either of the sin, or of the penalty, or of the person and thing involved in the criminality incurred (*Bleek* on Heb. ii. 15. II. 339 seq. cf. 552). As immediately before, the Supper is spoken of as a confession of the death of Christ, we cannot well understand body and blood of Christ otherwise than as referring to the death of Christ, in the sin of which the unworthy communicant makes himself guilty (Lev. v. 1–17 ; 2 Sam. xxii. 22 ; 2 Macc. xiii. 6). He who confesses the death of Christ unworthily is guilty of the death of Christ. All men are guilty of the death of Christ. But he who believes in Jesus Christ seeks from Jesus Christ forgiveness of the sin which crucified Christ. But he who receives forgiveness of his sin is thereby absolved from the guilt of the body and blood of Christ. He, consequently, who receives the Supper unworthily, really confesses : I have slain Christ, and does not receive forgiveness from that sin, and is, consequently, guilty of the body and blood of Christ. In this passage, beyond doubt, body and blood have the sense, death of Christ : ' Wherefore let a man examine himself, and so let him eat of that bread and drink of that cup. For he that eateth and drinketh unworthily, eateth and drinketh damnation to himself, not discerning the Lord's body. For this cause are many weak and sickly among you, and many sleep' (v. 28–30). The unworthy reception of the Supper, which involves so great a guilt, produces, also, a serious punishment. He who eats and drinks bread and wine in the Supper as if they were common food and common drink, without considering that bread and wine are the body and blood of Christ, draws upon himself, by so eating and drinking, a penalty. Upon the body into which he receives bread and wine he draws sickness and death. It is at once apparent that such results cannot be explained on the theory that this is a mere symbolical transaction, in which there lies just so much as faith puts into it. This feast, ordained and dispensed of God, through faith in Christ, has as its substance the divine word concerning the sacrificial death, which word, Jesus Christ, who has instituted this feast, imparts to the recipient. Inasmuch as the word of God, as spoken or written, never goes forth void, but is a savor of death unto death to every one to whom it is not a savor of life unto life, so in the Supper the word concerning the atoning death of Christ is not merely set forth, but Christ applies it, by the hand of the ministrant, to the recipient for bodily reception. But a visible word of God, which Christ applies to the individual after the manner of sensible reception, is a *sacramental word*. The same result is reached by attentively considering 1 Cor. x. 16, seq. The discourse is of sacrificial flesh. As in Israel those who ate of the sacrifice entered into the fellowship of the altar, so those who participated in the banquets on the Heathen sacrifices entered into the fellowship of the gods who are Demons. He who drinks the cup of the Lord cannot drink the cup of Demons, and he who participates at the table of the Lord cannot take part at the table of Demons. 'The cup of blessing which we bless, is it not the communion of the blood of Christ? The bread which we break, is it not the communion of the body of Christ? For we, being many, are one bread and one body: for we are all partakers of that one bread' (v. 16, 17). As the sacrificial flesh of the Jews and Heathen united them with the altar, and, consequently, with the God, or the gods, to whom the altar was reared, so is the bread of the Supper the communion, that is, the medium of communion (that through which the communion is made) with the body, the wine the communion with the blood. Body and blood of Christ cannot here mean the glorified corporeal nature of Christ, but only that which is sacrificed, that is, the death of Christ, because otherwise the point of comparison with the sacrificial feast is lost. The death of Christ is the sacrifice; bread and wine the sacrificial meal. But here again bread and wine are not a mere symbol, but a *sign* which is, at the same time, a *medium*. Not faith, but bread and wine, brings into union with the sacrificed humanity of Christ. As the sacrificial flesh is not ordinary flesh, but a medium of fellowship with the divine being to whom it pertains, so, also, in the Supper, bread is not ordinary food, but a medium of fellowship with the sacrificed corporeal nature of Christ, to whom it pertains. *Bread and wine, consequently, signs of the body and blood of Christ, are, in virtue of the institution of Christ, the sacramental word of the body and blood of Christ, which word, commanded by Christ, applies to the death of Christ.* The sacrificial death of Christ is a fact of the past, which abides only in its power, that is, in the reconciliation with God, which is its work. He, consequently, who partakes of the Lord's Supper worthily, that is, in faith, receives the virtue of the death of Christ, that is, forgiveness of sins. At this point Luther's doctrine is vindicated, according to which, forgiveness of sins is the proper fruit of the believing participation in the Lord's Supper. This doctrine Luther rested on the words: Broken for the forgiveness of sins, which he explained, not of the death of Christ, but of the impartation of the body of Christ in the Supper. This word concerning the forgiveness of sins, not the reception of the glorified body, is, to him, the main thing in the Sacrament. The body of Christ is to him but a pledge of the word. But in this mode of apprehending it, the exposition of *klōmenon* is surely not tenable, for that word can only refer to the sacrificial death of Christ, as even the Formula of Concord teaches (Abendm. 99, 209). But even if this exposition were abandoned, the relation of the word touching the forgiveness of sins to the glorified body would remain completely unadjusted (Abendm. 358). Finally, however, Luther's doctrine ignores the weight which is attached to the death of Christ both by the words of the institution and the apostle's doctrine of the Supper. In all the passages which we have just been considering, the language has reference, not to the glorified, but to the broken, or given body, that is, the sacrificed body. Even if the Supper was not instituted in connection with the feast of the Passover, yet Paul, in the words (1 Cor. v. 6, 7), ' Christ our passover is sacrificed for us,' and John (John xix. 36), by applying to the unbroken body of our Lord the Old Testament command that the Paschal Lamb must not be broken (Exod. xii. 46 ; Ps. xxxiv. 20), represent the death of Christ as a paschal sacrifice. We have seen (Dogm. I. 262 seq.) that in the Passover lay the germ of the later worship. It was a propitiatory sacrifice, and, at the same time, a sacrificial meal. The fulfilling has separated into two elements the two parts of the Paschal Feast, the offering and the eating. Christ, the Paschal Lamb, was sacrificed on Golgotha, at the time when the paschal lamb was offered in the temple. This sacrifice, which Christ offered in His own body to God, is the fulfilling of all sacrifices, and, consequently, the last sacrifice, and has an objective atoning efficacy for all men, and forever more. After this sacrifice has been made, the appropriation of it remains, until Christ's second coming, the essence of the Supper, the transfigured paschal festival. In the bread broken and the cup blessed, God imparts, through Jesus Christ, in whose name it is dispensed, not merely a sign, but a visible word, which, to the believing recipient, is a medium of communion, a word concerning the sacrificial death of Jesus Christ. He who, in faith, partakes of the bread and wine as the Sacrament of the body and blood of Christ, receives the fruit of the death of Christ, to wit, the forgiveness of sins.

" But even with this the significance of the Supper is not exhausted. To this the Passover, the type of the Supper, already points. The paschal supper was not a mere appropriation of the propitiatory virtue of the paschal sacrifice. It was the supper of the living fellowship of the people, of a unity of families, with God (Dogm. I. 262 seq). The Lord's Supper is, consequently, also, no bare appropriation of the propitiatory

virtue of the death of Jesus. The blood of the sacrifice which
was offered to God is the life which has passed through death,
and makes atonement for the sins of men (Dogm. I. 271 seq.,
and 584). In the New Testament, consequently, the blood of
Christ is not merely a concrete expression for death, but means
the life of this death, that is, the propitiatory power of it,
which forever dwells in the corporeal nature of Christ which
has passed through death (Rom. iii. 25; Eph. i. 7; 1 John
i. 7; Heb. ix. 25; xiii. 20, and see, on them, Olshausen, Harless, De Wette, Bleek: Abendm. 63 seq). He, therefore, who,
in faith, grasps the death of Christ, receives the propitiatory virtue of the blood of Christ — the virtue which dwells
in the glorified body of Christ. Hence St. John (1 John v.
6–8) styles the Supper simply 'the blood.' As the appearing
of Christ stood between water (Baptism) and blood (death),
thus water and blood still testify of Him. The blood which
testifies of Him can be nothing but the Supper. The substance of the Supper is, consequently, Christ's death as a
power of atonement. But he who receives this power of the
glorified bodily nature of Christ, receives in himself Christ's
bodily nature itself, and in and with it the entire living Christ.
This is the mystical meaning of the discourse of Jesus in John
vi. Jesus Christ calls Himself the bread which has come down
from heaven, which gives life to him who eats of it. From
this thought He advances in v. 51: 'And the bread which
I will give is My flesh, which I will give for the life of the
world.' After the offence which the people took at Him, He
expresses this thought still more strongly: 'Verily, I say unto
you, except ye eat the flesh of the Son of man, and drink His
blood, ye have no life in you. Whoso eateth My flesh, and
drinketh My blood, hath eternal life; and I will raise him up
at the last day. For My flesh is meat indeed, and My blood is
drink indeed. He that eateth My flesh, and drinketh My blood,
dwelleth in Me, and I in him. As the living Father hath sent
Me, and I live by the Father, so he that eateth Me, even he
shall live by Me. This is that bread which came down from
heaven: not as your fathers did eat manna, and are dead: he
that eateth of this bread shall live forever' (v. 53–59). The

bread of life which has come from heaven is the divine personality of Jesus Christ. To eat this bread can have no other
meaning than to appropriate Jesus in faith. Now, as Jesus
attaches to the eating of His flesh and the drinking of His
blood the same operations which are attributed to faith (v. 47)
and to the eating of the bread of heaven (v. 50, 51), namely,
eternal life, the eating of the flesh of Christ cannot be, specifically, anything else than the eating of the bread from heaven,
that is, the faith which unites with Christ. The flesh of Christ,
which He gives for the life of the world, is His body, which is
to be given in death, that is, is His death. Eating the flesh
and drinking the blood can, consequently, only mean the
receiving in us, in faith, Jesus as the Crucified for us. This
is the condition of salvation, of living fellowship with Christ,
of everlasting life, of the resurrection. He who receives in
himself Jesus Christ in His body and blood given to death,
receives, in this bodily nature, slain for us, the life of Jesus
Christ, which fills him with the powers of eternity. The unity
of this proposition lies, beyond doubt, in this, that the power
of the slain bodily nature of Christ is absorbed into the glorified bodily nature of Christ; so that he who grasps the sacrificed bodily nature of Christ with its propitiatory power,
together with the glorified corporeal nature, is filled, by it,
with the entire person of Christ. The discourse in John vi.
does not, primarily, treat of the Supper, but of that faith
which establishes a living fellowship between us and Christ.
But Christ, beyond doubt, designedly veiled the faith under
the image of an eating of His flesh and drinking of His blood,
in order to express the mystical thought which subsequently
was to be transferred to the body in the Supper, just as in
John iii. 5, He expressed the idea of Baptism. For the history
of the exposition, see Abendm. 114 seq. It is now alone that
we come to understand why Jesus calls bread and wine not
merely signs of His death, but of His body and blood, which
are to be given to death. Inasmuch as Christ designates His
death as a suffering which is to be endured by His body, His
blood, He means to express the thought that just as little as
broken bread ceases to be bread, and wine poured out ceases to

be wine, just as little does that dissolution destroy the substance of His body. He does not give us His death to eat, but His body. The bread signifies Christ's body, the breaking of the bread the killing of the body, the eating of the bread the appropriation of the slain body in faith. The Christian who grasps the slain body of Christ in faith, appropriates to himself the death of Christ, and the body of Christ also, as he who eats of the broken bread makes use of the breaking that he may receive into him the bread. He who eats the broken bread commutes it into his organism, consequently into his life. He who, in faith, grasps the slain body of Jesus Christ makes it living by receiving into himself its vital power, that is, its power of atonement. *If, now, that which the body of Christ suffered in death inheres in the glorified body, then he who receives the atoning power immanent in the glorified body receives into himself the glorified body itself, and in and with it the whole Christ.* This is the truth which lies in the Lutheran exposition of the words of institution. We cannot grasp the slain body in faith without receiving the glorified body into us, because the virtue of the slain body lies in the glorified body. This reception is, it is true, no eating and drinking, but a spiritual reception by faith as a medium. The Lord's Supper is a spiritual eating and drinking (1 Cor. x. 3, 4, 12, 13. See Abendm. 145, seq.) He who, in faith, receives Christ's body and blood, receives the whole Christ into himself (John vi. 59), which can take place in no other than a spiritual manner. As, finally, the feast of the Passover was a feast of fellowship in which the people of Israel were contemplated as one great family of God (Dogm. I. 263), so is the Lord's Supper a feast of fellowship in which they who eat of the one bread are one body (1 Cor. x. 17)."

Such, without abridgment, is Kahnis' own statement of his new faith, and of the argument for it. The feebleness, vacillation, and self-contradiction involved in it are beyond expression. At some point or other it exhibits the characteristic weakness of almost every false view which has ever been taken of the Supper. It is artificial, and yet not artistic; it is confused rather than complicated; for with all its elaboration it is not difficult to disentangle it. It wears the air of a self-tormented rationalism

44

which abandons the faith, and is ashamed of its apostasy. It does not propose a single new point. All its issues were long ago made and met. It is, in part, Zwinglianism tricked out with rhetoric; in part, Calvinism reached by circuitous by-paths; in part, a reproduction of the weak point in the Syngramma Suevicum — in short, a clumsy appropriation and fusion of exploded views, which yet assumes the air of original discovery. It distributes, after the manner of a huntsman, alternate lashes and morsels to Zwingli, Calvin, and Luther; but certainly has this merit, that it would unite them so far that they would perfectly agree that such a view, on such grounds, is untenable. Such of the points made by Kahnis as have not been anticipated in the previous part of our discussion will be taken up in what follows.

It will be noticed that KAHNIS takes the true view of the 1. "Is." De Wette, and others. necessary force of "is;" and in this is in complete conflict with the mass of rationalizing and rationalistic interpretation from Zwingli to this hour. The last refuge of this interpretation has been in the word which Kahnis surrenders.

Thus, DE WETTE's note on ἐστί is this: "In these contested words the ἐστί (which, in the Aramaic *denah hua gyphy*, was not expressed) is the bare logical copula, and can, in itself, just as well amount to a real is (so *Luther*) or a symbolic *is*, that is, *signifies* (so *Zwingli*). But, in fact, the latter sense alone is admissible; for the discourse and transaction is symbolical, like that in John xx. 22 (He breathed on them, and saith unto them, Receive ye the Holy Ghost), and in this instance, at least, the actual body of Jesus could not have been the subject of discourse. Eιναί has the latter sense in

"Luke xii. 1. Beware of the leaven *of the Pharisees, which is* hypocrisy.

"Heb. x. 20. Through the veil, *that is to say* (τουτ᾽εστι) (id est, das ist), His flesh.

"John xiv. 6. I *am* the way, the truth and the life: no man cometh unto the Father but by Me.

"John xv. 1. I *am* the true vine, and My Father is the husbandman.

" John xv. 5. I *am* the vine, ye are the branches: he that abideth in Me, and I in him, the same bringeth forth much fruit."

MEYER adds, as a proof-text, that ἐστί "is the copula of the symbolic or allegoric sense: "

Gal. iv. 24. Which things are an allegory. For these (αυται) are the two covenants.

LANGE, for the allegorical and symbolical occurrence of ἐστί, adds to Meyer and De Wette as proof, only Ex. xii. 11. Ye shall eat it (the lamb) in haste; it *is* the Lord's passover.

OLSHAUSEN, to show that the sense of " signifies " is *possible*, cites: 1 Pet. i. 28. The word of the Lord endureth forever. And this is (τουτο δε εστι) the word which by the gospel is preached unto you. Philem. 12. Thou, therefore, receive him, that is (τουτεστι), mine own bowels. John x. 7. I am the door of the sheep; x. 9. I am the door: by Me if any man enter in, he shall be saved.

In other writers, both of earlier and later date, we have these citations, as assumed parallels to the sacramental words: Gen. xli. 26. The seven good kine *are* seven years; the seven good ears *are* seven years.

With the Calvinists, in their theory of exhibitive sign, these texts were favorites: Titus iii. 5. The washing of regeneration — as if Baptism were called regeneration. 1 Cor. x. 4. They drank of that spiritual rock that followed them, and that rock was Christ. John i. 32. I saw the Spirit descending from heaven like a dove — as if it were said the Spirit is the dove. One of the most recent writers against the Lutheran view lays stress on the passage: " All flesh (is) grass," which he thinks indisputably means " All flesh *is* LIKE grass;" and thus proves that " is " may mean " is like," and that the proposition of the Supper, stated in full, is: " This bread is *like* My body." It is true the word " is " is not in the original of either Isaiah or Peter, but if it were, the interpretation proposed would stand, in general, where it now stands; for when we change such a phrase as: " All flesh *is* grass" into " all flesh *is like* grass," the word " *like* " is derived, not from the " is," (especially when it is not there,) but from the " *grass*." Consequently, we may

say: All flesh is *grass*-like; Napoleon is fox-like. The critic
fatally wounds his own theory, when, not at all to the point
for the purpose he has in view, he says: " The *mere juxtaposi-
tion* of the subject and predicate, *without the intervening copula*
(the ' is '), is common in most languages, particularly Hebrew,
and more *especially in metaphorical language ;*" that is, the word
in which the metaphor lies, according to the critic's theory, is
not only not necessary, but the very fact *that language is metaphorical leads to its omission.* The stress of the metaphor is so
violent upon the " is," as to squeeze it utterly out of the sentence.

1. Of the views of the critic in regard to metaphor, as
involved in the copula, with which the possibility
of his interpretation of " is " stands or falls, it is
enough to say that they are arrayed against the
universal judgment of rational men ; that they do
defiance alike to the statements of the most learned and of the
most popular works. He says that in such a sentence as this:
" Napoleon is a fox," Napoleon is literal ; which is very true ;
and so also, he says, is fox. The one would, consequently,
mean the man of that name, and the other would mean, literally, the animal of that name. Hence Napoleon *is like* " an
animal of the genus Vulpis, with a straight tail, yellowish or
straw-colored hair, and erect ears, burrowing in the earth,
remarkable for his cunning and his fondness for lambs, geese,
hens, and other small animals."*

(marginal note: 2. Of the nature of metaphor as affecting the force of " is.")

2. How will our critic resolve this sentence: " Napoleon *is*
Emperor of France, and a great fox?" If " *is* " be literal and
"*fox* " be literal, then he actually is a literal fox; if " *is* "
means *is like*, then Napoleon is like the Emperor of France.
If, moreover, when we say Napoleon is a fox, the word fox
means the literal animal, what is meant by it when some one
adds: That fox will be caught yet? Is it the literal animal of
the genus Vulpis, with the straight tail and the fondness for
geese, which is then meant? and yet cannot a child see that
the word fox is used in the second case as it was in the first?

3. The critic himself, when he comes to explain the phrase,

* Webster.

proves that "*is like*" is not sufficient as the meaning of "is," but that he must make it mean, "resembles in his reputed cunning." The verb "to be" means, then, "to resemble in reputed cunning" when it comes before the word "fox;" it also means "to resemble in reputed firmness" when it comes before "rock;" it means "to resemble in reputed feebleness" when it comes before "grass;" "to resemble in reputed sweetness" when it comes before "rose." In other words, it means everything conceivable which begins with "resemble," and has such a range of meaning that we might set aside a vast host of words with which our language is now encumbered.

4. To define, in a disputed case, the word "*is*" by "*is like*," is to do what, in its own nature, is inaccurate, and, in the present case, *is absurd*, for it repeats, in the definition, the word to be defined. If "*is*" by itself means "is like," what does it mean when combined with the word "like"? If, when it is said "Napoleon *is* a fox," it means "is like a fox," what does it mean in the sentence thus produced? Define the word "is" in the sentence: Napoleon *is* a fox. Now define the word "is" in the sentence: Napoleon is like a fox.

The same objection *virtually* holds against all the other proposed definitions of "is." "Signifies" means "*is* a sign of;" "symbolizes" means "*is* a symbol of." If This *is* my body means This *is* a sign of my body, then This is a sign of my body means This is a sign of a sign of my body; and this renewed "is" having the same force again of "is a sign," we have an interminable series in which nothing is or can be, but everything must be the sign of something else.

5. What does our critic, on his theory, make of such expressions as this: Louis Napoleon is like a lamb, but is a wolf, nevertheless? Why is it that when we ask what a thing is, and the reply is: It is like so and so, we rejoin: We did not ask you what it *is like*, but what it *is?* "He is not my brother, but he is exactly *like* him." How can terms which are the very opposite to each other in one case be synonyms in another?

6. How does this theory suit where the *article* is used in metaphor: "I am *the* door." I am like the door? What is *the* door Christ is like? And if He is only like that door, would

it not be better to find the door itself? "I am *the* vine." Who or what is that vine which Christ is merely like? "Yo are *the* branches." Who are the branches, in fact, if the disciples are merely like the branches? "I am *the* way, *the* truth, and *the* life." What is the real way, the real truth, the real life, which Christ merely resembles?

How does it suit when a *pronoun* is added in metaphor: "Israel is *my* flock;" Israel is like my flock? What is God's real flock which Israel is like?

How does it suit when an *adjective* is used in metaphor: "I am the *true* Shepherd"? Who is actually the true Shepherd whom our Saviour is merely like?

How does it suit when qualifying *nouns* are added: "The rock of *my strength;* rock of *salvation;* to come to the rock *of Israel;* upon this rock I will build my *church;* I lay in *Zion* .. a rock"? Where is the theory in these that the metaphor is not in the noun?

How does it suit in such phrases as: "*Blessed* be my rock"? Is some one who *is like* my rock the object of blessing? "Unto Thee will I *cry,* O Lord, my rock." If fox in metaphor is a literal fox, what does our Saviour mean when He says of Herod: "Go tell that fox"?

Can anything be more clear than that the metaphor, in such cases, lies not in the substantive verb, which is unchanging in its meaning, but in the noun?

Will the critic please tell us the canon by which he settles it, that, in a certain case, where "is" connects two nominatives, it means or does not mean "is like"? How does he know that, in the sentence: "Louis Napoleon is Emperor," the "is" does not mean "is like," and that, in the phrase: "Louis Napoleon *is* a fox," it does mean "is like"? Does not the *name* Emperor, in the one case, and the *name* fox in the other settle it? When he simply hears thus much: "Napoleon is," he cannot tell, on his own theory, whether "is" means "is," or "is like." The metaphor must, then, lie, not in the verb, but in the name; but it is conceded, that, in the Lord's Supper, it does not lie in the name; therefore it is not there.

When Wendelin (d. 1652) published his system he said

"The main controversy is on the meaning of the word ' is,' "
and then states what had then come to be the accepted position
of his party: " ' Is ' is taken for signifies: ' This is, that is, this
signifies my body.' *On account of this signification* (propter
hanc significationem) *of the copula,* or verb *is,* we say that
Christ's words: ' This is my body,' *ought not to be understood
literally* " (non debere intelligi proprie). From Zwingli's time,
in fact, this has been the position, almost without exception,
of all who have attempted to defend the metaphorical character of the words, and this is the position of most writers of that
school now. Yet so invincible are the facts and principles that
after the retreat to " is," as the point for a last struggle,
many of the best Zwinglian and Calvinistic writers   Concessions of
felt themselves compelled to abandon it. At the the point by Cal-
beginning of the controversy Carlstadt and Œco- vinists.
lampadius admitted that " is " has the exact force claimed for
it by Luther. *On this point* they stood with Luther against
Zwingli. They concurred with Zwingli's doctrine, but denied
the validity of his proof. They supposed him to have reached
the truth by a process of error. His conclusion was right,
though the reason which led him to it was wrong. The three
men reached a common result of inference, though each one of
the three premises implied the falsehood of the other two.
Even after the violent controversies of the sixteenth century,
when both parties had so many reasons which made the most
powerful appeal to natural pride not to abandon a position with
which their cause had been identified, Calvinistic theologians
of the first rank confessed the old position in regard to " is "
entirely untenable. Thus KECKERMANN (d. 1609) Keckermann,
says: * " Some maintain that there is a trope in Piscator.
the copula, a position which it is impossible to approve. . .
There cannot be a trope in it." Still more extraordinary is
the admission of PISCATOR of Herborn (d. 1626) who, following
Beza, in controversy with DANIEL HOFFMANN, of Helmstädt (d.
1611), had fully committed himself to the position whose falsity
he came to confess. In his first work he had said: " I affirm
that the metonomy lies in the substantive verb ' *is,*' and *I prove*

* System. Theolog. III. 8.

it in this way : That metonomy is either in the subject, **or in** the predicate, or in the copula of the proposition. But it is *not in the subject, nor is it in the predicate. Therefore* it is in the copula." The reply of HOFFMANN was so complete, that a result almost without parallel in controversy took place. Piscator acknowledged that his position was untenable : " I have been like a gladiator who, incautiously handling his sword, wounds himself with it. . . There cannot be a trope in the copula ' is.' In brief, before I enter on this third struggle, I RETRACT my former opinion."* The ripest scholarship of the most recent period, even under Calvinistic prepossessions, shows the wisdom of Piscator's retraction. Dr. EDWARD ROBINSON, for example, the greatest of American New Testament lexicographers, if, as a Puritan, he had been swayed by unconscious doctrinal influence (for of conscious misrepresentation he was incapable), would have been, of course, on this point, adverse to the Lutheran view. It is a happy thing for the truth here, that this eminent scholar, who so happily combined the results of English and German culture, saw and expressed the exact truth on this point. He says of *eimi* : " The verb *eimi* is the usual verb of existence, *to be ;* and also the usual logical copula, connecting subject and predicate : I. As the verb of existence, *to be, to exist,* to have existence. II. As the logical copula, connecting the subject and the predicate, *to be ;* where the predicate specifies who or what a person or thing *is* in respect to nature, origin, office, condition, circumstances, state, place, habit, disposition of mind, etc., etc. *But these ideas all lie in the predicate,* AND NOT IN THE COPULA, *which merely connects the predicate with the subject.*" What Robinson says is one of the elementary philological truths on which sound thinkers, when once the point is fairly brought before their minds, cannot differ. Thus, for example, we have in Bagster's Greek Lexicon : † " *Eimi,* a verb of existence, *to be, to exist ; a simple copula to the subject and predicate, and, therefore,* IN ITSELF *affecting the force of the sentence* ONLY by its tense, mood, etc." This same statement, word for word, is made by Green **in his** " Greek-English Lexicon to the New Testament."‡

(margin note: Robinson, Schaff, Kahnis.*)*

* Scherzer: Colleg. Anticalv. Lips. 1704, 4to, 574.   † London, 1852, 4to.
‡ London, Bagster and Sons, 12mo.

The point on which the confusion of imperfect or careless scholarship so often makes its blunders is brought out clearly by Dr. Robinson when he says: "The SUBSTANTIVE OF THE PREDICATE *often expresses* not what the subject actually *is*, but what it is like, or is accounted to be; *so that eimi* may be rendered to be accounted, etc."

Dr. PHILIP SCHAFF, in his note, in his translation of Lange's Matthew, says: "The exact nature of the relation" (expressed by the copula) "depends upon the nature of the subject and the predicate," that is, does not depend upon any mutations of meaning in the copula, and this, he says, "is an acknowledged law of thought and language." He adds: "It is, perhaps, more correct to say that the figure in these cases *does not lie, as is usually* assumed, in the auxiliary verb *esti*, but either in the subject, or *more usually* in the predicate."* KAHNIS, as we have seen, acknowledges that his new view can find no support in the copula, and says, very correctly: "From the copula 'is' the figurative no more than the literal can be proven, in the proposition. The copula allows of no change of meaning. Those who say that 'is' is equivalent to signifies, *mean to say* that either the subject or predicate of a proposition is to be taken figuratively."†

Because of this very inflexibility of meaning in the copula "is," the translations which desert the direct arrangement of the subject, copula, and predicate, drop the "is," and merge the whole thought in one complex. In this case the pretender to knowledge is apt to be drawn into the fallacy that the words which have the locality of the "is" translate the "is;" whereas, in fact, they translate, in whole or part, the subject or predicate. Let us take Luther's version to illustrate this. Where "is" stands in the original in various combinations, Luther's version has upwards of one hundred and sixty renderings, and yet "is" has, through the whole, its one fixed sense: all the diversities arising from the connection of the "is"—none from the "is" itself. Thus Gen. xxvii. 12 (Heb.): "I *shall be* in his eyes as a deceiver;" Authorized Version: "I shall *seem* to him as," etc.; Luther: "And

———
* Lange's Matthew, 471. † Dogmat. I. 617.

shall be *esteemed* (geachtet) before him," etc.   Does the Author
ized Version mean to translate "is " by " *seem;* " or does Luther
mean to translate it by " *esteemed* "?   Not at all ; but in both
cases the complete idea " *to* be in his eyes *as,*" is expressed in
the more indirect form, and it must be assumed that "is " is
perfectly literal in its meaning, in order that the complex idea
may be reached.   Jacob must really and literally *be as* a deceiver to justify the statement that he will be esteemed as such.
We are not aware of an instance in which Luther uses "bedeu-
ten" where "is " occurs in the original.   In Ezek. xlvi. 17
(Heb.) : " It shall *be* to him to the year of liberty ; " Authorized
Version : " It shall be his ; " Luther : " He shall *possess* (be-
sitzen)" ; not that "is " means to possess, but that to *be to him,*
or *be his,* does mean to possess.   The pronoun is involved in
the translation.   Deut. xxviii. 13 : " Thou *shalt be* above only ; "
Luther : " Hover above " (Schweben).   The adverb is involved.
Isaiah xv. 6 : " There *is* no green thing ; " " There *grows'*
(wächset).   The subject conditions the translation.

So inflexible is the substantive copula, that "is " may be

Inflexible char- written in a central column, and the ingenuity of
acter of the cop- man may be defied to write a rational subject on
ula.
the one side of it, and a rational predicate of that
subject on the other side of it, to connect which shall require
the addition of any word whatever to the "is," or the substitution of any other word for it.   Furthermore, we may add to
the word "is " such qualifying terms as will most distinctly
assert that it is to be understood, literally speaking, without
metaphor, dropping all symbolical, allegorical, or figurative
language, and it shall thereby only the more effectually answer
as proof that in the very cases of dreams, allegories, and parables, and such like, as are cited to show a departure from its
literal force, that literal force is actually — if such a thing be
possible — intensified.   " Is " is the great transmuter of the
figurative into the literal.

	is, are	
Seven ears	dropping symbol	seven years.
The eaven of the Pharisees	" allegory	hypocrisy.
The two women	" figure	tne two covenarts
The seed	literally speaking	the word.

The " is " is just as literal in a metaphor as in the plainest and most prosaic sentence. Those who deny this show that they do not see the real point. The seven ears *literally are* seven years, *though* the seven ears are not literal ears, but dream-ears. If they were literal ears, they could not be years. The leaven of the Pharisees *literally is* hypocrisy, but the leaven of the Pharisees is not literal leaven ; if it were, it could not be hypocrisy. The two women *literally are* the two covenants, but the two women are not literal women, but allegorical women. As natural women they could not be covenants. The seed *literally is* the word, but the seed is not literal seed, otherwise it could not be the word — it is Gospel-seed. Now, in the case of metaphorical leaven, seed or bread, there is a metaphor to drop, but in the case of literal leaven, seed, or bread, there is no metaphor to drop ; hence seven natural ears of corn cannot be seven years, nor can wheat or rye be the word, nor baker's bread be Christ's body. " This is My body " can mean but one thing, so far as the *is* is involved : This *literally is* My body. If there is a metaphor, it must lie in the word " body." Is it Christ's *literal body* which is meant ? If the body which is given for us be Christ's literal body, *then* the sentence can mean only one thing : This literally is My literal body. When we say " the " Church is Christ's body, we mean that the Church *literally is* Christ's body — literally is that which is called Christ's body by the apostle. Then the question; Is there a metaphor ? means, Is literal body meant ? The answer here is, No ; it is the assembly of believers in Christ. If the apostle had written, The Church is the body of Christ which was crucified, he would have written nonsense. Why ?

It seems incredible that on a basis so slight should have rested the opposition of millions, for centuries, to the doctrine of the Church. The whole thing is capable of a *reductio ad absurdum.* If " is " means " is a symbol of," then the right way for our Lord to have announced Reductio ad ab- surdum. the doctrine of a true presence would have been to say : " This is *not* My body ; " which would mean, " This is not a symbol of My body," the inference, of course, being that as it is not a symbol of the body, it is the body itself. On this style of interpretation, we are to go through the New Testament, and whatever it asserts " is," we are to declare is not, but is only a symbol ; and whatever it asserts is not, we are to declare is not a symbol, and therefore the reality.   God is not a Spirit, but is the symbol of a Spirit ; and they be no symbols of gods which are made with hands, and are, of consequence, real gods.   God hath chosen things which are not symbols to bring to naught things that are symbols — that is, He has chosen the things that are, to bring to nothing the things that are nothing already.   O glorious interpretation ! throwing into the shade the idea of the sceptic who wished to take all the " nots " out of the Commandments, and put them into the Creed — the matchless canon which covers all speech — the simple canon : whatever is, is not, and whatever is not, is.

" Naught is everything, and everything is naught."

As around the words of our Lord, uttered by His own lips, or breathed into His apostles by His Spirit, the controversy has gathered, so in those words alone can the solution of their own mystery be found.   The words themselves are a perfect rule of faith, and if they have not brought the whole Church to a unity, it is because not all have studied them enough in the right spirit.   God the Holy Ghost, in making a revelation to man by language, of necessity subjected His own words to the laws of language; and if the whole nominal Church of Christ ever agrees in the doctrine of the Eucharist, the agreement will be reached under the ordinary aid of the Spirit, by the right application of the laws of language to the inspired words.   The most vital question in the controversy is, indeed, one to which even now the Eastern Church, the unreformed Western Church, and the purified Church of the West — the Lutheran Church — return the same answer.   The doctrine of the objective presence of the body and blood of Christ in the Supper is the faith of a vast majority in Christendom now, as it has been from the beginning ; and mischievous as is the error of transubstantiation, it still leaves the foundation of the Eucharistic mystery undestroyed, while the rationalistic opposition destroys the foundation itself.

How the controversy is to be decided.

But rationalism itself cannot, without doing violence to the acknowledged ordinary laws of language, read into the words of the Supper a metaphorical sense. Handle these words of our Lord as boldly, construe them from as low a level as those of ordinary men, still no metaphor can be found in them. This assertion we hope to prove by a careful investigation of the fundamental principles of metaphor, which we shall reduce to thetical statements, and endeavor to illustrate. We shall try to present the rhetoric of the metaphor in the relation it bears to its logic.

I. The metaphor belongs, according to a distinction made by some writers, to the *rhetorical* figure, as distinguished from the *grammatical* figure. The distinguishing difference between the *rhetorical* figure and the *grammatical* is that the rhetorical is based upon an *ideal* relation, the grammatical upon a *real* one, or what is believed to be such. To say, He keeps a good table, this purse is gold, this cup is coffee, this bottle is wine, is to use a *grammatical* figure; for the relation of the subject to the predicate is that of *real* conveyance. There is a real purse and real gold, a real cup and real coffee, a real bottle and real wine ; and the figure turns simply upon the identification of the thing conveying with the thing conveyed, both being real, and the thing conveyed being communicated in some real respect by means of the thing conveying.

I. Grammatical and Rhetorical Figures.

Again, we say of particular books of the Bible: This book is Isaiah, this book is John. This is a grammatical figure, for the relation of authorship is real on which the identification rests. There is a real book, written by a real Isaiah, a real John, and hence we give the name of the author to his work. So we say: Here is my Milton, take down that Shakspeare, my Burke is in twelve volumes, I have read Homer through ; or of pictures: This is a Raphael, this is a Salvator Rosa, this is a copy from Titian, this is a Canova. Is your Madonna a Murillo or a Michael Angelo? All these are grammatical figures, for they imply a real relation between the author or painter who produces and the book, or work of art, produced.

Again, we say: His pen is able, his pencil is artistic : meaning that the writing, of which the pen is the instrument, the picture which is painted by the pencil, have these qualities.

Again, we say of a portrait or a statue : This picture is Washington, this statue is Napoleon. The figure is grammatical, for the identification is based upon a *real* likeness. We can say, Th s picture is *meant* for Washington ; but it is not Washington — it is no more Washington than it is any other man, that is, the identification lacks the *reality* of likeness.

Again, we say : His brain is clear, his hand is ready ; because of a *real* relation between the thought and its organ, the brain — the energy and its organ, the hand.

There are two kinds of figures which may be called grammatical. The one is Metonomy, based upon a *real* relation between cause and effect, or of subject and adjunct ; the second, Synecdoche, based upon a *real* relation of the whole and its parts, or of the genus and its species. The question here is not whether the words of the Supper contain a grammatical figure, but whether they contain a rhetorical one — not whether there is in them a metonomy, or a synecdoche, but whether there is in them a metaphor ?

II. Rhetorical figurative expressions, under whatever part of speech they are couched, or however modified in form, presuppose a starting proposition which may, ordinarily, be easily

II. Metaphors reduced to propositions. reduced to a noun subject, connected by the copula "is" with a noun predicate. The word of God is sharp, cutting to the dividing asunder of soul and spirit, implies : God's word is a sword. Man flourishes in the morning, in the evening he is cut down, and withereth : Man is a flower. The righteous grows in majesty, his roots spread forth by the river of life, and his fruits fail not : The righteous man is a tree. To this simplest form the words of the Institution are reduced, if they are metaphorical : This (bread) is My body.

III. In a metaphor, in the form of a noun subject, connected

III. Metaphor always in the predicate. by the substantive copula with a noun predicate, the metaphor *always* lies in the *predicate*, never in the subject.

1. This is so clear in the *crdinary arrangement* of metaphori-

cal propositions of this class, in which the subject comes first, that no one can dispute it. We will present a few illustrations in a

TABULAR VIEW.

Noun Subject.	Copula.	Noun Predicate.
God's word	is	a sword.
All flesh	"	grass.
Herod	"	a fox.
The usurer	"	a leech.
The slanderer of the dead	"	a hyena.

In all these propositions, in which the simple and usual form of the metaphor is presented, it will not be denied that the metaphor lies in the predicate.

2. The principle holds equally good — though an uncultivated reader may not, perhaps, as instantly and readily see it — in the *inverted arrangement* of poetical style, in which the *predicate* comes first: as, for example, if we say: A sword — is God's word; grass — is all flesh; a fox — is Herod, the subject and predicate are precisely the same as before. It is still God's word that is the sword, not the sword that is God's word, and so with the others. There is no new proposition; there is a mere change in the order of the old one.

3. The principle holds good — though it requires yet a little more reflection to see it — when the *words* which expressed subject and predicate recur in an inverted order, with a *new proposition* as the result. For example, in the sentence, " Love is heaven, and heaven is love," there are, undoubtedly, *two* propositions,—not one proposition with two arrangements, as in the examples under 2. " Love " has, under one genus, two specific senses in both propositions, and in the first, heaven is the *predicate*, and means exquisite happiness, and in the second it is the subject, and means the estate of angels and glorified men. The first proposition means that love, such as is felt by our race for each other, is exquisite happiness; the other means that the heavenly estate of angels and the glorified is heaven, indeed, because of the love they there cherish and the love **they** there receive.

4. The principle holds good, even in a case in which we seem to assert that the predicate ought to be the subject — the subject the predicate. " You say, the slanderer is a serpent; nay, rather say the serpent is a slanderer." Here, undoubtedly, there are *two* propositions, not a change of order in one proposition. In the first, slanderer is the subject, and is literal, serpent is the predicate, and is metaphorical; in the second, serpent is the subject, and is literal, and slanderer, the predicate, is metaphorical, precisely as our rule asserts. The force of the change turns on the thought: You speak of the serpent as that whose venom supplies the metaphor which intensifies our sense of the venom of the slanderer; but, in fact, the venom of the slanderer is that terrible thing which intensifies our sense of the venom of the serpent. Such examples, then, do not contradict the rule, but are very striking evidences of its truth.

5. The inflexible character of this rule is shown by the fact that if the noun which was the metaphorical predicate be actually made the subject of a proposition, the instant result is nonsense. Thus: My flesh is bread, has a clear sense; Bread is my flesh, if it be a mere inversion of order, with the subject and predicate unchanged, has the same sense, a little less clear and popular in the expression; but, Bread is my flesh, if bread be the true subject, is nonsense. *Here* applies what Kahnis has so miserably misapplied, in his argument on the Supper: Bread, *as such, cannot* be the flesh of Christ; and in metaphor, *because* the flesh of Christ is bread, it is impossible that bread should be the flesh of Christ.

We can say that a modest girl is a violet, but not that a violet is a modest girl; a feeble man is a bulrush, but a bulrush is not a feeble man; a politician is an eel, but an eel is not a politician; truth is a lamp, but a lamp is not truth; God is a rock, but a rock is not God; the Devil is a lion, but a lion is not the Devil; the promises are manna, but manna is not the promises; Christ is a lamb, but a lamb is not Christ; a gay woman is a butterfly, but a butterfly is not a gay woman; a proud man is a peacock, but a peacock is not a proud man; a church rebuilt is a phœnix, but a phœnix is not a rebuilt church ; a drunkard is a perfect fish, but a perfect fish is not a drunkard.

From all this it follows irresistibly that if there be a metaphor in the words of the Supper, it lies in the noun " *body*," which is the confessed predicate. The friends of the metaphor are compelled by the laws of language to maintain the proposition : This literal bread literally is something which is *metaphorically* styled the " body of Christ which is given for us." It is impossible that the proposition should be : The body of Christ which is given for us is something which is metaphorically styled, This bread : first, because they themselves declare that the This bread is literally, not metaphorically, so styled ; and second, if it were not so, because bread is the subject, and cannot involve the metaphor, body is the predicate, and must involve the metaphor, if there be one. So Œcolampadius contended at the beginning, and so Kahnis contends now. The latest opposition to the true view grants that the received argument on its own side has, for nearly three centuries, rested on a palpable fallacy. Kahnis picks up what Zwingli threw away, and ends where Œcolampadius begun. *So far* as this one point is concerned, to wit, that if there be a metaphor it must lie in the predicate, Œcolampadius and Kahnis are right — so far Luther agreed with Œcolampadius, and Zwingli differed from them both. Zwingli deserved the severest terms applied to him by Luther, for failing, in so unscholarly a manner, to see so obvious a point, and the long line of Zwingli's followers ought to be held accountable before the judgment seat of all earnest theological investigators of every school, for the slothful manner in which they acquiesced in so palpable an error. Right or wrong in itself, the current Zwinglianism rests on an assumption which is demonstrably false and preposterous.

IV. The Subject in a metaphor is always the PRIMARY OBJECT of thought : it is that *for which* the *predicate* and copula are brought in.* " Christ is the morning star : " Christ, *the*

---

* " The result which a spoken trope produces in the mind of the hearer is an image of the PRIMARY OBJECT under the change of aspect caused by its being viewed from the side of the *secondary* object ; and the emotion which is excited is consequent on this step." Spalding : Rhetoric, Enc. Brit. **xix.**, 132.

45

subject, is the primary object, and only to mark his majesty is the predicate, "morning star," brought in at all. If the words of the Institution are metaphorical, the "bread," as the subject, is the *primary object*, and the words are uttered for the sake of telling us what the bread is, and the body is brought in in a *secondary way*, to clear up the perception of the character of the bread. The body and blood are brought into the Supper for the bread and wine's sake, not the bread and wine for the sake of the body and blood.

V. This principle involves also that *the primary object* in a metaphorical proposition is always the SUBJECT. In the ordinary construction of sentences the subject comes first, the predicate last. But on this principle the inverted order will not obscure to us a perception of the real subject. "An open sepulchre is their throat," (Rom. iii. 13): throat is the subject, and in Luther's Version, and the King James', is put first. "The head of every man is Christ, the head of the woman is the man, the head of Christ is God," (1 Cor. xi. 3). Christ, man, God, are the subjects in the three propositions. In Luther's Version they come first. "He that soweth the good seed is the Son of man." Subject: Son of man. "The field is the world:" "world" is the subject; and so through that passage (Matt. xiii. 37–40) the devil is the enemy, the end of the world is the harvest, the angels are the reapers. The predicate is placed before the subject, in the explanation of a parable, because the object of the explanation is to show how those predicates *already mentioned* fit the subject, which now first comes into expression. A parable rests on a metaphorical proposition whose subject is not expressed.

If the words of the Institution be metaphorical, and if the *primary object* in it be the body and blood of Christ, they must, of necessity, be the *subject* of the proposition. Now they *are* the primary object, but they are *not* the subject. Therefore the words are not metaphorical. As the subject in the words is *expressed*, they are not of the nature of a parable.

VI. In a metaphor the subject, considered in itself, is related to the predicate, considered as metaphorical — as a whole is related to a part, or the greater to the less; the subject expresses the *whole* thing, the metaphorical predicate limits the mind to one part or aspect, either specific or generic, of that whole "Christ is a sun." Here Christ, the subject, expresses the whole being, Christ, and after it might follow a statement of *everything* that Christ is: the predicate limits the mind to the one aspect of that whole — Christ as the source of heavenly illumination, that is, to a part of what He is. And this holds good even when the predicate, in itself, *as literal*, is greater than the subject; as, for example, the sentence: " My lover is my God." Here still, lover, in itself, expresses *everything* that a lover is, while the term " my God," as metaphorical, expresses simply one part or aspect of the emotion by which he stands related to one person.

If the Eucharistic proposition be metaphorical, the bread, as a whole, is the subject. The metaphorical predicate, the body, limits the mind to this bread in one aspect. To what aspect of bread is bread limited by calling it the " body of Christ "? The bread is a whole, the body a part. What part? The bread is the greater, the body the less. In what respect ?

VII. In the resolution of metaphors into literal terms, the following principles are worthy of note:

1. In metaphor, there is a change of the ordinary signification of the word. In metaphor, " fox " is changed from its ordinary signification of a particular animal, and means a man of craftiness; " rock " means a support and stay; a " lion " means a hero; " Napoleon " means a man of distinguished ability and success. But in the Supper there is no change of meaning in the words. This means this, bread means bread, and body means body.

2. This change of ordinary signification is based on some similitude, or analogy, between the thing named in the new term and the thing to which that new term is applied. Herod is a fox, because an analogy to his craftiness is found in the cunning of the fox. It is not the man, as a man, with whom the animal, as an animal, is compared, but it is alone craftiness in the animal which is compared with craftiness in the man. Our God is a rock, because the mind traces an ideal resem

blance between the physical firmness of a rock and the moral
firmness of God. Now if there be a metaphor in the Supper,
it must be based upon some ideal similitude between bread and
Christ's body. The bread is called Christ's body because there
is some respect in which that bread resembles the body. But
the theory which accepts the metaphor makes the body resemble the bread, which is to subvert the metaphor. It is not the
fox that is Herod, the rock that is God, nor the body that is
bread; but Herod is the fox, God is the rock, and the bread is
the body.

3. In metaphor, the similitude is always *ideal*, either essentially or in the mode of regarding it. When this similitude
is a *real* one, both in essence and degree, there is no metaphor;
and hence a real similitude is expressed in different terms from
a metaphorical similitude. We say, A cat is like a tiger, because of certain points of real physical likeness. There is likeness, but no metaphor. We say, This cat is a tiger, she is so
fierce. Here there is metaphor; for though there is a real
likeness between a cat and tiger, and the fierceness of both,
yet it is the fierceness of the tiger, as idealized, that is imputed
to the cat. Or we may again say, This cat is like a tiger; but
if we wish to guard against the misconception that it is a *real*
similitude between the whole subject and the whole predicate,
we mean, we have to add "in fierceness." "Hegel is like Napoleon" might mean that he bore a real resemblance, physical
or otherwise, to him; "Hegel is a Napoleon" is open to no such
misunderstanding. "The bread is like the body of Christ"
may mean, grammatically, as well that there is a real likeness
as an ideal one. Hence, to clear the phrase with the resolution
proposed, it would be necessary to add to the words: "This
bread is like the body of Christ" some such phrase as "in nu-
tritiveness," or whatever may be assumed to be the matter of
analogy.

4. Hence it is a clumsy and inadequate mode of resolving a
metaphor simply to substitute "*is like*" for "is," because it
leaves it an unsettled question whether the likeness is real or
metaphorical. It both weakens and obscures the thought. If
for "John the Baptist is Elijah" we substitute "is like Elijah,"

it may mean like him in looks, or like him in various undefined respects, and the sentence is at once robbed of vigor and
clearness. If, to make it clear, we add " in the analogies of the
spirit distinctive of Elijah," it is not more clear, and is far less
strong than just as it stood : " John is Elijah." If the words
of the Supper be metaphorical, their obvious force is *weakened*
not *strengthened*, obscured not cleared, by substituting " is like "
for " is." But those who contend for the metaphorical sense
think their cause strengthened by this substitution. If this be
so, there can be no metaphor. They are met by the horns of
a dilemma. If " is like " *cannot* be inserted with advantage to
clearness, then, in the admission of their own argument hitherto, there can be no metaphor ; if " is like " *can* be inserted
with advantage to the sense, then, as we have just shown,
there can be no metaphor.

5. Furthermore, while in the case of a *naked*, unqualified,
metaphorical noun in the predicate " is like " may merely
weaken the sense, in the case of a metaphorical noun qualified
by terms which link it with higher associations " is like "
destroys the sense. We may say-: God is a rock, and then
God is like a rock ; but if we say, God is the rock of our salvation, we cannot interpret : God *is like* the rock of our salvation.
The Church is the body of Christ ; the Church is like the body
of Christ ; but not the Church *is like* the mystical body of
Christ. If we could say : Bread is body, and, consequently,
Bread is like body, it would not follow that we could say :
Bread is like the body of Jesus Christ which was given for the
remission of sins.

6. The RESOLUTION of a metaphor, by making " is like " the
copula, weakens it, at best, but the term " *signify* " does not
resolve the metaphor at all. Where " signify " can be substituted as a copula for " is," there is no metaphor. Leo (the
word) signifies a lion, that is, leo in one language and lion in
another, are verbal signs of the same thing, but Achilles does
not signify a lion. The seed of the parable is ideal seed, not
natural ; it does not *signify* the word, but that seed is the word,
and the word is that seed. *Natural* seed may be used as the
symbol of gospel seed, that is, of the parable seed ; but the para-

ble seed is not the symbol of anything else, but is itself the thing symbolized by the natural seed — it is the word. If we could say, *as in a parable:* This bread signifies the body of Christ, it would mean that real bread is the symbol of ideal bread, to wit, the communion bread, and that the thing idealized in the term communion bread is not the symbol, but the thing symbolized, and is identical with the body. It is a striking illustration of the way in which the extremes of exegetical absurdity meet, that to make a parallel between the language of the Supper and of a parable, would end practically in an error akin to transubstantiation. It would imply the *identity* of the thing expressed ideally in the word bread, with the thing expressed literally in the word body. It would leave, as the only literal elements in the Supper, body and blood — no real bread, no real cup; just as in the parable of the sower, the only literal elements left are the Son of man, the word, the world, the hearers.

7. Nothing is, *in itself*, metaphorical or symbolical. A lamb as a lamb, a lion as a lion, is not a symbol. Neither the real lion, nor the real lamb, is symbolical. It is the ideal lion or lamb that is symbolical. The mind makes it so. The mind recognizes and accepts the analogy on which the metaphor or symbol rests, and thus makes the symbol. Hence the bread, *as such*, can be no more a symbol of the body than it can be the body itself. Bread, as bread, is no symbol, but a literal reality. The moment we fix the fact that a piece of bread is to be regarded as a piece of bread, apart from the general analogies of all bread, we entirely exclude that bread from any possible relation to the symbol or metaphor. Christ could say, The bread which I will give is My flesh, but not, the baker's bread, the wheat bread, which I will give, is My flesh.

8. A *symbolical dream* and a *parable* differ essentially only in the manner in which they are brought before the mind. The dream is a parable pictured in sleep, and the parable is a symbolic dream stated in words. Suppose, with no antecedent dream, Joseph to have been inspired to say: The kingdom of Egypt is like unto seven ears of corn, etc., we would have, by a mere change of the manner of presentation, a parable; or if

the Son of God, with the same intent as in a parable, had, in a dream, presented to the minds of the apostles a man going forth to sow, or fishermen casting a net, there would have been a symbolic dream. Peter's vision can be shaped as a parable: The kingdom of heaven is like to a great sheet, which was let down, etc. In the explanation of a dream or parable, the *subject,* though it may come last in the order of words, is the real, literal thing which the dream or parable is meant to set forth. The seven years are the subject of the dream's explanation; the kingdom of heaven, and the Son of man, are the subject of the explanation of the parable, and what God hath cleansed is the subject of Peter's vision. In the explanation of dream and parable the subject is literal, and the predicate *purely ideal;* not a literal thing symbolizing, but an ideal thing symbolized. In the Supper, the subject is literal, and the predicate is literal. There is no dream-bread or parable-bread, no dream-body or parable-body. No matter how you arrange subject and predicate in it, you can find no parallel with the dream or parable.

9. As in metaphor the figure turns upon the predicate considered not in its natural character, but only as an ideal with a particular quality made prominent, the same noun predicate may be used with very different senses. Either the terms or associations will show, therefore, in every case, *what quality* in the predicate is the basis of a good metaphor. Achilles is a lion, for he is brave; the Devil is a lion, for he destroys; Christ is a lion, for He is majestic. Dan shall be a serpent in the way, for he shall be sagacious in strategy and resistless in attack; the Devil is a serpent, for he is the sagacious perverter of men — he is that "old serpent" which seduced Eve. Now, as a metaphorical predicate, the body of Christ fails to exhibit the particular quality in which the metaphor lies. It explains nothing, but needs explanation. *What* quality of Christ's body is imputed by metaphor to the bread? The most conflicting replies have been made to the question by those who insist that there is a metaphor. One says it is the quality of nourishment; Christ's body nourishes, therefore bread is called by its name. Another says: Christ's body is broken, and, as the bread is broken, it is called the body; and so on through a

range of conjectures ever increasing, and destined to increase, because the solution, in this direction, rests upon lawless conjecture — it gets no light from the text, and its sole limit is that of the ingenuity of man.

10. The *name* in the predicate in the metaphor is given to the subject, so that we can continue to conceive of the subject in all the aspects suggested by the name of the predicate within the whole range of the ideal analogy. Any adjective or verb that suits the predicate can so far be applied to the subject. The righteous man is a tree; God has planted that tree by the river of water; his leaf is ever green; his fruit is more and more abundant; his root is struck more and more firmly into the soil; if his branches are lopped off, it is to insure greater vigor; his shelter is pleasant to those who rest beneath it. Now give the name of the predicate, "body," to the subject, "bread," and attempt to carry out the figure in this way — apply to the bread adjectives and verbs derived from the body — and the impossibility of a metaphor is at once apparent. We can neither say, with a wider range, This bread is Christ's body, and has suffered for us, was crucified for us, has ascended to heaven; nor, with a narrower range, This bread is Christ's body, and nourishes us with heavenly strength — he that eats of it shall live forever — Christ gave this bread for the life of the world. Take John vi., where there is a metaphor underlying, in which Christ's flesh is the subject and literal, in which bread is the predicate and metaphorical, and contrast it with the words of the Supper, where the theory in question admits that bread is the subject and literal, and maintains that body, the predicate, is metaphorical. Now take Christ's flesh as bread, and see how the terms literally appropriate to bread adapt themselves metaphorically to the flesh; then go to the Supper, take bread as Christ's body, and see whether the terms literally appropriate to Christ's body adapt themselves metaphorically to the bread, and you cannot fail to see that there can be no metaphor here.

11. All figures *properly rhetorical* rise upon the common root of the *metaphor*, and are reducible ultimately to metaphorical propositions, that is, to propositions in which there *is* a subject

with a metaphorical predicate, capable, for the most part, of being linked to it by the substantive copula " is."

> " Though round his breast the rolling clouds are spread,
> Eternal sunshine settles on his head."

The good man is a mountain. " If he dare to light on me, I shall brush him off:" he is an insect. " The state is tossed on the waves of civil strife:" the state is a ship. " The sunshine of truth will scatter those falsehoods:" truth is a sun; falsehood is a cloud. " The diapason closing full in man:" nature is an instrument of music; man is the completion of nature's music. " From the egg to the apple, life is insipid:" life is a banquet. Hence all metaphorical language is but the evolution of the primary idea. It results from the ideal identification of the subject and predicate *throughout*, so far as that identification is *primarily* involved in the simple proposition.

Hence, after directly connecting the subject in a metaphorical proposition with its predicate, we can go on to apply to the subject the qualities of the predicate. The good man is a mountain, and though clouds are about his breast, eternal sunshine is on his head. The officious intermeddler is an insect, and if he dare to light on me, I will brush him off. The state is a ship, and is tossed on the waves of civil strife. Can we say, This bread is my body, and is given for you; this wine is my blood, and has been shed for many for the remission of sins? If we cannot, there is no metaphor.

12. In didactic metaphors, whose object is not so much to ornament as to make clear and vivify the meaning to the simple learner, predicates are chosen whose range of qualities is smallest, in fact, if possible, confined to one quality. The favorite popular metaphors turn very much upon the disposition to confine, as nearly as possible, the analogy to a single quality in a single predicate. A bee and a wasp both sting, yet if we say of a woman, " She is a bee," the first impression made is that she is industrious; if we say, " She is a wasp," the hearer supposes we attribute ill-temper to her. A bee is as provident as an ant, but when we wish to find an image of providence, we take the ant. A hare is both swift and timid,

yet, when we call a man a hare, every one at once supposes us
to mean that he is timid.   An elephant is sagacious as well as
ponderous, but when we say that a man is an elephant, we are
not thought to compliment his sagacity, but to allude to his
hugeness of body.   The torch was once an image of illumination, now it is an image of destruction.   We speak of the lamp
of knowledge, but of the torch of discord.   The spider has
many points of metaphor, but in popular language his image is
narrowed to the mode in which he ensnares his prey.   The ass
has had a varied fortune in metaphor.   Homer compares his
hero to an ass; yet, from being the image of enduring bravery,
of strength, of contentment, of frugality, of meekness under
wrong, the ass has come to be almost exclusively the image of
stupidity.   The dog once went into metaphor on the strength
of his worst points; he now generally goes in on his best.   Once
the question was put: Is thy servant a dog, that he should do
this thing?   Now institutions of trust paint upon their sign the
dog, who, as he watches the chest, is an image of the institution in the incorruptible fidelity it claims for itself.   If there
be a didactic metaphor in the Lord's Supper — and such it
would be most likely to be if there were any — it would select
the body of Christ as the predicate, because of one familiar quality which enabled it, more than any other, to make clear and
vivify the meaning of the bread.   Will any one pretend that
such is the case?

13. In a metaphor the adjectives and verbs appropriate to
the *predicate* are applied to the *subject*.   The adjectives and
verbs appropriate to the *subject* in a metaphor cannot be applied
to the *predicate*.   "The child is a flower; it opens its petals to
the dawning sun; it strikes its root into the green earth; it is
tender, sweet, fragile."   We cannot correctly apply in this
same metaphor any of the qualities of the child to the flower,
or mingle the attributes of the subject with those of the predicate.   We can simply and solely consider the subject under
the metaphorical conditions of the predicate.   We cannot say:
"The child is a flower; it strikes out its roots in the nursery;
that flower once had a father and mother, but, alas! the chill
wind came, and now the flower is an orphan."   If, therefore,

there were any warrant for the textual reading on which is based the interpretation: "This broken bread is my broken body," it would imply that the body is metaphorically broken, and that *because* the predicate body is identical in the metaphor with the bread, we can say that the bread is broken. But it is granted by all that the breaking of the bread is *literal*. It is *said* to be broken, because, and only because, it *is* broken. Hence the *a priori* presumption is entirely in accord with the external evidence that the true reading of 1 Cor. xi. 24, does not embrace the word "broken." If the word there were genuine, there can be no metaphorical relation between the breaking of the bread and the breaking of the body; but if there were, it would produce an idea exactly the reverse of that which the advocates of the metaphor desire. They wish the breaking of the bread to figure the breaking of the body, but, in fact, the breaking of the body would figure the breaking of the bread. If I say: "Hope is a broken reed," it is the "broken" of the predicate which we refer to the subject, not the reverse. It is not that hope is broken, and, therefore, we make it the image of a broken reed; but it is the reed that is broken, and we, therefore, make it the image of the broken hope. The words are not: My body is this broken bread, but (following the reading): This (bread) is my broken body.

14. A verbal SYMBOL is simply a *metaphorical* predicate, which is fixed in one determinate sense by general agreement and understanding. It must conform to all the laws of metaphor. When the symbolic idea of the verbal symbol is embodied in a representation, or associated with a natural object, apparent to the senses, a SYMBOL PROPER is the result. Thus, when, for the first time, it was said: "The brave man is a lion," there was but a metaphor. When the authority derived from a general use and agreement made the lion, by preëminence, and exclusively, the metaphorical representative of courage, the lion became the symbol of courage; and the carved or painted lion becomes the symbol proper of courage. Before a symbol can be assumed in language, there must be presupposed a metaphorical predicate, and a fixing of it by general agreement in one only sense. When there can be no metaphor,

there can, *a fortiori*, be no symbol. When we say: "The
lamb is the symbol of Christ," it implies, first, that the lamb is
a metaphorical predicate of all gentle human beings; second,
that because of the preëminent gentleness of Christ, God has
authoritatively, in his word, fixed the predicate as descriptive
of his Son. Hence, when the artist paints the lamb in sacred symbolism, we at once know he means Christ; he represents the lamb bleeding, it is Christ the Sufferer he means;
the lamb bears the banner, it is Christ triumphant.

15. A TYPE is a person or thing divinely foreappointed as the
symbol of a person or thing not yet revealed. It involves a
divine metaphor with the subject reserved for a future statement. The type is related to the antitype as the predicate to
the subject. The lamb is a symbol of Christ. The paschal
lamb is a type of Christ. For the same reason, as in the explanation of the parable and dream, the predicate, in the resolution of the type, is often placed first. We can say " Christ
is our paschal lamb," or " Our paschal lamb is Christ," but in
either case Christ is the subject.

16. The descriptive terms we add to a metaphorical noun to
make its nature apparent must be such as to imply that it is
metaphorical, not such as would apply to it as literal. Instead
of saying, " His wit is a dagger," we may enlarge by saying,
" His wit is the dagger of an assassin; he plunges into the
heart of every man who offends him; " but we cannot say;
" His wit is a dagger purchased at Smith's hardware store."
We do not say: " The law of God is a lamp of brass with a
cotton wick; " " our life is the flowing river Schuylkill, which
runs into the Delaware; " " he was clothed with the mantle
of humility, made of blue cloth." But to the words body and
blood are added just such terms as suit the literal body and
blood alone. It was the literal body which was given — the
literal blood which was shed for us and for many for the remission of sins. Contrast the words which in 1 Cor. xi. speak of
Christ's literal body with those which in chap. xii. speak of
His metaphorical body, His Church. Take the words : This
is my body which is for you — guilty of the body and blood of
the Lord — not discerning the Lord's body — which are found

in chap. xi., and lay them side by side with the terms in
which, in chap. xii., Christ's body, the Church, is spoken of;
the many members — the foot, the hand, the eye, the ear — now
ye are the body of Christ and members in particular, — and
note how striking the difference.   And in the Oriental cast of
thought, far more than in the Western, exists this very tendency to luxuriate in the details of metaphor.   The abstinence
from anything of the sort in the case of the Supper, which, if
it be metaphorical at all, involves the metaphor of metaphors,
is very significant.

Let us look for a moment longer at the bearing of these
principles on the Lord's Supper:

When the word *bread* is used metaphorically, or with a figurative allusion, it is a well established emblem of   I. "Bread" met-
food or of nutrition — intellectual, moral or spirit-   aphorically used.
ual.   As the fox is the emblem of cunning, the dove of gentleness, the rock of firmness, so is natural bread the emblem of
supernatural or spiritual nutriment.   The proposition " bread
is Christ's body," taken *figuratively*, would make bread the
literal thing, and Christ's body the emblem of it, and would
have to mean, " as Christ's body is supernatural or spiritual
food, so bread is natural bodily food."   The proposition,
" Christ's body is bread," on the other hand, makes Christ's
body the literal thing, and bread the emblem of it, and would
mean, " as bread is natural bodily food, so is Christ's body
supernatural or spiritual food."   If it be said, Bread is like
Christ's body, the question at once arises, In what respect?
What is the well-known property of our Lord's body to which
we find a likeness in bread?   If the reply is, Christ's body is
sacramentally eaten, and bread is like it, in that it is eaten
naturally, we would reply: The eating of Christ's body is a
recondite and imperfectly understood thing, — why, then, do
you take it as the illustration of something so simple and well
understood as the eating of bread?   Why illustrate the simple
by the obscure?   Why illustrate it at all?   Yet more, however, if the reply is, Christ's body is broken, and bread, like it,
is broken, we would reply, It is not characteristic of bread to
be broken; thousands of things equally with it are broken:

moreover, Christ's body is not naturally broken, but bread is; hence, instead of illustrating the supernatural by the literal, you are illustrating the literal by the supernatural. What you want to fit in with your theory is, that Christ should have said, Take, eat, my body is like this bread; or, the breaking of my body is like the breaking of this bread. But on this theory he exactly reverses the statement. He does not say, My body is this; but, This is my body. Here, too, is one of the sharp and noticeable distinctions between the thought in John vi. and the thought in the Lord's Supper. In John vi. he says: " My flesh is bread; my flesh is meat indeed." Here he says: " This is my body." If it were lawful to supply the word " bread," bread would here be the subject, as it is there the predicate. But, whether bread or the breaking of bread be considered as that with which the body or breaking of the body is to be compared, it would necessarily, to sustain the theory of metaphor, or symbol, be the *predicate*. But it is here manifestly the *subject*, as even the great mass of un-Lutheran expositors are forced to admit. But if bread or breaking of bread be the subject, it is compared with the body, or breaking of the body: that is, Christ is supposed to illustrate the natural and familiar action by the remoter and less intelligible — which is absurd.

Schwenckfeld * saw whither this false theory would drive him, to wit, that it would suppose that our Saviour, considering the eating of his body as the familiar thing, and the eating of the bread, the thing that required illustration, which is so manifestly false, that, to avoid it, he proposed to write the words thus: My body is this bread, to wit, is spiritual bread, as this is natural bread. If, now, the critic's view could be taken as to the force of " is," to wit, that it means " is like," he plunges headlong into the difficulty Schwenckfeld tried in vain to escape. Even if there were a metaphor, it would not have a parallel in the phrase, " Louis Napoleon is a fox;" but in this: " A fox is Louis Napoleon;" that is, a fox *is like* Louis Napoleon; or, a rock is God; or, grass is flesh; or, a door is Christ.

---

* The same view was maintained at a later period by John Lang.

Just as plain is it that the phrase "*breaking* bread," if figurative, is the well-established emblem not of the violent killing of a human being, but of supernatural or spiritual *distribution* or *communication.* Why is bread *broken ?* In order to its being *given, taken,* and *eaten.* Hence, when we speak figuratively of *breaking* bread, we mean this : the higher thing, of which the bread is the emblem, is *given, taken,* and *eaten* in some sense corresponding with the figure. Hence, in the Lord's Supper, it is inconceivable, if the *breaking* of bread have a figurative reference, that this reference should rest on the *breaking* of bread, *not* as the means of its *distribution,* in order to be taken and eaten, but on the *violent tearing* of it into pieces, as symbolical of crucifixion. If, therefore, the sole connection were, as the critic imagines, between *breaking* the body, the symbol would still contemplate the bread which we break as the communication of Christ's body.

II. The "Breaking of Bread" as metaphorical.

From these indisputable facts, as also from the sacred text, it is most clear that, as the "*breaking*" of the bread in the Supper was *distributive,* that is, the natural means necessary to its *distribution* or communication to the taker and eater of it as natural food, so, by consequence, the breaking of Christ's body, to which it would point, would be the communication of that body as supernatural food. The analogy is not this : That as bread may be considered as figuratively killed by breaking it with the hand into small pieces, so was Christ's body literally killed by piercing it with the nails and the spear, but is most clearly this : That as bread, in order to be naturally taken and eaten, must be physically communicated, (to which the natural breaking was necessary,) so the body of our Lord Jesus, in order to be sacramentally taken and eaten, must be supernaturally *communicated.*

III. The Breaking of Bread and the distributive character of the Supper.

The critic has said of the "resemblance in the fact that just as he had *broken* the bread, so his body *would be* broken," etc., that this is "the *only one* stated by Christ himself" in regard to the bread and the body. If we look at the sacred text, we find that the critic is at issue with it on three vital points :

IV. The "Breaking" of Bread not indicative of the mode of our Lord's death.

1. Our Saviour does not say "*would be* broken," "*would be* shed*," but uses the *present participle* in both cases: "*is* broken," "*is* shed." If the critic insists that the *present* participle has a future sense, he is bound to give reason for his departure from the letter. Till the critic proves this, he has against him the very letter of our Lord's word, testifying that he did not compare that *present* breaking of the bread with the *future* breaking of his body.

2. The sacred text, if we assume that the language is figurative, gives no warrant for the idea that the breaking of Christ's body, and the shedding of his blood, refer as their distinctive object to the *mode* by which his life was terminated, but both refer to the impartation or communication of the body and blood, as the applying organs of the redemption wrought through them. In other words, they are, in the Lord's Supper, contemplated distinctively in their sacramental application, and in their sacrificial character only as the sacrificial is to be presupposed, either in fact or in God's unchanging purposes, as the necessary antecedent and ground of the sacramental. Bread is broken in order to be communicated, and wine is poured out in order to be imparted. If these acts, then, are symbolical as regards the body and blood of Christ, they contemplate the one as broken, the other as shed, in order to communication and impartation; and then there is a parallel in the words of Paul: The cup of blessing, is it not the communion of the blood of Christ; the bread which we break, is it not the communion of his body?

3. Matthew says our Lord *brake* the bread, but does not think it necessary to record at all that our Lord said, My

V. None of the Evangelists connect the Breaking of the Bread with the Breaking of the Body. body *broken* — that is, according to the false theory, he failed to note the only resemblance which our Lord has authorized. Mark is guilty, on the same theory, of the same omission — not a word about the breaking of the bread as the point of comparison with the breaking of the body. Luke has: He *brake* it, and *gave* unto them, and said: This is my body which is *given* for you. Not a word about the breaking as a symbol of the crucifixion; but, as if the breaking were merely a necessary part of the communicative act ending in the *giving*, says: This is my body *given* for you. Is the *giving* of a piece of bread also an emblem of the crucifixion? Is it not evident that broken and given are considered as involving the same idea, and that the force is " so broken as to be given "? Is it not clear that the *giving* of His body is something which Christ himself does; that therefore the sacramental breaking or communication of it is His own act, and that if He symbolizes any acts, it is His own acts, and not those of His enemies? Who does not see, if we assume a figure, that the natural bread points to the supernatural bread, which He tells us is His body, and that the natural method by which the natural bread is communicated points to the supernatural method, by which the invisible sacramental bread, to wit, Christ's true body is given?

If in 1 Cor. xi. 24, we accept the Textus receptus, and read " broken for you," the meaning of the word broken is determined by the facts already stated. It is to be harmonized with St. Luke's "given," and with the omission of Matthew and Mark. But the best text sustained by the oldest manuscripts,[*] is without the word, and the editions of the greatest recent critics, as for example Lachmann, Tischendorff, and Alford, omit it. The attempt, therefore, to show that our Saviour put the *sole* stress on the *breaking* of the bread, is a complete failure, as is also the attempt to show that the breaking contemplates our Saviour's death in its mode, and not as the sacrificial pre-requisite, in the mind of God, to the sacramental communication. VI. The attempt to make the exclusive parallel in the Breaking, a failure.

The true view is strengthened by the fact that, although the three Evangelists say of the blood: " *shed* for you," not one of them speaks, nor does St. Paul speak, of the pouring, or shedding of wine at all; which would have been absolutely essential, had the breaking partaken, as the critic seems to suppose, of this pantomimic character. If Christ had broken the bread to symbolize, by that act, the breaking of His body, He must have poured the wine to symbolize, by that act, the shedding of His

[*] As the Codex Sinaiticus, א., 4th century; Alexandrinus, A., 5th century; Vaticanus, B., 4th century; Ephraem Syri, C., 5th century.

46

blcod. So absolutely necessary to his new theory does Kahnis see the *shedding* of the *wine* to be, that he goes completely out of the sacred record to assume that " the wine which is *poured* out of a large vessel into the chalice is the blood which is *shed* for us." This is not interpreting Scripture, but manufacturing it — and the manufactured Scripture directly contradicts the inspired Scripture. It is the cup of *blessing* which we *bless*, not the cup of wine already poured and consecrated in the Supper, not the skin-bottle of pouring which we pour before the Supper, which is the communion of the blood of Christ. It is not enough for Kahnis to add to St. Paul ; he feels himself forced to contradict him. But Kahnis is helpless. If the bread comes into the Supper solely to be eaten, and the breaking is but a natural mean toward the eating, a mean which can be used either before the Supper or in it ; if the wine comes into the Supper solely to be drunken, and the pouring is but a natural mean toward the drinking, a mean which can be used before or in it, Kahnis's theory of symbol goes by the board.

On the very word, then, on which the critic builds his whole theory, it goes to pieces. It is broken by "broken." Alike what the four narratives say, and what they omit, is decisive against him — as their words and their omissions strengthen the true view, the view of our Church.

The critic, as we have seen, formally abandons in great stress, VII. Summary in one important respect, the Zwinglian view of the of the false meaning of the word " is " in the Lord's Supper. theory.   He acknowledges that here it does not mean " symbolizes, represents." This he does, apparently, to avoid the rock on which we showed, and have again shown, that the old rationalistic symbolic theory struck and split, as soon as it was launched. He concedes that *the bread, as such, is not the symbol of the body of Christ.* So much for Zwinglianism. But, as he goes on to admit, there is a solitary point not peculiar to bread, in which there is a likeness to a solitary point, connected with the history of our Saviour's body, but not peculiar to it. His theory really is this : The bread does not here mean bread, but the breaking of the bread. The body of Christ does not mean His body, but the breaking of His body. The critic, with his theory of pronouns, gets the proposition: This bread (touto artos) is my body. Then, with his theory of the substantive verb, this is made to mean: This bread is like my body ; then, with the new theory of metaphor, bread means breaking of bread ; body means breaking of body ; and the sacred words mean this: This breaking of bread is like the breaking of my body broken for you, therefore take this breaking of bread and eat it. He abandons the argument on which the faith of our Church was originally assailed, and admits the untenableness of the philology of the anti-Lutheran rationalism of centuries.

Strange fallacy, which would make the *breaking* of anything, whatsoever, a title to its being called the Lord's body, which assumes that the bread as such, that is, as food, is not the symbol of Christ's body, but that the *breaking* of the bread is like the *breaking* of the body.

VIII. The false theory charac- terized.

This theory assumes that it would be as proper to affirm that a broken paving - stone, or a broken pane of glass, or a broken dish, or a broken rope, is Christ's body, as that the bread of His supper is ; for the parallel is between breaking and break- ing — broken bread and broken body. But if you concede that it is between bread and body, then you are drawn to the dreaded necessity of the true supernatural eating of the latter as the parallel to the true natural eating of the former. How pointless, too, opening in the lowest depth of Rationalism itself, a lower deep, is it to say that the breaking of bread is like the breaking of Christ's body, considering the breaking as the means of putting that sacred body to death. Bread is an inani- mate thing : how can breaking it be like the putting of a human being to death ? Breaking bread is the very symbol of quiet and peace. Who would dream of it as an appropriate symbol of the most cruel and ignominious death ? Bread is the representative food, and, used in metaphor, is the symbol of spiritual or supernatural food. The breaking of bread is the means to giving it as food, and taking it as food, and as a sym- bol, the symbol of giving and taking a higher food. No one would dream of the breaking of a piece of bread as the symbol of killing a human body ; and if so extraordinary a symbolic use of it were made, it would require the most explicit statement, on the part of the person so using it, that such was its intent; and when he had made it, the world would be amazed at so lame a figure.

We join issue, then, with this theory, and maintain that if there be a figure in the words, the figure must be this: that the bread is a figure of the body of Christ, as the true bread — and the breaking of that bread, so as to communicate it, a figure of the true communication of that body.   And thus our Lord did not mean, in the word " broken "—if he indeed used it at all — to point to the process by which His body was killed, but to His body as the bread of life, broken or given to be the nourishment of the divine life of the believer.   If His body be the broken bread, it is as the communication of that body of which He says: *Take, eat ;* this is my body given for you.

Utterly apart from the divine majesty and the plenary outpouring of the great Spirit of his prophetic office upon our Lord, it is a degradation to Him as the master of words,— Himself the incarnate Word and revealer of the mind of God, as the One who spake as never man spake, whose imagery combined, as they were never combined in human language, the most exquisite simplicity with matchless sublimity and appro priateness,—it is a degradation of our Lord to torture the whole drift of His words, so as to make them jejune and pointless, as the critic has done.   It sounds more like a Jewish taunt, than a sober Christian utterance, to say that, as an appropriate representation of a living body pierced by nails and spear, our Lord selected a loaf of bread, and brake it to pieces, and said: This bread is my body — not with allusion to the bread as food at all; not with allusion to the breaking as the great distributive and communicative act, but simply to the breaking as a means of destroying. We do not believe that from the Institution of the Supper to this hour the mere act of breaking the bread, as such, has vivified to any human creature the sacrificial agony and death of our Lord. We have searched the records of the ancient Church in vain for such an idea: it is not found· in any of the Fathers whom we have examined. It is modern, forced, and manifestly manufactured for certain doctrinal ends; is in conflict with all the laws of human speech; is insulting to our Lord, and is rejected by the best commentators of every school, even by some of the ablest Calvinists, Zwinglians, and Rationalists themselves.

The antithesis of the purified Church Catholic in modern times is strengthened by the fact that the Church Catholic, through its most ancient witnesses, asserts the same antithesis, and bases it upon the same doctrine. The Fathers are not authorities, but they are witnesses. The force of their testimony depends very much upon the nature of the thing to which they testify, whether it be something in regard to which they had ample opportunities of being informed. It depends also upon its clearness, its harmony with itself and with the testimony of others. The statements of a witness or of a body of witnesses may carry with them a moral force which is irresistible. The testimony of the Fathers of the earliest Church in regard to the Lord's Supper carries peculiar weight, because, from the nature of the case, the meaning of the Lord's Supper must have been asked for and determined at once. It is impossible that in the daily communion, with which the Church began, and the very frequent communion with which the Church continued, there should be no settlement of the question, What is the essential character of this Sacrament?

There are those now who think that the permanence of the Supper, and the practical fruits of it, are the only points of importance about it — its essential character may be left out of view. But in fact, from the beginning to this hour, it has not been possible to see why it should be permanent, or what fruits it is meant to have, without understanding *what* it is. In the very nature of the case, therefore, the essential character of the Lord's Supper was no matter of remote speculation. It came up instantly, and came up constantly. There are no two points on which we would expect the witness of the ancient Church to be more prompt and decisive than on the two Sacraments, Baptism and the Supper, and the fact corresponds with the anticipation. On nothing is the testimony of the primitive Church more full, more clear, and more decisive, than on Baptism and the Supper. The testimony begins very early. The first important witness is an Apostolic Father, IGNATIUS, for whom it is claimed that he saw our Lord, and who, beyond all dispute, was a pupil of the Apostles. He was consecrated pastor of the church of Antioch, by St. Peter, about A. D. 43; and was put to death as a Christian about A. D. 107.

The importance of the testimony of the early Church in regard to the Lord's Supper has been felt in all the churches. Extremists, in the churches most alien in their faith to the testimony of the Fathers, have tried to torture their declarations, if not so as to teach their own peculiar views, yet, at least, so as not directly to contradict them. Some, as for example, Marheineke, have claimed that the three leading views of modern times all have their representatives among the Fathers. In presenting the facts of most importance, it may be useful to premise the following principles: — *First.* For the early Fathers, Principles to be as mere thinkers, we need feel comparatively little observed in interpreting the Fathers. regard. It is only where they are competent witnesses that we attach great value to what they say. *Second.* We propose first to show, not what was the whole line of patristic thinking, but what was the original view, so early as to create a moral presumption that it was formed not by speculative thinking, but on the direct teaching of the Apostles. With this as a sort of patristic " Analogy of Faith," we shall assume that the later Fathers agree, if their language can be fairly harmonized with it. *Third.* The easiest and simplest interpretation of the Fathers is the best; the less use we make of the complex ideas and processes of the scholastic or modern theology the better. If we find our faith in the Fathers, we must not always expect to find it couched in the terms which we should now employ. It is their *faith* rather than their *theology* we are seeking; and we should compare our faith with their faith rather than our *dogmatics* with theirs. Systematic thinking and nicely balanced expression are the growth of ages in the Church. We must not suppose that the faith of the Church is not found in a particular writer, because we miss many of its now current phrases. No existing system of theology, and no dogmatic statement of a single distinctive Christian doctrine, can find its absolute fac-simile in form in the writ

ings of the Christian Fathers — not the doctrine of the Trinity
not the doctrine of Sin, not the doctrine of the person of
Christ, in a word, not any doctrine. The oak of a thousand
years is not a fac-simile of itself at a hundred years; yet less a
fac-simile of the acorn from which it grew. Yet the oak is but
the acorn developed, its growth is its history; and if the bond
with its past be broken anywhere the oak dies. *Fourth.* That
interpretation, all other things being equal, is best which most
naturally harmonizes all the sayings of a particular Father with
each other, or all the sayings of all the Fathers with each other.
We have no right to assume a contradiction in either case,
where a harmony is fairly possible. *Fifth.* That is the best
interpretation of the past which most naturally accounts for
the sequel. When a doctrine has taken an indubitable shape,
or even has undergone a demonstrable perversion and abuse,
we are to ask what supposition in regard to the precedent
doctrine best solves the actual development or the actual
abuse. *Sixth.* We reach the faith of a Father by the general
drift of his statements, although *seeming*, or even *real* contradictions with that general drift are to be found in his
writings. No man, perhaps, is perfectly self-consistent. The
reader may discover inconsistencies which the writer himself
has not noticed. The mass of mankind hold very sincerely
views which really involve a conflict. But in the ancient
Church, with the vast influx of men of every school of philosophy and of every form of religious education — with the ferment of the wonderful original elements which Christianity
brought into human thought — with Christian science hardly
yet in existence, we would expect many discrepancies, especially
where dogmatic accuracy is required.

THE TESTIMONY OF ST. IGNATIUS.

There are three passages in St. Ignatius confessedly bearing
upon the Lord's Supper. The *first* is from the [I. Ignatius, A. D.]
Epistle to the Smyrnians: "They (the Docetæ, [43-107.]
who denied that our Lord had a true body) abstain from the
Eucharist and prayer because they confess not that [1. To the Smyr]
the Eucharist is the flesh of our Saviour Jesus [nians. ¿7.]

Christ, which (teen) suffered for our sins, which (een) **the**
Father in His mercy raised again. They then who speak
against the gift (dorean) perish while disputing. Good had it
been for them to keep the feast of love (agapan), that they might
rise again." Agapan has been translated " to love it," but the
better rendering seems to be :" to celebrate it," agapee, *i. e.*, the
Lord's Supper, taking its name from the " agapee," or " love-
feast," with which it commenced in the earliest Church, as in
the following paragraph it seems to be defined by the terms
" agapee poiein," in the sense of " celebrating the Eucharist."

The *second* citation is from the Epistle to the Philadelphians,

2. To the Phila- " Haste ye then to partake of one Eucharist, for
delphians. ¿ 4.   there is (or it is) the one flesh of our Lord Jesus
Christ, and one cup for the uniting of His blood (enosin,) one
altar." The *third* citation is from the Epistle to the Ephe-

3. To the Ephe- sians, " Breaking one bread, which is the medicine
sians. ¿ 20.   of immortality ; the antidote that we should not
die, but live in Jesus Christ forever." It is very obvious, that
taking these words in their simple and native force, they best
accord with the doctrine of the Lutheran Church. In the *firs:*
place they affirm positively that the Eucharist is the flesh
(einai sarka) of our Saviour Jesus Christ; that it is the *one*
flesh of our Lord Jesus Christ which constitutes it. *Secondly.*
They distinctly affirm that the flesh meant is that which suffered for our sins, "which the Father in His mercy raised
again ; " thus overthrowing one of the most recent figments of
a very subtle, yet perverse interpretation, which, unable to
deny that there is an objective presence of Christ taught by the
Fathers, alleges that His body in the Eucharist is a body of
bread, or that the bread, as such, is His body; and that the
blood of Christ in the Eucharist is a blood of wine, that is,
that the wine itself is, as such, Christ's blood. Ignatius distinctly testifies that the body in the Eucharist is not a body
of bread, but is the body of that flesh which suffered for our
sins and was raised from the dead. EBRARD* himself says:
" The fundamental argument against the possibility of a tropi-
cal use of the word ' flesh' in Ignatius, lies in the fact that he

* Abendm. 1 254.

speaks distinctly of that very flesh which was put to death upon the cross, and was raised in glory by the Father." *Thirdly.* The effects imputed to the Eucharist by Ignatius are entirely inconsistent with the supposition of its being a mere memorial or a mere spiritual communion. He imputes to it the power of producing the resurrection to eternal life; not that he denies that the wicked shall rise again, but that like St. Paul, when he speaks of attaining unto the resurrection of the dead, he means the resurrection in its true glory, as a rising to eternal life. The medicine of immortality, the antidote to death, the spring of life in Christ forever, can be no other than Christ's flesh itself — the organ of His whole work. KAHNIS.*
" From these words it follows with certainty that Ignatius regarded the consecrated elements as the media of a Divine impartation of life, consequently as more than bare symbols ; " and EBRARD † admits, " When he calls the Eucharist a medium of immortality, it is clear that he was thinking not of a bare, subjective memory of Christ, but of an *actual appropriation* of Christ and of all His graces." *Fourthly.* So far from the early Church, as represented in Ignatius, being indifferent to the doctrine held in regard to the Lord's Supper, we find that it is distinctly marked as a heresy, practically resulting in the eternal death of those who held it, that the Eucharist is not the flesh of our Saviour. Taking then the simple and direct interpretation of Ignatius, we find him in perfect affinity with the Tenth Article of the Augsburg Confession: 1st. In the assertion that the true body and blood of our Saviour — that which suffered and that which was raised — is present in the Eucharist, actually constituting it. 2d. That true bread and true wine are present. 3d. That the bread and wine given and taken are the means by which the body and blood are imparted. When he says, That the cup is for the uniting (" enōsis ") of Christ's blood, the " enōsis " points distinctly to that specific idea which Paul expresses when he says, The cup is the communion of Christ's blood, and which our Church expresses by saying that the blood is *in, with, and under* the cup. The word " enōsis " is used by the Fathers to indicate the uniting of two things, and is most frequently used for the unit-

* Dogmat. II. 195.   † Abendm. I. 256.

ing of the human and divine natures in Christ. Whether we
interpret the "enōsis" here as implying that the cup is that
which unites, sacramentally, blood with wine, or blood with
the communicant, by impartation and reception, the great
idea remains unchanged, for either of these involves the other.
4th. Even the antithetical part of the Tenth Article has its
parallel in the condemnation of the Docetæ for denying that
the Eucharist is the flesh of Christ. That Ignatius teaches
the doctrine of the objective presence of the body and blood of
Christ in the Supper is shown among recent writers, by Engelhardt, Francke, Rudelbach, Semisch, and Kahnis.

THE TESTIMONY OF JUSTIN MARTYR.

The *second* testimony we adduce is that of JUSTIN MARTYR
II. Justin Mar- (converted A. D. 133, put to death as a martyr, 165).
tyr, A.D. 133. If the claim be doubtful which has been made for
him, that he was a disciple of the Apostles, the other claim
may at least be allowed, that he was a man not far from the
Apostles either in time or virtue. The extract we make is
from his Apology. "Having ceased from the prayers, we greet
Apology, I. c. one another with a kiss; then bread and a cup
66, 67. of water and wine are brought to him who presideth
over the brethren, and he, receiving them, sendeth up praise
and glory to the Father of all, through the name of the Son
and the Holy Spirit; and maketh at length an Eucharistic
prayer for having had these things vouchsafed to him. Those
called among us 'deacons,' give to each of those present to
partake of the bread and wine and water, over which thanksgiving has been made, and carry it to those not present; this
food, ('trophee,') is amongst us called 'Eucharist' (eucharistia),
whereof no one may partake save he who believeth that what
is taught by us is true, and hath been washed in that laver
which is for the remission of sins, and to regeneration, and
liveth as Christ hath delivered; for we do not receive it as
common bread (koinon arton) or as common drink (koinon
poma); but in what way (on tropon) Jesus Christ our
Saviour being, through the word (dia logou) of God, incarnate (sarkopoieetheis,) had both flesh and blood for our
salvation, so also have we been taught that the food over

which thanksgiving has been made by the prayer of the word (euchees logou), which is from Him — from which food our blood and flesh are by transmutation (metaboleen) nourished (trephontai) — is (einai) both the flesh and blood (kai sarka, kai aima) of Him, the incarnate Jesus (sarkopoieethentos)."

Applying here the same simple principle of interpretation, we find, *first*, that the flesh and blood of Christ are the sacramental objects; *second*, that they are distinguished from the bread and the wine; *third*, that they are so related to the bread and wine that the reception of the one implies the reception of the other — there is a sacramental unity and identification; *fourth*, that this relation is not one produced by the figurative character of bread and wine, as symbols of body and blood, but a relation subsequent to the consecration and produced by it; *fifth*, that a parallel of some kind is instituted between the two natures of Christ, conjoined personally in His incarnation, and the two elements, bread and body, cup and blood, conjoined sacramentally in the Supper. *Sixth.* The antithesis is implied when it is said, That no one may partake of this food among us save he who believeth that what is taught by us is true. This means that the rejecter of this doctrine of the Lord's Supper in common with the rejecter of any other article of faith is disapproved of and excluded from the Communion. Thus, again, is overthrown the false assumption that the ancient Church allowed of known conflicting views in regard to the Lord's Supper. *Seventh.* These words of Justin show that the supernatural character of the elements in the Supper is dependent upon consecration. He distinctly affirms that only after the word of God upon them do they possess their character as the flesh and blood of Christ. This alone overthrows the Zwinglian doctrine, for if the bread be the body of Christ symbolically, it is such, as bread, quite independently of any consecration. *Eighth.* Justin expresses the true doctrine of what it is that does consecrate in the Supper; gives the true answer to the question: What is it, by which that which was before mere bread, now becomes, in virtue of a supernatural relation, the body of Christ? He says, That the consecration takes place through the prayer of the word, which is from Him, *i. e.*, Christ, (di euchees logou tou par autou). This may include the Lord's Prayer, but by preëminence it expresses the words of the institution, which we know, in fact, constituted an essential part of the earliest liturgies; and St. Justin himself expressly mentions Christ's words as the words used in the consecration, and makes them parallel with the consecrating words used in the mysteries of "Mithra," which were a diabolic copy and parody of the Lord's Supper.

It has been asserted that the doctrine of Justin is that in the Supper a new incarnation of Christ takes place. This view has been maintained by Semler, Hahn, Neander, Baur, Engelhardt, and others. It has, following them, been most fully presented by Semisch, in his Justin Martyr.* "Justin," says Semisch, "regards the Supper as it were a repeated incarnation; as the incarnation was consummated in this, that the Divine Logos assumed flesh and blood, so he supposes that the presence of Christ in the Supper mediates itself in this, that the Divine Logos unites Himself with bread and wine as His body and blood. Bread and wine do not change physically in the Supper, but neither do they remain common bread and common wine. They are, after the Eucharistic prayer by which they are consecrated, as it were the vessel in which the Divine Logos dwells, and are, consequently, really, even if only figuratively, the body and blood of the Logos." This means that the bread is not the medium of the communication of the body of Christ, but is in some sense literally the new body of the unincarnate Logos. That is to say, that the Divine nature of Christ, *separate from His human body*, puts on the bread of the Eucharist as a new body; hence this bread is *a* body to the unincarnate Logos. That this is not Justin's view is very clear, *first*, because he connects with his own representation the words of the institution; clearly showing that he had in his mind the words, "my body, my blood," there occurring in that sense almost undisputed, in which they are accepted by universal Christendom, even by those who deny the doctrine of the true presence. When Justin speaks of the body of Christ he

---

* Semisch, C. A.: Justin der Märtyrer, 184)–42, (translated by J. F. Ryland, Edinb., 1843, 2 vols., post 8vo).

evidently has in view those words in which Christ says: "My body given — my blood shed for you." Who can believe that Justin imagined an impanate and invinate Jesus; and that he was so beclouded as to imagine that this bread-body could be the body which was given for men, this wine-blood, the blood which was shed for mankind for the remission of sins. The bread and the cup cannot be thought of as *that* body of Christ which was *given* and *that* blood which was *shed* for the remission of sins. Nothing, but the impossibility of any other view, would justify us in fixing so monstrous a theory upon the language of Justin. *Second.* Justin is very careful to express how far the parallel between the personal co-presence of the two natures of Christ and the sacramental co-presence of the two elements of the Supper goes and does not go. The "on tropon," which we have translated, "in what way," does not mean to state that the modes of the two things are identical, but simply to show that the first is a voucher for the second; that there is such a parallel; that the first authenticates and, to a certain degree, explains the second; but not at all that there is an identity of mode, still less that the second is a repetition of the first.

In the Septuagint and New Testament, "on tropon" has the sense, "As, even as, what manner, corresponding to," Ezek. xlii. 7: "After the manner of," Ezek. xlv. 6. "Outoos" has the sense, "So, even so, likewise, thus." There are passages in the Biblical Greek in which the two expressions are related precisely as in Justin. 2 Maccab. xv. 40, "*As* (on tropon) wine mingled with water is pleasant, *even so* (outoos) speech finely framed delighteth." Acts i. 11, "In like manner *as* (on tropon) ye have seen Him go into heaven, this same Jesus shall *so* (outoos) come." 2 Tim. iii. 8, "Now *as* (on tropon) Jannes and Jambres withstood Moses, *so* (outoos) these also resist the truth." Not identity but similarity is expressed in every case. Justin clearly says, that the "word," in virtue of which the Eucharist becomes Christ's flesh and blood, is the word of the prayer, or prayer of the word, "euchees logou." It is not the Logos which effects the change of which he speaks, but the prayer of the word which is from Him, to wit, from Jesus Christ, whom he has just styled the "incarnate Logos."

Finally, he says, in downright terms, that it (the bread and wine) are the flesh and blood of the *incarnate* Jesus, exactly the opposite of the position of Semisch, and of those who agree with him, which is, that the bread and wine are the body and blood of the unincarnate Logos. Now, could Justin call the unincarnate Logos Jesus? The Logos separated from the human nature is not Jesus. This manufactured theory represents Jesus as both incarnate and unincarnate, as having one abiding body of flesh, and innumerable ever-renewed bodies of bread, as approaching unincarnate the elements and taking them to Him, the bread as another body than His true body, the wine as another blood than His true blood. That great scholars should have acquiesced in a theory of such intrinsic absurdity — a theory which has nothing, in the language of Justin, to necessitate or even excuse it — can only be accounted for by the endemic disease of thought and feeling which in German theology so largely infects even those who most wish to escape it. The ambitious ardor of scholarship, the desire after originality, the love of novelty, the chaotic subjectivism which Rationalism, though baffled and defeated, leaves behind it, impair the solid judgment, and diminish the value of the labors of many of the greatest recent theologians.* Thiersch† says of this theory, "I declare that this whole statement is throughout fabulous. It has arisen from pure misunderstanding, and is undeserving of further notice. It would destroy the entire connection of the Christian faith, and annihilate the most hallowed doctrine of the ancient Church — the doctrine of the Incarnation." The Roman Catholic theology long endeavored to find in the words "kata metaboleen," that is, "by transmutation," a warrant for Transubstantiation; but these words so evidently refer to the transmutation of the bread and wine, as

---

* "Es will jedermann im Laden feil stehen, nicht dass er Christum order sein Geheimniss wolle offenbaren, sondern sein eigen Geheimniss und schöne Gedanken, die Er über Christi Geheimniss hält, nicht umsonst gehabt haben." — Luther. ("Everybody has his wares to offer — not that he wishes to reveal Christ and His secret, but that he is anxious that his secret and the beautiful idea he has about Christ's Secret shall not be lost.")

† In his able "Prelections on Catholicism and Protestantism," vol. ii., p. 247.

the sustenance of man, that Dœllinger, the ablest defender of the Romish views in our day, abandons the position. It is decisive against Romanism and Calvinism. "The Lutheran theologians," says Kahnis, "are justified in finding in this passage a testimony to the doctrine of the sacramental union of the body and blood of Christ with the elements; and in regarding this, not as the testimony of one Church teacher, but of the Church, as Justin represents it." "The least justification of all," says Semisch, "has the Reformed Church, in appealing to these words of Justin in defence of its views of the Lord's Supper; for not only is there throughout not a word in regard to a merely symbolical relation of the elements of the Supper to the body and blood of Christ, but the very opposite is clearly expressed in the declaration that the bread and wine of the Supper are not common bread, but the body and blood of Christ. The parallel which Justin draws between the incarnation of Jesus and the act of the Supper make it absolutely necessary to suppose that as the corporeal nature of the incarnate Redeemer was a real one, so also the bread and wine of the Supper are to be taken in a real sense for the body and blood of Christ." Even DORNER * says: "Although it is not strictly correct to identify his doctrine completely with the Lutheran, yet, from what has been said, it is evident that it stands most near to the Lutheran." EBRARD † puts the construction on the words: "As Jesus, supernaturally begotten, had His creaturely flesh in order to secure our redemption, so this Eucharistic food, which has been consecrated by prayer, — this food wherein we are nourished conformably to the transmutation of the creation, — is the body and blood of Christ (a supercreaturely food having respect to the Redeemer). Under metabolee, I believe, we are neither to understand the transmutation of bread and wine into the flesh and blood of Christ nor into our flesh and blood, but the world-historical fact of the transformation of the creaturely into the sanctified — the redeemed." On this, KAHNIS ‡ adds: "This exposition, and the argument for it, is to such a degree arbitrary and unhistorical, that we regard a refutation of it as unnecessary."

* Person Christi, II. 401.   † Abendm. I. 260.   ‡ Abendm. 186.

THE TESTIMONY OF IRENÆUS.

Our next great primary witness is St. IRENÆUS, martyr. He lived near the time of the Apostles. He was most intimate with Polycarp, who was one of the Apostle John's best beloved friends, and from Polycarp's own lips he heard what John told in regard to Christ: "Noting these things," he says, "in my heart." Tertullian styles Irenæus, "the most exact investigator of all doctrines." Erasmus says: "His writings breathe that ancient vigor of the Gospel, and his style argues a spirit ready for martyrdom." The school of Asia Minor, alike in the range of its science and the purity of its faith, was the great school of this era; and its most faithful and profound representative in its best tendencies is Irenæus. He has expressed himself in several passages with great clearness in regard to the Eucharist. The most important passage in regard to the essence and effects of the Eucharist is found in his "Book against Heresies," b. 4, ch. 18, § 45. He holds up against the *Gnostics* the confession of the Church as embodied in fact in the Supper. *First* of all, the offering of the products of nature — the bread and wine, which are the body and blood of Christ — is in conflict with the dualism of the Gnostics, according to which the world is not regarded as created by the Supreme God. *Second.* He urges against it the Church faith that our bodies, through the Supper, receive the potencies of the resurrection. This is opposed to the Gnostic dualism between matter and spirit. He speaks thus: "How shall they know certainly that that bread, over which thanks are given, is the body of their Lord, and that the cup is the cup of His blood, if they do not acknowledge Him as the Son of the Creator of the world, that is, His Word, through which Word wood yields fruit, and fountains flow, and the earth yieldeth blade, ear, and full corn. If the Lord belong to another Father, how was it just, that, taking bread of this our creation, He confessed that it was His own body, and He affirmed that the mingled drink of the cup was His own blood."

"Altogether vain are they who deny the salvation of the flesh and despise its regeneration, saying that it is not capable of incorruption. But if it will not be saved, in truth, the Lord

III. Irenæus, Fl., 176-202.

has not redeemed us by His blood, nor is the cup of the Eucharist the communication of His blood, nor the bread which we break the communication of His body; for blood is not save of veins and flesh, and of the rest of human substance, in which the Word of God was truly made."

"How say they that the flesh passeth to corruption, and partaketh not of life, the flesh which is nourished from the body of the Lord and His blood. Either let them (*i.e.* heretics) change their mind or abstain from offering the things above spoken of (that is, the Eucharist). Our doctrine harmonizes with the Eucharist, and the Eucharist confirms our doctrine, and we offer to God His own, carefully teaching the communication and union of the flesh and spirit, and confessing the resurrection. For as the earthly bread (literally, the bread from the earth,) (apo gees artos), receiving the invocation of God, is no longer common bread, but Eucharist, consisting of two things, an earthly and a heavenly, so also our bodies, receiving the Eucharist, are no longer corruptible, having the hope of the resurrection to eternal life."

Here we see distinctly, *First*, the doctrine of the copresence, really and truly, of the two elements, — the earthly one, true bread; the heavenly one, true body; the earthly one, the true cup; the heavenly one, the true blood. *Second.* We see that the earthly is regarded as the communicating medium of the heavenly, and a supernatural efficacy, reaching both body and soul, is connected with them. We see, moreover, that the consecration (the ekkleesis or epikleesis) of God produces the union of the earthly and heavenly. The doctrine of Irenæus alike is opposed to the Romish denial of the bread and the Reformed denial of the body.

Very violent is the pretext of Dœllinger and Möhler, who make the earthly part the body and blood of Christ, and the heavenly part, the Logos; but the passage says nothing about the Logos, nor would the Fathers call the Logos a pragma, a thing or part of the Eucharist. The "epigeion" (earthly) manifestly refers to the "apo gees," (just before,) *the earth*, from which the bread is said to come, and with reference to which it is called "earthly."

47

Some of the Reformed say that Irenæus means by the heav
enly element the *significance* of the elements: others maintain
that he means a certain virtue or operation supposed to be infused into the elements. But these evasions of the meaning of
Irenæus are, First, opposed to the direct *letter* of his statement:
the *significance*, or virtue, would not justify the word "consist."
Bread does not CONSIST of wheat and symbolic meaning, nor of
wheat and spiritual power. Second. To the argument of Irenæus: "Our bodies, *receiving the Eucharist*, are no longer corruptible, but have hope of the resurrection." Does he attribute
so great a thing to a *virtue* (not to speak of a *significance*) in
the bread and wine? Possibly the ardor of partizanship might
lead some to reply, He does; but such a reply is precluded by
his words in immediate connection: "How say they (the heretics) that our flesh comes to corruption, and does not receive
life, that flesh which is nurtured *by the body and blood of the
Lord.*" Third. To the *direct assertion* of Irenæus, in a parallel
place: * "Where the mingled cup and bread receives the word
of God, it becomes the Eucharist of *the body and blood of Christ.*"

Dorner,† after showing the untenableness of Semisch's theory, adds: "As Semisch concedes, the Catholic doctrine of Transubstantiation is excluded by the words of Irenæus, and no
less is the Reformed conception. This does not indeed demonstrate that the Lutheran view is that of Irenæus, yet it
cannot be denied that Irenæus stands more closely to it."
Thiersch says: "So much stands indisputably firm that the
body and blood of Christ is as certainly the 'ouranion' (the
heavenly thing) of the Eucharist, as the bread derived from
the earth, and the wine derived from the earth, is the 'epigeion' (the earthly thing) of the Eucharist." "But," adds
Kahnis, "this relation one to the other, of the heavenly and
earthly matter, is the characteristic feature of the Lutheran
doctrine."

On the meaning of the testimony of these earliest Fathers, a
most important concession is made by MARHEINEKE.‡
Marheineke's
Concession.   This concession is the more striking because it is
connected with his effort to establish the theory that the

---

* Adv. Hæres, V. 296.   † In his Per. Ch., vol. ii., p. 496.
‡ Sanctor. Patrum de Præsent. 22–31.

Reformed doctrine of the Lord's Supper was predominant in the first four centuries. Marheineke, after presenting the evidence on which he rests his theory, goes on to say : " There are other sayings of other Fathers (of this era), which, in whatsoever way they may be *tortured*, seem to admit of no other meaning than that of the real presence of our Lord." Such is that of JUSTIN MARTYR. " By no *force*, and by no *artifice* (nulla vi nulloque artificio), can his words be harmonized with the symbolic interpretation. The presence of Christ is true in the same sense in which the bread and wine are in themselves true, and there is a conjunction of Christ with them." " IRENÆUS does not say that the earthly is but the figure of the heavenly, but teaches that there is a conjunction of the heavenly, to wit, the Son of God, with that earthly nature, bread and wine. ' Christ declared that the bread is His *own proper* (idion) body, and the cup His own proper (idion) blood ; ' from which words ought to be gathered what he means by the ' earthly ' and ' heavenly ' things. The typical sense, therefore," (the Reformed) " and the hyperbolic " (the Romish) " Irenæus clearly excludes. Weighing with a just balance, we shall see that Irenæus held the middle view " (the Lutheran) " in regard to the real presence."

From the simple sense, then, of their own language, and from the concessions of men of eminence, who had reason to grant as little force as the testimony could possibly bear to our doctrine, it is fixed that the earliest witnesses of the faith of Christendom accord with the confession of the Lutheran Church in regard to the objective sacramental presence of the body and blood of Christ in the Holy Supper. They stand as a bulwark alike against the false spiritualism which reduces the Divine mystery to the level of nature, and that carnalism which makes it a prodigy arrayed against nature. They maintain, as our Church does, that the sacramental presence is neither natural nor unnatural, but supernatural, that is, is neither conditioned by the laws of the lower natures, nor contrary to them, but is conformed to the laws of the Supreme Nature.

The ancient Church Catholic professed to have one concordant faith. That interpretation, therefore, of the utterances of individual witnesses is most probable, all other things being equal, which best accords with the claim. The faith once delivered to the saints has abode through all time. By separating the testimony, and by *assuming* that the Christian Church for centuries had no fixed *doctrine*, no *faith* in regard to the Eucharist, but that there was a mere chaos of conflicting private opinions, the Fathers have been forced into contradiction of each other and of themselves. But if it first be allowed that the *whole* testimony of the Fathers, as adduced by Romanists, Lutherans, and Reformed, *may* be internally harmonious, and if that *possible* harmony be tested by the effort to arrange the whole in a self-consistent system, the Romish and Reformed views alike fail to meet the demands of the case; and the whole testimony, as a whole, corresponds from beginning to end with the Lutheran faith. We claim that the Latin and Greek Fathers had the same faith touching the Eucharist, and that the faith they held is identical with that confessed in the Tenth Article of the Augsburg Confession. This we shall endeavor to establish by a *Systematic Statement* of their views in their own words.

1. The Fathers clearly assert the *substantial reality of the bread* Systematic Statement of the views of the Fathers. *and wine* before, during, and after the Supper. Their utterances, decisive *against Transubstantiation*, have been perverted to a denial of the objective true presence, which they firmly held. They *call* these visible elements " bread and wine " throughout; they speak of them as " of the creature," " made of the fruits of the earth," as " the food of life," " the substance of bread and wine," (THEOPHYLACT in Marc. 14,) the bread is " made up of many united grains," is " wheat," " the nature of bread remains in it," (CHRYSOSTOM,) " not altering nature," (THEODORET).* The wine is " the blood of the vine," " fruit of the vine," " wine pressed out of many grapes," as conjoined with water it is " mixed," " the mystical symbols depart not from their own nature, for they remain still in their former substance," (ousia) (THEODORET).† So express is the language of THEODORET against Transubstantiation, that in the edition of his Dialogues, published in Rome, 1547, by

* Dialog. I., IV.   † Dialog. II.

Nicoliuus, printer to the Pope, it is admitted that his view is unsound (from the Romish point of view), and the apology is made for him that the Church had not yet fixed the doctrine by her decree. No less express is the language of Pope GELA SIUS (A. D. 492):* "Certainly the Sacraments of the body and blood of Christ are a divine thing, through which we are made partakers of the divine nature; and yet the substance or nature of bread and wine does not cease to be (tamen esse non desinit substantia, vel natura panis et vini)." So helpless are the acutest Romish controversialists, Baronius, Bellarmin, Suarez, and others, before this passage, that they try to prove that another Gelasius wrote the book. But not only have these arguments been overthrown by Protestant writers, but the Jesuit LABBE, renowned for his learning and his bitter antagonism to Protestantism, has completely vindicated the claim of Pope Gelasius to the authorship of the book.†

2. They sometimes speak of the elements, simply considered as bread and wine, in their natural relations and characteristics —as taken from the earth, nourishing the body, passing into the circulation of the blood. "Food by which our blood and flesh are nourished by transmutation," (Justin ;) "by which the substance of our flesh is nourished and consists," (Irenæus).

3. They sometimes speak of the elements, considered in themselves, as *natural symbols*; bread and wine as the most obvious symbols of spiritual nutrition and reviving, and this natural symbolism remains through the Supper. CYPRIAN: "As common bread, which we eat daily, is the food of the body, so that supersubstantial bread is the life of the soul, the healing of the mind." "Because, among all things that are the food of life, bread and wine seem most to strengthen and refresh our infirmity, it is with great reason that He was pleased through these two things to confirm the mystery of His Sacrament. For wine both gladdens us and increases our blood ; and, therefore, not unfitly the blood of Christ is figured by it." ‡ In *this aspect* the elements are sometimes styled symbols, signs, figures, types of the body and blood.

---

* De duabus natur. in Chr. adv. Eutych. et Nestor. in Bibl. Patr. Mag. IV., I 422.

† Cave: Hist. Lit. Ann. 492, p. 298. **Deyling: Obs. Misc. 361.**

‡ Druthmar (Christianus) **on Matt. 26.**

No passage in any of the Fathers asserts that the elements in the Supper are *merely* signs or symbols. The passages of TER-

Tertullian's application of the word "Figure" to the Lord's Supper TULLIAN, in which the word "figure" is applied to the Lord's Supper, have been the subject of much controversy. In the first of these passages,* he is speaking of the prophecies concerning Christ. He first urges Psalm xcvi. 10, according to a reading peculiar to some of the Greek writers, of which Justin also makes mention: "The Lord hath reigned *from the wood*." This "wood," says Tertullian, is "the wood of the cross." "This wood," he continues, "Jeremiah prophesies of (xi. 9) — that the Jews should say, ' *Come, let us put wood upon His bread ;*' undoubtedly meaning *upon His body*. For so did God reveal even in the Gospel, which you receive as genuine, calling bread His body ; so that, hence, already you may understand that *He* assigned to bread the *figura* of His body, whose body the prophet had *figurated* upon bread, of old, the Lord himself meaning in after time to explain the mystery." In this passage nothing seems to us more clearly Tertullian's train of reasoning than this: Jeremiah meant by "wood " the cross, by "bread " Christ's body. Christ, by calling "bread " His body, gave the key to Jeremiah's meaning. *This bread* is the *figura*, the real thing which Jeremiah *figurated*, or couched under a *figura ;* and this bread is *that* figure (now opened), because this bread is my body. Jeremiah calls Christ's true body, which was to have the cross laid upon it, *bread*. Why ? Because, replies Tertullian, there was to be a bread which should be Christ's true body. Jeremiah calls that bread which was true body — and Christ opens the mystery by declaring that there is a bread, to wit, the Eucharistic bread — which is His true body, "assigning *to bread* the figura of His body," as the prophet before had assigned to His body the figura of bread. He identifies the panis of the prophet with the panis of the Communion ; and, by consequence, as the panis of the prophet is really the body which was crucified, so is the panis of the Communion really the body which was crucified. That the Calvinistic interpretation is impossible, is very clear. As Tertullian reasons, if the panis in

* Adv. Marcion, III., XIX.

the Supper is not Christ's body, but the sign of it, then the panis in the prophet would not mean Christ's body, but would mean the sign of it; and the inference would be that he means, let us put the wood upon the sign of His body, that is, on the bread — which would make the inference exactly the opposite of that which Tertullian does make, would cause him to stultify himself and the prophet, and instead of confuting Marcion, he would play into his hands. Tertullian's whole point is this, what "bread" *means* in Jeremiah, it *is* in the Supper. It means Christ's body in Jeremiah, because it is Christ's body in the Supper. "To assign the (prophet's) figura of His body to the (sacramental) bread," means that what the prophet figured, that is meant by bread as a figura, to wit, Christ's body, is by Christ assigned to the sacramental bread — what the first means, the second is, to wit, Christ's body.

In another passage the same thought is repeated. He is showing that the "wood" of the cross is prophesied <small>Advers. Judæos.</small> of. He again quotes Jeremiah : "'Let us put wood <small>Chap. X.</small> upon His *bread.*' Assuredly wood was put upon *His body.* For so Christ hath revealed, calling bread His body, whose body aforetime the prophet figurated upon bread." The point again is, Why does the prophet give the name of bread to Christ's crucified body? The answer is, Christ gives the name of His crucified body to bread. But how does this answer meet the case? for the prophet, as Tertullian marks and emphasizes, has done exactly the opposite. The prophet calls Christ's body bread. Christ calls the bread His body. If Christ by this one phrase means that the bread is the sign of His body, the prophet by the other would of necessity mean that the body is the sign of the bread, which is absurd. The whole point of Tertullian rests again upon the supposition that it is one and the same thing which is called "bread" by the prophet and by Christ; and that because *Christ* calls *bread* His body, bread in the prophet means His body. On the contrary, if by "bread" Christ means not his body, but the symbolic signs of his body, then the prophet does not mean His body by bread, but the symbolic sign of His body; and Jeremiah's bread is bread.

These facts prepare us for a clearer view of the passage in

which this same argument is opened in its greatest fulness by Tertullian : " The law figurated Christ's passion. The bread re-

_{Adv. Marcion,} ceived and distributed to His disciples, He made that
_{IV. 40.} body of His own (illum suum), by saying, '*This is my body*,' that is, figura of my body. But there would not have been a figura unless there would be a body of verity. But an empty thing, which is phantasm, cannot receive a figura. Or if He feigned that bread was His body, because He lacked verity of body, it would follow that He delivered up bread for us. But why does He call bread His body? Marcion understands this to have been the ancient figura of the body of Christ, who said, through Jeremiah : 'They have thought a thought against me, saying, Come, let us cast wood upon His bread,' to wit, *the* cross upon His body. Wherefore, He who sheddeth light on the things of old, hath, by calling bread His own body, made sufficiently clear what He then meant ' bread ' to signify. That ye may also recognize the ancient figura of blood in the wine, Isaiah will aid." No passage in the most ancient Fathers has been so triumphantly appealed to by the rejecters of the objective presence as this; and yet, carefully examined, it is not for them; it is not neutral, but is utterly against them. The " figura " here is not a symbolic figure in the Supper, but is the " figura " of prophecy. This is most clear, First. From the whole drift of the argument, which turns upon the evidence that the Old Testament figurates, presents figures of the things of the New. Second. From the *tenses* of the verb which follows " figura of my body." " For there would not *have been* (non fuisset) a figure unless there *would be* (esset) a body of truth." " Fuisset " in the pluperfect, contrasted with " esset " in the imperfect, distinctly marks that the figura pertains to the past prophecy, as the esset does to the later Eucharist. Third. The figura is expressly said to be the ancient figura. " This to have been (fuisse, perfect) *ancient figura* (veterem figuram) of the body of Christ." Fourth. The figura of the blood is expressly called the " ancient figure." Fifth. The same argument which was used in connection with the other passages applies with equal force here. The thought is, Christ made the bread His body by the consecrating words; and thus this bread, now

by sacramental conjunction His body, is identified by Him with the ancient prophetic figura of His body. The thing which the prophet calls bread is literally Christ's body; the thing which Christ offers in the Eucharist is literally Christ's body. Hence, we recognize the ancient figura of the body in the bread, as we "recognize the ancient figura of the blood in the wine." "As now He hath consecrated His blood in wine, who under the Old Covenant figurated wine in blood," so now He hath consecrated His body in bread, as under the Old Covenant He figurated bread in His body. What is figure there is reality here — the figura and reality are thus identified — the bread of Jeremiah and the bread in the Supper are one and the same thing, to wit, the body of Christ.

4. They constantly distinguish between the elements considered as before the consecration and *after* it. IRENÆUS: "The bread which *receives the vocation* of God in the administration of the Supper." ISIDORE: "That which being made of the fruits of the earth is sanctified and made a sacrament, the Spirit of God operating invisibly." THEODORET: "*After* consecration, we call the fruit of the vine the Lord's blood." CYRIL of Jerusalem: * "The bread and wine of the Eucharist before the invocation is mere bread and wine."

5. They assert that the bread *after* consecration is *not* in every respect what it was before. IRENÆUS: "It is not common bread." "Though that bread be bread before the sacramental words, yet, when the consecration is added, of bread it becomes Christ's body."† "Our bread and cup is not mystical, but is made mystical to us by a certain consecration."‡ CYRIL of Jerusalem: "*After* invocation, the bread becomes the body of Christ, and the wine His blood."

6. They assert the presence of two elements; the first of which is earthly, the second, heavenly. IRENÆUS: § "It is a Eucharist consisting of two things, an earthly thing and hea-

* Cat. Myst. Prim.
† De Sacramentis, Lib. IV., imputed to Ambrose.
‡ Augustine, Contr. Faust. L XX. c. 13, fit non nascitur.
§ Adv. Hær. IV. 34.

venly thing." AUGUSTINE:* "It consists of two things, the visible species of the elements, and the invisible flesh and blood of our Lord Jesus, the Sacrament, and the thing of the Sacrament, the body and blood of Christ." HESYCHIUS: "At the same time bread and flesh." AUGUSTINE: "One thing is the object of vision, the other of the understanding."

7. They assert that the heavenly is received *in* the earthly. TERTULLIAN:† "*In* the bread is accounted the body of Christ. His blood He hath consecrated *in* wine." CYRIL ‡ of Jerusalem: "*In* the type of bread His body is given thee, and in the type of wine His blood, that thou mayest be of one body and of one blood with Him. His sacred flesh and precious blood we receive *in* the bread and wine." AUGUSTINE:§ "Receive *in* the bread that which hung upon the cross. Receive *in* the cup that which was shed from Christ's side." He severely reproves Urbicus∥ for "reproachful words against the whole Church of Christ from the rising of the sun unto the going down thereof;" and most of all because he does not believe that "now also the blood is received *in* the cup." CHRYSOSTOM:¶ "That which is *in* the cup is that which flowed from His side, and of it we are partakers." FACUNDUS: "The Sacrament of His body and blood, which is *in* the consecrated bread and cup. They contain *in* them the mystery of His body and blood."

8. They assert that the heavenly is received *with* the earthly. CHRYSOSTOM:** "*With* those things which are seen, we believe, are present the body and blood of Christ."

9. They assert that the heavenly is received *under* the earthly. HILARY:†† "*Under* the Sacrament of the flesh to be communicated to us, He hath mingled the nature of His own flesh... We truly *under* a mystery receive the flesh of His body." CYRIL of Jerusalem:‡‡ "*Under* the species of bread

---

* Apud. Gratian. II. 48. † De Oratione, IV. Adv. Marc. IV. 40.
‡ Cateches IV. Epist. ad. Cœlosyr. § Ad. Neophytos, I.
∥ Epist. LXXXVI. ¶ Hom. XXIV. in I. Cor.
** Hom. XXIV. in I. Cor. De Sacerdot. III. †† De Trinitat. VIII.
‡‡ Catech. Mystagog. 4.

the body is given there, and *under* the species of wine the blood is given there." BERNHARD: " What we see is the species of bread and wine: what we believe to be *under* that species is the true body and true blood of Christ, which hung upon the cross, and which flowed from His side."

10. They expressly deny that the elements, considered in their *distinctive* sacramental character, are figures of the body and blood. JOHN of Damascus : * " The bread and wine are not the figure of Christ's body and blood, but the very body of our Lord : inasmuch as the Lord himself has said, *This is* not the figure of a body, but *my body ;* not a figure of blood, but *my blood.* If some, as for example St. Basil, have called the bread and wine images and figures of the body and blood of the Lord, they have said it not after the consecration, but before it." NICEPHORUS : † " We do not call these things image or figure, but the body of Christ itself."

11. The Fathers considered the Lord's Supper as a great act in which believers alone could lawfully unite — those who received the pure faith, and who were regenerate of water and the Holy Ghost — none but the baptized, who were living as Christian men, were allowed even to look upon it. JUSTIN MARTYR : " Of the Eucharist, no one may partake save he who believeth that what is taught by us is true, and hath been washed in that laver which is for the remission of sins and to regeneration, and liveth as Christ hath delivered."

12. They applied to it *names* and epithets which imply its supernatural character. They call it " a mystery " in the latter sense, as a thing surpassing all grasp of reason — " a mystery before which we should tremble." IGNATIUS styles it " The medicine of immortality ; the antidote against death, which secures life in God through Jesus Christ ; the purifier ; the arrester of evil ; the bread of God ; the bread of heaven." JUSTIN calls it, " The assumption into the fellowship of the Son." DIONYSIUS : " The initiation into the mystery of mysteries." The NICENE CANON : " The viaticum ; the supply for the journey of life." DAMASCENUS : " The amulet against every evil ; the purifier from every spot ; the earnest of the life and

* De Fide Orthodox, IV. 13. † Allatius de perpet. Cons. III. 15

the kingdom yet to come." BASIL prays that he may receive it as the viaticum of life everlasting and the acceptable defence before the awful bar of God. CHRYSOSTOM calls it " The table which is the sinew of our soul ; the bread of the understanding ; the ground of confidence. It is hope, salvation, light, and life." " On account of this body, I am no longer earth and ashes — am no more captive but free; for its sake I hope for heaven, the life immortal, the state of angels, the near converse with Christ."

13. They find *prophecies* and *types* of it everywhere in the Old Testament. AMBROSE: " Hear holy David speaking of the table in (Ps. xxiii. 5), foreseeing these mysteries, and rejoicing : He that receiveth the body of Christ shall never hunger." The Fathers find types of the Eucharist in the Paschal Lamb, the manna, the blood of the Old Covenant, the shew-bread, and the flesh of the sacrifices.

14. They lay great stress on the *divinity* and *omnipotence* of Christ, as essential to the possibility of the sacramental presence and to the comprehension of its character. CHRYSOSTOM: " It is not man who makes the bread and wine the body and blood of Christ, but Christ himself, who was crucified for us. By the power of God, those things which are set forth are consecrated through the medium of the words, This is my body." IRENÆUS: " How shall they (the heretics) know that the Eucharistic bread is the body of their Lord, and the cup the cup of His blood, if they do not acknowledge Him as the Son of the Creator of the world, His Logos, through whom the tree grows fruitful, the fountains rise, and who giveth first the blade, then the ear, then the full corn in the ear." AMBROSE: " What word of Christ bringeth the Sacrament to pass ? That word by which all things were made — the heaven, the earth, the sea. The power of the benediction is greater than the power of nature." CYPRIAN: " That bread is made flesh by the omnipotence of the Word."

15. They insist upon following the *literal* force of the words, accepting them by faith, however the senses and natural reason may conflict with it; and declining even to attempt to define

*the *mode* of the presence. CHRYSOSTOM :* " Wc believe God everywhere, though to our senses and thougLt that which He says seems absurd. His word surpasses our sense and reason. In all things, but especially in mysteries, we regard not alone the things which lie before us, but we cling also to His words. Our senses are easily deceived ; His words cannot mislead us. When therefore He says: This is my body, there is no ambi· guity to hold us ; but we believe and perceive clearly with the eyes of the understanding." CYRIL of Alexandria: "*How* He can give us His flesh, it is impious to ask. He who asks it has forgotten that nothing is impossible with God. We, bringing to the mysteries a firm faith, never think or urge in such lofty matters that question, *How ?* It is a Jewish word. When God worketh, we do not ask: How ? but commit to Him alone the way and knowledge of His own work." DAMASCENUS : †
" Of the mystery, we know only that the word of Christ is true, and efficacious, and omnipotent — the mode is unsearchable."

16. They represent sacramental communion as *oral*, corporeal. IRENÆUS : ‡ " How say they that the flesh which is nourished by the body and blood of the Lord, falls to corruption ? How deny they that the flesh which is nourished by the body and blood of the Lord, is capable of receiving the gift of God, whicł. is life eternal." TERTULLIAN : § " The flesh is washed (in baptism), that the soul may be purified ; the flesh is fed with the body and blood of Christ, that the soul may be nurtured of God." CYPRIAN: | " Those mouths, sanctified by heavenly food — the body and blood of the Lord." CHRYSOSTOM : ¶ "Purify thy tongue and lips, which are the portals of the in-gress of the Christ. No common honor is it that our lips receive the body of the Lord.' CYRIL : ** " Christ dwelleth in us corporeally by the communication of His flesh." AUGUSTINE : ††
" It seemed fit to the Holy Ghost, that in honor of so great a Sacrament, the body of the Lord should enter the mouth of the

* Homil. in Matt. 83.
‡ Lib. IV. 34; V. 4.
| De Laps. ¿ 2.
** In John xiii., Lib. X.
†† Epist. 118, Contr. Adv. leg. et proph. II. 9.

† Orth. Fid. IV. 14.
¿ De Resurrect. Carn. 8.
¶ In I. Cor. xxvii.

Christian before any other food. Christ Jesus giving us His flesh to eat and His blood to drink, we receive with faithful heart and with the mouth ; although it seems more fearful to eat human flesh than to perish, more fearful to drink human blood than to shed (our own)." GREGORY: * " The blood of the Lamb is now upon the side - posts, when it is drunken not only with the mouth of the body, but also with the mouth of the heart." " His blood is poured into the mouths of believers." LEO: † " Doubt not of the verity of the body and blood of Christ, for that is taken by the mouth which is believed by faith."

17. They affirm that the *unworthy*, whether administrators or recipients, impart or partake of the body and blood of Christ. CYPRIAN: " They dare to profane the holy body of the Lord," (by giving it to the impenitent). " With polluted mouth he drinketh the blood of the Lord. With defiled hands he taketh the body of the Lord." CHRYSOSTOM: ‡ " How shall he dare to approach the judgment-bar of Christ who has dared with impious hands and lips to touch His body." " How can we receive the body of Christ with such reproach and contumely." AMBROSE said to the Emperor Theodosius: § " With what rashness dost thou take with thy mouth the cup of precious blood, when by the fury of thy words innocent blood has been spilt." AUGUSTINE: ‖ " Is it right, that from the mouth of Christians, when the body of Christ has entered, should come forth the wanton song, as it were the poison of the Devil ? " OECUMENIUS: ¶ " The unworthy with their impure hands receive Christ's most sacred body, and bring it to their execrable mouth." LEO: ** " With unworthy mouth they receive the body of Christ." THEODORETUS: †† " To Judas His betrayer, also, the Lord imparted His precious body and blood."

18. They institute a parallel, in certain respects, between the *incarnation* of the second person of the Trinity and the sacramental presence. JUSTIN: " As Jesus Christ, being through the wo d of God incarnate, had both flesh and blood for our salva-

---

* Hom. XXII., Pasch. Dialog. IV.   † De jejun. 6.
‡ Eph. Hom. I.   § Theodoret. Hist. Eccles. V. 17.
‖ De Tempor. Serm. 215.   ¶ In I Cor. xi.
** De Quadrag. Serm. iv.   †† I Cor. xi.

tion, so also, as we have been taught, the food . . . is the flesh and blood of the incarnate Jesus." HILARY : * " The Word was made flesh, and we through the food of the Lord truly receive the Word made flesh." AUGUSTINE : † " The Eucharist consists of two things — the visible species, and the invisible flesh and blood of our Lord — the Sacrament and the thing of the Sacrament, as the person of Christ consists and is constituted of God and man (sicut Christi persona constat et conficitur Deo et homine)." CYPRIAN : ‡ " As in the person of Christ the humanity was seen and the divinity was hidden, so the divine essence infuses itself ineffably by the visible Sacrament."

19. They affirm in the strongest manner the identity of the true body and blood with the body and blood which are given in the Supper. CHRYSOSTOM : § " That which is in the cup is that which flowed from His side ; and of that we are partakers." AMBROSE: ‖ " There is that blood which redeemed His people. . . . It is His own body and blood we receive." " The body (in the Eucharist) is that which is of the Virgin."

20. They compare the Eucharist with the most stupendous miracles under both dispensations, appealing to the miracles against the deniers or perverters of the sacramental doctrine. Such passages are so numerous and familiar as to require no quotation.

The *whole* testimony of the Fathers can be arranged into a self-harmonizing system accordant with the Lutheran doctrine. Neither Romanism nor Calvinism can make even a plausible arrangement of this kind on their theories. The Fathers held, in the Supper, to the true presence of the elements, and so cannot be harmonized with Romish Transubstantiation : they taught a true presence of the body and blood of Christ, and so cannot be harmonized with the Calvinistic spiritualism. Alike in their assertions and negations, they accord with the positive doctrine of the Lutheran Church, and the antithesis of that doctrine to error.

So steadfast was the faith of the Church on this point that

* De Trinit. VIII. 13.   † Apud Gratian. de Consecr. II. 48.
‡ Serm. de Sacra. Cœn.   § In I. Cor. Hom. XXIV.
‖ De Sacram. VI. 5.

the very heretics, to whose theory the doctrine of the **true** presence was most fatal, did not dare to deny it.

The Pagan revilers and persecutors of the Church, with their clumsy calumny, that the Christians in their assemblies ate human flesh covered with meal, bear witness to the truth they so coarsely misunderstood.

The profound impression made by the Christian faith in the Eucharistic mystery is shown in the attempts of idolaters to imitate and counterfeit it.

The superstitious views and practices which grew up in the Christian Church are evidence of the awful reverence with which the Eucharist was regarded. Abuses argue uses, superstitions imply truths, by which their characteristics are in some measure conditioned; and the history of errors in the doctrine of the Eucharist strengthens the evidence, already so strong, that the doctrine of the true objective presence was the doctrine of the earliest and purest Church.

The LITURGIES of the ancient Church testify to the same great fact; and their witness is the more important, as it shows in an official form the faith of the Church. In the most ancient Liturgy in existence, that contained in the APOSTOLIC CONSTITUTIONS, and which is the general model of all the others, the bishop of the congregation is directed, on delivering the bread, to say: The body of Christ. The deacon, at the giving of the cup, says: The blood of Christ—the Cup of
Liturgies. Life. The communicant replied, Amen. In the Liturgy of St. MARK,* the words are: "The holy body, the precious blood of our Lord and God and Saviour." The First Council of Tours, A. D. 460, directed these words to be used: "The body and blood of our Lord Jesus Christ profit thee to the remission of sins and everlasting life." In the Liturgy of St. JAMES, the bishop, before participating, prays: "Make me worthy by Thy grace, that I, without condemnation, may be partaker of the holy body and the precious blood, to the remission of sins and life eternal." In the Horologion of the Greek Church is the prayer: "Let Thy spotless body be to me for remission of sins, and Thy divine blood for the communication of the Holy Spirit,

---

* Renaudot. I. 162.

and to life eternal." In the Roman Canon : " Free me by Thy holy body and blood from all my iniquities, and all evils."

In the Service of GREGORY the Great, the formula of distribution is : " The body — the blood — of our Lord Jesus Christ, preserve thy soul."

In the time of Charlemagne, the form was : " The body — blood — of our Lord Jesus Christ, preserve thy soul unto everlasting life."

The Apostolic Constitutions direct that before the Communion, the deacon shall make proclamation : " Let none of the catechumens, none of the unbelievers, none of the heterodox be present. Let no one come in hypocrisy. Let us all stand before the Lord with fear and trembling, to offer our sacrifice." The prayer is made : " Send down Thy Holy Spirit, that He may show this bread (to be) the body of Thy Christ, and this cup the blood of Thy Christ (apopheenee ton arton touton sōma tou Christou sou)." Here, in the earliest form, the true function of the Holy Ghost in the Supper is clearly stated — *not* the consummation of the sacramental mystery, by His working, but the illumination of the soul, so that it may in faith grasp the great mystery there existent, and may have shown to it by the Holy Ghost that the bread and cup are indeed the body and blood of Christ.

After the Communion, the deacon says : " Having received the precious body and the precious blood of Christ, let us give thanks to Him who hath accounted us worthy to be partakers of these His holy mysteries." * In the Liturgy of St. JAMES, after the Communion, the deacon says : " We thank Thee, O Christ, our God, that Thou hast thought us worthy to be partakers of Thy body and blood, to the forgiveness of sins and everlasting life ; " and the bishop says : " Thou hast given us, O God, Thy sanctification in the partaking of the holy body and of the precious blood of Thine only-begotten Son, Jesus Christ." The Liturgy of St. MARK : " We render thanks to Thee, O Master, Lord our God, for the participation of Thy holy, undefiled, immortal, and heavenly mysteries which Thou hast given us."

---

* Clementis Opera Omnia. Paris, 1857.   Constitut. Apostol. L. VIII. xii –xiv.

The ANCIENT GALLICAN Missal: * " As we do now show forth the verity of this heavenly Sacrament, so may we cleave unto the verity itself of our Lord's body and blood." The MOZARABIC: † "Hail, sacred flesh! forever highest sweetness. I will take the bread of heaven, and call on the name of the Lord. . . . Having our strength renewed by Christ's body and blood, and being sanctified by the same, we will render thanks unto God." The AMBROSIAN: ‡ " What we have taken with the mouth, O Lord, may we receive with pure mind ; that of the body and blood of our Lord . . . we may have perpetual healing." Through the whole of the worship of the Christian ages runs the confession that it is the undivided person of Christ to which the heart of the Church turns: a Christ who is everywhere God, everywhere man ; a Christ in whom dwells the fulness of the Godhead bodily ; a Christ who has passed through all the heavens, and ascended up far above them all, that he might fill all things.

With these breathings compare the private prayers of the old saints which have been left on record,—the prayers of Ambrose, Basil, Chrysostom, Damascenus, and Aquinas,—which show how lowly, how tender, how trusting is the spirit inspired by a healthful recognition of the great abiding mystery of the New Dispensation.

> Jesu pie quem nunc velatum adspicio,
> Quando fiet illud, quod jam sitio,
> Ut te revelata cernens facie
> Visu sim beatus tuæ gloriæ? §

---

* Martene : De Antiq. Eccles. Ritibus. Ed. Noviss. Venitiis. 1783. 4 vols. **Fol.** I. 166. † Do. 171. ‡ Do. 175. Martene gives about forty orders of service, all having the common element of a complete recognition of the sacramental mystery.

§ [O holy Jesus, whom veiled I now behold, when shall that be for which I thirst, when, beholding Thee with open face, I shall be blessed in the sight of Thy glory?] The Hymn of Aquinas : Adoro te.

XIV.

OBJECTIONS TO THE NEW TESTAMENT DOCTRINE OF THE LORD'S SUPPER, AS CONFESSED BY THE LUTHERAN CHURCH.

THE objections to the Lutheran doctrine almost without exception involve the false DEFINITION of it which is couched in the words " Consubstantiation," " Impanation." From the time that the passions of men were roused in the Sacramentarian controversy, these terms of reproach were freely used against it. No man used such terms more bitterly than ZWINGLE. Yet not only did Zwingle, in his original doctrine, when he rejected Transubstantiation, accept, and for years retain, the same Eucharistic doctrine as Luther,* but even subsequently to his rejection of the doctrine he acknowledged that it had not the offensive characteristics he afterward so freely imputed to it. He wrote in 1526: " You steadfastly affirm that the true flesh of Christ is here eaten, under the bread, but in *an ineffable mode* " (sed modo quodam ineffabili).† But the moral descent of error is very rapid. Before Luther had written a line against him, Zwingle had styled the believers in the doctrine of the true presence, " Carnivoræ, Anthropophagites, Cannibals," " a stupid race of men ; " the doctrine itself he pronounced " impious, foolish, inhuman," and that its practical consequence was " loss of the faith." But so much is confessed

I. Objections derived from a false *definition*.

1. Not originally made.--Zwingle.

---

*See Lampe: Synops. H. E., 1721, 332. Cyprian, Unterricht, v. Kirchl. Vereinigung, 1726, 163. Zwingle: Comm. de ver. et fals. relig. Apolog. Libel. de Can. Missae.

†Ad Theod. Billican. et Urb. Rhegius Epistol. respons. Huld. Zwinglii. Cyprian : Unterr. 176.

that Zwingle when he held this doctrine, and Zwingle when he yielded it, and was yet comparatively just, acknowledged that it taught " *an ineffable mode.*"

The same is true of ŒCOLAMPADIUS. He not only at first held but zealously defended the same doctrine with Luther ; 2. Œcolampa- defended it against the very charge involved in dius. the name, " Consubstantiation." In his sermon on the Sacrament of the Eucharist, preached in 1521,* he says. " I do not pronounce it a mere figure, such as was the Paschai Lamb. Far from us be the *blasphemy* of attributing to the shadow as much as to the light and truth ; and to those figures as much as to the most sacred mystery. For this bread is not merely a sign, but is the very body of the Lord itself (sed est corpus ipsum Domini). We simply confess, therefore, that the flesh and blood of Christ are present and contained ; but in *what manner* (quo pacto), we do not seek to discover ; nor is it necessary nor useful that we should. . . In what mode, He who sits above the heavens, at the right hand of the Father, is truly present on the altars, inasmuch as it is a thing which it is impossible for us to know, is a matter which should not disturb us. What wonder is it since we know not in what mode Christ, after His resurrection, came into the presence of His disciples while the doors were closed? . . . What is that thing of inestimable price which is hidden within this covering (intra involucrum hoc delitescit)? It is the true body and true blood of our Lord Jesus Christ — that body which was born, suffered, died for us, and was afterward glorified in the triumph of the Resurrection and Ascension."

The attitude of CALVIN has been already illustrated. At Strasburg he took his place among Lutheran ministers, signed the Unaltered Augsburg Confession (1539), represented the Lutheran Church at various conferences, was charged with holding the doctrine of Consubstantiation, was complained of at a later period (1557), by the preachers and the Theological 3. Calvin. Faculty at Zurich, as " wishing to unite his doctrine with that of the Augsburg Confession, as in the very least degree unlike (minime dispares)." The same

* Cyprian: Unterr. 183.

Faculty, in 1572, wrote: "Calvin, of blessed memory, seemed, to pious and learned men in France, not to be in unity with our Churches in the doctrine of the Lord's Supper."

The reproach of teaching such a carnal presence as is involved in the word Consubstantiation is therefore an after-thought of opponents. How groundless it is, can be made evident by a long array of witnesses. " I will call it," says Luther,* "a Sacramental Unity, forasmuch as the body of Christ and bread are there given us as Sacrament: for there is not a Objection natural or personal unity, as in God and Christ; it answered. is perhaps also a different unity from that which 1. Luther the Dove had with the Holy Ghost, and the Flame with the Angel (Exod. iii. 2) — in a word, it is a Sacramental Unity." " We are not so insane," says Luther, elsewhere,† "as to believe that Christ's body is in this bread, in the gross visible manner in which bread is in a basket, or wine in the cup, as the fanatics would like to impute it to us. . . As the Fathers, and we, at times, express it, that Christ's body is in the bread, is done for the simple purpose of confessing that Christ's body is there. This fixed, it might be permitted to say, It is in the bread, or, It is the bread, or, It is where the bread is, or as you please (wie man will). We will not strive about words, so long as the meaning is fixed; that it is not mere bread we eat in the Supper, but the body of Christ." In 1537, he wrote to the Swiss: ‡ " In regard to the Sacrament of the body and blood of Christ, we have never taught, nor do we now teach, either that Christ descends from heaven or from God's right hand, or that He ascends, either visibly or invisibly. We stand fast by the Article of Faith, ' He ascended into heaven; He sitteth at the right hand of God.' And we commit to the divine omnipotence, *in what way* (wie, quomodo) His body and blood are given to us in the Supper. . . We do not imagine any ascent or descent, but merely hold fast in simplicity to His words, This is My Body; This is My Blood." Luther says, in his Larger

---

* Werke: Altenb. III. 364; Leipz. XIX. 496. (Bek. v. Abendm., 1528.)

† Werke: Altenb. III. 709; Leipz. XIX. 406. (Serm. v. Sacra., 1526.)

‡ Werke: Leipz. XXI. 108; Jena, VI. 507; Witteb. XII. 205; Altenb. VI. 4; Walch, XVII. 2594. Briefe: De Wette, V. 83; Buddeus: 258.

Confession: "It is rightly and truly said, when the bread is shown, touched, or eaten, that Christ's body is shown, touched, and eaten." This sentence, perhaps more than any he ever wrote, has been urged to show that he held the doctrine of Consubstantiation. But that he used these words in "no Capernaitish, or natural sense, but in a mystic and sacramental sense, to indicate that in the use of this Sacrament the bread and body are most presentially united and unitedly present," * is very clear from his whole train of thought and the words that follow: "This remains fixed, that no *one perceives the body of Christ, or touches it,* or bruises it with the teeth: yet is it most sure that *what is done to the bread,* is, in *virtue of the sacramental Union,* rightly and truly *attributed* to the body of Christ." It is very clear that Luther is availing himself, in this line of thought, of the distinction made in the doctrine of the person of Christ. That is affirmed of the body of Christ in the *sacramental Concrete* which is denied of it in the *natural abstract.* The consecrated bread is so far *sacramentally identified* with this body, of which it is the Communion, that in a *sacramental sense* that can be affirmed of this body which is not true of it in a *natural sense.* So in Christ Jesus we can say, speaking in the *personal Concrete,* God bled, God died; that is, such is the personal concrete that we can "rightly and truly" make personal affirmation in words which, if they expressed a *natural abstract,* would not be true. If the term God is used to designate this abstract of nature, it is thus equivalent to divinity, and it is heterodox to say divinity, or the divine nature, or God, in that sense, suffered. In sacramental concreteness then, not in natural abstractness, according to Luther, is the body of Christ eaten. What is eaten is both bread and Christ's body. Both are eaten by one and the same objective act; but because of the difference in the modes of their presence, and the nature of the object — the one being a natural object, present in a natural mode, the other a supernatural object, present in a supernatural mode, the one objective act is natural in its relation to the natural, and supernatural in its relation to the supernatural. So to the eye of the prophet's servant, by one objec-

* Hutter: Lib. Chr. Concord. Explicat., 625.

tive act there was a natural vision of the natural hills around the city, and a supernatural vision of the supernatural hosts — the horses of fire, and chariots of fire. So to the hand of the woman, by one objective act there was a natural touch of the natural garment of the Saviour, and a supernatural touch of the divine virtue, which the garment veiled. So to the blind man who washed in the Pool of Siloam, by one objective act of washing there was a natural removal of the clay, and a supernatural virtue which removed the blindness. In his Book: "That the words yet stand firm,"* Luther says: "How it takes place. . . we know not, nor should we know. We should believe God's word, and not prescribe mode or measure to Him."

The true intent of our Church, in the language used in regard to the Lord's Supper, is shown in the definitions used in connection with the early efforts at producing harmony with the Zwinglians. When the Landgrave of Hesse invited Luther to a Colloquy with Zwingle at Marburg (Oct. 1529), Luther replied: "Though I cherish little hope of a future peace, yet the diligence and solicitous care of Your Highness in this matter is very greatly to be praised. . . God helping me, I shall not permit those, of the adverse part, to claim with justice that they are more earnestly desirous of peace and concord than I am." In that Colloquy, the parties were agreed: "That the Sacrament of the Altar is the Sacrament of the true body and blood of Jesus Christ, and that the *spiritual* eating and drinking of the body and blood is specially (præcipue) necessary." When Melancthon drew up a brief statement of the points of difference between the view of the Zwinglians, he speaks of two general modes of the presence of the body of Christ, — the one local, the other the " mode unknown (arcano) by which diverse places are simultaneously present, as one point to the person Christ. . . Although we say that the body of Christ is really present, yet Luther does not say that it is present locally, that is, in dimension (mole), circumscriptively, but by that mode, by which the person of Christ, or the whole Christ, is present to His entire Church and to all creatures." The comparison of views finally led to the

2. Colloquies with the Zwinglians.

* Werke: Jena, III. 341.

Wittenberg Concord, touching the Supper of the Lord, entered into by Bucer, Capito, Musculus, and others originally of the Zwinglian party, and LUTHER, MELANCTHON, CRUCIGER, BUGEN-HAGEN, MENIUS, and MYCONIUS. In this CONCORD, both united in declaring: *

1. "That according to the words of Irenæus, there are two things in this Sacrament, — a heavenly and an earthly. They believe, therefore, and teach, that with (cum) the bread and wine, the body and blood of Christ are truly and essentially present, imparted (exhiberi), and taken.

2. "And although they disapprove of Transubstantiation, and do not believe that the body of Christ is locally included in the bread, or that it is in any other wise (alioqui, sonst) united corporeally with the bread, apart from the participation of the Sacrament, yet they confess and believe, that through the Sacramental Unity, the bread is Christ's body; that is, they hold that when the bread is given the body of Christ is truly present at the same time, and truly given.

3. "To the unworthy also are truly imparted (exhiberi) the body and blood of Christ; but such receive it to judgment; for they abuse the Sacrament, by receiving it without true repentance and faith.

4. "For it was instituted to testify that the grace and benefits of Christ are applied to those who receive it; and that they are truly inserted into Christ's body, and washed by His blood, who truly repent, and comfort themselves by faith in Christ.

5. "They confess that they will hold and teach in all articles what has been set forth in the Articles of the Confession" (the Augsburg) "and the Apology of the Evangelical Princes."

In the HEIDELBERG DISCUSSION (1560), the Fifteenth Thesis maintained by the Lutheran divines was this: "We repudiate Heidelberg also those gross and monstrous opinions which some Discussion, 1560. falsely impute to us, to wit, Popish transubstantiation, local inclusion, extension or expansion of the body of

* Chytræus: Hist. A. C. Lat., 1578, 680. Germ., 1580, 374. French, 1582, 497. Seckendorf: Hist. Luth., lib. iii., p. 133. Loescher: Hist. Motuum, 1. 205. Rudelbach: Ref. Luth. u. Union, 669.

Christ, mingling of the bread and wine with the body and blood of Christ." *

BRENTIUS † (1570) belongs to the first order of the men of his era, and, as an authoritative witness, is perhaps next to Luther himself. He says: " It is not obscure that a human body can, by its own nature, be in but one place ; Brentius, 1570. but this is to be understood as regarding the manner of this outward world. Whence also Christ himself, even when, after His resurrection, He was in the kingdom of His Father, yet when He appeared to His disciples in this world, appeared in one place only. But far other is the manner of the heavenly kingdom. For in it, as there is no distinction of times, but all are one eternal moment, so is there no distinction of places, but all are one place, nay, no place, nay, nothing of those things which human reason can think — ' which eye hath not seen (says Paul), nor ear heard, neither have entered into the heart of man.' Inasmuch, therefore, as Christ is in the heavenly kingdom, and the Supper of Christ also is heavenly, we are not, in the celebration of it, to think of a certain magnitude, or littleness, or even local position or circumscription of the body of Christ, but every carnal imagination being cast aside, we are to rest with obedient faith in the word of Christ." "As we have said before, there is here no magnitude or littleness, or length or thickness, or any sort of carnal tenuity to be imagined. Of a surety as bread and wine are truly present, so also the body and blood of Christ are truly present, but *each in its own mode :* the bread and wine are present in a visible and corporeal mode, the body and blood in a mode invisible, spiritual, and heavenly, and unsearchable by human reason. For as the capacity of man cannot grasp in what mode Christ, true God and true man, when He ' ascends above all heavens, fills all things,' so it cannot reach by its own thoughts in what mode the body and blood of Christ are present in the Supper." † " Christ's body and blood are present, not transubstantially (as the Papists

---

* Grundlich. Wahrhaftig. Historia d. Augs. Conf. Leipz., 1584, fol. 436. Do in Latin, ling. transl. per Godfried, Lipsiæ, 1585, 4to, 545.

† Catechesimus pia et util. explicat. illustrat. Witteberg, 1552, 12mo, 661-667. Cf: Evang. sec. Joann, Homil. explic. Francf., 1554, fol. 670.

dream), nor locally (as some calumniously assert we believe). . . .
Ours have often, and at large, testified in express words that
they in no manner attribute local space to the presence of the
body of Christ in the bread. We are therefore unjustly
accused of drawing down Christ's body from heaven, or including it locally in the bread, or of making a Christ of many bodies
and of many places." * "We do not deny that *there is a sense*
in which it can be truly said that Christ is on the earth, or in
the Supper, only according to (juxta) the divine nature . . . that
is, though Christ, true God and man, fills all things both by
His divinity and humanity, yet He has not the majesty originally from the humanity itself, which by its own nature can
only be in one place, but has it alone from the divinity, from
which however the humanity is in no place separated." † "As
a thousand years before God are scarce one day, nay rather,
not one moment, so a thousand places are before Him, not a
thousand places, but rather the minutest point." ‡ "All places
above and beneath are to Him one place, nay, no place, nay, no
point or place. . . Such terms applied to Him, as 'filling' the
heavens, 'being everywhere,' 'dwelling,' 'descending,' 'ascending,' are but transfers of metaphor." §

The FORMULA OF CONCORD ‖ (1580), in defining its own position, quotes and indorses Luther's words: "Christ's body has
three modes of presence: First. The comprehensible, corporeal
mode, such as He used when He was on earth, — the local. To
this mode of presence the Scripture refers when it says, Christ
Formula of has left the world. Second. In another incompre-
Concord, 1580. hensible and spiritual mode it can be present
illocally. Moreover, it can be present in a divine and heavenly
mode, since it is one person with God." The current error
about this view of our Church is, that she holds that the body
and blood of Christ are present in the first of these modes, —

* De personali Unione, Tübingæ, 1561, 4to, 1, 2.

† Sententia de Libello Bullinger, Tübingæ, 1561, 4to, XII. See also his book:
"De Majestate Domini et de vera præsentia Corp. et Sang. ejus Francofort,
1562, 4to;" and his "Recognitio Prophetic. et Apostol. Doctrinæ, Tübingæ, 156?."

‡ In Lib. I Sam. Hom. XIV.   § Contra Asotum. Peric. II.

‖ 667, 98–103

a view she entirely rejects. Though she denies that this presence is merely spiritual, — if the word spiritual means such as is wrought by our spirit, our meditations, our faith, — yet, over against all carnal or local presence, she maintains that it is spiritual. "When," says the Formula of Concord, * " Dr. Luther or we use this word 'spiritually,' in reference to this matter, we mean that *spiritual, supernatural, heavenly* mode, according to which Christ is present at the Holy Supper. . . . By that word 'spiritually,' we design to exclude those Capernaitish imaginings of a gross and carnal presence, which, after *so many public protestations* on the part of our Churches, the Sacramentarians still try to fix on them. In this sense we say that the body and blood of Christ in the Supper is received, eaten, and drunken *spiritually.* . . . The *mode is spiritual.*" "We reject and condemn, with unanimous consent, the Papal Transubstantiation." " We reject and condemn with heart and mouth, as false and full of fraud, first of all, the Popish Transubstantiation." " It is said that the body and blood of Christ are '*under* the form of bread and wine,' and '*in* the Supper,' not to imply a local conjunction or presence, but for other and very different reasons." " Our first reason for using the phrases, that the body of Christ is under, with, in, the bread, is by them to reject the Popish Transubstantiation, and to set forth that the substance of the bread is unchanged." The words " under " and " in " are meant to teach that " the bread which we break, and the cup we bless, are the *Communion* of the body and blood of Christ; " that is, communicate that body and blood to us, — or, in other words, we receive the body and blood, *with* the bread and wine, or " in " or " under " them as a *medium* By, in, with, and under the act of receiving the sacramental bread and wine truly and naturally, we receive the body and blood of Christ, substantially present, truly and supernaturally, after a heavenly and spiritual manner.

CHEMNITZ († 1586): † " All these passages of Scripture with wonderful accord show, prove, and confirm the proper and simple doctrine that the Lord's Supper consists Chemnitz, 1586 not only of the outward symbols of bread and wine,

* 670, 105, 108; 641, 34; 541, 22.   † De Fundam. SS. Cœnæ. ch. IX.

but also of the very body and blood of our Lord. . . . But by *what mode* (quo modo) this takes place, or can take place, it *is not for me to search out* (meum non est inquirere)."

ANDREÆ (†1590),[*] to whom more, perhaps, than to any other theologian, we owe the Formula of Concord, says: "From the Andreæ, 1590. sinister and perverted interpretation of Luther's meaning, as if he taught that Christ's body is affixed to the bread, or imprisoned in it, both he and those who stand with him are far removed. To say and teach that the bread signifies the body of Christ, is a figure, is also a sign of the body of Christ, if the terms be rightly understood, derogates nothing from the meaning of our Lord's words. For who denies that the bread is a figure or sign of the body of Christ? . . . But if any one contend that the bread is a naked sign, an empty figure, and signification, of a body not present but absent, he sets forth a doctrine at war with the teachings of Christ and of Paul. . . . The word 'corporeally' may be used in three ways: First. Naturally, as the Capernaites construed our Lord's words, when He spoke of 'eating His flesh and drinking His blood.' Second. To indicate that not naked signs and figures of the body of Christ are present, but that there is given to us with the bread that very body which was crucified for us. Third. To mark the outward and corporate signs, bread and wine, inasmuch as Christ imparts to us His body, spiritual food, corporeally; that is, with corporeal things or signs. For bread and wine are corporate things, with which at the same time is extended spiritual food and drink. . . . Luther used the terms to teach that with the bread and wine are imparted the body and blood of Christ as heavenly food, with which the soul is refreshed and the body strengthened to immortality. . . . By the word 'spiritually,' we understand is indicated a mode which is heavenly and spiritual, above the order of nature; a mode which can only be grasped by faith; a mode beyond the reach of our present reason and understanding — one of God's greatest mysteries. . . . The mode is no natural one, but recondite and heavenly. . . . With this mystery, locality has nothing to do. . . . If it had, one of these

* De Cœna Domini. Francof. 1559, 12mo. 27, 29, 33, 36, 40, 48, 72, 76

opinions would necessarily follow: Either that the body of Christ is extended into all places, or that it is hurried from one place to another, or that innumerable bodies of Christ are daily everywhere made from particles of bread (the Popish halucination). But *each one of these views* weakens and utterly takes away the presence of the body of Christ. If the body of Christ were expanded into all places of the world, it would not be communicated entire anywhere, but one part would be distributed here, another there. That the body of Christ is borne from place to place, and passes into the bread, is an affirmation which could only be made by one who had lost his senses ; and were this not so, the theory would imply that the body cannot be present in all places at the same moment. Add to this that such a doctrine is directly in conflict with Holy Scripture. As to the third view, we have shown in our previous discussion how contradictory, how abhorrent to the Christian religion and our faith, is the idea that many bodies are formed of the substance of bread, as by a prayer of magic.

"Set therefore before thee that Christ who is neither extended into all places nor borne from one place to another ; but who sitteth at the right hand of the Father, and there imparts to thee His flesh and blood. . . . Is it not possible for thee to understand this mystery, in what manner divine power effects this? This mystery faith alone grasps. In what way (quo pacto) body and blood are communicated to us in this Sacrament is so great a thing that the mind of man in this life cannot comprehend it. . . . The true body and blood of Christ are given in a heavenly and spiritual way which He knows, and which sorrowing and agitated consciences experience, and which surpasses the power of the mind of man. . . . The whole Christ is given to us in the Sacrament that we may be one flesh with Him."

In the COLLOQUY AT MONTBELIARD * (1586), between Beza, as the representative of Calvinism, and Andreæ, the great Lutheran divine laid down first in his Theses, and afterwards repeatedly in the discussion, the principle of a supernatural

* Acta Colloq. Mont. Belligart. 1594, 4to, 3, 5, 16, 17. Gespræch. etc., Tübing 1587, 4to, 4, 22, 25.

and heavenly presence over against a presence which is natural, physical, and earthly. In his conversation with the Baron de Cleroan, previous to the Colloquy, Andreæ said: "The mode of the presence, inasmuch as it is not natural or physical, but heavenly and divine, and the eating, not Capernaitish, is to be committed to God and His omnipotence. . . . Beza and his adherents charge the Churches of the Augsburg Confession with teaching a Cyclopian and Capernaitish eating — a bruising of Christ's body with the teeth, and a swallowing it. Such an idea never entered the mind of Luther, or of our Church. . . . From all the writings of our divines not a letter can be produced to sustain such a charge; on the contrary, they have constantly, in most unmistakable language, condemned the idea of such an eating." In the Theses prepared for the Wirtem berg Theologians by Andreæ, the Fourth says: "We do not hold a physical and local presence or inclusion of the body and blood of Christ." The Tenth, and last, affirms: "The MODE in which the body and blood are present is not expressed in Scripture; wherefore we can only affirm so much in regard to it that it is supernatural, and incomprehensible to human reason. . . . Therefore in this divine Mystery we lead our reason captive, and with simple faith and quiet conscience rest on the words of Christ."

HUTTER († 1611):[*] "When we use the particles ' in, with, under,' we understand no local inclusion whatever, either Transubstantiation or Consubstantiation." "Hence is clear the odious falsity of those who charge our churches with teaching that ' the bread of the Eucharist is literally and substantially the body of Christ; ' that ' the bread and body constitute one substance; ' that ' the body of Christ in itself (per se), and literally, is bruised by the teeth,' and all other *monstrous absurdities* (portentosa absurda) of a similar nature. For we fearlessly appeal to God, the searcher of hearts and the judge of consciences, as an infallible witness, that neither by Luther nor any of ours was such a thing ever said, written, or thought of." [†]

Hutter, 1611.

[*] Libri Christianæ Concordiæ, Explicatio, Witteberg, 1608, 669.
[†] Do. 525, 624.

ANDREW OSIANDER (Chancellor of the University of Tübingen) († 1617): "Our theologians for years long have strenuously denied and *powerfully confuted* the doctrine of a local inclusion, or physical connection of the body and bread, or consubstantiation. We believe in no impanation, subpanation, companation, or consubstantiation of the body of Christ; no physical or local inclusion or conjoining of bread and body, as our adversaries, in manifest calumnies, allege against us. The expressions in, with, and under are used, first, in order to proscribe the MONSTROUS DOCTRINE of TRANSUBSTANTIATION, and secondly, to assert a true presence over against the doctrine that the Lord's Supper is a mere sign." *

Osiander, 1617

MENTZER († 1627): † "There is no local concealment of Christ's body, or inclusion of particles of matter under the bread. Far from us be it that any believer should regard Christ's body as present in a physical or natural mode. The eating and drinking are not natural or Capernaitish, but mystical or sacramental."

Mentzer, 1627.

JOHN GERHARD († 1637): ‡ "On account of the *calumnies* of our adversaries, we would note that we do not believe in *impanation*, nor in CONSUBSTANTIATION, nor in any *physical* or *local* presence. Some of our writers, adopting a phrase from Cyril, have called the presence a *bodily* § one; but they use that term by no means to designate the mode of presence, but simply the object" (to show *what* is present, to wit, the body of Christ, but not *how* it is present), "nor have they at all meant by this that the body of Christ is present in a bodily and quantitative manner." "We believe in no consubstantiative presence of the body and blood. Far from us be that figment. The heavenly thing and the earthly thing in the Lord's Supper are not present with each other *physically and naturally*." |

Gerhard, 1637.

CARPZOV († 1657): ¶ "To compress into a few words what is

---

* Disputat. xiii., Ex Concord. Libro. Francoofurt, 1611, pages 280, 288.
† Exeges. Aug. Conf.   ‡ Loci (Cotta) x. 165.
§ Corporalem. | See also Harmonia Evang., ii. 1097.
¶ Isagoge, 345–350.

most important in regard to this presence, we would remark
1. That it is not finite, either physical, or local, or definite, but
infinite and divine.   2. That as there is not one
mode only of divine presence, but that presence
may be *general*, or gracious, or glorious, as the scholastics distinguish it, so this presence (of the body and blood of Christ)
is neither to be referred to the *general* nor the *glorious*, but to
the *gracious;* so that it constitutes that special degree of this
gracious presence which is styled *sacramental.* That which is
supernatural is also true and real. When this presence is called
substantial and *bodily*, those words designate *not* the MODE of
presence, but the OBJECT. When the words *in*, *with*, *under*,
are used, our traducers know, as well as they know their own
fingers, that they do NOT signify a CONSUBSTANTIATION, local
co-existence, or impanation. The charge that we hold a local
inclusion, or Consubstantiation, is a calumny. The eating and
drinking are not physical, but *mystical* and *sacramental.* An
action is not necessarily figurative because it is not physical."

margin note: Carpzov, 1657.

MUSÆUS († 1681): * " On the question, *By what mode* (quo
modo) that which we receive and eat and drink in the Holy
Supper is Christ's body and blood, we freely confess our ignorance." "The sacramental eating is sometimes
called spiritual, that is, an eating not gross, not
carnal, but wholly incomprehensible — the mode is supernatural,
and beyond the grasp of the mind of man. . . . That gross and
carnal eating which the Capernaites (John vi.) imagined is
denied by the Formula of Concord, and when Calvinists attribute this view to us, they are guilty of calumny."†

margin note: Musæus, 1681.

SCHERZER († 1683) : ‡ To the objection that the particles " in,
with, under, imply an inclusion of the body of Christ in the
bread, and a concealing of it under the bread, and
a consequent reduction of the body to the proportion and dimensions of the bread," he says : I. " From *presence*
to *locality*, no inference can be drawn. Those particles imply
presence, not locality. For they are *exhibitive*, not inclusive

margin note: Scherzer, 1683.

---

* De Sacra. Cœna. Jenæ, 1664, 85.

† Prælect. in Epitom. Formul. Concord. Jenæ, 1701, 4to, 259, 260.

‡ Collegium Anti-Calvinianum, Lipsiæ, 1704, 4to, 606, 630, 632.

II. Quantitative proportion is required to local inclusion, but not to sacramental presence. In the German hymn, the phrase : 'Hidden in the bread so small (Verborgen in brod so klein)', the 'Hidden,' notes a mystic hiding — that the body of Christ is not open to the senses ; not a physical one, which is local ; the words 'so small,' are a limitation of the *bread*, not of the body.' He shows that Calvin, Beza, and others of the Calvinistic school, use these particles also. "By *oral*, we do not mean corporeal, in the Zwinglian sense. . . . Corporeal eating, in the Zwinglian sense, we execrate (execramur)."

CALOVIUS († 1686): * "The *mode* is ineffable, and indescribable by us. We distinguish between a *natural*, a *personal*, and a *sacramental* presence, in which last sense only the body of Christ is present. . . . There is no question in regard to a *Capernaitish* eating and drinking, such as some of the hearers of our Lord at Capernaum dreamed of (John vi. 21); as if Christ had taught a deglutition of His body . . . a swallowing of His blood. This *delirium* our adversaries are accustomed to charge upon us falsely and calumniously. . . . The mode is not natural, but supernatural. . . . The bread is received in the *common*, *natural* manner; the body of Christ in the *mystic*, *supernatural* manner. . . . We do not assert any local conjunction, any fusion of essences, or *Consubstantiation*, as our adversaries attribute it to us; as if we imagined that the bread and the body of Christ pass into *one mass*. We do not say that the body is included in the bread, but only that there is a *mystic and sacramental* conjunction of substance with substance, without any *insubstantiation* or consubstantiation."

Calovius, 1686.

QUENSTEDT († 1688) † : "The manducation and drinking are called *oral*, not with reference to the *mode*, but to the organ. Luther calls it *corporeal*; but this form of expression is not to be understood of the *mode*, as if this spiritual food were taken in a natural mode as other food. . . Of the one sacramental or oral eating and drinking there are two modes — the *physical* and *hyper-physical*. . . . The body and

Quenstedt, 1688

---

* Synopsis Controversiarum, Wittenb. 1685, 4to. Pp. 793, 814. See also Calovii: Apodixis Artic. Fid. Wittenb. 1699, 4to. P. 385.

† Theologia. Didactico-Polem. Lipsiæ, 1715, Fol. II., 1223, 1231, 1232

blood of Christ are not eaten and drunken in a physical mode.
. . . The mode of the presence of the body and blood is mystic,
supernatural, and heavenly. . . . The body of Christ is spiritual
food, nourishing us not to this life, but to the spiritual and
heavenly life. . . . The body of Christ does not enter the mouth,
as if moved from without, it entered locally, deserting its former
place, and taking a new one in the mouth. . . . There is no distraction to be feared in that food which is present with a divine
presence. Each believer enjoys God as the highest good, but
the same presence is communicated to the flesh of Christ."

BAIER, J. G. († 1695)*: "The sacramental union is neither
substantial, nor *personal*, nor *local*. Hence it is manifest that
impanation and *Consubstantiation*, which are charged
upon Lutherans by enemies, are utterly excluded.
There is no sensible or natural eating of the body of Christ.
Alike the presence and the eating and drinking of the body
and blood of Christ are insensible, supernatural, unknown to
the human mind, and incomprehensible. As to the MODE in
which the body and blood of Christ are present and received in
the Supper, we may acknowledge our *ignorance*, while we firmly
hold to the *fact*." The same distinguished writer published a
dissertation on "Impanation and Consubstantiation," which is
entirely devoted to the vindication of our Church from the
charge of holding these errors. †

LEIBNITZ († 1716),‡ distinguished as a profound theological
thinker, as well as a philosopher of the highest
order, says: "Those who receive the Evangelical
(Lutheran) faith by no means approve the doctrine of CONSUB-
STANTIATION, or of impanation, nor can any one impute it to
them, unless from a misunderstanding of what they hold."

BUDDEUS († 1728) : "All who understand the doctrines of
our Church know that with our WHOLE SOUL WE ABHOR THE
DOCTRINE OF CONSUBSTANTIATION AND OF A GROSS UBIQUITY OF THE
FLESH OF CHRIST. They are greatly mistaken who suppose

---

*Theolog. Positiv. Lipsiæ, 1750, p. 661.

† Dissertatio Historica-theologica de Impanat. et Consubstantiat.

‡ Conformité de la foy avec raison, ₹ xviii. Dissertatio de Conformitate
Tübingen, 1771.

the doctrine of impanation to be the doctrine of **Luther and of our Church.** The doctrine of impanation, if we distinguish it from that of assumption, can mean nothing else than a local inclusion of the body of Christ in the bread. To admit such a doctrine would be to *admit the grossest absurdities;* they, therefore, who impute it to our Church, prove *only their ignorance* of our doctrine. In *either sense,* in which the word CONSUBSTANTIATION can be taken, the doctrine cannot, *in any respect,* be attributed to our Church; it was always far from the mind of our Church. The sacramental union is one which reason cannot comprehend, and the taking, eating, and drinking are done in sublime mystery."* Buddeus, 1728.

COTTA († 1779)† makes the following remarks upon the different theories of sacramental union: "By IMPANATION is meant a *local inclusion* of the body and blood in the bread and wine. Gerhard has rightly noted Cotta, 1779. that the theologians of our Church utterly abhor this error. The particles in, with, under are not used to express a local inclusion. As our theologians reject impanation, so also they reject the doctrine of CONSUBSTANTIATION. This word is taken in two senses. It denotes sometimes a *local conjunction* of two bodies; sometimes a *commingling* or *coalescence* into one substance or mass. But in *neither sense* can that MONSTROUS DOGMA of CONSUBSTANTIATION be attributed to our Church; for Lutherans believe neither in a local conjunction nor commixture of bread and Christ's body, nor of wine and Christ's blood."

We could multiply testimony on this point almost without end. No great dogmatician of our Church, who has treated of the Lord's Supper at all, has failed to protest in some form against the charge we are considering.

The less candid or less informed among the Roman Catholic writers have made the same groundless charge against our Church, while other writers in the same Church Roman Catholic writers. have acknowledged the falsity of it. One example of the former will suffice.

* Miscellanea, ii. 86, seq. Catechet. Theologia, ii. 656. Instit. Theol. Dogm. v. i. xv.

† In Gerhard's Loci, x. 165.

PERRONE* says of the Lutherans: "Some of them have brought in the doctrine of hypostatic union of the incarnate
Perrone. Word with the bread, which union *they call* impanation; others affirm a *consubstantiation*, as they call it, or a commixture or concomitance." Perrone has not only been following Romish guides, but he has selected the worst among them.

BECAN († 1624) † says: " Luther *seems* to assert impanation;" but even this, he goes on to show, is not true of the Lutheran
Becan, 1624. Church. BELLARMIN († 1621)‡: "Luther insinu-
Bellarmin, 1621. ates the impanation of Rupert and John of Paris, but does not state it explicitly." He then goes on to show that Martin Chemnitz and the other Lutherans did not hold this view.

MOEHLER §: " Luther had already rejected the doctrine of transubstantiation; but he still continued, with his accustomed
Moehler, 1838. coarseness and violence, yet with great acuteness and most brilliant success, to defend against Zwinglius the real presence of Christ in the Eucharist. For whenever the doctrinal truth is in any degree on his side, he is always an incomparable disputant, and what he puts forth on this subject in his controversial writings is still deserving of attention."

CARDINAL WISEMAN ‖ refers to " *consubstantiation* or *companation* in the chrysalis proposition*"* (the Tenth Article of the Augsburg Confession), " in which we must try to suppose it
Wiseman, 1865. originally contained." The cardinal means that the Confession " does not so much impugn the doctrine of transubstantiation as leave it aside;" but that if it does not leave transubstantiation an open question, it teaches *consubstantiation;* and that, out of deference to its friends, he is willing, in his good nature, to *try* to think the doctrine is there. But it is worthy of note that in the cardinal's whole argument in "The Real Presence *proved from Scripture,"* there is no posi-

---

* Prælect. Theologic. L. III.   † Manual Controvers. L. II.
‡ Lib. III. de Euch. Ch. XI.   § Symbolism. Transl. by Robertson. ₹ xxxv.
‖ The Real Presence of the Body and Blood of our Lord Jesus Christ in the Blessed Eucharist proved from Scripture. Lond. 1836. Lects. II. and VIII.

tion taken which involves the doctrine of *transubstantiation.*
The ablest parts of the book are a far better defence of the
Lutheran doctrine than of the Roman Catholic. Cardinal
Wiseman was too able a controversialist to attempt to *identify
in the argument* (whatever he might *assume* in the *definition*) the
doctrine of *transubstantiation* with the doctrine of a *real presence.* He argues exclusively from Scripture for the *latter,* and
merely takes for granted the former. This he admits in his
closing lecture: "In concluding these lectures on the Scriptural proofs of the real presence, I will simply say, that
throughout them I have spoken of the doctrine" (the real
presence) " *as synonymous* with transubstantiation. For as by
the real presence I have understood a corporeal presence, *to the
exclusion of all other substance,* it is evident that the one is, in
truth, equivalent to the other. On this account I have con
tended for the literal meaning of our Saviour's words, LEAVING
IT AS A MATTER OF INFERENCE that the Eucharist, after consecration, *is* the body and blood of Christ."

The most judicious Romish controversialists, like the cardinal, separate the two questions. BOUVIER * and Perrone,† for
example, prove, in the first article, " the real presence ;" in the second, they discuss the " *mode* of the Bouvier, 1854.
real presence — transubstantiation." The fact is that the two
lines of argument are directly contradictory. The processes
of exegesis which *establish* the doctrine of the true presence
overthrow the doctrine of transubstantiation. The Romanist
is on the Lutheran ground when he proves the first ; he is on
the Calvinistic ground when he attempts to prove the second.

Many of the ablest divines of the Calvinistic Churches have
acknowledged the libellous character of the charge Admissions of
that the Lutheran Church holds the doctrine of Calvinistic Di-
CONSUBSTANTIATION. While BUCER († 1551) was vines.
still with the Zwinglians, he wrote (1530) to Luther: " You do
not maintain that Christ is in the bread locally ; and you acknowledge that though Christ exists in one place of heaven in
the mode of a body, yet he can be truly present in the Supper,

* Institut. Theolog. Sept. Edit. Parisiis, 1850. III. 3, 31.
† Prælectiones Theologicæ. Paris, 1852. II. 155, 208.

through the words and symbols." In his Retractation he says: "To Luther, and those who stood with him, was attributed a grosser doctrine concerning the presence and reception of the Lord in the Supper than that which I afterwards found, and now testify, they ever held. I disapproved of certain forms of speech, as, that the sacraments confirmed faith and strengthened the conscience, that Christ was received in the sacrament, and that this reception was corporeal: which forms I now acknowledge I can use piously and profitably."[*] WOLFGANG MUSCULUS († 1563)[†]: "I do not think that any one ever said that the bread is naturally or personally the body of our Lord; and Luther himself, of pious memory, expressly denied both modes." WHITAKER († 1595)[‡]: "Luther taught no personal union of the flesh of Christ with the bread."

Bucer.
Musculus.
Whitaker.

SALMASIUS († 1653): [§] "Consubstantiation, or fusion of natures, is the commixtion of two substances as it were into one; but it is not this which the followers of Luther believe; for they maintain the co-existence of two substances distinct in two subjects. It is the co-existence, rather, of the two substances than their consubstantiation." Nothing would be easier than to multiply such citations. Some have been given in other parts of this work, and with one more we will close our illustrations of this point. We shall quote from STAPFER, who, probably beyond any other of the writers of Polemics, is a favorite among Calvinists. He first states [∥] the points in which Calvinists and Lutherans agree on the Lord's Supper: "They AGREE,

Salmasius.
Stapfer.

"*a.* That the bread is not changed into the body of Christ: after the consecration the outward signs remain bread and wine.

---

[*] Given in Verpoorten: Comment. Histor. de Martino Bucero. Coburg, 1709. § xx. xxiii.

[†] Loci Comm. Theolog. Bern, 1560, 1583. Folio, 771. Quoted in Baier: De Impanat. 13. Musculus was originally of the Strasburg school. His Loci are of the Helvetic type.

[‡] Præl. de Sacr. Franc. 1624, 561. Quoted in Baier, 13.

[§] Simpl. Verin. sive Claudii Salmasii De Transubstant. Ed. Sec. Lugdun. Bat 1660, p. 509.

[∥] Institut. Theolog. Polemic. Universæ. Tigur, 1748, 12mo, V. 227.

" *l.* The bread is not to be adored.

" *c.* The Sacrifice of the Mass is an invention which casts contempt on the Sacrifice of the Cross.

" *d.* The carrying about of the host in processions is absurd and idolatrous.

" *e.* The mutilation of the Supper, by giving only the bread, is impious, and contrary to the original institution.

" *f.* The use and virtue of the Sacrament is not dependent on the intention of the consecrator.

" *g.* The body and blood of Christ are present verily and really in the Eucharist, not to our soul only, but also to our body. They are present by power and efficacy.

" *h.* Only *believers*, by means of the right use of this Sacrament, are made partakers of the fruits of the sufferings and death of Christ; *unbelievers* receive no benefit.

" THEY DIFFER in these respects:

" *a.* The brethren of the Augsburg Confession teach: That the body and blood of Christ are present with the signs in the Supper substantially and corporeally.

" But here it is to be observed that these brethren do not mean that there is any *consubstantiation* or *impanation.* On the contrary, PFAFF, the venerable Chancellor of Tübingen, protests, in their name, against such an idea. He says: *
' All ours agree that the body of Christ is not in the Eucharist by act of that finite nature of its own, according to which it is now only in a certain " pou" (somewhere) of the heavens; and this remains that the body of Christ is not in the world, nor in the Eucharist, by diffusion or extension, by expansion or location, by circumscription or natural mode. Yet is the body of Christ really present in the Holy Supper. But the inquisitive may ask, How? I answer, our theologians, who have rightly weighed the matter, say that the body and blood of Christ are present in the Holy Supper according to the omnipresence imparted to the flesh of Christ by virtue of the personal union, and are sacramentally united with the Eucharistic symbols, the bread and wine; that is, are so united, that of the divine institution, these symbols are not symbols

* Instit. Theol. Dogm. et Moral. III. iii. 740, 748

and figures of an absent thing, but of a thing most present, to wit, the body and blood of Christ, which are not figurative, but most real and substantial.   Wherefore the body and blood of Christ are present, but not by a presence of their own — a natural and cohesive, circumscriptive and local, diffusive and extensive presence, according to which other bodies are said to be present — but by a divine presence, a presence through the conjunction of the Logos with the flesh of Christ.   We, rejecting all other modes of a real Eucharistic presence, hold, in accordance with our Symbolical books, that union alone according to which the body and blood of Christ, by act of the divine person, in which they subsist, are present with the Eucharistic symbols.   We repeat, therefore, all those of the Reformed do wrongly who attribute to us the doctrine of consubstantiation, against whom we solemnly protest.'

" *b.* The adherents of the Augsburg Confession hold that the true and substantial body and blood of Christ .. are received by unbelievers as well as by believers, orally.   Pfaff thus expresses it: ' Though the participation be oral, yet the mode is spiritual; that is, is not natural, not corporeal, not carnal.'"

Not only however have candid men of other Churches repudiated the false charge made against our Church, but there nave not been wanting those, not of our Communion, who have given the most effectual denial of these charges by approaching very closely to the doctrine which has been maligned, or by accepting it unreservedly.*

The Lutheran Church has been charged with *self-contradiction* in her interpretation of the words of the Eucharist in this respect, that, contending that the words " This is my body" are not figurative, she yet considers that there is a figure in the second part of the narrative of the Lord's Supper, as set forth by St. Luke, xxii.

II. Objection: That the exegesis is self-contradictory — answered.

---

* See, for example, the remarks of Theremin, the Fénelon of the Reformed Church (Adalbert's Confession), and of Alexander Knox, who was so profound and vigorous as a writer, and so rich in deep Christian experience: " Treatise on the Use and Import of the Eucharistic Symbols," in " Remains."   3d edition, London, 1844.

20 : that when our Lord says : " This cup (is) the New Testament in my blood," the word " cup " is used figuratively for
" contents of the cup ; " and that we do not hold that the cup
is literally the New Testament. If we allow a figure in the
second part, does it not follow that there may be a figure in
the first ? To this we answer, *First.* Either the modes of expression in the two parts are grammatically and rhetorically
parallel, or they are not. If they are not parallel, there not
only can be no inconsistency in different modes of interpreting,
but they *must* be interpreted differently. If they are parallel,
then *both* doctrines are bound to authenticate themselves by
perfect consistency in the mode of interpreting. Both agree
that the word " cup " involves " contents of the cup." Now
treat them as parallel, and on the Calvinistic view results logically , " The contents of this bread is my body, the contents of
this cup is my blood, or, the New Testament in my blood " —
that is, they reach the Lutheran view. If Lutherans are inconsistent here, it is certainly not that they fear to lose by consistency.

We at least accept the result of our exegesis of the word
" cup," (which our opponents admit is here right,) whether it
be consistent with our former exegesis or not. If any man
believes that the " contents of the cup " is the blood of Christ,
he can hardly refrain from believing that the bread is the Communion of His body. But our opponents will no more accept
the necessary consequence of our exegesis where it coincides
with their own, than where it differs ; for while on their own
exegesis, with which they claim that on this point ours is identical, the " cup " means " contents of the cup ; " to avoid the
necessary inference, or rather the direct statement, that the
" contents of the cup " is Christ's blood, they go on to say,
" the contents of the cup " we know to be wine ; the cup therefore really means, not in general the " contents of the cup,"
but specifically " wine." The word " cup," as such, never
means " wine." When Jesus says of the cup, " This cup
is the New Testament in my blood," the meaning they
give it is, after all, not as Lutherans believe, that the " contents of the cup " is the New Testament in Christ's blood,

but that "this wine is like the New Testament in Christ's blood, or the pouring out of this wine like the pouring out of the New Testament — or of the blood which is its constituting cause." The interpretation, therefore, of the word "cup," which they grant to be a correct one, if legitimately accepted, overthrows their doctrine.

But this still leaves untouched the point of the alleged *inconsistency* between the principles on which our Church interprets the "first" and "second" parts of the formula of the Lord's Supper. But our Church does not believe, as the alleged inconsistency would involve, that there is a *rhetorical* figure in the words, "This is my blood," or, "This cup is the New Testament in my blood." If, in a case fairly parallel, we acknowledge in the second part of the formula what we denied in the first, then, and then only, could we be charged with inconsistency. But in this case there is no parallel whatever, nor even the semblance of inconsistency. We do not interpret any word of the "second" part of the formula metaphorically, and therefore cannot be inconsistent with our denial of a metaphor in the "first." We do not interpret the word "cup" to mean "sign," "symbol," or "figure" of cup; but because a literal cup actually contains and conveys its literal contents, so that you cannot receive the contents without receiving the cup, nor the cup, without receiving the contents; they are so identified, that, without dreaming of a departure from the prose of every-day life, all the cultivated languages of men give the name "cup" both to the thing containing and the thing contained. There is, however, this difference — that the thing designed to contain bears the name "cup" even when empty, but the thing contained bears the name "cup" only in its relations as contained. A wine-cup may hold no wine; a cup of wine involves both wine as contained, and a cup as containing. The word "cup" may mean, without metaphor: *First.* The vessel meant to contain liquids, whether they be in it or not. *Second.* The liquid which is contained in such a vessel, or is imparted by it. *Third.* The vessel and liquid together. Before the sacramental cup was filled, the word "cup" would be applied to it in the *first* sense. In the words: "He took the cup," Luke

xxii. 17, the word " cup " is used in the *third* of these senses —
He took the cup containing, and through it the contents. In
the words : " Divide it among yourselves," the cup is conceived
of in the *second* sense — divide the *contained* cup, by passing
from one to the other the containing cup, with its contents. In
the words of the institution : " This cup is the New Testament," the contained cup, in the second sense, is understood —
the contained as mediated through the containing — that which
this cup contains is the New Testament in my blood. In such
a use of the word " cup " there is no metaphor, no rhetorical
figure whatever. It is a grammatical form of speech ; and if
it is called a " figure," the word " figure " is used in a sense
different from that which it has when it is denied that there
is a " figure " in the first words of the Supper. We deny that
there is a rhetorical figure in any part of the words of the
Institution.

While in the history of the second part of the Supper, Matthew and Mark upon the one side, and Luke and St. Paul
upon the other, are perfectly coincident in meaning, that is a
radically false exegesis which attempts to force the language
of either so as to produce a specific parallelism of phraseology.
According to Matthew and Mark, Jesus took the cup, and,
having given thanks, gave it to His disciples, saying, " Drink ye
all of it ; for this is that blood of mine, the (blood) of the New
Covenant, the (blood) shed for many for the remission of sins."
These words grammatically mean : " Literally drink, all of you,
of it. For it, this which I tell you all to drink, is that blood
of wine, the blood of the New Covenant ; the blood shed for
many for the remission of sins." So far as Matthew and Mark
are concerned, the exegetical parallel in the Lutheran interpretation of both parts is perfect. Their meaning is clear and
unmistakable. Luke and Paul state the same thought in its
Hebraizing form, which is less conformed than the Greek to
our English idiom. " In the same manner also, (taking, giving thanks, blessing,) He gave them the cup after they had
supped, saying : This the cup (is) the New Covenant in my
blood, which (cup) is poured out for you."

The grammatical differences between the two accounts are

several. First, in Matthew and Mark the subject is the demonstrative pronoun touto, this, which I command you to drink,* in Luke and Paul, the subject is: "This the cup" "poured out for you:" meaning of both, differently expressed, this which I command you to drink (Matt., Mark), to wit, the cup "poured out for you," (Luke,) the poured out, the shed contents of the cup, are the blood of Christ, (Luke, Paul). Second. The copula is the same: Esti, is. Expressed in Matthew, Mark, and Paul. *Understood* in Luke. But it can only be left unexpressed on the theory that the proper force of the substantive copula is *unchangeable.* It cannot mean, This which I tell you to drink is a symbol of my blood, or, This the cup is the symbol of the New Covenant. Third. The predicate is different grammatically, but identical really: In Matthew and Mark the predicate is, My blood; the blood of the New Covenant; the blood which is shed for many for the remission of sins. In Luke and Paul, the predicate is: The New Covenant in my blood. The blood constitutes the Covenant, the Covenant is constituted in the blood. In Matthew and Mark, our Lord says: That which His disciples drink in the Eucharist is the shed blood of the New Covenant. In Luke and Paul He says, That the cup poured out for them, which they drink, is the New Covenant (constituted) *in His blood.* Now, cup and that which they drink are two terms for one and the same thing; and blood of the New Covenant and New Covenant of the blood are one and the same thing, as an indissoluble unity. They are a cause and effect continuously conjoined. The blood is not something which originates the Covenant, and gives it a separate being no longer dependent on its cause; but the blood is forever the operative cause of the Covenant in its application, of which it was primarily the cause in its consummation. That which we drink in the Supper is the shed blood of Christ — and that shed blood is the New Covenant, because the Covenant is in the blood, and with the blood. This is the identity of

* So even Meyer: "Dieses was ihr trinken sollet." So far and so far only the Grammar carries him; but he presumes to add, not from any knowledge gained from the text, but from Lightfoot, that what they were to drink was "the (red) wine in this cup."

inseparable conjunction. Now attempt the application of the symbolical, metaphorical theory in this case. Can it be pretended that the symbolical or metaphorical blood of Christ, not His real blood, was shed for the remission of sins? * or that the symbol of the New Covenant, not the New Covenant itself, is established in the blood of Christ? As to the theory that "cup" does not mean generically "contents," but specifically "wine," it is at once arrayed against the laws of language; and, here, is specially impossible, because the cup-content is said to be shed or poured for us ("for the remission of sins"). *That* cannot be said of the wine. But as Matthew and Mark expressly say it is "the blood which is shed," and Luke and Paul say it is "the cup" which is shed, it is clear that cup is the content-cup, and that the content-cup shed for us is Christ's blood, not a symbol of it.

The cup is not said to be the New Testament simply, but the New Testament in *Christ's blood.* Now if the contents be mere wine, this absurdity arises with the metaphorical interpretation: Wine is the symbol of the New Testament in Christ's blood — but wine is also the symbol of the blood, on the same theory. In one and the same institution, therefore, it is a symbol, both of the thing constituting, to wit, the blood, and of the thing constituted, to wit, the New Testament. But if it be said, to avoid this rock, that it is a symbol of the thing constituted, because it is a symbol of the thing constituting, that implies that there is a grammatical metonymy of the effect for the cause it involves and includes; and this throws out the rhetorical figure, and admits just what the Lutheran Church claims here.

How completely different the use of "cup" in grammatical metonymy is from its use in metaphor, is very clear when we take a case in which the word "cup" is actually used in metaphor: "The cup which my Father hath given me shall I not

* This is not pretended even by the advocates of the symbolical theory. Meyer interprets: "'This is my blood of the Covenant;' my blood serving for the closing of the Covenant with God." He falls back upon esti, as what he calls "the Copula of the Symbolic relation." That such a character in the copula is a pure figment, we have tried to show in a previous dissertation.

drink it?" Here there is no literal cup, no literal contents; but anguish is figured under the word. Not so is it when our Lord says: "He that giveth a *cup* of cold water — " The containing cup is not of water, but of wood or metal: it is the cup contained, our Lord means; but He uses no figure, but plain every-day prose.

While metaphor proper is never used in a testament to directly designate the thing conveyed, the grammatical metonymy is constantly so used. A man may direct in a will that a cup of wine shall be given to every tenant on the estate, — so many barrels of ale, so many sacks of wheat, be distributed at a particular time.

The cup is called the New Testament, not because of the identity of sign and thing signified, but because of the identity of cause and effect — the cup contained is Christ's blood, and that blood is literally the New Testament causally considered.

It has been objected that, as our Saviour was visibly present, the disciples could not have understood that what they took from His hands and ate was truly the Communion — the com-

III. Objection. municating medium of His body. This objection
—The supposed reveals the essentially low and inadequate views of
impressions of the objector, both as to the person of Christ and
the first disci- the doctrine of the Church. *First.* It assumes as
ples.

a fact what cannot be proven, as to the understanding of the disciples. *Second.* Whatever may have been the limitation of the faith of the disciples at that time, when they were not yet under the full illumination of the Holy Spirit in the New Testament measure, and there was necessarily much they did not understand at all, and much that they understood very imperfectly, we have strong and direct evidence, as we have already shown, of their mature and final understanding of our Lord's words, to wit, that these words do involve a true, supernatural, objective presence of His body and blood. *Third.* All the earliest Fathers who were the disciples of the apostles, or of their immediate successors, show that it was their faith that in the Lord's Supper there is a supernatural, objective communication of the body and blood of Christ, and in connection with the other facts make it certain that this was the understanding and the faith of the apostles themselves. The more difficult to reason the doctrine of the true presence is shown to be, the stronger is the presumption that the doctrine was reached neither by the exercise of reason nor by the perversion of it, but by the witness of the New Testament writings and the personal teachings of the apostles.

It is objected that it is inconceivable that Christ, then present, visibly and locally, could have given His body sacramentally in a true, objective sense. There is a strong appeal made to the rationalism of the natural mind. Christ in His human form is brought before the mental vision, sitting at the table, holding the bread in His hand; and men are asked, "Can you believe that the body which continued to sit visibly and palpably before them, was communicated in any real manner by the bread?" It is evident at first sight that the objection assumes a falsity, to wit, that the body of Christ, though personally united with Deity, has no mode of true presence but the visible and palpable. The objection, to mean anything, means, "Can you believe that what continued in a visible and palpable mode of presence before their eyes, was communicated in a visible and palpable mode of presence with the bread?" To this the answer is: "We neither assert nor believe it!" If, to make the argument hold, the objector insists, "That, if the body were not communicated in that visible and palpable mode, it could be communicated in no true mode," he abandons one objection to fly to another; and what he now has to do is to prove that the palpable and visible mode of presence is the only one possible to the body of our Lord which is in personal union with Deity. It is interesting here to see the lack of consistency between two sorts of representations made by the objectors to the sacramental presence of Christ. The first is, We cannot believe that He was sacramentally present *then* at the first Supper because He was bodily so near. The second is, He cannot be sacramentally present *now*, because His body is so far off. But alike to the argument from mere natural proximity, or from mere natural remoteness, the answer is: The whole human nature of our Lord belongs on two sides, in two sets of

IV. Objection, from the visible presence of Christ.

relations, to two diverse spheres. That His body was before their eyes in the manner of the one sphere, is no reason why it should not be imparted to them, after the supernatural and heavenly manner of the other, in the sacramental mystery. If the local reality is not contradictory to spiritual reality, neither is it to the *supernatural*. If they could receive a body spiritually, they could receive it supernaturally. If they could have it imparted by the Holy Ghost, they could have it imparted by the Son. If the disciples could trust their eyes for the natural reality, and walk by sight in regard to it, they could trust Christ's infallible word for the supernatural reality, walking then, as we must ever walk in the high and holy sphere of the Divine, by faith, not by sight. The Lutheran doctrine of the Eucharist in no degree contradicts the testimony of the senses. Whatever the senses testify is in the Eucharist, it acknowledges to be there. We have the vision, feeling, and taste of bread and wine, and we believe there is true bread and true wine there. But body and blood, supernaturally present, are not the objects of the senses. The sight, touch, taste, are wholly incapable of testimony *to* such a presence, and are equally incapable of testifying *against* them. There are things of *nature*, *naturally* present, of which the senses are not conscious. There are probably things in nature which the senses may be entirely incapable of perceiving. How much more then may the supernatural be supernaturally present without affording our senses any clue. The senses in no case grasp substance; they are always and exclusively concerned with phenomena. What if the supernatural here be present as substance without phenomena? We deny that there is a phenomenal presence of the body and blood of Christ. We hold that there is a substantial presence of them. How little we may build upon the assumptions of human vision, is shown by the fact that the Docetists believed that the whole appearing of Christ was but phenomenal; that His divinity clothed itself, not with a true human body, but with a spectral and illusive form, which men took to be a real body; it was the substance of divinity in the accidents of humanity. The Romish view of the Supper is the Docetism of the earthly elements; the

Calvinistic view is the Docetism of the heavenly elements — the one denies the testimony of the senses in the sphere of the senses, and the other denies the witness of the faith in the sphere of faith. The senses are competent witnesses as to where bread is; but they are not competent witnesses for or against the supernatural presence of a body which is in personal union with God. We have no more right to reject the reality of the presence, which God's word affirms of Christ's body, after an invisible mode, than we have, with the Docetists, to reject the reality of His visible presence. We no more saw Christ at the first Supper than we now see Him at His Supper. We believe that He was visibly present at the first, on the same ground of divine testimony on which we believe that He was invisibly present in the sacramental communication. If the objector assumes that, on our hypothesis, the first disciples had a conflict between sight and faith, *we now*, at least, have no such conflict; for we have the same testimony in regard to both — the testimony of our senses — that the word of God declares both. With equal plausibility, if we are to reason from the limitations of our conceptions, it might be maintained that the divine nature of Jesus Christ could not be present at the first Supper. Was not that divine nature all in heaven? How then could it be all in the Supper? Was it not all at Christ's right hand, all at Christ's left hand, all above Him, all beneath Him? How could it be all *in* Him? How could the personal totality of Deity be present in Christ when the personal totality of Deity was present in each and every part of the illimitable? If the totality of the Deity could be really in the human nature of Christ, and at the same time really in the bread, could not that inseparable presence of the humanity which pertains to it, as one person of the Deity, be at once conjoined with the Christ visible before them, and the Christ invisible of the sacramental Communion? What the divine nature has of presence *per se*, the human nature has through the divine. We can no more explain the divine presence than we can the human. It is indeed easier, if the divine be granted, to admit the presence of a humanity, which is taken into the divine personality, than it is to rise from the original low plain

50

of natural thinking, to the primary conception of the omni-presence of the divine. The objectors admit the latter: they thus admit the greater mystery; yet they blame us for admit-ting the less. They admit the great fundamental cause of the mystery, to wit, the inseparable union of the human nature with the divine personality; and then deny the neces-sary effect and result of that cause. When Zwingle, at Mar-burg, declares that "God does not propose to our belief things which we cannot comprehend," Melancthon makes this indig-nant note: "Such foolish words fell from him, when in fact the Christian doctrine presents many articles *more* incompre-hensible and *more* sublime (than that article of the true pres-ence); as, for example, that God was made man, that this person Christ, who is true God, died."* The doctrine of the personal omnipresence of the humanity of Christ, *at the point at which it stands* in theology, is less difficult to receive than that of the essential omnipresence of God at the *place at which it stands* in theology. To the eye, the senses, reason, experience, Jesus Christ was but a man. He who can believe, against the appar-ent evidence of all these, that the bleeding and dying Nazarene was the everlasting God, ought not to hesitate, when He affirms it, to believe that what is set before us in the Holy Supper is more than meets the eye, or offers itself to the grasp of reason. The interpretation which finds mere bread in the Institution finds logically mere man in the Institutor. When Jesus sat visibly before Nicodemus, the palpable and audible Son of man, He said: "The Son of man" (*not* "the Son of God") "is in heaven." If that Son of man could be with Nicodemus in the manner of the lower sphere of His powers, and at the same time in heaven in the higher sphere, he could be with His disciples at the solemn testamentary Supper, after both manners, revealing the one to them in the natural light which flowed from His body, and the other in that truer light of the higher world of which He is Lord — the light which streams upon the eye of faith.

But there is an impression on the minds of many that the well-established results of *philosophical thinking* in the modern

---

*Chytræus: Hist. Aug. Conf. (Lat.), Frankf., a. M., 1578, 641.

world are in conflict here with the Church's faith. But those who are familiar with the speculations of the last three centuries are aware that so far from this being the case, v. Philosophy, Modern. the whole history of metaphysical thought during that era has shown, with increasing force, the entire inability of philosophy to disturb, by any established results, the simple faith which rests on the direct testimony of the word. A glance at the various modern schools will demonstrate this.

Why, then, if we ask for the light of that modern philosophy which it is thought can clear up the mystery left by revelation, why, in any case, do we believe, or know, or think we know, that there is a human body objectively in our presence? It is regarded by the mass of thinkers as certain that we never saw a human body, never felt it; but that the consciousness of the human soul is confined to its own modifications and impressions, and that our conviction that the modification we perceive, when we are convinced that a human body is before us, is the result of an objective body, and consequently presupposes its substantial existence, is an act not of cognition, but of faith — a faith which has been repudiated by the whole school of pure idealists, by many of the greatest European speculators, and in the philosophy of nearly the entire Orient. So far as philosophy, therefore, can determine it, we have no more absolute cognition of the objective, visible presence of a natural body than we have of the objective, supernatural, invisible presence of a supernatural body. Our persuasion of either presence is an *inference,* an act of *belief,* conditioned by testimony. We may think we have more testimony for the first inference than for the second; but it is none the less inference: it is not cognition. We *believe* that bread is there, on the *evidence* of the senses; we believe that Christ's body is there, on the *evidence* of the word. The knowledge or belief of the nonego, or external world, involves one of the grandest problems of speculative philosophy. The popular idea that we are cognizant of *the very external things* in themselves which we are said to see, hear, and feel, is entirely false. All accurate thinkers, of every school, admit this. This is the common ground of the extremest idealism and of the extremest realism.

Hegel and Hamilton stand together upon it. So much is not speculation: it is demonstration; and yet to the mass of minds this demonstrated fact in metaphysics seems as palpable and ridiculous a falsehood as could be devised.

What modern philosophy can do here will be best seen by looking at such of its results and efforts as most decidedly involve the matter under discussion.

The school of *theological idealism*, in which Berkeley is the great master, maintained that there is no substance proper except spirit, the divine Spirit, God, or created or finite spirits, among whom are men. While the common theistic view is that the will of God is the ultimate cause of properties or phenomena, and that he has made them inhere in substances, which thus become interme diate causes of the properties which inhere in them, Berkeley holds that there is no intermediate cause of properties, no substance in which they inhere, but that the ultimate cause, God's will, is the only cause, and that it groups them *without substance*, under the same laws of manifestation, as the common view supposes to be conditioned by substance. Spirit is the only substance; there is no essential nonego relative to an individual ego, except other egos. Objective reality presupposes originating mind, and mind acted upon. There are but two factors in all finite cognition: the ultimate causal mind, and the mind affected by it. Phenomena are but operations under laws of mind on mind, and in ultimate cause, of the infinite upon the finite. Annihilate spirit, and all reality ceases. The world which appeals to our consciousness is but the result of the operations of the Divine mind upon the human. Berkeley does not deny the reality of the phenomena, but he says that the solution of the phenomena is not the existence of a material substance — a thing which all philosophy grants that we can only conceive and can never reach — but the solution is the direct agency of that divine cause which, in the ordinary philosophy, is considered as a cause of causes, that is, what the ordinary philosophy says, God works through substance "intermediately," the idealist says God works through phenomena, without substance, "immediately." The whole

Theological idealism.—Berkeley.

question, therefore, between the Christian theological idealist and the Christian cosmo-thetical idealist is, really, whether God operates through phenomena, grouped simply by His causative will according to fixed laws, or, on the other hand, through objective substances in which attributes actually inhere; whether He operates upon our mind in producing impressions we connect with a supposed external world " immediately " or "mediately." It has been said by great philosophers, who rejected the former species of idealism, that though no man can believe it, no man can confute it; and it is claimed by its advocates that it never has been confuted. That no man can believe it, is certainly not true. We have the same evidence that confessedly deep thinkers have believed it that we have that men believe any other doctrine. But if the deepest thinking of some of the deepest thinkers can reach such a theory, where shall we place the crudities of the popular philosophy or want of philosophy? How little can it settle by *its* speculations.

The school of " *transcendental idealism,*" if it be proper to call it " idealism " at all, has its greatest modern representative in Kant; and it is said, " Kant cannot, strictly speaking, be called an idealist, inasmuch as he accepts objects outside of the Ego, which furnish the material for ideas, a material to _{Transcendental} which the Ego, in accordance with primary laws, _{Idealism.—Kant.} merely gives form."* The weakness of Kant's system was its arbitrary separation between the practical and the speculative. He held that the data of perception are valid in the practical sphere both of thought and action, but cannot be accepted as proven, and therefore valid, in the sphere of speculation. The practical here reached a result which *transcended* the powers of the speculative. To the speculative it was not, indeed, disproven, but only non-proven; yet, as non-proven, it made his system one which admitted, on one side, the speculative possibility of the purest idealism, while on the other, at the sacrifice cf internal consistency, he reached for himself a hypothetical realism, or cosmo-thetical idealism. All speculative thinking in Germany since has, more or less, turned upon the vindica

* Fürtmaier: Philosoph. Real Lexicon. Augsburg, 1854, Idealismus.

tion or repairing of this inconsistency, or the running out of one or other side of it to the exclusion of the other.

The school of *subjective idealism,* or *absolute subjectivity*, holds that all existence is subjective. Mind is the only essence. It sets aside a cosmos or external reality altogether, denies the objective existence of all matter, maintains that our seeming consciousness, through our senses, is not really the result of anything outside the mind. The assumed external thing, and the image of it, are one thing, and that is a modification of the mind. The conscious person, the *ego*, is the sole proper reality. This is Fichte's system in its entire form. Kant had avoided absolute idealism by granting the existence of sensuous intuitions to which real objects, distinct from the mind, correspond. But as the notions of pure reason, or universal notions, are not, according to Kant, to be styled objectively real because their objective reality cannot be demonstrated; and as it is equally impossible, on the principles of Kant, to demonstrate the objective reality of sensuous intuitions, Fichte drew the inference that these latter ought also to be regarded as mere subjective phenomena, and that consequently all so-called realities are but creations of the Ego, and all existence no more than thought.*

Subjective Idealism.—Fichte.

Fichte's later views are essentially different. He held in his riper period that it is not the finite *ego* or limited consciousness, but God the primary consciousness, whose life reveals itself in the infinite multiplicity of circumstances, who is to be regarded as the ultimate reason of all essence.

The school of *objective idealism* holds to the system of the *absolute identity* of the object supposed to be perceived, and the subject, the mind, perceiving. This school is represented in Schelling in his second stage, and Hegel in his first, and Cousin. Both the external thing and the conscious person are existences equally real or ideal; but they are manifestations of the absolute, the infinite, or unconditioned. Mind and matter are phenomenal modifications of the same common substance.

Objective Idealism.—Hegel.

* These views are developed especially in his work: Ueber den Begriff der Wissenschaftslehre (1794), 1798, and in his Grundlage der gesammten Wissenschaftslehre, Jena and Lpz. (1794), 1802.

The soberest and best form of idealism, which is indeed also realism, recognizes the external world as a real thing, but holds that we can have cognition of it, not as it is in itself, but as it is phenomenally, and that we reach a *"mediate* knowledge" of the phenomena by the direct cognition of consciousness. The mind is really modified by these phenomenal causes, and its inference, that its own states presuppose ultimate substantial realities without which these phenomena would not be, is a just inference. Hamilton calls this class "Hypothetical Dualists," or cosmothetic idealists, and says that to it "the great majority of modern philosophers are to be referred." It is an idealism which acknowledges realities which transcend the sphere of the senses, and which is thus compelled to admit that natural faith can challenge for its verities as just, if not as positive, an assurance as is given by direct cognition. All that the human mind immediately and absolutely knows is its own states of consciousness — everything else is inference, intuitive conviction, irresistible faith. "Mediate knowledge" is only intellectual faith.

Realistic Ideal-ism.

The greatest representative of another school in effect admits all this. Sir William Hamilton says: "The existence of God and immortality are not given us as phenomena, as objects of immediate knowledge." Metaphysics: Lect. VII. "The existence of an unknown substance is only an inference we are compelled to make from the existence of known phenomena." "Of existence absolutely and in itself, we know nothing." "All we know is known only under the special conditions of our faculties." "In the perception of an external object, the mind does not know it in immediate relation to itself, but mediately in relation to the material organs of sense." Lect. VIII. "Consciousness is a knowledge solely of what is now and here present *to the mind* . . comprehends *every cognitive act;* whatever *we are not conscious of, that we do not know.*" Dissert. Supplem. to Reid. "Consciousness is the condition of *all internal* phenomena . . comprises within its sphere the whole phenomena of mind." Lect. X. "Consciousness is an *immediate,* not a mediate, knowledge. We know the *mental representation* . . *immediately* . . the past *mediately* . . through the mental modification which **represents** it. Consciousness is co-extensive with our knowledge . . our special faculties of knowledge are only modifications of consciousness. *All real* knowledge is an immediate knowledge. What is *said* to be *mediately* known, is, in truth, NOT KNOWN to be, but only BELIEVED to be; for its existence is only an *inference*, resting on the *belief* that the mental modification truly represents what is *in itself* beyond the sphere of knowledge." Lect. XII.

The philosophical thinkers, whose leader we have just quoted, who claim to be the school of "Common sense," and vindicate their position as consonant with the popular interpretation of consciousness, are entitled by Sir William Hamilton,

Natural Realism. "Natural Realists." It is evident, in the Lectures of that illustrious philosophical scholar, that he started with one set of views, and experienced at least three changes before he reached his final position; and this final position is virtually a practical return to the first. These are as follows: 1. The mind has no immediate knowledge except of its own states. We only immediately know that of which we are conscious, and we can only be conscious of our own mental states. Our knowledge of the external world is therefore MEDIATED by our consciousness; it is an *inference* based on intuition and irresistible processes — is, strictly speaking, belief, not *cognition*. This is the first view, or Cosmothetic Idealism.

2. The *popular impression* of what consciousness affirms is the true standard of consciousness. We *are* conscious of whatever the mass of people think we are conscious of. But the mass of mankind suppose they are conscious of the very objects themselves in the external world. Therefore, we *are* conscious of the external verities themselves. This we may call Vulgar Realism.

3. The objective causes of *perception*, which is a form of consciousness distinct from *self*-consciousness, are only such parts of the nonego as come in *contact* with the sensorium, or bodily organ of perception. Of these the soul has immediate cognition. Organic Realism.

4. The soul and body are *personally* united, so that our perceptions are composite, embracing the *sensuous* organ as modified by the nonego in contact with it, and the mind as also modified in a manner which cannot be explained. The *nonego* outside of the man is, however, on this theory, still *hypothetical.*

For, first of all, it does not claim that we are conscious or perceptive of what is *outside* of the *individual*, as a total complex of soul and body ; and, secondly, to reach the nonego which it claims to establish, it is compelled to acknowledge that the ego is a personal unity — *both* soul and body. The *modified organ* is, therefore, a part of the ego; and the theory meets the horns of a dilemma. If it says the modification of the organ is within the man, though outside of the *mind*, and, *therefore*, is perceived as a *nonego*, it denies its own definition of the *complex person* on which the theory rests — for the *man* is the ego. But if the total *man* be the ego, then that which is within either part of his person is within the ego ; and the modifications of the man, be they where they may, are modifications of the ego, and not objective realities existent beyond it. This last view approximates the true view, which may be styled *Personal Realism.* It is in substance a renewal of the first theory, but with the great improvement of a true, yet still inadequate, view of the personality and unity of man. Personal Realism regards man as a being of two natures, inseparably conjoined in unity of person, so that he is not a soul *and* a body, but a psychical flesh, or incarnate soul. Apart from the personal relation of these two parts, there can be no man, no true human body, and no true human soul.

Between death and the resurrection there is only a relative, not an absolute separation between soul and body ; and the resurrection itself is a proof that the two natures are essential to the perfect, distinctive, human personality. A human spirit absolutely disembodied forever would not be a man, but only the spirit of a man. At the resurrection, in consequence of the changed condition of unchanged essences, man shall be a spiritual body, or an incorporate spirit. Before the resurrection, as the dead live " to *God*," both as to body and soul, both body and soul live to each other " to God," and still constitute one

person "to God." Man has the primary natural life, in which
he lives in both soul and body, to man and God, in the sphere
of nature. Man has the provisional, intermediate, and supernatural life, in which he lives no more to man, but "lives to
God" in both soul and body in the sphere of the supernatural.
Man has the ultimate eternal life, the resurrection life, which
is the natural life of heaven, in which he lives to God and
man. Then is he a spiritual body — an incorporate spirit.
Both natures in the highest perfection are forever in super-
organic union. Matt. xxii. 32, Luke xx. 38 : " God is not a God
of the dead, but of the living ; for all live unto Him," (*in* Him,
Arab. ; *with* Him, Æthiop.) This is to show, *not* that the soul
is immortal, but that the "dead are *raised*," 37. Marcion,
who acknowledged only the Gospel of Luke, rejected this whole
passage. He held to the immortality of the *soul*, but rejected
Christ's teaching of the immortality of *man*. The covenant
God is the God of the *whole person*. If God is the God of
Abraham, he is the God of the whole Abraham ; and the
whole Abraham, body and soul, lives. But as to the body he
is dead *to man ;* nevertheless, as to the body, he still lives to
God. Body and soul are *to God* a living inseparable, linked
even after death in the sphere of the supernatural — the sphere
which is *to God*. Between death and the resurrection, the body
and soul remain one person in the mind and in the hand of God.

The soul of the dead Christ was separated from His body,
so far as every natural and organic bond is concerned ; but His
body, through the three days, remained still in personal unity
with the divine nature, with which the soul also was united
personally ; and both, being held inseparably to the one person,
were *in it* held to each other still as parts of one person. So
that the body of Christ truly " crucified, dead, and buried,"
still lived *to God ;* and the personal union of the human nature,
body and soul, and of the divine nature, was unbroken. In
virtue of the mediatorial covenant, by which all who die in
Adam are made alive in Christ (1 Cor. xv. 22), the personal
relation of the bodies and souls of all the dead remains un-
oroken *to God*. But pre-eminently in the case of those who
are in " mystic union " with God — a union which involves

both body and soul — what is called death does not break that union with Him as regards *either part.* The body and soul, *separated* as to the old organic bond of nature, are united still to each other by being united to God — for all *live to Him.* The whole person in both natures lives to God, therefore the whole person in both natures lives forever — man is immortal. The intermediate relation must be provisional. Dead men can only live, even as to the body, to God, with a view to that direct reunion of the body with the spirit which takes place in the resurrection. Therefore, the "dead are *raised.*"

All, then, according to the theory which is the highest in its assumption as to our absolute knowledge of the "nonego" — or external world — all then that we know is so much of light, as is successively brought upon the optic nerve, so much of vibrating air as reaches the auditory nerve, and so through the little range of the other senses. The *objective reality*, which *causes* the undulation of light which produces the image on the retina ; the objective reality which *produces* the vibrations, which the tympanum communicates to the auditory nerve ; all this is equally, as on the second theory, to be accepted on the ground of intuitive *belief*, or of *logical* process ; it is *inferred* and *believed*, not *known.* How little then, on the showing of philosophy itself, even in its extremest pretensions, is it able to do in fixing or unfixing our faith in the testimony of God.

These views, which we have presented, are the sum of all the best philosophical thinking on the subject of the relation of the mind and its cognitions to the reality of an external world.

Our conviction then, that the causes of sensation have an objective substantiality, is at its root ethical rather than intellectual. It rests upon the veracity of God. No theist can deny that if God *will* so to do, every impression we now receive could be made upon us without the existence of matter. What we call the testimony of our senses is worth nothing whatever, except on the assumption that God is true ; and to take that very word of His — one of whose grand objects is to correct the mistakes of our natural senses and natural thinking — to treat this as a something whose plain teachings are to be set

aside by the very thing whose infirmity necessitates the giving
of it, is as unphilosophical as it is unchristian.

An objection which is a species under the metaphysical, and
which is, perhaps more frequently used than any other, is, that
it is impossible that a true human body should be really present
in more than one place at the same time — the
essential nature of the body, and the essential
nature of space, make the thing impossible. It is
worthy of note that the objection is usually put in the vague
assertion that *a* body, or *a human* body, cannot be thus present.
In this already lies a certain evasiveness or obscuration of the
real question. The incautious thinker is thrown off his guard,
as if the assertion controverted is that a body, or a human
body in general, that every and any body can be present in the
sense denied. There is a fallacy both as to *what* is present, and
what the *mode* of the presence is. As to the first, the question
fairly stated is : Can *Christ's* body be present? Can a body
which is in inseparable personal unity with the Godhead be
present? Can that, which no human body simply as such
could do, be done by the body of our Lord, whose relations and
powers are unique and transcendent? The question of possibility all through is not what is possible to a human body, in
its natural and familiar limitations, but what is possible to
God. Is there evidence that it is His will that the body of
our Lord should be sacramentally present at His Supper; and
if God wills it, is it possible for Him to fulfil it? If the evidence is clear that God does so will, *that* man is no Christian who denies that His will can be consummated; and *that*
man, who, because he thinks the thing is impossible, refuses to
accept what, but for that *difficulty*, he would acknowledge to be
invincible testimony as to God's will, is a Rationalist; his
mode of interpretation is Socinianizing, though he may be
nominally orthodox.

Objection from the nature of space.

On the question of possibility, it is well to remember, *first*,
that we do not know the absolute limits of the possible. All
sound philosophers acknowledge that there are incontrovertible
facts whose possibility not only cannot be demonstrated, but which are overthrown speculatively by

The Impossible. Self-existence.

all the logic which man is able to bring to bear upon the question. The philosophy of the world of thinkers has mysteries, which it accepts as irresistibly proven or attested to consciousness, which are as impossible, logically, as the doctrine of the Trinity, or the personal presence of the undivided Christ in His Supper. All systems of Christian theology, even the lowest, acknowledge that certain things, which seem to reason and logic impossible, are not only possible but actual; as, for example, that there should be a self-existent being. If there be one thing, which, beyond all others of its class, seems to the mind of man logically impossible, it is this very thing of SELF-EXISTENCE; yet it is most clear that we *must* choose between the idea of *one* self-existent or of a vast number of self-existents. The normal mind of man, on an intelligent presentation of the whole case, at once chooses the former, and thus concedes that the impossible, logically, is the presupposition of all that is possible and actual. *Because* self-existence seems to us impossible, we are compelled to believe in the self-existent. We have to choose between, once for all, accepting the seemingly impossible, and thus having a ground for all that is possible, or, accepting the same seemingly impossible, multiplied infinitely. But having accepted the seemingly impossible in *essence*, by believing in God, we are again compelled to acknowledge the seemingly impossible in *act*, by accepting the fact of *creation.*

Granted an infinite mind, yet does it seem impossible that by its mere will, material and intellectual being should come into existence. We are compelled to acknowledge that out of material nothing material something is brought to being. The lowest thing that is, we argue, must imply preexistent mind, to adapt it to its ends; yet the highest thing that is, God himself, though He be an entity of perfect adaptation, is not adapted, but is absolute.

Another mystery recognized in all Christian theology is that there should be a substantial PRESENCE of this Being, such that the whole of His essence shall be in each part of the universe; and yet that there shall be no multi-plication of essence or presence; that the entire essence should pervade infinity, and yet be indivisible; so that there is no part of God anywhere, and that the whole of God is every where, no less in the least than in the greatest, no less in the minutest part than in the absolute whole; in place, yet illocal, in all parts, yet impartible, in infinity, yet unextended.

The idea of ETERNITY, of something to which all time is unrelated, to which millions are no more than a unit, each being relatively to eternity nothing, of which a trillion

Eternity

trillion of years is no larger part than the minutest fraction of a second — a something of which we are compelled to conceive as back of us, and before us, but which is not back of us nor before us; in which we seem surely to have reached the middle point, this centre at which we stand, but which has no middle point; an infinite gone, and an infinite to come, but which has not gone and is not to come, but ever is, without past, or future, or proportion; this is a something which to reason and logic is utterly incomprehensible and impossible upon the one side, as on the other it is the irresistible necessity of our thinking. It is inconceivable *how* it is, or even *what* it is; but we can no more doubt that it *is* than we can doubt our own being.

If we come within the limits of the theology of the Catholic creeds, we find the seemingly impossible here also accepted as necessary truth. That the entire essence of the Godhead, the unity of the divine Being unimpaired, shall in its modi-

Trinity.

fications form the personality of the three persons, each person having the whole essence, yet being personally distinct from each of the others, not three essences, nor one essence in three thirds, but one essence entire in each — this swallows up the understanding of man. That the infinite Godhead should so take to itself a true human body, that the " human " and " divine " shall henceforth be one

Hypostatic union.

person, so that we can say, not by mere accommodation of language, but literally, " Christ made the universe, and God purchased the Church with His own blood " — this is fathomless. God is substantially present in every human creature: *How* is it then that but one of our race is God incarnate? However fathomless then, a doctrine whose basis is the truth, that the God of sternity, the God of omnipotence, the God of the unity in trinity, has a human nature, forming one person with His own, may be, we are bound to accept it, if His word teaches it; and we have seen that His word does teach it.

There has been great disingenuousness among some of the opposers of the Scripture doctrine of the Lord's Supper. They have first urged the speculative difficulties of natural reason against the direct sense of the text; then professing to be willing to bow before the Word of God with absolute submission, they yet claim to have shown, on the Onus probandi. ground of natural reason, that the Word does not teach the doctrine for which we here contend. Now the true mode of Scripture interpretation is: First. To fix the direct and literal sense of the words by the laws of language. Second. To adhere to that sense, unless, under a law acknowledged by God's Word itself, we are bound to accept a figurative sense. Those who depart from the literal sense in a disputed case are always by that fact thrown upon the defensive. He who has the literal sense of the text with him, is under no obligation to argue for his doctrine until it shall be shown that the literal sense is not tenable. On the main point of the objective presence, proven by taking the words in the literal sense, the immense majority of Christendom has been and is a unity. Those who deny the doctrine are bound to show that the literal sense *cannot* (not simply *may* not) be the true one. To say the literal sense cannot be the true one, because a small minority in the Christian Church think that sense involves something in conflict with *their* reason, is not only rationalistic, but egotistic and conceited in the last degree. Those who accept the literal sense have quite as much natural reason, quite as much power of seeing the difficulties it suggests, as the rationalizing minority. The question can never be settled on *that* ground. The attempt to do it has only wrought division. It has made chaos where Christendom before had order. The Reason, which has rejected the literal sense, has never been able to fix another. It has dropped pearl after pearl of truth into its vinegar, and the total result is spoiled vinegar and ruined pearls. The Reason has been injured by the abuse of the truth, and the truth has been perverted by the abuse of the Reason. But even on the low ground on which this rationalizing wishes to put this question, it has not the strength it claims for itself. If we consent, for argument's sake, to carry the question out of the sphere of the supernatural, where it belongs, to the sphere of the natural, where it does not belong, how little are we The natural. prepared to affirm of the ultimate power of God in Nature of things. the *natural world.* We indeed speak of the nature of things, and may say, the thing being so, its nature *must* be so; but we may not speak of a nature of things alien to and superior to the will of God. Even if we grant that there is a nature of things not the result of the *will* of God; as, for example, the nature of God himself, and the nature of the finite as finite, of the created as created, of the made as inferior to the maker; yet we cannot hold that the absolute *nature,* or the relative *nature,* is *contradictory* to the absolute *will.* God is not omnipotent as the *result* of His willing to be omnipotent; but neither is omnipotent *nature* possibly contradictory to the absolute *will.* The *nature* of the created as created, the *nature* by which the creature, in virtue of its being a creature, is of necessity, and not as a *result* of will, *not* creator, but creature, is not contradictory to the will of God. His will perfectly concurs, though it is not the cause of the *nature* of things, *abstractly* considered. But all things themselves exist by God's will. Without His will, therefore, there would be no things, and consequently no *concrete nature* of things. The concrete nature of things, therefore, is the result of God's will. While, therefore, the creature cannot be the creator, and, by the essential necessity of the presupposition, only the creature results from the divine will, and of *necessity* has a creaturely and finite nature, yet it is simply and solely because of the divine will that things exist, and that there is an *existent nature* of things. Whatever, therefore, may be the speculative relation into which the mind puts the *abstract* nature of things and the divine will, the *actual* nature of things and the divine will are in perfect harmony; and the actual nature would have no being without the will. Actual things and their actual nature, in a word, are so related to God's will that, knowing *them*, we know *it* — knowing *it*, we know *them*.

We admit that there are ideas, or what are called ideas, which are self-contradictory, and to which, therefore, there can be no corresponding realities. Yet, in regard to the great mass of things, which the uncultured mind would assert to be absolutely self-contradictory, and not necessarily merely such to our faculties, it may be affirmed, that the deepest thinkers would deny that they were demonstrably absolutely contradictory. Most things are said to be self-contra- Self-contradic-dictory because we have never seen them, nor are tion. we able to conceive of them, in harmony. But with finite faculties, this only demonstrates their relative, not their absolute, self-contradiction. Over an immense field of thought, we are not safe in affirming or denying certain things to be self-consistent or self-contradictory. Any man, who will take up the systems of human speculation wrought out by the greatest minds of all ages, will find that there is almost nothing, in the way of supposition, which can be set aside on the ground that the human mind invariably rejects it as impossible. It is wonderful how few things there are not only not demonstrably absolutely impossible, but which are relatively impossible to all minds.

John Stuart Mill (one of the most vigorous and most skeptical of the speculative thinkers of our day) maintains that, in a certain course which is conceivable, the human mind would come to consider the proposition that twice two are five as fixed, as it now considers the proposition that twice two are four. A few extracts from the examination of Hamilton's Philosophy, by this illustrious thinker, will show what results are compatible with the ripest philosophical thinking. He presents the following among the results of the latest speculation:

" If things have an inmost nature, apart, not only from the impressions which they produce, but from all those which they are fitted to produce, on any sentient being, this inmost nature is unknowable, inscrutable, and inconceivable, not to us merely, but to every other creature." " Time and Space are only modes of our perceptions, not modes of existence; and higher

51

intelligences are, possibly, not bound by them. Things, in themselves, are neither in time nor in space." Brown is "of opinion that though we are assured of the objective existence of a world external to the mind, our knowledge of this world is absolutely limited to the modes in which we are affected by it." "There may be innumerable modes of being which are inaccessible to our faculties. The only name we can give them is, Unknowable." Chap. II. Quoting Hamilton's Declaration,

Mill.   "There is *no ground* for inferring a certain fact to be *impossible* merely from our inability to conceive its possibility," Mill adds, "I regard this opinion as perfectly just. If anything which is now inconceivable by us were shown to us as a fact, we should soon find ourselves able to conceive it. We should be in danger of going over to the opposite error, and believing that the negative of it is impossible. *Inconceivability is a purely subjective thing*, arising from the mental antecedents of the individual mind, or from those of the human mind generally, at a particular period, and *cannot give us any insight* into the possibilities of Nature. But were it granted that inconceivability is not solely the consequence of limited experience, but that some incapacities of conceiving are *inherent* in the mind, and *inseparable* from it, this would not entitle us to infer that, what we are thus incapable of conceiving, cannot exist. Such an inference would only be warrantable, if we could know *a priori* that we must have been created capable of conceiving whatever is capable of existing; that the universe of thought and that of reality . . . must have been framed in complete correspondence with one another. That this is the case . . . is the foundation (among others) of the systems of Schelling and Hegel; but an assumption more destitute of evidence could scarcely be made, nor can we easily imagine any evidence that could prove it, unless it were revealed from above. What is inconceivable cannot, therefore, be inferred to be false. . . . What is inconceivable is not, therefore, incredible." Chap. VI. Furthermore, to argue from the *inconceivable* as deducible from the *supposed* properties of matter would be very fallacious in fact, while we see the idealism of Asia, part of Germany, and of New

England, denying at one extreme the very existence of matter and the materialism of part of Europe and America insisting, at the other extreme, that nothing exists but matter. A third tendency, represented in Locke and his school, throws a bridge by which men can pass over to the first or the second, by making the world of the senses the only world of cognition, and by maintaining that there is nothing in the nature of things, nothing in the nature of matter or of thought, to prevent matter from being endowed with the power of thought and feeling. But this is in effect to obliterate the essential distinction between spirit and matter. If matter can be endowed with the property of thinking, it can be endowed with all the other properties of mind; that is, mind can be matter, matter can be mind; but if the finite mind can be finite matter, the infinite mind can be infinite matter, and we reach a materialistic pantheism. The skeptical school of Locke itself being judge, we can, from the limitations usually belonging to matter, draw no inference against the presence of the body of Christ in the Supper.

While we repudiate all these extremes of speculation, we yet see in them that the human mind is unable to settle what are the precise limitations imposed by the *nature of things* on matter and spirit, or to say how much or how little of what is commonly considered the exclusive property of the one God may be pleased to give to the other. Sir William Hamilton says, " It has been commonly confessed that, as substances, we know not what is matter, and are ignorant of what is mind."* " Consciousness in its last analysis . . . is a faith." " Reason itself must rest at last upon authority; for the original data of reason do not rest on reason, but are necessarily accepted by reason on the authority of what is beyond itself. These data are, therefore, in rigid propriety, *belief or trust.* _{Hamilton.} Thus it is that in the last resort we must, perforce, philosophically admit that *belief is the primary condition of reason*, and not reason the ultimate ground of belief. We are compelled to surrender the proud *Intellige ut Credas* of Abelard, to content ourselves with the humble *Crede ut intelligas* of Anselm." " We do not in propriety *know* that what we are

* Discussions. Appendix.

compelled to perceive as not self is not a perception of self, and we can only on reflection *believe* such to be the case." * Mill sums up the opinion of Hamilton as this : " Belief is a higher source of evidence than knowledge; belief is ultimate: knowledge only derivative; knowledge itself finally rests on belief; natural beliefs are the sole warrant for all our knowledge. Knowledge, therefore, is an inferior ground of assurance, to natural belief; and as we have belief which tells us that we know, and without which we could not be assured of the truth of our knowledge, so we have, and are warranted in having, beliefs beyond our knowledge; beliefs respecting the unconditioned, respecting that which is in itself unknowable."

How little we are competent to decide on the metaphysic of a personal union, in which an infinite person takes to itself a human nature, is manifest when we attempt the metaphysic of that personal union with which we are most familiar — the union of soul and body in man. In our own persons, we are not always, perhaps are never, able to draw the line between what the body does through the soul, and what the soul does by the body. In ourselves there is a shadow of the marvel of the Communicatio idiomatum. The soul is not mechanically, nor merely organically, united with the body, but is incarnate, " made flesh." It takes the body into personal unity with it, so that henceforth there is a real fellowship of properties. What the soul has *per se*, the body has through the soul in the personal union. There is a real conjoint possession of powers by body and soul in the one human person. The body has real properties, by means of the union with spirit, which it could not have as mere matter. That which is *per se* but Fellowship of Properties in the human person. flesh, is, in the personal union, body ; and body is an integral part of the person of man. It receives personality from the spirit — not that the spirit parts with its personality so as in any sense to lose it, nor that the body receives it intrinsically, so as in any sense to hold it apart from the spirit, but that this one personality, essentially inhering in the spirit, now pertains to the complex being man ; **two natures** share in one personality, the one by intrinsic pos

* Note A, in Reed, pp. 749, 750.

session, the other by participation resulting from the unity
so that henceforth no act or suffering of the body is without
the soul, no act or passion of the soul is without the body; all
acts and passions are personal, pertaining to the whole man.
Though this or that be *relatively* according to one or other
nature, it is not to the exclusion of the other: "My soul
cleaveth to the dust" and "My flesh crieth out for the living
God." The human body has actual properties, in virtue of its
union with spirit, which are utterly different from and beyond
what matter, merely as matter, can possibly have. Because
this great truth has been ignored, philosophy stands helpless
before the question, How the soul can receive impressions by
the body? The attempts of the greatest of thinkers to solve
this problem seem more like burlesques, than serious efforts.
The *personal unity of man* alone solves the mystery. No theory
but this can meet the facts of our being. None but this can
avoid the two shoals of Absolute Idealism and Absolute Materialism. "The soul," says Tertullian,* "is not, by itself,
man, nor is the flesh, without the soul, man. Man is, as it
were, the clasp of two conjoined substances." "Man," says a
work attributed to Augustine, though evidently, in part, of
later date,† "consists of two substances, soul and flesh : the soul
with reason, the flesh with its senses, which senses, however, the
flesh does not put into activity (movet), without the fellowship
(societate) of the soul." "The soul," says the same ancient
book,‡ "is so united to the flesh, that it is one person with the
flesh. Of God as author, soul and flesh become one individual,
one man : hence, what is proper to each nature remaining safe,
that is added to the flesh, which is of the soul, and that is
added to the soul, which is of the flesh : according to the unity
of person, not according to the diversity of nature. What,
therefore, is proper to each, is common to both; proper according to nature, common according to person."

But if the body assumed by the soul has a new range of
properties, which give it a dependent exaltation, how much
more may we expect that when these conjoint natures, form

---

* De Resurrect. Carnis.   † De Spirit. et Anim., C. III.
‡ Augustini Opera, VI., App. 810. Liber de Spirit. et Animâ., C. XLI.

ing a human nature, are taken into personal union with the divine, there shall be a real *personal* participation by that human nature in the attributes of the divine. And if we may thus argue from the body that is, the natural body, how greatly is the argument strengthened by the fact that this same body, in its exalted attributes, as glorified at the resurrection, is so perfect an organ of the spiritual, so conformed to the spiritual in its unity, that St. Paul calls it "spiritual body." Now Christ's body is a spiritual body, and, by means of the Spirit whose organ it is, exercises spiritual functions; Christ's body is a divine body by means of the divine person it incarnates, and through that person exercises divine powers. A "spiritual body" is not a spirit which is a body, nor a body which is a spirit, but a true body, so pure, so exalted in its properties and in its glory, that it is more like our present conceptions of spirit than it is like ordinary matter, and is thereby fitted to be the absolute organ of the spirit. If we can limit the properties of a spiritual body by what we think we know of a natural body, the whole representation of the apostle is made void. "It doth *not yet* appear [is not yet manifested] what we shall be," but it is most certain that our conceptions of it are far more likely to fall below the truth than to rise above it.

It becomes us then to be modest in our affirmation as to what it is possible for God to do even with our natural bodies. Much more should we be modest in affirming what may be the possibilities of a body forming one part of a divine person. Let us acknowledge that we can no more comprehend how a spirit, even God himself, should be entire in more than one place at one time, than we can conceive of a body thus present. All thinkers acknowledge that in the actual conception, the definite framing to the mind of the presence alike of body or spirit, there is an invincible necessity of connecting locality with it. Now the presence of spirit demonstrates that presence and locality are neither identical nor inseparable; and if the argument, that they *seem* so, is demonstrative as to body, it is equally so as to spirit; but if it be granted that this seeming identity is false as regards spirit, then it may be false as regards body. Philosophy never has determined what space is — never has determined that it has an actual being — but be space what it may, the fact that our own souls are in our bodies, yet illocal, shows that there is no contradiction in the ideas of being in space, in locality, yet not having locality in it.

While, as regards the divine and human natures of Christ, we can, in both cases, define the *general kind* of presence, we cannot define in either the *specific mode.* It is so in the doctrine of the Trinity: we define the general kind of unity and threefoldness, but not *the mode.* We may thoroughly know up to a certain point what a thing is not, and yet be wholly ignorant beyond a certain other point what it is. We may know that a distant object is *not* a house, *not* a man, *not* a mountain, but be wholly ignorant what it is, or we may know what it is without knowing *how* it is. In the great mysteries we can know that they are *not* this or that. We may know further, to a certain extent, *what* they are (their *kind,*) but the *mode* of their being is excluded from our knowledge by the fact that they are mysteries. If we knew that, they would be mysteries no more.

Now the whole objection to the presence of Christ's body assumes a certain " *quo modo* " — starts with the assumption that Christ's body is limited as ours is, and that our doctrine assumes that it is present in *mode* and *kind* as ours is — both assumptions being absolutely false. Between the *kind* of presence which Christ's body has in the Supper and that which our body has in the world, there is a parallel in some part, but not in all; but as to the MODE, there is, so far as we know, no parallel whatever.

VI. There are several questions in the *metaphysic* of this doctrine which are entirely distinct, yet are often confounded; and as a result of this confusion, the doctrine of the true presence is thought to be encumbered with the same metaphysical contradictions as the figment of transubstantiation.

The first question is, do *attributes, qualities,* or *accidents inhere* in *substance?* To this the true reply is, They do. No *abstract* attribute, quality, or accident can have an objective existence.

Second. Is the *reason* of quality in the substance, so that essentially different qualities prove essentially different substances, and essentially different substances must have essentially different qualities ? The answer is *affirmative.*

Third. Does the character of a quality, as determined by the substance, have a real *correspondence* with the *phenomenon* in which the human mind is cognizant of the quality ? The answer is, Yes.

If these answers be tenable, then the doctrine of transubstantiation goes to the ground ; for it assumes that the *qualities* of bread and wine do not *inhere* in bread and wine, and may consequently exist *abstractly* fiom bread and wine: not only that a *something* which is not bread and wine may have all their qualities, but that a *nothing*, a *non-essence*, may have all their qualities. This theory, which is practically so materi-

VI. Objection: that alizing, runs out speculatively into nihilism. It as-
the same line of sumes that the *reason* of the qualities of bread and
argument can be
urged for tran- wine is not in the substance of bread and wine ;
substantiation. and that, consequently, the connection is purely arbitrary ; that the *reason* of the qualities of body and blood is not in the substance or nature of body and blood, and that consequently there is no reason in the essential nature of things why *all bread* should not have the *qualities* of human body and all body the *qualities* of bread. If the seeming loaf of bread may be Christ's body really, the seeming body of Christ might have been really a loaf of bread. We may be in a world in which nothing that seems is in correspondence with what is. The innocent family which thinks that it is eating bread is indulging in cannibalism, and some unfortunate wretch is hung on supposition of his having committed murder, when, in fact, what he plunged his knife into was but a loaf of bread, clothed with the accidents of a man. Transubstantiation unsettles the entire ground of belief and thought, and conflicts with the veracity of God in nature, as it does with His testimony in His Word.

A little reflection will show that not one of these metaphysical difficulties connects itself with the doctrine of the true sacramental presence. It grants that all the attributes of oread inhere in the bread, and all the attributes of Christ's body inhere in His body: the reason of this inherence is not arbitrary; but bread has its qualities because it is bread, and body has its qualities because it is body; bread cannot have the qualities of body because it is not body, and body cannot have the qualities of bread because it is not bread; and the *phenomena* by which the mind recognizes the presence of bread and body correspond with the qualities of each, so that the real *phenomenal* evidences of bread are proofs of true bread, and the phenomenal evidences of body are proofs of true body. So far, then, it is clear that the doctrine of the true presence is in perfect accord with the sound metaphysic with which the doctrine of transubstantiation conflicts. But it will be urged that the difficulty remains that the *phenomenal evidences* of the presence of true body are wanting in the Supper, and that our doctrine is so far in conflict with the *testimony* of the *senses*, equally with the Romish. This difficulty, which has often been triumphantly urged, has really no force. The senses may be competent to decide on the presence and reality of what is offered to them, but may be incompetent to decide whether a thing is really present, which does not come within their sphere. That I see the furniture in my room is proof that there is furniture there; but that I do not see the air in my room is no proof that air is not there. That I see the bread in the Supper is proof that bread is there; but that I do not see the body is no proof that the body is not there. But, says the objector, if the body be there, it must be clothed with the essential attributes of body, such as visibility and tangibility. You would see it and touch it, if it were there, on your own principles that properties inhere in substance. The *theological* answer to this is, that this objection assumes the natural presence of a natural body *per se*, while the doctrine to which it professes to be an objection is, that there is a supernatural presence of a supernatural body through the divine, with which it is one person. The metaphysical answer is, that though the properties which become known phenomenally, inhere in substance, the same substance, under different conditions, exhibits different properties. I take a compound substance which we call ice: it is visible, tangible, hard, and very cold. If it is struck, it returns a sound. It will not take fire, and puts out fire, and occupies in space a few inches. It melts and flows, and becomes warm; it occupies less space; it still will not take fire, but puts out fire — still visible, still tangible, still audible on a stroke, and can be tasted. I increase its temperature to a certain point, and it becomes invisible, intangible, intensely hot, inaudible; its volume has increased to between sixteen hundred and seventeen hundred cubic inches for every cubic inch as water. From its passivity it has become a force of the most tremendous potency, rivalling in its awful energy the lightning and the earthquake. The developed qualities of the substance which we first saw as ice, bear thousands swiftly over land and water, or, bursting their barriers, carry death and destruction with them. But science takes this substance and divides it into its elements. One of these is hydrogen. The heavy mass of ice has yielded the lightest of all known bodies; the extinguisher of combustion has given a substance of high inflammability; the hard has yielded one of the few gases which have never been liquefied. The other element, oxygen, is also one of the gases which have never been liquefied. The liquid of the world is produced by the union of two substances which cannot themselves be liquefied. The ice has no magnetic power, the oxygen has. Take the oxygen of our original lump of ice, and introduce the hydrogen of the same lump into it in a stream, and the two elements that quenched flame sustain it; or bring them together in a mass, and apply fire to them, and the union is one in which a terrific explosion is followed by the reproduction of the water which, under the necessary conditions, may become ice again. The circle has been run. Now if, under the changed conditions of nature, such marvellous phenomenal changes may take place in connection with the elements, with no change in their substance, who can say how far other changed conditions of nature may carry other substances in the sphere of nature? Yet more, who can say what the changed conditions in the supremest sphere of omnipotence may effect phenomenally in the sphere even of the natural, and, *a fortiori*, in the sphere of the supernatural? Qualities inhere in substance; but substance, under *changed conditions*, may put forth new qualities, or *withdraw* all the qualities that are objects of sense. That which can be seen, handled, and felt as a body, we may justly believe is a body; but that same body under *different conditions*, and *at the will* of Him it incarnates, may be present, yet neither be seen nor handled.

It is not logical to say, because what I see is matter, what I do not see is not matter. The senses only show us what is, not what must be. " What is visible is matter," is logical : " what is matter is visible," is sophistry. " What bears all the tests to which the senses can subject a true body is a true body," is logical : " what is a true body must be subject to all the tests of the senses," is sophistry. What bore all the tests of all the senses, as water, was fairly proved to be such ; but the same water passed into conditions in which it was attested by none of the senses, yet was none the less water. Hence our senses can and do prove that there is bread and wine in the Supper; but they do not and cannot prove that the body and blood of Christ are not there. The argument of the senses is conclusive against transubstantiation, but presents nothing whatever against the doctrine of the true presence.

VII. A seventh objection often urged, different in form from some of the others, yet essentially one with them, is, that " Jesus declares that He will leave the world, and has left the world ; therefore He is not present at His Supper." To this we answer, *First*, that if the expressions which speak of the absence of Jesus from the world are to be pressed without the Scriptural limitations as to the nature of His absence, it would follow that His divine nature is also VII. Our Lord's absent ; for these expressions, be their force what Declarations that He will leave the it may, always refer to his whole person. He never world. says, My body or My human nature will go away, but " *I* go away." Now the " I " expresses the person; if, therefore, the phrases are to be urged in such fashion as to preclude any sort of presence of His human nature, they will equally preclude any sort of presence of His divinity. Co-presence, that is, inseparable conjunction of the two elements of a person, is not only *an* essential of personality, but it is *the* primary essential element — such an element as is presupposed in every other, and without which the personal union could not exist. It is the minimum, not the maximum; the first, not the last, demand of personality. But the objector admits that Christ is present according to His divinity, and must, therefore, admit that He is present according to His humanity. *Secondly.* Our Lord, when He speaks of His absence, makes it antithetical, not to His essential presence, but simply to one kind of that presence, to wit, the continually visible or purely natural. So strongly is this the case, that after His resurrection, in view of the fact that, though yet visibly upon earth, He was even then no longer in the old relations, He speaks of Himself as in some sense not present with them: " These are the words which I spake unto you *while I was yet with you.*" (Luke xxiv. 44.) Here our Lord, after giving the strongest proof that He was then present bodily, expressly, over against a mere presence of His spirit, or disembodied soul, declares, at the same time, that He is in some sense no longer with them ; that is, after the former manner, and in the old relations. Already, though on earth, he had relatively left them. He thus teaches us that there may be an absence, even with the most positive tokens of natural presence, as there may be a presence, with the most positive tokens of natural absence. The incarnate Son of God is not excluded in the words, " I will *never leave* thee, nor forsake thee." He conforms to his own description of the good shepherd, as one who *does not leave* the sheep. (John x. 12.) When He says, " I came forth from the Father, and am come into the world," does it mean that he *so* came forth from the Father as no more to be present with Him, and so came into the world as to be absent from heaven (that Son of man who " is in heaven," John iii. 13) ? If it does not, then, when He adds, " I leave the world, and go to the Father," it does not mean that He *so* leaves the world as to be no more present in it, and so goes to the Father as to be absent from His Church. (John xvi. 28.) In a word, all the declarations in regard to Christ's absence are qualified by the expressed or implied fact that the absence is after a certain kind or mode only — a *relative* absence, not a substantial or absolute one. There is a *relative* leaving in human relations. " A man *shall* leave his father and mother, and cleave to his wife," and yet he may remain under their roof ; he leaves them relatively in rising into the new relation. As representatives of the supremest domestic obligation, the parents are left ; for his supremest domestic obligation is now to his wife. Hence, our Lord does not make the antithesis he shall *leave* parents, and *go to* his wife, but he shall *leave* father and mother, and shall cleave to his wife. A pastor may leave a congregation, as pastor, and yet remain in it as a member. A merchant may leave a firm, yet retain the room he had in their building. But these cases are not simply parallel. They illustrate the argument *a fortiori*.

The presence of God is regarded either as substantial or as operative and phenomenal. The substantial may exist without the phenomenal ; the phenomenal cannot exist without the substantial. God's substantial presence is alike everywhere — as complete in the lowest depths of hell as in the highest glory of heaven ; as perfect in the foulest den of heathen orgies as in the assembly of saints, or on the throne before which seraphim veil their faces. But His phenomenal presence varies in degrees. " Our Father who art *in Heaven*," marks His purest phenomenal presence, as making that Home to which our hearts aspire. As there is phenomenal presence, so is there phenomenal absence ; hence, God himself is frequently represented in Scripture as withdrawing Himself, and as absent, though, in His essence, He neither is, nor can be, absent from any part of the Universe. The absence of God is, so to speak, a relative absence, a *phenomenal* absence ; the tokens of Providence or grace by which this presence was actualized, not only to faith, but even to experience, are withdrawn. So the natural phenomenal tokens of the presence of the undivided Christ are withdrawn, yet is He substantially still present, and as thus present is operative in the supernatural phenomena of His grace.

Thirdly. Just as explicitly as Christ, the whole Christ, is said to be absent, is He affirmed to be present: " Where two or three are gathered together in my name, there am I in the midst of them." (Matt. xviii. 20.) " Lo, I am with you alway,—all the days,—even unto the end of the world." (Matt. xxviii. 20.) " If a man love me, he will keep my words: and my Father will love him, and *we will come* unto him, and make our abode with him." (John xiv. 23.)   The light of His presence shone around Saul, and the words of His voice fell upon Saul's ear. (Acts ix. 4–7 ; xxii. 6–11.) " The night following " Paul's appearing before the council, " *the Lord stood by him,* and said, Be of good cheer, Paul, for as thou hast testified of me in Jerusalem, so must thou bear witness also at Rome." (Acts xxiii. 11.)   Christ "filleth all in all." (Eph. i. 23.)   He is " in *the midst* of the seven candlesticks ; *walketh* in the midst of them ; holdeth the seven stars in His right hand ; and the seven candlesticks are the seven churches, and the seven stars are the angels of the seven churches." (Rev. i. 13 ; ii. 20 ; iii. 1.)   The glory of Christ ruling without vicars had been seen even by the Old Testament saints, and Jehovah had said to David's son, who was David's Lord, " Rule thou *in the midst* of thine enemies." (Psalm cx. 2.)

If, then, it be logical to say the Scripture declares He is gone, therefore He is not here, it is equally logical to say the Scripture affirms that He is here, therefore He is not gone. Both are meant, relatively, and both are true, relatively. Both are equally true in the sense, and with the limitation which Scripture gives to both ; both are untrue in the sense which a perverse reason forces upon them.   It is true both that Christ is gone, and that He is here ; he is gone, phenomenally, He is here, substantially.   It is false that Christ is either gone or here, as the carnal mind defines His presence or His absence. Absent in one sense, or respect, He is present in another ; both senses being equally real, though belonging to different spheres of reality.   The one belongs to the reality of the natural, in the sphere of the senses ; the other belongs to the reality of the supernatural in the sphere of faith.

Fourthly. If it be urged that Christ " *ascended into heaven,*" therefore He is not on earth, we reply, He not only has ascended into heaven, but, according to the apostle, He has passed *through* the heavens (Heb. iv. 14),* "is made higher than the heavens" (Heb. vii. 26), and has "ascended up *far above all* heavens" (Eph. iv. 10); but, with the apostle, we add, not that He may desert all things, or be absent from them, but "that He might fill all things." One of the grandest passages in CHRYSOSTOM † opens the true sense of these words : " Christ (at His Ascension) offered the first fruits of our nature to the Father ; and, in the Father's eye, because of the glory of Him who offered, and the purity of the offering, the gift was so admirable that He received it with His own hands, and placed it next to Himself, and said : 'Sit Thou at My right hand.' But to *which nature* did God say, 'Sit Thou at My right hand ? ' To that very nature which heard the words, ' Dust thou art, and unto dust thou shalt return.' Was it not enough for that nature to pass beyond the heavens ? Was it not enough for it to stand with angels ? Was not such a glory ineffable ? But it passed beyond angels, left archangels behind it, passed beyond the cherubim, went up high over the seraphim, speeded past the Principalities, nor stood still till it took possession of the Throne of the Lord. Seest thou not what lieth between mid-heaven and earth ? Or, rather, let us begin at the lowest part. Seest thou not what is the space between hell (adou) and earth, and from earth to heaven, and from heaven to the upper heaven, and from that to angels, from them to archangels, from them to the powers above, from them to the very Throne of the King ? Through this whole space and height, He hath carried our nature." ŒCUMENIUS : " With His unclothed Divinity He, of old, filled all things ; but, incarnate, he descended and ascended, that He might fill all things according to His flesh (meta sarkos)." THEOPHYLACT : " As before He had filled up all things by His divinity, He might now fill all things, by rule and operation, in His flesh." — GROTIUS : " That is above the air and ether, which

---

* This is the correct rendering of the passage. So the Vulgate and Arabic : penetravit Cœlos. (The Æthiopic makes it a passing through the heavens, in His coming into the world.) Von Meyer: Durch die Himmel gegangen. Stolz: gedrungen. Allioli, Gossner: die Himmel durchdrungen. De Wette · hindurch gegangen. So McKnight, Bible Union, Noyes, Alford.

† In Ascens. D. N. Jesu Christi. Opera, II. 534.

region is called the third heaven, and the heaven of heavens, and in the plural 'heavens,' and by pre-eminence ' heaven,' Acts ii. 34; i. 10; 1 Cor. xv. 47; Eph. vi. 9." Many of the Calvinistic divines appeal to this passage as proving the *omnipresence* of Christ, and, by consequence, His Deity.

But if Christ has *ascended* up far above all heavens, He has ascended according to the body. But if the body of Christ has ascended far above all heavens, by the processes of natural motion, it must have passed with a rapidity to which that of light is sluggish, and must have been capable of enduring processes which would not only have destroyed, but utterly dissipated, a natural body. But when a theory which calls in nature to its aid is compelled to acknowledge that a human body, fettered by the ordinary laws of natural presence, is hurried at a rate to which that of nearly twelve millions of miles in a minute is slowness itself, it asks for a trust in nature, what is harder to the mind than the most extreme demands of the supernatural. The nearest of the fixed stars, whose distance has yet been measured, is about twenty billions of miles from us, and requires three and a third years for its light to reach us. "It has been considered probable, from recondite investigations, that the average distance of a star of the *first* magnitude from the earth is 986,000 radii of our annual orbit, a distance which light would require $15\frac{1}{2}$ years to traverse; and, further, that the average distance of a star of the sixth magnitude (the smallest distinctly seen without a telescope) is 7,600,000 times the same unit, to traverse which, light, with its prodigious velocity, would occupy more than 120 years. If, then, the distances of the majority of stars visible to the naked eye are so enormously great, how are we to estimate our distance from those minute points of light discernible only in powerful telescopes? The conclusion is forced upon us that we do not see them as they appeared within a few years, or even during the lifetime of man, but with the rays which proceeded from them several thousands of years ago." * "The distance of a star whose parallax is 1″ is about twenty trillions of English miles. A spider's thread before the

---

* Hind's Astronomy, quoted in Chambers's Encyclopædia. Article: Stars.

eye of a spectator, at the same distance, would suffice to cancel the orbit of the earth; and the breadth of a hair would blot out the whole planetary system. But a star having this parallax is at a moderate distance in comparison of innumerable others, in which no parallactic motion whatever can be distinguished. Supposing the distance of one of them to be only a thousand times greater, a ray of light darted from it would travel between 3,000 and 4,000 years before it reached the earth; and if the star were annihilated by any sudden convulsion, it would appear to shine in its proper place during that immense period after it had been extinguished from the face of the heavens. Pursuing speculations of this kind, we may conceive, with Huygens, that it is not impossible that there may exist stars placed at such enormous distances that their light has not yet reached the earth since their creation." *

Now, if the presence of Christ is merely local, if He is above all heavens only by confinement to one place, His ascension to this one place involves something which may claim to be natural, but which is really super-supernatural. If the doctrine of the supernatural invites faith, the figment of the super-supernatural demands credulity. Calvin interprets "above all heavens" as meaning "beyond this created universe. The heaven in which Christ is, is a *place* above all the spheres. . . . Christ is distant from us by interval of space . . . for when it is said above all the heavens, it involves a distance beyond that of the circumference beneath sun and stars, and, consequently, beyond that of the entire fabric of the visible Universe."

VIII. Another shape which the same objection takes is: "Christ sitteth at the right hand of God, and therefore He is not on earth." This assumes that the "right hand of God" is a locality; and to this it is sufficient to reply, by asking the question, If the right hand of God be a place, in what place is God's left hand? Where is the place that God's right hand is *not*? If God's right hand means place *at all*, it means, not *one* place, but all place. If, moreover, Christ's human nature

---

* Encyclopædia Britannica (Eighth edition), Art.: Astronomy, iv. 81.

52

cannot be on earth, because it sitteth at " God's right hand,'
neither can His " divine " nature be present, for the same
reason; for Christ sits at the right hand of God in His whole
person, and according to *both* natures. If to sit at
God's right hand involves the limitations of locality, then the divine nature of Christ cannot be there.
But to sit at the right hand of God has no reference what
ever to locality. To sit at the right hand of a king is a
Biblical idiom for participation in the office, prerogatives, and
honor of a king. " To sit at the right hand of God " means,
therefore, " to be in that condition of plenary divine glory,
majesty, and dominion which belongs to God." We invert the
argument, therefore: we say, Christ is at the right hand of
God, therefore He is here. God is not mutilated nor divided;
He is without parts (impartibilis, Aug. Conf., Art. I.). Where-
ever God is, His right hand is; wherever His " right hand '
is, *He is ;* therefore the " right hand of God," so far as the
question of presence is involved, is everywhere. His throne is
as wide as the Universe! The " hollow of His hand " holds
creation! He who sits at God's right hand is omnipresent,
just as he who is sitting at the right hand of an earthly mon
arch is " *ipso facto* " where that monarch is. When Jesus rose
from the dead, He said, " All power is given unto me in heaven
and on earth ; " but the power of " presence " is a primary
part, a necessary element of all power or omnipotence ; that is,
omnipresence and omnipotence so cohere that no being can
have one of them without having both ; and as Jesus says this
power is *given* to Him, it must have been given to Him as
man, for, as God, He held it essentially and necessarily. Jesus
Christ our adorable Lord is not only essentially omnipotent
and essentially omnipresent as God, but is *personally* omnipotent and personally omnipresent in that human nature also
which has been taken into absolute and inseparable unity with
the divine. All objections vanish in the light of His glorious
and all-sufficient person. That the true and supernatural
communion with his Lord in His " Supper " — which is the
Christian's hope — *can be*, rests upon the fulness of the Godhead dwelling in Christ bodily; that it *will be*, rests upon the

VIII. Objection.
Christ is at God's
right hand.

absolute truth of Him who cannot deceive us. He who is incarnate God can do all things: He who is the Truth wil. fulfil all His assurances.

IX. It has been made an objection that the *Formula* in which the Lutheran theologians, combining different expressions in the symbols, usually set forth the truth of the presence, is not warranted, even if the Lutheran doctrine be true, inasmuch as the Scripture does not say that the body of Christ is " *in, with,* and *under* the bread." It is urged that _{IX. Objection : "in, with, under."} we ought to adhere to the Biblical phrase, nay, that we attempt to substitute for a Biblical expression, which allows of various meanings, one of our own, which can have but one sense. It has been asked, If our Lord meant that His body was to be given " in, with, and under the bread," why did He not say so in so many words? This feeble sophistry we have tried to dispose of, in a general way, in a previous discussion.* The men who urge it have their own phrases by which they ignore the direct teachings of the word of God. Let any man admit, without equivocation, *as the very letter of Scripture asserts,* I. That what Christ commands us to take, eat, and drink, is His body and blood, and II. That the bread we break is the communion of His body, and the cup we bless the communion of His blood, and we shall have no quarrel with him, as we are sure he will have none with us, about the phrase, " in, with, and under," which means no more nor less than the Scripture phrase. Bread and wine are there, Christ's body and blood are there; the bread and wine communicate the body and blood; that is what the Scripture says, and this, and no more, is what the Church says.

The implication that if Christ had used the phrase current in our Church, those who now reject our doctrine would have embraced it, was long ago noticed and answered by Luther. In his Greater Confession, he says: " If the text was, *In* the bread is my body, or, *With* the bread, or, *Under* the bread, then would the fanatics have cried, ' See! Christ does not say,

* Pp. 184–186.

The bread is my body, but *In* the bread is my body.' Gladly would we believe a true presence if He had only said, ' This is my body.' That would be clear; but He only says, ' *In* the bread, *with* the bread. *unde*·· the bread, is my body.' It consequently does not follow that His body is there. If Christ had said, *In* the bread is my body, they could more plausibly have said, Christ is in the bread spiritually, or by significance. For if they can find a figure in the words, This is my body much more could they find it in the other words, In the bread is my body; for it is a clearer and simpler utterance to say This is my body than to say In this is my body." Certainly it is a stronger affirmation of the divinity of Christ to say Christ is God, than to say God is in Christ, God is with Christ, or God is under the form of Christ.

No phraseology can be framed which *in itself* will shut up men to a fixed sense who are determined in advance not to accept that sense. The *history* of the terms must be brought in, in such case, to silence, if it cannot convince. Yet even the amplest history which fixes a sense beyond the cavil, which is restrained by an ordinary self-respect, is not sufficient to overcome the persistent obstinacy of determined perverseness. There are no words in the past whose sense is more absolutely fixed by every attestation of the letter and the history than the words of the Tenth Article of the Augsburg Confession. Yet in the face of those clear words, and of that ample history, men have done with that Article just as they have done with God's word : " The body and blood," say they, quoting it, " are truly present "— that is, by the contemplation of faith—" under the species of bread and wine," as symbols of an absent thing, and " are imparted " figuratively, spiritually, and ideally " to those who eat" with the mouth of faith. Hence the Confessors " disapprove of those who teach the opposite doctrine; " that is, disapprove of themselves and the Church they represent: " Wherefore also the opposite doctrine," to wit, the Lutheran doctrine, " is rejected," and the Zwinglian, Bucerian. Calvinistic, is accepted. We are making no humorous exaggeration. The Tenth Article of the Augsburg Confession has actually been manipulated in such a way, by the class whom Luther characterizes, as to make the object of it the rejection of the faith held by the Lutheran Church, the vindication of her enemies, and the stultification of her friends.

X. But it is argued that the doctrine of the continual personal presence of the humanity of Christ annihilates the very theory it is intended to aid ; for in making the body of Christ always present, everywhere, it renders impossible any special presence, such as the sacramental presence must be supposed to be. Hence it would follow that the Lord's Supper is no more a communion than any other supper is, and "*this* bread" no more than any other bread, the communion of Christ's body. This objection, if honestly urged, implies a complete ignorance of the doctrine of the true presence. The substantial presence, though presupposed in the sacramental, is not simply identical with it. The sacramental presence is the substantial presence *graciously operative*, in, with, and under the elements divinely appointed to this end. God is everywhere present, yet the Pagan cannot find Him for want of the divine means to actualize that presence. The Holy Ghost is everywhere present, but He can be found only in His Word and the ordinances, and cannot be found in nature, or in any book of man. The divine nature of the Son of God is personally present with every human creature, nay, is in every believer, yet no man thereby becomes incarnate God. All substantial presence, in the divine economy, becomes operative through means. The Lord's Supper is no exception to this rule. The relation of the supernatural reality conveyed, to the natural element conveying, is not that of mechanical union, or of passive copresence, but is that of sacramental union, of *voluntary* operativeness, in virtue of which the consecrated elements are the media of a communication which would not take place without them. Hence, while the generic, substantial presence of the whole Christ *perpetually* characterizes His state of plenary exercise of the prerogatives of His undivided divine-human person, the specific operativeness of that presence which renders it sacramental is dependent upon Christ's will, and is confined to the Supper. "Christ," says

X. Continual presence no argument against sacramental presence.

the Formula of Concord,* "can be with His body. . . *wner ever He wills* (wo er will — ubicunque voluerit), and there especially where He has promised that presence in His word, as in His Holy Supper."

XI. An objection is urged by Kahnis, that, "according to the Lutheran doctrine, there is but bread and wine, not the body and blood of Christ, before the eating and drinking," and therefore were that doctrine true, Christ would not have said, This *is* my body, "but would have had to say, This is *going to be* my body when you eat it." Were the point made by Kahnis correctly made, the inference justified would not be that the doctrine of the true presence is untenable, but that there ought not to be a limitation of the presence to the act of eating and drinking. But the point is not correctly made. The very opposite is the doctrine of the Lutheran Church. The Augsburg Confession says, "The body and blood of Christ

XI. Objection. Nothing sacramental apart from sacramental use.

are present *in the Supper*, and there communicated and received." The distinction is made between the generic presence which is "*in the Supper*," and the specific participation made by the reception of the sacrament imparted. From the *beginning* of the Supper, *strictly defined*, (that is, from the time when Christ's consecrating words are uttered in His name by His authority,) to *its end*, (that is, until the last communicant has received the elements,) or, in other words, from the first time to the last "*in the Supper*" in which, by Christ's authority, it is declared, "This is Christ's body, This is Christ's blood," that of which this affirmation is made, *is* His body, and *is* His blood. When He said, Take, eat, this is My body, undoubtedly He meant, Take, eat, *because* it is My body. The presence of the body in the *order of thought* precedes the command to Take, eat, though in point of time they are absolutely simultaneous. He imparts His presence that there may be a reason for the sacramental eating. But He imparts it with His word, by whose omnipotent force the element becomes a sacrament. Therefore, *when* He speaks, we know it is done. The mathematical moment need not concern us. We know the sacramental moment. But the

---

* 695, 92.

presence of the body is not mechanical, but *voluntary;* it is *conditioned* on the strict observation of the essentials of the institution. The body is present for sacramental impartation, and if the object of the external act of consecration *precludes* the *communion,* if the elements are merely to be reserved or carried about in procession for worship, there is no reason to believe that there is any sacramental presence of Christ's body whatever. Hence the emphasis of the Confession, " *in the Supper,*" cutting off in one direction an objection like that of Kahnis, and in another the Romish abuse of the reservation, procession, and worship associated with the elements.

In the Formula of Concord * the error of the Romish Church is defined as this: " They feign that the body of Christ is present under the species of bread, even *outside of the conducting of the Supper* (to wit, when the bread is shut up in the pyx, or carried about as a show and object of worship). For nothing has the character of a sacrament outside of God's command, and the use to which it has been appointed by Christ." This implies that within the entire conducting of the Supper, properly so called, as distinct from the mere preliminaries, or the things following it, the body of Christ is sacramentally present; and the principle that nothing has a sacramental character apart from the divine command and use, is properly limited by its antithesis to the abuses of the Romish Church. The doctrine of the Lutheran Church is, that the sacramental presence of the body and blood of Christ begins with the beginning of the Supper, and ends with the end of the Supper. The presence does not *depend* upon the individual eating; the eating simply actualizes a presence existing; that presence is vouchsafed on condition that the divine essentials of the institution be observed. " As to the consecration, we believe, teach, and confess, that the presence of the body and blood is to be ascribed solely to the Almighty power of our Lord Jesus Christ. . . The words of the institution are by no means to be omitted. . . The blessing (1 Cor. x. 16) takes place through the repetition of the words of Christ." † " The true presence is produced, not *by the eating,*

---

* 570, 108; 665, 82.   † Formula Concord. 530, 9

or the faith of the communicants, but simply and solely by the power of Almighty God, and the word, institution, and ordination of our Lord Jesus Christ. For those most true and omnipotent words of Jesus Christ, which He spake at the original institution, were not only efficacious in that first Supper, but their power, virtue, and efficacy abide through all .me; so that in all places where the Lord's Supper is cele-ɔrated in accordance with Christ's institution, by virtue of and in the power of those words which Christ spake at the first Supper, His body and blood are truly present, communicated, and received." * Luther says, " *When* (wenn-quando), according to His command and institution in the administration of the Lord's Supper, we say, ' This is My body,' *then* (so-tum) it *is* His body." † " Melancthon defines the sacramental action relatively to what is without, that is over against the inclusion and carrying about of the Sacrament; he does not divide it against itself, nor define it against itself." ‡ In a word, unless the sacramental action is entire, as Christ ordained it, His sacramental presence will not be vouchsafed at all; if it be entire, His presence is given from its beginning to its end. If it be argued, in a little sophistical spirit, that we cannot tell till the distribution whether the action will be complete, it is enough to reply that we have all the assurance that we have in any case of moral certainty. Christ himself knows the end from the beginning. At the beginning, middle, and end of the Supper, the minister need not fear to assert, nor the people to believe, the very words of Christ, in their simplest literal force. It is not *going to be* but *is*, when Christ says it is.

XII. The most extraordinary charge against the Lutheran doctrine of the Lord's Supper is that made by Roman Catholics

XII. Objection. That the doctrine is useless in the Lutheran System.

and by some of the Anglican High Church school, to wit, that the Lutheran doctrine, while it asserts the objective character of the presence of the body and blood of Christ, is able to make very little use

---

* Formula Concord. 663, 74, 75.

† Quoted in the Formula Concord. 664, 78, as confirmatory of its position. See also Gerhard: Loci. Loc. xxii., xvii., 194. (Ed. Cotta x. 327–329.)

‡ Luther. Opera Lat. Jen. iv. 586.

of the presence—in fact, might do as well practically without it. The objection urged, virtually is that the doctrine of justification by faith makes null the benefits of the Lord's Supper as involving a true presence.

On the general question of the efficacy of sacraments, Chemnitz* has expressed the doctrine of the Church with his usual judgment: "If regard be had to the necessary distinction, the explanation is not difficult as to the mode in which God does confer grace and the sacraments do not confer it?　God the Father reconciles the world unto Himself, accepts believers, not imputing their trespasses unto them.　Certainly the sacraments do not confer grace in this manner, as God the Father Himself does.　Christ is our peace.　The death of Christ is our reconciliation.　We are justified by His blood.　The blood of Christ cleanseth us from all sin.　He was raised again for our justification. Assuredly Baptism does not purge away our sins in that manner in which Christ Himself does.　There is the Holy Spirit's own proper efficacy in the conferring and application of grace. And the sacraments are certainly not to be put upon an equality with the Holy Spirit, so as to be regarded as conferring grace in an equal and, in fact, an identical respect with the Holy Spirit Himself.　Does it follow, then, that nothing is to be attributed to the sacraments?　Certainly the words of Scripture attribute something to the sacraments.　But most carefully and solicitously, when we dispute concerning the virtue and efficacy of sacraments, must we avoid taking from God, and transferring to the sacraments what properly belongs to the grace of the Father, the efficacy of the Spirit, and the merit of the Son of God: for this would be the crime of idolatry; nor are sacraments to be added as assisting and partial causes to the merit of Christ, the grace of the Father, and the efficacy of the Holy Spirit; for this would involve the same crime.　For there is no other name given under heaven among men. 'My glory will I not give to another.' How, then, does Baptism save us?　How is it the laver of regeneration? This, Paul explains very simply, when he says: 'He cleansed

Chemnitz on the efficacy of the Sacraments.

---

* Examen Concil. Trid. (Ed. Francof. a. M. 1707) 295 - 298.

the Church with the laver of water by the word.' Wherefore the Apology to the Augsburg Confession rightly says that the effect, virtue, and efficacy is the same in the word and in sacraments, which are the seals of the promises, in which respect St. Augustine calls them *visible words.* The gospel is the power of God unto salvation to every one that believeth, not because some magical power adheres in the letters, sylables, or sounds of the words, but because it is the medium, organ or instrument by which the Holy Spirit is efficacious, setting forth, offering, imparting (exhibens), distributing and applying the merit of Christ and the grace of God to the salvation of every one that believeth: so also to the sacraments is attributed power or efficacy, not that in the sacraments outside or apart from the merit of Christ, the pity of the Father, and the efficacy of the Holy Spirit, is grace to be sought unto salvation; but the sacraments are instrumental causes, so that through these means or organs the Father wishes to impart, give, apply, His grace: the Son to communicate His merit to believers: the Holy Ghost to exercise His efficacy to the salvation of every one that believeth.

" In this way God retains His own glory, so that grace is sought nowhere but with God the Father; the price and cause of the remission of sins and eternal life are sought nowhere but in the death and resurrection of Christ; the efficacy of regeneration unto salvation is sought nowhere but in the operation of the Holy Ghost. . . In the use of the sacraments faith does not seek or have regard to some virtue or efficacy in the outward elements of the sacraments themselves; but in the promise which is annexed to the sacraments, it seeks, lays hold on, and receives the grace of the Father, the merit of the Son, and the efficacy of the Holy Spirit. . . There is here a twofold instrumental cause. One is, as it were, God's hand, by which, through the word and the sacraments in the word, he offers, imparts (exhibet), applies, and seals to believers the benefits of redemption. The other is, as it were, our hand, to wit, that, by faith, we seek, lay hold on, and accept those things which God offers and imparts (exhibet) to us through the word and sacraments. There is no such efficacy of sacraments as if God, through them, infuses or impresses grace to salvation, even on those who do not believe or accept.   The meaning of the sentence: 'It is not the sacrament which justifies, but the faith of the sacrament,' is not that faith justifies without accepting the grace which God offers and imparts in the word and sacraments, or that it accepts the grace without the means or organ of the word and sacraments.   For the object of faith is the word and sacraments; nay, rather, in the word and sacraments the true object of faith is the merit of Christ, the grace of God, and the efficacy of the Spirit.   Faith justifies, therefore, because it lays hold of those things in the word and sacraments.   God does not impart His grace in this life all at once, so that it is straightway, absolute, and finished, so that God has nothing more to confer, man nothing more to receive; but God is always giving and man is always receiving, so as ever to be more closely and perfectly joined to Christ, to hold more and more firmly the pardon of sins; so that the benefits of redemption, which have been begun in us, may be preserved, strengthened, and increased.   Wherefore the sacraments are not idle or bare signs, but God, through them, offers to believers His grace, imparts it, applies it, and seals it. . . Between the promise and faith the relation is so close that the promise cannot benefit a man without faith, nor faith benefit a man without the promise. . . In this sense Luther says: 'The sacraments were instituted to excite, nourish, strengthen, increase, and preserve faith, so that whether in the promise naked, or in the promise in the vesture of the sacramental rite, it may grasp and accept grace and salvation.'"   In discussing more particularly the benefits of the Eucharist, the same great writer says: * "Faith, in the reception of the Eucharist, should reverently consider and, with thanksgiving, embrace all the riches and the whole treasure of the benefits, which Christ the Mediator, by giving up His body and shedding His blood, has purchased for His Church. . . That they also receive the remission of sins, who are conscious of grievous crimes, and do not renounce them, but cherish still the purpose of evil-doing, who bring no fear of God, no penitence or

* Examen Concil. Trid. (Ed. Francoff. a. M. 1707,) 364, 366.

faith, but knowingly persist in sins contrary to their con
sciences, is something which in no manner whatever is taught
by us. For among us men are seriously admonished that
those who do not repent, but who persevere in sins against
conscience, eat and drink judgment to themselves, and become
guilty of the body and blood of the Lord. For the offence
against God is aggravated by their taking the Eucharist in
impenitence, and treating with indignity the body and blood
of the Lord. In order that the eating may profit men, it is
necessary that they should have penitence, the fear of God,
which works dread of sin and of His wrath against it and
destroys the purpose of evil-doing. Faith also is necessary,
which seeks and accepts remission of sins in the promise."
"Inasmuch as in the Eucharist we receive that body of Christ
which was delivered for us, and that blood of the New Testament which was shed for the remission of sins, who can deny
that believers there receive the treasure of all the benefits of
Christ? For they receive that in which sins are remitted, in
which death is abolished, in which life is imparted to us; that
by which Christ unites us to Himself as members, so that He
is in us, and we in Him... 'Not only does the soul rise
through the Holy Ghost into a blessed life, but the earthly
body is brought back by that food to immortality, to be raised
to life in the last day' (Cyril). In the Eucharist, therefore,
we receive a most sure and admirable pledge of our reconciliation with God, of the remission of our sins, of immortality,
and of the glory to come. And in very deed Christ hath
abundantly poured out in this sacrament the riches of His
divine love toward men; for that body which He delivered for
us unto death, He gives to us in the Supper for food, that by
it, as divine and life-giving food, we may live, may be nurtured
and grow, and strengthen, and so turned to Him as never to
be separated from Him, as Augustine piously says, on the Person of Christ: 'Thou shalt not change me unto Thee, but
Thou shalt change Thyself unto me.'"

Gerhard sums up the benefits of the Lord's Supper as either
principal or secondary: "The principal fruits are: the showing of the Lord's death, the forgiveness of sins, the sealing of

faitL, spiritual union with Christ. The secondary are: re newal of the baptismal covenant, the arousing of love to God and our neighbor, the confirmation of patience and hope, the attestation of our resurrection, the serious amendment of life, public confession of Christ."*

It is not in the power of language to go beyond the state-ment of the blessings which the Lutheran Church believes to be associated with the believing reception of the Lord's Sup-per. The quarrel of Romanists and their friends with her is not that she diminishes the benefits of the Supper, but that she makes them conditioned on faith. The real thing with which they quarrel is the doctrine of justification by faith.

We have dwelt at what may seem disproportioned length upon the doctrine of the Lord's Supper; but we have done so not in the interests of division, but of peace. At this point the division opened, and at this point the restoration of peace must begin. Well-set bones knit precisely where they broke; and well knit, the point of breaking becomes the strongest in the bone. The Reformation opened with a prevailingly con-servative character. There lay before it not merely a glorious possibility, but an almost rapturous certainty, waiting upon the energy of Reform guided by the judgment of Conserva-tism. The Reformation received its first appalling check in the invasion of its unity in faith, by the crudities of Carlstadt, soon to be followed by the colder, and therefore yet more mis-chievous, sophistries of Zwingle. The effort at reformation, in some shape, was beyond recall. Henceforth the question was between conservative reformation and revolutionary radical-ism. Rome and the world-wide errors which stand or fall with her, owe their continued baleful life, not so much to the arts of her intrigue, the terror of her arms, the wily skill and intense devotion of Jesuitism and the orders, as they owe it to the division and diversion created by the radicalism which enabled them to make a plausible appeal to the fears of the weak and the caution of the wise. But for this, it looks as if the great ideal of the conservative reformation might have

* Gerhard's Ausf. Erklaer. d. heilig. Taufe u. Abendm. 1610, 4to, ch. xxiii. Do. Loci Theolog. Loc. xxii. ch. xx.

been consummated; the whole Church of the West might have been purified. All those mighty resources which Rome now spends against the truth, all those mighty agencies by which one form of Protestantism tears down another, might have been hallowed to one service — Christ enthroned in His renovated Church, and sanctifying to pure uses all that is beautiful in her outward order. The Oriental Church could not have resisted the pressure. The Church Catholic, transfigured by her faith, with robes to which snow has no whiteness and the sun no splendor, would have risen in a grandeur before which the world would have stood in wonder and awe. But such yearnings as these wait long on time. Their consummation was not then to be, but it shall be yet.

INDEX.

(The Roman Numerals indicate the entire Dissertations so numbered.)

PAGE

Adam, Original state............... 378
———— Fall................................ 379
———— Alone mentioned............... 380
Adiaphoræ 321
Aldine, Greek Text............... 96, 98
Allegory, Nature of 618
Allen, George, Prof., Communion
   of Priests .... 621, *n*
Alting, H., Lutheran and Re-
   formed Churches..................... 133
Ambrose, Lord's Supper..... 635, 675
America, Lutheran Church in,
   General Council of.................... 162
———————— Church in, the Fathers
   of.......................... . 218
American and German............. 208
Anabaptists, Pelagian............. 447
———— Infant Baptism.... 574-576, 581
Andreæ 297, 309
Anthropology, Original sin..... 365
Apology of Augsburg Confes-
   sion 275-280
———— Value of........................ 279
———— Original sin......... 373, 375, 378
———— Infant Baptism.................. 576
Aquinas, (Hymn,) Lord's Supper 754
Arnold, Dr., Germans............. 155
Articles, Electoral-Torgau 293
Audin, Cause of Reformation..... 3
———— History of Luther........... 10, 22
———— Luther's visit to Rome....... 25
———— Luther's Bible.................. 32
———— Luther and Madeleine....... 43
Augsburg Confession, 31, 179, VI.
———— Variata............... 180, 243-248
———— —— on original sin.......... 409
———— —— on necessity of Bap-
   tism...................... 562
———— —— Bibliography of...... 201, *n*
———— —— History of................. 212
———— —— Bibliography, 212, *n*. 220, *n*
———— —— Preparation of.................. 216
———— —— Preliminaries to......... 216
———— —— Bibliography of..... 216, *n*
———— —— Authorship of.................. 220
———— —— Luther's relations to......... 220

PAGE

Augsburg Confession,
———— Luther's opinion of 234
———— Object of......................... 242
———— Presentation of................. 242
———— Texts of..................... 242-258
———— Manuscripts of............ 244, *n*
———— Editions and Translations
   of................................. 248
———— Bibliography of............ 248, *n*
———— Structure of..................... 253
———— Divisions of..................... 253
———— Value of 255
———— Protest against Romanism.. 255
———— Interpretation of, Bibliogra-
   phy.......................... 255, *n*
———— Political value of.............. 257
———— Value as a Confession and
   Apology..................... 258
———— A centre of associations 259
———— A guide to Christ............... 259
———— Value for the future 260
———— Dogmatic works on, Bibli-
   ography.................... 260, *n*
———— as a creed, right reception
   of 260-267
———— Dr. Shedd on............. 332-337
———— "Romanizing Elements"... 342
———— Texts of Latin and German 356
———— —— Melancthonian & For-
   mula......................... 358
———— Papal Confutation.............. 360
———— Commission on.................. 361
———— Original Sin.................... 363
———— Article............II. 130, 244, IX.
———— —— ....III.   X.
———— —— .... IX. 130,   XI.
———— —— ....X.   XII.
———— —— ...."   XIII.
———— —— ...."   XIV.
———— —— —— Perversion of..... 820
———— —— "In the Supper" 823
———— —— ....XIII...... 339
———— —— ....XIX............ 374
Augustine, Original Sin 361, 362, 407
———— Traducianism 371
———— Pelagianism 447

Augustine, Person of Christ 469–510
------ Infants, believers.............. 581
------ Tree of Life...................... 588
------ Lord's Supper, 675,746, 749, 750
751.
---·--- (?) personal unity of man... 805
Augustus, Elector of Sax-
ony.................................. 296, 308

Baier, Lord's Supper 770
Baptism, Lutheran Doctrine of
129, XI.
------ Relations of, to Original Sin 427
------ Necessity of.............. 427, 557
------ ------ in what sense 430, 562
------ ------ not absolute........ 431, 563
------ ------ Luther...................... 431
------ ------ Bugenhagen.............. 432
------ ------ Hoffman................... 433
------ ------ Feuerlin 433
------ ------ Carpzov 433
------ Ordinary means of grace 439–444
------ ------ Alford......... 442, 443, 444
------ ------ Calvin...................... 444
------ only means of universal ap-
plication........................ 444
------ Disputes in regard to......... 519
------ Immersion not essential to 519
------ use of the word in Augsburg
Confession.................. 520
------ force of word "begiessen " 527
–531.
------ Luther, translation of words
connected with........ 531–536
------ Luther, Etymologies of
words 536
------ ------ did not regard Immersion as necessary 540–542
------ Mode in Lutheran Liturgies 541
542
------ Testimonies of Drs. Kurtz
and Schmucker.............. 543
------ views of the old Lutheran
Divines.................... 543, 544
------ Internal efficacy of 545–557, 583
584.
------ Not mere water 558, 583
------ Regeneration does not always follow.................. 559
------ Difference between " essential " and " necessary "... 562
------ Lutheran theologians on necessity of 564
------ Calvinistic and Lutheran
views compared 570–574
------ Infant, argument for... 576–581
Basis Confessional of Luther-
an Church, Reasons for............ 179

Bayle, Peter, Fathers on Lord's
Supper.................................. 663
Bellarmine, Romanism and
Calvinism............................ 628
------ Consubstantiation............. 772
Bible, Luther's.................. 8, 12, 32
------ in Middle Ages................. 7
------·--- First Polyglot 8
------ where it fell open............. 9
------ the only Rule 14
------ human explanations of...... 185
Birth, New, Necessity of abso-
lute.............................. 415–439
------ Infants need 416
------ Infants capable of 418
------ Holy Spirit, sole author of.. 420
------ Baptism one ordinary mean 439
–445.
Body, Spiritual...................... 806
Book of Concord.. .... 127, VII.
------ against persecution........... 144
Bread and Wine, Species of... 620
------ in what sense " the body and
blood of Christ "...... 673–678
------ metaphorically used.......... 717
------ breaking of 719
------ no symbol of crucifixion..... 723
Brentius, Hallam on.............. 76, *n*
------ Lord's Supper.................. 761
Buddeus, Lord's Supper.......... 770

Calovius, Consubstantiation 769
Calvin on Luther...................... 132
------ signed unaltered Augsburg
Confession 180
------ Infant Regeneration 420
------ Confession of Faith........... 490
------ Lord's Supper 493–495, 630, 636,
756.
------ Faith in Infants.......... 580
------ as a Lutheran Minister...... 756
Calvinism self-contradictory 435, 436
------ Socinianizing tendency of... 489
------ View of Baptism............... 570
------ ------ compared with the
Lutheran view   571–573
Carlstadt 27, 30, 608, 666
Carpzov, Consubstantiation 768
Catechism, Luther's................ 32
------ Heidelberg ... 351–353, 487, 488
------ Genevan........................... 483
Ceremonies, Ecclesiastical 321
Charles V., Reformation.......... 18
------ at Augsburg.:................... 31
------ at Luther's grave.............. 44
Chemnitz 309
------ on Personal Presence of
Christ.....................466–475

PAGE

Chemnitz, Body of Christ......... 469
——— meaning of Baptizo........... 543
——— Consubstantiation 763
——— Sacraments, efficacy of 825
Christ, Descent into hell... 320
——— Person of, Formula of Concord 316, 514–517
——— ——— Lutheran and Reformed Doctrine of........ X.
——— Sacramental Presence of.... X.
——— ——— Bibliography......... 456, n
——— Presence, Doctrine of ... 458, 469
——— ——— not local 458
——— ——— but true.............459–461
——— Ascension of.........466, 814–817
——— Body of........................... 469
——— inseparable unity of His person 481
——— in heaven.................. 483, 484
——— Resurrection Life of 484
——— Lutheran Doctrine Scriptural 501–507
——— ——— Sustained by the Fathers........... 508–510
——— ——— ——— Scholastics 510
——— ——— ——— some modern Romanists 511
——— ——— ——— Metaphysicians... 511
——— ——— ——— admissions of Calvinists 511, 512
——— Worship of, according to His human nature 512
——— body and blood of, Sacramental Communion 629
——— person, Unity of, not dissolved by death 794
Christianity, Essential idea of.. 113
Christians, whom may we recognize as.................................. 192
Chrysostom, Omnipresence of Christ...... 509
——— Tree of Life..................... 588
——— Lord's Supper 635, 660, 740, 746 748–751.
——— Ascension of Christ 815
Church 195
Church, Ancient, Sacramental presence........................ 657–663
——— sustains Antithesis in Art. X. 725–752
Church, Evangelical Protestant.. 114
——— Lutheran, Reformed Testimony to 132
——— ——— Controversies of 147
——— ——— Theological Science in 148 149, 151.
——— ——— in United States 150
——— ——— Education in 151

PAGE

Church, Missions in................. 152
——— ——— Church Constitution... 152
——— ——— Fidelity of, to her Confessions................. 196
——— ——— Acquaintance with, importance of............ 211
——— ——— Relations to Zwinglian-Calvinistic churches 325
——— ——— History and doctrines of, some mistakes in regard to............ VIII.
——— ——— not Romanizing......... 187
——— ——— Theological Seminary of, at Philadelphia ... 164
——— ——— Charity of................. 142
——— ——— Life in.................... 154
——— ——— Nationalities of.......... 155
——— ——— Mission of, in America 159
——— ——— Future of................. 161
——— ——— Relations to other Communions 138
——— ——— Worship, divine in 153
Church, Reformed, Importance of Lutheran Church to....... 311
Chytræus 311
Claude, Lutherans.................... 136
Cörner................................. 311
Communicatio idiomatum 476 –481.
Communion, Sacramental, in what sense oral...................... 461
——— ——— spiritual............ 462–465
——— ——— who receive ?............. 463
——— in one kind...................... 621
——— of the unworthy........ 641–648
——— (Koinonia, 1 Cor. x. 16.)
Force of word......... 629–641
——— Assembly, Westminster, annotat. 638
——— Baumgarten, S. J. 639
——— Bishop's Bible 637
——— Calovius........................... 639
——— Clarke, Adam 638
——— Conybeare and Howson...... 638
——— Coverdale 637
——— Genevan Version 637
——— Gill 639
——— Hall, Bp. 638
——— Hammond 638
——— Henry, Matthew 638
——— Hodge, Dr. 639
——— Hussey 637
——— Macknight 638
——— Nevin, J. W., Dr. 639
——— Olshausen 640
——— Parkhurst 639
——— Pool............................... 637
——— Rückert 641

53

Communion, Schmucker, S S.,
Dr. 639
—— Sharp, Arbp. 638
—— Tyndale 637
—— Wilson, Bp. 637
Complutensian Text........... 96, 99
Concomitance, Sacramental,
rejected 620
Concord, Book of.................... VII.
—— —— Contents of......... 268, 275
—— —— repressed multiplica-
tion of creeds......... 274
Concord, Formula of 288
—— —— History 289
—— —— Reception 302
—— —— Merits 305
—— —— Value 305, 328
—— —— plan...................... 312
—— —— doctrines 312, 348
—— —— Melancthon in 326
—— —— closing words of 328
—— —— Dr. Shedd on............. 345
—— —— " The Bread is Christ's
body " 677
—— —— modes of presence...... 762
—— —— When is the presence
vouchsafed ? 823, 824
—— —— *Suabian-Saxon* ... 294
Confession, what shall be our ?.. 167
Confessions, distinctive 168
—— Fidelity to...................... 169
—— —— object of theological
training 176
—— —— Ministerial efficiency
dependent on 177
—— Subscription to................... 177
—— not inconsistent with author-
ity of Rule of Faith 184
—— not Romanizing................. 186
—— Importance of.................... 204
—— Relations of, to Reformation 205
—— the Reformed 352
Confutation, Papal, of Augs-
burg Confession 624
—— History and Literature of 626, *n*
Consecration in the Supper 179
Conservatism of Lutheran Ref-
ormation ....: 49, 202
—— Ranke on...................... 84
Consubstantiation rejected by
Lutheran Church............. 130, 339
Proof of this:
1. From Confessions of Lutheran
Church, Formula, 130, 762.
2. Lutheran Divines: Luther, 130,
757; Brentius, 761; Chemnitz, 764;
Andreæ, 764; Hutter, 758, 766;
Osiander, 767; Mentzer, Gerhard,

340; Carpzov, 768; Musæus, Scher-
zer, 768; Calovius, Quenstedt, 769;
Baier, 340; Leibnitz, 340; Buddeus,
770; Cotta, 340, 771; Pfaff, 775;
Mosheim, 341; Reinhard, 341.
3. Roman Catholic Divines, 771;
Perrone, Beccan, Moehler, Wise-
man, 772; Bouvier, 773.
4. Calvinistic Divines, 755–757, 759:
Bucer, 340, 773; Musculus, Whit
aker, Salmasius, Stapfer, 774;
Waterland, 130; D'Aubigné, 131.
Copula................................ 696
—— interpretation of 696
—— Bagster's Gr. Lex. 696
—— Carlstadt 695
—— Green's Gr. Lex. 696
—— Hoffman, D. 696
—— Kahnis 696, 697, 704, 705
—— Luther 696
—— Keckerman 695
—— Œcolampadius 695, 705
—— Piscator 696
—— Robinson..................... 696, 697
—— Schaff 696, 697
—— Wendelin 694
Corpora Doctrinæ................ 291
Corruption, the state of......... 373
Cotta, Lord's Supper.......... 340, 771
—— salvation of Pagan infants.. 564
Council, General, of E. L.
Church in America, Fundamental
Principles................................ 162
Creation 797
Creationism, immediate........... 369
Creed, Apostles' 168
—— implies the Communicatio
idiomatum 316
Creeds, wide......................... 183
—— —— fallacy of argument for 190
—— may a church change......... 269
—— growth of..................... 270
—— defining of...................... 272
—— Formula of Concord on...... 313
Crypto-Calvinism 292
Cup in Supper.................... 777–782
Cyril of Jerusalem, Lord's
Supper 675

Dannhauer, Calvinistic view of
Christ's presence...................... 500
Death no regenerating power..... 426
Denmark 156
Development, Shedd on............ 330
Dreams, interpretation of. 614

Election, Calvinistic................. 434
—— Infant 435

PAGE

Election, unconditional, and Pelagianism.. 584
Elements, Worship of, or of Christ in....................................... 622
Emser, Counter-translation.. 104–107
Ephes. iv. 10., "above all heavens"..................................... 815–817
Erasmus, Greek Text.............. 97
———— Luther and....................... 66
Error and Errorists................. 143
———— Course of...................... 195
———— Formula of Concord on.. 325
Eternity 798
Eucharist 130, 314, 337, X., XII.-XIV.
Eutychianism, Lutheran doctrine not in affinity with..... 475, 476
Evangelical, name of Lutheran Church.................................. 116
Excommunication, Force and extent of 191
Exorcism................. 135, 136, 154

Facundus, Lord's Supper 675
Faith, Rule of................ 14–17, 165
———— —— Supreme Authority of. 184
———— —— Formula of Concord on 313
———— Fundamental principles of.. 163
———— Confession of..................... 166
———— Church, Restoration of...... 200
Fathers, use of, in Reformation.. 15
———— on Lord's Supper 635, 725, 740
———— Rules in interpretation of... 726
Figure, in what sense used by Fathers.................................. 741
———— use of word, by Tertullian.. 742
Figures, Grammatical and Rhetorical 701
Flacius, Illyricus, Baptizo......... 544
Fundamentals, union in......... 181
———— nature of 182, 183

Gaudentius, Lord's Supper 674
Geneva, Church of, Lutherans and Reformed......................... 137
Gerhard, Baptism..................... 544
———— "Touto" and "Artos"...... 671
———— "The bread is Christ's body " 677, 678
Gerhart, E. V., Dr., Article of, Reviewed .... X.
Gerlach, Stephen, Baptism......'.. 544
German Character 155
———— Language, Luther............. 13
Germany, Reformation in........ 17
God, Right hand of............ 485, 817
Goebel, Luther, author of Reformation 125
———— Lutheran Church 126, 151, 155

PAGE

Gospel and Law, Formula of Concord 314
Grauer, Baptism...................... 437
Gregory Nyssen, Lord's Supper 675
Gregory the Great, Lord's Supper........................... 750
———— Service of....................... 753
Grotius, "all heavens"............ 816
Guilty of the Body and Blood, (1 Cor. xi. 27–29).................... 642–648
———— Calvinists, Gualther, Meyer, Pareus on...................... 648
———— Syriac version 642
Gustavus Adolphus............... 156
Gustavus Vasa 156

Hamilton, Jas., Dr., Resurrection Life of our Lord............... 484
Hamilton, Wm., Sir, 791, 792, 803 804.
Hebrews iv. 14, "passed through the heavens"....................... 816
Hegel, Fall............................. 376
———— Philosophy 790, 802
Hell, Descent of Christ into 820
Heppe, Calvinistic view of Baptism 570
Heretics and Heresy.......... 143, 144
———— Ancient, Lord's Supper...... 752
High Churchism, Lutheranism not 141
Hollazius, Fall 377
Huguenots, Sympathy with, expressed in Book of Concord....... 145
Hunnius, Salvation of Pagan Infants................................ 564
Hutter, Baptism, necessity of.... 562
Huygens 817
Hypostatic Union................. 798

Idealism, Theological............. 788
———— Transcendental 789
———— Subjective 790
———— Objective 790
———— Realistic 791
Idiomatum Communicatio,
———— Formula of Concord.... 316–320
———— Apostles' Creed............ 316
———— Nicene Creed................. 317
———— Athanasian Creed............. 317
———— Augsburg Confession......... 317
Ignatius, Lord's Supper 635, 727 -730
Impossible, the..................... 796
Imputation 382
Infants, unbaptized, 431, 561, 582, 583
———— sin of .... IX.
———— elect 434, 571–574
———— of unbelievers................. 437

PAGE

Infants of heathens.......433, 561–564
—— salvation of...................... 434
—— regeneration of................. 569
—— —— consequences of deny-
ing...................... 570
—— —— faith of 578–581
—— —— defined by Chemnitz... 579
—— —— Calvinistic admissions
in regard to........... 580
—— —— held by Ancient Church 581
Integrity, the state of............. 371
Irenæus, Lord's Supper 635, 736–739
—— Doellinger...................... 737
—— Dorner 738
—— Moehler 738
—— Semisch 738
"Is" cannot mean "is a symbol
of"............................ 612–619
—— De Wette on...................... 690
—— Meyer, Olshausen, Lange,
the Calvinists 691
—— cannot involve Metaphor.... 692
—— Calvinistic theory involves
that it does................... 695
—— yet is abandoned by best
Calvinistic writers: Kec-
kermann, Piscator, Rob-
inson, Schaff........... 695–697
—— Luther's renderings of....... 697
—— inflexible character of....... 698
—— reductio ad absurdum 699
See "Copula."

Jerome, Lord's Supper 635, 674
John of Damascus, Lord's
Supper 635, 636
Judas at the first Supper 645
Judgment, private.................. 169
—— —— use and abuse of....... 171
—— —— limitation of...... 172, 175
—— —— abuse of, not to be re-
strained by persecu-
tion 173
—— —— —— how to be re-
strained......... 174
Justification, Formula of Con-
cord 813
Justin Martyr, Lord's Supper 635,
730–735.
—— Doellinger 735
—— Dorner 735
—— Ebrard 735
—— Kahnis 735
—— Thiersch........................ 734

Kahnis, Lutheran Church 146
—— Lord's Supper, on............. 678
—— —— controverted............. 690

PAGE

Kahnis adds to, and contradicts
Scripture........................... 722
—— misstates Lutheran Doc-
trine...................... 822, 823
Kind and Mode.................. 807
Knox, A., Lord's Supper....... 776, *n*
Kœllner, Augsburg Confession,
Luther's 238
—— Apology 276
Krotel, Dr., Schenkel's Article... 513
Kurtz, H., Lutheran Church...... 125

Law and Gospel, Formula of Con-
cord 314
—— third use of.................. 314
Life, Tree of........................ 586
—— Bush 589
—— Delitzch 588
—— Gregory Nazianzen 588
—— Vatablus 588
Light............................... 816
Lightfoot, Infant Baptism......... 577
Limborch, Calvinistic doctrine
of Lord's Supper.................... 499
Liturgies, Ancient, Sacramental
presence 752
Lord's Day........................ 132
Luther, Theses 1–4, 27
—— Bible, Translation of... 8, 12, 32
—— —— versions preceding..... 13
—— —— first sight of............. 9–11
—— New Testament, Transla-
tion of .... III.
—— Boyhood, preparation
for 89
—— Education.................. 89
—— Hebrew and Greek 90
—— Fritzsche.................. 90
—— Piety....................... 90
—— German Style........... 91
—— Translations, earliest 92, 93
—— First Draft.............. 93
—— Versions and texts
used 93–100
—— order of books......100, 101
—— Revision 101
—— Early impressions...... 102
—— enemies............. 103–107
—— latest revisions.......... 107
—— advances of literature 108
—— rival translations....... 109
—— defects and excellen-
ces 109, 116
—— Revision 111
—— early studies.................... 10
—— a Reformer because a Christian.... 18
—— pictured by pencil and pen IL

	PAGE
Luther, childhood	23
—— youth	24
—— university life	25
—— visits Rome	25, 26
—— begins the Reformation	27
—— at Diet of Worms	28
—— at the Wartburg	29
—— struggle with fanaticism	29
—— and Melancthon	30
—— Marriage	30
—— and Zwingle	30
—— Augsburg Confession	31, 221, 222
—— Catechisms	32
—— —— occasion	284
—— —— character	284
—— —— authority	285
—— opinions	286
—— Church Service	33
—— in private life	33
—— at Christmas	33
—— Letter to little Hans	36, 37, *n*
—— Madeleine	38–43
—— Last days and death	43, 44
—— Charles V. at his tomb	44
—— *Characterized,* Atter-	
bury	50
—— Audin	5, 25, 26, 32, 43
—— Bancroft, A., Rev	50
—— Bancroft, G.	72
—— Bayle	51
—— Bengel	31
—— Bossuet	53
—— Bower	53
—— Brewster	55
—— Buddeus	59
—— Bunsen	65 66
—— Calvin	132
—— Carlyle	23, 28, 39, 56
—— Chemnitz	57
—— Claude	57
—— Coleridge	58, 59
—— Cox	60
—— Coxe	59
—— Cyclopedia Br. Soc.	63
—— —— Rees'	65
—— D'Aubigné	60
—— Dictionnaire Historique	61
—— D'Israeli	61
—— Dœderlein	62
—— Dupin	63
—— Erasmus	66–70
—— Fritzsche	90
—— Gelzer	70
—— Gerhard	73
—— Guericke	71
—— Guizot	71
—— Hagenbach	73
—— Hallam	74

	PAGE
Luther, Characterized, Hare	78
—— Hase	78
—— Heine	45
—— Herder	80
—— Kahnis	82
—— Kidder	52
—— Kohlrausch	72
—— Lessing	45
—— Melancthon	85, 86, 89
—— Menzel	46
—— Palavicini	83
—— Ranke	84
—— Raumer, V. F	83
—— Reuss	109
—— Robertson	71
—— Schlegel	46–50
—— Smythe	71
—— Stang	85
—— Vaughan	70
—— Wieland	85
—— Zwingle	132
—— Character, Summary of	86, 87
—— unity, desire for	138
—— Swiss Church	139
—— Waldenses	140
—— on mode of Baptism	520
—— the Jewess	520–524
—— Catechisms, on Baptism	524–527
—— —— on Lord's Supper	819, 823
Lutheran, name	117–122
Lutheran Church, distinctive	
principle of	123
—— character and claims of	124
—— compared with other	
churches	125, 126
—— Doctrines of	126
—— —— misrepresented	129
—— neither Arminian nor Cal-	
vinistic	127
—— Rule of Faith, and Creed	128
—— Confessions of, Shedd on	345
Lutheranism, historical	180
Man, Fall of	376
—— personal unity	804
Manna, Type of Christ's Body.	
—— Cyril	598
—— Gerhard	598
—— Lombard	598
Marburg, Colloquy at, Arti-	
cles of	855
—— —— Original Sin	427
Marheineke, Fathers	726, 738
Martyr, Peter, Faith of Infants	580
—— Lord's Supper	636
Martyrs of the Word	8
Mary, the Virgin	381, 382
Matter and Spirit	486

PAGE

Maxentius, Lord's Supper 675
Melancthon, correspondence
with Luther............................ 227
——— Relations to Augsburg Con-
fession....................................... 219
——— Luther's admiration of 234
——— Formula of Concord.... 326, 327
——— Original Sin...................... 362
——— ——— definition of........ 407, 408
——— on inseparable unity of
Christ's person............... 482
Metaphor, none in the Lord's
Supper 613
——— nature and laws of............. 701
Metaphysic of doctrine of Sup-
per, distinct questions on.......... 805
——— sound, in harmony with doc-
trine of true presence 809–811
Metonymy 701, 702
Michelet, on Luther................. 3
Mill, J. Stuart 801, 802, 804
Mode and Kind.................... 807
Musculus 311

Name, Denominational............... 115
Natural.................................. 800
Nature of things 800
Navarre, King of............ 132
Nestorianism 475
Nevin, J. W., Dr., Lutheran Church 157
Nothing, privative and negative 397

Objects, the Sacramental 599–601
Œcolampadius, Lord's Supper 666,
756.
Œcumenius, Ascension............ 815
Omnipresence 797
Onus probandi rests on oppo-
sers of Scripture doctrine of Sup-
per 799
Oral Manducation........ 461–463
Original Sin, See Sin, Original.. 280
Osiander, A., Consubstantia-
tion..................................... 767

Pagans and Idolaters, calumnies
in regard to Lord's Supper....... 752
——— imitations of Supper 752
Paschal Lamb, type of Christ 592
–597.
Passover, a type of Lord's Sup-
per 592–598
Pelagianism 445–454
——— and unconditional election .. 584
Pelagius.......................... 445–447
Persecution......................... 144
Person, human, unity of, fellowship of properties in 804, 805

PAGE

Philosophy Modern, Doctrine
of true presence...................... 787
Pictetus, Lutherans and Calvin-
ists 137
Pietists, early......................... 196
Predestination, Formula of
Concord 321–327
Pre-existence of soul 368
Presence, the true............. 601–612
——— Sacramental, Lutheran Doc-
trine, summary view of... 650
–657.
——— Modes of 650, 812
——— History of Doctrine..... 657–668
——— Literature................... 657, n
——— Controversy on, how to be
decided......................... 700
——— Continual, no argument
against Sacramental....... 821
——— Sacramental, when does it
begin? 822
Progress, true, nature of 206
Propitiation and Sacramental
presence 654, 657
Protestant, name of Lutheran
Church............................... 117
Pusey, Dr., Testimony of the
Fathers 658–663

Quenstedt, Fall................. 377
——— Baptism 544
——— Consubstantiation 769

Race, Human, unity of 366
Rationalism, character of 197
——— and Romanism 627
Realism, Natural 792
——— Personal........................ 793
Reformation, Church of the,
Conservative .... IV.
——— Early efforts for.............. 19
——— Era, characteristics of... 12, 18
——— Festival of...................... 4
——— Lessons of, for our time... 19–21
——— Occasion and cause 1–21
——— Providence and Word in... 17
——— Results of....................... 32
——— Solutions of its cause........ 5
——— Value of.................... 20, 21
——— Confessional Principle....... V
——— ——— Confession of..... VI., VII.
——— ——— Primary Confession of VI.
——— ——— Secondary Confessions
of.......................... VII.
——— Spirit of........................ 201
——— Conservatism of 203
——— Specific Doctrines of IX.
X., XI., XII., XIII., XIV., XV

PAGE

Regeneration, Baptismal... 564–570
Reuss, Luther's Translation...... . 109
Romanism and Rationalism..... 627
—— Lutheran Church, great bulwark against.................. 187
——— and Augsburg Confession... 228
255.
Rome, Church of, originally pure 14
——— —— Christians in 194
——— —— Creeds...................... 215
Rückert, Augsburg Confession... 228
239.
——— Lord's Supper.. 641

Sacramental character............ 622
Sacraments, efficacy of............ 825
——— —— Chemnitz on........ 825–828
——— ——⊥ Gerhard on......... 828–829
Salvation, Infant, Lutheran System 434–439
——— —— Calvinistic System 434–436
——— —— Pelagian System........ 434
——— —— Romish System 436
"Sanctified," (1 Cor. vii. 14)
sense of...................... 424
Saviour, a living.................... 652
Scandinavians .. 152, 153, 156, 157
Schaff, Lutheran piety 155
Schelling 790, 802
Schenckel, Communicatio Idiomatum................................ 513
Schmalcald Articles 280
——— Origin of 281
——— Necessity of 281
——— Value 283
Schwabach Articles....... 356, 409
Schwenckfeld, Lord's Supper.. 610, 666, 718.
Scriptures, not a Creed............ 183
——— interpretation of............... 799
Self-contradiction................. 801
Self-existence......................... 796
Selneccer 310
Shedd, History of Christian Doctrine...... .... VIII.
Sin, Original................... 280, IX.
——— Formula of Concord.......... 313
——— not a creature.................. 354
——— unity of Church 364
——— time of operation............ 378
——— involves all men 381
——— imputation 382
——— mode of perpetuation......... 384
——— fact of 385
——— result............ 386
——— truly sin....................... 391
——— names........... 391
——— morbus and vitium............ 392

PAGE

Sin, Original, analogies 394
——— relations and connections... 399
——— synonyms 400
——— essence 400
——— attributes........... 402
——— acts............... 403
——— penalties....................... 404
——— remedy....................... 405
——— definition 406
——— natural consequence 408
——— Scripture proof of 409
——— new birth....................... 415
——— relation of Baptism to........ 427
——— no man lost for, only 429
——— practical uses of doctrine... 454
–455.
Soul, propagation of................. 368
Space, nature of...................... 796
Spanheim, Lutherans and Calvinists 134
"Species," meaning of............. 620
Spirit and matter.................... 486
Stapfer, Lord's Supper....... 774–776
Stars................................... 816
Supper, Lord's, Lutheran doctrine of................ .. 192
——— Formula of Concord.......... 314
——— Reformed and Lutheran doctrines of 465
——— differences noted......... 491–493
——— Reformed theory of, objections to.................. 496–501
——— two views of 500
——— doctrine of, thetically stated XII.
——— —— in its antithesis....... XIII.
——— —— who are meant ? 665
——— objections to .... XIV.
——— I. False definition........ 755
——— II. Self-contradiction..... 766
——— III. Impressions of Disciples.................. 782
——— IV. Visible presence....... 783
——— V. Modern philosophy... 787
——— VI. Transubstantiation... 807
——— VII. Christ has left world 811
——— VIII. Right hand of God... 817
——— IX. "In, with, under,"... 819
——— X. Continual presence... 821
——— XI. Sacramental use...... 822
——— XII. Efficacy................ 824
——— Old Testament foreshadows of.......................... 585–598
——— New Testament doctrine..... 599
——— Fathers' Interpretation of... 635
——— Non-Lutheran Reformers of... 636
——— English and American writers.. 637–640
——— German interpreters......... 640

PAGE

Supper, superstitions in............ 752
—— doctrine, importance of 829
Symbol, Symbolical Books... 715, 716
Synecdoche 702
Systems, Lutheran and Calvinis-
tic, difference of, source............ 457

Tertullian, Lord's Supper.. 675, 742
–745.
—— personal unity of man........ 805
Testament,   New,   Luther's
translation............................. III.
—— defects in.......................... 110
—— order of books in 100
—— revision and publication...... 101
—— early impressions 102
—— enemies of....................... 103
—— counter-translations ... 104, 109
—— growth of literature of...... 108
—— merits of........................... 111
Texts, Greek, Luther's............ 96
Theodoret, Lord's Supper.. 635, 675
Theophylact, Lord's Supper.... 635
—— Ascension.......................... 815
Theremin, Lord's Supper ..... 776, *n*
Theses, Luther's...................... 2
Thirty Years' War 20, 156
"This" (touto) 667–673
—— Alford 673
—— Hammond 672
—— Hengstenberg.................... 672
—— Lange 672
—— Maldonatus...................... 673
—— Schaff 673
Thoroughness, spirit of our
time, adverse to...................... 207
Torgau, Book of..................... 298
Traducianism 371
Transubstantiation, Formula
of Concord............................. 315
—— Dr. Shedd......................... 343
—— rejected..................... 623–629
—— Fathers, testimony against.. 740
—— opposed to sound metaphysic 808
Trinity................................. 798

PAGE

Turretin, J., Lutherans and Reformed 137
Type 716

Ubiquity of Christ's body not
held by Lutheran Church........... 131
—— Dr. Shedd........................ 349
—— Dr. Gerhart............... 495, 496
Unionism 198
Unity, Church. true 137, 141, 142, 182
Unworthy, Communion of the... 641
–648.
Ursinus, faith of infants........... 580
—— Romish and Lutheran inter-
pretation...................... 628

Vœtius, faith of infants............. 580
Vulgate, Luther's New Testament 93
–96.

Wiggers, Lutheran Church........ 125
—— Denmark 156
—— Sweden...................... 156, 157
Will, Free, Formula of Concord 313
—— conditions of.................... 450
—— Pelagian views of........ 453–454
Winer, Apology 276
Wittenberg, beginning of Ref-
ormation................................ 1
Word of God, cause of the Ref-
ormation................................. 6
Works Good, Formula of Con
cord 313

Ximenes,   Cardinal,   Polyglos
Complutensian 8, 96, 99, 108

Zwingle, Luther.................... 133
—— Pelagian..................... 447–450
—— —— denial of................. 448
—— on Lord's Supper 607, 611, 615
–618, 629, 630, 636.
—— original doctrine of.......... 755
—— gave a check to Reformation 829

THE END.